Encyclopedia of the

AMERICAN LEGISLATIVE SYSTEM

ASSOCIATE EDITORS

Allan G. Bogue
Professor of History, University of Wisconsin–Madison

David W. Brady
Professor of Political Science, Stanford University

Joseph Cooper
Provost and Professor of Political Science, Johns Hopkins University

Garrison Nelson
Professor of Political Science, University of Vermont

Gary W. Reichard
Professor of History, Florida Atlantic University

Encyclopedia of the

AMERICAN LEGISLATIVE SYSTEM

Studies of the Principal Structures, Processes, and Policies
of Congress and the State Legislatures
Since the Colonial Era

JOEL H. SILBEY

Editor in Chief

Volume I

CHARLES SCRIBNER'S SONS/NEW YORK
MAXWELL MACMILLAN CANADA/TORONTO
MAXWELL MACMILLAN INTERNATIONAL/NEW YORK OXFORD SINGAPORE SYDNEY

Charles Scribner's Sons   Maxwell Macmillan Canada, Inc.
Macmillan Publishing Company   1200 Eglinton Avenue East

866 Third Avenue   Suite 200
New York, New York 10022   Don Mills, Ontario M3C 3N1

Macmillan Publishing Company is part of the Maxwell Communication Group of
Companies.

Library of Congress Cataloging-in-Publication Data

Encyclopedia of the American legislative system / Joel H. Silbey,
    editor in chief.
        p. cm.
    Includes bibliographical references.
    ISBN 0-684-19243-8 (set)—ISBN 0-684-19601-8 (vol. 1)—ISBN 0-684-19602-6
    (vol. 2)—ISBN 0-684-19600-X (vol. 3)
    1. Legislative bodies—United States—Encyclopedias. I. Silbey,
Joel H.
JF501.E53 1994
328.73′003—dc20   93-35874
                                                                 CIP

1 3 5 7 9 11 13 15 17 19 V/C 20 18 16 14 12 10 8 6 4 2

PRINTED IN THE UNITED STATES OF AMERICA

The paper used in this publication meets the minimum requirements
of American National Standard for Information Sciences—Permanence
of Paper for Printed Library Materials. ANSI Z3948-1984. ⊚™

EDITORIAL STAFF

CONTENTS

Volume I

CONTENTS

Volume II

CONTENTS

CONTENTS

Volume III

CONTENTS

PREFACE

Legislatures have been an integral part of the government process in much of the Western world since the Middle Ages. In England, as the prime example, Parliament early on established a crucial, ultimately a dominant, role within the nation's political system. In the American colonies, stimulated by the English example, legislative assemblies appeared very soon after settlement, to be followed by state legislatures, the Continental Congress, and then the Congress of the United States at the end of the eighteenth century. All but one of America's legislatures after independence contained two houses, usually differently constituted, but sharing equal responsibility with each other at the center of government activity. From the first, these legislatures had enormous powers which were enumerated in written constitutions. Article I of the United States Constitution, for example, provides not only a list of extensive lawmaking, oversight, and policy-monitoring powers enjoyed by Congress, but also empowers that body "to make all Laws which shall be necessary and proper" for the carrying out of its responsibilities. At the same time, other articles in the Constitution reserve to the states and their legislatures another array of governing powers. As a result, throughout American history, the Congress and the state legislatures have been very busy, and usually quite contentious, places.

From elections, through organization for business, through the developing and debating of different policy initiatives, legislatures have acted and reacted, followed well-developed and/or more confused lines of behavior, tried to read the world around them and react to it effectively. The influence on legislatures of external forces—interest-group pressures, demands from constituents, the test of frequent elections that determine their makeup, and the initiatives of the other branches of government—has been constant. Because of all of these pressures and processes, legislatures have been part of, and often determinative of, larger political processes in the United States.

From the beginning, in order to carry out their many functions, the United States' various legislative institutions developed their own internal processes and rules in order to facilitate their activities. At the same time, they have always had to deal with the co-equal executive and judicial branches of government which shared much more of the responsibility for policy development—first in a new, and then in a rapidly developing, continental nation. Finally, all legislatures have histories, that is, memories of past events and long-established ways of doing things that have continued to shape the way that they have operated. Still, legislatures have never been static institutions. They have repeatedly changed to meet new conditions, pressures, expectations, and demands in the larger society. All of these many elements come together to form the legislative experience. Spelling out and interpreting all of these factors, their nuances, and their differences contribute to an understanding of the role and nature of the legislative system in its entirety.

The *Encyclopedia of the American Legislative System* is designed to provide a convenient reference work about the nation's legislatures in all of their dimensions which is accessible to a general audience of students and nonprofessional readers and useful to scholars seeking information outside their own area

PREFACE

of expertise. It contains authoritative articles on a range of topics that together provide an understanding of legislatures in the United States, their membership, processes, powers, and accomplishments since their colonial beginnings. The editors believe that these thematic essays provide the kind of in-depth treatment of each topic, providing a foundation for understanding the range of events and processes that are on display on any given legislative day, or in any particular legislative episode. Obviously there has been a great deal of selectivity in deciding which topics to include. Nevertheless, we believe that the essays included here cover all of the major aspects of the American legislative experience.

At the same time, the editors wished to establish a balance between important historical information concerning a specific theme or topic and the tracing of its development over time on the one hand, and the current status or condition of the various legislative institutions and processes discussed on the other. As a result, the editorial board and the contributors are made up fairly evenly of historians and political scientists, all of whom have their own perspectives and an appreciation of the other's disciplinary perspectives as well. Each contributor is an expert on the matter that he or she has discussed. The editors provided the authors with a specific format to follow and acquainted them with the general aims and shape of the whole work, but they did not insist on a single common approach or on a correct perspective to be followed.

Finally, the editors suggest that the vast number of elements comprising the legislative experience readily divide into six sub-areas: first, the story of the way in which Congress and the state legislatures have developed over two centuries, with particular concern for the similarities and differences in legislative activity in distinct chronological eras; second, an account of the nature of the membership of legislatures, who legislators were and are, demographically, socially and politically, and how they have come to be members; third, a review of the nature of the internal structure and organization of the legislatures once they meet, their specific rules, leadership arrangements, committees and support staffs; fourth, an analysis of the way that the legislators have behaved as they go about their business, their reactions to pressure groups, party demands, and constituency needs; fifth, consideration of some of the main policy areas that legislators address and the policies that they are able to, or fail to, enact; and, sixth and finally, the external relations that legislatures have—that is, their interaction with the other branches of government and the important informal institutions of the political world (such as pressure groups). The *Encyclopedia* is organized into these six specific areas and the essays included are presented chronologically and/or topically within each section. In most cases, Congress, state, and local legislatures are dealt with in separate entries owing to the quite different situations each of them represents. In other cases, where appropriate, the various legislative levels are treated together. Allan G. Bogue took primary responsibility for section one, Garrison Nelson for section two, Joseph Cooper for section three, David Brady for section four, Joel H. Silbey for section five, and Gary Reichard for section six. The editor in chief and each associate editor also contributed substantially to the shaping and direction of all the other sections as well.

The editors are grateful to a number of scholars who gave them advice on broad issues of coverage and inclusion. Yvonne Vallely of Cornell University's History Department provided major assistance to the editor in chief. The staff at Scribner Reference Books, led by Karen Day, publisher, and Sylvia Miller, managing editor, significantly aided in bringing the work to completion. It has been a pleasure for the editors to work with all of them.

Joel H. Silbey

Part I

THE AMERICAN LEGISLATIVE SYSTEM IN HISTORICAL CONTEXT

REPRESENTATION

Samuel C. Patterson

The democratic government of national political communities would be awkward and incomplete, if not impossible, without some system of representation. Representation is a central ingredient of democratic politics, for it allows the will of a nation's citizens to mold and shape public policies through the deliberation and actions of representatives voters have chosen. But to say that a political institution is "representative," or that a legislator "represents" his or her constituents, is to imply a rather subtle complex of relationships. What is meant, then, when an individual or an institution is called a "representative"?

THE MEANINGS OF REPRESENTATION

Political representation concerns individuals and institutions. On the one hand, representation may be said to characterize a relationship between a representative and his or her individual constituents. This may be thought of as a causal relationship in which constituents bring influence to bear upon their representative, or in which the representative educates or persuades his or her constituents to accept a particular preference or solution. But the nexus between each representative and those whom he or she represents may be mainly symbolic or stylistic. On the other hand, representation may be understood in largely holistic terms, so that the central questions turn on the functions of the representative assembly—for example, what authority does the representative body possess in law and custom, or how well does the legislature as an institution represent the nation as a whole? Discussions of representation do not always make this micro/macro distinction clear.

By the same token, the substantive connotation of *representation* is often obscured. When one asks, "Who is the representative around here?" or "What is the representative institution here?" the object of inquiry depends on various implicit meanings. What follows are brief explanations of the different aspects of representation as it is used in widest currency.

Status

Determining who the representative is depends upon the status of the individual or institution. For instance, we may designate as "the representative" that person who has been authorized to serve in this capacity—an agent empowered by law or an individual elected to office. But the authorized person may not be considered representative by any particular constituent, who may regard some other person as properly "standing for" his or her own political position. The latter indicates that individuals may enjoy the status of symbolic representatives. Alternatively, the instrumental representative, the one who "acts for" another, may be neither elected in that other's constituency nor the symbolic representative.

Policy Process

Representation is commonly understood in regard to a policy process, that is, the linkage between the attitudes, desires, interests, or needs of a constituency and the policy decisions of a policy-making body. This nexus is often dealt with as a matter of "congruence": What is the degree of similarity or dissimilarity in the policy stances or demands of the public and the decisions of the legislative body? Or, alternatively, to what extent are individual legislators and their own constituents in accord on issues of public policy? But the question of "responsiveness" in analyzing representation need not be limited to policy responsiveness; representatives may respond to constituents in a number of other ways, including providing services or winning "pork" (special benefits) for their districts.

Support from the Constituency

According to some, representation refers to a systemic configuration in which the representative body enjoys the support of its constituents; citizens adhere to laws enacted by that body and are strongly committed to nurturing and perpetuating it. Emphasizing the supportive input of the public, this understanding of representation derives partly from the recognition that few citizens have the resources to make complex policy demands.

Role of the Representative

Since the eighteenth century, conceptions of representation have often concerned the political role of the representative. The representative is defined as the person who plays a representative role—embracing the style of "delegate" or "trustee," and the purview of "district" or "nation." This concern with the style and focus of the representative role derives from the seminal observations of English parliamentarian Edmund Burke (1729–1797), who told his constituents in Bristol in 1774 that the representative should be a trustee, not a delegate bound by their instructions: "Your representative owes you not his industry only, but his judgment; and he betrays, instead of serving you, if he sacrifices it to your opinion." Burke argued further that the representative should focus on the national interest, and not be bound by the interests of his constituency: "You choose a member, indeed; but when you have chosen him he is not a member of Bristol, but he is a member of *Parliament*."

Procedure

Whether or not an individual or an institution is regarded as representative may depend upon procedures. Representation has been intimately tied to processes of free elections, and the legitimacy of representatives and legislatures has hinged on elections that are free and frequent. Other conditions may apply to elections, for example, equal population apportionment and districting, party competi-

tion, the absence of corruption, regulation of campaign practices and expenditures, and so on. Americans often seem to regard their legislatures as representative if their members are elected in districts drawn so that all are of equal population.

Composition of the Membership

The degree to which a body of political decision makers is representative may, alternatively, turn on the composition of that body. For example, many understand a legislature to be representative to the extent that its membership mirrors the citizenry (a "representative sample"). In this case, the thrust of representation lies in the sociological, ideological, or partisan makeup of the membership. At the same time, some argue that a representative assembly must have an educational, occupational, or social class composition parallel to that of the overall population (rather than, for example, a subregion)—with all kinds of groups and interests present, if not proportionally. To others, the representative body must perfectly reflect the partisan division of the popular vote in the last general election. This normally implies proportional representation (PR), an electoral system whose rules assure proportionality in party representation. Women and minority groups often argue for compositional representation, claiming that a percentage of the legislative membership should mirror the size of their respective groups in the population.

Structural Representation

Although in the American experience legislative institutions have been regarded as central to political representation, other institutions may be regarded as representative. In communist systems, the Communist party has been regarded as the primary representative entity. In some countries the army is seen as the most representative institution. The executive branch or the bureaucracy may be regarded as representative in some senses. Certainly it is true that, in the United States, the president is considered a representative of the people. However, because this essay is concerned with legislative representation, these and other forms of structural representation will not be discussed.

Virtual Representation

Theoretically, a person may be represented by someone other than his or her respective elected representative. Accordingly, conservatives in many parts of the country may think of themselves as best represented by someone like conservative Senator Jesse Helms (R.-N.C.), and many liberal Democrats may similarly regard Senator Edward M. Kennedy (D.-Mass.). Such symbolic representation must be commonplace in congressional politics, in which each constituency elects only one representative, and the minority partisans may feel under- or unrepresented in some respects. Many times constituents are "free riders" whose political or economic interests are served or advanced by representatives not of their own choosing.

"Virtual" representation surely is widespread and unavoidable in all political systems. In the eighteenth century, however, the doctrine of virtual representation provided a justification for depriving any direct representation in the Parliament to large proportions of the citizenry. In England, Edmund Burke invoked this doctrine to argue that "rotten borroughs"—communities under- or unrepresented in Parliament—were effectively (or virtually) represented by members of Parliament from other communities with the same or similar interests. Burke argued that "virtual representation is that in which there is a communion of interests, and a sympathy in feelings and desires, between those who act in the name of any description of people, and the people in whose name they act, though the trustees are not actually chosen by them." At the same time, Burke took the side of the American colonists when he agreed that they were not even virtually represented in the British House of Commons, despite claims to the contrary made by some members of the British Parliament.

Thus because the concept of representation is ambiguous and admits of various definitions and emphases, it is important to keep in mind what conception is involved when undertaking an analysis of representation.

THE AMERICAN REPRESENTATIVE TRADITION

Colonial Americans inherited two lines of thinking about political representation. One, the doctrine of virtual representation, was firmly accepted in English governmental practice from at least the sixteenth century, when Sir Thomas Smith wrote (in 1583) that "the consent of Parliament is taken to be every man's consent." The other, a concept of "actual" representation, flowed from the thinking of the Levellers, a group of seventeenth-century Puritans who advocated direct democracy and accepted the authority of representatives only if these individuals spoke unequivocally for the people.

Although English Whigs of the eighteenth century, such as Edmund Burke, believed that the people should share in the governmental process, and that Parliament should take constituents' desires and interests fully into account, they also took the elitist view that considerable distance should separate the rulers and the ruled. The citizenry could have its voice in Parliament, but Parliament's role should be limited: Parliament should, the Whigs thought, meet briefly to authorize taxes and vent grievances, but should not take a substantial role in the processes of governing. This old-fashioned view is, in essence, still held by some of the English in the early 1990s.

REPRESENTATION EMERGENT

Representation in America emerged over one and a half centuries of colonial, state, and early national experience. American ideas and practices of representation grew directly from this long experience, rather than from theory or doctrine laid down for implementation by representatives and represented. British parliamentary customs and representational expediencies influenced American development, but practices of representation in America were substantially homegrown. This owed in part to the long distances between colonies and imperial headquarters in London: colonial political development was, for much of the emergent period, left to its own devices. In part, independently developed colonial practices of representation reflected the colonial politicians' vigorous and persistent claim to the rights and privileges of the English, including the privilege of real, immediate, and direct representation in lawmaking.

By the eve of the American Revolution, legislative representation was very well known to Americans. By the 1690s the legislatures had become a well-established feature of colonial government, remarkably similar institutions bicameral in structure and exercising law-making powers, including the power of the purse.

The Colonial Assemblies

Representative assemblies emerged, stabilized, and took permanent shape within about two decades after the colonies were established. The first colonial assemblies met in Virginia in 1619; in Massachusetts, Maryland, and Connecticut in the 1630s; in Rhode Island in 1647; in North and South Carolina and the Jersey proprietaries between 1665 and 1681; and in New Hampshire, Pennsylvania, and New York in the 1680s. An assembly emerged much later in Delaware in 1729, and in Georgia in 1755. These new legislative bodies were small (ranging in size from ten to twelve members in Connecticut, North Carolina, East Jersey, and New Hampshire to forty-two members in Pennsylvania). All except for the Pennsylvania legislature became bicameral in the seventeenth century. Although these assemblies developed somewhat differently in different colonial settings and were variously affected by English parliamentary practices and forms, historian Michael Kammen notes that "beginning with the 1690s, the representative assembly can be said to have become a fixed feature of English colonial administration" (*Deputyes and Libertyes,* p. 57).

By the middle of the eighteenth century, the houses of representatives in Massachusetts and Pennsylvania had become the most powerful of the colonial assemblies, with the South Carolina Commons and the New York House of Assembly running close seconds. These representative bodies exercised almost complete political authority in their colonies, including fiscal power, and they eclipsed those institutions—royal or proprietary governors or their appointed councils—intended by the British crown to wield authority.

Although executive-legislative relations were fairly conflictual in the eighteenth-century colonies, by and large the colonial assemblies attained hegemony by conducting routine legislative business, enacting legislation and establishing governing practices. Pragmatically, the colonists claimed their political rights as Englishmen, including the privilege of representation. William Smith, a New York assembly member in the 1750s, epitomized the colonists' viewpoint when he asserted, "Our representatives . . . are tenacious in their opinion that the inhabitants of this colony . . . have a right to participate in the legislative power, and that the . . . assembl[y] here is wisely substituted instead of representation in parliament which . . . would, at this remote distance, be extremely inconvenient and dangerous."

These assemblies sunk deep roots into their colonial constituencies. They came to show remarkable self-confidence, and firm willingness to assert and protect their autonomy and authority. As they became important training grounds for leadership the colonial statehouses gave rise to leaders such as Richard Henry Lee, Thomas Jefferson, and Patrick Henry in Virginia; John and Samuel Adams in Massachusetts; and John Dickinson and Benjamin Franklin in Pennsylvania.

The colonial assemblies emerged and developed without the benefit of a sophisticated theory of political representation. The populism of colonial politics and the rivalry between colonial and imperial interests encouraged governing practices that fostered representative democracy. Representatives were allocated to communities—towns and counties—two from each town or county in Massachusetts and Virginia, a larger number for more populous counties in colonies such as New York (where New York city and county was accorded four representatives).

In general, members of the colonial assemblies were elected annually by the adult male "freeholders," or property owners, of each county or town. These freeholders often constituted a sizable majority of a given region's male population, so participation in elections was potentially quite substantial (although actual turnout for elections was often modest). Representatives were required to be residents of their constituencies, and it was commonplace for constituents to "instruct" their representatives how to vote in the assembly.

Eighteenth-century colonial politics came to gravitate around a growing belief that the colonists could not properly be represented "virtually" in the British House of Commons, on the one hand, and the emerging practices of representative democracy. Colonial charters and laws came under increasing pressure to widen the suffrage by relaxing property qualifications and extending fair representation to the growing frontier regions.

The idea of actual (as opposed to virtual) representation gradually gained currency, and some leaders advocated an assembly composed in a way that would mirror the socioeconomic diversity of a colony's adult male population. By the time of the American Revolution in 1775, elected representative assemblies operated in every colony, taking the lion's share of governmental power and practicing representative politics in a manner quite similar to today.

Representation in the State Legislatures

By the outbreak of the revolutionary war, colonial governments were already effectively in the hands of the politicians who controlled the colonial assemblies. The new state constitutions were written in the midst of intensified discourse over the proper representation of citizens in the state legislatures.

The leaders in some of the new states called for legislatures composed in a way so that their memberships would be a "mirror image" of the public. One such leader, John Adams, argued that "the greatest care should be employed in constituting [the] representative assembly." He advised that "it should be in miniature an exact portrait of the people at large," so that it would "think, feel, reason, and act like them." This Populist spirit was echoed in the pages of the *Essex Result,* a Massachusetts newspaper:

> Representatives should have the same view, and interests with the people at large. They should think, feel, and act like them, and in fine, should be an exact miniature of their constituents. They should be (if we may use the expression) the whole body politic, with all its property, rights, and privileges, reduced to a smaller scale, every part being diminished in just proportion.

Political realities prevented this mirror-image understanding of representation from serious implementation. But almost immediately after independence, the new states increased the numbers of representatives from towns and counties, substantially enlarging the state legislatures. In the eight states that increased representation, legislatures were enlarged from 53 to 121 in average membership.

The enlargement of legislatures opened them to representatives from the lower social orders. In a number of states, greater representation was accorded frontier areas, producing a westward shift in the balance of political power and increasing the political influence of small farmers. By 1780, a large majority of the representatives in states such as Massachusetts, New Jersey, and Pennsylvania were of only moderate economic status. In occupational terms, farmers, shopkeepers, and artisans came into the state legislatures in greater proportions than was true during the colonial era. Consequently, the early state legislatures represented their citizens far more accurately than had the colonial assemblies.

Representation was democratized in the post-Revolutionary state constitutions by relaxing qualifications for both holding public office and voting, and by making a greater number of offices elective. And politics became more public: the publicity given to laws and legislative activity increased, legislative politics were conducted in secrecy less often, and recorded votes taken in the legislative chambers were more often required and published.

To say that the early state legislatures were roughly representative of their citizenry does not mean that they would have met current equal population standards of legislative apportionment, although some of the early legislative bodies—even some state senates—were not far from such a standard. Many of the post-Revolutionary state constitutions and laws provided for fixed representation for counties or towns, following the practice of the colonial assemblies. In some states, though, additional representatives were provided to towns or counties on a population basis, usually determined on the basis of the taxpaying citizenry.

In the 1780s and 1790s the apportionment formulas sometimes produced quite representative legislative houses on the basis of the population's geographical distribution. In Massachusetts, for instance, the four most overrepresented counties in 1784 contained 48 percent of the apportionment population, and were apportioned 52 percent of the legislative seats. In fact, a number of communities failed to send their full number of delegates and, while Maine (then part of Massachusetts) was considerably underrepresented, the western counties actually were represented in excess of their populations.

Nonetheless, the extent of malapportionment with respect to population was considerable in the early state legislatures. Representation was yet to be understood primarily in equal population terms, and population was seldom considered the major basis for allotting representation. Indeed, apportionments tended to be resolved not on principle but rather in light of pragmatic political considerations. In some states this meant, in effect, that apportionments were unchangeable because opening the issue of representation would have produced unwanted conflicts that were better left alone, or because the mobilization of bias was rigid enough to prevent change.

Thus, in Connecticut, King Charles's charter of 1662 served as the state's constitution until 1818; it provided for one or two assembly members per town, in an arrangement that was not altered until 1874. Although this kind of apportionment was apparently viable in the 1780s and 1790s (when the population was fairly widely dispersed among the towns), by the late 1880s it meant that sixty small towns with an aggregate population of less than twelve thousand had seventy-six representatives while New Haven, with nearly eighteen thousand people, had only two.

In other states, reapportionment struggles were persistent and bitter. Adherence to the imperial charter's apportionment formula precipitated Dorr's Rebellion in Rhode Island in the 1840s. In Virginia, persistent attempts to reapportion the legislature were made after 1782. That state, like many others, was apportioned on an ad hoc basis, and the legislature was not willing to establish a regular population basis for reapportionment, despite efforts by Thomas Jefferson, James Madison, and many of their successors in the House of Burgesses to do so. Until 1830, the apportionment allocated two burgesses per county, and then awarded additional representatives to the cities. From the post-Revolutionary days, representatives from the counties west of the Blue Ridge Mountains favored straight-population apportionment (based upon the census of the white population, called the "white basis"), and the eastern delegates insisted on a property or taxation basis for representation in order to protect their slave property. The reapportionment issue in Virginia was a part of a more general struggle for political power, with the cleavages over the issue reflected also in interparty turmoil concerning fiscal and monetary policy, internal improvements, and the broader issue of slavery.

The post-Revolutionary state legislatures did not do much to alter their basis of representation in laws regulating citizens' right to vote in elections. Enlargement of the legislatures was not matched in the states by measurable expansion of the suffrage. In any event, voting was restricted to white males who were twenty-one years old or older. (Universal women's suffrage was not accepted in the United States until the passage of the Nineteenth Amendment in 1920; nationally, the voting age was reduced to eighteen years of age when the Twenty-sixth Amendment was passed in 1971; and voting by blacks was not effectively protected nationally until the enactment of the voting-rights legislation of the mid-1960s.) Property or taxpaying qualifications for voting prevailed in all of the early states, but because most white men were freeholders or taxpayers, the electorates of the states were, in fact quite large.

That political activists and citizens in the post-Revolutionary states understood their representatives as delegates—that is to say, bound to present the opinions and desires of their constituents—is evidenced by the commonplace practice of "instructions" or "mandates." In New England, for instance, town meetings frequently adopted instructions for the town's delegate to the state assembly. This practice was not an innovation of independence and statehood—seventeenth-century colonials in Virginia and Massachusetts often instructed their representatives.

In a celebrated instance, Massachusetts towns instructed their colonial assembly members on the Stamp Act question; John Adams drafted the instructions for the town of Braintree in 1765.

Adams wrote in his diary: "I prepared a draught of instructions at home and carried them with me. The cause of the meeting was explained at some length, and the state and danger of the country pointed out; a committee was appointed to prepare instructions, of which I was nominated one. We retired to Mr. Niles' house, my draught was produced, and unanimously adopted without amendment, reported to the town, and accepted without a dissenting voice."

In 1776, the Massachusetts House of Representatives adopted a resolution calling on towns to instruct their representatives as to whether or not they supported the Declaration of Independence. In the same year, the Boston town meeting instructed its representatives regarding several detailed provisions of the new state constitution, including favoring the wider representation of citizens and the separation of powers between the legislative, executive, and judicial branches of the state government.

It may well be true that instructions from constituents to state representatives were frequently putative, instruments of leadership control as often as straightforward expressions of constituents' preferences. Accordingly, historian Ralph V. Harlow has argued that the instructions for Boston state legislators were hammered out by a clique of leaders—Samuel Adams, his cousin John Adams, and other lieutenants—of a political club, the Caucus Club, that met in Tom Dawes's garret. Harlow claimed that this club was

> responsible for the pronunciamentos issued by the town meeting. . . . [C]aucus, town meeting, and House of Representatives were all linked together in the person of Samuel Adams. Such being the case, instead of being bona fide instructions from constituents to representatives, these publications of the town were nothing but the declaration of the policies of the leaders. Measures recommended by a machine-controlled town meeting were consistently ratified by the House of Representatives, directed by the same power. (p. 31)

While constituent instruction of delegates to the state legislatures was quite commonplace in the early history of the United States, it operated most effectively and persisted longest where representatives were chosen by town meetings. In other areas the practice of instruc-

tions gradually fell into disuse, owing to the difficulty of assembling constituents, although it persisted in states such as New Hampshire for many years.

The Continental Congress

The first national legislature, the Continental Congress, was a "revolutionary legislature," first convened in 1774 in the aftermath of restrictive new British laws involving trade regulations, governmental structure, the administration of justice, and British military prerogatives in the colonies (colonial radicals called these the "intolerable acts"). Its fifty-six members had been selected by the colonial assemblies (but only in Pennsylvania were they chosen directly by the legislature) or by conventions especially designated to select delegates.

From the beginning, the unit rule prevailed in decision-making—the congressmen from each colony (and later, each state) together cast one collective vote. The issue of representation was debated earnestly in Congress, and there were those who advocated so-called equal representation, apportioning the number of delegates from each colony on the basis of population. However, in the absence of a population census for the colonies, population-based apportionment of the congressional membership was not practical. More important, political considerations (anxieties of the small states about domination by the large states; the view that effective action required the agreement of all colonies) dictated that each colony should be entitled to cast one vote apiece.

The representation question underwent serious debate and discussion when the nation's first national constitution, the Articles of Confederation, was considered. But in October 1777, Congress rejected proposals to apportion congressional membership on the basis of population or the state's contribution to the national treasury. Each state would continue to have one vote in congressional decision-making. Article V provided that

> delegates shall be annually appointed in such manner as the legislature of each State shall direct, to meet in Congress. . . .
> No State shall be represented in Congress by less than two, nor by more than seven

members; and no person shall be . . . a delegate for more than three years. . . .

Each State shall maintain its own delegates in a meeting of the States, and while they act as members of the committee of the States.

In determining questions in the United States, in Congress assembled, each State shall have one vote.

The ideas of equal population representation and popular election of members of the national legislature were not very seriously entertained until the late 1780s, when a new national constitution came under fervent discussion.

The most far-reaching legislation enacted by the Continental Congress was the Northwest Ordinance of 1787, which provided for the establishment of new states in the West. Among other things, the ordinance called for the creation of bicameral legislatures in which membership in the house of representatives would be allocated on the basis of population.

The ordinance read that "For every five hundred free male inhabitants, there shall be one representative, and so on progressively with the number of free male inhabitants shall the right or representation increase, until the number of representatives shall amount to twenty-five, after which the number and proportion of representatives shall be regulated by the legislature."

In addition to restricting the suffrage to males, eligibility to vote required property ownership—"a freehold in fifty acres of land." Representation on the basis of population, which was the basis for practice in each state, garnered widespread support, and the anomaly of equal representation of the states, rather than of people, in the Continental Congress, became increasingly unacceptable to citizens and uncomfortable for the political leadership.

REPRESENTATION AT THE FOUNDING

While the Continental Congress met in New York, the Constitutional Convention had convened in Philadelphia. Congress found it difficult to maintain the quorum needed to complete action on the Northwest Ordinance because a number of congressmen also served as delegates to the Philadelphia convention. Moreover, the conflicts that marked the deliberations of Congress—between large and small states, and between north and south—were reflected in the debates and decisions of the convention. Issues of representation were central to the deliberations of the convention, and to its aftermath in the ratification debates in the states.

The Distribution of Seats

When the Continental Congress debated the Articles of Confederation, the nation's first constitution, it rejected proposals that the confederate Congress be based upon population representation or representation based upon taxpaying, and provided one vote for each state regardless of its population or the size of its congressional delegation. The Constitutional Convention of 1787, in effect, reopened the whole question of representation in a national legislature, and the resolution of the representation question provided the most significant political compromise at the convention. The so-called Virginia Plan provided for a bicameral legislature with population-based representation in both houses; the New Jersey Plan provided a unicameral body with equal representation of the states. The New Jersey Plan was defeated early in the convention, but representation nevertheless remained the focus of extended debate. "The great difficulty," said James Madison, "lies in the affair of representation; if this could be adjusted, all others would be surmountable."

The great compromise of the convention was the decision to create a bicameral Congress, with a House of Representatives based upon population and a Senate upon equal state representation. This agreement came to be called the Connecticut Compromise because the motion to adopt it was offered by the Connecticut delegation. House members were to be allocated to each state on the basis of an apportionment standard—which, in the beginning, would be one representative for every thirty thousand people in the state. But all states would receive at least one representative, and in those states entitled to more than one representative, districts would be created, their boundaries drawn by the state legislatures. And what would be the term of office of representatives? Some delegates favored annual elections, following the practice in the states at the time; others, including James Madison, favored three-year terms. The convention compromised, agreeing to a two-year term for representatives.

The Senate was to be a federal house, where each state would be represented by its two senators. The Constitution provided that a state's U.S. senators would be selected by the state legislature, not by the voters directly. This was the practice until 1913, when the Seventeenth Amendment to the U.S. Constitution was ratified, providing for the direct popular election of senators. Some delegates at the convention preferred a seven-year term for senators; a six-year term was finally agreed on, with a third of the members being chosen every second year.

The Composition of Congress

What kinds of people should serve as representatives? The Constitution required only that members be residents of the state they represent, and that representatives and senators be at least twenty-five and thirty years old, respectively. Life expectancy being what it was two hundred years ago, thirty-year-olds were then regarded as relatively old.

But the founders thought that the constitutional rules would induce a congressional composition well beyond the matters of age and residency. It was important that, somehow, the wisest and best be elected to serve as representatives. This, in turn, hinged partly on the nature of elections, and partly on claims about the varying effects of the size of the legislative body.

The founders had agreed that the first sitting of the House of Representatives should include sixty-five members, who were distributed among the states in accord with their estimated population sizes. (The decision to give the original thirteen states two senators each meant a first Senate of twenty-six members.) They provided for a decennial census of population so that, every decade, the house could be reapportioned, and they assumed that the house would grow in size as new states came into the federation.

Some politicians thought the larger legislative assembly would tend to bring prudent individuals to its membership. Melancton Smith told the New York ratifying convention that, "by increasing the number of representatives, we open a door for the admission of the substantial yeomanry of our country who, being possessed of the habits of economy, will be cautious of imprudent expenditures. . . ." But Smith and others also made the "mirror-image" argument. He averred that "the idea that naturally suggests itself to our minds when we speak of representatives is that they resemble those they represent." He thought a proper blend of men from the "natural aristocracy" and representation of the yeomanry would make for an ideal legislature.

But opponents of the new constitution—antifederalists—took a different view. In general, they argued that a House of sixty-five members and a Senate of twenty-six members were too small for proper representation. These, they argued, would be elitist bodies. The minority report of the Pennsylvania ratifying convention gave the crux of the argument:

> Men of the most elevated rank in life will alone be chosen. The other orders in the society, such as farmers, traders, and mechanics, who all ought to have a competent number of their best informed men in the legislature, shall be totally unrepresented. . . . [Congress] will consist of the lordly and high minded; of men who will have no congenial feelings with the people, but a perfect indifference for, and contempt of them; [it] will consist of those harpies of power that prey upon the very vitals, that riot on the miseries of the community.

John Jay, Alexander Hamilton, and James Madison defended the prospective composition of Congress in articles supporting the ratification of the new Constitution; and Madison and Hamilton further defended it in the New York and Virginia ratifying conventions.

In *The Federalist,* no. 57, Madison argued that the new Constitution provided for such widespread participation in elections and opportunity for office-seeking that the House of Representatives would not be "taken from that class of citizens which will have least sympathy with the mass of the people." Hamilton tackled the issue at the New York ratifying convention. "Who are the aristocracy among us?" he exclaimed rhetorically. He answered that "there are men who are rich, men who are poor, some who are wise, and others who are not—that indeed every distinguished man is an aristocrat."

Besides, he argued, "if the people have it in their option to elect their most meritorious men, is this to be considered an objection?" Both Madison and Hamilton asserted that Congress would be no more or less elitist in its makeup than the state legislatures—the national House of Representatives would be chosen by the same electorate selecting state legislators; and, U.S. senators would be picked by the state legislatures directly.

Constituency Representation

When the U.S. Constitution was framed and implemented in the 1780s, populism was a widespread and growing tendency. In keeping with this sentiment, the founders advocated a constitutional system they thought would both keep government close to the people and prevent ill-considered legislation, control by unscrupulous majorities, or rule by the mob.

Free and frequent election of representatives was viewed as the cornerstone of true democracy. Said Hamilton, "the true principle of a republic is that the people should choose whom they please to govern them." But free elections occur in a constitutional system "where, in the organization of the government the legislative, executive, and judicial branches are rendered distinct; . . . the legislative is divided into separate houses; and the operations of each are controlled by various checks and balances, and . . . by the vigilance and weight of the state governments. . . ."

It was widely agreed by the founders, underscored by straightforward advocacy on more than one occasion by both Madison and Hamilton, that in a representative democracy (a "republic") close ties would bind representative and constituents together. Yet, by the 1780s, citizens had come to distrust their state legislatures, much as before the Revolution they distrusted the colonial governments. Some sought a cure for wayfaring or self-serving representation in constituency mandates. When the First Congress met in 1789, a constitutional amendment was proposed that would have permitted a constituency to instruct, or issue mandates to, its representatives in Congress. When what ultimately would become the Bill of Rights' First Amendment was debated, Congressman Thomas T. Tucker (Fed.-

S.C.) proposed to amend the freedom of assembly clause in a way that would have guaranteed the right of the people "to instruct their representatives." The proposal failed by a vote of 41–10, perhaps largely because of Madison's opposition. But the practice of constituents' instructing representatives and senators was not so unusual throughout the nineteenth century. Until the Civil War period, state legislatures commonly instructed the U.S. senators they had chosen, and this practice remains vestigially today in state legislatures' adopting resolutions memorializing Congress to take, or refrain from taking, some action.

Madison's theory of representation embodied constraints and practices aimed at ensuring, as much as humanly possible, that the elected representatives would be men of wisdom and virtue. He favored large-sized constituencies because he thought small constituencies would be too prone to elect representatives with narrow, selfish interests at heart. The purpose of a proper system of representation, Madison argued in No. 57 of *The Federalist,* ought to be "first to obtain for rulers men who possess most wisdom to discern, and most virtue to pursue, the common good of society; and in the next place, to take the most effectual precautions for keeping them virtuous whilst they continue to hold their public trust."

Virtual Representation in a Federal Senate

The Connecticut Compromise, providing for equal representation of the states in the Senate regardless of population variations, to some extent allayed the fears of the small states that they would, in the new government, be swamped by large states like New York and Virginia. Madison did not favor such a senate, and accepted the compromise only because such a federal house had the support of a majority at the Constitutional Convention, and "that which has been proposed by the convention is probably the most congenial with the public opinion." His argument in *The Federalist,* nos. 62 and 63, in defense of equal state representation in the Senate and selection of senators by the state legislatures was rather diffident and tepid. His case for the Senate was even more subdued in the Virginia ratifying convention.

REPRESENTATION

In the Virginia convention, firebrand Patrick Henry framed the issue. He thundered at Madison:

> The honorable gentleman was pleased to say that the representation of the people was the vital principle of this government.... We contended with the British about representation. They offered us such a representation as Congress now does. They called it virtual representation.... Is there but virtual representation in the upper house?

Henry's contention was, of course, that citizens from populous states, like his own Virginia, would only be virtually and not "actually" represented in a body in which "the two petty states of Rhode Island and Delaware" would have the same number of senators as Virginia. Madison skirted the issue, saying only that Thomas Jefferson, absent from the country in France, approved the new Constitution. In fact, Madison said, Jefferson admired several parts of the new constitution "which have been reprobated with vehemence in this house," and, in particular, "he is captivated with the equality of suffrage in the Senate, which the honorable gentleman [Mr. Henry] calls the rotten part of this Constitution."

In *The Federalist*, no. 62, Madison made his case in support of representation in the Senate:

> If ... it be right that ... every [state] ought to have a *proportional* share in the government, and that among independent and sovereign states bound together ... [the states], however unequal in size, ought to have an *equal* share in the common councils, it does not appear to be without some reason that in a compound republic, partaking both of the national and federal character, the government ought to be founded on a mixture of the principles of proportional and equal representation.

He thought of the new system of congressional representation as mainly a matter of political compromise, not theory, "called for by the voice, and still more loudly by the political situation, of America."

Today, of course, senators are elected directly by the people, and the Senate is much less clearly a strictly federal house than was intended two hundred years ago. Accordingly, equal representation of the states in the Senate has come to seem increasingly anomalous in today's world of insistence on the precision of equal population representation in most environments. Still, even today, demands for reapportionment of the Senate are never discussed or even voiced.

The Represented

One matter upon which there was little controversy among the founders concerned the electorate, that is, the represented. It was widely agreed that the qualifications for voting in national elections should be those provided in state laws governing voting eligibility for membership in the state legislatures. To Madison this was largely a practical matter—"to have reduced the different qualifications in the different states to one uniform rule would probably have been as dissatisfactory to some of the states as it would have been difficult to the convention" (*The Federalist*, no. 52).

A more controversial concern regarding the represented was the issue of property. In the late eighteenth century it was widely believed that in a true republic both population and property would be represented in the councils of government. In general, the founders agreed that population could serve as a surrogate for wealth, inasmuch as property and taxpaying were quite widely distributed among men. Moreover, the founders made sure that the Constitution provided for the apportionment of direct taxes—levies on the states—on the basis of population. But the slave states of the South presented a special problem: how were slaves to be counted?

The founders agreed to a Three-fifths Compromise; as long as slavery existed, only three-fifths of the black population of slave states would be counted for the purpose of representation and the apportionment of direct taxes. This appealed to the southern slave states because, although their representation in the House was smaller than it would have been if slaves had been counted as free men, their collective tax liability would be discounted according to the three-fifths ratio.

Some northern politicians swallowed this reluctantly. Thomas Dawes of Boston, delegate to the Massachusetts ratifying convention, bemoaned the racial prejudices of southerners, but conceded that "it would not do to abolish slavery by an act of Congress in a moment, and so destroy what our southern brethren consider as property." Hamilton argued similarly in the New York ratifying convention, "it is the unfortunate situation of the southern states to have a great part of their population, as well as property, in blacks"; he acknowledged, however, that without the three-fifths compromise "no union could possibly have been formed." Despite its practical necessity at the time, in retrospect we can reflect soberly on the nearly two centuries it took to begin to deal properly with the representation of blacks in American politics.

This method of counting only three-fifths of the black population for purposes of representation ended when the Fourteenth Amendment was added to the Constitution in 1868, following the Civil War. That amendment provides that representatives are to be distributed among the states "according to their respective numbers, counting the whole number of persons in each state, excluding Indians not taxed." (For apportionment purposes, there were no "Indians not taxed" after 1940.)

REPRESENTATIVE PRACTICE UNFOLDING

The Constitution of 1789 established the framework around which issues of political representation would be debated and determined in the future. Yet as the new nation experienced steady population growth, a vast continent had to be absorbed, and representation accorded to new states. Political parties came, unexpectedly to some, to provide a crucial vehicle for representation, mediating between citizens and government. Populist demands for political equality grew to a crescendo after the Civil War. Demands were voiced for popular election of senators, for actual representation of blacks and women, for constraints on the representation of interests, for reapportionment and "one person, one vote" in devising constituencies, and even for direct representation through adoption of the devices of the referendum and recall. Increasingly, citizens looked to the presidency, rather than to Congress, to represent their demands, interests, and concerns.

Apportionment and the Size of Congress

In defense of the new Constitution, both Madison and Hamilton argued in behalf of the decision to set the size of the first House at sixty-five members. They argued that sixty-five members was a reasonable size, large enough to ensure diversity and prevent undue influence on the part of narrow, selfish, or imprudent interests. As Madison predicted, the size of the House grew rapidly in the early years of the Republic; there were 106 House members throughout the 1790s, and by 1800 the House, with 142 members, had more than doubled its original size. House membership grew steadily until 1910 when it reached its present size, 435 members.

Because the Constitution was vague on the appropriate procedures and methods for electing members of Congress, congressional apportionment was an episodic problem throughout the nineteenth century. Of course, the Senate grew by two as each new state was admitted to the Union. (Since the apportionment of the Senate, so to speak, is etched into the Constitution at two senators per state, its size and apportionment have never been at issue.) But House membership, apportioned to the states on the basis of their census populations, presented sometimes knotty questions for the distribution of seats.

Representation based upon population apportionment, rather than upon territory alone, was a new and untried system. None of the colonial assemblies had practiced population apportionment. Even after the Revolution, fewer than half of the states reapportioned their legislatures on a population basis. So practical experience with population apportionment of legislatures was rather scarce. Little wonder, then, that various experiments with apportional practices and formulas were tried over the course of the nineteenth century.

The original House membership was distributed among the thirteen states in accord with their estimated populations: one congressman for every thirty thousand people. After the census of 1790, it was decided to increase this number to thirty-three thousand in order to slow the growth of the House; that yielded a House of 105 members. The apportionment formula was seemingly simple—divide each

REPRESENTATION

state's census population (counting slaves at a three-fifths discount, and excluding nontaxpaying Indians) by thirty-three thousand to derive the number of House members to which it would be entitled. But what if this formula results in a fraction?

The founders were unable to work out the apportionment rules in detail, so the Constitution is silent on the specific method of apportioning the House. In the early decades of congressional struggle with apportionment, members tended to think about the problem as a matter of setting the number of persons who would be represented by each congressman—just as the Constitution had required that there be no more than one congressman for every thirty-thousand souls. Having set the ratio, the size of the House was allowed to float upward. But from the beginning, members were well aware that different ratios and the handling of fractions could variously affect the representation of large versus small states.

In 1792, Congress passed the first apportionment act after spirited debate. It provided for rounding upward of fractions of .5 at least one-half, giving a state an additional representative in such a case; and this method of apportionment came to be called the "method of major fractions." As it happened, President George Washington vetoed the bill on rather technical grounds (at the advice of Secretary of State Thomas Jefferson), in the first congressional enactment to suffer a presidential veto. The House attempted, but failed, to override the president's veto. Then, Congress passed a new apportionment bill that contained a formula recommended by Jefferson. It apportioned House membership to the states based solely on the whole number obtained when a state's population was divided by the representation ratio; this came to be called the "method of rejected fractions."

After every decennial census, Congress again agonized over the apportionment rules. Jefferson's method was continued through the 1830s, but the fact that it seemed to favor the larger states precipitated objections to it. After the 1840 census, Congress changed the apportionment rules, providing that, first, the size of the House be determined; then, divide that figure into the total apportionment population of the nation to derive the apportionment ratio; then, divide each state's population by this

ratio, and award congressmen to each state based on the resulting whole number and fraction more than one-half. Proposed by Senator Daniel Webster (Whig-Mass.), this became known as the "Webster method." These three apportionment methods—major fractions, rejected fractions, and Webster's—were variously reinvented later in European countries, and are known under various aliases (most commonly as the "method of greatest remainders," the "d'Hondt rule," and the "Sainte-Lague method," respectively).

Beginning in 1850, six reapportionments were conducted following what was called the "Vinton method" after its sponsor, Representative Samuel F. Vinton (Whig-Ohio). This involved a variant of Webster's method, using a priority list of fractional sizes to determine which states would get additional House seats. In practice, though, Congress departed from the prescribed procedure to enlarge the size of the House so that no state would lose members following a federal census. By 1920 it had become clear, on the one hand, that the House would grow to unacceptable proportions if its size were not fixed, but on the other, that fixing it would mean that states might lose House seats in future reapportionments. Congress could not agree on a reapportionment of the House after the 1920 census, and there followed a sequence of debates, proposals, and votes on a number of apportionment schemes.

Finally, in 1929, Congress enacted an apportionment law that established a permanent and automatic method for redistributing House seats every ten years. The size of the House was fixed at 435 members. House membership was then reapportioned, in 1930 and 1940, on the basis of a modified method of major fractions. In 1941, Congress established a new apportionment formula called the "method of equal proportions," which yields priority values for each state indicating its entitlement to representation in the House. This method minimizes the differences between any two states in the average population per representative.

Only after 1842 did Congress require that states establish single-member congressional districts; until then most of the small states elected House members statewide (although congressional seats are allocated to the states under congressional legislation, congressional district boundary lines are drawn by the state legislatures). Thereafter, apportionment legislation often contained language requiring districts that are equal in population size. Notwithstanding the prevailing law, the differences between the largest and the smallest congressional districts in a state were often very large, a condition called malapportionment.

By the 1960s, disparities in both national and state legislative district sizes had grown dramatically, partly because of population migration and partly because of the inaction of state legislatures. In Texas, for instance, the largest congressional district embraced 951,527 people, while the smallest had a population of only 216,731; some state legislative districts were even more disparate in population size. Such inequalities led the U.S. Supreme Court to render several historic decisions between 1962 and 1964 dealing with malapportionment (the pioneer state-legislative case is *Baker* v. *Carr*, 1962; the key congressional case is *Wesberry* v. *Sanders*, 1964). The Court held that a state legislature must draw boundary lines so that legislative districts are substantially equal in population. Thus, the Court established the doctrine of equal-population apportionment, or "one person, one vote."

Spatial and population considerations have always marked the representation debate in the United States. In the case of state legislatures, distributing members over the territory and drawing district boundaries is a single process. In contrast, congressional representation depends on two separate processes: apportionment of seats to the states, done by Congress; and districting, done by the state legislatures. Congress never has been substantially malapportioned—considering that the Constitution entitled every state to at least one representative (and two senators), House members have always been distributed among the states according to population, at least within policymakers' best efforts. Districting, required of the state legislatures, was sometimes neglected or done so as to produce disparities between rural and urban areas, resulting in maldistricting. The "reapportionment revolution" of the 1960s succeeded: today, Congress and the state legislatures conform to the equal population standard.

The population deformity of legislative districting may or may not have political consequences; the partisan deformity of districting does. "Gerrymandering" occurs when constituency boundaries are drawn deliberately to advantage one political party over another. (The term *gerrymander* was coined when the Massachusetts legislature drew a salamander-shaped district in 1812 to benefit the Democratic party led by Governor Elbridge Gerry.) The federal courts have hesitated to enter this redistricting thicket because gerrymandering can be hard to prove, is often ineffective, and submits to no easy standard. (It is relatively easy to require all districts to be equal in population, but how could a standard political party composition be required?) In a recent case (*Davis* v. *Bandemer*, 1986) the U.S. Supreme Court held that partisan gerrymandering could be unconstitutional, but no such gerrymander has, in fact, been invalidated. So-called racial gerrymandering—discrimination against racial or ethnic minorities in the drawing of district boundaries—has been more amendable to judicial or legislative regulation.

Constituency and Party Representation

In legislatures, two combinations of influences affect how representatives conceive their job and what they do, once elected. One of these is political party influence; the other is constituency influence. These two bases of representation operate in tandem and in tension. The two may go hand in glove, as when a partisan constituency chooses an ideologically sensitive representative; or, alternatively, the two may conflict, as when representatives perceive contradictions between the demands of their party and the interests of their constituents.

In the United States, constituency representation has been the dominant ethos. In the formative years of the Republic, colonial assemblymen, state legislators, and congressmen propounded the ideal of constituency loyalty. The practice of "instructions" epitomized faith in the delegate or agency representation that adherence to constituency interests implies. Madison opposed instructions because he believed that the representative must be able to rise above narrow and selfish constituency interests to support what is best for the nation as a whole. He favored large districts because they would likely be diverse, and the representative would be less prone to being controlled by any single interest. Madison sought to frame and defend a constitutional system that could cure "the mischiefs of faction" through the representation of many interests.

Constituency representation has referred to complex networks tying representatives and represented together, and invoking all of the modern technologies of mass communications and campaigning. The contemporary representative is a professional, serving in a highly institutionalized legislature, and confronting a large number of very technical issues. When the representative's constituents are uninterested or uninformed, he or she is called upon to make judgments about what is in the public interest. Elections assure that, in those cases when constituents care or can be aroused about an issue (for instance, civil rights or social welfare issues in recent decades), representatives tend to be highly responsive to constituency preferences; but when issues are highly technical or remote (for instance, science policy or foreign policy), representatives are likely to be quite free to make decisions outside the orbit of constituency considerations.

Whether grounded in constituencies, ideology, or organizational politics, political party representation has been practiced in the United States for a long time, certainly since the 1830s at the national level and much earlier in many states. In New York and Pennsylvania, two-party politics was firmly established in the state legislatures well before the adoption of the national Constitution in 1789. In New York, legislative partisan cleavage arose between supporters and opponents of Governor George Clinton. The two New York legislative parties differed sharply over key political issues, and their memberships were quite dissimilar in socioeconomic, cultural, and sectional backgrounds. In Pennsylvania, legislative parties were institutionalized by the mid-1780s. Historian Jackson Turner Main found that, "by 1786, at least, every member of the legislature had to openly reveal his party affiliation because the delegates seated themselves in two opposing groups."

The few studies of party voting in nineteenth-century state legislatures demonstrate the substantial impact of party on voting cleavages. For instance, Peter D. Levine has been able to demonstrate the pervasiveness of party competition and party legislative voting in the New Jersey legislature of the Jacksonian era (*The Behavior of State Legislative Parties in the Jacksonian Era* [1977]). And Ballard C. Campbell's research on legislative politics in Iowa, Illinois, and Wisconsin in the 1890s underscores the profound influence of partisan cleavage (*Representative Democracy* [1980]). Both these studies amply demonstrate the important role that party voting in the state legislatures played in establishing more or less viable linkages for political accountability and representation.

There is ample evidence of sharp partisan cleavage at the national level by the time of the Fourth Congress, as Federalist and Democratic-Republican congressmen polarized into two distinct voting blocs. Over Congress's two-century history, party polarization has waxed and waned. In studying congressional representation in the 1840s and 1850s, Joel H. Silbey has found "a stable, wide-ranging, and large-scale system of national parties." He found that the division between the Whig and Democratic parties often transcended sectional differences, survived the Wilmot Proviso of 1846 (forbidding slavery in southwestern territories won after the Mexican War), and persisted through the sectional compromises of the early 1850s.

At the end of the nineteenth century, as David W. Brady has so amply demonstrated, congressional voting was highly partisan, pitting Republicans led by powerful speakers—"czars" Thomas B. Reed and Joseph G. Cannon—against Democrats (*Congressional Voting in a Partisan Era* [1973]). In the twentieth century, the variety and complexity of congressional issues expanded enormously and the scope of party voting diminished. Nevertheless, partisanship today remains the single most substantial basis of policy cleavage in Congress, and party voting increased in the 1970s and 1980s in the wake of divided party control of the legislative and executive branches as well as partisan stimulation by the president.

Political party organization and interparty conflict have been important features of representative government in Congress and in the state legislatures. Because parties provide a basis for aggregating interests and citizens' preferences, they have served an important representative function in American democracy. As such, the legislative parties have allowed for greater accountability in the relationship between representatives and the represented. Although variable over time in strength and across the subnational legislatures, party representation provides an important ingredient to effective democratic government.

Rolling Representation: New States and New Senators

Party and constituency representation are rooted in geographical units—in precincts, counties, legislative districts, or states. American politics has always been a politics of territory, and territorial politics have remained important. The Northwest Ordinance and the U.S. Constitution provided rules and procedures for the absorption of new territory, first by establishing the minimum standards for intermediate, *territorial* status, with establishment of territorial assemblies and representation in Congress, and then by providing for statehood.

The steady growth of the republic in the nineteenth century maintained the pressure on Congress to devise ways to distribute seats in the House of Representatives on a population basis while regulating the size of the House to maintain its viability as a deliberative assembly. The original sixty-five-member House more than doubled in size, to 141 members, after the second federal census in 1800, although only three states had been added to the Union by that time. The House had more than doubled in size again, to 292 members, after the post–Civil War federal census in 1870, by which time the federation included thirty-seven states. Since the Sixty-third Congress sat (1913–1915), there have been 435 House members, except for a brief period after Alaska and Hawaii were admitted to statehood in 1959, when 437 members served in the House.

The Senate grew inexorably in size, inasmuch as each additional state brought two new senators to its membership. By 1900, the number of states had grown from thirteen to forty-five, and there were ninety members in the U.S. Senate. In the twentieth century, five states were admitted: Oklahoma in 1907, Arizona and New Mexico in 1912, and Alaska and Hawaii in 1959. At present, fifty states provide the Senate complement of one hundred members.

By dint of changes in the apportionment formulas and a rapid population growth, the average constituency for each member of the House of Representatives has regularly grown in size—from thirty to forty thousand for the first congresses, to more than one hundred thousand by 1863, to more than two hundred thousand by 1913, to more than five hundred thousand today. Because the Constitution allots two U.S. senators to each state, from one state to another, senators have always represented widely varying numbers of constituents. In the early 1990s, the senators from California, the largest state, Alan Cranston (D.) and John Seymour (R.) represented nearly thirty million people, but Senators Malcolm Wallop (R.) and Alan K. Simpson (R.) from Wyoming, the smallest populated state, have represented fewer than a half-million people.

Until the Seventeenth Amendment was added to the U.S. Constitution in 1913, the two senators from each state were elected by their respective state legislatures. By the middle of the nineteenth century, though, it was apparent that election of senators by the state legislatures was fraught with difficulties. Because the houses of the bicameral legislatures were often controlled by different political parties, Senate representation to a number of states was delayed. By the 1890s, the problem had become acute. For example, between 1891 and 1905 fully forty-five legislative deadlocks over the election of senators transpired in twenty states.

A fairly typical deadlock occurred when the Missouri legislative houses met in joint session in 1905, a scene colorfully portrayed by historian George H. Haynes:

> The Missouri election of a senator in 1905 took place in the midst of a riot. Lest the hour of adjournment should come before an election was secured, an attempt was made to stop the clock upon the wall of the assembly chamber. Democrats tried to prevent its being tampered with; and when certain Republicans brought forward a ladder, it was seized and thrown out of the window. A fistfight followed, in which many were involved. Desks were torn from the floor and a fusillade of books began. The glass of the clockfront was broken, but the pendulum still persisted in swinging until, in the midst of a yelling mob, one member began throwing ink bottles at the clock, and finally succeeded in breaking the pendulum. On a motion to adjourn, arose the wildest disorder. The presiding officers of both houses mounted

the speaker's desk, and, by shouting and waving their arms, tried to quiet the mob. Finally, they succeeded in securing some semblance of order. (*The Election of Senators*, 1906)

Finally, after deliberating for two months and sixty-seven calls for ballots, the legislature elected Republican William Warner to serve as U.S. senator.

Political pressures rose in the states for a direct-election amendment, and a number of states enacted legislation providing popular-nomination processes binding on the legislature. Finally, in May 1912, after a legislative struggle of several years in Congress, the direct-election amendment was enacted. Three-quarters of the state legislatures had ratified the Seventeenth Amendment by the spring of 1913, and the first popularly elected U.S. senator, Blair Lee (D.-Md.), was chosen in a special election the following November.

Although U.S. senators have been popularly elected in the states, strictly speaking, the Senate has been grossly (and constitutionally) malapportioned. Obviously, it never would pass a test of "one person, one vote." Oddly enough, given Americans' populist predispositions regarding legislative representation, no hue and cry has gone up concerning representation in the Senate. Americans accept its federalist origins, and its special function as a second legislative chamber. Moreover, because many states have large metropolitan areas to which senators relate, the Senate has come to be quite representative of major contemporary American political problems. There has been no public demand for Senate reform, or for reapportionment of the Senate, akin to the demand for a reallocation of the membership of other American legislatures meticulously on the basis of population.

Representation of Interests

In *The Federalist*, no. 10, Madison theorized about ways of controlling interests in a new constitutional regime. Since those seminal days of the late eighteenth century, the role of interest representation in American politics has been heatedly debated and cautiously analyzed. By the end of the nineteenth century, when the industrial revolution had produced both a vibrant, diverse economy and inherent pressures for government regulation of its

might and abuses, interests became highly organized and widely politicized.

Representation of organized political interests means overrepresentation of business interests, whose individual and corporate motivations and resources facilitate mobilization and political activity. Many interest groups, including the disadvantaged, have representation in Washington, D.C., and in state capitals, but the playing field of interest representation has not been level. In *Organized Interests and American Democracy* (1986), political scientists Kay L. Schlozman and John T. Tierney argue that what they call the "Washington pressure community" has been "tilted heavily in favor of the advantaged, especially business, at the expense of the representation of broad publics and the disadvantaged." E. E. Schattschneider has put it more colorfully: "The flaw in the pluralist heaven is that the heavenly chorus sings with a strong upper-class accent."

This does not mean that the disadvantaged—racial or ethnic minorities, the poor, the homeless, the infirm, or the aged—have not been represented. Political leaders and parties have often championed their causes. It has remained true, however, that the structure of interest representation has been skewed or biased in the direction of a higher socioeconomic station and individuals with relatively high educational achievement, income, and occupational prestige.

Moreover, organized-interest representation has not been pervasive across issues, but has tended to be most influential regarding policies whose costs and benefits are highly concentrated, such as those benefiting a particular business or industry. Where costs and benefits flowing from public policies have been widely distributed, as with social welfare or national defense policies, organized-interest representation has tended to be subsidiary. Distributive politics tends to arouse political party–dominated, often ideological, representation.

THE AMERICAN WAY OF REPRESENTATION

In the early days of the Republic, discourse and disagreement about representation took shape in ways that have remained largely familiar. The founders, especially James Madison and Alexander Hamilton, understood very well the main theoretical features of representative government. The constitutional system they helped to invent fit quite comfortably with American ideas about representation through politics. Over the years since the founding, the American way of representation has emerged along familiar lines. Legislatures became well institutionalized, and they sheltered legislative power. At the same time, features of direct democracy—the initiative, referendum, and recall—became a fixture in a number of states, mostly those west of the Mississippi River. Yet legislative representation has remained robust: the strength of constituency ties, the populist insistence on legislative apportionment on the basis of population, the emphasis on popular elections, and the determination to preserve legislative power have all epitomized the diverse character of representation in the United States.

Political representation in America is multifaceted and complicated. Highly Populist in its political culture, the United States is a place where representation by the legislatures is grounded in a variety of ways: in direct linkage between individual representatives and their constituents; in the systemic representation of the legislative body as a whole; in the connections between organized interests and legislatures; and in the aggregative function performed by political parties and their leaders.

Patterns of representation in the United States have emerged over several hundred years of experiment and practice. The historical experience has not ironed out all of the contradictions in representative politics. In a highly Populist system, though, the fulcrum of representation lies in *responsiveness*, in the emergence of institutions (legislative, executive, judicial, and so on) capable of responding to citizens' demands for policies, services, allocations of public projects, and symbols. Scholars continue to investigate how such institutions work in order to achieve a better grasp of what Heinz Eulau so felicitously calls "the puzzle of representation."

BIBLIOGRAPHY

The best philosophical analysis of representation is to be found in HANNA FENICHEL PITKIN, *The Concept of Representation* (Berkeley, Calif., 1967). The theory of political representation is also perceptively analyzed in HEINZ EULAU, *Politics, Self, and Society: A Theme and Variations* (Cambridge, Mass., 1986).

Because the problem of representation often appears in American politics as an exercise in legislative apportionment and districting, scholars have focused upon these processes. Following on the seminal research of LAURENCE F. SCHMECKEBIER, *Congressional Apportionment* (Westport, Conn., 1941), apportionment schemes and alternatives are adumbrated thoroughly in MICHEL L. BALINSKI and H. PEYTON YOUNG, *Fair Representation: Meeting the Ideal of One Man, One Vote* (New Haven, 1982). A broader historical analysis is ROBERT G. DIXON, JR., *Democratic Representation: Reapportionment in Law and Politics* (New York, 1968).

The U.S. Constitution
For fascinating treatments of representational issues emerging before the adoption of the U.S. Constitution, turn to ALFRED DE GRAZIA, *Public and Republic: Political Representation in America* (New York, 1951); H. JAMES HENDERSON, *Party Politics in the Continental Congress* (New York, 1974); MICHAEL KAMMEN, *Deputyes and Libertyes: The Origins of Representative Government in Colonial America* (Philadelphia, 1969); JACKSON TURNER MAIN, *Political Parties Before the Constitution* (New York, 1973); J. R. POLE, *Political Representation in England and the Origins of the American Republic* (Berkeley, Calif., 1966); and GORDON W. WOOD, *The Creation of the American Republic, 1776–1787* (New York, 1969).

Discourse about the meaning of political representation and its best application to American circumstances abounded during the period of the formation of the U.S. Constitution. The relevant debates at the Constitutional Convention are recorded by MAX FARRAND, *The Records of the Federal Convention of 1787*, 3 vols. (New Haven, 1911), and the defense of the Constitution's provision for representation is recounted in ALEXANDER HAMILTON, JAMES MADISON, and JOHN JAY, *The Federalist Papers*, Introduction by CLINTON ROSSITER (New York, 1961). The theoretical underpinning for the provision of representation in the Constitution is dissected in ROBERT J. MORGAN, "Madison's Theory of Representation in the Tenth Federalist," *Journal of Politics* 18 (1988). The debates at the state-ratifying conventions illuminate the meaning of representation in the founding era, recorded in JONATHAN ELLIOT, *The Debates in the Several State Conventions on the Adoption of the Federal Constitution*, 5 vols. (New York, 1965 [Philadelphia, 1907]).

Theory and Practice

A number of empirical studies of representation shed light on its theory and practice, including DAVID W. BRADY, *Congressional Voting in a Partisan Era: A Study of the McKinley Houses and a Comparison to the Modern House of Representatives* (Lawrence, Kans., 1973); BALLARD C. CAMPBELL, *Representative Democracy: Public Policy and Midwestern Legislatures in the Late Nineteenth Century* (Cambridge, Mass., 1980); HEINZ EULAU and JOHN C. WAHLKE, *The Politics of Representation* (Newbury Park, Calif., 1978); JOHN F. HOADLEY, *Origins of American Political Parties, 1789–1803* (Lexington, Ky., 1986); RALPH VOLNEY HARLOW, *The History of Legislative Methods in the Period Before 1825* (New Haven, 1917); PETER D. LEVINE, *The Behavior of State Legislative Parties in the Jacksonian Era* (Rutherford, N.J., 1977); JOEL H. SILBEY, *The Shrine of Party: Congressional Voting Behavior, 1841–1852* (Westport, Conn., 1967); and ROSEMARIE ZAGARRI, *The Politics of Size: Representation in the United States, 1776–1850* (Ithaca, N.Y., 1987).

Issues of suffrage, direct legislation, and party representation are considered in THOMAS E. CRONIN, *Direct Democracy* (Cambridge, Mass., 1989); GEORGE H. HAYNES, *The Election of Senators* (New York, 1906); SAMUEL C. PATTERSON and GREGORY A. CALDEIRA, "Party Voting in the United States Congress," *British Journal of Political Science* 18 (1988); and CHILTON WILLIAMSON, *American Suffrage from Property to Democracy, 1760–1860* (Princeton, N.J., 1960).

SEE ALSO Colonial Assemblies; Constituencies; Federalism and American Legislatures; The Origins of Congress; The Origins and Early Development of State Legislatures; AND Pressure Groups and Lobbies.

COLONIAL ASSEMBLIES

Jack P. Greene

The territorial, demographic, and economic growth of Great Britain's North American colonies during the first three-quarters of the eighteenth century was remarkable, so much so, that when the Scottish moral philosopher and economist Adam Smith wrote his *Inquiry into the Nature and Causes of the Wealth of Nations* in the mid-1770s, he felt compelled to try to explain it. "The two great causes of the prosperity of all new colonies," he suggested, are "plenty of good land, and liberty to manage their own affairs their own way." Because the Spaniards, Portuguese, and perhaps even the French colonists all enjoyed a comparative advantage over the British in terms of the amount of good land available to them, Smith concluded that the superior performance of Great Britain's North American colonies must be attributable to the fact that their political institutions had "been more favourable" to the improvement of their lands. Britain, Smith emphasized, permitted its colonies more self-government than any other European power. He observed:

> The government of the English colonies is perhaps the only one which, since the world began, could give perfect security to the inhabitants of so very distant a province. . . . In every thing, except their foreign trade, the liberty of the English colonists . . . is complete. It is in every respect equal to that of their fellow-citizens at home, and is secured in the same manner, by an assembly of representatives of the people. (vol. 2, pp. 572, 584–586)

Smith's association of British colonial prosperity with self-government was common in his generation. Self-government was also associated with the elected legislative assemblies, underscoring the vigor of the traditions of legislative government and the institutions that embodied those traditions in British America during the late colonial era.

ORIGINS

By the fall of 1774, when the Continental Congress met in Philadelphia and effectively rendered itself the first "national" American legislature, the American legislative tradition was already more than one and a half centuries old. Virtually contemporaneous with the beginnings of English colonization in America, the first legislative assembly met at Jamestown, Virginia, in 1619, and the second, in Bermuda in 1620. Between 1630 and 1690, every English colony except Newfoundland (which remained primarily a seasonal base for fishermen) acquired a legislature, usually within a few years of that colony's establishment: Massachusetts (1634), Connecticut (1637), Maryland (1638), Barbados (1639), Plymouth (1639), New Haven (1639), Saint Kitts (1642), Antigua (1644), Rhode Island (1647), Montserrat (post-1654), Nevis (1658), Jamaica (1664), North Carolina (1665), East Jersey (1668), South Carolina (1671), New Hampshire (1680), West Jersey (1681), Pennsylvania (1682), and New York (1683). All over the English-American empire, legislative government had become a standard feature of English colonial governance and an integral component of colonial political culture by the end of the seventeenth century.

The sources of this development were complex. The earliest legislative assemblies—in Virginia, Bermuda, and Massachusetts—all emerged in colonies under the control of chartered commercial trading companies; some scholars have traced this development to the self-governing traditions of English corporations. "Adventurers," or shareholders, in such corporations or their representatives gathered at set times to determine company policy, according to their government-issued charters. The distinguished constitutional historian Andrew C. McLaughlin stressed "the connection between the corporation, as a quasi-body-politic, and the beginnings of representation, by deputies and proxies" in the colonies (p. 58).

But two other sets of conditions would seem to have been even more significant in the emergence of powerful legislative institutions in the colonies: the circumstances in which the colonies were established and the inherited English legal and political traditions the settlers brought with them to America.

Chief among the circumstances that helped shape colonial governance was the scarcity of financial resources for American colonizing projects. Without funds for such enterprises, the crown, in effect, delegated projects to private companies and proprietors, both of whom were incapable of sustaining for more than a short period the costs of American settlement, administration, and development. Nor did their limited funds provide either the metropolitan government or its private surrogates with the means to enforce their will and authority in distant overseas polities.

Britain's need for money to finance its activities in America had first forced colonist authorities to seek contributions and cooperation from the settlers, while the weakness of their coercive resources meant that effective governance in the English-American empire would necessarily be consensual. Along with the vast distance of the colonies from England, these circumstances powerfully nudged those who were nominally in charge of the colonies toward the establishment and toleration of political structures that involved consultation with, and the consent of, local settlers. Prior approval by their representatives meant that local populations would more willingly both acknowledge the legitimacy of social and other regulations and contribute to local costs.

The widespread process of individual empowerment that occurred during the colonization process stimulated the emergence of participatory government in the colonies. In early modern England, that is, the period 1458–1842, only a tiny fraction of the male population ever managed to rise out of a state of socioeconomic dependency to achieve the civic competence—the full right to have a voice in political decisions—that was the preserve of independent landowners. By contrast, as a consequence of the easy availability of land, a very large proportion of the adult male

colonists acquired land, built estates, and achieved individual independence. This development gave rise to strong demands by large, empowered settler populations for Britain to extend to the colonies the same rights to security of property and civic participation that appertained to independent English property holders. In their view, English domestic and colonial government should guarantee that men of their standing would be neither governed by laws nor subjected to taxes enacted without their consent. Without promises of such guarantees, colonial sponsors found it difficult to recruit settlers.

The form through which colonial property holders extended their consent depended heavily upon the settlers' English inheritance. In contrast to the heavily populated areas that the Spanish had encountered in New Spain and Peru, North America presented itself to aspiring colonizers as an immense, sparsely populated, and bounteous territory that was open for experimentation. Between 1607 and 1750, what would become English North America seemed to offer fertile soil for people to try out a great variety of advanced political ideas that were then circulating in England. These included unicameral legislatures, secret ballots, and rotation in office. Yet, however experimental their initial designs for their respective colonies, no group of colonial sponsors departed radically from the traditional institutional arrangements that had long operated in the English polity. Sponsors intended many of their specific innovations as devices for better implementing the fundamental values long associated with that polity. Especially included were the interrelated principles of limited government, representation, consent, rule by law, local control, and the sanctity of private property, including property in individual legal and civil rights as well as in land and other forms of wealth. New York was the only one of these new polities that was not founded on traditional English ideas of law and liberty, of limited and representative government. The New York colony's absolutist cast was the result of efforts by the proprietor, the future James II, to implement the sort of absolutist polity Louis XIV was then fashioning for France.

The importance of this English inheritance in the development of colonial legislative institutions can scarcely be overemphasized. Long before John Locke's elegant formulation of the theory of emigration in his *Two Treatises of Government* (1688), colonial leaders had developed the view that the English had a right to migrate to a new country; to take their country's constitutional rights with them into the new political entities that they founded overseas; and to establish local institutions as well as local customs to secure those rights to themselves and their posterities.

From the colonists' point of view, the crown seemed to have recognized the legitimacy of this theory by its charters. Beginning with the charter issued for Maryland to Lord Baltimore in the mid-1630s, royal authorities in England usually required proprietors to seek the advice and consent of the freemen in making laws for their colony. Yet, colonial spokesmen invariably insisted that, so far from conferring rights upon them, charters did nothing more than acknowledge the colonists' entitlement as English people to all the traditional rights, privileges, and immunities of Englishmen.

The founding and development of the colonies occurred during a period of great constitutional change in England. During the late Middle Ages, both the House of Lords and the House of Commons functioned less as modern legislative bodies with independent initiating powers than as advisers of or counselors to the king. The two centuries after 1540 witnessed a shift in the balance of authority between king and Parliament—from a situation of royal absolutism under Henry VIII to one of parliamentary omnicompetence by the time of George III. During the seventeenth century, Parliament had sought to diminish the relative authority of the crown, and developments set in motion by the Glorious Revolution of 1688–1689 ensured that future sovereignty in England would reside not in the king alone, but in the king-in-Parliament. The crown, Lords, and Commons would be coordinate branches in a tripartite and sovereign legislature.

The structure of colonial governments reflected these inherited arrangements. Each of the three most important political institutions—governors, councils, and lower houses of assembly—constituted a distinct branch of the colonial legislature and was roughly analogous to an institution in the parent state. The governorship was the provincial equivalent of the crown. Except in Connecticut and Rhode Island, where it was elective, this office was filled by royally approved appointees, usually from England. As viceroys for the crown, governors were theoretically invested with, and expected to defend, all of the crown's vast prerogative powers. As the chief representatives of the metropolises in the colonies, governors were responsible for the execution of laws, appointment of judicial and executive officers, and all matters of defense and local diplomacy. As one of three coordinate branches of the legislature, the governorship had veto power over all colonial laws.

The governors' councils took on the multiple functions performed in Britain by the Privy Council and the House of Lords. Like the Privy Council, the governors' councils served as an advisory body whose approval was required for most executive actions and, in a few colonies, acted as a superior court. Like the House of Lords, they constituted (in every colony except Pennsylvania) an upper house of the legislature whose consent was necessary for the passage of all legislation. In the two corporate colonies and in one royal province—the former corporate colony of Massachusetts—these bodies were elected by the lower houses of the legislature. Elsewhere, they were composed of a small number—usually twelve—of royal and proprietary appointees. These men were usually drawn from the wealthiest and most prominent colonists but, unlike members of the House of Lords, they enjoyed no legally privileged status and did not constitute a hereditary aristocracy.

Composed of elected representatives from an expanding number of localities, the representative lower houses of assembly—the third major political institution—were the colonial counterparts of the House of Commons. Unlike the English body, however, they mostly met together with the colonial councils in a single body during their early years and only gradually established their right to deliberate separately. Meeting for short periods and, in most colonies only irregularly, the lower houses handled a wide array of judicial and administrative matters referred to them by their constituents; house consent was required to approve all laws and taxes.

Colonial assemblies were always both far more representative of the voting population and far more directly responsive to the wishes of their constituents than was the House of Commons. In a few colonies, the first assemblies seem to have been composed of all the freemen, but the dispersion of settlement rapidly led to the practice of constituents' sending deputies to represent them. Within a few years, the chief unit of local administration—the county in the colonies from New York south to North Carolina, the town in New England, and the parish in South Carolina and Georgia—also became the unit of representation, each constituency sending a set number of delegates to the assembly. In contrast to English practice, colonial assemblies tended to require representatives to be either residents or property holders in the communities they represented.

THE FRANCHISE

The franchise by which representatives were elected to the colonial assemblies was limited. Initially, there was often some confusion about who was eligible to exercise the suffrage. Within a few decades, however, all colonies followed traditional English practice by establishing property requirements for voting. A majority of colonies required voters to own freehold property, with the requirements varying from a freehold of a specific worth (£40 to £50) to one of a specified number of acres, to one producing a certain amount of annual income (40 shillings in the English fashion, for example), but several colonies provided legal alternatives to a freehold possession in the form of a personal property or a taxpaying qualification.

The Virginia legislature spelled out part of the logic behind these property requirements in 1670 when it prefaced a law with the statement that "the laws of England grant a voice in such election only to such as by their estates real or personal have interest enough to tie them to the endeavour of the public good" (Pole, *Political Representation*, p. 138). Just as it was widely assumed in English and colonial law that membership in a corporation should be restricted to those with a full legal share, so citizenship in a polity—as symbolized by the right to vote—should be limited to those with a permanent attachment in the form of property.

But the lack of sufficient property was not the only criterion for exclusion from the franchise. In both Britain and its colonies, whole categories of people were denied the franchise whether or not prevailing property stipulations were met. Women, minors, aliens, Catholics, Jews, and nonwhites all belonged to social categories that could not be excluded on the grounds of property requirements alone or by the stake-in-society argument. Like slaves, servants, short-term tenants, the poor and the indigent, and even sons over twenty-one years of age who still resided with their parents, most married women and most minors could be denied citizenship on these grounds, but for unmarried women and any other members of these groups who may have met the property requirements, the grounds for denial had to lie elsewhere.

Sir William Blackstone elaborated precisely what these grounds were in the 1760s in his *Commentaries on the Laws of England*: "The *true* reason of requiring any qualification, with regard to property, in voters, is to exclude such persons as are in so mean a situation that they are esteemed to have no will of their own" (vol. 1, p. 171). Property, then, was an essential precondition for the suffrage not only or even primarily because it demonstrated a permanent attachment to the community but because it alone conferred personal—as well as economic and political—independence. Those who were without property and those who, because of religious, legal, or family obligations, were subject to the will of others simply did not have the degree of autonomy necessary for full civic rights. One corollary of this assumption that justified the exclusion of women, minors, nonwhites, and Jews who could meet the property requirements and therefore presumably had the requisite personal independence, was that groups with presumed emotional, physical, or "natural" disabilities were incapable of controlling themselves. For that reason, they also lacked the competence to be accorded full civil status in society.

If, however, the political systems of the Anglo-American colonies were just as exclusivist as that of the metropolis in their assumptions about who was entitled to the full rights of political participation, a considerably larger proportion of colonial populations actually enjoyed those rights. Because of the relative ease of availability of property throughout most of the colonial period, a large majority (up to 90 percent in some colonies) of free white adult males could expect to acquire enough property during their lifetimes to secure the personal independence necessary to meet the suffrage requirements. The population of no other extensive political societies during the early modern era had so large a proportion of voters.

ELECTIONS

The frequency and form of elections varied considerably from one colony to another. Five colonies had regularly scheduled elections: Rhode Island (before 1727) and Connecticut had semiannual elections; and Rhode Island (after 1727), Massachusetts, Pennsylvania, and Delaware had annual elections. In all other colonies elections were held irregularly, whenever the governors called them. Although officials in England were careful to disallow statutes by which the assemblies sought, in the manner of similar statutes in Britain, to require elections at least once every three or seven years, no governors after 1675 went more than seven years before calling an election.

Mostly characterized by open voting in the English tradition, elections could be rowdy affairs. Candidates appeared personally and solicited votes through promises and treating voters to food and drinks. Before 1725, voter turnout seems to have been relatively high; contested elections were normal; the social basis of candidates was comparatively low; and turnover among representatives was very high. With such extensive popular involvement in the electoral process, voters often expressed their preferences aggressively, and legislative leaders frequently found that they had to accede to the articulated wishes of the larger political communities that they served.

A conspicuous feature of the period after 1725 was the contraction of the role of the electorate. Suffrage remained high. Within the limits imposed by the franchise requirements on which they were based, colonial political systems were extraordinarily inclusive. Lower voter turnout did not result from the systematic exclusion by the leadership of any segment of the traditional electorate. Rather, a larger proportion of voters seemed merely to have withdrawn from active involvement in the political process and neglected to participate in elections. Unless a vital public issue was involved, voters simply did not vote in large numbers. As long as "government did not threaten burdensome taxes, military duty, or religious restrictions," Gary B. Nash noted, "most of the people found no need to engage actively in politics" (pp. 335–338), even though they retained the passive authority to thwart any political action that seemed to be inimical to their interests.

One effect of the phenomenon of political demobilization was the relative turnover rates (the percentage of new people returned) in elections to the colonial legislatures during the eighteenth century. At the beginning of the century, these rates were high everywhere, frequently reaching as much as 80 percent, but rates declined over the following seventy-five years as the electoral systems of the colonies became more settled. One group of colonies, Massachusetts, South Carolina, and Virginia, was characterized by a relatively steady long-term decline. Turnover in Massachusetts, where elections were annual, fell from an average of 55 percent in the 1720s to 45 percent in the period 1730–1759, 32 percent in the 1760s, and 28 percent in the 1770s. In Virginia, where elections were irregular but never at intervals of more than seven years, turnover dropped from an average of approximately 50 percent in the 1720s and 1730s to 45 percent in the 1750s, 33 percent in the 1760s, and 26 percent in the 1770s.

In a second major pattern, found in Maryland, New Hampshire, New Jersey, New York, North Carolina, and Pennsylvania, turnover rates fell much earlier and more abruptly than elsewhere and then began to rise more or less steadily after midcentury, though not to the levels at the beginning of the century. Thus, in New York, for example, the turnover rate precipitously declined to an average of just 29 percent in the 1710s and 27 percent in the 1720s. Though they rose to slightly more than 40 percent during the 1730s, these rates fell again to 22 percent in the 1740s and 1750s before rising dramatically beginning in 1759 to an average of more than 40 percent for the remainder of the colonial period. Whatever the variations, the generally declining trend in legislative turnover may serve as a measure of the increasing passivity of the electorate.

This passivity may also have been a function of the growing distance between leaders and constituents. During the first seven decades of the eighteenth century, the ratio of representatives in the legislature to potential voters (adult white males) rose—relatively slowly in South Carolina, Rhode Island, Massachusetts, Connecticut, and Virginia and much more rapidly in Delaware, North Carolina, New Hampshire, Maryland, Pennsylvania, New Jersey, and New York. Especially in these last four colonies, the distance between voters and representatives was growing rapidly. By 1770 the legislatures in these colonies were both less representative than those of other colonies and probably less in touch with their constituents' needs. In addition, these colonies were less able to absorb new people with political ambitions.

LEADERSHIP

Another effect of the demobilization of the broad body politic that occurred after 1725 was the emergence and popular acceptance of the legitimacy of a growing elitist leadership structure. Increasingly, a broad electorate composed overwhelmingly of medium- and small-property holders routinely exercised their franchise to return their social and economic betters to office. Before about 1720, many men from modest estates had served in, and occasionally even played a conspicuous role in, the assemblies. As the historian William Smith, Jr., later complained in commenting on the character of the members of the assembly in the early days of New York, they were mainly "plain, illiterate husbandmen whose views seldom extended farther than to the regulation of highways, the destruction of wolves, wildcats, and foxes, and the advancement of the other little interests of the particular counties, which they were chosen to represent" (vol. 1, p. 259).

Smith was correct to emphasize the parochial and basically utilitarian orientation of most legislators. From the beginning, colonial politics had been expressive of a fundamental preoccupation with the protection and facilitation of group interests and individual enterprise. The colonists, wrote Governor William Gooch of Virginia, assumed they had "a Natural Liberty of pursuing what may promote their own benefit," and they expected the colonial assemblies to encourage them in that pursuit (Byrd, vol. 2, p. 230). Indeed, throughout the colonial era, men went into the legislature in quest of direct economic and social benefits for themselves and their associates in the form of easier access to land, special business or professional advantages, remunerative public offices, or higher social status. Increasingly thereafter, however, seats in the legislatures went to wealthy men, members of the nascent elites who began to appear in Virginia, Massachusetts, and Connecticut near the end of the seventeenth century and in the other colonies in the 1730s and 1740s.

By European standards, these elites were peculiar. At their core was a group of first families or descendants of first families who, having successfully established themselves during the first or second generation after settlement, managed to retain their wealth and social standing in the discordant years of the late seventeenth and early eighteenth centuries. But, especially in colonies such as South Carolina, which experienced extraordinary economic booms after 1740, and in Pennsylvania and New York, where rapid commercial expansion opened up widespread new opportunities in commerce and the professions, the elites were, in large part, nouveau riche. Even in older colonies like Virginia and Massachusetts there was always room for the talented newcomer or upstart who, through education, industry, patronage, or marriage, managed to pull himself up the economic ladder.

Membership in the elite therefore depended at least as much upon achievement and merit as upon traditional ascriptive criteria such as family and inherited status. With such origins and with no legally sanctioned sphere of influence, colonial elites, unlike their metropolitan model, never developed an exclusive function or that well-developed and secure sense of identity that derives from longevity and its illusion of permanence. To a large extent, the colonial elites remained loose categories and did not become sharply defined corporate groups.

But these emergent elites did acquire a high degree of coherence and visibility within their respective societies early in their history. Through intermarriage and personal and social ties, the elite developed the close family and personal relationships and informal, inter-elite communication patterns that characterize this group in every society. Such ties, like their great estates, more liberal and extensive educations, and closer connections to metropolitan culture, helped to set them apart from men in other social categories. The imposing houses of the elite, built in country and town in increasing numbers through the middle decades of the eighteenth century, expressed their accomplishments and standing in monumental form for all to see.

Although the majority of legislators continued to be men of lesser property and learning and of narrower experience and vision, these cohering elites, spreading, as one contemporary remarked, in size and influence as the colonies became more wealthy, provided a growing reservoir of political leaders who more and more dominated the colonial assemblies. The progenitors of these elites—the men who between 1640 and 1720 had established and consolidated the positions of the elites in colonial life—had fulfilled themselves by acquiring estates, obtaining status in the community, and enhancing the family name. But their extraordinary success meant that their heirs who were just coming into manhood during the 1720s and 1730s—members of the second generation in newer colonies like South Carolina, New Jersey, and Pennsylvania, and of the third generation in older provinces such as Virginia, Massachusetts, Maryland, and New York—had to look elsewhere to find a suitable outlet for their energies and talents.

For men whose wealth and security of position provided them with the necessary leisure to direct at least part of their attention into noneconomic channels, politics provided the most satisfying opportunities in mid-eighteenth-century colonial America. Many men, for the most part first-generation arrivistes, like the Massachusetts merchant Thomas Hancock (1703–1764), still entered public life primarily for economic or material gain. For many of the established elite, however, and even many of the more thoroughly socialized among the new men, politics was becoming an absorbing activity to which they devoted much of their time. In most colonies between 1720 and 1740, these elites had transformed themselves into communities of expert legislators who enjoyed the challenges and responsibilities found in the political arena and used their superior learning and political skills to influence the back-benchers in the legislature and men of lesser rank and knowledge in their constituencies. The influence of such men far surpassed their numbers.

The domination of the assemblies by these emerging colonial elites cannot be explained by the coercive models employed by earlier generations of historians. There were simply too many instances of tenants voting against landlords, of clients rejecting patrons. More recently, historians have tended to attribute this development to the fact that the political systems of the colonies, like that of Britain, operated within a deferential, rather than a democratic, political culture. Prescriptively at least, colonial systems functioned within an integrated structure of ideas that was fundamentally elitist in nature and also assumed that government should be entrusted to men of merit; that merit was very often associated with wealth and social position; that men of merit were obligated to employ their talents and greater learning and expertise for the benefit of the public; and that deference to them was the implicit duty of the rest of society. But the extent of deferential behavior in the colonies seems to have been limited. Voters often rejected representatives who acted against public wishes and otherwise treated unpopular elite figures in ways that reflected neither awe nor respect. Dominance by the elite may well have been more a function of political disinterest than of either deference or elite control. In ordinary times in a society that provided such broad scope for engagement in the private realm, interest in public affairs seems to have been low.

CONSTITUENT-REPRESENTATIVE RELATIONS

Elite dominance did not mean that legislatures could ignore the opinions of their constituents. Rather, legislatures showed considerable responsiveness to the needs of the empowered populations that they served. In addition to having to win the approval of voters at periodic elections, individual legislators sometimes found themselves also charged with carrying out the specific and formal instructions of their constituents. This practice had clear English precedents. Not just on local matters but, especially after 1640, during times of crisis on great national issues, English voters often instructed their representatives how they were to comport themselves on specific questions that came before Parliament. Colonial constituencies employed the same device on similar occasions, especially in New England and other colonies where elections were annual or semiannual, but also occasionally elsewhere. The implicit theory behind such instructions was that a representative was a delegate for a particular constituency and ought to be bound by the specific directions of his electors.

Not all representatives acceded willingly to this theory. With the Virginia legislator Landon Carter, some questioned "whether a Representative was obliged to follow the directions of his Constituents against his own Reason and Conscience." Arguing that it was "absurd to Suppose one part of the Community could be apprized of the good of the whole without Consulting the whole," representatives contended that they had to be free to make up their own minds after consulting with legislators from "other parts of the Community" (Greene, ed., *Diary of Landon Carter*, vol. 2, pp. 116–117). Responsible politics, they thereby suggested, was not always representative politics.

Petitioning was a much more widely used way for the electorate to make its sentiments known to legislatures. Again, following English practice, colonial voters frequently petitioned legislatures on particular issues and problems. The right of petition was one of the hallowed liberties of the English, and over time, colonists seemed to have used that right to an increasing degree. In most colonies, the number of petitions grew substantially during the eighteenth century. Petitions most often involved matters of local concern, but they occasionally also extended to provincewide concerns. As many as half the laws in some colonies originated in petitions.

Legislatures, when uncertain about how the electorate felt on a given issue, used various devices to consult with their constituents; these included two principal devices. The first was to print and circulate a controversial bill for public response to be taken into account at a subsequent session. The second was to adjourn, permitting representatives to return to their constituencies for direct and immediate consultation with voters. Through these devices, colonial legislatures kept in touch with, and endeavored to stay in tune with, popular opinion.

INSTITUTIONAL DEVELOPMENT

The emergence of communities of expert legislators also produced important changes in the character of the colonial assemblies. By the 1730s, some of these bodies were a century old. Although their roles in the colonial political system were enhanced by the demands of the first two intercolonial wars between 1689 and 1713, as late as the 1720s some of them still lacked the independence, the guarantees of regular meetings and frequent elections, the regularity of procedures, the continuity of leadership, and the intense self-consciousness that characterized the House of Commons after, if not to a great extent also before, the Glorious Revolution.

Under the guidance of more-expert leaders through the early and middle decades of the eighteenth century, the lower houses consolidated their position within the colonial governments and acquired greater autonomy, developments that were greatly accelerated in most colonies by the exigencies of the last two intercolonial wars between 1739 and 1763. Recruited from a rising leadership pool, assembly Speakers frequently served for many years, the longest tenure being the twenty-eight years that Virginia speaker John Robinson, Jr., served between 1738 and 1766. Exerting far more power than the speakers of the British House of Commons, such men resembled British prime ministers in their political influence, which often surpassed that even of royal and proprietary governors.

As the growing complexities of the political process made them indispensable to the functioning of the political systems, the colonial lower houses met more regularly and for longer periods; passed a greater quantity of less ambiguous legislation; defined their procedures more clearly; established permanent standing committees; exhibited more continuity in leadership; developed a much more articulate sense of their corporate rights; abandoned their judicial functions in favor of executive and administrative ones, and otherwise sought to give substance to the ideal that as the sole givers of all statutory law operating inside a colony and as the presumed equivalents of the House of Commons, they were endowed with charismatic authority and held in trusteeship all of the sacred rights and privileges of the public.

Notwithstanding this lofty self-conception, colonial assemblies continued to spend most of their time acting upon a wide range of mundane concerns of the large and broad-based landowning class they served. Assemblies took responsibility for initiating a large assortment of political and social institutions, including counties, towns, parishes, courts, churches, and hospitals; and social services such as the production of roads, ferries, lighthouses, fortifications, canals, and public buildings. Conferring a variety of privileges, benefits, and exemptions upon the creators of those institutions and the provision of those services, colonial assemblies sought to foster the economic well-being of the citizenry through regulations to produce new staples and improve the quality of old ones, enhance the competitive advantage of the inhabitants in trade or at markets, and relieve chronic shortages in the cash supply. Assemblies assumed responsibility for local defense against Native Americans or rival European colonies, for maintaining social order, and for defending local rights against challenges from the metropolitan government and its representatives.

CONSTITUTIONAL STATUS

Though limited in every colony by the governor's veto power and in the royal colonies and Pennsylvania by the requirement that all statutes be transmitted to Britain for review and possible disallowance by the crown-in-council, the lawmaking power of these colonial bodies was as extensive in each of their respective spheres as was that of the House of Commons in Britain. Nevertheless, the legal and constitu-

tional status of the colonial assemblies was always in dispute between their adherents and metropolitan officials in London and the colonies.

The colonists' right to legislative assemblies and the legislative power of those assemblies were not in dispute. Those rights and powers had been conveyed to most colonies by their early charters from the crown or, for those few colonies (like Jamaica and New Hampshire) that never had charters, by the royal commissions to the first governors. Moreover, the crown repeatedly reaffirmed these early concessions in all royal colonies by clauses in the governors' commissions empowering them to call and use assemblies to exercise full authority to make laws for their respective colonies. Except for the brief experiment with absolute government for the Dominion of New England under James II from 1684 to 1689, metropolitan officials never attempted to govern in the colonies without representative institutions, generally agreeing that the colonists' rights and properties should be preserved for them through their assemblies.

The question was not whether the assemblies had lawmaking power, but how extensive that power was and whether those bodies enjoyed the same status in the colonial constitutions as the House of Commons did in the British constitution. The crown in a sustained way first raised these issues during the Restoration, through a concerted effort to consolidate royal authority over the colonies and retrench the authority of colonial legislatures. As colonial leaders came to realize that the crown's actions challenged their claims to English rights, these leaders began to demand explicit guarantees of those rights. Between 1675 and 1695, colonial legislatures repeatedly tried to pass measures that would serve as formal legal protections of their constituents' rights to English liberties and privileges.

But crown officials never accepted the colonists' demands for explicit statutory guarantees of their rights and took special pains to deny the assemblies' strident and often reiterated claims to constitutional authority within their respective jurisdictions equivalent to that of the House of Commons. Crown officials always insisted that the assemblies were subordinate institutions, much like the governing bodies of English corporations, and did not enjoy the full rights and privileges of the House of Commons.

Three conditions combined to undermine the crown's position. First, the colonies were too distant from Britain to be closely and effectively supervised. Second, the colonies needed a broad range of laws and regulations to help settlers organize and develop the new and expanding areas in which they lived. Third, the assemblies controlled the power of the purse, and colonial governors found it impossible to govern without their consent. As a result, the assemblies gradually succeeded in obtaining, in practice, the authority that crown officials denied them in theory.

Working out the logic of the analogy between the assemblies and the House of Commons, colonial legislative leaders not only copied the forms and procedures of the metropolitan body but insisted that on the basis of both their inherited rights as Englishmen and of local custom, they were constitutionally vested with the same powers and privileges in the colonies as was the House of Commons. With this goal before them, colonial legislators gradually extended their financial authority over every phase of raising and distributing public revenue. Colonial legislative leaders acquired a large measure of legislative independence by winning control over their proceedings and obtaining guarantees of basic English parliamentary privileges. Finally, they extended their power well beyond that of the House of Commons by gaining extensive authority in handling executive affairs, including the right to appoint not just officials concerned with collecting and handling local revenues but many other executive officials and to share in formulating executive policy.

These specific gains were symbolic of a fundamental shift of the constitutional center of power in the colonies from the executive to the elected branch of the legislature. As the House of Commons had itself done during the seventeenth century, the colonial assemblies effectively managed, through precedent and custom, to establish their authority and status as local parliaments as the most important institutions in the colonial polities and the primary guardians of the colonial rights, especially including the right not to be subjected to any taxes or laws relating to their internal affairs without the consent of their representatives in assembly.

EXPANSION OF POLITICAL CONSCIOUSNESS

Under the influence of the new communities of expert legislators, traditional configurations of political consciousness also underwent important changes. During the seventeenth century, prevailing English conceptions of political life as a perpetual struggle between prerogative and privilege, between a grasping and arbitrary monarch and a beleaguered House of Commons fighting valiantly to preserve the rights of the people, were transferred to the colonies, where they were given additional power and acquired a continuing hold on the minds of colonial legislators because of the crown's exaggerated claims for prerogative in the colonies.

In Britain, under the later Stuarts and increasingly during the first half of the eighteenth century, fears of prerogative were supplanted by fears of corruption. "Court Influence or Ministerial Corruption," a "hydra-headed monster" whose heads were the standing army, "Placemen, Pensioners, National Debt, Excise, and High Taxation," came to be set in opposition to the ideal of the virtuous, uncorrupted, and independent (preferably landed) proprietor whose economic independence, active patriotism, and sense of civic responsibility were the primary bulwarks against the subversion of liberty by the minions of corruption and, ideally, the prerequisites for the exercise of a voice in the political system (Pocock, pp. 119–124).

For aspiring colonial political elites whose major claim to social position rested upon the amount of property at their command and for many of whom propertied independence was an undeniable reality, the appeal of this conception of politics was irresistible. But the ideal of the vigilant, independent, and patriotic landholder had far greater resonance—and a deeper and more lasting impact upon colonial political consciousness—than did the fears of corruption. With no standing army and as a small civil establishment, without sinecures, pensions, secret-service funds, or, indeed, much patronage, colonial administrations simply lacked the means for effective corruption through the distribution of offices and pensions in the style of Sir Robert Walpole. Colonial political leaders did indeed worry about corruption, but it was the more primitive form of corruption arising from the evil and avarice of individual governors and other officials—not corruption deriving from court or administrative "influence." Only in places such as Massachusetts during the 1740s and early 1750s, or in proprietary Maryland, where the governors did have some patronage at their disposal, did the fears of "ministerial corruption" achieve much appeal or frequency of expression.

But there was an additional reason why this newer conception of politics as an adversary relationship between virtue and corruption did not gain wider acceptance and why the older notion of politics as conflict between privilege and prerogative lost some of its appeal through the middle decades of the eighteenth century. With the gradual relaxation of pressure from London, beginning in the 1720s, colonial politics, under the accommodative ministrations of men like Virginia governor William Gooch, came to be seen more as a cooperative and less as an antagonistic process. No longer faced with claims for excessive prerogative powers from the governors, many of whom were becoming increasingly domesticated, a rising community of expert legislators could feel free to cultivate a pragmatic concern for compromise and accommodation with the executive in the pursuit of the public weal. In Virginia and Massachusetts, where, for somewhat different reasons, political stability lasted for several decades, a vital tradition of such cooperation even developed, along with a habit of following executive leadership that was not too dissimilar from the tradition of routine obedience to the crown among the British parliamentary elite. The revival of prerogative claims by authorities in the metropolis beginning in the late 1740s seriously undermined this tradition.

CHANGING PATTERNS OF LEGISLATIVE POLITICS

Struggles between governors, councils, and assemblies, concerning both the nature of colonial constitutions and the status of assemblies, were not the only areas of contention within colonial politics. Initially the colonial assemblies, like all colonial political institutions, op-

erated on a relatively primitive level. Leadership and institutional structures were weak and undefined, levels of political expertise and socialization were low, and political consciousness was inchoate and undeveloped. Under such conditions, political life was usually brittle, often even explosive, as would-be leaders in the legislatures jockeyed with each other in a sometimes ruthless competition for power, wealth, and prestige. This primitive "politics of competition" characterized the polities of Pennsylvania, South Carolina, New Hampshire, Rhode Island, and New Jersey until the 1730s and 1740s, and North Carolina until the eve of the American Revolution. As long as social status and claims to leadership were unclear, political life remained chaotic and unsettled.

But the vigorous competition that characterized the politics of most colonies during the earlier generations of settlement was only one of two predominant patterns that marked the primitive stages in the development of colonial politics. A second was the "politics of oligarchy," a situation in which the legislature and other institutions were dominated by a single, unified group. Bound together by common religious beliefs, economic interests, patronage and kinship ties, or a combination of these factors, these dominant groups monopolized all avenues to political power and to most of the primary sources of wealth. This type of politics was possible only in very special circumstances in which small groups could monopolize political and economic power. During the eighteenth century, such a situation existed only in the relatively small and undeveloped colony of New Hampshire. Between 1741 and 1767, its governor, Benning Wentworth, constructed an extraordinarily close-knit oligarchy that exerted an almost exclusive control over both the most lucrative segments of the New Hampshire economy and most aspects of provincial political life.

Beginning in the 1720s and 1730s, these primitive forms of politics began to give way to more traditional modes that were more closely approximated to the politics of the metropolitan state of Great Britain. The hallmarks of this traditional politics, as it developed in the colonies during the early- and middle-eighteenth century, were the muting of fundamental issues that deeply divided the polity; the visible dominance of broad-ruling elites that were roughly representative of, or sensitive to, the needs and interests of all important segments of society; and the reduction of factional strife to levels at which it became relatively unimportant, thus no longer disruptive.

With these developments, public life became more settled, levels of political socialization and consciousness became much higher, and institutional and leadership structures were more clearly articulated. The result was an era that, in comparison to earlier periods, was one of considerable political coherence, continuing in most colonies until at least into the 1760s and 1770s. Virginia, South Carolina, Pennsylvania, and Massachusetts all exhibited genuinely impressive stability through the middle of the eighteenth century; only North Carolina and New Hampshire did not participate in this development.

In colonies where levels of, or the potential for, conflict remained high, a political system emerged that in its development of informal structures for the routinization of conflict, such as interest groups or parties, was peculiarly modern in form and represented a transition from traditional to modern politics. This transition was most evident in New York and Rhode Island after the mid-1740s, though it was also manifest to a lesser extent in Connecticut and Maryland. The central feature of this new political mode was a vigorous, functional, and strikingly modern rivalry among a multiplicity of interests within clearly defined— and agreed-upon—political boundaries. Such rivalry routinized and, through the eventual creation of loose and semipermanent parties, institutionalized competition at the same time that it discouraged or diminished the possibilities for explosive open conflict, civil disorder, and political disruption. In a complex political society, such as that of New York, parties were perhaps a necessary precondition for the achievement of a functional political order.

To a modest extent, these embryonic political parties in late-colonial New York, Rhode Island, Maryland, and Connecticut developed rudimentary organizations, and they systematically cultivated support among the electorate. Elsewhere, however, political groups were small, closely knit, and ephemeral. Even in New York

and Rhode Island, where an interest-group theory of representation was most thoroughly developed, there were no well-defined or reasonably permanent pressure groups, public associations, or other organizations to process demands and proposals from the citizenry, which continued to rely on petitions and instructions to make its wishes known to its representatives.

CONCLUSION

If, as Adam Smith noted with an air of national pride in 1776, Britain had "dealt more liberally with her colonies than any other nation" (vol. 2, p. 583), the most dramatic testimony to that liberality in the political realm had been the emergence of the colonial legislatures as vigorous, effective, and, by contemporary standards, extraordinarily representative institutions. "The case of a free country branching itself out in the manner Britain had done and sending to a distant world colonies which have there, from small beginnings and under free legislatures of their own, increased and formed a body of powerful states likely soon to become superior to the parent state," echoed the English philosopher Richard Price during the same year, was unprecedented "in the history of mankind" (Peach, ed., p. 82).

For one and a half centuries in colonial British America, free government had been synonymous with legislative government. Through the colonial assemblies, the broad property-owning, empowered, and rights-conscious settler populations of the colonies had developed powerful traditions of self-governance. The colonial legislatures were both fertile training grounds for political leaders and the principal arenas for the emergence and expansion of political consciousness. Generally, the legislatures enjoyed the confidence of the electorate, knew how to cope with internal contention, and exhibited impressive political expertise. That expertise, as well as the institutions that sustained it, represented a major development of political resources that contributed significantly to the successful efforts of the colonies to secure their independence, establish republican governments, and join together in a national political union.

BIBLIOGRAPHY

General Studies

The best general studies of the political context of colonial legislative development are LEONARD W. LABAREE, *Royal Government in America* (New Haven, 1930); BERNARD BAILYN, *The Origins of American Politics* (New York, 1968); and JACK P. GREENE, "The Growth of Political Stability: An Interpretation of Political Development in the Anglo-American Colonies, 1660–1760," in JOHN PARKER and CAROL URNESS, eds., *The American Revolution: A Heritage of Change* (Minneapolis, 1975). JACK P. GREENE, "Changing Interpretations of Early American Politics," in RAY A. BILLINGTON, ed., *The Reinterpretation of Early American History* (San Marino, Calif., 1966), analyzes the literature published before the mid-1960s.

Assemblies and Colonial Constitutions

The debate over the place of the assemblies in the colonial constitutional order may be followed in ANDREW C. MCLAUGHLIN, *Foundations of American Constitutionalism* (New York, 1932); GEORGE DARGO, *Roots of the Republic: A New Perspective on Early American Constitutionalism* (New York, 1974); and JACK P. GREENE, *Peripheries and Center: Constitutional Development in the Extended Polities of the British Empire and the United States, 1607–1788* (Athens, Ga., 1986).

The Franchise

The franchise and the logic behind it are discussed in CHILTON WILLIAMSON, *American Suffrage: From Property to Democracy, 1760–1880* (Princeton, N.J., 1960) and JACK P. GREENE, *All Men Are Created Equal: Some Reflections on the Character of the American Revolution* (Oxford, 1976). ROBERT J. DINKIN, *Voting in Provincial America: A Study of Elections in the Thirteen Colonies, 1689–1776* (Westport, Conn., 1977), analyzes voting patterns. EDMUND S. MORGAN, *Inventing the People: The Rise of Popular Sovereignty in England and America* (New York, 1988); J. R. POLE, *Political Representation in England and the Origins of the American Republic* (New York, 1966); ALLAN TULLY, "Constituent-Representative Relationships in Early America," *Canadian Journal of History* 11 (1976); RAYMOND

C. BAILEY, *Popular Influence upon Public Policy: Petitioning in Eighteenth-Century Virginia* (Westport, Conn., 1979); and J. R. POLE, *The Gift of Government: Political Responsibility from the English Restoration to American Independence* (Athens, Ga., 1983), examine aspects of relationships between legislators and their constituents. JACK P. GREENE, "Legislative Turnover in British America, 1696–1775: A Quantitative Analysis," *William and Mary Quarterly*, ser. 3, 38 (1981), studies changing patterns of electoral turnover and BRUCE C. DANIELS, ed., *Power and Status: Officeholding in Colonial America* (Middletown, Conn., 1986), provides a series of prosopographical studies of colonial legislators and other political leaders.

The Development of Colonial Assemblies

The institutional development of colonial assemblies is analyzed in MICHAEL KAMMEN, *Deputyes and Libertyes: The Origins of Representative Government in Colonial America* (New York, 1969); JACK P. GREENE, *The Quest for Power: The Lower Houses of Assembly in the Southern Royal Colonies, 1689–1776* (Chapel Hill, N.C., 1963); and MARY PATTERSON CLARKE, *Parliamentary Privilege in the American Colonies* (New Haven, 1943).

Colonial Political Ideology and Legislative Behavior

Significant general studies of political ideology in colonial America are J. R. POLE, "Historians and the Problem of Early American Democracy," *American Historical Review* 67 (1962); RICHARD BUEL, JR., "Democracy and the American Revolution: A Frame of Reference," *William and Mary Quarterly*, ser. 3, 21, no. 2 (1964); JOY B. GILSDORF and ROBERT B. GILSDORF, "Elites and Electorates: Some Plain Truths for Historians of Colonial America," in DAVID D. HALL, JOHN M. MURRIN, and THAD W. TATE, eds., *Saints and Revolutionaries* (New York, 1984); and J. G. A. POCOCK, "Virtue and Commerce in the Eighteenth Century," *Journal of Interdisciplinary History* 3 (1972).

The intellectual context of legislative behavior is analyzed by JACK P. GREENE, "Political Mimesis: A Consideration of the Historical and

Cultural Roots of Legislative Behavior in the British Colonies in the Eighteenth Century," *American Historical Review* 75 (1969); PAUL LUCAS, "A Note on the Comparative Study of the Structure of Politics in Mid-Eighteenth Century Britain and Its American Colonies," *William and Mary Quarterly*, ser. 3, 28 (1971), and RICHARD L. BUSHMAN, "Corruption and Power in Provincial America," in *The Development of a Revolutionary Mentality* (Washington, D.C., 1972).

Individual Colonies

The most important studies of political life in individual colonies are BERNARD BAILYN, "Politics and Social Structure in Virginia," in JAMES M. SMITH, ed., *Seventeenth-Century America: Essays on Colonial History* (Chapel Hill, N.C., 1959), pp. 90–115; PATRICIA U. BONOMI, *A Factious People: Politics and Society in Colonial New York* (New York, 1971); TIMOTHY H. BREEN, *The Character of the Good Ruler: A Study of Puritan Political Ideas in New England, 1630–1730* (New Haven, 1970); RICHARD L. BUSHMAN, *From Puritan to Yankee: Character and the Social Order in Connecticut, 1690–1765* (Cambridge, Mass., 1967); JERE R. DANIELL, *Experiment in Republicanism: New Hampshire Politics and the American Revolution, 1741–1794* (Cambridge, Mass., 1970); A. ROGER EKIRCH, *"Poor Carolina": Politics and Society in Colonial North Carolina, 1729–1776* (Chapel Hill, N.C., 1981); JACK P. GREENE, "Foundations of Political Power in the Virginia House of Burgesses, 1720–1776," *William and Mary Quarterly*, ser. 3, 16 (1959), and "Society, Ideology, and Politics: An Analysis of the Political Culture of Mid-Eighteenth Century Virginia" in RICHARD M.

JELLISON, ed., *Society, Freedom, and Conscience: The American Revolution in Virginia, Massachusetts, and New York* (New York, 1976); GARY B. NASH, *Quakers and Politics: Pennsylvania, 1681–1726* (Princeton, N.J., 1968); THOMAS L. PURVIS, *Proprietors, Patronage, and Paper Money: Legislative Politics in New Jersey, 1703–1776* (New Brunswick, N.J., 1986); ALAN TULLY, *William Penn's Legacy: Politics and Social Structure in Provincial Pennsylvania, 1726–1755* (Baltimore, 1977); ROBERT M. WEIR, "'The Harmony We Were Famous For': An Interpretation of Pre-Revolutionary South Carolina Politics," *William and Mary Quarterly*, ser. 3, 26 (1969); and Robert Zemsky, *Merchants, Farmers, and River Gods: An Essay on Eighteenth-Century American Politics* (Boston, 1971).

Contemporary Sources

Contemporary sources cited in this essay are SIR WILLIAM BLACKSTONE, *Commentaries on the Laws of England*, 4 vols., 6th ed. (London, 1774); WILLIAM BYRD, *History of the Dividing Line, and Other Tracts*, 2 vols. (Richmond, Va., 1866); JACK P. GREENE, ed., *The Diary of Colonel Landon Carter of Sabine Hall, 1752–1778*, 2 vols., (Charlottesville, Va., 1965); BERNARD PEACH, ed., *Richard Price and the Ethical Foundations of the American Revolution* (Durham, N.C., 1979); ADAM SMITH, *An Inquiry into the Nature and Causes of the Wealth of Nations*, in R. H. CAMPBELL and A. S. SKINNER, eds., *The Glasgow Edition of the Works and Correspondence of Adam Smith*, 6 vols. (Oxford, 1976–1983); and WILLIAM SMITH, JR., *The History of the Province of New York*, 2 vols., edited by MICHAEL KAMMEN (Cambridge, Mass., 1972).

CONSTITUTIONAL CONVENTIONS

Christian G. Fritz

Constitutional conventions have played an essential part in a major American innovation in political governance: the practice of writing constitutions designed to serve as frames of government and to restrict governmental powers. The idea of imposing structural limitations on the power of the state drew heavily on English history, in that the English constitutional tradition had developed a notion of *fundamental law*—associated with the ancient heritage of the English common law—that implied such limitation of governmental power. While fundamental law had originated as a means of checking royal power, constitutional arrangements in England eventually placed absolute power with Parliament. However, instead of a fundamental law in the form of a written constitution, English constitutional history developed the theory of parliamentary sovereignty. Although the theory made Parliament supreme, English constitutional law created constitutional understandings (called "conventions"—a term referring here to the implicitly understood observance of common precepts as opposed to the deliberative meetings that are the main topic of this essay) that implicitly restrain governmental power and form an unwritten constitution.

In contrast, the constitutionalism that developed in the United States after the American Revolution significantly differed from the English tradition. American constitutionalism was unique not only in adopting the practice of writing constitutions but also in pioneering the use of a deliberative body specially designed to draft fundamental law as written constitutions—namely, the constituent assembly that came to be called a "constitutional convention." Moreover, apart from the use of such conventions, a practice developed of requiring popular ratification of the document produced by a convention before it attained binding force—a step implied by the theory of popular sovereignty.

The justification of the American Revolution and republican government—as opposed to the monarchical forms of government in Europe—rested on the theory of popular sovereignty. In essence, that theory established the basic premise of American political life: the ultimate and sole legitimacy of government rests on the consent of "the people." Defining "the people" became one of the central issues in the development of the American experience, but soon after declaring independence, American revolutionaries came to agree that popular sovereignty underlay America's republican governments. If identifying "the people" and their role in changing government took many decades, the problem of how to locate popular sovereignty was solved relatively quickly by the institutional device of the constitutional convention.

Popular sovereignty served well as a theory, but it lacked a mechanism by which the people's sovereign political power could be exercised to produce a tangible structure of government having the legitimacy required by that theory. The English civil wars of 1642–1651 and the potential Catholic succession to the English throne that led to the so-called Glorious Revolution of 1688 raised ideas that prefigured the American solution. Nonetheless, only in America were these ideas—independently arrived at—put into practice. The American answer was a convention, called for the purpose of drafting a constitution, whose delegates represented the people and whose work could be submitted to them for ratification.

Although the federal constitutional convention in 1787 has dominated studies of American constitutional history, the most dynamic users of constitutional conventions have been the states. Indeed, while only one federal constitutional convention has ever been held whose product has experienced relatively little formal amendment, state constitutional revision has been nearly continuous from the Revolutionary period to the present day. More than 220 American state-constitutional conventions have been called, and many thousands of state constitutional amendments have been adopted. In contrast, constitutional adjustments at the federal level have mainly occurred through judicial interpretation, giving rise to President Woodrow Wilson's claim that the U.S. Supreme Court functions, in part, as a continuing constitutional convention.

Why constitutional revision took such different directions on the state and federal levels has long intrigued scholars. One explanation is the greater difficulty of amending the federal constitution than most state constitutions. Moreover, a reluctance to disturb the delicate compromises struck in the federal constitution has also been suggested. Certainly some of the Founding Fathers sought to avoid extensive or frequent revision of the federal constitution. James Madison was not alone in hoping that judicial interpretation would prove an adequate and more conservative means of adjusting the federal constitution than its revision by amendment or convention. Ultimately, such considerations help explain the dearth of federal constitutional change but fail to account for the extensive revision of state constitutions.

After all, many obstacles have stood in the way of state constitutional revision. State constitutions, like the federal model, have revealed a desire to prevent their too frequent or easy revision. Indeed, state constitutions have often required successive legislatures to pass proposed amendments by special majorities—sometimes two-thirds—before such proposals could be submitted to the voters. Moreover, many of the earliest state constitutions even lacked provisions for their amendment, a pattern that continued well into the nineteenth century. When existing constitutions failed to provide for their revision, constitutional reformers had to convince legislators of the desirability of a constitutional convention. Finally, even when procedures existed for the calling of a convention, the legislature not only needed to initiate the process of revision by placing the issue of whether to call a convention on the ballot but also had to organize the convention through an enabling act.

Ultimately, the different experiences with constitutional revision at the federal and state levels produced two distinct traditions of constitutional revision. While the two traditions were closely related and rested on a shared commitment to popular sovereignty, ideas about revising the fundamental law of the states developed differently from notions about revision of the federal constitution. Federal constitutional revision was obviously linked with the experience and product of the first and only national constitutional convention (1787). The federal constitution described the structure of the federal government and its relationship with the state governments in broad terms. The decision to submit this document for state ratification—as well as to draft the constitution by a convention—had been pioneered by Massachusetts when that state created its constitution of 1780. Thus, the federal constitutional convention emulated a state model that became the paradigm for future state constitutional conventions.

Although no other federal constitutional conventions have been held, numerous efforts have been made to call for a new convention. Indeed, at the beginning of the 1990s an attempt was made to hold a federal convention, ostensibly to force the federal government to balance its budget. In the absence of any other conventions, the combination of infrequent amendment and frequent constitutional interpretation of the existing document has characterized the process of federal constitutional revision. The flexibility of the national constitution as a frame of government to accommodate to changes over time distinctly contrasts with the frequency of state constitutional revision both through conventions and the amendment process. Moreover, while the federal tradition emerged quickly and experienced little change after the eighteenth century, the state tradition has undergone a dramatic evolution.

The basic reason that the states departed from the federal tradition of constitutional revision and developed their own distinct tradition was rooted in how Americans in the eighteenth, and especially in the nineteenth century, understood the nature of constitutionalism and federalism. For them, the essence of American constitutionalism implied that popular sovereignty was the basis and justification for change in government. Virtually all of the Revolutionary states' constitutions proclaimed the republican principle that the people had the inherent right to alter their government and urged a frequent recurrence to fundamental principles. Recurring to fundamental principles did not imply a reexamination of specific rights so much as it symbolized the power of the people to change their government at will. It also suggested the principle (that eventually became the practice) that state constitutional revision was the norm rather than the exception. As the president of the Massachusett's constitutional convention said in his opening address to the assembled delegates: "An occasional revision of the institutions of government, and a frequent recurrence to its fundamental principles, is in accordance with the maxims of its founders..." (*Official Report of Debates and Proceedings in the State Convention*, vol. 1, Boston, 1853, pp. 9–10). This heritage marked a clear departure from the federal constitutional tradition, which came to view the continual tinkering with state fundamental law as unfortunate, if not inappropriate.

Within the state constitutional tradition, however, theory fully supported the reexamination and refinement of fundamental law. The language in state constitutions declaring the people's right to alter their governments expressed an important attitude about constitution making. No constitutional principle was more fundamental to Revolutionary theory and nineteenth-century practice than the idea that constitutional revision was inherent in popular sovereignty. Indeed, the absence of provisions for constitutional revision underscored the fundamental nature of such a right of revision: its existence did not depend on a constitutional provision.

To the extent that popular sovereignty implied the right to change government, the state level was the logical, natural location for constitutional revision during the eighteenth and nineteenth centuries. The relationship between individuals and government during this period was overwhelmingly cast in terms of local and state government rather than the federal government. Indeed, even on the eve of the Civil War, the national government lacked the power to act in such basic matters as health, education, morals, safety, sanitation, welfare, and local transportation. Virtually all activities that affected the day-to-day lives of Americans were the province of their local or state governments. Therefore, it made compelling sense that in the course of altering the powers and practices of government, constitutional revision would focus on state constitutions.

Even as the struggle over the institution and spread of slavery helped define federalism, by which governmental powers are divided between federal and state levels, underlying that sectional dispute and ultimately, the Civil War was the deeply held concept of independent statehood. The fact that the Civil War repudiated the theory of states' rights associated with the doctrine of nullification (that is, states did not have the power to declare federal laws unconstitutional) and confirmed the national character of sovereignty underlying the federal constitution should not obscure the fact that the states remained the primary governmental unit in the lives of Americans. Although the Civil War and, even more, Reconstruction did lay the foundations for the power the federal government would later exert over the lives of individuals, that potential would only be realized in the twentieth century. Thus, the Civil War did not mark a radical break in the natural focus that state constitutions had as the most important source of fundamental law for Americans. Throughout American history, state constitutions offered the most fruitful arena within which to exercise the power of popular sovereignty that underlay American constitutionalism.

THE FUNCTION OF CONSTITUTIONAL CONVENTIONS

Within the federal and state traditions of constitutional revision, constitutional conventions have played different roles as well as undergone a shift in function at the state level. The federal constitution and many of the early state constitutions established a pattern of short documents with broad statements allocating governmental structures, powers, and restrictions. This pattern would later be seen as the appropriate or correct nature and function of written constitutions. Nonetheless, challenges to this approach of making constitution quickly emerged in the nineteenth century as constitutional conventions developed different roles and the function of state constitutions changed. The blurring of distinctions between the two traditions has led to a recurring tendency to compare the products of state constitutional conventions with the federal constitution, a comparison that ignores both the functional differences of constitutions in American federalism and the dynamic tradition of state constitutional revision.

Departing from the federal model, nineteenth-century state constitutions increasingly grew in size and began to incorporate matter that many described as legislative detail inappropriate for a constitution. The general trend in the course of the nineteenth century was from pithy constitutions to documents of substantial length. The type of documents produced illustrated the resemblance that constitutional conventions increasingly bore to quasi-legislative bodies. Few contrasts greater in style or substance existed than between the brief U.S. Constitution (a mere 5,000 words, excluding amendments) and the mammoth Louisiana Constitution of 1921, which by 1969 had grown to more than 250,000 words and had acquired over five hundred amendments.

The resulting form of state constitutions reflects the important, if strange, dual role that constitutional conventions have played in American history: they have served both as the institutional means through which popular sovereignty is expressed and as deliberative bodies frequently engaged in constitutional legislation. This historic combination of political theory and pragmatic politics existed in some measure from the start of constitution making in the United States. Even the federal constitution—frequently described as a classic product of "pure" constitution making—contains matters of legislative detail that reflected contemporary political concerns. The oblique but numerous provisions dealing with slavery, for example, were hardly matters of constitutional structure or theory. Likewise, the first generation of state constitutions contained references to such matters as the specific county organization for the militia (Georgia, 1777), the establishment of universities (Massachusetts, 1780), and the illegality of contracts for the sale of Native American land (New York, 1777)—all of which hardly was consistent with the idea of fundamental law as substantively distinct from ordinary legislation. Nonetheless, both the federal constitution and the first state

constitutions contained significantly less legislative detail than would subsequent nineteenth- and twentieth-century constitutions. Thus, American fundamental law has always contained some degree of constitutional legislation.

Still, scholars have lamented the transition from the relatively brief constitutions of the Revolutionary period to the long and detailed nineteenth-century constitutions. To some, the trend demonstrates a decline in the quality of framing constitutions. The federal constitution and some of the early state constitutions are cited as correct examples of constitutions, after which the art of constitution making evidently diminished during the nineteenth century.

This characterization, however, fails to recognize the eventual function state constitutional conventions served as a major political process related to, and supplementing, the normal, legislative processes. Although constitutions' forms changed, the fact that many state constitutions evolved into codelike documents hardly proved a degeneration in the making of a constitution. Indeed, approached as a historical process, the increasing length and greater legislative detail of state constitutions merely reflected a shifting understanding of the function and purpose of state constitutions. Ultimately, then, a comparison of nineteenth-century constitutions with the federal model is inappropriate because the purposes of state and federal constitutions were significantly different.

It is a truism of constitutional law that the federal constitution created a national government of limited, delegated powers and that the states, as plenary governments, automatically possess unlimited powers, except as limited by their own constitutions and the federal constitution. This truism clearly affected the course of nineteenth-century constitutionalism. Federalism, as understood throughout most of the nineteenth century, meant that individuals would interact most extensively with their state and local governments. Since state governments inherently had potentially vast general powers, it followed for nineteenth-century constitution makers that the constitutions they were framing needed to be explicit about limiting and defining the scope of governmental powers, especially on behalf of individual liberty. Thus, the logic of constitutional theory dictated the increased length and comprehensiveness of state constitutions, as compared to the federal constitution.

Indeed, most state constitutions eventually defined the powers and limits of government through a variety of means. State constitutions included an explicit declaration or bill of rights, and this statement of rights was usually broader than the first ten amendments of the federal constitution. For example, states' bills of rights were often more detailed in regard to their protection of the freedom of religion and speech. In addition, they came to include guarantees for certain, free, and swift legal remedies; a broad right to bail; and provisions against the forfeiture of property. Moreover, state constitutions routinely included thorough definitions and provisions regarding the structures, powers, and procedures of the three branches of government; limits on the power to tax, borrow, and spend; the state's obligations and powers in such areas as education, incorporation, voting, and banking; the state's powers to exploit its natural resources and oversee local government; and unique local state circumstances, such as arid conditions in the southwestern states.

Concepts of how state constitutions ought to be framed and what they should contain underwent significant shifts from the Revolutionary period through the twentieth century. From the start, state delegates questioned the propriety of including legislative matters in a constitution. Indeed, even in the conventions of the late nineteenth century, clearly the era of code-like constitutions, delegates still complained about legislative detail finding its way into state constitutions. Nonetheless, such occasional complaints hardly stopped the practice, and by the latter half of the nineteenth century, most delegates justified the inclusion of legislative detail because of its intrinsic importance. Detailed provisions governing the creation and operation of corporations and banks were defended as appropriate constitutional provisions because the legislatures had not, would not, or could not address these issues. To some extent, this inclusionary practice reflected a growing lack of faith in the legislative process and the desire to safeguard controversial political objectives within state constitutions. For example, by inserting provisions that regulated business

or voting rights, delegates succeeded in achieving political goals that were less subject to change than ordinary statutory law.

Even though the desire to entrench political choices in state constitutions may have initially motivated delegates, proponents of constitutions as detailed documents developed broader theoretical justifications. Those justifications reflected the collective sense by convention delegates that constitution making was an evolving science and thus naturally created improved constitutions over time. Far from feeling inferior to their constitutional Founding Fathers, nineteenth-century convention delegates displayed abundant self-confidence that they understood the nature of making constitutions much better than their ancestors. Although respectful of the patriotism and sacrifices of the Revolutionary generation, most nineteenth-century constitution makers believed that their era's constitutions reflected considerable improvement over older models and that future constitutions would likewise improve.

A belief in progress not only suggested that newer constitutions were improvements on older models but also accounted for the expansion of subject matter that nineteenth-century constitutions embraced. Nineteenth-century delegates explained much constitutional legislation in terms of a growing enlightenment about the principles of republican government. The expansion of political participation, for example, demonstrated how the nineteenth century had moved beyond a more limited understanding of representative government held by eighteenth-century constitution makers. Moreover, changes in the nature of government (influenced by changes in American society) presented both new problems and new opportunities for constitution makers. Delegates noted that earlier constitution makers had not been faced with the complex issues of nineteenth-century business regulation and economics. The combination of refining older constitutional provisions and creating new ones required of constitutional government in the nineteenth century accelerated the process of constitutional legislation.

All conventions, of course, reflected the political and economic environment within which they labored, but the different types of conventions produced distinctions. Conventions framing a state's first constitution faced different challenges than those conventions called to reconsider and reexamine an existing constitution. Conventions charged with the reexamination of constitutions spent much time debating the perceived merits and deficiencies of the existing document. Delegates frequently departed from the present constitution and adopted the constitutional practices of other states on the grounds of updating the constitution. In this context, delegates often spoke of making the new constitution reflect "the spirit of the age." Given the sparseness of many of the initial, Revolutionary constitutions, subsequent constitutional conventions often produced more detailed and certainly more self-consciously created constitutions. While the Revolutionary constitutions were often created in a short period of time, conventions meeting in the nineteenth century often sat for many weeks or months. The Pennsylvania convention of 1837–1838, for example, deliberated for eight months and produced debates that ran to fourteen volumes. In contrast, New Jersey created its 1776 constitution in twelve days.

GENERAL THEMES IN CONSTITUTION MAKING

To a significant extent, the history of constitutional conventions in the United States has paralleled the democratization of American politics. An inherent and unanswered question in the concept of popular sovereignty was the definition of "the people." Defining the electorate and debating the meaning of representation occupied the attention of many delegates during the nineteenth century. Indeed, one underlying impetus for the call for many conventions—as well as a principal theme in their proceedings—was the desire to increase the political participation of underrepresented groups or to include groups not yet represented.

An even broader theme at the level of state constitutional conventions has been the ambivalence apparent in the process of constitutional revision. Despite the extraordinary number of state constitutional conventions that have been convened, neither the Revolutionary generation nor later generations eagerly embraced constitutional revision and change. In fact, the broad history of American constitutional revision reveals a pronounced tension between those who sought to resist constitutional revision on the grounds of maintaining stability and those who insisted that change was needed to improve the nature of government and society. This tension, however, underlay the level of express debate in which all participants acknowledged the political axiom of popular sovereignty and the people's right to revise, if not abolish, their existing governments. The wisdom of making a constitutional change, not the right to do so, was the perennial issue.

One symptom of misgivings about the desirability of constitutional change was the reluctance that legislatures in the nineteenth and twentieth centuries have displayed about calling conventions. Indeed, that reluctance occasionally developed into active resistance to popular demands for constitutional revision. For example, Virginia's 1829 convention, no less than Maryland's 1967 convention, met only after many years of agitation for a new convention. In Virginia, constitutional revision required a convention because the 1776 constitution contained no provisions for constitutional amendment. In Maryland the constitution in force in the twentieth century, dating back to 1867, provided for an automatic referendum on the issue of constitutional revision at twenty-year intervals, but the legislature declined to organize a constitutional convention even after the electorate voted by substantial majorities in favor of constitutional revision in 1930 and 1950.

Reluctance to engage in constitutional revision also produced an interesting dimension of the history of nineteenth-century constitutional conventions—namely, the appearance of the so-called circumvention convention, an extralegislative body designed to pressure recalcitrant legislatures into calling for a constitutional convention. The most dramatic example of such extralegal pressure to prompt constitutional revision (for the purpose of broadening the suffrage) was the struggle in Rhode Island leading to a People's Convention and culminating in Dorr's Rebellion (1841–1842). Thomas Dorr and his followers took the strategy of circumvention conventions to the point of revolution by framing a constitution and attempting to put it into operation in defiance of the existing government.

CONSTITUTIONAL CONVENTIONS

Underlying much of this resistance to constitutional revision was a reluctance by groups who enjoyed political dominance under existing state constitutions to relinquish some of their power or respond to the efforts to expand political participation. The 1820s and 1830s, in particular, saw a growing pressure for wider political participation. Thomas Jefferson's election to the presidency in 1800 initiated a movement—which bore fruit only decades later—to democratize government. This process often found its expression in the calls for, and the process of, constitutional revision. Some of the bitterest struggles took place in Virginia, where critics assailed the alleged aristocratic nature of government under the first state constitution and its perpetuation of unequal representation. Repeatedly frustrated by the Virginia and North Carolina legislatures, reformers held circumvention conventions, whose pressure eventually resulted in constitutional conventions (Virginia's in 1829 and North Carolina's in 1835). Thus, a common theme in state constitutional revision from the 1820s to the Civil War was the powerful impulse for greater political democracy (at least for adult white males) epitomized by a movement toward more elections, fuller participation, and fairer representation.

In the course of efforts to expand political participation, the character of constitution making and constitutional conventions began to change. To the extent that conventions had been devoted to the formulation of fundamental principles outlining governmental powers, they shifted to arenas for the resolution of particular ongoing political conflicts. By the 1830s, constitutional revision was deeply involved in party politics and competing social and economic interests. Some scholars have characterized this transition as a shift from constitutionalism to administrative instrumentalism. Although conventions never lost a sense of their theoretical role of framing the organic law of the state—designed to last for many years—they increasingly became conscious of their role in making political decisions in lieu of the legislature.

One external factor affecting all state conventions was the legislation, or enabling act, that brought the convention into being. Such acts often detailed how the convention should be organized and sometimes directed the convention's attention to specific issues or questions for constitutional revision. In territories, however, a different dynamic existed because of the issue of statehood. Delegates to territorial constitutional conventions were acutely aware that the U.S. Congress would sit in judgment of their final product. Congressional enabling acts usually dictated the terms and conditions under which Congress would be willing to admit the would-be state. Apart from that difference, however, territorial conventions often resembled state constitutional conventions and frequently raised similarly wide-ranging questions about what was constitutionally appropriate.

The question of what power conventions had to depart from the acts of the legislature that called them into being forced delegates to struggle with the theoretical basis of constitutional conventions. Furthermore, if the convention embodied or represented popular sovereignty, could its work ever be restrained? Delegates to numerous nineteenth-century conventions—including those in New York (1821), Illinois (1847), Kentucky (1849), and Massachusetts (1853)—concluded that constitutional conventions could not be limited. Delegates often pointed to the classic example of the federal constitution, the product of a convention that clearly exceeded its legislative mandate, but became fundamental law with popular ratification. Restraints on the action of constitutional conventions, they argued, were incompatible with the American political theory of popular sovereignty, since the electorate could always validate any action of the convention through the process of ratification.

What had largely been accepted in theory and practice came under attack in the wake of the Civil War when a Chicago judge and later law professor, John A. Jameson, sought to repudiate the idea that constitutional conventions represented the unrestrainable sovereignty of the people. Jameson initially responded to the use of such illimitable power by delegates to the 1862 Illinois constitutional convention, who had gone well beyond the drafting of a new state constitution to reapportion congressional districts and ratify an amendment to the federal constitution. Jameson blamed such misguided views about the power of conventions on proslavery groups and their theories of secession. Eventually Jameson published his *Treatise on Constitutional Conventions* (1866), which sought to establish the idea of limited conventions and stressed the limits on state powers and the subordination of the states to the federal union.

Jameson's *Constitutional Conventions* proved enormously influential and went through four editions by 1887. Despite the influence of Jameson's work and its attraction to conservatives, the notion of the convention-as-sovereign persisted. Especially as the concerns of the Civil War faded, many commentators suggested that while state constitutional conventions might not produce results repugnant to the federal constitution, they might ignore the legislative act calling them into existence. Indeed, some prominent lawyers and constitutional commentators writing in the early twentieth century, such as Walter F. Dodd, Yale law professor and attorney, and Roger Sherman Hoar, a Massachusetts assistant attorney general, argued that extraconstitutional conventions were valid because they were drawn from the highest source of political power: the people.

While the idea of the convention's power has underlain much state constitutional revision, the factor of regionalism has also exerted a broad influence on constitution making. Delegates frequently responded to regional circumstances in their constitutions. Particular natural and economic environments often gave rise to particular constitutional provisions dealing with eminent domain, water rights, and corporate regulation. Ethnic demographics influenced provisions dealing with the requirements that educational instruction and the publication of statutes occur in other languages in addition to English. Obviously, other significant regional factors, such as the institution of slavery in the South, left their marks on some constitutions.

Nonetheless, nineteenth-century constitutions looked more like each other than like documents representative of specific regions. Even more telling, while the content of documents revealed regional or local circumstances, the deliberations of delegates—how they approached and understood their task as American constitution makers—revealed a shared constitutional tradition that cut across regions of the country. For all of the substantive issues that varied from convention to convention, nineteenth-century constitution makers revealed a remarkable awareness of the practices and approaches of other states to the process of constitution making. There were common constitutional ideas and behavior, and both the products and especially the process of nineteenth-century constitution making had a distinct national dimension.

In drafting and revising constitutions, state constitutional conventions engaged in much borrowing from other state constitutions. This borrowing, however, had a strong dimension of creativity and self-conscious reflection that is apt to be overlooked if only the texts of various state constitutions are compared. While it often happened that one state incorporated provisions (sometimes verbatim) from earlier constitutions, the borrowing convention delegates often spent considerable time discussing the merits of various options. Thus, the derivative aspects of nineteenth-century constitutions can obscure the true nature of the process of constitution making unless one examines the debates, not just the final product.

Furthermore, nineteenth-century delegates worked in a context of heightened awareness of the broad constitutional tradition of state revision. Many conventions had access to all the existing models of state constitutions (collected in numerous editions of pocket-sized compilations), and many delegates were aware of contemporaneous state constitutional conventions or practices. Rarely did constitutional conventions in the nineteenth century approach the task of constitution making in isolation from, and in ignorance of, the constitutional practices of other states. Even on the western frontier, such as California in 1849 and South Dakota in 1889, delegates displayed extensive knowledge of the constitutions in other states and a sophisticated level of understanding about constitutional experience and practice in general. An examination of constitution making across the broad sweep of the nineteenth century prompts the conclusion that a national ideology of constitutionalism existed that transcended regions and individual states.

THE POLITICAL CONTEXT OF MAKING A CONSTITUTION

State constitution making came to embody an extremely dynamic concept of constitutionalism. Nonetheless, despite the evolving uses of constitutional conventions, one can detect broad waves of constitution making and general trends in constitutional revision. Considering constitution making in distinct periods helps identify the substantive concerns of delegates and the broader political context within which they worked. Moreover, the shifts in institutional arrangements and allocation of governmental powers can also be traced in the nature of the constitutions produced. It is useful to consider state constitution making in seven periods: Revolutionary, 1776–1800; early national, 1800–1830; antebellum, 1830–1860; Confederate, 1860–1864; Reconstruction, 1864–1870; late nineteenth century and territorial; and twentieth century.

Revolutionary Period, 1776–1800

The American Revolution made it necessary for the colonies to create new republican governments. All but two former colonies engaged in this process by drafting constitutions; only Rhode Island and Connecticut kept their colonial charters as the basis of their government. These first efforts at Revolutionary constitution making shared a number of common characteristics. Most significant from the standpoint of later constitutional theory and the history of constitutional conventions was the failure to distinguish clearly between statutory and fundamental law. Many of the first state constitutions were the products of legislatures (not specially created constitutional conventions), some of which were concurrently engaged in passing ordinary legislation. Beyond the general absence of constitutional conventions, few of these early states submitted their first constitutions to the people for ratification. Indeed, among the early state constitutions, the Massachusetts (1780) and New Hampshire (1784) constitutions were the only ones to be drafted by constitutional conventions and submitted for popular ratification.

In part, the blurred distinction between legislation and fundamental law and the failure to abide by the implicit requirements of popular sovereignty stemmed largely from the exigencies of the Revolution. The desire to make a smooth transition from colonial status to statehood and to avoid potential internal disputes—including trouble from Tories, or British sympathizers—helps explain a preference for framing governments by sitting legislatures. Moreover, the distinction between normal legislation and the process of making constitutions was not uniformly well understood in 1776. Indeed, in the 1780s, Jefferson reflected that Virginia's 1776 constitution had been formed when the Founding Fathers were inexperienced in the science of government. Given a colonial experience that had strongly identified the legislature with the people, the fact that American legislatures wrote and adopted constitutions in the name of the people seemed unremarkable. Only when the people began to insist that constitutions be submitted directly to them for ratification would the process of constitution making attain a modern characteristic.

The republican legacy of the American Revolution dictated that governments in the United States would divide governmental power among the legislature, the executive, and the judiciary. The combination of popular sovereignty and republicanism led to the incorporation of a new version of the concept of separation of powers in the early state constitutions. By accepting "the people" as the ultimate sovereigns, early constitution makers rejected the European pattern of dividing governmental power in accord with social divisions.

Although the Revolutionary state constitutions separated powers, they allocated wide powers to the legislatures and limited the power of the executive. These early state constitutions trusted the legislative branch to determine community goals. The establishment of governments that nearly created legislative supremacy reflected colonial distrust of the executive powers of royal governors. Conversely, the legislative branch, in the form of the popular assemblies, had long been identified with the interests of the people. For this reason, excessive power placed in the hands of the legislature under the new state constitutions seemed unlikely to produce a dangerous governmental arrangement.

Massachusetts pioneered the modern practice of a special constitutional convention followed by popular ratification, yet states did not completely embrace the full implications of fundamental law requiring popular ratification until well into the nineteenth century. Not only did some eighteenth-century constitutions permit the legislature alone to change the fundamental law (e.g., the South Carolina [1790] and Georgia [1798] constitutions), but in some states that same power remained in the hands of the legislature well into the nineteenth century (as in the Arkansas [1836] and Florida [1838] constitutions). Indeed, even as late as 1897, Delaware's constitution did not formally require popular ratification before the legislature could alter the constitution. By then, of course, the constitutional tradition of popular ratification was well established, but the Delaware example illustrates the length of time it took for the formal requirements of popular sovereignty to penetrate into the written fundamental law of all the states.

Thus, the period of eighteenth-century state constitution making reflected the growing understanding of the distinction between statutory and constitutional law, as well as a growing sophistication about the mechanics of constitutional revision. In addition, the frequency of such conventions mirrored the active nature of state constitutional revision. Between 1776 and 1798, sixteen states drafted twenty-nine constitutions. The longevity of these first efforts was mixed: although seven of the first states replaced their initial constitutions within ten years, the average state constitution written in that period remained in force for more than sixty years.

In terms of brevity, eighteenth-century state constitutions compared favorably with the model of the federal constitution. Most contained little of the type of detail that would later characterize state constitutions. By the end of the eighteenth century, the shortest constitution was that of New Jersey (about twenty-five hundred words) and the longest that of Massachusetts (about twelve thousand words).

In general, the earliest state constitutions drew more heavily upon a colonial tradition of covenants and compacts than did the federal constitution. As a result, those early state constitutions had a different philosophical orientation, manifested by a greater emphasis than the federal model's on the direct and continuing consent of popular majorities. This goal was sought by providing for short tenures, elective offices, and the instruction of representatives by their constituencies. Absent were provisions for amendment in some of the Revolutionary constitutions (e.g., New York, Virginia, North Carolina, and New Jersey). Implicitly, the omission of such provisions assumed that the people retained the inherent right to change their government. Indeed, in 1789 the people of both Delaware and Pennsylvania demonstrated the strength of their belief in this inherent right of popular sovereignty when in both states the methods of amendment set out by their respective constitutions were disregarded.

Early National Period, 1800–1830

Constitutions of the early national period bore the marks of the first decade of experience of government under the Revolutionary constitutions. Between the Revolution and the federal Constitutional Convention of 1787 many influential leaders became disenchanted with what they viewed as the ill effects of excessive legislative powers in state governments. Indeed, many of the delegates who gathered in Philadelphia to draft a new federal constitution were, like Madison, strongly affected by state laws that they believed were blatant violations of property rights and republican principles and by their perception of a rise in legislative demagoguery. This reaction against legislative supremacy ultimately led to a better institutional balance between the three branches of government in the federal constitution. Likewise, state constitutions drafted in the early national period reflected a shifting of power away from the legislature (including more restrictions on its powers) and a conferral of greater power on the executive branch. Still, none of the state constitutions (Massachusetts, perhaps, came the closest) provided for a degree of executive power or of judicial independence equal to that found in the federal constitution.

This second period of constitution making also saw what might be considered the first "western" wave of constitution making, with the drafting of constitutions for eight states created out of lands on the frontiers of the original states—namely, Louisiana, Ohio, Indiana, Mississippi, Illinois, Alabama, Maine, and Missouri. In addition, the period saw the revision of two eastern constitutions: Connecticut's in 1818 and New York's in 1821. Western migration and expansion, of course, gave impetus to these new constitutions, but the increasing growth of a western population, even in existing states, produced a constitutional tension of its own.

The combination of this growing western population with a broader vision of political participation initiated by Jefferson's election in 1800 found expression in constitutional revision. One of the broad trends in this period was the increasing pressure on the propertied minority (holding most of the political power) to accept government that entailed majority rule. This process of democratizing state governments often became extremely bitter and heated, since it inevitably challenged constitutionally entrenched political interests. Some of the bitterest struggles occurred in the South, where political debate focused on efforts for constitutional revision. In Virginia and North Carolina, opponents of the existing constitutions were especially vocal in their call for creating procedures for constitutional amendment, a key issue because no methods for amendment were currently provided by their constitutions.

These struggles, particularly in Virginia, led to the appearance of the technique of the circumvention convention, which was, as described above, a strategy designed to pressure recalcitrant legislatures into calling constitutional conventions. From 1806 onward, the western portion of the state petitioned yearly for a constitutional plebiscite, but to no avail. Eventually, western reformers, frustrated by the legislature's unwillingness to revise the 1776 constitution, threatened to bypass that obstruction and secede from the state. Their frustration led to counter, or shadow, conventions, the so-called Staunton Conventions in 1816 and 1825, which eventually coerced the state government into calling a constitutional convention in 1829.

One of the significant substantive differences between constitutions created or revised in the Revolutionary period and those produced in the early national period was that the latter documents all provided for a means of amendment. The procedures for amendment varied widely and included Missouri's 1820 constitutional provision for amendment that did not require popular ratification. Instead, two successive legislatures in Missouri could amend the constitution by approving changes with a two-thirds majority. The first several dec-

ades of experience with constitutional government underscored the importance of an institutionalized process of revision. That Americans began to place such provisions in their constitutions reflected not only the fear or threat posed by circumvention conventions but also the explicit recognition of the revolutionary implications of popular sovereignty. Moreover, the shift to constitutional revision procedures marked a successful transition from theory to practice in American constitutionalism. Such procedures demonstrated how popularly based governments could accommodate political change without violence. That achievement, more than the existence of written constitutions, gave the American experiment with republican government a chance for survival and an institutional structure within which to accommodate shifting political parties and regimes.

Collectively, the conventions that met during this period—in particular, the important regionally representative conventions of Virginia (1829–1830), Massachusetts (1820–1821), and New York (1821)—had little substantively in common with one another, except for a shared split within their ranks between conservative and democratically oriented delegates. Each of these conventions wrestled with the broad issues of accommodating democracy, liberty, and property with republican government. Moreover, they marked the first effort to reform the Revolutionary constitutions of those states. The support for established churches stimulated serious debate, as did the issues of representation in the legislature and judicial independence. Despite a large presence of reform-minded delegates, conservatives managed to hold sufficient sway to ensure that property requirements for voting and election to the upper legislative houses remained intact, to deflect efforts to elect judges, and to discontinue government support of religion.

Thus, even though circumvention conventions introduced a radical new twist into the state tradition of constitutional revision, thoroughgoing constitutional revision did not occur in the early national period. Virginia's 1829 convention, for example, while bringing together some of the most accomplished figures of the period, including James Madison, James Monroe, and John Marshall, did not result in a revised constitution that marked a significant shift of political power from that which existed under the 1776 constitution. More sweeping change, however, would occur after the 1830s, accompanied by a more extensive use of circumvention conventions to pressure for constitutional change.

Antebellum Period, 1830–1860

The antebellum period marked the high-water mark of constitution making in American history. Some fifty constitutional conventions were held in the three decades between 1830 and 1860. By 1860, more than half the states had framed new constitutions or revised existing ones. More than any previous time, this period marked a heightened awareness of the process of constitution making and the variety of existing constitutional arrangements. The sheer number of constitutional conventions helped create this general awareness, but in addition, improvements in communication—through railroads, the telegraph, and a better postal service —made it possible to take a wider interest in constitution making. The result of a broader discussion and exchange of constitutional ideas promoted a growing commonality of ideas about the fundamentals of governmental organization and standards for state constitutions. Indeed, one of the first convention manuals—a compilation of comparative constitutional data distributed to delegates—appeared in 1846 to assist New York's revision of its constitution.

This period also saw the continued and enhanced use of the circumvention convention, culminating in the dramatic events of Dorr's Rebellion in 1842. Earlier, in 1833, Pennsylvania had used the circumvention technique to pressure the calling of a constitutional convention that ultimately met in 1837. Moreover, circumvention strategies were also successfully used to force constitutional conventions in North Carolina, Georgia, and Maryland. Nonetheless, Dorr's Rebellion marked the start of a distinct phase of constitution making that inspired other radicals in other states, in part, because it prompted individuals to consider the logic and implication of circumvention. Earlier circumvention techniques simply had not resulted in resistance that pitted the inherent "right of revolution" against the stability of existing institutions.

Events in Maryland and Virginia exemplify how both conservatives and radicals reacted to, and used, the Dorr incident. In Maryland, Democrats sought revision, but the Whigs, citing provisions of the state's 1776 constitution, claimed that only the legislature could amend the fundamental law. The Democrats, however, invoked the inherent right of the people to change their government and eventually, after much pressure, a constitutional convention was called in 1850. In Virginia, a circumvention strategy was used in 1842 when a shadow convention gathered in Lewisburg. Eventually that pressure gave impetus to the 1851 constitutional convention. Between 1840 and 1853 eleven other states held constitutional conventions that resulted from tensions similar to those in Maryland and Virginia. The influence of Dorr's Rebellion on constitution making peaked when eight states held conventions between 1849 and 1852.

The Far West—California, Oregon, and Nevada—also experienced inaugural efforts in constitution making during this period. Delegates to these constitutional conventions were principally concerned with creating a political community and achieving the goal of statehood. In the final analysis, the differences between the three far western conventions was a reflection of the different political cultures of their frontier societies. Even though their frontier cultures had differing degrees of stability and continuity, the constitutional conventions in Oregon, Nevada, and California reflected strong similarities in the self-perceptions of, and in the approach taken by, antebellum delegates in the process of constitution making.

In the last decades of the antebellum period, constitutional conventions emerged as the means of overcoming what many regarded as an unresponsive political system. Constitution making during this period reveals the ongoing process of democratization and popular control of government as well as a trend toward restricting legislatures, especially with regard to the incurring of state debt following the internal-improvement fiascos and bank failures of the late 1830s. Moreover, many of the new constitutions provided for general, rather than special, charters of incorporation, taking away earlier legislative discretion. These concerns also reflected a general desire to shift power from the legislative to the executive branch. Increasingly, state constitutions enhanced the authority of governors through the veto and pardoning powers and the ability to make appointments, once the exclusive province of the legislature.

Another important substantive issue during this period was the role and composition of the judiciary and, in particular, the power of judicial review, by which courts can examine legislative and executive actions to determine their constitutionality. Even as the idea of judicial review found growing acceptance, substantial disagreement existed over how that power ought to be applied. That disagreement in turn stemmed from fundamental differences over the purpose of written constitutions. Conservatives thought judges should review constitutions and statutes with the purpose of protecting minority rights (particularly with respect to property), while radicals wanted judges to render decisions that popularly interpreted constitutions as expressions of political principles. The explicit debate that reflected these underlying attitudes concerned the selection and tenure of judges—whether judges should be appointed or popularly elected and have limited or life tenure on good behavior. For the radicals, elective judges would be free from the oversight of governors and legislatures and more able or willing to interpret newly fashioned constitutions vigorously. At the end of the period, those who sought an elective judiciary clearly carried the day: on the eve of the Civil War twenty-one of the thirty states had adopted popular election.

Confederate Constitutions, 1860–1864

The delegates from the seceded Southern states who met to form a new federal republic in February 1861 at Montgomery, Alabama, produced constitutions that reflected dualities in their thought. (Two constitutions were produced: a provisional one drafted in less than a week and a subsequent permanent constitution that was debated, revised, and finally approved on 11 March 1861.) Their concerns over slavery and states' rights found clear expression in their constitutions: property in slaves was expressly placed beyond the control of the Confederate congress, and the constitutional preambles sounded the central theme that their government was a confederation of sovereign states, with each state acting in its sovereign and independent character. And yet, the delegates largely patterned their fundamental law after the federal constitution. In this sense, it is fair to describe the Confederate constitutions as the result of both imitation and innovation.

The influence and hold that the federal constitution had on the Southern delegates was hardly surprising, since their quarrel was not with the federal constitution but with how it had been interpreted. Secession in their view was necessary to preserve the true principles of American constitutionalism. The Southern delegates saw themselves as defenders of traditional constitutional rights who had been forced to become revolutionaries and builders of a new political order. They clearly identified with the Founding Fathers.

The principal departures from the federal constitution model—apart from the establishment of a slaveholding republic founded on state sovereignty—were institutional. The Southern constitution provided for the establishment of a court to handle claims against the government (an omission clearly felt under the original federal constitution). Moreover, the allocation of powers among the branches of government followed the general nineteenth-century theme of strengthening the executive at the expense of the legislature. One example of such a shift was the provision that the president under the Confederate government would exercise an item veto.

Perhaps the most striking characteristic of the Confederate constitution that suggested the strong attachment Southern delegates had to the tradition of American constitutionalism was the extent to which they constructed a government that sought to preserve a nation. Despite all of the concern with states' rights as a foundation for the new republic (reflected, in part, by the provision that constitutional amendment would exclusively rest with the states), the existing document left intact powers that evidenced a desire to create a national government. For example, the Confederate constitution did not eliminate two provisions that had successfully been used to promote a strong American national state: the "supremacy clause" (Article VI, Section 2) and the "necessary and proper" clause (Article I, Section 8). Moreover, despite vigorous debate over the matter, Southern delegates did not provide for a mechanism for nullification or provide for a right of secession in their Confederate constitutions.

The paradox in the thought of Southern delegates was indeed reflected in the fundamental law they produced. The Confederate constitutions stand as the ultimate nineteenth-century constitutional expression of states' rights philosophy and the concept of state sovereignty; yet, they embodied the hopes for a perpetual national union, albeit with a Southern vision of American nationalism. The outcome of the Civil War, of course, buried these documents, but not—as the postwar experience would show—the desire for state control over the constitutional order.

Reconstruction Period, 1865–1870s

The wave of constitution making stimulated by the end of the Civil War and Reconstruction broadly reflected the struggles between the opposing forces of restoration and change. The central dynamic in the movement for constitutional revision in this period was the political parties', or factions', desire for power. Behind the calls to revise constitutions were the issues of maintaining the ascendancy of existing parties, frustrating political opposition, and seeking to forge new political alliances or parties. Politicians understood how constitutions could affect political-party patronage by mandating electoral districts, the number of elected versus appointed offices, and the amount of pay for public service.

The first Reconstruction conventions were obviously concerned with the steps necessary for reintegrating the Southern states into the Union: abolishing slavery, imposing certain obstacles for political participation of former Confederates, and paying off the war debt; the Reconstruction conventions also occasionally dealt with the issue of providing freed black slaves with certain civil rights. However, the perception among Republican congressmen that President Andrew Johnson had not required sufficient steps by the Southern states before their reintegration into the Union led Congress to require Southern states to revise their constitutions again in 1867 and 1868 in politically decisive ways. Congressional insistence that state constitutions include black suffrage resulted in giving the new Southern Republican parties control over all of the five South Atlantic constitutional conventions that met in 1867–1868.

The Republican party's desire to maintain political control can be traced in the provisions inserted in the new constitutions, particularly concerning the process of constitutional revision. Essentially, the new constitutions were changed to make constitutional revision more difficult, with the clear intent of preventing conservatives from overturning the constitutional provisions ensuring Republican political primacy. The strategy was initially successful, since every South Atlantic state was readmitted by 1870 and the Republicans remained firmly in control in all those states. Eventually, however, the defeated Democrats reacted and employed the tactic of constitutional revision to their own ends.

North Carolina's 1875 convention illustrates one of the first successful efforts of the Democrats to reverse the results of the post–Civil War reconfiguration of political power. As the North Carolina Democratic party gathered strength after 1870, it still lacked the necessary two-thirds majority required in both houses to call a convention. After disputed efforts by the legislature to call for a popular referendum on the issue of a convention, Democrats flirted with the idea of invoking the power of a constituent assembly and thereby circumventing the constitutionally entrenched Republicans. Ultimately, in 1875 a convention was called that proposed numerous amendments to the Reconstruction constitution.

Most important, the struggle by the Democrats to regain political control generated a debate over whether and how a new convention might be limited in its agenda and what exactly constituted the legitimate means of calling for a convention. While contemporary political control was the ostensible concern, the struggle raised the issues of circumvention, extralegislative calls for a convention, and the role and power of Congress and the president to ensure and maintain republican forms of government. Interestingly enough, one of the amendments proposed by the 1875 North Carolina convention (and ratified by the electorate) was designed to prevent the Republicans from undoing the remaining amendments. The amendment mandated a two-thirds vote in the legislature, and the approval of a majority of the people before a convention could be called, and it limited constitutional amendment, except by a three-fifths vote of the legislature and a majority of the voters.

Collectively, the Northern-state constitutions framed or revised in the 1870s were designed to check and restrain legislative action, apparently in reaction to the war-induced tendency toward the creation of a strong and active national government. It is clear that by the end of the nineteenth century, state constitutions were serving very different purposes than the federal constitution, in terms of form and function. More like codes than charters, state constitutions increasingly served a negative function in terms of declaring what government—and especially the legislature—could not do. In this respect, state constitutions generally reflected the popular hostility to the active or bureaucratic state.

The Late Nineteenth Century and the Territorial Period

Many of the conventions that gathered to form constitutions in the late nineteenth century were held by territories seeking to submit a constitution as part of admission into the Union. This type of constitution making was dominated by the Rocky Mountain states, which collectively seemed to respond to a series of factors. The greatest influence on the nature and content of the documents these states developed was their territorial experience and the law that governed territories. In addition, the physical environment of the region, particularly its aridity, left distinctive marks on the fundamental law that such states as Utah, New Mexico, Colorado, Idaho, Montana, Wyoming, and Arizona created in the late nineteenth century and the early twentieth century. The Idaho Constitution of 1889, for example, drew detailed distinctions on water priorities based on specific environmental needs. In general, delegates to these conventions had faith in the judiciary, suspicion of the legislature, and increasing confidence in governors.

The new western states that drafted constitutions in the 1880s and 1890s also reflected a suspicion of big business. Frequently, their constitutions contained restrictions on railroads and corporations and responded to the concerns of labor. For example, the Washington Constitution (1889) forbade free railroad passes and called for the legislature to set reasonable maximum-rate charges. A number of the constitutions inserted provisions designed to ensure safety in working conditions and imposed minimum-age limitations. For example, Wyoming's 1889 constitution outlawed labor of women and children in mines and called for the establishment of a state mining inspector. In the process of enumerating specific economic regulations, these constitutions continued the nineteenth-century pattern of constitutional legislation and ever-increasing length.

Some of these constitutions also reflected a trend toward public expropriation of property that coincided with the late nineteenth and early twentieth centuries. In the late nineteenth century a number of legislatures in the West experimented with the law of eminent domain by authorizing private corporations to take private property for private purposes. Delegates to Colorado's 1875–1876 constitutional convention placed such a provision in that state's fundamental law. Mining companies of the state especially benefited by this provision.

The South, too, saw its share of constitutional conventions during this period. Late-nineteenth-century southern constitutional revision had in common the desire to ensure legal and social supremacy for whites. This objective was sought through constitutional provisions that prohibited interracial marriages (as in South Carolina's 1895 constitution) and diminished the political participation of blacks. For example, Mississippi's 1890 constitution established a poll tax and required every elector to be able to read or give a reasonable understanding or interpretation of any section of the state's constitution. It required little imagination for local officials to use these provisions selectively. Louisiana's 1898 constitution contained a provision that excused from the stiff educational or property requirements all males entitled to vote in 1867 (one year before ratification of the Fourteenth Amendment to the U.S. Constitution), their sons and grandsons, and naturalized persons and their sons and grandsons. In effect, the failure to meet the voting requirements remained, but it worked only against blacks.

The Twentieth Century

What is most striking about twentieth-century constitution making is the relative dearth of such activity when compared to earlier periods in American history. Indeed, close to 80 percent of the more than two hundred state constitutional conventions occurred before the twentieth century (66 percent in the nineteenth century). There was a brief continuation of the progressive spirit of state constitutional revision in the first decade of the twentieth century as three states, Virginia, Alabama, and Oklahoma, revised their constitutions. But from 1910 to 1945 only one state, Louisiana, revised its constitution (indeed, it did so twice). Then in 1945 two more states, Georgia and Missouri, adopted new constitutions and, three years later, so did New Jersey.

The 1960s brought a renewed spirit of constitution making, particularly from 1964 through the 1970s. This spate of constitution making drew much of its stimulus from the series of one-person, one-vote decisions rendered by the Supreme Court beginning with *Baker* v. *Carr* in 1962. Malapportionment of state legislatures had perpetuated unequal political advantages, and a number of state conventions were called to correct the imbalances created by apportionment schemes. Although bringing state constitutions into line with the Supreme Court's interpretation of the equal protection clause of the Fourteenth Amendment to the federal constitution may have been an initial objective, conventions frequently extended their consideration to a variety of other topics.

With the increasing use of a variety of other mechanisms for state constitutional revision—initiatives, referendums, and amendments—and a more conservative attitude toward wholesale constitutional revision, states have been more reluctant to convene a constitutional convention. Constitution making in the 1960s and 1970s reflects the knowledge that constitutional conventions are potentially double-edged affairs. While conventions may accomplish constitutional reform and political gains, they also have the potential of upsetting existing political advantages enjoyed by various interests. As a result, numerous states have rejected calls for conventions since the 1950s.

Where called, such conventions have often involved the increased use of limited conventions. Constitutional conventions have traditionally been assumed to have plenary powers to propose such revisions as they considered appropriate. Since World War II, however, a practice has developed of using conventions whose authority was limited in advance to the consideration of specific subjects. The modern practice of limited conventions began in the 1940s with Virginia and Rhode Island; of the thirty constitutional conventions called between 1938 and 1970, twelve were limited and eighteen were unlimited. The political advantages of a limited convention—especially their greater control by the legislature—evidently have made them increasingly attractive as a means of constitutional revision.

Another indication of this trend away from the nineteenth-century use of full-scale constitutional conventions can be seen in the increasing use of auxiliary techniques for constitutional change, perhaps the most significant of which has been the constitutional commission. These extraconstitutional bodies are essentially staff arms of the legislative branch, since their work is invariably advisory and preliminary in nature. During the 1950s, almost one-fourth of the states established constitutional commissions or used existing legislative staff to consider constitutional revision. Given the rise of the use of the constitutional commission and the existence of numerous clearinghouse organizations dealing with the improvement of state government, increasing information and comparative data are available to guide modern constitutional revision, with the result that the fundamental laws of the various states have become more and more similar.

BIBLIOGRAPHY

Most studies of American constitutionalism have focused on the federal constitution framed in 1787, with much less attention on the process by which Americans made, amended, and remade their state constitutions.

General Studies

On the background of American constitutionalism, see DANIEL J. ELAZAR, *The American Constitutional Tradition* (Lincoln, Nebr., 1988); DONALD S. LUTZ, *The Origins of American Constitutionalism* (Baton Rouge, La., 1988); and EDMUND S. MORGAN, *Inventing the People: The Rise of Popular Sovereignty in England and America* (New York, 1988).

On Revolutionary background and constitution making, see WILLI PAUL ADAMS, *The First American Constitutions: Republican Ideology and the Making of the State Constitutions in the Revolutionary Era* (Chapel Hill, N.C., 1980); RONALD M. PETERS, *The Massachusetts Constitution of 1780: A Social Compact* (Amherst, Mass., 1978); and GORDON S. WOOD, *The Creation of the American Republic, 1776–1787* (Chapel Hill, N.C., 1969).

Despite its having been written in the wake of the Civil War with the objective of establishing that constitutional conventions had limited powers, the best overview of the institutional operation of state-constitutional conventions remains JOHN A. JAMESON, *A Treatise on Constitutional Conventions* (4th ed., facs., New York, 1972).

On the general experience of constitution making in America, see WALTER F. DODD, *The Revision and Amendment of State Constitutions* (Baltimore, 1910); KERMIT L. HALL, HAROLD M. HYMAN, and LEON V. SIGAL, eds., *The Constitutional Convention as an Amending Device* (Washington, D.C., 1981); ROGER SHERMAN HOAR, *Constitutional Conventions: Their Nature, Powers, and Limitations* (Boston, 1917); MERRILL D. PETERSON, ed., *Democracy, Liberty, and Property: The Constitutional Conventions of the 1820s* (Indianapolis, 1966); and ALBERT L. STURM, *Thirty Years of State Constitution Making, 1938–1968* (New York, 1970).

Regional Studies

Much work on American constitution making has a state or regional focus. For example, see GORDON M. BAKKEN, *Rocky Mountain Constitution Making, 1850–1912* (New York, 1987); ELMER E. CORNWELL, JR., JAY S. GOODMAN, and WAYNE R. SWANSON, *State Constitutional Conventions: The Politics of the Revision Process in Seven States* (New York, 1975); DON E. FEHRENBACHER, *Constitutions and Constitutionalism in the Slaveholding South* (Athens, Ga., 1989); FLETCHER M. GREEN, *Constitutional Development in the South Atlantic States, 1776–1860: A Study in the Evolution of Democracy* (New York, 1966); KERMIT L. HALL and JAMES W. ELY, JR., eds., *An Uncertain Tradition: Constitutionalism and the History of the South* (Athens, Ga., 1989); JOHN D. HICKS, *The Constitutions of the Northwest States* (Lincoln, Nebr., 1923); and DAVID ALAN JOHNSON, *Founding the Far West: California, Oregon, and Nevada, 1840–1890* (Berkeley, 1992).

The Confederacy

On the creation of the Confederate constitution, see CHARLES ROBERT LEE, *The Confederate Constitutions* (Chapel Hill, N.C., 1963). On the Dorr War, see GEORGE M. DENNISON, *The Dorr War: Republicanism on Trial, 1831–1861* (Lexington, Ky., 1976) and WILLIAM M. WIECEK, "'A Peculiar Conservatism' and the Dorr Rebellion: Constitutional Clash in Jacksonian America," *American Journal of Legal History* 22 (1978).

Bibliographies

For the most useful bibliographies of the subject, see CYNTHIA E. BROWN, *State Constitutional Conventions from Independence to the Completion of the Present Union, 1776–1959: A Bibliography* (Westport, Conn., 1973) and ALBERT L. STURM, *A Bibliography on State Constitutions and Constitutional Revision, 1945–1975* (Englewood, Colo., 1975).

THE ORIGINS OF CONGRESS

Jack N. Rakove

From fall 1774 until early spring 1789, the effective powers of national government of the Revolutionary American colonies (states) were lodged in a unicameral Congress. The authority of both the First Continental Congress, which met in Philadelphia in September and October of 1774, and its successor, the Second Continental Congress (May 1775–February 1781), rested on revolutionary necessity, popular support, and the willingness of state governments to carry out congressional decisions. Thereafter, the United States in Congress Assembled —to use its formal title—derived its authority from the thirteen Articles of Confederation, which had been proposed to the states in November 1777 but were only ratified on 1 March 1781, as the American republic was entering the decisive seventh year of its military struggle for independence. By 1787, the "imbecility" (this term was commonly used to describe the Congress and the Confederation in the 1780s) of the Confederation led to the appointment of the federal convention that proposed replacing the existing federal government with a bicameral legislature and constitutionally independent executive and judiciary. The framers of the Constitution designed the new federal Congress to remedy many of the defects that had hampered the Continental Congress. But they also drew crucial lessons from their observations of the "vices" (as James Madison had once called them) of legislative governance within the individual states under the new constitutions drafted in conjunction with independence.

REVOLUTIONARY BEGINNINGS

In its origins, the Continental Congress was not conceived as a legislative body in the strict sense. Americans used the word *congress* to describe an extraordinary meeting of delegates from individual colonies who convened to deliberate on issues of common concern. At the Albany Congress of 1754, for example, commissioners from seven colonies had discussed frontier defense and relations with Native American nations. Eleven years later, the Stamp Act Congress drafted resolutions opposing the new tax levied by the Parliament of Great Britain. Although by 1773 a few American leaders believed that the colonies should hold regular congresses to consult on matters of mutual concern, the decisive impetus for the First Continental Congress came only when Parliament passed the Coercive Acts punishing Massachusetts for its defiance of imperial policy. In one sense, this new congress resembled its predecessors: it was still an extraordinary meeting called to adopt measures to be implemented by the individual colonies. Yet the severity of this new crisis gave Congress a stature and authority that few colonial legislatures had ever enjoyed. During its seven weeks of deliberations, the First Continental Congress endorsed positions that denied Parliament any right to legislate for America. It also proposed a new commercial boycott of Britain, to be enforced by a network of locally elected committees. These resolutions were treated as sacred commandments by the apparatus of local committees, county conventions, and provincial congresses that formed throughout the colonies in 1774 and 1775. Just as these bodies looked to Congress for guidance, so did Congress understand that its future authority would depend on the vigor with which these committees and conventions carried out its decisions.

Before adjourning in late October 1774, the delegates to the First Congress recommended that a Second Congress should convene in Philadelphia the next spring. Meeting only weeks after civil war erupted in Massachusetts in April, the Second Continental Congress immediately transformed itself from a consultative body into the nucleus of an intercolonial (or, in effect, national) government. It took control of the army that had already gathered outside Boston, issued paper currency to support that army, and opened diplomatic relations both with Native American nations, whose neutrality it sought, and with foreign powers, whose aid it needed. At the same time, the Second Continental Congress continued to debate great issues of policy and strategy, from the prospects for reconciliation with Britain to the case for independence. Congress was both a deliberative and an administrative body; delegates divided their time between meetings of the whole house, which were devoted to debate and decision, and committees charged with a host of urgent tasks.

These dual responsibilities persisted throughout the war. In appearance and operations, Congress resembled a representative legislature—but with important qualifications. Its procedures generally followed the familiar rules under which the colonial legislatures had long operated. Resolutions were read, referred to standing or select committees for further consideration, reported to Congress for debate, and then acted upon or recommitted. But the decisions produced by these deliberations were often not strictly legislative in nature. Much of the routine business of Congress—and too much of the delegates' time—was devoted to approving expenditures of funds, both great and small, for military operations, supplies, and other costs of war. More important were decisions relating to issues of foreign policy, the conduct of the war, and military appointments—matters that many eighteenth-century commentators would have classified as executive in nature. The greater part of the output of Congress took the form of recommendations and requisitions directed to the state legislatures, who were expected to enact the actual laws required to raise taxes, recruit soldiers, and carry out every other vital task.

In discharging these duties, members of Congress acted both as delegates from their respective states and as officials of a national government that was more than a diplomatic assembly. As delegates, they were bound to obey the instructions and advance the interests of their constituents; they were paid by the states and subject to annual election and the possibility (never exercised) of recall. But in practice delegates often knew little of what their constituents wanted and found themselves acting less as ambassadors from semisovereign states than as members of a national government, with separate duties of their own.

CONGRESS UNDER THE ARTICLES OF CONFEDERATION

The most important rule under which Congress acted was the rule of voting that it adopted at its opening debate on 5 September 1774. Enormous disparities of population and wealth set colonies like Massachusetts, Pennsylvania, and Virginia apart from the colonies of Rhode Island, Delaware, and frontier Georgia (which first appeared in Congress in 1775), and large state delegates argued that Congress should adopt some scheme of proportional voting. But this demand foundered on two objections: first, that Congress lacked the information needed to fix any formula for allocating votes; and second, that Congress represented the colonies as corporate units with an equal stake in its decisions, regardless of a colony's size. This second objection was reinforced by the recognition that successful resistance to Britain required decisions based not on mere majorities but on broad consensus. If unanimity was the goal, any apportionment of votes seemed superfluous. Members of Congress voted as individuals only when committees were chosen by ballot; on all other issues, they voted as the majority of each state delegation decided.

This initial decision did not conclusively settle the issue of voting: it was bound to recur whenever Congress attempted to place its authority on a more secure constitutional footing than what public support alone had provided. As part of the movement toward independence in the spring of 1776, American leaders concluded that legal governments had to be reconstituted in the individual colonies to replace the effective but extralegal committees and conventions that had exercised power since 1774. Members of Congress reached similar conclusions about their own authority; thus, when Congress launched its final preparations for independence on 7 June 1776, it appointed three committees to draft a declaration of independence, a plan for treaties with foreign powers, and articles of confederation.

Most of the states quickly adopted written constitutions restoring legal governments, which were dominated by popularly elected legislatures. The progress of the Articles of Confederation was more labored. On 12 July 1776 the committee chaired by John Dickinson of Pennsylvania reported a draft set of articles that Congress considered over the next six weeks. Some of the most important aspects of the proposed federal union were relatively noncontroversial. There was broad agreement that Congress should direct war and foreign relations and that the states should retain exclusive control over their internal police and domestic legislation, including the right to levy all taxes and to determine how to mobilize other resources required for war. The one area where consensus about the respective spheres of national and state authority proved elusive involved the control of western lands. Here the states were divided into two blocs: those with claims to the interior lands lying beyond the Appalachian chain and those with colonial charters that definitively limited their western boundaries, which accordingly favored the creation of a national domain whose sale would ease the financial burden the war promised to impose.

This dispute over western lands was one of three issues that led Congress to defer further action on the Articles from 20 August 1776 until the spring of 1777, and then again until the fall, when the delegates finally mustered the will to complete the Confederation and submit it to the states. The other two issues—the apportionment of representation in Congress and of the expenses of the union among the states—were similarly intractable, in that they pitted blocs of states sharing well-defined interests against each other over issues where there would be clear winners and losers. On the questions of western lands and representation, the respective winners were the landed states, which defeated every proposal to vest Congress with power that would threaten their claims, and the small states, which retained their equal vote in Congress over heated objections from such powerful opponents as James Wilson and John Adams. (Because small states were landless states, this result was an implicit compromise—though that was not in fact how either the delegates or their constituents regarded it.) On the issue of expenses, however,

a sectional deadlock between northern and southern states persisted until the New Jersey delegation promoted an unwieldy scheme to apportion the costs of the war on the basis of the value of each state's settled lands "and the buildings and improvements thereon."

In their final push to complete the Articles, the delegates recognized that the political imperative to establish a permanent union outweighed whatever flaws they thought the Confederation contained. Similar considerations prevailed in most of the states, ten of which had ratified the Articles by the late summer of 1778. But opposition from the landless states—New Jersey, Delaware, and especially Maryland—kept the Confederation unratified until 1781, when cessions of western land claims by New York and Virginia pointed the way toward the creation of a national domain above the Ohio River.

Two broad sets of assumptions defined the basic conditions and limitations under which Congress exercised its power both before and after the Confederation was ratified. The first was that the sphere of national government was largely confined to great affairs of state—that is, war and foreign relations. Within this sphere, Congress could be said to be sovereign and its decisions, binding. But because these responsibilities were historically associated with the prerogative powers of the British crown, Congress could not be easily thought of as a legislative body, even if that was what it resembled. Observers revealed the confusion that arose from this anomalous combination of executive power and legislative form when they sometimes described Congress as a "supreme executive" or a "deliberating executive assembly" (quoted in Rakove, *The Beginnings of National Politics*, p. 383).

The second broad set of assumptions shaping the exercise of congressional power concerned the relation between Congress and the states. The framers of the Articles assumed that the states would faithfully execute whatever Congress asked them to do—so long as Congress acted within its own proper sphere of government. In requiring congressional resolutions to be translated into state legislation, the basic concern of the framers of the Articles was not to encourage the state assemblies to protect their rights against congressional abuse but rather to enable the legislatures to determine how best to accommodate those resolutions to their particular circumstances. This assumption, though naive, was consistent with the political experience of the early years of the Revolution, when provincial authorities had obeyed congressional directives scrupulously. But as the war ground on indecisively, and as the states proved unable and occasionally unwilling to implement the resolutions of Congress, this dependence on the states exposed the central constitutional flaw in the architecture of union. True legislative power in America—that is, the ability to use law to command the obedience of citizens—was an attribute of the state governments alone.

THE CONTINENTAL CONGRESS: A BALANCE SHEET

Often hailed in the early years of its existence as "the collected wisdom of America," Congress saw its reputation decline sharply as the war dragged on. Issues of financial and foreign policy proved particularly damaging. Lacking the authority to levy taxes, Congress relied upon emissions of paper currency to pay for the spiraling costs of the war, hoping that taxes laid by the state legislatures would draw enough of this money out of circulation to prevent or limit its inevitable depreciation. This hope proved naive. For political and other reasons, the states were unwilling and unable to act as Congress had desired, and the rate of inflation mounted rapidly, finally forcing Congress to halt further emissions of currency in 1779. But this decision and other expedients it adopted to cope with the ensuing crisis came too late to redeem Congress from the political damage inflation imposed. At the same time, a bitter dispute that was provoked when France asked Congress to specify American terms of peace spilled over into the press, sullying the image of Congress further.

For all the criticism to which Congress was subjected after 1779, its real achievement cannot be measured in terms of the success or failure of particular policies—especially given the sheer scope and novelty of the problems it confronted. The crucial test of a revolutionary leadership lies instead in the success of the revolution it directs. Relying, in part, on the

enormous political capital it acquired during the early years of the Revolution, Congress kept the conduct of the American war effort sufficiently cohesive to maintain the struggle at an adequate level through eight years of a burdensome war that left many of its countrymen exhausted. During the war, its detractors often faulted Congress for failing to establish distinct departments to carry out executive functions: only in 1781 did it establish departments of finance, foreign affairs, and war. But criticisms of its administrative inefficiency and shortsighted policies need to be weighed against the constraints under which Congress operated. These included the ideological animus against the bureaucratic apparatus of a nation-state that American Whigs shared with the opposition tradition of Georgian Britain, the necessary reliance Congress placed on the separate states, and sheer inexperience.

Beyond presiding over the successful struggle for independence, the other great achievement of the Second Continental Congress derived from its territorial policies. Just as the war was winding down, Congress began to implement a shrewd policy to convert the contested claims of states to territory north of the Ohio River into a national domain whose settlement would anticipate the crucial role that the federal government was to play in the development of the West. Without attempting to adjudicate the merits of these conflicting claims, Congress encouraged the landed states to cede their rights to the Union. With the Virginia cession of 1784, Congress acquired authority over millions of acres of land; soon afterward, it wrested title to this vast expanse through peremptory treaties dictated to the resident Native American nations that had allied themselves with Britain in the war. Those treaties marked a low point in relations between Americans and native peoples, leading to the destructive frontier wars of the early 1790s, but Congress soon after sought to redeem the promise of the West through the adoption in 1787 of an enlightened ordinance regulating the government of the new territories. In all accounts, the Northwest Ordinance remains one of the most notable pieces of legislation adopted by any Congress in American history. It provided an enlightened model of government to smooth the transition of frontier territories into nascent states that would be admitted to the Union on terms of political equality with its original members.

LEGISLATIVE POWER IN THE STATES

Congress could legislate for the Northwest Territory only because the states had surrendered their prior claims to its governance. Before power to legislate for Americans resident in already established states could be vested in Congress—or rather, in the union it embodied—crucial shifts had to occur in American ideas about both national and state government. These shifts involved more than specifying individual legislative powers that Congress could usefully exercise; they also required explaining why state legislatures were failing to meet their federal obligations. Equally important, Americans had to reconsider fundamental ideas about representation and to overcome doubts about the feasibility of implementing any scheme of national political representation that would not be consistent with essential republican principles. Those principles were most clearly expressed in the state constitutions that were drafted in conjunction with the decision for independence. But their application after 1776 depended on the interplay between two sets of historical experiences: a tradition of political and institutional development in both the colonies and Britain, and the lessons that Americans learned only after the Revolution subjected individual legislatures to extraordinary stresses.

Americans drew their ideas of legislative power from a rich and decidedly Whiggish history that reached back to the meeting of the first representative assembly in Virginia in 1619 and across the Atlantic to the centuries-long rise of Parliament. Political elites in all the colonies had made the lower houses of assembly the principal institutional focus of their quests for power, and in seeking to consolidate their authority they had naturally insisted that these bodies should enjoy all the privileges that the House of Commons had struggled to wrest from the crown. The vindication of parliamentary authority in the Glorious Revolution of 1688–1689 lit a beacon for colonial legislators; what they learned to dread, however, were the

tools of patronage and influence that successive British ministries had used to subvert the theoretical independence of Parliament. By the eve of the imperial crisis of 1765–1776, colonial legislatures had secured many of the rights and privileges they desired, although they could not prevent royal governors from arbitrarily proroguing, or dissolving, their sessions or the crown itself from vetoing legislation that the assemblies desired.

When independence allowed the early constitution writers to reform the balance of power within the state governments, they accordingly confined executive power within a narrow sphere. The central characteristic of those constitutions was the effective concentration of power in the legislative branch of government. Recalling the abuses the colonies had suffered from royal and proprietary governors and the even longer history of the struggle between crown and Parliament, the early constitution writers stripped the executive branch of anything that smacked of the prerogative power of the crown. Executive power became merely that: it existed to carry out the legislative will, not to embody a separate authority of its own. Though most of the constitutions affirmed the principle of the independence of the executive and the judiciary, in practice these two branches lacked both the constitutional power and the political resources to resist legislative control or influence. Only in New York and Massachusetts—two states whose constitutions were written after the first flushes of republican enthusiasm had begun to fade—was the executive given a limited veto over legislation and the political influence that came with election by the people rather than the legislature.

Most Americans looked elsewhere—to republican principles and the institutional security of bicameralism—for protection against the abuse of legislative power. Annual elections and rotation in office could render lawmakers both responsive to their constituents and responsible in their duties (because they would soon return to private life to be governed by the very laws they had framed). Dividing the legislature into two houses could further diminish the danger of hasty legislation. As a question of representation, the existence of a senate posed a problem: if the lower house was meant to provide a "mirror" or "miniature" of the people and if no legally privileged estate existed in America to form a house of lords, it was not entirely clear what a senate would represent. But on functional grounds, the value of an upper house was demonstrated by the example of the House of Lords, which was widely credited with preserving the vaunted balance of the British constitution.

As much as these ideas shaped the ways that Americans thought about legislative power, its actual exercise was even more strongly influenced by the political circumstances and exigencies under which the assemblies operated, as the war created problems that no one had foreseen. In most states, legislative leaders who had held power before 1776 retained influence after independence. But the participatory politics of a popular revolution challenged their influence in several ways. Constituencies that had previously not been represented in the colonial assemblies or that had simply ignored provincial politics altogether were first caught up in the enthusiasm of resistance and then alarmed enough by the burdens of the war to send a delegate to the two or three sessions that the press of business obliged most legislatures to hold each year. Not only did the state assemblies contain more members than their colonial forerunners, but they also were increasingly composed of amateur lawmakers who faced the staggering problems of mobilizing American society for a prolonged war. The overriding circumstance to which every legislature had to adjust was that this mobilization required a massive use of legislative power unprecedented in the colonial past, for the assemblies had to struggle to raise the men and supplies that the war required while feebly attempting to control all the financial and economic dislocations that paper currency and wartime shortages generated.

Under these conditions, continuity of legislative leadership masked a more fundamental shift in legislative politics. The problem was not just that larger assemblies were more difficult to manage or even that continuous turnover made inexperience the most conspicuous characteristic of many legislators. The deeper transformation lay in the nature of legislative activity itself. Before the Revolution, positive lawmaking was not regarded as the sole or even most important responsibility of the legislature. Americans were still attached to the traditional theory that representative legislatures existed as much to check the exercise of arbitrary power by the executive as to enact general legislation. Most colonial legislation involved parochial matters. Many acts were framed as responses to petitions in which a community or its more notable members requested permission to undertake some useful activity; other acts resolved disputes or reviewed judicial decisions in a manner that illustrated why a legislature could still be regarded as a "general court." Colonial legislatures passed general statutes as well, of course, and a good case can be made that the pace of social and economic development in the New World led the assemblies to play a more active role in American governance than the role Parliament played in Britain. But many Americans still clung to the traditional image of the legislature as less a lawmaking body than as the watchguard of the rights and liberties of its constituents.

The Revolution sorely tested that notion in two ways. First, it required all American legislatures (including Congress) to conduct massive experiments in economic regulation and the distribution of resources. Second, the Revolution made the legislatures the natural butt of the complaints that this regulatory legislation inevitably generated. With the power of the other branches of government so reduced, the assemblies stood alone in the public eye as the real locus of government. And the more representative they became, the more exposed they were to the grievances of ordinary citizens who felt that their rights were being violated, not protected, by duly elected lawmakers.

MADISON AND REPUBLICAN LEGISLATION

The most acute observer of these developments was James Madison, the young Virginian who in 1787 set for himself the task of preparing an agenda of radical reform for the Constitutional Convention he was so instrumental in calling. As a member of the Virginia Council of State (1778–1780), the Continental Congress (1780–1783), and the Virginia House of Delegates (1784–1786), Madison came to see the failings of state legislatures, legislators, and legislation in a doubly critical way—as evidence of underlying weaknesses in both the

Articles of Confederation and the new state constitutions. All of the key elements of his thought—his ideas of representation, the separation of powers, federalism, and rights—can be traced to his analysis of the sources and consequences of legislative misrule in the states. The lessons he drew from these observations were, in turn, incorporated into the Virginia Plan, which the convention immediately accepted as its working draft of a constitution.

As a constitutional thinker, Madison had little use for the trite axioms of conventional political science, and he was never happier intellectually than when he could draw a finely nuanced distinction. Even so, the crucial considerations that informed his thinking about the reconstitution of the national Congress can be summarized fairly succinctly. Assessing the state and federal constitutional experiments of the mid 1770s, Madison concluded that their framers had committed two natural but dangerous errors. The drafters of the state constitutions had failed to provide adequate institutional means for assuring "*wisdom* and steadiness" in legislation, largely because their backward-looking preoccupation with remedying evils inflicted by generations of royal governors prevented them from anticipating the problems that unchecked legislatures might create (Madison to Caleb Wallace, 23 August 1785, in Robert Rutland et al., eds., *The Papers of James Madison* (1962–) vol. 8, pp. 350–351). The "compilers" of the Articles of Confederation had erred in another way (Rutland et al., vol. 9, p. 351). The patriotism that flourished in America at the crisis of independence had convinced them that the state assemblies would always implement congressional decisions faithfully, without needing to be goaded by the coercive authority that governments ordinarily relied upon to secure obedience.

As successive efforts to amend the Articles of Confederation by granting Congress modest incremental authority to collect an impost (a levy) or regulate foreign trade failed to surmount the hurdle of unanimous state ratification, Madison perceived that the discrete problems of strengthening the Union and correcting the internal "vices" of the state constitutions were closely linked. The same causes explained why the states would rarely comply with national policy and why their domestic legislation was ill-conceived and unjust. Madison faulted both the character of state legislators and the excessive influence that the interests and passions of their constituents exerted on public policy. Just as the parochialism and demagoguery of state politics assured that provincial interests would always prevail over the national good, so the free play of majoritarian populism left Madison fearful that rights of property would no longer be secure within the narrow compass of the states. In opposition to the familiar view that republican government could operate only in relatively small, homogeneous societies, Madison formulated his radical hypothesis that an enlarged sphere would work both to improve the quality of representation and to lessen the danger that the wrong kinds of majorities would coalesce to ignore the public good and trample on private rights.

This analysis defined the program that Madison carried to Philadelphia in May 1787. Believing that the states could never be expected to implement federal decisions uniformly and punctually, he concluded that the national government should be empowered to act directly on the population through its own statutes and taxes. This crucial decision, in turn, led to equally momentous conclusions about the structure of the government the convention would have to propose. Because orthodox theory held that legislative power could be safely vested only in a bicameral assembly, Congress itself would have to be reconstructed into two chambers. Further, because this legislature would act directly upon the people and their property—but not upon the states as such—Madison believed that it would become both theoretically possible and politically necessary to apportion voting within Congress on some principle other than the equal state vote required by the Confederation. Justice demanded the adoption of some system of proportional representation, but so did the political calculation that the large states would reject any radical change in the power of the national government unless proportional principles applied to both houses.

From his criticism of the state legislatures, Madison drew one other noteworthy conclusion about bicameralism. Since 1785 he had believed that the best institutional solution to the problem of improper legislation required creating genuine senates capable of bringing "wisdom and steadiness" to American lawmaking. But Madison did not regard the upper house of the legislature as a representative body in any substantive sense. Should a proper scheme of apportionment be adopted, the people and their interests would be sufficiently represented in the lower house alone; the upper house 'existed to check its more numerous and impetuous colleagues in the "popular" chamber. Insofar as the kind of legislation that most merited checking was that which adversely affected rights of property, Madison thought of the Senate as a body that would somehow represent property interests. But the protection it offered would result not from any electoral scheme that would tie senators directly to large landholders and wealthy merchants but rather from its institutional character as a small body of sober statesmen, serving long terms and detached from any political obligations to constituents.

CONGRESS AT THE FEDERAL CONVENTION

The Virginia Plan, which Governor Edmund Randolph presented to the convention on 29 May 1787, supported Madison's general ideas of representation in every respect. Article 2 proposed that "the rights of suffrage in the National Legislature" should be "proportioned" to either state contributions to the national treasury or "the number of free inhabitants" (Farrand, ed., vol. 1, p. 20). Rather than risk an early discussion of specific modes of apportionment, Madison quickly offered a resolution affirming "that an equitable ratio of representation ought to be substituted" for the equal state vote of the Confederation (Farrand, ed., vol. 1, p. 36). Succeeding articles of the Virginia Plan divided the legislature into two houses and provided that members of the lower house would be "elected by the people of the several States," while the members of the second chamber would "be elected by those of the first, out of a proper number of persons nominated by the individual Legislatures"—thereby honoring the principle of proportionality, not by apportioning senators among the states, but by simply giving the right of election to a proportionally constituted house. Finally, the Virginia Plan authorized the national legislature

"to legislate in all cases to which the separate States are incompetent, or in which the harmony of the United States may be interrupted by the exercise of individual [state] legislation." As a notable extension of this principle, Article 6 of the Virginia Plan also proposed allowing Congress to "negative" all state laws contravening "the articles of Union" (Farrand, ed., vol. 1, pp. 20–21).

These sweeping proposals ran far beyond anything that had been seriously discussed either publicly or privately prior to the convention—which helps to explain why the first fortnight of debate at Philadelphia sometimes seemed tentative and cautious. Even so, the most important implications of both the Virginia Plan and Madison's political strategy were readily apparent. Where many delegates expected the convention to begin its work by asking what particular additional powers needed to be vested in the Union, the sweeping language of the Virginia Plan directed their attention to the radical changes it proposed in the institutional structure of national government through the creation of three independent branches—including, most important of all, a bicameral legislature. From the start, too, it was apparent that the crucial test would come over the composition of the upper house. For while Madison and his allies—most notably, James Wilson of Pennsylvania and Rufus King of Massachusetts—insisted that some scheme of proportional representation had to be applied to both houses of the new national legislature, their leading opponents—John Dickinson of Delaware, Roger Sherman and Oliver Ellsworth of Connecticut, and William Paterson of New Jersey—argued with equal passion that the small states could never completely abandon the principle of state equality enshrined in the Confederation.

From 29 May until 16 July, this single issue overshadowed everything else; though other matters were discussed, everyone understood that their resolution somehow depended on the outcome of the conflict over the Senate. The strategy pursued by Madison and his allies presumed that the opposition of the small states would eventually collapse in the face of superior arguments and the perceived need to preserve the Union. For all the passions it evoked and all the threats, bluffs, and conciliatory pleas it inspired, the debate over legislative apportionment was very much concerned with fundamental principles of representation.

On one side, the large-state delegates argued that both individuals and the interests they possessed (primarily economic) were true constituent elements of the polity and the principal objects of legislation; states, as such, did not possess interests distinct from those of their own inhabitants, who should be represented in the national government in proportion to their aggregate numbers, though some consideration might also be given to the value of their property. Perhaps a case could be made for representing states as equal corporate entities, Madison conceded, if the new government were to act through the state governments in the same way as had the Continental Congress; but that claim was undercut by the same considerations that held that this dependence on the states was the fatal debility in the whole structure of the Confederation. Depriving the states of their national administrative functions thus also worked to eliminate their claim to representation. As the large-state delegates repeatedly argued, any scheme of representation that gave the small states of Rhode Island, New Jersey, and Maryland an equal vote with their respective populous neighbors—Massachusetts, Pennsylvania, and Virginia—was simply unjust.

These were powerful arguments that the leading spokesmen for the small states could not easily rebut on their merits. Their case for retaining an equal state vote in one house of the legislature took a different cast. At times they insisted that the convention lacked the authority to abandon the essential principle of the Confederation or that the states were simply the primordial sovereign elements from which any American union must be immutably composed (a point belabored by Luther Martin of Maryland, who was the most persistent advocate of state sovereignty present at the convention). But, in practice, their most potent arguments revolved around claims of security. The interests of the small states could never be protected in a legislature in which they would always be outvoted; simple arithmetic suggested that the large states could coalesce to rule the nation, glibly equating their interests with the good of the whole. At other times, the small-state delegates argued that without an equal vote the very existence of the states would

somehow be jeopardized or, again, that without the cooperation of the state governments no federal system could work, a cooperation that could only be assured by allowing the upper house to represent the state governments (each of which possessed equal sovereign rights, regardless of the number of citizens they represented).

Madison, Wilson, King, Gouverneur Morris, and Alexander Hamilton labored earnestly to explain why these fears and claims were both unreasonable and unjust. Against the specter of large-state domination, they argued that the disparate interests of Virginia, Pennsylvania, and Massachusetts—differences rooted in economics, history, geography, and religion—would prevent their coalescing on any improper basis. Ironically, the only issue on which the large states were likely to agree lay in their common interest in proportional representation. The security the small states sought could be obtained simply through a well-designed constitution; but it should not be purchased at the expense of allowing overrepresented minorities to thwart the desires of proper majorities, which finally deserved to rule.

Powerful as these arguments were, the large-state delegates found themselves vulnerable on several counts. One involved the difficulty of imagining what an upper house would represent if it did not represent the states. As early as 7 June, the convention decisively approved a motion substituting election by the state legislatures for the original method proposed in the Virginia Plan. Though states could presumably elect different numbers of senators, reconciling legislative election with the principle of proportionality would threaten the character of the Senate in two ways. How could a senate generate broad-minded, cosmopolitan thinking about the great national problems that it was supposed to provide if it was made politically accountable to the very institutions where parochial concerns flourished so freely? And how could it deliberate soberly and prudently if the larger numbers required to honor the dual principles of proportional and state representation made a senate resemble an ordinary assembly more than a select council of deliberation?

The key tests of strength on the character of the Senate took place during the second fortnight of June. On 19 June the large states easily turned back the alternative New Jersey Plan, which called for modestly augmenting the powers of the existing unicameral Congress. But, far from being discouraged, delegates from the small states seized the initiative by pressing a series of motions designed to legitimate the claim for an equal state vote in the upper house. On 2 July they secured the deadlock they sought when, by a tie vote, the convention rejected Ellsworth's motion to that effect. Mounting pressure for accommodation thereupon led the convention to appoint a committee (one member from each state) to frame a compromise; even more revealing, the delegates selected from the large states (by ballot of the entire convention) were those who had appeared most sympathetic to the small states' claims: Elbridge Gerry, Benjamin Franklin, and George Mason.

With great difficulty, good conscience, and modest enthusiasm, the committee fashioned an ostensible compromise with three major elements: representation in the lower house would be apportioned by population, with slaves counting for three-fifths of free inhabitants; the states would have an equal vote in the Senate; and the lower house would have the exclusive right to introduce and amend revenue bills. This last provision, which was presented as a concession to the large states, appealed strongly to those delegates—such as Mason and Gerry—who regarded popular control over revenue acts as one of the exalted principles of Whig constitutionalism; but it was denounced with equal vigor by Madison and Wilson, who argued that the nominal concession was useless because the Senate could simply reject measures it disliked until the lower house amended them to its satisfaction.

By endorsing the equal state vote, the committee's report of 5 July clearly placed the large-state leaders on the defensive; but, in fact, the issue of the apportionment of representation in the lower house dominated the debates that preceded the climactic decision of 16 July. The central problem was whether to count slaves for purposes of representation and, if so, on what basis. The resolution of this problem was not made easier by the moral embarrassment that some delegates felt, but the political complexities of accounting for slavery ran even deeper. The question of counting slaves for purposes of representation could, for

example, be used to buttress the argument that the size of a state would be irrelevant to its political behavior or interests once a new constitution went into effect and thus to undermine the small states' claim to equal representation. As Madison had already noted, future divisions between the states were far more likely to revolve around the presence or absence of slavery in their social systems than the extent of their territory or population. If one purpose of representation was to provide security to particular interests, as the small-state delegates repeatedly asserted, did it not make more sense to extend special protection to the slave states in order to enable them to defend their peculiar form of property against the free northern electorate, which might otherwise control the national legislature?

Paterson inadvertently confirmed the theoretical uses to which the slavery issue could be put when, on 9 July, he opposed any counting of slaves on the grounds that "the true principle of Representation" was simply to provide an "expedient" mechanism to take the "place of the inconvenient meeting of the people themselves." If slaves could not vote when the citizens did assemble, why should they be represented at all, when the law treated them only as property, not citizens? Madison immediately reminded Paterson that this definition of representation, "which was in its principle the genuine one, must for ever silence the pretensions of the small States to an equality of votes with the large ones" (Farrand, ed., vol. 1, pp. 561–562).

If the specific question of slavery thus implicated the general theory of representation in this surprising way, the delegates nevertheless understood that the real challenge they faced was to balance gross sectional interests. Southern delegates knew that their region would be in a minority at the inception of the new government, but adoption of some formula to count slaves for representation would move their states closer to parity with the northern states. Moreover, many Americans expected future migrations to carry settlers southwest toward New Orleans rather than northwest toward the Great Lakes, so that the initial imbalance of free population between the sections would narrow even further. But for these developments to have appropriate political consequences, southern delegates could not leave the later reapportionment of seats to the discretion of a legislature in which they would be at an initial disadvantage. Accordingly, the pressure for both a constitutionally mandated census and a constitutional rule of apportionment came from the southern delegates, led by Edmund Randolph. Yet while northern delegates were willing to accede to the claims of the southern states in order to persuade their southern colleagues to grant the legislature broad regulatory powers over commerce—the issue that mattered most to their constituents— they remained reluctant to allow the proposed constitution to imply that the southern states were being rewarded politically for their sordid reliance on slavery. Rather than avow that slaves were being counted primarily for purposes of representation, the convention approved a clever circumlocution stating that when direct taxes were levied on the states—through requisitions similar to those used by the Continental Congress—each state's quota would be proportioned to its free population plus three-fifths of inhabitants of other descriptions and that representation in the lower house of the new legislature would be allocated by this same formula. In fact, few delegates thought the national legislature would ever levy taxes directly on the states; all understood that this language was meant to legitimate the southern states' claim to additional protection for slavery.

Only after the convention resolved the apportionment of representation in the lower house did it muster the courage to return to the crucial issue of the Senate. By this point, it was apparent that the political advantage had shifted to the small states. In the climactic debate of 14 July, Madison and Wilson professed willingness to telescope representation in the upper house so that the largest states would have five senators, the smallest, one—a compromise that would preserve the institutional intimacy an ideal senate should possess. But the small states refused to bargain. When the delegates reassembled on Monday, 16 July, the ostensible compromise passed by the narrow margin of five states to four, with the key vote of Massachusetts being divided, and thus lost, when Gerry and Caleb Strong chose to elevate the appeal of the small states above the apparent interest of their own constituents.

The margin of this vote alone suggests why it is something of a misnomer to recall it as the Great Compromise: all along the issue had been whether the principle of proportionality would be honored in the upper house, and on this point one side had lost, the other won. The case for security prevailed over the argument for justice; the advantage the small states enjoyed in defending a right they already enjoyed proved more potent than the rhetorical appeals of Madison, Wilson, and Rufus King. Though the convention was indeed free, as the large-state delegates repeatedly noted, to propose whatever solutions it wished for the problems of federalism and republicanism, it could ignore persisting structural features of the Union only by jeopardizing the adoption of any revised compact. Just as in the composition of the Senate, concessions had to be made to the history and corporate integrity of the states, so the delegates also offered equivalent gestures of "security" toward the slaveholding interests of the South.

It took the convention nearly another month, however, to begin examining the implications that these decisions about the structure of representation would have for the substantive powers to be vested in the legislature. Here, two developments were of seminal importance. First, the convention replaced the open-ended grant of legislative authority implied in the Virginia Plan with a more carefully worded list of enumerated powers—a process that began in the five-member Committee of Detail, whose report of 6 August converted the resolutions previously adopted into the working draft of a constitution. Second, concerns about both the "aristocratic" character of the Senate and its dependence on the states led the delegates to consider distributing powers they initially anticipated vesting in the upper house elsewhere within the government. In addition, several other discrete decisions had noteworthy implications for conditions of membership within the new "Congress"—as it was called for the first time by the Committee of Detail for the new bicameral legislature.

For all the attention it devoted to issues of representation in June and July, the convention had spent remarkably little time considering the scope of legislative power, primarily because the large states insisted that decisions on this point had to follow the resolution of the dispute over representation. None of the delegates assumed that national legislative power would reach all objects of government; the residual authority of the state legislatures would still embrace most of the ordinary activities of Americans. That presumption informed even Madison's radical plan for a congressional veto on state laws, which had to be unlimited precisely because the positive legislative authority of the states would remain so substantial. Yet even if the Virginia Plan did not envision absolute national legislative supremacy, it would still have allowed Congress to exercise enormous discretion in setting the perimeters of its authority.

By contrast, the enumeration of legislative powers proposed by the Committee of Detail was clearly a formula for a government that could be at once supreme yet limited. Conceivably, this was the conception of legislative power that even the large-state delegates expected to adopt all along: once the principle of proportional representation was vindicated, the convention could proceed to specify the "cases" to which national legislative supremacy would extend. Yet it is also possible that resentment over the decision of 16 July left the large-state delegates less willing to delegate power so freely to a legislature where the "vicious" principle of equal state representation would still operate.

In either case, the shift in the image of legislative power implicit in the report of the Committee of Detail was material. Its list began with the powers of taxation and commercial regulation that Americans generally expected the convention to propose, and it then specified which powers vested in Congress by the Confederation would be retained by the new legislature. Though this enumeration narrowed the potential scope of national legislative power, the revised article reported by the committee still authorized Congress "to make all laws that shall be necessary and proper for carrying into execution the foregoing powers, and all other powers vested, by this Constitution, in the government of the United States" (Farrand, ed., vol. 2, p. 182). So, too, rather than authorize the new Congress to legislate in areas where the states were "incompetent" or where state legislation would threaten national "harmony"—as the Virginia Plan proposed—the committee supplemented the existing restrictions on state power contained in the Confederation with a handful of additional prohibitions on the power to "coin money," "emit

bills of credit, or make any thing but specie a tender in payment of debts," or "lay imposts or duties on imports" (Farrand, ed., vol. 2, p. 187).

During the debates of August, the convention revised and augmented the enumerated powers of Congress to compile the final list that eventually became Article I, Section 8, of the Constitution. A few delegates initially wondered whether Congress would need to legislate all that much; in a revealing debate on 7 August, the convention considered whether annual meetings of Congress would be necessary and eventually approved a clause to that effect only after Mason and Nathaniel Gorham argued that the legislature should sit regularly to monitor the conduct of the executive—rather than to enact positive legislation.

Some of the most important debates about legislative power centered on issues of national security. After a brief but momentous debate on 17 August, the delegates replaced the language empowering Congress "to make war" with a new clause allowing it "to declare war," thereby suggesting that while decisions about going to war were fundamentally legislative in nature, the power to determine how war was to be conducted belonged elsewhere, in the executive. Of course, through its appropriation power Congress could still influence how Americans would fight, and in theory, it could use the power of the purse to constrain executive war making in other ways. More controversial were the clauses empowering Congress to call forth and regulate the militia of the states. The traditional Whig view that many delegates held regarded the militia as both a political safeguard against tyranny and a reserve army; allowing Congress to control its organization would, they alleged, sap the independence of the states. After strenuous debate, the convention agreed that Congress should be able to set rules of discipline, organization, and training for the militia, while reserving the appointment of officers to the states.

The two sets of legislative powers that most concerned the delegates, however, involved taxation and the regulation of commerce. The two were related in one obvious way: most delegates anticipated that duties on imported foreign goods and commodities would offer the most convenient and valuable source of public revenues. But southern delegates feared that a northern majority in Congress might use these powers for regional advantage by levying duties on the export of agricultural commodities or on the importation of finished products and luxuries desired by the planter class of the Chesapeake and the Carolinas or by taxing or even prohibiting the importation of slaves. After several sharp debates, the convention reached decisions that amounted to an explicitly intersectional bargain—though a few delegates still dissented from particular elements of it. Acts regulating commerce, like other acts, would be passed by simple majorities rather than the two-thirds vote avidly sought by Mason and the South Carolina delegation. In deference to the presumed labor needs of Georgia and South Carolina, laws prohibiting the importation of slaves would not be permitted before 1808—the convention again adopting a circumlocution to avoid using the words *slavery* and *slaves*. A flat prohibition against taxing the exports of any state was also added to reassure the South, while a further prohibition on laws giving "preference . . . by any regulation of commerce or revenue to the ports of one State over those of another" was similarly designed to assuage lingering doubts that majority coalitions in Congress could pursue schemes to aggrandize their states at the expense of others (Farrand, ed., vol. 2, p. 618).

Through all these decisions, the delegates were consciously bargaining on behalf of their constituents—and this, at last, made it easier to treat the vote of 16 July as a compromise too. Yet, ironically, even as the delegates became more accommodating, other concerns made them less comfortable with the institution whose character had been at the core of the disputes of June and July: the Senate.

One element of the Great Compromise—the restriction on the power of the Senate to amend or alter revenue bills—was now abandoned, because key large-state leaders saw no value in the nominal concession it offered. As far as Madison and Wilson were concerned, the benefits to be gained in this area of legislation, from allowing the Senate to check the impetuosity and relative inexperience of the House, far outweighed their resentment over its composition. After complicated maneuvering, the convention agreed to require revenue bills to originate in the lower house but be subject to the same amending power that the Senate would exercise over all other legislation.

Where the institutional competence of the Senate became far more problematic was in those areas where its powers would not be merely or essentially "legislative" in the strict sense of the term. From the start, most delegates apparently assumed that powers of appointing major officers and negotiating treaties (and therefore conducting foreign relations) would be vested in the Senate. The report of the Committee of Detail was drawn accordingly. But when its relevant provisions were taken up in late August, ambivalence about the character of the Senate quickly percolated to the surface. The sources of these doubts were multiple and not wholly consistent. Some delegates wondered whether a body elected by the parochial state legislatures would have the requisite independence of mind and cosmopolitan view to frame the wise foreign policies the country needed; this concern was reinforced by lingering resentment over the fact that the small states would enjoy an equal vote in its decisions. By contrast, other delegates worried that the Senate's small size and six-year terms would convert it into a conspiratorial den of intriguing aristocrats whose special powers would enable them to dominate the government.

These reservations led the delegates to consider dividing the special powers intended for the Senate between it and another branch of the government. Though a few delegates suggested that these powers could be shared with the House, two decisive objections weighed against that position. First, the more numerous and presumably impulsive chamber would not be a fit repository for authority over foreign affairs. Second, allowing both houses to share in appointments to office was like a formula for endless conflict and stalemate. So it was that in the final weeks of debate, dissatisfaction with the Senate led to an enhancement of the power of the executive substantially beyond what most of the delegates had initially envisioned. In its critical report of 4 September, the Committee on Postponed Parts (or Unfinished Business) proposed giving power over appointments and treaties to the president, acting with the "advice and consent" of the Senate. Though the framers clearly expected the Senate to play an active consultative role in both matters, rather than merely ratify executive decisions, this shift nevertheless prefigured a significant transfer of governing authority and political initiative to the executive.

Even more important, the convention also accepted the committee's proposal to have the president chosen by an electoral college rather than by joint ballot of Congress. Many delegates doubted that the electoral college would ever produce a majority, however, and three days of debate (4–6 September) were required before it was finally agreed that the eventual election of the president would fall to the House of Representatives, if needed, voting by states, rather than the Senate, as originally proposed. But the clear purpose and consequence of this scheme were again to enhance the political independence of the executive at the expense of Congress. Coupled with an earlier decision of 4 June giving the president a veto over legislation, the framers had significantly circumscribed legislative power by restoring to the executive a substantial measure of political autonomy and influence.

In addition to enumerating the powers of Congress and allocating particular duties among the two houses and the executive, the convention in its final weeks of debate also considered the social characteristics it desired of congressmen—or their electors. Many delegates hoped to insulate both houses of Congress against the populist pressures and demagogic impulses that they ascribed to state legislative politics. To secure this end, and especially to encourage Congress to protect rights of property, some of the framers thought the Constitution should contain explicit qualifications either for membership or for the exercise of the suffrage in the election of representatives. Under instructions from the convention, the Committee of Detail had tried, but failed, to devise appropriate standards of wealth or property. As its members explained when queried about their inaction, no satisfactory standard could be found that could be uniformly applied to the disparate societies of the states. Rather than trust Congress to set qualifications for membership at its own discretion, the framers adopted only minimal standards of age, residence, and citizenship for election to Congress, allowing the same electorate that chose the lower houses of assembly in the states to vote for members of the House of Representa-

tives. Far from setting requirements to assure elite rule, the relevant clauses of the Constitution left competition for office and rights of suffrage open and democratic. Delegates, such as Madison, hoped that the relatively small size of both houses would lead to the election of distinguished candidates, while the longer term of senators would foster the independent judgment desired for the upper house; but these were only hopes, not constitutionally mandated rules.

THE RATIFICATION DEBATES

A strong argument can be made that the course of debate at the Constitutional Convention had carried the delegates away from the most radical (or, in a sense, reactionary) implications of the Virginia Plan. Even so, critics of the Constitution and many wavering citizens still feared that the new Congress would quickly evolve into an aloof and even aristocratic institution whose membership would be drawn primarily from the upper strata of American society. Simple arithmetic and repeated comparisons with the state legislatures seemed to prove that only wealthy and prominent individuals could have any hope of election. One of the recurring charges that anti-Federalists leveled against the Constitution was that congressmen drawn from large electoral districts would know little of the needs and concerns of their countrymen.

Other critics worried that the roots of a different, but no less dangerous, aristocracy could be found in the Senate. With their six-year terms, senators would gain the experience needed to dominate their colleagues in the lower house, while the special powers over treaties and appointments that they shared with the president would enable them to influence the conduct of the executive branch just as effectively.

Nor did criticism of Congress stop there. Notwithstanding the enumeration of specific legislative powers in Article I, Section 8, of the Constitution, anti-Federalists argued that the potential reach of its authority was limitless. Just as the necessary and proper clause seemed to invite Congress to enact any law it desired, so too, the grant of a general power of taxation, reinforced by the supremacy clause, suggested that the national government could sap the power of the state legislatures by monopolizing the most accessible and remunerative sources of revenue. Even the clause authorizing Congress to alter the procedures fixed by the states for the election of senators and representatives, it was charged, could be exploited to thwart the political desires of the states.

Federalists responded to these complaints by emphasizing both the checks and balances of the Constitution and the political influence that could still be exerted by the popular electorate for the House of Representatives and the state legislatures for the Senate. In his concluding contributions to *The Federalist* (essays 52–58, 62–63), for example, Madison carefully refuted anti-Federalist charges by examining each of the provisions regulating the construction and powers of the two houses. All the dire predictions about Congress, Federalists argued, assumed that the electorate and the state legislatures would passively acquiesce in the nefarious schemes of congressmen who would no sooner take office than begin to conspire to subvert the liberties of the people.

As extravagant as many anti-Federalist criticisms and predictions seemed to be, the belief that a relatively small Congress could never fairly represent so extensive and diverse a country as the United States did strike a sensitive nerve in the American body politic. Had the ratifiers of the Constitution been permitted to vote on its individual provisions instead of having to approve or reject the document as a whole, it is entirely possible that any of a number of alterations affecting the character of Congress and its members might have been proposed and adopted. But under the rule of decision that the Constitutional Convention successfully imposed on the ratification process, no single objection or set of objections could ever outweigh the simple choice that required determining whether the nation would be better off with the proposed Constitution or without it.

In a deeper sense, both Federalists and anti-Federalists—and many later commentators as well—were inclined to ascribe greater benefits and dangers to the Constitution than any formal document could, of its own authority, provide. The actual uses to which the legislative powers of Congress have been put, like the social characteristics and political ambitions of its members, have always been determined by factors lying well beyond the control of the formal provisions of the Constitution. As James Madison soon discovered, many of his new colleagues in the First Congress (1789–1790) resembled the state legislators whom he had come to disdain before the convention. So, too, notwithstanding the broad interpretation of the necessary and proper clause that Secretary of the Treasury Alexander Hamilton invoked to persuade Congress to adopt crucial elements of his financial program, it took the upheaval of the Civil War and the transformation of the United States into an urban industrial society for Congress to begin to realize its potential as the leading source of American legislation.

BIBLIOGRAPHY

General Studies
Voluminous scholarly literature traces the "rise of the assembly" in colonial and Revolutionary America. JACK P. GREENE, *Peripheries and Center: Constitutional Development in the Extended Polities of the British Empire and the United States, 1607–1788* (Athens, Ga., 1986), provides a synthetic overview of the relation between claims for provincial legislative autonomy and demands for imperial or national supremacy under both the British Empire and the Revolutionary American union. An earlier work by GREENE, *The Quest for Power: The Lower Houses of Assembly in the Southern Colonies, 1689–1776* (Chapel Hill, N.C., 1963), similarly offers the most detailed analysis available of the institutional and political development of legislative power before independence.

The Continental Congress
The history of the Continental Congress is best approached through three scholarly monographs. JACK N. RAKOVE, *The Beginnings of National Politics: An Interpretive History of the Continental Congress* (New York, 1979), emphasizes the political concerns and constraints

that continually shaped the exercise of congressional power; it also includes a close analysis of the drafting of the Articles of Confederation and later efforts at its amendment, culminating in the movement that led to the Constitutional Convention. H. JAMES HENDERSON, *Party Politics in the Continental Congress* (New York, 1974), relies on roll-call analysis in tracing the factional dimensions of congressional politics. JERRILYN GREENE MARSTON, *King and Congress: The Transfer of Political Legitimacy, 1774–1776* (Princeton, N.J., 1987), argues that Americans initially regarded Congress more as a successor to the crown than as a national legislature in any substantive sense.

The starting point for all inquiries into Revolutionary constitutionalism in general and American ideas about legislative power in particular is GORDON S. WOOD, *The Creation of the American Republic, 1776–1787* (Chapel Hill, N.C., 1969). Wood shows how an initial confidence in the representative capacities of popular assemblies was challenged both by mounting populist demands on government and elite criticisms of the character of state legislation. JACKSON T. MAIN, *The Upper House in Revolutionary America, 1763–1788* (Madison, Wis., 1967) is an important study.

State Constitutions

To examine how the legislatures actually framed public policy under the intense pressures generated by the Revolution, it is necessary to turn to studies of particular states. Especially useful are RONALD HOFFMAN, *A Spirit of Dissension: Economics, Politics, and the Revolution in Maryland* (Baltimore, 1973); EDWARD COUNTRYMAN, *A People in Revolution: The American Revolution and Political Society in New York, 1760–1790* (Baltimore, 1981); and RICHARD BUEL, *Dear Liberty: Connecticut's Mobilization for the Revolutionary War* (Middletown, Conn., 1980). For the 1780s, JACKSON T.

MAIN, *Political Parties Before the Constitution* (Chapel Hill, N.C., 1973) and NORMAN K. RISJORD, *Chesapeake Politics, 1781–1800* (New York, 1978), emphasize patterns of partisan alignment within the state legislatures.

Critical Studies

All students of the framing of the Constitution should be encouraged to read the notes of debates, principally, but not exclusively, kept by James Madison and readily accessible in MAX FARRAND, ed., *The Records of the Federal Convention of 1787*, rev. ed., 4 vols. (New Haven, Conn., 1937), reissued with a new *Supplement* (1987), edited by JAMES H. HUTSON. The interpretations of the convention developed in this essay draw extensively on two essays by JACK N. RAKOVE: "The Great Compromise: Ideas, Interests, and the Politics of Constitution Making," *William and Mary Quarterly* 44 (1987), and "The Structure of Politics at the Accession of George Washington," in RICHARD BEEMAN, STEPHEN BOTEIN, and EDWARD C. CARTER II, eds., *Beyond Confederation: Origins of the Constitution and American National Identity* (Chapel Hill, N.C., 1987). In the same volume, PAUL FINKELMAN, "Slavery and the Constitutional Convention: Making a Covenant with Death," provides an acute analysis of the network of sectional bargains. The famous dispute between large and small states is also ably treated in PETER S. ONUF, *The Origins of the Federal Republic: Jurisdictional Controversies in the United States, 1775–1787* (Philadelphia, 1983) and ROSEMARIE ZAGARRI, *The Politics of Size: Representation in the United States, 1776–1850* (Ithaca, N.Y., 1987). Also useful is MICHAEL J. MALBIN, "Congress During the Convention and Ratification," in LEONARD W. LEVY and DENNIS J. MAHONEY, eds., *The Framing and Ratification of the Constitution* (New York, 1987).

SEE ALSO Colonial Assemblies; Legislatures and Slavery; The Origins and Early Development of State Legislatures; AND Representation.

FEDERALISM AND AMERICAN LEGISLATURES

Ballard C. Campbell

Civic authority in a federal system is divided between central and numerous subnational governments. This arrangement occupies an intermediate position between a unitary political structure, which concentrates authority in a single government, and a confederation, which disperses authority among coequal sovereignties. The amount of power allocated to a country's political subunits (for example, provinces and states) varies among federal systems, such as those of the United States, Canada, and Switzerland. The jurisdiction of their central governments extends over all territory in the nation, while the authority of each subunit applies only within its own borders. Federalism also apportions authority by legislative subjects. In the United States the national government performs certain functions, such as the maintenance of national security and the printing of paper currency, while state and local governments handle other tasks, such as schooling, sanitation, and public safety. Although the central and state governments in the United States can act independently of each other, they also legislate in similar fields and now administer jointly many programs.

The mix of independent and coordinated policy-making has changed since the American federal system began. The Constitution of the United States, which outlines federalism's legal foundation, does not clearly define the scope of national power or enumerate the powers reserved to the states. Federalism was born amid considerable theoretical ambiguity, which has persisted since 1789. Woodrow Wilson noted the enigmatic nature of the system. "The relation of the States to the federal government," he wrote shortly before becoming president, "is constantly changing, for it is the life of the nation itself" (*Constitutional Government in the United States,* 1908, p. 173). A complete description of American federalism must take account of this history, comparing the propor-

tion of governance performed at each level at particular times in the past. Governance encompasses all dimensions of public activity, including constitutional law, civic ideology, and patterns of politics and policy-making. These developments will be summarized in this essay within four historical eras, beginning with the period of constitutional formation (1775–1788). Each stage exhibited a distinctive style of governing, although the national government gained power in every period. This centralization of authority increased markedly after 1887 and in conjunction with the growth of government.

Federalism affected the way these processes evolved. The creation of the system itself was a reflection of democratic theory, called "republicanism" by early Americans. This philosophy located the supreme sovereignty of the civil regime in "We the People," as the Preamble to the Constitution expresses the idea. As a practical matter, citizens gave their "consent" to be governed by delegating authority to elected and appointed officials. Legislators were regarded as the people's principal representatives during the nation's first century. By providing for a dual system of legislatures—Congress and the several state legislatures—federalism duplicated republicanism's insistence on rule by elected lawmakers.

Provisions in the Constitution concerning the selection of national officials create channels of influence in the federal system. Each state, regardless of its size, sends two senators to Congress. State legislators chose these lawmakers until 1913, when the popular election of senators began under the Seventeenth Amendment. Seats in the House of Representatives are distributed according to the populations of the states, respectively, and districts are drawn wholly within them. Many members of Congress first gained law-making experience in their own state legislatures. Presidents are chosen by electors, who were selected by state legislators during the early years of the nation, and now are elected by the voters of each state. Political parties, which are primarily state and local organizations, put up candidates for both federal and state positions. Shared partisanship among officeholders and civic activists at both levels of government have built many political bridges across federalism's structural divisions.

Federalism affects policy in other ways besides the selection of officeholders. The existence of numerous states, each possessing authority to formulate law in numerous fields, creates an arena conducive to policy diversity. Before 1863, for example, fifteen states legalized slavery, while the other nineteen prohibited it. Some, but not all, jurisdictions forbade the sale of alcoholic beverages, enacted antimonopoly laws, and regulated small-loan contracts during the late nineteenth and early twentieth centuries. Eastern states continued English precedents regarding the use of water, but western states revised these standards to accommodate their region's aridity. The states manifest many variations in their revenue arrangements and expenditure habits, administrative practices, relations with local government (including the allocation of fiscal responsibilities), and statutory law concerning most aspects of civic life.

While federalism has facilitated creation of a mosaic of policy variations at the state level, its structure can also intimidate policymakers. Competition between states to attract and hold business, for example, has discouraged certain kinds of legislation, principally rigorous commercial regulation and taxation. Matters assigned to national jurisdiction are off limits to the states, and the range of these issues has widened in recent decades. The two levels of government also share "concurrent" jurisdiction over similar subjects, such as public health and transportation, and now administer many programs collaboratively. Early in the nation's history, state legislators attempted to "instruct" U.S. senators on key votes; this has developed into the modern practice in which state and local officials routinely lobby Congress. The federal system also contains state and federal courts, which allow a double review of the constitutionality of state legislative action. In various ways, the structure of federalism influences the pattern of politics and the design of public policy in the United States.

CONSTITUTIONAL FORMATION, 1775–1788

The institutional roots of American federalism extend back to colonial assemblies, which functioned as semiautonomous regimes under nominal British authority. During the American Revolution these indigenous institutions were converted into permanent state governments whose authority was outlined in written constitutions. These documents "consecrated" the principles of republicanism, which began with the axiom that the purpose of government was the protection of individual liberty. But the power needed to achieve this objective was inherently liable to abuse by officials who succumbed to temptations of self-interest. Consequently, state constitutions contained declarations of rights that enumerated the liberties of individuals, limited the authority of executives and courts, and entrusted extensive power to legislatures.

Americans formed a national league under the Articles of Confederation during the revolutionary war, but gave little power to its Congress, which could not regulate commerce, raise an army, or levy taxes. Critics worried that the Confederation's inability to deter foreign threats and temper "domestic dangers" undermined liberty. They urged restraint of the "unruly men" in the state legislatures, which had issued paper money, repudiated debts, and engaged in other purportedly wicked projects. A stronger central government, they believed, would restore "public virtue."

The delegates sent to Philadelphia in 1787 to revise the Articles resolved to recast the whole basis of the Union. This task was complicated by two issues, the first of which concerned the power of the central government and the second, the basis of representation in Congress. Delegates from small states advocated equality of representation among the states, while members from large states wanted legislative seats distributed according to population. The resulting "Great Compromise" combined both plans in a bicameral Congress, in which each state had equal representation in the Senate and population was the criterion for representation in the House.

This accord facilitated compromise concerning the apportionment of power between the central government and the states. The delegates invented a constitution "of a mixed nature" that awarded selective powers to the national government and reserved others to the states. National authority was limited to certain enumerated powers, yet acts of Congress were designated the "supreme Law of the Land," which officials at every level were "bound by Oath" to support. Congress was allowed to tax, borrow money, regulate commerce with foreign countries and among the several states, coin money and punish counterfeiting, declare war, raise an army and maintain a navy, call up the militia (now called the National Guard), and suppress "Insurrections." The latter grant was related to the Constitution's "guarantee to every state . . . a Republican Form of Government." Congress could "make all Laws which shall be necessary and proper" to execute these powers, admit new states, and make "Rules and Regulations" respecting the territories.

The enhanced authority of the Congress alarmed anti-Federalists, who opposed ratification of the Constitution on grounds that its centralization of power would have tyrannous consequences. Advocates of a stronger Union, who cleverly called themselves "Federalists," worked diligently to rebut this apprehension. On behalf of ratification, James Madison, Alexander Hamilton, and John Jay collaborated on *The Federalist* (1788), a collection of essays that remains a classic treatise on American government. Madison emphasized in *The Federalist*, no. 46, that the two levels of government are "instituted with different powers, and designated for different purposes." National powers, he wrote, are "few and defined" (no. 45) and extend to "certain enumerated objects only" (no. 39). The Constitution also prohibits the states from coining money, taxing imports, impairing the obligation of contracts, and a few other matters. Yet, Hamilton observed (no. 9), the states retain "certain exclusive and very important portions of sovereign power."

Madison agreed that the new "compound republic" preserved the largest quotient of power to the states, which he predicted (no.

46) would command "the first and most natural attachment of the people." In his famous tenth *Federalist* essay, he argued that a large republic increased the "obstacles" for a majority faction to subvert private rights. Elaborating in *The Federalist,* no. 51, Madison explained that the division of power between "two distinct governments" and then among the central government's "separate departments" afforded a "double security" for liberty. As a further conciliation, federalists agreed to append a Bill of Rights to the Constitution. The last of these ten amendments (ratified in 1791), adopted by the First Congress, formalized Madison's and Hamilton's contention that the residue of powers "are reserved to the States respectively or to the people."

DUAL FEDERALISM, 1789–1887

By creating a national government and by acknowledging the existence of the states, the Constitution established a federal union but offered little guidance on how power was apportioned between jurisdictions. The charter did not elaborate on the scope of congressional authority, nor did it enumerate the powers of the states, other than to itemize certain prohibitions and assign responsibility for the election of national officials. It remained for the participants in politics to define federalism's practical form.

Ideological deference to the link between federalism and liberty created a standard for the conduct of public affairs. Presidents repeatedly saluted the connection in their major addresses, beginning with George Washington's characterization of the "union" as "a main prop" of liberty. Thomas Jefferson was the first of many presidents to embrace explicitly the principle of separate but interdependent sovereignties, which constituted the philosophic essence of dual Federalism. In his first inaugural address (1801), he pledged his "support of the State governments in all their rights, as the most competent administrations for our domestic concerns" and of "the preservation of the General Government in its whole constitutional vigor." John Quincy Adams agreed in his inaugural address (1825) that the central and state governments were "all sovereignties of limited powers" that cohabited "a confederate representative democracy." Maintaining this duality, James Polk opined in his inaugural address (1845), preserved "the blessings of liberty."

Even as Abraham Lincoln poised to break the Southern siege at Fort Sumter, he reaffirmed at his inauguration (1861), the "right of each State to . . . control its own domestic institutions," slavery included. The Civil War confirmed the supremacy of the national government, but it did not repudiate federalism as the cradle of American liberty. James Garfield reiterated the axiom at his inauguration (1881), venerating "the manifold blessing of local self-government." Perpetuating the "priceless benefits" of the Union, as Grover Cleveland announced at the next presidential induction (1885), required "a careful observance" of the constitutional foundations of dual federalism. Several corollaries clung to this ideological scaffold: congressional authority was limited to its enumerated powers, the states retained wide policy-making discretion, all power should be used sparingly (especially regarding taxation), and special-interest favoritism ("class legislation") was subversive of the public good.

Governance in practice conformed closely to these prescriptions. Congress's chief duties before 1860 centered on foreign relations, the maintenance of a small army and navy, the exploration and distribution of public lands, the operation of a rudimentary postal system, the collection of tax duties (or tariffs) on imported articles, the provision of a few aids to business, the regulation of several navigational activities, and the support of a tiny administrative regime. Although limited in scope, federal powers were sufficient to assist in the economic development of the nation, as federalist proponents of a new constitution in the 1780s had hoped. The national government acquired a vast territorial domain, defended it from foreign threats, removed native Americans from it, and transferred it to various public and private interests. Congress gave sections of the public domain to states for the support of schools and, in 1862, for land-grant colleges. National lawmakers encouraged commercial development by making land affordable to settlers, protecting commercial ideas with patents and copyrights, improving navigable waterways, subsidizing railroad construction, regulating currency, promoting the formation of capital, and maintaining a legal system that protected private property.

The states played an equally important commercial role. They chartered business ventures (and later incorporated them) and regulated business and labor, although more on paper than in practice. States developed a body of statutory and judge-created law concerning commercial transactions, property rights, and indebtedness. States offered various subsidies, including loans and the expropriation of private land (via eminent domain) to stimulate entrepreneurial projects, and invested directly in banks and transportation companies. Beginning with New York's decision in 1817 to construct the Erie Canal (opened in 1825), many states, primarily in northern locations, built and operated transportation facilities, chiefly canals. Cities, as well as states, offered various financial inducements to railroads during their initial decades of activity. Charges of political favoritism and strains on state finances, brought on in part by the depression of 1837–1843, produced a wave of changes in state constitutions beginning in the mid-1840s that restricted state-sponsored enterprise. Limitations on the amount and purpose of, and method of incurring, state indebtedness were imposed, and public investment in private ventures or public internal improvements was prohibited altogether in some places. New constitutional provisions permitted or instructed legislatures to enact analogous controls over municipal finance.

State and federal policymakers shared jurisdiction over commercial subjects, but subnational officials made most social policy. This activity included life-cycle matters such as marriage, orphans, divorce, and burial, as well as education, care of the poor, and punishment of immoral conduct. The protection of people and property lay with the states, which delegated the administration of most criminal and civil law to local government. The workhorses of the era, the county, town, and municipal governments, financed and managed most civic affairs, from the maintenance of police, fire protection, and schools, to the registration of land deeds, the construction of roads and streets, and the regulation of health and safety. State lawmakers created and empowered these local jurisdictions and instructed city and county officials on election and administrative procedure.

FEDERALISM AND AMERICAN LEGISLATURES

The allocation of responsibilities between the national government and the states usually proceeded uneventfully; yet, occasional controversies disrupted the routine. Alexander Hamilton's proposal in 1791 to charter a national bank, which would hold federal revenues and offer loans to private entrepreneurs, provoked the first major debate in Congress over the scope of national jurisdiction. Taking a strict-constructionist position, Thomas Jefferson opposed the bill because the Constitution did not explicitly provide for the creation of a bank. Hamilton replied that the "necessary and proper" clause (in Art. I, Sect. 8) empowered Congress to use any constitutionally permissible means to carry out objectives clearly specified in the Constitution. The Jefferson-Hamilton debate laid out the essentials of the strict- and broad-constructionist views of congressional power that surfaced repeatedly in the era of dual federalism and afterward. In 1791, Congress and President George Washington sided with Hamilton, as did the Supreme Court, which later upheld the constitutionality of the first Bank of the United States (*McCulloch* v. *Maryland* 4 Wheaton 316, 1819). Yet, the dispute persisted. President Andrew Jackson vetoed a bill to recharter the second Bank in 1832, citing Jeffersonian reasoning in declaring the measure unconstitutional. Congressional hostility to federal banks prevailed as policy until the Civil War, when lawmakers authorized a system of national banks and used the tax power to coerce many state banks to join. The Federal Reserve System, which was founded to reform national banking in 1913, showed the influence of federalism on its policy design in its reliance on a noncentralized financial structure.

Strict constructionists sometimes turned to the states to support complaints of illegal congressional actions. Jefferson and Madison drafted charges that Congress had exceeded its authority in enacting the Alien and Sedition Acts (1798). Adopted by the legislatures of Kentucky and Virginia, these resolutions asserted the right of states to refuse enforcement of unconstitutional laws that threatened personal liberty. The War of 1812 provoked disgruntled New Englanders to contemplate manifestos that elevated states' rights over national power. South Carolina's Ordinance of Nullification (1832), issued to condemn high tariff rates, claimed that the Union was a voluntary compact among states, which retained the right to declare congressional actions null and void. President Andrew Jackson, who accepted the theory of dual federalism, nevertheless rejected South Carolina's threat to render federal tax power impotent.

Congress and presidents repeatedly debated the extent of national powers, but the Supreme Court became the arbiter of their limits. The Constitution did not explicitly provide for this prerogative, called "judicial review," but most attorneys believed that the power was implied. The Supreme Court first disallowed a state statute (*Ware* v. *Hylton,* 3 Dallas 199) in 1792 and upheld an act of Congress (*Hylton* v. *United States,* 3 Dallas 171) in 1796. In 1816 the Supreme Court asserted its authority to review the decisions of state courts on constitutional issues (*Martin* v. *Hunter's Lessee,* 1 Wheaton 304). The Court took its boldest step in 1803 when it overturned a national law (*Marbury* v. *Madison,* 1 Cranch 137). The invalidated legislation was minor, but the ramifications of the action were immense. By claiming the right to legitimize federal statutes as well as to overturn state actions, the justices acquired a formidable weapon with which to enhance national power.

John Marshall, chief justice of the Supreme Court from 1801 to 1835, used this legal sword in just such a fashion. A Hamiltonian in outlook, Marshall led the Court in developing a firm constitutional foundation for congressional authority, usually at the expense of state discretion. In *Gibbons* v. *Ogden,* 9 Wheaton 1 (1824), Marshall struck down a New York statute concerning navigational rights around Manhattan on the ground that Congress had already legislated on the subject and states must yield to national law. Marshall adopted Hamilton's reasoning in confirming the legality of the Bank of the United States. A state tax on the bank was invalid, he held in *McCulloch* v. *Maryland,* 4 Wheaton 316 (1819), because it "involves the power to destroy" a legitimate instrument of the United States.

Roger Taney, Marshall's successor as chief justice until 1864, assumed a more balanced position on the relationship between state and nation. Beginning with the *Charles River Bridge,* 11 Peters 420, and *New York* v. *Miln,* 11 Peters 102, decisions in 1837, Taney gave greater latitude to state actions than had Marshall. The Taney Court did not embrace a compact theory of the Union, but it emphasized subnational prerogatives. Under an emergent doctrine of police powers, states possessed inherent authority to legislate on "everything essential to public safety, health, and morals." So long as they did not violate federal law or their own procedural guidelines, states had extensive discretion to regulate "for the good and welfare" of their citizens. Conflicts between state use of their police powers and congressional power to regulate interstate commerce produced a complex history of litigation in the hundred years after Taney's elevation to the Court. Despite some restrictions, federal jurists generally acquiesced in state and municipal regulation of social and commercial activity in the late nineteenth century.

The Civil War posed the ultimate challenge to comity between the states and the nation. Jurisdiction over slavery served as the nominal provocation for the breakdown of the Union. Few Americans before 1861 questioned the ability of the states to legalize slavery or of Congress to legislate for the return of runaways. The Constitution then prohibited a state from freeing a slave who had fled from another state, but left, according to the theory of dual federalism, the principal prerogative of protecting property rights and defining social relations to the states. The constitutional battle over who controlled slavery focused on the Union's fringes—the territories. Congress had the indisputable right to regulate affairs in the territories and to admit new states. The prospect that non-slaveholders would dominate newly settled areas and then request admission as "free" states moved Southerners to demand protection of slavery in the territories. In one of its most controversial decisions, *Dred Scott,* 19 Howard 393 (1857), the Supreme Court said that the Fifth Amendment provided such a constitutional guarantee. The ensuing outrage in the North generated support for the new Republican party, which rejected the legitimacy of the ruling. Election of the Republican Abraham Lincoln to the presidency prompted Southerners to vote secession from the Union. Lincoln called the action "legally void" and the Union "perpetual." Federalism and liberty were inseparable to him.

The Civil War sustained the inseverability of the Union, confirmed federal supremacy, and ended slavery (Thirteenth Amendment, 1865). During Reconstruction, the Congress treated the states of the Confederacy as conquered provinces and demanded that these states write new constitutions according to specifications set by Republican lawmakers. The Southern states were also forced to ratify the Fourteenth Amendment (1868), which provided that persons born or naturalized in the United States were citizens of both the United States and their respective states. The amendment prohibited denial to "any person of life, liberty, or property without due process of law" or "the equal protection of the laws." The Fifteenth Amendment (1870) prohibited state abridgment of the right to vote due to race.

In theory, these so-called Civil War amendments gave Washington substantial authority to curtail state or local actions that deprived ex-slaves of their civil liberties. In practice, national lawmakers used their new power sparingly, and the courts emasculated the legislation they did enact. In a series of rulings in the 1870s and 1880s, federal jurists narrowed the applicability of the Fourteenth and Fifteenth Amendments. This trend culminated in *Plessey* v. *Ferguson,* 163 U.S. 537 (1896), wherein the Court ruled that state-mandated segregation of the races did not deny the equal protection under the law to African Americans.

GROWTH OF GOVERNMENT SINCE 1887

The states and Washington, observed James Bryce, noted British student of nineteenth-century America, operated like "two sets of machinery...each set doing its own work without touching or hampering the other" (vol. 1, p. 319). Although exaggerated, Bryce's metaphor captures the essence of dual federalism. This divided structure of government reflected American insistence on limiting power, an ideology that the judiciary consistently reaffirmed. The small scale of public activities before 1887—the year in which the Interstate Commerce Act inaugurated the modern era of national commercial regulation—helped to sustain this arrangement by minimizing intrusions between the levels of government. The failure of political parties to develop cohesive national organizations to overcome regional and state loyalties lent further support to the pattern. Small, noncentralized governance, moreover, was compatible with the rural and localized economy, individual self-reliance, and simple commercial relationships.

The expansion of the public sector after 1887 changed the face of federalism. The growth of government over the next century was visible in the creation of new civic functions, larger public expenditures, and the increasing complexity of administration. The centralization of power in Washington both reflected these trends and helped to drive them. Congress designed many of its new programs after 1887 as cooperative undertakings that engaged two or three levels of government. As state and national policymakers broadened their agendas and coordinated administrative activities, the gears of dual government increasingly meshed and eventually produced a complex pattern of "intergovernmental relations."

The addition of eight new federal functions illustrates the pace and substance of this growth (see Table 1), beginning with the Interstate Commerce Act of 1887. At the turn of the century, federal policymakers extended ser-

Table 1
EVOLUTION OF FEDERAL FUNCTIONS SINCE 1887

Function and Formative Period	Symbolic Entry Action
Commercial regulation, 1887–1916	Interstate Commerce Act, 1887
Social control and services, 1891–1918	Federal immigration regulation, 1891
Civil liberties, 1918–1935	Sedition Act, 1918
Economic stabilization, 1933–1946	National Recovery Act, 1933
Income assistance, 1933–1939	Federal emergency relief, 1933
Global stability, 1940–1949	Atomic bomb project, 1940
Nondiscrimination, 1954–1968	*Brown* case, 1954
Environmental, worker, and consumer protection, 1962–1972	Drug pretesting, 1962

vices to millions of individuals and regulated aspects of social behavior, such as prohibiting the interstate transportation of lottery tickets and prostitutes. Officials laid the foundations of modern civil liberty and internal-security policy during the years between World War I and the early 1930s. During that period Washington accepted responsibility for stabilizing the economy and providing financial assistance to individuals. In the 1940s the United States commenced its modern quest to achieve political stability in the world, a role that required the maintenance of a large military establishment. National officials reentered the field of civil rights in the 1950s and fashioned broad nondiscrimination policies during the subsequent decade. Congress also developed comprehensive protections for the environment and for workers and consumers during the 1960s and later. Because each function became a permanent addition to the national role, the scope of congressional policy-making and administrative oversight expanded during successive stages of federalism after 1887. By 1980, no major field was immune from national intervention.

The cost of government rose in tandem with this functional transformation (see Table 2). Expenditures measured in per capita constant dollars (dollars adjusted for inflation) tripled between the 1880s and 1920s, doubled during the 1930s, and increased more rapidly in the 1940s when war and defense consumed billions of additional dollars. Higher spending on social programs, such as Social Security, was a primary cause of the doubling of public outlays between 1962 and the mid-1980s. Government spending in per capita constant dollars was twenty-eight times greater in 1980 than in 1890. The rise in national wealth influenced this fiscal expansion, yet the rate of government expenditure climbed faster than economic growth. Public expenditures equaled 7 percent of the gross national product (GNP) in 1890 and grew to 36 percent by 1980. Prior to 1930, state and local governments accounted on average for two-thirds of public outlays, financed largely by local property taxes. The Great Depression and World War II shifted fiscal dominance toward Washington, which controlled about 64 percent of public finance in the late twentieth century. The new fiscal relationship was evident in federal grants-in-aid to

Table 2
GOVERNMENT SPENDING AND FEDERAL GRANTS

	Total expenditures		Federal grants	
	Per capita Constant 1958 dollars	Percent federal spending	Amount (in billions of dollars)	Percent state and local revenue*
1890	56	36	.002	.3
1927	188	31	.1	1.6
1936	306	55	.9	13.
1962	893	64	7.7	16.
1980	1,584	64	94.6	27.
1988	1,761	63	115.3	19.

*State and local own general revenue.

Sources: U.S. Bureau of the Census, *Census: 1890, Report on Wealth, Debt, and Taxation,* pt. 2 (Washington, D.C., 1895), p. 417; U.S. Census, *Historical Statistics of the United States* (Washington, D.C., 1975), pp. 1114–1115; U.S. Census, *Historical Statistics on Governmental Finances and Employment* (Washington, D.C., 1985), tables 10–12; Advisory Commission on Intergovernmental Relations, *Significant Features of Fiscal Federalism 1990,* vol. 2 (Washington, D.C., 1990), tables 21, 37, 51. Expenditures on federal grants in 1890 determined from relevant statutes. The author calculated all indices.

the state and local government (see Table 2). These intergovernmental transfers were negligible before the 1930s, but by 1980 they grew to $94.6 billion, which equaled 27 percent of the general revenue raised by state and local governments.

Numerous factors caused the growth of government. The primary stimulants were social and economic changes wrought by industrialization. This transformation raised the standard of living, including expectations about the quality of life, but it also created new problems. The rise of large business firms and labor unions disrupted the classical understanding of how a free-market economy worked. The emergence of sprawling metropolitan regions, mass migrations of people, and pollution from modern productive and consumption habits typify developments that triggered demands for public intervention. The industrial transformation spawned the formation of innumerable commercial and nonprofit organizations that lobbied government on behalf of their respective special interests. Political parties contributed to policy expansion by marketing problem-solving and risk-reduction proposals to voters. Public officials in all units of government, including administration, contributed to the dynamics of growth. Their initiatives stemmed from various motives, such as a desire to improve society and to promote their own careers. Public opinion has played a role too, although its influence lies more in ratifying the policy decisions of officeholders than in proposing new programs. Contrary to eighteenth-century apprehensions that government would compromise liberty, Americans in the late twentieth century have expected government to use power actively to solve society's problems. In fueling the growth of the federal government's role, these dynamics altered the nature of federal relations in the twentieth century.

THE TRANSITIONAL ERA, 1887–1932

Between the presidencies of Grover Cleveland and Herbert Hoover, government entered a transition period, when debates raged about appropriate public responses to new social and economic conditions. Out of this dialogue came the initial steps toward modern governance. With the enactment of the Interstate Commerce Act and the inauguration of ongoing federal grants of money to the states, governments expanded their activities and adopted new forms of policy management. Although not abandoned, dual federalism was strained by these developments.

State and local governments were in the vanguard of these innovations. Acting under state authority or instruction, municipal officials established kindergartens and built high schools, engineered water-purification and sewer systems, lighted and paved streets, collected garbage, staffed public-health commissions, organized police and fire departments, created parks, zoned land use, and provided other services. State lawmakers had traditionally delegated most civic tasks to local officials, but during the transition era they assigned greater administration to states. This trend toward state centralization is illustrated by public-utility commissions, created to regulate railroads, trucks, gas, electric, and telephone companies. State economic legislation ranged from antimonopoly laws and regulation of insurance companies to the protection of worker safety and the licensing of trades (e.g., barbers) and professions (such as the practice of medicine). States also widely legislated concerning the moral and social behavior of individuals (for example, gambling, marriage) and sought improvements in public health. They lengthened the list of criminal offenses, created more courts, and expanded correctional facilities.

Emergent concepts of "scientific" administration and popular resentment of partisan politics generated pressures to reform governmental procedures. Election balloting was placed under state supervision, and the adoption of primary elections was intended to democratize the nomination process. The U.S. Senate was made a popularly elected office (Seventeenth Amendment, 1913), and women were included in the electorate, first in the states and later nationwide (Nineteenth Amendment, 1920). The ragtag arrangement of state agencies was streamlined, and cabinet-style departments were placed under gubernatorial control. A variety of revenue innovations, including the taxation of income and motor fuels, substantially redesigned state finances. This burst of state lawmaking produced a diversity of policies, including the failure of some states to legislate on certain subjects. Critics predicted that federal preemption would occur if states did not coordinate their policy efforts. Attorneys spearheaded a "uniform state law" campaign (sponsored after 1935 by the Council of State Governments) that sought to reduce statutory diversity and deter national intervention.

The modest success of the uniform-law effort failed to halt the expansion of national policy-making. After Congress created the Interstate Commerce Commission in 1887, it went on to establish broader controls over the use of natural resources (as in the creation of forest reserves), subsidized entrepreneurial groups (such as in loans to farmers), and invested in infrastructure (for example, highway construction). By 1930, Washington was regulating various economic sectors, such as railroads, banks, shipping, and manufacturing (the latter via antitrust policy) and was offering entrepreneurs and farmers a variety of services that ranged from the collection of price data to tips on how to increase the yield of field crops. Congress moved into social policy too. Lawmakers set cultural standards for immigration to the United States, authorized the free delivery of mail and packages to rural residents, and prohibited the interstate transportation of prostitutes. The Eighteenth Amendment (1919, repealed 1933) permitted Congress to prohibit the manufacture and sale of alcoholic beverages, thereby interjecting Washington into a field historically reserved for the states. World War I occasioned a further expansion of national power, as Congress drafted men into the military, increased the income-tax levy (exercising a power authorized by the Sixteenth Amendment, 1913), penalized unauthorized speech, and delegated wide discretion to the president to manage the economy.

Greater national activism increased areas of concurrent policy-making between governments. Federal grants-in-aid, whereby Washington subsidized programs managed by the states, represented a cooperative form of intergovernmental overlap. The Hatch Act of 1887 established the first permanent cash transfer to the states. The law awarded $15,000 annually to each state in support of "original researches" in agriculture. The act stipulated that the work must be carried out by an "experiment station" that operated under the supervision of the state agricultural college. The states without such research facilities had soon created them in order to qualify for funding. In 1894, Congress ordered periodic audits of research expenditures and in later laws further tightened control over the use of grant monies. Legislators increased the stipend in 1906 and in subsequent Congresses and added agricultural economics, rural sociology, and marketing to eligible areas of research. By 1981, the secretary of agriculture had wide discretion to distribute $290 million to state agricultural stations.

Experiment-station grants established a precedent, whereby Washington funded a specific category of activity on an ongoing basis, subject to increased federal supervision and larger appropriations as time progressed. A dozen such programs existed by the end of the transition era. Cash stipends for the state agricultural colleges began in 1890, for protection against forest fires in 1911, and for local demonstration of modern farming techniques in 1914. The last act required each state to match its federal allotment, a condition repeated in the Federal Aid Road Act of 1916 and many subsequent programs, including the 1935 expansion of aid to agricultural experiment stations.

Federal grants derived from Congress's willingness to enter new fields of civic activity and to design policies in ways that conformed to the federal structure of government. The widening range of congressional statutes enacted during the transition era foreshadowed lawmakers' later tendency to respond to innumerable problems by creating new programs, many of which were cast as grants. Several arguments bolstered proposals for federal aid to other governments. For example, policy diversity among the states made a case for common national standards that grant provisions could set; yet, wide economic and fiscal inequalities existed between states. In 1929 New Yorkers, for example, were four times wealthier on the average than Mississippians, which meant that the Empire State could raise more public money with less effort than the Magnolia State. The possibility of fiscal redistribution was especially attractive to southerners, whose region was the poorest in the nation, as well as being solidly devoted to the Democratic party. The seating of Democratic majorities in Congress, beginning in the 1930s, politically facilitated grant enactments. The widening gulf in wealth, between the central cities and the suburbs in the post–World War II years created similar political trends that fed the development of urban grants.

The tradition of dual federalism influenced Congress to package many domestic programs as grants. Doing so deferred to local control and minimized expansion of the federal bureaucracy, both popular objectives in Congress. Moreover, Washington's authority to legislate in many fields was doubtful before the 1940s. Grants skirted these constitutional uncertainties. By the time this legal issue was re-

solved, grants had already become a precedent. The structure of congressional representation gave grants a political appeal. Traditional ideology condemned special-interest favoritism, historically called "class" legislation. But lawmakers had a legitimate obligation to act on behalf of their constituents, who were defined in geographic terms. Grants enabled national legislators to address modern policy needs and simultaneously secure financial benefits for their individual districts.

The increased activism in the public sector stimulated challenges to its legality. Litigation centered on two questions. First, where was the dividing line between state-police powers and congressional control over interstate commerce? As economic regulations proliferated, more possibilities arose that one government, usually a state, could intrude on the jurisdiction of another. Second, when did society's right to legislate in the public interest give way to the rights of private property and individual freedom to engage in commercial transactions? These two questions were conjoined for many jurists, who saw federalism, personal liberty, and classical economic theory all interweaving to form a philosophic standard.

Between 1874 and 1930 the Supreme Court struck down 460 state statutes, of which many were judged to intrude on national jurisdiction over interstate commerce. The decision in *Wabash, St. Louis, and Pacific Railroad* v. *Illinois,* 118 U.S. 557 (1886), which disallowed an Illinois regulation of railroad charges, rested on this ground. With state regulation of transportation restricted to each state's own territory, Congress filled the void in 1887 with the Interstate Commerce Act. This sequence, in which a federal court's prohibition of a state action had stimulated Congress to enter the field, was repeated for the regulation of liquor, the trucking industry, and other subjects. The Fourteenth Amendment, which prohibited states from depriving "persons" of their property without "due process of law," offered another legal rationale for constraining state actions. Businesses, once they were deemed "persons" under the amendment, found constitutional protection from many state regulations, especially regarding rates and prices, wage and labor provisions, and taxation.

Congressional actions also ran afoul of the Court. In *United States* v. *E. C. Knight Com-*

pany, 156 U.S. 1 (1895), the Court held that manufacturing was not a part of interstate commerce, a verdict that narrowed the application of the Sherman Antitrust Act (1890) for some years. The decision in *Pollock* v. *Farmers Loan and Trust Company,* 157 U.S. 429 (1895), struck down a national income tax because it was not "apportioned among the states" as the Constitution dictated. The Sixteenth Amendment (1913) rectified this constitutional problem and inaugurated competition between the federal and state governments over this source of revenue. In *Hammer* v. *Dagenhart,* 247 U.S. 251 (1918), the Court rejected a law that limited the use of child labor, on grounds that Congress had intruded on the reserved power of the states, which the Tenth Amendment protected. "Our federal government is one of enumerated powers," wrote Justice William R. Day for the Court, which demonstrated that it continued to embrace the interdependency of traditional federalism and liberty. But *Dagenhart* and kindred decisions were exceptions. The usual outcome of litigation over the constitutionality of state and federal actions upheld the use of legislative power. Still, the courts erected enough legal hurdles to temper the zeal of the lawmakers who designed economic policy through the 1930s.

CENTRALIZING FEDERALISM: THE NEW COOPERATION, 1933–1963

The Great Depression and World War II had profound impacts on federalism. During these crises and their immediate aftermath, the national government inaugurated three major functions and established numerous cooperative programs with the states and municipalities. The depression, an economic decline of unprecedented severity and duration, set many of these changes in motion. The average purchasing power of individuals fell by 28 percent and unemployment rose between 1929 and 1933 to one quarter of the work force, with conditions in industrial cities becoming even worse. These numbers spelled fiscal calamity for local governments, whose revenues plummeted but whose welfare obligations soared. Local government, which collected half of all public revenue in 1929, depended on property taxes for most of its funds. But unemployed workers and bankrupt farmers could not pay, and local government had little authority to tap alternative sources of revenue. With cities bankrupt or insolvent, mayors pleaded with state officials for help.

The states delayed property foreclosures and expanded local revenue authorities, but states provided only token financial assistance to destitute families during the critical years 1930–1933. This parsimony was partially the result of the underdeveloped condition of state finance before the depression. An array of constitutional limitations restricted the taxation, borrowing, and budgetary prerogatives of state officials. Equally confining regulations, some constitutional and others statutory, hamstrung local finance. These structural constraints, which had evolved since the 1840s, manifested long-standing apprehensions about the financial capriciousness of state legislators. Many state officials, as well, clung to old beliefs of strict fiscal economy and of antipathy to bureaucracy, attitudes not conducive to a speedy bailout of local government. Constitutional straitjackets on state legislatures limited most assemblies to short biennial sessions. These legislatures paid their part-time lawmakers a pittance and seldom hired professional staff, contributing to the policy lethargy in the states. Frustrated mayors urged Washington to act.

Despite unprecedented steps to contend with depression, President Herbert Hoover resisted broad intervention into the economy and opposed direct federal assistance for the unemployed. The Republican party's minimalist approach to governance during the depths of the depression assured victory for Democrats, who won control of the White House and both houses of Congress in the 1932 election. President Franklin D. Roosevelt and congressional Democrats collaborated to create the New Deal which between 1933 and 1938 extended federal powers substantially and established new relations with state and local officials. Meeting annually without limit, drawing a livable salary, and facing few restrictions on national fiscal powers, congressional delegates served in a more hospitable lawmaking environment than did state legislators. These incentives for the use of power were magnified by Roosevelt's unprecedented leadership of Congress and by his charismatic personality, which directed popular attention toward national politics.

The New Deal concentrated on stimulating the recovery of the economy and providing relief to unemployed workers. Initially conceived as mainly interim measures, many legislative experiments evolved into permanent federal undertakings. The first hundred days of the new administration signaled the breadth of its policy actions: Congress delegated broad authority to the executive to negotiate cooperative agreements between businesses and their employees (National Industrial Recovery Act), control agricultural production (Agricultural Adjustment Act), regulate banks (Banking Act) and the stock market (Securities Act), refinance home mortgages (Home Owners Loan Act), underwrite loans to business and financial institutions (Emergency Banking Act and prior authorizations to the Reconstruction Finance Corporation), sponsor massive public works projects (Public Works Administration under Title II of the National Industrial Recovery Act and the Tennessee Valley Authority Act), and support job programs (Federal Emergency Relief Act and Civilian Conservation Corps Act). Eventually, Washington extended controls over many sectors of the economy, including transportation, communications, power, wholesaling, and labor. By the end of the 1930s, the administration had abandoned classical political economy and acknowledged that deficit financing could be an asset in stabilizing the economy. Emergency-relief efforts of 1933–1935 grew into permanent income-assistance programs, anchored by the Social Security Act (1935) that provided benefits to retired workers, public assistance for the poor (welfare), and compensation for the unemployed. Other income-assistance measures set minimum wages and maximum hours for workers, experimented with the resettlement of poor farmers, and subsidized the construction of low-income housing.

Many of these programs were formulated as grants to state and local government. Public assistance under the Social Security Act took the form of categorical programs to assist dependent children, the blind, and the elderly poor. States set both eligibility and benefit levels for each welfare program, administered them, and defrayed part of their cost with federal reimbursements. Other grants subsidized public health activities, city roads, new areas of agricultural research and market services, flood and land management, public housing, and un-

employment offices. National administrators drafted many of the enabling acts by which states joined particular programs. With federal dollars equivalent to one quarter of state revenues in the mid-1930s, there was a strong financial inducement for state participation.

Many traditionalists were distressed by the scope of this federal expansion. The Supreme Court shared this alarm in 1935 and 1936 when it struck down the centerpieces of New Deal policy. The majority held in *Schechter Poultry Corporation* v. *United States,* 295 U.S. 495 (1935), that the National Industrial Recovery Act delegated an unreasonable amount of authority to the executive and exceeded congressional jurisdiction over commerce. "Extraordinary conditions" did not suspend constitutional federalism, Chief Justice Charles Evans Hughes replied to administration arguments that the economic emergency justified unconventional countermeasures. The Court decided in *United States* v. *Butler,* 297 U.S. 1 (1936), that regulation of agricultural production by means of taxation misused this power and also intruded on state powers protected by the Tenth Amendment. By clinging to a historical conception of dual federalism, the Court had provoked a major political impasse with the Roosevelt administration.

The Court retreated from this confrontational position in 1937 when it upheld federal regulation of union-employer relations (the *National Relations Labor Board* v. *Jones and Laughlin Steel Corporation,* 301 U.S. 1, 1937) on the basis of an expansive definition of interstate commerce. This shift in the Court's thinking and Roosevelt's appointment of liberal justices after 1937 resulted in judicial approval of New Deal regulatory and income-assistance measures enacted after 1934. This was a momentous shift, because thereafter the Court ceased to issue constitutional objections to national management of the economy. This new judicial tolerance toward economic management also encompassed the states, whose legislatures expanded their activities in "little New Deals," enacted partly at federal prompting.

World War II replaced the domestic emergency with an international crisis as the rationale for uncapping federal power. Besides mobilizing a military of twelve million people, Washington established a sort of "command economy," in which it planned and supervised military production and research, allocated labor, resources and transportation, set prices, and rationed certain essential domestic goods during the war. Output soared, many businesses thrived, unemployment evaporated, and personal income rose, in large part because of Washington's unprecedented use of its powers to tax and to borrow. Congress transformed the income tax from a levy on the upper-middle class to a levy most workers paid. In addition, Congress elevated all rates and instituted employer withholding. Income-tax receipts in 1945 were twenty times higher than those in 1940. Borrowing as much as it taxed, Washington spent eleven times more in 1945 than in the most lavish year under the New Deal.

The policy innovations of 1933–1945 profoundly affected postwar federalism. The precedent of deficit spending established during the depression and the fiscal leverage afforded by the new tax structure laid the foundations for economic stabilization policy after 1945. The Kennedy-Johnson tax cut of 1964, designed to stimulate business activity, evolved from these policy developments and new macroeconomic theory. Furthermore, Washington never relinquished its revenue superiority, which it gained during the war, over state and local governments. Citing the need to prevent deficits, control inflation, and fight communism, the Truman, Eisenhower, and Kennedy administrations resisted efforts to reduce taxes toward their prewar levels. Federal coffers grew fuller during these years because the income tax's graduated-rate schedule reaped higher returns from both economic growth and inflation, both of which had remained robust in the postwar era. The resulting federal affluence underwrote a major expansion of intergovernmental aid, especially in the 1960s and 1970s. Grant expenditures increased from less than one billion dollars in 1946 to $94.6 billion in 1980, when federal aid represented a large fraction of subnational revenues (see Table 2).

After the war, grant enactments resumed with the funding of school lunches, hospital construction, and airports in 1946. Adoption of "urban renewal" in the Housing Act of 1949 forged a closer relationship between national and municipal officials. Although opposed to "needless federal expansion," President Dwight D. Eisenhower signed many new grants, including the massive Interstate Highway Act of 1956.

Washington put up 90 percent of the funds (eventually, more than $100 billion) for multilane freeways, of which many intersected metropolitan areas. The same year, Congress authorized subsidies for local sewer-treatment plants, rural libraries, and conservation on the Great Plains. President John F. Kennedy signed grant funding for worker training, air-pollution control, college classrooms, health facilities, and the economic redevelopment of the Appalachian region.

CENTRALIZING FEDERALISM: REGULATORY EXPANSION, 1964–1978

Lawmakers broadened the range of national programs, greatly increased expenditures on grants, and imposed new regulations on the public and private sectors between 1964 and 1978. Federal judges played a leading role in the last development. The new judicial federalism had two dimensions, one grounded on the due process clause of the Fourteenth Amendment and the other on the amendment's equal-protection clause. Abandoning its earlier position, the Supreme Court, between the 1930s and the 1950s, interpreted the due-process test for state action to embrace the individual liberties protected in the First Amendment, such as freedom of speech and religion, and in the Fourth, Fifth, Sixth, and Eighth amendments, which concern criminal-justice practices. By the 1960s this "nationalization" of the Bill of Rights in the Constitution of the United States established uniform standards of conduct for state and local officials on matters such as the right to counsel, unreasonable search and seizure, and double jeopardy. Federal courts discovered new rights, such as privacy, and redefined old ones, such as the meaning of "cruel and unusual punishment." It was commonplace in the 1970s and 1980s for federal courts to order subnational officials to remedy "unconstitutional" conditions in correctional and mental-health facilities and in housing, police, and educational policy.

The Court also breathed new life into the "equal protection" clause. In a series of decisions that culminated in *Brown* v. *Board of Education of Topeka*, 347 U.S. 483 (1954), it held that racially segregated schools violated the Fourteenth Amendment. Southern and conservative opposition prevented Congress from enacting enforcement mechanisms until the Civil Rights Act of 1964. This law outlawed racial discrimination in public accommodations and racial and gender discrimination in private employment practices (state- and local-governmental employment was added in 1972), directed administrators to issue rules for compliance with these standards, and authorized the termination of federal funds to violators. The adoption of federal aid to schools in 1965 gave Washington potent leverage to force recalcitrant southern school districts to end dual systems of education. Administrative strategies to reduce racial and gender discrimination (and their effects) were usually sustained by federal judges, who often proved more courageous than Congress in ordering remedial steps, such as busing to integrate schools, or curtailing sex discrimination in the workplace and in educational institutions.

Articulating new standards of equality was part of the quest to achieve a "Great Society." Its goal, President Lyndon Johnson exclaimed in 1964, was "to enrich . . . and to advance the quality of our American civilization." Congress responded to the challenge by legislating civil rights protections such as the Voting Rights Act (1965), the expansion of income-assistance programs (such as Medicaid and Medicare, 1965), and a series of regulations that concerned the environment, workers, consumers, and public health. Unlike earlier rules governing commercial transactions, which focused on specific sectors of the economy, the "new" regulations set social as well as economic goals and encompassed broad segments of society, including state and local government. These and other Great Society enactments substantially widened the radius of federal influence.

An explosion in the number and cost of grants during the Johnson, Nixon, Ford, and Carter administrations was a by-product of this national activism. Federal-aid programs grew from 181 in number in 1964 to 387 in 1969 and 539 in 1981, with outlays that had increased four times in inflation-adjusted dollars. Spread across twenty-nine substantive categories in 1981, intergovernmental-aid programs ranged from highways and housing to energy and the arts. New initiatives during Johnson's years (1963–1969) included "War on Poverty" programs

(such as Head Start and Legal Services), urban mass-transit projects, aid to schools, housing assistance, health care for low-income and elderly persons, air- and water-pollution control, college facilities, and local policing. Until 1967, each grant was a categorical program—which restricted the subsidy to a designated activity. After decades of complaints from state and local officials about the restrictiveness of categorical programs, Congress consented to five block grants (relatively unrestricted federal grants), which permitted recipients some discretion concerning the allocation of funds. Major block grants were the Crime Control and Safe Streets Act (1968), the Comprehensive Employment and Training Act (1973), and the community-development program (1974), which aided cities. General revenue sharing (1973–1986) took this trend a step further and provided $83 billion, with few programmatic restrictions, to every state and local government.

Besides this programmatic expansion, the grant system evolved into a complex network of allocational options and regulatory purposes. Two-thirds of revenue sharing went directly to local government, an arrangement reflective of Congress's willingness since 1964 to bypass state government. Revenue-sharing dollars were distributed automatically according to a formula that weighted population, income, and level of taxation. Most grants were assigned by similar statutory formulas, which ensured a wide geographical distribution of money. Project grants, by contrast, were awarded by federal administrators, who selected proposals that applicants had submitted. Revenue sharing required no fiscal contribution from recipients, but most grants stipulated some proportionate expenditure from state or local government. Program-related conditions, such as the designation of a state agency to administer grant funds, had long been attached to intergovernmental subsidies, but in the 1960s, Congress began to make generalized policy standards applicable to all intergovernmental transfers. The most pervasive of such "crosscutting" regulations prohibited discrimination on the basis of race and gender and required compliance with environmental protection rules.

The attachment of performance guidelines to grants was one of various methods by which Washington preempted state prerogatives. In some instances, Congress authorized the reduction of aid if a state failed to meet national policy standards. The full allocation of highway assistance became contingent on state enforcement of truck weight limits on interstate highways (1956), highway safety (1966), the fifty-five-miles-per-hour speed limit (1976), and a mandatory drinking age of twenty-one years (1984). Inadequate state performance could trigger greater federal involvement within a field. Both the Clean Air Act (1970) and the Water Pollution Control Act (1972) provided for such conditional preemption by federal officials. And both laws allowed suits in federal courts against states for failure to meet national environmental standards.

Conditional policy designs, in which states were allowed to administer a function subject to strict federal guidelines, increased after 1964. In the instance of the Occupational Safety and Health Act (1970), which required employers to remove hazards from the workplace, some states elected to administer the regulations while others let Washington handle the job. The "preclearance" section of the Voting Rights Act of 1965 required states to remove discriminatory features from their election laws and to submit the revised versions to national officials for approval. Other preemptive legislation established national standards that states could not exceed or reserved areas of policy-making to Congress exclusively. The 1970 amendment to the Cigarette Labeling and Advertising Act (1965), for example, prohibited all state and local health-related regulations of cigarette advertising. Sought by the tobacco industry, this restriction on state action illustrates private-sector strategy to prevent potentially harmful legislation. Federal preemptions took various forms, but collectively they spread national regulation into every civic area by 1978.

CENTRALIZING FEDERALISM: PRAGMATIC ADJUSTMENT, 1979–1992

The federal system entered a period of adjustment after 1978 as a mood of caution slowed the growth of government. Demands for moderation were fueled by a stagnant economy, chronic federal deficits, and hostility to new social policies, such as legalized abortion and affirmative action for minorities. Complaints centered on national domestic policy, including its methods of delivery. The Advisory Commission on Intergovernmental Relations (ACIR), created in 1959 to monitor developments affecting federalism, concluded after several comprehensive studies that governmental relations had become "overloaded" and "dysfunctional." Washington's mode of governing, in the commission's view, was increasingly intrusive, unmanageable, ineffective, costly, and "above all ... unaccountable" (*An Agenda for American Federalism,* p. 101). Ronald Reagan agreed and pledged in his presidential campaigns to reduce the burden of government and to expand the "privatization" of public services. He drew on ACIR language to promote his effort in 1982 to decongest the grant system by placing numerous programs under total state control. In 1991, President George Bush proposed a similar idea, which he predicted would encourage "creative experimentation" in the states. The proposition that states could function as "laboratories" of policy innovation had initially surfaced early in the twentieth century when expansion of Washington's role began to erode dual federalism.

Steps to curb public expenses and reduce regulations on business and government began in the Carter administration and blossomed during Reagan's years in the White House. Outlays for federal grants peaked (in inflation-adjusted dollars) in 1978, the year that Californians voted in Proposition 13 to limit local property taxes. Reagan's 1981 "economic recovery program" reduced federal taxes and modified the grant system. Some aid programs were terminated, others revised, and seventy-seven categoricals consolidated into seven new and two existing block grants. Cuts in intergovernmental assistance fell disproportionately on the poor and the cities. Between 1978 and 1987, federal aid to local government fell in terms of purchasing power by 50 percent and to state government by 14 percent. The states reacted by increasing their own taxation and intergovernmental assistance during the 1980s, which partially offset local losses of federal money. Greater state spending, along with higher national outlays for defense, Social Security, and interest on the federal debt, pushed up the cost of government by 10 percent (in inflation-adjusted dollars) during the Reagan years.

THE SHAPE OF CONTEMPORARY FEDERALISM

Has modern governance altered the allocation of power in the federal system and diminished the importance of the states? Scholars agree that traditional dual federalism is dead but give conflicting answers to this question. One interpretation contends that the states have retained considerable autonomy and influence despite Washington's policy expansion. Daniel Elazar argued that federal grants represent an enabling, rather than a coercive, development, because subnational officials negotiated their enactment and oversaw their implementation. Grant regulations are more bark than bite in Thomas Anton's opinion (1984), as Washington has neither the technical means nor the political will to monitor subnational activities closely. Michael Rich concluded that local political influence was a key factor in the distribution of grants to localities.

This point of view emphasized federal stimulation of policy innovation in the states, including the reform of state political machinery. A major improvement in state policymaking and administrative capacity has occurred since the 1950s. State constitutions have been modernized, executive structures reorganized, legislatures professionalized, and revenues enhanced. The states now collect more taxes than do local governments. These innovations have established the states as the new workhorses of the federal system, with responsibility for directly administering or overseeing the local implementation of numerous human-resource, social-service, and regulatory programs. State courts have rediscovered protections for the rights of individuals in their own constitutions and, in some instances, have articulated safeguards that exceed federal standards.

An alternative perspective sees fundamental changes in the character of federal relations. Ever since Woodrow Wilson wrote that "the central government is constantly becoming stronger," resulting in the "declining status of the states," later observers have repeated his conclusion (*Congressional Government,* pp. 205, 38). Unless abated, "the March of Power to Washington" would render the states "hollow shells," predicted Leonard White (*The States and the Nation,* p. 3). The contemporary tendency to intergovernmentalize virtually every domestic problem was "dysfunctional," David Walker concluded in *Toward a Functioning Federalism* (1981), because it strained state finances, distorted local priorities, and overloaded the servicing system. The centripetal tendencies of the Reagan-Bush era, he observed a decade later in a 1991 essay "American Federalism from Johnson to Bush," continued the "counterproductive" consequences of "permissive federalism."

The contention that the role of the states has diminished comparatively is illustrated by four developments. First, a fiscal imbalance prevails in the federal system. Washington has captured the nation's most lucrative revenue sources: high tax rates on individual income and Social Security levies. State and local governments are left with inferior revenue choices, which constitutional and statutory restrictions adopted since 1978 have limited further. National outlays for just two federal functions, defense and Social Security, equal all state and local revenues, which pays for a myriad of obligations. Some state-run programs, such as health care for low-income persons (Medicaid), came to depend heavily on federal assistance. Congress trimmed back on aid to the states in the 1980s as part of its deficit-reduction effort. Yet Congress may borrow with virtual impunity, while state lawmakers face less hospitable credit markets, balanced-budget requirements, and hostile voter referenda.

Second, "regulatory federalism" has imposed numerous performance standards on state officials. Some regulations appear as conditions to grants, while others are expressed as general policy statements. Together they placed a "mandate millstone" around the necks of local officials in the opinion of Edward I. Koch in 1980, mayor of New York City. Federal jurists can be as insistent as legislators and administrators in their directives to subnational officials. In 1991, Massachusetts state mental-health facilities, county jails, the Boston school system, and the agencies in charge of cleaning up Boston and New Bedford harbors all were under federal district court orders that mandated remedial actions. Each policy directive implied higher costs for subnational government.

Third, public attention has shifted toward the nation's capital and away from statehouses. Signs of Washington's political magnetism abound. The National Conference of State Legislators (founded in 1948), for example, has set up shop in Washington to lobby Congress, which in turn often instructs or bypasses state lawmakers. The contemporary Congress exercises its powers under the supremacy clause of the Constitution with few legal checks. A split majority of the Supreme Court held in *Garcia v. San Antonio Metropolitan Transit Authority,* 469 U.S. 528 (1985) that concerns about the preemption of state functions are matters for Congress and the voters, rather than for the judiciary, to resolve. The decline of state and local political parties has further undercut intergovernmental control of Congress and tipped the balance of power toward the center. While congressional incumbents direct their own campaigns for reelection and presidents bask in the attention of the media, state legislators face anonymity, a legacy of popular mistrust, and, more recently, federal prosecution when Federal Bureau of Investigation "sting" operations uncover wrongdoing.

Fourth, contemporary ideology has discounted the importance of federalism. The states were once considered vital components in a system designed to disperse power in order to contain its misuse. States were judged less by the effectiveness of their response to social and economic problems than by their existence as semisovereign polities within a federal division of authority. Pragmatic considerations have replaced this philosophical rationale as the standard for assessing the governmental system. Power is now viewed as a practical instrument for social betterment and reduction of individual risk. Federal relations in this new political culture are assessed according to economic efficiency, administrative effectiveness, and fiscal equity. Federalism has gravitated toward becoming a set of technical considerations regarding the implementation of policy, which increasingly is shaped by officials in the national government.

BIBLIOGRAPHY

General Studies

General overviews of federalism are THOMAS J. ANTON, *American Federalism and Public Policy* (New York, 1989); W. BROOKE GRAVES, *American Intergovernmental Relations: Their Origins, Historical Development, and Current Status* (New York, 1964); M. J. C. VILE, *The Structure of American Federalism* (London, 1961); and DAVID B. WALKER, *Toward a Functioning Federalism* (Cambridge, Mass., 1981).

Historical developments are discussed in BALLARD C. CAMPBELL, *The Growth of American Government: From Grover Cleveland to Ronald Reagan* (Bloomington, Ind., forthcoming 1955); JAMES T. PATTERSON, *The New Deal and the States: Federalism in Transition* (Princeton, N.J., 1969); MICHAEL D. REAGAN and JOHN G. SANZONE, *The New Federalism* (New York, 1981); HARRY N. SCHEIBER, "Federalism and the American Economic Order, 1789–1910," *Law and Society Review* 10 (1975), and "American Federalism and the Diffusion of Power: Historical and Contemporary Perspectives," *University of Toledo Law Review* 9 (1978).

On legal-judicial trends, see PHILLIP J. COOPER, *Hard Judicial Choices: Federal District Court Judges and State and Local Officials* (New York, 1988); ALFRED H. KELLY, WINFRED A. HARBISON, and HERMAN BELZ, *The American Constitution: Its Origins and Development* (New York, 1991); and BENJAMIN F. WRIGHT, *The Growth of American Constitutional Law* (Chicago, 1942).

Federalism

On the origins of American federalism, see JACOB E. COOKE, ed., *The Federalist* (Cleveland, 1961); CATHY D. MATSON and PETER S. ONUF, *A Union of Interests: Political and Economic Thought in Revolutionary America* (Lawrence, Kans., 1990); HARRY N. SCHEIBER, "Federalism and the Constitution: The Original Understanding," in L. FRIEDMAN and H. SCHEIBER, eds., *American Law and the Constitutional Order* (Cambridge, Mass., 1978); and GORDON S. WOOD, *The Creation of the American Republic, 1776–1787* (New York, 1969).

Classic assessments of federalism are JAMES BRYCE, *The American Commonwealth* (New York, 1888); LEONARD D. WHITE, *The States and the Nation* (Baton Rouge, La., 1953); DANIEL J. ELAZAR, *American Federalism: A View from the States* (New York, 1972); and WOODROW WILSON, *Congressional Government: A Study in*

American Politics (Boston, 1885; New York, 1956). Important studies by the Advisory Commission on Intergovernmental Relations are *Categorical Grants: Their Role and Design* (Washington, D.C., 1978) and *An Agenda for American Federalism: Restoring Confidence and Competence* (Washington, D.C., 1981); other titles in the same series are valuable.

Views on modern federalism include THOMAS J. ANTON, "Intergovernmental Change in the U.S.: An Assessment of the Literature," in TRUDI MILLER, ed., *Public Sector Performance* (Baltimore, 1984); DONALD F. KETTL, *The Regulation of American Federalism* (Baltimore, 1988); RICHARD P. NATHAN, FRED C. DOOLITTLE, et al., *Reagan and the States* (Princeton, N.J., 1987); MICHAEL J. RICH, "Distributive Politics and the Allocation of Federal Grants," *American Political Science Review* 83 (1989); THOMAS R. SWARTZ and JOHN E. PECK, eds., *The Changing Face of Fiscal Federalism* (Armonk, N.Y., 1990); and DAVID B. WALKER, "American Federalism from Johnson to Bush," *Publius: The Journal of Federalism* 21 (1991).

SEE ALSO Colonial Assemblies; The Historiography of the American Legislative System; Legislatures and Bureaucracy; AND Legislatures and the Judiciary.

CONGRESS IN THE FEDERALIST-REPUBLICAN ERA, 1789–1828

Norman K. Risjord

In the thirty years following the adoption of the U.S. Constitution, American political leaders converted that piece of parchment into an enduring stable government. During that period differences in political opinion crystallized into political parties, which vied with one another for popular support. Central to this developmental process was the institutional evolution of the U.S. Congress.

FEDERALISTS AND JEFFERSONIANS, 1789–1809

Federalist-minded New York City joyously celebrated the ratification of the Constitution in the summer of 1788 and eagerly looked forward to the arrival of the new Congress, scheduled to convene on 4 March 1789. The capital city ushered in the day with the booming of cannons and the ringing of bells, but the jubilation subsided quickly when only twelve House members and eight senators appeared at Federal Hall to present their credentials. The House of Representatives did not achieve a quorum until 1 April, and the Senate had to wait three more days before the twelfth senator arrived to make a quorum.

Senate Committees to 1809

As members straggled into the city, some of the more eager federalists began to fret that the new government was already infected with the same lackadaisical attitude that had brought the old Congress into disrepute. Once quorums were achieved, however, the two houses quickly settled down to business. The vice president presided over the Senate; a president pro tem was elected at the beginning of each session to preside in his absence, but this office had little or no political significance and was not even the subject of a contest in the first two decades of the Senate's history. The Senate was small enough (twenty-two members in 1789, thirty-two by 1801) to work virtually as a committee, and it met behind closed doors in its first few years. The Senate did not create any standing committees in its first twenty years; bills were drafted by select committees with three to five members. By rules adopted in its first session, the Senate appointed committees by ballot, specifying that "a plurality of votes shall make a choice."

The choice by ballot quickly led to the practice of excluding opponents of a measure from the committee named to consider that measure, a procedure that had been adopted by the British House of Commons earlier in the century. This, in turn, led to the exclusion of the minority party from committees when parties began to appear. The first Senate consisted almost exclusively of supporters of the Constitution; the only anti-Federalists in the body were the senators from Virginia—Richard Henry Lee and James Monroe. During its three sessions (1789–1791) the Senate of the First Congress set up a total of 131 committees with 544 seats. Six senators (23 percent of the whole) held 45 percent of the seats. All but one had been prominent members of the Constitutional Convention; all but one had served in the Continental Congress. The Senate, in short, relied for daily work on men with experience, on men with whom such work was familiar. Oliver Ellsworth of Connecticut alone held 13 percent of the committee seats, a work load that would not be matched in the first half century of the Senate's existence—perhaps not ever. The North predominated: three of the six leaders were from New England and only one came from the South. It was not long before those who found themselves in the minority felt the Senate's partisan bias. William Maclay, the waspish senator from Pennsylvania who broke with the administration over Alexander Hamilton's fiscal policies, grumbled in mid-1790 that "I cannot see that I can do any further good in this place. Everything, even to the naming of a committee, is prearranged by Hamilton and his group of speculators" (*Journal of William Maclay*, 1890, p. 376).

By 1791, those in opposition to the Washington administration had begun referring to themselves as the "republican interest," or simply "Republicans," an indication of an emerging sense of identity. Consequently, beginning with the Second Congress, it is possible through roll-call analysis to identify congressmen as Federalists or Republicans (although there were waverers or independents in every Congress of the decade). In the Second Congress (1791–1793), Federalists in the Senate outnumbered Republicans 15–10, with 4 independents and 1 seat vacant. In the Third Congress (1793–1795) the ratio was 17, 12, and 1, and in the Fourth Congress (1795–1797) it was 21 Federalists to 11 Republicans. In the last two congresses of the decade Federalists outnumbered Republicans, 22–10.

The committee work load became more evenly distributed in the Second Congress, but the ratio held steady thereafter. The top six senators held 40 percent of the committee seats in the Second Congress, 36 percent in the Third Congress, 36 percent in the Fourth Congress, and 40 percent in the Fifth Congress. The regional and partisan distribution of the leadership was also remarkably stable. In each of these Congresses the leadership consisted of five Federalists and one Republican. Usually three were from New England, two from the Middle Atlantic states, and one from the South. And the same people took the lead—session after session: Oliver Ellsworth, Caleb Strong (Mass.), George Cabot (Mass.), and Rufus King (N.Y.) early in the decade; Samuel Livermore (N.H.), Uriah Tracy (Conn.), Benjamin Goodhue (Mass.), and William Bingham (Pa.) in the middle of the decade.

Most of the committee work, to be sure, was routine (such as providing revolutionary-war pensions) and of little partisan significance. But when an important political issue was referred to a committee, the Federalists made sure they controlled it. The committee to consider Jay's Treaty in 1795, for instance, consisted of five high-powered Federalists. Toward the end of the decade, amid the politically charged atmosphere of the Quasi-War with France (1798–1800), the Federalists took the final step in ensuring partisan control of the Senate's institutional machinery. At the opening of the Sixth Congress in December 1799, a Federalist caucus named committees to consider the various points in President John Adams's annual message, and it systematically excluded Republicans from every one of them. The purpose, explained one Federalist, was "to shew them that they have no confidence in them and are afraid to trust them at this crisis: there is not a man in the minority on any one committee" ("South Carolina Federalist Correspondence," p. 789).

Both the election of Thomas Jefferson as president in 1800 and the accompanying Republican sweep of Congress reversed the party ratio in the Senate. In the Seventh Congress (1801–1803), Republicans outnumbered Federalists, 18 to 14, and in the Eighth Congress (1803–1805), 25 to 9. That ratio held firm until the War of 1812. Not surprisingly, the Republicans took control of the committee structure, and the work load was more concentrated than in the Federalist years. Six senators held 50 percent of the committee seats in each of Jefferson's Congresses, and, in each session, 5 of the 6 were Republicans. Geographical influence shifted toward the South and West but not to the exclusion of New England. Abraham Baldwin (R.-Ga.) had the heaviest work load in the Seventh Congress, followed by Uriah Tracy (Fed.-Conn.), Stephen Bradley (R.-Vt.), and Wilson Cary Nicholas (R.-Va.). In the Eighth Congress the leaders were Abraham Baldwin, Stephen Bradley, Samuel Smith (R.-Md.), and John Breckinridge (R.-Ky.). In his diary entry for 4 January 1805, freshman Senator John Quincy Adams described the system as it stood during Jefferson's presidency: "As our committees are all chosen by ballot, the influence and weight of a member can very well be measured by the number and importance of those of which he is a member." Having received only 14 assignments in his first two years, Adams added, "In this respect I have no excitements of vanity."

HOUSE COMMITTEES AND THE SPEAKER TO 1811

The development of a committee system in the House of Representatives paralleled that of the Senate, but House members were slower in perceiving the partisan advantages to be gained in controlling committees. One reason is that the House adopted a rule authorizing the Speaker to make committee appointments, and the Speakers in the early Congresses—Frederick A. Muhlenburg of Pennsylvania in the First and Third Congresses, Jonathan Trumbull of Connecticut in the Second—made an effort to be impartial arbiters. There was sound British precedent for this, with which Americans were quite familiar. The Speaker of the House of Commons was expected to be an impartial arbiter. Although he had power to appoint committees, the Speaker almost always followed the recommendations of the partisan leaders of the House.

Their prior legislative experience had acquainted the U.S. House members with the concept of "the committee of the whole," in which the Speaker yielded to a committee chairman and the House engaged in informal discussion with unrecorded roll calls. Soon after it began its proceedings, in May 1789, the House engaged in a discussion of the functions of such a committee. Elias Boudinot of New Jersey observed that "it seemed to be a settled point in the House that a Committee of the Whole was the proper place for determining principles before they were sent elsewhere" (for example, to a select committee). James Madison agreed, pointing out that "it was much better to determine the whole outlines of all business in a Committee of the Whole" (*Debates and Proceedings in the Congress of the United States* [*Annals of Congress*], 1st Cong., 1st sess., p. 370).

Unlike the Senate, the House felt the need for standing committees, although initially they dealt with administrative detail rather than public policy. The First Congress created two of them, namely, the Committee on Elections and the Committee on (i.e., to proofread) Enrolled Bills. The House added the Committee of Claims in 1794 to handle the avalanche of petitions stemming from revolutionary-war veterans. Like the Senate, the House in its first twenty years relied primarily on select committees to consider matters of public policy and to draft resolutions or bills. Madison was the workhorse of the initial session of the First Congress in the summer of 1789, introducing bills on revenue and amendments to the Constitution, and serving on committees. In the second and third sessions, however, after he broke with the administration on Hamilton's fiscal policy, Madison's committee service dropped markedly. In his place, William Loughton Smith of South Carolina emerged as both the spokesman for the presidential administration and the dominant figure on committees.

Except for some twenty congressmen who grouped around Madison on issues of fiscal policy and who ultimately formed a nucleus for the Republican party, it is hard to discern partisanship in the First Congress. Roll-call analysis reveals a division that was essentially sectional, North versus South, but the reason for that, one suspects, is that debate over the permanent location for the seat of government generated a disproportionate number of roll calls. By the beginning of the Second Congress, however, party lines were taking shape, as they did in the Senate. Roll-call analysis indicates that there were 37 Federalists, 26 Republicans, and 6 independents in that Congress (that would have been the tabulation if all members were present on any given day; attendance, as well as deaths, resignations, and by-elections, or special elections held between regular elections in order to fill a vacancy, affected the tally on any given vote). In the next three Congresses the party balance was almost even, so House decisions depended on daily attendance and the swing vote of independents: there were 47 Federalists, 48 Republicans, and 10 independents in the Third Congress; 45 Federalists, 56 Republicans, and 4 independents in the Fourth Congress; and 53 Federalists, 51 Republicans, and 1 independent in the Fifth Congress.

Throughout these years, Republicans were hampered by absenteeism. In the Third Congress average party strength on three partisan roll calls (construction of frigates, denunciation of the Whisky Rebellion, and passage of the carriage tax) was 47 Federalists and 34 Republicans. In the Fourth Congress, where Republicans seemed to have a plurality of 10 at the outset, Federalists won a crucial vote on

91

Jay's Treaty, 51–48. In the Fifth Congress, where parties at the outset appeared to be evenly matched, party strength on fifteen party-determining roll calls (ranging from military preparations to the four bills that became the Alien and Sedition acts) was an average of 47.4 Federalists to 39.6 Republicans.

There are several possible explanations for Republican absenteeism. The most likely one is that Republicans had a long distance to travel to reach the seat of government. Reports of southern congressmen shipwrecked "off the capes" and making their way to Philadelphia by wagon were not uncommon. Another factor may have been low morale due to Federalist control of the committee machinery. Even in the Third Congress, where Federalists at the outset (December 1793) unsuccessfully tried to replace the nonpartisan Muhlenburg with the ferocious partisan Theodore Sedgwick (Fed.-Mass.), committee appointments went to Federalists. This was particularly important because crises at home and abroad (the Whisky Rebellion of 1794 and deteriorating relations with Great Britain) induced the House to create select committees to consider important and highly partisan issues of public policy. There were four of these committees, staffed by twenty-five Federalists, seventeen Republicans, and two waverers, whose party loyalty was indeterminate.

Republicans did achieve one victory in institutional development in this Congress, but artful management by the Federalists turned it to their own advantage. Ever since the First Congress, when all the initiatives on fiscal policy had emanated from Hamilton, Madison had been looking for some way to recover congressional control over public finance. The war scare caused by British seizures of American ships in the spring of 1794 presented a prime opportunity. The House approved a resolution (the *Journal of the House* does not reveal its origins) to create a committee of fifteen members (one from each state) to look into revenues, public credit, and report "the ways and means" of raising further revenues. Committees of Ways and Means were nothing new. State legislatures had used them during the Confederation period, and the House had created one in its first session, only to dissolve it upon the appointment of Hamilton as secretary of the Treasury. Speaker Muhlenburg proceeded to appoint a committee consisting of ten Federalists, four Republicans, and one independent. Chairing the Committee of Ways and Means was a staunch ally of Hamilton's, William Loughton Smith of South Carolina. Madison was named to the committee, but after a week of meetings he reported his disappointment to Jefferson: "The committee on ways and means was unfortunately composed of a majority infected by the fiscal errors which threaten so ignominious and vexatious a system to our country" (*Madison Papers*, XVI, 306–307). Mistrusting the mails, Madison rarely mentioned names in his letters, but Jefferson would understand that they had been thwarted by the appointive power of the Speaker.

Although viewed as an ad hoc select committee when it was established, the Committee on Ways and Means quickly became something different as it took on additional assignments through the session. In December 1795, Albert Gallatin, newly elected Republican from western Pennsylvania, successfully moved to give it formal status. It was treated as a standing committee thereafter, although it was not formally made a standing committee by House rules until 1802.

In the meantime, the hardening of party lines bent, and ultimately shattered, the self-imposed impartiality of the Speaker. In the Third Congress the response to the president's annual address became a subject of partisan confrontation. At the opening of its second session in November 1794, Muhlenburg alienated Federalists by voting against a Federalist amendment to the reply denouncing the Democratic Societies that had sprung up across the country in sympathy with the cause of France in the European war. When the Fourth Congress opened in December 1795, Federalists held the first party caucus on record to fix on an alternative candidate for Speaker. Although most of them favored Theodore Sedgwick, they decided that the more moderate Jonathan Dayton of New Jersey had a better chance of being elected in a closely divided House. The Republicans, equally cautious, backed Muhlenburg rather than one of their more ardent adherents. Because Republicans were late in arriving, Dayton won, 46 to 31. At this point in party development, each side was willing to accept a moderate rather than risk having an active enemy in the Speaker's chair.

The Ways and Means Committee achieved more formal standing in that session, and Dayton gave it a Federalist majority, 9 to 6, with arch-Federalist William Loughton Smith again in the chair. The House created a fifth standing committee—the Committee on Commerce and Manufactures—in that session. It was established in response to the numerous petitions from merchants and tradesmen seeking relief from some provision or other of the navigation or revenue laws. The Speaker staffed it with members who had mercantile experience, most of whom also happened to be Federalists.

Dayton aided the Federalists by helping them win an appropriation to carry out Jay's Treaty in 1796, and he worked for John Adams in New Jersey in the presidential election later that year. He was accordingly reelected Speaker at the opening of the Fifth Congress. The Republicans, even more hampered than usual by absenteeism at the opening of the session, did not even bother to contest Dayton. The political importance of the Speaker became even more evident in that Congress. The crisis with France in 1798–1799 necessitated the appointment of a number of politically sensitive select committees. Although most select-committee chairmen were routinely given power to report by bill, this was conspicuously withheld from a committee to consider the national emergency. When its chairman, Samuel Sewall (Fed.-Mass.), requested this authority two weeks later, his motion gave rise to an extraordinary debate on the purpose and power of select committees. A tie vote (45 to 45) was broken by Speaker Dayton in favor of the committee. Once empowered to draft bills, Sewall did exactly what the Jeffersonians had feared. His committee continued in existence for seven months, submitting a total of twenty bills, fifteen of which became law. Sewall's committee was the spearhead for the Federalist program: it drafted bills on military and naval appropriations, increased the size of the army and navy, suspended commerce with France, and drafted the Alien and Sedition acts. Never before had a committee made itself into such an independent source of power, nor had any earlier committee so blatantly used that power for partisan purposes.

The mask of neutrality was stripped altogether from the speakership in the Sixth Congress (1799–1801). The midterm election of 1798, held amid the uproar over the XYZ affair regarding France's attempt to gain concessions from the United States that some viewed as extortionary, was a major victory for Federalists in Congress. Modern roll-call analysis indicates that they controlled the House of Representatives in the Sixth Congress, 58 to 43, with four independents. At the opening of the first session in December 1799, Federalists put up Sedgwick for Speaker. Republicans, who, according to Federalist newspapers, had made a concerted effort to arrive in Philadelphia on time, countered with nominating Nathaniel Macon of North Carolina. The election took three ballots because some members were still not ready for so stark a choice, but in the end, Sedgwick won.

Sedgwick as Speaker represented a new order; he was the forerunner of the nineteenth-century czars of the House of Representatives. He not only loaded the important committees with Federalists but also chose men from his own party whom he knew to be of the same opinion on French policy as himself. He advised fellow Federalists on legislative tactics and noted smugly, "My wishes were submitted to." He even drafted a bill to accomplish one of his own pet projects, a national road system, and gave it to a crony to steer through the House (Sedgwick Papers, Massachusetts Historical Society). Although he yielded to presidential pressure in the first session and chose Robert Goodloe Harper (Fed.-S.C.) as chair of the Ways and Means Committee, he dropped Harper (whom he considered lazy) in the second session and chose his friend and ally, Roger Griswold of Connecticut. As a measure of the extent to which Sedgwick had polarized the House, Republicans decided at the end of that Congress in March 1801 to make an issue of the traditional vote of thanks to the Speaker, considered to have been previously a mere formality. The resolution passed the House by a vote along party lines, 40 to 35.

The election of 1800 gave Republicans control of the House as well as the Senate. The House in the Seventh Congress (1801–1803) numbered 68 Republicans and 37 Federalists; in the Eighth Congress the disparity climbed to 103 Republicans to 39 Federalists. (The House increased in size owing to the census of 1800.) Federalist ranks dwindled to about 25 in the following Congress and remained in that range (increasing slightly during the embargo of 1807–1809) until the War of 1812.

During Jefferson's presidency the House established four new standing committees (Accounts, Post Office and Post Roads, Public Lands, and the District of Columbia), bringing the total to nine. As with several of the earlier standing committees, these were primarily set up to handle the numerous memorials and petitions that annually flooded the House. Matters of public policy remained in the hands of select committees. Even so, the standing committee as an institution was winning new respect. Given this changing attitude, the establishment of standing committees to consider matters of public policy, such as foreign affairs and military preparedness, was only a matter of time. There was also a growing appreciation of the powers and responsibilities of committee chairmen. Senator William Plumer (Fed.-N.H.) noted in his diary in November 1804, "The business of a chairman of a standing committee is very arduous & attended with much labour. His duty is to call the Committee together, draw up the report in writing, which frequently is prolix & argumentative—And in the House he must support & defend the Report."

At the opening of the Seventh Congress in 1801, the House chose Nathaniel Macon as Speaker, by a vote of 53 to 26, over Federalist candidate James A. Bayard of Delaware. Macon followed the Federalist practice of giving Republicans control of both the standing committees and the politically significant select committees. However, he was more evenhanded than the Federalists had been. On the politically important select committees in the Seventh Congress (committees to investigate past Treasury practices, revise the naturalization law, reduce the military establishment, alter the judiciary, and reduce the number of government employees), Republicans outnumbered Federalists 25 to 16, a ratio that gave Federalists a bit more voice than their numbers warranted.

Macon also followed the Federalist practice of naming the party's most prominent spokesman as chair of the Ways and Means Committee. Macon's choice was John Randolph of Roanoke (R.-Va.), a surprise to some because Randolph was a relative newcomer to the House. However, he had been prominent in debate during the previous Congress, his first term, and was a close friend of

Macon's. They also lived in the same boardinghouse, as did two other members of the Ways and Means Committee, Joseph H. Nicholson (R.-Md.) and Joseph Clay (R.-Pa.). Macon favored his housemates in making committee appointments. In the Eighth Congress, Randolph, Nicholson, or Clay—and sometimes two of the three—served on almost half of the 107 select committees set up by the House. Three other friends of Randolph's were not far behind in committee assignments. These six members (in the following Congress, Randolph's following would be dubbed the "Tertium Quids") held 111 seats (14 percent) of the 772 committee assignments in that Congress. Years after the Macon-Randolph-Nicholson-Clay quartet was broken up by Randolph's eccentricity and Nicholson's appointment to the federal bench, correspondence among the four revealed a nostalgia for the early years of Jefferson's presidency, when they had spent long evenings in the boardinghouse talking politics and plotting strategy (Nicholson Papers, Library of Congress). This is not to say that the living arrangement itself governed their politics; rather, they chose to live together because they were politically and personally congenial. Significantly, when Randolph broke with the Jefferson administration over policy toward Britain and the Embargo Act of 1807, he moved into a boardinghouse dominated by Federalists.

This apparent southern control of the House did not go unnoticed by northern Republicans, especially after Randolph accused several of them in the spring of 1805 of having been involved in the Yazoo land-speculation scandal of 1795–1796, in which Georgia sold lands in present-day Mississippi to speculators before ceding its claim over the territory to the federal government. At the opening of the Ninth Congress in December 1805, discontented northerners pushed the candidacy of Joseph B. Varnum of Massachusetts for the speakership. On the first ballot, Macon received fifty-seven votes; Varnum, twenty-seven; Federalist John Cotton Smith (Conn.), sixteen; and John Dawson (Va.), a brother-in-law of James Madison, ten. This ratio held firm through a second ballot, but on the third, Dawson's supporters shifted to Macon, who was reelected. The *Richmond Enquirer* expressed the opinion in its 29 November 1805 issue that Varnum's support came from congressmen "professedly jealous of the southern influence."

Randolph broke openly with the administration during that Congress, using his power as chair of the Ways and Means Committee to delay an appropriation of money for the acquisition of West Florida and criticizing the president's policy toward Great Britain. By the end of that Congress in April 1807, Macon realized that his support for the eccentric Randolph would cost him the speakership in the next Congress.

When the Tenth Congress opened the following October, Macon tactfully arrived late, pleading illness as an excuse, and the House chose Varnum as Speaker. The new Speaker replaced Randolph as chair of Ways and Means with George Washington Campbell of Tennessee. Otherwise, he continued Macon's policies. Indeed, he favored the South and West in committee appointments even more than Macon had (whether consciously or not cannot be determined). Of the fourteen men who received the most committee assignments, only five came from New England or the Middle Atlantic states. Varnum's nominations to the standing committees in the Tenth Congress revealed the new perception that experience and expertise on those committees were important. Except for the newly created District of Columbia and Post Office committees, thirty-five out of forty-one standing-committee members served in both sessions.

The speakership "revolution" of 1807 may well be viewed as the end of the first phase of institutional development in the House of Representatives. A political party had ousted a Speaker and replaced him with another from within its own ranks, and it did so primarily to secure a change in membership of House committees. And the purpose of the change was to secure committee leadership that was willing to coordinate party policy with members of the executive branch. A second phase in House development would begin with the election of Henry Clay as Speaker on his first day in the House in November 1811.

CONGRESS AND ITS CONSTITUENTS

The constitutional provision that the House of Representatives be based on population was a landmark in political development. The state legislatures and their colonial assemblies antecedent had followed the British example, representing places (counties or towns) rather than people. Even so, American legislators, beginning in colonial times, were acutely aware that they drew their strength from the fact that they voiced the concerns of their constituents. The Constitution transferred this relationship to the federal arena and institutionalized it.

From the outset, House members were determined to maintain close contacts with their constituents. At the beginning of the First Congress, the House adopted a rule that its doors would be open to anyone wishing to attend debates. Newsmen, already familiar with the openness of state legislatures, began recording and publishing the proceedings. In the first session of the First Congress, South Carolina anti-Federalist Aedanus Burke offered a resolution for the appointment of an official stenographer to record House debates. His reasoning was that newspaper reports of state proceedings in the past had been inaccurate. Opponents pointed out that newsmen could not be barred from the House and they would record debates, whether or not there was an official version. Burke withdrew his resolution.

Congressmen nevertheless complained constantly of newspaper summaries of their speeches. During the debates on Jay's Treaty, New England Federalist Roger Griswold complained to his wife that a "blundering short hand writer" had condensed an hour-long speech into a single newspaper column, and his constituents would be able to make little sense of what he said. He noted, however, that most members had begun the practice of writing their own speeches for the press, "by which means a very indifferent speech when delivered has appeared correct and respectable on paper" (Roger Griswold Papers, Manuscripts and Archives, Yale University Library). At some point in the 1790s, the House authorized the clerk of the House to designate an official recorder with a printing contract for House debates. In 1801, Republican John Beckley, who had replaced a Federalist as clerk, took advantage of this authority to give the printing contract to Samuel Harrison Smith, publisher of the newly founded *Washington National Intelligencer*. This made that paper the official record of House proceedings as well as the semiofficial organ of the Republican party.

The Senate represented states rather than people, and those who gathered in New York for the first session of Congress in 1789 seemed to take it for granted that that body would function behind closed doors, as had the Continental Congress. The Senate also perceived itself as a council to the president, and that executive function also seemed to demand privacy. The practice quickly ran into criticism, however, for the vision of legislators meeting in secret conclave was reminiscent of the practices of European monarchies. The Senate yielded and opened its doors in 1794, and the result was almost one of comical anticlimax. No more than a handful of spectators appeared in the newly built gallery, and they soon disappeared. Viewed as theater, a handful of urbane and courteous senators, discussing public policy in conversational tones, could not compete with the boisterous and highly partisan House. Journalists did not record the debates, in part because of a lack of public interest but also because the acoustics were so poor in the gallery that they could not hear the debates. In 1802, Samuel Harrison Smith, armed with his contract for the printing of congressional debates, asked for authority to post a reporter on the Senate floor. He got it by a vote along party lines, and a new era in public relations opened for the Senate. By 1805, the gallery had become so crowded that listeners overflowed onto the Senate floor. Because the audience often included women, the Senate engaged in factional, though not bellicose, discussion that year as to whether women ought to be allowed on the floor. Exclusionists argued that women ought to be confined to the galleries because they were a distraction on the floor, that some senators directed their remarks at the women rather than at fellow senators. It was not recorded who won, the exclusionists or the egotists.

The publication of debates was only one of the ways in which members of Congress interacted with their constituents. From the outset, they commonly solicited the opinions of friends and acquaintances about specific measures before them. In 1789, Senator Richard Henry Lee of Virginia sent copies of the judiciary bill to several prominent Virginians to solicit their opinions. Although Lee himself had been an opponent of the Constitution, the people he consulted were Federalists who favored the law. To cite just one other example, William Loughton Smith in 1790 was contemplating drafting a federal bankruptcy act, and he wrote to his friend Edward Rutledge, asking him to sound out the merchants of Charleston on the subject. Rutledge consulted some of the large international traders who were creditors of small retailers and hence were opposed to such a law. Smith confessed that Rutledge's reply "came upon me like a Clap of thunder & overturned in an instant all my projects" (quoted in Rogers, ed., p. 101).

The Republican victory in the election of 1800 (a landslide in the congressional races) induced Federalists to take a new look at their relations with their constituents. "We shall probably pay more attention to public opinion than we have heretofore done," James A. Bayard of Delaware, wrote to Hamilton, "and take more pains not merely to do right things, but to do them in an acceptable manner." Even so, Republican congressmen remained a step ahead of them in devising ways of interacting with their constituents. A device commonly used after 1800 was the circular letter. Posted under congressional franks, they were two to four pages long and contained news of national politics, particularly congressional affairs. Noble E. Cunningham, Jr., has discovered and published 250 of these documents written by 112 different congressmen between 1800 and 1829. A few were from Federalists, but the great majority were drafted by Republicans, particularly men from distant districts in the South and West. They were often timed to arrive near election day, and many included a reminder that the member was seeking reelection. Most circulars centered on claiming credit, through members' votes and committee work, for benefits to constituents. The credits most frequently claimed were influences on policy regarding land, internal improvements, the economy, the military, Native Americans, post roads and offices, and the judiciary. This sort of advertising—much of which is still employed by members of Congress—goes a long way toward explaining the political success and long-range influence of the Jeffersonian Republican party.

CONGRESS IN THE FEDERALIST-REPUBLICAN ERA

CONGRESS AND THE EXECUTIVE

In most of the American colonies, the upper house of the assembly also served as a council of advisers to the governor. The drafters of the Constitution envisioned a similar role for the Senate, and many senators took this function seriously. When George Washington, in the summer of 1789, submitted the names of 102 appointees to various Treasury and naval posts, the Senate quickly confirmed all but one of them. (Washington chided them for rejecting even one!) However, some senators were unhappy with this arm's-length method of submitting nominations and wanted the president to appear before the Senate in person with his list. A delegation waited upon the president with this suggestion. Washington agreed that a personal appearance would be useful when he submitted a treaty for Senate approval, but he thought his presence while the Senate discussed his nominees might hamper debate or even force him to defend his selections. The practice of written nominations continued; however, Washington did try to consult the Senate in person on a question of foreign relations. The occasion was a proposed treaty with the Creek Indians. On 22 August 1789, Washington appeared in the Senate with Secretary of War Henry Knox with a set list of questions. Not having thought about the matter, the senators sat in embarrassed silence and finally referred the questions to a committee, which defeated the very purpose of the president's coming. The president departed and never returned. The incident ended any further thought that the Senate might function as an executive council.

The creation of a new government naturally meant that there were many offices to fill. The Treasury Department, largest employer of civilians, had more than one thousand openings for collectors and surveyors. President Washington was swamped with applicants, many of whom used members of Congress as references. Washington accepted congressional recommendations but regarded them as merely that. He had no concept of "senatorial courtesy" (a later rule that nominees from a given state would not be confirmed unless approved by the senators of the president's party from that state); recommendations from members of

the House of Representatives carried as much weight with him as those from the Senate. In confirming the president's nominations, the Senate followed an unwritten rule that they would be accepted unless found actually unfit for office. Of the hundreds of nominations submitted to the Senate by Washington in eight years, it rejected only five. The most famous instance was its rejection of John Rutledge of South Carolina as chief justice of the Supreme Court in 1795. Jefferson thought the rejection by the Federalist majority in the Senate was due to Rutledge's criticism of Jay's Treaty. His "sottish" drinking habits and shady finances may also have been factors.

Washington's social relations with Congress took two forms: a weekly levee and a weekly dinner party. The former was a formal occasion that did little for executive-legislative relations. Republicans were suspicious of these meetings because they were reminiscent of the practices of European monarchs. Congressmen of both parties found them dull. It was a matter, explained one Federalist, "of being introduced into an elegant apartment, making a bow and talking nonsense with a large collection of well dressed People" (Roger Griswold Papers). The dinner parties, held every Thursday, were more successful. A congressman described one occasion as including a company of twenty-eight, "his usual number," among them three Republicans. Other guests included a relative of Martha Washington and the president's private secretary, Tobias Lear, together with Lear's "beautiful and amiable" wife (Dwight Foster Papers, Massachusetts Historical Society). In such mixed company, political subjects were probably avoided, but Washington was certainly capable at such occasions of letting his feelings be known. After a forensic duel with Madison on the House floor in 1792, Theodore Sedgwick reported to a friend that Washington had paid him "particular attention" when Sedgwick came to dinner.

John Adams began his presidency on good terms with Congress. Federalists were particularly pleased with his firm stand on France, and both chambers moved with alacrity in naming committees to consider his recommendations. A few weeks after the opening of the Seventh Congress in December 1797, Sedgwick wrote home: "The President since I have been here I have seen more than any other man—have dined with him twice & shall again today." Adams also followed Washington's practice of inviting Republicans to dinner; Albert Gallatin of Pennsylvania reported an invitation only a few weeks after Adams was inaugurated. In the spring of 1798, while Republicans in Congress were calling for publication of the XYZ dispatches, Adams let Sedgwick have a look at the dispatches, seeking advice from him on the subject.

In 1799, relations between Adams and the Federalists in Congress cooled markedly. After preparing for war by authorizing huge increases in the army and navy in 1798, some congressional Federalists, with verbal encouragement from Hamilton, wanted to take the final step and declare war. Adams, however, wanted to make a final effort at peace, and without consulting anyone, he nominated William Vans Murray (Fed.-Md.) as envoy to France in February 1799. He later explained that he consulted no one because the cabinet would have opposed it and that Hamilton would have learned at once of his plans. The Senate could not bring itself to reject the nomination, but to Adams's chagrin, it added two other envoys to the delegation. As relations between the president and Congress deteriorated, Adams began complaining publicly of the "combinations of senators, generals, and heads of department" arrayed against him. In conversation with one Federalist senator, he accused the Senate of having "crammed Hamilton down his throat" as second in command of the army. When the Senate rejected the nomination of Adams's son-in-law as adjutant general, Adams accused it of having figuratively "killed his daughter" and brought ruin to his family. In early 1800, Sedgwick reported that he rarely saw the president, and when he did visit, Adams's "conduct was as cold as his heart."

Jefferson believed that the executive branch under President Adams had drifted, with each department head running his "fief" without regard to the others. After taking office in 1801, Jefferson sent a memorandum to all department heads, informing them that he intended to be "a central point for the different branches." He expected to be kept informed of all correspondence and to participate in all important decisions. A similar attitude governed his relations with Congress. Jefferson worked closely with congressional leaders, informally communicating information and detailed proposals for legislation. However, he was always careful to warn those in whom he confided to keep his role hidden, fearing he would be accused of meddling in legislative business. Jefferson's influence in Congress was nonetheless an open secret, and it was one reason behind John Randolph's defection in 1806.

The president's cabinet had worked closely with Congress during the Washington and Adams administrations and continued to do so under Jefferson. By 1800 it had become almost standard procedure for a committee chairman to whom a measure had been referred to seek information and recommendations from the head of the relevant executive department. Cabinet officials never appeared on the floor of Congress, and most of their communications were in writing. However, they occasionally testified before committees of both the House and the Senate.

Jefferson's best-known contacts with Congress were the small dinner parties that he gave on a regular basis when Congress was in session. The dinner parties were an important part of the process of government because Jefferson used them to get personally acquainted with members of Congress and to clear up bits of misinformation or minor misunderstandings. Dinner-table conversation commonly ranged from science to music and literature, but politics must have intruded. Early in his presidency Jefferson mixed Federalists and Republicans, as his predecessors had, but by the end of his first term he had adopted the practice of inviting only Federalists or only Republicans.

Jefferson's cabinet also invited congressmen to dinner, a practice that, if it had occurred at all during the Federalist years, had not occasioned much comment. Senator Samuel Latham Mitchill (R.-N.Y.), a favorite invitee of both Jefferson and Madison because of his wide-ranging scientific interests, thought Madison's dinner parties furthered his presidential aspirations because they extended his contacts in Congress. Treasury secretary Gallatin had fewer dinner parties (an average of only one per week), but he had a circle of congressmen who regularly visited his house after dinner, spending the evening discussing the doings of Congress. Since most congressmen lived in boardinghouses where their own opportunities for entertaining were limited, the role of the executive officers in the social life of Washington, D.C., was an important part of the governing process under Jefferson.

RECONSTITUTION OF THE SENATE AFTER 1809

In its first twenty years the Senate was de facto the lesser of the two houses of Congress in that it was utterly subservient to the executive. It confirmed almost all of the president's appointments, including those to the cabinet, Supreme Court, and high-level military and diplomatic posts. It rejected only one of Washington's high-level appointments, none of Adams's, and only one of Jefferson's. The Senate also yielded to the House in work load. In the second session of the Second Congress (1793), for instance, the House originated thirty-three public bills, to the Senate's seven; and in the second session of the Eighth Congress (1805), the House originated fifty-seven, to the Senate's seventeen. Contemporaries also felt the House was the more visible chamber. Congressman Samuel L. Mitchill (R.-N.Y.) wrote to his wife upon his election to the Senate, "Henceforward you will read little of me in the Gazettes. Senators are less exposed to public view than Representatives" (Mitchill Papers, City Museum of New York). Mitchill was correct. Even after the Senate removed all restrictions on newspaper coverage of its debates, reporters paid less attention to it than to the House. In the second session of the Eighth Congress, the country's leading newspapers devoted only about fourteen out of eleven hundred inches of their coverage to the Senate (about 1 percent), compared to approximately three hundred inches (27 percent) devoted to the House of Representatives.

Political scientists have defined "reconstitutive change" as "a marked and enduring shift in the fundamental dimensions of the institution." In the Senate this change began with the presidency of James Madison. A senatorial faction led by William Branch Giles of Virginia and Samuel Smith of Maryland (dubbed "the Invisibles") began carping at Treasury secretary Albert Gallatin in the last years of Jefferson's term. When Madison took office, he found that in order to retain Gallatin at the Treasury, he had to appease the Invisibles by naming Senator Smith's brother Robert secretary of state. Robert Smith proved utterly incompetent, and Madison eventually replaced him with James Monroe. The Invisibles resumed their attacks on Gallatin and eventually drove him from office.

The Senate gave President James Monroe less trouble, but it came into its own during the four-year presidency of his successor, John Quincy Adams. Under the guidance of Martin Van Buren (D.-N.Y.), the Senate wrecked the Adams presidency by pouring ridicule on his proposals for federally sponsored scientific expeditions and national astronomical observatories ("lighthouses in the sky"), and it rejected administration-sponsored bills for a national university and establishment of a department of the interior.

The Senate shouldered more of the congressional work load after 1809. By the 1820s, the number of bills introduced in the Senate averaged one per senator in a session, whereas the average in the House was about half that per congressman. Of equal importance is that, in contrast to its first twenty years, the Senate initiated a greater share of important legislation. For instance, the Missouri Compromise of 1820 (permitting Missouri to enter the Union as a slave state, admitting Maine as a free state, and forbidding slavery in the Louisiana Purchase), was essentially fashioned in the upper chamber. The evolution of a system of standing committees was further evidence of the Senate's emergence between 1809 and 1829.

SENATE COMMITTEES AFTER 1809

The Senate had no standing committees until the second session of the Fourteenth Congress (December 1816). However, it is possible to discern the forerunners of such important standing committees as Foreign Affairs, Military Affairs, and Naval Affairs in the preceding congresses. In his first annual message in December 1809, President Madison outlined the critical condition of Anglo-American relations. The following day, William Branch Giles, a Republican veteran of fifteen years of service in the House and Senate, introduced a resolution that portions of the president's message involving foreign relations be submitted to a select committee. The Senate agreed and named a committee of six Republicans and one Federalist, chaired by Giles. All were prominent members with many years of service in the Senate and House. The committee sat throughout the session and drafted numerous bills and resolutions. It was reestablished in each succeeding session, with Giles retained as chairman each time. By 1812, senators were commonly referring to it as the "Committee on Foreign Relations." In the final session of the Thirteenth Congress (December 1814) the Senate reduced the size of the committee to five (a number that would become standard for Senate standing committees), and four of the five had previous experience on the committee. George W. Campbell (R.-Tenn.) served as chair in the second session of the Twelfth Congress and first session of the Thirteenth. William W. Bibb (R.-Ga.) replaced him and served through the first session of the Fourteenth Congress.

Select committees on military and naval affairs also assumed semipermanent status during the War of 1812. Both met throughout each session and handled numerous bills and reports. Military Affairs had virtually no continuity of membership, and when it became a standing committee in 1816, only two members had prior experience on the committee. Naval Affairs, on the other hand, had more continuity than even the Foreign Relations Committee. By the end of the Thirteenth Congress, four out of five members had prior experience on the committee, and all five were placed on the standing committee when it was created in the following Congress.

Shortly after the opening of the second session of the Fourteenth Congress on 5 December 1816, Senator James Barbour (R.-Va.) offered a resolution to erect eleven standing committees, and the Senate approved the idea five days later. Several of the new committees—Claims, Public Lands, and Judiciary—paralleled standing committees previously established by the House. Others—indeed, the most important ones—covered areas, such as foreign relations and military and naval affairs, for which the House had as yet no standing committee. The Senate added new standing committees in nearly every Congress thereafter until by the end of the Twentieth Congress in 1829 it had a total of eighteen with eighty-six seats. Since there were only forty-eight senators

in that year, the committee work load must have been quite onerous. However, it was evenly distributed. Every senator had at least one committee assignment, and only three sat on as many as three committees.

Table 1 traces the growth of continuity in committee service in the Senate. It reveals a growing perception that experience and tenure were important criteria in committee assignments. This was particularly true of committee chairmen. By the Twentieth Congress every one of the eighteen committee chairs had prior experience on his committee, and five-sixths of them had served as chair in the previous Congress. The Senate rewarded talent as well as experience. The most prominent members of the Senate were assigned to the most important, policy-making committees, and after the Federalist party collapsed, politics did not play a role in committee assignments. James Barbour served on the Foreign Relations Committee from 1816 to 1824 and was chairman for six of those years. Nathaniel Macon (R.-N.C.) was a member for twelve years and three times was its chairman. Rufus King (Fed.-N.Y.) served on the committee from 1815 to 1823. Samuel Smith (R.-Md.), a fixture in Congress since the 1790s, chaired the Committee on Finance from 1823 to 1829, and the workhorse Nathaniel Macon also worked for eight years on that committee.

HOUSE COMMITTEES AFTER 1811

Henry Clay's election to the office of Speaker on his first day in the House of Representatives in November 1811 is a familiar story. Equally well known is his placement of prominent war hawks on the policy-making committees for foreign affairs and military affairs. As this narrative has sought to make clear, Clay's use of his appointive powers to further a policy goal was nothing new; the practice dated back to the Federalist Speakers of the late 1790s. Clay nevertheless brought a level of charisma to the office that it had previously lacked, and he used his authority to influence executive decisions in ways no previous Speaker had done. In March 1812 he wrote to Secretary of State James Monroe to recommend that the president consider a thirty-day embargo to be "followed by war." He thought this would "give

Table 1
GROWTH OF CONTINUITY IN COMMITTEE SERVICE IN THE SENATE: FIFTEENTH TO TWENTIETH CONGRESSES

Congress	Standing Committees		Experience on Same Committee		Chair with Experience		Holdovers from 1st to 2d Session	
	No.	Seats	In Previous Congress	Previous Two or More	As Past Chair	As Committee Member	Chair	All Members
Fifteenth (1817–1819)	11	55	20 (36%)	2 (4%)*	6 (55%)	8 (73%)	9 (82%)	49 (89%)
Sixteenth (1819–1821)	12	60	27 (45%)	7 (12%)	2 (17%)	8 (67%)	9 (75%)	46 (77%)
Seventeenth (1821–1823)	13	65	36 (55%)	14 (22%)	6 (46%)	11 (85%)	13 (100%)	63 (97%)
Eighteenth (1823–1825)	15	71**	29 (41%)	14 (20%)	5 (33%)	9 (60%)	15 (100%)	62 (87%)
Nineteenth (1825–1827)	17	81	35 (43%)	17 (21%)	8 (47%)	14 (82%)	12 (71%)	50 (62%)
Twentieth (1827–1829)	18	86	54 (63%)	17 (20%)	15 (83%)	18 (100%)	Not available	

*Includes service on a select committee in the Twelfth or Thirteenth Congress
**Two new committees established in the Seventeenth Congress had only three members.

tone to public sentiment" and "powerfully accelerate preparations for war" (Hopkins, ed., p. 637). President Madison agreed, recommending an embargo in April and sending his war message to Congress on 1 June. During the War of 1812, Clay did not hesitate to make recommendations for field commanders to the president and the secretary of war. William Henry Harrison acknowledged Clay's role in winning for him the command of the western armies in August 1812. John Randolph, a perceptive though bitter foe of Clay, referred to the Speaker as "the second man in the nation," and other congressmen agreed that Clay's authority was second only to that of the president (Langdon Cheves to Clay, 30 July 1812, quoted in Hopkins, ed., p. 700).

During the War of 1812, the select committees on Foreign Affairs, Military Affairs, and Naval Affairs became standing committees in all but name. Appointments to them were regularly made at the beginning of each session in response to the president's message, and they had some continuity of membership as Clay came to realize the importance of experience. John C. Calhoun (R.-S.C.), though only in his first term, was a prominent member of the Foreign Affairs Committee in the Twelfth Congress and chaired it in the Thirteenth. John Forsyth (R.-Ga.) chaired the committee in the Fourteenth and Fifteenth congresses. There was little continuity in the membership of the Military Affairs Committee, but the chair was invariably handed to a man with military experience. Richard M. Johnson (R.-Ky.), who led the cavalry charge against the British and Indian army at the battle of the Thames and took credit for killing Tecumseh, the Shawnee chief, chaired the committee from 1815 to 1819. William Eustis, Madison's onetime secretary of war, was made chair of the Military Affairs Committee when he entered Congress in 1821 and retained the post when the committee at last became a standing committee (along with Foreign Affairs and Naval Affairs) in 1822.

Except for Ways and Means, the standing committees of the House dealt mostly with routine matters, such as petitions from constituents and claims against the government. To the nine standing committees in place by the end of Jefferson's presidency, the Thirteenth Congress (1813–1815) added three new ones: Judiciary, Pensions and Revolutionary Claims, and Public Expenditures. On 30 March 1816, the Fourteenth Congress created six new standing committees that were all three-man administrative committees that oversaw the accounts of the executive departments. The membership of these committees changed with every session for the first few years; evidently, their duties were so routine that it was thought best to rotate the burden. By the mid-1820s these accounts-oversight committees were serving Congress by Congress, with a complete membership turnover every two years, rather than annually, as in session-by-session appointments.

The growth in importance of standing committees shifted the work load within the House. During the 1790s, select committees had handled the most important business and drafted most of the legislation. By the 1820s these functions had shifted to the standing committees. A few statistics show the trend. In the first session of the First Congress the single standing committee reported no bills, while select committees fashioned 32; in the second session of the Fifth Congress (1797–1798) standing committees reported 61 bills, and select committees reported 65; in the first session of the Fifteenth Congress (1817–1818) standing committees reported 127 bills and select committees were responsible for 70; and in the first session of the Twentieth Congress (1827–1828) standing committees reported 264, while the number emerging from select committees dropped to 37.

The evolution of the committee system, together with the rapid growth of the country, led to an explosion in congressional business. But the busy nature of the House also meant that a lower percentage of measures actually won approval. In the earliest congresses the House normally agreed to the general principles of a bill before it was drafted. As a result, a full 75 percent of the bills introduced in the first session of the First Congress were signed into law. This figure dropped steadily with each succeeding Congress until by the Twentieth Congress only 32 percent of bills that were reported to the House floor were enacted. Few of these were actually defeated; the most common action was to leave a bill pending in the Committee of the Whole. Nevertheless, the approval rate of bills drafted by standing committees was consistently greater than that of select committees.

Table 2 charts the growth of continuity of membership in the House standing committees from 1809 to 1829. Because membership on the three-man administrative committees appears to have been deliberately rotated, the table charts only the seven-man policy-making committees. As in the Senate, the most dramatic increase was among committee chairmen, although the degree of continuity and level of experience did not at any time equal that of the Senate.

After returning from Ghent, Belgium, where he had taken part in the negotiations to end the War of 1812, in 1815, Clay resumed the post of Speaker and held it until he resigned in December 1820, midway through the Sixteenth Congress. Clay seems to have had little perception of the value of continuity, though he did retain some committee chairmen from one Congress to the next. John W. Taylor (R.-N.Y.) succeeded Clay, but he yielded to Phillip Pendleton Barbour (R.-Va.) at the opening of the Seventeenth Congress. Taylor was a northern nationalist, and Barbour, an Old Republican who venerated states' rights (and ultimately became a Jacksonian). Clay returned to the Speaker's chair in the Eighteenth Congress (1823–1825). When Clay left Congress in 1825 to become John Quincy Adams's secretary of state, the National Republican majority in the House returned Taylor to the Speaker's chair. In 1827, at the opening of the Twentieth Congress, the emerging Jacksonian wing of the Republican party placed Andrew Stevenson (R.-Va.) in the Speaker's chair. Stevenson, like Barbour before him, was an Old Republican and a foe of the Adams-Clay brand of nationalism. He remained Speaker through the early years of Andrew Jackson's presidency, and in 1834, Jackson appointed him minister to Great Britain.

Given the dramatic shifts in politics and personality among Speakers during the 1820s, it might seem surprising that there was any continuity at all in committee membership. Perhaps the continuity that did exist, imperfect though it was, is testimony to the rising perception that experience, particularly among committee chairmen, is an important asset. It also is true that the disintegration of the first party system removed any pressure on the Speaker to reward party loyalty with political preferment. Although a few congressmen continued to regard themselves as Federalists, the great majority of them were Republicans after 1815, even though they might differ ideologically among themselves.

Table 2

GROWTH OF CONTINUITY IN COMMITTEE SERVICE IN THE HOUSE OF REPRESENTATIVES:
ELEVENTH TO TWENTIETH CONGRESSES

Congress	Number of Standing Committees*	Policy-making**		Experience on Same Committee		Chair with Experience		Holdovers from 1st to 2d Session	
		No.	Seats	In Previous Congress	Previous Two or More	As Past Chair	As Committee Member	Chair	All Members
Eleventh (1809–1811)	9	7	59***	24 (41%)	5 (8%)	3 (43%)	7 (100%)	7 (100%)	45 (76%)
Twelfth (1811–1813)	9	7	59	10 (17%)	0	4 (57%)	5 (71%)	7 (100%)	34 (58%)
Thirteenth (1813–1815)	12	7	49	20 (41%)	4 (8%)	2 (29%)	6 (86%)	6 (86%)	16 (33%)
Fourteenth (1815–1817)	19	10	70	20 (29%)	2 (3%)	2 (20%)	4 (40%)	9 (90%)	38 (54%)
Fifteenth (1817–1819)	19	11	77	10 (13%)	2 (3%)	6 (55%)	7 (64%)	7 (64%)	49 (64%)
Sixteenth (1819–1821)	21	11	77	25 (32%)	5 (6%)	4 (36%)	7 (64%)	10 (91%)	47 (61%)
Seventeenth (1821–1823)	25	17	119	33 (28%)	8 (7%)	9 (53%)	10 (59%)	13 (76%)	88 (74%)
Eighteenth (1823–1825)	25	17	119	41 (34%)	19 (16%)	7 (41%)	8 (49%)	14 (82%)	102 (86%)
Nineteenth (1825–1827)	27	17	119	53 (45%)	20 (17%)	13 (76%)	14 (82%)	12 (71%)	85 (71%)
Twentieth (1827–1829)	27	19	133	43 (32%)	18 (13%)	10 (53%)	15 (79%)	13 (68%)	104 (78%)

*Includes standing committees established during that Congress

**Seven-man committees as distinguished from the three-man committees that handled accounts and House routine

***Until the Thirteenth Congress the newly established Post Office and Roads Committee had seventeen members (one from each state).

THE COMPENSATION CONTROVERSY OF 1816–1817

The Constitution was formed, and Congress was born, in the eighteenth-century atmosphere of deferential politics. Congressmen in the 1790s consulted their constituents, but they did not hesitate to vote their consciences when the occasion demanded. Even senators, who were subject to instruction by state legislatures, occasionally went their own way. The Virginia assembly was perhaps the most adamant of all in keeping a leash on its U.S. senators, but when Senator Richard Brent violated his instructions and voted in favor of rechartering the Bank of the United States in 1811, he received only a mild rebuke from his legislative constituency. With the advent of the second party system in the late 1820s, however, popular politics was the order of the day, and most politicians subscribed to the slogan *vox populi, vox Dei*—the voice of the people is the voice of God. A milestone in this transition was the controversy over the Compensation Act of 1816.

The Compensation Act arose out of a perceived need to raise the pay of congressmen and to regularize it. Since 1789, congressmen had been paid on a per diem basis at the rate of $6 per day. By 1816 the cost of living had doubled, and virtually every member of Congress regarded the pay as inadequate. In March of that year, Richard M. Johnson (R.-Ky.) proposed an annual salary instead of the per diem rate, "nothing extravagant, nothing prodigal," perhaps comparable to the pay of a government clerk. The debate over Johnson's measure in the House involved only the amount of pay; virtually everyone agreed that the change to an annual salary was necessary. Robert Wright (R.-Md.) reflected the prevailing philosophy when he recalled that in the old days Maryland delegates "lived like gentlemen and enjoyed a glass of generous wine, which cannot be afforded at this time for the present compensation" (*Annals of Congress*, 14th Cong., 1st sess., p. 1182). A figure of $1,500 was agreed upon, President Madison signed the measure into law, and congressmen began to draw salary that very session.

Someone had suggested in the course of debate that Congress approve the principle but delay the actual pay raise until after the approaching election of 1816. The idea was rejected, and that was the biggest mistake of all. Letting the voters consider the merits of a legislative pay raise was not a new idea. It was among the many amendments to the Constitution suggested by the states during the ratification debate, and it was one of the twelve approved by Congress and submitted to the states in 1789. (In that age of deferential politics the states had failed to approve it, and thus it did not become part of the Bill of Rights.)

The public uproar was immediate, spontaneous, and deafening. Federalist and Republican newspapers blamed each other for inciting the public wrath, but, in truth, the pay increase had had bipartisan support in Congress. Arch-Federalist Timothy Pickering was one of many congressmen who declined to run for reelection for fear of being defeated. Resolutions adopted by public meetings all over the country had a common theme: the act was "high-handed and arbitrary" and was a "profligate trespass against . . . the *morals* of the *Republic*." Voters saw it as antithetical to republican virtue and an open door to creeping corruption in the national legislature. Richard M. Johnson complained that "the poor compensation bill excited more discontent than the alien or sedition laws, the *quasi* war with France, the internal taxes of 1798, the embargo, the late war with Great Britain, the Treaty of Ghent, or any one measure of the government, from its existence" (*Annals of Congress*, 14th Cong., 2d sess., p. 237). In the election that year, while James Monroe was winning handily over the Federalist Rufus King, only 30 percent of members in the House of Representatives retained their seats, the highest turnover of any election in American history.

When the chastened Congress assembled for its lame-duck session in December 1816, an extraordinary debate occurred. Congress knew it was forced to act, but a majority still believed that the people were wrong. The issue was whether the people and their legislatures could instruct their representatives and senators to vote against their consciences. Unable to agree, even on raising the per diem, Congress simply repealed the Compensation Act and left the question of setting compensation to a future Congress. (The next Congress set it at $8 per day.) The concept that a representative was fundamentally a servant of the people, not some imperial official whose work was impeded by popular will, was at the root of the popular politics of the second party system (dominated by the Whig and Democratic parties). The remaining question is, What impact did the reemergence of political parties have on the institutional development of Congress?

EMERGENCE OF THE SECOND PARTY SYSTEM

George Nielsen, the leading authority on congressional voting behavior during the Era of Good Feeling, stated that party-line voting declined after the War of 1812 and was nonexistent from 1817 to 1824. During that time, the Federalists virtually disappeared and Republicans split into several voting blocs. Congressional waters were far from calm, as issues such as the tariff and internal improvements, as well as the controversy over slavery in Missouri, kept things in turmoil, but roll-call voting did not follow party lines. The election of John Quincy Adams, Nielsen argued, changed all this and triggered the birth of the second party system. Nielsen discerned that two partisan blocs had formed in the House of Representatives by January 1825, specifically, an Adams-Clay bloc and a Jacksonian bloc. The election of John W. Taylor as Speaker in the Nineteenth Congress suggests that the Adams-Clay faction had the upper hand, but there was no party discipline and the roll calls were too disparate to permit modern quantitative analysis.

Instead, it was the Senate that became the focal point of partisan opposition to the Adams administration. There, Martin Van Buren, making political capital out of such seemingly routine matters as the nomination of delegates to a Pan-American conference in Panama, single-handedly created the nucleus of what would become the Jacksonian Democrats. According to Nielsen, a solid bloc of antiadministration "Democratic Republicans" had formed by 1826.

By December 1827, when the Twentieth Congress opened, Vice President Calhoun was in the Jacksonian camp. As presiding officer, he controlled committee appointments, and his nominations reflected the restoration of partisanship in the committee structure. Without violating the rule (unspoken, but by then, well established) that chairmen have experience on the committees that they head, Calhoun put Jacksonians in control of all the key policy-making committees. To head the Foreign Relations Committee, he chose the venerable Nathaniel Macon. Macon had served on the committee for twelve years (though only once before as chair); he was also an Old Republican staunchly opposed to the administration. Jacksonians outnumbered Adams supporters on the committee by three to two. Acknowledging the value of experience, Calhoun reappointed William Henry Harrison to be the chair of the Military Affairs Committee, but he loaded it with powerful Jacksonians, such as Richard M. Johnson and Thomas Hart Benton (D.-Mo.). To chair the Naval Affairs Committee, he named a sectionalist cohort from South Carolina, Robert Y. Hayne, who, incidentally, had chaired the committee in the previous Congress. To chair the less-sensitive, but nonetheless important, committees on Commerce, Manufactures, and Agriculture, Hayne named Levi Woodbury (D.-N.H.), Mahlon Dickerson (D.-N.J.), and John P. Branch (D.-N.C.), all of whom would later serve in President Jackson's cabinet.

Andrew Stevenson, Speaker in the Twentieth Congress, was much less inclined to use his office for party advantage, although at least one of his appointments revealed a curious ideological nostalgia. To chair the Ways and Means Committee, he named John Randolph of Roanoke, who had not served on the committee since his ouster in 1807. Randolph lasted for only one session before succumbing to one of his periodic fits of insanity, but Stevenson replaced him with Alexander Smyth, another Old Republican from Virginia. Stevenson also placed the Calhounite George McDuffie of South Carolina on the committee, but the remainder of the committee comprised Adams supporters whose chief qualification appears to have been prior service. He named Edward Everett, an Adams supporter from Massachusetts, to be the chair of the Foreign Affairs Committee, and he gave future Whigs a four-to-three majority on the committee. In chairs of other committees Stevenson gave deference to experience. If his record in this regard (see Table 2) was less effective than his predecessor, it may have been attributable to high electoral turnover as political parties once again took shape.

In summary, the institutional framework of the modern Congress was largely in place by 1829. The Speaker of the House was the "second man in the nation," with broad power to promote party interests and influence public policy. In the Senate the power of the vice president to name committees may have given him more influence than has hitherto been supposed. Both houses had come to recognize the value of tenure and experience, especially among committee chairs. Committees were not yet the fiefdoms they would become later in the century, but the foundation for that trend was there.

BIBLIOGRAPHY

Congress: 1789 to 1828
Sources for the institutional development of Congress between 1789 and 1828 include ALLAN G. BOGUE, JEROME M. CLUBB, CARROLL R. MCKIBBIN, and SANTA A. TRAUGOTT, "Members of the House of Representatives and the Processes of Modernization, 1789–1960," *Journal of American History* 63 (September 1976): 275–302; NOBLE E. CUNNINGHAM, JR., *Circular Letters of Congressmen to their Constituents, 1789–1829* (Chapel Hill, N.C., 1978) and *The Process of Government Under Jefferson* (Princeton,

N.J., 1978); MARY P. FOLLETT, *The Speaker of the House of Representatives* (New York, 1896); PATRICK J. FURLONG, "The Evolution of Political Organization in the House of Representatives, 1789–1801" (Ph.D. diss., Northwestern University, 1966); RALSTON HAYDEN, *The Senate and Treaties, 1789–1817* (New York, 1920); GERALD R. LIENTZ, "House Speaker Elections and Congressional Parties, 1789–1860," *Capitol Studies* 6 (Spring 1978): 625–645; RONALD M. PETERS, JR., *The American Speakership: The Office in Historical Perspective* (Baltimore, 1990); DAVID M. PLETCHER, "What the Founding Fathers Intended: Congressional-Executive Relations in the Early American Republic," in MICHAEL BARNHART, ed., *Congress and United States Foreign Policy* (Albany, N.Y., 1987); NELSON W. POLSBY, "The Institutionalization of the U.S. House of Representatives," *American Political Science Review* 62 (1968): 144–168; ROY SWANSTROM, *The United States Senate, 1787–1801* (Washington, D.C., 1962); ELAINE K. SWIFT, "The Electoral Connection Meets the Past: Lessons from Congressional History, 1789–1899," *Political Science Quarterly* 102:4 (1987): 625–645; and JAMES S. YOUNG, *The Washington Community, 1800–1828* (New York, 1966).

Congressional Committees

For the origin of congressional committees see JOSEPH COOPER, "The Origins of the Standing Committees and the Development of the Modern House," *Rice University Studies* 56:3 (Summer 1970): 3–163, and "Jeffersonian Attitudes Toward Executive Leadership and Committee Development in the House of Representatives, 1789–1829," *Western Political Quarterly* 18 (March 1965): 47–55; PATRICK J. FURLONG, "The Origins of the House Committee of Ways and Means," *William and Mary Quarterly*, 3d ser., 25 (1968): 587–604; GERALD GAMM and KENNETH SHEPSLE, "Emergence of Legislative Institutions: Standing Committees in the House and Senate, 1810–1825," *Legislative Studies Quarterly* 14 (February 1989): 39–103; J. FRANKLIN JAMESON, "The Origin of the Standing Committee System in America," *Political Science Quarterly* 9 (1894): 245–267; and THOMAS W. SKLADONY, "The House Goes to Work: Select and Standing Committees in the U.S. House of Representatives, 1789–1828," *Congress and the Presidency* 12 (Autumn 1985): 33–47.

Congress and Political Parties

The relationship between political parties and the development of Congress is explored in ALLAN G. BOGUE and MARK MARLAIRE, "Of Mess and Men: The Boardinghouse and Congressional Voting, 1821–1842," *American Journal of Political Science* 19 (1975); JOHN F. HOADLEY, *Origins of American Political Parties, 1789–1803* (Lexington, Ky., 1986); GEORGE NIELSEN, "The Indispensable Institution: The Congressional Party During the Era of Good Feelings" (Ph.D. diss., University of Iowa, 1968); and NORMAN K. RISJORD, *The Old Republicans: Southern Conservatism in the Age of Jefferson* (New York, 1965).

Primary Sources

Published primary sources used in this essay are ALBERT BONI and CHARLES BONI, eds., *Journal of William Maclay* (New York, 1927); JOSEPH F. HOPKINS, ed., *The Papers of Henry Clay*, vol. 1 (Lexington, Ky., 1959); ULRICH B. PHILIPS, ed., "The South Carolina Federalist Correspondence, 1789–1797," *American Historical Review* 14 (July 1909): 529–543, 731–743; GEORGE C. ROGERS, ed., "Letters of William L. Smith to Edward Rutledge, 1789–1794," *South Carolina Historical Magazine* 69 (1968): 1–25, 101–138, 225–242; and 70 (1969): 38–58; ROBERT A. RUTLAND, ed., *The Papers of James Madison* 12 (Charlottesville, Va., 1979); and J. C. A. STAGG, ed., *Papers of James Madison* 16 (Charlottesville, Va., 1989).

SEE ALSO The Congressional Committee System; The Historiography of the American Legislative System; AND The Role of Congressional Parties.

THE U.S. CONGRESS: THE ERA OF PARTY PATRONAGE AND SECTIONAL STRESS, 1829–1881

Allan G. Bogue

The years 1829–1881 comprise a period in American history in which there was great territorial expansion, much growth in the population and change in its composition, significant industrial development, and conflict between the northern and southern sections of the country that culminated in civil war and important constitutional readjustments. The Congress of the United States reflected and helped shape these developments in many respects. Some scholars have pictured the federal lawmakers working out their peculiar visions of American republicanism. Others have seen Congress as a stage on which appear the great orators and problem solvers of U.S. history. Still others have offered the insights of modernization theory in explaining congressional development. To some, the changing agendas and recurrent realignments of political parties provide the driving forces that underlie activity in the federal legislature. In varying degrees all of these approaches have merit, but each has limitations. The approach of this essay, therefore, will be essentially functional, focusing on major elements in congressional development during the period under study and drawing on the insights of various interpretive approaches as appropriate. We shall not, however, consider in detail the changing personal and social characteristics of members of Congress, since Jerome Clubb discusses that topic elsewhere in this encyclopedia.

WASHINGTON, D.C., AND THE CONGRESS OF 1830: FOREIGN OBSERVATIONS

The representatives and senators who came to Washington to serve in the Twenty-first Congress (1829–1831) distributed themselves among approximately fifty boardinghouses, several hotels, and a few private residences. Although many of the lawmakers had left their families at home, some brought their wives or other relatives for company or to join them in savoring cosmopolitan society. The grandeur that Washington's architect, Pierre-Charles L'Enfant, had visualized was still a dream. "The houses," reported one traveler, "are scattered in straggling groups . . . and ever and anon our compassion is excited by some disconsolate building, the first and last born of a square or crescent yet in *nubibus,* suffering like an ancient maiden in the mournful solitude of single blessedness" (Hamilton, pp. 223–224). Pennsylvania Avenue joined two clusters of buildings, one surrounding the White House and including various departmental buildings, the other adjacent to the Capitol. Washington, some thought, resembled a watering place rather than a national metropolis.

Visitors remarked that accommodations in Washington were shabby and cramped, but most congressmen appeared to be agreeable, chatty, and cooperative. There were numerous receptions, parties, and balls, and respectable visitors easily obtained invitations. Social life spilled into the Capitol: congressional wives and daughters, visitors, and local belles sometimes packed the galleries, and visiting clerics, lecturers, and entertainers were allowed to use the Hall of the Representatives, where on Sundays the congressional chaplains might offer service.

According to one visitor, Thomas Hamilton, the House Chamber was a

splendid semicircular saloon, around the arc of which is a range of anomalous columns, composed of breccia, found in the neighbourhood, with a highly-decorated entablature of white marble. In the centre of the chord is the chair of the Speaker, from which radiate seven passages to the circumference, and the desks and seats of the members are ranged in concentric rows. Behind the chair is a sort of corridor or gallery, with a fireplace at either end, and furnished with seats and sofas, which serves as a lounging-place.

(Actually the acoustics in this "splendid" chamber were poor and the representatives rejoiced when they moved into a new one in 1857.) The assembly room of the senators was "a good deal smaller than that of the Representatives" but "very elegantly fitted up" and "also arranged in a semicircle, with desks at convenient distances for the members who sit uncovered" (pp. 110, 222, 225).

Visiting Washington during the Twenty-second Congress (1831–1833), the French historian Alexis de Tocqueville decried the "vulgar demeanor" and "poverty of talent" discernible in the House of Representatives, while lauding the Senate for containing "within a small space a large proportion of the celebrated men of America" (de Tocqueville, *Democracy*, vol. 1, pp. 233–234). Thomas Hamilton described many representatives as "well dressed and of appearance sufficiently senatorial to satisfy the utmost demands of a [severe] critic" but found "a large proportion . . . vulgar and uncouth." Some members—particularly westerners—were seen as being strangely dressed. Debate in the House, Hamilton believed, "though often troubled and vehement" was "rarely violent" (Hamilton, pp. 224–225). In the Senate the demeanor was "grave and dignified. . . . the tone of debate . . . pitched higher than in the more popular House." English writer Harriet Martineau affirmed that "a nobler legislative body, for power and principle, has probably never been known," although she believed that the method of selecting senators was a republican anomaly (Martineau, vol. 1, p. 72). These commentators did not fully understand the American political system. The House of Representatives, faulted by de Tocqueville, included a former president, a future president, a major contender for that honor, and others destined for public fame.

Foreign observers of the early 1830s looked in vain for well-defined political parties with contrasting philosophies of government. "Now," said one informant, "there are scarcely more than those who defend and those who attack the measures of government to gain office and bring public opinion over to their side" (quoted in de Tocqueville, *Journey*, p. 273). Nor was agreement between the Congress and the President essential. The American "political machine . . . can work by itself," noted the eminent banker Nicholas Biddle (quoted in de Tocqueville, *Journey*, p. 88). The President, Joel Poinsett informed de Tocqueville, was without power; Congress governed. To Hamilton it appeared that the "important functions" of government were "practically engrossed by the House of representatives." In both houses, standing committees managed "the whole business of the executive departments."

These committees have separate apartments, in which the real business of the country is carried on, and from which the heads of the executive departments are rigidly excluded. The whole power of the government is thus absolutely and literally absorbed by the people; for no bill, connected with any branch of public affairs could be brought into Congress with the smallest prospect of success, which had not previously received initiative approbation of these committees. (Hamilton, pp. 242–243)

REPRESENTATIVES AND SENATORS

The reapportionment, based upon the national census of 1830, provided 242 congressional seats. A decade later the representatives seriously discussed the merits of smaller and larger units of population and called for the general use of single-member districts, but members kept the number of seats approximately the same through the 1860s. Following the census of 1870, 293 seats were created, the first in a series of increases that continued until the 1910 census, after which 435 seats were allocated. In the Senate each entering state automatically increased the membership by two. There were forty-eight senators in 1829; by 1876, when Colorado was admitted to the Union as the fourteenth new state since 1829, the number of senatorial desks had increased to seventy-six. But even this growth in membership posed few organizational problems.

Nelson Polsby has estimated that in the Congresses between 1829 and 1881, only two times did first-time representatives constitute less than 40 percent of the total; in eleven assemblies more than half of all the members were freshmen (Polsby, pp. 144–148). In the Twenty-eighth House (1843–1845), two-thirds of the members were serving their first term, 58 percent of the representatives in the second Civil War Congress. Most representatives served for only one or two terms in the House during this era.

The most significant difference between a representative and a senator lay in the greater amount and diversity of the latter's political training and in his expectations of continuing public service. For both a representative and a senator, holding state office was the most important source of experience. Although senators apparently served less frequently in local office than did representatives, they compensated for this loss in training by gaining experience in the House of Representatives. Service in the judiciary was more than twice as common for a senator than for a representative. Not all of the additional experience was obtained prior to entering the Senate. After an unprecedented thirty years as a senator, Thomas Hart Benton (1782–1858) appeared in the House to represent Missouri for a term. Some of the judicial service recorded by senators followed their senatorial terms. However, for politicians from new states, federal service as a territorial governor, council member, or judge might lay the foundation for election to the Senate.

Senators took their oaths at a somewhat more advanced age than did representatives. As in the larger chamber, service in the Senate of the American Middle-Period and Reconstruction eras was short by twentieth-century standards. Only twelve out of one hundred senators who had served during the years 1829–1851 had enjoyed terms longer than ten years (Price, p. 35). Various reasons may be given for the relatively short congressional careers during these years. The Jacksonian commitment to frequent rotation of political offices was of some influence, but rotation was not universal in mid–ninteenth-century politics. The highly competitive nature of political life was a more important source of short tenure. National parties formed during the 1830s, reformed during the 1850s, and confronted the exigencies of civil war during the 1860s. Following the war, federal agencies rebuilt the politics and delegations of the Confederate states, and the process of reorganization began again as other elements of the local populace took control.

During this era parties did not have the resources or continuity of control that might have created large numbers of safe seats in the House or produced legislatures that were prepared to give long-term commitments to senators. There also were apparently some attractive alternatives: in the antebellum South the post of governor was considered prestigious enough to be regarded sometimes as a superior obligation. Throughout the nation, politicians might regard the lifelong possession of a post in the federal judiciary (subject to good behavior) as more desirable than the more limited guarantee of tenure in the Senate. Highly charged and volatile ideologies were very apparent by the 1850s, and within such a context short congressional careers were not surprising.

Citizens of the federal Union shared a common political culture of republican institutions based upon a British colonial heritage. But there were subregional variations. Those who represented the residents of the newer states in the West took somewhat different agendas to Washington than did those who represented the original thirteen states. Westerners, however, understood the eastern position; in many cases they had been born or reared in the older states. For example, only 43 percent of the members of the Senate sample from 1830 to 1850 represented the state of their birth. In general the migration streamed from east to west. The congressional delegations of the Northwest usually traced their roots to Yankee and Mid-Atlantic states' origins, and those from the Southwest found their roots in older Southern states. Thus long-standing cultural differences and institutions were perpetuated, most notably slavery and related attitudes, in the Northwest and Southwest.

The biographical patterns of Southerners in the House differed somewhat from other members. A higher proportion of Southern members had relatives who had served or who also would sit in the Congress. Southern-state delegations included larger proportions of agriculturists; among the Northern delegations were more businessmen. Southern members of the Congress tended to serve for somewhat longer terms than did Northern ones, although comparisons of North and South are skewed by the tendency of New Yorkers and Pennsylvanians to serve for shorter terms than other representatives. In comparison to Northerners, Southerners expressed greater commitment to patriarchal family values, esteemed military service more highly, drew upon the concept of chivalry in their references to themselves and to colleagues, and emphasized the importance of honor to the point of resorting to armed duels. Southerners subscribed to states'-rights doctrines to an extent that a eulogist of Senator Andrew Pickens Butler (D.-S.C.) affirmed that he "loved the union of the Constitution only less than South Carolina" (quoted in Allan G. Bogue, *The Congressman's Civil War* [New York, 1989], p. 25). Northerners, however, represented a more varied industrializing economy and a more ethnoculturally diverse constituency swept by reform-inducing revivalism, nativism, and its own variety of racism, and flavored by the New England sense of mission.

Most representatives and senators during the years 1829–1881 could anticipate only a short stay in Washington. But many politicians enjoyed multiple-level political careers for large portions of their working lives. Those whose stay in Washington was brief did not necessarily consider their time wasted. The majority were lawyers who acquired knowledge or a reputation in politics that helped them further their professional careers and gave them additional political influence at the local level. For the abler or more fortunate, service in the House of Representatives opened the doors of the Senate or enabled access to local, federal, or territorial appointments. A senator after loyal party service might find cabinet offices, the federal judiciary, or consular or diplomatic posts open to him. It was not unusual for a senator to hold four or more public positions during the course of his career. Congressional office was integral to a kind of multilevel professional politics during the years 1829–1881.

THE FORMAL RULES

The representatives and senators of this period worked within a framework of rules and precedents inherited from their predecessors; this framework was interpreted by the Speaker of the House and the president of the Senate, and changed or elaborated over time within the chambers. The representatives of the Twenty-first Congress (1829–1831) approved 106 standing rules and orders. By the time of the Forty-fifth Congress (1877–1879) there were 166 standing rules and orders. Although a new member in 1829 might have easily comprehended the basic order of business in the House—the Speaker's call for order; the chaplain's prayer; the reading of the previous day's journal; the calls for petitions; committee reports; and resolutions in the morning hour, the dispatch of business on the Speaker's table; and then the call for the orders of the day—he might have served his terms without ever fully understanding the rules upon which the basic order was based.

During the 1830s and early 1840s considerable change occurred in the House rules. This development, in part, mirrored the emergence of well-organized national political parties whose leaders wished to focus the energies of Congress on their legislative agendas. The rule-changing activity reflected both the high emotional or ideological charge that some issues of the decade carried as well as the increasing volume of legislative business. The chronological annotations in the *Standing Rules and Orders* of the Thirty-first Congress (1849–1851) show several dozen changes made during the 1830s and early 1840s. Some of the alterations were relatively unimportant; for example, the members' decision in 1837 to remove their hats. The real challenge was providing mechanisms by which more important measures could be identified and perfected. Throughout, the right of critics to be heard had to be balanced by the need to get on with the business of governance, appropriating funds, and providing legislative solutions of major public problems.

Although the motion for the previous question (requiring an immediate vote on the subject under debate) appeared in the initial House *Rules* of 1789, many representatives considered it to be an unfair means of stilling critical voices. Congressional leaders of James Madison's administration, however, used it to silence the vituperative criticism during John Randolph and others. Rule changes made in 1837, 1840, and 1848 clarified the status of pending amendments and roll-call procedure when the motion was put, making it so useful that by the 1850s even members who submitted resolutions in the morning hour were using it to protect their measures from amendment or other parliamentary action.

A new member of 1829 learned that Fridays and Saturdays were normally restricted to the consideration of private business unless otherwise decided by a majority of members. After the first thirty days of a session members could present petitions only on Mondays. In the face of conflicting rules, Speakers of the House increasingly held that departures from the normal order of business required a two-thirds majority. In the Twenty-fourth Congress (1835–1837) the chairman of the Ways and Means Committee suggested that uncontroversial private bills be grouped and handled en masse. This basic principle was written into the rules of the Twenty–fifth Congress (1837–1839) and later applied to other aspects of House business. The Twenty-fifth House provided an alternate method of accepting petitions: direct referral to the clerk of the House who entered the petition in the *Congressional Journal*. In the Twenty-eighth House (1843–1845), this became the standard procedure, and ultimately the principle was expanded to other types of documents. The members of the Twenty-fifth House also ruled that petitions should be accepted only on alternate Mondays, the other first days of the week being reserved for resolutions.

At an early date congressmen and executive officers recognized the key role of the Committee of Ways and Means. Although not authorized to report at his own pleasure until the late 1850s, its chairman became recognized as administration floor leader. Colleagues also understood that he could withhold submission or delay the call of appropriations bills for political purposes, scheduling his presentations to deny the floor to other business. The members of the Twenty-fifth House agreed that Ways and Means should submit its appropriations bills within thirty days of the formation of the committees, but the instruction proved to be wishful thinking.

In theory, the order in which legislative measures were introduced into the House and reported back by the appropriate committees determined the order in which they were made final in the Committees of the Whole and the House. Even in the 1830s, however, so simple a formula was utterly inadequate to the volume of bills handled by the committees. Committee

chairs increasingly tried to perfect legislation in the morning hour as part of the committee-reporting process. Considering the Twenty-third through the Twenty-fifth Congresses, Marvin Downey maintained that "the most significant development in the House in the sphere of procedure was the extended use of the special order." He estimated that members sought at least one-hundred special orders during the years 1833–1839, authorizing consideration of a particular measure at a given time with indefinite continuance (Downey, pp. 108–109). By the Twenty-fifth House there was general agreement that a two-thirds majority was necessary to create a special order. More difficult to obtain were motions for unanimous consent to consider or to suspend the rules, devices that broke the lockstep of a special order.

As these developments occurred in the Congresses of the 1830s and early-1840s, a representative's opportunity to obtain the floor diminished. Rule 23 of the Twenty-first House stated, "No member shall speak more than twice to the same question. . . ." Ten years later the members of the Twenty-sixth House (1839–1841) decided that no member might speak to any question for longer than an hour, although the committee member in charge of a measure was also allowed a closing response. The hour-rule was also applied in the Committee of the Whole and, as the use of the previous question gained ground in the House, minority-party members fought to preserve the freedom of maneuver allowed in Committees of the Whole, where motions of the previous question, adjournment, referral, postponement, and other motions to lay on the table were not used. Clever floor managers, however, still curtailed discussion in the Committees of the Whole. In 1847 the members responded by agreeing that at the closing of debate any member should "be allowed, in committee, five minutes in which to explain any amendment he may offer."

During the 1850s, complaints about the inadequacy of House procedures were more common than specific changes in work ways. By then, however, members were handling petitions by requesting the clerk of the House to record them in the House *Journal*. Committee chairmen who had in the past extended their reports through numerous morning hours were now limited to two days of the House's attention before the roll call of committees was resumed. Members disregarded the recommendations of select committees that were attempting general revision of the House rules during the years 1849–1859, although the decision in the Thirty-fifth House (1857–1859) —to have the Speaker head such a committee—faintly forecasted the future.

Members of the Thirty-sixth House approved a general revision of the rules in 1860, involving considerable simplification and rearrangement. Use of the previous question was clarified and made less destructive of amendments to the initial legislative proposal. House rejection of the Committee of the Whole's action in striking out the enacting clause of a bill now returned that measure to the deliberative body rather than providing it a fast track to the statute book. Members of all standing committees now sat for the duration of the Congress rather than for the session. Henceforth, the rules of one House were to be those of the next, "unless otherwise ordered." The principle of grouping noncontroversial measures for speedy action was extended. The revision of 1860, primarily consolidative in nature, highlighted the trends of the previous thirty years curtailing members' access to the floor. Dissidents still could foil or delay proceedings in the House, however, by putting procedural motions leading to roll calls or verifying the existence of a quorum (the number of members necessary for the transaction of business).

In one respect representatives' options expanded significantly during the years 1829–1861. Rule changes of 1837–1838 encouraged representatives to introduce bills by leave of the House on their own responsibility, rather than instructing committees to do so. There were no members' bills of this sort introduced in the Twenty-second House (1831–1833), but 71 percent of those introduced in the Thirty-sixth House (1859–1861) were of this nature. Following a further relaxation of procedures since the 1860 rules revision, members directly introduced 99 percent of all public bills during the Forty-seventh House (1881–1883). Although most of these bills were never seriously considered, members could point to them when justifying their stewardship among constituents.

During the Civil War the lawmakers found it unnecessary to make sweeping changes in the rules, although the definition of a quorum presented a problem. Considering that the standard of a quorum was one-half of all possible members plus one, the absence of Southern members required high levels of attendance for the passage of legislation. Speaker Galusha A. Grow (R.-Pa.) decided in 1861 that the quorum requirement was satisfied when a majority of those members chosen to serve in Congress were present. During the second Civil War Congress, the senators agreed to the understanding that "chosen" should be qualified by "and alive." To challenge the credentials of Reconstruction delegations, in 1868 the senators added further restrictions by adding the words "and sworn" to their definition. Some Democrats and moderate Republicans questioned the Republican radicals' insistence that all members take the "iron-clad oath" of allegiance that Congress imposed upon federal officeholders in 1862, in addition to their conventional oath of office.

Even during the 1850s the practice of adding unrelated measures to appropriations bills as riders was well established and frequently criticized. As House business increased after the Civil War, competition among the committee chairmen for floor time became intense. The appeal for unanimous consent, the creation of special orders, requests to suspend the rules, and the appropriations rider were commonplace. The "watchdog of the Treasury," William S. Holman (D.-Ind.), won approval of a provision that ran, "nor shall any provision in any such bill or amendment thereto, changing existing law, be in order except such as, being germane to the subject of the bill, shall retrench expenditures" (in other words, changes shall be germane and reduce expenditures). Nevertheless the Democrats, holding a narrow majority in the House in the late 1870s, attempted to repeal aspects of Republican reconstruction by attaching riders to appropriations bills, but their efforts were vetoed by President Rutherford B. Hayes. The Holman rule enhanced the legislative authority of the Appropriations Committee and inspired counterattacks. Beginning with the Commerce Committee chairman in 1877, others won the right to introduce their own budget bills. Growing dissatisfaction with House procedures led the representatives to create a revision committee in 1879 and to approve its work in 1880, a compilation best considered with the reforms of the next twenty years.

In contrast to the curtailment of floor access that had occurred in the House during the previous twenty years, a Senate rule of the 1850s ran, "No member shall speak more than twice, in any one debate, on the same day, without leave of the Senate." In the smaller chamber, where elaborate rules were believed unnecessary, deference and courtesy were expected to prevail. Oratory worthy of Virginia patriot Patrick Henry greeted Kentucky senator Henry Clay's suggestion of the early 1840s that the senators use the call for the previous question; a decade later Stephen A. Douglas encountered similar opposition. In 1856 the senators agreed that special orders were to be considered in the order of their creation, and in 1826 required a two-thirds majority for their approval.

An 1858 legislative manual lists fifty Senate rules; the House had begun the decade with more than 150. As a continuing body the Senate did not need to adopt its rules anew in each Congress as did the House through much of this period. Only one systematic revision of senate rules took place during the period under review, a task completed in 1868 and producing a revised set of fifty-three rules. Headed by Senator Henry B. Anthony (R.-R.I.), chairman of the Republican Caucus, the Select Committee on Rules in charge of the revision produced sections dealing with the addition of nongermane riders to appropriation bills, specified procedures for the handling of special orders, elaborated the procedures under which nominees for office were considered, and codified acceptable decorum within the chamber.

Anthony and his colleagues, Samuel C. Pomeroy (R.-Kans.) and George F. Edmunds (R.-Vt.) proposed procedural changes that appeared in the 1868 revision or were accepted in following years. Under these changes amendments could be tabled without affecting the status of the bill and remarks upon amendments were to be limited to five minutes in length. The "Anthony Rule" established a half-hour period at the conclusion of the business of the morning hour during which uncontroversial measures might be perfected under the five-minute rule. Edmunds's proposition laid down the order of priority under which the senators considered bills in the absence of special orders, with appropriations measures given first preference. But an observer of the late

1890s would find that the order of business of 1828 was still basic to chamber procedures.

The Senate Rules Committee was established as a select committee during the Fortieth Congress (1867–1869), and retained that status until the Forty-third Congress (1873–1875), when it became a standing committee. Never as powerful as its counterpart in the House, this committee nonetheless became an integral part of the enhanced power structure that Senate leaders developed during the late nineteenth century.

COMMITTEES AND LEGISLATIVE LEADERS

"The necessities of his office" made the Speaker "a despot," argued the Ohio Democrat Clement L. Vallandigham in 1860, the standing committee chairmen being "sub despots." Members merely registered "the decrees of committees" rather than engaging in "collective thinking upon public issues" (*Congressional Globe,* 36th Cong., 1st sess., p. 1182). Although the members of the early national House relied heavily on select committees chosen to work upon specific legislative matters, the first standing committee (Elections) appeared in 1789, and others followed. In the Twenty-first House (1829–1831) there were nineteen, each with seven members, plus two three-person committees (Revisal and Unfinished Business, and Accounts)—all serving on a session-by-session basis. Six additional committees consisting of three members supervised the public accounts and expenditures of various executive divisions and were organized for the duration of any given congress. The rules of the Twenty-fifth House (1837–1839) described the duties of twenty-two standing committees with nine men each, and five committees for which the membership was five. There were then five members on the committees supervising the public accounts. During the 1830s the members added committees on the militia, roads and canals, patents, public buildings and grounds, and mileage, as well as dividing the duties of the earlier Committee on Military Pensions. Only one additional standing committee was added in each of the next two decades.

In 1865 a new era of committee formation began when the House separated Appropriations, Banking and Currency, and Pacific Railroads from Ways and Means. Two years later the Committee on Education and Labor appeared. By the end of the Forty-sixth Congress (1879–1881) the Speaker apportioned members among forty-two standing House committees (most with eleven members) and an additional three joint committees; others were added by the end of the century. Thus the institutional structure of the House was considerably elaborated during the last thirty-five years of the century. The subdivision of Ways and Means reflected the heavy work load of its members during the Civil War as well as some dissatisfaction with its administration. The general postwar growth in the number of committees in part reveals the impact of the Civil War and its residual effects upon congressional business, and also stems from the reaffirmation of national powers and the complexities of a rapidly growing industrial economy.

The freshman senator of 1829 found twenty-three standing committees, a number that was only increased by two during the next twenty years. By the Thirty-sixth Senate (1859–1861) the number had been cut to nineteen—committees on Manufactures, Agriculture, Roads and Canals, Retrenchment, and Printing having been eliminated and the Military Affairs and Militia committees combined. The senators created new standing committees during the 1860s and 1870s, but some, such as those for Agriculture and Manufacture, represented restoration rather than innovation. A Pacific Railroad Committee (its name soon changed simply to Railroads) reflected the changing nature of the senatorial constituency, as did that on Mines and Mining, and the short-lived Committee on Education. Other committees were efforts to meet the challenge of much heavier flows of legislation and federal appointments. These included an Appropriations committee to assume part of the labors of the Finance committee, one on Laws Revision, a short-lived Investigation and Retrenchment committee, and committees on Privileges and Elections, Rules, Engrossed Bills (those in final approved form), and Enrolled Bills.

Forty-five select committees have been identified in the Ninth House (1805–1807), and forty-eight in the Fourteenth House (1815–1817). In the following years the number of committees generally fell; in the Forty-fourth House (1875–1877), for example, there were fifteen committees (Stubbs 1985). The select committee nonetheless remained useful as an investigatory agency or as a means of dealing with troublesome legislative issues. The experience in the Senate was similar.

Some select committees of the Civil War era were particularly notable. During the Thirty-sixth Congress (1859–1861), John Covode (R.-Pa.) headed a select House committee that investigated wrongdoing in the James Buchanan administration, providing ammunition for the next presidential campaign. Early in the war the two houses established a unique Joint Committee on the Conduct of the War which generated few legislative proposals but energetically investigated military disasters and errant generals. In the House, select committees investigated the loyalty of government employees, government contracting, and other matters. There was similar activity in the Senate chamber. The senators placed their version of the controversial Confiscation Act of 1862 in the hands of a select committee and, during the Thirty-eighth Congress, the Massachusetts Republican Charles Sumner circumvented the Senate Standing Committee on the Judiciary by winning approval of a Select Committee on Slavery and the Treatment of Freedmen. In their conflict with President Andrew Johnson, the houses created a joint committee that developed reconstruction legislation under which national reunification was to be affected. The select committee was a discrete entity, designed to solve a problem and then to vanish—the antithesis of a formal structure prepared for a particular type of business, or of a system based on standard procedures.

The Speaker and the various committee chairmen provided leadership in the chamber. The speakers of this era, however, on the average served only three years; the most common length of service was but two years. Of the pre-Civil War presiding officers in office, Andrew Stevenson (D.-Va) served for seven years (1827–1834) and James K. Polk (D.-Tenn.) and Linn Boyd (D.-Ky.) each held office for four years (1835–1839 and 1851–1855). Schuyler Colfax (R.-Ind.) presided for six years (1863–1869), as did James G. Blaine (R.-Maine, 1869–1875). Michael C. Kerr (D.-Ind.) died in 1876 after a year in office but his successor, Samuel J. Randall (D.-Pa.), enjoyed five years at the helm. Although Stevenson's service was the longest, in general the Civil War and post-bellum years fostered longer terms for the Speakers.

As a group, the eighteen Speakers of the years 1827–1880 were slightly more than forty-one years of age when they took office, just slightly below the median age of entry for representatives during the same period. But their mean term of prior legislative experience was seven years, in an era when only about 6 percent of members served for more than eight years. Sixteen speakers had been members of state legislatures or constitutional conventions, five of them speakers at the state level. These men had displayed political talents that brought them into the Congress at a relatively early age. At the extremes stood Robert M. T. Hunter (D.-Va.) and William Pennington (W., N.J.), aged twenty-nine and sixty-two years, respectively, when they became Speaker. Hunter had two years of previous experience in the Congress and Pennington had none (although he was a former governor of New Jersey). Eleven of the speakers were lawyers and two had both legal and editorial experience. Two were newspaper editors and others had backgrounds in medicine, agriculture, and merchandising. Seventy-two percent of the group had attended college.

Individuals most frequently left the post of Speaker when their party lost control of the House, as happened with seven speakers. Five retired for other reasons, and some Speakers later held government posts. Two others ran successfully for governor in their states, and Schuyler Colfax became vice president. Pennington and Grow met defeat in the general election subsequent to their service. Kerr died in office.

The chairman of the Ways and Means Committee had long played the role of floor leader in the House, but not until the Thirty-sixth House (1859–1861) did he win the unquestioned right to report appropriations measures at any time, although the chairmen of Enrolled Bills, Elections, and Printing had already enjoyed that privilege. Twenty members held the post of chairman of Ways and Means between 1827 and 1881, averaging only 2.7 years of service, although seven had each served total terms of four years. (One of these chairmen was Thaddeus Stevens, who moved to the newly created Committee on Appropriations, where

he continued as floor leader until his death three years later. Therefore Stevens was the longest serving floor leader of the period.) When they took office, the chairmen of Ways and Means were significantly older—between forty-seven and forty-eight years of age on average—than the speakers of the same era, and their average service in the chamber was almost two years longer. Eight-five percent of them were trained in the law.

Party turnover accounted for the departure of seven of the twenty chairmen of Ways and Means; four met electoral defeat and the Speaker passed over or removed four others. Three went to the Senate, while James K. Polk took the Speaker's chair and Stevens moved to the Appropriations Committee, as noted. Six other members chaired the latter committee before 1880. Their educational attainments and professional backgrounds were similar to those of the chairmen of Ways and Means, but they were somewhat more experienced and older, reflecting the graying of House leadership subsequent to the Civil War. Of the seven, Stevens died, two lost their positions due to the turnover of party control in the House, one became secretary of state, one became speaker, another assumed the chair of Ways and Means, and one met defeat in a general election.

With only a few exceptions the Speakers named the members of committees and designated the chairs. In theory they matched talent to position, but they also considered length of service, eminence in the majority party, the preferences of other party leaders, sectional background, and prior commitments made in seeking support for the speakership. By the 1850s Speakers usually honored the wishes of the minority-party caucus in assigning minority representatives to committees, but the first Speaker of the Civil War, Galusha A. Grow (R.-Pa.), did not. Supporters and opponents of slavery viewed seats on the committees on Territories, the District of Columbia, Public Lands, and the Judiciary as particularly vital to their interests.

The Speaker chose committee chairmen from a core membership of veterans, a group not large enough to provide experienced individuals to head every committee. Six of the twenty-seven committee chairmen of the Twenty-first House had served in the House for ten years or more, but 55 percent of the group had only been in the House for two terms or less, and four were freshmen. In the Thirty-sixth House only two chairmen had as much as eight years of experience, 88 percent had previously served four years or less, and nine were in their first terms. After ten years of Republican dominance the picture was changed, but seventeen chairmen in the Forty-first House (1869–1871) were entering their second term as members. Members without prior experience appeared on even important committees, although generally more impressive credentials were needed to obtain the chair of such groups.

Seniority as understood in the mid-twentieth century did not prevail in the allocation of chairmanships and committee seats in either house. Loyal party members with substantial prior service in the House received consideration from the Speaker, but there was no general understanding that the more experienced man must be accommodated, or that the second-ranking majority-party member in the preceding Congress automatically assumed direction in the absence of a former chairman.

From the mid-1840s on, the party caucus determined the allocation of committee assignments in the Senate, with the party majority automatically approving these choices on the floor. But caucuses might punish dereliction from the administration line, as Stephen A. Douglas, the former chairman of the Senate Committee on Territories, learned in 1859, and Republican supporters of President Ulysses S. Grant emphasized when they refused to retain Charles Sumner as chairman of the Senate Foreign Relations Committee in 1872.

The prevalence of congressional inexperience enhanced the importance of the Speaker and the chairman of Ways and Means. Andrew Stevenson, his successors, and their colleagues recognized the Speaker's power to shape legislative outcomes through both his selection of committee members and his role as presiding officer. In theory the Speaker could be nonpartisan, actively support the administration, ally himself with party colleagues, or advance his own agenda. Stevenson strongly supported President Andrew Jackson's administration, a fact reflected in his committee selections. By naming John Quincy Adams head of the Committee on Manufactures he balanced Adams with low-tariff Democrats. He dropped a four-year chairman of Ways and Means to align that committee more closely with President Jackson's views. His successors were even more partisan; members making the traditional motion of thanks to the Speaker at the conclusion of a congress came to avoid the use of the word "impartial," fearing raucous reaction.

Charles G. Sellers has argued that James K. Polk was the "first speaker to be regarded frankly as a party leader, responsible for pushing a party program through the House" (p. 304). Polk's rulings during the years 1835–1839 were challenged by militant Whigs who excoriated him. Just when abolitionists were deluging Northern congressmen with petitions pleading for the elimination of slavery in the District of Columbia, Polk ruled that the House could refuse to receive a petition. Members approved an infamous gag rule, which provided that petitions and other matters concerning slavery "shall, without either being printed or referred, be laid upon the table, and that no further action . . . be had thereon" (pp. 304, 314–315). John Quincy Adams and others fought the application of this rule until it was discarded in 1844.

Although able men, none of the presiding officers of this period shaped the powers of their position as had Henry Clay or some later Speakers. One scholar has characterized Galusha A. Grow and Schuyler Colfax, who both held office during the Civil War, as "figureheads." Postbellum speakers like James G. Blaine and Samuel J. Randall faced accusations that they used their powers to advance private agendas, and that their relations with private interests were unethically close.

In selecting the chairman of Ways and Means the Speaker usually first offered the post to the man who had been his leading rival for the speakership, although not everyone accepted the offer. Charles H. Jones, the biographer of J. Glancy Jones, chairman of the Ways and Means Committee in the Thirty-fifth House (1857–1859), described the duties of the chairman:

> [He] has charge of all the legislative measures that are necessary for the administration of the Government. . . . He encounters difficulties at every step, in the form of amendments, opposition, and criticism. He must be equipped with a thorough knowledge of the workings of the Government in all its departments. . . . He

must be prepared with readiness to repel the attacks of the skilful and able members of the opposition, who at every turn seek to embarrass the party in power, and he must also be prepared to answer those who seek for information. The arrangement of the business of the House is largely under his control, and he must see to it that the time of the House is not wasted, and that the measures in his charge get through without hindrance or delay. (Jones, vol. 2, pp. 2–3)

Thaddeus Stevens was the best known of the chairmen of Ways and Means during this era, in part, because of his domineering and sarcastic style and because of the importance of the problems that he and his colleagues faced. Stevens is noteworthy for his efforts to provide leadership in war-policy areas lying outside his committee's fiscal and monetary mandate. His motions elicited a relatively large number of roll-call votes, with about one-third of them going against him.

The structure of leadership in the Senate was less well-defined than in the House of Representatives. A favorite analogy in descriptions of the nineteenth-century Senate is to liken it to the Sacred College of Cardinals. Neither the vice president of the United States as president of the Senate, nor the president *pro tempore,* wielded power comparable to that of the Speaker. It is true that the president and president *pro tempore* did appoint Senate committees in some Congresses before 1845, but from then on party caucuses generally assumed this power.

The chairman of the Senate Majority Caucus is considered generally to have been the most powerful figure in the Senate during this era, an officer most easily identifiable because he moved for approval of the committee slate early in the proceedings of a new congress or session (McConachie, 1898, pp. 265–266). But this was not always the case. During the Civil War, William Pitt Fessenden, the chairman of the Finance Committee, was certainly more powerful than Senator Henry B. Anthony of Rhode Island, the Republican Caucus Chairman. Finance chairmen, usually among those with the lengthiest prior service in the majority party, played a major role in setting the order of floor business.

Senators differed in interpreting their roles. Sumner noted that Fessenden "rarely spoke except for business, what he said was restrained in its influence, but it was most effective in this Chamber." The Massachusetts senator, however viewed his Senate seat as a "lofty pulpit with a mighty sounding board, and the whole wide-spread people is the congregation" (*Memorial Addresses,* pp. 12–13). Fessenden himself professed willing "to work like a dog" and leave "the jabber to others" (Fessenden to Elizabeth F. Warriner, February 8, 1862). Thus were contrasted the opinion-shaping and reputation-building opportunities of the Senate with the approach of the legislative craftsmen.

THE PARTY AS LEGISLATIVE FORCE

Leaders, rules, and committees provided guidance for the members of the House. Members had various ambitions in coming to Washington and surely understood that their congressional careers would probably be short, but in seeking the favor of the chief executive or congressional leaders they kept in mind their standing at home. The roll-call evidence suggests that representatives during the nineteenth century voted in line with their party affiliation, state or regional interests, the specific needs of their home district, or perhaps, idiosyncratic personal objectives. What most clearly predicted voting behavior was party affiliation, followed sometimes by sectional origin. By 1835 the ranks of the Democratic and Whig parties were clearly identifiable in the House and Senate.

The respective party positions can be briefly summarized: the Democrats inveighed against special privilege and lauded the right of the common people to rule and to improve themselves in a society of equal opportunities, while the Whigs endorsed governmental action designed to develop the nation and to assist disadvantaged groups. Politicians drew on elements of ideology that reflected the views of specific sectors of American society, such as the frontier farmers or the increasingly self-aware labor groups of the developing industrial centers. The national platforms constituted the official party agendas—mixtures of ideological justification and policy commitments upon which political managers obtained broad agreement within their party and which, they believed, would attract the most voters. In the national assembly the majority party's elaboration of policy was found in the body of law seriously proposed and passed.

The 1830s were years of hardening party lines, the 1840s a period of intense partisan commitment and rather evenly balanced party competition, and the 1850s years of party disintegration and realignment. Nevertheless, during all these decades the two major parties never completely dominated the national system nor their own members. Marginal groups or unattached figures were almost always present in the Congress. Multiple ballots were needed in the election of seven speakers between 1834 and 1861; those of 1839, 1849, 1855, and 1859 involved 11, 63, 133, and 44 political factions. External events, the vote-drawing potential of military heroes like Andrew Jackson, William Henry Harrison, and Zachary Taylor, the increasing effectiveness of campaign organizations, unique needs of a constituency, or the persistence of stubborn regional or ideological commitments all complicated efforts to maintain party discipline.

Since the 1950s, historians have used the record of roll-call voting to show that there were gradations of opinion on major and minor issues within the parties (see Alexander 1967 and Silbey 1967). Different matters typically produced different alignments. Voting on economic subjects, for example, was strongly influenced by regional considerations. The problem of slavery and its related concerns also eroded party solidarity during the 1840s and 1850s, but politicians kept working to find nationally acceptable positions even on this explosive issue. Members and senators sometimes changed party allegiance to match perceived changes of opinion in their constituencies, but for the most part new faces reflected the changing perceptions of the national constituency. Increasingly, however, Southerners dominated the Democratic party in the congresses of the 1850s.

Constructive lawmaking was easiest when the same national party held sizable margins in both chambers and had elected its presidential and vice-presidential candidates, an alignment achieved in only twelve of the twenty-six congresses convening between 1829 and 1881. In eleven cases control of the two branches was divided, and in three congresses, former vice presidents John Tyler and Andrew Johnson were repudiated by the party that had elected them. In only one of the four Jackson con-

gresses was control split, but even in the other three the administration majority in the Senate was paper-thin.

The regional background of the Speakers and of the chairmen of Ways and Means reveals the crosscutting influence of geography. Between 1829 and 1861 nine Southern Speakers served for a total of twenty-four years. Four Northerners held the office during the same period, each for two years. The selection of the chairmen of Ways and Means was somewhat different. Of the fourteen men who chaired the Committee of Ways and Means between 1831 and 1861, seven were Southerners serving for a total of seventeen years and seven were Northerners serving for fifteen years. Between 1816 and 1881 all Speakers and chairmen of Ways and Means were from a Northern state. Sectionalism colored the representation and internal structure of the Senate as well, where through the antebellum period Southerners endeavored to maintain an equal balance of slave states and free states.

During these years a controversy arose over the right of "instruction." That is, was the representative or senator the delegate of his constituency, pledged to represent its views faithfully, or was he a trustee, free to use his best judgment? Particularly in the South, Jacksonian majorities in various state assemblies instructed Whig senators to help expunge the resolution censuring President Jackson from the Senate *Journal*. (Jackson's veto of a bill in 1832 rechartering the Second Bank of the U.S. caused great political conflict). Because those rejecting the instructions sometimes felt obliged to resign, the process might terminate a senatorial career, but some senators were politically secure enough to disregard such commands. Instruction was most commonly invoked during the 1830s and early 1840s but some Northern state legislators tried to use it in the Civil War years.

Some scholars have argued that the members of Congress who were messmates, living in the same boardinghouse, displayed sufficient solidarity to influence congressional proceedings, but the evidence for this relationship is doubtful. Senators and representatives gravitated to houses occupied by those with similar state, sectional, and party affiliations; floor activity reflected these underlying loyalties rather than the disciplined marshaling of fellow boarders. Particular boardinghouse groups might, however, contain important party leaders who counseled each other as did the so-called F Street Mess of the Thirty-third Congress (1853–1855).

THE CAUCUS

As the Jacksonian era opened, the party convention was displacing the caucus as a forum where electoral candidates were anointed, but the latter's use continued in the selection of Speakers of the House of Representatives. During the 1840s and 1850s multiparty or factional arrays impeded the evolution of binding party-caucus designations of Speaker candidates. During the fall of 1863, however, Republican leaders came to fear that the clerk of the House was plotting with Democrats and border-state members to select the Speaker of the Thirty-eighth Congress, and the caucus united in support of Schuyler Colfax. From then on caucus selection of the party's choice for Speaker prior to the formal House vote became customary. In the Senate the practice of caucus selection of committee members dates from 1845, with the majority party usually accepting the minority's suggestions for a party complement proportional to its numbers.

The caucus was an important forum in which to map party strategy and encourage support of party goals. During the third session of the Thirty-seventh Congress (1861–1863) radicals in both the House and Senate caucuses sharply criticized President Lincoln and his moderate cabinet members. The Republican Senate caucus sent a delegation to demand that the president reorganize the cabinet—an unprecedented action, believed William P. Fessenden. It was not only the parties that found caucusing useful. Disaffected groups met in Capitol committee rooms or boardinghouse rooms to lay plans or draft agenda. State delegations or their party components caucused concerning appointments or other matters of state interest.

THE LOBBYISTS

The representatives and senators arrived in Washington with a keen sense of what their districts or states expected. The chief executive, his cabinet members, and administration leaders in the House made their wishes clear. As national parties emerged, their platforms articulated common objectives for the lawmakers. But much congressional business involved private claims or local issues, such as authorization of new postal routes or harbor improvement. "Village lawyers," or solons, from unaffected regions might not understand the details or implications of tariffs, land policy, or major fiscal measures. Here entered the lobbyist. By the 1830s so-called claim agents were fixtures of the Washington scene. Government clerks also accepted fees for advancing claims in government agencies or explaining the circumstances of would-be pensioners.

Influential state-party leaders and former federal legislators or cabinet officers began to make lobbying forays to Washington. Deputations of businessmen intent on changing federal law to their benefit became common during the thirty years prior to the Civil War. President Polk reported manufacturers "swarming" in Washington in opposition to the Tariff Reduction bill. Federal subsidies to companies carrying the mail in steamships and land grants to railroads opened new opportunities for lobbyists. The pleas of those claiming reimbursements for French spoliation during the early nineteenth century still echoed in congresses of the 1850s. During the same decade, the United Brethren of the War of 1812 successfully sought to equalize their veteran's land bounties with those of the soldiers of the Mexican War. The Civil War opened more opportunities for the lobbyists, as the government contracted with industry to supply the Union armies and Congress developed tariff, taxation, and banking policies that affected the business community. In evaluating private legislation the congressmen followed the lead of more-informed colleagues. By the end of the Civil War some lobbyists were happy to advise the Speaker even regarding the placement of new congressmen on committees.

It has been suggested that the period 1830–1880 was one of transitional corruption in a Congress responding to the growth of a large and complex industrial economy. For example, congressmen accepted loans from the Second Bank of the United States while its rechartering was at issue. (One Washington banker, W. W. Corcoran, was found to be particularly accommodating.) Lawyer members of the House or Senate represented interests seeking favorable action from the Congress. Until the early 1850s the fact that bribery or attempted bribery of federal lawmakers was considered criminal behavior under the common law was believed to restrain improper behavior adequately. But as the pressure of the lobbies increased the federal lawmakers sought to control abuses. In 1853 the senators restricted access to the floor of their chamber, and members of both houses barred themselves from serving as agents of private claimants. Yet the lawmakers still could press private claims in Congress if they did not accept pay. In the next year, however, House members recommended the expulsion of four of their colleagues for improper behavior. Upon the initiative of senators James F. Simmons (R.-R.I.) and John P. Hale (R.-N.H.) during the Civil War, federal lawmakers forbade accepting remuneration for helping obtain government contracts and for representing constituents before government departments.

During the scandals of the Grant administration, the House expelled members for unethical relations with business interests, and Vice President Schuyler Colfax, among others, suffered damaged reputations. Although the letters of lobbyists suggest that federal lawmakers commonly accepted some form of material consideration, the details usually are unclear, some of the correspondence perhaps reflecting the lobbyist's effort to demonstrate his worth rather than votes actually purchased. As the era ended, the federal legislator's need for information continued to increase. He was still his own secretary or information gatherer, unless, as a committee chairman, he was fortunate enough to have the services of a clerk. Therefore by this time the lobby was an essential part of the lawmaking process, as well as a more obvious one, with veterans and growing industrial corporations, most notably the railroads, increasing and refining their lobbying efforts. Despite the passage of rules regarding ethical behavior, the activities of the railroad corporations in particular convinced many in the general public that Congress was for sale.

AGENDAS

Resolutions, petitions, memorials, public and private bills, and presidential messages formed the raw material of the congressional agenda in any session—a slate of business that was refined by committee action and debate and voting in the chambers. Such agendas reflected constituency concerns, administration initiatives, the policies of foreign powers, the activity of lobbyists, and the individual objectives of members. In the broadest sense the lawmakers of 1829–1881 were building the nation. They helped expand its boundaries, encouraged vast settlement in its distant regions, and provided answers to two threatening questions that the Founding Fathers had left unanswered: How could a nation proclaiming the individual's inalienable right to liberty and the pursuit of happiness also nurture the institution of slavery? How could sovereign states share their powers with a central government whose policy objectives might be inimical to the residents of individual states? Although later viewed as costly and incomplete, the answers ensured that the America of 1881 was vastly different from that of 1829.

Floor activity involving far-reaching political issues was not the only concern of the representatives and senators. During each session members promoted the passage of private bills, of interest primarily to their constituents and sometimes to themselves. At times the floor oratory and maneuvering was, as one observer put it, mere "president-making." Occasionally the legislators spent frustrating hours wrangling over procedural matters. The work of those serving on standing or select committees has been little noticed, but in exercising oversight the lawmakers in committee could have a significant influence on events. They pressed the claims of constituents in the executive departments or at social gatherings. And sometimes when the proceedings were routine or boring, members listened to speeches in the other house or went to the races.

The public bills and joint resolutions offered during Congress' major sessions during this period can be categorized under as many as three-dozen subject headings. One sampling of five peacetime Congresses from 1830 to 1870 shows that most measures fell in the following areas: military affairs (15.4 percent of the total); internal improvements and transportation (14 percent); public lands (11.7 percent); appropriations (7.6 percent); judiciary (6.1 percent); commerce (5 percent); revenue and tariff (4.4 percent); District of Columbia (4.3 percent); and territories (3.3 percent).

One measure of legislative activity, albeit a somewhat crude one, is the number of bills and joint resolutions introduced during the course of a congress. During the Twenty-first Congress (1829–1831) 856 such documents appeared. From the mid-1830s to 1853 the number of bills and joint resolutions totaled some 1,200 items per Congress. Between 1853 and the end of the Civil War the mean number of bills was 1,678, with somewhat more activity displayed during the late 1850s than in the war years. During the Thirty-ninth Congress (1865–1867) the lawmakers introduced more than 2,000 measures and thereafter the course was steadily upward, standing at 10,067 in the Forty-sixth Congress (1879–1881).

The number of laws actually passed was more modest: the Twenty-sixth Congress (1839–1841) approved fifty public acts, an unusually low figure, and the legislators of the next Congress wrote 178 measures into law. The number of public measures passed during other congresses between 1829 and 1861 falls within these bounds. Most congresses of the troubled 1860s added more than 300 measures to the statute books and the Forty-second Congress (1871–1873) produced a grand total of 515. However, the congressmen in each of the last three congresses of the 1870s failed to produce as many as three-hundred public acts. If one examines legislative output per congressman, there were 3.3 public measures introduced and .55 public bills or joint resolutions approved for each senator and representative serving in the Twenty-first Congress (1829–1831). Their counterparts of the Forty-sixth Congress (1879–1881) on average introduced 27.3 public measures and perfected one.

At the beginning of this article's period of discussion, private legislation was generated almost solely by the referral of petitions for committee action. Until the Civil War the members of each congress usually approved more private statutes than public ones. The Civil War congresses devoted little attention to private bills, but thereafter the amount of such legislation again was sometimes greater than the total number of public acts.

Examination of House resolutions provides a different picture. In part, these initiatives encouraged committees to produce legislative measures. Some measures lubricated the legislative process—as when they were used by committee chairs to change the order of business or to advance the progress of particular bills. Lawmakers offered resolutions to instruct executive officers or obtain information from them, to establish investigatory committees, or to enunciate policy positions in the House. From the Twenty-first through the Twenty-fifth Congress (1837–1839) the number of resolutions of the House ranged from 856 to 1,631. During the next eleven Congresses (1839–1861) internal resolutions in the House of Representatives only once exceeded 900 and in one instance (1851–1853) totaled only 263. After 1860, resolutions were more common, totaling more than 1,000 in three of the Congresses between 1861 and 1871 and never falling below 798. But in the Forty-fifth Congress (1877–1879) the number of resolutions was only 448. It can be observed that members offered resolutions most frequently during the period of party formation in the 1830s and during the turmoil of the 1860s. But the postbellum decline in the number of internal resolutions also reflected the culmination of the representatives' tendency to introduce bills directly rather than by resolutions instructing committees to do so.

Given that the House of Representatives has a constitutional mandate to introduce financial measures, contemporaries initially assumed that it would be the most powerful chamber. But by the 1830s the senators had demonstrated that their power of amendment made them as important in fiscal matters as congressmen. Senators were initiating increasing amounts of legislation and had shown that they could substantially modify executive initiatives by rejecting presidential nominees or agreements with foreign powers. A senator's six-year term guaranteed him tenure well above the average service in the lower house. Moreover, in his forum he competed for public attention with a only a few dozen others. Senators could hold the floor at length, sometimes spelling out personal, sectional, and party positions in orations that attracted wide attention during the great crises of the era. Senators thus could develop national reputations relatively quickly, and could be seen as logical candidates for positions in the cabinet, important legations, or the presidency.

CONFRONTING PRESIDENTS AND CRISES

Congress and the Executive Branch

In his various way, every president of this era was a distinguished man. All but Zachary Taylor and Ulysses S. Grant—both generals—had served in Congress; Millard Fillmore had been a capable chairman of Ways and Means. But developments abroad, economic depressions, the balance of parties, the ambitions and plans of other leading politicians, the legacy of predecessors, and other factors might influence a president's ability to achieve his purposes. Consider the case of Andrew Jackson, who demonstrated that he, rather than his cabinet, spoke for his administration. Although the extent to which Jackson introduced the spoils system has been exaggerated, he favored rotation in office, and congressmen understood the opportunities that this offered them and their job-hungry constituents. Old Hickory vigorously pressed his views upon the Congress, and his opposition to the efforts of the National Republicans to have the federal government more actively encourage economic growth helped crystalize the national Democratic and Whig parties at both the congressional and electoral levels. When he vetoed the bill rechartering the Second Bank of the United States and transferred the government's deposits to approved state banks, his Whig opponents in the Senate charged executive ursurpation and approved a resolution censuring him—an act of disrespect unparalleled in congressional history, although Thomas Hart Benton (D.-Mo.) later won approval of an expunging resolution. In another sign of increasing independence, during Jackson's presidency the Senate for the first time rejected a presidential nomination to a diplomatic post.

Congressional leaders expressed their disapproval of other presidents as well. Whig congressional leaders persuaded most of the members of John Tyler's cabinet to resign when his opposition to their fiscal and monetary policies became clear. The Covode Committee probed for evidence that President Buchanan had failed to execute the laws. A delegation from the Republican senatorial caucus sought to have Lincoln dismiss moderate members of his cabinet. By passing a Tenure of Office Act, radical Republicans in the Congress attempted to restrict Andrew Johnson's power to dismiss members of his cabinet, and the House later tried to impeach him.

By the beginning of the Jackson administration the various parts of presidential messages to Congress were routinely referred to appropriate standing committees, as were resolutions for legislative action, introduced by individual representatives or senators, and petitions. Committee members drafted appropriate bills or reworked tentative drafts prepared in the executive departments, returning them to the chambers for consideration and amendment, along with the increasingly common bills or joint resolutions from the late 1830s on. Although Lincoln noted that in drafting platforms the national parties made commitments that elected presidents should honor, he did not consider himself bound by them in the civil arena. Moreover, the Civil War demanded legislation undreamed of by those who framed the Republican platform of 1860. Despite his problems with radical Republicans, Lincoln was the only president during the years 1829–1881 whose party was in the majority and generally united in his support from both houses.

Prior to the presidency of Andrew Johnson, Jackson's twelve vetoes of congressional measures and Tyler's ten vetoes had set the upper limit for such action. (Pierce had vetoed nine and both Buchanan and Lincoln seven congressional measures. Lincoln also sent a veto message to Congress, which he had prepared in anticipation that the Confiscation Act of 1862 would be unacceptable to him.) Andrew Johnson rejected twenty-nine proposed laws, of which fifteen were passed over his veto, an unsurpassed number. Grant vetoed ninety-three measures, including many private bills, but was overridden only four times. Although vetoes did not necessarily reflect disagreement over major policy issues, they usually signaled tensions between the executive and legislative branches. On average, twentieth-century presidents have vetoed many more bills than their nineteenth-century predecessors. But presidential nominees to the Supreme Court were treated less sympathetically by senators of the Middle Period and Reconstruction eras. Of the twenty-five nominees who withdrew or were rejected by vote between 1794 and 1970, fifteen saw their hopes dashed between 1829 and 1874.

Congress and Crises

Congress was involved in four major crises during the years 1829–1881: the so-called nullification crisis of the Jackson presidency; the troublesome issues precipitated by the territorial accessions of the 1840s; the secession of the Southern states following Lincoln's election; and the problem of postwar reunification, involving both the impeachment of Andrew Johnson and congressional reconstruction of the defeated Confederacy.

The Crisis of Nullification   In the first major national crisis since the Missouri Compromise, Jackson firmly opposed the efforts of South Carolina to proclaim a state's right to nullify federal statutes and to reject current tariff schedules. Jackson sought congressional support for a bill, implemented partial mobilization, and threw a defiant toast in the faces of sectionalists: "the National Union it must be preserved." Meanwhile Senator Henry Clay developed a bill that reduced the tariff to more acceptable levels. In defusing the crisis Congress and the president shared honors, and the reputation of the Senate as a legislative command post was enhanced. The nullifiers in the Congress faded from view but not from Southern memory.

Nullification was the response of the agrarian South to a nationalizing economic agenda. Victorious in 1840, the Whigs again tried to implement a program of high tariffs, national banking, and federal aid for the building of canals and railroads. Drawn to the Whigs as an opponent of Jackson rather than as a supporter of their policies, President Tyler vetoed vital elements of the Whig agenda. Not surprisingly, most congressional Whigs then deserted him. The president sought to rally an independent following in Congress but this experiment in executive-legislative relations failed. The Tyler administration was disastrous both for the president and for Whigs hoping to build an impressive legislative record.

The Crisis of Expansion   Supported by solid majorities in both houses during the Twenty-ninth Congress (1845–1847), Polk suc-cessfully advanced the low-tariff and independent-treasury measures that Jacksonian orthodoxy dictated, while also conducting an active foreign policy that led to the northern boundary's projection to the Pacific along the forty-ninth parallel and to the acquisition of the Mexican cession. Polk, however, misread the sectional implications of these acquisitions and left his successors and Congress confronting a major crisis.

The legislators were faced with a host of difficult issues: Northern complaints about the presence of slavery and the slave trade in the District of Columbia; Southern complaints about the inadequacy of federal statutes mandating the return of fugitive slaves from Northern states; the problems of establishing the western boundary of Texas; the status of slavery in the newly acquired territory; and whether California was to be admitted as a free state. During the Thirty-first Congress (1849–1851), Henry Clay and other congressional leaders attempted compromise in a Congress where neither major party had a clear majority, and in the face of President Taylor's determination to bar slavery from the new western acquisitions. When the Kentuckian's omnibus bill failed, Stephen A. Douglas and others worked various compromise measures through the chambers, each bill receiving somewhat different majorities. In the end, California was admitted as a free state; residents in the Utah and New Mexico territories were allowed to decide the status of slavery, thus implementing the principle of squatter sovereignty; Texas was provided with an acceptable western boundary and reimbursed for surrendered claims on New Mexico; the slave trade, but not the institution of slavery, was eliminated in the District of Columbia; and a fugitive-slave law more acceptable to Southerners was provided. President Fillmore's cooperation facilitated the legislative process. Members of this Congress supported a "finality resolution," pledging that the Compromise of 1850—as these combined measures were called—was the final word on these matters.

The Crisis of Secession   During the 1850s recurrent economic depression and the increasing flow of immigrants threatened the livelihood of native-born workers. Nativism was becoming a potent national force, in contrast to its more restricted manifestations in earlier decades. Endeavoring to foster the building of railroads and settlements beyond the Missouri River, Stephen A. Douglas and his legislative colleagues revived the slavery issue when they won approval of the Kansas-Nebraska Act in 1854, establishing the Kansas and Nebraska territories and replacing the territorial formula of the Missouri Compromise with the concept of popular sovereignty. Although antislavery forces had been active in Northern politics during the 1840s, they were significant mainly for their diversion of votes from the major parties. With the passage of the Kansas-Nebraska Act the restriction of slavery's westward expansion became a major political issue—potent both as a moral and ideological cause and as a bread-and-butter issue. Northern farmers wished to preserve the West for freehold farming; laborers, both native and immigrant, feared the potential of the African American labor pool. The organization of anti-Nebraska or Republican-party tickets to contest the congressional elections of 1854 signaled the beginning of a national party realignment. In the Kansas Territory free-state and proslavery settlers clashed physically in guerrilla activity and sometimes even on the floor of constitutional conventions and legislative chambers: the South Carolina representative, Preston Brooks, once caned Charles Sumner at his Senate desk over the latter's "Crime against Kansas" speech, which bitterly attacked Southern slave-power conspiracy. Other inflammatory developments followed both within and without the Congress, including the Supreme Court's Dred Scott decision in 1857 that validated the right of slaveholders to take their bondsmen into free territory.

Strained beyond tolerance, the Whig party disintegrated and its Northern elements metamorphosed into the Republican party, which also incorporated significant numbers of antislavery Democrats, and nativist American party members, as well as smaller numbers of abolitionists. Rebellion spread among the Northern Democrats in the Congress as President Buchanan tried to force acceptance of a Kansas state constitution legitimizing slavery. From the Thirty-fourth (1855–1857) through the Thirty-seventh (1861–1863) Congresses significant numbers of men in both chambers were unaligned with the major parties. In all, four national tickets contested the presidential election of 1860. Although obtaining a minority of votes cast, Abraham Lincoln won this contest on a Republican platform that advocated a free Kansas and restriction of the spread of slavery, along with various developmental policies in the Whig tradition. By Lincoln's inauguration in March 1861 Southern states had seceded and war was imminent.

When the members of the Thirty-seventh Congress assembled in emergency session on 4 July 1861, Lincoln and the members of his administration had begun mobilization, proclaimed a blockade of the Southern coastline, and acted to suppress disloyalty in various areas. The war in the North, Lincoln informed the legislators, would be waged to save the Union. Members of the emergency summer session of 1861 confined their attention to war measures. But when the second session of the Thirty-seventh Congress met in December 1861, the Republican majority broadened its legislative activity. The members of standing committees found their work loads greatly increased and select committees labored on various fronts. Initially many representatives and senators assisted directly in the recruitment of troops in their states, with matters relating to the state regiments demanding their attention throughout the war. Place-seekers (job hunters), contractors, and constituents seeking special treatment besieged the federal lawmakers, who were pursued by lobbyists from the corridors of the Capitol to their boardinghouses.

The Thirty-seventh Congress was one of the most productive in the nation's history. In uneasy cooperation with Lincoln and his cabinet, its members created the budgets and other legislation necessary to mobilize the people and industries of the Northern states. In doing so they passed a major revision of the Militia Act of 1791, and in March 1863 Congress passed a federal conscription law. The Senate approved the appointments of legions of officers. Together the houses approved a direct levy on the states, an income tax, and a sweeping internal-revenue act. They approved bond issues and the issue of United States notes. Reacting to charges of fraudulent contracting, the Thirty-seventh Congress passed an elaborate statute to eliminate malfeasance in supplying the government's myriad needs.

The representatives and senators also produced an impressive array of other measures. Honoring the 1860 Republican platform and the homestead and transcontinental-railroad laws, they acted on the provision calling for a protective tariff. The National Banking Act restored the federal government to the national banking scene, as Congress sought to stabilize the banking system and stimulate the sale of government bonds by requiring the new banks to hold reserves against notes issued in government securities. To nurture agrarian interests, Congress adopted the Land Grant College Act of 1862, which provided for the organization of colleges of agriculture and mechanical arts, and a Department of Agriculture was created. This Congress also revised the federal judiciary system and provided the District of Columbia with a new legal code.

The lawmakers of the Thirty-seventh Congress admitted the free state of Kansas to the Union, abolished slavery in the District of Columbia and within the territories of the United States, and admitted West Virginia as a new state. Contention developed across and within party lines when Republicans, alleging military necessity, recommended measures threatening the institution of slavery in the loyal border states as well as in the Confederacy. The authorization provided in the Act to Amend the Militia Act of 1791 to use blacks in the military forces and the emancipation provisions of the confiscation acts passed in the first and second sessions were particularly divisive. During the third session, Congress specifically approved the enlistment of black soldiers. Pressed by radical senators and representatives, Lincoln issued the preliminary Emancipation Proclamations of September 1862 and its final form in January 1863.

Scholars have stressed that the Democratic minority provided a loyal opposition during the war. Nonetheless, members of both chambers expelled some who they believed to be traitors and considered charges of disloyalty against others. As demonstrated by Senator Jesse Bright's (D.-Ind.) expulsion on the basis of thin evidence and the near-escapes of Senator Benjamin Stark (D.-Ore.) and Representative Benjamin Wood (D.-N.Y.) from the same fate, the Republican majority would not tolerate anything less than complete fidelity.

The Thirty-seventh Congress girded the Northern states for war and resolved policy issues that had concerned a generation of national lawmakers. Their successors of the Thirty-eighth passed the additional legislation necessary to grind the Confederacy into subjection and amended or amplified important laws passed by its predecessors. The lawmakers of the second Civil War Congress were less productive than their predecessors, in part because much of the Republican program already had been written into law, and in part because there were significantly more Democrats in the fray. In addition, the lawmakers were to a greater degree moving into uncharted territory, mounting direct attacks on slavery and devising plans under which Confederate states might be brought back into the Union. The Thirty-eighth Congress passed the Thirteenth Amendment and provided for the organization of a Freedmen's Bureau to assist the freed blacks of the South, but Congress dissolved in March 1865 in deep disagreement with the chief executive over Reconstruction.

Although sorely tested, the system of republican governance created by the Founding Fathers survived the Civil War. Among the Northern states the electoral process continued without major challenge. Beginning early on in the war, however, radical Republicans in Congress faulted Lincoln's moderate course designed to keep the support of the loyal border states and his commitment to middle-of-the-road constitutionalism. Wishing to move rapidly toward emancipation and to punish Southerners harshly, and frustrated by recurrent military failures, radical Republicans aimed much of their criticism and investigative activity in the Congress at Lincoln's moderate cabinet members.

Major legislative confrontations between Lincoln and the radicals occurred when the president forced changes in the text of the Confiscation Act of 1862 and when he vetoed the Wade-Davis Reconstruction Act in 1864, preferring the gentler system of executive reconstruction that he had initiated in various Southern areas. The radicals led their colleagues in refusing to seat delegations from Southern states reconstructed under Lincoln's direction. Nonetheless Lincoln tried to work with all elements of his party; although radicals always constituted a majority among the congressional Republicans, the possibility that party moderates, border-state legislators, and Democrats might unite in voting on key measures forced compromise on controversial issues.

The Crisis of Reunion The crisis of the Civil War changed rapidly into a crisis over reunification. In the 1860s Lincoln had outlined a plan of reconstruction that required 10 percent of the voters in each ex-Confederate state to swear loyalty to the Union and to elect members for a convention that was to produce a new constitution. Though eminent Confederates were not to be forgiven immediately, Lincoln was prepared to pardon generously, restoring all rights in property—excepting slaves—to those involved. The Wade-Davis bill, however, required that 50 percent of the 1860 electorate attest to their loyalty, electors for the constitutional conventions swear they had never supported the Confederacy voluntarily, and delegates repudiate secession and abolish slavery. Other provisions safeguarded various civil rights of the freedmen.

Welcomed by radical congressional leaders as a kindred spirit, President Johnson disappointed the lawmakers by endorsing the Southern governments organized under executive aegis and by overusing his pardoning power. The radicals noted that the Southern governments Lincoln had approved were developing laws highly restrictive to blacks. The Republicans of the Thirty-ninth Congress (1865–1867) refused to seat Southern delegations, establishing a Joint Committee on Reconstruction that developed its own plans for reunification. Johnson vetoed an act extending the life and jurisdiction of the Freedmen's Bureau as well as a civil rights act designed to protect the Southern freedmen from intimidation. But the Congress prevailed and the Joint Committee steered the Fourteenth Amendment through both houses by mid-June 1866. Johnson unwisely took his differences with congressional Republicans into the campaign of 1866, after which the Northern electorate returned Republican majorities sufficient to override presidential vetoes.

Johnson's efforts to obstruct congressional reconstruction and defend his presidential prerogatives convinced radical Republicans that he should be impeached. The House Judiciary Committee reported against impeachment in 1867, but agitation against Johnson continued. Johnson's efforts to dismiss Edwin Stanton as Secretary of War, in contravention of procedures enunciated in the Tenure of Office Act, led the House in February 1868 to approve a resolution calling for impeachment. From early March to late May of 1868, the House managers argued the articles of impeachment that they had prepared before the Senate, with Salmon P. Chase, chief justice of the Supreme Court, presiding. In brief, the questions were these: Was it legitimate for a president to disobey a law to test its constitutionality? Did the Tenure of Office Act apply to Stanton, a Lincoln appointee? Could a president be impeached for an act that was not a crime in a court of law? There were enough Republican senators who believed impeachment unwarranted to deny Johnson's opponents the necessary two-thirds majority.

According to a modern authority, "the record of the impeachment process in Congress ... reached a nadir in the vindictive ordeal of Andrew Johnson" (Swindler, p. 24). Although the radical Republicans failed to impeach Andrew Johnson, they effectively asserted the dominance of Congress in the federal government. With initial support from Republican moderates and many Democrats, Johnson faced a situation by no means as hopeless as had been John Tyler's a generation earlier. But he drove most Republican moderates into the radical wing and aroused the hostility of the Northern electorate, which was seasoned with Union veterans.

As noted above, the Thirty-ninth Congress rejected the approach of Lincoln and Johnson to Reconstruction by renewing and strengthening the Freedmen's Bureau, passing a Civil Rights Act (1866) to safeguard the rights of freedmen, and enhancing the act's provisions by passing the Fourteenth Amendment. Their numbers enlarged in the congressional election of 1866, the congressional Republicans reimposed martial law on the Southern states and required the states to elect conventions by universal manhood suffrage (excepting ex-Confederates disqualified under the terms of the Fourteenth Amendment), conventions that would draft constitutions providing for black suffrage. The Southern states also were required to ratify the Fourteenth Amendment. When they failed to act, Congress passed supplementary legislation that authorized the federal military commanders in the South to implement the required constitutional provisions and allowed new state constitutions to be approved by a simple majority vote.

By June 1868 the Congress had readmitted to the Union seven states of the rebel Confederacy. Passage of the Fifteenth Amendment, which bars voter discrimination on the basis of race, followed in 1869 and in the next year Mississippi, Texas, and Virginia approved the Amendment and were readmitted. Although restored to the Union in 1868, Georgia was again put under military rule when it expelled black members from the state legislature. Subsequent to the restoration of the black lawmakers and ratification of the Fifteenth Amendment it was readmitted in July 1870. Efforts of white Southerners to restore their control by using violence led the Congress to pass the Ku Klux Klan acts of 1870–1871, designed to secure enforcement in the South of the Fourteenth and Fifteenth amendments. In 1872 the national lawmakers restored the civil rights of former state and federal officeholders or military personnel who had supported the Confederacy, excepting only the most prominent. After President Hayes removed federal troops from the South, problems there lost their urgency in the Congress. The Southern electorate, reconstituted by constitutional amendment and federal force, was now to be reshaped by intimidation and state law.

The congressional delegations whose members initially spoke for the returning Southern states were transitional groups. Highly diverse in social origins and composed of transplanted Northerners, Southern Unionists, and black leaders, they failed to survive popular elections once the U.S. Army left the South. Later, however, their members often obtained appointive federal posts when the Republicans held the White House. Both the Southern Republicans of the Reconstruction era and the Democrats who replaced them strongly supported economic measures that would aid in rebuilding the devastated Southern economy.

Although alignments varied on particular issues, Southerners tended to vote with westerners in the Congress rather than with Republicans from the northeast centers of capital and industry. Southerners complained of poor committee assignments, insensitivity to Southern needs for additional currency and tariff adjustments, the need for levee and channel improvements, lack of campaign funds, for example. When the Electoral Commission was weighing the claims of various presidential electors following the contest of 1876, some Southern legislators tried to negotiate terms for accepting a verdict favorable to Rutherford B. Hayes. The degree of Republican commitment to Southern developmental projects or the extent to which Southern congressmen felt bound by the parleying is unclear. Decisive in their grudging acceptance of the findings of the Electoral Commission, however, was the understanding that Hayes would restore home rule in the South.

The Republican effort to remake the political geography of the South was now over. The Republican party became anathema in the South, where methods of voter exclusion perfected during the next several decades produced monolithic Democratic control. In Congress the resultant increase in tenure was a precedent for the overall lengthening of the average congressional term by the close of the century. In the aftermath of war, old sectional alignments died hard. In 1877 a representative from Tennessee did chair the Appropriations Committee, but it was not until Charles F. Crisp of Georgia became Speaker in 1891 that a member from the Confederate heartland held a major leadership position in the House. And throughout, Congress continued to wrestle with monetary and fiscal problems rooted in Civil War policies and with other issues generated by an expanding and industrializing nation.

All of the great congressional crises of the era ran along the economic, institutional, and ideological fault lines separating the Northern and Southern states. At the root of each crisis were material issues, although leading actors on the political stage developed elaborate constitutional justifications for their positions. The first three major congressional crises—nullification, expansion, and secession—threatened the very existence of the Union, while the fourth—reunification—placed the constitutional balance of power in jeopardy. The events were complex, and one must carefully weigh the historical influence of any one or two actors in arriving at solutions. Although each crisis had unique characteristics, each helped set the stage for the next, and in each there was a complex interaction between the executive and legislative branches.

CONCLUSION

The challenges facing the national legislators during the years 1829–1881 reflected the ever-expanding area of the country, the mutual interactions of increasing technological change, urbanization, industrialization, immigration, and population, and the increasing diversity of regional and material interests represented in the Congress. Values also were changing and the imperative of events forced reconsideration of constitutional interpretations and regional positions. The institutions of politics as a whole—the nature of the electorates, the mode of representation, and in the ways in which elected representatives performed their duties —were all modified. Although no period in congressional history differs completely from another in terms of its institutional activity, this one is set apart by the extent of the partisan use of patronage, the establishment of precedent, the forging of unique work ways, and the building of self-identity. The various crises alone did not contribute solely to the process. One must bear in mind that the social charac-ter of the lawmakers themselves changed, albeit slowly, as did the methods by which they were recruited.

This era was a watershed in congressional development because the conflict between states' rights and centralization ostensibly ended with the affirmation of the powers of the central government. The implications of the postwar settlement, however, were to be problematic in both the nation and the Congress. Southern problems of race relations and economic dependency took on new form, and the new one-party South affected future congressional development in manifold ways. Political parties emerged as the great shapers of political and national development and as the dominant feature of the political landscape. In doing so they had greatly changed the nature of service in the U.S. Congress and were to change it still more in years to come.

BIBLIOGRAPHY

General Studies

A number of general studies of the U.S. Congress or its individual houses contain useful information concerning congressional development during the years 1829–1881. Notable among these are DeAlva S. Alexander, *History and Procedure of the House of Representatives* (Boston, 1916); Joseph Cooper, *The Origins of the Standing Committees and the Development of the Modern House* (Houston, 1971); Mary P. Follett, *The Speaker of the House of Representatives* (New York, 1896); George B. Galloway, *History of the House of Representatives*, rev. by Sidney Wise (New York, 1976); George H. Haynes, *The Senate of the United States: Its History and Practice*, 2 vols., (New York, 1938); and Lauros G. McConachie, *Congressional Committees: A Study of the Origins and Development of our National and Local Legislative Methods* (New York, 1898). Joel H. Silbey, *The American Political Nation, 1838–1893* (Stanford, Calif., 1991), provides useful background for any study of the Congress during this period.

Early Firsthand Accounts and Biographies

Many visitors to the Congress recorded their observations of congressional issues and proceedings in travel narratives or social analyses. Among the best of these for this period are Thomas Hamilton, *Men and Manners in America* (Philadelphia, 1833); Harriet Martineau, *Society in America*, 3 vols. (London, 1837); and Alexis de Tocqueville, *Democracy in America* (New York, 1961, edition), and de Tocqueville, *Journey to America*, J. P. Mayer, ed. (New Haven, Conn., 1960). Of accounts of congressional activity by participants during this period, the best are Thomas H. Benton, *Thirty Years View: or, A History of the Workings of the American Government for Thirty Years, from 1820 to 1850*, 2 vols. (New York, 1854–1856, repr. ed., Westport, Conn., 1968); James G. Blaine, *Twenty Years of Congress: From Lincoln to Garfield with a Review of the Events Which Led to the Political Revolution of 1860*, 2 vols. (Norwich, Conn., 1884); and James A. Garfield, "A Century of Congress," *Atlantic Monthly* 40 (July 1877): 49–64. The memorial eulogies given in the Congress for senators and representatives who died in office provide interesting insights; see, for example, *Memorial Addresses on the Life and Character of William Pitt Fessenden (A Senator from Maine,) Delivered in the Senate and House of Representatives . . .* (Washington, D.C., 1870).

THE U.S. CONGRESS, 1829–1881

Although there are fewer good biographies of mid-nineteenth-century senators and representatives available than desirable, some are excellent. See particularly: CHARLES G. SELLERS, *James K. Polk, Jacksonian, 1795–1843* (Princeton, N.J., 1957) and DAVID H. DONALD, *Charles Sumner and the Coming of the Civil War* (New York, 1960) and *Charles Sumner and the Rights of Man* (New York, 1970). Some older works are useful, including, for example, CHARLES H. JONES, *The Life and Public Services of J. Glancy Jones*, 2 vols. (Philadelphia, 1910).

Modern Studies

A number of authors approach aspects of the congressional history of this period from specialized perspectives. NELSON W. POLSBY, "The Institutionalization of the U.S. House of Representatives," *American Political Science Review* 62 (March 1968): 144–168, is concerned with the development of an institutionalized legislative body as were ALLAN G. BOGUE, JEROME M. CLUBB, CARROLL R. MCKIBBIN, and SANTA A. TRAUGOTT, "Members of the House of Representatives and the Processes of Modernization, 1789–1960," *Journal of American History* 63 (September 1976): 275–302. The emergence of the professional politician is the concern of H. DOUGLAS PRICE, "The Congressional Career Then and Now," in NELSON POLSBY, ed., *Congressional Behavior* (New York, 1971), 14–27 and "Congress and the Evolution of Legislative Professionalism," in NORMAN ORNSTEIN, ed., *Congress and Change: Evolution and Reform* (New York, 1975), 2–62. Another approach is provided by SAMUEL KERNELL, "Toward Understanding 19th Century Congressional Careers: Ambition, Competition, and Rotation," *American Journal of Political Science* 21 (November 1977): 669–693. DAVID W. BRADY related congressional change to electoral realignments in *Critical Elections and Congressional Policy Making* (Stanford, Calif., 1988). DAVID J. ROTHMAN discusses the acquisition and uses of power in *Politics and Power: The United States Senate, 1869–1901* (Cambridge, 1966).

Various authors have treated congressional procedures. Particularly useful are the following: JOSEPH COOPER and CHERYL D. YOUNG, "Bill Introduction in the Nineteenth Century: A Study of Institutional Change," *Legislative Studies Quarterly* 14 (February 1989): 67–105; GARRISON NELSON, "Change and Continuity in the Recruitment of U.S. House Leaders, 1789–1975," in NORMAN ORNSTEIN, ed., *Congress and Change: Evolution and Reform* (New York, 1975), 155–183; and MARVIN DOWNEY, "The Rules and Procedure of the United States House of Representatives, 1789 to 1949," Ph.D. diss., University of Chicago, 1952.

WILLIAM F. SWINDLER, "High Court of Congress: Impeachment Trials, 1797–1936," *American Bar Association Journal* 60 (April 1974): 1–25, and MARGARET S. THOMPSON, *The 'Spider Webb' Congress and Lobbying in the Age of Grant* (Ithaca, N.Y., 1986), consider the interaction of the Congress with the executive and the private sector.

The authors of specialized monographs treat important elements in the political history of the Congress during this period. Among such contributions are THOMAS B. ALEXANDER, *Sectional Stress and Party Strength: A Study of Roll Call Voting Patterns in the United States House of Representatives, 1836–1860* (Nashville, Tenn., 1967); ALLAN G. BOGUE, *The Earnest Men: Republicans of the Civil War Senate* (Ithaca, N.Y., 1981); WILLIAM E. GIENAPP, *The Origins of the Republican Party, 1852–1856* (New York, 1987); TERRY L. SEIP, *The South Returns to Congress: Men, Economic Measures, and Intersectional Relationships, 1868–1879* (Baton Rouge, La., 1983); and JOEL H. SILBEY, *The Shrine of Party: Congressional Voting Behavior, 1841–1852* (Pittsburgh, 1967).

We have been able to mention here only a few of the articles that are relevant to this essay in some respect and therefore refer the reader also to the collection of 356 articles on the history and operation of the United States Congress in JOEL SILBEY, ed., *The Congress of the United States, 1789–1989*, 23 vols. (New York, 1991).

SEE ALSO African American Legislators; Congressional Reform; The Historical Legislative Career; Legislating: Floor and Conference Procedures in Congress; Legislatures and Impeachment; The Motivations of Legislators; AND The Social Bases of Legislative Recruitment.

THE MODERNIZING CONGRESS, 1870–1930

Garrison Nelson

Reconstruction, the closing of the American frontier, the Spanish-American War, World War I, the stock market crash of 1929, and the Great Depression were the defining events of American life in the years between 1870 and 1930. The American Congress moved through those six decades, sometimes as the nation's dominant political institution, at other times not always sure of its power or of its capacity to deal with acute crisis. The years preceding the Civil War had revealed the difficulty of Congress in peacefully resolving national divisiveness on a grand scale, and the war itself raised questions about how effectively a legislative body could deal with a conflict that threatened the very existence of the nation.

The Congress had its triumphs in the decades between 1870 and 1930. In domestic policy it was most effective dealing with issues upon which negotiation was possible and time was available—currency reform, tariff revisions, economic development, appropriations, and taxes. Legislative solutions to changing economic circumstances involved the process of compromise and conciliation, which was the strength of the congressional arena. Nonnegotiable moral issues, such as slavery, and acute foreign policy crises necessitating unified command, such as wars, worked against the compromising tendencies of collective decision-making bodies such as the Congress.

CONGRESS IN TRANSITION

The years from Reconstruction to the Great Depression saw a number of conscious changes designed to enhance congressional responsiveness in a transforming United States. Some of the changes were internal to the Congress, such as more clearly defined roles for its leaders, more orderly leadership-succession systems, the greater specialization of the standing-committee structure and the growth of legislative staff. Other changes affected Congress in its dealings with the executive branch including more specific guidelines concerning the nation's finances and the refining of the executive-oversight function.

The Constancy of Change

The sixty years between 1870 and 1930 transformed the United States from a scattered rural and agricultural nation to a major urbanized industrial one experiencing the greatest economic growth and expansion of any country in modern history.

A bloody four-year civil war that left more than 620,000 soldiers dead had answered the question of whether or not a nation founded on principles of self-determination and freedom could exist with the institution of slavery. With slavery abolished, the United States resumed the journey of consolidation of its westward settlements and the urbanization of tens of millions of people which would change the nation and the North American continent forever. It was a time when the United States moved well beyond its relatively minor world status as a refuge for Europe's dispossessed to one of the world's premier economic forces and a model for the new nations of the twentieth century.

Another era and World War II were necessary for America to reach its apex of economic and military power. But none of this could have happened without the growth and development of American political structures from the highly fragmented and turbulent bodies that existed before the Civil War to the sophisticated and differentiated institutions they would become by 1930.

Five amendments were added to the Constitution during the six decades from 1870 to 1930; four of those amendments changed the

Congress. The Fifteenth Amendment (passed in 1870) guaranteed voter eligibility to black males and the Nineteenth (passed in 1919) extended it to women. The passage in 1913 of the personal income-tax amendment (the Sixteenth) provided Congress with a major new source of revenue that made possible government spending programs capable of redistributing the wealth of the nation's citizens between regions and population subgroups.

The amendment with the clearest impact on Congress was the Seventeenth, passed in 1913, which eliminated the indirect election of the U.S. Senate by the state legislatures and made the Senate directly elected by the people of the various states.

Most of the congressional changes of this era were accomplished through the auspices of the Republican party, which had successfully led the nation through the Civil War. It was the enormous economic and industrial power of the urban centers of the Northeast and the Midwest that gave the Union forces the might to win the war. But following the war, Republican leaders saw an immediate convergence of interest in the reconstruction of the South and the settlement of the West. To these enlightened mid-nineteenth-century politicians, commerce and progress coincided. What better way to heal the wounds of the Civil War than to encourage the individual entrepreneurial spirit and to further economic expansion? These forces would better the existence of the returning soldiers, the newly enfranchised blacks, and Southern farmers whose lands had been ravaged in the war.

Industrialism would unite the country and bind its wounds. And as the nation's single largest spender, Congress was uniquely situated to spur its industrialization and to develop its rich natural resources for export to the world. This was a time when the nation's economic agenda supplanted its social agenda.

Demographic Factors

Population Growth and Diversity The census of 1870 enumerated the population of the nation at slightly less than 40 million. This was the first census that did not include a slave category. In this enumeration, there were 5.4 million "Negroes" in the nation—a ratio of 6.3 whites for every black. Most of these were the former slaves whose destiny had played such a large part in the traumatic decades leading to the Civil War, but who would virtually disappear from the national political arena in the decades following it. The racial composition of members of the Congress reflected this shift— sixteen native blacks sat in the Congress during the 1870s; five in the 1880s and 1890s; but none between 1901 and 1929.

By 1930, the number of enumerated Americans would more than triple from the 1870 census's total to 122,775,046 in the continental United States. Much of the growth was due to immigration, which brought an increase in the degree of ethnic and religious diversity as well as an increase in population. The white immigrants from central, southern, and eastern Europe would swell the masses of the nation's cities and decrease their open spaces. But racial diversity declined as the nation's racial composition increased to 8.8 whites for every nonwhite.

Growth was particularly explosive in the metropolises of the Midwest. In the sixty years between 1870 and 1930, the population living in Chicago grew from 298,977 to 3,376,438; in Detroit, from 79,577 to 1,568,662; in Cleveland, from 92,829 to 900,429; in St. Louis, from 310,864 to 821,960; in Milwaukee, from 71,440 to 578,249; and in Cincinnati, from 216,239 to 451,160. By 1920, four of the nation's six largest cities were in the Midwest.

These newer metropolises, which had earlier been forced to occupy positions of deference to the eastern cities of New York, Philadelphia, Boston, and Baltimore, became the centers of a revitalized American economy. Their convenient access to the nation's agricultural heartland and their own burgeoning industrialization gave them positions of economic and political power. Thanks to the congressionally sponsored growth of the railroads and the development of a transportation infrastructure along the Great Lakes, the Midwest prospered and blossomed in this era.

The House grew by 198 seats from the 1850 census through the 1930 census. Almost 40 percent of this growth came from the Midwest—76 seats in all. The industrializing east north-central states—Ohio, Indiana, Illinois, Michigan, and Wisconsin—accounted for 42 seats while the more agricultural west north-central states of Iowa, Minnesota, Kansas, Missouri, Nebraska, and the Dakotas added another 34 seats to the mix. (See Table 1.)

The controlling Republican party took note of this shift as both the presidency and the speakership came to be dominated by the men of the Midwest.

Economic Factors: Transportation and Commerce

The years following the Civil War were characterized by immense economic expansion and marked most dramatically by the construction of the railroads that transformed the western landscape of "wide-open spaces" into an elaborate steel network of resource development and commercial enrichment.

In 1870, 5,658 miles of railroad track were built—the highest annual number of new miles recorded to that date. Twelve times in the next twenty years, more than 5,000 new miles were added annually to the nation's railroads. In 1887 alone, 12,878 miles were constructed. Seventy-four percent of the railroad miles that were ever built were constructed by 1900. The urban landscape was similarly transformed by the bridges, roadways, and subways designed to move the nation's millions of new industrial workers in and out of the cities.

In 1900 only 8,000 automobiles were registered. Thirty years later, that figure jumped to 26,749,853—an increase 3,344 times that of 1900. The technological transfer of the nation's transportation sector from its railways to its highways was in full swing by 1930.

The gross national product of the 1869–1873 period was averaged by Simon Kuznets at 6.71 billion dollars annually. By 1929, the year of the stock market crash, that number stood at 104.4 billion. The per-capita growth in those sixty years increased from $165.00 in the 1869–1873 period to $857.00 on the eve of the 1929

Table 1
HOUSE APPORTIONMENT BY REGION, 1860–1930

Region	House Seats by Selected Census							
	1860		1890		1910		1930	
	Number	Pct.	Number	Pct.	Number	Pct.	Number	Pct.
New England	27	11.1	27	7.6	32	7.4	29	6.7
Middle Atlantic	61	25.1	73	20.4	92	21.1	94	21.6
Northeast	88	36.2	100	28.0	124	28.5	123	28.3
East North-Central	56	23.0	79	22.1	86	19.8	90	20.7
West North-Central	19	7.8	50	14.0	57	13.1	47	10.8
Midwest	75	30.9	129	36.1	143	32.9	137	31.5
Solid South	53	21.8	80	22.4	94	21.6	93	21.4
Border	22	9.1	31	8.7	41	9.4	39	9.0
South	75	30.9	111	31.1	135	31.0	132	30.3
Mountain	1	.4	6	1.7	14	3.2	14	3.2
Pacific	4	1.6	11	3.1	19	4.4	29	6.7
West	5	2.1	17	4.8	33	7.6	43	9.9
Totals	243		357		435		435	

Note: Due to rounding, not all totals equal 100.0 percent.
Regions are defined as follows:
New England (Conn., Me., Mass., N.H., R.I., Vt.)
Middle Atlantic (Del., N.J., N.Y., Penn.)
East North-Central (Ill., Ind., Mich., Ohio, Wisc.)
West North-Central (Iowa, Kans., Minn., Mo., Neb., N.D., S.D.)
Solid South (Ala., Ark., Fla., Ga., La., Miss., N.C., S.C., Tex., Va.)
Border (Ky., Md., Okla., Tenn., W.Va.)
Mountain (Ariz., Colo., Ida., Mont., Nev., N.M., Utah, Wyo.)
Pacific (Calif., Ore., Wash.)

Source: Seat numbers come from U.S. Congress, *The Biographical Directory of the American Congress, 1774–1989* (Washington, D.C., 1989), p. 47. The regional divisions are those used by the Interuniversity Consortium for Political and Social Research at the University of Michigan.

crash. The percentage growth of the gross national product was more than four times (13.6) greater than the growth of the nation's population (3.1). Prosperity had been broadened rather than narrowed by increases in population.

Despite the steady growth of these indicators of economic expansion, uncertainty persisted. Swings in the economy from prosperity to depression occurred in each of the decades from 1870 to 1930, particularly those of the 1870s and 1890s. Legislative solutions were regularly proffered by Congress to insulate the nation (or electorally significant portions of it) from financial hardship. Among these solutions was currency reform. The battles between the forces of hard and soft currency were often decided at the ballot box when good financial times would favor creditors eager to be repaid in hard currency and the poor financial times when the economically distressed were able to mount majorities for supporters of soft currency. The gold-silver bimetallism debate of the 1890s was the most dramatic of the currency conflicts but it was not the only one of the era.

The Civil War's Prelude to Congressional Modernization
The Congress was affected greatly by the Civil War decade of the 1860s. Three developments that were prefatory to the modernizing era included: (1) the 1863 selection of nominees for the House speakership in separate party caucuses; (2) the creation of the standing committees of Appropriations in the House in 1865 and in the Senate in 1867; and (3) the congressional impeachment trial of President Andrew Johnson in 1868.

In the decade before the war, multiballot conflicts on the House floor to fill the House speakership had tied up congressional business for weeks and sometimes months as internal party mechanisms had failed. In 1863 the two major House parties began to rely regularly upon the caucuses before each Congress convened to nominate candidates for Speaker of the House. Moving the conflicts between rival members of the same party for leadership from floor contests to the caucus room eliminated multiballot speakership contests and provided the presiding officer with near-unanimity from his own party—a small but clear sign of growing party discipline.

The war's extraordinary financial pressures made particularly heavy demands upon the House Ways and Means Committee, which was legislatively responsible for the nation's fiscal policy, consisting of both revenue and spending measures. Dividing the budgetary power into revenue functions and spending functions was essential during the war as Congress scrambled to find the funds and gain the credit it needed to cover the mounting debts it incurred equipping and feeding a massive one-million-man army. It was especially difficult in the midst of a major disruption of the nation's industrial output. In order to deal with growing financial responsibilities, the House in 1865 created the Appropriations Committee from Ways and Means. Thaddeus Stevens (R.-Penn.) moved from the chair of Ways and Means to assume the initial chairmanship of Appropriations.

Two years later in 1867, the Senate made a similar effort and created its own Appropriations Committee. In 1869, the Senate followed the House's lead as Senator William Pitt Fessenden (R.-Me.) moved from chairing the tax-writing Finance Committee to chair Appropriations. The two Appropriations Committees gained the primary congressional power to oversee federal spending.

Presidential-congressional relations were most influenced later in the decade by the successful effort of the Radical Republicans in the House in 1868 to bring impeachment charges against President Andrew Johnson. Johnson's failing was his insufficient commitment to the Reconstruction-era policies that the Radical Republicans had promulgated. The legal technicality used was Johnson's "violation" of the Tenure of Office Act by his firing of Secretary of War Edwin Stanton without congressional approval. The real concern among Republicans in the Congress was to prevent the seceded states from imposing statutory restrictions—the Black Codes—on the recently freed slaves, which would have returned them to a degree of servitude. However, the impeachment failed by a single vote in the Senate to convict Johnson and have him removed from office, but the seriousness of the effort made future presidents wary of congressional power.

The modernizing Congress built off these changes in committee differentiation and leadership selection. The next decades saw further refinements in the congressional leadership structure and its committee system. In the words of James L. Sundquist in *The Decline and Resurgence of Congress* (1981), the last third of the nineteenth century would become "the golden age of congressional ascendancy" (p. 25).

1870–1895: DIVIDED GOVERNMENT

The House of Representatives

Electoral Politics The Republicans, the party of the Union, organized the House for eight consecutive Congresses from 1859 until 1875. Apart from the Civil War Congresses, the Republican majorities were not large.

The first cracks in post–Civil War Republican party hegemony occurred in the election of 1874. Democratic Representatives elected from the returning Southern states, combined with the growth of urban electorates, enabled the House Democrats to organize eight of the Houses in the following ten Congresses from 1875 to 1895.

A deep economic recession in President Grant's second term and intraparty bickering over flagrant pension scandals within the administration gave the Democrats control of the House of Representatives in the 1874 election for the first time since 1856. This placed them in a position where they could speed the departure of Northern troops from the Southern states and return their fellow partisans to seats in the Congress.

The evenness of party competition in the House reflected the extraordinarily tight series of contests for the presidency in the elections marking the end of the Reconstruction and its aftermath. Only one Republican presidential candidate won a popular-vote victory (Garfield in 1880) in the five elections from 1876 to 1892. However, the Republican-controlled Electoral Commission of 1877 installed Governor Rutherford B. Hayes of Ohio as president, and an Electoral College fluke gave the White House to Republican Benjamin Harrison of Indiana in 1889.

With party control of the presidency in relative turmoil, it was not surprising to find that in the eleven Congresses elected from 1874 to 1894, party control of the House alternated between the two major parties five times. Only three of the eleven Houses (27 percent) were organized by the party that simultaneously held the presidency and the Senate. (See Table 2.)

Third-party politics played an intermittent role throughout this era with the soft-money Greenbackers able to capture some House seats in the 1870s. But the most successful of the third-party movements was the Populist party of the early 1890s, which gained a number of House seats in the agricultural plains and the silver-rich regions of the new western states.

House Leaders and Party Organization

James G. Blaine of Maine, "The Plumed Knight," was the most dominant House politician of the immediate post–Civil War Congresses. Born in Pennsylvania, Blaine relocated to northern New England in early adulthood. Blaine was a protégé of Thaddeus Stevens (R.-Penn.), with whom he served on the House Appropriations Committee and whose leadership he followed in the effort to impeach President Johnson.

Like Stevens, Blaine understood that directing the reconstructed nation could be best managed through the spending power of the Congress. Blaine became Speaker of the House in 1869 when General Ulysses S. Grant chose as his vice-presidential running mate the relatively young and vaguely competent Speaker Schuyler Colfax (R.-Ind.).

Blaine was made of greater resolve and intellect. He took control of the House and placed his friends in key positions of power. During his six years as Speaker (1869–1875), he used the power of committee assignments to consolidate Republican gains in the House and to further the goals of the commercial interests of the Northeast. This was most evident in the case of the Appropriations Committee where his best friend and closest political ally, James Garfield of Ohio, was seated as chair (1871–1875). Blaine's fusion of commercial and political power gave the Republicans a guaranteed source of financial support in congressional elections, but it opened the door to potential scandals. Blaine was personally impli-

Table 2
PARTY-SEAT PERCENTAGES AND FLOOR-PARTY VOTING IN THE U.S. CONGRESS, 1871–1897

Election Year	Congress	Presidential Administration	House Seats Rep.				Senate Seats Rep.				Floor-Party Voting	
			R.	D.	Other	Pct.	R.	D.	Other	Pct.	House	Senate
1870	42d	Grant (R.)	134	104	5	55.1	52	17	5	70.3	74	na
1872	43d	Grant (R.)	194	92	14	64.7	49	19	5	67.1	73	na
1874	44th	Grant (R.)	109	169	14	37.3	45	29	2	59.2	71	na
1876	45th	Hayes (R.)	140	153	—	47.8	39	36	1	51.3	73	65
1878	46th	Hayes (R.)	130	149	14	44.4	33	42	1	43.4	76	74
1880	47th	Garfield (R.)/ Arthur (R.)	147	135	11	50.2	37	37	1	49.3	69	81
1882	48th	Arthur (R.)	118	197	10	36.3	38	36	2	50.0	65	64
1884	49th	Cleveland (D.)	140	183	2	43.1	43	34	—	55.8	67	63
1886	50th	Cleveland (D.)	152	169	4	46.8	39	37	—	51.3	53	78
1888	51st	Harrison (R.)	166	159	—	51.1	39	37	—	51.3	83	80
1890	52d	Harrison (R.)	88	235	9	26.5	47	39	2	53.4	43	59
1892	53d	Cleveland (D.)	127	218	11	35.7	38	44	3	44.7	47	72
1894	54th	Cleveland (D.)	244	105	7	68.5	43	39	6	48.9	70	56

Sources: The seat numbers and percentages are adapted from Congressional Quarterly, *Guide to U.S. Elections,* 2d ed. (Washington, D.C., 1985), pp. 1116–1117. The party-vote (50 percent of one party opposing 50 percent of the other party) data come from Jerome M. Clubb and Santa A. Traugott, "Partisan Cleavage and Cohesion in the House of Representatives, 1861–1974," *The Journal of Interdisciplinary History* VII (Winter 1977): 382–383; and Patricia A. Hurley and Rick K. Wilson, "Partisan Voting Patterns in the U.S. Senate, 1877–1986," *Legislative Studies Quarterly* XIV (May 1989): 225–250. Additional data were provided by Patricia A. Hurley.

cated in the "Mulligan Letters" railroad scandal, and Garfield narrowly escaped prosecution in the Crédit Mobilier incident, in which influential members of the House were given underpriced stock in a Union Pacific holding company in exchange for their legislative support of the railroad's expansion.

The House Democrats were led through much of the 1870s by Samuel J. Randall of Philadelphia, an urban protectionist in a rural free-trade party. Randall successfully parlayed his chairmanship of the House Appropriations Committee into the speakership upon the untimely death in 1876 of Michael Kerr of Indiana, the first post–Civil War Democratic Speaker.

As Speaker in 1880, Randall transformed the House Rules Committee from a select procedural body into an effective policy-making agent of the leadership by placing himself at its helm and making it a standing committee of the House. Prior to Randall's speakership, the Rules Committee had existed as a standing committee for only two prewar Congresses (1849–1853). Randall put this committee to-

gether with only five members, three from the majority and two from the minority. With the Speaker as its chair and accompanied by senior members of the Ways and Means and Appropriations committees, the Rules Committee controlled floor business until the 1910–1911 revolt against Speaker Joseph G. Cannon (R.-Ill.).

The political reintegration of Southern Democratic members moved slowly at the start of the 1870s, but when Randall gave the chairmanship of the Appropriations Committee to John D. C. Atkins (D.-Tenn.) in 1877, Randall gained the loyalty of many newly seated Southern Democrats. Their support enabled Randall to become the first Democratic Speaker elected three times since Andrew Stevenson of Virginia (1827–1834).

Randall was displaced as Democratic House leader in 1883 by John G. Carlisle (D.-Ky.) but he surrendered little of his power as he returned to chair the Appropriations Committee. Writing in his classic analysis of the time, *Congressional Government,* after Randall had resumed the chair, Professor Woodrow Wilson concluded in 1885 that "all [House chairmen] are subordinate to the chairman of the Committee on Appropriations."

House Republicans suffered under the lackluster leadership of J. Warren Keifer of Ohio and they replaced him in 1885 with Thomas B. Reed of Maine. Although Reed came from the same state as James G. Blaine, he and Blaine were cordial with each other but not politically close. Reed was a protégé of Senator William Pitt Fessenden, a leader of the Senate's Civil War moderates, and the Bowdoin College roommate of the senator's son, Sam. Reed was elected speaker once the Republicans regained control of the House in 1889 and is considered to have been the most powerful of the post–Civil War Speakers. An acerbic wit and portly body made him a favorite of both the political humorists and cartoonists of the day.

The "Reed Rules" It was under Reed that House rules were dramatically changed. To thwart the small Republican majority in the late 1880s, Democratic members of the House used obstructionist tactics to slow legislative business to a crawl. The most obvious tactic of the Democratic minority was not responding to a roll call. When the number of responding members fell below half the House's membership, a member would arise and call for an adjournment based on the lack of a quorum. The "disappearing quorum" was regularly used to delay Republican tariff and currency measures. Reed eliminated this practice by ordering the clerk to record the names of all members who could be seen in the hall of the House but who refused to answer the roll call. Democrats, indignant over this move, would head for the lobby. Reed then ordered that the doors be locked. One member, Constantine ("Kicking Buck") Kilgore (D.-Tex.), kicked the door open so as to escape the Speaker's recitation of his name. These actions and his marked disdain for motions that he refused to entertain and peremptorily ruled out of order earned for Reed the nickname of "Czar."

The vote to institutionalize the "Reed Rules" took place on 14 February 1890. By a vote of 161–144, the House adopted the rules, which provided that a quorum would consist of those present in the chamber; that one hundred would constitute a quorum in the Committee of the Whole; that the Speaker could disallow motions that he considered dilatory; and that the Committee of the Whole could close debate on any paragraph or section of a bill under consideration.

Membership The composition of the House became more professionalized during the years following the Civil War as the mean terms of service rose dramatically from 1.92 terms (3.84 years) in 1875 to 2.65 (5.30 years) by 1893—a relative increase of 38 percent.

The Northeastern states gained only twelve House seats—a relative percentage drop from 36.2 percent to 28.0 percent—between 1860 and 1890. The Midwest, which gained 54 House seats—a relative percentage increase from 30.9 percent to 36.1 percent—emerged as both the nation's largest region and the source of its leading politicians. The South maintained its relative numeric position in the House— 30.9 percent of the seats in 1860 and 31.1 percent in 1890.

Floor Voting Roll-call voting patterns on the floor of the House indicated a clear break along party lines. The twelve Congresses between 1871 and 1895 reported a median of 70 percent of the floor votes cast divided along the lines of opposing party majorities. Party voting reached as high as 83 percent in the Fifty-first Congress (1889–1891) led by Speaker Reed early in Benjamin Harrison's presidency.

Committee Structure Committee growth in the House during these Congresses was steady. There were forty-five standing and select committees with 370 places in the Forty-second Congress (1871–1873)—an average of 1.52 places per member. By the Fifty-third Congress (1893–1895), the number of committees had grown to fifty-five and the number of places to 666—an average of 1.87 places per member.

Among the standing committees added to the House during these years were War Claims, Civil Service Reform, Rivers and Harbors, Interstate and Foreign Commerce, and Alcoholic Liquor Traffic. But only two of the 1871–1893 additions—Rules (1880) and Merchant Marine and Fisheries (1887)—have continued to the 1990s.

Congressional Staffing and Support The most telling statistic of congressional change in this era was the enormous increase in the legislative payroll. In 1871 there were only 618 federal legislative employees. Within ten years the number had quadrupled, to 2,579 in 1881 and to 3,867 by 1891. A more professional congressional membership required larger support services in the Library of Congress and staff posts.

The Senate

Electoral Factors   The Senate was an exception to the competitiveness of this era. It was consistently, if not overwhelmingly, Republican in the years between 1870 and 1894 with Republicans capturing the Senate eleven times out of thirteen (85 percent). Only the elections of 1878 and 1892 had Democrats winning the Senate.

Five of the Congresses convened with a Democratic Speaker and a Republican Senate. Divided-party control of the Congress in this era was attributable to two major factors. Republicans dominated a disproportionate number of small states, such as the five in New England—Connecticut, Maine, New Hampshire, Rhode Island, and Vermont. These states combined sent fewer than half the number of Representatives to the House than the neighboring state of New York but five times the number of senators. However, with one exception, every Senate election in these states between 1868 and 1908 was won by a Republican. New England's small states gave the Senate Republicans a solid base of ten seats throughout the era prior to the passage of the Seventeenth Amendment.

The other factor giving Republicans power in the Senate, but not in the House, was related to the rural-dominated and malapportioned state legislatures, which elected the Senate at the time. Many of these state legislatures were often susceptible to pressures from commercial interests and accommodated them by returning more Republicans than Democrats to the Senate.

Senate Leaders and Party Organization
The years following the Civil War marked a relative decline in the Senate's political prestige if not in its power. In 1874, Charles Sumner of Massachusetts, the last of the giants of the pre–Civil War Senate, died. The newer senators were much more in the model of New York's dapper Republican Roscoe Conkling. Less interested in social betterment, they were ambitious and eager to protect their political bases

with patronage appointments. This was what Mark Twain would call the Gilded Age.

The Senate's loss of luster was owed, in part, to the emergence on the national agenda of narrow commercial issues such as currency reform and railroad expansion and also the ongoing debate over civil-service reform. Unlike the pre–Civil War debates over slavery and the maintenance of the Federal Union, the post–Civil War issues lacked moral passion and eloquence was seldom forthcoming.

Strong personalities continued to populate the Senate, such as John Sherman (R.-Ohio), author of the Sherman Antitrust Act of 1890, and Arthur Pue Gorman (D.-Md.), the longtime leader of the Democrats. However, others left the Senate out of frustration. In 1881 former House Speaker Blaine left the Senate after five years to become secretary of state. After his years in the House, Blaine found himself very exasperated by the arcane rules of the "other body," which permitted egotistical senators such as Conkling, his despised fellow Republican, to use unlimited debate to delay national business interminably in order to pursue their local interests. The ever-sardonic "Czar" Reed observed at the time that the Senate was the place where "good Representatives go when they die."

Thus, it was not surprising that during the last quarter of the century, no single member or faction assumed a consistent leadership role. As Woodrow Wilson observed in *Congressional Government* (1885): "No one is *the* Senator. No one may speak for his party as well as for himself; no one exercises the special trust of acknowledged leadership. The Senate is merely a body of individual critics."

Membership   Another source of the Senate's relative loss of prestige was due to the arrival in Washington of a number of senators whose elections from the state legislatures had been engineered by political bosses and industrial robber barons who expected federal patronage and contracts in return. Owing their elections to strong party organizations back home, these newer senators were very eager to demonstrate the depths of their partisanship and to consolidate their state's "machines."

Even without its spoilsmen and partisans, the late-nineteenth-century Senate was a very difficult body to lead. Born out of the fierce egalitarianism among the several states which marked the American Revolution, the Senate's structure worked against cooperation.

Committee Structure   The Senate's collection of committees grew throughout this period from 27 standing and 4 select committees in the Forty-second Congress (1871–1873) to 46 standing and 13 select committees in the Fifty-third Congress (1893–1895). In 1871, 197 committee places were filled by 74 senators —an average of 2.7 places per senator. By the Fifty-third Congress in 1893, 84 senators were assigned to 459 committee places—an average of 5.5 each. There were more Senate committees than there were majority members to chair them. Senate committee power was far more fragmented than that of the House.

Among the standing committees added to the Senate roster were Civil Service and Retrenchment (1873), Census (1887), Interstate Commerce (1887), and Pacific Railroads (1893). Few of the 1871–1893 additions survived the 1923 Senate committee reorganization and only Agriculture and Forestry (1884), among this era's new committees, survived the 1946 reorganization.

Executive-Legislative Relations

Divided government and the relative institutional weakness of the presidency disrupted party continuity and created major difficulties for the presidents in developing coherent legislative agendas. Republican presidents Ulysses S. Grant, Rutherford B. Hayes, James A. Garfield, and Chester A. Arthur (from the years 1869– 1885) were reluctant to confront Congress.

Conflict between Congress and the presidency became more pronounced with the inauguration of Grover Cleveland in 1885. In the twelve years between 1885 and 1897, President Cleveland, a Democrat, and Benjamin Harrison, a Republican, vetoed 628 bills between them —a rate of rejection of legislation that was more than three times the total of 203 in the nation's first ninety-six years.

Because of the frequency of divided government and the possibility of an assassin's bullet reversing the outcome of an election, the Presidential Succession Act of 1886 took congressional officers such as the Senate President pro tempore and the Speaker of the House out of the line of succession and placed the officers of the cabinet right below the vice

president. President Garfield's assassination in 1881 by the rejected office seeker Charles Guiteau, a member of an opposing Republican faction, inspired that legislation. The Pendleton Act of 1883 which reformed the Civil Service to lessen patronage appointments also derived its impetus from that murderous event.

Major Legislation

Bringing an end to Reconstruction shaped the social-policy legislation of the era under discussion. In an effort to reintegrate those white Southerners who had fought in the War, the Amnesty Act was passed in 1872. It removed political and civil disabilities from all Southerners except those who held major political rank in the Confederacy. The Civil Rights Act of 1875 attempted to guarantee access to jury duty and public accommodations for the newly freed blacks. However, once full Southern representation in Congress was established, these issues disappeared from the legislative agenda. And it was not until 1964 that another Civil Rights Act guaranteeing minority access to public accommodations was passed.

People of "color" did not seem to benefit from legislation in this era. The Western territories were opened for white settlement through the combination of the Chinese Exclusion Acts of 1882, 1884, and 1892 and in efforts to break tribal hegemony over Native Americans in the Dawes Severalty Act of 1887, which "bought" Native Americans off the land, and the establishment of the Oklahoma Territory in 1890 from land that had belonged to the Five Civilized Tribes.

Post–Civil War economic dislocations led to surpluses and depressions. The major source of governmental revenue was the tariff. There was a rhythm to tariff reform, veering from Republican high-tariff protectionism to Democratic tariff reductions. The rhythm related to political factors as well as to currency ones. When party control of both houses of Congress and the presidency was united, tariff reform was more likely because the respective institutions presumably agreed upon its intended beneficiaries.

The reductionist Dawes Tariff of 1872 was reversed by the Tariff of 1875 that restored the high Morrill Tariff rates of 1861 and other increases. The Tariff Commission of 1882 created by Congress suggested lowering duties by 25 percent, but the "Mongrel" Tariff of 1883 reduced rates by only a net of 5 percent. This was followed by the highly protectionist McKinley Tariff of 1890, which raised rates by almost 50 percent and imposed the first duties ever on agricultural products. The era closed with the Democratic Wilson-Gorman Tariff of 1894, that lowered rates by almost 40 percent. The revenue shortfall was to be made up with a federal income tax, which was declared unconstitutional by the Supreme Court a year later in *Pollock* v. *Farmers' Loan and Trust Co.,* 158 U.S. 601 (1895).

Currency questions were resolved most often in favor of "hard-money" creditors rather than "soft-money" debtors. The Coinage Act of 1873 discontinued the widespread coinage of silver dollars while the Specie Resumption Act of 1875 reduced the value of "greenbacks" in circulation. Democratic congressional gains and the efforts to counter economic depression led to the passage of the Bland-Allison Act of 1878 which made silver legal tender. The growth of western-state representation led to the Sherman Silver Purchase Act of 1890 which confirmed a bimetallist monetary policy.

The unbridled capitalism of the late nineteenth century had its casualties among small businessmen and farmers who needed to ship their products along the railways to eastern markets. Two pioneering pieces of federal legislation were designed to help these groups. The first was the Interstate Commerce Act, which created the Interstate Commerce Commission in 1887 to monitor railroad rates. Although not initially powerful, it would become the prototype for other congressionally created federal regulatory commissions. The other was the Sherman Anti-Trust Act of 1890, authored by Senator John Sherman of Ohio, which sought to prevent the concentration of economic power and regulate unfair business practices.

1895–1911

The House of Representatives

Electoral Politics   The election of 1894 gave the House Republicans a resounding net gain of 117 seats—a 92-percent increase over the preceding Congress. Combined with their gain of 32 seats in the 1892 election, the Re-

publican party had almost tripled its numbers in the House from the 88 seats following the 1890 disaster to 244 in just four years. The Fifty-fourth Congress was the first of eight consecutive Congresses that the Republicans controlled. For the next sixteen years, there was no partisan division between the House and the Senate in these Congresses.

William McKinley's presidential victory in the 1896 election, combined with the Republican congressional landslide two years earlier, ended the twenty years of divided government and led to the emergence of the Republican-dominated "fourth party system." The presidency and the House would remain in the same partisan hands, if not the same philosophical ones, for the next fourteen years.

For the congressional Democrats, it was a disastrous combination of financial depression and party factionalism which crippled them early in the 1890s. Southern and western Democrats, caught up in the Populist fervor of the times, were led by Representative William Jennings Bryan of Nebraska. Bryan, who would be nominated for president in 1896, 1900, and 1908, was a spokesman for the agricultural Midwest and the silver miners of the Mountain states. He blamed many of the nation's problems on eastern banks and urban immigrants. In so doing, his campaigns mobilized the West but antagonized eastern voters leading to the Democratic party's self-isolation from the popular votes of the nation's largest cities and the electoral votes of its largest states.

The election of 1896 was memorable for many reasons. Earlier that year, the Supreme Court decided to legalize racial segregation in the "separate but equal" case of *Plessy* v. *Ferguson,* 163 U.S. 537 (1896). This eventually led to the disenfranchisement of Southern blacks in those states where they still could vote. With Republican blacks steadily removed from the voting rolls, Democratic landslides in the South were assured. Also, the regional East-West conflict fostered in this election led to the creation of large one-party multistate enclaves that lowered overall turnout and resulted in more competitiveness between regions than within them. This was what Walter Dean Burnham called "the system of 1896." (See Table 3.)

Third-party seats swelled to forty in the Fifty-fifth Congress (1897–1899). But the fusion of the Populist program within the Bry-

Table 3
PARTY-SEAT PERCENTAGES AND FLOOR-PARTY VOTING IN THE U.S. CONGRESS, 1897–1911

Election Year	Congress	Presidential Administration	House Seats Rep.				Senate Seats Rep.				Floor-Party Voting	
			R.	D.	Other	Pct.	R.	D.	Other	Pct.	House	Senate
1896	55th	McKinley (R.)	204	113	40	57.1	47	34	7	53.4	79	76
1898	56th	McKinley (R.)	185	163	9	51.8	53	26	8	60.9	75	77
1900	57th	McKinley (R.)/										
		T. Roosevelt (R.)	197	151	9	55.2	55	31	4	61.1	67	76
1902	58th	T. Roosevelt (R.)	208	178	—	53.9	57	33	—	63.3	90	79
1904	59th	T. Roosevelt (R.)	250	136	—	64.8	57	33	—	63.3	74	66
1906	60th	T. Roosevelt (R.)	222	164	—	57.5	61	31	—	66.3	57	65
1908	61st	Taft (R.)	219	172	—	56.0	61	32	—	65.6	80	80

Sources: The seat numbers and percentages are adapted from Congressional Quarterly, *Guide to U.S. Elections,* 2d ed. (Washington, D.C., 1985), pp. 1116–1117. The party-vote (50 percent of one party opposing 50 percent of the other party) data come from Jerome M. Clubb and Santa A. Traugott, "Partisan Cleavage and Cohesion in the House of Representatives, 1861–1974," *Journal of Interdisciplinary History* VII (Winter 1977): 382–383; and Patricia A. Hurley and Rick K. Wilson, "Partisan Voting Patterns in the U.S. Senate, 1877–1986," *Legislative Studies Quarterly* XIV (May 1989): 225–250. Additional data were provided by Patricia A. Hurley.

anite Democratic party led to the virtual disappearance of third-party politics from the House by the turn of the century.

House Leadership and Party Organization Republican gains in the House in the election of 1894 led to the return of "Czar" Reed to the chair in 1895. This ascension was marked by another change in House party organization. Reed greatly valued party discipline on the House floor and to maintain it in the Fifty-fourth Congress (1895–1897), he appointed James A. Tawney of Minnesota to be the first Republican party whip. Borrowed from the British Parliament and based on a hunting term, the whip is responsible for making sure that there are enough party members on the floor at the time of a key vote to guarantee victory for the party.

Prior to that time, whips were appointed on an ad hoc basis with responsibility for specific roll calls. Tawney was followed as whip in 1905 by James E. Watson of Indiana, and since then the position has become a permanent post among the House Republicans and has subsequently been adopted by the other congressional parties.

Like many other House Republican floor leaders of this era, such as Colfax, Blaine, and Garfield, Reed entered the presidential arena. However, Reed's quest for the 1896 Republican presidential nomination ended when he fin-

ished a dismal second, 577 votes behind William McKinley, the governor of Ohio and onetime chair of the House Ways and Means Committee. Reed had appointed McKinley to chair the Ways and Means in 1889 and was not pleased when the highly protectionist McKinley Tariff of 1890 contributed substantially to the loss of 78 seats in the House, including McKinley's own.

Following McKinley's inauguration in 1897, Speaker Reed found himself in the uncomfortable position of having to deliver House votes for presidential programs that he did not favor. Clearly, the power that he had enjoyed while leading the congressional opposition to Democratic president Grover Cleveland had been severely diminished. The outbreak of the Spanish-American War in 1898 led to a rupture between McKinley and Reed, and the Speaker left the chair in 1899 in opposition to both the war and the annexation of Hawaii.

Republican senators, who had just recently organized themselves, took advantage of the turmoil among the House Republicans and helped the speakership candidacy of David B. Henderson (R.-Iowa). Henderson's passivity as Speaker (1899–1903) enabled the Senate to gain ground relative to the House. Henderson's speakership ended in 1903 amid a flurry of rumors of bad health and the shadow of a scandal involving a senator's daughter.

Henderson's successor was Joseph G. ("Uncle Joe") Cannon of Illinois who chaired the House's powerful spending committee, Appropriations. Cannon was sympathetic to Reed and appreciated Reed's efforts to preserve the power of the House speakership both with regard to the chamber itself and relative to the Senate and the presidency. In 1903 Cannon became Speaker and used his power of committee assignments, the chairmanship of the Rules Committee, and control over the floor to further the fortunes of his fellow conservative Republicans. These actions brought him into conflict with many insurgent members of his own party and also with President Theodore Roosevelt, a Republican of a different philosophical cast.

Leading the minority House Democrats were relatively junior southerners such as Joseph W. Bailey of Texas, James D. Richardson of Tennessee, and John Sharp Williams of Mississippi. Electoral reversals had lessened the size and effectiveness of the House Democrats and had forced them back into their southern enclaves to find leaders.

The Cannonites felt very secure in their power and asserted themselves in very arbitrary ways, particularly in the assignment of committee places. However, times had changed.

The Revolt Against Speaker Cannon
By 1909, Progressive Era constitutional amendments such as the popular election of the Senate and the imposition of a federal income tax had successfully moved through the state legislatures. To many House members, the leadership of Speaker Cannon and his lieutenants, Sereno Payne (R.-N.Y.) and James Tawney (R.-Minn.), was hopelessly out of touch with the times. The insurgent midwestern Republicans, led by George Norris of Nebraska and John Nelson of Wisconsin, believed that their party's philosophical agenda had become too narrow in scope and too self-protective of its leadership.

House membership had became more senior. The Sixty-first Congress (1909–1911), Cannon's last as Speaker, was made up of only 23 percent freshmen. This meant that three-quarters of the House had come to appreciate the benefits of seniority and were not willing to let an arbitrary and capricious Speaker deprive them of those benefits.

Speaker Cannon's power over committee assignments derived from the First Congress (1789–1791), when the House decided it was easier to give the Speaker the power to name committee members than to have time-consuming floor votes to fill the slots.

Studies of committee seniority in the House indicate that Cannon's overall removal rate of chairs, while not unusually high, differed from those of his predecessors in that it increased as his speakership continued. As Nelson Polsby, Miriam Gallaher, and Barry Rundquist discovered, "Cannon committed a higher proportion of violations on major and semi-exclusive committees after his first term than any Speaker . . . more post–first-term violations of the seniority of incumbents than anyone, . . . and more uncompensated violations after his first term than anyone" (p. 801).

Speaker Cannon used his assignment power to punish progressive Republicans and to divide the Democrats. But at the close of the Sixtieth Congress in 1909, the House adopted Calendar Wednesday in an effort to permit committee bills to come to the floor. This reform and the adoption of the Consent Calendar, which gave individual members an opportunity to move consideration of bills, were attempts to limit Cannon's control of the floor.

The new leader of the Democrats, James B. ("Champ") Clark of Missouri, allied himself with the insurgent Republicans to topple Cannon's autocracy. In a series of moves beginning on 16 March 1910, the insurgent Republicans and their allies in the Democratic party voted to enlarge the Rules Committee from five members to ten, to remove the Speaker from the Rules Committee, to eliminate his power to name committee chairs, and to assign other members to committees. In an effort to regain control of the House, Cannon attempted to have the speakership declared vacant, but he was rebuffed as the House voted to keep him in his much-diminished office.

Champ Clark's efforts to exploit the breach within Republican ranks had a more personal political dimension. Clark had hoped to be nominated as president, and it was clearly in his long-term interest to weaken the power of the speakership lest he find himself, as president, hamstrung by a strong Speaker. This alliance of dissident Republicans and the Democrats forever altered the power of the speakership.

Membership
The regional composition of the House was relatively unaffected by census returns from 1890 through 1910. The Mid-

west remained the largest region (32.9 percent of House seats) relative to the South (31.0 percent) and the Northeast (28.9 percent). However, within the regions, the urbanizing states such as Massachusetts, New York, Pennsylvania, Illinois, and Missouri gained at the expense of their rural regional neighbors.

House seniority was on the rise as a result of the regional stabilization of the party system and as more members chose to move their families to Washington. This made them more electorally secure and less tolerant of the abuses of "Cannonism." Members of the Fifty-fourth Congress elected in 1894 had already served an average of 2.25 terms (4.50 years) in the House but by the Sixty-first Congress, elected in 1908, average previous service had lengthened to 3.84 terms (7.68 years).

Committee Structure   By 1909, the fourth and final House over which Cannon presided, the number of committees had increased from 55 in 1894 to 62 and the number of places available had grown from 666 to 812—an average of 2.08 places per member.

Among the standing committees added to the House roster during these years were four Elections Committees; Insular Affairs, to deal with the Hawaiian and Philippine islands; and Census. None of these survived the 1946 committee reorganization intact.

Party Voting   The most distinctive feature of this era was the prevalence of party voting on roll calls. It was during Cannon's speakership in the Fifty-sixth Congress (1903–1905) that party voting reached a high of 90 percent as opposing majorities of the two major parties found little agreement. The median percentage of party-divided roll-call votes in the eight Houses between 1895 and 1911 was 74.5 percent—the highest incidence of party voting ever recorded in the House.

The Senate

Electoral Politics   The Senate remained safely in control of the Republican party from 1894 until Woodrow Wilson's election in 1912. Republican senators comprised more than 60 percent of the membership for six consecutive Congresses in this era (1899–1911). Republicans were able to consolidate their power in the Northeast and the industrial Midwest and to gain the majority of Senate seats elected by the seven new states added to the Union between

1889 and 1896—Idaho, Montana, North Dakota, South Dakota, Utah, Washington, and Wyoming. From 1895 to 1911, Republican senators held 78 percent of these new seats.

The Democrats were primarily confined to their southern and border-state enclaves as a number of Populist and independent senators were seen as the more credible challengers to Republicans in the Plains and Mountain states. Democratic gains outside the South in the 1900s came at the expense of third-party senators, not the Republicans.

Senate Leadership and Party Organization   By the 1890s, Republicans in the Senate had finally recognized the need for some semblance of leadership structure. Historian David J. Rothman contends that it was the poker-playing gatherings at the Washington home of Senator James McMillan (R.-Mich.) that led to the initial creation of formal floor-leadership posts. Republican Senators William B. Allison of Iowa, Nelson Aldrich of Rhode Island, Orville Platt of Connecticut, and John Coit Spooner of Wisconsin chose the post of Republican caucus chairman to provide party leadership. In 1897, Senator Allison assumed the post and used it to provide legislative direction for the party.

Each of the others took his turn in time as chair of the Republican caucus, but it was Nelson Aldrich who was to emerge as this era's *primus inter pares,* or the first among equals. His fiscal agenda, with its commitment to gold-backed hard currency, would be the dominant Republican position on this issue.

The Democrats were clearly outnumbered throughout these Congresses and relied heavily upon their southern and border-state core to find their leaders. Only twenty-six Senate Democrats sat in the Fifty-sixth Congress (1899–1991). Their preeminent spokesman throughout the 1890s was Arthur Pue Gorman of Maryland, a protégé of Senator Stephen A. Douglas (D.-Ill.), who was occasionally able to thwart Aldrich with the support of the silver Republicans. During the first decade of the twentieth century, the diminished Senate Democrats were led by Joseph C. S. Blackburn of Kentucky, Charles A. Culberson of Texas, and Thomas S. Martin of Virginia. However, only Senator Gorman was ever considered a match for the Republican powerhouses.

Membership   The composition of the Senate underwent changes as well. The closing of the frontier in the 1890 census, which historian Frederick Jackson Turner saw as a major turning point in American history, had a direct impact on the Senate. The seven states that entered the Union between 1889 and 1896 contributed only eight new members to the House, a slight increase of 2.3 percent, but they added 14 new members to the Senate, a sizable increase of 18.4 percent.

These states had been carved out of the silver-rich Rocky Mountains and sent to the Senate men with a commitment to improve the lot of the region's silver miners. With their new compatriots from the Dakotas, they also sought to help the financially distressed farmers. The clubbiness of the Senate was jeopardized by these men of the West.

Committee Structure   Although the Senate's leadership structure had gained some coherence, its committee system lurched dangerously out of control. By 1911, the ninety-two senators in the Sixty-first Congress served in 700 places on 71 separate committees—an average of 7.6 places per senator, which was an average gain of 2.1 committee places per member in less than twenty years and 4.9 places in forty years.

The largest growth of Senate standing committees occurred in 1909 when eight of the executive-oversight expenditures committees were converted from select to standing committees.

The Senate added new committees on the University of the United States (1896), Relations with Cuba (1899), the Philippine Islands (1899), the Pacific Islands and Puerto Rico (1899), and Coast and Insular Survey (1899). None of these survived the committee reorganization in the Sixty-seventh Congress (1921–1923) and only Interoceanic Canals (1899) made it to 1946.

Presidential-Congressional Relations   An aggressive foreign policy greatly changed the nature of the U.S. political process. The Spanish-American War of 1898 brought the United States into the Age of Imperialism. The successful efforts of the American military in annexing the remains of Spain's crumbling empire in the Caribbean Sea and the Philippines had long-term domestic ramifications on American politics.

In the U.S. political system, the president is granted preeminence in matters of foreign policy, and the legislative body that gains most from that concern is the Senate with its power to approve treaties and confirm ambassadors. Senate attention fastened upon the opening of the Pacific to American investors, the extension of U.S. influence from the Hawaiian to the Philippine islands, the control of the Caribbean Sea, and the growing debate about constructing an interoceanic canal through Central America.

McKinley gained politically from the Spanish-American War and his reelection in 1900 was the first successful continuation in the White House since Grant's reelection in 1872. Both of his immediate successors, Theodore Roosevelt, the hero of the Battle of San Juan Hill in Puerto Rico, and William Howard Taft, who administered the postwar fortunes of the Philippines, were beneficiaries of this shift in national attention.

President Theodore Roosevelt's expansive personality led him to involve himself in a host of domestic issues such as antitrust legislation and labor-management disputes, and the resolution of international conflicts such as the Russo-Japanese War, for which he won the 1906 Nobel Peace Prize. His photogenic smile and indefatigable energy made the presidency the center of government power. Roosevelt's immense presence clearly detracted from the nation's awareness of congressional politics.

Woodrow Wilson, the president of Princeton University from 1902 to 1910 who had lamented the weakness of presidential authority in the 1880s, now saw the presidency as the major engine of change.

Major Legislation   On the economic front, tariff and currency questions continued to dominate. The highly protectionist Dingley Tariff of 1897 imposed the highest duties ever assessed to that time. As foreign policy became more important to America's role in the world, tariffs were lowered in the Payne-Aldrich Tariff of 1909. By 1900, silverite sentiments had declined and it became possible to pass the Gold Standard Act (1900), which placed gold as the standard of American currency.

Regulatory activities grew as the Hepburn Act of 1906 empowered the Interstate Commerce Commission to fix uniform railroad rates. Also that year, the Meat Inspection and the Food and Drug acts were passed to deal with meat-packing abuses discovered by "muckraking" journalists.

THE MODERNIZING CONGRESS, 1870–1930

As the United States became more involved in international affairs, the Congress passed the Teller Amendment (1898) recognizing Cuban independence from Spain; the Hawaiian Annexation Act (1898); the Foraker Act (1900) establishing a civil government in Puerto Rico; the Hay-Pauncefote Treaty (1901), in which Britain gave the United States the right to build a canal across the Isthmus of Panama; the Hawaiian Organic Act (1900); the Platt Amendment (1901) regulating Cuba's external relations; the Spooner Amendment (1901) establishing civil government in the Philippines; and the Hay-Bunau-Varilla Treaty (1904), which confirmed American diplomatic hegemony over the Panama Canal Zone.

The restrictive social policies of the previous era prevailed and little that was new happened apart from the creation of the Bureau of Immigration and Naturalization, which standardized the naturalization procedures of the increased number of immigrants.

Institutional Support   The growth of legislative personnel continued throughout these years. By 1911 there were 5,902 federal legislative employees—almost a tenfold increase over the 618 employees reported in 1871. Many were employed within the Library of Congress. However, enough were employed as staff to warrant the construction of the House Office Building (later to become the Cannon House Office Building) in 1905 and the Senate Office Building (renamed the Russell Senate Office Building) in 1906. These were concrete monuments to the growing institutionalization of the Congress.

1911–1919: WILSON AND THE GREAT WAR

The House of Representatives

Electoral Politics   Conflict within the Republican party erupted when it became clear that President William Howard Taft had little of the reformist spirit of Teddy Roosevelt. Taft's apparent philosophical capture by the Republican party's more ardent conservatives jeopardized party control of the House. Democrats took advantage of the discord and gained a slight edge in the 1910 elections. It was their first congressional victory of any sort since 1892 when they were brought into office on the coattails of Grover Cleveland.

Four House elections were won by the Democrats in this decade. Building upon their initial victory in 1910, the Democrats had a resounding success in 1912 as the Taft-Roosevelt conflict spilled into contests for the House. They also were able to capture the Senate and hold it for three consecutive elections, the first time that had happened since the 1850s. (See Table 4.)

Third-party House seats were held primarily by Progressives in these Congresses but only in the Sixty-fifth (1917–1919) did they hold enough seats to tilt the balance between the two major parties.

House Leadership and Party Organization   The House Democrats elected "Champ" Clark to be Speaker in 1911. Ironically, Clark found himself presiding over the House from an office that he had helped to emasculate.

Table 4
PARTY-SEAT PERCENTAGES AND FLOOR-PARTY VOTING IN THE U.S. CONGRESS, 1911–1919

Election Year	Congress	Presidential Administration	House Seats Rep.				Senate Seats Rep.				Floor-Party Voting	
			R.	D.	Other	Pct.	R.	D.	Other	Pct.	House	Senate
1910	62d	Taft (R.)	161	228	1	40.3	51	41	—	55.4	60	56
1912	63d	Wilson (D.)	127	291	17	29.2	44	51	—	45.8	62	73
1914	64th	Wilson (D.)	196	230	9	45.1	40	56	—	41.7	58	60
1916	65th	Wilson (D.)	210	216	6	48.6	42	53	—	44.5	45	44

Sources: The seat numbers and percentages are adapted from Congressional Quarterly, *Guide to U.S. Elections,* 2d ed. (Washington, D.C., 1985), pp. 1116–1117. The party-vote (50 percent of one party opposing 50 percent of the other party) data come from Jerome M. Clubb and Santa A. Traugott, "Partisan Cleavage and Cohesion in the House of Representatives, 1861–1974," *Journal of Interdisciplinary History* VII (Winter 1977): 322–323; and Patricia A. Hurley and Rick K. Wilson, "Partisan Voting Patterns in the U.S. Senate, 1877–1986," *Legislative Studies Quarterly* XIV (May 1989): 225–250. Additional data were provided by Patricia A. Hurley.

By this time, the Speaker had lost his power to name all of the committee members, and a reconstituted Rules committee had excluded the Speaker from its membership. Command of the House floor was lost to Speakers with the establishment of the Consent Calendar for minor bills; the discharge petition for legislation blocked in committee; and Calendar Wednesday.

Speaker Clark accepted the new constraints of his office and concentrated instead on obtaining the 1912 Democratic nomination for president. Party changes in the presidency had often been preceded by changes in party control of the House of Representatives, and Clark wished to position himself for that likely eventuality. However, Clark's ambitions were blocked by Woodrow Wilson, the governor of New Jersey, and he had to preside over a House that answered to the legislative agenda of his presidential rival. Unlike "Czar" Reed, Speaker Clark remained loyal to the policies of his party and its president.

The Democratic caucus emerged as the legislative force within the House and the chair of the Ways and Means Committee, Oscar W. Underwood (D.-Ala.), as its leading actor. For the next eight years (1911–1919) the Democrats elected the chair of the Ways and Means Committee as floor leader. This move gave the majority leader independence from the Speaker. With the post-Cannon speakers unable to make committee assignments, the Democratic members of the Ways and Means Committee became the "committee on committees" for the Democratic party. Concerns that members had about the arbitrariness of committee assignments were resolved to some degree by the strengthening of the "seniority system," which automatically elevated the majority members with the longest continuous service to chairmanships.

Also in 1911, the minority leaders of the House were clearly identified for the first time in official documents. Prior to that time, the minority leadership was associated with the minority party's losing candidates for Speaker. Since 1911, all minority floor leaders have been elected within their caucuses to represent their party's interests on the floor. And for most of this time, they have not served on any of the House's standing committees, thereby separating their jobs from the committee system.

The leader of the House Republicans throughout these eight years in the minority was James R. Mann of Illinois, a protégé of Joe Cannon and the author of the Mann Act (1910), which prohibited the transportation of women across state lines for immoral purposes.

Membership Following the 1910 census, the membership of the House was stabilized at 435, a number that has remained constant for more than eighty years. The post-1910 reapportionment remained in place for twenty years, permitting the regions that had gained in population to consolidate power.

The arrival of millions of European immigrants to the cities of the Atlantic Seaboard led to an increase of 19 seats for the Middle Atlantic states between 1890 and 1910. It was the largest growth for any region and it tilted the politics of the nation toward its urbanizing areas.

Although seniority had become more important, the average number of terms already served by House members increased only slightly from 3.62 (7.24 years) of those members elected in 1910 to 3.83 (7.66 years) of those elected in 1916.

Committee Structure The number of House committees remained at around sixty and committee places hovered at 850, slightly less than two for each House member. The stability of House committee places contrasted dramatically with the unchecked growth of Senate committees during this era. The only standing committees added to the House roster with any continuity were Roads (1913), Flood Control (1916), and Woman Suffrage (1917).

Party Voting Fewer roll-call votes divided along party lines during the Wilson administration than in those of his predecessors. Opposing-party majorities appeared in 62 percent of the House roll calls in his first Congress—the Sixty-third (1913–1915)—and dropped to only 46 percent in his last Congress—the Sixty-sixth (1919–1921). The diminished speakership and the loss of its power to enforce party discipline through committee assignments is cited by David Brady as a major reason for the decline in House partisanship.

The Senate

Electoral Politics As the power of the House declined with the diminution of the speakership, the Senate gained. The passage of the Seventeenth Amendment in 1913 altered the relationship between the House and the Senate. The popularly elected Senate made its politics more similar to that of the House. From the Sixty-third to the Seventy-first Congresses (1913–1931), the House and the Senate were ruled by the same majority parties. Both chambers were now subject and accountable to the same electoral forces.

The Seventeenth Amendment had little direct impact on renominated incumbents, as all twenty-three senators previously elected by the state legislatures won popular-vote victories in 1914. However, political change was already in process as the seats that came open fell to the resurgent Democrats.

From 1910 through 1914, Democrats made a net gain of twenty-four seats in the Senate. It was a nationwide trend as Democratic seats were won in the Republican strongholds of Maine and New Hampshire as well as in the urbanizing states of New York, Illinois, Ohio, and Missouri.

New rules for admittance to the exclusive Senate changed the nature of its role and that of its leaders.

Senate Leadership and Party Organization

In 1913, John Worth Kern of Indiana became the new leader of the Senate Democrats. With President Wilson's help and urging, Kern changed both the direction of the floor leadership and the course of the Senate. Kern had been the Democratic vice-presidential nominee in Bryan's third ill-fated presidential campaign in 1908. As a result, he was more sympathetic to presidential prerogatives in legislation than had been his predecessors among Democratic floor leaders. In her analysis of their relationship, in "Origin and Development of the Party Leadership in the United States Senate" (*Capitol Studies*, 1974), Margaret Munk argued that

> the Kern-Wilson alliance established one of the most important precedents in the history of Senate leadership. Never before had the president's party in the Senate, backed by the president's approval and perhaps his direct influence, intentionally elected a floor leader for the primary purpose of implementing an executive-initiated legislative program.

Kern, who was only a third-year senator at the time, set a precedent for ignoring seniority in the choice of a floor leader. The "seniority rule," which placed the majority committee member with the longest continuous service at the helm of Senate committees, was apparently waived in the case of the floor leaders. The Wilson legislative agenda in the Senate benefited from Kern's astute guidance.

It was also under Kern that the Senate Democrats began to identify and fill the post of party whip continuously. James Hamilton Lewis of Illinois was chosen in 1913 to assist Kern. Two years later, the first Republican whip, James Wadsworth, Jr., of New York, was selected.

Wadsworth served for only one year under New Hampshire's Jacob Gallinger, who led the Republican minority from 1913 to 1919. Wadsworth was succeeded by Charles Curtis (R.-Kans.) who would serve as whip for nine years, 1915–1924, and later become Majority Leader (1924–1929) and Herbert Hoover's vice president (1929–1933).

Membership

The Senate's membership stabilized at ninety-six with the admission of Arizona and New Mexico to the Union. Senate changes in this era were not attributable to the admission of new states.

Progressive reformers had hoped for years that the Seventeenth Amendment's requirement of popularly elected senators would dramatically alter the membership of the Senate, but its initial impact was less than expected. While the Senate elections of 1914, the first under the amendment, may have continued all renominated incumbents in office, retirements increased and the nature of the membership changed.

In 1913, Maryland Democrat Blair Lee became the first senator elected after the ratification of the Seventeenth Amendment. Other Democrats who entered the Senate in the 1911–1914 period were to shape the institution for years to come. The new southerners such as Joseph Robinson of Arkansas, Hoke Smith of Georgia, former House Minority Leader John Sharp Williams of Mississippi, and Morris Sheppard of Texas were more electorally sophisticated than their predecessors from the Confederacy.

In addition to Indiana's John Kern, elected in 1910, and Illinois's Ham Lewis, elected in 1912, other talented new Democrats who understood the Senate's new electoral politics were James Reed of Missouri, Thomas J. Walsh of Montana, Gilbert Hitchcok of Nebraska, and Key Pittman of Nevada, all of whom would play a role in the modernization of the Senate.

Committee Structure The pace of committee growth slowed as the only new standing committees added to the Senate were Expenditures in the Department of Commerce and Labor (1912), which was separated in 1914, and Banking and Currency (1913). But there were no reductions.

The *Congressional Directory* of December 1917 reported that the ninety-six senators of the Sixty-fifth Congress served in 772 places on 75 separate committees—an average of 8.04 places per senator. Senator James D. Phelan (D.-Cal.), the chair of Irrigation and Reclamation of Arid Lands, served on eleven committees. He was not unusual: nine other senators had at least ten committee assignments. The Senate's committee system strained under its multiple memberships and overlapping jurisdictions.

Party Voting As had happened in the House, party differentiation on roll-call voting declined. However, the drop in the three Democrat-controlled Senates of President Wilson was less steep than that in the House. The 1913–1919 Senate average for party voting was 59 percent—a drop of only 11 points from the 70 percent recorded in Theodore Roosevelt's three Republican Senates (1903–1909). The House rates changed more dramatically from 73.7 percent (1903–1909) to 55.0 percent (1913–1919).

Presidential-Congressional Relations President Wilson, whose original model for effective governance had been the British parliamentary system, saw that the revitalized presidency and enforceable party discipline in the Congress could create a de facto responsible party government. To demonstrate his commitment to legislative involvement, Wilson revived the practice of delivering the State of the Union Address in person to a joint assembly of both houses of Congress. President Thomas Jefferson had abandoned the practice more than a century earlier and his nineteenth-century successors had followed the example. Wilson sought to tie his prestige to a specific legislative agenda; in this way, he opened the door for the executive-driven legislative agendas of the modern Congress.

Major Legislation Progressive gains in both Congress and the White House led to an expansion of legislative activity. Regulatory policies appeared in a number of forms. The Mann-Elkins Act of 1910 placed communications under the control of the Interstate Commerce Commission. In 1914 the Federal Trade Commission was created to outlaw unfair methods of business competition. The Clayton Act of 1914 prohibited price discrimination intended to diminish competition.

The Federal Reserve Bank Act of 1913 brought the federal government into the banking business for the first time since the time of Andrew Jackson. It created the Federal Reserve Board, which was able to alter the supply of money through adjustments to the discount rate for member banks.

Revenue measures shifted from tariffs to taxes with the passage of the Sixteenth Amendment in 1913. With a new source of federal revenue, the Underwood-Simmons Tariff of 1913 was able to lower the overall average of duties from the 38 percent of Payne-Aldrich to less than 30 percent. And it contained new levies on annual incomes more than $2,000.00. Changing major revenue sources from tariffs to taxes greatly augmented the federal government's cash flow. In 1910, internal-revenue receipts accounted for $289,934,000—42.9 percent of total government receipts. By 1915, the figure had grown to $415,670,000—59.6 percent of the total. And wartime revenue measures pushed the total take from taxes to $5,405,032,000—80.7 percent of the total.

Corporations came under greater legislative control in 1914 with the passage of the Federal Trade Commission Act, which established the FTC and regulated advertising; and the Clayton Antitrust Act, which prohibited price discrimination, gave injured parties the right to sue through the FTC, and limited the use of court injunctions to outlaw labor union activities. Another major piece of labor legislation was the Adamson Act of 1916, which established the eight-hour workday and provided for overtime wages for laborers on interstate railroads.

During the early phases of the war in Europe, President Wilson was able to gain from the Congress a series of defensive legislative measures, including the Coast Guard Act of 1915, which created that service; and the National Defense Act of 1916, giving the president greater control over the National Guard, establishing officer-training programs at colleges, and approving the construction of airplanes. The Senate authorized the purchase of the Virgin Islands from Denmark in 1916 and passed the Jones Act (1916) which gave more autonomy to the government of the Philippine Islands.

The Impact of the First World War With the outbreak of war in Europe in 1914, pressure upon the United States to become involved was immense. Emissaries from Great Britain and France hoped fervently for American participation, while emissaries from Germany, Austria-Hungary, and Italy were equally desirous of continued U.S. neutrality.

Congress felt this pressure directly. Within both of the congressional parties, factions supporting involvement and neutrality emerged. President Wilson was justifiably fearful that this intraparty conflict would disrupt his legislative agenda, and he hoped that the conflict would be contained by Speaker Clark and Democratic floor leaders Underwood in the House and Kern in the Senate.

Underwood's departure from the House for the Senate in 1915 left the Democratic party's reins in the hands of Claude Kitchin of North Carolina, whose support for the Wilson agenda was not so committed. Wilson's own narrow reelection victory over Charles Evans Hughes in 1916 and the loss of some key Democratic members of Congress had weakened the party's position in the House.

Wilson's goal of "armed neutrality" as a way of keeping the United States out of the war ended in April 1917, when the nation joined the side of Great Britain and France. War was declared on 4 April 1917 by a vote of 82–6 in the Senate, and two days later the House agreed, 373–50.

Wartime Legislation A series of wartime acts approved by Congress in 1917 included the Liberty Loan Act for financing the war; the Selective Service Act for providing registration and classification of men between ages 21 and 30; and the Lever Food and Fuel Control Act, giving the president the power to ration foodstuffs and fuel. The War Revenue Act of 1917 greatly increased corporate and personal income taxes for the war effort.

Legislation affecting civil liberties included the Trading With the Enemy Act (1917), the Espionage Act (1917), the Sabotage Act (1918), and the Sedition Act (1918). Dissent and antiwar protests were sharply curtailed with these legislative acts. The Federal Bureau of Investigation, originally created in 1908, used these acts to broaden its mandate and to investigate a number of citizens who opposed the war.

Congress itself was not immune from such sentiments, and on three occasions the House tried to prevent the seating of Victor L. Berger, an elected Socialist from Wisconsin, who had challenged American involvement in the conflict.

Congress's cooperation with the war effort led to further financial assistance through the War Finances Corporation with money for banks to loan to war industries. Further executive authority was granted by the Overman Act of 1918, which gave the President the power to reorganize the bureaucracy of the executive branch for more efficient prosecution of the war, and by the Railroad Control Act of 1918 which created a government-appointed director general for the nation's railroads. Congress thus acted quickly and unhesitatingly to provide President Wilson with the authority and the revenues that he felt were necessary for the war effort.

1919–1931: THE RETURN OF THE REPUBLICANS AND THE RETREAT FROM POLITICS

The House of Representatives

Electoral Politics The victory for the Allied forces in 1918 resulted in a personal triumph for President Wilson on the international stage but a political disaster at home. In spite of the successful conclusion to the war, both chambers of Congress fell to the Republican party in the 1918 election.

The congressional election of 1918 broke the slender hold that the Democrats had on the houses of Congress. Agricultural policy disagreements in the Sixty-fifth Congress (1917–1919) split the Democratic party between its southern and western wings in the election and led to the Republicans' recapture of both chambers of Congress. They would hold the

House until 1931 and the Senate until 1933. (See Table 5.)

Congressional Democrats made substantial gains in the 1922 off-year election and were poised to capitalize on the obvious ethical inadequacies of the Harding administration. But Harding died late in 1923 and removed a clear target from Democratic sights. With the succession of Calvin Coolidge, a flinty Vermonter and incorruptible former governor of Massachusetts, the smell of scandal had been removed from the administration and the Democrats fell into disarray.

Coolidge's decision not to run in 1928 opened the Republican presidential nomination for Secretary of Commerce Herbert Hoover. Democrats rallied behind their clear front-runner, New York's Governor Alfred E. Smith, the first Roman Catholic to receive a major party nomination. However, the nation was not ready to abandon religious prejudice. As a result, anti-Catholicism swelled Republican electoral vote totals as five states of the Old Confederacy joined traditional Republican strongholds in the Midwest and Northeast.

Hoover's first Congress, the Seventy-first (1929–1931), which convened on 4 March 1929, found the Republicans with 61 percent of the House seats and 58 percent of the Senate seats. But before the year was out, the stock market great crash and the ensuing Great Depression helped make that Congress the last one in this century with that commanding degree of Republican control.

House Leadership and Party Organization   Upon resuming their majority status in the House in 1919, Republicans were eager to avoid a repeat of the autocratic Joe Cannon era, which had cost them control of the chamber eight years earlier. The Republican caucus rejected the speakership candidacy of Cannon's protégé, James R. Mann of Illinois, the party's minority leader in the previous eight years. Instead, they installed a phlegmatic Massachusetts member of the Appropriations Committee, Frederick Gillett, in the speakership, and after an angry Jim Mann rejected the offer, Franklin Mondell, a relatively obscure Wyoming member, was named majority floor leader.

After his election as floor leader, Mondell abandoned his seat on the Appropriations Committee. The modern majority leadership, elected independently of the Speaker and separated from the standing-committee system, stems from this era.

The speakership of Gillett was challenged by liberal and moderate Republicans following the 1922 House elections. Republicans remained in control of the House, but their mar-

Table 5
PARTY-SEAT PERCENTAGES AND FLOOR-PARTY VOTING IN THE U.S. CONGRESS, 1919–1935

Election Year	Congress	Presidential Administration	House Seats Rep.				Senate Seats Rep.				Floor-Party Voting	
			R.	D.	Other	Pct.	R.	D.	Other	Pct.	House	Senate
1918	66th	Wilson (D.)	240	190	3	55.4	49	47	—	51.0	46	64
1920	67th	Harding (R.)	301	131	1	64.5	59	37	—	61.5	60	76
1922	68th	Harding (R.)/ Coolidge (R.)	225	205	5	51.7	51	43	2	53.1	59	47
1924	69th	Coolidge (R.)	247	183	4	56.9	56	39	1	58.3	45	44
1926	70th	Coolidge (R.)	237	195	3	54.5	49	46	1	51.0	53	42
1928	71st	Hoover (R.)	267	167	1	61.4	56	39	1	58.3	59	66
1930	72d	Hoover (R.)	214	220	1	49.2	48	47	1	50.0	59	40
1932	73d	F. Roosevelt (D.)	117	310	5	27.1	35	60	1	36.5	73	68

Sources: The seat numbers and percentages are adapted from Congressional Quarterly, *Guide to U.S. Elections,* 2d ed. (Washington, D.C., 1985), pp. 1116–1117. The party-vote (50 percent of one party opposing 50 percent of the other party) data come from Jerome M. Clubb and Santa A. Traugott, "Partisan Cleavage and Cohesion in the House of Representatives, 1861–1974," *Journal of Interdisciplinary History* VII (Winter 1977): 322–323; and Patricia A. Hurley and Rick K. Wilson, "Partisan Voting Patterns in the U.S. Senate, 1877–1986," *Legislative Studies Quarterly* XIV (May 1989): 225–250. Additional data were provided by Patricia A. Hurley.

gin over the Democrats had diminished from an intimidating 170 seats to a less fearsome 20 seats. Restive at what they felt was a House leadership out of touch with the nation's needs, twenty rebellious Republicans cast their votes for Representatives Henry A. Cooper of Wisconsin and Martin B. Madden of Illinois and forced the speakership contest to nine ballots before giving way to Gillett. It was the first open-floor fight for the speakership since the Civil War and the only one that has occurred since 1863.

Nicholas Longworth (R.-Ohio) succeeded Mondell as floor leader in 1923 and Gillett as Speaker in 1925. Longworth, who had married the notorious Alice Roosevelt, Teddy Roosevelt's oldest daughter, had little sympathy for the La Follette Progressives and dispatched them summarily from committee assignments. Their challenges to Speaker Gillett in 1923 and to President Coolidge in 1924 were not forgotten.

Longworth had served as majority floor leader prior to his election as Speaker in 1925. In the 1920s, Republican power had been lodged in an extra-institutional body, the Steering Committee, which set the party's agenda. First appointed in 1919 upon the party's recapture of the House, this group operated separately from the standing-committee system. As floor leader in the previous Congress, Longworth had chaired the Steering Committee; when he became Speaker, he said, "I was able to take the majority leadership from the floor to the Chair." It was Longworth who turned his informal drinking hideaway in the Capitol into the first "Board of Education." He understood clearly that his power would have to rely more upon personal influence than upon institutional authority.

Leading the Democrats in the House during this time of Republican ascendancy was Claude Kitchin of North Carolina and Finis Garrett of Tennessee. The party's irreducible southern wing had become dominant as Democratic districts elsewhere disappeared. Kitchin died in 1923 and a possible fight for the minority leadership was averted when Tennessee-born caucus chair Samuel Rayburn of Texas rebuffed the entreaties of John Nance ("Cactus Jack") Garner (D.-Tex.) to lean in his favor. Garrett found life leading the House minority frustrating and sought a seat in the Senate in 1928. He failed in his quest and was replaced as minority floor leader by his old rival Garner. It took six years of waiting, but in 1929, Garner finally gained the post that would take him to the speakership two years later and to the vice presidency in 1933.

Another important sign of institutional development was the regular naming of a Democratic whip. The post was initially filled in 1900 by Oscar W. Underwood, but it was not consistently filled until 1921, when William Oldfield (D.-Ark.) assumed the title under the minority leadership of Claude Kitchin.

Committee Structure   As the decade of the 1920s opened, the internal organization of the House was impeded by its large number of standing committees. Sixty standing and four select committees met during the Sixty-sixth Congress (1919–1921) with 909 places—2.1 per member. By 1930 the number of House standing committees had been reduced to 47, but the number of committee places remained relatively constant at 850, or 1.98 per member. The surviving committees had become larger.

With the 1921 creation of the Bureau of the Budget in the executive branch as a central location for fiscal management, it became necessary for the House to locate its executive-oversight activities in fewer places. By 1927, sixteen committees had been eliminated, most through the creation of the Committee on Expenditures in the Executive Departments, which merged eleven committees. Two committees, Alcoholic Liquor Traffic and Women Suffrage, had paved the way for the Eighteenth and Nineteenth constitutional amendments respectively and were no longer needed. Joining the committee casualties were Industrial Arts and Expositions, Mileage, and Railways and Canals. Only two committees, World War Veterans Legislation and Memorials, were added to the House roster.

Membership   Stability in the membership of the House and its districts was made possible by the absence of new states to admit and by the lack of a reapportionment following the 1920 census. Thus, the size of the House and the shape of its districts remained intact for twenty years (1913–1933). With greater stability, House members stayed longer. The average number of terms served by members increased from 3.74 (7.48 years) in the Sixty-sixth Congress (1919–1921) to

4.49 terms (8.98 years) by the Seventy-first Congress (1929–1931).

During the 1920s the composition of the House began to change. The first female member of the House was Jeannette Rankin of Montana, who served her first term during the war (1917–1919) and was defeated for reelection. Twelve other women from nine different states saw House service in the years from 1921 through 1931. Included among them were Mary T. Norton (D.-N.J.) and Edith Nourse Rogers (R.-Mass.), who would chair standing committees of the House in the next congressional era.

Oscar DePriest, a Republican from Chicago, was elected to the House in 1928 and became its first black member in twenty-eight years.

Party Voting Party voting continued to decline in the House as scarcely more than half of the roll calls in the six Congresses from 1919 through 1931 divided the floor votes along party lines (a per-Congress mean of 53.7 percent and a median of 56.0 percent). As parties became less important, committees became more important.

The Senate

Electoral Politics The Republican recapture of the Senate in 1918 created the most difficulties for Wilson. The return to the majority leadership of Henry Cabot Lodge (R.-Mass.) brought an old Wilson nemesis into a post where he could derail Wilson's dreams for a postwar government for Europe. The inability of Wilson to get Senate confirmation of the Treaty of Versailles with its League of Nations provision in 1919 led to his most serious personal and political crisis. And as happened in the post–Civil War period, Congress reasserted itself and trimmed the expansiveness of the executive branch.

Press coverage of the Senate during its battles over the League of Nations had given it greater prominence. Ironically, its prominence contributed to the nomination and election in 1920 of one its lesser lights, Warren G. Harding (R.-Ohio), the first president ever to be elected directly from the Senate.

Senate Leadership and Party Organization It was during the 1920s that the Senate leadership was first named in the official minutes of the party conferences conferring floor leadership on the Democratic caucus chair in 1921 and on the Republican conference chair in 1925.

Legislative leadership of the Republican party fell to the Senate where majority leaders Henry Cabot Lodge (Mass., 1919–1924) and Charles Curtis (Kans., 1925–1929) regularly parried the verbal thrusts of Democratic floor leaders Oscar Underwood (Ala., 1919–1923) and Joseph Robinson (Ark., 1923–1937). Three of these leaders were directly involved in presidential politics as Underwood was a finalist for the 1924 presidential nomination and Robinson was nominated as the vice-presidential "dry" (pro-Prohibition) balancer for New York governor Al Smith's "wet" (against Prohibition) presidential nomination in 1928. Both vice-presidential nominees in 1928, Robinson for the Democrats and Curtis for the Republicans, were their party's Senate floor chieftains.

This was clear evidence of the Senate's increasing role in presidential politics, with the leaders of the president's party leading the fight for his programs and those of the opposing party often becoming the president's most vocal critics. Senate involvement in presidential politics, so pronounced in present times, thus had its beginnings in the 1920s.

Membership The Senate's new public prominence focused newspaper attention upon its more colorful members. The western Senators did not disappoint them. Hiram W. Johnson (R.-Calif.) and William P. Borah (R.-Idaho) played important roles in shaping an isolationist foreign policy while Montana's two Democratic senators, Thomas J. Walsh and Burton K. Wheeler, led investigatory attacks on the Harding administration. Wheeler's efforts exposed the corruption within the office of Harding's campaign manager and attorney general, Harry M. Daugherty, while Walsh was able to investigate the widely publicized Teapot Dome oil-leasing scandal. This scandal, which led to the indictment of two other cabinet members and the ultimate jailing of Secretary of the Interior Albert Fall, was a model of the aggressive investigative power that the Congress could exercise over an aggrandizing executive branch.

Progressive Republicans such as Robert M. La Follette (R.-Wis.) and Independent Republican George W. Norris (R.-Nebr.) continued to bedevil the conservative Republican presidencies of Harding, Coolidge, and Hoover, but presidential requests were too few in number for their opposition to make much of a difference.

Diversity has come slowly to the U.S. Senate. Only Rebecca L. Felton (D.-Ark.), who served two days in 1922, broke the all-male ambience of the Senate. No black members were seated in the Senate between 1881 and 1967.

Committee Structure   The Senate reorganized its committee system much more quickly and effectively than the House. On 21 April 1921, Senate Majority Leader Lodge arranged the consolidation of ten separate expenditures committees into one committee, Expenditures in the Executive Departments, reducing the number of places from 50 to 7. Thirty-two other standing committees were also eliminated. With the notable exceptions of Private Land Claims (1826) and Transportation Routes to the Seaboard (1879), most had been created in the previous thirty years. They had become sinecures for empty prestige and occasional staff with only a minimal impact on legislative business.

The Senate's committee system shrunk from 75 committees with 757 places in 1919 to 34 committees with 401 places in 1921. No new standing committees were added to the Senate roster in that decade.

Although the Senate's rigid seniority system and its propensity to tolerate filibusters remained in place, its extensive committee reorganization and its executive focus made it a more modern chamber than the House.

Party Voting   With individualism running rampant, Senate party voting continued to decline. Four of the six Congresses in this latest Republican era had party-voting percentages under 50 percent. Light presidential legislative agendas and the lack of an acute crisis provided no incentive to tighten party reins on the Senate.

Presidential-Congressional Relations The whirlwind Wilson years gave way to the Harding and Coolidge administrations. Neither president had a lengthy legislative agenda. With little leadership emanating from the White House, both the House and the Senate relied upon their legislative leaders for guidance.

The war highlighted the need for an integrated budget process for both the executive and legislative branches. In 1921, Congress passed the National Budget and Accounting Act, which created both the Bureau of the Budget in the executive branch and the General Accounting Office in the legislative one.

While President Wilson had failed in 1919 to get the Senate to ratify the League of Nations, Presidents Harding and Coolidge were more successful. The Four-Power Pacific Treaty (1921) recognizing each nation's Pacific possessions, the Five-Power Naval Limitation Treaty (1922) that sought to control military shipbuilding, the Nine-Power Treaty (1922) protecting China's sovereignty, and the Kellogg-Briand Pact (1928) that renounced war as an instrument of national policy were all passed overwhelmingly.

Major Legislation   While battles over farm bills and foreign policy engaged the interest of the congressional parties, politics virtually disappeared as American social events careened from one dramatic sideshow to another. Pole sitters, midgets, and fiery evangelists all captured more interest from a public exhausted by the righteous fervor of President Wilson and his "war to end all wars." Prohibition and the blatant efforts to circumvent its stringent requirements had created a decade of cheery cynicism that rendered legislation irrelevant and political events secondary. It was the Roaring Twenties.

Returning veterans were to be accommodated by the Veterans Bureau (1921), but President Coolidge was markedly unsympathetic and vetoed the Soldiers Bonus Bill in 1924, which was later overridden. The president was more sympathetic to the plight of the wealthy and their taxes, and corporate taxes were reduced in the Revenue Act of 1926.

Immigration restriction became a major focus of public policy through the passage of the Immigration Quota acts of 1921 and 1924. The latter act reduced annual immigration to 150,000 and completely excluded the Japanese.

As was often the case with Republican Congresses, tariff rates rose with the Fordney-McCumber Act of 1922 and the Hawley-Smoot Act of 1930.

The postwar farm depression persisted in spite of the efforts of "farm bloc" members of Congress to protect farmland in the Agricultural Credits Act of 1923 and timberlands in the Clarke-McNary Reforestation Act of 1924 and to encourage cooperative marketing in the Capper-Volstead Act of 1922. The Flood Control Act of 1928 was an effort to spare Mississippi Valley farmers future harm to their crops. And President Hoover, an Iowa farm boy, successfully urged Congress to pass the Agricultural Marketing Act in 1929. All of this was prelude to what the 1930s would bring.

Institutional Support As the 1930s opened, federal legislative employment stood at 11,192, almost twice the number of legislative employees reported in 1911. Even after the number of committees in the Congress had been reduced, the legislative payroll, both in congressional offices and in the Library of Congress, continued to grow. Ground was broken for a second House office building in 1933, which would be named for Speaker Longworth, another concrete monument to congressional institutionalization.

A MODERNIZED CONGRESS AWAITS A MODERN PRESIDENT

By 1930 the U.S. Congress had brought about major reforms in its leadership structure and its committee system. Floor leadership posts in both parties had been established and institutionalized. The legislative payroll had been expanded, and office buildings had been constructed. The unchecked proliferation of standing committees had been stopped, and serious efforts at committee retrenchment and jurisdictional reorganization had begun. The passage of the Twentieth Amendment—called in 1929 (and ratified by 1933) shortened the time between the November elections and the convening of Congress from four months to two months and enabled the newly elected members to begin work on the public's business at the opening of the next calendar year.

In October 1929, the stock market crashed and the Great Depression began. Like the Civil War, the depression represented one of those acute crises that legislative authority could not handle effectively without strong executive guidance. Because this was a domestic economic crisis, the Seventy-first Congress was reluctant to share its authority with President Hoover. The president's inability to convince the overwhelmingly Republican majorities in both chambers to put aside their noninterventionist market philosophies and use the power of the federal government to overcome the economic dislocations of the depression undermined the Republican party's hold on power. Instead, they reacted, as they had previously to economic dislocations, by raising tariff rates. In this case it was the Smoot-Hawley Tariff, which brought rates to the highest levels seen since 1828.

By November 1930 it was clear that this latest era of Republican dominance was close to cracking. In spite of the horrendous economy, congressional Republicans held narrow postelection majorities in both houses. But they were robbed of the right to organize the House of Representatives when seven newly elected Republicans (including Speaker Longworth) died between the election of the Seventy-second Congress and its convening in 1931.

In 1931 the Democrats organized the House of Representatives for only the fifth time in the twentieth century. But they went on to increase their margin of seats in each of the next three elections and to keep the House of Representatives in Democratic hands for sixty of the next sixty-four years—forty of those years in a row. It would become the longest period of single-party domination of any national political institution in the history of American politics. In the November 1932 elections, the Democrats extended their control to the Senate and the presidency.

With Franklin Roosevelt's New Deal on the horizon and united congressional government to buttress it, the modernizing era had ended and the modern one had begun.

BIBLIOGRAPHY

Statistics
The economic and demographic statistics used in this essay can be found in U.S. BUREAU OF THE CENSUS, *Historical Statistics of the United States, Colonial Times to 1957* (Washington, D.C., 1960). The political statistics are in CON-

GRESSIONAL QUARTERLY, *Guide to U.S. Elections,* 2d ed. (Washington, D.C., 1985).

Historical congressional statistics were taken from CONGRESSIONAL QUARTERLY, *Guide to the Congress of the United States: Origins, History, and Procedure,* 3d ed. (Washington, D.C., 1982); NELSON W. POLSBY, "The Institutionalization of the U.S. House of Representatives," *American Political Science Review* 62 (March 1968): 144–168; NELSON W. POLSBY, MIRIAM GALLAHER, and BARRY SPENCER RUNDQUIST, "The Growth of the Seniority System in the U.S. House of Representatives," *American Political Science Review* 63 (September 1969): 787–807; and MICHAEL ABRAM and JOSEPH COOPER, "The Rise of Seniority in the House of Representatives," *Polity* 1 (Fall 1968): 52–85.

Membership information can be found in MURRAY G. LAWSON, "The Foreign-Born in Congress, 1789–1949: A Statistical Summary," *American Political Science Review* 51 (December 1957): 1183–1189; and CONGRESSIONAL QUARTERLY, *American Leaders 1789–1987: A Biographical Summary* (Washington, D.C., 1987).

The best compilation of voting records can be found in the twenty-one articles contained in JOEL H. SILBEY, ed., *The Rise and Fall of the Political Parties in the United States, 1789–1989: The Congressional Roll Call Record* (Brooklyn, N.Y., 1991). A summary of the development of the selection systems for congressional leaders can be found in GARRISON NELSON, "Party Selection of Congressional Leaders," in L. SANDY MAISEL, ed., *Encyclopedia of American Political Parties and Elections* (New York, 1991), Vol. 2.

Useful introductions to institutional party leadership may be found in RANDALL B. RIPLEY, *Power in the Senate* (New York, 1969) and *Party Leaders in the House of Representatives* (Washington, D.C., 1967).

Committees

Information on committee assignments can be found in the various editions of the *Congressional Directory.* Dates for resolutions creating committees and terminating them can be found in WALTER STUBBS, comp., *Congressional Committees, 1789–1982: A Checklist* (Westport, Conn., 1985).

Data on the number of congressional committees and their places come from GARRISON NELSON, *Directory of Committee Assignments in the Historic U.S. Congress, 1789–1946* (Washington, D.C., forthcoming).

Legislation

A valuable source for legislation passed in each Congress is the compilation prepared for the Congressional Research Service of the Library of Congress by CHRISTOPHER DELL and STEPHEN W. STATHIS, *Major Acts of Congress and Treaties Approved by the Senate, 1789–1980* (Washington, D.C., 1982).

The party-system approach to political change and the economic backdrop can be found in EVERETT CARLL LADD, JR., *American Political Parties: Social Change and Political Response* (New York, 1970); RICHARD L. MCCORMICK, *The Party Period and Public Policy: American Politics from the Age of Jackson to the Progressive Era* (New York, 1986); JAMES L. SUNDQUIST, *The Dynamics of the Party System: Alignment and Realignment of Political Parties in the United States,* 2d ed. (Washington, D.C., 1983); and WALTER DEAN BURNHAM's classic article, "The Changing Shape of the American Political Universe," *American Political Science Review* 59 (March 1965): 7–29.

Autobiographies

Useful autobiographies of key congressional actors during these years include JAMES G. BLAINE, *Twenty Years of Congress: From Lincoln to Garfield,* 2 vols. (Norwich, Conn., 1884–1886); JOHN SHERMAN, *Recollections of Forty Years in the House, Senate, and Cabinet,* 2 vols. (Chicago, 1895); GEORGE F. HOAR, *Autobiography of Seventy Years,* 2 vols. (New York, 1903); JOSEPH G. CANNON, *Uncle Joe Cannon: The Story of a Pioneer American as Told to L. White Busbey* (St. Clair Shores, Mich., 1970); OSCAR W. UNDERWOOD, *Drifting Sands of Party Politics* (New York, 1928); and CHAMP CLARK, *My Quarter Century of American Politics,* 2 vols. (New York, 1920).

Biographies

Biographies of some of the more influential individuals include WILLIAM A. ROBINSON, *Thomas B. Reed, Parliamentarian* (New York, 1930); JAMES BARNES, *John G. Carlisle, Financial Statesman* (New York, 1931); CLAUDE BOWERS, *The Life of John Worth Kern* (Indianapolis, 1918); CLARA LONGWORTH DE CHAMBRUN, *The Making of Nicholas Longworth: Annals of an*

American Family (New York, 1933); BLAIR BOLLES, *Tyrant from Illinois: Uncle Joe Cannon's Experiment with Personal Power* (New York, 1951); FESTUS P. SUMMERS, *William L. Wilson and Tariff Reform* (New Brunswick, N.J., 1953); ALEX M. ARNETT, *Claude Kitchin and the Wilson War Policies* (Boston, 1937); KARL SCHRIFTGIESSER, *The Gentleman from Massachusetts: Henry Cabot Lodge* (Boston, 1944); and LEROY ASHBY, *The Spearless Leader: Senator Borah and the Progressive Movement in the 1920's* (Urbana, Ill., 1972).

Historical Accounts and Critical Assessments
Valuable assessments of Congress with overviews of this period are DAVID J. ROTHMAN, *Politics and Power: The United States Senate, 1869–1901* (Cambridge, Mass., 1966); DAVID W. BRADY, *Critical Elections and Congressional Policy Making* (Stanford, Calif., 1988); JAMES L. SUNDQUIST, *The Decline and Resurgence of Congress* (Washington, D.C., 1981), Chapter 2; and MARGARET R. MUNK, "Origin and Development of the Party Leadership in the United States Senate," *Capitol Studies* 2 (Winter 1974): 23–41.

Contemporaneous accounts of the years between 1870 and 1930 can be found in the 1880s essays of FRANK G. CARPENTER, *Carp's Washington* (New York, 1960); O. O. STEALEY, *Twenty Years in the Press Gallery* (New York, 1906); WOODROW WILSON, *Congressional Government* (Boston, 1885); and ARTHUR WALLACE DUNN, *From Harrison to Harding: A Personal Narrative, Covering a Third of a Century, 1888–1921,* 2 vols. (New York, 1922).

The Reconstruction Congresses are described in MARGARET SUSAN THOMPSON, *The "Spider Web": Congress and Lobbying in the Age of Grant* (Ithaca, N.Y., 1985). The post-Reconstruction Congresses are assessed in TERRY L. SEIP, *The South Returns to Congress: Men, Economic Measures and Intersectional Relationships, 1868–1879* (Baton Rouge, La., 1983). DAVID W. BRADY deals with the McKinley years in his *Congressional Voting in a Partisan Era: A Study of the McKinley House and a Comparison to the Modern House of Representatives* (Lawrence, Kans., 1971). The Congresses of the Taft and Wilson years are assessed in KENNETH W. HECHLER, *Insurgency: Personalities and Policies of the Taft Era* (New York, 1940) and SEWARD W. LIVERMORE, *Politics Is Adjourned: Woodrow Wilson and the War Congress, 1916–1918* (Middletown, Conn., 1966).

Economic-policy linkages and their congressional impact can be found in TOM E. TERRILL, *The Tariff, Politics, and American Foreign Policy, 1874–1901* (Westport, Conn., 1973) and LLOYD J. MERCER, *Railroads and Land Grant Policy: A Study in Government Intervention* (New York, 1982).

The best recent compilation of academic articles on the Congress is JOEL H. SILBEY, ed., *The United States Congress in a Partisan Political Nation, 1841–1896,* 3 vols. (Brooklyn, N.Y., 1991) and JOEL H. SILBEY, ed., *The United States Congress in a Nation Transformed, 1896–1963* (Brooklyn, N.Y., 1991).

SEE ALSO Congress, the Executive, and War Powers; The Congressional Committee System; The Historical Legislative Career; The Historiography of the American Legislative System; Legislatures and American Economic Development; Parties, Elections, Moods, and Lawmaking Surges; AND Party Coherence on Roll-Call Votes in the U.S. House of Representatives.

THE CONTEMPORARY CONGRESS, 1930–1992

David W. Rohde

The account of the history of the U.S. Congress between 1930 and 1992 is a chronicle of enormous changes. Responses to the Great Depression and World War II vastly increased the scope of congressional policy-making, which grew further still under the Democratic administrations of the 1960s. Also during these six decades, the weakening of ties between voters and parties, and the growth of electronic media transformed electoral politics. The expansion of government activity was accompanied by an increase in executive-branch power, which led to greater presidential-congressional conflict —a situation that was exacerbated by frequent division of control of the branches between the parties. In the 1970s and 1980s, the Congress underwent major institutional changes that seemed to decentralize further the already decentralized legislative system, increasing concerns about Congress's inability to act. Later developments indicate, however, that congressional change has been more subtle and more consequential than observers had anticipated.

The Congress had already undergone significant transformations in the early years of this century. The House of Representatives had rejected the "boss rule" of Speaker Joseph Cannon (R.-Ill.), replacing it with committee dominance based on the seniority system. Through almost inviolate observance of the seniority norm, committees and their leaders grew progressively stronger through the 1920s, at the expense of party leaders and party organizations. The Senate also was changed, as the Seventeenth Amendment to the Constitution shifted the election of senators from state legislatures to direct popular election. Within the Senate, committees began to assume a stronger role in the legislative process. By 1930, the Congress had arrived at the point where its processes deserved the commonly applied phrase of "committee government."

1930–1945: DEMOCRATIC DOMINANCE AND THE SEEDS OF CHANGE

The New Deal and Agenda Change

The principal formative event of this period was the political realignment resulting from the Depression. Until 1930 the Republicans had long been the majority party, dominating with occasional interruptions both the presidency and Congress. During the early 1930s, the situation was transformed: Franklin Roosevelt's overwhelming victories in the presidential races of 1932 and 1936 were coupled with tremendous Democratic gains in Congress. In 1930, seats were almost evenly divided between the parties in both the House and Senate; by 1936 the Democrats held three fourths of the seats in both chambers.

The Depression and other developments created widespread demands for government action on many fronts. The Democratic party was more prepared than the Republican party to respond to these demands, and so it benefited electorally. This realignment produced an expansion and transformation of the agenda of the national government: new issues were considered, and old issues changed. Throughout the period, Congress grappled with the new agenda, and this process set the stage for changes within the Congress itself.

As one would expect, much of the political conflict early in the decade revolved around direct responses to the Depression. While Herbert Hoover was president, congressional Democrats sought to involve the government in providing direct relief to citizens, but he resisted those efforts. Under Roosevelt, though, the Congress adopted a wide range of proposals intended to manage various aspects of the economy, to prevent future economic catastrophe, and to help individuals. Democrats and Republicans had long been distinguished by their attitudes toward big business, but in this regard the innovation of the the New Deal was the Democrats' advocacy of an activist federal government role in regulating business and the economy. This was reflected, for example, in the Emergency Banking Relief Act (which authorized the reopening of banks under Treasury Department licenses and gave new powers to the Federal Reserve Board), and the National Industrial Recovery Act (which created industrywide boards made up of management and labor to stabilize wages and prices).

The other thrust of the New Deal, toward direct assistance, amounted to another new kind of activity for the federal government. Major programs of this type included the Social Security Act, the Works Progress Administration, and the Civilian Conservation Corps (the latter two provided millions of jobs to the unemployed). Another aspect of individual economic protection was legislation to protect the members of organized labor, such as the National Labor Relations Act.

The expansion of the congressional agenda during this period was not limited to economic issues. Questions of American international involvement began to come to the fore in the late 1930s. In addition, civil liberties issues—particularly civil rights for blacks and restrictions on "subversive activities"—began to receive significant attention, notably in the 1938 establishment of the House Un-American Activities Committee. For example, the House passed an antilynching bill in the Seventy-fifth Congress (1937–1939), and five times in the 1940s it passed bills barring the poll tax as a voting requirement; however, none of these bills passed the Senate.

The Decline of Party Government

For decades before the 1930s, the usual political situation was a partisan majority controlling both chambers of Congress working in tandem with a president of the same party and political orientation. This American version of party government flourished during Roosevelt's first term, under the president's vigorous leadership. Most major New Deal bills were Roosevelt's proposals, which were quickly guided to congressional approval by the Democratic leaders in both houses. An extreme example is the Emergency Banking Bill, which passed both chambers in less than eight hours when the Seventy-third Congress convened on 3 March 1933—even though few members had seen a printed copy.

The great majority of these proposals received strong Democratic support, with sometimes muted and always ineffective Republican opposition. Partisan divisions on economic issues tended to be very sharp. In the House, institutional arrangements were used to reinforce partisan control. In 1933–1934, the Rules Committee gave most economic recovery measures a "closed rule," a procedural arrangement that barred any amendments on the House floor. The primary responsibility of this committee was to prescribe the amount of time for debate and the floor procedures to be used for most significant bills that were to receive floor consideration. In this period, the Democratic members of the Rules Committee saw it as the arm of the party's leadership, and those leaders understood their responsibility to be the passing of the president's program.

This situation began to change, however, early in Roosevelt's second term, catalyzed by his 1937 proposal to expand the membership of the Supreme Court. The Court had declared a number of important pieces of New Deal legislation unconstitutional, and the president proposed to appoint new justices to compensate for the older ones who had voted against his programs. The "court-packing" plan touched off a firestorm of controversy, and it was openly opposed by a number of prominent conservative Democrats in both chambers, as well as by Republicans. Opposition increased when Roosevelt pressed ahead with the bill despite a shift in the Court's voting patterns in favor of the New Deal, but his proposal was defeated in the Senate. This conflict revitalized and united conservative opposition, creating the legislative alliance of southern Democrats and Republicans that came to be known as the "conservative coalition." This alliance frustrated much of Roosevelt's domestic program throughout the remainder of his presidency, and was to be a strong influence on congressional politics for decades to come.

One consequence of Congress's above-mentioned rejection of strong, centralized party leadership early in the century was the elaboration and strengthening of the seniority system. Seniority on a committee became the sole basis for awarding the committee's chair. In addition, party leadership posts also tended to go only to senior members of Congress. Thus power followed seniority, and under Democratic majorities that meant it went to southerners, many of whom were conservative. Moreover, this shift in power from party leaders to committees permitted the latter much independence of action within their policy domains. During Roosevelt's second term, most of the major committees were dominated by southerners, and the conservative coalition asserted itself on many of them to block the president's proposals. A particularly salient example was the House Rules Committee, which was transformed from an arm of the leadership into a roadblock for party programs. Southern Democrats who opposed New Deal initiatives joined with conservative Republicans to form a coalition to block action or an effective majority on many major bills. The Rules Committee frequently gave unfavorable procedural arrangements to administration proposals or flatly refused to let them be debated on the floor.

As conservative resistance to Roosevelt's programs grew, conflict between the administration and Democratic dissidents grew more personal. It went so far that in the 1938 congressional primaries the president unsuccessfully opposed a number of conservative Democratic senators. This failed effort to purge the conservatives serves as a vivid illustration of their electoral and policy independence.

International Affairs and World War II

While in the domestic arena the president went from dominance to weakness over the years he served, the reverse was true in international affairs. Roosevelt had sought to strengthen America's international role during his first term, but his efforts were overwhelmed by isolationist sentiment in Congress and in the country. For example, the Congress passed an embargo on arms sales to any belligerent, regardless of whether its actions were offensive or defensive, and the president acquiesced. As war in Europe became more likely in the late 1930s, Roosevelt sought to persuade Congress to adopt a less neutral stance, and in 1939 the arms embargo was repealed.

In 1941, after the onset of war and the fall of France to Germany, Roosevelt proposed to go further. The lend-lease bill, which granted the president wide powers to transfer arms to friendly governments, encountered strong resistance. Vigorous efforts by new Speaker Sam Rayburn (D.-Tex.) guided the proposal through the House, and soon thereafter it passed the Senate. Ironically, one of the Senate leaders who supported the president was Walter George (D.-Ga.), chairman of the Foreign Relations Committee and one of the conservatives Roosevelt had sought to purge in 1938. Later in the same year, extension of the army draft was authorized, though it passed the House by a single vote.

After the Japanese attack at Pearl Harbor and the subsequent declaration of war, isolationist sentiments ceased to matter. Congress granted the president wide-ranging powers to create war agencies, enforce rationing, and regulate international commerce. His hand was not entirely free though: Congress repeatedly attempted to influence those wartime policies related to domestic issues, and by the time of Roosevelt's reelection to his fourth term in 1944 there was widespread opposition to his postwar reconstruction proposals. But the New Deal and World War II had expanded the power of the president and the executive branch vis-à-vis the Congress, which would ever after prevent the legislative branch from resuming the dominant position it had once held in national politics.

1946–1960: DIVIDED GOVERNMENT AND A DIVIDED CONGRESS

Institutional and Electoral Change

Responses to the depression and involvement in the War had expanded the size and scope of the national government; but with economic improvement and the end of hostilities, new conditions gave rise to new changes. One momentous change was the death of Roosevelt in 1945, and the succession of Harry S. Truman. Soon thereafter came the election of 1946, which produced Republican majorities in both houses of Congress. The result was a divided partisan government, a condition that had been rare in the past—between 1897 and 1946, America had experienced divided government in only three of twenty-five Congresses—but one that would become the norm in the years to come.

With the arrival of peace, the size of the federal establishment began to shrink. Civilian federal employment was reduced by almost half between 1945 and 1947, from 3.8 million to 2.1 million persons. Shrinkage of a different sort occurred in Congress in 1947, when the issue of congressional reorganization was taken up. Many members were concerned that the expansion of federal responsibilities had weakened the Congress relative to the executive branch. A joint select committee was created to look into issues of congressional structure, and the result was the Legislative Reorganization Act of 1946.

The primary aim of the reformers was to strengthen Congress's ability to make and evaluate governmental policy by streamlining the committee system. In many cases, committees were inactive, and in others control over the same policy area was divided among many committees. The act didn't entirely eliminate these problems, but it did improve matters by reducing the number of committees in the House from forty-eight to nineteen, and in the Senate from thirty-three to fifteen. Committee procedures were regularized by the act, although a number of committees paid little attention to the new rules. The reforms also sought to improve congressional staffing, and this began the staff expansion that would continue for the next three decades.

Other aspects of the reorganization were more directly targeted at executive-legislative relations. Committees were encouraged to increase oversight activities, and in the years following passage they did so. The law also provided for the creation of a legislative budget to correspond to the president's budget. This was a move to restore congressional control over the government's purse strings, although the joint budget committee that was set up did not work out. Finally, the act also imposed regulations on lobbyists, increased congressional salaries, and established a congressional retirement system.

The restoration of Republican congressional majorities in the 1946 elections marked the onset of electoral changes that would also profoundly influence the operation of the Congress. These GOP gains and the presence of an unelected president in the White House convinced many observers that full Republican control of government would return in the 1948 elections. This anticipation was reinforced by the divisions among the Democrats that resulted in two splinter parties in 1948: the Progressives on the left, and the southern States'-Rights party on the right. While the Democrats won a surprise victory in 1948, the divisions within the party remained and undermined their ability to govern.

The Democrats' luck ran out in 1952, when Dwight Eisenhower won a solid presidential victory and carried with him narrow GOP majorities in the House and Senate. Of signal importance for the future was Eisenhower's success in the South: he carried four of the former Confederate states in 1952, and he increased this to five in 1956. The solidly Democratic South was no longer solid, although the Republicans made little progress in southern congressional seats during the 1950s. The elections of 1954 saw another important development: the return of Democratic congressional majorities and divided government, which were maintained in 1956 and 1958. The 1956 outcomes were particularly significant, because they marked the first time since 1876 that a president was elected without majority control of Congress.

Division on Domestic Policy

As the Congress grappled with domestic issues in the postwar period, it became clear that the New Deal's response to the economic emergency of the 1930s had permanently expanded the scope of the national government's activities. The Employment Act of 1946 stated that it was "the continuing policy and responsibility of the Federal Government . . . to promote maximum employment, production and purchasing powers." To further those ends, the act, among other provisions, established the President's Council of Economic Advisors, and the congressional Joint Economic Committee. Precisely what the government was to do within its expanded scope, however, was a matter of great conflict between the parties and among the Democrats.

THE CONTEMPORARY CONGRESS, 1930–1992

The Republican Congress elected in 1946 was able to block most Truman initiatives, but it was usually unable to enact proposals of its own. One exception was the Taft-Hartley bill, which was passed over Truman's veto. Bitterly opposed by organized labor, the bill outlawed the closed shop and placed restrictions on union activity. The situation was somewhat better for the Democrats after they regained control of Congress in 1948. A few of Truman's Fair Deal proposals were enacted, but most (including aid to education, the repeal of Taft-Hartley, and a Fair Employment Practices Commission) failed to pass. For the remainder of his tenure, the president and his liberal supporters were unable to overcome the resistance of the conservative coalition. The divisions between and among the parties, moreover, were sharpened by the hunt for domestic subversives that was intensified by Senator Joseph McCarthy's (R.-Wis.) charges of communist infiltration of the State Department and the ensuing investigations.

When the Republicans regained the White House under Eisenhower, they did not mount a wholesale effort to repeal the New Deal's innovations. By and large, the GOP and their Democratic allies were content with retaining the status quo and preventing liberal initiatives. This pattern continued to hold even after the Democrats regained control of Congress in the 1954 elections. The effectiveness of the conservative coalition in using its dominance on major committees, particularly on the House Rules Committee, to prevent passage of liberal initiatives continually frustrated northern Democrats. After the Democratic party won almost two-thirds majorities in both chambers in 1958, House liberals considered launching an effort to break the power of conservatives on Rules by changing the party ratio on the committee and adopting rules to bypass it if necessary. Speaker Rayburn, however, persuaded the liberals not to propose these changes, by assuring them that he would get party proposals to the floor. Nevertheless, over the next two years Rules again often acted as a roadblock, and the conservative coalition still managed to prevent passage of most liberal proposals.

One liberal initiative that did pass during the late 1950s intensified the divisions among Democrats—the first major civil rights bill of the century, adopted in 1957. In the wake of the school desegregation decisions by the Supreme Court, the symbolism of the bill's passage was more important than its direct effects. The House had passed a number of civil rights proposals over the previous twenty years, so the real stumbling block was the Senate, under whose rules the minority party can use extended debate to prevent a floor vote on proposals it opposes (in a maneuver known as a "filibuster"). The chief architect of the bill's passage was Senate Majority Leader Lyndon Johnson (D.-Tex.), who managed, by offering judicious compromises to southern Democrats, to secure an agreement not to filibuster the bill. In its final form, the Civil Rights Act of 1957 created the Commission on Civil Rights in the executive branch and empowered the attorney general to seek court injunctions when individuals were denied the right to vote. This success irrevocably put the national Democratic party on the side of protecting the civil rights of black Americans—and later, other minority groups—and as a consequence served further to undermine support for the party among white conservatives in the South.

Cold War Politics

Foreign policy and defense issues were far less partisan and ideological than were domestic matters. During this period, these policy areas were characterized by substantial bipartisan consensus. This is not to say that there were no disagreements, or that there were never conflicts across party lines; yet most of the time strong majorities in both parties lined up behind the president on most significant matters.

Despite Republican control of Congress in 1947–1948 under the Democratic President Truman, for example, major international initiatives moved forward. Perhaps the most remarkable of these was the Marshall Plan, a massive aid program designed to rebuild the economies of Europe, and thereby to enhance political stability and Western security. The member of Congress most responsible for the passage of the plan was Senator Arthur Vandenberg (R.-Mich.), the chair of the Foreign Relations Committee. Strongly committed to the bipartisan ideal and to the view that America had major international responsibilities in the postwar world, Vandenberg assuaged the doubts of many opponents through compromise, secured unanimous approval of the plan by his committee, and engineered a substantial majority on the Senate floor in March of 1948; the House quickly followed suit. Another major initiative was the Vandenberg Resolution, adopted by the Senate in June of 1948, which called on the U.S. government to pursue arrangements for international collective self-defense under the United Nations Charter, setting the stage for the creation of the North Atlantic Treaty Organization. The Senate ratified U.S. participation in NATO in 1949.

In the remainder of the Truman years there was some partisan conflict over Korea, and over who "lost" China to the communists, but bipartisanship was largely restored under President Eisenhower and Secretary of State John Foster Dulles. Majorities of both parties in Congress remained committed to communist containment, collective security arrangements, and substantial defense expenditures.

1961–1966: UNITED PARTY GOVERNMENT RETURNS—BRIEFLY

Enacting a Domestic Agenda

The elections of 1960 returned simultaneous control of the presidency and Congress to the Democrats. The Democratic congressional leadership recognized that rather than merely reacting to a Republican president, they would now have the responsibility of moving their own president's agenda through the legislative process. Many of the items President Kennedy supported were similar to proposals that conservatives had blocked in previous Congresses. As a consequence, Speaker Rayburn realized that he could no longer tolerate an independent, conservative-dominated Rules Committee, and at the opening of Congress in 1961 he moved to change the situation.

Instead of seeking to alter the formal powers of the committee, though, Rayburn supported the milder action of expanding the membership from twelve to fifteen members, two new Democrats and one additional Republican. The plan was that two more Democrats loyal to the party would enable the committee Democrats to outvote the conservative coalition there. After a month of maneuver and debate, the proposal was approved by a narrow 217–212 margin, with a majority of southern Democrats opposed. Conservatives of both parties recognized this effort to undermine their power, and the narrowness of the victory illustrates the divisions among Democrats.

President Kennedy was able to exploit his "honeymoon" period with Congress to secure passage of certain domestic proposals he supported. The minimum wage was increased, as were Social Security benefits. Also passed were a major housing bill, increased grants to fight water pollution, and a large public works program. There were also failures: no aid to education bill passed, and an effort to create a Department of Urban Affairs was defeated. After the 1962 elections, even though the Democrats' losses were relatively minor, the conservative coalition asserted itself more strongly, and Kennedy's program bogged down.

Most of the president's major initiatives were blocked in 1963. He proposed a significant tax cut and a major civil rights bill but neither passed. There was much conflict over spending priorities: as of the beginning of December, most of the appropriations bills for the fiscal year that began the previous July 1 had still not reached the president. Some critics attributed much of the problem to the change in the Democratic congressional leadership from Johnson and Rayburn to Sen. Mike Mansfield (D.-Mont.) and Speaker John McCormack (D.-Mass.). McCormack, old and frail, lacked Rayburn's forceful personality; Mansfield did not believe in trying to pressure senators to take any particular action.

When Kennedy was assassinated in November 1963, Lyndon Johnson succeeded to the presidency. Johnson had come to the House of Representatives in 1937 as a committed New Dealer, and he quickly made the main features of Kennedy's agenda his own—particularly the tax cut and the civil rights bill. The former passed in February of 1964, and the latter in July. The Civil Rights Act was a very broad piece of legislation, including protections for voting rights, access to public accommodations and facilities, and equal job opportunities. Other legislation passed in 1964 included a permanent food stamp program, a program to attack poverty, and a mass transit bill. The political agenda continued to broaden with the adoption of a number of major conservation bills. Johnson overwhelmed conservative opposition partly because of his personal legislative skills and knowledge of the process, and partly by using Kennedy's memory to marshall support.

After the 1964 elections, Johnson had additional assets: a personal landslide victory and a large number of new supportive members of Congress. Against Sen. Barry Goldwater, (R.-Ariz.), the president had carried all but six states. In addition, the Democrats won two-thirds majorities in the House and Senate. Goldwater had opposed the Civil Rights Act, and five of the states he carried were in the deep South. Until 1964, none had voted Republican since Reconstruction. At the same time, despite the large national congressional gains for the Democrats, the GOP achieved a five-seat net increase in House seats from the South. The result was a Congress in which liberal voting strength was vastly increased, and in which many Democrats felt an electoral debt to President Johnson.

Johnson took advantage of the situation by proposing an ambitious agenda of domestic legislation, almost all of which passed. The conservative coalition reacted very negatively in 1965–1966—for example, over half of southern Democratic representatives sided with the Republicans more often than with their own party on votes that divided party majorities—but they were simply outvoted time after time. Among Johnson's successes were Medicare, a housing bill, aid to higher education, a doubling of the size of the poverty program, and auto and highway safety bills. Perhaps most significant in the long run was the Voting Rights Act of 1965, the most comprehensive effort to protect the right to vote in ninety years. It authorized the federal government to send voting registrars into the South. An additional half-million black voters were registered in the South in just the first year of the law's operation.

The Undermining of International Bipartisanship

Kennedy's presidency illustrates the strength of the two-party consensus on foreign policy and defense issues, yet it was in those years that the seeds of its dissolution were sown. Shortly after taking office, Kennedy authorized an invasion of Cuba to overthrow Castro, an effort that be-

came the ill-fated Bay of Pigs. He supported increases in defense spending, resumed nuclear testing, and compelled the Soviets to remove their missiles from Cuba. His foreign policy was not, however, solely motivated by anticommunist sentiments; it also exhibited a strong internationalist flavor, as illustrated by the creation of the Arms Control and Disarmament Agency, the Alliance for Progress, and the Peace Corps.

Of greatest historical importance, however, was Kennedy's decision to expand America's role in Vietnam and others parts of Southeast Asia. This too became a part of the legacy passed on to Lyndon Johnson, which the new president also felt obliged to pursue. In a series of fateful steps, President Johnson introduced ground-combat troops to South Vietnam in 1965, gradually increased the number of U.S. troops to 181,000 by year's end, and initiated large-scale bombing raids against North Vietnam. In 1966, troop strength was further increased to over 389,000. Also during 1965, Johnson sent 30,000 American troops to the Dominican Republic to end a civil conflict that, he claimed, threatened to result in a communist government.

While among the general public and in the Congress there was widespread support for Johnson's moves in Vietnam and the Dominican Republic, there were also signs of dissent, and significantly they came largely from within the Democratic party. Sen. J. William Fulbright (D.-Ark.), chairman of the Foreign Relations Committee, was only the most prominent Democratic congressional critic of administration policies in these areas. Along with the civil rights issue, the Vietnam War would become a fulcrum for major changes in congressional politics over the next decade.

1967–1976: INTERBRANCH CONFLICT AND THE ERA OF REFORM

The Conservative Coalition Restored

The last Congress of Johnson's tenure and Richard Nixon's first term as president was a time of sharp conflict over policy and general stalemate in the domestic arena. The GOP gained forty-seven House seats in the 1966 elections, depriving liberals of their solid voting majority in that body, although the change in the Senate balance was small. Johnson's programs bogged down in Congress due to opposition from the revitalized conservative coalition, and existing programs were scaled back. Environmental policy remained one of the few areas in which a consensus could be built, and some new initiatives passed there.

In Vietnam, the number of American troops peaked at over 585,000 in 1968, as opposition to the war within the Democratic party continued to grow. Successive candidacies for the Democratic presidential nomination were launched by Senators Eugene McCarthy (D.-Minn.), Robert Kennedy (D.-N.Y.), and, after the second Kennedy assassination, George McGovern (D.-S.D.). All of these candidacies were founded in part on opposition to the administration's policies in Southeast Asia. In addition, the Vietnamese communists launched the infamous Tet Offensive in February 1968, which showed the enemy to be far more capable than the American public had been led to believe. In the face of these events and mounting U.S. casualties, support for the war declined, and President Johnson chose not to seek reelection.

However, the election of President Nixon only intensified the domestic stalemate and the foreign policy conflict. The first session of the Ninety-first Congress (1969) was the sixth longest in American history, but it had the lowest legislative output in thirty-six years. The president and Congress struggled constantly over spending priorities, and Nixon attacked the Democrats for not passing his new proposals for consolidating grant-in-aid programs and for revenue sharing, two types of programs designed to shift money and responsibility away from the federal government and to the states. Another point of conflict was the Senate's rejection of two of Nixon's nominees to the Supreme Court. Notably, though, one of the few areas where significant legislation did pass was control of air and water pollution.

With a Republican in the White House, Democratic opposition to the Vietnam War became the majority position among northern Democrats. Congress restricted the use of ground troops in Cambodia, and repealed the Gulf of Tonkin Resolution, which had granted President Johnson almost a blank-check authorization on the use of force in Vietnam. The defense budget was intensely scrutinized, and final appropriations were substantially below administration requests. In an effort to reassert a congressional role in foreign policy, the Senate passed the National Commitments Resolution in 1969 by a vote of seventy to sixteen: it expressed the Senate's sense that the commitment of U.S. troops abroad required congressional approval, but it was not binding on the president.

Electoral Changes

Due to deep splits over domestic policy and foreign affairs, this period was the nadir of Democratic party unity in Congress. The constituencies of northern and southern Democrats were very different demographically—the former was primarily urban, the latter predominantly rural. Southern conservatives voters were turning away from the Democratic party in large numbers—in reaction to the national party's support for civil rights, large social-welfare programs, and opposition to the Vietnam War—as was reflected in the fact that the Democrats lost all but one southern state in the 1968 presidential election, and failed to carry any of them when Nixon won reelection in 1972. The Republicans also increased their share of congressional representation in the South, from eleven House seats in 1962 to thirty-four seats ten years later, and from one Senate seat to seven in the same period. In Congress, substantial majorities of southern Democrats in both the House and Senate voted more often with the Republicans than with their own party.

Meanwhile, however, other electoral developments were taking place that would profoundly affect congressional politics. In 1962, the Supreme Court's ruling in *Baker* v. *Carr* reversed long-standing precedent in holding that legislative districting was in fact a proper matter for judicial consideration. This was followed in 1964 by the decision in *Wesberry* v. *Sanders*, which ruled that congressional districts in each state must contain the same number of people; this had not been the practice in many states, where rural-controlled state legislatures frequently drew districts with large population disparities or chose not to redraw congressional districts as population densities shifted. For example in 1962 in Georgia (which hadn't redistricted since 1931), the largest district, centered on Atlanta, had three times the population of the smallest. Under the *Wesberry* ruling the result—especially in the South—was many more districts with an urban or suburban population base, and fewer rural districts.

The factors that influenced voters in congressional elections were also changing. Elections were centered less on a candidate's party affiliation and more on specific candidates. The strength of voters' identification with the two major parties declined, and any given level of attachment became a weaker predictor of voting behavior. Independent sources of information about congressional candidates, especially television, became more widely available. In 1950, only 9 percent of American households had television, but by 1960 the figure was 87 percent and by 1970 it was 95 percent.

These new sources of information provided voters with an opportunity to see incumbents and candidates as individuals rather than simply as members of a party. Furthermore, the expansion of the scope of government activity, particularly in the Johnson years, meant that government touched peoples' lives in many more ways than in the past. Citizens frequently had problems with these programs, and they sought the assistance of their senators and representatives in rectifying the problems. This enabled members of Congress to serve further their constituents' interests and thereby to develop positive attachments with voters which were independent of party or ideology. Moreover, as attachments to parties declined, so did party organizations, which meant that each candidate had to construct his or her own personal campaign organization. To develop these organizations and encourage citizen participation, candidates for Congress became political entrepreneurs, developing and publicizing attractive issue positions to stimulate voter interest. The consequences of all these developments were two: first, more and more voters chose which candidates to support based on those candidates' individual qualities; and second, presidents were less likely to have "coattails" to pull their party members into office, and thus members had weaker ties to presidents and to their parties.

Congressional Reform

By late in the Johnson administration, liberal Democrats in the House had become very frustrated. They believed that procedures in the House granted disproportionate power to senior conservative Democrats, thus enabling the conservative coalition to block those policies that liberals favored. Their concerns were intensified after Nixon's election, because they feared he would seek to undo the gains they had achieved under Democratic presidents, and that congressional conservatives of both parties would help. Therefore they set out to change House procedures in order to remove the perceived bias against them.

Some initial steps were taken in the Legislative Reorganization Act of 1970. Like the Act of 1946, the new law was primarily concerned not with the distribution of power but with congressional efficiency. Some of its provisions encouraged open committee meetings, in some cases even permitting them to be televised; others were intended to streamline floor procedures. One significant move that had serious implications was a new rule permitting record votes (votes on which the positions of individuals are recorded and made public) on amendments on the House floor. Previously such votes were rare, which made it difficult to overturn on the floor decisions committees had made. Relatedly, it was difficult for voters to know where their representatives stood on many specific issues. As a result of the rules change, then, committees were now more dependent on majority sentiment, and representatives' positions were more visible to voters.

The Reorganization Act was a regular piece of legislation passed in both houses, with Republican participation. However, liberal Democrats realized that their strength would be magnified if matters were decided only among party members; so most subsequent reforms involved changing the rules not of the House but of the Democratic Caucus. The reforms followed three tracks. Initially, most visible and fundamental were changes that undermined the independent power of committee chairs. First the Caucus adapted procedures for an automatic, secret-ballot vote on committee chairs at the beginning of every Congress. This reform abolished the automatic nature of the seniority system, and with it the guarantee of independence for chairs. In the future they would have to take account of caucus sentiment in running their committees, or risk losing their positions. This was no empty threat, for in 1975 three southern Democratic chairs were deposed by the caucus.

Another set of changes, collectively known as the Subcommittee Bill of Rights, limited the exercise of power by chairs. They were deprived of the ability to name subcommittee chairs and subcommittee members, or to determine the jurisdictions of those subordinate organs. Subcommittees were guaranteed an adequate budget and some independent staff, and committee chairs were obliged to assign bills to the unit with jurisdiction over the matter.

The second track of reform sought to strengthen the powers of the party leadership, compensating for the weakening of committees and their chairs. A Steering and Policy Committee was created, made up of party leaders, members elected by the rank and file, and members appointed by the Speaker. The committee was intended as a forum for discussing party policy and strategy, and it was also vested with the power to make Democratic committee assignments—which gave the leadership much more influence over the distribution of that valuable commodity. In another move, the Speaker was empowered to refer bills to more than one committee, and to set deadlines for their consideration. Perhaps the most important change was to empower the Speaker to appoint and to remove the chair and Democratic members of the Rules Committee. This ended, once and for all, the independence of that frequently recalcitrant body and made it firmly an arm of the party leadership.

The last track of the reforms was the effort to make members who were granted positions of power through the party responsible to the rank-and-file members. New rules for votes on chairs constituted one such measure. Similarly, the Subcommittee Bill of Rights created Democratic caucuses on every committee, which could block certain arbitrary exercises of power by their chairs and could ratify or remove subcommittee chairs. In addition, special procedures were adopted to foster caucus influence over the most important committees, such as Appropriations, Rules, and Ways and Means.

The discussion of reform has, to this point, focused on the House. Reform efforts were much more limited in the Senate, partly because that body has always operated in a less formal manner, making procedural rules less consequential, and partly because power in the Senate, as it is distributed between parties or along seniority lines, has always been more egalitarian than in the House. For example, Senate committees had long been less influential and less independent than their House counterparts. Nevertheless, reform actions were undertaken in the Senate as well. Procedures were adopted that would permit the removal of a chairman by the Democratic Caucus (although the power was never exercised); junior senators were given greater staff resources; and, in a matter that had long been a source of conflict between Senate liberals and conservatives, the number of votes required to cut off a filibuster was changed from two-thirds of those voting to a flat sixty in all cases.

There was one other set of reforms that affected members of both bodies—those involved in the rules governing campaign financing. Growing out of a desire to limit the influence of wealthy individuals on politics, the new laws limited the amount each person or group could give to any one candidate, or (for individuals) to all candidates combined. Procedures were adopted to gather and disclose information on the source of all but the smallest campaign contributions. The laws also made it easier to form and operate nonparty committees, popularly known as political action committees or PACs.

The Reassertion of Congressional Power

The years of Nixon's second term saw continued stalemate on many domestic issues, but significant congressional action on other fronts. In previous years, Nixon and Congress had clashed over their respective powers regarding war-making and control of the federal budget. Many members of Congress had proposed legislative resolutions to these conflicts, and as the Watergate scandal weakened the president's political power, these proposals moved through Congress.

The first of these measures to pass was the War Powers Act, adopted over Nixon's veto in 1973. American forces had withdrawn from Vietnam in March, but later in the spring the country learned that the United States was still bombing Cambodia. Congress forced Nixon to stop the bombing, and the administration's secrecy gave impetus to passage of the War Powers Act, which required the president "in every possible instance" to "consult with Congress" before introducing troops to areas where hostilities were occurring or likely to occur. Should Congress refuse to authorize the commitment of troops within sixty days, they would have to be withdrawn; alternatively, Congress could terminate the action even sooner by concurrent resolution. Nixon claimed that the bill was an unconstitutional restriction of the president's power, but both chambers overrode his objections.

Another major dispute involved the congressional "power of the purse." Inflation had became a salient political issue, and Nixon and Congress continually clashed about the aggregate amount of federal spending and budget priorities. The president criticized Congress for the Democrats' overspending and the institution's lack of any mechanism to create a coherent fiscal policy (the budget was simply the sum of what Congress decided to spend through its separate appropriations bills each year). Nixon sought to solve the problem by asserting that he could simply refuse to spend congressionally appropriated funds, an action termed "impoundment."

These impoundments caused bitter conflict, because they struck at the very core of Congress's power. Democrats and even many Republicans did not believe a president could be permitted to exercise such power unchecked. On the other hand, though, many members of both parties did agree that spending had to be brought under control by improving congressional procedures for creating a budget. The solution was the Budgeting and Impoundment Act of 1974, which created a Budget Committee in each house and set up a Congressional Budget Office. The latter was intended to provide the Congress with an independent source of information, equivalent to what the Office of Management and Budget gave the president. The vehicle for Congress's budget was to be an annual concurrent resolution, passed by the House and Senate but not requiring the president's signature; it would set limits on the spending decisions of authorizing and appropriating committees. The law also provided that the president could propose to impound appropriated funds, but these impoundments could be blocked by Congress.

In the midst of these interbranch disputes, the Congress also waded through the Watergate scandal, which entailed the involvement of executive-branch and Republican-campaign of-

ficials in a break-in at the headquarters of the Democratic National Committee, and in the cover-up of that and other crimes. The Senate held investigative hearings in 1973, and the House considered the matter of impeaching the president in 1974. In July, the House Judiciary Committee voted three articles of impeachment, Nixon resigned shortly thereafter, and Vice President Gerald Ford (R.-Mich.) formerly the minority leader of the House, succeeded to the presidency. The brief Ford administration was marked by continuing conflict with Congress over domestic and foreign policy, especially after the Democrats made major gains in the 1974 elections. Ford frequently exercised his veto on spending bills, only some of which were overridden. Congress blocked further American aid to South Vietnam and U.S. involvement in the Angolan Civil War. There were also disputes over defense spending, although by Ford's last year, evidence of a Soviet arms buildup led Congress to support defense increases.

1977–1980: THE CARTER PRESIDENCY

Congressional politics in the Carter years was in some ways similar to the previous decade, and in others very different. Some observers might have expected that the restoration of united party control of both the presidency and Congress would have created the conditions for vigorous joint action and a coherent political program, but that was not to be.

The trend toward more individual-oriented congressional campaigns continued as voters' attachment to the two major parties declined further. Campaigns for Congress became more expensive, requiring entrepreneurial members and aspirants to spend more time raising campaign funds. One prominent source of campaign money was the PACs that proliferated in the wake of the campaign-finance reforms. In 1974 there were only 608 registered PACs, but by 1980 there were more than 2,500. The aggregate amount of funds they contributed grew during that period from $12.5 million to more than $55 million.

Legislative resources available to members also increased, particularly in the realm of staff. At the time of the Legislative Reorganization

Act of 1947, representatives' personal staffs numbered 1,440. Twenty years later this had increased to 4,055, and by 1980 it had grown further to 7,371. The corresponding numbers for senators were 590 in 1947, 1,749 in 1967, and 3,746 in 1980. These employees worked on legislative matters or on constituents' problems with government, all of which helped members build support among voters. In addition, the ability of representatives to reach their constituents directly was further enhanced when the House began televising its proceedings in 1979 (the Senate did not follow suit until 1986).

The reforms of the early 1970s had two major affects: they reduced the power of committee chairs to provide centralized direction to the bodies they headed, and they also protected the independence and the resources of subcommittees. This encouraged legislative lethargy and stalemate in Congress—a result made even more likely because conflicts within the Democratic party in Congress and between the president and congressional Democrats deprived party leaders of a policy consensus that would have permitted them to exert centralizing leadership. These trends caused many observers to label this as the era of "subcommittee government" in Congress, characterized by conflict, inaction, and frustration.

The policy conflicts of this period primarily stemmed from the continued existence of serious divisions between northern and southern Democrats, and from the fact that the political preferences of President Carter—a southern moderate—were often different from those of the dominant liberal faction of the party in Congress. Carter wanted to reduce the budget deficit and reform the operation of government programs, not a set of priorities that would excite Democratic liberals. He was an outsider with no direct experience with the federal government, and he regarded himself as a proponent of the national interest but saw Congress as responsive to special interests—as evidenced by his efforts to block congressional water projects that he saw as porkbarrel programs. On defense and foreign policy, he supported increased spending on conventional defense programs (which many liberals disliked), while he favored cuts in strategic weapons, increased humanitarian foreign aid, and the return of the Panama Canal to the Panama-

nian government. These latter positions all caused him trouble with conservatives.

These problems were exacerbated by the increased prominence of issues, such as energy and the environment, that cut across partisan and ideological lines, making it more difficult to build political coalitions. Carter's situation was made even worse when the 1978 elections brought a new group of aggressive conservative Republicans to the House and Senate, and when economic decline and the Iranian hostage crisis (involving the Iranian government's holding of American embassy officials) undermined his standing with the public. The eventual result was the first defeat of an elected incumbent president since Herbert Hoover in 1932.

1981–1990: THE RESURGENCE OF PARTISANSHIP

President Reagan and the Ninety-seventh Congress

The 1980 elections not only produced a Republican president, but also gave the GOP control of the Senate for the first time in twenty-six years. In addition, the Democrats suffered a net loss of thirty-three House seats. President Ronald Reagan came to office with a strongly conservative agenda that included tax cuts, reductions in domestic spending, increases in defense outlays, and the trimming of federal regulatory activity. Despite continued Democratic control of the House, the Ninety-seventh Congress (1981–1983) gave the president most of what he wanted, as perceptions of constituent pressure revitalized southern Democratic participation in the conservative coalition.

The elections of 1978 and 1980 raised fears among southern Democrats of a full-scale partisan realignment, as GOP representation from the region grew from twenty-seven to thirty-nine in the House, and from five to ten in the Senate. Reagan had beaten a southerner, carrying every state in the region but Georgia in the process. Many southern Democrats, made sensitive to constituency preferences by the increasingly candidate-centered electoral process, saw the election outcomes as an endorsement of Reagan's conservative agenda, and provided the margin of votes necessary for the enactment of his major proposals. Spending for defense increased substantially, while there were sharp cuts for domestic programs. Simultaneously, a major tax cut was passed, and tax rates were indexed to the cost of living, blocking continued automatic increases in government revenues—which meant that future expansion of programs would have to be paid for by larger deficits, increased taxes, or cuts elsewhere. This turned congressional politics into more of a zero-sum game: the role of representatives and senators as brokers among competing interests was intensified.

During 1982, however, a serious recession set in, and Reagan's approval ratings began to drop. Meanwhile, members returned to their districts and interacted with their constituents, and many southern Democrats discovered that their constituents did not necessarily endorse all of the president's programs.

Further Effects of Electoral Change

By the time of the 1982 congressional elections, the cumulative effects of electoral changes in the 1960s and 1970s were being felt, especially in the South. Population migration from North to South, and within the South, coupled with court-mandated redistricting created more urban-oriented House districts in that region. The effects of the Voting Rights Act substantially increased the number of black voters, most of whom identified with, and participated in, the Democratic party. Meanwhile, white conservative Democrats continued their exodus from their old party. The increase in black voters and the decrease in conservative whites both contributed to a liberalization of the southern Democratic electorate. The result was that the constituencies of southern Democrats were more like those of northern Democrats, and less like those of Republicans. It also shaped the nomination process for southern Democrats, creating conditions less hospitable for conservative candidates but more favorable to moderates and liberals.

In 1982, these changing circumstances combined with economic conditions that were politically unfavorable to the GOP: the Democrats gained twenty-five House seats, while the Republicans won one additional Senate seat. Thus, the GOP retained their Senate control, but more politically important were the House

results: in the South the Democrats defeated six Republican incumbents, held many open seats, and won in a ratio of five to two the new districts transferred to the region through reapportionment. The result was a class of twenty freshman southern Democrats, most of whom had a strong inclination to support the positions of their party and its congressional leadership. The Republicans regained some ground in southern House seats in 1984, but the Democrats bounced back in 1986, and the regional division of seats remained unchanged through the 1990 elections. Meanwhile, the GOP experienced their most painful reversal in 1986, when the Democrats took back control of the Senate (partly through the gain of four southern seats) and held it in subsequent elections.

These electoral outcomes gave the Democrats solid numerical control of Congress. More politically significant, though, these altered underlying conditions meant that the policy preferences among congressional Democrats were more homogeneous than they had been at any time since early in the century. (For example, in the One-hundredth Congress of 1987–1989 unity in floor voting among Democratic representatives on issues that split the two parties was at the highest level since the Sixty-first Congress of 1909–1911.) This did not mean that the views of northern and southern Democrats in Congress were identical—far from it—but it did mean that their preferences were far more similar than they had been in the divisive days of the 1960s and 1970s, and that the views of southern Democrats were less like those of Republicans.

The changes in the South interacted with other, more general electoral trends, some of which mitigated and some of which reinforced them. The net population gains of the South were paralleled by substantial gains in the Southwest and West as well, but these came at the expense of midwestern and northeastern states, which experienced modest economic growth and even some population losses. These growth differences led to the shifting of congressional seats from the Rust Belt to the Sun Belt. California, for example, grew from thirty House seats in 1960 to forty-five in 1982 (and then to fifty-two in 1992).

Republicans had believed that these trends would bring them majority status, since their party was stronger and growing in the areas of population gain—but this was not to be. Except for the above-mentioned gains in the South, the GOP did not do particularly well in the Sun Belt, at least not well enough to compensate for net losses they experienced elsewhere. As a result, in 1986 the Republicans held 177 seats, only one more than the 176 they had in 1962.

On the other hand, the population changes of the 1960s and 1970s had resulted in shifts in the nature of the Democratic congressional coalition. The decline of union strength in the United States, as measured by the size of unions' membership and their political influence, was coupled with declining loyalty of voters who belonged to unions to the Democratic party. In addition, the number of congressional districts centered on major cities in the North also was reduced. Consequently, there was a smaller base of Democrats whose districts led them automatically to support traditional Democratic programs. Meanwhile, a number of the northern Democrats who were elected from former Republican districts took relatively moderate positions on some issues. These members found some common ground with the new, more liberal southern Democrats, forming a stronger moderate base among House Democrats, especially on fiscal matters.

House Reform Revisited

As noted earlier, many observers believed that the reforms of the 1970s, particularly in the House, had further decentralized congressional policy-making, and thereby perhaps even paralyzed it. The altered electoral conditions in the 1980s produced results that indicate that judgment may have been premature: more homogeneous preferences among congressional Democrats made it easier to find common ground on previously divisive issues, and more difficult to reactivate the conservative coalition.

In the House, this increased cohesiveness made it more feasible for the party and its leadership to employ the tools granted through the reform process. A responsive Rules Committee shaped the terms of floor consideration for major bills so that Democratic positions were protected, and opportunities for Republican counterattacks were restricted. Party loyalty was taken into account to a greater degree in assigning members to major committees. The Democratic Caucus's ability to remove committee chairs continued. In two consecutive Congresses (in 1985 and 1987), the Caucus voted down different chairs of the Armed Services Committee, in part because of their perceived failure to protect the Democratic majority's positions on defense issues. Greater party homogeneity and enhanced powers also permitted a more forceful leadership style, as when Speaker Jim Wright (D.-Tex.) fashioned an independent Democratic position on America's involvement in the civil conflict in Nicaragua. Against much opposition from the Reagan administration, this position became government policy.

Thus, in the 1980s the previous decade's reforms in the House enhanced the chances for passing Democratic policy proposals and reinforced electoral incentives for individual Democrats to support those positions. Moreover, committee leaders lost some of their power to frustrate those party proposals with which they did not sympathize. Meanwhile in the Senate, the changed electoral conditions also improved Democratic cohesion, although the party apparatus lacked powers equivalent to those held by House leaders, so the results were less powerful.

Divided and Unified Government

This improved homogeneity among congressional Democrats arose within the context of continued partisan division of government control, and it made that condition extremely important. If party divisions in Congress are muted, and the president is able to build legislative coalitions across party lines (as Reagan was so frequently able to do in 1981), then divided government may not be of much practical consequence. Divided government mattered from 1981 through 1992 because Republican presidents and most congressional Democrats represented fundamentally different constituencies with different policy preferences, which led them to respond very differently on most important policy issues.

On the civil rights issue, the historic divisions within the Democratic party had almost entirely disappeared, while the GOP took more conservative positions. In the realm of budget politics, southern Democrats became more supportive of domestic spending, and an increasing number of northerners became sensitive to the economic (and political) detriments of large deficits. Homogeneity even increased on defense matters, long a source of regional conflict for Democrats, as more southerners supported cuts and were also increasingly prepared to express their will over and against the president's on specific military issues, such as the Strategic Defense Initiative (the defense system intended to shoot down hostile strategic nuclear warheads).

It appears that the existence of divided government stems in part from voters expecting different things from presidents and members of Congress. They want presidents to speak for the broad national interest, and they have tended to conclude that Republicans do this better; on the other hand, they want the programs that benefit them and their localities protected, and they see this task better performed by Democrats, who tend to personally favor such programs. Relatedly, division also seems to stem from the voters being offered different types of candidate choices for the offices they must fill. For president, the choice (in the voters' perception) is often between an extremely liberal Democrat and a moderately conservative Republican, while for Congress it is often the Democrat who appears to be more moderate and the Republican to be more extreme.

The 1992 elections ended twelve consecutive years of divided government, the longest such period to that point in U.S. history. The poor performance of the economy and the electorate's concerns about other domestic issues appeared to overcome, perhaps only temporarily, the causes of divided government outlined above. The similarity between the electoral coalitions of President Clinton and congressional Democrats made it appear that it would be possible for them to find common ground on many (albeit not all) issues. Constituency differences, on the other hand, would likely lead to frequent friction between Republicans and Democrats, in the White House and in Congress. These conditions would create the possibility of significant policy changes, but only if the entrepreneurial politicians in the Democratic party perceived electoral incentives that induced them to stick together, and that permitted them to overcome Republican resistance. Furthermore, if the public remained dissatisfied with government performance and held the Democrats responsible, it seemed that divided government—and its related "gridlock"—could be restored by a Democratic loss of control of Congress in 1994, or of the White House in 1996.

BIBLIOGRAPHY

Elections and Their Consequences
DAVID W. BRADY, *Critical Elections and Congressional Policy-making* (Stanford, Calif., 1988), is a study of policy innovation in the House during three periods of electoral realignment, including the New Deal era. EDWARD G. CARMINES and JAMES A. STIMSON, *Issue Evolution: Race and the Transformation of American Politics* (Princeton, N.J., 1989), analyzes the impact of the race issue on the restructuring of American electoral politics. Of particular interest is the effect of congressional decisions on civil rights legislation on partisan attitudes.

RICHARD F. FENNO, *Home Style* (Ann Arbor, Mich., 1978), offers generalizations based on the author's travels with representatives in their districts. He argues that members face a variety of constituencies, and they develop different relationships with them. Of particular import is the effort to establish trust between representative and represented.

BRUCE CAIN, JOHN FEREJOHN, and MORRIS FIORINA, *The Personal Vote: Constituency Service and Electoral Independence* (Cambridge, Mass., 1987), is an analysis of the ways in which legislators in the United States and Great Britain earn personal support from voters, thereby weakening their ties to national leaders and parties. MORRIS P. FIORINA, *Congress: Keystone of the Washington Establishment*, 2d ed. (New Haven, Conn., 1989), is an expanded version of an earlier statement of the thesis that representatives derived electoral support independent of their policy views by solving constituents' problems with the bureaucracy. GARY C. JACOBSON, *The Electoral Origins of Divided*

Government (Boulder, Colo., 1990), argues that the Republicans are disadvantaged in congressional elections for political rather than structural reasons, particularly when weak challengers run against Democratic incumbents. Data cover the entire postwar period. BURDETT LOOMIS, *The New American Politician: Ambition, Entrepreneurship, and the Changing Face of Political Life* (New York, 1988), describes the ambitious, issue-oriented congressional entrepreneurs who came to office in the 1970s and 1980s.

DAVID R. MAYHEW, *Congress: The Electoral Connection* (New Haven, Conn., 1974), is an analysis of the ways in which the electoral self-interest of representatives shapes the institutional structure of the House and its operation, and BARBARA SINCLAIR, *Congressional Realignment, 1925–1978* (Austin, Tex., 1982), uses House roll-call data to describe and explain shifting alignments within and between parties on various issues, and the emergence of new issue dimensions.

Internal Politics of Congress

DAVID W. BRADY, JOSEPH COOPER, and PATRICIA A. HURLEY, "The Decline of Party in the U.S. House of Representatives, 1887–1968," *Legislative Studies Quarterly* 4 (1979), documents the long-term decline of partisanship in floor voting in the House, and argues that it is the consequence of both external and internal forces. JOSEPH COOPER and DAVID W. BRADY, "Institutional Context and Leadership Style: The House from Cannon to Rayburn," *American Political Science Review* 75:3 (1981), argues that the transition from a hierarchical pattern of leadership in the House to a bargaining pattern was primarily the consequence of external electoral forces that produced internal divisions within the legislative parties. RICHARD F. FENNO, *Congressmen in Committees* (Boston, 1973), is a classic study of Senate and House committees which demonstrates that members join committees, and structure their operations, in order to serve a variety of personal goals. FRANK H. MACKAMAN, ed., *Understanding Congressional Leadership* (Washington, D.C., 1981), is a collection of articles dealing with congressional leadership in the postwar era. DONALD R. MATTHEWS, *United States Senators and Their World* (New York, 1960), is the classic study of the membership and politics of the Senate of the 1950s.

JAMES T. PATTERSON, *Congressional Conservatism and the New Deal* (Westport, Conn., 1967), documents the rise of the conservative coalition in response to the New Deal policy agenda. NELSON W. POLSBY, "The Institutionalization of the U.S. House of Representatives," *American Political Science Review* (1968), describes the development of the House as an institution, including data on the increasing length of congressional careers, the decline of membership turnover, and the elaboration of a leadership structure. RONALD M. PETERS, *The American Speakership: The Office in Historical Perspective* (Baltimore, 1990), is an account of Speakers of the House from the beginning through Jim Wright. LEROY N. RIESELBACH, *Congressional Reform* (Washington, D.C., 1986), describes the reforms of the 1970s and discusses their impact on the House and Senate.

DAVID W. ROHDE, *Parties and Leaders in the Postreform House* (Chicago, 1991), argues that electoral changes and internal reforms have combined to produce more homogeneous congressional parties and stronger party leadership. DAVID W. ROHDE, NORMAN J. ORNSTEIN, and ROBERT L. PEABODY, "Political Change and Legislative Norms in the U.S. Senate, 1957–1974," in GLENN R. PARKER, ed., *Studies of Congress* (Washington, D.C., 1985), contends that some norms in the Senate served the general interest, while others served only the interests of senior conservatives, and that the latter ceased to control behavior when the conservatives could no longer impose effective sanctions for their violation. BARBARA SINCLAIR, *The Transformation of the U.S. Senate* (Baltimore, 1989), describes the development of the Senate into a more open, egalitarian institution from the 1950s to the 1980s.

STEVEN S. SMITH, *Call to Order: Floor Politics in the House and Senate* (Washington, D.C., 1989), analyzes the shift in congressional policymaking toward a greater role for individual members on the floors of the House and Senate. See also STEVEN S. SMITH and CHRISTOPHER J. DEERING, *Committees in Congress*, 2d ed. (Washington, D.C., 1990), an analysis of contemporary committee politics in the House and Senate.

Congressional-Executive Relations

JOEL D. ABERBACH, *Keeping a Watchful Eye: The Politics of Congressional Oversight* (Washington, D.C., 1990), describes the growth of congressional oversight of the executive since the 1960s, presenting a fairly positive view of developments. JON R. BOND and RICHARD FLEISCHER, *The President in the Legislative Arena* (1990), is an analysis of congressional roll calls on which the president took a position, from Eisenhower through Reagan. The focus is on the conditions that determine whether the president wins or loses.

GARY COX and SAMUEL KERNELL, eds., *The Politics of Divided Government* (Boulder, Colo., 1991), is a collection of readings dealing with the causes and consequences of divided government in the second half of the twentieth century. Some comparisons with earlier historical periods are included. CECIL V. CRABB and PAT M. HOLT, *Invitation to Struggle: Congress, the President and Foreign Policy*, 4th ed. (Washington, D.C., 1992), deals with presidential-congressional interactions in foreign affairs since World War II. LAWRENCE C. DODD and RICHARD L. SCHOTT, *Congress and the Administrative State* (New York, 1979), is an extensive historical and analytical treatment of congressional-bureaucratic relations. GEORGE C. EDWARDS III, *At the Margins: Presidential Leadership of Congress* (1989), examines under what conditions presidents lead Congress, and argues that such leadership usually occurs only at the margins.

General Works

GEORGE B. GALLOWAY and SIDNEY WISE, *History of the House of Representatives* (New York, 1976), is a good, one-volume history of the House, updated through the early 1970s, and JAMES L. SUNDQUIST, *The Decline and Resurgence of Congress* (Washington, D.C., 1981), discusses the shifting balance of power between the branches, with emphasis on the efforts by Congress in the 1970s to reassert itself in a variety of areas.

SEE ALSO Congress, the Executive, and Foreign Policy; Congress, Sectionalism, and Public-Policy Formation Since 1870; The Congressional Committee System; Congressional Reform; Constituencies; Constitutional and Political Constraints on Congressional Policy-Making: A Historical Perspective; Executive Leadership and Party Organization in Congress; Legislative-Executive Relations; AND Parties, Elections, Moods, and Lawmaking Surges.

THE ORIGINS AND EARLY DEVELOPMENT
OF STATE LEGISLATURES

Peter S. Onuf

The early U.S. state legislatures drew on the institutional and procedural legacies of their predecessors, the colonial general assemblies. Traditions of representative government were well established in all the colonies, including the British West Indies, long before the Declaration of Independence. Scholars have drawn the natural conclusion that the development of colonial self-government, and particularly the rise of the assemblies, prepared the way for the break with Britain. The state constitutions confirmed the dominant position of the legislatures in governing republican America. Yet, conventional scholarship explains, conservative constitutionalists soon sought to restrain the excesses of popular government by strengthening the executive branch, establishing an independent judiciary, and supplanting the most radical, unicameral legislatures with bicameral systems. After enjoying only mixed success at the state level, constitutional reformers finally found an effective remedy for the "democratic despotism" of the state legislatures in the creation of a powerful national government.

This standard account makes good sense either from a narrowly institutional or from a broadly historical perspective. Certainly the state legislatures, which included substantial numbers of former assemblymen, borrowed liberally from colonial practices and procedures; and in the larger scheme of things, the legislators' contributions to the progress of freedom and constitutional government seem unassailable. But just as contemporary critics saw legislative pretensions in a less flattering light, a closer look at the immediate historical context of legislative behavior and at the ideas and intentions of Revolutionary state-makers suggests alternative lines of interpretation.

First, the political and social aspirations of colonial legislators before the onset of the resistance movement and the deterioration of British imperial rule are best understood in terms of a powerful anglicizing impulse in provincial America. The self-styled "better sort," the would-be aristocrats who aped British metropolitan taste and fashion, attempted to make their assemblies into "little Parliaments." Far from representing themselves as typical colonists, the more sophisticated and cosmopolitan representatives sought to differentiate and distance themselves from common folk. For the upwardly aspiring, the challenge to imperial rule constituted a genuine crisis: patriot leaders who sought to mobilize constituency support against British policy sacrificed all hopes for royal patronage or preference, relying instead on the popular perception of their merit or virtue to sustain their social pretensions and political power.

The Revolutionary crisis transformed the premises of representative government even while old institutions were adapted, sometimes with little change, to new conditions. State-makers had to reconcile their conceptions of constitutional government and the rule of law with the destruction of royal prerogative, which had been the foundation of the monarchical and aristocratic elements in the colonies' mixed governments. The challenge was to "constitutionalize" the new state legislatures—to construct limited, legitimate governments that could rule effectively while commanding broad popular support. The succession of the state legislatures to power may have been logical, even inevitable, but it was deeply problematic. As a result, and in the midst of an often-desperate war for national independence, Revolutionary leaders in every state (except Connecticut and Rhode Island) made extraordinary efforts to draft constitutions that would establish their right to rule.

As the states emerged from their Revolutionary and constitutional crises, the legislatures consolidated their jurisdiction and expanded the scope of their governing authority far beyond that claimed and exercised by their colonial predecessors. But the problems of the American Union under the Articles of Confederation and the movement for a strong federal constitution have overshadowed and distorted these developments. In fact, nationalist attacks on state sovereignty reflected a begrudging recognition that the state governments were operating effectively and stood poised to move into the jurisdictional vacuum caused by the deterioration and apparently imminent collapse of congressional authority. Astute reformers understood that the need was not so much to check or change the state governments, as to confine their power within the limits set forth in the Articles—and generally observed in the informal constitution of the old British Empire—by establishing an independent constitutional government for the union as a whole.

As Federalist proponents of the Constitution predicted, the institution of the new federal regime strengthened republican government in the states by preempting the external challenges—from other states or foreign powers—that would have justified the states' assumption of full sovereign powers. If the state legislatures were thus precluded from developing into little Parliaments, they were free to move decisively into a wide range of policy areas. The progressive development of legislative power, already apparent in the so-called critical period before the Philadelphia Convention of 1787, was not reversed, but rather reinforced by the establishment of the federal regime. The early national period was the golden age of state legislative government in U.S. political history.

THE RISE AND FALL OF THE COLONIAL ASSEMBLIES

The lower, representative houses of the colonial assemblies played a leading role in the coming of the American Revolution. Representatives presented themselves as guardians of their constituents' rights as Englishmen in America, identifying the corporate claims of the assemblies with individual property rights. They argued that representative institutions constituted the only effective guarantee of liberty against power, the property owners' best defense against the depredations of rapacious and irresponsible crown officials.

The colonial assemblies' pretensions in the imperial crisis prepared them to assume a dominant position under the Revolutionary state constitutions. From a narrowly institutional perspective, the continuities are striking. The rise of the assemblies long antedated belated efforts of British reformers to rationalize imperial governance and curb the corporate privileges that impeded efficient administration. In every colony, the lower house effectively asserted the power of the purse, thus gaining a decisive advantage over royal governors and the crown appointees in the upper houses. Drawing inspiration from the British House of Commons, the assemblies successfully asserted a wide array of claims—over members' privileges and immunities, internal organization, and relations with the executive—that in some cases exceeded the British model. It was hardly surprising that in Virginia, for instance, the House of Burgesses would reconstitute itself as a "convention" with extraordinary powers, or that colonial representatives elsewhere would be elected to new state legislatures that bore such a striking resemblance to their colonial predecessors.

Yet this traditional, Whiggish view of growing legislative competence and self-confidence seems less straightforward and more problematic from a broader historical perspective. By British standards, the scope of the assemblies' authority was radically limited. If royal governors were vanquished—or at least neutralized—on various constitutional fronts, it did not follow that the assemblies were ready to fill the resulting vacuum of authority. Adhering to the traditional idea that government and the executive branch were synonymous, colonial assemblymen disavowed any inclination to govern. In Britain, by contrast, the newly orthodox conception of "king-in-Parliament" effectively obliterated the distinction between representatives and government. The king was considered part of the legislature, and ministerial appointments were drawn increasingly from the Commons.

Colonial assemblymen often occupied key positions in local government, most notably in county courts in the South, but the assemblies as such did not govern locally, even if they controlled the purse strings. Except in New England, where towns governed themselves, local officials were gubernatorial appointees; governors exercised at least nominal control over the court systems in all the colonies. Nor did legislators presume to encroach on crown jurisdiction over external trade and foreign policy. Patriot polemicists sought to modify or nullify British mercantile policy by arguing that regulatory duties were "taxes," but they disclaimed any right to interfere in the management of empire-wide concerns.

The rapid expansion of transatlantic trade and credit relations undercut the independence of colonial economies and increased pressures for imperial regulation and control even as the assemblies rose to preeminence. In the final phases of the imperial crisis, British policymakers increasingly sought to circumvent recalcitrant colonial legislatures. Direct rule over the colonists through revitalized executives and a more effective imperial bureaucracy threatened to marginalize the assemblies. The *proroguing*, or suspension, of the New York Assembly in December 1766 after its refusal to comply with Parliament's Quartering Act was the first in a series of direct assaults on the integrity of representative institutions in the colonies. Governor Francis Bernard suspended successive assemblies in Massachusetts (in March and July 1768) after legislators sent out the famous circular letter denouncing the Townshend duties of 1767, and governors elsewhere were ordered to suspend any assembly endorsing the letter. The most sustained impasse took place in South Carolina, where the Commons House was repeatedly suspended beginning in 1769 after voting to give public funds John Wilkes, the English radical who refused his seat in Parliament because of his opposition to ministerial policy. No legislation of any sort was enacted in South Carolina from February 1771 until independence. It was a short step to the complete supersession of representative government, culminating in Massachusetts with the abrogation of the charter and the institution of military rule under General Thomas Gage in 1774. Struggles over assembly rights helped promote mass mobilization and the creation of revolutionary political structures—but they also showed that the colonies could be governed quite effectively without representative institutions.

The imperial crisis transformed representative-constituent relations. As was the case with Parliament in Britain, the institutional ethos of the assemblies had long fostered their corporate identification with the defense of English rights in America. In Britain, however, this rights-consciousness combined with expanding legislative competence to validate parliamentary claims to sovereignty. The colonial assemblies moved in the opposite direction. As they were marginalized and immobilized, assemblymen strengthened constituency ties by emphasizing their role as guardians of popular rights. The irony of these appeals is that they ran counter to the tendency of colonial legislatures before the imperial crisis to become *less* representative of the common folk. The parliamentary privileges asserted and assumed by assemblymen may have protected them from executive interference and therefore rendered the property and liberty of all colonists more secure, but these pretensions also underscored the growing social distance between a self-consciously anglicizing elite and the mass of voters. Although intra-elite competition in colonies such as Pennsylvania and New York periodically prompted appeals to constituents, the quasi-aristocratic tendencies of provincial politics were only reversed when patriot leaders began to mobilize popular resistance to imperial policies that jeopardized their political power and social status.

The transformation of representative-constituent relations was equally apparent in theory and practice. British ministerial writers who argued that colonists were "virtually represented" in Parliament, claiming that members "represented" the entire empire, not simply the few electors who voted for them, provided a convenient foil for patriots who celebrated the direct, "actual" representation the colonists supposedly enjoyed in their own legislatures. The absence of highly differentiated social structures in the colonies, long a sore point for would-be aristocrats, could now be portrayed as the best guarantee of communal harmony and virtue. Representatives were attached to the represented by the strongest ties, symbolized and strengthened by election rituals and the drafting of instructions by town meetings and other constituent bodies. As the history of the Boston Committee of Correspondence, an arm of the town meeting, demonstrates, these "spontaneous" initiatives were often orchestrated by patriot leaders anxious to bolster their increasingly tenuous position in the struggle against imperial authority.

CONSTITUTIONAL CRISIS

Colonial polemicists challenged the legitimacy of the old regime, demonstrating the "unconstitutionality" of innovations in British imperial policy. But patriots sought a popular mandate to resist the encroachments of British power on American rights, not to justify the creation of new governments. By focusing on individual rights, the rule of law, and constitutional first principles, resistance rhetoric made the assumption of authority profoundly problematic. Widespread misgivings were apparent in the colonists' reluctance to declare independence until the war had been in progress—and the Continental Congress had been exercising extensive powers—for more than a year. Even then, large numbers of Americans across the continent refused to abjure (formally renounce) the king, including Whig Loyalists, like Daniel Dulany of Maryland, who had taken an active role in earlier phases of the resistance movement.

The current conventional view of loyalists is that they were alienated and marginalized by the increasingly radical character of the patriot coalition. Arguably, however, John Dickinson, author of *Letters of a Pennsylvania Farmer* (1768), and other scrupulous colonists immobilized by the independence crisis were most sensitive to the contradictions at the heart of Anglo-American constitutionalism. The question was not whether Americans were capable of governing themselves—they were doing that already—or even whether they had the abstract right to do so. The idea of popular or community sovereignty was deeply embedded in Anglo-American political theory and practice. But how could independent Americans establish durable, legitimate governments that would secure their fundamental rights? Patriot leaders had deduced or abstracted rights from the British constitution in order to justify resistance to imperial authority; now they had to move from this heightened consciousness of rights to the construction of new constitutions that would

permit American legislatures to exercise extraordinary, unprecedented powers.

Well before the effective collapse of imperial government in America in 1775, colonists had demonstrated their organizational genius in the proliferation of radical institutions and associations. Wherever possible, patriots transformed local governments into agencies of revolutionary persuasion and coercion; committees, conventions, and congresses linked communities and quickly filled the vacuum of power at the colonial and intercolonial level. To a remarkable extent, this outburst of political activity made the "fiction" of popular sovereignty plausible, reassuring optimistic patriots that the empire's demise would not lead to anarchy and social chaos. Yet this revolutionary infrastructure could not by itself resolve the succession crisis; to the contrary, the legitimacy of these institutional expedients depended on their provisional and ad hoc character. The defense of fundamental rights and the redress of constitutional grievances justified extraordinary and extraconstitutional measures. But the final move toward independence subverted the conditions that had permitted radicals to assume power without confronting its problematic implications.

The authors of the first state constitutions thus faced formidable challenges. The perceived legitimacy of the new regimes was crucial to the continuing success of mobilization efforts, particularly where popular loyalties were contingent and contested. The resistance movement politicized an expanding and demanding electorate, raising popular expectations about the responsiveness of the new state governments and their conformity to exalted constitutional standards. At the same time, of course, these governments had to manage the war effort efficiently and expeditiously. But many Revolutionaries wondered whether the inevitable concentration of power that war entailed was compatible with the preservation of liberty.

The conditions under which the first state constitutions were drafted were hardly propitious. In some states, including Massachusetts, political leaders invoked the wartime emergency in urging that constitution writing be delayed. At the national level, the protracted drafting of the Articles of Confederation (sent out to the states in 1777) and their belated ratification (in 1781), were justified on these grounds. Yet every state (except Connecticut and Rhode Island, which continued to operate under their colonial charters) drafted a constitution during the war years. It might even be argued that wartime conditions made the writing of constitutions imperative, and that these documents were fundamentally shaped by both the ongoing struggle of provisional state governments for popular loyalty and a legitimating mandate in the face of powerful foreign and domestic enemies. State-constitution writing was integral to the conduct of the war and the definition of war aims, not a sideshow or afterthought. If there had been no war and American independence had been uncontested, it is highly unlikely that state leaders would have felt compelled to go to such extraordinary lengths.

The precise sequence of the final moves toward independence confirms the importance of the state constitutions in the context of the war. Throughout 1775 and early 1776, patriot leaders in the various colonies had effectively assumed governing power. In some places, notably in New York and Pennsylvania where Loyalist sentiment neutralized the assemblies, resistance leaders had created parallel governing structures; elsewhere, where the popular party was well entrenched, the assemblies reconvened on an ad hoc, extraconstitutional basis. But everywhere, the Revolutionaries' right to rule was doubtful, and no more so than in the minds of the more scrupulous of the Revolutionaries themselves. Patriot leaders thus turned to the Continental Congress, both for practical support in efforts to supplant uncooperative assemblies and for authorization to take the decisive step in establishing independent state governments. If the decision for independence presented a crisis of conscience for individual Americans, the break with Britain underscored the need to reconstitute legitimate authority for leaders who sought to sustain the war effort through makeshift arrangements in the various colonies. Thus on 10 May 1776, Congress called on the states to constitute new governments where existing arrangements had proved unsatisfactory. Congress's resolution for independence on 2 July reaffirmed the transformation of colonies into states, and that change was defined in terms of writing constitutions.

That the early political history of the new states should be dominated by constitutional issues is not surprising given the central preoccupations of the resistance movement. These preoccupations help explain why Revolutionaries were so troubled by their own assumption of power, notwithstanding such extensive social and institutional continuities with the old regimes. Indeed, the challenge was to rationalize and reconstitute government in ways that would accommodate the Revolutionary mobilization of political society and conform to the lofty standards and rising expectations generated by resistance constitutionalism.

The Revolutionary legislatures that drafted the first state constitutions confronted a thicket of theoretical and practical problems. Once they overcame scruples about their own authority to act, legislators had to define future limits on legislative power. Where could such limits be found? Independence eliminated the royal prerogative, represented in most colonial constitutions by governors—who controlled the timing and duration of assembly sessions, vetoed legislation, and dispensed patronage—and by appointed royal councils that functioned as upper houses in the provincial legislatures. How could American constitution-writers create mixed or balanced governments and thus secure their liberties when the social and political foundations of the colonial governors and royal councils were so completely destroyed? How, with the empire's demise, could American constitution-writers institute checks on their own power (as legislators) that would secure their right to rule?

Few American constitutionalists were opposed to monarchy or aristocracy on principle. Before independence, patriot polemicists attacked corrupt royal governors who allegedly perverted and misrepresented the king to his American subjects. When he asserted that George III was "king of the Massachusetts, king of Rhode Island, king of Connecticut, &c.," John Adams (writing as "Novanglus" in 1775) was attempting to redeem royal authority from ministerial corruption, with the intent to reconcile the monarchical principle with American liberties. Similarly, the most devastating charge against the colonial councils was that they were merely tools of court corruption; they lacked the "independence" of truly aristocratic bodies that could have checked the excesses of royal—or popular—power.

The metaphorical "killing of the king" through the Declaration of Independence in 1776 effectively suppressed monarchical sentiment—though it would reappear in the critical period leading up to the Philadelphia Convention of 1787—and the egalitarian ethos of mass mobilization precluded the creation of legally privileged classes. But a radically idealized British constitution continued to epitomize good and legitimate government to American constitutionalists. The shadows of monarchical and aristocratic authority were apparent in most of the new constitutions, not only in the attenuated form of impotent executives and popularly elected senates, but also in the extraordinary efforts the framers made to guarantee against abuses of power by the people's representatives—the same people, in many instances, who wrote the constitutions.

American Revolutionaries had clear ideas about the dangers of unrestrained legislative power in their recent experiences with the corrupt and supposedly sovereign British Parliament. The problem with Britain, Thomas Paine charged (and his fellow patriots were finally forced to agree), was that its constitution was "sickly" beyond rehabilitation. When the colonial assemblies had made their bid for power in constitutional conflicts with royal governors, they liked to think of themselves as little Parliaments. But during the imperial crisis such comparisons ceased to be flattering to patriot legislators. They saw themselves as guardians of popular rights, not as legitimate successors to the unlimited authority claimed by the imperial legislature. Far from authorizing the assumption of absolute power, the Revolutionaries' idea of popular sovereignty mandated the kinds of constitutional limitation that balanced government had once supposedly guaranteed in the uncorrupted British constitution.

Even if the theoretical dilemma of regime succession could be resolved by relocating sovereignty from monarch to people, practical problems yet remained. How could representatives portray themselves to skeptical constituents as the embodiment of the sovereign people, with a right to constitute new governments? In practical terms, how could the governmental institutions they created be made both responsive and responsible to a mobilized political public? The paradoxical answer to these questions resided in the fact that the new governments invited challenges to their authority, both by frequent elections and, in several states, by developing progressively more elaborate mechanisms for ascertaining the will of the sovereign people. If constitutional experimentation and flux made the authority of the new state governments seem tenuous and contingent, it was only on such a provisional basis that many Americans, with their republican scruples and constitutionalist principles, were prepared to submit to popular government. Constitution writing perpetuated the extraordinary conditions that had justified patriot mobilization—and coercion—before independence.

CONSTITUTIONAL EXPERIMENTS

When the revolutionary war was going badly on all fronts during late 1776 and early 1777, most of the United States (as well as the independent republic of Vermont) began drafting constitutions. Their main provisions were remarkably similar. They all authorized the people's representatives to exercise extensive authority and deprived executives of the kinds of powers royal governors had deployed against the assemblies during the imperial crisis. In New Jersey, the new governor was stripped of his predecessor's veto and appointment powers: sheriffs, coroners, and council members were now chosen by popular election, while important state officials—including supreme court justices and the governor himself—were elected by joint ballot of the assembly and council, the lower and upper legislative bodies, respectively.

The supersession of executive authority was most complete in Pennsylvania and Georgia, where the "president" or governor was chosen by a unicameral legislature. Such drastic curbs on gubernatorial power were designed to preempt the inevitable threats to liberty and property that occurred when government was not responsible to the people or to the people's representatives. But this did not mean that the assemblies could be entrusted with unlimited power. As John Adams wrote in

Thoughts on Government (1776) in response to Thomas Paine's iconoclastic assault on constitutional government in *Common Sense*, "a single assembly is liable to all the vices, follies, and frailties of an individual." Collapsing all the branches of government into one was a prescription for despotism: popular assemblies were dangerously "unfit to exercise the executive" or "judicial power."

Yet Adams did not propose to create an independent executive by raising it over the people, as the British king had once exercised authority over his American subjects. Adams's answer was instead to expand the *electorate's* power and responsibility: he advised constitution writers to divide their legislatures into two popularly elected houses that would check each other and thereby guarantee the executive a degree of independence. Legislative, judicial, and executive powers "ought to be in different hands," agreed Theophilus Parsons in the "Essex Result" (1778); they should be "independent of one another, and so ballanced, and each having that check upon the other, that their independence shall be preserved." The independence of the respective branches—the hallmark of Anglo-American constitutionalism—would be secured through mobilizing the electorate.

In order to justify balanced government in independent America, constitutional theorists had to jettison traditional ideas of mixed government based on distinct social orders. The solution was to ground the authority of the respective branches in distinct acts of electoral will. After all, a South Carolina writer explained in 1784, "every officer, from the Governor to the constable, is, so far as the powers of his office extend, as truly the representative of the people, as a member of the legislature." In this way, the idea of popular sovereignty, made manifest in frequent elections, could be invoked *against* the lower houses' pretensions.

In that bicameralism—the doubling of popular representation—was the most ideologically acceptable way for early constitution writers to preempt legislative excesses, the direct election of governors represented the next logical step. New York took the lead in its 1777 constitution by providing for the triennial election of a governor who, significantly, could exercise a modified veto (which could be overturned by a two-thirds vote of the legislature)

and a share in state appointments. George Clinton was repeatedly reelected, thus becoming one of the most powerful and effective state executives.

All the new states relied on an active electorate to sustain constitutional government. Everywhere, whether or not a new constitution was implemented, representatives were chosen annually. Members of upper houses were also elected every year, except in South Carolina (with two-year terms), Delaware (three years), Virginia and New York (four years), and Maryland (indirectly, by an electoral college, every five years). The pace of legislative activity thus quickened—elections in most colonies had been considerably less frequent and regular—while the scope of legislative power expanded dramatically. Meanwhile, voters were called on regularly to choose a wide range of local officials, thus participating directly in what had generally been an executive prerogative.

One of the most striking and significant results of expanding electoral activity was to explode the fiction, so crucial to parliamentary pretensions to supreme power, that political society was embodied or immanent in the legislature itself. The American idea, articulated so eloquently by Adams, that a legislature "should be in miniature an exact portrait of the people at large," betrayed fundamental misgivings about the actual representativeness of any representative body. By setting up a standard of representation external to the legislature, Adams underscored the potential differences between constituents and delegates. Popular vigilance and frequent elections made possible the constant readjustments necessary to guarantee the faithfulness of representation and the exactness of the portrait. The "sacred depositum" of liberty, Adams's cousin Zabdiel Adams told the Massachusetts General Court, "cannot be watched with too great attention." The legislature's natural tendency to abuse power was most effectively offset or balanced by "vigilancy on the side of the people."

Early state legislators called attention to the ambiguities of their status as representatives when, as constitution writers, they attempted to justify their assumption of power. The misgivings of Revolutionary leaders were particularly conspicuous in North Carolina, South Carolina, and New Hampshire, where provisional governments held the reins of power until permanent constitutions were enacted in late 1776, 1778, and 1784, respectively. The most common practice was to call special elections for special congresses or conventions that would draft charters. But representatives in Virginia, New Jersey, and New York simply assumed constituent powers, and assemblies that were specifically empowered to write constitutions (Maryland, North Carolina, and Georgia) also enacted routine legislation during their sessions. Only Pennsylvania and Delaware clearly distinguished constituent and legislative authority. In Pennsylvania the independence crisis immobilized the colonial assembly, and a province-wide convention of committees seized the initiative by drafting a constitution; in Delaware, widespread Loyalist sentiment encouraged patriots in the assembly to seek a popular mandate through special elections.

Analyses of the early state constitutions usually emphasize the extent of popular power in the governments they established. "Democratic" Pennsylvania and other states with unicameral legislatures are compared to the more Whiggish "aristocratic" regimes established in Maryland and New York. A complementary, chronological approach shows the democratic constitutions of 1776, most notably those of Pennsylvania and Georgia, giving way to progressively more complex systems that curbed popular power: this story climaxes with the drafting of the federal Constitution in 1787 and the subsequent move to bicameralism in Georgia (1789) and Pennsylvania (1790). These accounts make considerable sense, particularly in places like Pennsylvania, where partisan debate between constitutionalist defenders and republican opponents of the 1776 Constitution focused on the putative excesses of unrestrained democratic rule. At the same time, however, a taxonomy based on the presence or absence of "democratic" elements in the new state charters distorts the intentions of their authors and obscures the distinctive political conditions within which they had to operate.

A more useful comparative scheme focuses on the difficulties faced by resistance leaders in making the transition to independence. Where internal opposition to the move was limited and provincial institutions could be adapted to revolutionary purposes, the succession was smooth. Neither Connecticut nor Rhode Island, relatively autonomous charter colonies where bicameral assemblies and governors were popularly elected, saw any need to draft new state constitutions.

The Revolutionary situation in Massachusetts and New Hampshire, two other New England colonies with similarly strong traditions of local self-government, differed significantly. Royal governors in both colonies dispensed considerable patronage and commanded strong "court parties," or loyal supporters of the administration, in the legislature; recently settled frontier communities were often not represented in the assemblies and would later respond eagerly to court-closing or separatist appeals. Loyalist tendencies in Massachusetts were powerfully reinforced by the British occupation of Boston throughout the first year of the war.

The tradition of town sovereignty in New England, when combined with cross pressures that immobilized provincial government and divided the old ruling elites, created optimal conditions for the development of more elaborate and politically responsive procedures for constitution writing. Town meetings accustomed to instructing representatives—and to sending delegates to ad hoc county and provincial conventions—had no difficulty in recognizing what Berkshire County constitutionalists defined as the "essential Distinction . . . between the fundamental Constitution, and Legislation." The government set up under the old, superseded charter of 1691 was obviously provisional and "unconstitutional." Therefore, Concord in October 1776 called for a special "Convention, or Congress . . . to form and establish a Constitution." Taking this logic a step further, dissidents in the western part of the state demanded that the new compact be ratified by the people: "to suppose the Representative Body capable of forming and imposing this Compact or Constitution without the Inspection and Approbation Rejection or Amendment of the people at large would involve in it the greatest Absurdity."

Deference to the popular will, manifested in town meetings, led to the rejection of proposed constitutions in Massachusetts in 1778 and in New Hampshire in 1779 and 1781. The documents finally adopted in 1780 in Massachusetts (by an equivocal interpretation of town-election returns on specific provisions) and in New Hampshire in 1784 vindicated the steps taken to ascertain the sovereign will of the people and, by general agreement, represent the Revolutionaries' greatest contribution to constitutional theory and practice. But ratification also meant closure on a period of extraordinary, extraconstitutional popular political activity: once the people had finally and deliberately acted, their further action was confined to regular constitutional channels. By the same token, a legislator was no longer merely the creature of his constituents but was sworn to uphold a new constitutional order that defined the rights and responsibilities of governors and governed alike. "All power indeed flows from the people," Marylander Alexander Contee Hanson conceded in an important and revealing debate over the status of constituent instructions in 1787, "but the doctrine, that the power actually at all times resides in the people, is subversive of all government and law."

The political infrastructure of resistance and revolution was contained and to some extent suppressed in constitutional procedures, particularly in New England. During the war, extraconstitutional conventions filled a power vacuum, authorizing radical measures in defense of fundamental rights where existing institutions no longer functioned effectively. By contrast, the conventions that drafted new state constitutions sought to eliminate the occasions for further popular agitation. The sovereign people were acknowledged as the ultimate source of the legitimate authority that they routinely reaffirmed through regular elections, but they were now expected to defer to government. "Of [extraconstitutional] combinations there can be no need," Zabdiel Adams concluded, "where our rulers are so immediately under our controul, where they are elected once a year, and where every corporate body may meet as often as they please, to give instructions to those whom they have deputed from their number."

The politics of constitution writing in Massachusetts and New Hampshire is as important and interesting as the charters themselves. By contrast, Revolutionaries in states to the south implemented new constitutions in 1776 and 1777 without protracted preliminaries. This did not mean, however, that the decision for independence—much less the creation of widely acceptable new regimes—was straightforward and unproblematic. New York, New

Jersey, Pennsylvania, Maryland, and Delaware were all afflicted to varying degrees by factional and sectional conflict, ethnic animosity, widespread loyalism and, except for Maryland, protracted British military occupation. None could rely on a highly developed tradition of local self-government to foster mobilization efforts or to provide a broad popular foundation for their new regimes. (The expansion of New England institutions into the contested New Hampshire Grants region enabled Vermont separatists to conduct a successful revolution against New York.) The collapse or inertia of provincial legislatures required decisive action and radical institutional innovations. It was crucial for the patriots' success that they justify their moves in constitutional terms.

Yet for all their common problems, state makers in the Middle Atlantic region moved in significantly different directions. While Pennsylvanians constructed the most radically democratic new government, constitution writers in the other states crafted Whiggish documents that sought to reconcile balanced government and popular sovereignty. The Pennsylvania Constitution was controversial throughout its relatively brief life, while less "popular" systems gained broad acceptance and support. The conformity of these new regimes to conventional expectations—their ostensibly conservative character—combined with popular tax and fiscal policies to preempt widespread dissidence and sustain the patriot coalition. In Maryland, Charles Carroll of Carrollton told his recalcitrant father that wealthy planters in Maryland had to be prepared to sacrifice their class interests in order to conciliate popular opinion: "No great revolutions can happen in a state without revolutions or mutations of private property." Despite an aristocratic senate that was the envy of Whig constitutionalists across the continent, Maryland's new government worked well enough for Samuel Chase and other self-styled tribunes of the people. Similarly, the complex system set up under the New York Constitution worked effectively because of the pragmatic leadership of conservative assemblymen such as Egbert Benson and the popular governor George Clinton.

Pennsylvania patriots took a radically different approach to managing their internal revolution. The premium there was on mobilizing popular support against deeply entrenched resistance to the independence movement. In effect, the 1776 Constitution transformed the Revolutionary infrastructure into a plan of government; a vigilant citizenry would prevent internal enemies from seizing the reins of power. Pennsylvanians who refused to support the Revolution and submit to popular control faced the choice of accepting severe civil disabilities or leaving the state. The exclusion of nonjurors, or those who refused to take oaths of allegiance to the state government, including large numbers of Quakers and other sectarian pacifists as well as a sizable contingent of Loyalists, radically limited the size of the Pennsylvania electorate, notwithstanding the constitution's liberal provisions for taxpayer suffrage.

The apparent rejection of balanced government and the creation of a powerful unicameral legislature in Pennsylvania defined the radical limit of constitutional experimentation in 1776. But it would be a mistake to exaggerate the differences between Pennsylvania and its neighbors. The practical and theoretical challenge for state makers everywhere was to redefine the relationship between the institutions of government and a mobilized electorate. The premium in most states was on sustaining fragile coalitions among patriot factions; Pennsylvania patriots, by contrast, had to create and sustain a popular revolutionary force to smash the old regime and suppress internal enemies.

The authors of the Pennsylvania charter eschewed a conventionally balanced system because they relied so heavily on regular appeals to active and informed citizens. The Pennsylvania Constitution required publication of all bills and approval by a subsequent and newly elected assembly before becoming law, thus institutionalizing a kind of referendum system. Legislative responsibility was further guaranteed by a Council of Censors, a popularly elected body who met once in seven years, that would pass on the constitutionality of previous legislation and, by two-thirds vote, could recommend constitutional amendments to a special convention. By the mechanisms of publicity, instruction, annual election, referendum, and review, the people would virtually become a second branch of the legislature, as well as the periodic source of constituent power.

Despite its apparent simplicity, the Pennsylvania system was no less complex than those fabricated in other states, nor were the characteristically constitutionalist obsession with checks and balances and radical-republican suspicion of legislators and legislative supremacy any less conspicuous. The difference in Pennsylvania was that the Revolutionaries sought to obliterate the traditional distinction between governors and governed that in other states was reconciled with the concept of popular sovereignty through the process of constitution writing. In other words, if state makers elsewhere sought to republicanize inherited constitutional structures, Pennsylvanians set out in the opposite direction: they would constitutionalize republican society. "The law is king" in republican America, Paine asserted in *Common Sense*, because an active citizenry was vigilant in defense of its rights, not because legislators exercised power in the people's name. But the different approaches dictated by distinctive political situations should not obscure the similarity of impulses and intentions from state to state. Whatever intentions guided state makers, the lower houses inevitably exercised preponderant and unprecedented power.

The history of the Pennsylvania Constitution of 1776 is replete with ironies. The partisan differences that were supposed to be so dangerous to the revolutionary republic, and that the constitution was designed to suppress, reemerged with a vengeance. Critics of the constitution, the self-styled "republicans," launched scathing attacks on the document's alleged defects, particularly the provision for a unicameral legislature, and quickly demolished its defenders' insistence that patriotism and submission to the new regime were synonymous. While the constitution itself provided a polarizing issue, constitutional provisions for virtually continuous electoral activity facilitated party mobilization. "Either from the disposition of its inhabitants, its form of government, or some other cause," wrote historian David Ramsay, "the people of Pennsylvania have constantly been in a state of fermentation." However excellent in theory, the Council of Censors in fact simply "opens a door for discord, and furnishes abundant matter for periodical altercation."

Pennsylvania republicans had little difficulty in depicting their constitutionalist opponents as a narrowly based, unrepresentative legislative faction—the "Presbyterian party"—that was unwilling to risk putting the constitution to the test of popular approval. Constitutionalist majorities in the legislature repeatedly rejected referendum calls, and the Council of Censors elected in 1783 refused, by a party vote, to call a constitutional convention. Not surprisingly, proponents of constitutional reform quickly learned to exploit the political and rhetorical opportunities provided by the system they sought to overturn. Arguing for the reintegration of nonjurors in the polity after the Revolution, republicans could represent themselves as proponents of truly popular government; linking their opponents' power to partisan organization and manipulation of the electorate, republicans could show the inefficacy of constitutional mechanisms that were supposed to curb legislative excesses. The people could not take the place of the upper house in a bicameral legislature because they lacked "independence." It was precisely because he "abhor[red] every species of aristocracy" that republican Arthur St. Clair "object[ed] to a single branch in a legislature." Pennsylvanians would be best served by a "double representation" that would prevent the assembly from assuming "aristocratic" powers and thus secure the essential rights and interests of the people-at-large. Not coincidentally, constituents would no longer be expected to perform the extraordinary constitutional role assigned to them in radical-republican theory, but subverted by partisan practice.

The effect of party competition in Pennsylvania was to replicate and perpetuate the debate over constitutional first principles that preceded and accompanied constitution writing elsewhere, most notably in Massachusetts and New Hampshire. These debates resulted in wide agreement on the essential components of constitutional government in republican societies. Bicameralism, a double representation of the people, alone could assure that republican lawmakers would proceed with due deliberation and with respect for the people's liberty and property rights. As South Carolinian Thomas Tudor Tucker wrote in 1784, "subject as we all are to be influenced by interest, by passion, and by the sentiments of a few leading men, the division of the legislative power seems necessary to furnish a proper check to our too hasty proceedings." The constitutionalist consensus emerging in the states was re-

flected in the Philadelphia convention's plan for a new federal government. There may have been serious misgivings about the relations among the branches of the new federal government and about that government's relations with the states, but few voices were raised for a powerful unicameral national legislature. Anti-Federalists instead echoed their Revolutionary predecessors in seeking guarantees of individual rights against a potentially despotic central government.

The great achievement of state-constitution writers was the incorporation of popular political power into durable institutional frameworks. Their success is apparent is apparent in the subsequent histories of the fourteen constitutions that were in place after the period of drafting and revision was complete in 1798 (with new charters adopted in South Carolina in 1790, New Hampshire in 1792, Vermont in 1793, and Georgia in 1798). The longest-lived, the Massachusetts Constitution of 1780, is still in operation today; the other thirteen, superseded between 1821 and 1865, had an average life of 57.8 years.

LEGISLATORS AND VOTERS

The durability of the state constitutions depended upon confining popular political activity to acceptable channels. On the theoretical plane this meant distinguishing between the primary constituent activity of the people in establishing constitutions and the ordinary business of making and enforcing laws. In practical terms, the governments—and particularly the legislatures—that gained effective power under the new constitutional dispensation had to demonstrate their responsiveness to public opinion and their competence to govern. The democratization of the legislatures as well as the gradual expansion and redefinition of the electorate was crucial to this process.

By drawing new men into politics and driving many prominent colonists into political exile, at home or abroad, the independence movement transformed the social character of the legislatures. This was most conspicuously true in the case of the upper houses, where more than three-quarters of the royally appointed provincial councillors became Loyalists or neutrals. Although a few of the state constitutions set high property requirements for senators—the highest were in Maryland and South Carolina, at one thousand and two thousand pounds, respectively—electoral competition and the need to expand the pool of eligible candidates made the new upper houses much more representative bodies. The most comprehensive study of the upper houses shows that men from the wealthiest and most socially prestigious families held about half of the provincial council seats but made up only one quarter of the new senates; 45 percent of the state senators were upwardly mobile (defined as surpassing their parents' economic rank), compared with 24 percent of the councillors. The senates' larger size and more rapid turnover meant that there were three times as many senators in the twelve years after 1775 than provincial councillors in the previous twelve.

Changes in the composition of the lower houses were also striking. If the social profile of the new senates closely resembled that of the old assemblies, the new lower houses became still more broadly representative. The House of Burgesses, a sympathetic Virginian noted in 1776, was "composed of men not quite so well dressed, nor so politely educated, nor so highly born as some Assemblies I have formerly seen." After independence the proportion of great planters in the Burgesses decreased slightly (from 60 percent to 50 percent), but common farmers doubled their representation (from 13 percent to 26 percent).

The transformation of the assemblies was more pronounced in colonies where the transition to statehood was contested. The displacement of Loyalists and the recruitment of marginal and excluded groups into the Revolutionary coalition provided unprecedented opportunities for ambitious outsiders. In New Hampshire, for instance, the proportion of assemblymen with estates valued at two-thousand pounds or more dropped from 70 percent to 30 percent after independence; more than half of the new legislators were yeomen farmers with modest property holdings. Middling farmers (owning farms of less than 2,000 pounds value) in Maryland comprised 28 percent of the representatives in 1785 compared with 18.5 percent twenty years earlier; over the same period, representatives' median holdings in New Jersey dropped from one thousand to three hundred acres.

The practical needs of military mobilization converged with the ideological imperatives of republican constitutionalism to guarantee that the new state legislatures would be considerably more representative than their colonial predecessors. "An ample Representation in every Republick," wrote a South Carolinian in 1778, "constitutes the most powerful Protection of Freedom, the strongest Bulwark against the Attacks of Despotism." Accordingly, the South Carolina Assembly more than doubled in size, to more than 200 members, and for the first time included a contingent of westerners. There were comparable increases in New Hampshire (from 34 to more than 80 assemblymen) and Massachusetts (from 110 to approximately 350). The number of counties sending representatives to the Pennsylvania Assembly increased from eleven to nineteen, while the number of counties and towns claiming representation in North Carolina grew from forty-three to more than sixty. Even where representation was not extended to newly organized—or formerly unrepresented or underrepresented—counties, towns, and parishes, state makers enlarged the legislatures: the number of representatives per county in Delaware was increased from six to seven, and in New Jersey from two to three.

Continuous pressure to extend and reapportion representation to reflect population distribution reinforced the closer identity of representatives and their constituents under the new republican regime. In Pennsylvania, where the western counties had been notoriously underrepresented in the colonial assembly, constitution writers staked out the most advanced ground: "representation in proportion to the number of taxable inhabitants is the only principle which can at all times secure liberty, and make the voice of a majority of the people the law of the land." Other states, including New York, South Carolina, and Georgia, also provided for proportional representation and periodic reapportionment. In Massachusetts, where the principle of corporate equality was well established, a proportional scheme was superimposed on the old system of town representation and was a factor in the enormous increase in the size of the assembly. Under the 1780 constitution, every existing town could claim at least one representative, as could any new town with 150 "rateable polls," or male taxpayers more than sixteen years of age; for every additional 225 polls a town was entitled to another representative. Virginia and North Carolina did not join the general move toward proportional representation, but redressed perceived inequities through county division and creation.

Because the franchise was already so broadly distributed in colonial America, changes in the electorate are less obvious than those in the composition of the legislatures. According to the best studies, qualified voters in the various colonies comprised between 50 and 80 percent of all white male adults, and the range increased to between 60 and 90 percent under the new state constitutions. The variation is less a measure of democratic tendencies than one of resistance to the independence movement. Where the transition was smoothest, in Connecticut and Rhode Island, there was little reason to enlarge electorates that included 60 percent and between 60 and 70 percent of white male adults, respectively. In Pennsylvania, by contrast, the expanded electorate created by taxpayer suffrage—an estimated 90 percent of the relevant population—played an important role in the internal revolution.

Constitution writers devoted considerable energy to establishing the qualifications of electors as well as elected officials. They all paid their respects to the conventional idea that political participation should be confined to those with a stake in society since, as John Adams put it, "very few who have no property have any judgment of their own." But the broad distribution of wealth in America eliminated any plausible threat from a propertyless mob, particularly where the prospects for acquiring property were so favorable.

Property qualifications occasionally drew adverse comment. Pennsylvania radicals believed that propertyless soldiers deserved the vote: "Every man in the country who manifests a disposition to venture his all for the defence of its Liberty should have a voice in its Councils." Petitioners from nearby Salem County, New Jersey, asked if God intended that "a certain quantity of the Earth on which we tread should be annexed to Man to Compleat his dignity and fit him for society." But the suffrage in both states was virtually universal (for males; unmarried, property-holding women in New Jersey voted until 1807), and stiffer qualifications elsewhere rarely generated significant debate. Few white male adults were barred from

political life, even when limitations were enforced—which was by no means always the case. As a result, and despite the anxieties of John Adams, Edmund Pendleton, and numerous other conservative constitutionalists, the supposedly conflicting interests of propertied and propertyless never amounted to much. Instead, splits *within* the propertied classes generated much more serious controversy. The most divisive conflicts over the limits of citizenship had nothing to do with property, but were instead provoked by the campaigns to reenfranchise loyalists and neutrals, which culminated in the repeal of the Pennsylvania Test Acts in 1785.

Solicitude for property explains some of the peculiarities of the state constitutions, most notably Adams's misguided design for a senate in Massachusetts that would represent and protect "property," but the tendency of revolutionary politics was toward the expansion and homogenization of the electorate. Property could not function as an effective surrogate for the aristocratic principle in America. Nor, as the behavior of wealthy Loyalists made clear, did a stake in society necessarily guarantee patriotism and good citizenship. Instead, American state makers had to fashion new relationships between more democratic representative bodies and an inclusive, undifferentiated electorate that would sustain constitutional government and the rule of law.

The move toward proportional representation guaranteed wider access to power. Most states also decided to relocate their capital cities in order to make attendance at legislative sessions less onerous for delegates from distant hinterlands. According to a typical complaint from the Little River District in South Carolina, the present "Seat of Government" at Charleston "is very inconvenient on account of loss of time and expence . . . to those Inhabitants who are obliged to attend on public or private business." The solution was to establish the capital "as near the Center of the State" as possible, in this case at Columbia (removal act passed in 1786).

Virginia, which extended its jurisdiction west to the Mississippi, was the first large state to move its capital (to Richmond, act of 1779), followed by Georgia (Louisville, act of 1786; Milledgeville, act of 1804), North Carolina (Raleigh, act of 1788), and New York (Albany, act of 1797). The location of the capital was a perennial bone of contention in Pennsylvania until the move to Lancaster (act of 1799) and finally Harrisburg (act of 1810). Of all the large states, only Massachusetts—where complaints from the western counties were offset by those from the Maine District—resisted relocation pressures. It is significant that legislators in smaller states also honored the equal-access principle: the site of legislative sessions rotated in Rhode Island and Connecticut, and it was moved toward more central locations in Delaware (to Dover, 1777), New Jersey (Trenton, 1790), and New Hampshire (Concord, 1808, after prior moves).

The moving of state capitals reflected population shifts that, under more equitable schemes of representation, gave delegates in rural districts more voting power in the legislatures. Challenges to state authority in contested frontier regions strengthened the hand of relocation advocates. Frontier settlers repeatedly raised the access issue, threatening to form their own new states if legislators failed to guarantee law and order, confirm their land titles, and give them a voice in their own government. With state boundaries, state capitals, and electoral districts all contingent and negotiable, government was stripped of much of its traditional authority, just as representation was demystified by frequent elections, bans on the accumulation of power and prestige through plural office holding, and the diminishing social distance between representatives and constituents.

Consent could not be taken for granted. Republican governments that could command popular loyalties had to be convenient and responsive. It was not enough simply to assert the popular foundation of political authority (as constitution writers soon discovered), nor were provisions for an "ample representation" sufficient without being reduced to practice. In addition to making the legislatures accessible to countryfolk of relatively humble means, a functioning representation system depended on facilitating popular participation. Voters in the middle states were accommodated with more polling places (increasing in New Jersey, for example, from thirteen to fifty-three between 1776 and 1788); southern voters were given extended periods to get to centrally located polling places in parishes or counties (polls remained open for up to four days in

Maryland and Virginia); and several states introduced the secret ballot in place of viva voce, or oral, voting.

The success of these measures in securing popular support for the new state governments was apparent in higher voter turnout, increased electoral competition, and the formation of coherent, issue-oriented factions or "parties" in the postwar legislatures. Although fragmentary data make generalizations about voting hazardous, the best study suggests that turnouts of 10 to 15 percent in the years 1776 to 1779 rose to from 20 to 30 percent in the late 1780s. Contemporary observers were impressed by the increased bustle of election campaigns: Virginian Archibald Stuart reported in 1785 that "Competition for seats in the house run[s] higher than ever they Did under the Old government." Candidates canvased and provided lavish hospitality to voters, emphasized their common touch—if not common origins—and pledged to promote popular issues. In politically precocious areas, ad hoc conventions endorsed slates of candidates, and published "tickets" were distributed among electors.

Electioneering practices during the 1780s pointed toward the more highly organized party system emerging in the 1790s. But they are less indicative of a newfound enthusiasm for partisanship, which righteous republicans continued to condemn, than of the effects of popular constitutionalism on American state politics. The premium on constituency vigilance and representative accountability promoted electoral activity. Ironically, constitutional provisions that preempted the formation of an elective aristocracy—rotation in office, separation of powers, and bans on multiple office-holding—encouraged candidates to make promises to voters that could only be fulfilled by concerted action of a legislative party. In effect, candidates' promises extended the logic of constituency instructions but substituted a sense of trust—the fellow-feeling and like-mindedness of truly representative representatives—for the suspicious distrust that the act of instruction presupposed. The development of such protopartisan practices in the political realm thus paralleled the incorporation—and containment—of popular political power in state constitutional settlements.

The primary impetus toward partisanship in post-Revolutionary America came from a wide array of conflicts over fiscal and economic policy, the status of Loyalists, and federal-state relations. In some cases, notably the agrarian disturbances associated with Shays's Rebellion in Massachusetts (1786–1787), an uprising of embattled debtors who forced the courts to close down, these conflicts appeared to threaten fragile constitutional settlements. But Thomas Jefferson's sanguine view that "a little rebellion now and then" was symptomatic of republican good health, was—beneath the characteristic hyperbole—more astute than generally reckoned. With independence secured and broadly acceptable political structures in place, the states could accommodate unprecedented levels of conflict.

Political mobilization around controversial issues reinforced the legitimacy of the new state regimes. Voters who saw legislatures as arenas for issue-oriented conflict and believed that representatives could protect or promote their interests were inclined to accept the rules of the game. Even in Massachusetts, the Shaysites—who had proven so ineffectual on the battlefield—had their revenge at the polls. With the rebellion safely suppressed, Bay State voters turned fiscally conservative legislators out of the General Court and elected John Hancock as governor in place of the unpopular James Bowdoin. In other states, "popular" or "localist" parties enjoyed considerable success in mitigating the impact of postwar economic dislocations on indebted farmers. At the same time, however, a wide range of interest groups looked to the state legislatures for support or relief and the opportunities for coalition building increased accordingly. With electoral competition centered on policy issues, conservative "cosmopolitans" became more and more adept at conciliating and exploiting public opinion.

The redefinition of representative-constituency relations under the new state constitutions combined with controversial policy questions to foster partisan political activity across the continent. But few commentators were intellectually prepared to welcome these developments. For Edmund Pendleton, post-Revolutionary electioneering seemed all too reminiscent of the provincial practice of treating voters to food, drink, and riotous frolics: "I had hoped that our annual elections would have put a stop to every Species of bribery, and Restored perfect freedom to the choice of our representatives in General Assembly, but am sorry to find myself disappointed." The corruption that had once emanated from King George and his governors simply had been displaced and democratized.

Rather than deferring to merit and virtue at "perfectly free" elections, the common folk expected to be courted. They also expected republican government to serve their interests by promoting policies that conservatives, such as Pendleton, feared would subvert the social order and jeopardize the American union. Anxious aristocrats certainly exaggerated the dangers of popular power: partisanship and other symptoms of corruption were the inevitable concomitants of the adaptation of American political societies to republican constitutionalist regimes. But Pendleton's friend James Madison and his fellow national constitutional reformers had good reasons to fear for the future of the union. One of the most pressing was the success of the states in establishing legitimate and effective governments.

INTERGOVERNMENTAL RELATIONS

The relationships between the development of the state legislatures and other branches and levels of government are complex. Certainly the tendency of later state constitutions was to enhance executive authority, though this tendency was retarded in practice where governors were not popularly elected. State courts were also beginning to move hesitantly toward judicial independence as American concern about preserving a separation of powers shifted from the dangers of plural office holding to the differentiation of legislative, executive, and judicial functions. The emerging distinction between constitution writing and mere legislation, reflected in the increasing use of prescriptive ("shall") rather than permissive ("ought") language in state bills of rights, enabled judges to present themselves as custodians of the higher law.

Yet constitutional developments in the states did not jeopardize the dominant role that the legislatures assumed during the Revolutionary crisis. To the contrary, the legislatures' authority was enhanced by their new aura of constitutional legitimacy. The emergence of effective upper houses—whose independence was grounded in popular elections—was most crucial to this process of legitimation. The sovereignty of the people, expressed through acts of electoral will, was in this way reconciled with balanced, constitutional government. But institutional innovations and conceptual transformations could not by themselves secure broad popular acceptance of the new state regimes. Voters also expected responsive representatives to act in positive ways to promote and protect individual and collective interests. Such instrumental attitudes fostered partisanship; they also tended to neutralize the fears about the abuse of governmental power that had fueled resistance to British tyranny before independence.

The legislatures consolidated their dominant position by curbing the power of subordinate jurisdictions and securing their states' territorial integrity. The capacity to create counties, towns, and other corporate entities was now clearly within the legislative domain. Legislatures could determine the conditions of corporate existence, including town and county boundaries, the organization of local government, and the extent of legislative representation. If constitutional provisions or extraconstitutional conventions guaranteed equitable representation to new electoral districts, reapportionment and redistricting diminished the relative power, and sometimes subverted the corporate identity, of older districts. Legislative control of state court systems reinforced the tendency to reduce local governments to administrative units with limited and derivative authority.

Representation should "be so equally and impartially distributed," wrote Theophilus Parsons, "that the representatives should have the same views, and interests with the people at large." This principle of equal, or proportional, representation implied both a direct relationship between voters and delegates—unmediated by towns or other corporate entities—and the collective identity of the people at large. But the corporate integrity of local communities was well established, particularly in rural New England where town governments routinely defied or ignored state government during the early years of the Revolution. In the upper Connecticut Valley, for instance, towns voted on whether to be part of Massachusetts, New Hampshire, New York, or

the renegade republic of Vermont. Vermont annexed adjacent regions by legislative unions with sixteen and thirty-five New Hampshire towns in 1778 and 1781, respectively, and with twelve New York towns in 1781. Though a tradition of local self-government was less well developed in other frontier regions, legislatures in all the large "landed" states had to enforce their authority against a wide range of jurisdictional competitors.

Massachusetts and New Hampshire secured their boundaries through the drafting and popular ratification of state constitutions and the normalization of relations with Vermont. New York also eventually negotiated an accord with the new state, which was finally admitted to the union in 1791. Bilateral agreements also resolved boundary disputes elsewhere, but the most important device for defining jurisdictional limits was the unilateral cession of the states' western-land claims to Congress. Cessions by New York (1782), Virginia (1784), Massachusetts (1785), Connecticut (1786), North Carolina (1790), and Georgia (1802) created a national domain (and an independent source of revenue for the central government), strengthened state titles in unceded areas, and preempted separatist movements.

Under the Northwest Ordinance of 1787, the process of creating new states was nationalized. Congress would govern embryonic new states or territories until they were sufficiently developed to enjoy the privileges of legislative representation and self-government. The right of frontier settlers to constitute their own political societies was thus suppressed, a development that replicated the containment of popular political initiatives under settled state constitutions. These settlers were carefully distinguished from the sovereign people of future states, just as the sovereign people who authorized state constitutions were distinguished from the electoral or legislative majorities who exercised power in accordance with their provisions and limitations.

The resolution of the western-lands controversy and the implementation of a national territorial policy enabled the state legislatures to move effectively, and without interference from other states, against separatist challenges to their authority. Vermonters mounted the only successful new-state movement in the

Revolutionary period, though the Kentucky District of Virginia and western North Carolina (Tennessee)—both sites of earlier separatist activity—achieved independent statehood in 1792 and 1796, respectively. Without the patronage of states with competing claims or from a coalition of landless states in Congress, separatists could not hope to sustain popular support. Neither the confederation nor particular state governments were willing to receive separatist representatives or representations.

But the consolidation of state jurisdiction and the new regime of interstate comity promised by western-land cessions depended upon the survival and strengthening of the union. During the critical period of the mid-1780s, the failure of repeated efforts to amend the Articles of Confederation and the irruption of deeply divisive foreign-policy issues threatened to immobilize Congress and fracture the union. In the absence of a national commercial policy that could protect American traders against British discrimination—or domestic manufacturers against cheap imports—state legislatures began to fashion distinctive, potentially conflicting, mercantilist policies. Where import and tax revenues permitted, legislators also began to assume responsibility for federal as well as state debts held by their citizens. Even while the new national domain held out the prospect of an expanding and prosperous union, the state governments appeared all too ready to exercise the full range of sovereign powers on behalf of distinctive state interests.

Many national constitutional reformers attributed the crisis of the confederation to the dangerously excessive pretensions of the state legislatures. Attacks on the "democratic despotism" of the assemblies drew attention to the supposed failure of the states to construct balanced, constitutional regimes that guaranteed law and liberty. But the reformers' brief against the legislatures, most memorably catalogued in Madison's "Vices of the Political System" (1787), was in fact eloquent testimony to their increasing effectiveness and popular legitimacy. The problem was with the constitution of the national government, not with the state constitutions.

In the ensuing ratification campaign, Federalists recognized that gratuitous attacks on the state governments would alienate voters.

Their solution was to focus instead on the limited efficacy of the states' power in the crucial areas of defense, commercial policy, and foreign relations generally. The state legislatures could only continue to function effectively if they were not forced to fill the political vacuum that the collapse of the central government would create. Federalists could thus conclude that the establishment of a "more perfect union" would preserve and strengthen the states.

The connections between the national reform movement and the development of the state legislatures were reciprocal and complex. The framers of the federal Constitution certainly drew on constitutional experimentation and development at the state level in designing the new federal regime; proponents of ratification had to convince skeptical voters that their system satisfied the highest standards of American constitutionalism. Furthermore, constitutional settlements in the states that were premised on the distinction between the sovereign people and their governments opened the way for the direct delegation of authority to a reformed national government. Therefore the argument for the independence of the respective branches of state government could be invoked on behalf of the national government, which Federalists insisted could not function effectively—or constitutionally—as the dependent creature of the state legislatures.

Federalist arguments were designed to justify a significant redistribution of power, most notably from the state legislatures to the new Congress. But to a large extent this was power, particularly in the realm of external affairs, that legislators were in any case reluctant to exercise. Anti-Federalists disclaimed dis-unionist sentiments, distinguishing the kind of sovereignty they insisted should remain in the state governments from the sovereign powers that properly appertained to the government of the union. Federalists exploited this conceptual confusion: the states were *not* sovereignties, and if they became sovereignties because of the breakup of the union, they would cease to be constitutional republics. Membership in a federal union could thus be portrayed as a fundamental limitation on legislative power in the states, confining representative, republican governments to the sphere of authority delineated by their own constitutions. Simply stated, reformation of the national government would preempt the transformation of the state legislatures into American parliaments with dangerous delusions of their sovereign omnipotence.

As all participants in the debate over the federal Constitution recognized, the long-term expansion and development of state legislative power did not necessarily or naturally lead toward parliamentary sovereignty. To the contrary, the early history of the state legislatures was dominated by the efforts of constitution writers to reconcile the principles of limited constitutional government with active, expanding, and increasingly undifferentiated electorates. State constitutional settlements effectively enlarged the scope of legislative power, but only within well-defined and generally recognized limits. The collapse of the union threatened those limits, thus calling into question the legitimacy of legislative power.

The ratification campaign had a more practical and immediate impact on state politics by raising the level of partisan polemics and electoral competition. If conflicts between "cosmopolitans" and "localists" helped organize and normalize post-Revolutionary state politics, the national debate over the future of the union lent unprecedented rhetorical and ideological coherence to the projects and programs of interest-group coalitions. Party polarization at the national level—beginning with the ratification struggle and soon reemerging with divisions over commercial, fiscal, and foreign policy in the Washington administration and the early congresses—thus served to reinforce the development of political parties in the states. Party development in turn facilitated the formulation and implementation of legislative policy, thereby extending the competence of positive state government.

The growing effectiveness of the legislatures in the years leading up to the reconstitution of the central government prepared the way for a remarkable outburst of activity in the early national period. Halting efforts by the state governments in the waning years of the confederation to promote the interests of traders, manufacturers, and land speculators pointed toward more coherent and successful state programs for internal improvement and economic development after ratification. State legislators could act more effectively and command broader popular support within the limits of a new federal regime that guaranteed free trade within the union and preempted destructive conflicts over national commercial policy. As Vermonter Nathaniel Chipman wrote in 1793, the new national government "added, at the instant of organization, a degree of energy to the state governments." At least in part because of the constitutionalist vigilance of the anti-Federalists and their strict constructionist successors, the federal government did not become the engine of "consolidation" and despotic power that opponents of ratification had feared it would. Voters therefore became accustomed to looking to their state legislatures for positive action. The often frenetic pace of state-sponsored activity in the decades after 1789 stands in striking contrast to the limited role of a national legislature inhibited by conflicting sectional interests and constitutional scruples.

BIBLIOGRAPHY

For a fuller discussion of the development of the colonial assemblies see the essay in this encyclopedia. The analysis presented here draws heavily on JACK P. GREENE, "Political Mimesis: A Consideration of the Historical and Cultural Roots of Legislative Behavior in the British Colonies in the Eighteenth Century," *American Historical Review* 75 (December 1969): 337–367; his essay, "The Growth of Political Stability: An Interpretation of Political Development in the Anglo-American Colonies, 1660–1760," in JOHN PARKER and CAROL URNESS, eds., *The American Revolution: A Heritage of Change* (Minneapolis, Minn., 1975), pp. 26–52; and GREENE, *Peripheries and Center: Constitutional Development in the Extended Polities of the British Empire and the United States, 1607–1788* (Athens, Ga., 1986). American concepts of representation are discussed from various, sometimes conflicting, perspectives in

RICHARD BUEL, JR., "Democracy and the American Revolution: A Frame of Reference," *William and Mary Quarterly* 21 (April 1964): 165–190; BERNARD BAILYN, *The Ideological Origins of the American Revolution* (Cambridge, Mass., 1967); and JOHN PHILLIP REID, *The Concept of Representation in the Age of the American Revolution* (Chicago, 1989).

The state constitutions may be found in FRANCIS N. THORPE, ed., *The Federal and State Constitutions, Colonial Charters, and Other Organic Laws of the United States, Territories, and Colonies Now or Heretofore Forming the United States of America*, 7 vols. (Washington, D.C., 1909). For systematic commentaries on their provisions see DONALD S. LUTZ, *Popular Consent and Popular Control: Whig Political Theory in the Early State Constitutions* (Baton Rouge, La., 1980), and WILLI PAUL ADAMS, *The First American Constitutions: Republican Ideology and the Making of the State Constitutions in the Revolutionary Era*, translated by RITA and ROBERT KIMBER (Chapel Hill, N.C., 1980). Important earlier studies include ELISHA P. DOUGLASS, *Rebels and Democrats: The Struggle for Equal Political Rights and Majority Rule During the American Revolution* (Chapel Hill, N.C., 1955), and FLETCHER M. GREEN, *Constitutional Development in the South Atlantic States, 1776–1860* (Chapel Hill, N.C., 1930). Valuable discussions of constitution making may also be found in vol. 1 (pp. 213–235) of R. R. PALMER, *The Age of the Democratic Revolution: A Political History of Europe and America, 1760–1800*, 2 vols. (Princeton, N.J., 1959–1964), and J. R. POLE, *Political Representation in England and the Origins of the American Republic* (New York, 1966).

The most wide-ranging and influential study of the development of political and constitutional ideas in the states is GORDON S. WOOD, *The Creation of the American Republic, 1776–1787* (Chapel Hill, N.C., 1969). Many of the important sources are collected in CHARLES S. HYNEMAN and DONALD S. LUTZ, eds., *American Political Writing During the Founding Era, 1760–1805*, 2 vols. (Indianapolis, 1983). See also OSCAR HANDLIN and MARY HANDLIN, eds., *The Popular Sources of Political Authority: Documents on the Massachusetts Constitution of 1780* (Cambridge, Mass., 1966), and MELVIN YAZAWA, ed., *Representative Government and the Revolution: The Maryland Constitutional Crisis of 1787* (Baltimore, 1975).

The best general introduction to suffrage, electioneering, and party development in the states is ROBERT J. DINKIN, *Voting in Revolutionary America: A Study of Elections in the Original Thirteen States, 1776–1789* (Westport, Conn., 1982). The analysis presented above relies heavily on data assembled and analyzed by DINKIN. The definitive work on suffrage requirements is CHILTON WILLIAMSON, *American Suffrage: From Property to Democracy, 1760–1860* (Princeton, N.J., 1960). The changing social profile of American legislatures is discussed in JACKSON TURNER MAIN, "Government by the People: The American Revolution and the Democratization of the Legislatures," *William and Mary Quarterly* 23 (July 1966): 391–407, and MAIN, *The Upper House in Revolutionary America, 1763–1788* (Madison, Wis., 1967).

For the general history of early state politics see MERRILL JENSEN, *The Articles of Confederation: An Interpretation of the Social-Constitutional History of the American Revolution, 1774–1781* (Madison, Wis., 1948), and JENSEN, *The New Nation: A History of the United States During the Confederation, 1781–1789* (New York, 1950). PETER S. ONUF, *The Origins of the Federal Republic: Jurisdictional Controversies in the United States, 1775–1787* (Philadelphia, 1983) focuses on state making, new-state movements, and interstate relations; for further discussion of national territorial policy see ONUF, *Statehood and Union: A History of the Northwest Ordinance* (Bloomington, Ind., 1987), pp. 1–87. On the location of state capitals see ROSEMARIE ZAGARRI, *The Politics of Size: Representation in the United States, 1776–1850* (Ithaca, N.Y., 1987), pp. 8–35. The most comprehensive work on incipient party divisions is JACKSON T. MAIN, *Political Parties Before the Constitution* (Chapel Hill, N.C., 1973). Debates over political economic issues in the states and changing conceptions of the federal union are also surveyed in CATHY D. MATSON and PETER S. ONUF, *A Union of Interests: Political and Economic Thought in Revolutionary America* (Lawrence, Kans., 1990).

The monographic literature on political and constitutional development in particular states is voluminous. Some of the best work is collected in RONALD HOFFMAN and PETER J. ALBERT, eds., *Sovereign States in an Age of Un-*

certainty (Charlottesville, Va., 1981), and in PETER S. ONUF, ed., *The New American Nation, 1776–1820*, vols. 3 and 10 (New York, 1991), 12 vols. The leading studies of political mobilization are RICHARD D. BROWN, *Revolutionary Politics in Massachusetts: The Boston Committee of Correspondence and the Towns, 1772–1774* (Cambridge, Mass., 1970); RICHARD ALAN RYERSON, *"The Revolution Is Now Begun": The Radical Committees of Philadelphia, 1765–1776* (Philadelphia, 1978); RICHARD BUEL, JR., *Dear Liberty: Connecticut's Mobilization for the Revolutionary War* (Middletown, Conn., 1980); and EDWARD COUNTRYMAN, *A People in Revolution: The American Revolution and Political Society in New York, 1760–1790* (Baltimore, 1981).

Valuable state histories for the period include RICHARD P. MCCORMICK, *Experiment in Independence: New Jersey in the Critical Period, 1781–1789* (New Brunswick, N.J., 1950); ROBERT L. BRUNHOUSE, *The Counter-Revolution in Pennsylvania, 1776–1790* (Harrisburg, Pa., 1942); RONALD HOFFMAN, *A Spirit of Dissension: Economics, Politics, and the Revolution in Maryland* (Baltimore, 1973); and JEROME J. NADELHAFT, *The Disorder of War: The Revolution in South Carolina* (Orono, Maine, 1981).

The multitude of studies on Revolutionary Massachusetts includes VAN BECK HALL, *Politics Without Parties: Massachusetts, 1780–1791* (Pittsburgh, Pa., 1972) and, for an insightful commentary on constitutional development, RONALD M. PETERS, JR., *The Massachusetts Constitution of 1780: A Social Compact* (Amherst, Mass., 1978). OSCAR HANDLIN and MARY FLUG HANDLIN provide an excellent introduction to the development of state economic policy in *Commonwealth: A Study of the Role of Government in the American Economy, Massachusetts, 1774–1861,* rev. ed. (Cambridge, Mass., 1969).

GORDON WOOD's *The Creation of the American Republic, 1776–1787* (Chapel Hill, N.C., 1969) features an extensive and illuminating discussion of constitutional developments in Pennsylvania. The interpretation presented in this essay differs from WOOD's, particularly on the relation of republicanism and constitutionalism. See also ERIC FONER, *Tom Paine and Revolutionary America* (New York, 1976), and O. S. IRELAND, "The Crux of Politics: Religion and Party in Pennsylvania, 1778–1789," *William and Mary Quarterly* 42 (October 1985): 453–475. DONALD S. LUTZ offers a sympathetic account of the Pennsylvania Council of Censors in *Popular Consent and Popular Control: Whig Political Theory in the Early State Constitutions* (Baton Rouge, La., 1980), pp. 129–149.

SEE ALSO Colonial Assemblies; Federalism and American Legislatures; The Origins of Congress; AND Representation.

STATE LEGISLATURES IN THE NINETEENTH CENTURY

William G. Shade

Although historians disagree about many aspects of the American Revolution, they recognize that the rise of the legislative assemblies in every colony epitomized the process and that it was the provincial gentry in the colonial legislatures who led the uprising against the king and Parliament. The new state constitutions institutionalized revolutionary republicanism by placing primary responsibility for governing in the hands of representative assemblies that exercised many judicial and executive powers, dominating those branches of government. Historians' excessive emphasis on the politics and policies of the federal government has obscured the importance of the state legislatures in nineteenth-century America.

The well-known eighteenth-century contrast between the "court" and the "country" entailed a general distrust of government and a willingness to see party prejudice in any decision adverse to interests that were easily equated with those of the people. So embedded in American political culture are these republican myths, that the history of American state legislatures has been characterized by persistent charges of corruption—usually lodged by those whose ox had been gored—accompanied by cycles of reform that loaded state constitutions with negative provisions designed to restrain powers that have been abused rather than to establish new areas of legislative activity.

At the time of the Revolution, the Old Dominion, Virginia, epitomized the very ideal of the "country" ideology. The planter elite who had controlled the colonial assembly led the resistance to the crown, drew up the Virginia Bill of Rights and the Constitution of 1776, constructing a government in which the legislature predominated over the Governor and the General Court. The bicameral assembly was composed at a House of Delegates, in which each county and the boroughs of Williamsburg and Norfolk were represented, and a Senate based on a smaller number of districts. Members of both houses had to be resident freeholders; senators were required to be more than twenty-five years of age. House members were elected annually, senators were elected on a rotation of "four classes," so that six members were elected annually for what amounted to four-year terms. Although the Virginia Bill of Rights emphasized the separation of powers, the Assembly was essentially the government of the Old Dominion.

All of the other states except Pennsylvania followed Virginia in adopting bicameral legislatures. The debate over balanced government led to the construction of upper and lower chambers that represented the people in different ways. Not only did members of each house have different terms, and different age and property requirements, but in some cases they were chosen by different electorates. In general, the states retained a connection between property holding and suffrage. The provision in the Virginia Constitution of 1776 that the right be extended to "all men, having sufficient evidence of permanent common interest with and attachment to the community" was interpreted to include only the freeholders who had voted before the Revolution.

The social and economic composition of the state assemblies underwent a modest democratization that loosened the grip of the colonial elite. The proportion of extremely wealthy lawmakers fell from nearly half to less than one-quarter. In the northern states, men of more moderate means gained a majority of the seats. The number of seats increased; the proportion of merchants and lawyers declined. Farther south there was less change. Seventy percent of the seats remained in the hands of the wealthy planters.

The patterns of eighteenth-century politics lingered into the nineteenth century. Electoral practices continued basically unchanged. Voters chose their social superiors to represent local interests and to exercise independent judgment. In theory, they employed their education, talents of persuasion, and political expertise for the benefit of the people of the state. In practice, conflicting interests extended the factionalism of the colonial assemblies into the Confederation period. Voting blocs reflecting regional interests often overlapped the feuds of leading families and the ethnic and religious conflicts that dominated the legislative politics of the new states.

FEDERALISTS AND REPUBLICANS

In the 1950s and 1960s critics of the paradigm of American political history constructed by the Progressive historians early in this century emphasized the functional importance of political parties in establishing stable and legitimate government in the new nation. These historians replaced the drama of the economic and ideological conflict between the Hamiltonian Federalists and the Jeffersonian Republicans with the calm of a liberal capitalist consensus. They focused upon the relationship between party structure and political participation, while marveling at the irony of the Founding Fathers both constructing a constitution against parties and inventing the apparatus for relatively modern electoral machines.

Like their Progressive predecessors, these historians centered their work on the new arena of national politics created by the Constitution, analyzing elections for federal offices and the formation of voting blocs in Congress. In sketching the parameters of the first party system, historians became increasingly aware of the spasmodic nature of party conflict during these years. Partisan activity within Congress was most pronounced in the periods of crisis from 1794 to 1801 and 1807 to 1815. At these times intermittent organization of electoral politics focused on federal policy. The Federalists and Republicans were, at best, protoparties that only barely penetrated the surface of the federal system.

From the Peace of Paris to the War of 1812, American state governments expanded their activities at a snail's pace. The states established twenty-two banks in the last two decades of the eighteenth-century, and the number grew to eighty-nine before the War of 1812. At the same time the total number of roll calls—while differing from year to year and state to state—hardly increased at all. For example, in the nine years before the establishment of the U.S. Constitution, three hundred votes were recorded in the New Jersey Assembly—approximately thirty-three votes per session. This changed very little over the next two decades. Between 1801 and 1805 the state's upper house held only ninety-one votes on matters other than patronage, such as finances, slavery, roads, and corporations. The state council—the upper house of state government (the assembly, the lower)—was extremely active in 1811, but had averaged only sixteen such votes in each of the four sessions.

The degree to which partisanship affected the behavior of the New Jersey legislators is problematic. Alexander Hamilton was a "Jerseyman," and friends of George Washington's administration dominated state politics in the 1790s. Although actual returns for legislative elections are far from complete, historians have estimated that the Federalists held two-thirds of the seats in the state legislature in 1800. Their majority disappeared abruptly the next year, and, from 1801 to 1815, the party gained a majority in the assembly only twice. To limit sectional conflict over patronage and to control elections, the Republicans first employed a caucus and then a parallel convention system. With the exception of patronage votes, scant evidence exists that shows the caucus controlled voting behavior, even in the small Legislative Council. Positions taken on federal issues determined party affiliation.

The relationship between national issues and factions in the state legislatures can be illustrated by the development of the Republicans and the Federalists in Virginia. The conflict over ratification of the Constitution reflected factional differences that existed in the 1780s and continued into the early 1790s on issues involving amendments to the Constitution, a second Constitutional Convention, and Hamilton's proposal on the assumption of state debts. In the five sessions from 1788 to 1792, however, these issues yielded eight roll calls that permitted Norman Risjord and Gordon DenBoer to identify one-third of the members of the House as "Federalists, 41; leaning Federalist, 10; middle of the road, 5; leaning anti-Federalist/Republican, 6; and anti-Federalist/Republican, 88." The anti-Federalist majority included about one third of those who had earlier favored the Constitution.

In the mid-1790s, the response to the French Revolution and the international situation divided the Virginia Assembly into pro-British and pro-French factions. Republicans opposed the Washington administration on Citizen Genet, the Whisky Rebellion, and the Jay Treaty, which provided for the restoration of loyalist property and the collection of British debts while remaining silent on the matter of slaves liberated by John Murray, Earl of Dunmore, the British commander. Although the number of roll calls continued to be small, more and more were being contested. By the end of the decade about four-fifths of the members could be identified with one of the parties. Sixty percent of these men were Republicans. The final vote on the adoption of the Virginia Resolutions against the Alien and Sedition acts that had been passed by the Federalists in Congress in 1798 was 100 to 63.

Throughout the 1790s the assembly continued to send former anti-Federalists to the Senate, but the vote for governor was not a partisan matter until 1799, when James Monroe defeated his Federalist opponent by a vote of 111 to 44. Partisanship during that session affected the election of the Speaker and the choice of the states printer. The Republicans also moved to deprive President Adams of two electoral votes he had received in 1796 by abolishing the district system and mandating the choice of electors in 1800 on a general ticket. Finally, the divisions on national issues also influenced a small number of roll calls on economic issues involving state matters of taxation and debtor relief. The Republicans were more united than the Federalists and favored the reduction of taxes and postponement of the collection of debts. The new factional alignment in the assembly was merged with the one that had appeared in the fight over ratification.

During the 1780s new members made up slightly more than half of Virginia's House of Delegates for each session, but the following decade brought a decline in the number of freshmen, with approximately 60 percent of the legislators in the Old Dominion holding their positions from one year to the next. During the 1790s, the number of nonslaveholding farmers doubled, but they made up only one-tenth of the members. The majority of Virginia legislators were small planters. As in the colonial period, a small group of legislators was regularly reelected. According to Richard R. Beeman, "Thirty-three men dominated the business of the House of Delegates between the years of 1788 and 1800" (*The Old Dominian*, p. 46). The stable core controlling Virginia's lower house, however, contained the wealthiest men elected to the legislature. They were overwhelmingly English by family origin, Episcopalians, and well connected to the First Families of Virginia. Nearly two-thirds of them owned more than twenty slaves each. Marriage and economic interests tied the large number of lawyers to the planters.

The Federalists were strongest in the upper Tidewater and in the area west of the Blue Ridge Mountains where they outnumbered their opponents by more than two to one. The Republicans controlled the Piedmont and nearly all of the seats from the planter-dominated Southside. Jeffersonian party leaders included the wealthiest men from the oldest families in the state. On average they owned more land and held more slaves than did their Federalist opponents. Half of the nonslaveholders in the legislature in the 1790s were Federalists, while more than 80 percent of the planters were Republicans.

The situation in Massachusetts differed in several particulars reflecting general differences between New England and the Chesapeake. Farmers made up the majority of the Massachusetts legislature, but one-fifth were businessmen. There were actually fewer lawyer-politicians in Massachusetts than in Virginia. There were also slightly fewer college graduates, and family origin was far less important. The New England legislators had much more previous governmental experience—there were more local offices to hold—and they were generally older. Like the Virginians, the New England legislators were former Revolutionary officers, overwhelmingly English in family origin, generally affiliated with the publicly supported church (in this case Congregationalist).

The majority of legislators in Massachusetts were Federalists.

When the parties were poorly organized and the opposition Republicans posed only a minor threat to Federalist control of the Massachusetts legislature, about half of the members of the General Court were freshmen. From 1807 to 1815, when there was an increase of partisan activity, the proportion of incumbents jumped to two-thirds. More than half of the Massachusetts legislators in the first two decades of the nineteenth century were farmers; merchants and other businessmen made up nearly one quarter of the members of the assembly. One in ten were artisans and "mechanics." The average legislator was in his mid-forties.

Although there are no precise figures, the number of dissenters—Baptists, Methodists, and the unchurched "Nothingarians"—grew along with the Democratic-Republican party that supported disestablishment. The main differences in the occupational profile between Federalists and Republicans were that the former included three times as many lawyers as the latter as well as a larger proportion of merchants and a smaller proportion of farmers. As James Banner, Jr., pointed out, however, "Not only were 55 per cent of the farmer-members with ascertainable political loyalties Federalists, but over 42 per cent of the Federalist delegations in the fifteen years after 1800—more than double the proportion of merchants—were farmers" (*To the Hartford Convention*, p. 290).

A somewhat similar pattern occurred in the Middle States, where the Federalists became a minority party after 1800. These states differed from both Virginia and Massachusetts because of the more cosmopolitan nature of their population. Legislators from Pennsylvania, New York, and New Jersey represented a greater diversity of national origin. In Pennsylvania there were more people of Scots–Irish than English descent, and a sizable number of Germans. Those of Dutch stock held the same number of seats in New York as those with English backgrounds. Religious diversity was also evident. In New York, Pennsylvania, and New Jersey, Presbyterians were the largest group, but there were significant numbers of Quakers and Dutch Reformed, as well as Episcopalians, Baptists, and Methodists.

The occupational profile of the New Jersey legislators resembled that of their Massachusetts counterparts in the 1780s, and did not change greatly in the era of the Republican ascendancy after 1800. Fragmentary evidence indicates that during the era of the first party system the Federalists were somewhat older than their Republican opponents and were more strongly tied to the Revolutionary elite, having "old stock family origins, membership in established religious groups, college degrees ... high status occupations such as the law, and involvement in manufacturing and transportation projects" (Pasler and Pasler, p. 53) As was the case in Massachusetts, Federalist legislators in New Jersey were less likely than Republicans to be farmers and more often were manufacturers and lawyers. Presbyterians, who made up the largest denomination in the Garden State's legislature were split evenly among the parties: the Dutch Reformed, Episcopalians, and Quakers tended to be Federalists, while the Baptist and Methodists generally were Republicans.

The level of incumbency in New York showed a slow decrease from 1780 through the first decade of the nineteenth century. The proportion of first-term members in the assembly of New York increased from one-third to one-half. In Pennsylvania each new legislature during this era included about fifty percent freshmen, but typically a core of members who had at least a few years of experience served as the most important leaders to the Republican party.

The Pennsylvania legislative caucus appeared to unify the Republicans on candidates for offices and to mediate the factional controversies to which the politics of the Middle States were prone. The movement of the capital to Lancaster added to the power of the legislative caucus by putting "the legislature another step away from the nonlegislative party leaders and newspapers editors, many of whom resided in Philadelphia" (Bowers, "From Caucus to Convention," p. 283).

The major effect was to make legislative experience necessary for advancement to the offices of governor and U.S. senator. Throughout the 1790s, such experience had not been necessary; five of the seven U.S. senators had little connection with the legislature. Simon Synder, however, who defeated incumbent

Thomas McKean in 1805, had been Speaker before assuming the governorship for nearly a decade. His successor, William Findlay, who served from 1817 to 1820, had been closely associated with the legislature as state treasurer. The next two treasurers, three governors, and seven of the nine senators selected between 1803 and 1827 all previously had been legislators.

Pennsylvania parties basically were defined by federal politics, and there was little attempt to control issues other than those relating directly to party matters. Practically no Federalists were left in the legislature after 1800. Even the years just before and during the War of 1812—a period of high excitement—showed relatively low levels of party unity. Questions such as the embargo, federal judges, the rechartering of the Bank of the United States, and support for Madison's foreign policies drew the Republicans together, but there is little reason to believe that the caucus produced this cohesion. On banking and internal improvements the Republicans were sharply divided.

In the southern states the effect of party on legislative voting was even more limited. After the so-called Revolution of 1800, Federalism practically disappeared from Virginia and the Carolinas. The Federalist party was able to win only one-fourth of the seats in the Virginia House of Delegates in 1800. The portion fell the following year and never again exceeded one-fifth of the seats. The party fared best in North Carolina, although even there, a permanent minority held only 23 percent of the state's legislature seats, with its low point in 1805. In South Carolina Federalist influence dropped steadily each year. By 1812 there were only four Federalists in the lower house.

The southern states were characterized by an absence of contests over the speakership and partisan control of the major committees. The roll calls reveal extremely low cohesion, especially among the Republican majority. In the average roll call in the Virginia house during these years, 40 percent of the Republicans stood against the majority of their party. Federalist unity was a product of the fact that most were from the western counties of the Commonwealth. Although members considered themselves either Federalists or Republicans on federal matters, this rarely affected decisions on state issues. The conflict between Federalists and Republicans had no relation to state matters such as slavery, internal improvements, education, taxation, and public morals. Partisans clustered together only on the few votes dealing with patronage, election laws, and redistricting.

THE SECOND AMERICAN PARTY SYSTEM

The years following the War of 1812 are usually subdivided into (1) the Era of Good Feelings in which previous party controversies were laid aside in a rush of nationalism associated with the Missouri Compromise (which included the admission of Missouri as a slave state and a limit to the entrance of slavery above a line drawn across the Louisiana Purchase), the rulings of the Supreme Court, under Chief Justice, John Marshall, and the American System, a term used to describe the economic principles envisioned by Henry Clay; and (2) the period of Jacksonian Democracy ushered in by Andrew Jackson's victory over John Quincy Adams in the presidential election of 1828. The democratic trend of the times was based on earlier changes in the constitutional rules of the game.

Between 1815 and 1821, five new states entered the Union, and New York, Connecticut, and Massachusetts revised their own constitutions. The extension of suffrage, an increase in the number of elective offices, the lowering of qualifications for office, and attempts to provide more equitable representation opened up the political process to almost all adult white men. Increased acceptance of political individualism moved the political culture toward a more modern conception of representation and a more positive evaluation of the democratic potential of political parties.

Since Richard P. McCormick coined the term in the 1960s, the "second American party system" has served to describe the new electoral organization that appeared in the 1830s with the advent of the Democratic and Whig parties. Although McCormick realized the critical importance of organization at the state level, he focused upon presidential elections and applied the electoral-machine model to

American parties. From this perspective the desire to gain and control political power led to the invention of popular parties and produced both the substantial increase of voter turnout in the late 1830s and the new system.

Both Whigs and Democrats developed a faithful following throughout the country, yielding an era of highly competitive elections. One of the features that distinguished the second party system from its predecessor was its penetration into the affairs of the state legislatures. As governmental activity in antebellum America expanded, parties began to influence policy-making in the states to an unprecedented degree, so much so that the last two-thirds of the nineteenth century has been called the "party period" of American history.

At that time, the idea that laissez faire characterized American economic policy ignores the significant degree of government participation in economic development. It is misleading to focus solely on the federal government, where the activist tendencies associated with Henry Clay were reversed by the Jacksonian Democrats in the name of states' rights and individual liberty. The states played an important role because they controlled many aspects of business, particularly in the areas of transportation and banking. Economic policy in the states involved the cooperation of public and private enterprise through the device of the mixed corporation to create what may be called social overhead capital. The primary function of the state legislatures was the allocation of public resources.

Conflict within the state legislatures on these matters involved the clash of regional interests and those of groups of private entrepreneurs. The politics of internal improvements often determined the future economic life of a town or a district. Just as delegations in the U.S. Congress acted in the interest of their states in such matters, state legislative coalitions were formed for similar purposes: they determined where extensions to the "main line" would be constructed in Pennsylvania and the representatives of various Ohio towns worked together to gain routes favorable to their localities. Similar geographical and personal-interest groups struggled to obtain bank charters. The interests were often mediated by legislative cliques centered in the capitol, such as the Albany "Regency" in New York and the "Family Party" in Pennsylvania. Roll calls on these matters reflected regional differences. In Virginia, the Richmond "Junto" resisted demands from outlying areas for credit facilities and state aid in enlarging their access to markets.

The number of roll calls doubled between the 1820s and 1830s and then leveled off in the 1840s; during this decade in New Jersey, for example, there were four times as many roll calls per session than in the decade following the Revolution. The distribution of legislative business was roughly the same from state to state. In the Virginia House of Delegates of 1840–1841, more than half of the one hundred thirty-one roll calls concerned governmental matters such as elections, legislative procedures, and public printing. Issues related to business, banking, transportation, and state-financial policy took up another one-third of the legislators' time. The New Jersey legislature presented a slightly different pattern. One-third of roll calls pertained to control of the government. One-fourth dealt with business and commerce, about 20 percent involved counties and townships, and 15 percent concerned social issues. Pennsylvania differed in that there were twice as many roll calls compared to New Jersey, with 40 percent of the legislators' time devoted to transportation, because of its state works, or transportation systems owned by the state.

Profiles of the Legislators

The men who deliberated on these issues and essentially made policy in nineteenth-century America were truly "delegates fresh from the people," as Andrew Jackson once said in 1835. Yearly elections and the high number of freshmen each session meant that a sizable proportion of the white male population not only voted and served on election committees, but actually took a direct part in governing their states. Levine's examination of 561 men who made up the Council and the Assembly of New Jersey between 1829 and 1844 showed that none served more than six terms, 233 men sat only once, and another 216 sat only twice. Of the known candidates for the legislature, one-fifth ran for office on three or more occasions, but most ran only once.

Turnover in New Jersey was in fact quite low during these years. Of the 548 men who served in the North Carolina House of Commons between 1836 and 1850, 61 percent served only one term. In the New York Assembly in the 1830's, two-thirds of the legislators were freshmen, and in the following decade three-quarters were freshmen. Most states fell somewhere between these extremes, yet most had an increase in the number of freshmen during the 1840s.

These years also brought a further democratization of the state legislatures in terms of the changing socioeconomic status of their members. The common man may not have ascended to the throne, but quintessentially middle-class white men were in power in the mid-nineteenth century. In every state the men who sat in the legislatures were approximately forty years old, better educated than the average citizen, well connected in their local communities, engaged in high-status professions, and moderately wealthy (or at least on the way to becoming so). Yet in terms of social status they were clearly a cut below their predecessors of the Jeffersonian era.

Because of the variation in regional economic development in antebellum America, the occupational profiles of legislators in the South and North show clear differences. A simple contrast between Virginia and Massachusetts reveals the differences: in Virginia more than half of the legislators in 1850 were primarily in agriculture, nearly a third were lawyers, and fewer than one-fifth pursued nonagricultural occupations; in Massachusetts 60 percent of the legislature were from nonagricultural professions, and only about one-fourth were farmers, and none were planters. It must be borne in mind that this divergence, which would be even more stark were it drawn between South Carolina and New York, hides regional differences within the North.

Although they are most often conceptualized as a contrast between the East and the West, basic differences existed between the predominately agricultural states and those that had more complex economies and populations increasingly concentrated in urban centers. Nearly 60 percent of the men who served in the lower house of New Jersey between 1829 and 1844 were farmers, at a time when about two-thirds of the entire state's work force were still employed in agriculture. Businessmen made up 25 percent and lawyers just under 20 percent of the New Jersey lawmakers. In con-

trast, Pennsylvania, New York, and Massachusetts had fewer farmers and more businessmen in their legislatures. These states also had slightly more lawyers and more members of the working class. Almost half of the Massachusetts legislators were in some form of business; artisans and laborers held one-tenth of the seats in Pennsylvania. There were distinctly fewer farmers and more lawyers in the upper houses of all of these three states. Half of the New York state senators were professionals of one sort or another, 35 percent of whom were lawyers.

In the more agriculturally oriented states of the Old Northwest, farmers made up a larger portion of the legislators than they did in the industrializing states. In Indiana, for example, three-fifths of the legislators were farmers, one-fifth were lawyers, six members were physicians, and the remainder were small businessmen and artisans. The mean age was thirty eight, and practically all resided in the state for at least ten years. In Illinois, Rodney O. Davis found fewer farmers and more lawyers. Yet, an examination of the personnel of the Illinois legislature shows that "not quite half of the senators and slightly more than half of the representatives claimed farming as their primary occupation." About one-fourth were lawyers ("others" make up the rest). Missouri, a slave state, had an occupational profile quite similar to that of Illinois.

In the antebellum South, the clearest indicator of wealth and status was slaveholding. Using this standard legislators in the 1840s were men of status in their communities and most were on their way to increasing their position in Southern society. The populous states of the upper South from Maryland to Missouri contained most of the cities and the industry of the Old South, but they all had predominately agricultural economies and slavery remained firmly entrenched. In these states farmers and planters made up nearly three-fifths of the legislators. More than half of the members held slaves and one-sixth were planters possessing twenty or more. One-quarter of the legislators in the upper South were lawyers; Kentucky had the most lawyer-legislators in the country.

The legislators of the lower South generally differed from those of the upper South in that they were younger and wealthier. In both regions almost exactly the same proportion was in agriculture, but in the lower South a much higher percentage held slaves, and twice as many were planters. Lawyers made up one-fifth of the legislators although 26 percent of the lawmakers in the planter state of Alabama practiced law. The proportion of slaveholders was highest in South Carolina, but it exceeded two-thirds in Georgia, Alabama, and Mississippi, as well. While planters possessed more than half of the seats in South Carolina's legislature, they held only one-third of those in Georgia, Alabama, and Mississippi. As to age, in 1850 three-quarters of the members of Mississippi's lower house were under forty years of age, but that was only a slightly higher proportion than Louisiana.

Whigs and Democrats In terms of economic and social status, the Whigs and the Democrats sent similar men to the Southern legislatures. Farmers and planters made up the majority of both Whig and Democratic legislators throughout the South, but the ratio of slaveholders and nonslaveholders varied from state to state. In all of the states of the upper South except Maryland, the party of Jackson and Polk sent a slightly larger percentage of slaveholders to the state capitals than did their opponents. In Georgia and Florida a larger proportion of Whigs owned slaves, but in Mississippi and Louisiana the situation was reversed. In 1850 in Alabama nonslaveholders made up almost exactly one-third of both parties, while one-third of the Whigs and slightly more than one-quarter of the Democrats were planters. Throughout the South, however, Whig legislators came disproportionately from the nonagricultural sector of the economy; there were larger proportions of Democrats among farmers. In the Virginia House of Delegates lawyers who were *not* also planters or farmers or who combined the law with nonagricultural interests were overwhelmingly Whigs.

In most of the Northern legislatures, lawyers were generally split evenly between the parties, with farmers making up a slightly higher portion of the Democrats, and businessmen were more often Whigs. The differences were usually rather small. Of the three hundred forty men identified in New Jersey's General Assembly, 64 percent of the Democrats but only 54 percent of the Whigs farmed. Two-thirds of Indiana's Democratic legislators in the 1840s were farmers while only 47 percent of

the Whigs were in agriculture. The lawyers in New Jersey divided equally between the parties, but Whigs clearly outnumbered Democrats among businessmen-legislators. About one-quarter of the Indiana Whigs were lawyers and 30 percent were involved in nonagricultural occupations as merchants, small businessmen, and craftsmen.

Although there have been a number of studies of ethnic and religious differences among voters, there is only scattered material on the backgrounds of legislators. Illinois had cultural differences between the party leaders that reflected those of their constituents. A slightly higher proportion of New Englanders were Whigs, and they have been described as more "overtly religious" (although this may simply be because it is easier to find information on them). Those from the northern part of the state showed a tendency toward an "evangelical" orientation, with a higher percentage of "Presbygational" legislators. They also had a much larger number of Methodists while the Democrats had an equally sizable advantage among the Baptists. Foreign-born legislators were more likely to be Democrats than Whigs. These findings coincide with Michael F. Holt's study of Pittsburgh candidates for office that shows the Whigs much more likely to be Presbyterians and all of the Catholics to have been Democrats.

Party played a primary role in determining the behavior of state legislators in the era of the second party system. Southern Democrats and Whigs opposed each other on issues similar to those contested in the Northern state assemblies. A study by Herbert Ershkowitz and William G. Shade of the voting in the Jacksonian-era legislatures examined the results of two hundred fifty selected roll calls from six states during the decade from 1833 to 1843. The study showed that party conflict existed in the 1830s on matters related to banking and currency, internal improvements, business corporations and social issues, particularly questions relating to slavery and the rights of blacks, but that after 1837 it increased greatly.

Studies of roll calls from additional states from 1829 to 1853 permit an extension of this picture. All of the states followed the same pattern from moderate party disagreement in the 1830s, once elections for legislatures began to be contested, to high levels of party cohesiveness and conflict in the 1840s. In the New Jersey assembly the mean index of disagreement on all of the nonunanimous roll calls taken in the five sessions from 1833 to 1837 was 39. This figure jumped to 60 for the sessions between 1838 to 1844. From 1835 to 1837 the same index was 30 for the Mississippi house; mean disagreement increased to 43 for the sessions from 1838 to 1844.

Partisanship varied from issue to issue. The divisions in the Virginia House of Delegates in 1840 to 1841 were similar to those found in New Jersey, Mississippi, Illinois, and North Carolina at the same time. The mean disagreement on all the roll calls was 50. The mean cohesion scores for the Whigs and the Democrats were 62 and 54.* On a majority of the votes, three-quarters of one party opposed three-quarters of the other. The clearest conflict came on money and banking; the dozen roll calls produced a mean disagreement of 73. The votes related to government control yielded a mean disagreement of 64; on the seven roll calls on railroads the mean was 48. Four of the seven roll calls on the treatment of free blacks and slavery and six out of eight on taxes revealed a mean disagreement of more than 40.

The most consistently partisan matters were national resolutions and issues related directly to control of the government. Yet votes on economic issues—banking and currency, business incorporations, internal improvements—all produced clear party conflict during the depression of the late 1830s and early 1840s. Fewer roll calls were taken on social issues and the results were less divergent; however, they show the Whigs and Democrats at

swords' point. In Michigan, roll calls on slavery, the clergy, capital punishment, and prohibition set the "anti-evangelical" majority of the Democrats against the "evangelical" Whigs. Whigs in the General Assembly of Illinois came out much more strongly in favor of temperance and sabbatarianism than did their Jacksonian opponents. These differences were most clear on questions relating to slavery and free blacks, which were matters of partisan contention in both the North and the South.

The Whigs were unified in favor of banks and the credit system, while the Democrats were equally decisive in their opposition to limited liability and paper currency. Internal improvements caused slightly less conflict. The Whigs generally supported the use of corporations and mixed enterprise and the Democrats opposed them. Local pressure in favor of such projects strained Democratic unity, a situation seen even more clearly on social issues. Whigs generally favored "reform"; Democrats opposed governmental interference with personal freedom. Lee Benson has contrasted the negative liberalism of the Democrats with the positive liberalism of the Whigs and related these to the cultural constituencies of the parties in New York. Voting studies of other Northern states confirm this initial description of the cultural differences between Whig and Democratic voters.

Half of the American states wrote new constitutions in the decade from 1845 to 1855. The constitutional conventions of the time provided a forum for detailed debate on banking, internal improvements, blacks' rights and slavery, taxes, and the role of government, in general. The result was the extension of limits on legislative power and governmental activism. In most states the power to extend the states indebtedness was restricted and the way cleared to divest state interest in transportation projects. Private and local legislation was restrained. While only Iowa and Arkansas actually prohibited banks, other states outlawed lotteries and gave the power to grant divorces to the courts. Several Southern states banned the emancipation of slaves. A number of states adopted biennial sessions and limited them to a certain number of days. These changes were resisted by the Whigs even though they did not go nearly as far as most Democrats wished. The party program for reform widely circulated by

---

* Historians and political scientists examine partisan conflict as reflected in roll-call voting in a variety of ways. Two simple measures are used. The index of party cohesion yields a score for each party on each roll call. It is the difference between the percentage of the party members voting "yea" and the percentage of the party members voting "nay" on a roll call. The *mean party cohesion* is the average of cohesion scores for each party on all of the roll calls within a group. An *index of disagreement* shows the relationship between the parties on each roll call. It is the difference between the proportion of each party voting "yea" on a particular roll call. The *mean disagreement* is the average of disagreement scores over all of the roll calls in a set. Each of these measures may be used in relation to any subset of votes such as those on a single issue. The index of cohesion measures intraparty unity; the index of disagreement measures interparty conflict.

the *Democratic Review* and in the party press constituted a stern invocation of the Jeffersonian maxim that "the world is too much governed." Insisting that excessive legislation endangered individual liberty and fostered special privilege, the Democrats called for the total elimination of banks and corporations and for greater separation of powers, to be achieved by increasing the independence of governors and judges from legislative control. Democrats focused Americans' long-standing distrust of government on the legislatures that already were associated with corruption, while their opponents insisted that the problem was excessive partisanship.

In the late 1840s and the early 1850s partisanship deteriorated somewhat and levels of party disagreement in the state legislatures declined. After 1847 the mean for disagreement on all roll calls in Pennsylvania fell, but it remained relatively high from 1848 to 1853. This modest movement toward consensus was the product of a decline in Democratic cohesion within business and commerce as the economy improved. Throughout the country, Democratic "softs," pro-bank Democrats, split with their party and joined with the Whigs to pass free-banking and free-corporation laws. At the same time, the decline in the level of partisan conflict in states such as Virginia was the product of a large increase in the number of roll calls on traditionally nonpartisan questions. In the 1848–1849 session of the Virginia House of Delegates the mean index of disagreement was only 29, down from 50 in the 1840–1841 session, but on governmental matters such as elections, national resolutions, banking and currency, and slavery, high levels of conflict between the Whigs and Democrats continued.

The Realignment of the 1850s The crisis of the 1850s had profound effects on the state legislatures that reflect the political changes during the decade that led to the Civil War. Historians have focused on the electoral realignment in the North that gave birth to the Republican party. The legislatures have drawn less interest. Small changes in the electorate, however, caused sizable shifts in the partisan balance in state assemblies because of the adherence to single-member districts. In Pennsylvania, for example, the proportion of Democrats in the lower house fell from one-half in 1849 to one-third in 1859, even though the Democrats claimed 44 percent of the vote the following year.

A sizable number of new men entered the Northern legislatures in the 1850s. The mean percentage of first-term members in the New York Assembly jumped to 83 percent, the highest in the state's history. These new men were younger and from slightly different economic backgrounds than their predecessors. Between 1850 and 1860, the proportion of farmers held steady in the lower house and went up in the senate. The number of lawyers declined in both houses, while the number of businessmen increased dramatically from 27 to 38 percent.

The most striking aspect of the realignment of the 1850s was the outburst of nativism that led to the sudden disappearance of the Whigs and the meteoric career of the American party. The nativist program mixed demands for temperance and opposition to the extension of slavery with warnings about the effects of immigration. In 1854 and 1855 this party, or Know-Nothings as Horace Greeley named them, won majorities in the legislatures of six Northern states. In 1855 all of the senators and nearly all of the 390 members of the Massachusetts General Court supported the new party. Of these men nearly 90 percent were serving their first term, and have been described by historians as "new men" in terms of their lack of political experience and lower social status in comparison with their predecessors. They included far fewer lawyers and wealthy businessmen. Most were entrepreneurs, shopkeepers, and skilled workers, and they passed an ambitious program of social reform.

Legislative output continued to grow. In Pennsylvania the number of session laws increased to nearly 800 by 1859. Although party conflict in general declined because of the lack of Republican cohesion on transportation issues, disagreement continued to be high on votes affecting the control of the government, business and banking, as in the other Northern states. Social issues, most obviously those related to slavery, but temperance as well, split the parties internally, although the Republicans were more cohesive than the Democrats.

As in the North, the number of laws increased as the demands for internal improvements, particularly railroads, spread across the South. Alabama's legislature chartered forty new corporations per session during the 1850s.

At the same time, turnover in the Southern legislatures also increased. The proportion of freshmen in the Georgia legislature went from two-thirds in 1851 to three-fourths in 1859. Even in Virginia nearly 60 percent of the House of Delegates members during the decade served only one term, and most states saw even fewer incumbents elected.

In the slave states these new men were strikingly older and wealthier than those who had held office the previous decade. The change was most pronounced in the lower South, where the average amount of real property held by legislators more than doubled. The proportion of slaveholders and planters in the legislatures of these states increased, although the percentage of slaveholders in the general population of the states declined between 1850 and 1860. Three-quarters of the men who sat in the legislatures of South Carolina, Georgia, Alabama, and Mississippi on the eve of secession were slaveholders, and 42 percent of them owned more than twenty slaves.

Partisan behavior in the legislatures all but disappeared. In the Alabama legislature the vigorous two-party system of the 1840s had disappeared by the end of the next decade. The number of votes in Georgia that set 60 percent of the Democrats against an equal proportion of their opponents fell from half in the 1840s to 14 percent in 1859. This was also the case in states of the upper South, such as North Carolina and Virginia, where electoral competition continued to exist. The mean index of disagreement in the Virginia House of Delegates fell to a low point of 15 in 1859, when the Democrats controlled 60 percent of the seats. Only national resolutions showed partisan conflict, with the Democrats united in support of the cause of the South.

REPUBLICAN RECONSTRUCTION

Although the Republicans had established themselves as the majority party in the North by 1860, it was not until the 1870s that the third party system became institutionalized. Its dominant characteristics included a high degree of participation and party identification, and a one-party Democratic South combined with an extremely close balance of power in presidential elections and in Congress. The Gilded Age was a period of persistent partisanship, ineffective government, and political cynicism—especially when seen from the perspective of its Progressive critics.

Two images of state legislatures dominate the traditional view of the postwar era: the "blackout of honest government" in Southern states during Radical Reconstruction and the "moral collapse" of Northern state government in the era of "the boss and the machine." While the ex-Confederate states suffered under "foreign" legislatures composed of corrupt "carpetbaggers, scalawags and ignorant blacks," their Northern neighbors had to endure state legislatures dominated by "politicos" acting at the bidding of the "robber barons" who controlled emergent industrial capitalism.

The Radical Republicans in Congress resisted President Andrew Johnson's efforts to quickly bring the rebellious states back into the Union. Under their auspices conventions of "black and tan" (blacks and their allies) met in 1867 to draw up new constitutions to reconstruct the ex-Confederate states. The new documents incorporated into their work progressive provisions from contemporary Northern state constitutions and brought uniformity grounded upon the acceptance of universal manhood suffrage and representation based on total population or registered voters. What most distinguished the reconstructed governments from their antebellum predecessors, however, were their makeup and their expanded conception of social responsibility.

The same Republican coalition that had written these constitutions was elected to run the governments created under them. Blacks, Northern carpetbaggers, and Southern-born white "scalawags" took control of the governments of the ex-Confederate states. In contrast to the myths spread by Democrats of outside agitators and black rule, a majority of all the Republicans that sat in Southern legislatures during Reconstruction were Southern-born whites. Ex-slaves received fewer than one-fifth of the places in the new governments. Carpetbaggers made up slightly less than one-third of the Republican officeholders.

The scalawags were primarily former Unionists and ex-Whigs who had been reluctant Confederates at best. Their greatest strength was in the upland counties of western Virginia and of North Carolina, eastern Tennessee, and the northern portions of Georgia and Alabama. Most owned medium-sized farms and harbored hostility toward the planter-elite. Their white allies differed in ways other than simply their Northern birth. The carpetbaggers had moved south to seek their fortunes. Some invested substantial sums in cotton planting, but most were professionals and businessmen. They were well educated and vocal advocates of modernization of the South.

Most black Republican leaders, of course, were amateurs, marginal men, poor, and uneducated. The majority had been slaves. Southern-born "free blacks," generally mulattoes, also played an important role during Reconstruction, and made up about one-quarter of the African American lawmakers. Another 10 to 15 percent of these black leaders lived most of their lives or were born outside the South. Because of the presence of these black carpetbaggers and the freeborn element, more than four-fifths of the black legislators were literate, and a significant number were college graduates or had professional training.

The makeup of these groups differed from state to state. Sixty-nine blacks sat in the Georgia legislature, but information is available on about half of them. More than 80 percent had been slaves and there were only a handful of mulattoes and carpetbaggers. One-quarter were illiterate and many others almost so; only 40 percent owned land. Most had become preachers after the war, including the famous Henry M. Turner. On all counts, Georgia's black political elite was less well-off than its counterparts in South Carolina and Louisiana. Between 1868 and 1876, blacks held a majority of the seats in the lower house of the South Carolina legislature. Approximately one-third of these men were ministers and teachers, a third were artisans and small entrepreneurs, and a third were farmers, the majority of whom owned their land. Color and class conflict caused tension between the freeborn mulattoes and the dark-skinned ex-slaves.

The different elements of the Republican coalition responded differently to the major work of the Radical legislatures. The Radicals brought public education to the South as an integral element in the modernization of the region. Reconstruction was practically synonymous with railroad development, although the gospel of progress preached by the Republi-

cans also included boomtowns, expanding industries, and diversified agriculture. Aid for internal improvements was hardly new to the South, but the scale and scope of the Republican program far exceeded that proposed by any of its predecessors.

Public support of internal improvements and new social programs such as the first public, or common, schools, meant the mounting of state debts and skyrocketing taxes. At the outset of Radical rule, the ex-Confederate states had a total indebtedness of $175 million, which after four years had jumped to $305 million. Increased taxes hit all landowners, because the states relied almost exclusively on land taxes, often giving tax breaks to businesses to lure capital. Rates were three or four times higher than before the war and conflicts over these issues further strained the Republican coalition.

During these years there was a high turnover of legislators and relations became strained between the members of the Republican majority. Even in South Carolina, where the Republicans retained control the longest, nearly two-thirds of the legislators served only one term. The mean cohesion scores for the minority Democrats never fell below 68, but the majority Republicans never exceeded 50. In fact from 1872 to 1874 a majority of the whites opposed a majority of the blacks on 60 percent of the crucial votes, and there were also splits among the blacks, as usual between the ex-slaves and freeborn mulattoes.

North Carolina from 1868 to 1870 provides an example of a radical Republican legislature at work. Its makeup was quite different from that of South Carolina. In North Carolina there were 39 white Democrats and 87 Republicans. The latter group was overwhelmingly white; two-thirds of them were Southern-born scalawags. Eighteen of these Republicans were native blacks and only eleven were white carpetbaggers. The legislature's record was one of activism and impressive achievement, establishing legal and political equality, public schools, and an array of social services. The Radical legislators are remembered, however, for their zeal for internal improvements that plunged the state deeply in debt.

Radical legislation included questions of blacks' rights and the handling of ex-rebels, but the largest number of roll calls taken during these sessions involved taxes. Voting and debating on taxes, as well as on issues of internal improvements, chiefly railroads, occupied half of the legislature's time. Smaller but significant matters were education, government spending on social services, and matters relating to debtors and the poor. The Republicans were distinctly more radical than the conservative Democrats on every category of legislation. The scalawags split; about two-fifths of them made up a moderate voting bloc.

Yet, given this division within the Republican party, the mean disagreement between Democrats and Republicans in North Carolina was quite high (52), comparable to the peak reached during the second party system. The sharpest disagreement was shown in matters relating to elections, schools, civil rights, and local government, but railroads, taxes, and expenditures were clearly partisan matters as well. The questions relating to black equality caused the greatest chasm between the parties, but the Democrats also resisted all Republican efforts to expand education, were less willing than Republicans to take a pro-debtor position, and solidly opposed Republican taxes. All in all, the postwar Southern Democrats voted a consistently negative and typically Jacksonian position.

Democratic Redemption

Redemption in North Carolina involved constitutional amendments cutting the pay of legislatures and limiting legislative powers by adopting biennial sessions for specified short periods. North Carolina Democrats in the late nineteenth century were fairly typical of Southern Redeemers as a whole. In their emphasis on privatization, they sold off the state's interest in the railroads at bargain-basement prices. They passed the notorious Landlord and Tenant Act in 1877, which put the crops in the hands of the landlord, who served as "the court, sheriff and jury" in determining the tenant's shares after rent, fees, and loans had been paid to him. Two years later the Democratic legislature repudiated the Reconstruction debt and refunded the remainder of the states' debt at a rate of four cents on the dollar. An array of amendments to the state constitution and specific legislation mandated segregated schools, outlawed miscegenation, and limited black influence by abolishing the elective county commissioners.

Elsewhere, the Redeemers drew up new constitutions to replace the Radical documents written in the 1860s and to limit the excesses of government associated with them. Redeemers curtailed the size of government, slashed salaries, limited legislative sessions, and barred public aid to corporations. Democratic advocates of "retrenchment and reform" cut back spending on education—described by Virginia governor Frederick W. M. Holliday as "a luxury" his state could ill-afford—and eliminated the social services established under the Republicans.

The Southern Democrats oversaw the wholesale repudiation of their respective state's debts to the tune of approximately $150 million and made a fetish of economy in government. Louisiana reduced state expenditures from $7.6 million in 1871 to $1.6 million in 1882 and instituted a lottery. Extreme measures enabled Alabama to cut expenditures in half in just two years, 1874 to 1876, and hold them below $1 million for the next decade. Most of the state's money went to pay pensions to Confederate veterans.

The Redeemers slashed taxes everywhere when they returned to power. They reduced the rates and shifted the tax burden from the shoulders of the large landowners. Planter property that had been seized by the Republicans for nonpayment of taxes was returned by the Democrats. Southern legislatures imposed new assessments on storekeepers, insurance agents, traveling salesmen, liquor dealers, moneylenders, and other urban occupational groups. Tools, animals and even the furniture of tenants, small farmers, and laborers were taxed. The convict-lease system was typical of the Democratic solution to the fiscal mess: rather than using taxpayer money to incarcerate criminals the states "leased" prisoners to private businessmen and planters.

These paternalistic patricians did not immediately institute the Jim Crow system, but throughout the ex-Confederate states black influence was "controlled." Local autonomy was eliminated. Districts were gerrymandered to reduce Republican strength. In the upper South, blacks continued to vote and sit in the legislatures, and the Republicans remained competitive into the 1890s. Throughout the lower

South, fraud and violence restricted black participation; the Republican party became a hopeless minority. Even before constitutional disfranchisement other methods were devised to limit black voting.

These Bourbon Democrats, a term referring to their French ruling-class ancestry, prided themselves on their service in the cause of the Confederacy. As late as the mid-1890s nearly three quarters of the Democrats in the Alabama legislature were Confederate veterans and 40 percent of those had served as officers. An examination of nearly seven hundred leading Confederates shows that nine-tenths held office after the war and practically all were Democrats. In Tennessee and North Carolina, where there had been significant Whig parties before the war, the Redeemers included a sizable number of ex-Whigs, but in general they came from Democratic backgrounds. In the 1880s half of the South Carolina Democratic legislators were planters, and the landholding interest played a large role in the party in Alabama, Mississippi, and Louisiana.

The most common occupation other than those related to farming in the Southern legislatures was the law. In Alabama in 1894 lawyers accounted for half of the Democratic legislators while only a quarter were farmers and planters. These townsmen, however, came from planter-dominated counties where large landholders were their kin as well as clients, if they themselves were not economically involved in agriculture. Businessmen made up only 15 percent of the Democratic legislators at the time. Especially in the lower South, representatives of the Black Belt, or slaveholding, planters dominated the Democratic party that served their interests.

Southern populism was essentially an anti-Redeemer movement directed primarily against the influence of the large landholders, although its agrarian attack often focused on town influence and business interests. In the Alabama legislature in 1894 the Populists came from a lower social strata than the dominant Democrats. Among the handful of Populist leaders about whom there is biographical information, one finds five farmers, a planter, a doctor, a real-estate agent, and a businessman. None had attended college, and of the six who had served the Confederacy only one had been an officer. One Alabama newspaper described the Populists as "the plain farmers, the country

store keepers, the skilled mechanics and workmen . . . country doctors, preachers and lawyers" (from the *Choctaw Alliance*, 15 April 1894, quoted from Hackney, p. 30). The profile of Oklahoma legislators, for example, reveals almost exactly this picture of the forty-five Populists who served in the 1890s; two-thirds were farmers and one-fourth were professionals. Only three of these men were lawyers—while lawyers made up a third of both the Democrats and Republicans.

THE GILDED AGE

The "Genteel Reformers" in the North, like Redeemers in the South, combined their criticism of corruption and hostility to partisan politics with a generally antigovernmental stance that focused on the restriction of legislative power in the name of democratic government. It involved a revival of Jacksonian ideals and a return to power of the Democratic party rooted, as was the original party of Jackson, in its hold on the solid South. As a Southern Democratic newspaper, editor, Henry Watterson, wrote in the *Louisville Courier Journal* in 1875: "There is so much to undo . . . [and] so little to do."

Between 1864 and 1879, thirty-seven states wrote and ratified new constitutions. Those written in the 1860s reflected the Republican acceptance of positive government as well as the altered attitudes toward race relations. In response to a postwar explosion of private and local legislation, the economic depression of the 1870s, and the Democratic resurgence, the new constitutions written in the Northern states during the 1870s reduced legislative authority by enhancing judicial power and prohibiting local and private laws in wide areas. From New York to Nebraska Northern voters embraced "a grand design to reduce the field of state law and withhold from it every subject which it is not necessary to concede" (Keller, *Affairs of State*, p. 112).

Liberal reformers extolled this antigovernmental trend but increasingly saw the state legislatures as an arena of corruption and cupidity manipulated by the monied interests. The author of one of the classics of muckraking literature, *Wealth Against Commonwealth*, social critic Henry Demarest Lloyd quipped that Standard Oil had "done everything with the Pennsylvania legislature but refine it" (quoted in "The Story of a Great Monopoly, *Atlantic*, March 1881, 318). In the late 1870s a Philadelphia reform editor described Harrisburg's capitol, as a "hornets' nest" and his city's delegation as "rum-shop bummers, political rounders and petty jobbers . . . a herd of legislative incompetents and corruptionists."

The Pennsylvania legislature typified those of the Northern industrial states in terms of the social and economic makeup of its members, the nature and scope of its output, as well as the degree of its corruption. Legislative output doubled from 1860 to 1870, when the legislature passed more than 1,200 public and private acts per year on an incredible range of subjects, from the establishment of 270 private corporations to a private bill that enabled a married woman to buy a sewing machine without her husband's approval. Such private legislation added to the widespread belief that the legislators auctioned to the highest bidder franchises and public offices, including Pennsylvania's seats in the U.S. Senate.

A diverse coalition of upper-class Philadelphia reformers, dissident Pittsburgh Republicans, and frustrated Democrats joined to thwart the control of the commonwealth's government by the Pennsylvania Railroad and the machine of Simon Cameron, who was in Lincoln's cabinet. Reform journals congratulated the members of the convention of 1872–1873 on their "wealth and prestige" as well as their conservative mission. The resulting constitution of 1873 basically aimed to circumscribe the power of the vested interests by curtailing special and local legislation. Sessions were made biennial and penalties for bribery increased. Limits were placed on the public debt, and the governor was granted the power to veto special items.

Even after the new conservative constitution, the state remained within the grip of the most powerful political machine in the country, and the influence of lobbyists seemed to grow even stronger. On most matters of public policy, however, partisan affiliation continued to dominate legislative behavior from the 1870s through the 1890s. In 1877, 16 percent of the roll calls met A. Lawrence Lowell's extremely restrictive criterion of "party votes" (90% or more of members vote together). The effects of the machine most clearly prevailed on those is-

sues relating directly to the party organization, such as the selection of the House Speaker or the U.S. senators. Cohesion and conflict were nearly as important on fiscal policy and were present, but less striking, on matters of local option and mine safety.

By the 1890s the proportion of Lowell-type "party votes" dropped in Pennsylvania, but there and in the other four Northern states he studied one finds levels of party conflict that are very similar to those for the 1840s. Half of all of the roll calls taken in seven sessions set a majority of the Republicans against a majority of the Democrats, and (excluding nearly unanimous votes) the proportion jumped above two-thirds in all of the states. The mean index of disagreement was 40. The greatest difference occurred over governmental matters such as elections, legislative procedure, and personnel. Social questions, particularly liquor control and women's rights, were the second-most contentious issues, while regulation of business, railroads, and taxes all elicited lower but significant partisan strife.

Reformers and historians have emphasized the importance of the lobby in the Gilded Age. Organized groups had influenced legislation before the Civil War, but in the late nineteenth century the lobbying activities grew in size and visibility, leading to widespread charges that large corporate interests, specifically Pennsylvania Railroad and Standard Oil, "owned" the legislature. Yet, most of the activities of the Pennsylvania legislature extended far beyond what concerned these two corporations. Although no one would deny that individual corruption existed in the 1870s, the reformers' "evidence" usually took the form of disapproval of the fact that assemblymen regularly voted the party line.

The main charge that can be arrayed against Northern legislators is that they were amateurs. In the late 1870s, after the new constitution expanded the size of the Pennsylvania house, freshmen made up three-quarters of its members. In New York's lower house in the mid-1870s, about 60 percent were new members each year. By the end of the century half of the lower houses of both states were incumbents, but at that time, in Connecticut, Michigan, and Wisconsin more than 70 percent of those in the lower houses were serving their first term.

The socioeconomic makeup of the Pennsylvania legislature during the Gilded Age, which reflected changes in society, was characteristic of the northeastern states. Approximately three-fifths of the members of the Pennsylvania legislature in the late 1870s were businessmen, lawyers, and other professionals, and only one-fifth were farmers. The percentage of farmers in the Pennsylvania legislature continued to decline throughout the last quarter of the nineteenth century. By the 1890s businessmen accounted for 40 percent of the members, about one-fourth were lawyers, and 10 percent were workers.

A similar shift could be seen in other states as well. The percentage of farmers in the lower houses of Massachusetts and New York fell below 10 percent in 1890. Slightly more than half the members were businessmen in Massachusetts as were two-fifths of members in New York. The most striking shift by the end of the century was the great increase in the number of lawyers in New York's lower house, where their portion of seats jumped from 25 to 40 percent. At the same time, the working classes were underrepresented in both states.

In the midwestern states the percentage of farmers was higher, generally making up about one-third of the legislators. A quarter to one-third were businessmen and a similar proportion were lawyers. Illinois had the largest percentage of both businessmen and lawyers and the lowest number of farmers (although the three groups each held the same proportion of seats). Iowa had the largest percentage of farmers (47 percent) and lowest of lawyers (10 percent). Interestingly, Indiana had the same percentage of working-class legislators as did Massachusetts, but trailed behind Wisconsin. Illinois had nearly twice as many working-class members as Indiana or Wisconsin—about the same percentage as Pennsylvania.

The best predictors of party affiliation for the midwestern legislators in the 1880s were religion and ethnicity. While 92 percent of the Catholic legislators were Democrats and 85 percent of Methodist and Congregationalists were Republicans, no denomination had fewer than 62 percent in one party or the other. Even two-thirds of the "nothingarians," a nineteenth-century term meaning unchurched, were Democrats. Ballard C. Campbell's study of 847 legislators from Illinois, Iowa, and Wisconsin divided them into three cultural groups: a core made up of Yankees, British, and Scandinavians and smaller kindred groups; the periphery composed of Germans, eastern- and central-Europeans and Irish; and a residual intermediate group that included those who migrated from the Southern states. Seventy-eight percent of the core legislators were Republicans; 90 percent of those from the cultural periphery were Democrats.

Given this sort of division of the legislators and the sharp ethnoreligious split among their constituents, it is not surprising that issues affecting the regulation of community mores and social behavior set midwestern Republicans against that region's Democrats. Conflict was most common concerning community mores, particularly liquor control legislation, and nearly as important on questions that were directly related to the parties' control of the government. Contested roll calls concerning government, business and transportation, and fiscal policy, however, consumed most of the legislators' time. In all of these areas partisanship structured legislative behavior.

The parties did differ clearly on specific issues and the behavior of midwestern legislators was like that of their fellow partisans in other regions of the country. Republicans favored compulsory school attendance and restrictions on the sale of liquor and tobacco. They supported blue laws to sustain the social values of the core culture. Republicans also waved the "bloody shirt," blaming Democratic ex-Confederates for the bloodshed, and protecting the pensions of veterans with far greater zeal than the Democrats. On fiscal policy and taxes, the heirs of Jefferson and Jackson took a far more parsimonious position than the party of Lincoln. Like the Southern Redeemers, the midwestern Bourbon Democrats were the party of retrenchment and reform.

A wide variety of groups lobbied the legislators for their special interests. The representatives of the railroad rings and other corporations competed for the legislators attention with the Knights of Labor, stockbreeders' associations, veterans' organizations, and even groups such as the Bee Keepers or the Wheelmen of America, who wanted better roads for their bicycles. Legislation often pitted one set of entrepreneurs against another. Matters such as railroad regulation and antitrust legislation were nonpartisan, although in the midwestern states these were favored by the representatives of rural Protestant districts and the core cultural groups.

The political pattern in Nebraska, for example, was similar to that in its midwestern neighbors except that it was more solidly Republican in the 1880s and fell into the hands of the Populists in 1891. During the Gilded Age, ethnoreligious conflict in the state set the core culture against the periphery. The minority Democrats represented the "ritualist" denominations (Catholics, Lutherans) among the Germans, the Bohemians, and the Irish, and struggled against the cultural imperialism of the "devotionalist" (Presbyterians, Methodists) Republicans. In the legislature in the 1880s, the GOP leaders were split almost equally between farmers representing rural districts and professional and business people from the towns. The Democrats who were strongest in the state's two largest cities—Lincoln and Omaha—sent twice as many businessmen and professionals as farmers to the state capitol, although they only held one-fifth of the seats.

The Populist victory in 1891 brought about dramatic change. In the state house the Republicans lost seventy-seven seats, most of which went to the sixty-nine new Populists, who had won a slim majority. Because all but one of the Nebraska Populists were farmers, the proportion of businessmen and professionals in the legislature plummeted. These third-party legislators formed a strong bloc, voting against railroads and to restrict interest rates. At the same time, the People's party took a pietistic cultural position in favor of woman suffrage and blue laws that represented the cultural values of their constituents.

CONCLUSION

By the end of the nineteenth century when Lowell looked at American state legislatures, they had certain definable characteristics all of which would change dramatically in the course of the next century. Those changes paralleled the institutionalization of the U.S. House of Representatives and the growth of the American bureaucratic state. Although some men persued legislative careers, most nineteenth-century legislators were amateurs. Turnover rates were much higher than what they have now become in the second half of the twentieth century. Our legislators are significantly older, even when elected for the first time, and, by and large, we are governed by lawyers. In occupational terms the state legislators in the nineteenth century more accurately mirrored their society. Yet it must be asked: Was it a more democratic system even though women and blacks were excluded for most of the century? It seems to have represented the concerns of its constituents quite well, basically through the agencies of parties that were clearly more important to the process than they have become. Lobbyists were less well-organized and represented sporadic (yet very specific) efforts to introject influence into the legislative process.

When one compares the state legislatures of the nineteenth century with those of the late twentieth, several things stand out. Less intrusive into citizens' lives for good or ill, the nineteenth-century legislatures commanded far more limited resources. Nineteenth-century governments in America did not accomplish very much, and policy-making in the legislatures tended to be incremental, building relatively slowly upon previous decisions that possessed an ad hoc quality. Yet, legislators were far less fearful of using the government to solve their public problems and were far more confident that by doing so they were expressing the "will of the people." James Madison had worried that the new government under his Constitution faced the dilemma that newly elected representatives might lack the legislative skills derived only from experience such as his own. Nineteenth-century legislators were amateurs. Turnover was high, and most of these men returned happily to their farms and businesses, perhaps wiser, but no richer in the goods of this world. The governing elite was not a separate order in nineteenth-century society. It is hardly clear that the quality of our laws has improved or that today's professionals provide more democratic government than did the amateurs of the nineteenth century.

HISTORICAL CONTEXT

BIBLIOGRAPHY

Early National Period

In effect the nineteenth century began in 1789 when the states were forced to forge a new relationship with the national government created by the Constitution and construct the first "new federalism." The best studies of state legislative activity and makeup in the post-Revolutionary years are those of JACKSON TURNER MAIN: "Government by the People: The American Revolution and the Democratization of the Legislatures," *William and Mary Quarterly* 13 (July 1966): 391–407; and *Political Parties Before the Constitution* (Chapel Hill, N.C., 1973).

In the era of the conflict between the Federalists and the Jeffersonian Republicans—that dominated by the first party system—development of parties in the state legislatures was limited. The two best studies deal with two of the largest states, Massachusetts and Virginia: JAMES M. BANNER, JR., *To the Hartford Convention: The Federalists and the Origin of Party Politics in Massachusetts, 1789–1815* (New York, 1970); and RICHARD R. BEEMAN, *The Old Dominion and the New Nation, 1788–1801* (Lexington, Ky., 1972). They include excellent material on the social and economic backgrounds of legislators. Some comparable material is found in RUDOLPH J. PASLER and MARGARET C. PASLER, *The New Jersey Federalists* (Rutherford, N.J., 1975). CARL E. PRINCE, New Jersey's Jeffersonian Republicans: The Genesis of an Early Party Machine, 1789–1817 (Chapel Hill, N.C., 1964) is a good study of functioning of party-in-the-legislature at this time. DOUGLAS E. BOWERS draws on his dissertation on the Pennsylvania legislature in his article, "From Caucus to Convention in Pennsylvania Politics, 1790–1830," *Pennsylvania History* 56 (October 1989): 276–298. Party development in the Virginia Assembly in the late eighteenth century is the focus of NORMAN K. RISJORD and GORDON DenBOER, "The Evolution of Political Parties in Virginia, 1782–1800," *Journal of American History* 60 (March 1974): 961–984; while the story for Virginia and the Carolinas is carried forward in JAMES H. BROUSSARD, "Party and Partisanship in American State Legislatures: The South Atlantic States, 1800–1812," *Journal of Southern History* 43 (February 1977): 39–58.

Antebellum America

The literature on legislative policy in antebellum America evolved from the debate over laissez faire in early America. The classic studies are those of Massachusetts and Pennsylvania: OSCAR HANDLIN and MARY FLUG HANDLIN, *Commonwealth: A Study of the Role of Government in the American Economy: Massachusetts, 1774–1861* (New York, 1947); and LOUIS HARTZ, *Economic Policy and Democratic Thought: Pennsylvania, 1776–1860* (Cambridge, Mass., 1948). An excellent general study of state economic activity is CARTER GOODRICH, *Government Promotion of American Canals and Railroads, 1800–1890* (New York, 1960). LANCE E. DAVIS and JOHN LEGLER, "The Government in the American Economy, 1815–1902: A Quantitative Study," *Journal of Economic History* 26 (December 1966): 514–552, is more statistical and theoretical. HARRY N. SCHEIBER details the evolution of the law in "Federalism and the American Economic Order, 1789–1910," *Law and Society Review* 10 (March 1975): 57–118. The focus of recent work has shifted to political development as seen in the work of L. RAY GUNN: "Political Implications of General Incorporation Laws in New York to 1860," *Mid-America* 59 (October 1977): 171–191; "The Crisis of Authority in Antebellum States: New York, 1820–1860," *Review of Politics* 41 (April 1979): 163–202; "The New York State Legislature: A Developmental Perspective," *Social Science History* 4 (Summer 1980): 267–294; and *The Decline of Authority: Public Economic Policy and Political Development in New York, 1800–1860* (Ithaca, N.Y., 1988). ANN MARIE DYKSTRA, *Region, Economy, and Party: The Roots of Policy Formation in Pennsylvania, 1820–1860* (New York, 1989), traces the evolution of the legislative agenda in response to economic development in a single Northern state.

The Jacksonian Era

Our understanding of partisan conflict during the period of the second party system—the Jacksonian era—has grown tremendously since the publication of LEE BENSON, *The Concept of Jacksonian Democracy: New York as a Test Case* (Princeton, N.J., 1961), and RICHARD P. McCORMICK, *The Second American Party Sys-*

212

tem: *Party Formation in the Jacksonian Era* (Chapel Hill, N.C., 1966), although neither focused specifically on legislative behavior. The most extensive study of any state legislature during this period is that of PETER LEVINE in his book, *The Behavior of State Legislative Parties in the Jacksonian Era: New Jersey, 1829–1844* (Rutherford, N.J., 1977), a portion of which is briefly summarized in "State Legislative Parties in the Jacksonian Era: New Jersey, 1829–1844," *Journal of American History* 62 (December 1975): 575–590. RODNEY O. DAVIS studied both the composition and the behavior of the Illinois legislature in his articles: "Partisanship in Jacksonian State Politics: Party in the Illinois Legislature, 1834–1841," in ROBERT P. SWIERENGA, ed., *Quantification in American History: Theory and Research* (New York, 1970); and "The People in Miniature: The Illinois General Assembly, 1818–1848," *Illinois Historical Journal* 81 (November 1988): 95–108. More specific in focus are: JOHN R. REYNOLDS, "Piety and Politics: Evangelism in the Michigan Legislature, 1837–1860," *Michigan History* 61 (Winter 1977–1978): 322–361; and DOUGLAS E. BOWERS, "From Logrolling to Corruption: The Development of Lobbying in Pennsylvania, 1815–1861," *Journal of the Early Republic* 3 (1983): 439–474. HERBERT ERSHKOWITZ and WILLIAM G. SHADE, "Consensus or Conflict? Political Behavior of State Legislatures During the Jacksonian Era," *Journal of American History* 58 (December 1971): 591–621, examines partisan response to selected major issues in the legislatures of five states from 1833 to 1845.

Legislative Behavior

Most of the studies of the second party system emphasize electoral behavior, but J. MILLS THORNTON, *Politics and Power in a Slave Society: Alabama, 1800–1860* (Baton Rouge, La., 1977), MARC W. KRUMAN, *Parties and Politics in North Carolina: 1836–1865* (Baton Rogue, La., 1983), and DONALD A. DE BATS, *Elites and Masses: Political Structures, Communication and Behavior in Ante-bellum Georgia* (New York, 1990), include chapters on legislative behavior. Two studies focusing on the primary economic issue of the day, money and banking, that deal extensively with legislative behavior are: JAMES ROGER SHARP, *The Jacksonians Versus the Banks: Politics in the States After the Panic*

of 1837 (New York, 1970); and WILLIAM G. SHADE, *Banks or No Banks: The Money Issue in Western Politics, 1832–1865* (Detroit, 1972). An early study of the socioeconomic character of the members of one legislature at the time is GRADY McWHINEY, "Were the Whigs a Class Party in Alabama?" *Journal of Southern History* 23 (November 1957): 510–525.

Realignment

The period of realignment from the late 1840s to the Civil War is treated generally in MICHAEL F. HOLT, *The Political Crisis of the 1850s* (New York, 1978), which emphasizes legislative behavior. Similarly the books by THORNTON, KRUMAN, and DE BATS mentioned above deal with this topic in the 1850s. Two excellent specialized studies of the brief career of the Know-Nothing party that analyze the makeup of the party's legislators and their behavior are: JEAN H. BAKER, *Ambivalent Americans: The Know-Nothing Party in Maryland* (Baltimore, 1977); and VIRGINIA C. PURDY, *Portrait of a Know-Nothing Legislature: The Massachusetts General Court of 1855* (New York, 1989). In two books, RALPH A. WOOSTER has examined in detail the socioeconomic background of state legislators in the Southern states in 1850 and 1860: *The People in Power: Courthouse and Statehouse in the Lower South, 1850–1860* (Knoxville, Tenn., 1969); and *Politicians, Planters and Plain Folk: Courthouse and Statehouse in the Upper South, 1850–1860* (Knoxville, Tenn., 1975).

ERIC FONER, *Reconstruction: America's Unfinished Revolution, 1862–1877* (New York, 1988), is a mine of information on all topics relating to its subject including legislative behavior and the makeup of the Southern legislatures at the time. HOWARD N. RABINOWITZ, ed., *Southern Black Leaders of the Reconstruction Era* (Urbana, Ill., 1982), is concerned primarily with legislators. An excellent state study is ALLEN W. TRELEASE, "Republican Reconstruction in North Carolina: A Roll-Call Analysis of the State House of Representatives, 1868–1870," *Journal of Southern History* 42 (August 1976): 319–344.

The Gilded Age

The Gilded Age or the period of stabilization of the third party system is synonymous with partisanship and corruption in the state legislatures. An excellent general study covering many aspects of governance in the late nineteenth century that is also a mine of information on all matters, particularly the powers of state legislatures, is MORTON KELLER, *Affairs of State: Public Life in Late Nineteenth Century America* (Cambridge, Mass., 1977). ROBERT HARRISON, "The Hornets' Nest at Harrisburg: A Study of the Pennsylvania Legislature in the Late 1870s" is a recent study that represents a modest revision of the traditional view.

Late Nineteenth Century

The classic study of roll-call behavior in the late nineteenth century is A. LAWRENCE LOWELL, "The Influence of Party upon Legislation in England and America," *Annual Report of the American Historical Association for the Year 1901* (Washington, D.C., 1901): vol. I: 321–542. The best contemporary work in the field of legislative history is that of BALLARD C. CAMPBELL: "Ethnicity and the 1893 Wisconsin Assembly," *Journal of American History* 62 (June 1975): 74–94; "Did Democracy Work? Prohibition in Late Nineteenth-Century Iowa: A Test Case," *Journal of Interdisciplinary History* 8 (Summer 1977): 87–116; and *Representative Democracy: Public Policy and Midwestern Legislatures in the Late Nineteenth Century* (Cambridge, Mass., 1980). PHILIP R. VANDERMEER has produced two excellent studies of Indiana politics that relate to legislative history: "Bosses, Machines, and Democratic Leadership: Party Organization and Managers in Indiana, 1880–1910," *Social Science History* 12 (Winter 1988): 327–348; and *The Hoosier Politician: Officeholding and Political Culture in Indiana, 1896–1920* (Urbana, Ill., 1985). JAMES TICE MOORE surveys the literature on the Southern states in his thoughtful historiographical article, "Redeemers Reconsidered: Change and Continuity in the Democratic South, 1870–1900," *Journal of Southern History* 44 (August 1978): 357–378.

Populism

Populism, like nativism, was primarily a state movement in the 1880s and 1890s, but it has captured historians' imaginations. There are several excellent state studies that include material on legislative behavior and social profiles of Populist legislators and their opponents: SHELDON HACKNEY, *Populism to Progressivism in Alabama* (Princeton, N.J., 1969); STANLEY B. PARSONS, *The Populist Context: Rural Versus Urban Power on the Great Plains Frontier* (Westport, Conn., 1973); JAMES E. WRIGHT, *The Politics of Populism: Dissent in Colorado* (New Haven, Conn., 1974); and WORTH ROBERT MILLER, *Oklahoma Populism: A History of the People's Party in the Oklahoma Territory* (Norman, Okla., 1987).

General Studies

There are a number of studies that relate to the topic of nineteenth-century legislatures that are general in nature. The various general issues concerning legislative history are discussed in ALLAN G. BOGUE, "American Historians and Legislative Behavior," in LEE BENSON et al., eds., *American Political Behavior: Historical Essays and Readings* (New York, 1974), and BALLARD C. CAMPBELL, "The State Legislature in American History: A Review Essay," *Historical Methods Newsletter* 9 (1976): 185–195. Although the title indicates an emphasis on electoral politics, the essays in PAUL KLEPPNER, et al., *The Evolution of American Electoral Systems* (Westport, Conn., 1981), discuss legislative behavior during the first, second party and third party systems. RICHARD L. MCCORMICK touches on matters related to legislative history in several of the essays in *The Party Period and Public Policy: American Politics from the Age of Jackson to the Progressive Era* (New York, 1986). In a similar fashion, JOEL H. SILBEY interweaves legislative and party history in his collection of essays, *The Partisan Imperative: The Dynamics of American Politics Before the Civil War* (New York, 1985), and his excellent revisionist study of nineteenth-century political development, *The American Political Nation, 1838–1893* (Stanford, Calif., 1991). An unusual source because of its chronological scope is HORACE B. DAVIS, "The Occupations of Massachusetts Legislators, 1790–1950," *New England Quarterly* 24 (December 1951): 89–100. See also MARGARET SUSAN THOMPSON and JOEL H. SILBEY, "Research on 19th Century Legislatures: Present Contours and Future Directions," *Legislative Studies Quarterly* 9 (May 1984): 319–350.

STATE LEGISLATURES IN THE TWENTIETH CENTURY

Thomas G. Alexander
David Roy Hall

Although state legislatures have preserved substantial control over their three main functions—lawmaking, constituent representation, and monitoring of the executive—throughout the twentieth century, they have also become increasingly subject to standards dictated by Washington. In large part, this shift of power from the state legislatures to Congress has resulted from the national response to constituent demands. During the Progressive Era in the early twentieth century, powerful business interests preferring uniform regulations throughout the United States lobbied for national laws on matters as diverse as corporate regulation and food and drug control. As Congress cut the national budget during the 1920s, state legislatures—afraid to pay for needed services by increasing taxes—incurred large debts in an attempt to fund constituent demands.

Burdened with heavy debts as the Great Depression of the 1930s deepened, state legislatures reached the limits of prudent borrowing and failed to meet the needs of the unemployed and destitute. Taking a note from the businessmen's book, in that those with enough clout can get what they want from Congress, the people turned to the federal government. Members of Congress responded to their constituents and, with the federal government's larger size and borrowing power, began to fund various economic recovery and relief programs. Transferring money to the states, Washington also attached compliance standards in a carrot-and-stick approach. Grateful for relief from boosting taxes or borrowing money, the state legislatures swallowed their pride and took the federal handouts in return for compliance.

Since World War II, the variety of carrots has continued to proliferate as Congress has sought to achieve technological, social, and even aesthetic goals. State legislatures have to take the medicine of a large number of federal standards many would rather not have, but they take a deep breath and swallow.

Although the desire to avoid the loss of federal money may explain much of the state response to federal offers of help, the inability of the legislators to meet local needs derives in part from the composition of the legislatures themselves. Most states have preferred economical amateur legislatures. In practice, however, citizens of the states pay for these legislatures, perhaps not in higher taxes but in other ways, such as the loss of authority to the federal government and domination by powerful local interest groups.

In 1991, forty-one states elected only semiprofessional or amateur legislators, to whom they need pay only a pittance. Legislators in some states, such as New Mexico, receive only travel and per diem allowances (in New Mexico's case, $75 per day). Some states like Hawaii, which pays $15,600 per year, could be considered semiprofessional, though the salaries rank only slightly above the poverty level. Only nine states consider their legislators to be professionals. They pay only modest salaries, ranging from $33,000 to $41,000 per year plus per diem and travel allowances.

Given the generally low salaries, state legislatures have tended to attract those with independent means or compliant employers. Beholden to powerful interests for their seats and heavily reliant on lobbyists for information, they have tended to respond reluctantly to the underprivileged. In practice, it seems almost as though John C. Calhoun's concept of the "concurrent majority" as a criterion for passing legislation had achieved a new life in the state legislatures. However, legislators have tended to respond more quickly to powerful and conservative interests. Many scurry to provide tax breaks for business, particularly if they promise economic development, shifting the tax burden to lower-income groups.

It is not at all certain that higher legislative salaries and professional legislatures would solve the problems created by powerful interest groups, since they tend to have enormous influence with the well-paid Congress as well. The major difference, however, is that the range of interest groups that can successfully lobby Congress tends to be broader than in the states (especially in states with small populations), and thus, the range of politically possible choices for Congress tends to be larger. In a real sense, James Madison judged correctly when he argued that republics covering large areas with a broad range of interests work more effectively than small ones.

THE PROGRESSIVE ERA

In the face of a generally conservative mood, the twentieth century opened with popular pressure on the state legislatures to enact democratic reforms. As the American economy recovered from the depression of the 1890s, the legislatures began to grapple with the complex issues associated with modernization, such as industrialism, urban development, extremes of wealth and poverty, the influence of large corporations, environmental deterioration, disease, and political graft and corruption. Appalled by the corruptive influences of powerful economic interests, the majority of Americans became dismayed, and then outraged, at the decadence they found among their elected representatives.

Under pressure from their constituents, legislators added corporate regulation and the creation of state public-utilities commissions to the agenda. In the South, reform sentiment resulted from the Populist agitation against monopolies and railroads, and North Carolina created a commission to regulate corporations in 1899. Virginia set up a similar agency three years later.

Sentiment for regulating railroads abounded throughout the South, but the issue of monopoly proved more significant in some states than in others. Between 1897 and 1902, a number of southern state legislatures created railroad commissions. In some states, notably Virginia, Tennessee, and Louisiana, these became relatively ineffective. The Louisiana legislature, for instance, established a commission in 1898 and augmented its powers in 1902. Still, the commission was ineffective because the state set a higher priority for creating a pro-business atmosphere. In desperate need of capital, legislators often willingly risked the disapproval of Progressives to avoid driving business away with strong regulatory commissions.

Nevertheless, a relatively great degree of Progressive sentiment appeared in Alabama, Georgia, North Carolina, Florida, Kentucky, Arkansas, and Texas. Georgia's legislature, for example, strengthened its railroad commission between 1905 and 1907, making it an elective body and investing it with power to regulate securities as well as rates.

In contrast, some states in the Far West lagged far behind in the regulation of public utilities. Dependent upon the export of the products of such extractive industries as mining and agriculture, states like North Dakota, Utah, and Wyoming, did not create regulatory commissions until well into the twentieth century. By 1916, Utah and Wyoming were the only states with no public-utilities regulation.

Following and improving upon the southern lead, Progressives in a number of other states often tried to wrest control of their state governments from the forces of political corruption and corporate influence. In some cases, voluntary organizations became vehicles for reform agendas.

Reform in Wisconsin, for instance, had its origin in the efforts of the Milwaukee Municipal League to change a civil-service system riddled with graft and corruption. Using public education to call attention to the abuses of the spoils system, the league brought intense pressure for political reform upon state lawmakers. Under this pressure, in 1897 the legislature passed some of the desired laws, including civil-service reform and a corrupt-practices act.

After the turn of the twentieth century, Progressive forces in the Wisconsin legislature gained an important ally with the election of Robert M. La Follette as governor. Feisty and determined, La Follette's leadership assured that the Progressive program would continue as a priority in the state. Nevertheless, even with La Follette's support, Progressives in the legislature had a difficult time battling conservative forces. The 1901 legislature disappointed Progressives, since a "combination of politicians, railroad henchmen, and conservatives" killed efforts to reform taxation for railroads (Maxwell, p. 37).

In 1903 and 1905, however, the people elected Progressive majorities to the legislature, and members passed a large number of reform laws. The Progressives held a majority in Wisconsin's 1903 house, and a small group of liberal Democrats held the balance of power in the state senate. Adopting the recommendation of a temporary tax commission, the legislature based tax rates on the physical valuation of railroad properties. In 1905 a Progressive majority established a railroad commission, a state board of forestry, and a permanent tax commission. The trend continued in later sessions. In 1907 the legislature passed several bills regulating the insurance industry. Four years later, the lawmakers revoked perpetual utility franchises and provided that public authorities could revoke future franchises if the utilities abused the public.

In some cases, well-placed individuals worked for the legislature in investigating and proposing reforms. In New York, for instance, a series of scandals reached the public attention between 1905 and 1907 when the Consolidated Gas Company sought the contract for lighting New York City's streets. A joint committee, chaired by Progressive state senator Frederick C. Stevens, hired Charles Evans Hughes as counsel. The revelation of such abuses as monopolistic discrimination, tax evasion, and irregular bookkeeping led to a public outcry and the creation of a state public-utilities commission.

Hughes also served as counsel for a committee chaired by State Senator William W. Armstrong that investigated New York's massive insurance industry. Revealing misuse of policyholders' premiums, questionable lobbying, excessively large executive salaries, and fraudulent bookkeeping, Hughes's investigation also uncovered an industry-supported "house of mirth" that catered to the legislators' more worldly tastes. Public pressure, then, led to regulatory legislation that set standards for permissible investments and required standard

forms for policies. New York followed with legislation that regulated campaign contributions from corporations. Often, as in cases of utility, insurance, and campaign regulation, other states followed New York's lead. By 1907, fifteen states had outlawed corporate contributions to political campaigns.

California reformers organized their campaign for Progressive reform in May 1907 through an improvement league. The league proposed a list of reforms that provided one of the most comprehensive Progressive Era programs. Relying on public pressure, the league secured legislation that created and strengthened a state public-utilities commission in 1909 and 1911.

In some states, regulation and reform resulted from multiparty coalitions. Reformers in New Jersey formed a coalition of Progressive Democrats and independent Republicans backed by the force of public opinion. Together they challenged a state government dominated by corporate interests accustomed to complete control of the political process. Reformers held considerable power in the Democratically controlled lower house, but the conservative Republican state senate and governor successfully opposed Progressive legislation. Thus, while achieving some reforms, they failed to provide equitable taxation of corporate interests.

Progressives also sought reform of the tax structure to transfer the burden from the poor to corporations and the wealthy. Most sought to accomplish this goal through a graduated income tax, corporate income taxes, and inheritance taxes. The Wisconsin legislature, for instance, enacted a graduated income-tax law during its 1911 session and an inheritance tax in 1912.

Even as Progressive forces united to take control of their legislatures from powerful corporate influence, they also sought to extend democratic power to the average voter. They passed a number of measures to accomplish this goal, including direct primaries; direct election of senators; initiative, referendum, and recall; and women's suffrage.

Responding to the Populist heritage, southern legislators passed some popular democratic reforms. Most southern states adopted the direct primary, limited and publicized campaign expenses, restricted lobbying by corporations and other vested interests, and outlawed free railroad passes. Most also adopted the direct primary. The South Carolina legislature seems to have become the first to adopt the direct primary, in 1896. During the next decade, however, legislatures throughout the South passed similar laws, and by the end of the Progressive Era, the direct primary extended to all candidates at every level of government in the region.

Direct-primary reform was perhaps more important in the South than in any other region because of the domination by the Democratic party in a one-party system. By passing direct-primary laws, the southern state legislatures tried to ensure competition already provided, to some degree, by two parties in the remainder of the nation. Many southern states also adopted the direct election of U.S. senators before the ratification of the Seventeenth Amendment in 1913, usually by amending the rules of the Democratic party's primary.

At the turn of the century, a number of states began to consider the passage of direct legislation like the initiative and referendum. In Oregon a legislative coalition headed by William S. U'Ren and Jonathan Bourne organized the Direct Legislation League in 1898, secured the passage of amendments to the state constitution for the initiative and referendum in 1899, and lobbied successfully for their ratification in 1902.

In many states, conservative interests overcame popular democratic measures. In Wisconsin, for instance, the 1903 legislative assembly quickly passed a direct-primary law. In the state senate, however, Republican stalwarts managed to keep the bill bottled up for more than a month. After public opinion forced the passage of the act, the stalwarts fought a rearguard action by requiring a referendum on the bill, delaying inauguration of the measure until after the 1904 election.

More than a dozen states followed this lead within the next five years by enacting laws establishing direct legislation or extending existing provisions to form a complete system. In California, direct-primary legislation became an issue during the 1909 and 1911 sessions. Lobbying by corporate interests almost killed a proposed bill until the state supreme court provoked public furor by overturning San Francisco boss Abraham Reuf's graft conviction. The

resulting uproar and ensuing protest by the state attorney general forced the assembly to pass the bill by a lopsided vote.

Woman suffrage proved a divisive issue among Progressives in some states. Following the lead of Wyoming and Utah, a few western states had extended the franchise to women during the 1880s and 1890s, and several others adopted woman suffrage in the early twentieth century. Most of the legislatures in the older states refused to act, however, until the ratification in 1920 of the Nineteenth Amendment, which granted woman suffrage.

Since many Progressives came from the business classes, they often divided on Progressive social legislation. Though they generally supported laws to protect women and children, they remained ambivalent about acts to defend the interests of workers against their employers. Divisions occurred on such issues as workers' compensation and the right to strike or boycott. Ironically, labor leaders found themselves lined up with business interests on occasion. Both groups generally opposed binding arbitration of labor disputes—business leaders because they thought it interfered with property rights, and labor leaders because they thought it the opening wedge to prohibiting strikes.

State legislatures passed laws protecting women and children. Utah passed laws regulating working conditions of children in 1896, when it forbade their employment in mines and factories and limited the hours they could work at other jobs. Utah gave similar protection to women by 1900. In 1911 that state's legislature passed the first of a series of laws that eventually established the eight-hour workday for women. During its 1911 session, Washington's assembly passed similar legislation, including an eight-hour day for women and workers' compensation. Colorado led in the creation of courts to treat juvenile offenders differently from adults. The legislature enacted these reforms largely because of the work of Judge Ben Lindsey of Denver. Massachusetts broke the path in the passage of a minimum wage for women, and other states followed. By 1913, Utah had set up a minimum-wage law for women, and in 1911 it established pensions for mothers and children.

California provides a good example of the mixed responses by the public to labor legislation. In the Golden State, labor opposition killed a voluntary-arbitration bill in 1911 because it was viewed as a precursor to compulsory arbitration. At the same time, Progressive opposition killed a bill that would have limited the use of injunctions in labor disputes. Progressive governor Hirum Johnson vetoed a bill creating free state employment bureaus. State progressives did support some legislation to protect women. Despite continued opposition from Los Angeles merchants and hotel operators, the California legislature set a maximum eight-hour day for women in all industries except canning and packing. Both Progressives and conservatives opposed workers' compensation, which passed in 1911 only after Governor Johnson supported a compromise bill.

The enactment of labor legislation also proved difficult in New Jersey. As with regulation of utilities, Progressives in New Jersey faced hard fights to enact any reforms, and in the end often had to accept watered-down measures. Between 1903 and 1909, New Jersey passed a series of laws that eventually prohibited labor by children under sixteen. Facing strong opposition from manufacturing interests, the legislators bottled up some legislation until public outcry had created a scandal.

Progressives also looked for a governmental role in the protection and management of natural resources. Utah created a conservation commission in 1903. Wisconsin established a state board of forestry in 1904. A number of states passed legislation taking state control of undeveloped water resources.

Many Progressives sought to regulate morals, but this proved nearly as divisive as labor legislation. While California reformers had little trouble enacting legislation against racing and gambling, attempts to deal with moral issues split the more conservative southern and rural delegations from the more cosmopolitan cities surrounding San Francisco Bay. A slot-machine bill passed, but a racetrack measure failed. A number of states with large evangelical Protestant populations, especially in the Midwest and South, passed prohibition legislation.

Rounding out many of the Progressive agendas in the states were bills aimed at establishing standards of purity in food and drugs. Utah began the passage of such legislation during the first decade of the twentieth century. North Dakota followed quite rapidly.

Some states also began to deal with problems of legislative efficiency. Beginning in 1908, the Wisconsin legislature set up annual budget estimates and a central accounting system. In 1917, Illinois reformed its administrative structure.

Following the lead of Texas and Iowa, a number of states adopted legislation to reform their urban governments. Utah and North Dakota, for instance, provided for commission government (modeled on the business corporation) during the early twentieth century.

Progressivism had its darker side as well, as legislatures enacted racist legislation. In the South, the Democrats used the direct primary to disfranchise blacks. Democratic party rules barred blacks from voting in primaries, which in one-party states essentially replaced the general election. The South Carolina legislature, for example, required every black to "produce a written statement of ten reputable white men ... that they know...that the applicant... cast his ballot for General [Wade] Hampton in 1876 [and] has voted the Democratic ticket continuously ever since" (quoted in Grantham, pp. 119–120). Some states aimed legislation at other minorities. Reflecting anti-Japanese prejudice, the 1913 California legislature passed an alien land bill prohibiting first-generation Japanese-Americans from owning land.

During World War I the states retreated somewhat from the Progressive impulse, aiming their legislative activities at foreigners and radicals. States passed laws setting up councils of defense designed to protect defense installations and to eliminate pro-German and other supposedly subversive sentiments. Some states passed antisyndicalist laws aimed at labor coalitions, and others prohibited the teaching of German in the schools.

Despite these and other problems and despite uneven reforms among the states, state legislatures played an important role in beginning to deal with problems caused by modernization. Many of the attempts proved ineffective or discriminatory. Corporations continued to wield considerable power in the states, and legislation such as that concerning the direct primary was turned against minorities. In contrast, legislation protecting women and children, setting standards for pure food and drugs, and regulating public utilities often served the public interest.

THE TWENTIES

After the flurry of Progressive reform, many state legislatures retreated to a period of relative calm during the 1920s. In the wake of World War I, the Treaty of Versailles, the controversy over U.S. membership in the League of Nations and increasing radicalism, many people had become disillusioned. Moreover, reformers had enacted the majority of their common agenda, leaving little in the way of additional measures on which they could agree.

Some reform obviously continued during the 1920s. One prominent example was the adoption of old-age pensions. Montana passed the first law setting up old-age pensions in 1923, and by 1931 the reform had spread to seventeen more states. The pensions were far from generous. The largest annual payment in any state was only $390, and by 1931, payments were being made to a mere seventy-five thousand persons nationwide under the plans.

Administrative reform took place during the 1920s as well. By 1928, seventeen states had adopted measures for administrative reorganization. These laws sought to eliminate waste in state governments, strengthen the powers of state governors, and coordinate staff services.

Civil service reform made little headway, and this failure ran at cross-purposes with the rapid increase in state expenditures. While total federal expenditures tended to decline during the decade, state budgets rose. Legislatures increased total state expenditures from $400 million in 1913 to $1.2 billion in 1921 and to nearly $2.1 billion in 1929. Per capita state spending rose 60 percent between 1922 and 1929.

The most significant increases came in education and highway construction, the latter necessitated by the rapid increase in automobile ownership. The cost of building highways rose from an annual per capita cost of 59 cents in 1919 to $2.06 in 1930. A number of states enacted compulsory-education laws during the Progressive Era and followed these with the creation of increasingly diverse high school and college curricula during the 1920s. All of these activities demanded increased expenditures. While revenues rose dramatically during the decade—from $1.1 billion to $2.1 billion—they remained inadequate to cover the rising costs of state services. State legislatures turned to gasoline taxes as a source of revenue for highway construction, but revenues proved inadequate to cover the costs.

Although Congress decreased the federal income tax during the 1920s, state legislatures (with the exception of New Hampshire) declined to increase state income taxes, and budget deficits mounted. During the 1920s, states contracted debts at a faster rate than either the national or local governments and, indeed, faster than ever before. The increase in indebtedness placed many states on an extremely precarious financial footing when the Great Depression hit the nation.

In the broader sweep of things, the 1920s saw little other progressive legislation. Social legislation especially suffered. Because of the pro-business sentiment, states tended to ignore existing laws designed to protect women and children, and the Supreme Court undermined some enforcement by declaring child-labor legislation unconstitutional in *Hammer* v. *Dagenhart*, 247 U.S. 251 (1918).

Legislatures were even more reluctant to enact new labor legislation. By the early 1930s, eighteen states had adopted anti-injunction legislation, but these laws were poorly enforced. Generally ambivalent about labor legislation, business-oriented progressives became even more hostile during the 1920s.

Legislatures resisted reform of public utility regulation as well. Although most states had created public-utilities commissions, the commissions' mandates proved inadequate to deal with the proliferation of increasingly powerful interstate holding companies.

In practice, citizens had considerable difficulty in holding on to the gains of the past in the face of a conservative backlash. In Massachusetts, for example, legislators had to fight bills that would have outlawed labor unions, imposed mandatory labor-dispute arbitration, weakened existing workers' compensation, and undermined child-labor laws. The 1920s became the heyday of the so-called American Plan that aimed at breaking labor unions by creating open shops in all industries.

On balance, the record of state legislatures during the 1920s remains mixed. In a period much like the 1980s, except that deficits grew on the state level rather than on the federal level, state legislatures declined to deal with problems created by inequities in the social system. Legislators did increase expenditures for education and highways, but only by incurring large debts.

THE GREAT DEPRESSION

During the 1930s, power shifted away from the state legislatures. Since most legislators were amateurs and met in sessions for only a few weeks annually or even biennially, the members were unable to devote a sustained period of time to solving economic and social problems. Leadership responsibility thus fell at first on the state governors. In those states where the governors provided effective administration, the legislatures proved effective as well. Where executive direction failed, the legislatures also generally failed.

Other factors influenced the effectiveness of state governments as well. Legislatures in urban states with high voter turnouts tended to act more rapidly than rural states with low voter participation. States with interparty conflict also seemed to enact more creative social programs. Few one-party states dealt effectively with depression problems. Some states like Indiana and Michigan compiled effective records in part because they traded Republican domination in the 1920s for greater political diversity in the 1930s. Higher per capita income and previous reform traditions also promoted successful change. The legislatures voted money for more generous services in those states with broad tax bases (e.g., New York and Wisconsin) than in poorer states (e.g., Alabama and Mississippi).

A tradition of reform helps explain disparities among states with a similar socioeconomic makeup. States successful in coping with depression conditions, such as New York, Wisconsin, and Minnesota, had histories of reform stretching back to the Progressive Era. Conservative Republican administrations had dominated New Jersey and Ohio, neither of which achieved as much success in solving economic problems.

With the onset of the Great Depression, most people still looked to the state or local governments to aid the poor and indigent and to address serious social and economic problems. Spending at the state level made up 74 percent of total governmental expenditures during the era. Unfortunately, the heavy financial burden of meeting problems caused by the depression, coupled with the indebtedness that the states had incurred during the 1920s, eventually forced a reconsideration of state-federal relations. The force of circumstances led to the expansion of the role of the national government.

From the time of the stock market crash in 1929, most states tried to help their own unemployed and destitute. Many legislators felt they had the resources to deal with distress in their states, and most people protested little at President Herbert Hoover's limited attempts to manage the crisis.

Some states, notably Minnesota and Wisconsin, enjoyed considerable success. Despite a hostile legislature, Minnesota's Governor Floyd Olson secured $15 million for highway construction. Wisconsin's chief executive, Philip La Follette, convinced the legislature to appropriate $8 million in unemployment relief, increase taxes, and approve a plan for voluntary unemployment compensation.

Franklin Roosevelt of New York proved one of the most effective governors in the early years of the depression. The positive role he played in New York foreshadowed in many ways the approach he would take after his election to the presidency. Working with a number of legislative leaders during a special session in August 1931, he secured the appropriation of $20 million and the creation of the Temporary Emergency Relief Administration to coordinate relief activities in the state.

Although Governor Gifford Pinchot of Pennsylvania proposed solutions to deal with the depression in the Keystone State, he achieved only minimal success, largely because of his inability to work effectively with the legislature. Calling a special session in November 1931, Pinchot asked the lawmakers to create a system of state grants for unemployment relief by creating public-works jobs. Because of intraparty divisions, the legislature deadlocked. Unable to act creatively, the legislators fell back on the old remedy of a dole, which Pinchot derided as "stage money." Later Pinchot secured legislation funding road construction.

Other chief executives worked with legislators in formulating positive and innovative responses to the crisis. Connecticut's Wilbur

Cross persuaded the legislature to pass a public-works bill with increased state expenditures. Oklahoma's William ("Alfalfa Bill") Murray prevented the arrest of vagrants and established relief stations while obtaining the support of the legislature for a moderately progressive tax levy.

As unemployment rose and businesses failed, tax revenues fell. In response, legislatures enacted measures for strict economy, and many passed new tax laws to try to make up for lost revenues. Trying to provide for the destitute, some states added higher expenditures and new debt to the deficits already created during the 1920s.

In 1931, states continued to expand their relief efforts. The legislatures in Oklahoma and Maryland appropriated the modest amounts of $300,000 and $24,000, respectively. The West Virginia and Ohio legislatures permitted counties to issue relief bonds. Legislatures appropriated increases for relief that, on the average, rose from $1 to $3.50 per capita between 1927 and 1932. As a result, expenditures for relief in all states grew from less than $500,000 by mid-1931 to almost $100 million by the close of 1932.

Some governors who achieved the least success either faced badly divided legislatures, as did Pinchot, or refused to offer leadership, as with California's James Rolph. Rolph left legislators to deal with the crisis on their own. Unwilling to move in advance of the governor, the legislators essentially neglected the unemployed. One impotent chief executive complained he had "picked a bad year to be governor" (quoted in Patterson, p. 38).

In some states, the governor's fear of the legislature led to inaction. Mississippi's Theodore Bilbo almost forced the state to default on a $500,000 debt when he refused to call a special session of the legislature; he feared that state lawmakers might impeach some of his cronies for political corruption in such a session. The governor finally came to terms with the legislative leaders and called a special session, saying that for his part, the state could "go to the damnation bow-wows."

While most states attempted in some way to solve the economic crisis, legislators often seemed unsure of themselves. Some lawmakers fell into a self-defeating cycle of handwringing, factionalism, and partisan politics, twisting and turning to shift blame to someone else. Certainly the attitudes engendered during the laissez-faire 1920s had not equipped the legislators to deal with the problems of massive unemployment, social dislocation, and economic collapse.

As the depression deepened, most legislatures continued to fund relief efforts, but they simultaneously cut their overall budgets. Instead of responding to a plea from the Reconstruction Finance Corporation to appropriate more for jobs, they continued to provide doles and passed a new round of regressive (i.e., falling more heavily on those with lower incomes) sales, gasoline, and excise taxes to make up for lost revenues. Although these taxes helped balance budgets, they also decreased consumer purchasing power and likely lengthened the depression.

The cuts tended to be, according to James Thomas Patterson, as indiscriminate as they were drastic. Several states cut their budgets as much as 25 percent, while the Arizona legislature trimmed a whopping 35 percent.

Education suffered particularly. South Carolina suffered particularly. South Carolina reduced its aid to schools and universities by 19 percent; Maryland, by 40 percent; Wyoming, by 53 percent; North Carolina, by 42 percent; Mississippi, by 40 percent; New Hampshire, by 32 percent; and Washington, by 34 percent. Cuts of this sort would have made Grover Cleveland proud, who favored less government spending, but they did little to solve problems created by a massive economic heart attack. Moreover, they indicate the degree to which the state governments—legislative and executive departments alike—had simply lost the will to search for solutions to the economic problems their citizens faced.

Prior to the depression, most legislatures had not prepared for the adverse conditions that existed during the 1930s. As 1931 began, most states lacked even a rudimentary apparatus to administer effective relief, and none had a centralized unemployment-relief commission. In most states, the poor could only resort to private agencies or local governments staffed by people who condescendingly equated unemployment with laziness.

In many states, politics tied up the 1932 and 1933 legislative sessions. After the 1932 election, many legislatures had an unusually large number of new and inexperienced members as the result of the Democratic sweep. Unsure of themselves, many willingly waited for the federal government to act. Under these conditions, someone had to step in to perform corrective surgery, and the buck stopped on Franklin Roosevelt's desk. Confusion, political factionalism, and harsh economizing by state legislatures greeted Roosevelt when he took office in March 1933.

Roosevelt believed that the federal government had to help the states, and he responded by offering the Federal Emergency Relief Administration (FERA). Congress approved $500 million in FERA aid for the states, half for matching grants at a ratio of one federal dollar for each three state dollars. The Congress gave FERA administrator Harry L. Hopkins almost complete discretion in dispersing the remaining $250 million in response to state emergencies. The FERA was the first step in Roosevelt's New Deal, and like later programs, it fundamentally and irreversibly affected the relationship between the federal government and the states. Most important, FERA required the states to provide close administrative supervision of the funds, forcing legislators to adopt centralized professional administration.

It is not surprising that Hopkins faced an enormous task in getting the state legislatures to appropriate funds for the matching grants. Stretched to the fiscal limits and heavily in debt, some states simply refused to raise the funds, many passed them quite reluctantly, and others used them ineffectively.

Kentucky's legislature followed the last course. Legislators refused to discuss appropriations and hesitantly agreed to turn over $280,000 in beer and whiskey taxes to the state for relief. After threats from Hopkins's agents, state lawmakers finally enacted a regressive sales tax to provide $2.4 million to the state relief commission. After the legislature made the appropriation, Governor Ruby Laffoon reportedly ignored the unemployed by keeping the relief money for political payoffs.

Like a teenage driver aiming headlong at a rival, the Colorado legislature decided to play chicken with Harry Hopkins, and Hopkins swerved first. Convinced that Hopkins would not dare cut off funds for the needy, the legislature appropriated only $60,000 for the state's share of relief in 1933. Calculating the ravages of the dust bowl in eastern Colorado, Hopkins provided $330,000 per month to the state, with additional aid for transients in the form of surplus commodities. Hopkins then tried to pressure the legislature into appropriating the matching funds. Colorado lawmakers eventually responded with an auto-license tax, which the state supreme court promptly invalidated. When a special legislative session failed to appropriate funds, Hopkins met the challenge head-on, this time cutting off aid during the middle of a cold January. This action caused a swift backlash from the unemployed and forced the legislature to appropriate the money in another special session.

After two years of fighting with state legislatures over matching funds, Congress created the Works Progress Administration (WPA) in 1935 to administer emergency employment under federal auspices. Although requiring consultation with the states in planning projects, Congress asked for no obligatory state match. Holding an unprecedented $4.8 billion for work relief and with Hopkins at its head, the WPA provided employment for as many as three million people per year during 1935–1938. In addition to relieving the state legislatures of appropriating matching funds, the WPA reduced further hardships by constructing projects such as schools, town halls, and sewer systems that the states would ordinarily have built themselves.

Despite their newly limited responsibilities, many of the state legislatures continued to balk at providing adequate relief to the unemployed poor. A May 1936 federal report characterized relief in many of the states as "inadequate," "critical," and "chaotic."

If the FERA and WPA provided employment for jobless workers, Social Security revolutionized the way states helped the unemployable and retired. State legislatures had appropriated only meager amounts for the aged or disabled prior to federal action. Only twenty-four states had voted money for poor blind people in 1934; only twenty-eight helped the aged. While dependent children received support in forty-five states, most were provided inadequate assistance. Assistance to the aged in 1934 averaged just $16.21 per month and benefited only 400,000 people nationwide. Further, only Wisconsin had a state unemployment-compensation system in place by 1933, and it had paid no benefits.

Conservative attitudes and competition for industry had made state legislatures wary of adopting unemployment-compensation plans before the federal government inaugurated Social Security. Not until 1935 did some legislatures begin to act, and they operated in expectation of federal relief. Seven more state legislatures provided assistance for the aged by August 1935, and fifteen others added provisions that were more liberal to existing aid. Seven states adopted unemployment compensation.

Since the federal social-security tax applied to all businesses in the nation with eight employees or more, most states eagerly took advantage. By 1937 every state legislature had adopted a plan. Similarly, by 1939, every state had adopted plans to aid the elderly through central administration. Though the Social Security Act affected unemployable dependents unevenly, it encouraged state legislatures to liberalize benefits. Under the act's provisions, state legislatures had to aid the blind, the indigent aged, and dependent children, generally on a two-to-one or three-to-one matching-fund basis. In many states, however, legislatures responded with stingy contributions to the federal match. Because "the extent of need was . . . the least important part of the formula," Patterson has concluded that "the system continued to widen rather than narrow the gap between rich and poor states" (p. 93). Despite these inequities, the effort to aid the dependent poor grew dramatically during the decade. State contributions grew from $9 million in 1930 to $479 million in 1940.

Because of federal pressure, the state legislatures drafted budgets providing for increased spending. In 1930 the states appropriated about $2 billion for public needs. Between 1930 and 1933, austerity measures had caused a leveling off of state expenditures. After 1933, however, state appropriations increased, reaching $3.8 billion by 1940. Moreover, between 1932 and 1942, the proportion of state expenditures for welfare rose from 5 percent to 13 percent.

Roosevelt achieved less success in obtaining cooperation from the state legislatures with some other New Deal programs, particularly the National Recovery Administration (NRA). The National Industrial Recovery Act of 1933 allowed industries to establish codes of fair competition, fix prices, and ignore the antitrust laws, while guaranteeing labor's right to organize. After passage of the act, the administration encouraged the state legislatures to set up smaller-scale, state-administered NRA's to encourage local businesses in fair competition. Regular sessions of most of the state legislatures had already adjourned by the summer of 1933 when the NRA field agents lobbied to secure the passage of model bills. Nevertheless, the legislatures of Washington, Indiana, New Mexico, and Wyoming passed such acts. Ten additional states had similar legislation by 1934.

To Roosevelt's chagrin, by the time the various state legislatures began to meet again early in 1935, businesspeople had already attacked the act's constitutionality. In *Schechter Poultry Corporation* v. *United States*, 295 U.S. 495 (1935), the Supreme Court accepted an appeal from the Schechter company and shot NRA's symbolic blue eagle from the air in a unanimous decision in May 1935.

The federal government experienced a mixed response to calls for cooperation from state legislatures in regional planning to conserve and develop natural resources. After the federal government inaugurated the Tennessee Valley Authority in 1933 and began considering similar authorities for other drainage systems including those of the Missouri and Columbia rivers, some states paid lip service to regional planning, appearing eager to accept federal funds for that purpose. In practice, however, legislatures cooperated less in carrying out such experimental programs, especially when they had to contribute state funds.

As they had done in promoting relief, most state legislatures chalked up improved scores in reforming conditions in the workplace. During 1933, seven legislatures approved minimum-wage laws for children and fourteen ratified a proposed federal child-labor amendment to the Constitution. Within the next three years, four more ratified the amendment, bringing the total to twenty-four, and six states reinforced existing child-labor laws.

In part because of New Deal support, labor conditions had steadily improved by 1937 when a series of strikes produced a conservative backlash that cooled the ardor for reform. By the end of the decade, despite the efforts of federal officials, the gap between the provisions of federal and state labor laws had widened considerably.

On the positive side, the New Deal had benefited most citizens by prodding the state legislatures to reorganize their state governments for greater efficiency. By the end of the 1930s, a total of twenty-six states had reorganized their governmental agencies. Many also inaugurated civil service reform.

It is significant, Patterson noted, that the New Deal changed the idea of "states' rights" from a negative to a positive concept. While the role of the federal government expanded dramatically during the era, so too did that of state governments. Though increasingly dependent on the U.S. Treasury to meet the demands upon them, the states offered a larger scope of services and assumed responsibilities that made them better able to function in dealing with social and economic problems.

WORLD WAR II

As economic conditions improved during 1939–1941, war drums sounded abroad, and those who longed for a reduction of national influence over the states reaped disappointment. Americans experienced even more regimentation as the nation prepared for war. Mobilization ensured that the states would continue along the path of growing dependency upon federal funds and regulation. But the war was only one of the factors that drove this trend of expanding federal influence. Many Americans had begun to favor positive governmental action to deal with serious problems. During the Progressive Era and the Great Depression, the populace had come to expect a more active role—first from the state government and then from the federal—and as time passed legislatures became increasingly willing, if not able, to try to meet their constituents' new expectations.

Despite a common desire to put partisanship aside during the crisis, party activists exhibited the normal degree of bickering. Whether from motives of patriotism or personal advantage, one Wyoming legislator suggested—without success—that the state authorize

officeholders to run unopposed in the 1942 elections.

Intensely interested in contributing to national defense, state legislatures assisted the war effort. The legislatures of New York, Iowa, and Nebraska led in creating state councils of defense to coordinate the activities of the national, state, county, and local levels of government. The response of New York's legislature to the wartime crisis seems typical. The lawmakers passed bills to protect against sabotage by regulating admission to defense installations and punishing those who damaged war materiel. Other proposals facilitated cooperation with other states in the conservation of oil, provided for absentee voting by servicemen, created recreation centers near military bases, established a commission to facilitate military transportation, regulated the manufacture and sale of explosives, and extended the functions of the state health commission.

As mobilization began, American citizens began to see major shifts in population as millions entered the armed services and industry expanded to meet defense needs. After the attack on Pearl Harbor in December 1941, massive dislocation became commonplace. Wartime reshuffling of industry led to unprecedented growth in many parts of the country with accompanying demands on housing and services. Federal, state, and local governments worked together to alleviate shortages of housing, transportation, clothing, and food. Like the legislatures in many states, the Connecticut legislature tried several times to control skyrocketing rents and provide new housing for the large influx of defense workers. Ultimately, the state housing authority proved ineffective, and the federal government stepped in, declaring the entire state a rent-control area in 1942.

Connecticut authorities proved nearly as ineffective in building new housing. Fearing postwar slums and continued growth of governmental power at individuals' expense and believing that existing housing would meet future demands, the state housing authority ignored the rapid population growth and recommended as early as 1943 that the state stop sponsoring the construction of new housing units.

Many states found that the large influx of workers created both an economic miracle and a social disaster. Their economies were stimulated by additional dollars as the demand for services grew, but people with little attachment to the community flooded the cities. Legislatures then had to provide additional social services to meet the problems caused by dislocation.

As the federal government began to plan new defense installations, conflict between the states to milk the federal cow became inevitable, and a fierce competition developed. Westerners saw the war as an opportunity to diversify economies heavily dependent upon extractive industries. North Dakota, Wyoming, New Mexico, Utah, Arizona, and Nevada all received their share as the government built war plants and military installations in the West. In addition, the vast expanses of undeveloped land made the West an ideal area for training installations, which benefited the region's economy with more federal jobs and funds, introducing at the same time hazardous chemical, biological, and atomic weapons.

The Pacific Coast and the Northeast fared especially well. Shipyards, steel plants, and airbases dotted the landscape of California and Washington, encouraged by those states' well-established industrial base and strategic location near the Pacific theater. Industrialized states like New York, Pennsylvania, Michigan, and Connecticut benefited from various other contracts.

As millions joined the military service, the growth of defense industries and the need for food and fiber created a shortage of workers. In response, state legislatures relaxed their maximum-hour and child-labor laws. New York's legislature suspended its laws for six months in 1942 and then extended the suspension during its 1943 session. The new laws permitted men and women to work extra hours and seven days per week. The demand for workers had grown so great by 1943 that legislatures allowed sixteen- and seventeen-year-olds to work for long hours as well.

Western farmers, especially in Arizona and California, lobbied for the importation of Mexican braceros: between 1942 and 1947, more than two-hundred thousand Mexican farm workers entered the United States to work in the fields. The use of compliant migrant and foreign workers, coupled with an already existing housing shortage, brought abuses in housing and working conditions. Alone among

western states, California's legislature enacted minimum standards for sanitation and housing for its migrant workers. In the East, after three years of study, the New York legislature enacted statutes designed to make contractors responsible for workers' health and safety.

In general, the labor shortage also led to a degree of improvement in employment opportunities for minorities and women during the war. As the federal government acted, the state legislatures also recognized the need to utilize all available sources of labor. States passed laws establishing fair-employment boards and gave them power to arbitrate cases of discrimination. New York provided a model when it passed permanent legislation in 1945 creating the State Commission Against Discrimination.

Even with such legislation, states achieved only halting and uneven progress in fighting discrimination. Minorities usually remained in jobs on the lowest rungs of the ladder, exploited by business and despised by labor unions. Significant steps to correct these abuses had to await the civil rights movement in the postwar decades.

Beyond the exploitation of braceros, a racial problem of a different sort appeared on the West Coast. California and Washington had the largest Japanese American communities at the beginning of the war, and the surprise attack on Pearl Harbor spawned a wave of paranoia that fed on racism. Citing potential sabotage, California's governor Culbert B. Olson, Attorney General Earl Warren, and legislative leaders demanded Japanese American removal. In response to such concerns, President Roosevelt issued Executive Order 9066 authorizing evacuation of Japanese Americans to inland concentration camps. Some western states sought to avoid playing host to the internees. Idaho's governor Chase Clark said he wanted to send them back to Japan rather than locating them "in our state." Utah's governor Herbert Maw expressed a somewhat more tolerant attitude, but the state legislature had already passed an alien land law modeled on California's 1913 statute. In 1943, Wyoming's legislature passed a bill prohibiting Japanese American detainees from voting or obtaining property in the state. Subsequent events proved the loyalty of these people and revealed the racism that lay behind their incarceration.

Relatively early in World War II, a number

of state legislatures became concerned with providing opportunities for returning veterans. Legislatures set up departments to look after the well-being of returning soldiers by providing educational and economic opportunities. To show their appreciation and patriotism, legislatures commonly voted for veterans bonuses and other benefits. Wyoming, for instance, exempted its veterans from payment of certain taxes and fees, gave them, or their widows, preference in contracts, counted extra points on state civil-service exams, and gave teachers credits for wartime service.

When the war ended, the soldiers flooded home, and the housing shortage worsened. Some states responded with an increase in housing subsidies; others failed to assist in providing housing for the veterans. New York lawmakers devoted $135 million to slum clearance and low-rent housing. Connecticut's legislature, still hampered by political conflict, proved more interested in appearances than in building houses. Instead of voting money for new housing, it enacted a bill reimbursing up to $5 million to localities for emergency housing for veterans.

As the war drew to a close, many state legislatures created planning boards to guide the development of postwar state economies. Assessing the economic and social changes caused by wartime conditions, these boards tried to plan for growth and diversity.

STATE LEGISLATURES SINCE WORLD WAR II

After the war, Congress expanded the practice of appropriating funds and mandating standards in an increasingly large number of fields. These standards fell most heavily on state legislatures that had discriminated against the poor, urbanites, the mentally retarded, minority groups, and women or had allowed their citizens to pollute land, water, or air. Although these laws restricted the discretion of state lawmakers in fashioning solutions to problems, they also forced the legislators to address matters they had previously chosen to ignore.

Following World War II, the national government increasingly acted to protect rights traditionally denied by state laws. Perhaps the most dramatic example attacked state-legislated segregation. By the early 1950s, eighteen states had laws making racial segregation mandatory among school children, and six others left local school boards free to do so. Previous Supreme Court decisions had begun to chip away at state practices, but the Court dealt a death-blow to legislated segregation in *Brown* v. *Board of Education of Topeka*, 347 U.S. 483 (1954). The decision, written by Earl Warren, overturned the legal framework of *Plessy* v. *Ferguson*, 163 U.S. 537 (1896), ruling that school segregation based on race violated the equal-protection clause of the Fourteenth Amendment. *Brown* was only the first of a number of court rulings mandating the protection of civil rights.

Conservative majorities in these states fought a rearguard action, trying to maintain traditional class and racial distinctions. Southern legislators and governors couched their efforts to stop the wave of racial equality in high-sounding doctrines, interposing state authority between their citizens and the federal government. The Supreme Court considered this sophistry and struck down state objections. In succeeding years, the courts and Congress reduced the power of state legislatures to pass laws discriminating against citizens on the basis of race or gender. Congressional action culminated with the Civil Rights Act of 1964, which established guidelines for protecting citizens and required compliance in order to receive federal funds.

The federal government extended its protection to other citizens as well. The decision in *Baker* v. *Carr*, 369 U.S. 186 (1962), for instance, attacked the tendency of conservative rural minorities to dominate state legislatures. As urban population grew during the twentieth century, many legislatures failed to redistrict to make representation more equitable. In Tennessee, where the case originated, the legislature had refused to reapportion either house since 1901, despite a requirement in the state's constitution.

Tennessee did not stand alone. In 1960, thirty-six states had provisions in their constitutions requiring periodic reapportionment based on the national census. In six of these states, lawmakers had not acted for a quarter of a century or more, and in fourteen others, the legislatures violated their constitutions in varying degrees. The *Baker* decision caused a flurry of suits aimed at correcting malapportionment. Within five months, citizens in twenty-two of the fifty states had filed suits. Federal courts in twelve states declared existing modes of apportionment unconstitutional. In five states, the legislatures had begun to reapportion under threat of suit. By the end of 1963, citizens had instituted federal suits in thirty-one states, while similar suits had been initiated in the state courts of nineteen other states.

In more recent years, decisions in an increasingly conservative Supreme Court have begun to undermine the protections guaranteed in the *Baker* decision. The decision in *Mahan* v. *Howell*, 410 U.S. 315 (1973) allowed substantial variation between Virginia legislative districts, and a decision in a Wyoming case following the 1980 census allowed a disparity ratio of three to one between the largest and smallest legislative districts. Nevertheless, some legislatures, as in Arizona and New Mexico, reapportioned under threat of suits, and some states established extralegislative reapportionment commissions.

As the Supreme Court has undermined legislative discretion in redistricting, federal laws have restricted the states in other areas as well. Using a carrot-and-stick approach, Congress has influenced state legislatures to take action in such diverse matters as highway construction, control of water and air pollution, waste disposal, pesticide and herbicide use, and facilities for the mentally and physically handicapped. Ordinarily Congress offered matching funds for state action in selected areas and threatened loss of funds for inaction.

Some conservatives thought the return of a Republican administration in 1953 would reverse this trend, and soon after taking office, President Eisenhower appointed the Commission on Intergovernmental Relations to suggest policy on the division and cooperation between states and the federal government. The commission's final report disappointed conservatives by recommending federal-state cooperation. Rather than occupying separate spheres, the report suggested, the state and federal governments should cooperate "in meeting the growing demands on both."

Following these recommendations, Eisenhower and the Congresses that served with him continued to offer money to the states in return for compliance with federal regulations. By 1961, federal domestic aid had increased to $7.3 billion annually—triple the amount expended in the last year of Truman's term.

Federal contributions to highway construction mushroomed after World War II, especially when the Eisenhower administration undertook what was at the time the nation's largest public works program, the 1956 Federal-Aid Highway Program. Between 1947 and 1950, the number of private vehicles had increased by 30 percent to 48.6 million, and mileage driven had grown proportionally, especially on urban roads. Reports from the states showed not only a shortage of highways but inadequate standards on existing roadways.

State needs staggered the imagination. California's legislature estimated that it would need $1.7 billion over a ten-year period to bring the state's roads up to standard. Estimates in other states seemed nearly as unimaginable: Washington, $509 million; Oregon, $468 million; Michigan, $1.75 billion; Connecticut, $400 million; and Massachusetts, $700 million.

Given the limited revenues then available and the reluctance of states to incur new debt or increase taxes, needs far exceeded money available for construction. Consequently, the states began to pressure Congress to increase the federal share of the burden. Thus, state demands, coupled with a heightened awareness of the need for adequate highways for national defense, led to congressional action, the Interstate Highway Act of 1956, authorizing appropriations totaling $25 billion through fiscal year 1969. Channeling federal taxes on fuel and tires and certain vehicle excise taxes into the Highway Trust Fund, the act departed significantly from previous federal highway legislation.

In return for taking responsibilities from the legislatures for funding the highway system, Congress mandated construction standards and regulations in labor relations. The law applied provisions to wage rates for all contracts, including those funded by the states' matching portion. Though popular with laboring people, this provision caused considerable discomfort for conservatives. In general, other measures inaugurated by the Eisenhower administration, such as aid for education and water-pollution control, paled beside the Interstate Highway Act of 1956.

STATE LEGISLATURES IN THE TWENTIETH CENTURY

During the 1960s the Johnson administration began the programs of the Great Society. These led to an unprecedented expansion of federal activity in social programs. As a result, federal grants-in-aid grew from $10.9 billion in 1965 to $20.2 billion in 1969. Largest among Johnson's programs was Medicaid, an entitlement program that allowed the states some flexibility in determining benefits and eligibility. Medicaid expenditures have continued to grow over the years, increasing from $741 million in 1966 to nearly $19 billion by 1984.

During the Johnson administration, Congress passed a number of other acts that had significant impacts upon the states and their legislatures. The Education Act of 1965, the Job Corps, and the Neighborhood Youth Corps all increased federal activities.

Although federal grants to the states continued during the early 1970s, the Nixon administration became concerned with the bewildering proliferation of grant programs. In an attempt to simplify the procedure, Nixon began to design programs to give states greater flexibility by making block rather than specific grants. Included in the block grants were the Comprehensive Employment and Training Act (CETA) and the community-development program, both of which consolidated a number of previous programs.

Behind Nixon's proposal for block grants lay an idea he called "the New Federalism." Most state observers hoped the New Federalism would reverse the continuing trend of centralization of government functions and return some of the initiative for programs to the state legislatures, along with money to fund them. Nixon tried to implement this vision through general revenue sharing, through which he hoped to distribute funds without strings directly to the states. As adopted in 1972, revenue sharing provided more than $5 billion in funds per year for five years.

In practice, however, Congress and Nixon further centralized certain programs and reduced the discretion of the state legislatures in establishing local standards. For example, the supplemental security income (SSI) program placed administration of aid for the needy aged, blind, and disabled under federal jurisdiction. Although this program eliminated many of the disparities between the states in the size of grants, it also reduced the authority of state legislatures. Additionally, while the block grant and revenue-sharing programs enacted during the Nixon-Ford years did allow a much greater degree of flexibility to the states, the trend toward greater state dependency on federal funds continued throughout the period. Total grants-in-aid grew from $20 billion in 1969 to more than $68 billion by 1977.

THE POST-VIETNAM YEARS

Although it is tempting to see the administration of President Jimmy Carter as continuing the policies of Johnson's Great Society and Nixon's New Federalism, the former Georgia governor actually reversed rapid budgetary expansion and began a trend that continued into the Reagan years. Early in his administration, Carter convinced the Congress to increase grants in an attempt to reverse the effects of a nationwide recession that began shortly after the end of the Vietnam War. Midway through Carter's term, however, a national tax revolt began with the passage of Proposition 13 in California. This proposition and laws imitating it in other states limited the discretion of state legislatures in raising taxes. In its wake, some local governments found themselves unable to maintain basic services. The national backlash forced Carter to retrench, leaving many of his plans, including a major new urban program, at the mercy of an increasingly cost-conscious Congress. Thus, as the nation moved into the Reagan years, government expenditures for grants-in-aid, as measured in dollars of constant value, were already beginning to decrease.

Ronald Reagan entered the White House emphasizing a return of authority and responsibility to the states. In practice, however, given the conservative mood, most state legislatures remained timid about increasing taxes. Moreover, unlike the U.S. Constitution, many state constitutions required balanced budgets so that legislatures could not follow the federal pattern of continuous borrowing, spending, and reelection. Thus, instead of responding to the challenge by funding programs dropped by the federal government, the state legislatures dropped public-works programs and left public needs underfunded.

In many ways, the federal government made the burden upon the states more difficult during the Reagan years. Instead of funding programs as it did during the Johnson and Nixon years, Congress laid additional burdens on the states through mandated activities and standards without providing the revenue to meet the requirements. Thus, while state revenues rose during the 1980s, mandated activities ate up a large part of the increases, and the state legislatures struggled to fund needed programs, such as welfare, education, and highways. In 1990 alone, Congress put in place an additional twenty federal mandates—ranging from an expansion of the Social Security system to environmental regulations—estimated to cost the states $15 billion over five years.

Over the years, states have become increasingly dependent upon federal grants. At the same time, legislatures have suffered from the burden of complying with federal standards. The Supreme Court undercut state-sovereignty arguments against such compliance when it ruled in *Oklahoma* v. *United States Civil Service*, 330 U.S. (1947) that such standards did not constitute undue coercion because the states could simply refuse to accept the federal funds.

Legislatures in western states with substantial proportions of federal land have tried to resist increasing federal control over land management. Attempts to secure transfer of federal lands to the states date from the 1920s and saw their most recent expression in the Sagebrush Rebellion, beginning in 1979. Led by Nevada, with 85 percent of its land under federal ownership, a number of western legislatures laid claim to federal lands or tried to restrict federal management options within their borders. Although the efforts failed in practice, they received the verbal support of the Reagan administration and engendered considerable western hostility to federal management.

Although, as the Supreme Court indicated in the *Oklahoma* case, states can break some federal tethers by refusing to accept the funds to which the strings are tied, legislators have been reluctant to force their citizens to accept additional tax burdens in order to furnish services otherwise funded by dollars from Washington.

The federal highways program provides an excellent example. Although each state is entitled to certain funds based on a congressionally mandated formula, the Federal Highway Administration has long withheld funds in order to force state compliance with uniform standards in the construction of the interstate system.

In 1965, however, with the passage of the Highway Beautification Act, a new type of federal control—the so-called crossover sanctions—was introduced. This legislation authorized a new grant with added requirements by threatening to withhold up to 10 percent of highway appropriations to any state that failed to comply with national guidelines for the control of billboards and junkyards.

The effectiveness of this technique led Congress in 1974 to threaten to cut off all highway funds for any state that failed to enact a maximum speed limit of fifty-five miles per hour. Within two months every legislature in the Union had complied. In 1977, as part of the Clean Air Act, Congress required the secretary of transportation to withhold approval for some highway projects in states that had not submitted an air-quality improvement plan. Three years later, it threatened loss of 10 percent of federal highway funds to states inadequately enforcing the fifty-five-mile limit.

Again, in 1984, Congress used similar sanctions to force state compliance with minimum-drinking-age legislation. Eight state legislatures failed to comply with the law, feeling they were justified in determining their own standards under the Twenty-first Amendment. In *South Dakota* v. *Dole*, 483 U.S. 203 (1987), the Supreme Court ruled in favor of the federal government.

The success of the federal government in using sanctions in the disbursement of funds will no doubt ensure its continuance. Consequently, state legislatures continue to find themselves increasingly under federal domination. As one observer recently remarked, "the states are treated more and more like administrative units of the national government" (quoted in Sevin, p. 28). Thus, near the end of the twentieth century, the reduction in the autonomy of local legislatures continued.

Finally, studies published in 1987 and 1990 suggest that the twentieth century has also seen an increasingly rapid shift in power from the legislative to the executive branch. Several factors seem responsible. These include the enhanced role of state governors and their staffs in the budget-making process, the executive appointive and veto powers, and the amount of party influence governors can wield over legislators. The 1990 study also says something about the relative power of the executive and legislative branches by ranking governors from very strong to weak according to their institutional powers. According to the study, Maryland, Massachusetts, New York, South Dakota, and Virginia had very strong or strong governors. The study found weak governors in North and South Carolina, New Hampshire, Nevada, Rhode Island, Texas, and Vermont. Governors of other states tended to rank in between. The relative power of the legislatures seems to have varied in inverse proportion to that of the governors.

In the years since *Baker* v. *Carr*, institutional changes have modernized the apparatus of most state legislatures, including elimination or relaxation of state constitutional limits on lengths of legislative sessions, improvement in the salaries of legislators, the adoption of procedures encouraging greater public participation, the increase in legislative oversight over state budgetary expenditures, and more careful attention to the ethics of legislators.

These changes would seem to parallel changes in the U.S. Congress. The power of state legislatures has tended to diminish, just as Congress has lost influence to the president. Legislatures tend to follow the federal example in the use of committees to complete their work. In some states where the length of sessions are limited by law, legislative committees are often in session outside the prescribed time for such purposes as preparing bills for upcoming sessions, conducting oversight functions, and working on such problems as redistricting.

BIBLIOGRAPHY

General Studies

THAD L. BEYLE, "The Governors, 1988–1989," *The Book of the States: 1990–1991 Edition*, vol. 28 (Lexington, Ky., 1990); WILDER CRANE, JR., and MEREDITH W. WATTS, JR., *State Legislative Systems* (Englewood Cliffs, N.J., 1968); MARTHA FABRICIUS, "More Dictates from the Feds," *State Legislatures* 17:2 (1991): 28–31; RICH JONES, "The State Legislatures," *The Book of the States: 1990–1991 Edition*, vol. 28 (Lexington, Ky., 1990); ALFRED H. KELLY and WINFRED A. HARBISON, *The American Constitution, Its Origins and Development* (New York, 1963); GABRIEL KOLKO, *The Triumph of Conservatism: A Reinterpretation of American History, 1900–1916* (New York, 1963); RICHARD P. NATHAN, FRED C. DOOLITTLE, et al., *Reagan and the States* (Princeton, N.J., 1987); JAMES T. PATTERSON, *The New Deal and the States: Federalism in Transition* (Princeton, N.J., 1969); CARL TUBBESING, "Passing the Buck to the States—Without the Bucks," *State Legislatures* 17:1 (1991): 23–25.

Regional Studies

CALLIS BLYTHE AHLSTROM, "Utah and Colorado During the Reform Era, 1890–1917," (Master's thesis, Columbia University, 1960); WALTON BEAN and JAMES J. RAWLS, *California: An Interpretive History* (New York, 1983); BERNARD BELLUSH, *Franklin D. Roosevelt as Governor of New York* (New York, 1955; repr., 1968); MONROE LEE BILLINGTON, *The Political South in the Twentieth Century* (New York, 1975); GORDON B. DODDS, *Oregon: A Bicentennial History* (New York, 1977); MARTHA FABRICUS, "More Dictates from the Feds," *State Legislatures* 17:2 (1991): 28–31; CHARLES N. GLAAB, "The Failure of North Dakota Progressivism," *Mid-America* 39:4 (1957): 195–209; GRANTHAM W. DEWEY, *Southern Progressivism: The Reconciliation of Progress and Tradition* (Knoxville, Tenn., 1983); JOSEPH J. HUTHMACHER, *Massachusetts People and Politics, 1919–1933* (Cambridge, Mass., 1959); WILLIAM T. KERR, JR., "The Progressives of Washington, 1910–1912," *Pacific Northwest Quarterly* 55:1 (1964): 16–17; GABRIEL KOLKO, *The Triumph of Conservatism: A Re-interpretation of American History, 1900–1916* (New York, 1963); T. A. LARSON, *Wyoming's War Years, 1941–1945* (Laramie, Wyo., 1954); ROBERT S. MAXWELL, *La Follette and the Rise of the Progressives in Wisconsin* (Madison, Wisc., 1956); GEORGE H. MAYER, *The Political Career of Floyd B. Olson* (Minneapolis, 1951); RICHARD L. McCORMICK, *From Realignment to Reform: Political Change in New York State, 1893–1910* (Ithaca, N.Y., 1979); FRANKLIN D. MITCHELL, *Embattled Democracy:*

Missouri Democratic Politics, 1919–1932 (Columbia, Mo., 1968); GEORGE E. MOWRY, *The California Progressives* (Berkeley, Calif., 1951); GERALD D. NASH, *The American West Transformed: The Impact of the Second World War* (Bloomington, Ind., 1985); RANSOM E. NOBLE, *New Jersey Progressivism Before Wilson* (Princeton, N.J., 1946); DAVID P. THELEN, *The New Citizenship: Origins of Progressivism in Wisconsin, 1885–1900* (Columbia, Mo., 1972); CLIVE S. THOMAS, ed., *Politics and Public Policy in the Contemporary American West* (Albuquerque, 1991).

War Periods

ALAN CLIVE, *State of War* (Ann Arbor, Mich., 1979); KARL DREW HARTZELL, *The Empire State at War: World War II* (Albany, N.Y., 1949); JOHN W. JEFFRIES, *Testing the Roosevelt Coalition: Connecticut Society and Politics in the Era of World War II* (Knoxville, Tenn., 1979); RICHARD POLENBERG, *War and Society: The United States, 1941–1945* (Philadelphia, 1972).

Environmental and U.S. Infrastructure Concerns

WILLIAM L. GRAF, *Wilderness Preservation and the Sagebrush Rebellions* (Savage, Md., 1990); M. NELSON McGEARY, *Gifford Pinchot: Forester-Politician* (Princeton, N.J., 1960); ALI F. SEVLIN, "Highway Sanctions: Circumventing the Constitution," *State Legislatures* 15:2 (1989): 25–28; UNITED STATES DEPARTMENT OF TRANSPORTATION, *America's Highways, 1776–1976* (Washington, D.C., 1976).

SEE ALSO The Congressional Budget Process; The Contemporary Congress, 1930–1992; Legislatures and Civil Rights; Legislatures and the Environment; Legislatures and Political Rights; Legislatures and Social Welfare Policy; AND The Modernizing Congress, 1870–1930.

LOCAL LEGISLATIVE INSTITUTIONS

Jon C. Teaford

Separation of powers is a cardinal tenet of political faith in the United States. Since the founding of the nation, American schoolchildren have been taught the constitutionally prescribed division of authority among the executive, legislature, and judiciary, and textbook charts of the federal and state governments have been drawn to distinguish clearly between the three branches. Admirers of American government have praised the resulting system of checks and balances as a pillar of liberty without which the whole structure of freedom would collapse. American dogma has demanded that the three branches remain separate, independent, and ever vigilant in checking the abuses of one another. Concentration of executive, legislative, and judicial authority in a single person or agency has been considered anathema; power divided among jealous rulers has been envisioned as the ideal.

Yet, at the local level, Americans have shown a remarkable willingness to ignore the concept of separation of powers and tolerate institutions that deviate markedly from the precepts that have determined the organization of the state and federal governments. Drafters of city charters have most often attempted to create a clear division between executive and legislative institutions, but other local government structures have driven devotees of separation of powers to despair. At the county level, the governing board generally has exercised executive, administrative, and legislative functions and, in many instances, judicial duties. Some cities have even been willing to experiment with schemes that mix legislative and executive functions, making the same person lawmaker and administrator. Local legislative institutions, then, have not always been little Congresses, replicating in counties and townships the structure of the federal government. In fact, local government has not necessarily included distinctively legislative institutions.

Generalizations, however, are difficult, for diversity rather than uniformity has been the norm. At various times in various localities, Americans have experimented with direct democracy, small boards with executive-administrative-legislative authority, large representative assemblies, and district-based councils modeled on the U.S. Congress. To some degree, the county's state legislative delegation has also acted as the local legislature. Thus, local governments have defied both the traditional vertical divisions (federal, state, and local) and the long-honored horizontal distinctions (executive, legislative, and judicial) of American government. In the minds of chart makers and those fond of structural neatness, local rule has been a disgrace. But fixed formulas have simply not applied.

THE COLONIAL ERA

During the colonial era, Britain's various New World provinces developed different structures of local rule, thus laying the foundation for the diversity of forms that followed. Throughout most of the South, the county was the principal unit of local government, and the justices of the peace sitting together as the county court were the chief officials.

The County Court

As its name implies, the county court was a judicial body, trying both criminal and civil cases. Yet it was also the chief administrative agency of the county, charged with the power to issue licenses to tavern keepers, regulate weights and measures, fix prices for certain commodities, and appoint persons to lay out and maintain bridges and roads. Moreover, it performed some functions usually associated with the legislative branch of government, such

233

as levying taxes and appropriating funds. The very idea of division of powers was antithetical to the county court. All the functions of local government were under its control.

Not only did the institution of the county court defy the concept of separation of powers, but it also conflicted with later notions of representative rule. The colonial governor had the formal authority to select the justices. But in Virginia and, to a large degree, North Carolina, he followed the recommendations of the county's incumbent justices in making his appointments; in other words, their county courts were actually self-perpetuating bodies, for vacant judgeships were filled by those named by the remaining members of the court. The general body of county residents had no voice in the choice of local rulers. Instead, the county gentry, those with the most land and slaves, appointed themselves to the court and maintained a firm control over county government.

During its early years, the Pennsylvania colony also relied on the county court composed of appointed justices as the principal institution of local government. Yet in the first half of the eighteenth century, Pennsylvanians developed a rival body that robbed the justices of some of their authority. This was the three-member board of county commissioners. Created in 1711 by the provincial assembly to collect provincial taxes at the local level, the commissioners gradually acquired additional powers, including the authority to determine the county tax rate and to order county expenditures. They were originally appointed by the assembly, but in 1722 became elective. Although the justices of the peace continued to exercise administrative as well as judicial powers, the commissioners generally gained the upper hand in county affairs during the remainder of the colonial period.

In New England, by contrast, the county court and its appointed justices of the peace continued to dominate county government throughout the decades prior to the American Revolution. Yet the county was not the chief unit of local government for New Englanders. Instead, the town was the basic building block in the structure of local rule and the principal agency for ensuring order. The town maintained roads, operated schools, provided relief for the poor, and assumed responsibility for a range of other services and regulations.

The Town Meeting

Ultimate authority in the New England town rested with the town meeting. This gathering of enfranchised residents elected the town officers, approved town tax levies, and adopted the bylaws necessary for the good conduct of the community. A board of elected officials, known variously as selectmen, townsmen, or councilmen, were responsible for administering the town during the intervals between meetings. During the course of the colonial era, these officers seem to have assumed increasing power, with the town meetings often endorsing whatever the selectmen proposed. But the white males who composed the local electorate and gathered at the town meetings continued to enjoy the final say on community policy.

In American mythology the town meeting has become a symbol of civic-minded democracy, a much-heralded forum for hardy, independent yeomen speaking their minds and steering the course of government. In reality the town legislature fell far short of the ideal. Apathy rather than civic diligence seemingly prevailed in most New England towns, and the typical Yankee yeoman was more concerned with plowing than with governance. Normally, towns held only a few meetings each year, and in one community after another, most eligible voters avoided even these infrequent gatherings. Unless the town faced a crisis or was embroiled in a lively controversy, relatively few New Englanders seemed eager to perform their civic duty and vote on town issues. In Newport, Rhode Island, a town with a population of more than nine thousand, only eight voters were present at a meeting in 1769 and only five were present for a session in 1776. In some cases, the poorly attended meetings adjourned until additional bodies could be rounded up, but sometimes business proceeded with the few present deciding all questions. "The inhabitants . . . have wholly failed in attendance," reported the town records of Pomfret, Connecticut, but the town agreed that the bylaws adopted by those few who did attend were as binding "as if all were present" (Daniels, *The Connecticut Town*, p. 84). Such apathy only strengthened the hand of the selectmen, who were able to make decisions without interference from an interested electorate.

234

LOCAL LEGISLATIVE INSTITUTIONS

The Municipal Corporation

The town was the unit of local government for both the farming and commercial communities of New England. In the middle and southern colonies, however, America's nascent trading centers adopted the English institution of the municipal corporation as the principal instrument of local rule. Most colonial municipalities had a mayor and a body of councilmen or aldermen, but the concept of separation of powers was as alien to municipal corporations as it was to county governments. The mayor was a member of the common council and basically served as its presiding officer. He performed certain ceremonial duties that distinguished him as the municipality's executive, but he had no veto over the actions of the council and little or no authority to appoint subordinate officials. Moreover, both the mayor and the aldermen exercised judicial power, trying a wide range of civil and criminal cases. These city officers also performed administrative tasks and were charged with guaranteeing the implementation of municipal policy. In New York City, for example, each alderman was responsible for enforcing within his ward (the subdivision of the city each represented) the requirement that householders maintain streetlights. Each was also in charge of administering ward elections: he determined the polling location, registered the voters, and recorded the ballots. Like the county justice, the colonial mayor or alderman was, then, a combination legislator, judge, and administrator, performing his tasks without any concern for the notion of a tripartite division of powers.

Yet the origins of certain common legislative practices were evident in these early municipalities. For example, the custom of aldermanic courtesy seems to date from the pre-Revolutionary decades, for in the eighteenth century, as in the nineteenth, the city councils appeared willing to defer to the judgment of the ward alderman on any issues that affected his ward only. It was his bailiwick, and he enjoyed the right to make policy for his small political domain. Thus, in 1750, New York City's common council adopted a standing rule that "whenever a Committee shall be appointed for the future for any matter or thing to be done in any of the wards of this City that the alderman of such ward shall be Chairman of such Com-

mittee" (quoted in George W. Edwards and Arthur E. Peterson, *New York as an Eighteenth Century Municipality*, 1917, p. 231). Eventually the practice would result in the ward alderman becoming virtually a one-person legislature for all measures affecting his ward. In New York and later in other municipalities, he determined whether his constituents won favors from the city.

The municipal aldermen, county justices, and town meetings all to some degree laid down the rules regulating the local communities they presided over. Yet to speak of legislative bodies at the local level during the seventeenth and eighteenth centuries is in large measure misleading. Throughout the colonial period there were actually few local legislative institutions per se. One might classify the town meeting as a legislative body, but in cities and counties, judicial, administrative, and legislative functions were inextricable, providing for no neat division of powers among governing institutions. Judges exercised powers usually associated with legislators, and aldermen and mayors performed tasks latter-day observers would view as judicial. Local governing bodies were most frequently all-purpose agencies that, it would be more accurate to say, ruled rather than legislated.

THE NINETEENTH CENTURY

During the century following the American Revolution, local institutions adapted to the nation's changing political ideology, its rapid urban growth, and its expansion westward. Concentration of authority in the hands of a single body of governors offended the post-Revolutionary mentality and led to a separation of powers in some local units. At the same time, the rising power of plebeian politicians catering to foreign-born urban voters caused some to favor a periodic reordering of the structure of municipal rule. Moreover, in the region west of the Appalachians, freshly minted states faced the problem of determining the proper mode of rural government. During the colonial era, Americans had experimented with a variety of alternatives. Throughout the nineteenth century the issue was whether to adopt any of these Atlantic-seaboard creations and, if they were adopted, how to adapt them to the needs of the trans-Appalachian West.

Urban Rule

In the post-Revolutionary era, heightened suspicion of concentrated government authority clearly influenced the changing structure of America's municipal corporations. Gradually the framework of urban rule came to resemble more closely that of the national government, with legislators no longer exercising judicial powers and executives becoming independent of the local legislature. During the 1790s both Philadelphia and New York City began to develop a municipal judiciary whose magistrates were not members of the city council.

City Councils During the nineteenth century, in one city after another, mayors ceased to serve simply as chair of the city council and instead became independent of that ordinance-making body, exercising both veto power over council measures and enhanced authority over appointment of municipal officials. Some nineteenth-century cities even opted for bicameral (two-house) city councils comparable to the U.S. Senate and House of Representatives. Increasingly, a system of checks and balances became the norm at the municipal as well as the state and federal levels. With his veto the mayor could check the council, and the upper house of the municipal legislature could check the lower house and guard against the overhasty passage of measures of doubtful wisdom.

By the second half of the nineteenth century, however, measures of doubtful wisdom seemed to be the specialty of American city councils. Cries of corruption were heard in major cities throughout the country, and most critics regarded the municipal council as the rotten core of urban rule. In New York City the culprits on the board of aldermen won the nickname the "Forty Thieves," and in Chicago the corrupt pack of municipal legislators ravaging that city were called the "Gray Wolves." In part, the opprobrium heaped upon city councils was owing to the relatively undistinguished social standing of council members and their role as servants of neighborhood interests. Usually elected by wards, late-nineteenth-century councilmen were most often grocers, livery-stable owners, or saloon keepers with a neighborhood reputation sufficient to get them elected to the municipal assembly but without the distinction enjoyed by the city's leading professionals and business chieftains. Moreover, council members conceived of themselves largely as spokesmen for their wards, charged with winning favors for constituents. They were not primarily policymakers for the city as a whole but representatives of the various urban districts, seeking to obtain as much as possible for their friends and neighbors. affluent and socially prestigious city dwellers with a broader vision of the role of urban government deplored these plebeians and their parochial outlook on municipal legislation. Heightening the sense of outrage among the "better sort" were repeated stories of public utility companies paying handsome bribes to council members for the privilege of operating streetcars or laying gas mains. According to critics of the municipal legislature, council members were "peanut politicians" who took advantage of public office to line their own pockets and who lacked an adequate comprehension of citywide problems.

Independent Commissions Attacks on the city councils led to a shift in authority to the executive branch of municipal government and to the creation of independent commissions. For example, in the 1880s and 1890s the mayors of New York City and Brooklyn—which were separate cities until 1898—acquired absolute appointive power, their selections for public office no longer requiring the consent of the city councils. Moreover, in a number of cities mayors won the authority to remove appointed officials; thus, executives could hire and fire at will, without regard for the opinion of the municipal legislature. During the late nineteenth century some mayors further secured the power to exercise the item veto, allowing them to strike down sections of ordinances without voiding the entire measure. At the same time state lawmakers established independent park boards and library commissions in a number of urban areas, thereby ensuring that certain local government services were free from the control of supposedly venal city councils. Composed of appointees of higher social standing than the members of the city council, these boards were charged with governing urban America's institutions of truth and beauty.

LOCAL LEGISLATIVE INSTITUTIONS

Rural Institutions

Although cities were home to an increasing share of the nation's population, throughout the nineteenth century an overwhelming majority of Americans were rural dwellers. Outside of New England, where the town remained preeminent, the county was the chief unit of rural government, yet the structure of county government varied widely. No uniform desire to copy the three-branch federal structure produced a standard framework at the county level. Instead, the states demonstrated considerable ingenuity in fashioning a confusing diversity of institutions.

County Commissioners In the southern tier of midwestern states, the Pennsylvania system of county commissioners prevailed. Thus, in Ohio, Indiana, southern Illinois, Iowa, and Kansas a board of from three to seven commissioners administered the county and levied the county tax. Like their Pennsylvania forebear, these boards were the combined executive, administrative, and legislative branches of government. Moreover, the three-to-seven-member county commission became the most common form of local government in the region stretching from the Great Plains to the Pacific Coast. Ohio, Indiana, Iowa, and Kansas also divided their counties into townships, with township trustees exercising control over local roads and bridges, schools, relief for the poor, and cemeteries. Like the county commissioners, the township trustees were multipurpose officials who did not conform to any model of separation of powers.

Townships The northern tier of midwestern states also created townships within their counties. Each township in Michigan, northern Illinois, and Wisconsin elected a supervisor to oversee its business, and the chief governing body of the county was the board of supervisors, an assembly of all the township chieftains. Sizable cities within the counties usually elected more than one supervisor to the board. Since the typical county included more than a dozen townships, the boards of supervisors were considerably larger than the county commissions of Pennsylvania and the southern Midwest. For example, in 1895, Wisconsin's Fond du Lac County contained twenty-one townships and three cities with a total of fifteen wards. Since each township and

ward had a representative on the county board, that body consisted of thirty-six supervisors. Some Wisconsin county boards had as many as sixty members. Because of their relatively large size, these boards more closely resembled legislative assemblies than the smaller county commissions. Yet like the commissions, the boards exercised executive and administrative powers as well as the legislative authority to levy taxes and appropriate funds. To facilitate administration, the larger boards were divided into committees, each charged with supervising a certain function. The board as a whole virtually always approved the decisions of these committees.

In this northern tier of states, the township meeting was formulated as the township's legislature. Like the New England town meeting, it was ideally a gathering of all eligible electors, who were given the opportunity to express their views and vote directly on the township levy and elect the supervisor and other officers. Yet by the close of the century, participation in township meetings had fallen to such a point that in many areas they seemed to have a minimal role in policy-making. In townships with five hundred to six hundred voters, it was commonplace for only ten to twenty persons to show at annual meetings. Some communities had more active meetings, and a heated controversy could swell attendance figures, but few such controversies seem to have stirred township voters. Without a vigilant and concerned electorate, the supervisor and other officers enjoyed a freer hand over township affairs.

The County Court Whereas the northern states opted for boards of supervisors or county commissions, the county court continued to dominate local government in much of the South during the first half of the nineteenth century. The Revolution wrought little change in the structure of local government in Maryland, Virginia, and North Carolina, where the justices remained life-tenure appointees of the governor or legislature, and Virginia's governors continued to make their appointments on the basis of recommendations from the county court itself. Moreover, this system spread westward to Kentucky, Tennessee, and Arkansas, though Arkansas's first constitution (1836) provided for the popular election of justices. Not until 1850–1851, however, did democratic sentiments finally force Virginia, Maryland, and

Kentucky to require the election of county magistrates. Until that time, the traditional local oligarchy remained relatively undisturbed. With no regard for separation of powers, these county justices continued to try suits, supervise elections, dole out poor relief, regulate taverns, appoint slave patrols, levy taxes, and oversee all the other functions of county government. Whereas northern commissioners or supervisors only combined the duties of executive and legislator, their southern counterparts remained judicial officials as well throughout the first half of the century.

Although the Revolution caused no upheaval in the structure of southern local government, the Civil War did force marked change. During Reconstruction, carpetbaggers imposed midwestern forms of government on much of the South, transplanting the county-commission structure in Virginia, North Carolina, and South Carolina. Unlike earlier county courts, these commissions did not exercise judicial power. In Kentucky, Tennessee, and Arkansas, however, the traditional framework survived throughout the remainder of the century and justices of the peace retained their executive, legislative, and judicial authority.

The School District   During the nineteenth century an additional unit of government appeared throughout the nation. This was the school district, often a subdivision of the township and thus the smallest unit of local rule. A county superintendent or county board of education generally exercised some supervisory authority over schools, as did township trustees in those states where they existed. But the district's board of directors or trustees had primary responsibility for education. As with so many local institutions, the school board enjoyed both legislative and executive authority, though in the typical large district, administrative responsibilities devolved on a school superintendent appointed by the board.

In many states the school board had to answer to the system's most basic decision-making body, the school-district meeting. Similar to its township counterpart, this meeting was a congregation of the district's eligible voters. Yet it was actually more democratic than the town meeting, for by the close of the century many states had extended voting rights in school matters to women. Both mothers and fathers were to have a voice in the education of their children, determining how much should be spent for schooling, who should serve as district school directors and trustees, and how school property should be managed and maintained.

As with the other examples of direct democracy, the school-district meeting had many defenders who lauded it as the purest form of grass-roots rule. Yet by the late nineteenth century, a number of critics viewed it as an obstacle to achieving higher professional standards in education and as an obsolete relic of pioneer existence. Moreover, as with township meetings, attendance was uneven. In the 1880s, New Hampshire's state superintendent of education said of the school district that "it was difficult to secure a quorum at its meetings, and when secured, if there was not some quarrel on the carpet, they were generally very stupid affairs" (quoted in M'Donald, "Independent District System," p. 217). In 1891 a Kansas critic described one meeting, at which "there were present three persons, the director *ex officio* occupying the chair, a husband and wife constituting the deliberative assembly, supreme council or parliament of the district." This Kansan also reported that, "the husband offered the resolutions, the wife seconded them, the director put them, and they were carried unanimously." This same critic also claimed, however, that the meetings had been "the source and generator of perennial feuds, the focal point to which all neighborhood animosities converge, the storm centre of every district" (quoted in M'Donald, p. 217). According to his critical eye, both apathy and chaos characterized the district meeting.

The County Delegation to the State Legislature   The school-district meetings, county commissions, and city councils each laid down rules and regulations for their governmental units and imposed the taxes to pay for local services. But perhaps as important a local law-making body as any of these was the county delegation to the state legislature. During the nineteenth century, state legislatures passed thousands of local laws authorizing public improvements for specific municipalities, additional public offices or boards for individual localities, and special levies applying to only a single city or county. Such local laws filled volumes, and in actuality they were the product of the county legislative delegation. In state legislatures as in city councils, measures applying to only one locality were the responsibility of the legislators from that locality. They reviewed such proposals, and if they endorsed the local bills, these measures usually passed the legislature as a whole. For example, in 1875 the Saint Louis delegation in the Missouri House and Senate made thirty-one recommendations regarding bills dealing with the local government of Saint Louis, and in every case the legislature accepted the cues of the delegation and acted according to the recommendation. In two-thirds of the votes, the Missouri House or Senate unanimously endorsed the will of the local delegation. According to prevailing legislative etiquette, the Saint Louis delegation was in charge of legislation dealing solely with Saint Louis, and as a result of this etiquette, the legislative delegation played a significant role in the resolution of local questions.

In a few states, the county legislative delegation even determined county appropriations and fixed the county tax levy. Both Connecticut and New Hampshire granted control over county finances to an institution known as the county convention. In Connecticut, each county convention consisted of the members of both houses of the state legislature from that county, and in New Hampshire it comprised all of the county's members in the lower house of the legislature. By the close of the century, county delegations in South Carolina wielded similar power. That state's legislature enacted the annual supply bill for each county in the state. This bill was basically the county budget, specifying the appropriations for the coming year. Although such measures required the formal approval of the entire legislature, in fact, each county legislative delegation fashioned the supply bill for its own locality and it alone determined how county officials spent tax dollars. As in Connecticut and New Hampshire, the power over the county purse rested with the locally elected state senators and representatives and not with county commissioners or supervisors.

By the close of the nineteenth century, it seemed as if American localities had tried virtually every form of government. America's large municipalities adopted the federal model of separation of powers and created a distinct legislative branch. Yet during the latter half of the century power gravitated to the executive, as many city dwellers came to equate the mu-

nicipal council with parochialism, incompetence, and corruption. Boards or commissions combining legislative, administrative, and executive authority presided over the government of most northern and western counties. In the South, however, the all-purpose county court survived, and during the first half of the century this meant a concentration of power in the hands of a self-appointed body of leading landholders. For Virginians, Kentuckians, and many other southerners, the principles both of democracy and separation of powers simply did not apply at the local level. In much of the nation, though, the direct democracy of the town or township meeting maximized the voice of the individual elector. And in school government, the district meetings perpetuated this tradition. From oligarchy to direct democracy, from separation of powers to concentration of authority in a single body, the institutions of American local government ran the entire gamut.

THE EARLY TWENTIETH CENTURY

Although American localities in the past had employed a wide range of governmental forms and procedures, by the beginning of the twentieth century an increasing number of observers seemed dissatisfied with all the varied efforts at structuring local rule. A chorus of critics loudly attacked city government and called for a restructuring of the municipal framework. Something had to be done about the city legislature, with its tobacco-spitting, saloon-owning aldermen. County government also was the target of criticism. Lacking a single executive and without a true legislative body, it seemed unable to handle the problems confronting it. In the eyes of many observers, even the time-honored town meeting appeared in need of an overhaul. During the first two decades of the twentieth century, interest in restructuring government thus reached a peak. In one state after another malcontents were crying for new forms of local rule and more effective legislative institutions at the city, county, and town level.

City-Government Reforms

The Commission Plan   In an effort to improve city government, some urban reformers attempted to reverse the long-term trend toward an increasing separation of powers based on the model of the federal government. Beginning with Galveston, Texas, in 1901, cities across the nation experimented with the commission plan, which placed executive, administrative, and legislative authority in the hands of a single body. Although individual cities modified the plan in various ways, in its purest form the scheme provided for a council of five commissioners elected from the city at large rather than from wards or districts. Each commission member was responsible for one division of city government. Thus, one member of the small council supervised finances, another public safety, and another public works. Proponents of the plan claimed that it guaranteed more efficient and responsible administration. Voters could readily pinpoint praise or blame, defeating the commissioner charged with public safety in the wake of a crime wave or the commissioner of public works when the sewers backed up. Moreover, elections at-large eliminated rule by neighborhood representatives concerned only with the parochial demands of a single ward. The reform scheme sought to ensure that the ablest figures with citywide appeal would take charge, displacing the saloon keepers and ward heelers.

By the beginning of the second decade of the twentieth century the commission plan was all the rage in reform circles. At the close of 1913, 337 municipalities had embraced the scheme, with 245 adoptions in the previous three years alone. Small cities were more likely to adopt the commission plan than were large metropolises, but the converts did include such prominent municipalities as Jersey City, Omaha, New Orleans, Denver, Oakland, and Portland, Oregon.

As an increasing number of cities turned to commission rule, the scheme began to garner some sharp criticism. A growing number of observers lambasted the multiheaded commission, claiming that a city needed a single executive to guide its course. "Think of running a ship with five captains," remarked the mayor of Wichita, Kansas. "No marine insurance company would take such a risk, and the boat would in all probability drift on the rocks while the captains were trying to settle their differences as to how the boat should be run" (Rice, p. 91). Moreover, critics claimed that

elected commission members lacked the expertise necessary to administer their departments effectively. One detractor noted simply, "When you want representation, elect. When you want administration, appoint" (Rice, p. 93). In the minds of many concerned citizens, then, a single elected body of administrator-legislators did not appear to be the best solution to municipal ills.

The City-Manager Plan   As flaws in the commission scheme became apparent, the city-manager plan developed as a reform alternative. Under this form of government, the city council retained full legislative authority and was responsible for determining municipal policy. Control over day-to-day administration, however, rested with a single appointed expert known as the city manager. In 1913, Dayton, Ohio, became the first major city to adopt the plan, and by the end of 1923, the number of cities employing managers had risen to 269. Again the scheme seemed best suited to smaller municipalities, yet during the 1920s Cleveland, Cincinnati, and Kansas City, Missouri, all joined the list of manager cities.

Manager rule was supposed to enhance the significance of the council, for that body was to be the undisputed local policymaker and no powerful mayor existed to infringe on council authority. In fact, the council often followed the lead of the city manager, and municipal legislators did not necessarily assume a commanding role in policy determination. In 1923 one observer remarked, "The success of the manager plan is due largely to the complete separation of the legislative from the executive function . . . [yet] because of the mediocre ability of the leaders of the legislative body, the executive [the city manager] now is frequently the chief legislative officer of the government" (Stone, Price, and Stone, p. 253). Specifically, in the manager city of Cleveland, many complained that the council members were so preoccupied with running constituent errands and with serving the interests of their wards that they could not possibly direct the affairs of the city as a whole. Cleveland's dynamic city manager filled the void left by the parochial legislators and, in the process, usurped much of the policy-determining power of the council.

In many smaller cities, and especially in suburban municipalities, the city-manager plan proved satisfactory to voters, and the number of communities adopting the scheme continued to increase throughout the 1920s and 1930s. Meanwhile, the commission plan grew less popular, and many commission cities eventually switched to manager rule. In any case, the traditional mayor-council form of government was no longer the unchallenged framework for municipal rule in America.

Changes in the Mayor-Council Plan
Even where the mayor-council plan survived, there were often changes in this traditional scheme. In many cities, reformers fought for the creation of a small council of seven or nine members to supplant the unwieldy larger bodies of the nineteenth century. Ideally, these councils would also be elected at large, not by wards. To further cleanse the political system, good-government crusaders argued for nonpartisan elections. According to reform elements, citizens needed to vote for the best person, regardless of party label. Party tags, it was argued, threatened the quality of city government, for they diverted voters' attention from the serious issues under debate and enhanced the role of corrupt party bosses. By 1934, of the twenty-four mayor-council cities with populations over two hundred thousand, fifteen elected council members on a nonpartisan ballot and four had councils of seven to nine members elected at large. Two others had nine-member councils elected by wards. Yet New York City's board of aldermen still had more than seventy members, and fifty persons served in Chicago's legislative body. Moreover, political reality could differ from the official blueprint. In some purportedly nonpartisan cities the party organizations continued to determine who would run for council, and voters were well aware which candidates were Republicans and which were Democrats.

The Initiative and Referendum Procedure
Although council members were seen as the principal molders of municipal policy, reform-minded Americans were not content to give these legislators a monopoly over policy determination. Instead, in the first two decades of the twentieth century, many civic crusaders sought to transfer some legislative authority to the individual voters and consequently included initiative and referendum in their reform package. Under the procedure of initiative and referendum, voters could initiate charter proposals or ordinances by submitting a petition signed by a specified percentage of the electorate. The proposal would then appear on the ballot, and if ratified by a majority of the voters, it would become law, no matter what the city council thought. In other words, the electorate could legislate without relying on their elected representatives. Municipal charters also could require that certain council-initiated measures won the approval of a majority of the electorate. No matter whether the measure was initiated by the voters or the municipal legislature, the referendum procedure granted the electorate a new and enhanced role in the legislative process.

Yet initiative and referendum were intended to be exceptional safeguards, rather than the legislative norm. Supporters of these reforms believed that the procedures could be used to protect the electorate from an incompetent or corrupt legislative body, but the council or commission was still expected to enact the overwhelming majority of all ordinances and to determine basic municipal policy. "Advocates of the initiative and referendum staunchly defend the representative system of legislation," wrote the reformer C. F. Taylor, "but recognize that its operations, for reasons of dishonesty or lack of understanding, may not be truly representative of the sentiments, desires and welfare of the represented" (quoted in Woodruff, ed., *A New Municipal Program*, p. 160). Initiative and referendum were, then, proposed as checks on existing legislative institutions and were not introduced to supplant municipal councils or commissions.

Home Rule Another popular reform of the early twentieth century further revised the framework of lawmaking in American cities. For decades reformers had complained about state legislative interference as a source of corruption and irresponsible government at the local level and, by the turn of the century, increasing numbers of good-government devotees were sponsoring home-rule amendments to state constitutions. These constitutional provisions deprived state legislatures of the authority to enact municipal charters for cities desiring home rule. Instead, in each such city, a locally elected charter commission fashioned the framework of government, and the new charter took effect after it won the approval of the city's electorate. Moreover, the provisions gave city governments authority to handle all municipal affairs, subject only to the general laws of the state. Although courts differed in their interpretation of home rule, for the most part state legislatures could no longer legislate on specific local questions. Such questions were exclusively a municipal responsibility. By 1920, thirteen states had adopted home-rule articles in their constitutions and more than two hundred municipalities were operating under charters framed in accord with these provisions. Among the municipalities were fifteen of the thirty largest cities in the nation.

Because of the prevailing state-legislative practice of deferring to a local delegation on issues affecting its district only, home rule did not shift authority from outsiders in the state capital to locals. Instead, it transferred authority from one set of locally elected officials to another. Home rule robbed the local delegation to the state legislature of some of its clout by attempting to ensure that the delegation would no longer make municipal policy. The goal was to heighten public scrutiny and control of the lawmaking process by limiting behind-the-scenes dealings with the local delegation and by empowering popularly chosen charter commissions and enhancing the role of municipal councils. To a large degree, home-rule provisions realized this aim. State measures affecting only a single locality diminished in number, and municipal bodies assumed greater control over local policy.

Thus, home rule closed one alternative channel for lawmaking at the same time initiative and referendum opened a new one. No longer could one readily obviate the will of the municipal council by appealing to the state legislature. But one could bypass the local lawmakers by initiating a proposal and winning voter approval. This latter means of evading the authority of the council did not lend itself to surreptitious action. Unlike the traditional recourse to the legislative delegation, the process of initiative and referendum took place in the open, before the public's eyes.

Reforms in County Rule   Although reformers targeted city government for their heaviest blasts, they did not overlook the shortcomings of county rule. Many civic crusaders believed the structure of county government was as rotten as the urban framework and as much in need of a thorough overhauling. In 1917, H. S. Gilbertson titled a book describing the backward and insufficiently explored institution of county government *The County: The "Dark Continent" of American Politics*, and his chapter on the seeming irrationalities of the county structure is titled "The 'Jungle'." Others also castigated the senile institutions of county government and the inefficiencies produced by a framework that lacked any sense or reason. One reform-minded critic was so disgusted by county rule that he suggested virtually abolishing the county as a political unit. For him "no county at all" was the "theoretically perfect county" ("County Government," p. 278).

Basic to the complaints of reformers was dissatisfaction with the headless form of county rule. There was no single executive coordinating county affairs, and the elected county clerks, auditors, assessors, and sheriffs acted independently of the county boards or commissions. The boards or commissions did not appoint such officials, who ran their offices as they wished. Without a separation of powers, it seemed unclear who actually made policy for the county and who ultimately was in charge of executing it. In the words of H. S. Gilbertson, county government was a "wilderness of conflicting responsibility" with "no single officer who could be called the executive" (pp. 35–36).

The solution seemed to be to restructure the county, with executive and legislative authority more clearly allocated to specific officers or bodies. As early as 1901, in an article entitled "Responsibility in County Government," one student of local rule, Samuel E. Sparling, suggested: "A separation of legislative and executive functions, accompanied by popular control over the fiscal affairs of the county by a widely representative body, seems to be the more probable solution of the difficulties surrounding our county government" (p. 449). Twelve years later, a study of Illinois local government likewise urged passage of a law that would grant executive authority to the county clerk or some other county official, and would create county councils empowered to levy taxes, make appropriations, and enact local legislation.

The County-Manager Plan   During the second decade of the century, an increasing number of commentators felt adaptation of the manager plan to county government would provide the necessary leadership. For example, an Oregon reformer proposed a board of directors to serve as the county's legislative body, and a "county business manager" who would "hire all the other county officers and hold the same position towards county business that . . . the general manager of an American private corporation holds towards the business of his company" ("County Government," p. 272). The leading promoter of the city-manager plan, Richard Childs, also recommended the hiring of county managers who "should be expert, experienced and reasonably permanent." According to Childs, the county board or commission "would then be purely the policy-determining body . . . with full power to levy the taxes" ("County Government," p. 277). Thus, one reformer after another suggested unraveling the tangled lines of county authority and creating a legislative branch restricted to policy determination, and a single official responsible for policy execution.

County Home Rule   During the early twentieth century, the traditional structure of county rule proved much more resistant to innovation than the city framework. Reform rhetoric produced little change, and civic crusaders scored few victories. Most encouraging was the development of county home rule, permitting individual counties to create their own governmental structure rather than conform to a blueprint drawn by the state legislature. In 1911, California became the first state to provide for county home rule, and Los Angeles County's home-rule charter of 1912 won reform applause. It concentrated authority in the five-member board of supervisors and reduced the number of elected county officers. Henceforth, the supervisors would appoint the principal officials and thus would have greater control over county affairs. Yet still the idea of separation of powers was ignored. The supervisors were both executives and legislators, determining and executing policy. Chosen by district, like a member of Congress, each supervisor was in fact recognized as virtual mayor of the area electing him or her.

Before 1930 Maryland alone joined California in adopting a county home-rule provision in its constitution. Moreover, the county-manager idea only slowly won adherents. Iredell County, North Carolina, was the first to try this scheme, adopting it in 1927. Yet, as late as 1950, only sixteen of the more than three thousand counties in the nation had appointed administrators comparable to city managers. During the early twentieth century, reformers laid the foundation for future changes in county rule, but the construction of a new framework on that foundation proceeded at a snail's pace before World War II.

Changes in the New England Town Meeting

Reform sentiment not only affected cities and counties but also produced some changes in the New England town meeting. As many New England towns grew more populous, it became increasingly difficult to assemble all qualified voters. Generally, no building existed to accommodate such a congregation, and since no one knew every town resident in the larger communities, outsiders could wander into meetings and vote illegally. Excessive attendance, however, was only an occasional problem. Most often, a small percentage of the eligible voters attended meetings, and consequently the few concerned citizens, together with those who had a special interest to pursue and those who had nothing better to do, decided local questions. In other words, at the beginning of the twentieth century, the traditional town meeting could prove ungainly and most often was unrepresentative of the entire community.

The Representative Town Meeting   To remedy these problems, in 1915 the suburban town of Brookline, Massachusetts, with a population of thirty-three thousand, created the limited or representative town meeting. Henceforth, Brookline voters were to elect approximately 240 "town meeting members" who were charged with attending the meetings and voting for those whom they represented. Every voter could show up at the meetings and participate in the debates, but only the elected members could vote on the issues. In Brookline, then, a representative form of government supplanted the traditional direct democracy. Other towns followed Brookline's example, and by 1930 eighteen Massachusetts towns had adopted the representative town meeting.

Therefore, during the early twentieth century, reformers had finally modified the ancient institution of the town meeting and challenged the confusing but venerable structure of county rule. Civic-minded citizens achieved their most notable changes in the cities, but in city, suburb, and countryside there was action to rectify the shortcomings of local legislative institutions. Commission rule, the city-manager plan, initiative and referendum, home rule, separation of powers at the county level, and the representative town meeting were all legacies of this reform era.

THE LATE TWENTIETH CENTURY

Following World War II, there was no revival of the earlier enthusiasm for restructuring local government. Changes occurred, but the crusading spirit of the first decades of the twentieth century had disappeared. Most institutional adaptation in the last half of the twentieth century was a pragmatic response to suburbanization and changing population patterns. Although a new concern for ethnic equality resulted in some revisions, the desire for better services, rather than any demand for a purer democracy, most often motivated the creation of new local units and the rehabilitation of older ones.

Institutional Continuity at the Town Level

As in previous eras, there was a notable degree of institutional continuity as Americans demonstrated a preference for tradition and a suspicion of the novel. At the town level this was especially evident, for despite repeated testimony to its impracticality and unrepresentative nature, the traditional New England town meeting open to all voters proved remarkably durable. Many towns refused to switch to the representative town meeting and, by 1984, only forty-nine Massachusetts towns had adopted this reform, with just nine adoptions in the previous twenty-five years. Massachusetts law authorized any town of six thousand inhabitants or more to install the representative form, but 113 of the communities in this category chose not to do so. Not until 1935 did any Maine town adopt the representative town meeting, and twenty-two years passed before another town in that state opted for the reform. By the early 1980s, only seven towns in Connecticut and one in Vermont had representative town

meetings, and no communities in Rhode Island or New Hampshire had such governing bodies. Clearly, the open town meeting had proved a survivor, tenaciously deflecting the criticisms that threatened it.

Both the city-manager and mayor-council schemes also survived intact, remaining the two principal plans of city government. Moreover, manager rule still proved more popular in smaller cities, whereas mayor-council government was the norm in the largest municipalities. Meanwhile, the commission plan of city government continued to lose support. In 1960 its birthplace city of Galveston even discarded the plan, and only inertia seemed to keep other communities in the commission fold. By the late 1980s only 171 of the nation's cities with populations of more than twenty-five hundred still had a commission form of government. In comparison, 3,664 cities adhered to the mayor-council scheme and 2,385 municipalities employed a city manager.

At-Large Elections versus District Elections During the decades following World War II, debate continued as well over at-large versus district election of the municipal legislature. In the 1940s and 1950s, good-government advocates won many supporters to the at-large option by raising the old specter of ward-boss rule. But by the 1970s and 1980s a new emphasis on neighborhood power and adequate representation for ethnic minorities resulted in revived demands for election by district. One study found that during the 1970s a switch from at-large to district representation either took place or was attempted in fifty cities having populations greater than one hundred thousand. The shift was especially notable in southern cities, where blacks felt at-large systems had been part of the longstanding legal structure of racial discrimination. The white majority in the city as a whole traditionally elected white members to the city council or commission, denying black neighborhoods within the community an effective voice in public affairs. In 1980 the U.S. Supreme Court upheld at-large elections in Mobile, Alabama, but the fight persisted. In the minds of many voters in the 1970s and 1980s, equality outweighed efficiency, and the parts were as important as the whole. Consequently, it was felt that neighborhood representation deserved renewed support.

LOCAL LEGISLATIVE INSTITUTIONS

Changes in County Government

The most noteworthy changes in local government institutions occurred at the county level. Massive postwar migration to the metropolitan fringe resulted in a sharp increase in the number of Americans living in unincorporated areas outside the boundaries of any municipality, and dependent chiefly on county services. In addition, as an increasing proportion of America's population moved to the myriad of small suburban municipalities, county governments provided some needed coordination among the cities and villages and offered some services that smaller units could not afford to supply on their own. At the same time, beleaguered central cities faced with declining populations and rising costs sought to transfer some of their responsibilities to the counties and allowed county governments to assume new tasks that the cities might have been willing to shoulder in earlier decades. These changes resulted in an unprecedented expansion of county government and new demands for the modernization and reform of the structure of county rule. Whereas the expenditures of America's cities rose 126 percent between 1977 and 1978 and 1987 and 1988, the outlay of the nation's counties increased 138 percent during this same decade. America's counties were no longer simply supplying minimal services to rural areas. By the late 1980s they spent more than $100 billion annually, and they needed governments capable of administering effectively their manifold programs.

Separation of Powers   Responding to the new imperative, an increasing number of counties turned to the time-honored idea of separation of powers, creating for the first time distinct executive and legislative branches. In the 1930s suburban Nassau and Westchester counties in New York each decided to establish an elected chief executive comparable to a mayor, and suburban Saint Louis County, Missouri, did likewise in 1950. But as late as 1960, only eight counties in the United States had an elected chief executive. During the ensuing two decades the situation changed rapidly. By 1987, at least 391 counties in thirty-one states had a council-elected executive scheme of government similar to the mayor-council form found in cities. As an increasing number of

states adopted provisions for county home rule, counties were able to eliminate the standard commission structure and adopt in its place this new framework. In some cases the state had to impose the council-elected executive form on its counties. In 1974 a constitutional amendment required all 75 of Arkansas's counties to install council-elected executive arrangements. Four years later the Kentucky legislature mandated that every county maintain a chief executive officer and a legislative body known as the fiscal court. That same year, a Tennessee constitutional amendment specified that each county establish a legislature of nine to twenty-five members and an executive with veto power over local legislative measures.

Moreover, by 1987 at least 422 counties in thirty-six states had adopted a council-administrator structure approximating the city-manager framework. As in the case of the elected executive structure, the majority of these adoptions occurred after 1960. Supporters of the administrator and executive schemes proved so successful that by the 1980s a majority of Americans lived in counties with either an elected chief executive or an appointed manager. The commission or board form was no longer the norm.

Thus after more than three centuries, counties were finally moving toward the creation of distinctively legislative institutions charged with determining policy but without executive or administrative authority. Strict separation of powers did not necessarily prevail, for in many counties the elected executive was also a member of the council or commission. Yet the clear trend was toward imitating the structure of city government and discarding the venerable peculiarities of the county framework.

Reapportionment   During the 1960s the reapportionment decisions of the U.S. Supreme Court also forced changes in county institutions. This was especially true in such states as New York, Michigan, Wisconsin, and Illinois, where each township, regardless of population, had equal representation on the governing board of supervisors. Population was not the basis for apportionment; instead, the township was the basic unit of representation and the county board was an assembly of emissaries from equally powerful townships. Consequently, in the mid-1960s in Kent County,

Michigan, Vergennes Township, with 945 residents, had a single board member, as did Plainfield Township, with fifteen thousand inhabitants. After the Supreme Court's adoption of a "one person, one vote" standard, such arrangements were no longer constitutional and had to yield to county boards or commissions whose members represented districts of equal population without regard for township boundaries. Henceforth county board members would represent people rather than townships.

Special Districts Not only did Americans of the late twentieth century witness dramatic changes in county government institutions, but they also experienced the proliferation of special districts. Although many school districts disappeared owing to consolidation, there were thousands of new fire protection, drainage, park, soil conservation, cemetery, and water supply districts as well as other small units charged with limited tasks. Specifically, between 1952 and 1987 the number of school districts dropped from 67,355 to 14,721, whereas the figure for nonschool special districts rose from 12,340 to 29,532. By the late 1980s nonschool special districts constituted more than one third of all local government units in the United States.

The governing structure of these special districts closely resembled that of the school district. A board was empowered to make basic policy but usually hired a manager or director comparable to a school superintendent to administer the district's business. As was often the case with school superintendents and city managers, in many districts this hired administrator actually determined policy, with the board generally acquiescing to its employee's initiatives. Board meetings were usually open to the public, but few citizens attended or seemed to understand what the board did, if in fact they even realized it existed. Performing mundane chores and attracting little media attention, the districts operated in relative obscurity, unknown elements in the complex puzzle of American local government.

CONCLUSION

From the colonial era through the close of the twentieth century, then, the people of the United States experimented with many units and forms of local government. Unlike at the federal or state levels, where the principle of separation of powers exercised a powerful influence, at the local level Americans were more flexible, sometimes embracing the principle, sometimes not. In the traditional governing structure of American counties, there was no strict separation of powers. Instead, county rule conformed to patterns that had developed during the colonial period, and this early framework remained remarkably durable. Not until the late twentieth century did distinctively legislative institutions develop in a large number of American counties. Meanwhile, urban Americans tried a wide range of formulas for better municipal government. Some communities adhered to the model of mayor-council government, with its distinct legislative and executive branches. Others turned to the commission plan or city-manager scheme. The local legislative process also included attempts at direct democracy. From the colonial town meeting to the twentieth-century practices of initiative and referendum, direct legislation played a role in the American governing process at the local level. Variety seemed to be one constant in American local government. Cities, counties, townships, and districts pursued a multitude of structural alternatives, in some cases displaying an unthinking reliance on past forms no matter how irrational, and in other instances demonstrating a remarkable ingenuity in developing novel schemes.

BIBLIOGRAPHY

County Government
Basic to the study of county government in the South are RALPH A. WOOSTER, *The People in Power: Courthouse and Statehouse in the* *Lower South, 1850–1860* (Knoxville, Tenn., 1969) and *Politicians, Planters, and Plain Folk: Courthouse and Statehouse in the Upper South, 1850–1860* (Knoxville, Tenn., 1975). An excel-

lent account of nineteenth-century county government in one state is found in ROBERT M. IRELAND, *The County Courts in Antebellum Kentucky* (Lexington, Ky., 1972) and *Little Kingdoms: The Counties of Kentucky, 1850–1891* (Lexington, Ky., 1977). CLAIR W. KELLER, "The Pennsylvania County Commission System, 1712 to 1740," *Pennsylvania Magazine of History and Biography* 93 (1969) is very useful on the origins of the county commission. "County Government," *Annals of the American Academy of Political and Social Science* 47 (1913) is a volume of articles offering an overview of county government in the United States during the early twentieth century.

For a brief summary of the state of county government in the mid-twentieth century, see CLYDE F. SNIDER, "American County Government: A Mid-Century Review," *American Political Science Review* 46 (1952). SAMUEL E. SPARLING, "Responsibility in County Government," *Political Quarterly* 16 (1901) offers a reform-minded critique of county rule at the turn of the century. For a short overview of the changes in county government, see VICTOR S. DESANTIS, "County Government: A Century of Change," *Municipal Year Book, 1989* (1989). The classic work on county government is H. S. GILBERTSON, *The County: The "Dark Continent" of American Politics* (New York, 1917). A fine account of the "county oligarchies" in colonial Virginia appears in CHARLES S. SYDNOR, *Gentlemen Freeholders: Political Practices in Washington's Virginia* (Chapel Hill, N.C., 1952).

Municipal Government

For information on the development of American municipal government, see JON C. TEAFORD, *The Municipal Revolution in America: Origins of Modern Urban Government, 1650–1825* (Chicago, 1975) and *The Unheralded Triumph: City Government in America, 1870–1900* (Baltimore, 1984). CLINTON R. WOODRUFF, ed., *A New Municipal Program* (New York, 1919) is a reform-minded publication of the National Municipal League. GEORGE W. EDWARDS and ARTHUR E. PETERSON, *New York as an Eighteenth-Century Municipality* (New York, 1917) is a detailed study of the government of colonial New York City. EDWIN A. GERE, JR., *Modernizing Local Government in Massachusetts: The Quest for Professionalism and Reform* (Lanham, Md., 1984) is a useful source on the twentieth-century New England town. Studies of local government in the colonial period include BRUCE C. DANIELS, *The Connecticut Town: Growth and Development, 1635–1790* (Middletown, Conn., 1979), *Dissent and Conformity on Narragansett Bay: The Colonial Rhode Island Town* (Middletown, Conn., 1984), and, as ed., *Town and County: Essays on the Structure of Local Government in the American Colonies* (Middletown, Conn., 1978). HAROLD A. STONE, DON K. PRICE, and KATHRYN H. STONE, *City Manager Government in the United States: A Review After Twenty-five Years* (Chicago, 1940) presents the successes and shortcomings of city-manager rule during the first quarter century of its existence. BRADLEY R. RICE, *Progressive Cities: The Commission Government Movement in America, 1901–1920* (Austin, Tex., 1977) presents the best account of the rise of city-commission government. JOHN FAIRFIELD SLY, *Town Government in Massachusetts, 1620–1930* (Cambridge, Mass., 1930) is a reliable account of the Massachusetts town.

Districts

JOHN C. BOLLENS, *Special District Governments in the United States* (Berkeley, Calif., 1957) is the standard work on special districts. JOHN A. M'DONALD, "The Independent District System," *Journal of Proceedings National Educational Association* (1891) offers insights into nineteenth-century school-district government. PEGGY HEILIG and ROBERT J. MUNDT, *Your Voice at City Hall: The Politics, Procedures, and Policies of District Representation* (Albany, 1984) deals with district representation in the late twentieth century.

SEE ALSO Colonial Assemblies AND Representation.

TERRITORIAL LEGISLATURES TO 1862

Jo Tice Bloom

Following independence in 1776, the new American politicians, in and out of Congress, knew that they would be dealing with the acquisition and government of new lands to the west. All of the new national politicians, except for a few conservatives, envisioned some form of western expansion—perhaps not the continental expansion envisioned by such dreamers as Benjamin Franklin and Thomas Jefferson—but they hoped at least to make the Mississippi River the western boundary of the new United States. These practical men, who had already created a revolution, then went on to create a new republic with its own colonial system. The framers of this colonial system had a major advantage over previous imperialists, for they had been colonials themselves and knew the problems of empire from the perspective that had brought about rebellion. They thus set out to devise a system of empire that would not provoke rebellion and that would function in a manner satisfactory both to the "mother Congress" and to the colonials.

One of the first steps was to employ a new terminology to refer to temporary government and, shortly thereafter, to territorial government, thus removing the stigma of such terms as *colony* and *empire* from the system. It was provided that the system would include some degree of self-government early in the territorial or colonial period through an elected legislature. But the executive power would be vested in officials appointed by the central government, which would bear much of the cost of the territorial governments. The American system offered the territories and their residents other features not usually available in empires: a congressional delegate, a guarantee of individual rights similar to those in states' bills of rights, and a guarantee of republican government and full membership in the Union as a state.

EARLY ORDINANCES AND TERRITORIAL EXPERIENCE

Ever since they first thought about the development of government for western lands, political thinkers and congressional leaders assumed that an elected legislature would be part of the temporary, or colonial, government in unincorporated territory. The Ordinance of 1784 provided that the "free males of full age" of a "state" could establish a temporary government, "adopt the constitution and laws of any one of the original states; so that such laws nevertheless shall be subject to alteration by their ordinary legislature; and to erect, subject to like alteration, counties, townships, or other divisions, for the election of members for their legislature."

The Northwest Territory

Since the Ordinance of 1784 was never used in the West, the drafters of the Northwest Ordinance of 1787 drew on their experiences as colonists themselves, as well as the express desires of land speculators, in shaping a more explicit law. Thus, in the second instrument, the framers started with rough outlines from the 1784 ordinance and added details that proved quite workable in the long term.

The newly created Northwest Territory was bounded by the states of New York and Pennsylvania on the east, the Ohio River on the south, the Mississippi River on the west, and the international boundary with Canada on the north. This vast area included all or parts of the future states of Ohio, Indiana, Illinois, Michigan, Wisconsin, and Minnesota. Initially the 1787 ordinance applied only to this area, although later legislation with amendments extended its basic provisions throughout the U.S. territories.

Under the Northwest Ordinance, the original legislature of a territory consisted of the governor and three judges, all of whom had the power to "adopt and publish in the district such laws of the original States, criminal and civil, as may be necessary and best suited to the circumstances of the district . . . [but after the elected legislature is established] the Legislature shall have authority to alter them as they shall think fit." In the Northwest Territory, the legislative power rested with these appointed officials from 1787 until 1797, when residents first elected a lower house. During those years, there was considerable controversy over the powers of the appointed "legislature."

The first question of dispute, and one that remained unresolved, was over the meaning of *adopt*. Did this term give the legislature the right to adapt or alter the laws of other states? Or did this mean that the laws must retain their original wording when adopted in the Northwest Territory? During the ten-year period of 1788–1798, this controversy was never settled satisfactorily for those espousing either interpretation. The fact that the legislature "adapted" laws was a basis for charges that Arthur St. Clair, governor of the Northwest Territories, was a tyrant, as will be described below.

By 1797 the population of the territory had increased significantly, election districts were laid out, and a lower house was elected by the residents. Then an upper house was appointed by President John Adams from a list of names submitted by the lower house, and the first legislature came into existence in the Northwest Territory. It was given power to regulate and define the duties of magistrates and other civil officers and to make "laws in all cases, for the good government of the district." The governor's powers were similar to those of colonial governors, including an absolute veto and power to convene, prorogue (to terminate by executive prerogative), and dissolve the general assembly. In many respects, the territorial general assembly resembled the old English colonial legislature: the lower house was elected by the residents; its members were required to own property, as were the members of the upper house, or council; and the voters also had to meet a property-holding requirement.

A difference from colonial practice existed in the makeup of the council, in that the lower house nominated ten persons for appointment as councilmen. In practice, this usually meant that the governor recommended candidates to the president, who recommended to Congress, which made the final appointments. In colonial times, in contrast, the lower house had no power over the appointment of council members in royal and proprietary colonies.

In the Northwest Territory the establishment of an elected legislature provided a new forum for open opposition to the governor, and in the first session a struggle began in 1798 between Governor St. Clair and the elected representatives. An early battle concerned the election of the territorial delegate to Congress. St. Clair's son was a leading candidate, as was William Henry Harrison, scion of a prominent Virginia family and son-in-law to John Cleves Symmes, a territorial judge who often opposed St. Clair. The election resulted in Harrison's victory, reflecting the increasing number of Virginia land speculators in the territory and the developing Jeffersonian Republican party.

Another conflict between the governor and members of the legislature surfaced over the method of voting. In 1800, Governor St. Clair recommended that secret paper ballots be used instead of voice voting. The lower house opposed this and continued voice voting on the grounds that "if a man is not strong enough to stand up for his opinions openly he doesn't deserve the vote."

As the population increased, the movement for statehood gained momentum, especially among former Virginians and Republicans. Both Governor St. Clair and the Federalists opposed statehood and controlled the legislature. Congress eventually admitted Ohio over the protests of the territorial delegate, the governor, and a majority of the territorial legislature.

The Southwest Territory

Although government in the Northwest Territory was the first to be organized, the first elected territorial legislature met in Knoxville in the Southwest Territory in 1794. In ceding this land to the United States, North Carolina had provided that "the inhabitants shall enjoy all the privileges, benefits and advantages set forth in the ordinance of the late Congress for the Government of the Western territory of the United States . . . *Provided always* that no regulations made or to be made by Congress shall tend to emancipate Slaves." The 1790 organizing act for the Southwest Territory simply stated that the inhabitants of the new territory would enjoy all the same privileges, rights, and form of government as established in the Northwest Territory and as provided for in the act of cession. Thus, the Southwest Territory was similar to the Northwest Territory, with the major exception of the legal status of slavery.

The first territorial legislature met in the late summer of 1794 and began the process of providing the Southwest Territory with more counties and better roads and solving the myriad of other issues that it could address by legislative actions. It elected the first territorial delegate to sit in Congress, Dr. James White, a prominent longtime resident and a supporter of territorial governor William Blount. There was little conflict within the two houses of the legislature or between the legislature and the governor because most of the members were land speculators, as was Blount. Many of these leaders, including Blount and White, had been involved in the earlier state of Franklin, which existed between 1784 and 1787, and were old political friends. They were of one mind in seeking to achieve statehood. White went to Philadelphia with that primary goal and recommended to Blount in the spring of 1795 that the general assembly of the territory should take the initiative. Accordingly, the legislature called for a census and a constitutional convention at its second session, in late summer 1795. The following year, the Southwest Territory entered the Union as the state of Tennessee.

POWERS AND DUTIES OF TERRITORIAL LEGISLATURES

Most territorial legislatures were bicameral, although Florida and Michigan had unicameral legislatures throughout their territorial periods. The duties and responsibilities of the legislatures were similar, calling for the general assemblies to legislate on local matters and to pay the cost of local officials, roads, and buildings from taxes levied on the residents by the legislature or county courts.

A major responsibility of the general assembly of every territory was to establish counties. As territorial populations grew, the number of counties increased. Since most representatives in the legislatures were chosen by counties, their boundaries were of great importance to the legislature and to the citizens. Most of the local officials were county officials, such as sheriffs, judges, and tax collectors, and the creation of additional counties meant more government jobs, even though many did not pay well.

The establishment of lower courts and their jurisdictions were significant matters to the residents. The most common courts, those of quarter sessions, often had typically legislative and administrative responsibilities to levy taxes, build roads, issue licenses, and carry out other such duties normally beyond the role of a court of law. The legislature had the privilege of creating the lower-court system and determining the jurisdiction of lower courts in accord with English common law (judicial decisions based on custom or precedent, unwritten in statute or code), and American tradition. In addition to courts of quarter sessions, there were courts of common pleas, probate courts, and justices of the peace. In some territories, justices of the peace were elective, but often they were appointed, along with other judges, by the legislature or the governor. In some territories, there were also superior courts, on which the members of the territorial supreme court sat. Because of sparse population, court sessions were held infrequently. The judges traveled throughout the territory, holding court sessions on a regular schedule in various communities—riding horseback around a set circuit of towns.

One of the first obligations of a territorial legislature, whether appointed or elected, was to draft civil and criminal codes. At first, they were adopted from other states, as noted above. For instance, the first legislature in Kansas Territory simply took the Missouri Code and changed the name from the "State of Missouri" to the "Territory of Kansas" wherever appropriate throughout both civil and criminal codes. As the years passed, each general assembly would alter its codes to meet the needs of its respective territory.

General assemblies were also responsible for organizing the militia. The senior officers were usually appointed by the governor, and junior officers were elected by the troops. The militia was a vital matter in terms of defense against Indians in the early territories. Occasionally a legislature would pass laws applying to Indians, as in Arkansas Territory. Here the legislature not only prohibited the sale of liquor to Native Americans, a common state and territorial law, but even prohibited the sale of horses to them. The criminal code stated that any person with one quarter or more Native American blood could not give testimony in court in criminal cases.

The territorial legislatures regulated marriage and divorce; in 1848, for example, the Wisconsin General Assembly granted twenty-four divorces by private bills. The general assemblies also provided for the establishment and maintenance of schools, incorporated cities and towns, established prisons and asylums, and built the territorial capitol. They authorized the building of roads, ditches, bridges, and ferries and licensed the ferries and toll-road operators. They legislated on issues such as fences, horses running loose, and many other mundane matters of life.

General assemblies had great economic influence. They could charter banks and other businesses and could establish tax rates. During its territorial period (1836–1848), the Wisconsin General Assembly chartered seventy-three businesses, with twenty-nine in 1848 alone. The charters included forty for such internal improvements as the construction of new piers, bridges, canals, steamboats, railroads, plank roads, and turnpikes. Eleven insurance companies were chartered, as were eleven mining companies. Manufacturing companies received six charters. In addition to controlling licenses for transportation facilities such as ferries, territorial legislatures also licensed taverns, inns, and other public houses.

The banking business was a major concern, for the territories initially were without banks and often without ample currency or, of course, credit. Banks not only provided ease of business transactions, but were usually authorized also to issue bank notes, which eased the currency shortage. Since each bank received an individual legislative charter, banks were often the "pets" of members of the legislature and were not financially sound, leading to unwelcome additional difficulties in the economy. Although the Wisconsin territorial legislature chartered only seven banks, legislation concerning one of them was disallowed by Congress, which was the only time such action was

taken by the national legislature in regard to Wisconsin. This suggests the tenuous nature of territorial banking procedures. Through regulation of mortgages, bankruptcies, and debtor punishment, the legislatures exercised additional economic influence.

Territorial legislatures sent petitions and memorials to Congress on a regular basis, requesting aid of all kinds, mostly legislative or economic. They requested federal funds for roads, river improvements, bridges, prisons, courthouses, capitol buildings, and printing costs. They asked for protection against Indians. The Arkansas General Assembly petitioned the federal government to control Native Americans by surrounding them with white settlements, calling the Cherokee "a restless, dissatisfied, insolent, and ambitious tribe, engaged in constant intrigues with neighboring tribes, to foment difficulties." The memorials protested gubernatorial actions, asked for the recall of governors and judges, and requested authority for popular election of delegates and other officials. They sought better postal service, more liberal land laws, and compensation for those who suffered depredations during the War of 1812 and subsequent white-Indian conflicts. The Michigan legislature sought aid from the federal government to establish a silkworm industry, since the territory had a native species of mulberry tree. Every issue of concern to a territorial legislature usually found a place in a petition to Congress at some time.

Another such issue involved the question of who should finance the costs of territorial legislatures. Until 1822, territories paid the expenses of their legislatures, a burden often cited in trying to delay the change to an elected legislature. Although the amounts pale beside those of twentieth-century legislatures, they loomed as substantial expenditures to the territories, which always suffered a lack of cash and had great difficulty in tax collecting. After receiving territorial petitions, Congress agreed to pay legislative expenses in Florida in 1822, in Michigan in 1823, and in Arkansas in 1828. This included not only the $3 daily attendance salary of legislators but also their traveling expenses of $3 for each twenty miles "by the most expeditious route." After 1828 all expenses of territorial legislatures were paid by the federal government, thereby easing a financial burden on the residents.

DEVELOPMENTS IN THE ROLE OF LEGISLATURES IN TERRITORIAL GOVERNMENTS

By the time a Dr. William Lattimore, delegate from Mississippi Territory (created in 1798), reached Washington in 1805, territorial politicians were seeking changes in the structure of territorial government. The presence of three delegates upon his arrival made possible more concerted efforts to achieve change. Controversy in Orleans Territory over the makeup of the council and conflicts between legislatures and governors in the Northwest, Mississippi, and Indiana territories led to a drive for greater power for the legislatures and more responsiveness to the citizens by territorial government. The growing number of territorial delegates and their activism in the U.S. House of Representatives led to changes, although they were slow in coming.

A first step was to provide for the election of members of the upper house, achieved first in Indiana Territory in 1809. Previously members of the upper house, or council, had been appointed by the president or governor from a list submitted by the lower house, producing a council that often reflected the governor's position. Popular election of the council added to the power of the legislature and the people at the expense of the governor. Not until 1816 did voters in Missouri Territory gain the right of an elective upper house, but from then on, all upper houses of bicameral legislatures were elected. In 1826 and 1827 the unicameral legislatures of Florida and Michigan, respectively, became elective, and territorial voters everywhere then had control over the membership of their entire legislatures.

Under the Ordinance of 1787, each territorial legislature was empowered to elect a delegate to Congress. This delegate, the old colonial agent now given official status, had the right to debate on the floor of the House of Representatives and to serve on committees, but could not vote on the floor of the House. Reinforced by the promise of statehood, the delegate as a voice of the people functioned to reduce impatience or even the possibility of rebellion by territorial residents. As the legislative election of the delegates was practiced originally in the Southwest, Northwest, Mississippi, Indiana, and Orleans territories, the members of the lower house quickly became dissatisfied with the process because they had to compromise with the upper house on candidates. Many residents and several delegates also supported popular election as a means of providing more opposition to the governor. As a result of lobbying by territorial delegates, Congress granted the Mississippi and Indiana territories the right of popular election of their delegates in 1809, a right slowly extended to other territories until all had it by 1825. With an official elected by the voters and representing the entire territory, a new and powerful instrument was created for possible opposition to the governor. Over the years, a party split in the territories would mean that a territory's delegate and governor might often be in opposing parties. Both officials would have supporters in the legislature. Conflicts between the parties focused on local patronage, influence in Washington, access to economic opportunities, and appointments to political positions in the territories and new states.

Relations with Governors and with Congress

In the beginning of territorial government, in 1787, the governor of a territory wielded an absolute veto over legislation. Often it was used to defeat the creation of more counties or designation of county seats, the governor viewing such legislative action as a challenge to his executive authority. Vetoes were often designed to prevent local appointive offices from becoming elective, the governor usually claiming that such action by the general assembly was unconstitutional. In 1799, in the first session of the General Assembly of the Northwest Territory, Governor St. Clair vetoed eleven measures, six of which were to create new counties. He probably saw the prospective increased membership in the lower house as a challenge to his power, and he claimed that only the governor had the power to designate new counties. The tremendous uproar that followed these vetoes led to unsuccessful attempts to have him removed. Later governors were usually more judicious in their use of the veto, having St. Clair's example before them.

As the territorial system matured and residents became more sensitive to their subordinate colonial status, pressure built to abolish the absolute veto, although territorial politicians apparently never advocated a system without a veto. They did seek the same privilege as that afforded the U.S. Congress—the right to override an executive veto. In 1823, Congress finally granted the Florida legislature the right of overriding the governor's veto with a two-thirds vote. Slowly other territorial legislatures were granted this right—Arkansas in 1829, Wisconsin and Iowa in 1839. After 1860 the power of all territorial governors to veto legislation was limited by organic acts or by supplemental legislation, except in Utah.

Territorial legislatures also faced vetoes by Congress, for Congress reserved the right to review, approve, or disapprove all territorial legislation. Congress first took such action in 1805, disapproving a bank charter in Michigan Territory. In the period prior to 1862, few pieces of territorial legislation were disapproved, and most of those originated in Florida. Most of these laws concerned banks, railroads, and the lower courts. Congress never relinquished this right of approval or disapproval.

In the Ordinance of 1787 the governor was also given power to convene, dissolve, and prorogue the legislature. Ultimately, only the governors of the Northwest, Southwest, Mississippi, Indiana, Illinois, and Alabama territories had this power. Although there was a little vocal opposition, Congress readily granted the general assemblies of the territories the right to determine their own meetings, beginning with Missouri in 1812. This provides a good illustration of the pragmatic nature of the territorial system: the governor's powers were modeled after the old British colonial system and adapted the new American system. When experience proved that the territorial legislatures were responsible bodies and that the governors did not need this power, Congress removed this vestige of British colonialism.

Requirements to Vote or to Serve in Legislatures

The Ordinance of 1784 had provided that all "free males of full age" resident in the territories could vote, reflecting the early liberalism of the United States (although women were denied the vote in the territories until Wyoming provided for female suffrage in 1869). By 1787 a trend toward conservatism had set in, and the Northwest Ordinance reinstated property requirements for voters and officeholders. In order to vote, the free male of full age had to be a citizen of a state, own a freehold of at least fifty acres, and be resident in the territory. American citizenship, which was determined by state citizenship at this time, was not required. Noncitizens could vote if they had been resident for two years or more.

To serve in the legislature, the free adult male must have been a citizen of a state for three years, be resident in the territory, and own in fee simple (that is, with no limitations to any classification of heirs) a minimum of two hundred acres of land. No serious discussion of this property-holding requirement surfaced until Mississippi residents were confronted with long delays in gaining title to land because of conflicting British, Spanish, and American claims, and the controversial Yazoo land grants made by Georgia in areas of Mississippi Territory. Conditions were such that few residents could vote, and they thus began petitioning Congress to broaden the franchise. The petitions were granted in 1814 when Congress granted taxpayer suffrage, a privilege already extended to Indiana (1811) and Illinois (1812) territories. Other territorial residents were occasionally granted this privilege until 1836, when Congress standardized voting requirements in all territories: only free white adult males who were U.S. citizens, residing in the territory at the time of the first elections, were eligible to vote.

In the Missouri Organic Act of 1812, Congress not only provided for taxpayer suffrage but also allowed any qualified voter to sit in the lower house. Attainment of the age of twenty-five and a two-hundred-acre freehold were required for membership in the council. In 1826, while making the legislative council in Florida elective, Congress removed all property requirements for office holding in the territory. This was standardized in the Wisconsin Organic Act of 1836, which required that the members of both houses of the general assembly have the same qualifications as voters. This organic act also provided that after the legislature was established, it had the right to determine suffrage requirements for residents of the territory. Rights and privileges that had become common to the territories at this point were applied consistently in all future territories.

The terms of office for members of territorial legislatures were usually two years for the lower house and four years for the upper house. Congress required that both the elected representatives and the councillors be apportioned by population. The elections were set by the governor initially and then by the territorial legislature. When Congress set the election of territorial delegates to occur in the same year as that of other members of the House of Representatives, many territories followed suit and held their legislative elections at the same time as the delegate election.

Political Parties and Partisanship

The political parties in territories were based on land speculation, office patronage, economic development, and especially personalities. Often they reflected the national alignments, although more often they were founded in conflicts within the territories. It was often personality and the exercise of local power, rather than ideology, that brought on partisan politics. But to have lasting influence in a territory, which was so dependent upon the national government, local politicians had to align themselves with a national party, even one that might not be their natural choice. Thus, in the Northwest Territory, the struggles between St. Clair and his opposition were not originally along the lines developing in the national legislature. But the opposition was heavily dominated by Virginians who had lines of communication to, and had influence over, Thomas Jefferson and James Madison. Thus, St. Clair and his group were forced into the Federalist camp. In terms of ideology, they really were Federalists, but in reality they had no choice.

Two or more local partisan groups might have ties to the same national party. Debate over which group had more influence with that national party often led to territorial partisan politics. Both parties in Missouri Territory between 1812 and 1821 supported the national administration of National Republicans, arguing over which had better access to the president and congressional leaders. On the national scene, they were united in favor of statehood for Missouri and slavery. Within the territory, there was a struggle for political supremacy when the new state came into being, and con-

flicts over land speculation and other economic endeavors continued.

Much of the partisanship in Wisconsin Territory was based on the personal animosity between Judge James D. Doty and General Henry Dodge. Doty was deeply involved in land speculation and banking, while Dodge lived in the mining area and had political ties to Missouri and Iowa through family relationships. They both used national alliances to further their own power in the territory and to maintain themselves and their supporters in power. In Minnesota the rivalry of Henry M. Rice and Henry H. Sibley dominated territorial politics. Both men had been fur traders, and it was in that trade that their personal animosity began. Throughout the territorial period they both remained Democrats, disagreeing over railroads, Indian affairs, the Kansas-Nebraska Act, the delegateship, and the governor—everything except statehood. Similarly, in Kansas politics revolved about slavery and landownership, and the local groups looked to Washington primarily for support for their issues. Since Washington did not give much help, the Kansans fought their own political battles in a violent civil war.

Boundary Disputes

Occasionally the governor and legislature united in pushing policies of general interest to their territory. When Michigan Territory and the state of Ohio became embroiled in a boundary dispute, the governor and legislature of Michigan unsuccessfully worked together to defeat Ohio. The issue stemmed from 1803 when Ohio was admitted to the Union with a northern boundary that placed Toledo within the new state. This line was farther north than the line established by the Northwest Ordinance. As the economic potential of Toledo and the Maumee River developed, and as Michigan approached statehood, the territory decided to extend its claims to include Toledo. At one point, officials of both governments were operating within the disputed area, eventually leading to an armed confrontation referred to as the Toledo War of 1835–1836. Only a horse was injured; no one was killed. Congress settled the dispute by leaving Toledo in Ohio and giving the Upper Peninsula to Michigan.

The Northwest Territory was involved in an earlier boundary dispute. During the last years of territorial status, the governor and his supporters sought to maintain Federalist control and to destroy the power of the Virginian land speculators who were allied with the Jeffersonian Republican party. The Federalists, St. Clair's supporters, were strong along the eastern side of the territory, centered in Marietta, the territorial capital. The other Federalist stronghold was in Cincinnati and the surrounding Miami River valley. In between, along the Scioto and Muskingum rivers, were the Virginians. Much jockeying over setting boundaries was carried out through actions of St. Clair, the territorial delegate William Henry Harrison, and residents from the Scioto River valley, rather than in the general assembly itself. St. Clair proposed to divide the territory along the Scioto River, creating two territories with capitals at Marietta and Cincinnati; naturally the Republicans opposed this. When Indiana Territory was created, Congress ordered the western boundary of the Northwest Territory to be fixed upon the mouth of the Kentucky River rather than the mouth of the Miami, as provided under the Ordinance of 1787. However, when Ohio became a state, the boundary was to revert to the mouth of the Miami. As the battle for statehood increased, St. Clair strove to stop the proceedings toward statehood, divide the territory again, maintain Federalist control, and continue colonial status. Opponents of St. Clair successfully pressured Congress to keep the boundaries as they had been established in 1787 and to create the state of Ohio within those boundaries.

Boundary questions continued to be raised involving various territories during the ensuing years and were usually fought among the land speculators and politicians rather than on the floors of the general assemblies. Many times, the territorial legislatures were uninvolved and did not even instruct their territorial delegates on the disputes. None of the other disputes reached the level of confrontation of the Toledo War or the factional rancor exhibited in the Northwest Territory.

TERRITORIAL LEGISLATURES AND CONFLICTS OVER SLAVERY

Early on, the territories became involved in conflicts relating to slavery. The Northwest Or-

dinance of 1787 prohibited slavery in the territory northwest of the Ohio River and east of the Mississippi River. There was little debate over this article and equally little debate when the organic (organizing) act for the Southwest Territory allowed slavery in accordance with the North Carolina cession. Although at first it seemed that no one really questioned the right of Congress to legislate on slavery in the territories or objected to the right of the Southwest Territory and later southern territories to continue slavery, the issue was present and building up throughout much of the early national period.

Early Examples

Many early settlers in the Northwest Territory were from the South, chiefly Kentucky and Virginia. These people settled along the Ohio River, some bringing slaves with them. In 1799 some of the former Virginians and Kentuckians petitioned the General Assembly of the Northwest Territory for a slave code or an indenture law to protect the status of slaves already in the territory. After some debate, the legislature took no action, believing that the proposal was incompatible with the Ordinance of 1787.

Not until the creation of Indiana Territory in 1800 did the issue become a serious legislative matter. Beginning in 1804, the Indiana legislature regularly petitioned Congress to allow slavery, and it was a cause for the early partisan split in Indiana. Territorial delegate Jonathan Jennings led the heavily Quaker antislavery group in opposition to the proslavery southerners, who had support from Governor William Henry Harrison. The presence of slaves in the territory was never disputed. President Thomas Jefferson and Congress consistently refused to listen to any petitions on slavery.

In 1805, however, the Indiana General Assembly specifically protected slavery by passing indenture laws. If slaves brought into the territory were over fifteen years of age, the owner could make an indenture contract for any length of time and register it with a county clerk within thirty days of entering the territory. If the slave refused the terms of the contract, the owner could remove the slave within sixty days without losing title. Slaves under the age of fifteen were to serve until age thirty-five if they were male and age thirty-two if they were female. Children born to slaves in the territory were to serve the owner of their parents until age twenty-eight for females and thirty for males. In 1806 the General Assembly permitted the unexpired time of service of "Negroes and mulattoes" indentured under the 1805 law to be sold as part of a person's estate. When there were political changes in the elections of 1810, the antislavery party led by Jonathan Jennings took control of the legislature and repealed the indenture laws, effectively ending slavery in Indiana Territory.

The Indiana situation was exacerbated by the fact that the earliest Euro-American inhabitants had held slaves for decades. Slaveholding French immigrants settled along the Mississippi River bottoms opposite Saint Louis and in Missouri at Cape Girardeau, Sainte Genevieve, and Saint Louis. The Illinois settlements of Kaskaskia and Cahokia, in particular, dated to the years prior to the American acquisition of French, Spanish, and British territories. The French felt they had been guaranteed their property rights, including slave property. Because they were not very vocal and lived quite distant from the seats of territorial government, Cincinnati and Vincennes, their proslavery advocacy received little attention. But the proslavery arguments of the residents of southern Indiana awakened French voices, and the creation of Illinois Territory in 1809 brought the seat of government much closer to them. They were joined by southerners who had migrated into southern Illinois Territory from Kentucky and Tennessee with their slaves. From then until 1824, the legalization of slavery in Illinois was a significant issue in Illinois territorial and state politics, although it was never legalized through a slave code or indenture laws. The defeat of a constitutional amendment in 1824 ended the open political debate over slavery in the state, although the decennial census continued to list slaves in Illinois and other parts of the Old Northwest Territory.

It was the role of free African Americans, rather than slaves, which was an issue in statehood debates regarding the admission of Orleans Territory as the state of Louisiana. In the territory, it had been provided that free men of color could participate in the militia and vote in local elections, continuing traditions from French and Spanish days. Opposition developed in Congress at the thought that such persons might be elected to Congress. Several members, notably Pleasant Miller of Tennessee, felt that they would not be able to serve in the same legislative body with a "person of color." Thus, the constitution of the state of Louisiana provided that free persons of color could not vote.

The status of African Americans in Orleans Territory had been determined largely by the traditional racial attitudes of the French and Spanish Creoles prior to acquisition by the United States, and it was a matter of discussion at times in the territory. The "invading" Americans opposed the tolerance of the Creoles and eventually came to dominate territorial and state governments and to change the racial policies of the area.

The slavery issue erupted at the time of Missouri's drive for statehood, partly because Missouri was farther north. There had not been any opposition to slavery in Orleans Territory when it was created after the vast trans-Mississippi purchase in 1804 or when Missouri was organized in 1812 at the time of Louisiana's statehood. In fact, when Arkansas Territory was organized in 1819 in response to Missouri's request for statehood, there was no debate over slavery in Arkansas. Therefore, the controversy over slavery in the state of Missouri was due partly to geography and partly to a rising opposition to slavery in the northern states. Within the territory, there had never been discussion of the question, and the legislators and territorial delegates had all assumed that slavery would continue under statehood. In the end, the Missourians preserved their peculiar institution.

"Bleeding Kansas"

The issue of slavery in Kansas Territory not only became violent and bloody, but it also affected national politics and was part of the process leading to the disastrous Civil War. The organic act for Nebraska and Kansas territories provided that the determination of being a free or slave state would be left up to the residents of the territories. There was no real issue in Nebraska, as everyone assumed it would be a free state. Kansas became the issue because both free-soil and proslavery settlers moved into the territory and each group worked to make its position prevail.

Within a year after the organic act, elections were held for a legislature. In the 1855 election, proslavery groups from Missouri swarmed into Kansas Territory, stuffed ballot boxes, and intimidated Free-Soilers. When the first legislature met in July 1855 in Pawnee, the proslavery group had a majority. It proceeded to investigate the conduct of the election and declared that the Free-Soilers had been fraudulently elected. Thus, the Free-Soilers were unseated and replaced with proslavery men, all within the space of four days. The legislature promptly voted to move to Shawnee Mission, more hospitable country than Pawnee, but Governor Andrew Reeder vetoed the bill authorizing the move. When his veto was overridden by the Kansas General Assembly, he appealed to the territorial supreme court, which upheld the legislature. The governor resigned. A pattern thus began in Kansas of governors' vetoes regularly being followed by legislative overrides. Reeder's short tenure as governor was typical: six governors served in the seven-year existence of that tumultuous territory.

As mentioned above, the first Kansas General Assembly adopted the Missouri civil and criminal codes simply by changing references to "Missouri" to "Kansas" wherever appropriate. However, proslavery advocates felt it necessary to strengthen the slave code. Thus, it became illegal to read a free-soil newspaper. A person could lose his vote by refusing to take an oath to support the Fugitive Slave Act of 1850 or could lose his property for questioning the right of slaveholding. It became a capital offense to aid an escaping slave. And the new code provided that the governor was prohibited from pardoning a person for a violation of the slave code.

These actions of the recognized legislature prompted the Free-Soilers to establish their own legislature, which they determined to do at a meeting on 4 July 1855. In October their rump Free State legislature (i.e., a fragmentary group claiming to represent the full legislature) met in Topeka and declared the proslavery legislation of June to be nonbinding. In passing their own laws, however, the rump representatives declared that no black, free or slave, could reside in Kansas when it became a state. This followed a pattern being set in eastern states and shows vividly the racism that permeated American culture. The Free Staters also agreed to elect their own delegate to Congress and to establish their own legal code. Thus, a pattern was set with two legislatures governing the territory, the legal one regularly overriding the governors' vetoes. Both sides indulged in such violence until very soon Senator Charles Sumner (R.-Mass) could rightfully refer to "Bleeding Kansas."

President Franklin Pierce took a stand in January 1856 when he endorsed the proslavery legislature, called the creation of the Free State legislature "an act of treason," and asked Congress to authorize a constitutional convention. The Senate did not agree to the convention. Pierce also issued a proclamation forbidding a meeting of the Free State legislature on 4 July 1856 and authorized the U.S. Army, stationed at Fort Leavenworth, to stop it. When the Free-Soilers met, they lacked a quorum. Colonel Edwin Vose Sumner appeared with an army detachment and ordered them to disperse. They adjourned, scheduling another meeting for January 1857, but again a quorum failed to appear.

At the same time, the legal, proslavery legislature met in the new territorial capital, Lecompton, and did little work. Most of their time was spent issuing resolutions denouncing the governor, John Geary, and raising issues to embarrass him. For example, they granted judges the power to set bail for any offense, whether or not the offense was bailable, and the governor's veto of this bill was overridden. The assembly also enacted a bill to take a census and call for a new constitutional convention. Governor Geary vetoed this bill because there was no provision for a referendum on the constitution, and this veto, too, was overridden.

The June 1857 election for a constitutional convention led to the Lecompton Constitution, which was never accepted by Congress or by the Free-Soilers in the territory. While the proslavery voters were electing proslavery members of the convention, the Free-Soiler party met in convention along with their rump legislature; little action was taken.

By October 1857 the territory had acquired a firm governor, Robert Walker, who used the army to enforce fair elections that fall. Fraudulent returns from McGee County and the town of Oxford led the governor to throw out those returns. The result was that the Free-Soilers controlled the General Assembly by ten votes in the lower house and five votes in the council. The new legislature met in special session in December to consider various matters, especially setting a referendum on the Lecompton Constitution. They also made the Free State Militia the territorial militia by overriding the acting governor's veto; Governor Walker had already left the territory forever.

About the same time, members of the new legislature met with members of the Free State legislature. The Free Staters urged the regularly elected representatives to vote themselves out of existence and grant all legislative powers to the Free State group. Wise minds prevailed, and the legal legislature refused to do this, realizing that such action would completely discredit the Free-Soilers.

In February 1858 the General Assembly met in regular session and repealed the 1855 laws punishing offenses against slave property by overriding the governor's veto. The capital was moved to Mineola, a town that had just been created, and the governor refused to move himself or the territorial records, even though his veto had been overridden on this bill as well. The legislature also did some less controversial work, it should be noted, such as incorporating towns and cities and issuing business charters. On the last day of the session, the legislature passed a bill calling for a constitutional convention, which was vetoed and the veto overridden. When Governor James Denver, who still had the original bill, proved that the bill returned to him from the General Assembly was not the original, the fraudulent one was burned. The legislature again overrode the veto. The convention was held, but the resulting constitution was defeated by the electorate in a referendum.

There was much political bickering over appointments. Divorce bills were passed and the Atchison and Pike's Peak Railroad was chartered. A thousand dollars was voted to provide legal support for Doctor John Doy and his son Charles, who had been captured and held by proslavery forces when they were conducting thirteen free African Americans to Iowa for safety reasons.

In typical fashion, the legislature passed a bill abolishing slavery, but it was promptly vetoed by Governor Samuel Medary, who argued that the legislature did not have power to do this. The legislature overrode his veto. The governor did receive legislative support in his

efforts to maintain peace. A new election was authorized for another constitutional convention. The resulting constitution, the Wyandotte Constitution, was approved by the voters and Congress, and in 1861, Kansas finally achieved statehood and relative peace.

ISSUES IN OTHER TERRITORIES

New Mexico Territory

New Mexico Territory, created in 1850, presented a different problem to the federal government. Hispanics made up a majority of the population and were accustomed to a degree of self-government because they were so distant from the Mexican cities of Durango and Mexico City. A weak tradition of legislative assemblies existed in the Spanish and Mexican administrations, and it was not strengthened appreciably by constitutional conventions convened in the fruitless hope of attaining statehood by preemptive action, as the 1850 compromise was being thrashed out in the national capital.

During the 1850s, as reflected in the makeup and actions of the territorial legislative assembly, a new New Mexico was taking shape through the mixing of different cultures, Hispanic Mexican and Yankee American, that would not become homogeneous. The assembly has been characterized as marked by "complicated factions and elaborate disunity," because of family feuds, personal dislikes, and disagreement over the desired degree of Americanization. It consisted chiefly of Hispanics inclined to delay on any action involving change and to favor actions that served to preserve the cultural status quo.

Concepts of slavery, American style (based on race and chattel property), for instance, seemed irrelevant in the early 1850s, for there were very few African Americans in the territory. But the legislators were accustomed to peonage and Indian slavery, and these practices became more formalized under territorial government. The increase of population brought more proslavery residents from the South, and by 1859, political support for slavery led to the enactment of a slave code. When Congress abolished slavery in all existing and future territories in 1862, New Mexico was the only territory with a slave code. The New Mexicans did not take the matter seriously, so Congress specifically abolished slavery in the territory in 1863 and again in 1867.

The work of the assembly was carried on in Spanish, and in 1859 there were fewer Anglo-American members than there had been in 1851. Unaccustomed to paying taxes, the legislators consistently opposed taxes, forcing the administration to use warrants to pay expenses. Viewing a public school system as a threat to their church and culture, they opposed effective school organization and its adequate funding. The fifteen or twenty established, prosperous, native New Mexican families that dominated legislative work were a constant check on the Americanizing pressures that were manifested, especially by the governors imported from Washington. Fortunately for all concerned, the decade of the 1850s was relatively prosperous. The gold seekers rushing to California merely passed through, for the most part, and the influx of new American residents was not so large as to be broadly disruptive. Because New Mexico was dominated by Hispanic culture and politicians, it was still basically New Mexican (not Mexican) in 1862. The stage was set for drastic and difficult government and cultural developments as the Anglo-American presence increased. New Mexican statehood would be delayed for several generations.

Utah Territory

Utah Territory presented different circumstances to the federal government and provided a real test for the territorial system. Mormons, through their main instrumentality, the Church of Jesus Christ of Latter-day Saints, completely dominated the legislature and the territorial government until 1858. Brigham Young, president of the church, sought complete control of the government in order to protect Mormon culture and religion in Utah. His work had led to the migration of the Saints to Utah in 1847. Two years later, a formal constitution laid the groundwork for the state of Deseret, which the church hoped Congress would approve without benefit of a territorial period. However, Congress saw fit to establish Utah Territory in 1850 with the traditional government. Unlike the governors of New Mexico Territory (also estab-

lished in 1850) and other existing territories, the governor of Utah Territory was granted an absolute veto. Congress was obviously chary of what might happen in the territory.

Mormons and their friends in Washington, D.C., succeeded in having Brigham Young appointed governor of the new territory, a position he held until 1858 when the first non-Mormon, or "gentile," governor arrived. Most of the other territorial officials were gentile from the beginning, laying the basis for contentious territorial politics. Young moved swiftly to convene the legislature in March 1851, a month after being sworn in as governor. The representatives had been handpicked by Young or the church leadership and elected in some irregular procedures. Often a meeting on church matters would be turned into a caucus to elect members of the territorial legislature and the territorial delegate. The vote in these circumstances was usually unanimous. Since the population was almost totally Mormon, there was no objection to such procedures. The first legislature established the courts, ordered a census, and adopted civil and criminal codes of law before gentile appointees even arrived in Salt Lake City.

Throughout the 1850s, there was no opposition party and the legislature consisted exclusively of Mormons, to whom the thought of contravening church leadership seemed never to occur. The Utah War of 1858 between the federal government and Mormons and the arrival of the new gentile governor that year, Alfred W. Cumming, along with U.S. Army support, led to further confrontation. The legislature specifically prohibited anyone from voting who had not been a resident or taxpayer for a year. This was to prevent soldiers from voting. Another act attempted to prevent Utah lands from becoming part of the public domain. In 1859, Governor Cumming asked the Utah General Assembly to clarify the jurisdiction and powers of the probate courts; to pass laws on land, water, and grazing that would be easier to enforce; and to provide better funding for the schools. The legislature, in a sincere gesture of noncooperation, did nothing.

As the 1850s ended, the federal government and gentile governors had to confront the territorial laws that protected polygamy and other practices of the church. Not until 1862 did Congress act. Then Congress disapproved an 1851 law of the state of Deseret incorporating the Church of Jesus Christ of Latter-day Saints that had been repassed in 1855 and all laws passed to "establish, support, maintain, shield or countenance polygamy." The lines were drawn for future conflicts with the territory.

The difficulties with gentiles in the territory, from governor to settlers, led the general assembly to enact a bill calling for a constitutional convention in 1861. This bill was promptly vetoed by Governor John W. Dawson, who was soon forced to flee east for personal reasons. His successor, Stephen S. Harding, asked the 1862 legislature to revise the court system, to grant him power to commission and remove officers in the Nauvoo Legion (a militia sanctioned and operated by the Mormon church), and to abolish polygamy. The general assembly very carefully replied. First, in revising the court system, it assigned the new federal judges to the wrong districts. The governor's message was lost, so that further action following his advice could not be taken. By the end of the session, Harding, using his absolute veto, had killed fourteen bills and truly raised the hackles of the Mormon community. He was removed.

By 1862, tension was very high between the church and the federal government over polygamy, land speculation, and noncooperation between the legislature and the governor. The Mormons, in vain hope, established a de facto "shadow" state of Deseret. But it would be another thirty years before Congress would seriously consider statehood for the Utah territory.

CONCLUSION

Since the ultimate goal of Congress and most territorial politicians and residents was statehood, in most cases the territorial general assemblies led the struggle for statehood. There were always some residents opposed to statehood because of the additional expenses of state government. And governors occasionally opposed statehood for personal or political reasons. For the most part, however, the opposition came from the federal government, either through dilatory tactics by presidential administrations or through reluctance in Congress.

The general assembly of the Southwest Territory, on advice of the governor and the territorial delegate, took its own initiative to begin the statehood process. This method, the "Tennessee Plan," was used by a minority of territories to achieve statehood. In this case, the territorial legislature called for a census, authorized a constitutional convention, and presented Congress with a constitution and a full slate of elected state officals.

For most territories, however, the process was to convince Congress to authorize a census and constitutional convention. Here the general assemblies played an important role in regularly submitting petitions setting forth the justifications for immediate statehood. Since the actuality of statehood, the enabling act, was passed at the whim of Congress, territorial politicians could do only so much. When the governor, legislature, and delegate of the Northwest Territory opposed statehood for political reasons—namely, their potential loss of power—the opposition simply took its case directly to Washington and carried the day through an "old-boy network" of Virginians. Such gubernatorial opposition was rare, however. Kansas and Utah sought statehood to achieve independence of action, but although the legislatures called conventions and provided for the drafting of constitutions, Congress was unwilling to act for two reasons—slavery and polygamy. The role played by the legislatures was that of advocacy rather than action in most cases.

Up to 1862, Congress provided the framework for territorial residents and legislatures to develop local governments and to increase their participation in national politics. The Ordinance of 1787 provided the basis—three-branched republican government, individual civil rights, and a congressional delegate. The basic principles remained the same over the years, but both Congress and the territories changed the working details. By 1836 the Wisconsin Organic Act incorporated the many significant changes of the early years, providing a more detailed framework for the future. Yet all the organic acts and amending congressional legislation constituted variations on the theme, and no organic act was an exact duplicate of another. Each territory was unique in its inception, its geography, its demographics, and its operation, and the organic acts and amendatory legislation reflected that.

Territorial legislatures dealt primarily with local issues—courts, taxes, economic development, county boundaries, and officials—rather than national issues. They often clashed with the governors over these issues. These clashes were primarily local in nature and, more often than not, concerned personalities and personal power rather than ideology as such. Many of the men in the factions that developed had common philosophies or similar pragmatic approaches to issues, but their differences were usually not based on the platforms or programs of national parties. The national parties were ordinarily important only in the respect that alliance with them could give territorial factions access to national political power and patronage. The local general assemblies provided an opportunity for self-government, for maturing political strategies, and for young men to become successful. For the territorial residents, they were important, for these general assemblies controlled many aspects of daily living. In the long run, these local legislative bodies provided the kind of government their constituents wanted, concentrating their energies on territorial needs and trying to work with or control the appointed territorial officials for efficient, inexpensive government.

In the first seventy-five years of the American empire, the system worked effectively. Sixteen territories graduated from territoriality into statehood (see Table 1). Seven more, listed in Table 2, would achieve statehood after varying lengths of "colonial" political status. Still others, occupying lands emcompassed by territories just named, plus Alaska and Hawaii, were yet to be given separate status as territories and elevated to statehood.

In this three-quarters of a century the colonial territorial government became more democratic, giving territorial residents more voice in their legislatures and more opportunity to direct their own affairs. Some of the worst features, such as the governor's absolute veto, had disappeared. The territorial delegate was an

Table 1

U.S. TERRITORIES THAT ACHIEVED STATEHOOD, 1787–1862

State	Date of Territorial Establishment	Entry into Statehood
Ohio	1787	1803
Tennessee	1790	1796
Mississippi	1798	1817
Indiana	1800	1816
Louisiana	1804	1812
Michigan	1805	1837
Illinois	1809	1818
Missouri	1812	1821
Alabama	1817	1819
Arkansas	1819	1836
Florida	1822	1845
Wisconsin	1836	1848
Iowa	1838	1846
Oregon	1848	1859
Minnesota	1849	1858
Kansas	1854	1861

Table 2

U.S. TERRITORIES IN 1862 THAT LATER ACHIEVED STATEHOOD

State	Date of Territorial Establishment	Entry into Statehood
New Mexico	1850	1912
Utah	1850	1896
Washington	1853	1889
Nebraska	1854	1867
Colorado	1861	1876
Nevada	1861	1864
Dakota	1861	1889

important fixture in Washington, and the general assembly worked well with both governor and delegate. The framers of the Ordinance of 1787 had been successful.

BIBLIOGRAPHY

General Sources and Studies

The best sources on territorial legislatures are the journals and laws of the general assemblies of individual territories, along with local newspapers. The best general secondary accounts are JACK ERICSON EBLEN, *The First and Second United States Empires: Governors and Territorial Government, 1784–1912* (Pittsburgh, 1968) and JOHN PORTER BLOOM, ed., *The American Territorial System,* (Athens, Ohio, 1973). The best documentary collection is CLARENCE E. CARTER and JOHN PORTER BLOOM, eds., *The Territorial Papers of the United States*, 28 vols. (Washington, D.C., 1934–1975), covering the territories through Wisconsin. Focusing on legal background are MAX FARRAND, *The Legislation of Congress for the Government of the Organized Territories of the United States, 1789–1895* (Newark, N.J., 1896) and WILLIAM WIRT BLUME and ELIZABETH GASPAR BROWN, comp., *Digest and Lists Pertaining to the Development of Law and Legal Institutions in the Territories of the United States: 1787–1954* (Ann Arbor, Mich., 1965).

Monographs pertaining to specific topics are MALCOLM J. ROHRBOUGH, *The Trans-Appalachian Frontier: People, Societies, and Institutions, 1775–1850* (New York, 1978); JOHN WELLING SMURR, "Territorial Constitutions: A Legal History of the Frontier Governments Erected by Congress, 1787–1900" (Ph.D. diss., University of Wisconsin–Madison, 1958); and NANCY JO TICE (BLOOM), "The Territorial Delegate, 1794–1820" (Ph.D. diss., University of Wisconsin–Madison, 1967).

Individual Territories

Studies of individual territories that discuss the territorial legislatures include THOMAS P. ABERNATHY, *From Frontier to Plantation in Tennessee* (Chapel Hill, N.C., 1932) and *The Formative Period in Alabama, 1815–1828* (University, Ala., 1965). These are early studies of territorial history and are models. The classic study of the Northwest Territory is RANDOLPH C. DOWNES, *Frontier Ohio, 1788–1803* (Columbus, Ohio, 1935). ANDREW R. L. CAYTON emphasizes economic history in *The Frontier Republic, 1780–1825* (Kent, Ohio, 1986). FRANCIS S. PHILBRICK is primarily concerned with legal history, but these two studies of his include good material on the territorial legislatures and their development: *The Laws of Indiana Territory, 1801–1809* (Springfield, Ill., 1930) and *The Laws of Illinois Territory, 1809–1818* (Springfield, Ill., 1950). Indiana Territory has been well studied; the best monographs are JOHN D. BARNHART and DOROTHY L. RIKER, *Indiana to 1816: The Colonial Period* (Indianapolis, Ind., 1971) and R. CARLYLE BULEY, *The Old Northwest: Pioneer Period, 1815–1840* (Bloomington, Ind., 1950, 1983). Good monographs on other territories are THOMAS PATRICK COFFEY, "The Territory of Orleans, 1804–1812" (Ph.D. diss., St. Louis University, 1956); WILLIAM E. FOLEY, *A History of Missouri*, vol. 1 (Columbia, Mo., 1971); WILLIAM W. FOLWELL, *A History of Minnesota* (St. Paul, Minn., 1921); ALEC R. GILPIN, *The Territory of Michigan* (East Lansing, Mich., 1970); ROBERT V. HAYNES, "A Political History of the Mississippi Territory" (Ph.D. diss., Rice Institute, 1958); MARIETTA M. LeBRETON, "A History of the Territory of New Orleans, 1803–1812" (Ph.D. diss., Louisiana State University, 1969); ROBERT W. LARSON, *New Mexico's Quest for Statehood, 1846–1912* (Albuquerque, N. Mex., 1968); JAMES B. POTTS, "Nebraska Territory, 1854–1867: A Study of Frontier Politics" (Ph.D. diss., University of Nebraska–Lincoln, 1973); and ALICE E. SMITH, *The History of Wisconsin*, vol. 1, *From Exploration to Statehood* (Madison, Wis., 1973). WILLIAM F. ZORNOW, *Kansas: A History of the Jayhawk State* (Norman, Okla., 1957), covers the territorial period as part of a larger state history. In *The Far Southwest, 1846–1912* (New Haven, Conn., 1966), HOWARD R. LAMAR discusses the territorial history of Arizona, Colorado, New Mexico, and Utah.

THE TERRITORIAL SYSTEM SINCE 1862

Gordon Morris Bakken

The territorial system of 1862 was part of what Jack Ericson Eblen has called "the Second United States Empire," a part of the territorial system established by the Northwest Ordinance of 1787, but clearly not its clone. The Ordinance of 1787 created a fully centralized, and nondemocratic form of colonial government similar to the British system. By 1862, Congress had moved away from its original model and had created territories with more-democratic institutions. As a result, home rule characterized the Second Empire as appointed governors lost much of their appointive and patronage powers. Legislative authority increased and often conflicted with the territorial supreme courts and, less frequently, with Congress.

Congress also gave territorial legislatures more power to govern in the Second Empire. Washington gave the western territories, with the notable exception of Alaska, extensive legislative power to apportion the territory, to regulate elections, and to establish the location of the capital of the territory. Federal statute authorized general incorporation laws for industrial purposes and, in 1885, general laws for the incorporation of banks and canals. At the same time, Congress was active nullifying territorial laws that were in conflict with federal statute or policy, that had technical defects, and that were undesirable. Washington nullified, for example, the Utah statutes regarding the Mormon church and polygamy, in its effort to rid the country of plural marriage; struck down laws granting special privileges contrary to the organic act or federal statute; disallowed two New Mexico laws dealing with slavery; and voided three sessions of the Montana territorial legislature for its failure to reapportion the territory.

Territorial governors also used their veto power to impact legislative behavior, but in the Second Empire, federally appointed governors only faced their locally elected solons (members of a legislative body) for about one month

per year. In 1869, Congress made biennial sessions uniform throughout the territories and in 1873 limited sessions to forty days. In 1880, Washington decreed that those sessions could now be for sixty days. After 1862, governors had limited veto power but still exercised it, increasingly citing conflict with organic acts or federal provisions. The veto power was in turn limited by politics. As the territorial experience unfolded in the period, governors increasingly tried to accommodate legislators. Some of the compensation received by territorial governors came from territorial coffers subject to legislative action. Territorial politics could also coerce governors. Governor Sidney Edgerton of Montana decided to leave the territory permanently when threatened with mob violence after vetoing a reapportionment bill. Governor Caleb Lyon of Idaho slipped out of the territory to avoid a mob because he refused to veto a bill to move the capital from Lewiston to Boise.

Territorial government faced new challenges during the Second Empire owing to some dramatically changed circumstances. The environment west of the Mississippi changed rapidly to a sea of grass and then an arid landscape. The West depended upon transportation, mining, and ranching for its livelihood. Mining rushes to Pikes Peak, Last Chance Gulch, the Comstock, and Alaska added a new dimension to legislative challenge. Mining towns sometimes became instant cities, and other times, ghost towns. Irrigation became a way of life; a hydraulic society emerged. The territorial enterprise after 1862 was truly different.

These environmental differences posed new questions for territorial legislators. Miners formed local mining districts and legislated for themselves. Territorial legislators found a need to give uniformity to some provisions and the force of law to the regulations. The aridity challenged lawmakers to provide for the distribution of a scarce natural resource in the face of the established English common-law concept of riparian rights, which regulated the use of water along banks of streams. These would be some of the many issues that brought law and politics together in Second Empire territories. To explore these developments, one needs first to look at political structure and then at selected topics of territorial law.

PARTY SYSTEMS

The early territorial politics in the states that were admitted after 1862, with the exception of Utah, was characterized by a chaotic factionalism focused on personality rather than on party. As Kenneth N. Owens has so insightfully noted, this chaos was replaced by a one-party, two-party, or no-party system. Territorial legislatures operated within these political realities to work out some of the most basic aspects of government, provide for an economic infrastructure, and tend to the social fabric. One of the continuing items of legislative, as well as political, business in the territories was statehood. For some, like Nevada, statehood came quickly, but for Arizona, New Mexico, Alaska, and Hawaii, admission to the Union was a long political journey.

Early territorial political chaos stemmed from the scattered and geographically isolated populations, primitive communications systems, and subsistence or extractive economies. Political appointees to territorial office were generally of the national party in the White House. Regardless of political affiliation, the appointees and the few politically active members of early territorial communities focused on the politics of personal advantage. Many of these political activists were newly arrived frontier entrepreneurs. In Utah, territorial government was delivered into the hands of the Mormon church by appointment. Control of the legislature and local government by church officials became a fact of territorial life. The church and territorial government, prior to the intervention of the federal government, worked in partnership.

Hawaii became a territory in 1900, and its first territorial legislature exhibited many of the characteristics of chaos, despite the long experience with government and politics. Native Hawaiians did not support Republican or Democratic party nominees, but turned to the Home Rule party under Robert Wilcox. Wilcox told voters to look at the skin of candidates when they voted. Home Rule candidates won fourteen seats in the territorial house and nine in the senate—a majority in both. They also sent Wilcox to Washington as the territorial delegate. The legislature spent a great deal of its time over language, in that Home Rulers insisted on speaking Hawaiian even though English was the official language of the legislature, and wrangled over trivial issues. In 1902 the Republicans invited Prince Jonah Kuhio Kalanianaole to run for delegate, thereby splitting the native vote and putting Republicans in power for decades.

Alaska's first territorial legislature was not chaotic, but exhibited the no-party tendency, with legislators considering themselves independents. The first Alaska Organic Act of 1884 had ended military rule but expressly forbade a legislature. Rather, Congress gave Alaska the code of Oregon to operate under. In 1899, Congress amended the criminal code and passed a tax statute. The next year, it amended the civil code and created two judicial districts. Congress also provided for the incorporation of towns, thus providing a minimal form of self-government and legislative power. In 1912, Congress passed a second organic act, authorizing a legislature, but expressly forbade any legislative action relating to fish and game or the primary disposal of the soil. Further, Congress retained authority to legislate on divorce, gambling, liquor sales, and municipal incorporation. The Alaska territorial legislature had to petition Congress on the creation of county government, could not borrow money, and had to limit its property taxes to 1 percent of assessed valuation. The first legislature, although independently minded, was far from independent of Congress.

The gradual movement to stable political-party systems came with the development of local interest groups. Mine owners and operators found a community of interest in preventing unfavorable tax legislation. Cattlemen formed associations to protect their interests and to move into territorial politics. Farmers and laborers followed. Pioneer-community leaders formed alliances with these groups to sustain political advantage.

The one-party system emerged in territories with relatively homogeneous populations, a degree of control over patronage, and politicians who welcomed positive interaction with local social- and economic-interest representatives. As Kenneth N. Owens, Howard R. Lamar, and Carlos A. Schwantes have demonstrated, the Washington and Dakota territories exhibited this pattern. Dominated by Republican appointees, Washington Territory's governors Elisha P. Ferry and Watson C. Squire manipulated politics from the vantage of Northern Pacific Railroad interests and maintained Republican control until statehood. Dakota Territory Republican appointees of the 1860s, including the governors Newton Edmunds and Andrew J. Faulk and the delegate Walter A. Burleigh, controlled territorial politics until the early 1870s, when the opening of the Black Hills introduced new, heterogeneous elements into politics. In the 1880s politics centered on interests in Yankton and Bismarck. The Farmers' Alliance challenged the dominant Republican party and ultimately convinced the Yankton politicians that division into North and South Dakota would preserve their political futures. They were correct in that vision as pro-Alliance men dominated the constitutional convention and elected a pro-Alliance governor. Despite these gains, the North Dakota Republican party, led by Alexander McKenzie, maintained its allegiance to the Northern Pacific Railroad and elected a Republican delegation to Congress.

Oklahoma politics were likewise dominated by Republican territorial appointees, with the brief exception of Grover Cleveland's administration. Oklahoma voters sent Republican delegates to Congress every election except one. After 1889 these Republican appointees were residents who attached themselves to such popular local issues as Indian land allotment, free homesteads, and joint statehood with Indian territory. When Oklahoma Democrats became organized in 1906, they were able to turn the territory and then the state to their party.

Hawaii's Republican domination was not altered by Democratic presidential appointees or anything else until 1954. Republicans outnumbered Democrats sometimes five to one, and the party was closely allied with the most powerful economic interests on the islands, "the Big Five," which owned most of the sugar and pineapple land on the islands, maintained interlocking directorates, and bought control of significant transportation companies. As a result, more than half the total land area of the islands was in the hands of fewer than eighty private owners. The Alexander and Baldwin Company had directors in common with American Factors and with Castle and Cooke, as did other of the Big Five companies. Four of the Big Five owned 74 percent of Matson Navigation Company and had nine Big Five directors on its board. Those nine also were directors of sixty-seven other Hawaiian companies. Republican party politics was dominated by business interests.

Territorial politics in Colorado was more of the two-party variety. Republicans were firmly entrenched by 1864, but were challenged by Democrats who gained office when Republican factional struggles sapped party resolve. In the 1870s the Grange (an independent third party, originating from the Patrons of Husbandry, that advocated state regulation of railroad and warehouse rates and prices) agitated from the agricultural sector, but the Republicans waved the bloody shirt, attacked the Chinese "threat," and got on the prohibition bandwagon to maintain the clear political edge in the territorial period. Regardless of a two-party system, Colorado's politicians, as Carl Abbott has demonstrated, still attended more to personalities than to issues.

Alaska and Hawaii also had some of the characteristics of the two-party system, much of them coming well into the twentieth century. Alaska's first territorial governor, John H. Kinkead, had been a delegate to the 1863 and 1864 Nevada constitutional conventions and was president of the October 1869 "People's Convention" at Sitka prior to his appointment in 1884. Like Walter A. Burleigh of the Dakota and Montana territories, he had migrated. Kinkead's term was filled with conflict with the local missionary and gave way in 1885 to Alfred P. Swineford, who built political support among the miners. The third Republican appointee to the post, Lyman Knapp, spent most of his time in conflict like Kinkead's feuds. And so it went until the second organic act. James Wickersham ran for delegate on a "Bull Moose" Progressive ticket opposed by a Republican, two Democrats, and a Socialist. Similarly, the first legislature was populated by those who ran as nonpartisans or Republicans and Democrats opposed to the Socialists. The Republican party emerged from these electoral battles to consolidate and maintain power until the Great Depression. Democrats then had their turn.

Hawaii's Republicans maintained their hold on island politics and offices until 1954. Supported by a growing middle class in the Japanese and Chinese communities, the Democrats kept before the voters the fact that the Big Five owned the land on which their homes stood. Once in power, Democrats moved "Maryland bills" to allow lessees to "redeem" the fee interest in their house lots from their landlords. They passed such a bill in 1967, but not until 1975 was implementation legislation passed. Land and politics were very much the business of the modern legislature.

No-party systems are managed by a coalition of local interests that transcend party lines. In Utah the Church of Jesus Christ of Latter-day Saints came to dominate politics even after 1890, when the church decreed political affiliation to be permissible. As Edward Leo Lyman makes clear, whether a no-party system or a two-party system, the object of politics was the protection of Mormon interests and deliverance from territorial status.

POLITICAL OLIGARCHY

In New Mexico, the "Santa Fe Ring" dominated territorial politics. Led by Stephen Benton Elkins and Thomas Benton Catron, the ring was preoccupied with the control of land grants, statehood, open-range cattle ranching, railroads, and mining. As Howard Roberts Lamar has so ably demonstrated, the ring assembled a powerful coalition of judges, politicians, businessmen, and journalists united in their personal desire to run the territory and to make money out of their enterprises. So effective was the ring that from 1865 until 1885 it had nearly every territorial governor, several federal judges, and other federal officials as members.

In Montana, as Clark C. Spence has so effectively demonstrated, Samuel T. Hauser, Martin Maginnis, and Benjamin Potts used government and politics to safeguard their immediate economic interests and develop the territory. They built coalitions of upper-class interests

whose public positions were supported by the electorate. Their effective control of territorial politics minimized the impact of the transient electorate as well as federally appointed officials. Mining, cattle, and railroad interests mixed well in Montana politics, with something for all to gain.

Francis E. Warren and Joseph M. Carey similarly ran Wyoming politics, as Lewis L. Gould has shown. During the territorial governorship of John A. Campbell (1869–1875), personalities, rather than party or issues, dominated politics, but with increased economic stability Warren and Carey, pioneer resident politicians, emerged with a booming cattle industry and a prosperous Union Pacific Railroad. Republican identification with the interests of the Wyoming Stock Growers Association helped keep the Republicans in power.

The Idaho and Arizona territories had what Owens has called a mixed-party system evolving into a no-party system. Local issues, such as anti-Mormonism and anti-Apache sentiment, shot across party lines and changed positions and politics dramatically.

In Idaho, Democrats dominated territorial office, despite Republican appointees holding office and dispensing patronage. Democratic legislatures and Republican governors worked out a tradition of accommodation and shared power until the 1880s. Fred T. Dubois began anti-Mormon agitation in the decade from his position as U.S. marshal. The anti-Mormon movement gained momentum, split the Democratic party, and forced anti-Mormonism on the Republicans. Conservative Democrats joined Republicans in anti-Mormonism in the legislature to disfranchise Mormons. As Merle Wells has so thoroughly documented, Dubois used anti-Mormonism to win election as territorial delegate and chairmanship of the constitutional convention. Anti-Mormonism, rather than party affiliation, became the politics of Idaho on the eve of statehood.

In Arizona, Republicans held a near monopoly on the appointive governorship, and Democrats normally held the elective offices. Often they were unified in their desire to develop the territory and to profit personally in the process. As Howard R. Lamar and Jay J. Wagoner have so ably explicated, nineteenth-century territorial politics revolved around economic development, home rule, and the

Indian threat. The first two governors, John N. Goodwin (1863–1865) and Richard C. McCormick (1866–1868), worked to build up a Republican party. Anson Peacely-Killen Safford (1869–1877) spent most of his time dealing with the Apache threat, tax-supported public schools, and fighting crime. Party politics gave way to concern with self-defense and economic development—so much so that starting with the delegate election of 1874, Democrats won the post three times. These Democrats ran as "Independents," and it was not until 1880 that Republicans started adopting the party designation on a regular basis.

Party designations emerged during the administration of John Charles Frémont (1878–1881), the governor that Jay J. Wagoner has argued did the least for the territory of all its territorial governors. Frémont linked up with Associate Justice Charles Silent of the territorial supreme court and territorial assembly member Thomas Fitch to promote their personal fortunes. When Frémont left, the *Tombstone Epitaph* asked on 18 October 1881 that the president not send "another eleemosynary barnacle to be fed from the public crib." Frémont's successor, Frederick A. Tritle (1882–1885), restored public sympathy for the Republican hopefuls sufficiently to have Curtis C. Bean elected delegate in 1884. He was the first to hold that office in a decade.

Party labels were given increased strength with the election of Grover Cleveland as president and the appointment of the first Democratic territorial governor, Conrad Meyer Zulick (1885–1889). Zulick's term was concurrent with the Republican territorial secretary Nathan O. Murphy's arousal of public sentiment against the Apache and against Democratic inaction against Geronimo. General George Crook's inability to catch the Apaches resulted in public outcry and Cleveland's removal of Crook in favor of a Democrat, General Nelson A. Miles. Zulick's departure with the change of president in Washington brought in a bevy of short-termers.

Amid populist agitation in several parts of the territory, Marcus Aurelius Smith emerged as a unifying force in Democratic politics. Building on the anti-Apache sentiment started by Murphy, Mark Smith won the delegate election in 1886 and held that post until elected U.S. senator from Arizona in 1912. Smith established a Democratic machine known as Corporation Democrats, mixing economic expansion with eight-hour-day legislation to attract the rank and file. In Arizona, as in Idaho, the politics were those of accommodation and economic expansion. Most important, economic expansion in Arizona became tied to home rule. Statehood as a goal unified Republican, Democrat, and Progressive after 1900. Mark Smith spent most of his time in Washington opposing federal land-and-water policies, and George W. P. Hunt, a Progressive and Arizona's first state governor, focused upon statehood as a means of putting progressive policies into law. In statehood, they were unified.

THE POLITICS OF STATEHOOD

For territorial legislators and many of their constituents, statehood was a high priority throughout the territorial period. There were many who saw territorial status as vassalage. Some thought that popular sovereignty should prevail throughout government and objected to the bevy of appointed federal officials, too often carpetbaggers. Others thought territorial officials were unresponsive to local needs. There were, in many territories, opposition groups who valued the patronage that territorial status brought, counted upon the federal contracts that fattened bank accounts, and assumed that political control from outside was better than the possible political chaos that could result from local control. In some ways, the two poles of thinking were the ins and the outs of power arguing about political advantage as well as unknown futures.

The politics of statehood frequently involved the holding of constitutional conventions, with or without congressional approval, sometimes with legislative support, and always with the sure and certain hope that Congress could give the endeavor its blessing in statehood. Hawaii's tradition of holding constitutional conventions went back to 1840 with subsequent conventions in 1852, 1864, 1887, 1894, and 1950. In 1947 the legislature established the Hawaii Statehood Commission, gave it a six-figure budget, and committed the political and financial future of the territory to statehood. Utah held its first constitutional convention in 1849, like Hawaii, before territorial status, to avoid territorial status, but had to repeat the constitutional convention ritual six more times before gaining statehood in 1896. The state of Deseret, proclaimed in the 1849 constitution, became the territory of Utah the next year and was, like the 1859 Territory of Jefferson, proclaimed under a constitution before Congress could establish the Territory of Colorado. These earliest attempts at constitution making were clearly attempts to escape vassal status and to join the union as an equal.

The reason for this premature constitution making was the history of statehood politics at the national level. The Northwest Ordinance of 1787 had prescribed specific stages for statehood. The third stage entailed passage of a congressional enabling act authorizing the holding of a constitutional convention and submission of that document to Congress for action. In territorial legislatures, the petitioning for an enabling act became a device to legitimize statehood movements. Ohio had set the pattern under the ordinance. In 1802 its territorial legislature petitioned for authorization to write a constitution. Congress had responded with an enabling act establishing the rules for the election of constitutional convention delegates and the limits of power of those delegates. Ohio elected delegates, held a convention, wrote a constitution, submitted it to Congress, and won admission to the Union. So it went with Indiana, Illinois, Alabama, Mississippi, Missouri, and Louisiana; but between 1836 and 1848, the tradition changed.

Congress admitted Arkansas, Michigan, Iowa, Florida, and Wisconsin in that period, but only Wisconsin wrote its constitution under an enabling act. This shift to territorial initiative in the period was part of a more general congressional tendency to give the territories more power to rule at home. The net impact was for territorial politicians to see a laissez-faire attitude in Congress and great latitude for territorial action. The 1850s and 1860s gave territorial politicians little clear guidance and every reason to believe that the Northwest Ordinance formula was honored in the breach. California, Oregon, and Kansas wrote constitutions and organized state governments without enabling acts. Nebraska and Minnesota petitioned Congress and received the blessing of an enabling act prior to calling a constitutional convention. Nevada's enabling act, given to a territory in

the stage of chaotic factionalism, validated a statehood movement, and after two constitutional conventions the territory gave President Abraham Lincoln the desired electoral votes. This ambivalent heritage resulted in numerous statehood movements and constitutional conventions in the territories. For most, the politics of statehood had the highest priority.

FINDING AND MAKING LAW

The territorial legislatures had the initial responsibility of lawmaking for the people. While Congress usually had the law of the territory from which a new one was sliced to pass on to the new territory in its organic act, such was not always the case. A drafting oversight in the creation of Idaho Territory failed to carry over the laws of Washington Territory, resulting in one homicide case being dismissed on the ground that there was no crime in law against homicide. In the Alaska Organic Act of 1884, Congress created the Territory of Alaska and thereby ended military rule, but it imposed the code of Oregon and forbade the creation of a legislature. In 1899, Congress made changes in the Alaska criminal code and passed a law of taxation for its distant land. The next year, Congress revised the civil code, created two judicial districts, and provided for the incorporation of towns. Finally, in 1912 a second Alaska Organic Act authorized a territorial legislature. Idaho had no law, and Alaska had no authority.

The more usual case found territorial legislatures searching statute books to create law for what most legislators saw as their unique situation. As noted, Alaska had a long heritage of law before a legislature could act. Hawaii also had decades of lawmaking before the creation of a territorial legislature. Regardless of existent law, most territorial legislatures enacted the English common law to the extent that it applied to their conditions. Utah and New Mexico territories refused to enact the English common law because of their respective unique social institutions. Plural marriage in Utah and peonage in New Mexico were very much a part of the social fabric. Mormon territorial legislators wanted to give the gentile minority no leverage in law to attack polygamy. That would come later with federal legislation, but in 1850 the Mormon theocracy controlled the legislature. New Mexico's first families in its first territorial legislatures wanted protection for a labor system that was both traditional and economically beneficial to their interests. But in 1867, Congress again stepped in to end peonage in New Mexico Territory.

In addition to the broad provisions of English common law, first legislative sessions had to deal with the immediate problems of creating the offices of government and its infrastructure. They also had to deal with inherited statutes. Such was the experience of Arizona, created from New Mexico Territory in 1863. Governor John N. Goodwin's message to the first territorial legislature called for the immediate repeal of the New Mexico territorial statutes authorizing peonage and imprisonment for debt. Goodwin found these statutes repugnant to the great principles of liberty then being contested on the battlefields of North and South. Further, Goodwin stressed the need for a code commission to bring law to Arizona Territory and to assure the people that the law was suited to their condition. The legislature followed his advice, and also incorporated six tollways and two railroad companies.

The Arizona code commission was made up of Associate Justice William T. Howell of the territorial supreme court and Coles Bashford, both relative newcomers to the territory. Bashford was the first lawyer admitted to the Arizona bar, first president of the territorial council, and first territorial attorney general. He had been a district attorney in his native New York before moving to Wisconsin, where he won election to the state senate as a Whig. He was active in the formation of the Republican party and in 1855 gained the Wisconsin governor's seat. Howell, in addition to having judicial experience, had been a member of the Michigan legislature. Howell and Bashford started work on the code six months before the legislature convened on 26 September 1864 to authorize their work or to devise a compensation scheme. Howell, in particular, had seen the need for a code and a comprehensive means of superseding New Mexico territorial statutes at the first legislative session.

Howell's Code, as it came to be known, was eclectic. Working from available statute books from California, New York, and several other states, its authors found law. They also held hearings to find out the opinions of interested citizens. Ninety days later, they had compiled a four-hundred-page comprehensive code. After the legislature authorized Governor Goodwin to appoint a code commissioner, he selected Howell and two days later presented the code to the solons. The legislature provided $2,500 for his services as code commissioner, and he drew a judicial salary of $2,500 per year beginning on his date of appointment, eleven months prior to his arrival in the territory. As Jay J. Wagoner has observed, this compensation scheme was one of the most lucrative in the history of the territory. His service as code commissioner, however, did give the territory a comprehensive statutory basis for governing.

Other territories were not as fortunate to have the foresight of a Howell. The first legislative session, usually too brief for comprehensive lawmaking, made efforts to deal with the highest-priority issues. Most legislatures created governmental offices, taxing systems to pay for them, civil and criminal codes, and statutes for special interests. For legislatures meeting before 1872, the central problem of the economy and a large constituency was the creation of mining law. Howell took most of his language from California and Mexican law, with parts of the New York code salted in in places. Legislators looked, as Howell had, to California and their own experience because the Congress did not enact a comprehensive statute until the Mining Act of 1872. The first legislative session usually ratified the local mining district rules and gave them the sanction of territorial legislation for judicial scrutiny. The reason for this form of legislation was the respect legislators had for the local rules and their efficacy. Subsequent legislative sessions started tinkering with local rules to give them uniformity for future application.

The reason for the early attention to mining law was the vast wealth that the mineral enterprises represented. Gold and silver strikes were spectacular news, but the mineral industry meant jobs and economic growth. Arizona and Montana would benefit not only from the glint of precious metals but also from the copper deposits in their ground. Coal was abundant in Utah, Montana, and Wyoming. Even the lignite deposits of Dakota Territory would attract notice as cheap fuel. Territorial legislation would control the location by prospectors of these minerals and provide for their exploitation.

TAXATION

Territorial legislators early on had to confront the question of taxing mines and the public policy issue of whether to favor the mining enterprise over others. One of the problems that legislators faced was how to assess value for tax purposes. Local tax assessors had the burden of looking at a mine in various stages of development and establishing a value for the tax rolls. Mine owners argued that such assessment was unfair because the value of a mine could only be determined as the enterprise unfolded and the ore was converted into bullion. With mine owners in legislatures, these arguments carried a good deal of weight and limited the tax man's burden.

Arizona's experience perhaps best illustrates the shaping of tax legislation in a territorial legislature. The Howell Code provided that mines were to be taxed as property, but mine owners were permitted to pay, instead of property taxes, an annual tax of 5 percent on the net proceeds and 50 cents on every hundred dollars of value of real estate owned. The 1866 legislature tinkered with this provision, repealing it and replacing the concept of value with one based on invested capital and capital stock. That concept lasted until the 1868 session, when the legislature provided that all mining companies were relieved of the payment of taxes in 1868 beyond those assessed on their real and personal property. In 1875 the legislators hit on the concept of net proceeds, with the provision that operating expenses could not exceed 90 percent of the gross proceeds of ore for ore valued at $30–$90 per ton and a similar sliding scale for ores of greater value. Ore with a value of less than $30 per ton was exempt from taxation. Two years later, the legislature tinkered with the distribution of the 2-percent net-proceeds tax, with 25 percent going to territorial coffers and the remainder to the county. In 1881, the 1875 net-proceeds tax was repealed and mining companies were taxed under the corporation tax scheme. By the end of the nineteenth century, the complaint that the mines were not bearing their fair share of the tax burden had surfaced.

Governor Nathan O. Murphy's 1899 message to the territorial legislature painted a grim picture. Small farmers and cattlemen were paying their fare share of the tax burden, but the great mining companies were extracting their gold, silver, and copper to the great profit of eastern investors but not the territorial coffers. He estimated that the $100-million worth of mining properties in Arizona were assessed and taxed at a value of $2 million. He called on the legislature for action and got nothing. The net-proceeds tax bill failed, as did a bill to create the office of territorial mine inspector and to regulate the hours of underground miners. The mining bloc, or the "copper collar," of the Phelps-Dodge Company was a very effective lobby against any unfavorable legislation. But the Arizona Progressives, under George W. P. Hunt, were building popular momentum by singling out corporate favor and abuse for political and constitutional action.

These Progressives captured the 1910 constitutional convention, determined to stamp out graft and corruption and to eradicate all special favors, including bounties, subsidies, and taxes for any purpose other than revenue. The Progressive's philosophy of taxation for revenue purposes did not question tax policy in varying the burden for economic or social goals. Rather, they wanted to ensure equality and uniformity and to stamp out the sordid legislative past. They reasoned that with equality and uniformity, the burden of taxation would be based on the ability to pay and would reflect the relative benefit received from the state. Further, they wanted a tax commission to oversee the system. The scheme was to overturn the territorial legislative system that had allowed mines and railroads to escape most taxation.

The Progressives got what they wanted. In 1912 the tax commissioner more than doubled the assessed valuation of mines. The year before, Arizona's mines had paid 19.3 percent of Arizona's taxes. In 1912, mine owners would contribute 31.7 percent of the tax revenues and 37.2 percent the year after. With statehood came a new dawn for revenue enhancement.

Alaska's first territorial legislature started where the Arizona Progressives left off with statehood. Although hampered by an organic act that limited the taxing power, Alaska's first territorial legislature established a tax system and the office of territorial treasurer. Included in the tax system was a license tax on salmon canneries. The second territorial legislature created the first old-age pension system in the United States, created four road districts, amended the banking code, placed a bounty on wolves, provided for the government of Indian villages, enacted a voluntary workers'-compensation system, but was unable to improve the taxing system, because of the effectiveness of the canned salmon lobby.

And so it went until 1949. Taxation was minimal, and much of the wealth of Alaska was being transported elsewhere. Further, tax reform was important because it was a signal to Congress that Alaskans were willing to tax the special interests and themselves. The 1949 legislature rose to the occasion to pass a comprehensive revenue code and to become what Governor Ernest Gruening termed the best legislature in territorial history.

WATER LAW

The arid environment also created a challenge for the Rocky Mountain territorial legislatures. The scarcity of water and the increasing demands for water from farmers, ranchers, and city dwellers put pressure on legislators for innovative action and consequently on legal tradition. The law of the East was riparian rights: under that English common law of waters, the owners of a stream bank could take water for agricultural, domestic, and other purposes to a reasonable extent. The amount of water taken could not diminish the interests of downstream riparian users, nor could the upstream riparian decrease the quality of the water by use of that water. Riparian rights assumed a steady and dependable supply of water. In the rainy parts of the East, as in England, nature provided and the law gave rights to property owners.

In the arid West, nature did not so provide. Rain was a sometime thing in many parts of the Rocky Mountain territories, and Native Americans, like the Spanish, had found that irrigation was necessary to sustain agriculture. So, too, the region's placer (a deposit of gold in sand, gravel, or disintegrated rock along the course or under the bed of a watercourse) miners had diverted water from streams and conducted it great distances to wash their pay dirt and ex-

pose a little color in the sluice. Faced with the environmental necessity and the practices of the region, legislators and territorial judges altered the law of England and created a law of waters to fit their condition. This new water law came to be known as prior appropriation.

Prior-appropriation doctrine held that the first to appropriate water for a beneficial purpose had a right to that amount of water. "The first in time is the first in right" became a legal precept in the region. What this meant in practical terms was that any person, not just the owner of the bank of a stream, could access water for beneficial purposes such as agriculture, industrial, and domestic applications. Riparians could not close out those that came later. There would be no staking out of the water hole to monopolize the only means to agricultural or ranching success on the arid lands.

The doctrine found its way into territorial legislation and forced another innovation in property law. For a person remote from a water source to access water, the appropriator had to cross the lands of others to bring water to the land. The appropriator had to trespass, but legislators worked a revolution in the concept of eminent domain to eliminate the problem of trespass. Eminent domain gave government the authority to take private property for a public use with just compensation being paid to the property owner. This concept had roots in the colonial experience and had been included in the Fifth Amendment to the U.S. Constitution. Private parties had no such authority. A person owning land remote from water could only attempt to negotiate easements with each and every property owner in the path to the water. One property owner could frustrate the effort to irrigate. But Rocky Mountain territorial legislators declared such takings by private parties to be for a public purpose, thereby putting the power of government in the hands of entrepreneurs.

The public policy goals were simple and dynamic. The application of water to the soil or to industry had the necessary multiplier impact of producing goods or services that enhanced economic growth. Eminent-domain provisions allowed for access to water and protected property owners by requiring the payment of just compensation for the property taken in the process of digging an irrigation ditch or laying a pipe across the land. Natural resources were to be used, but individuals were not always able or willing to use water as efficiently as possible.

Early territorial legislation legitimized the taking of water by appropriators and established procedures for subsequent appropriations. The procedures usually treated water as property requiring appropriators to file notices of intent to take water at a certain place and time. These notices were to be filed with the local recorder. This filing requirement gave other appropriators opportunity to challenge the filing appropriator and judges certainty regarding the time, place, and amount of the appropriation. As quickly became obvious, conflicts arose and people appropriated more water than the streams carried. Utah Territory did not follow this recording system in early legislation, but gave to the Mormon hierarchy rights in land and water that enabled it to control those natural resources. Territorial legislation required that in addition to filing requirements, the appropriator start work within a statutory period of time and continue work on the irrigation facility with due diligence. The public policy objective was to exploit the resource as quickly as possible.

Another area of legislative attention was the definition of "beneficial use." In the abstract, the declaration of beneficial use for water was simple; however, in conflict situations, competing interests required legislative definitions and priorities. Territorial legislators easily defined domestic applications of water to have the highest priority. Not as easily defined were the agricultural, ranching, industrial, and urban interests. Legislative preferences changed with time, but early statutes exhibited the farming and ranching preferences, yielding in the twentieth century to urban and industrial uses.

Territorial legislation also provided for the institutional means for dispute resolution. Most frequently, legislation directed parties to the court system, but legislators often aided the judicial process by authorizing special investigations and by expanding jurisdiction. Colorado, Montana, and New Mexico territories were particularly active legislatively. Utah Territory was the least active because Mormon church officials often adjudicated disputes between church members. Gentiles went to court. Wyoming territorial legislation was the most far-reaching in the early movement toward adjudication by an administrative agency.

Territorial lawmakers gave the irrigators' business organization form in the irrigation district. Early legislation gave irrigators the authority to define a geographic area as an administrative entity with quasi-governmental powers. Generally, the legislation provided that a certain number of freeholders or a majority thereof could define a geographic area as an irrigation district. The statutes described the government of that district. A board of trustees, elected under statutory procedures, was vested with administrative authority, including the taxing power. This power to tax enabled the district to raise capital sufficient for the location, construction, and maintenance of canals and pipelines. Again, legislators had delegated the sovereign power to tax to a private entity for the public policy purpose of economic expansion. Ultimately, legislators extended the authority to issue bonds to irrigation districts. These water bonds created liens upon district lands and tax revenues were used to pay bondholders. Tax-exempt status for irrigation districts further enhanced the investment value of the bonds and the viability of the districts.

Territorial legislation also insinuated itself into the governance of the irrigation of the districts. The legal privileges extended in organization, administration, and taxation carried with them certain duties. Districts were to keep their canals in repair to prevent seepage and overflow. Headgates were to be maintained in good order. Waters were not to be polluted. Statutes authorized a structure of enterprise, but held it to basic levels of responsibility. Unfortunately, in the area of water pollution, legislators did not quickly respond to the coal slack, animal carcasses, and mine tailings that befouled the waters of the West. Therefore, victims turned to courts, often finding common-law remedies less than satisfactory.

WOMEN'S RIGHTS

Women in the territorial West found legislative progress moving with glacial slowness in some areas and with volcanic speed in others. In the area of property rights, women made substantial gains. Building upon gains in the East, territorial legislatures early extended property rights to women. For example, Colorado's first territorial legislature granted women rights in property conveyances and inheritance. In 1874 the lawmakers expanded those rights to include *feme sole*, the right of married women to conduct business independently of their husbands. Arizona's Howell Code and early Wyoming and Montana statutes made similar provisions. Women in other territories had to wait much longer for such rights.

Utah, New Mexico, and Hawaii had cultural constraints on legislative action that delayed the extension of property rights to married women. Hispanic pressure and political influence delayed statutory revision until 1884 in New Mexico. Utah's Mormon heritage retarded reform in the territory until the 1880s. Similarly, Hawaii's ruling family hindered reform until 1888, when the kingdom passed the Married Women's Property Act, bringing it into line with states that had passed similar laws in prior decades. Not surprisingly, the legal status of women in Hawaii changed little after annexation in 1898. Two years later, Hawaii became a territory, and in 1907 and 1919 the territorial legislature opened higher education to women. In the latter year, the legislature provided for a Board of Child Welfare to give money to women with dependent children. Six years earlier, the lawmakers had passed protective labor legislation for women limiting the place of employment and forbidding women to work on graveyard shifts. Change was slow, but change it was.

Change for women in Wyoming moved at volcanic speed. The 1869 territorial legislature, borrowing a statute from Colorado, adopted an act to protect married women in their separate property, as well as an antidiscrimination school-employment law and a law giving women the right both to vote and to hold office. William H. Bright, the president of the territorial council, offered the bill giving women of eighteen years of age the right to vote. In the Wyoming House of Representatives the bill was amended to change the age limit to twenty-one. Governor John A. Campbell signed the bill into law on 6 December 1869.

Woman suffrage in the West was clearly ahead of its time, but Wyoming was not alone. The Dakota territorial legislature had failed by a single vote to enact woman suffrage in January 1869. The Utah territorial legislature gave women the vote in February 1870. Change was under way, but slow in arriving in the statute books. For Utah, woman suffrage lasted little more than a decade, being stamped out by federal legislation designed to end the power of the Mormon church in the territory. The movement was not to end in Utah or any other territory. Ultimately, a constitutional amendment would endorse what Wyoming had brought to territorial statute.

INERTIA AND THE PORK BARREL

Other aspects of territorial legislation were far less forward looking. The simple question of where the capital should be located engaged several territorial legislatures for extended periods of time and illustrates the nature of politics and its intersections with law.

The Oklahoma territorial legislature's fixation with the location of the capital cost the people of the territory dearly. The lawmakers took so much time debating capital location that they had to stay in session without pay to pass a code of laws. That code of laws was eclectic and somewhat incongruous because of its patchwork nature. The public schools were unable to open until January 1891 because of legislative ineffectiveness, and the county governments started out in debt. The legislature created counties that were compelled to run for a year or more after organization without tax revenues, because of the failure of the legislature to authorize the counties to tax. Warrants and bonds had to hold together the fabric of local government, pending legislative action.

Idaho's first territorial capital was Lewiston, a handling center for the mining region. The second session of the legislature wanted to move the capital to Boise because of its burgeoning population. This naturally embittered Lewiston and northern Idaho residents. Governor Caleb Lyon became embroiled in the hot political debate, but eventually escaped it by leaving the territory; his absence left the territory without a governor for two months. Territorial secretary Clinton Dewitt Smith was appointed acting governor, but he took eight months to reach Idaho and soon died of alcoholism. Amid this turmoil, the Boise County treasurer absconded with $14,000 in tax receipts, only to be bested by Horace Gilson, who looted the territorial treasury of $41,000. Lyon returned to Idaho eleven months later to complete his term and to return east with $46,000 in Indian funds that were later allegedly stolen from him on his way to Washington. The capital made it to Boise, but governmental stability did not seem to accompany it.

Montana's first legislature met in Bannack and, as part of its first session, moved the capital to Virginia City. Virginia City, like Lewiston, started to lose population, thereby giving other cities hope of becoming the capital and reaping the economic benefits. Helena and Deer Lodge worked hard to gain legislative favor. In 1869 the legislature provided for an election contest to determine the capital. Helena and Virginia City voters apparently turned out unusually large numbers in the August election, returning more votes than their populations seemed to justify. The returns were sent to Virginia City for tabulation, but mysteriously the votes were burned. Virginia City remained the capital, and the struggle continued.

In 1874 the legislature sent the issue to the people for a fourth time. This time the statute provided for electoral controls. The law provided harsh penalties for voting fraud and for dishonesty by election officials. County commissioners were charged with the responsibility of counting the ballots and sending them to the territorial secretary. The territorial secretary then, with the U.S. marshal and in the presence of the governor, was to canvass the election results and to declare a winner. That was the law on the books. The law in action—or, more precisely, Montana territorial politics in action—was another matter. The vote of Gallatin County was not in its proper form. The unofficial tabulation of Meagher County gave the capital to Helena, 561 to 29, but when the vote emerged from the canvassing board, Virginia City had 561 and Helena 29.

The public and government reactions were immediate. Helena denounced the electoral theft. The Meagher County clerk and recorder declared the returns to be a forgery. Marshal William Wheeler agreed and sought to postpone the official canvass. The territorial secretary refused. Wheeler and Governor Benjamin Franklin Potts appealed to the U.S. attorney general for a ruling. They were rebuffed on jurisdictional grounds, and the issue went to

court in the form of a mandamus action (a writ issued by a superior court commanding the performance of a special official act or duty) against the canvassing board.

The issue before the Montana Supreme Court was whether the canvassing board had the power merely to count the returns and inform the governor of the result or also to determine the validity of the returns and compel the governor to proclaim the results. The court decided that the territorial legislature had the authority to require federal appointees to perform duties not set out with specificity in the organic act. Given this state of the law, the court ordered a recanvassing based on the true vote and instructed the governor to proclaim the result based on that vote. This decision was appealed to the U.S. Supreme Court, with James A. Garfield representing the territory. In Washington the justices declared that they had no jurisdiction to hear the case and dismissed. With judicial finality in hand, territorial secretary James E. Callaway conducted the recanvassing. With Governor Potts absent, Callaway declared Helena to be the capital. Another long and costly fight over the spoils of government ended—at least until statehood.

Wyoming's capital politics was somewhat more sophisticated. Cheyenne and Laramie competed in the territorial legislature for favor and the prize of governmental operating expenses. An 1875 effort to shift government to Evanston failed, but it reminded Cheyenne politicans how weak their hold on territorial politics could be. Governor Francis E. Warren pushed to end the divisive atmosphere by assuring Cheyenne the permanent site. In 1886, Warren moved with his trusted lieutenant, Willis A. Van Devanter, to end the controversy. On 24 February 1886, Warren had Nick O'Brien introduce a bill to erect a capitol building in Cheyenne. Van Devanter moved to quiet Laramie's cries with a bill to build the University of Wyoming in Laramie. To keep Evanston in line, legislation directed the building of an asylum for the mentally ill there. The logrolling was successful, and all three of the competitors got something that brought jobs and prosperity in the public mind.

Arizona's capital politics were protracted and, like Wyoming's, filled with logrolling. When the first territorial legislature met on 26 September 1864 in Prescott, the "capitol building" was a two-room log cabin with a dirt floor and pine logs so freshly hewn that balsam still speckled the beams. In 1867 the solons designated Tucson the capital, and in November 1868 they occupied Hiram S. Stevens's adobe on Main Street. Tucson had no sidewalks, lawns, paved roads, or trappings of governmental splendor. The 1877 session of the legislature moved the seat of government back to Prescott, but the pressure was still on for change. The 1885 session took some steam out of the capital campaigns by spreading the spoils. Yuma got a prison. Phoenix won the prized asylum and an appropriation of $100,000. The legislature gave Tempe the state teachers' college and $5,000 to get the urgent job of training teachers under way. The University of Arizona went to Tucson with a grant five times that of Tempe's, but only one-fourth that of Phoenix.

Tempe's normal school resulted from the work of Charles Trumball Hayden, father of Carl Hayden, Arizona's longtime U.S. senator. Hayden worked to have one of his employees, John S. Armstrong, elected to the legislature on a platform that pledged to get an asylum and a university for the county. Armstrong got legislators to consider Tempe for the asylum, but Hayden considered the asylum a liability and sent Armstrong back to Prescott to support Phoenix for the plum. So it was that Tempe got what became Arizona State University.

But the Phoenix campaign continued, for despite having the asylum in town, the city fathers still wanted the capital, and in 1889, they got it. The fifteenth legislative session opened in Prescott on 21 January 1889, and Governor Conrad Meyer Zulick, a lame-duck Democrat, signed a bill five days later declaring that the capital was Phoenix and that the legislature would convene there on 4 February 1889. While Zulick's ink was drying on the act, the legislators started packing their bags for a ride on two Pullman cars to Phoenix via Los Angeles. The citizens of Phoenix picked up the tab for the junket and welcomed government to town.

THE DEATH OF THE TERRITORIAL SYSTEM

Territorial legislatures, like many of their state counterparts, spent too much time on the im-

mediate. As Carlos A. Schwantes has so ably put it regarding Washington Territory's legislators, they seldom raised their sights beyond narrow, partisan, and material ends. The capital campaigns could, however, focus the people upon the shortcomings of territorial status and their politicians. As Lamar has described Dakota Territory's experience, such campaigns could carry the seeds of the demise of the territorial system.

Even before the first Dakota territorial legislature met in 1862, Governor William Jayne and Yankton politicians were working to assure Yankton capital status. Sioux Falls, Vermillion, and Bon Homme saw themselves as fine capital cities. But spoils could cross party lines and soothe city fathers. Agreeing to leave the capital in Yankton, George M. Pinney of Bon Homme accepted the speakership of the House, and his Bon Homme neighbor J. H. Shober became president of the council. Vermillion became the site of the territorial university, and Bon Homme got the territorial penitentiary. But the factionalized politics of the Yankton Oligarchy, the Custom House Gang, and the Railroad Combination and its attendant corruption gave the local press fodder aplenty.

Yankton and the railroad lobby became closely identified. One way to break railroad domination, some thought, was by moving the capital away from it, and Ansley Gray's 1879 bill to move the capital to Bismarck was designed to do exactly that. The Yankton forces won the 1879 fight, but capital removal indicated that division was inevitable. Governor Nehemiah G. Ordway became the force that broke the Yankton machine. Appointed in 1880, Ordway was ready by 1882 to move the capital to Pierre, where his son was railroad agent, or to Bismarck, where he owned property. Ordway also had his spoilsmen in place under federal patronage as well as a press beholden thereto.

Ordway forces used the legislative stratagem of proposing Huron as capital. Failing that, the Huron and northern Dakota legislators got behind a capital-removal commission bill. Not surprisingly, the 1883 commission report recommended Bismarck as the new capital. That recommendation set off a political struggle that would result in division of the territory. As Lamar has pointed out, this struggle was in fact three movements: a statehood movement, a crusade for social reform, and a farmers' revolt. Ordway had linked up with another political boss, Alexander McKenzie of Bismarck and the Northern Pacific Railroad, in the capital-removal scheme. The three movements would diverge from the bosses and converge in statehood.

Ordway and McKenzie controlled much of the territorial press, but the anti-Ordway forces built up a press seeking his removal and the defeat of every legislator from southern Dakota who had voted for capital removal. The anti-Ordway forces were successful on both counts. President Arthur removed Ordway on 25 June 1884 and replaced him with Gilbert A. Pierce, a Chicago journalist and playwright. In the 1885 elections the people returned only one of the capital-removal legislators to the assembly. The 1885 assembly withheld funds for the building of the new capitol at Bismarck and flatly refused the capital commission report. Rather, they reported a bill establishing the capital at Pierre. Pierce vetoed it. In 1887 the legislature, calmed with time, accepted the report of the commissioners, and thus Bismarck became the capital.

The chaos flowing from the capital controversy and the legislative behavior regarding it created a negative idea in the public mind. The territorial system seemed corrupt, but the Yankton men had won the political wars, despite losing the capital. The people elected southern Dakotans as the territorial delegate until statehood and gave Dakotan southerners the edge in the assembly. Further, the corruption increased hatred of the territorial system. Reformers, Grangers, and statehood advocates came to see that they had common ground in statehood.

Given this territorial experience, legislators and politicans were very much a part of their times and environment. They were making law for a new land in most cases and bringing the politics of the East to the West. The new land impacted both in most cases. As shown, politics and law are not the same, although certain themes give both an American flavor. The spoilsmen of the East sent retainers to the West with their carpetbags carefully packed, but there they met newly arrived settlers and old families wanting to participate in the territorial experience for personal gain. As a result, the rise of rings, oligarchies, and gangs in politics is not particularly surprising. The late-nineteenth-century experience of spoils and protest was mirrored, in part, in the West. But territorial legislators had more to do than participate. They had to give law to this new land.

CONCLUSION

The lawgivers were not particularly innovative in the first sessions of territorial legislatures. Generally, they borrowed from what they knew best and what had stood the test of time. The English common law and eastern codes quickly found their way into statute books. But territorial lawgivers also faced challenges unknown in the East. An arid frontier and a hard-rock mining industry required innovation or at least action to validate the actions of local lawmakers, and so there emerged a new water law that had vast impact in the Rocky Mountain states. For the miners, territorial legislators gave sanction to their actions in local mining-district meetings. Territorial legislators also provided civil and criminal codes for the general governance of the jurisdiction. Much of this law was borrowed, but so, too, was the structure of government. What most legislatures struggled with was a taxing system for their fiscal needs. Those struggles continued into statehood and will persist into the future. Much of this responsible lawmaking exhibited innovation as well as petty politicking. Wyoming was able to be the first state to give women the right to vote, but would play politics with the location of the capital. Arizona would give life to a major Progressive movement, but have a prolonged season of wrangling over the location of a capitol.

Territorial legislators and officials were among the famous and the obscure. Willis A. Van Devanter of Wyoming proved an accomplished politican and jurist for the territory and sat on the U.S. Supreme Court. Coles Bashford was an experienced politician, officeholder, and lawyer in New York and Wisconsin before arriving in Arizona. Walter A. Burleigh appeared in both Dakota and Montana territories during his career. John H. Kinkead sat in the Nevada constitutional conventions of 1863 and 1864, held the presidency of the People's Convention of Sitka, Alaska, in 1869, and served as that state's governor in 1884 and 1885. Some of these men were clearly the wanderers of the western territorial experience.

The man to examplify the wanderer in territorial politics and law was John C. Frémont's right-hand man in Arizona Territory, Thomas Finch. Finch was an editor, attorney, and politician on the fly. He was the editor of the *Milwaukee Free Democrat* in 1859, but a law student in San Francisco in 1860. In 1861 he returned to journalism to edit a paper in the Bay City. The next year found him editing the *Placerville Republican*. In 1863–1864 Fitch edited the *Virginia City Union* in Nevada and was a member of the Nevada constitutional convention of 1864. He turned to law in Belmont, Nevada, in 1869; in Salt Lake City in 1871; in San Francisco in 1875; in Prescott, Arizona, in 1877; in Minneapolis in 1880; and in Tucson in 1881. Finch was a frontier cruiser with the famous and the infamous.

But the flighty politician was not the one that took a territory to statehood. Rather, the men and women who persisted and worked diligently for change and statehood eventually prevailed. The business of many a legislator and politician was the struggle for political deliverance. In statehood and the idea of popular sovereignty, many thought they had found liberation from the bonds of congressional oversight. The politics and law of the territorial experience were carried into statehood, along with their attendant problems.

One of the key reasons for the conception of statehood as deliverance was the omnipresent hand of the federal government in the appointment of officials, the setting of legislative limitations, and bureaucratic intrusion. Whether the heavy hand of federal intrusion in shared governance was real or not, the fact that people in the territories wanted liberation from it is critical. Complete democracy and discretion in statehood was a watchword of statehood movements, but the hand of the federal tax man, bureaucrat, and administrator was never really withdrawn. Statehood changed the relationship and put these territories on a new footing and gave them a voice in Washington, where they could continue to be heard.

BIBLIOGRAPHY

The Northwest

For a general work relating to territorial legislatures in the U.S. Northwest, see CARLOS A. SCHWANTES, *The Pacific Northwest: An Interpretive History* (Lincoln, Nebr., 1989). On Washington politics, see ROBERT W. JOHANNSEN, "National Issues and Local Politics in Washington Territory, 1857–1861," *Pacific Northwest Quarterly* 42 (January 1951): 3–31 and WILLIS A. KATZ, "Benjamin F. Kendall, Territorial Politician," *Pacific Northwest Quarterly* 49 (January 1958): 29–39. For a discussion of sentiments against Mormonism in Idaho, see MERLE W. WELLS, *Anti-Mormonism in Idaho, 1872–1880* (Provo, Utah, 1978) and "Origins of Anti-Mormonism in Idaho, 1872–1880," *Pacific Northwest Quarterly* 47 (October 1956): 107–116. MICHAEL P. MALONE and RICHARD B. ROEDER, *Montana: A History of Two Centuries* (Seattle, 1976); and CLARK C. SPENCE, *Territorial Politics and Government in Montana, 1864–89* (Urbana, Ill., 1975), relate to Montana, while Wyoming is discussed in T. A. LARSON, *History of Wyoming*, 2d ed. (Lincoln, Nebr., 1978) and LEWIS L. GOULD, *Wyoming: A Political History, 1868–1896* (New Haven, Conn., 1968). The Dakotas are covered in HOWARD ROBERTS LAMAR, *Dakota Territory, 1861–1889: A Study of Frontier Politics* (New Haven, Conn., 1956); THOMAS W. HOWARD, ed., *The North Dakota Political Tradition* (Ames, Iowa, 1981); and ALAN L. CLEM, *Prairie State Politics: Popular Democracy in South Dakota* (Washington, D.C., 1967).

The Southwest

HOWARD ROBERTS LAMAR, *The Far Southwest, 1846–1912: A Territorial History* (New Haven, Conn., 1966), contains information on the "Four Corners" states of Arizona, Colorado, New Mexico, and Utah. Also discussing those states are JAY J. WAGONER, *Arizona Territory, 1863–1912: A Political History* (Tucson, Ariz., 1970); JAMES W. BYRKIT, *Forging the Copper Collar: Arizona's Labor-Management War of*

HISTORICAL CONTEXT

1901–1921 (Tucson, Ariz., 1982); CARL ABBOTT, STEPHEN J. LEONARD, and DAVID MCCOMB, *Colorado: A History of the Centennial State* (Boulder, Colo., 1982); JACK ELLSWORTH HOLMES, *Politics in New Mexico* (Albuquerque, N.Mex., 1967); and EDWARD LEO LYMAN, *Political Deliverance: The Mormon Quest for Utah Statehood* (Urbana, Ill., 1986).

Other works on specific states in this region are RUSSELL R. ELLIOTT, *History of Nevada*, 2d ed. (Lincoln, Nebr., 1987); GRANT FOREMAN, *A History of Oklahoma* (Norman, Okla., 1942); and ROY GITTINGER, *The Formation of the State of Oklahoma* (Norman, Okla., 1939).

Alaska and Hawaii
The forty-ninth state's history can be found in ERNEST GRUENING, *The State of Alaska* (New York, 1954); CLAUS M. NASKE, *An Interpretive History of Alaskan Statehood* (Anchorage, Alaska, 1973); TED C. HINCKLEY, *The Americanization of Alaska, 1867–1897* (Palo Alto, Calif., 1972); GERALD A. MCBEATH and THOMAS A. MOREHOUSE, eds., *Alaska State Government and Politics* (Fairbanks, Alaska, 1987); and KERMIT SYPPLI KYNELL, *A Different Frontier: Alaska Criminal Justice, 1935–1965* (Lanham, Md., 1991).

Hawaii's path to statehood can be traced in GAVAN DAWS, *Shoal of Time: A History of the Hawaiian Islands* (Honolulu, 1968); RICHARD H. KOSKI, "Constitutions and Constitutional Conventions in Hawaii," *Hawaii Journal of History* 12 (1978): 120–138; ROGER BELL, *Last Among Equals: Hawaiian Statehood and American Politics* (Honolulu, 1984); and GEORGE COOPER and GAVAN DAWS, *Land and Power in Hawaii: The Democratic Years* (Honolulu, 1985).

Other Topics
For the American territorial system in general, see JACK ERICSON EBLEN, *The First and Second United States Empires* (Pittsburgh, Pa., 1968); EARL S. POMEROY, *The Territories and the United States, 1861–1890* (Seattle, 1969); and KENNETH N. OWENS, "Pattern and Structure in Western Territorial Politics," in JOHN PORTER BLOOM, ed., *The American Territorial System* (Athens, Ohio, 1973): 161–179.

To read more on the woman-suffrage movement, see BEVERLY BEETON, *Women in the West: The Woman Suffrage Movement, 1989–1896* (New York, 1986); JUDITH R. GETLING, "Christianity and Coverture: Impact on the Legal Status of Women in Hawaii, 1820–1920," *Hawaiian Journal of History* 11 (1977): 188–220; and PAULA PETRIK, *No Step Backward: Women and Family on the Rocky Mountain Mining Frontier, Helena, Montana, 1865–1900* (Helena, Mont., 1987).

A legal history of the Rocky Mountain region in particular is discussed in GORDON MORRIS BAKKEN, *Rocky Mountain Constitution Making, 1850–1912* (Westport, Conn., 1987) and *The Development of Law on the Rocky Mountain Frontier: Civil Law and Society, 1850–1912* (Westport, Conn., 1983).

Also see ROBERT W. LARSON, *Populism in the Mountain West* (Albuquerque, N.Mex., 1986); and LEWIS EMANUEL YOUNG, *Mine Taxation in the United States* (Urbana, Ill., 1916), for further research on specific topics discussed in the above essay.

SEE ALSO Constitutional Requirements for Legislative Service; Legislatures and the Environment; Legislatures and Gender Issues; AND The Social Bases of Legislative Recruitment.

THE HISTORIOGRAPHY OF THE AMERICAN LEGISLATIVE SYSTEM

Joel H. Silbey

For more than a century, there have been repeated attempts by journalists, scholars, and other observers to describe and analyze the American legislative experience in all its complexity. These efforts to comprehend the dynamics of legislative life by now include a very large list of books and articles—a legislative historiography that has ranged from memoir and the retelling of anecdotes and morality tales, to scientific examination, nuanced description, sophisticated theory building about legislative activities, and, at present, the attempt to grasp the legislative experience as a total system of predictable behavior.

The first observers who described American legislatures were involved partisans, journalists, and foreign travelers seeking to understand the dynamics of American democracy in the nineteenth century. Their efforts were usually anecdotal and largely addressed to a single aspect of legislatures in action, such as a dramatic debate, the activities of a prominent representative, or the way some legislative office operated. Frequently, they had either a partisan or a reformist agenda and thus graded American legislatures on their policies or compared them to some ideal form and almost always found them wanting. Moralizing, often hyperbolic in tone, these writers usually ended with a number of specific prescriptions for improvement. Over time, however, the participatory style of these observers gave way to a more systematic and empirical approach, ultimately with more scientific, generalizing purposes, as political scientists, historians, and occasionally economists and sociologists channeled legislative research in new directions and far beyond its original boundaries.

The styles of investigation—scholarly, partisan, popular, reformist—were never mutually exclusive. In the latter half of the nineteenth century, for example, amid much partisan description and reformist prescription, scholarly endeavors were also well under way. And even as scholarly norms came to dominate the more and more professional endeavor to understand legislatures in the twentieth century, a variety of more popular journalistic material continued to appear, along with partisan and reformist tracts and even several novels about Congress and state legislatures.

FROM PARTICIPATION TO SCHOLARSHIP

When scholarly interest in legislatures began to develop during the birth of history and political science as professional disciplines at the end of the nineteenth century, there already was at hand an extensive list of personal memoirs by legislators, some studies of great moments of political history as acted out in Congress, and collections of raw material drawn from legislative activities on which to base scholarly legislative studies. In the 1830s, Alexis de Tocqueville discussed Congress's contribution in *Democracy in America*. As far back as 1856, Thomas Hart Benton of Missouri published his *Thirty Years View* of life in the U.S. Senate. Similar autobiographical efforts by other congressmen—James G. Blaine, Samuel Sullivan Cox, Shelby Cullom, George Frisbie Hoar, and John Sherman, among others—followed, along with views of Congress in action by journalists and other observers of the Washington scene, both native and those from abroad who followed Tocqueville's path. The clerk of the House of Representatives during the Civil War era, Edward McPherson, compiled an impressive array of descriptive materials about congressional activities, first published in a single volume in 1866 and thereafter presented in his annual political almanacs. None of these, of course, laid any claim to scholarship or dispassion, but they provided some of the basic raw material of, and useful insights into, legislative life to go along with the plentiful records compiled by the legislatures themselves, such as the reports of their debates, and with descriptive material published in contemporary newspapers and other publications.

Woodrow Wilson's *Congressional Government*, originally published in 1885, marks the real beginning of scholarly analysis of the American legislative process. As a political scientist with a doctorate from Johns Hopkins University, Wilson successfully demonstrated the disciplined research commitments of the new social sciences rapidly emerging within American universities at the end of the nineteenth century. In *Congressional Government* he focused a great deal of attention on its committee system as the fulcrum on which legislative activity turned on Capitol Hill, traced the institutional apparatus as it had developed, then evaluated the role Congress played within the political system as a whole, and finally warned against the growing dominance of Congress over the other branches of the federal government, all with the disciplined eye for detail of the scholar that Wilson was and with the progressive stance of the reformist that he also considered himself to be. He boasted that he had never visited Congress or seen it in action. But he painted a picture of the institution as it then was with unerring care and discipline, relying heavily on written records and reports of its activities. It was a tour de force of research, description, and analysis.

Wilson's pioneering effort did not stand alone for very long. Over the next decades students trained in the new graduate programs in politics and history produced an impressive array of additional studies, most focused on the key institutional elements of legislative life. In 1896, Mary Follett published *The Speaker of the House of Representatives*; two years later, Lauros McConachie published *Congressional Committees*. Also in the 1890s, A. Lawrence Lowell produced the first serious examination of roll-call voting in Congress, measuring the influence of political parties on Congress's recorded decisions and comparing that to the role played by parties in England's House of Commons. At the same time, the historian

Frederick Jackson Turner's interest in the influence of sectionalism on American politics led him and several of his students to look at legislative battles, to confirm his notions that sectional pressures overrode all other influences present in serious legislative battles. In 1916, De Alva Alexander brought out what was to be the first of a number of descriptive overviews of individual legislative bodies produced over the years, *The History and Procedure of the House of Representatives*.

The sum of these early scholarly efforts was heavily weighted toward Congress, the most visible legislative institution, in contrast to state and local legislative bodies. Still, the latter received some attention as well. Of course, local and state legislatures are different from Congress in many ways, none more important than that they represent much smaller constituencies. But the similarities in the legislative process, objectives, and structures, regardless of level, were also important. From the beginning, it was recognized, if not always formally stated, that the study of all legislatures, federal, state, and local, encompassed three dimensions: the external environment (political conflict, societal differences, elections), their internal structures (committees, leadership, caucuses, individual and group voting), and, finally, the results of their activities (laws passed, their relations with other branches).

As a result, no part of the legislative experience escaped intense scholarly investigation. Among professional scholars, with all of their differences, there was continuous interest in a number of similar questions, questions that in turn echoed an earlier tradition of more-amateur endeavors: What are legislatures like? Who serves in legislatures, and how do they get there? How do Congress and state legislatures go about their business of representing, investigating, overseeing, and enacting policies? What resources are available to them? How are these resources organized and utilized? Who sets the original legislative agenda and how is the final result achieved? What understandings and customs are part of the scene, and what external influences from the political world at large are most important in shaping and affecting legislative behavior?

To be sure, the overwhelming interest of scholars in this early period lay in what has been called institutional studies (as against studies of informal processes, covert interactions, and personal behavior by individual legislators). These efforts concentrate on the formal arrangements of American legislative institutions—their organization and procedures, the committees and their jurisdictions, the number and responsibilities of leaders—cataloging and describing the architecture of legislatures, their internal construction, and the way these elements had changed over time. These scholars looked primarily at constitutions and statutes to define the legislature's tasks, the formal institutions set up within the legislatures to carry them out, and the written rules by which they were supposed to operate. All of this provided a clear geography—a set of maps that located each part of the legislative structure and how it had come to be what it was.

The formulation of the questions asked and the ways then used to arrive at answers to them were always rooted in what Dorothy Ross refers to as the "descriptive empiricism" of early professional social science. First, there was a strong commitment to the collection of information (empiricism), out of which to construct the formalistic descriptions of institutions. Scholars re-created the record of what happened as legislatures went about their business and tried to assess why it happened as it did. Many of these studies focused on a crucial indicator episode to follow the ways that legislatures specifically responded to the external political pressures affecting them.

A certain degree of quantitative analysis— the systematic manipulation of numerical data —appeared as well. Turner, Orin Libby, and the political scientist Lowell all looked at Congress's recorded roll-call votes to measure the relative strength of the two main influences present in American politics—political parties and sections. Although the results were intriguing and formed the basis for many subsequent explanations of legislative activity, the methodology of Turner, Lowell, and Libby was simple, and the data they collected ultimately proved to be too numerous to analyze successfully with the statistical tools then at hand.

As noted, many of these early studies included the strong hortatory quality that characterized Wilson's *Congressional Government.* Their focus was not on "government as it was, but government as it was supposed to be." Wilson and others, often progressives to the core, joined such nonscholarly reformers as David Graham Phillips in *The Treason of the Senate* (1906) and James Bryce in *The American Commonwealth* (first edition of many, 1888), with its dozen chapters on Congress and another on the state legislatures, in pointing out the imperfections, lapses, and corruption apparently endemic to the legislative process and in painting a contrasting picture of the ideal type of legislature. As one scholar later wrote about these efforts, "legislative scholars were confident that they knew what a really good legislature would be like and they thought it useful to measure the real article against the models they constructed."

THE DESCRIPTIVE-FORMALIST ERA (1900–1950s)

The work of Wilson, Follett, Alexander, Turner, and the rest formed the basis of the descriptive-empiricist tradition that dominated scholarly studies of legislatures for about fifty years after the first published efforts appeared at the end of the nineteenth century. During and after World War II, scholars continued to produce an array of similar studies that, as this approach emphasized, described the legislature, delineated its component elements, and evaluated its effectiveness. One or two followed Alexander's example and cataloged and described the whole institution, as in Lindsay Roger's *The American Senate* (1926) and George H. Haynes's *The Senate of the United States: Its History and Practice* (1938). Most continued the institutionalist focus and described one formal element of the whole, notably Ralph V. Harlow's *The History of Legislative Methods in the Period Prior to 1825* (1917), Ada McCown's *The Congressional Conference Committee* (1927), Chang-Wei Chiu's *The Speaker Since 1896* (1928), Marshall E. Dimock's *Congressional Investigating Committees* (1929), and George R. Brown's *The Leadership of Congress* (1922). Some examined the structure of deci-sion-making, as in Paul De Witt Hasbrouck's *Party Government in the House of Representatives* (1927) and in Edward Pendleton Herring's *Group Representation Before Congress* (1929), the pioneering description of organized nonpartisan interests in the legislative process. Among studies of state legislatures of this era, Belle Zeller's *Pres-

sure Politics in New York (1937) marked an ongoing style pursued at the same level of analysis.

Each of these writers continued to reflect the particulars of the formalist tradition of scholarship. They detailed the laws establishing the particular institution being described, arguing that tracing its evolution back into the colonial period and even earlier into the British experience provided the kind of information needed to understand the workings of the institution in the present day. The authors defined the institution and diligently detailed all that could be found in a specific case study or two that revealed the way it operated. In the end, they provided an extremely thoroughly drawn description of the structure and characteristics of a specific institution, of an aspect of American legislative life. Finally, each usually ended with some comment about the institution's effectiveness, coupled with a direct or implied suggestion for reform. As descriptive geography and programmatic advocacy, they filled out the boundaries of the prevailing institutional approach to legislative historiography.

Biographies also played an important role in legislative scholarship in this era, particularly among historians. Studies of the lives of prominent politicians who had made their marks on state legislatures and Congress, from James Madison through Henry Clay, John C. Calhoun, Daniel Webster, to Robert La Follette, appeared, as did the memoirs of Senator Oscar Underwood and Speaker of the House Champ Clark. Less interested than their political scientist colleagues in the details of legislative institutions, historians found in such biographical studies an important means of understanding a time, such as the antebellum era; through such biographies they could illuminate an episode, such as the passage of a particular piece of progressive legislation, and come to grips with the interaction between individuals and their goals and the impersonal elements that affected the legislative scene at a particular moment, such as sections and political parties.

Finally, historians also published many studies of particular legislative moments of some note—for example, the dramatic episodes of the 1770s, 1790s, 1830s, and later—as well as studies of particular pieces of legislation or policy areas in which Congress played an especially central or important role and in

which, again, the focus was less on legislatures as institutions and more on how they demonstrated the force of important elements at play in American politics. A few scholars also examined the external dynamics that led to the creation of legislatures themselves. Colonial historians, for example, spent much time tracing—and arguing about—the origins of legislative bodies in seventeenth- and eighteenth-century America.

At the same time, political scientists undertook a number of case studies of the contemporary legislative process in action. They traced, in particular, how a specific piece of legislation was shaped, the role of organized groups and of party leaders in the outcome of the legislative process, as in E. E. Schattschneider's investigation of the passage of the protectionist Smoot-Hawley Tariff Act of 1930 (1935) and Roland Young's examination of congressional politics during World War II (1956), or they explored a particular policy complex or interest group within a set of chronological boundaries, as in Roland Pennock's close analysis of the framing of agricultural policies (1956) or George L. Grassmuck's *Sectional Biases in Congress on Foreign Policy* (1951). In these studies, scholars generally saw legislatures as reflectors of society's problems and politics, as receivers of pressures from their society, and then described the way that these pressures are translated into legislation and other outcomes. Legislators did not act in a vacuum. They were aware of, and in some way affected by, a range of elements, from impending elections to interest-group pressures.

In the 1930s and 1940s, as the American government on all levels demonstrated an unprecedented policy-making energy in reaction to depression and war, a number of monographs traced the evolution of critical legislative policy initiative over the course of time. David M. Schneider's *History of Public Welfare in New York State* (2 vols., 1938–1941), is one example: it is a highly detailed legislative history of one particular set of initiatives in the social realm. Schneider and others whose work was of a similar nature underscored the quite prominent role played by legislatures, particularly at the state level, as major incubators of vigorous government activity and responsibility.

In sum, then, the authors most interested in legislatures during the first half of the twentieth century produced empirical studies that amassed an enormous amount of descriptive detail about the various components of American legislatures, from committees and leadership positions, to the development of legislation and who shaped particular outcomes, as well as about the relations between legislatures and the other branches of the state and national governments. These studies rarely attempted to draw a complete picture of legislatures in action. The authors of these case studies drew few generalizations from the individual topics covered. That was not their intention. Rather, what characterized empirical legislative studies during this era was the desire to describe an event, institution, or personality; to draw a lesson from a small-scale, in-depth description; and to follow an issue or a crisis—to place each brick correctly, but not necessarily to build a total structure or to understand its informal dynamics. Finally, these scholars did not systematically gather large amounts of measurable data that would support their ideas or that would have allowed comparisons across time to be made, even though in the 1920s social scientists such as Stuart Rice and Herman Beyle developed and demonstrated increasingly sophisticated quantitative methods designed to handle amounts of data about legislative activity unattainable by Turner and Lowell thirty years before. Usually, after collecting information, the authors assessed how well legislatures performed their constitutional functions to oversee and to check and balance, as well as their political functions of representing constituencies and making useful policy.

The reformist impulse in legislative studies, earlier represented by Woodrow Wilson and David Graham Phillips, continued. A new generation of scholars saw it as part of their responsibility to assess legislative effectiveness and commitment to doing the right things, and as in earlier days, they usually found that each institution hesitated, turned away, or did not meet a challenge. Legislatures often sought responsibility, but, just as often, failed. In the work of such distinguished scholars as George Galloway in the 1940s and, somewhat later, James MacGregor Burns, Congress was always at the crossroads, usually on trial. State legislatures fared not much better: they were usually found to be corrupt, always inefficient and unable to do their job. In such studies, in Nelson

Polsby's terms, "what is communicated is not information about how things work, but rather information about whether the author approves or disapproves of what he has seen."

CONGRESS MAKES A LAW

Although research about legislatures was a vigorous enterprise in the years before World War II, the number of studies produced proved minuscule compared to that of the following decades. From the 1950s on, legislative research became a very large, very wide-ranging component of the scholarly study of politics generally—much larger and much more wide-ranging than ever before. As one scholar summed up the pattern of development, "research on legislatures is essentially a post–World War II phenomenon. As recently as the early 1950s, the legislature—its practice and politics—was an unexplored wilderness.... In the ensuing years, an ever-growing army of scholars marched boldly into this virgin territory, producing literally thousands of studies that illuminated many dark corners of the forest." Further, "in sheer volume, the scholarly production on Congress from the 1960s forward probably exceeds that for any political institution ever."

It was not only the quantity of the scholarly output after World War II that was noteworthy, however. In the twenty years after 1945, a major methodological and philosophical revolution occurred in the social sciences and directly affected such subdisciplines as the scholarly study of legislatures. Stephen K. Bailey's *Congress Makes a Law* (1946) signaled a major turning point in legislative historiography. In its emphasis on a single episode, one could argue that it was among the best, certainly the most sophisticated, in an older tradition. But it differed from earlier work in important respects. Bailey's book was neither fully in the formalist-descriptive nor the reformist tradition. His work focused, most critically, on how the individual legislators acted and reacted, defined and moved, as each of them concentrated their attention on a single bill. Rather than rely primarily on the written record, he interviewed members of Congress and other participants in the drafting of the Full Employment Act (enacted in 1946), and from that direct evidence, he carefully analyzed a process at work, in all of its behavioral messiness; he did not report a set of procedures and events, nor did he call for improvements. As Ralph Huitt wrote about it, "the idea of paying attention to what legislators do was revolutionary."

What Bailey represented was the culmination of growing dissatisfaction with the existing approaches to studying American politics and an awareness of new methods and organizing conceptions developed in psychology and sociology that promised to open up the understanding of legislatures in profound ways. Led in the 1940s and 1950s by such scholars of popular voting, political parties, and the governmental process as Robert Dahl, Angus Campbell, and David Truman, the behavioral approach, or "persuasion," as it was sometimes called in its early years, provided the impetus to move beyond the simple description of political events toward firmer, more empirically rooted scientific analysis of the legislative system as a whole—its members and its actual elements, how they functioned, and what they did.

The social sciences revolution in the years after 1945 was stimulated by the growth of psychology and its widespread application during World War II to test and measure soldiers' attitudes and behavior. Pioneers in the field argued that the focus of scholarly research into human institutions had to shift. Raw, empirical description and romantic reformism were to be replaced by a theory-driven, analytic, objective, scientifically correct understanding of how individuals in politics behaved. Legislative scholarship, along with studies of popular-voting behavior, became a primary focus for such behaviorally driven scholarship. Both had at their disposal an enormous data bank that could be drawn on to test and extend behavioral propositions.

From social science generally, legislative scholars reiterated, and made more central than it had ever been, the need for precise observation and systematic classification. Moreover, the legislator, both as an individual and as part of specific groups, became the primary focus of scholarly attention. From psychology and sociology, the behavioral scholars drew notions and theoretical propositions about the internal thought processes and long-standing group associations that shaped the values, ideas, commitments, and decisions of individuals, from voters to decision-makers. Further, behavioral scholars argued that not everything that happened was haphazard and unrelated to other elements. Rather, there were strong, dominant, and evolving patterns in human behavior, and in such an aspect of it as the legislative process, that transcended the individual episode. Details of an episode were always crucial, but not for themselves alone or to demonstrate the legislature's role in larger political affairs. Rather, the details were building blocks for an understanding of the whole system (for example, a legislature) and for the formulation of theoretical propositions that would further refine and develop scholarly understanding of human behavior.

The result of this shift in emphasis and perspective was startling. For scholars of American legislatures, it meant a clear turn away from anecdote and unadorned description of institutions. Rather, the major scholarly current now concentrated on elucidating the internal dynamics shaping legislative action, particularly those affecting individual legislators; on cataloging more systematically the external factors at work, both specific societal interests and particular group values and prejudices; and on discovering what was persistent, illuminating the continuities present in the behavioral dimension. The behavioral revolution in political science, in short, sought to improve and expand the discipline's commitment to developing a genuine science of politics.

THE BEHAVIORAL ERA
(1950s–1970s)

Evidence of the behavioral revolution was everywhere in the 1950s, appearing first in journal articles and then in monographs and collections of essays. In 1959 a pioneering compilation by John C. Wahlke and Heinz Eulau, *Legislative Behavior*, presented some of the major findings and approaches of this new scholarly persuasion. Roland Young's *The American Congress* (1958) tried to develop a more general understanding of congressional behavior out of systematic research. Four years later, Wahlke, Eulau, and several colleagues, in *The Legislative System*, brought the new research approach into the world of state legislatures.

These efforts were largely preliminary probes and suggestions of what was to come, indicating that a significant research corner had been turned.

The behavioral revolution in legislative analysis, first glimpsed in Bailey's work, largely took off from the pioneering efforts of Ralph Huitt, who, in a series of articles in the 1950s and early 1960s, "brought the internal structure and culture of Congress to the top of the academic agendas." Early explanations of causal relationships had emphasized the direct importance of such external forces as party, section, and constituency on individual legislative behavior. But Huitt and others argued from the theories available to them that what went on was not simply a reaction to external pressures directly applied on the legislators. Rather, it was the result of the impact of a range of not always conscious elements affecting each individual.

The key issue was understanding how legislators perceived their roles and opportunities and how they weighed the constraints placed on them. Huitt focused his attention on how such externalities were received and reshaped by internal legislative norms and structures. He argued that legislatures worked within boundaries, but not the formal institutional and legal ones usually stressed as much as those set by norms—the personally internalized expectations, assumptions, and perceptions of the legislative actors on the stage. Each house of Congress, Huitt wrote, "is a human group, with leadership, a hierarchy of influence, and a set of norms that 'control,' more or less, the behavior of its members." As time passes, certain practices become stabilized and routinized parts of the culture of legislatures. These norms helped define the limits of individual and institutional behavior and clearly bounded the legislative arena in which such behavior took place and thus limited the unadorned impact of the external pressures working on them.

The original research approach of the behavioral scholars emphasized close observation of legislators at work. Various outside institutions, from the Social Science Research Council to the American Political Science Association, proved willing in the 1950s and 1960s to provide financial support to invigorate and advance the emerging field and its particular research approach. In the 1950s, therefore, hordes of scholars crisscrossed legislative halls "in the manner," one wrote, "of the anthropologist studying an unfamiliar tribe," observing, interviewing, trying to tease out the norms of behavior that Ralph Huitt had articulated as the key to understanding, and to define the resulting whole worldview of a legislative group. Such observations became a "window through which . . . enduring aspects of legislative politics are viewed."

The result of these efforts was a range of studies of legislators at work, particularly in their committee roles—the key to so much legislative activity. (Woodrow Wilson had written that Congress "in its committee rooms is Congress at work.") The predominant theme of these studies is power—the rise, activities, and patterns of a legislature's leadership; the role of committees and their chairs; the relative power of individual legislators; and the way all legislators are constrained, or provided opportunities, by the behavioral dynamics at play. Among the many studies that appeared, Richard Fenno's analysis of the House Appropriations Committee, originally published in 1962, became a classic of the genre.

Fenno, in his "plunge into the forest of internal congressional life," used extensive interviewing as well as formal records to build up his case study. More important, perhaps, was his approach, borrowed from social psychology, to the behavior of people in groups and their interaction with each other and the existing institutional structure of which they were a part. Fenno saw the committee as "a political subsystem" that, in order to meet its functional responsibilities, had to mesh together a number of subgroups and individuals. Committee members shared certain consensual outlooks that provided an opportunity to accomplish the committee's goals. Finally, Fenno made it plain that his goals went beyond the description of the committee at work: "Functional classification of committees (i.e., well or poorly integrated) derived from a large number of descriptive analyses of several functional problems, may prove helpful in constructing more general propositions about the legislative process."

Other scholars adopted Fenno's approach, "following politicians around and talking with them," as the latter went about their normal, day-to-day activities. (The U.S. House of Representatives received more attention than the Senate or state legislatures in these efforts, probably because house members proved to be particularly accessible to scholars.) More critically, these scholars also adopted the kind of theoretical apparatus and outlooks that Huitt, Donald Matthews in his seminal *U.S. Senators and Their World* (1960), and Fenno had introduced, following the same behavioral pathways into the inner life of legislatures and legislators and arguing that they were doing so in order to improve not only the descriptive capacity of scholars but also their ability to theorize about legislative activity more generally.

Underlying all of these studies was a particular sociological theory of human behavior within institutions called "structural-functionalism." Each component of a system, structural-functionalists argued, served a specific purpose; each had its place and role within the larger institution. If it existed, it must be functional in some way to someone. Legislators tended to accept what was there and adapt themselves to already working institutions. Such adaptive necessities took precedence over the purposive pursuit of whatever policy opportunities were present to individual legislators. In this, legislators took to heart House Speaker Sam Rayburn's dictum that "if you want to get along, go along." Conflict was normal and usually well contained within the process. Only when things failed to mesh as they should (that is, became dysfunctional) did destabilizing conflict emerge. At such times, the tendency was for the system and its members to try to adjust and move back toward institutional stability. In short, everything was tied together by the need for legislatures to operate effectively and to persist as important functioning political institutions.

These scholars were also much influenced by a pluralist conception of the American political process. Pluralists stressed, as David Truman did in *The Governmental Process* (1951), that Congress and the other parts of the government were a continuous battleground of competing, usually well-organized interests, each of which had as good a chance as any other of getting some part of the legislation they desired. No one group or combination of groups could dominate the floor of Congress or the state legislatures more than briefly. Thus, the most useful focus for legislative scholarship lay in tracing the interplay of these forces at work, as Truman himself did in *The Congressional Party* (1959).

In delineating these processes, legislative scholars renewed an earlier interest—the manipulation of large amounts of data through increasingly sophisticated quantitative means. In contrast to the behavioral studies of individual legislators and committees, these efforts produced macrolevel analyses of the patterns of behavior of whole legislatures and provided guides to what legislators responded to in their sustained behavior in a particular episode, in a legislative session, or over a number of years. As Turner, Libby, and Lowell had originally argued, parties and sections were significant influences on the course of legislative activities, and their rise, fall, and comparative importance could be measured by analyzing roll calls as a prelude to explaining their roles and persistence. Legislative roll calls were plentiful and systematically well recorded, and they remained the basic public expression of the policy attitudes of all legislators. In the work of Truman, Julius Turner, and Duncan MacRae in the 1950s and 1960s and in the conscious use of measuring devices borrowed from psychology (scaling, cluster bloc analysis, and, later, factor analysis), the definitional clarity of roll-call analysis was effectively demonstrated, helped in great measure by the availability of increasingly sophisticated computer technology. In particular, these studies reaffirmed the notion that the role of political parties was central to any description and understanding of American legislative behavior, that party labels provided a persistent classifying and ordering force and, although never alone, an explanatory one as well. Partisan behavior always affected whatever legislatures did.

A similar strain of macrolevel analysis, utilizing large amounts of quantitative data, involved studying the underlying personal conditions shaping individual legislators, including their social backgrounds and experience before they entered the legislative halls, the length of their tenure once there, and their experiences therein, such as their committee assignments and leadership positions. Great masses of personal data were brought together to test the assumption that there was a direct relationship between social background, political structures, and electoral success and career patterns.

Donald Matthews devoted several chapters of his *U.S. Senators and Their World* to exploring this issue. Heinz Eulau and a number of colleagues did a similar analysis for state legislators in *The Legislative System* (1962). In an extension of this approach, some scholars compared voters' choices in legislative elections to their choices in presidential and gubernatorial contests, bringing large masses of numerical data into play as the centerpiece of their analysis.

Finally, an emerging theme of quantitative description and analysis emphasized the importance of change in shaping legislative behavior. Early in the behavioral era, some scholars criticized structural-functionalist assumptions in individual studies for their lack of a sense of historical change, sequential development over time, and the very important differences present in function and capability at different moments. The behavioral approach, it was said, was "largely ahistorical"; its purpose was "the search for general explanations that transcend[ed] time and place." In such an approach, the changing, always-in-motion external environment faded away almost totally. But such timelessness did not allow for an accurate understanding of legislative life. To be sure, legislatures manifested great stability in their norms, activities, and behavior. Yet, every American legislature has changed a great deal in structure, personnel, and scope of concern over two hundred years. Did that matter? Some political scientists said yes, to some degree, to be sure, but not in any important ways. Others, however, insisted that changes in size, the growth of operational complexity, and the institutionalization of legislative processes illuminated not only the context of particular actions but also something about legislative boundaries and behavior at a single point of observation and a great deal about the limits of generalizing propositions about legislative patterns and behavior.

In the 1950s and 1960s, Polsby led the way among political scientists in focusing on changes over time, in order to place current practices in some sort of chronologically comparative context. He and others adapted notions not only of evolution from simple to more complex forms of development but also of modernization theory, borrowed from economic analysis and the study of international relations, in suggesting the limits and boundaries set by variations in historical condition. Polsby's studies of the internal development of congressional structures, the patterns of seniority, and the institutionalization of leadership, for example, became seminal analyses of the ever-shifting nature of legislative life over time. Similarly, Garrison Nelson traced shifts in congressional leadership patterns over long chronological periods, David Mayhew explored changes in the qualities defining congressional membership over time, and David Brady and his students looked outside of Congress and traced the shift in the power of such pressures as party loyalty over the course of the twentieth century.

These behavioralists described their subject much as earlier students had done, albeit with greater rigor and precision and by using a much larger body of data than had ordinarily been the norm. To them, however, the description was raw material for a more precise understanding of the process of legislating. Research topics were chosen less for their intrinsic interest or drama and more for the role they could play in clarifying and extending a particular understanding or explanation of legislative behavior. Scholars considered themselves to be "practicing normal science," in their emphasis on "replication, refinement, revision and extension of dominant models."

Studies of state legislatures were quite numerous in these years of great vigor and change in legislative research. But scholars of the states often tended to go their own way in the 1950s and thereafter. Some infused their studies with the new behavioralism as in Malcolm Jewell's *The State Legislature: Politics and Practice* (1962) and Samuel C. Patterson's *Midwest Legislative Politics* (1967), both of which were heavily descriptive as well. Some essayed a comparative approach as in *American State Legislatures* (1954), edited by Belle Zeller. Most state-level scholars focused on one or another central concern of state political analysis, such as the divisive presence of rural-urban conflict, as reported by Gordon Baker in *Rural Versus Urban Political Power* (1955); the related question of legislative apportionment, as in *The Politics of Reapportionment* (1962), edited by Jewell; and the variety of partisan conflicts present on the state level. Reformism appeared as well, as in *Strengthening the*

States: Essays on Legislative Reform (1971), edited by Donald G. Herzberg and Alan Rosenthal. Finally, city councils were occasionally treated, as in Heinz Eulau and Kenneth Prewitt's *Labyrinths of Democracy* (1973).

Although political scientists led the way in the behavioral revolution in legislative research, they were never alone. Some historians adopted the methods and approaches of behavioral analysis to decipher patterns of behavior at critical moments in the past. They used quantitative methods to assess the accuracy of the belief in the importance of parties and sections on legislatures over long periods of time. As Turner and Libby had argued long before, roll-call analysis was particularly useful in delineating the strength of partisan commitments both at a single moment and over a period of time. Now, utilizing improved means of measuring very large amounts of data, Thomas B. Alexander and I, in books published in 1967 that represented the first efforts of this type of exploration of the American scene, delineated systematically the relative influence of parties and sections on congressional behavior in the pre–Civil War era and traced the changes over time in such influences. Other historians followed our pioneering efforts. In particular, the Era of Good Feelings, the Civil War years, and Reconstruction drew a great deal of attention from roll-call analysts. These discrete studies began to add up to all but complete coverage of congressional roll-call voting, at least for the nineteenth century. Still other historians, led by Ballard Campbell and Rodney Davis, began to look at state legislative behavior over time as well. Finally, a number of historians, most notably Allan Bogue and Jerome Clubb, picked up other aspects of the behavioral revolution, examining recruitment, the patterns of leadership, and the psychosociological underpinnings of individual legislators' behavior, from the colonial legislatures to the Confederate Congress, to the House of Representatives since 1789.

These historical studies were not particularly theoretical. While they effectively addressed historical controversies of some importance and fleshed out in more systematic and thorough style the existing historical record, they made few, if any, contributions to understanding the dynamics of the legislative experience as such. Still, their findings complemented the contemporary focus of the political scientists. The importance of partisan behavior in nineteenth-century legislatures, for example, helped establish firm descriptive baselines from which such political scientists as David Brady could trace the decline of partisanship over the course of the twentieth century. Historical findings also contributed to the assessment of the problem of contextual impact on general theories of legislative behavior—how much of legislative behavior was universal and how much was critically affected by change over time.

All of these analyses were made possible by the systematic collection of large amounts of quantitative data and their processing into machine-readable form by the Interuniversity Consortium for Political and Social Research (ICPSR) established at the University of Michigan. Begun by the students of popular-voting behavior in the 1960s, the collections had originally been largely limited to the popular-election data and the county-level census material that election analysts needed. But it then extended its reach into legislative analysis by collecting both roll-call data and biographical material about individual legislators going back to the eighteenth century.

By the 1980s the ferment of the behavioral revolution in legislative studies produced an unprecedented number of scholarly analyses. Some political scientists went further than ever before in deciphering yeas and nays, as in Donald Matthews's *Yeas and Nays* (1975), Aage Clausen's *How Congressmen Decide* (1973), and John Kingdon's *Congressmen's Voting Decision* (2nd ed., 1981). Richard Fenno extended his analyses of congressional committees, and Joseph Cooper and David Brady examined committee and leadership behavior and the patterns of roll calls well back in American history. Behavioral historians such as Allan G. Bogue, in *The Earnest Men* (1981) and *The Congressman's Civil War* (1989), and Margaret S. Thompson, in *The Spider Web: Congress and Lobbying in the Age of Grant* (1985), moved beyond roll-call data to build on the approach of the inside-the-chambers studies of legislative behavior pioneered by Huitt, Matthews, Fenno, and other political scientists.

Throughout the years of the behavioral revolution and even later, much of the more traditional approach to legislative scholarship continued to appear, from popular studies such as the newspapermen's William Smith White's informative study of the Senate in the 1950s, *Citadel* (1957), and Neil MacNeil's study of the House, *Forge of Democracy* (1963), to historian Alvin Josephy's popular *American Heritage History of the Congress of the United States* (1975), to Senator Joseph S. Clark's reformist analysis based on his own service, *Congress, the Sapless Branch* (1964), Richard Bolling's similar *House Out of Order* (1965), and John J. Rhodes's *The Futile System* (1976), to Elizabeth Drew's study *Senator* (1979).

Studies of the relationship between legislatures and the other branches of government in America's separation-of-powers system were also frequent throughout these years. Since the American system apparently leads inevitably to competition between legislatures and other parts of the government, illumination at critical moments reveals much about what is at stake, the way matters come out, and the pattern evident at a given moment. In general, the many studies produced fell into two categories: descriptive-evaluative and topic-specific. In the first case, the object was to determine who the dominant partner was in what was seen as an unceasing battle between legislatures and other branches. (This had been one of the major themes of Woodrow Wilson's original investigation; Congress was then emerging as the dominant force in national government and successfully and, unfortunately, in Wilson's view, taming the presidency and whatever administrative apparatus then existed.) But such power relationships, scholars discovered, vary over time, first toward the executive and then toward the legislature. Some scholars suggested in the 1960s, as James L. Sundquist later did in *The Decline and Resurgence of Congress* (1981), that such relationships have been cyclical in nature, not random or owing to particular personalities or situations. They move in a uniform rhythm from one pattern of dominance to another as pressures that are energized by one pattern build up, and then produce a counterreaction, restoring a balance toward the other pattern.

Second, a number of topic-specific studies of legislative relations with the other parts of the government focused on specific historical episodes in which interbranch power relationships significantly varied. T. Harry Williams's excellent tracing of the conflict in *Lincoln and the Radicals* (1941) is a prototypical example of such description, and Seward Livermore's

Politics Is Adjourned (1966), another, as were parts of John Morton Blum's *The Republican Roosevelt* (1954). Similar studies covered a wide range of other topics, including the relationship between the president and Congress in the foreign policy arena from the 1940s onward.

Historians continued to describe other crucial legislative episodes in the more-traditional prebehavioral manner. Holman Hamilton's examination of the Compromise of 1850 in *Prologue to Conflict* (1964), James T. Patterson's investigative *Congressional Conservatism and the New Deal* (1967), and Roy Nichols's masterly analytic essay about the Kansas-Nebraska Act of 1854 published in the *Mississippi Valley Historical Review* in 1954 were all excellent examples of an enduring genre. The biographical tradition, with its emphasis on great or important leaders and its case-study approach, also remained prominent. Fine examples have included David H. Donald's study of Charles Sumner (1960), Robert Johannsen's work on Stephen A. Douglas (1973), and Richard Lowitt's recounting of the life of George Norris (1963). Richard Baker's 1977 bibliographic compilation *The United States Senate* lists hundreds of such studies completed over the years. In these, the ferment unleashed by the behavioral revolution, with its systematic, generalizing, theoretical analyses, was rarely present. Rather, these studies continued to meet the needs of their particular audience and contributed something to the data pool drawn on by the more behavioral analysts in their midst. Perhaps their most interesting dimension was the unconscious suggestion of the widening gap between the approaches of most political science students of legislatures with their theoretical, generalizing purposes, on the one hand, and on the other, those followed by many historians interested in Congress and state-legislative activity, largely focusing on specific nontheoretical goals. Emerging out of the same influences in an earlier era, most now followed quite different scholarly pathways.

OUTSIDE THE HALLS (1970s–1990s)

Toward the end of the twentieth century, scholars of legislative research maintained their vigorous pace and output. Description and analysis continued to accumulate and conceptual breakthroughs sharpened, extended, and became better detailed as more data were produced in their support. At the same time, important changes continued to occur in the thrust of many of the scholarly efforts. First, in the 1970s, there was a shift in scholarly focus toward paying more-systematic attention to the role played by the external dimension of the legislative world. There had always been something of an inside-outside dichotomy in studies under the behavioral persuasion. Behavioralists had stressed the norms, rules, and leadership structures developed within legislatures as the main shapers of individual careers and successes, the way the chambers acted, and their policy outputs. Scholars certainly had not ignored the roles played by parties, interest groups, and constituencies in shaping legislative behavior. The linkages between legislators and their constituents formally expressed in elections and informally articulated in many other ways, had also always drawn a certain amount of attention. But the behavioralists had taken many of these relationships for granted or considered them to be conceptually less interesting than the inside-the-chamber focus they stressed in their work.

Richard Fenno took the lead shifting perspective, as he had in an earlier orientation shift. Legislators have always paid close attention to their districts. But the way that they did so, and its meaning and relevance, had never received systematic scholarly attention as an object of great importance. In a series of articles and in *Home Style* (1978), Fenno explored in great detail the way that individual congressmen went about their day-to-day activities in Washington and especially in their home districts. Until Fenno, the critical nature of this latter activity was dimly understood, if at all. In his home-style studies, the behavioral notion of looking at matters through the eyes of the participants once again became the dominant research style. Fenno used interviews and observation to spell out a "web of relationships" that had a powerful impact on individual behavior. Beginning with his close observation, scholars learned important ways of understanding how legislators worked to keep this critical external constraint on their career and behavior aligned with their inside-the-chamber behavior. In pointing out the interaction of the personal and

the institutional, the pressures of home and workplace, he produced an extraordinary range of findings that reoriented understanding and served as a powerful reminder of how much individual micro-level observation contributed to a more general understanding of larger patterns and dynamics.

Another aspect of this focus on the relationship between external considerations and legislative activities was the scholarly attention paid to voters and elections, an old approach revived in the 1970s with great vigor and important results. As had always been accepted, elections crucially determined much about legislatures. Competition between political parties with different policy orientations for each legislative seat had been seen as a key determinant of legislative behavior in the behavioral era. Parties influenced national and state policy by determining the strength of party majorities, dictating committee majorities and chairs, and selecting party leaders.

The particular outcomes of electoral activity had been organized by scholars working under the rubric of electoral realignment theory as originally developed by students of American popular-voting behavior. Electoral realignments have occurred at distinct, quite rare moments of great upheaval and change. The long-term result of each realignment, notably in the 1850s, the 1890s, and the 1930s, was a major shift in the power of different parties and social groups and a sharp regeneration of policy energy and initiatives within the political system generally as well as within legislatures. David Brady and Jerome Clubb, for example, found that the closer legislators were to an electoral realignment, the more ideological they were and the more committed to the passage of specific policy initiatives. At the same time, as the political impulses unleased by electoral realignments waned, so did the policy energy within the American legislative system. In short, as Clubb summed up, scholars had to focus on the shape of the popular-electoral cycle to understand what was happening inside legislatures:

> Patterns of voting behavior observed in particular Congresses cannot be taken as simply a reflection of the responses of members of Congress to the specific issues and personalities of the day. Rather, such patterns must also be seen in relation to long-term decline in

party voting and to the location of these Congresses in the realignment cycle.

But from the 1970s on, scholars detected a major shift in the pattern of electoral results in the United States. The influence of party loyalty in helping voters make electoral choices has ebbed considerably. The decline of party in the electorate contributed in turn to the shifting outlooks of those elected to Congress and their willingness to let party institutions within Congress decline as well. Ongoing research, originally undertaken by David Mayhew in *Congress: The Electoral Connection* (1974) and then pursued by Gary Jacobson and Morris P. Fiorina, among others, demonstrated that the outcomes of congressional elections owed less and less to party competition and more and more to what came to be labeled "the incumbency factor." The extent of member turnover in each successive election to the U.S. House of Representatives declined precipitously in the 1970s and thereafter. Federal and state legislators could routinely expect to be reelected to their seats, apparently because of the extraordinary power of incumbency and the sapping of the influence of party competition on the competition for legislative seats.

These scholars attempted to explain why this should be so and what its impact was as legislatures turned both to policy-making and its relationships with the rest of the government. No single element explained the power of incumbency. Voter perception of candidates remained central, but voters no longer looked at legislative candidates primarily through partisan lenses. The extremely favorable electoral climate for incumbents in the late twentieth century was connected rather with the shift in legislators' roles vis-à-vis their constituents. Legislators, in a nation increasingly dominated by a large governmental system that provided various kinds of services to individuals, helped their constituents by serving as "ombudsmen," interceders between bureaucratic agencies and individual supplicants for some denied or lost service or for remedy for some injustice.

Second, legislators became masters of using their financial and publicity advantages effectively to discourage strong challenges or to overwhelm any that were offered. The high cost of election campaigns and the increasing publicity resources available to incumbent legislators (government-financed and -mailed newsletters, radio and especially television) to provide a forum for an announcement of some gain for a district gave those already in office an immediate advantage even before an electoral campaign began against a usually lesser known, more-poorly financed challenger. Finally, incumbents learned that their major electoral vulnerability lay in demonstrating unappealing personal characteristics and behavior in an era of intense media scrutiny. They therefore spent much time managing their appearance or striking out at similar vulnerabilities in their opponents. All of this implicitly acknowledged the reality that in the modern bureaucratic age political parties had lost a great deal of their ability to influence popular-voting behavior.

Scholars such as Jacobson and Fiorina argued that the impact of this new electoral connection on legislators' behavior inside their particular chamber was direct and critically important. First, they noted how much the staying power of legislators over long periods of time affected the power roles and effectiveness of legislative committees and subcommittees as individual federal and state legislators pushed to get the share of power they believed their tenure deserved. Second, it became clear that it was to the benefit of individual legislators to proceed inside the chamber in ways that maximized incumbency benefits—that is, to get on the right committee and expand the reach of the government's largesse to constituents. In doing all of this, legislators became individual entrepreneurs, free of constraints from groups, rules, or the demands of the leadership, except when such were useful to them.

All of this paid off at the polls, but led to massive increases in legislative activity, the length of sessions, and the amount of incumbent-friendly legislation that was passed. In Barbara Hinckley's summary, since voters support incumbents, the outcomes of legislative elections support seniority and continuity within legislatures. The latter, in turn, support stable patterns of interaction between committees and bureaucratic agencies and a pattern of incremental policy-making. Nothing could more directly demonstrate the immense power of external forces to shape the activities, directions, and goals of legislatures or demonstrate the importance of changes over time in influencing legislative behavior.

ACTING RATIONALLY (1980s–1990s)

At the same time that legislative research was shifting its focus, it was also growing more sophisticated methodologically. Election analysts and other legislative scholars had a variety of data at their disposal (voting returns, public opinion surveys, and demographic data), supported by their own systematic observations and interviews conducted in various districts over the course of a campaign. Inside-the-chamber data—from roll calls to observation, to interviews—had also grown enormously in quantity. Classifying and interpreting these data were no longer the problems they once had been, for quantitative analysis had been the hallmark of the behavioral revolution and had not remained static as major advances in the statistical sciences were absorbed into political analysis. In the 1970s and 1980s, various forms of regression statistics were becoming the standard scholarly way to organize and analyze electoral, demographic, and polling data, as well as roll-call responses.

There was also a major shift in the organizing conceptions that scholars brought to the data. The emphasis on psychologically rooted norms, constraints, and perceptions as the key to understanding functionally-directed legislative behavior waned significantly. Stimulated by the work of William H. Riker, the focus of explanation shifted to theories derived largely from economics, particularly from analyses of the business cycle and an understanding of the utility-maximization impulses shaping individual entrepreneurs and the business firm. As early as 1957, Anthony Downs argued that political phenomena were the sum total of individual choices and behavior that resulted more from calculated self-interest than from ethical or ideological factors or those rooted in tribal or institutional loyalties. In the early 1960s, Riker extended these ideas into *The Theory of Political Coalitions* (1962).

Scholars of legislatures picked up the idea and extended it, no one more cogently than Morris P. Fiorina, beginning with his *Congress, Keystone of the Washington Establishment* (1977; 2nd ed., 1989). "Most people most of the time," he argued, "act in their own self-interest." Individual legislators are power-oriented. They want to succeed—to be re-elected, to get their legislation through. When confronted by choices and decisions to be made, therefore, legislators consciously act strategically so as to maximize their self-interests, rather than in response to their values, ideologies, or partisan commitments. In fact, rational-choice theorists found an instrumentalist basis for social-psychological legislative norms. Whatever norms or group commitments exist in a legislature are themselves the product of strategic, conscious, rationally defined choices.

Researchers believed that they could coherently operationalize the theory by compiling numerical data about voting and policy outcomes and then testing the theory's relevance through quantitative analysis. Such analytic capabilities meshed nicely with the long-standing but increasing tendency among many scholars to make the study of legislatures (and politics more generally) more and more scientifically rooted and theory-driven, which had been the dominant goal certainly since the 1950s at least. As a result, the utility of rational-choice theory was widely accepted, its utilization becoming more and more the norm in legislative studies.

Rational-choice theories affected other areas of legislative studies as well. Rooted in notions derived from theories of coalition behavior and games, as reported in the work of Kenneth Arrow and Oskar Morgenstern, formal theorists, or modelers, of legislative behavior began to emphasize social-choice theories of individual and, ultimately, institutional behavior. From the mathematics used in macroeconomics, scholars borrowed formulas describing institutional behavior centering on the attempt to build majority coalitions for a specific purpose by rationally acting participants.

Modelers and theorists isolated the essential elements in the process, simplified them, and subjected them to intensive logical and mathematical analyses. William Riker, Morris Fiorina, John Ferejohn, and Barry Weingast, among others, followed this logic. They argued what the expected voting behavior of legislators should be if everyone acts rationally with perfect information; it could be projected mathematically, because strategic choices derive from the need to build minimum-winning coalitions on each action taken and no more than that. The result is that legislative behavior can be seen as an effort to induce, in the modeler's terms, preference-induced equilibriums in a legislative situation. As Barry Weingast wrote, "the legislature can be modelled as an n-person cooperative game." Such a mathematical model provides estimates of likely behavior, given the numbers present and the observable factors in play. The theoretical formulation was then tested against what occurred in given situations. A number of studies—led by Kenneth Shepsle in *The Giant Jigsaw Puzzle* (1978), and by Keith Krehbiel and Barry Weingast, in a series of articles—tried to operationalize these conceptions in real-world legislative situations, such as the construction of committees or the victories of particular groups in certain situations.

Such rational-mathematical-ordering notions became increasingly commonplace in legislative studies. Their scope widened as they became institutionalized by researchers. Legislatures, as noted earlier, are not alone in government. They and the other branches of the state and federal governments remain inevitably intertwined in many ways in a system that emphasizes checks and balances between them in a range of guises. Scholars had always used many case studies of legislative relations with administrative agencies, especially formal interaction and oversight activities, budget hearings, investigations, and the confirmation process. The traditional results of these analyses had often suggested great shortcomings in the respective legislature's ability to oversee and constrain administrative activities effectively. These scholars also discerned a long-term pattern of an apparently irreversible growth in executive dominance over the legislature in both foreign and domestic affairs.

Utilizing rational-choice theory, students of oversight began to discern a stronger legislative control in the relationship with the executive than earlier studies had detected. Some researchers argued that legislatures made preferred choices as to how they would exercise their oversight function, choices that made sense to them and that did provide an effective but often more subtle form of control than scholars had usually looked for. "Our analysis suggests," one group wrote, that "when the interests represented on the relevant congressional committees change, so will [bureaucratic] policy. If regulatory agencies were substantially independent of Congress, such changes in

Congress would have little connection with agency decisions." In short, they argued, officials in various agencies administered programs strategically for their own rational purposes. They wanted to keep on the right side of Congress (and state legislatures) and not be hampered by the great potential that exists for legislative constraint on their activities. Some scholars have argued that in relations between the executive and legislature, the notion of one-way presidential dominance is not as accurate as an exchange-bargaining model based on market relationships, in which both sides have needs and something to offer, prompting a willingness to trade with one another in the pursuit of each other's particular goals.

As rational-choice notions became the norm among many legislative scholars in the 1980s, other scholars reawakened interest in measuring change over time in legislative structure and behavior. The behavioral political scientists had tended to emphasize the stable dimension, the persistent elements of legislative life as they closely delineated it in the 1950s and 1960s. But, in the 1970s, there was an increasing awareness of a decline of, or important shifts in, many of the previously immutable elements that scholars had argued defined legislatures. Congress, for one, moved from an institution of apparently permanent and inflexible modes to one that proved always to be in flux. Donald Matthews summarized the matter:

> The picture of the Senate we painted in the 1950s was that of a relatively stable and bounded system, with reasonably clear norms, informal but effective sanctions, and a clear hierarchy (or two) of power. Today's Senate is characterized by extreme individualism, lack of hierarchy, and a style of unrestrained activism which was frowned upon in the 1950s.

Clearly, institutions such as legislatures were not fixed entities, as they had seemed to be. Seniority, party loyalty, the role of committees, the size of the work load, and the role of constituencies and election behavior had not remained immutable from one decade to the next.

In addition to short-term changes, there were longer-term shifts. When researchers probed the past, they found significantly different legislative worlds from those that existed in the behaviorally stable 1950s or the rapidly fluctuating 1970s. In legislatures, political parties remained important because where organizational matters were concerned, party influence and direction still held. In contrast, party lines on policy voting have very clearly followed a long-term pattern of declining importance. To scholars, history was important not because things always change but because shifts over time illuminate the shape and nature of contemporary practices with sharper insight then provided by the snapshot approach. Thus, as David Brady suggested, if Speakers of the House of Representatives once were strong and had grown weak, historical research suggests a useful causal analysis for understanding that shift.

Given the existing scholarly behavioral emphases, drawn from immutable theories of behavior, it was not possible to explain such changes and explore their impact. In Lawrence C. Dodd's terms, scholars had to find ways of "solving the puzzle of change" by developing understanding of the cyclical histories of legislatures. In such bodies, self-correcting mechanisms and forces existed that worked to restore stability to the way legislatures acted. These self-correcting mechanisms, Dodd argued, appeared in an inevitable, rhythmic fashion once the forces of change had reached a certain level. Other scholars followed Dodd's lead by exploring various ways of catching shifting patterns and following their impact on legislative activities, behavior, and outcomes. Some investigators suggested that in fact Dodd's cyclical analysis was as time-bound as other theories of legislative behavior were once considered immutable.

This change occurred in an institutional context. Legislatures were not simply atomistic epiphenomena of self-interested individuals and groups in action. The shape and structure of an organization affects behavior within it by setting boundaries, providing certain channels and not others. First, institutions helped to define the outlooks of people working within them. What resources were present defined individual strategies and choices. Brady and Ettling suggested that in the middle of the nineteenth century, "rational candidates saw their electoral fate tied to the fate of their party and its presidential candidates, rather than to

their ability to service constituents." Second, institutions always had needs that could conflict with an individual legislator's particular goals. Individual-oriented models of behavior could not help in understanding and explaining some phenomena affected by institutional processes. Individual-oriented models did not explain larger, more complex systems.

These "endogenous structural factors" had immense impact on behavior and policy outcomes. The chronological context in which events occurred led people to adopt certain strategies, whatever their specific preferences in a given situation might be. As parties declined in the electoral arena, an institutional shift of some magnitude inside legislatures permitted individuals to act in certain ways not acceptable or available in a strong party era. Thus, "from a behavioral point of view, formally organized social institutions have come to be portrayed simply as arenas within which political behavior, driven by more fundamental factors, occurs." But "organizations have an impact on their environments; they do not simply respond to them." They evolve as members learn to cope, as the external environment shifts, and as adjustments are made. Brady and Morgan pointed out how the decentralizing of the appropriations process from an earlier, more tightly controlled situation had led to what its proponents wanted—an increase in expenditures. Given such examples (and there were many), the study of legislatures clearly required comparative historical evidence.

Rational-choice theorists also found utility in historical analysis and the new institutionalism, focusing on the obvious change in, and constraints on, individual-goal achievement by the particular institutional context. To Kenneth Shepsle, legislative "outcomes appeared to track the preferences of distinguished actors upon whom institutional structure and procedure conferred disproportionate agenda power." Outcomes, in short, were not the results of a straightforward aggregation of preferences. The contriving hand of legislative leadership—the premier institution of all—was still at work in shaping outcomes by building and utilizing particular kinds of strategically important structures to accomplish certain goals or by basing their strategies of action on the nature of the institutional structures present. A theory of legislative behavior would therefore include both rational actors and institutional structures. Rational decisions, plus legislative rules and processes, led to predictable policy outcomes, or, over time "structual-induced-equilibria" in legislative activities.

AN INCOMPLETE PICTURE

In the late 1980s and early 1990s, the study of the American legislative system constituted one of the largest enterprises undertaken by researchers into the political system. Since 1976, a journal, *Legislative Studies Quarterly*, published at the University of Iowa in Ames, has had little trouble filling its pages with research presentations. Such legislative research also continued to attract a wide variety of different practitioners. As Keith Krehbiel has written, there was at the beginning of the 1990s, a "healthy heterogeneity within the legislative research community," which included "politicians, anecdotists, soakers-and-pokers, number crunchers, and proposition provers." Both behavioral researchers and those of a more traditional bent continued to pursue their own interests, delineating patterns, measuring influences, exploring individual "critical" episodes, and writing biographies of the great and near-great. Popular books about Congress continued to appear as well. The reformist tradition was also present, as were memoirs of legislators reporting on what they had seen and done, and often—echoing an age-old theme—offering suggestions for improving the workings of the legislative branch.

Finally, studies of the state legislatures continued to appear, reflecting both an individual focus, as in Malcolm Jewell and Penny Miller's *The Kentucky Legislature: Two Decades of Change* (1988), and more macrocosmic analyses, as in Alan Rosenthal's several studies, such as *Legislative Life: People, Process, and Performance in the States* (1981) and *Governors and Legislatures: Contending Powers* (1990). Time-honored subjects also continued to merit attention, as in Jewell's *Representation in State Legislatures* (1982). These authors pursued long-standing agendas, from description to reformism, while mixing in up-to-date approaches to legislative analysis.

Complementing the vigorous research activities was a great deal of effort in support of scholarly endeavors. A large amount of raw material for the historical study of legislatures continued to be collected in such places as the ICPSR archive at Ann Arbor. A number of publications of the latter's data were essayed. The most ambitious of these was Stanley Parsons's collection delineating and describing all of the congressional districts formed since 1789. Other such compilations, guides, and bibliographic aids included the collection on microfilm of state legislative journals and records, a massive gathering-together of the records and activities of the First Congress, and Kenneth Martis's two-volume historical atlas of congressional districts (1982) and of political party strength in Congress since 1789 (1989). Norman Ornstein and several colleagues began in 1980 to produce regular editions of *Vital Statistics on Congress*. The U.S. Senate and House of Representatives both established historical offices that began to publish a range of useful guides and bibliographies, including a new edition of the *Biographical Directory of the American Congress* (1989). A number of similar efforts for state legislatures has also appeared. Research institutions focusing on Congress, such as those associated with the names of former Speaker of the House Carl Albert and former Senate Minority Leader Everett Dirksen were established and engaged in vigorous programs promoting research and the diffusion of knowledge about Congress.

What does all of this activity add up to after forty years of intense scholarly examination? Certainly, students know more, look for more, and clearly now have a wealth of information and theoretical propositions unavailable to earlier generations. Anyone entering the field can readily find much guidance on how to proceed methodologically and substantively. All of this historiography has been accumulated into a massive intellectual data bank. At the same time, among the social scientists, all of these presentations together suggest how much the study of legislatures has become both coherent and divided. It is coherent because of scholars' commitment of scientific method, the systematic search for casual explanations. It is divided in that there are strong disagreements over how to proceed under the general rubric of science. Barbara Sinclair has summed this up:

> Two very different approaches to understanding and explanation are identifiable. At one extreme are the modelers, who focus upon a few variables assumed to be key (ruthlessly ignoring others) and made often-heroic assumptions that allow the derivation of clear and frequently testable propositions; on the other are scholars, who, taking their cue from historians rather than economists, attempt to include all possibly relevant variables in their analysis and to explain phenomena in all their complexity.

To be sure, nothing has stood still. The behavioral approach still has its champions, although rational-choice analysis had by the 1990s clearly become the preferred organizing scholarly conception. Some legislative scholars have remained critical of the latter, because, in their view, it could not explain a wide range of behavior without expanding and diluting what was included within the term. Nor were such students convinced that rational-choice theories could ever adequately account for the differences observed over time in the way legislators went about their business. In short, once again, as researchers learned more about their subject, what had appeared to be clean-cut, universalist explanations began to lose some of their force and persuasiveness.

More critically, some analysts remained dissatisfied with many of the fruits of the larger efforts. Students of legislatures had pursued case studies designed to illuminate larger processes, they had forged links between individual studies and across time in order to get a better handle on the whole, and they had filled in thousands of details that, taken together, formed building blocks for a greater understanding. But, as early as the 1960s, some scholars warned that the ongoing legislative research, no matter how behaviorally oriented and scientifically pursued, remained largely descriptive and fragmentary studies of processes at work rather than of the nature of the legislative process itself. Although more information is available than ever before, it has not provided a better understanding of the totality of the process being investigated. Such approaches as rational-choice theory and the new institutionalism have provided some of the general statements about the legislative proc-

ess. But, in the 1980s, critics still made the charge of mere description and fragmentation, because still lacking was a clear understanding of the legislature as a system operating in certain well-understood ways, not only as the sum of its parts but as a whole constantly interacting with its parts.

The publication, in 1985, of the *Handbook of Legislative Research*, edited by Gerhard Loewenberg, Samuel Patterson, and Malcolm Jewell, underscored this criticism. The volume marks a massive stocktaking of several generations of scholarly research effort. Its main themes are the successful accumulation of much descriptive knowledge, the continued presence of many gaps in that knowledge, and the significant lack of well-developed theories to integrate the findings and explain the nature of legislatures as a whole. No one, it seems, felt able to pull everything that was known together and write a comprehensive theoretical statement about legislatures or a full-fledged history of the legislative process, despite thirty fruitful years of research activity.

It was therefore not surprising that as the research material accumulated and discontent was expressed, scholars essayed several times to link it all together. Legislative analysts began to try to draw a clearer picture (or paradigm) of what legislatures are and how they act in toto and to place each new quantum of data within a persuasive conceptual framework. The notion that individual, group, and systemwide activities, choices, and behavior had an underlying definable logic to them grew quite strong among a growing bloc of mathematical modelers of the whole legislative process. A level of generalizing and abstraction of great ambition entered the literature. Titles such as *The Logic of Lawmaking* (Gerald S. Strom, 1990) and *The Logic of Congressional Action* (R. Douglas Arnold, 1990), appeared as guides to, and explanations of, something much greater than the behavior of a single committee or the particular pattern discerned in a sample of roll-call behavior. But such efforts remained controversial and problematic because some judged them too ambitious for what the evidence, with all its variety and inconsistency, could bear.

An intermediate effort between paradigmatic modeling and individualistic description was under way contemporaneously with the grander attempts at synthesis. That effort involved the compilation of large-scale collections of essays covering the whole legislative experience diachronically and cross-sectionally and the publication of several encyclopedias written by scholars that attempted to bring available knowledge together in somewhat organized form, if not yet in an integrated one.

This stocktaking of all that has been learned was perhaps the last necessary step toward the elaboration of a fully textured, full detailed, sharply focused, well-integrated, and theoretically compelling picture of the American legislative system.

BIBLIOGRAPHY

The intellectual development of the social sciences at the end of the nineteenth century is nicely detailed in DOROTHY ROSS, *The Origins of American Social Science* (New York, 1991). On Woodrow Wilson as scholar, see HENRY W. BRAGDON, *Woodrow Wilson: The Academic Years* (Cambridge, Mass., 1967). The evolution of political science as a discipline is traced from empiricism to behavioralism and beyond in ALBERT SOMIT and JOSEPH TANENHAUS, *American Political Science: A Profile of a Discipline* (New York, 1964), and ADA FINIFTER, ed., *Political Science: The State of the Discipline* (Washington, D.C., 1983). The development of the historical profession is described in JOHN HIGHAM, *History: Professional Scholarship in America* (Baltimore, 1983, 1989), and, particularly relevant to this essay, ALLAN G. BOGUE, *Clio and the Bitch Goddess: Quantification in American Political History* (Beverly Hills, Calif., 1983).

Reviews of Research
Since the 1960s there have been a number of historiographic reviews of legislative scholarship, beginning with NORMAN MELLER, "Legislative Behavior Research," *Western Political Quarterly* 13 (March 1960): 131–153 and "'Legislative Behavior Research' Revisited: A Review of Five Years' Publications," *Western Political Quarterly* 18 (December 1965): 776–793. See also HEINZ EULAU and KATHERINE HINCKLEY, "Legislative Institutions and Processes," in James A. Robinson, ed., *Political Science Annual*, vol. 1 (1966); NELSON W. POLSBY, "Legislatures," in FRED I. GREENSTEIN and NELSON W. POLSBY, eds., *Handbook of Political Science,* vol. 5 (Reading, Mass., 1975); ROBERT L. PEABODY, "Research on Congress: The 1970s and Beyond," *Congress and the Presidency* 9

(1981–1982): 1–16; LEROY RIESELBACH, "The Forest for the Trees: Blazing Trails for Congressional Research," in FINIFTER, *Political Science*; BARBARA SINCLAIR, "Purposive Behavior in the U.S. Congress: A Review Essay," *Legislative Studies Quarterly* 8 (February 1983): 117–131; and CHRISTOPHER J. BAILEY, "The U.S. Congress: An Introductory Bibliography," *American Studies International* 28 (April 1990): 185–194.

Historians' interest in legislative behavior is reviewed in ALLAN G. BOGUE, "American Historians and Legislative Behavior," in LEE BENSON et al., eds., *American Political Behavior: Historical Essays and Readings* (New York, 1974); ROBERT ZEMSKY, "American Legislative Behavior," in ALLAN G. BOGUE, ed., *Emerging Theoretical Models in Social and Political History* (Beverly Hills, Calif., 1973); BALLARD C. CAMPBELL, "The State Legislatures in American History: A Review Essay," *Historical Methods Newsletter* 9 (September 1976): 185–194; JOEL H. SILBEY, "Congressional and State Legislative Roll-Call Studies by U.S. Historians," *Legislative Studies Quarterly* 6 (November 1981): 597–607, and "'Delegates Fresh from the People': American Congressional and Legislative Behavior," *Journal of Interdisciplinary History* 13 (Spring 1983): 603–627.

In a class by itself for the extent, depth, and completeness of its historiographic review is GERHARD LOEWENBERG, SAMUEL C. PATTERSON, and MALCOLM E. JEWELL, eds., *Handbook of Legislative Research* (Cambridge, Mass., 1985), which contains analytic articles by distinguished scholars covering every phase of legislative studies.

Collections of Essays
In addition to the historiographic reviews, there are also several collections of essays

that effectively demonstrate the dominant approaches to legislative research since the behavioral revolution. JOHN C. WAHLKE and HEINZ EULAU, eds., *Legislative Behavior: A Reader in Theory and Research* (Glencoe, Ill., 1959), was the first such stocktaking collection, followed by JOHN C. WAHLKE, HEINZ EULAU, WILLIAM BUCHANAN, and LeROY C. FERGUSON, eds., *The Legislative System: Explorations in Legislative Behavior* (New York, 1962), which focuses on state legislatures. Several of these publications have Congress, not legislatures generally, as their focus, including ROBERT L. PEABODY and NELSON W. POLSBY, eds., *New Perspectives on the House of Representatives* (Chicago, various editions, 1963–); RALPH HUITT and ROBERT L. PEABODY, eds., *Congress: Two Decades of Analysis* (New York, 1969); and NORMAN J. ORNSTEIN, ed., *Congress in Change: Evolution and Reform* (New York, 1975). Particularly illuminating are the successive editions of LAWRENCE DODD and BRUCE OPPENHEIMER, eds., *Congress Reconsidered* (New York, 1977; 4th ed., Washington, D.C., 1989). Historians are represented first in WILLIAM O. AYDELOTTE, ed., *The History of Parliamentary Behavior* (Princeton, N.J., 1977), which deals with more than the American legislative system; and JOEL H. SILBEY, ed., *The Congress of the United States, 1789–1989* (New York, 10 vols. in 23, 1991), which reprints more than three-hundred-fifty scholarly articles covering every phase of congressional activities since the beginning.

Current Research Directions

Many essays and essay collections focus specifically on some of the main approaches to legislative analysis in the behavioral and post-behavioral eras. RALPH HUITT's articles are collected in *Working Within the System* (Los Angeles and Berkeley, 1990); RICHARD FENNO constituency-based analysis is looked at in MORRIS P. FIORINA and DAVID ROHDE, eds., *Home Style and Washington Work* (Ann Arbor, Mich., 1989); rational-choice and new institutional approaches are presented in MATHEW D. McCUBBINS and TERRY SULLIVAN, eds., *Congress: Structure and Policy* (New York, 1987); and JOSEPH COOPER and DAVID W. BRADY call for more-historical focus by political scientists in legislative analysis in "Toward a Diachronic Analysis of Congress," *American Political Science Review* 75 (December 1981): 988–1006.

BARBARA HINCKLEY, *Stability and Change in Congress* (4th ed., New York, 1988), is a marvelous presentation of what scholars know about Congress in all of its facets, revealing a great deal in its presentation about historiographic trends.

Bibliographies

Finally, there are three excellent bibliographies of research on Congress that strive for completeness in their coverage: RICHARD BAKER, ed., *The United States Senate: A Historical Bibliography* (Washington, D.C., 1977); ROBERT U. GOEHLERT and JOHN B. SAYRE, eds., *The United States Congress: A Bibliography* (New York, 1982); and DONALD R. KENNON, ed., *The Speakers of the House of Representatives: A Bibliography, 1789–1984* (Baltimore, 1986).

Part II

LEGISLATIVE RECRUITMENT, PERSONNEL, AND ELECTIONS

CONSTITUTIONAL REQUIREMENTS FOR LEGISLATIVE SERVICE

Paul S. Rundquist

The requirements determining who may serve in a legislative body determine as much about the policies that emerge from that body as does any other factor. The U.S. Congress was not crafted by the delegates to the Constitutional Convention in a vacuum, in that the leading delegates were experienced students of the governments of classical antiquity and had read of, or seen at firsthand, the British Parliament at Westminster. Most had served in their own colonial legislatures and many had served in Congress of the Articles of Confederation, which they sought to supplant. These varied experiences with the composition of legislatures inevitably influenced their judgments concerning appropriate qualifications in the U.S. Constitution for service in the House and Senate.

Foremost among the powers to be acquired by a legislative body is the right to determine the qualifications for service in that body. In Britain this right was not clearly established until late in the seventeenth century. When King James I summoned his first Parliament, he directed that returns be filed with the Chancery, thereby giving agents of the crown the authority to rule on the validity of election results. The Commons challenged this authority immediately by voting to seat an outlaw, Sir Francis Goodwin, who was elected in the face of the king's command in the election writ banning criminals from serving in the assembly. The House of Lords sought a conference with the Commons on the matter, but the Commons refused. Later the king summoned the speaker who, along with a large delegation from the Commons, was informed that the king desired that the Commons confer with the Chancery judges about the election returns. No compromise was reached, and the king ordered new elections. But the standoff was viewed as a

victory for the Commons, so that by 1625 Commons members boasted, according to Robert Luce, that the review of election credentials was one of their "antient and natural undoubted privileges and powers."

FORMAL CONSTITUTIONAL REQUIREMENTS

Minimum-Age Standards

In Britain, the matter of appropriate age for members of Parliament was not settled clearly or consistently for centuries. Under British common law, a man reached full legal age at twenty-one, although some legal rights could be exercised at a younger age. At twelve, one might undertake the oath of allegiance; at seventeen, one could become an executor of an estate; and by the age of twenty-one, one acquired the full rights to dispose of property. Logically, therefore, the age of twenty-one might be an acceptable entry age into the national legislature.

During the reign of James I (1603–1625), the issue of a formal age qualification apparently was raised for the first time. Secondary parliamentary sources indicate that during one of James's parliaments, more than forty members of the Commons were under the age of twenty, and some public complaints were heard that minors ought not to be legislating on matters to which they were not themselves liable.

In 1621 the Commons debated (but did not pass) an amendment to an election bill setting the age of twenty-one as the minimum for service in Parliament. Underage Commons representation continued to be a problem, even after Parliament acted in 1695 to set the membership-age minimum at twenty-one. As late as 1787, two members of Parliament long noted in history—Charles James Fox and Anthony Ashley Cooper, the future Lord Shaftesbury—served in the Commons before their twenty-first birthdays, and in the nineteenth century, Lord John Russell, a future prime minister, entered the Commons one-month shy of twenty-one. In her classic treatise on British parliamentary practice, Erskine May, the former clerk of the House of Commons notes no breach of the age minimum since the passage of the Reform Act of 1832.

The American Revolution was the work of young men; and it was therefore unlikely that the newly independent states would greatly restrain political involvement because of age. The early constitutions of the newly independent colonies followed the practice of the British Commons, setting twenty-one as the minimum age for membership in the lower chamber. In the elected upper chambers, however, widespread diversity was the rule, although only three states—Virginia, Maryland, and South Carolina—set a higher age limit (twenty-five for Virginia and Maryland; thirty for South Carolina). In addition, New Hampshire inserted a requirement of thirty years of age for its senators in its second constitution (1784).

The Congress of the Articles of Confederation was silent on age or other qualifications for delegates. Presumably, the drafters of that document believed that the state legislatures, which chose the national Congress delegates, ought to be trusted to send only well-qualified members, and that the Articles ought not limit state discretion in the matter very much. Of course, the Articles did limit the states in sending delegates by restricting a delegate to service for only three years out of any five.

In the federal Constitutional Convention, the issue of age requirements for representatives played, at most, a minor role. In Governor Edmund Randolph's Virginia Plan, the original proposal contained a phrase that required members of the first branch (the House of Representatives) "to be of the age of———years at least." On 12 June 1787 the Committee of the Whole struck out the age-requirement phrase, seemingly endorsing no minimum-age standard. On 22 June, George Mason of Virginia moved that the draft be revised to reflect a minimum-age standard of twenty-five years. Al-

though he admitted that members below that age had served in the Articles of Confederation Congress, Mason contended that youthful political views are often vastly different from those one later develops, and so he suggested that the very young should attain greater maturity and until then be barred from national councils. James Wilson of Pennsylvania opposed the higher age requirement, claiming that it tended to damp the efforts of genius and laudable ambition, and noted the singular influence held by William Pitt the Younger and Lord Bolingbroke (Henry St. John) before their own twenty-fifth birthdays. But Mason's argument held sway in the convention; the amendment to set the age requirement at twenty-five was adopted by a vote of seven states to three, with one state (New York) divided.

Randolph similarly had contained no age specification for senators in his Virginia Plan. On 12 June 1787, the Committee of the Whole approved a motion to set thirty years as the minimum-age requirement. Madison's journal does not report the slightest discussion of this issue, as the amendment was agreed to, seven states to four.

During the ratification process, the differential age restrictions established for the House and Senate elicited no major controversy. In *The Federalist*, Number Sixty-two (attributed to Madison), the author points to the quasi-executive role of the Senate as grounds for the higher age requirement: "The propriety of these distinctions is explained by the nature of the senatorial trust; which requiring greater extent of information and stability of character, requires at the same time that the senator should have reached a period of life most likely to supply these advantages."

Max Farrand's *Records of the Federal Convention* reveal little formal discussion of the age requirement for either the House or the Senate in state conventions called to ratify the Constitution. In the Maryland ratification convention, James McHenry, a member of the Philadelphia convention, while examining the draft constitution point by point, declared that twenty-five was "deemed a necessary age to mature the judgment (of Representatives) and form the mind by habits of reflection and experience." McHenry's journal noted that "little was said on this subject; it passed without any considerable opposition and therefore I was not at the pains to note any other particulars respecting it." This reaction was typical of that in all state ratifying conventions.

In the early Congresses, the minimum-age standard was violated at least a dozen times. The most notable case involved Henry Clay, who was chosen at age twenty-nine by the Kentucky legislature (in which he served as speaker) to fill a senatorial vacancy. No challenge was made to his seating in 1806. In the House, William Claiborne was elected from Tennessee at the age of twenty-one or twenty-two in 1797. More-stringent standards of enforcement later developed, however, and in the Thirty-sixth Congress (1859), Representative-elect John Young Brown (D.-Ky.) refrained from taking his seat during the first session as he had not yet reached the age of twenty-five.

Citizenship

The national legislature of a nation of immigrants faced a problem relatively unknown to the British Parliament: whether to permit naturalized citizens to serve in the Congress, and if so, under what conditions. In Britain, during the late eighteenth century, naturalized citizens were banned from election to the House of Commons. It was not until the establishment of local self-government in Canada in 1847, and other dominions later in the nineteenth century, with the inclusion of vast numbers of new British "subjects" not born in the British Isles that the question of naturalized citizens and their eligibility for Parliament was raised anew. By the Status of Aliens Act of 1914 and the British Nationality Act, all British subjects either by birth or by naturalization are eligible for election to Parliament upon reaching the age of twenty-one.

At the time the U.S. Constitution was framed, widespread legislative service by naturalized citizens was virtually unheard of outside the New World. The Constitution gave the federal Congress the authority to establish a uniform national standard for naturalization. Previously, the colonies and the newly independent states had established their own standards for granting citizenship to immigrants, and the diversity of those standards led to many complications. Madison, in *The Federalist*, Number Forty-two, notes contemptuously the confusing protections afforded to adopted citizens under the Articles of Confederation:

> In the 4th article of the confederation, it is declared "that the *free inhabitants* of each of these States, paupers, vagabonds, and fugitives from justice excepted, shall be entitled to all privileges and immunities of *free citizens,* in the several States, and *the people* of each State, shall in every other, enjoy all the privileges of trade and commerce, &c." There is a confusion of language here, which is remarkable. Why the terms *free inhabitants,* are used in one part of the article; *free citizens* in another, and *people* in another, or what was meant by superadding "to all privileges and immunities of free citizens,"—"all the privileges of trade and commerce," cannot easily be determined.

In contemplating citizenship requirements for the Congress, the convention attempted to steer a middle course—one that continued to encourage immigrants to join in the political life of the new nation, while simultaneously attempting to assure that only those naturalized citizens with established affinity for their adopted nation were admitted into its highest legislative councils.

The citizenship issue was first raised by Charles Pinckney of South Carolina, who suggested that four years of citizenship be required for senators, and some lesser, unspecified number of years be required for representatives. The Committee on Detail suggested three years for House members, but George Mason of Virginia believed this to be inadequate. He thought that three years would not ensure sufficient local knowledge on the part of the naturalized representative. Mason also feared organized foreign influence: "[A] rich foreign nation, for example, Great Britain, might send over her tools, who might bribe their way into the legislature for insidious purposes." He suggested a seven-year requirement, but significant opposition arose. Oliver Ellsworth of Connecticut suggested that one year was sufficient, while Madison announced his opposition to any such restriction in the Constitution. Benjamin Franklin of Pennsylvania opposed anything in the Constitution that smacked of "illiberality," but he announced his willingness to support reasonable restrictions. James Wilson of Pennsylvania spoke against restrictions, noting that as he was foreign-born himself, he might be barred from legislative service under a constitution he had helped to write.

Gouverneur Morris of New York moved that a fourteen-year citizenship requirement be imposed on naturalized senators, but the motion was defeated: four states voted for, and seven against, that measure. Morris then suggested thirteen years and lost again. Pinckney suggested ten years, and his motion was defeated. A proposal of nine years finally secured the support of six states, a majority.

Attention then turned to citizenship requirements for federal representatives. Surprisingly, in view of his varied opposition to Senate restrictions, Elbridge Gerry of Massachusetts announced his support for only native-born representatives. Several members supported the Senate's nine-year citizenship requirement for the House. But Alexander Hamilton and James Madison both supported leaving any citizenship requirement to action by the individual state legislatures. Wilson and Randolph endorsed a four-year requirement for representatives that had been supported earlier in the Committee of the Whole, but ultimately the convention rejected all proposals except for the final adopted provision of seven years of citizenship.

The first test of this standard occasioned one of the most heated early debates in the U.S. Senate and ultimately led to greater public accountability from the Senate. In 1793 the Pennsylvania state legislature elected Swiss-born Abraham Alfonse Albert Gallatin to the Senate. Gallatin had been a leader of the Whisky Rebellion, an agrarian western Pennsylvania protest in 1794 against federal excise taxes imposed on distilled-grain products. Imposing the tax successfully was a major early test for the federal government, and a detachment of federal and state troops put in a show of force to break up the protest movement. The anti-Federalists had a hero in Gallatin, and the Federalists who controlled both houses of Congress viewed him as a threat to the operation of the government.

Gallatin had come to Massachusetts in 1780, during the latter stages of the American Revolution. He seemingly renounced his Swiss allegiance in 1783, but did not actually take an oath of allegiance until 1785, when he became a citizen of Virginia. Under the terms of the Articles of Confederation, however, free inhabitants of any state were to be entitled to all the privileges and immunities of free citizens in the several states. Arguably, Gallatin as a free resident was entitled to be treated as a citizen in any of the thirteen independent states, regardless of whether he had actually taken the oath of allegiance to any one of them. A related legal issue concerned whether the new Constitution could overturn the legal standing that an individual possessed prior to its ratification.

Gallatin presented his credentials on 2 December 1793. Immediately, questions were raised about his eligibility to serve, as he had not yet been formally a citizen of a component state of the United States for the nine years requisite for Senate service.

Until that time, the Senate had met in closed session, ostensibly because its first meeting place in New York City lacked a gallery for attendance by the press and public. Although its Philadelphia chamber had a perfectly usable gallery, the Senate continued to meet in secret. So great was public interest in the seating of Gallatin that the Senate decided, for the first time, to open its doors to the public during debate on his qualifications.

By a vote of fourteen to twelve, the Senate refused to seat Gallatin. But, finding that having let in the public once it could not easily close its doors again, the Senate voted less than six months after the Gallatin debate to open its legislative sessions permanently to the public. By their actions, the Federalists had also unwittingly made a hero out of Gallatin. In the autumn of 1794, Gallatin was elected to the House and became the leading spokesman for the Jeffersonian Republicans, moving on to serve as treasury secretary in the Jefferson and Madison administrations.

The interpretation of the citizenship qualification was rarely thereafter an issue in the Congress. In 1849 Irish-born Senator-elect James Shields (D.-Ill.) was initially excluded from the Senate because he had not then completed nine full years of naturalized citizenship. Later that year, the Illinois legislature reelected him after he had satisfied the requirement. The Senate seat remained vacant during this hiatus. In 1906 the House voted to seat a foreign-born representative-elect, Anthony Michalek (R.-Ill.), born in Bohemia, who had always assumed the fact of his naturalization through his father, but could not produce any naturalization records to substantiate this assumption. Representative-elect Henry Ellenbogen (D.-Pa.), born in Austria, did not take the oath of office until 3 January 1934, some ten months after the Seventy-third Congress convened, because he had not until then satisfied the seven-year citizenship requirement. A memorial from citizens of Pennsylvania challenged his right to the seat based on his noncompliance with the constitutional requirement at the time of his election. The Committee on Elections reported on this development and the House agreed to a resolution stating that Ellenbogen "was qualified to take (the) oath" on 3 January 1934, and was duly elected and entitled to retain the seat.

Residency Requirements

In the sixteenth century, the Commons was subject to a local residency requirement. Election writs to sheriffs in the reign of King Henry VIII (1509–1547) directed the selection of qualified residents of the county or borough to serve in Parliament. By the reign of Queen Elizabeth I (1558–1603), the residency requirement was widely ignored and, by an Act of 1784, it was formally abolished. In most Commonwealth countries, residence in the electoral district is not generally required.

In the American colonies, a local residency requirement was not uniformly required at first. In Luce's view, the size of the colony often determined the need for a residency standard. In smaller colonies, he claimed, a local residency requirement was often imposed, as in the case of the Plymouth colony. In larger colonies, with greater distances between the capital and outlying areas, residency requirements were generally abandoned. In the first quarter of the eighteenth century, colonial assemblies came to require local-district residence or, failing that, an appropriate freehold in the district represented as a condition of membership.

The Constitutional Convention did not trouble itself much on this issue. As the Virginia Plan and others submitted to the convention did not specify the creation of electoral districts within a state, it was generally viewed that the interests of republican representation could be satisfied merely by a requirement that the representative or senator be "an inhabitant of that State" from which he was elected.

When challenged on the issue of residence qualification, the House and Senate have generally interpreted the standard loosely. Evidence of a legal connection to the state has generally been sufficient for both the House and Senate in these matters. In 1824 the House seated Representative-elect John Forsyth (R.-Ga.) who, at the time of his election, was U.S. minister to Spain. A majority of the House concurred that absence owing to government service did not sever one's former state inhabitancy. In 1929 the House seated Representative-elect Louis Ludlow (D.-Ind.), a Washington-based journalist, on the grounds that he had retained sufficient connection to Indiana as a property owner, taxpayer, and registered Indiana voter to qualify as an inhabitant of that state.

In 1964 the Senate agreed to seat Pierre Salinger (D.-Calif.), who was appointed to the Senate to fill a vacancy. At the time, Salinger was press secretary to President Lyndon Johnson, and his formal "inhabitancy" in California was questioned. The Senate declined to exclude Salinger when satisfied that he had established a legal residence in California at the time he appeared to take the oath of office.

District residence has always been a matter of local political importance, however. Most states with more than one House seat have consistently elected their House members from single-member districts, rather than in an at-large manner. However, it was not until the Act of June 25, 1842, that the Congress imposed upon the states guidelines directing the establishment of single-member districts. Thereafter, the House was reluctant to enforce the single-member-district standard, voting several times to seat state delegations elected at-large. In some states, it was common for several seats to be chosen at-large at the same time that other representatives from the state were elected from single-member districts. The reapportionment rulings of the Supreme Court in the 1960s effectively ended the practice of at-large representation, except in those states entitled to only one House seat.

Members of the House generally must be clearly identifiable as having a connection to the district they represent, however tenuous it may be. Failure to maintain such a legal connection (through home ownership, voting registration, parental homestead, or some other such tie) has often been a major political issue in House election campaigns. (Noteworthy exceptions include the election of James Michael Curley, former mayor of Boston, to the House in the 1940s even though he lacked formal residence in the district, and the election of John F. Kennedy to the House from a Massachusetts district in which his voting residence was a rooming house.) But the House has consistently failed to enforce state efforts to impose a residency requirement different from that contained in the Constitution.

INFORMAL QUALIFICATIONS AND EXCLUSIONS

Wealth and Income Qualifications

There was initially no wealth qualification for service in the British House of Commons, but no formal salary was attached to service as a member of Parliament, and the informal custom of constituencies paying salaries to their members began to die out early in the seventeenth century. Thereafter, competition for the available seats increased electioneering expenses to such a degree that a poor man was unlikely to be able to afford to campaign for, much less serve in, the Commons.

In 1710, Parliament passed an act requiring that a member of the Commons have an income of at least £600 annually if elected from a county constituency, and £300 annually if elected from a borough. In both cases, the income was required to be derived from landownership. The law was widely evaded, either by outrightly false asset oaths, or by fictitious property transfers from large landowners to worthy candidates so that the formal income threshold could be reached. In 1838 income from personal property was permitted to qualify for the first time, and it was not until 1858 that the property qualification was abolished forever in the Commons.

In the American colonies, property qualification for membership in the legislature was generally the same as the property qualification for the electoral franchise. Only three states made a distinction in the value of property for legislators: both South Carolina and New Jersey

required £1,000, and New Hampshire £300. In most of the colonies, a land freehold was normally required, and in New Jersey, Connecticut, and South Carolina the land freehold was required to be in the district that the member represented. Georgia's short-lived colonial assembly featured a unique property qualification in order to promote the development of the silk industry. Initially, a deputy there was required to have planted "a hundred mulberry trees . . . upon every fifty acres he possessed." Later, this requirement was changed to stipulate that the deputy produce at least fifteen pounds of silk for every fifty acres of land he owned.

After independence, the new states redrafted their constitutions, and most retained some form of property qualification for service in the state legislature. Only Pennsylvania and Vermont omitted such a property qualification, although Pennsylvania limited election to office only to taxpayers, which constituted an implicit property qualification.

In the Constitutional Convention, George Mason strongly advocated a property qualification for senators. Gouverneur Morris thought senators should serve without pay, thereby ensuring that only independently wealthy senators would be chosen. However, he later formally opposed any explicit property qualification for senators or representatives because such qualifications in Britain had been so widely evaded. Pinckney said that executive, legislative, and judicial officers should possess sufficient property as to make them "independent and respectable." Pinckney's proposal was defeated by a voice vote, and thus the Constitution came to require no formal property qualification for membership, explicitly authorizing Congress, in fact, to set a legally payable salary for senators and representatives.

Traditionally, members of Congress have come from the ranks of the comfortably affluent farming, business, and professional classes whose income-producing activities would be little impaired by prolonged absences for congressional sessions. During the Gilded Age of the nineteenth century, many seats in the Senate were held by business tycoons who, some charged, had bought the necessary votes in their state legislatures. During the Progressive Era, David Graham Phillips wrote *The Shame of the Senate,* an exposé of the influence of money on the election and votes of senators. Its publication renewed public interest in a constitutional amendment for the popular election of senators. But even after the Seventeenth Amendment's passage to that effect in 1913, a significant number of wealthy individuals campaigned successfully for the Senate.

In the 1920s the Senate considered charges of excessive campaign expenditures by three senators or senators-elect. In 1922 Truman Newberry (R.-Mich.) resigned from the Senate while it was inquiring into his campaign expenditures of two years before. In 1929 the Senate voted to deny seats to two senators-elect, William S. Vare (R.-Pa.) and Frank L. Smith (R.-Ill.), because of excessive campaign expenditures. Nevertheless, the Senate continued to attract a relatively affluent membership. A study in the early 1980s showed that a majority of senators had a net worth in excess of $1 million.

Ethics regulations adopted during the 1970s reflected the influence of established congressional wealth as representatives and senators were limited in the amount of money they could earn from work while in Congress; at the same time, there was no limit imposed on "unearned income" from investments. Salary increases after World War II gave members an annual income that placed them in the upper 5 percent of all American wage earners.

Religious Tests for Membership

In Britain, the Tudor dynastic wars following Henry VIII's break from Rome in 1534 led to Parliament's passing of a series of measures debarring Catholics from holding office. This began a period in which only adherents to the Church of England could be elected to the Commons. Jews had been banned from elective office because of required oaths signifying a belief in the divinity of Christ. The Anglican monopoly on political power was undercut in practice, as Protestant religious dissenters (after the "Glorious Revolution" of 1688, which entailed the abdication of the Catholic king, James II) were normally not challenged, so long as their religious observance was not a matter of widespread public comment. The ban against Catholics (and the formal ban against dissenting Protestants) was lifted by the Act of 1829.

In 1847, Lionel Rothschild was elected to the Commons, but his seating was refused on the ground that he could not in conscience take the parliamentary oath, as the law required, "on the true faith of a Christian." John Russell, the Liberal party prime minister, placed a bill before Commons action to remove all civil disabilities against Jews. The House passed the bill, but it was rejected in the House of Lords, a situation that recurred twice more during the 1850s.

It was not until 1858 that the Commons and Lords reached a compromise in which each house would be permitted to set its own form of the oath of membership. Thus, by standing order, Jews were permitted to sit in the Commons, although all remaining civil disabilities understand, and membership in the House of Lords would not be reached, until the twentieth century.

Religious tests were commonplace in American colonial legislatures and in the earliest state constitutions. In Massachusetts Bay and in Virginia, where the earliest colonial legislatures emerged, representation was limited to those who adhered to mainstream Protestant groups, such as the Anabaptists. In the General Court of 1654, according to Robert Bruce, membership was limited to those with sound "judgment concerning the main points of the Christian Religion as they have been held forth and acknowledged by the generality of the Protestant Orthodox writers." In 1663, John Porter was expelled from the House of Burgesses for his association with Quakers and his personal objections to the baptism of children.

Pennsylvania, though a haven for Quakers, was less tolerant of elected legislators; under a 1705 election law, assembly members-elect had to swear their adherence to a series of religious doctrines that effectively barred many radical Protestants, as well as Catholics and Jews. However, the Pennsylvania Constitution of 1790 opened the door wider by permitting membership to anyone who "acknowledges the being of a God and a future state of rewards and punishments." With the ratification of the federal constitution with its ban against religious tests, the states moved generally to follow suit. In 1792, Delaware's new constitution stated that "no religious test shall be required as a qualification to any office, or public trust, under this State." The language of this Delaware document was included in six new constitutions established through 1820, and by the twentieth century more than two-thirds of the state constitutions exempted religious belief as a test for officeholding.

The language of Article VI of the federal Constitution comes from Charles Pinckney of South Carolina: "No religious Test shall ever be required as a Qualification to any Office or public Trust under the United States." Debate on Pinckney's amendment was brief. Roger Sherman of Connecticut thought it unnecessary, as "the prevailing liberality" would be a sufficient guard against the establishment of a religious test. But Gouverneur Morris spoke for it as a necessary statement in a nation with so many different religious sects present. In the end, the Pinckney amendment was agreed to without formal objection being noted. During ratification, the religious-test provision received little attention. Only in Massachusetts did it become an issue, and none of the seventeen ministers serving as convention delegates objected to the Constitution because of its ban on religious tests.

In the First Congress, Protestant and Catholic members of both chambers were selected. It was not until 1841 that a Jew, David Yulee, was elected as a delegate from Florida. Upon Florida's admission to the Union in 1845, Yulee was elected to the U.S. Senate and served separate six-year terms.

The relative strength of the various religious denominations in Congress has shifted. Historically, Episcopalians once predominated, but over time, their relative numbers in Congress have declined compared with the more evangelical Protestant groups. With increased immigration from Catholic European countries, the number of Catholic members of Congress has substantially risen. With the election of Senator John Kennedy of Massachusetts to the presidency in 1960, reservations about electing Catholics to high office dissipated. Within a year of Kennedy's inauguration, the Senate elected its first Catholic majority leader, Michael Mansfield (D.-Mont.), and the House elected its first Catholic Speaker, John W. McCormack (D.-Mass.).

Members of Congress have generally been affiliated with some organized religion. Even if they were not active churchgoers, they have tended to announce a preference for one denomination or another. Only in the late twentieth century have noticeable numbers of members of Congress publicly stated that they held no religious affiliation.

The Mormon religion has, from its inception, been a matter of some public controversy in the United States. In seating adherents of the Church of Jesus Christ of Latter-day Saints as members of Congress, the House and Senate have become embroiled in controversy as well. The challenges to seating Mormon members of Congress focused on allegations that certain members-elect or senators-elect had practiced polygamy. In 1873 an attempt was made to exclude George Q. Cannon (R.-Utah), delegate-elect from Utah Territory. The issue of his alleged polygamy was further complicated by the fact that he was a delegate and not a representative, during a period when the privileges and benefits of delegates were substantially different from those of representatives. The House took no action against Cannon during that Congress, but when he was reelected as a delegate in 1881, the House did vote to exclude him.

In 1900, with Utah admitted as a state, the issue presented was clearer. That year, the House conducted an exhaustive investigation into charges that Representative-elect Brigham H. Roberts (D.-Utah) was an acknowledged polygamist, and that such conduct was improper for a member of the House. The committee found that the charges were accurate, and later the House agreed to a resolution by a 268 to 50 vote declaring that Roberts "ought not to have or hold a seat." The House rejected by a vote of 81 to 244 an amendment that would have cited polygamy as grounds for expulsion but not for exclusion from House membership.

The Senate was again faced with the issue of Mormon beliefs in 1906 in a challenge to the seating of senator-elect Reed Smoot. The Senate elections committee ruled that Smoot, an elder in the Church of Jesus Christ of Latter-day Saints but not a practicing polygamist, nevertheless tacitly endorsed the practice as an inevitable consequence of his church office. The full Senate, however, did not concur in that view, and rejected attempts to exclude or to expel Smoot.

Loyalty

Among the unwritten qualifications for service in the House and Senate is the presumed national loyalty of the member. William Blount, a senator from Tennessee, was expelled from the Senate in 1797 on the grounds that his involvement in a plan to incite the Creek and Cherokee Indians to aid the British in conquering Spanish West Florida was inconsistent with his duty as a senator. Initially, the Congress had been intent upon impeaching him, and the House had formed an investigative committee to inquire into his conduct. However, an opinion by Attorney General Charles Lee to the effect that bills of impeachment were only to be directed against judges and officials of the executive branch stayed the House's hand.

The Civil War tested the ability of Congress to function during a period of political disorder. In 1861, during the second session of the Thirty-sixth Congress, a number of Southern representatives and senators announced their retirement from the Congress in view of their states' action on instruments of secession. When the new Congress (elected with Lincoln) convened, most Southern representatives-elect were understandably absent, and failed to take the oath of office. There was some question as to whether a quorum could be maintained solely by the representatives present. To abolish the representation status of Southerners in the House formally would have been to acknowledge the Confederacy's secession as legally valid. To promote a workable quorum, and simultaneously to cancel the status of Southern representatives who had joined the Confederacy, the House voted to declare the seats of absent Southerners vacant. In the other body, senators who were absent because they supported secession were expelled. These actions maintained the legal argument that the Confederate states remained part of the Union, but were currently and temporarily unrepresented; it also reduced the size of an effective working quorum in both chambers.

By the Act of 2 July 1862, the Congress required the admission of a so-called test oath for its members in order to ban from Congress (and from many professions as well) individuals who had once supported the Confederacy. A minority of members in both chambers challenged the constitutionality of this measure as an ex post facto law that also attempted (without constitutional amendment) to add to the qualifications for members of the House and Senate. After the war the Supreme Court, in *Ex parte Garland* (4 Wall. 333, 1867), found the ban for professions to be just such a law, but the Congress insisted on its enforcement for members of Congress until the end of Reconstruction.

The issue of disloyalty again arose during World War I. The Congress, in the Espionage Act of 1917 and the Sedition Act of 1918, prohibited speeches, writings, and actions that undermined the war effort, particularly the enforcement of compulsory military service laws. A leading member of the American Socialist party, Victor Berger, who had served previously in Congress from 1911 to 1913, was elected to the House in November 1918. In December 1918, Berger was convicted of violating the Espionage Act. When Congress assembled in March 1919, his right to the seat was challenged. In November 1919 the House voted 311 to 1 to declare Berger ineligible for the seat because of his conviction for encouraging disloyalty and disobedience to the government of the United States. By giving such "aid and comfort" to the enemies of the U.S., Berger would not be eligible for election to the House until the Congress, by a two-thirds vote, reinstated his rights as sanctioned by the Fourteenth Amendment.

Later that Congress, Berger was victorious in a special election to fill the vacant seat and was again excluded by vote of the House. When elected again in 1920, there was no objection to his taking the oath when he presented his credentials in 1921, as the Supreme Court had voided his conviction earlier that year (*Berger et al.* v. *U.S.*, 255 U.S. 22, 1921).

Acceptance of an Incompatible Office

The Constitution prohibits members of Congress from holding an office of trust or profit under the United States while also serving as a member of Congress. Similarly, a member may not, during his term of office, accept appointment to a civil office that is created, or its "emoluments," or perquisites, increased during his term. The evolution of these concepts is relatively clear.

The ban on the acceptance of an incompatible civil office derives from the practice of the British Parliament. It has long been established that, once chosen, a member of the House of Commons may not resign his seat. However, the inability of a member to resign occasionally embarrassed the Commons when one of its number was the subject of a scandal. Bankruptcy, public corruption, and other such unsavory incidents had to be dealt with in a reasonably expeditious manner, and so the practice of disgraced members' accepting a "place of profit under the Crown" became the favored manner of departure from the Commons. In a truly scandalous episode, however, it was not advisable that this post actually be one of importance. Over time, a number of formal posts with no duties and no salary attached to them evolved in Great Britain, most notably stewards of the Chiltern Hundreds—crown lands and manors in Oxfordshire and Buckinghamshire. Since the eighteenth century, a member seeking to leave the Commons has requested the chancellor of the exchequer to arrange for his or herappointment to the Chiltern Hundreds. On receiving the formal commission from the crown, the individual automatically ceases to be a member of the Commons.

At the U.S. Constitutional Convention, there was little discussion of the "incompatible offices" provision, its purpose apparently being self-evident. In *The Federalist*, Number Seventy-six, Alexander Hamilton explains the role of the Senate in consenting to presidential appointments, and notes that the Constitution provides "some important guards against the danger of executive influence upon the legislative body," as no senator or representative may be appointed to any civil office that is created or the pay of which is expanded during the member's term. In his *Commentaries on the Constitution of the United States* (1833) §867, Justice Joseph Story notes a complex set of incentives and constraints in this ban:

> The [Constitution] take[s] away, as far as possible, any improper bias in the vote of the Representative, and to secure to the constituents some solemn pledge of his disinterestedness. The actual provision, however, does not go the extent of the principle, for his appointment is restricted only "during the time for which he was elected"; thus leaving in full force every influence upon his mind, if the period of his election is short, or the duration of it is approaching its natural termination.

This notion of a duality and incompatibility of function between legislative and executive or judicial responsibilities was not always clear during the colonial period. For example, the speaker of the Pennsylvania assembly for many years also served as treasurer of the colonial government. Moreover, the Congress of the Articles of Confederation combined both legislative and executive functions in one body.

The Constitution does not bar members of Congress from holding simultaneous State office. Although the Congress has never formally ruled on this matter, it appears settled from a series of congressional debates on the issue that the requirement that members be present for sessions of the House or Senate would be an effective, informal ban on such dual position-holding. However, in 1866 the House and Senate voted to seat members from Illinois who, as state judges, had been banned by state law from election to any state or federal office during their elected judicial terms or for one year after their completion.

Relatedly, several representatives and senators have begun their sworn congressional service late in order to remain in other elective positions until their departure was more convenient or their current terms had expired. Huey Long (D.-La.), elected to the Senate in November 1930 for a term beginning in March 1931, did not take the Senate oath of office until 25 January 1932, preferring to remain governor of Louisiana until the completion of an important legislative assembly session. In 1957, Senator-elect Jacob K. Javits (R.-N.Y.) took the oath of office a week late, in order to complete his elective term as New York attorney general. In 1985, Senator-elect Jay Rockefeller (D.-W. Va.) and in 1987 Representative-elect Joseph Brennan (D.-Maine) took the oath late to complete their elected terms as state governors. In such instances, congressional salaries are not paid until the oaths of office have been formally sworn.

The issue of appointments to offices for which members of Congress have voted to increase salary or other benefits has occasioned several controversies and some creative solutions to the constitutional problem. In 1937 several senators opposed the nomination of Senator Hugo Black (D.-Ala.) to the Supreme Court because during Black's Senate term a pension program had been established for retired Supreme Court justices. The Senate rejected that argument as a bar to his appointment, as did the Supreme Court when it effectively denied the standing of a private citi-

CONSTITUTIONAL REQUIREMENTS FOR LEGISLATIVE SERVICE

zen challenging Black's eligibility (*Ex parte Levitt,* 302 U.S. 633, 1937).

Just after World War II, Congress agreed to legislation permitting members of Congress to serve simultaneously as delegates to the United Nations. The measure specifically precluded members from receiving additional salary for the U.N. service, but it did make them eligible for various expense allowances provided to the delegation. Interestingly, Senator Wallace White (R.-Maine), one of the opponents of Black's nomination on constitutional grounds, was one of the first members of Congress to serve additionally at the United Nations.

In the late twentieth century, members of Congress have increasingly served on presidential advisory commissions. Private citizens appointed to such boards are typically paid a daily salary for their service, but members of Congress are not, so as to avoid constitutional problems. In 1969, Representative James Battin (R.-Mont.) resigned from the House and took the oath of office as a federal judge on the afternoon of 27 February, in order to assume office on the day before a judicial pay raise enacted by Congress became effective. Earlier, in January 1969, Representative Melvin Laird (R.-Wis.) took the oath of office as secretary of defense, and later was permitted to accept a salary increase that was proposed and pending before Congress at the time of his nomination. In 1974, Senator William Saxbe (R.-Ohio) was confirmed as attorney general, but could not accept the current salary for the post since he was a senator when the salary was raised. He was the only cabinet member at the time to be paid a salary lower than that of his colleagues.

Holding a congressional seat at the same time as a position in the military has been viewed differently by Congress at various times. For most of its history, Congress viewed active military service to be incompatible with congressional service. On several occasions in the nineteenth and early twentieth centuries, the House or Senate acted to declare vacant (or assume the vacancy thereof) a seat held by members who accepted military commissions. This practice was not uniform, however. The issue was further complicated by the small size of the federal armed forces for most of the nineteenth century and by the frequent use of state militia forces to augment federal forces. As a commission in the militia was clearly a

state office, acceptance of militia office was arguably compatible with congressional service, even when (as frequently occurred during the Mexican War and the Civil War) the state militias were federalized.

When several members accepted active-duty commissions during the Mexican War, the House declared their seats vacant. In the earliest battles of the Civil War, several members of Congress fought with volunteer and militia regiments from their states. Senator Edward Baker (R.-Oreg.) was killed leading his troops in October 1861 at the Battle of Balls Bluff. Ultimately, Lincoln banned sitting members of Congress from serving in any active military units. Later, in the Spanish-American War, attempts were underway to declare vacant the seats of House members who had active-duty service, but the Congress adjourned before acting on these resolutions, and the quick termination of hostilities rendered the issue moot by the time the new Congress convened.

In 1917 the House voted to declare vacant the seats of members of Congress whose national guard (the modern name for the militia) units had been federalized for service in World War I. It had been previously agreed upon that a temporary absence for training exercises and other short-term military responsibilities would be permitted, but that extended absence, especially potential absence on foreign fronts, could not be excused.

By 1941 military preparedness directly intruded upon the House. On several occasions, the House voted "leaves of absence" for members to train with their military reserve units. With the outbreak of war, many younger members of Congress were torn between their desire to serve the nation in Congress and the desire to serve it in the military. Twenty House members took leaves of absence from the Congress in early 1942 to begin active military service, with their congressional salaries blocked by action of the comptroller general. In June 1942 the president ordered these members of Congress to return to their jobs. A dozen members of the House refused to return to Washington, and resigned from the House or urged the House to declare their seats vacant so that they could remain on active duty. A similar number of members determined not to seek reelection to the House in 1942 in order to begin active military service. Military service by members of

Congress is governed by a Department of Defense directive dated 16 January 1965 reclassifying all members of Congress out of the active reserves and into the standby or retired reserve, thereby generally limiting their military role to annual training exercises. Several members of Congress trained with their reserve and National Guard units in the Middle East during the 1990–1991 conflict with Iraq.

Status of Extraconstitutional Qualifications

For most of their history, the House and Senate have informally added to the constitutional requirements for legislative membership. This was evident with regard to the issues of Mormon religious beliefs and charges of disloyalty and financial improprieties. The courts, especially the U.S. Supreme Court, studiously avoided intruding into the internal operations of the Congress, at least as far back as *United States* v. *Ballin* (144 U.S. 1, 1892), which decided that the courts would not review the methods by which the House determined the presence of a quorum.

A landmark Supreme Court case challenged the validity of any standard for admission to membership that was not explicitly sanctioned by the Constitution. In *Powell* v. *McCormack* (395 U.S. 486, 1969), Representative-elect Adam Clayton Powell (D.-N.Y.) brought suit against the speaker of the House and the officers of the House for the House's action in denying his eligibility for a seat.

Various allegations against Powell surfaced during 1966, but he was nevertheless elected to his twelfth term in the House. On 10 January 1967, Powell's right to the seat was challenged, and the House agreed to a resolution directing a select committee to review his eligibility. The committee determined that Powell, in the previous Congress, had improperly claimed immunity from prosecution in a New York State court and had misused his congressional expense funds. On 1 March 1967, the House voted 307–116 to exclude Powell from the House. Powell thereupon sued the speaker and the clerk and doorkeeper of the House, charging that he had been improperly denied the seat to which he was elected, and demanded back pay and benefits dating from the beginning of that Congress. Both the U.S. District Court and the U.S. Court of Appeals rejected Powell's suit, claiming in the words of the Supreme Court decision in *Colegrove* v. *Green* (328 U.S. 459, 1946), that the matter was a "political issue" into which the courts should not enter. Powell appealed to the Supreme Court.

In rendering its 7–1 decision in *Powell* v. *McCormack,* the Court ruled that legislative immunity protected Speaker McCormack from being sued under the speech-and-debate clause. But the Court maintained the suit against the elected officers of the House and declared that the House had acted improperly in attempting to add to the formal qualifications of membership. The Court reasoned that voters had a right to be represented by someone of their choosing and that the Congress had no authority to establish standards for admittance to membership higher than those the Constitution set. If the House or Senate found improper a member's conduct—either past or present, or internal or external to the Congress—they had an unfettered right to attempt to expel the offending member by a two-thirds vote, and not by the simple majority vote permitted on a motion to exclude.

Powell was reelected to the House in 1968, and no challenge was made to his seating, in return for an agreement by Powell to relinquish his committee chairmanship and to repay the House the funds he allegedly misused. However, the issue was so clearly adjudicated by the Court that challenges in the future to the qualifications of members-elect are likely to be more narrowly drawn than in the past.

MINORITIES IN CONGRESS: BREAKING THROUGH IMPLICIT BARRIERS

African Americans in Congress

Until the Civil War, American blacks existed under a dual legal status. In the states of the North and in certain territories, they were free citizens, and in most of these designations they held the voting franchise, especially after most states abolished property qualifications to vote. In the South they were slaves, and after the passage of the Fugitive Slave Act of 1850 they could not acquire the status of freedom even by escaping to states where slavery was barred.

CONSTITUTIONAL REQUIREMENTS FOR LEGISLATIVE SERVICE

The Supreme Court, in the *Dred Scott* v. *Sanford* case (19 How. 393, 1857), asserted that blacks had no standing as citizens of the United States.

With the passage of the Fourteenth Amendment in 1868, blacks and all other persons born in the United States and subject to its jurisdiction (an attempt to exclude Native Americans still living autonomously on their own lands) were recognized as citizens of the United States. With the ratification in 1870 of the Fifteenth Amendment, which banned franchise discrimination based on race or previous condition of servitude, the Constitution was revised to protect blacks' political rights. In the Southern states that were "reconstructed" back into the Union, newly enfranchised blacks became a major voting block. For example, in Mississippi, blacks made up more than 60 percent of the postwar population. In other states the black population tended to be concentrated in several regions of the state. In this postwar environment, blacks could and did win election to the House and Senate from the Southern states.

The first black members were seated in 1870. Hiram Revels, a Republican, was chosen by the Mississippi state legislature to serve the last two years of a term in one of the state's two Senate seats. Revels took the oath of office on 25 February 1870, thereby giving him the distinction of being the first black member of either congressional chamber. Revels's credentials were challenged in the Senate on the grounds that he had not been a citizen for nine years, but the Senate ruled that as a free black before the Civil War and a voting resident of Ohio for nearly twenty years, his citizenship was clearly established without reference to the Thirteenth Amendment. Joseph Rainey of South Carolina and Jefferson Long of Georgia were elected to the House, taking their seats in December 1870 for the remainder of the Forty-first Congress. Rainey was elected to the House for four additional terms. In 1874, Mississippi elected another black senator, Blanche K. Bruce, who served the full six-year term. With Bruce's retirement from the Senate, black congressional representation was confined to Southern districts in the House. The number of black representatives was as high as eight in the period 1873–1877, but then began to decline as the reconstructed Southern states slowly began to impose restrictive-franchise tests that systematically reduced, or eliminated outright, black-voting rights, and consequently, the electoral chances of black candidates. The last black from the South to be elected to the House for more than seventy years was George White (R.-N.C.), who served from 1897 to 1901.

There followed a period of nearly three decades during which no black was elected to Congress, and during which much debate existed within the black community about how to restore black political strength. During World War I, an enormous migration of blacks began from the rural South to the industrial cities of the North. Chicago, New York, and Detroit, among other cities, experienced a significant increase in black population. In many cities, racial tensions exploded, but the nucleus of black political power and influence was created. In 1928 a black Republican from Chicago, Oscar DePriest, was elected to the House—the first black to represent a Northern district. Segregated facilities had grown up in the Congress since 1901, and DePriest was initially prohibited from eating in the members' dining room, until President Hoover personally protested to the congressional leadership. DePriest was the last black Republican to be elected to the House until 1990, when Representative Gary Franks of Connecticut was chosen.

Franklin Roosevelt's landslide presidential victory in 1932 upset traditional political alliances, blacks—when they could vote—had traditionally voted Republican, the party of Lincoln, but New Deal social programs were attractive to blacks hard hit by unemployment during the Great Depression. In 1934 DePriest was challenged by Republican-turned-Democrat Arthur Mitchell. Mitchell won a narrow victory and for four terms turned his Chicago district into a dependable Democratic voting block. Mitchell was succeeded in the House by William L. Dawson, who served nearly twenty-eight years in the House and became the first black member to chair a standing committee, Government Operations.

Illinois' monopoly on black House membership was broken in 1945 with the election of Adam Clayton Powell of New York. Until 1955, Dawson and Powell were the only black members of Congress, until they were joined by Charles Diggs, Jr., of Michigan, and three years later by Robert N. C. Nix of Pennsylvania.

In 1963 California elected its first black representative, Augustus Hawkins, and in 1965, Michigan became the first state since Reconstruction to elect two black members when John Conyers joined Representative Diggs in the House.

The Supreme Court reapportionment decisions of the 1960s increased the likelihood that a greater number of predominantly black population districts would be created at city, state, and national levels. The election of greater numbers of blacks to state and local office expanded the pool of experienced black politicians who would ultimately seek election to the Congress. Black members of the House increased from four in 1959 to nine in 1969 to twenty-one in 1983 to twenty-four in 1989.

The passage of time, the growth in black population throughout the country, and the enactment of aggressive civil- and voting-rights legislation all combined to increase black political participation and electoral success. At the same time, the political attitudes of blacks and whites were changing.

In 1967, Edward Brooke of Massachusetts became the first black senator since Reconstruction, and the first black Republican elected to Congress in more than thirty years—all this from a state that was overwhelmingly white in its racial mix and Democratic in its voting patterns. Brooke served for twelve years in the Congress.

Shirley Chisholm of New York became the first black woman elected to the Congress in 1969, and in 1992, Carol Moseley-Braun became the second black to be elected as U.S. senator (D.-Ill.), as well as the first black female senator.

Political reapportionment following the 1990 census has promised to increase the number of districts having a sizable black population, and with it the likelihood of additional black members of Congress. However, despite changes in past attitudes, black Americans are still substantially underrepresented in the House.

Women in Congress

Women were largely denied a role in electoral politics until the late nineteenth century. In Britain there is evidence that women peers (especially abbesses who held an ecclesiastical rank equivalent to that of a bishop) occasion-
ally sat with the House of Lords up through the end of the sixteenth century. But it became commonplace, according to Luce, for women peers to enlist male proxies, and by the beginning of the Stuart dynasty, the crown ceased issuing summonses for women peers. British women were denied the franchise, and even after gaining the vote in 1918, could not sit in the Commons at Westminster until another law was changed in 1919. Later that year, Lady Nancy Astor was chosen in a by-election (a special election called to fill a vacancy) as the first woman member of Parliament.

Women won the right to vote in a half dozen U.S. states before the adoption of the Nineteenth Amendment in 1920. One of the earliest such states was Montana, which in 1916 elected Jeannette Rankin, a Republican, to the House of Representatives. Rankin, a committed pacifist, voted against U.S. entry into World War I. She ran for the Republican senatorial nomination in 1918, losing by a mere seventeen hundred votes. Out of electoral politics for two decades, she was reelected to the House in 1940, and was the only member to vote against entry into World War II, making her the only member to vote against entry into both world wars.

The first woman senator held a totally honorific appointment when Georgia governor Thomas Hardwick appointed Rebecca Felton, at eighty-seven years old an experienced advocate of woman suffrage, to the post, and the newly elected senator, Walter George, agreed not to present his credentials immediately to the Senate. On 20 November 1922, Felton took the oath of office. In her brief speech that afternoon, Felton acknowledged the tribute paid her by her appointment and predicted the selection of more women in the future. The next day George presented his credentials and was sworn.

By 1929 the number of women representatives had grown to nine, but the number of women elected to the House rose slowly thereafter, not reaching 18 until 1961 (plus two senators). Thereafter, a precipitous decline set in with the number of women representatives falling to ten in 1969. The numbers rebounded to nineteen in 1981 and twenty-nine in the 101st and 102d Congresses, respectively. Women's entry into Congress was slow in large part because many women first ran for Congress to succeed their deceased husbands. For most, the election (or appointment to the Senate) was honorific and temporary; for a few, it was the beginning of a long congressional career. For example, Representative and later Senator Margaret Chase Smith (R.-Maine), Representative Corinne "Lindy" Boggs (D.-La.), and Representative Leonor K. Sullivan (D.-Mo.) were all elected to the House to succeed their deceased husbands, and all went on to serve two decades or more in their own right.

As greater professional opportunities were opened up to women after the 1960s, women began to enter politics as a career. Greater numbers of women were elected to state and local office, thereby enlarging the pool of experienced women candidates for election to Congress. Moreover, increasing numbers of women began entering politics as the family business. Generations of male Adamses, Frelinghuysens, Fishes, Lodges, Kennedys, Tafts, and Goldwaters have served in Congress. In the 101st Congress, Representative Susan Molinari (R.-N.Y.) became the second woman elected to succeed her father in the Congress, and in the 102d Congress, at least a half-dozen women members of Congress were the second- or third-generation politician in their families, among them Senator Nancy Landon Kassebaum (R.-Kans.), the daughter of Kansas governor Alfred Landon; Representative Barbara Kennelly (D.-Conn.), the daughter of former Democratic National Party chairman John Bailey; Representative Nancy Pelosi (D.-Calif.), daughter of former Maryland representative Thomas D'Alesandro; and Representative Elizabeth Patterson (D.-S.C.), daughter of former senator Olin Johnston. Despite these advances, women members of Congress are still vastly underrepresented as a proportion of the voting-age population.

Other Minorities in Congress

An analysis of the representation of some minority groups in Congress is problematic. Hispanics and American Indians, for example, may be difficult to identify from historical records owing to intermarriage with the Anglo population and a reluctance on the part of members to claim such heritage publicly for fear of discrimination. It is thought that Senator Matthew Quay (R.-Pa.), who served in the late nineteenth century, was of American Indian ancestry, as was Charles Curtis (R.-Kans.), a senator and vice president.

Members of Congress of Hispanic ancestry are even more difficult to identify, especially as many surnames originating in the Iberian Peninsula are similar to surnames occurring in other Mediterranean countries. Latino ancestry among members of Congress became quite evident with the admission to the Union of former Spanish and Mexican territories in the Southwest, and establishment of commonwealth or territorial status for Puerto Rico, Guam, the Virgin Islands, and the Philippines (prior to 1946). Among the first Hispanic Members was Delegate Trinidad Romero, a Republican elected from the New Mexico Territory in 1877. Representative and Senator Dennis Chavez (D.-N.Mex.) served in the House and Senate for a combined more than thirty-one years beginning in 1931. By 1990 Hispanic members of the House had risen to positions of prominence, such as Representatives Kika de la Garza and Henry Gonzales, both of Texas, who chaired the Agriculture and Banking committees, respectively; Representative Edward Roybal of California, a senior member of the Appropriations Committee; and Representative Tony Coelho of California, of Portuguese ancestry, who served as Democratic majority whip.

Members of Asian ancestry have been slower to gain election to the Congress since immigrants who were not "free white persons or persons of African nativity or descent" could not become naturalized citizens before 1943. Hawaii was represented by a nonvoting House delegate for many years, and that territory elected Asian Americans occasionally to that post. The most notable was Jonah Kuhio Kalanianaole, a native Hawaiian, who served as its House delegate from 1903 to 1922. It was not until Hawaii's admission as a state that larger numbers of Asian Americans were elected to the House and Senate, with Hiram Fong being chosen as the first Chinese American to serve in the Senate, and Daniel Inouye the first Japanese American to serve in that body. With the growth of Asian-ancestry population, especially in the western United States, the number of Asian Americans in Congress is sure to grow.

CONCLUSION

The formal constitutional qualifications of members of Congress regarding age, citizenship, and state residence have not changed since the adoption of the Constitution. However, the accessibility of various groups—blacks, Native Americans, and women, in particular—to a full role in the political process has changed, making these groups implicitly eligible for congressional service. The informal standards for membership have also changed, both by action of the Congress and by court interpretation.

Further changes are possible in the future. Some interest has been expressed in lowering the age standard to reflect the Twenty-sixth Amendment's giving eighteen-year-olds the vote. Others have suggested that increasing the size of the House would result in smaller-population districts that would be more likely to elect women and ethnic minorities to Congress. Still others, (particularly, Delegate Eni F. H. Faleomavaega of American Samoa), have proposed reserving several nonvoting delegate seats for Native Americans. Term-limitation proposals, pending in 1993, may also add to the diversity of congressional membership by mandating more-frequent changes in House and Senate membership. The Constitution, although changing little in the way of formal qualifications, grants the American people enormous latitude in selecting representatives and senators. Over time, ethnic and racial diversity in the Congress has come closer to, but has not yet matched, the diversity of the people the Congress represents.

BIBLIOGRAPHY

Primary Sources

The standard reference works on constitutional requirements for legislative service are the volumes of printed congressional precedents. These works reprint major portions of congressional debates, excerpts from congressional documents, and review relevant court decisions. For the House of Representatives, these documents are *Hinds' Precedents of the House of Representatives* (Washington, D.C., 1907), covering the period 1789–1903; *Cannon's Precedents of the House of Representatives* (Washington, D.C., 1936), covering the period 1903–1935; and *Deschler's Precedents of the U.S. House of Representatives* (Washington, D.C., 1977), covering 1935–1975. The counterpart Senate volume is FLOYD M. RIDDICK, *Senate Procedure* (Washington, D.C., 1985). Together, these volumes summarize major challenges to the seating of senators and representatives on constitutional grounds, and on various extra-constitutional standards surveyed in the preceding essay. Similar references to membership standards in the British Parliament are provided in SIR CHARLES GORDON, ed., *Erskine May's Treatise on the Law, Privileges, Proceedings, and Usage of Parliament,* 20th ed. (London, 1983).

Secondary Sources

The most comprehensive secondary work on the development of constitutional standards and their interpretation by the Congress and the courts is ROBERT LUCE, *Legislative Assemblies: Their Framework, Make-up, Character, Characteristics, Habits, and Manners* (New York, 1924; reprinted, 1974). This volume is one of four produced by Luce, a college professor and long-serving member of Congress from Massachusetts, on the organization, structure, and rules of procedure of the U.S. Congress, with additional references to comparable issues in foreign legislatures and to U.S. state legislatures. A number of other secondary works—many of them long out of print—discuss the institutional evolution of the U.S. Congress and historical antecedents. Among these are DEALVA S. ALEXANDER, *History and Procedure of the House of Representatives* (Boston, 1916); GEORGE H. HAYNES, *The Senate of the United States: Its History and Practice,* 2 vols. (Boston, 1938); ROY SWANSTROM, *The United States Senate, 1787–1801,* Senate Document 99-19 (Washington, D.C., 1985); RALPH V. HARLOW, *The History of Legislative Methods in the Period Before 1825* (New Haven, Conn., 1917); and George B. Galloway, *History of the*

House of Representatives (New York, 1961). The magisterial history of the U.S. Senate by Senator ROBERT C. BYRD, *The Senate, 1789–1989: Addresses on the History of the United States Senate,* 2 vols. (Washington, D.C., 1988–1991), includes a lengthy review of the work of the Constitutional Convention in framing qualifications for Senate service, the controversy surrounding the seating of Gallatin and Smoot, and discusses the entry of women, blacks, and other minority groups into the Senate.

For a general treatment of the role of blacks and women in the U.S. Congress, including brief (and generally uncritical) biographical treatments of each such member of Congress, see U.S. Congress, Joint Committee on Arrangements for the Commemoration of the Bicentennial of the United States of America, *Women in Congress,* House Report 94-1732 (Washington, D.C., 1976); and, from the same source, *Black Americans in Congress,* House Report 95-208 (Washington, D.C., 1977). Other secondary treatments, generally of a supportive and laudatory nature, include HOPE CHAMBERLAIN, *A Minority of Members: Women in the U.S. Congress* (New York, 1973), Samuel D. Smith, *The Negro in Congress* (Chapel Hill, N.C., 1940), and MAURINE CHRISTOPHER, *Black Americans in Congress* (New York, 1976). More-analytical work—generally in article form—on blacks and women in Congress has been done by MARGUERITE ROSS BARNETT, ARTHUR LEVY, and SUSAN STOUDINGER.

SEE ALSO African American Legislators; Representation; AND Women in Legislatures.

THE SOCIAL BASES OF LEGISLATIVE RECRUITMENT

David T. Canon

The questions of who governs and who should govern have been central to the study of politics since Plato and Aristotle's time. An interest in the social backgrounds of political leaders springs naturally therefrom. Do elected officials differ from the people they represent? If so, do these differences influence their behavior in office? This essay examines these questions and places them within the context of various approaches to studying political recruitment. It also offers a new perspective that combines assumptions of rational behavior with an analysis of social backgrounds of political leaders. Though the essay focuses primarily on members of Congress, studies of legislative recruitment that examine the careers and backgrounds of lower-level politicians are also essential for developing broader theoretical issues.

DEFINING RECRUITMENT

Most broadly conceived, political recruitment begins with the preliminary sorting of the politically active members of society from the inactive members and culminates with the election of a relatively small number of individuals to public office. Scholars who study this process focus on political socialization, social backgrounds of leaders, the structure of political opportunity, psychological traits of the politically active, institutional arrangements, and the incentives for participation. A narrower conception of recruitment begins with the subset of people who are already politically active and examines the "intramural sorting and screening" that identifies political candidates (Prewitt and Eulau, p. 293). This essay examines recruitment in the most general terms but focuses on the social and political roots of recruitment.

Within this broad perspective, an important distinction must be made between initial recruitment and promotion or advancement. Initial entry into politics is very different from the subsequent process of climbing the political ladder, both in terms of social backgrounds and the strategic calculus of office-seeking. Early studies of the social backgrounds of political leaders demonstrated that the opportunity to enter politics is strongly skewed toward highly educated, upper-middle-class professionals (Matthews, 1954). However, social backgrounds do not help predict which lower-level politicians will seek higher office. Thus, the analysis of social background provides little analytical leverage in explaining patterns of advancement to the U.S. Congress. Theories of the strategic calculus of office-seeking have the opposite problem: they do an excellent job of explaining the logic behind promotion to higher office (Jacobson and Kernell), but they provide little assistance in helping explain which of eligible millions will enter politics.

The relatively clear distinction between initial recruitment and promotion quickly becomes muddied upon further scrutiny. First, the context of initial recruitment varies greatly with the level of entry into the career structure. The barriers to entry are much lower at the local level than at the national level. This simple observation is a central insight of Joseph Schlesinger's seminal work on political careers, *Ambition and Politics;* the tiering of local, state, and national offices, with hundreds of thousands of opportunities at the bottom of the pyramid and only a handful at the top, charts out the path of least resistance to aspiring politicians. The relative openness of the career structure, however, makes it difficult to generalize about initial entry. A majority of those who make it to Congress climb their way up, but a sizable number of political amateurs do not follow the typical path (Canon).

Second, the term *initial entry* is inherently ambiguous. Do people enter politics when they volunteer to work for a political campaign, when they hold their first part-time appointive or elective office, or when politics becomes their full-time vocation? The sociologist Max Weber offered a definition in 1921 in his classic essay, "Politics as a Vocation." Professional politicians, by definition, must be continuously engaged in politics, but Weber did not make distinctions based on the motivations of individuals: professional politicians may either "live for" or "live off" politics.

The other distinction between professional and amateur politicians typically used in American politics is based on James Q. Wilson's analysis of politicians' motives. Amateurs are those who receive intrinsic emotional reward from politics and base their involvement on principle rather than on the professional politician's extrinsic rewards of power and material gain. Wilson's definition overlaps with Weber's: the amateur typically "lives for" politics, while the professional "lives off" politics. However, the professional may gain some intrinsic rewards from politics, and the amateur may be fully engaged in politics.

For the purposes of analyzing recruitment to Congress, Weber's definition is more useful. Motives are not as critical as the full-time commitment to politics. Certainly by the time a politician reaches Congress, he or she must be a professional in Weber's sense. Few part-time Weberian amateurs will make it to Washington; those who do will not last long.

THE SOCIAL-BACKGROUND APPROACH AND ITS CRITICS

An interest in the backgrounds of political leaders stems from both normative and analytical concerns. From a normative perspective, democratic theorists are concerned that government should represent the will of the people. If leaders come from higher social strata, have different occupations, and go to different churches than do the masses, the broader interests may not be served. The analytical perspective evolved in American political science in the 1950s and 1960s. In a break with previous institutional studies, the scholars Donald Matthews, Heinz Eulau, and Herbert Jacob (among many others) argued for a focus on individual politicians—for the study of members of Congress rather than congressional rules and institutions. Many behavioralists, as they came to be known, shared the democratic theorists' normative concern that representatives should reflect the broader population, though this assumption generally was left unspoken.

Social Backgrounds and Representation

Direct democracy skirts any potential problem of unrepresentative leaders by having the people determine policy. The ancient Athenians used random selection to choose representatives of the *boule*, or council, of Athens. Its five hundred members were paid for attending and were chosen by lottery from the ten "tribes" of Athens to serve one-year terms. Direct democracy has been used at various times in Venice, Florence, various cantons of Switzerland, Basque communities in Spain, and New England town meetings. In his 1984 book, *Strong Democracy*, Benjamin Barber called for the random selection of representatives for some local offices.

The Founding Fathers believed direct democracy unwise and unworkable and so opted for representative democracy. The "Great Compromise" at the Constitutional Convention that in 1787 established Congress as a bicameral legislature reflected an understanding of the impact that the backgrounds of leaders and the selection process could have on representation. In the Great Compromise, the Senate was removed from direct public selection, instead being elected by the state legislatures to serve as a check on the more responsive, popularly based House. John Adams hoped that the House would replicate the population in terms of demographic characteristics, saying that a legislature "should be an exact portrait, in miniature, of the people at large, as it should think, feel, reason, and act like them" (quoted in Ernest Callenbach and Michael Phillips, *A Citizen Legislature* [Berkeley, Calif., 1985], p. 1).

THE SOCIAL BASES OF LEGISLATIVE RECRUITMENT

The behavioralists were interested in the empirical questions of whether Congress is in fact an "exact portrait" and how backgrounds affect recruitment and political behavior. Matthews noted the significance of variables such as occupation and social standing: "Subtle processes may eliminate a far larger number of potential decision-makers than do primaries and elections. . . . Regardless of democratic institutions and values, political decision-makers will tend to be chosen from among those ranking high in America's system of social stratification" (1954, pp. 4, 23).

That members of Congress are not cut from the same cloth as the broader public is well established, but the link between background variables and behavior has been more difficult to determine. Elite theorists maintain that the ruling class serves its own interests. Political thinkers as varied as Karl Marx, Vilfredo Pareto, and Gaetano Mosca all emphasize the power of the elite in political affairs. Charles Beard's famous "economic interpretation of the Constitution" argued that the Founding Fathers acted primarily from self-interest to protect their property and positions of power.

Sociologists Floyd Hunter and C. Wright Mills present a more sophisticated argument. Mills rejects the view of the power elite as an economic class based on the ownership of property. But he does see a certain unity within the ruling elite based on a "coincidence of interests" rooted in shared educational (Ivy League or military academy), occupational (top executives in business, military, and government), religious (Episcopalian and Presbyterian), ethnic (Anglo-Saxon), and social origins (old family, upper-class). Mills does not provide much evidence for the link between background and behavior. Furthermore, in his view Congress is not even part of the power elite; its members do not make the central decisions of government concerning war and peace or the economy.

The behavioralists, operating more in the pluralist tradition than on elite theory, believed that Congress is a central actor and that socioeconomic background helps explain legislative behavior. At first glance, this link seems obvious. Politicians who represent a working-class ethnic background, such as former Congressman "Tip" O'Neill (D.-Mass.), or who are a product of a political machine, such as Congressman William Lipinski (D.-Ill.), are likely to have a very different outlook on politics than, for example, Rudy Boschwitz (R.-Minn.), who became a millionaire by selling plywood and then was elected to the Senate. However, separating the influence of one's constituency from personal-background variables is difficult. Was Tip O'Neill a supporter of the "common man" because his father was a bricklayer or because his district shared his ethnic working-class background?

The Critics

Do the backgrounds of members of Congress contribute to an understanding of how they got to Washington and how they behave in office? Sifting through the data on members' age, occupation, religion, and education left Herbert Jacob "wondering about the significance of it all" (p. 706). There are so many other rival explanations for why members behave as they do—constituency, party, the president, interest groups, the media, and staff—that background variables get lost in the shuffle.

Donald Matthews, the father of the social-background approach, retreated from his early work, saying, "After hanging around Capitol Hill for a few weeks—just watching and talking to a few Senate staff members—it was apparent that social background variables did not make as much difference in the behavior of senators as the immediate context within which they lived and work" (1971, p. 16). In a comprehensive survey of the field, Moshe Czudnowski is even more blunt: "There is little of interest for the study of recruitment that one can hope to find in general and noncontexually interpreted indicators of social background" (p. 186).

From the perspective of recruitment, social backgrounds are not very useful. That 45.6 percent of all members of Congress were lawyers, and 26.5 percent were Roman Catholics in 1992, and that all but a few have college degrees says little about recruitment. That is, such data do not indicate why the hundreds of thousands of other people who are similarly situated did not pursue a career in politics or why the handful who are elected to Congress every two years did. Thus, social-background data are useful primarily in providing longitudinal information (data over a period of many years) about descriptive representation, in setting the broad parameters within which recruitment operates, and perhaps in giving some clues about substantive representation.

However, there are other reasons to study the backgrounds of leaders. Whether sanctioned by political scientists or not, practitioners of politics care about descriptive or symbolic representation. African American leaders push strongly for redistricting that would create more districts with a black majority. The National Women's Political Caucus and other women's groups urge more women to get involved in politics and run for office. The media pay attention to the backgrounds of the nation's leaders, and every textbook on Congress has the obligatory chapter on the social composition of its members.

The remainder of this essay will review the evidence concerning the social bases of recruitment. Each section will examine the questions of how elected leaders differ from the people they represent and whether differences in backgrounds have any impact on their behavior in office.

RACIAL AND ETHNIC BACKGROUND

Most studies of the racial backgrounds of members of Congress examine the careers of African Americans, but even these are relatively scarce. Indeed, Czudnowski's comprehensive review of the recruitment literature concluded, "No empirical studies of the recruitment of black politicians are available" (p. 202). This dearth of research can be explained by a simple historical fact: the peak of social-background analysis occurred in the late 1950s and early 1960s, when fewer than 1 percent of the members of Congress were black. Later studies of black political leaders focused on issues such as discrimination, biased electoral practices, and social justice rather than recruitment.

However, early studies of black leaders at the local level and more recent analysis of minorities in Congress provide some insights. First, African American and other minorities are severely underrepresented at the national level. Second, the political opportunities available to minorities who aspire to Congress differ radically from those available to others. Finally, proportional ethnic and racial representation in

Congress today is probably more important symbolically than substantively.

The composition of Congress does not reflect the "melting pot" image of America. Ethnic and minority groups have always been underrepresented in Congress, although the situation has improved since the 1960s. No blacks served in Congress between 1901 and 1929, and no more than two served at one time until 1955. In the 1960s, black representation in Congress slowly increased (see Table 1). By 1993, blacks constituted about 7.5 percent of the congressional membership (40), though this is far short of their 12 percent of the U.S. population.

Similar patterns hold for other minorities.

Table 1
WOMEN AND AFRICAN AMERICANS IN THE U.S. CONGRESS, 1941–1994

Year	% of Members who were:	
	Women	African American
1941–1942	1.9	0.2
1943–1944	1.7	0.2
1945–1946	2.1	0.2
1947–1948	1.5	0.2
1949–1950	1.9	0.2
1951–1952	2.1	0.2
1953–1954	2.8	0.2
1955–1956	3.4	0.4
1957–1958	3.0	0.6
1959–1960	3.4	0.6
1961–1962	3.7	0.6
1963–1964	2.6	0.7
1965–1966	2.4	0.9
1967–1968	2.1	1.1
1969–1970	2.1	1.9
1971–1972	2.6	2.5
1973–1974	3.2	3.4
1975–1976	3.6	3.4
1977–1978	3.4	3.0
1979–1980	3.4	2.8
1981–1982	3.9	3.2
1983–1984	4.5	3.7
1985–1986	4.5	3.7
1987–1988	4.7	4.1
1989–1990	5.0	4.3
1991–1992	5.8	4.9
1993–1994	10.1	7.5

The percentages reflect the number of women and African Americans who were serving at the beginning of each Congress.

Only 3.5 percent of the members of the 103d Congress were Latino, while they constituted about 7 percent of the population. Nine members of Congress (1.7 percent) were Asian Americans, which is less than a third of their proportion in the population. Similarly, despite the success of Italian, Polish, and Irish Americans in urban-machine politics, immigrant groups have never had proportionate representation in Congress.

Ethnic Representation

A massive literature on ethnic politics in America examines the mobilization and recruitment of immigrants. Lacking the necessary resources to become easily integrated in the new society, immigrants have turned to political machines that offer them patronage and the means for social mobility. However, two factors have limited their numbers in Congress: first, like blacks, new immigrants have been victims of discrimination outside of their areas of urban concentration and second, the machines that have channeled their political activity have been primarily interested in state and local politics rather than national. Consequently, the proportion of first- and second-generation immigrants in Congress has always lagged behind their proportion in the nation. Matthews shows that in the periods of peak immigration in the early twentieth century, 12 to 15 percent of the population, but only 3 to 5 percent of senators, were foreign-born. In 1940, only six House members were foreign-born. In contrast, 75 percent of urban-machine bosses were either foreign-born or second-generation Americans (1954, p. 25).

What are the consequences of underrepresentation? Were the needs of ethnic groups ignored in national politics? Evidence on this question is mixed. LaGumina's study showed that the Italian American congressmen from New York from 1888 to 1950 were primarily interested in issues of central importance to their constituents, such as immigration quotas, naturalization, and alien policies (p. 80). Obviously, many ethnic politicians have served both local and national constituencies from their positions of leadership in Congress (John McCormack, Tip O'Neill, Tony Coelho, and Dan Rostenkowski, just to name a few). On the other hand, Leo Snowiss (1966) showed that machine congressmen from Chicago were less active and less effective than their counterparts from Detroit and Los Angeles. The same relationship between recruitment and behavior has been established for other urban areas as well.

Though ethnic identification has always been a major force in American politics, its influence has waned since the 1960s. The peak decade from 1901 to 1910 saw the arrival of 8,795,000 immigrants, an annual rate of 10.4 per 1,000 of the existing population; another 9,843,000 came in the next twenty years. The large number of immigrants made them a potent political force as leaders attempted to win their emerging loyalties. By the 1970s and 1980s the rate of immigration had dropped to about 2 per 1,000 with most of the recent immigrants coming from Asia and Latin America, groups that historically have not been as politically active as their European counterparts. Furthermore, social mobility has eroded the homogeneity of most ethnic neighborhoods, and ethnic roots are not as deep as they once were. Today most members of Congress with ethnic backgrounds are third- and fourth-generation Americans, rather than first- or second-generation (however, there were still five foreign-born members of the House in 1991). These observations are reflected in the scholarship on Congress. The ethnic backgrounds of members of Congress are rarely mentioned in current textbooks; even Matthews's comprehensive 1984 review of legislative recruitment failed to mention this topic.

One ethnic group, Latinos, merit special attention. Latinos are an important political group in American politics, partly because their numbers, which are growing at a faster rate than the general population, are concentrated in states that are pivotal in presidential elections (Florida, Texas, California, and New York). However, this concentration serves as a ceiling for the potential impact of Hispanic representation in Congress. According to Susan Welch and John R. Hibbing, about 71 percent (308) of all congressional districts in the 1980s had constituencies that are less than 5 percent Latino. The greatest potential for Latino representation occurs in less than 2 percent (8) of all districts where Latinos comprise at least half the population. Only 6 percent (27) of all congressional districts have constituencies that are at least one-fourth Latino.

African American Representation

Many of the same observations hold for African Americans. Until the 1960s, underrepresentation could largely be explained by overt discrimination and racism that barred blacks from the political process in the South. Poll taxes, racially applied literacy tests, grandfather clauses (which exempted whites in seven states from the first two devices by enfranchising those individuals whose ancestors voted before 1867), and white-only primaries disenfranchised blacks for nearly a century after they had the constitutional right to vote (black men were given the right to vote in 1870, women in 1920). With a majority of blacks living in the South, it was not surprising that only a handful were elected to Congress between Reconstruction and the Voting Rights Act of 1965.

Today, voting along racial lines, electoral laws, and redistricting limit the number of black officeholders, especially at the state and national levels. Racial voting makes it almost impossible for blacks to win in white-majority districts. Therefore, because blacks do not control a majority in any state, most black politicians are limited to serving as mayor, state legislator, city councillor, school-board member, or county commissioner. As with Latinos, black-majority districts in the House provide limited national opportunity. Politicians such as former Senator Edward Brooke of Massachusetts and Representative Ronald Dellums of California show that this is not an ironclad rule, but the proportion of minority population is the best predictor of success for minority office seekers.

The impact of electoral laws and redistricting on the success of black politicians is less clear. Some studies show that structural features such as at-large elections, small city councils, and runoff elections hurt black candidates. Others claim that these structural biases are small. Runoff elections, which exist only in the South, are the most controversial of these institutions. In many instances the black candidate wins the first election with 40–45 percent of the vote against two white candidates, only to lose in the runoff. Black leaders have lobbied for the abolition of runoff elections or weakening their bias by dropping the winning percentage from 50 to 40.

In the past, redistricting limited black representation in Congress by disenfranchising blacks and diluting their voting power. Intentional discrimination in redistricting was ruled unconstitutional in *Gomillion* v. *Lightfoot* (364 U.S. 339, 1960), and the Supreme Court ruled that racial votes cannot be diluted, even if there is no demonstrable intent to discriminate, in *Thornburg* v. *Gingles* (478 U.S. 30, 1986). The *Thornburg* decision has been widely interpreted as a mandate for the creation of more black-majority districts. By the early 1990s an odd alliance to pursue this mandate had been forged between black leaders and Republicans, who were willing to sacrifice a few districts to dilute the Democratic strength in many others. As a result fifteen new African American and nine new Latino members were elected to the 103d Congress through redistricting.

Political opportunities for African Americans differ in several subtler ways. Because of more-limited political opportunities, blacks have used alternative career paths. Many black leaders served their political apprenticeships in the civil rights movement rather than in low-level political office; others, such as William Gray (D.-Pa.), the former House majority whip and an ordained minister, used their large urban congregations as a political base. Blacks also express different motives in running for office. Whites are more likely to claim that "serving the nation" is their primary motivation for running, while blacks typically cite "correcting social injustice." Finally, several studies such as Robert C. Smith's, show that black challengers and incumbents cannot raise as much money in House elections as their white counterparts, even after accounting for differences in electability. Given the central role of money in politics today, this could severely constrain future increases in black representation in Congress.

As with most studies of recruitment and the backgrounds of leaders, the central unanswered question remains of what the consequences of the underrepresentation of minorities in Congress are. Can black Americans be represented fairly only by other blacks? Proponents of creating more black-majority House districts point to the importance of symbolic representation. Black role models in the political arena bring more black voters and activists into the political process and provide a feeling of empowerment.

The argument that only black politicians can represent the interests of black constituents is not so clear. As recently as the 1960s, white politicians in the South ignored black voters, but today that attitude is a recipe for political suicide. Support from black constituents provides the winning margin for many white southern Democrats. Senator Wyche Fowler (D.-Ga.), for example, won only 41 percent of the white vote but more than 90 percent of the black vote, which gave him a narrow 51–49 percent victory in 1986.

Given this type of loyalty among black voters, southern Democrats have become increasingly responsive to the views of their black constituents. Issues such as the failed confirmation of Robert Bork's appointment to the Supreme Court and sanctions against South Africa were widely perceived as civil rights issues by southern Democrats. By the late 1980s, according to David W. Rohde, southern Democrats' voting records were virtually indistinguishable from their nonsouthern counterparts. Despite the evidence that white politicians have become increasingly sensitive to black concerns, whites representing black-majority districts, such as Peter Rodino (D.-N.J.), who had represented his black urban district for forty years, were urged to retire, and so Rodino was replaced by a black, Donald Payne, in 1988. When Lindy Boggs of New Orleans was succeeded by William Jefferson in 1990, no black-majority districts in the House were represented by whites.

From the perspective of aggregate representation, one could argue that blacks in Congress are not representing the full range of their black constituents' views. In the early 1990s, exit polls showed that 22 percent of blacks identified themselves as Republicans, yet only one black House member, Gary Franks of Connecticut, was a Republican. (In 1990, Franks became the first black Republican elected to Congress since Oscar De Priest, who represented Illinois from 1929 to 1935.) Black House members vote with the Democratic party 90 percent of the time.

However, district-level analysis reveals that blacks' views are in fact being represented. Most blacks in Congress come from urban districts that are liberal and heavily Democratic, which explains their liberal voting records. When a black member of Congress represents a more conservative district, he or she reflects those views, as any politician would. For example, Mike Espy represents a rural Mississippi Delta district that is half black and half white. He requested an assignment on the Agriculture Committee, which is shunned by urban blacks, and appeared in an ad for the National Rifle Association toting a shotgun. Espy has won the support of conservative white voters through aggressive constituency service and bringing home his district's share of the pork barrel (in this case a huge army contract for catfish raised in his district). Substantive representation, it appears, is driven primarily by constituency rather than race.

WOMEN

Matthews's 1984 review of legislative recruitment began its section on women by noting, "The big losers in legislative recruitment everywhere have been women" (p. 551). However, the 1990 elections continued a decade-long trend of increasing the number of women in politics: women held a record 17 percent of statewide offices, including three governorships; 18 percent of state legislative seats (2,063 women ran for state legislatures in 1990); and a record thirty-one seats in Congress (the same number as at the end of the 101st Congress, but four more than were elected in 1988). Maintaining the thirty-one seats was deceptively difficult because five congresswomen announced their retirements or sought higher office in 1990.

Looking forward to the large number of open seats arising from redistricting and retirements in 1992, Sharon Rodine, the president of the National Women's Political Caucus, was quoted in the 18 November 1990 *Durham Morning Herald* as saying, "The rules of the political game have changed. The good old boys better watch out." Midway through the primary process in 1992, it appeared Rodine was right. In a year of the "political outsider," many women candidates billed themselves as the "ultimate outsiders." About twice as many women ran for the Congress in 1992 than in the previous election, and fifty-four were elected with record highs of forty-eight in the House and six in the Senate.

This success has been a long time coming. From the mid-1940s until 1970, the proportion of women in Congress was stuck at about 2 percent. Then, through the 1970s it inched up to 3.5 percent, but many women were still being elected to Congress by replacing their deceased husbands. From 1920 to 1979, 41 percent of all women reached Congress "over his dead body." Typically, these women did not have long or distinguished careers, although Sala Burton (D.-Calif.) and Lindy Boggs (D.-La.) were notable exceptions. Finally, by the mid-1980s, most women were being elected in their own right, and their proportion in Congress had reached 4.5 percent (see Table 1). The number of women in Congress should continue to grow.

The volume of research on women in politics has followed a similar trajectory. In 1975 a major eighty-page essay on political recruitment did not even mention women and an eight-page bibliography had no citations about women (Czudnowski). While this was an oversight, the literature was thin until the 1970s, when more women were elected to office. In the 1980s the topic received a flood of attention.

The driving question of most of this work is why there are so few women in politics. Three explanations have been offered: discrimination, characteristics of women candidates, and structural factors.

Early studies indicated that voters, the media, contributors, and parties all discriminated against women candidates. Gallup polls in the 1970s revealed that between 9 percent and 13 percent of all voters said they would refuse to vote for a qualified women candidate in their party. Another national poll in 1983 showed that 87 percent of the public would vote for a woman nominee of their party for president. Rather amazingly, in that same survey, only 77 percent said that a women should work outside the home if her husband is capable of supporting the family!

More recent studies show that there is no evidence of discrimination against women running for office at the state or local level (Darcy, Welch, and Clark) or for national office (Gertzog). In fact, in House races, women tend to be viewed more favorably than men by voters, and voters perceive themselves closer to women on the issues than to men.

However, gender discrimination in politics is still evident. The gender gap that received so much attention in the 1980 and 1984 presidential races has appeared with a vengeance in some state races involving women. In Texas, Ann Richards won the governorship with 61 percent of the women's vote in 1990, while Dianne Feinstein drew 58 percent of the women's vote in a losing effort for the governorship of California; two years later, however she was elected to the U.S. Senate. While these figures are viewed with great pleasure by women's groups, the other side of the coin shows that many men are still not willing to support women candidates. In the gubernatorial race in 1990 in Texas, for example, Clayton Williams won 55 percent of the men's vote.

Virginia Sapiro offered additional evidence that sexual stereotyping in politics is not dead. Sapiro noted that survey data are unreliable indicators of prejudice against women because people may not reveal socially unacceptable views to a pollster. (The same problem is evident in polls involving campaigns with black candidates). Furthermore, subconscious prejudices cannot be revealed in standard surveys. To test for this bias, Sapiro asked students to evaluate a speech by Senator Howard Baker, under the guise that this was a campaign speech by a candidate for the U.S. House. Half of the class received the speech with the name Joan Leeds, and the other half with the name John Leeds. With this limited information, students were quick to use gender as a cue in evaluating the candidates: 15 percent more of the students thought that John would win than Joan, perhaps projecting their own subconscious prejudices or at least exhibiting expectations that the rest of the electorate has such prejudices.

The media and campaign contributors are other potential sources of discrimination. The media often perpetuate stereotyped female roles, as when the Democratic vice-presidential candidate Geraldine Ferraro was asked about her favorite recipes on the campaign trail in 1984. Evidence from the early 1970s indicated that financial contributors discouraged women from running for office by refusing to support them. More recent studies show this is no longer true. Several of them have found that women do as well as men in raising money for congressional campaigns, even after accounting for varied campaign contexts and the strengths of one's opponent, as did Carole Uhlaner and Kay Schlozman. Women in the Democratic party have taken steps to make sure this trend continues, by establishing their own fund-raising network, EMILY's List—Early Money Is Like Yeast (it raises the dough).

Characteristics of women candidates also help explain the dearth of women in Congress. Women running for Congress are often handicapped by their lack of previous elective experience. Women's political base, appointive office, or local political activism are better stepping-stones to state and local office than to the U.S. House or Senate. Women are also hurt by their underrepresentation in the two occupations that are the most common bases for political service, law and business. Only 10 percent of all women members of Congress are attorneys, while close to half the men are. Occupations dominated by women, such as nursing, secretarial work, and teaching have never produced many members of Congress. Women are obviously also disadvantaged by societal expectations concerning families and children. Though traditional roles are slowly changing, women still have primary responsibility for child rearing, which often forces them to postpone careers.

The most important barriers to women in politics are structural: the incumbency advantage, the problems of raising money as a challenger, fickle voters, weak parties, the infrequency of open seats, and the intense competition when an incumbent does retire. These roadblocks to office are equally obstructive to both men and women, but because the barriers protect the status quo, which is a male-dominated Congress, women are disproportionately disadvantaged. The best hope for women to gain access to Congress is to amass efforts in reapportionment years such as 1992, when there were a large number of open seats, and to continue to build a base in state and local offices that will serve as springboards to Congress.

The consequences of the underrepresentation of women in Congress is as unclear for women as it was for African Americans. Clearly an important benefit of having more women in Congress is symbolic. One common bumper sticker says it all: "A WOMAN'S PLACE IS IN THE HOUSE...AND IN THE SENATE." Women should play a larger role in politics to help break down remaining stereotypes about the "proper place" for women in American society. However, substantive arguments for increasing representation are not so clear. Policy differences between men and women legislators, while evident, are not dramatic. Again, the power of constituency influences dominate in a reelection-minded legislature.

RELIGION

There are two distinctive features of the religious affiliations of members of Congress. First, 99 percent of them claim some religious affiliation (though 5.6 percent label themselves "unspecified Protestant" or "other Christian," which implies inactive involvement), compared to roughly two-thirds of the general population. Whether this high level of participation among members of Congress can be attributed to an intense and ongoing interest in religion or to the perceived political benefits of being a church member is not clear.

Second, there has been a gradual but significant shift in the denominational distribution of congressional religious affiliations. In the 1940s, Protestant denominations associated with high social status (Episcopal, Congregational, and Presbyterian) were very overrepresented in Congress. Between 1941 and 1946 they had about 29 percent of all members of Congress, but only about 7 percent of the population. (Unitarians were also considered high-status Protestant by Matthews, but since the merger of the Unitarians and the Universalists in 1961, the Protestant roots of the church have become weaker, though there is still variation between congregations). The number of House members and senators from other Protestant denominations was about what would have been expected given their proportions in the population in the 1940s. Jews and Catholics were underrepresented; Jews constituted 3 percent of the population, but had only 1 percent of the members of Congress; Catholics represented about a fourth of the population, but only had about 12 percent of the members (Matthews, 1954, pp. 26–27; Matthews's figures for religious affiliation of the general population do not include those who express no preference. The figures presented here include the entire population as the denominator).

Several shifts were evident by the 103d Congress (see Tables 2 and 3). Jews were by then one of the most substantially overrepresented groups (they constituted 2.5 percent of the population, but 7.9 percent of Congress), and there were slightly more Catholics in Congress than would be proportional. At the same time, the representation of high-status Protestant churches had fallen, though they still were very overrepresented. Episcopalians and Presbyterians each constituted about 2 percent of the population, but they had 9.3 percent and 10.1 percent, respectively, of the members of the 103d Congress. However, the all-time record for overrepresentation goes to the 2,748-member Schwenkfelder church of Pennsylvania. Thanks to Richard Schweicker (R.-Pa.), the Schwenkfelders were overrepresented by a ratio of about 800–1 for twelve years.

What implications does the religious affiliation of members of Congress have for substantive representation? Given the constitutional "wall of separation" between church and state, one would expect to find little relationship between a member of Congress's religious beliefs and his or her actions in Congress. Indeed, during the 1960 presidential campaign, Catholic John F. Kennedy had to assure Protestant voters that he would serve the people, not the pope. Yet Catholic members of Congress may be expected to be strong opponents of abortion, Jewish members strong supporters of Israel, and Protestant members opponents of aid to parochial schools.

Surprisingly little research has been done on the link between religious affiliation and behavior in Congress. The studies that do exist are limited studies of religious-bloc voting on roll calls, and the evidence here is mixed. One study found no differences between Catholic and Protestant House members in their support for legislation on civil rights, foreign aid, and organized labor. Another study found that between 1934 and 1964, Catholics were more supportive of foreign-aid bills than their colleagues. (Wald, pp. 156–160, reviews this literature.)

Table 2
RELIGIOUS AFFILIATIONS OF MEMBERS OF THE U.S. HOUSE, 1959–1994

	Jewish	Catholic	High-Status Protestant[1]	Other Protestant	Other[2]	None
1959–1960	2.3	20.7	29.0	45.5	1.8	0.7
1961–1962	2.5	20.2	30.1	44.0	2.5	0.7
1963–1964	2.1	20.0	30.1	43.4	2.8	1.4
1965–1966	3.2	21.6	28.5	40.2	4.4	1.8
1967–1968	3.4	21.8	29.9	40.1	3.9	0.9
1969–1970	3.6	22.0	30.3	38.4	4.1	1.6
1971–1972	2.8	23.2	31.0	37.0	5.1	0.9
1973–1974	2.8	22.8	28.3	39.7	5.3	1.1
1975–1976	4.6	25.3	25.7	38.0	5.3	1.1
1977–1978	5.3	27.4	24.1	37.0	5.1	1.1
1979–1980	5.2	26.7	26.0	35.7	5.3	1.1
1981–1982	6.2	27.4	24.6	35.8	5.1	0.9
1983–1984	6.7	28.5	23.0	35.8	5.3	0.7
1985–1986	6.9	28.7	22.8	35.8	5.3	0.5
1987–1988	6.7	28.3	21.8	37.0	5.5	0.7
1989–1990	7.1	27.6	21.1	37.8	5.5	0.9
1991–1992	7.6	28.0	20.2	37.4	5.7	1.1
1993–1994	7.4	27.1	20.2	38.4	5.1	1.8

1. Includes Episcopalians, United Church of Christ and Congregationalists, and Presbyterians.
2. Includes Christian Scientists, Eastern Orthodox, Mormons, and Unitarian-Universalists.

Table 3
RELIGIOUS AFFILIATIONS OF MEMBERS OF THE U.S. SENATE, 1953–1994

	Jewish	Catholic	High-Status Protestant[1]	Other Protestant	Other[2]	None
1959–1960	2	12	31	46	8	1
1961–1962	1	12	31	45	9	2
1963–1964	2	11	32	45	9	1
1965–1966	2	14	31	41	11	1
1967–1968	2	13	33	44	7	1
1969–1970	2	13	34	42	9	0
1971–1972	2	12	40	36	10	0
1973–1974	2	14	38	35	11	0
1975–1976	3	15	37	35	10	0
1977–1978	5	13	35	36	11	0
1979–1980	7	13	31	38	11	0
1981–1982	6	17	33	35	9	0
1983–1984	8	17	33	34	7	1
1985–1986	8	19	34	31	6	2
1987–1988	8	19	36	30	7	0
1989–1990	8	19	34	32	7	0
1991–1992	8	20	34	31	7	0
1993–1994	10	23	30	29	7	1

1. Includes Episcopalians, United Church of Christ and Congregationalists, and Presbyterians.
2. Includes Christian Scientists, Eastern Orthodox, Mormons, and Unitarian-Universalists.

The central problem with this work, as previously noted, is that it is very difficult to disentangle the influences of constituency from a member's personal religious views. For example, if a Jewish member of Congress is a strong supporter of Israel, is it because of personal views or pressure from the constituency? Simple controls for the proportion of a given religious group in a member's constituency must be introduced. The best attempt to sort out these major influences on voting behavior concluded that religious background had little general impact, except for abortion measures, which were strongly opposed by Catholic members, even when the study controlled for plausible alternative explanations (Page, Shapiro, Gronke, and Rosenberg).

A few studies have gone beyond roll-call analysis to probe the relationship between religious background and political behavior through personal interviews. However, these studies have not developed sophisticated designs that would allow firm conclusions about the causal sequence of the relevant variables.

SOCIAL BACKGROUND

No myth dies harder in American politics than the log-cabin, rags-to-riches notion that anyone can be elected president or a member of Congress. As will become evident by the end of the essay, this simply is not true. The variables considered in this section—age, father's occupation, family connections, and education—are some of the most important in terms of screening people from careers in politics, but they are the least helpful in explaining behavior in office.

Age is a good example of this pattern. At least at a superficial level, age restricts entry into Congress: very few people under the age of 30 or over the age of 65 are initially elected to Congress. The average age of members in the 103d Congress (1993–1995) was 52.1 years, an increase from 47 years in the Ninety-eighth Congress (1983–1985). However, age is not very important in explaining behavior in Congress. Far more crucial is a member's seniority. In 1991, Tom Downey (D.-N.Y.), an important member of the Watergate generation, was in his seventeenth year in the House, but was only 42 years old. Harry Johnston (D.-Fla.), who had yet to make his legislative mark, was in his third year in the House and was 59 years old.

However, age can be significant in terms of cohort effects (behavior that is influenced by generational differences). Politicians who were born in the 1920s and grew up during the Great Depression were likely to have a different attitude about the role of government than those born in the post–World War II baby boom. The latter have a distinctive profile as well: having been raised with television, they tend to be more adept at using this important political medium.

The occupation of the fathers of decision makers is typically used as an indicator of social class and social mobility. As with other social indicators, the father's occupation reveals the upper-class tilt of members of Congress. Tip O'Neill's father was clearly the exception; very few fathers had working-class origins. However, when compared to Supreme Court justices and executive-branch officials (president, vice president, and cabinet members), leaders of the House had more middle-class origins; 90 percent of the justices' and 72 percent of executive branch officials' fathers had professional backgrounds, compared to 58 percent of congressional leaders' fathers (Nelson, 1975, pp. 165–168).

Family dynasties are another important source of political leaders. As of the early 1990s, sixteen American families had produced eight presidents, three vice presidents, thirty senators, twelve governors, fifty-six House members, and nine cabinet officers. In another study, 54 percent of one group of eighty-five members of Congress said they had relatives in politics. However, the proportion of representatives who have had a close relative in the House fell from 20–24 percent in the first five Congresses to 5–6.8 percent in the Eighty-sixth Congress (Czudnowski, p. 188).

Higher education is another screening device for limiting who can run for Congress. Though it is obviously not a fixed rule, no senator and only 3 percent of members of the House did not attend college at all. In the Ninety-sixth Congress, 87 percent in the House and 92 percent in the Senate actually received a degree. This compares to 70 percent of the general population who never attended college and 17 percent who have a degree (from the 1980 census). However, apparently there have been no studies that have examined the behavioral consequences in Congress of educational attainment.

Prewitt and Eulau attempted to link socioeconomic background to recruitment, but they found it of limited use. They found that there is a relatively strong correlation between the social status of the community and the politically active stratum, but they could not predict who within the active stratum will actually run for office.

GEOGRAPHIC REPRESENTATION

All of the indicators thus far have described an unrepresentative, upper-class, highly educated, white, male institution. But the geographic backgrounds of members of Congress show that they have stronger local roots than the people they represent. *The Federalist*, no. 56, argues that this is the way it *should* be; House members should have a "considerable knowledge of [state] laws and a local knowledge of their respective districts."

Two types of data are typically presented to demonstrate geographical representation: whether the member of Congress still lives in his or her home state and whether the hometown was urban or rural. Members of Congress often tout their local roots during campaigns. In many districts, being an "outsider" (defined as someone who was not born in the state and did not go to college or serve previously in elective office in the state) can be a real political liability. Since the Reconstruction era, the charge of "carpetbagger" has brought down many candidates. In 1988, for example, Pete Dawkins, an All-American football player and decorated army general, suffered from this charge in the New Jersey race for the U.S. Senate. Dawkins, who did not have any strong roots in the area, had apparently been shopping for a state in which to run for the Senate.

Only 6 percent of senators and 7 percent of House members in the Ninety-sixth Congress (1979–1981) were outsiders. Approximately three-fourths of the members of that Congress had been born in their home states, compared with 68 percent of the U.S. population (as of the 1980 census). In the 102d (1991–1993) Congress, only sixty-five of the hundred senators had been born in their home states. The pattern is stronger in the South, where 80 percent have strong local roots, compared to 61 percent outside the South.

The distinctiveness of the local roots of members of Congress becomes more apparent when contrasted with the backgrounds of non-political elites. Hacker's 1961 analysis of the hundred senators and the presidents of the hundred largest American corporations revealed that the only significant difference between the two groups was their local roots: 71 percent of the senators lived in their hometown or within a hundred miles of it, compared to only 30 percent of the corporate presidents. Furthermore, 52 percent of the corporate presidents had been born in large metropolitan areas, while 64 percent of the senators were from rural areas.

Despite the implication of these findings, rural areas are not overrepresented in Congress. In the Ninetieth Congress (1967–1969), only 36 percent of House members and 52 percent of senators had been born in rural areas, compared with 57 percent of the population of comparable age as a whole (Rieselbach, p. 325). In almost every other category related to city size, however, members of Congress closely matched the general population.

Many critics of Congress believe strong local roots contribute to parochial, provincial, and conservative views. Rural members of Congress are indeed more conservative, according to Rieselbach, but this pattern cannot be attributed to geographic background. As with previous variables, it is difficult to disentangle the impact of constituency from personal factors. A city slicker from Chicago representing a downstate rural district would probably vote for agricultural concerns, as would a representative who had been raised on a farm.

Garrison Nelson developed an interesting angle on the geographical backgrounds of members of Congress in his 1978 study of "matched lives." He argued that geographical proximity is an important determinant of friendships in Congress, which in turn help explain patterns of leadership succession and policy outcomes. One of the first questions usually posed to a visitor on Capitol Hill is, "Where are you from?" This query is more than a polite conversation starter, for it reflects a deep and enduring pattern of social interaction in Washington.

The often noted Austin-Boston connection in Democratic leadership in the twentieth-century House is the most obvious example of the importance of geographically based relationships. The careers of the Texans Joseph Bailey, John Nance Garner, Sam Rayburn, Jim Wright, and Carl Albert (Albert was actually from Oklahoma, but his district was directly across the Red River, only ten miles from Sam Rayburn's home), and of the Bostonians John McCormack and Tip O'Neill were intertwined, with the older generation helping their protégés get a headstart in Congress, according to Nelson.

OCCUPATION

The occupations of members of Congress are dutifully reported in all the textbooks on Congress and, every two years, in the *Congressional Quarterly Weekly Reports*, as well as in other national publications, without any indication of the significance of the data. Certainly it is interesting that in the 102d House there were more engineers than doctors (seven and five, respectively), that there were two actors (Fred Grandy, R.-Iowa, and Ben Jones, D.-Ga.), and that lawyers still dominated Congress (lawyers constituted 0.1 percent of the workforce, but nearly half of the membership of Congress). In general, the data provide more evidence of the upper-class bias of Congress: blue-collar workers, the service sector, and farmers are underrepresented. However, the data reveal little about recruitment to Congress.

Occupational data are of limited value because they do not explain why similarly situated people choose to enter politics or not. Also, most background analysis depends on self-supported data, which often may be very biased. Just as a politician in a European workers' party may label himself a "worker," even though he had been a labor union official for twenty years before entering politics, so a congressman from a farm state may call himself a farmer, even though he has not been on a tractor since he was seventeen.

But most significant, most members of Congress refuse to admit they are politicians, even if they have been in politics most of their adult lives. Running for Congress by running against the "Washington establishment" is a time-honored tradition, but it reached new heights in the 102d Congress. In the wake of the savings-and-loan scandal and the anti-incumbency sentiment that swept the nation in 1990, forty-nine fewer incumbents were willing to admit that "public service or politics" was their career. In the 101st Congress (1989–1991), ninety-four House members and twenty senators said politics was their career; two years later, these numbers fell to sixty-one and four. This change cannot be explained by the freshman members, 16 percent of whom named politics, compared to 12 percent of Congress as a whole. It is interesting that *Congressional Quarterly* casually mentioned this change without commenting on its significance. Two years later (in the 103d Congress), 86 House members and 12 senators claimed public service as their careers. Clearly, self-reported data must be viewed with caution.

Lawyers in Congress

A separate discussion of lawyers in Congress is warranted here, if for no other reason than the amount of attention the topic has drawn from political observers for 150 years. Elite theorists, looking to find the "ruling class" in the military-industrial complex, the business world, or the halls of the Ivy League, need look no further than their local American Bar Association. Lawyers have quite literally ruled the United States since its inception. (Of course, elite theorists argue that Congress only plays a middle-level role: it decides how the pie is divided, but it cannot determine the size of the pie or what type it will be.) The "high priests of politics" constituted 37 percent of the combined houses of Congress in 1790; 70 percent in 1840; 54 percent in 1957; and 44.7 percent in 1993. The downward trend has been more apparent in the House since the early 1970s (Table 4). The proportion of lawyers in the Senate, though falling from its peak of 68 percent in 1977–1978, has remained relatively stable. There is no conclusive reason for the decline, but it may be explained by the growing gap between the earnings of top-level lawyers and members of Congress or by the generally negative view of lawyers among the broader public. In 1963 a

Table 4
LAWYERS IN THE U.S. CONGRESS, 1953–1992

	House	Senate
1953–1954	56.8%	59%
1955–1956	56.3	60
1957–1958	53.8	59
1959–1960	55.6	61
1961–1962	56.1	63
1963–1964	57.5	66
1965–1966	56.8	67
1967–1968	56.5	68
1969–1970	55.6	68
1971–1972	54.2	65
1973–1974	50.8	68
1975–1976	50.8	67
1977–1978	51.0	68
1979–1980	47.1	65
1981–1982	44.6	59
1983–1984	46.0	61
1985–1986	43.7	61
1987–1988	42.3	62
1989–1990	42.3	63
1991–1992	42.1	61
1993–1994	41.6	58

National Opinion Research Poll showed that lawyers received the highest score on the Socio-economic Index, 93, just ahead of doctors, who scored 92. However, a more recent national poll placed lawyers in the bottom ten professions in terms of respect —down with used-car salesmen and politicians.

Two questions are central in the literature: Why do lawyers have such an advantaged position, and does it make any difference that there are so many of them in Congress? The answers to the first question are varied and numerous (for a review of this massive literature, see Czudnowski, pp. 204–209; Eulau and Sprague; Cohen; and Wells). Alexis de Tocqueville saw lawyers as the logical political rulers in democracies that did not have a landed aristocracy or hereditary elite. James Bryce noted a natural fit between law and politics that was encouraged by legal questions rooted in tensions between state and national government and the private sector. Increasing government regulation of railroads, communications, banking, oil interests, insurance, and mining through the late nineteenth and early twentieth centuries placed public attorneys and judges at the center of many policy issues. Benjamin Twiss expanded this view in his "client-group" approach:

> The bar has represented clients of such a type and in such a way that broad issues of public policy are necessarily raised and resolved. Lawyers are, then, representatives in a mosaic of private groups, associations and interests that characterizes American politics. They are only slightly different from the [lawyers who are actually elected to public office]. (quoted in Wells, p. 171)

Since the writings of Bryce and Twiss appeared, the "natural fit" between law and politics has become even tighter because of the growth of large corporations, labor-management disputes, and an explosion in the number of administrative regulatory agencies.

James March and Herbert Simon make a similar but more general argument about movement in and out of careers based on the relative visibility of the organization and the individual. This resembles proximity-affinity theories of social relations in which the frequency of contact creates opportunity for interaction. In the case of political careers, the mutual visibility of politics and law creates mobility between the two professions. As noted above, lawyers are naturally involved in the subculture of politics through their contacts with judges, district attorneys, and prosecutors. Thus, it is not surprising that lawyers are more aware of political opportunities and more heavily recruited for legislative service than other professionals (Cohen, pp. 573–574).

A slightly more cynical view of the client-group and visibility perspectives has a conspiratorial air. Lawyers dominate politics, and therefore all laws are written in a legal jargon that requires the interpretation of other lawyers. One could ascribe causal motivations to the recruitment side of this observation and assert that lawyers enter politics to create more demand for their profession and that legislation does not need to be so complex. As with most conspiracy theories, there is probably a kernel of truth in it.

Max Weber developed a "dispensability" hypothesis, arguing that lawyers have a professional mobility that allows them to move easily between private practice and politics. Movement back into law after serving in politics is facilitated by new clients and the access that an attorney can bring back to his or her firm. In

1954, Matthews refined this point by noting that the law changes so slowly that even an extended tour in Washington will not professionally handicap an attorney. Indeed, retiring members of Congress are often eagerly recruited by large Washington law firms. While the dispensability hypothesis helps explain why lawyers are more suited to politics than doctors or businesspeople, who would find it more difficult to leave their careers for an extended period, it does not explain their comparative advantage over other flexible professions, such as teaching, the clergy, or many service jobs.

In a precursor to his more fully developed theory of political careers, Joseph Schlesinger showed in 1957 how lawyers' domination of law-enforcement offices, an important stepping-stone to higher office, gives them a structural advantage in seeking a governorship. Between 51 percent and 68 percent of governors elected between 1870 and 1950 had been lawyers; of these, 56–85 percent had held law-enforcement positions (primarily as judges and public attorneys). In 1966, Schlesinger showed that more than a quarter of all U.S. senators had held a law-enforcement position.

Eulau and Sprague suggested that some lawyers may be willing to enter a race to advertize their practice and meet new clients. This probably is a better explanation for the presence of frequent amateur challengers who have no chance of winning than it is for the career of a successful politician. Eulau and Sprague also presented a more convincing explanation for the preponderance of lawyers in politics, based on lawyers' relatively intense political socialization: when compared to non-lawyers, lawyers in state legislatures show an earlier interest in politics, they have more relatives in other political and judicial offices, they are more active in party politics, they have more ambition for higher office, and they are more likely to identify themselves as "self-recruited."

There is obviously no definitive explanation for the abundance of attorneys in politics. The truth lies in some combination of the above hypotheses. One fertile ground for future research lies in comparative analysis: as with many political phenomena, America is somewhat unique in its love for lawyers. Only 4 percent of the members of the Danish parliament are lawyers, while other European countries vary from 10 percent to 25 percent (Matthews, 1984, p. 551; Czudnowski, pp. 207–209). Differences in party systems and institutional arrangements account for some of these differences, but more definitive research is needed.

A strong argument can be made that all of this research is merely for the entertainment of social scientists. It has been nearly impossible to establish the significance of the overrepresentation of lawyers in politics. Early theorists were concerned that lawyers introduced a conservative bias into politics, that their narrow legal training did not prepare them for a career in politics (indeed, the paradigm of confrontation in the adversarial process is inimical to the necessities of bargaining and compromise that politics requires), and that overly complex and technical legislation can be attributed to the legal backgrounds of its authors.

Research that attempted to establish a link between prepolitical careers in law and political behavior came up empty. Lawyers do not vote in blocs in legislatures, and they do not dominate leadership positions. Subsequent work hypothesized that earlier studies did not uncover distinctive behavior by lawyers because the studies were too crude. But even tailoring analysis to issues that should be of central concern to lawyers showed no distinctive patterns of behaviors. On a series of roll-call votes from 1937 to 1968 in the House and Senate concerning support for the judiciary against various bills to curb the power of the courts, lawyers were statistically indistinguishable from their nonlawyer counterparts (Green, Schmidhauser, Berg, and Brady).

The absence of behavioral differences between lawyers and nonlawyers led Eulau and Sprague to conclude that the legal profession and politics had become "isomorphic," as a function of their historical and functional "convergence." That is, if law and politics have responded in similar ways to the increasing complexities of society, it is not surprising that lawyers do not have a distinctive pattern of behavior.

Several questions about the links between previous occupations and recruitment remain unanswered. First, if politics and law have converged, what was the nature of the assimilation? Which profession dominates the other? Do lawyers have to act like politicians, or have lawyers defined politics in their terms? Second, what is the interaction between political and prepolitical careers? Matthews (1954, 1960) and Eulau and Sprague touched briefly on this question. Lawyers and farmers are more likely to start their careers early, while businesspeople are more likely to enter politics later in life. Schlesinger demonstrated in 1957 that lawyers are more likely to be careerists in politics. Of those who are elected to high office without any previous political experience, only 20 percent are lawyers, but for those with at least fifteen years of prior experience, 61 percent are lawyers. An approach that examines this question from the perspective of the individual politician holds the most promise for resuscitating the study of the backgrounds of members of Congress.

Political Careers

The most important aspect of occupational data from the perspective of recruitment studies is whether or not the congressional aspirant is a current officeholder. This is a key variable in the motivational approaches to studying recruitment, according to Jacobsen and Kernell, but it is not emphasized in social-background research, which tends to focus on occupations at the time of entry into politics. This approach makes sense for studies of lower-level offices, by way of which most people enter politics from other careers. But most new members of Congress are "promoted," rather than recruited; that is, they enter Congress from some lower office. How does the electoral process differ between those who are promoted and those who are recruited? Do those who try to make Congress their first office have a chance?

Survey research indicates that voters value political experience in candidates for public office. Of thirty desirable qualities for political candidates ranked in various polls, ranging from youth and good health to courage and intelligence, political experience was the only one consistently mentioned as the "most important characteristic" (Leuthold, pp. 24–25). Consequently, previous political experience is typically viewed as a necessary requirement for serving in Congress. V. O. Key stated the prevailing view of recruitment to the Senate: "Commonly, nominations for the Senate go to

THE SOCIAL BASES OF LEGISLATIVE RECRUITMENT

men who have achieved eminence in the party in their state. By their performance in other public offices and by their ascent up the ladder of party status, men make themselves 'available' for the senatorial nomination" (p. 436).

As can been seen in Table 5 and Figure 1, previous experience has not always been a requirement for service in the House or Senate. Though previous work showed no pattern in levels of previous experience (Bogue, Clubb, McKibbin, and Traugott), Canon's study discovered that more amateurs are elected during periods of increased political opportunity, such as the 1930s for the Democrats and the 1980s for the Republicans (see chap. 3).

Schlesinger built a theory of ambition on the notion that political opportunities are structured by ambitious people looking to further their political careers. When each of a series of challengers uses a state legislative seat as a stepping-stone to the House, it becomes more firmly entrenched as the preferred route—or, as he calls it, the "manifest office." The use of manifest offices for the House and Senate have undergone significant changes since the post–World War II years. More House members have been elected from a manifest office in a state legislature (about half in Congresses of the 1980s, compared with 30 percent in the 1930s and 1940s), while fewer senators have used the

common stepping-stone of a governorship (13.7 percent between 1960 and 1987, compared with 23.2 percent between 1913 and 1959).

Candidates who have previous political experience, especially if they have served in the manifest office, have many advantages: an existing vote base that leads to greater name recognition, a campaign organization and fundraising network in place from previous races, and greater attention from the media, who are more likely to treat their candidacies seriously. Aggregate-level results provide some evidence for the link between experience and votes. On the average, between 1972 and 1978, experienced challengers received 7 percent more of the two-party vote than inexperienced candidates (Jacobson and Kernell, p. 31). Of course, experienced candidates are more likely to run against vulnerable incumbents, because they have more at stake than amateurs, but even after researchers control for other variables that would reduce the incumbent's vote, the relationship between previous experience and votes remains strong. Another study showed that a highly experienced challenger receives 10 percent more of the vote than a complete amateur, even after one controls for the candidates' relative ability to raise campaign money (Green and Krasno, p. 990).

Table 5
NUMBER OF YEARS IN OFFICE FOR SENATORS: ELECTED AND TOTAL PUBLIC

		1913–1923	1924–1933	1934–1943	1944–1953	1954–1963	1964–1973	1974–1983	1984–1987
Number of	0	2.4%	6.5%	5.6%	6.0%	3.3%	3.8%	14.1%	0%
years in	1–5	18.3	18.2	20.8	12.0	14.8	15.4	15.5	15.0
public	6–10	37.8	28.6	31.9	22.9	26.2	34.6	40.8	15.0
office (%)	10+	41.5	46.8	41.7	59.0	55.7	46.1	29.7	70.0
Average (yrs.)		9.93	11.49	10.22	12.62	12.89	10.94	8.80	13.40
Number of	0	13.4%	28.6%	26.4%	16.9%	11.5%	13.5%	32.4%	0%
years in	1–5	35.4	32.5	31.9	21.7	21.3	19.2	15.5	20.0
elected	6–10	34.1	15.6	20.0	27.7	27.9	40.4	32.4	30.0
office (%)	10+	17.1	23.4	20.9	33.1	39.4	26.9	19.6	50.0
Average (yrs.)		6.48	5.98	5.78	7.98	8.92	7.75	6.59	11.35
No legislative experience		28.0%	42.0%	47.2%	44.6%	29.5%	28.8%	49.3%	25.0%
No legislative or executive experience		18.3	32.5	27.9	22.9	16.4	15.4	36.6	5.0
Column (n)		82	77	72	83	61	52	71	20

RECRUITMENT, PERSONNEL, AND ELECTIONS

Figure 1
PRIOR OFFICE EXPERIENCE (U.S. HOUSE)

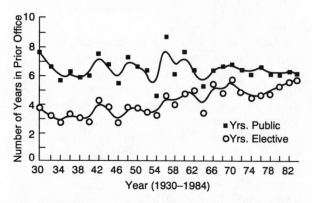

The interaction between gender and previous experience must also be examined in the study of recruitment to Congress. Women are more dependent on the advantages of having held prior office than men. For decades political observers have noted that the representation of women in Congress will not increase until they win more state and local offices. Bledsoe and Herring explained:

> Men are more likely to have the social and business connections or networks that facilitate their candidacies. Thus, males are less likely to need an at-large council seat as a platform for higher office. Males are less in need of a political party to win higher office because they have these other resources. (p. 221)

Even among men, the well-connected amateur is the exception. Most inexperienced candidates run poorly funded campaigns that have almost no chance of success. Amateurs are at a disadvantage for several reasons: the lack of campaign experience, little name recognition (unless one is well known in another field), and most voters' preference for experienced candidates. These disadvantages were offset in the campaigns of Senators Herbert Kohl (D.-Wis.) and Frank Lautenberg (D.-N.J.) and of former Representative Ed Zschau (R.-Calif.), among many others, by spending large sums on consultants, staff, and advertising. The impact of voters' preferences for experience can also be overstated. The career structure in the United States is relatively open. Compared to nations with stronger party systems, the United States requires little in the way of party or office apprenticeship, even for the highest offices. Furthermore, all voters do not automatically prefer experience. Indeed, the suspicions held by many Americans of career politicians and the long-standing tradition of "running against Washington" can be exploited by amateurs who can credibly claim that they are not "one of them." Independent candidate Ross Perot's success in the 1992 presidential campaign is the most recent evidence for this claim.

Although an amateur's deficiencies in electoral politics can be overcome with money and an effective campaign strategy, nonpolitical backgrounds may be more of a liability in Congress. Robert Dahl said, "To suppose that one can run a complex political system without first learning the trade is, as Plato pointed out, as

Table 6
CHANGES IN THE MANIFEST OFFICES: PROPORTION OF SENATORS ELECTED FROM GOVERNORSHIPS AND THE HOUSE

	Years		
	1913–1959	1960–1987	Totals
Senators elected from:			
House of Representatives	32.7% (117/358)	36.9% (59/160)	34.0% (176/518)
Governorships	23.2% (83/358)	13.7% (22/140)	20.3% (105/518)

338

THE SOCIAL BASES OF LEGISLATIVE RECRUITMENT

Table 7
MANIFEST OFFICE USE IN THE U.S. HOUSE, 1930–1986

	Years						
	1930s	1940s	1950s	1960s	1970s	1980s	Total
Previous state legislative experience	30.5% (191)	29.4% (164)	36.7% (140)	38.8% (145)	45.1% (175)	49.3% (133)	36.5% (948)
% of those with state legislative experience who move directly to the House	35.6% (68)	33.5% (55)	53.6% (75)	71.0% (103)	84.0% (147)	74.4% (99)	57.7% (547)
Former House members who return to House	9.6% (60)	13.3% (74)	9.7% (37)	7.0% (26)	3.4% (13)	3.1% (8)	8.4% (218)

Numbers are precent of newly elected House members in each category.
Ns are in parenthesis.
Source: David T. Canon, *Actors, Athletes, and Astronauts* (Chicago, 1990). © 1990 by The University of Chicago. All rights reserved.

silly as to suppose that one can be a doctor or a carpenter without prior training," and another political observer commented, "The sooner we spurn celebrity and revert to expertise the better" (quoted in Canon, p. 3). Tip O'Neill argued that the decade he spent in the Massachusetts state legislature before arriving in Washington put him several terms ahead of those who did not have that experience. Others do not share this concern. Richard Fenno spoke favorably of Jim Johnson (R.-Colo.), a "citizen-legislator" in the early 1970s who became interested in politics because of the Vietnam War. Once in Congress, he brought substantial skill and energy to bear on the issues that concerned him (for a more complete discussion of amateurs in Congress, see Canon).

In general, as with most background variables, simple distinctions between members of Congress based on previous political experience do not reveal significant differences in institutional behavior. A more promising route is to examine the goals members seek, and the interaction between goals, previous experience, and electoral context.

New Approaches to Social-Background Research

No theory of recruitment will ever be able to predict with precision which individuals will run for office. Within broad categories, there is simply too much individual variation. Even so,

the social-background approach can be made more useful in two ways.

First, analysis of the backgrounds of candidates and incumbents should be done contextually, identifying similarities and differences with their district-level constituencies. Typically, studies report aggregate statistics on the composition of the House or Senate and compare these figures to the nation as a whole. Tip O'Neill's oft-repeated observation that "all politics is local" should be taken to heart. District-level analysis could provide insights into recruitment and representation (for work on local office done from this perspective, see Prewitt and Eulau). For example, at the aggregate level, Jews have enjoyed record levels of representation in Congress. However, a contextual perspective would show that a liberal Jewish college professor probably still could not win in a rural Maine congressional district (Maisel). Similarly, a white conservative from downstate Illinois might as well save his or her filing fee in the First Congressional District of South Chicago.

A contextual approach also would reveal whether social backgrounds really make a difference in congressional elections. The massive literature on congressional elections has largely ignored the topic of social backgrounds. An analysis of the 1988–1992 National Election Study Senate surveys and the 1978 House survey reveals how important the age, race, gender, occupation, and religion of candidates are to voters; some of these variables would have to be added to the contextual file. Analysis of the issue positions of voters and candidates vis-à-vis their respective demographic characteristics may provide some insights into patterns of substantive representation. Most of these relationships will probably be relatively insignificant, but sophisticated analysis should be done before the social background approach is abandoned completely.

Second, studies need to focus more on losing candidates and potential candidates who decide not to run. How do losing candidates differ from successful ones? Since Huckshorn and Spencer's 1971 study of the 1962 congressional elections, there has been very little on this side of the equation, and their analysis did not pursue the contextual approach outlined above. Similarly, very little is known about potentially strong candidates who do not run. In every congressional district there are many state legislators and other elected officials who never run for Congress. Understanding the motivations of these noncandidates gets at the heart of the recruitment problem: Why do similarly situated people in the political-career structure reach different decisions about pursuing higher office?

Finally, the sociological tradition of examining politicians' backgrounds and the rational-choice approach of looking at political actors' goals and incentives should be combined. This can be done by examining some background characteristics as strategic variables rather than static descriptive items. Conceptually, variables can be divided into those over which the actor has control (strategic) and those over which he or she does not have control (descriptive). Race, gender, age, and ethnic background must be taken as givens. (There are some rather humorous examples of older incumbents trying to demonstrate their youth, such as Senator Alan Cranston of California dying his hair orange, and it is at least technically feasible to change one's sex, but it is safe to assume that these variables are fixed.)

Occupation and, to some extent, religion are the central strategic variables, though they have been taken as given in the social background research (i.e., one has a better chance of being elected to Congress if one is an Episcopal lawyer). From the rational-choice perspective, these variables become strategic resources. There is some evidence that aspiring politicians join the Episcopal church because of the opportunities to make social and political contacts. There is convincing evidence that people regularly choose certain occupations because it will help their political careers. The most quoted example is Woodrow Wilson, who said, "The profession I chose was politics; the profession I entered was law. I entered one because I thought it would lead to the other. It was once the sure road; and Congress is still full of lawyers." The irony is that Wilson became unhappy with the "scheming and haggling practice" of his profession and stayed in law school only one year, at which point he entered graduate school at Johns Hopkins University to study political science.

From this perspective, it is not so important to note whether someone is a lawyer, but why he or she has chosen that profession. By looking at the goals of politicians, one may be able to discern links between goals, background, and behavior in office. Lawyers seem to fit the mold of ambitious career politicians, whereas those with stronger policy and ideological commitments would not be as likely to be found in the law or business.

It is clearly important to know about the backgrounds of leaders—"who they are"—on several different levels. Symbolic representation remains important to African Americans, women, and other groups. Yet it is equally important to know why they are in politics. Combining these two approaches should yield important new insights into legislative recruitment and representation. Most important, the linkages between social background and policy representation would be illuminated by examining the motivations and goals of politicians in their prepolitical careers.

THE SOCIAL BASES OF LEGISLATIVE RECRUITMENT

BIBLIOGRAPHY

General Studies of Recruitment

On theories and general studies of congressional recruitment see HERBERT JACOB, "Initial Recruitment of Elected Officials in the U.S.—A Model," *Journal of Politics* 24 (November 1962): 701–716; ROBERT J. HUCKSHORN and ROBERT C. SPENCER, *The Politics of Defeat: Campaigning for Congress* (Amherst, Mass., 1971); GARY C. JACOBSON and SAMUEL KERNELL, *Strategy and Choice in Congressional Elections* (New Haven, Conn., 1983); DAVID LEUTHOLD, *Electioneering in a Democracy* (New York, 1968); SANDY L. MAISEL, *From Obscurity to Oblivion: Running in the Congressional Primary* (Knoxville, Tenn., 1986), and LEO M. SNOWISS, "Congressional Recruitment and Representation," *American Political Science Review* 60 (September 1966): 627–639.

For excellent reviews of the recruitment literature see MOSHE M. CZUDNOWSKI, "Political Recruitment," in FRED I. GREENSTEIN and NELSON W. POLSBY, eds., *Handbook of Political Science*, vol. 2 (Reading, Mass., 1975), 155–242; and DONALD R. MATTHEWS, "Legislative Recruitment and Legislative Careers," *Legislative Studies Quarterly* 9 (November 1984): 547–585.

The Social-Background Approach

On the social-background approach to studying recruitment see DONALD R. MATTHEWS, *The Social Backgrounds of Political Decision-Makers* (Garden City, N.Y., 1954), and *U.S. Senators and Their World* (New York, 1960). For a retreat from his earlier work see DONALD R. MATTHEWS, "From the Senate to Simulation," in OLIVER WALTER, ed., *Political Scientists at Work* (Belmont, Calif., 1971); also see C. WRIGHT MILLS, *The Power Elite* (New York, 1956). For an analysis of the social background of congressional leaders see GARRISON NELSON, "Change and Continuity in the Recruitment of U.S. House Leaders, 1789–1975," in NORMAN J. ORNSTEIN, ed., *Congress in Change: Evolution and Reform* (New York, 1975), 155–183. See also KENNETH PREWITT and HEINZ EULAU, "Social Bias in Leadership Selection, Political Recruitment, and Electoral Context," *Journal of Politics* 33 (May 1971): 293–315.

Minorities and Women in Congress

On racial and ethnic groups in Congress, see SALVATORE J. LAGUMINA, "Ethnicity in American Political Life: The Italian-American Experience," *International Migration Review* 3 (Spring 1969): 78–81. For the response of congressional Democrats to the changing importance of the black vote in the South, see DAVID W. ROHDE, *Parties and Leaders in the Postreform House* (Chicago 1991); ROBERT C. SMITH, "Financing Black Politics: A Study of Congressional Elections," *Review of Black Political Economy* 16 (Summer 1988): 5–30; and SUSAN WELCH and JOHN R. HIBBING, "Hispanic Representation in Congress," *Social Science Quarterly* 65 (June 1984): 328–335.

On women in Congress see TIMOTHY BLEDSOE and MARY HERRING, "Victims of Circumstances: Women in Pursuit of Political Office," *American Political Science Review* 84 (March 1990): 213–223; ROBERT DARCY, SUSAN WELCH, and JANET CLARK, *Women, Elections, and Representation* (New York, 1987); IRWIN GERTZOG, *Congressional Women: Their Recruitment, Treatment, and Behavior* (New York, 1984); VIRGINIA SAPIRO, "If U.S. Senator Baker Were a Woman: An Experimental Study of Candidate Images," *Political Psychology* (Spring/Summer 1981–1982): 61–83; and CAROLE UHLANER and KAY SCHLOZMAN, "Candidate Gender and Congressional Campaign Receipts," *Journal of Politics* 48 (February 1986): 30–50.

Particular Traits of Lawmakers

On the religious backgrounds of members of Congress see BENJAMIN I. PAGE, ROBERT Y. SHAPIRO, PAUL W. GRONKE, and ROBERT M. ROSENBERG, "Constituency, Party, and Representation in Congress," *Public Opinion Quarterly* 48 (1984): 741–756; and KENNETH D. WALD, *Religion and Politics in the United States* (New York, 1987).

On lawyers in Congress see MICHAEL COHEN, "Lawyers and Political Careers," *Law and Society Review* 3 (May 1969): 563–574; HEINZ EULAU and JOHN D. SPRAGUE, *Lawyers in Politics: A Study in Professional Convergence* (Indianapolis, 1964); JUSTIN J. GREEN, JOHN R.

SCHMIDHAUSER, LARRY L. BERG, and DAVID BRADY, "Lawyers in Congress: A New Look at Some Old Assumptions," *Western Political Quarterly* 26 (1973): 440–452; JOSEPH A. SCHLESINGER, "Lawyers and American Politics: A Clarified View," *Midwest Journal of Political Science* 1 (May 1957): 26–39; and RICHARD S. WELLS, "The Legal Profession and Politics," *Midwest Journal of Political Science* 8 (May 1964): 166–190.

On the geographic backgrounds of members in Congress see ANDREW HACKER, "The Elected and the Anointed: Two American Elites," *American Political Science Review* 55 (September 1961): 539–549; GARRISON NELSON, "The Matched Lives of U.S. House Leaders: An Exploration," paper presented at the Annual Meeting of the American Political Science Association, New York, August 31–September 3, 1978; and LEROY N. RIESELBACH, "Congressmen as 'Small Town Boys': A Research Note," *Midwest Journal of Political Science* 14 (May 1970): 321–330.

On the political careers of politicians before they are elected to Congress see ALLAN G. BOGUE, JEROME M. CLUBB, CARROLL R. McKIBBIN, and SANTA A. TRAUGOTT, "Members of the House of Representatives and the Processes of Modernization, 1789–1960," *Journal of American History* 63 (June 1976): 275–302; and DAVID T. CANON, *Actors, Athletes, and Astronauts: Political Amateurs in the United States Congress* (Chicago, 1990). For an analysis of the impact of previous experience on fund-raising capabilities and electoral success, see DONALD P. GREEN and JONATHAN S. KRASNO, "Salvation for the Spendthrift Incumbent: Reestimating the Effects of Campaign Spending in House Elections," *American Journal of Political Science* 4 (November 1988): 884–907. See also V. O. KEY, JR., *Politics, Parties, and Pressure Groups*, 5th ed. (New York, 1964), and JOSEPH A. SCHLESINGER, *Ambition and Politics: Political Careers in the United States* (Chicago, 1966).

SEE ALSO African American Legislators; The Motivations of Legislators; AND Women in Legislatures.

THE MOTIVATIONS OF LEGISLATORS

Burdett A. Loomis

Political scientists have long pondered what motivates legislators and prospective lawmakers to run for office and once there, to remain ensconced, or to exit voluntarily, thus providing opportunities for other citizens to serve. At the dawn of the behavioral era around 1930, political scientist Harold D. Lasswell helped establish an academic field studying these motivations that many others have sought to address, built upon, and modified. In many ways the question of motivation lies at the very heart of democratic theory. The framers of the U.S. Constitution, for example, had clear views about politicians' motivations, which led them to propose an intricate system of checks and balances. Their assumptions remain relevant, since most work on legislative motivations is still based on suppositions rather than on firm empirical evidence.

That no definitive studies have been carried out to probe legislators' motivations is simultaneously surprising and yet unremarkable. It is surprising that, given the amount of attention accorded the Congress since the late 1950s, we have so little good empirical evidence on what motivates legislators. At the same time, why should anyone expect that political elites would willingly subject themselves to the intense scrutiny that a sophisticated, systematic study of motivation would require?

Still, students of Congress and other legislatures have not allowed a dearth of information about motivations to hinder their use of the concept of motivations, broadly defined, as a centerpiece in analyses of legislative behavior and policy outcomes. Formal modelers of political science assume by definition a rational-actor mind-set; key theorists have noted the power and utility of assuming that a reelection motivation is dominant among members of Congress. Richard Fenno has initiated several rich lines of congressional research with his suggestion that members of Congress have a limited number of motives/goals (namely, reelection, power, and the formulation of good public policy).

In a similar vein, other academics have proposed that the motivation of advancement —ambition—is central to understanding legislative behavior. But ambition has often been defined in the relatively limited terms of progressive office-seeking. The very prominence of ambition among most national-level politicians has hindered the empirical examination of this notion, in that most scholars have merely assumed its existence rather than seeking to flesh out its various implications.

In short, motivations play a major role in shaping how political scientists think about the legislature, but scholars have not spent commensurate resources in exploring their nature and impact. For example, state legislatures have become much more professional through the years and have required more time and effort from their members since the 1950s, but we know little about what motivates the state legislators beyond what James David Barber found in the early 1960s in a small-state body (Connecticut's) that harbored mostly part-time citizen lawmakers who frequently sought a high level of self-esteem.

Within the legislative context, motivations overlap considerably with incentives and goals. Although not exactly synonymous, the concepts of motivations, incentives, and goals have all been used to explain why legislators behave as they do. In an extensive comparison of these notions, James Payne argues that goals and motivations are less useful concepts than incentives are in understanding what propels politicians' actions. For Payne, the study of "motivations" is too broad in its characterization of forces that shape political lives. In addition, he is troubled by the a priori nature of the concept, which encourages a heavy reliance on ideal types articulated by theorists from Aristotle to Lasswell. In *The Motivation of Politicians* (1984) Payne writes, "The scholar who seeks to detect political types would do best if he put aside all he thought he knew and simply interviewed a number of politicians and then began generalizing."

Conversely, goals may be excessively specific in a consideration of motivations. Inherent in the notion of a goal is the implication that it can be achieved, which might well lead a legislator to abandon public life for other challenges. Thus, David R. Mayhew's emphasis on the reelection goal might well be better understood as an incentive that needs to be addressed every two years for a member of the House. Payne argues that most politicians have only a single incentive (e.g., status), which motivates various forms of behavior, such as seeking reelection or running for higher office. Although this essay will not take up the debate relating to the concepts of motivations, goals, and incentives, it will side with Payne in interpreting motivations broadly, thus including goals and incentives, rather than narrowly, which would limit us to sketchy evidence, inconclusive findings, and a series of research dead ends. As with Payne's work, incentives will be the organizing concept of this essay. Still, treating motivations, goals, and incentives as rough equivalents allows for an examination of the major research and literature on contemporary legislative behavior.

We will first examine psychological approaches to motivations, then turn to broad incentive/goal approaches to legislative activity, with a special focus on ambition as an important motivating force, concluding with considerations of changes in politicians' motivation over time. In addition, we will pay some attention to citing evidence for motivations, goals, and incentives from various sources, including biographies.

WHY RUN? WHY SERVE?

In the study of American legislative politics, all considerations of motivations are ultimately based on Lasswell's initial formulation that "Private Motives [are] Displaced on Public Objects [and] Rationalized in Terms of Public Interest." For example, a personally ambitious minister might embark on an election campaign for Con-

gress that would emphasize pro-life policies in terms of the broad public interest. Political life, in general, and legislative life, in particular, are seen in terms of this motivation-displacement-rationalization sequence. For Lasswell, power is expected to overcome a low estimation of oneself, although this expectation does not derive from any systematic direct observation of legislators. Indeed, legislators, who must act as members of teams (political parties, committees, and so forth) and who will ordinarily find it very difficult to exercise unilateral power, are not the politicians most likely to experience the displacement that Lasswell hypothesized. The uncertainties and fluidity of legislative life may well encourage extended cooperation among individuals who have well-integrated personality structures.

Some students of legislative recruitment and behavior have sought to test this notion of ego compensation. For the most part, the little available evidence does not definitively support the displacement thesis. Rather, a sample of South Carolina legislators given psychological tests in 1950 proved somewhat less neurotic and more self-sufficient than the population as a whole. Subsequent evidence from Pennsylvania, while impressionistic, does offer support for Lasswell's thesis, though. Still, most successful candidates are incumbents, and Frank Sorauf in *Party and Representation* (1963) points out that for these individuals the motivation to serve may be largely vocational—running for reelection is what career legislators do. If this was true in the 1950s, it is surely all the more the case in the 1980s and 1990s, when careerism in state legislatures has become increasingly common.

Occupying a substantial niche in the examination of legislative motivations is the early work (*The Lawmakers*, 1965) of Barber, who developed a four-celled framework (based on permutations of active/passive and positive/negative dichotomies) for linking motivations to subsequent behavior, as shown in Table 1. Both high self-esteem and a need to compensate can lead individuals to seek legislative office. Most optimistically, legislators take an active and positive approach to their jobs; those who are either passive or negative or both toward their work as legislators tend to contribute less to the instrumental ends of legislative life.

THE MOTIVATIONS OF LEGISLATORS

Table 1
FOUR PATTERNS OF ADAPTATION

	Activity	
	High	Low
Willingness to Return (Positive/Negative)		
High	Lawmakers	Spectators
Low	Advertisers	Reluctants

Source: James David Barber, *The Lawmakers: Recruitment and Adaptation to Legislative Life* (New Haven, Conn., 1965), p. 20.

The active/positive (as empirically measured by a willingness to return to the legislature for three more terms) legislators, called Lawmakers in Barber's study, come to politics with a reservoir of personal strength, as opposed to needs that they seek to fulfill in a public arena. Those who are active/negative (unwilling to return to office) initially seek office to join those who have frustrated them in their occupations (often lawyers or real-estate agents), but for these individuals, labeled Advertisers, there is no long-term commitment to lawmaking; instead, they wish to gain attention for their extralegislative careers. The passive/positive type (the Spectator) is essentially a follower who seeks approval from others. Finally, the passive/negative legislators, or Reluctants, tend to avoid conflict and by definition have short careers.

Although Lawmakers dominate the legislative process and care for the institution of the legislature, the others—Spectators, Reluctants, and Advertisers—can play significant roles in a body that values followership, a skepticism toward change, and at times, the energy of self-promotion.

Such motivational diversity among legislators helps explain why some have high self-esteem while others are much less sure of themselves, to the point that legislative service acts as a form of psychological compensation. For the latter, becoming legislators can overcome substantial self-doubt, even though such a career choice is often highly disruptive. The compensations are significant enough to outweigh the disarray and difficulties of seeking legislative office. For Lawmakers, however, compensating for self-doubts is not the major element of a legislative career. Rather, their high level of self-esteem allows them to manage and overcome the strains of legislative service.

Alternatively, self-esteem may mesh with other personality characteristics to generate successful legislative personalities. For example, high self-esteem, when linked to a low complexity of self-concept, may produce a confident legislator much like the Lawmaker. And high complexity, coupled with low self-esteem, may lead to a compensating legislative style, somewhat akin to that of Barber's Advertiser.

Finally, in the South Carolina study mentioned above and in other works, there is some evidence that American legislators are, in comparison with nonpoliticians, less dogmatic and authoritarian. This is consistent with the Lawmaker notion and the general expectation that legislative life benefits from compromise and the ability to adapt.

The entire ego-compensation approach to motivation, as initially articulated by Lasswell and developed unsystematically by others, has produced very little in the way of definitive conclusions about legislators' behavior. Recruitment patterns, the demands of legislative life, and diverse constituencies all contribute to the election of individuals with a variety of personality structures, each of which affects lawmaking differently within a wide range of legislative situations (e.g., in committee work, as opposed to the floor). It remains unclear how (or whether) motivations affect the legislative process and its outcomes in systematic ways.

Incentives and Goals

Moving beyond questions of ego strength and compensation, we now begin a less judgmental approach toward motivations focused on politicians' emotional needs, labeled "incentives" in the work of Payne; these incentives include status, program (preferred policies), conviviality, obligation, game, mission, and adulation, although the last two are uncommon in the United States among elected officials. As recruitment patterns have changed from relying on party selection to seeking office on one's own, more status-oriented individuals may have found their way into the legislature. This pattern of initiative might help explain the decreasing significance of legislative behavioral norms that contribute to stability and organizational maintenance, to say nothing of those that support a general level of civility within the Congress.

At the same time, as Donald Matthews speculates in *U.S. Senators and Their World*, status incentives can coexist with strong institutional norms, as occurred in the Senate of the 1950s. Indeed, Matthews finds a certain irony in the denigration of politicians in general, in contradiction with the high standing that many individual senators enjoy. Going a bit further, Matthews anticipates behaviors of successful business and civic leaders entering public life as amateurs. "Where does [such a local figure] turn to assuage his lofty ambitions? Politics is always a possibility," in that it requires no formal prerequisites. Like most other legislative scholars, however, Matthews merely speculates on motivations, rather than actually pursuing a line of empirical research.

The status incentive may lead candidates to seek legislative office, but once in office legislators often disparage the institution as a whole. Almost every member of Congress is highly regarded by his or her own constituency, but the institution itself is negatively perceived. And most representatives contribute to this perception by resolutely running against the Congress as a whole. The ultimate message is that each individual member of Congress is great, at least as perceived by his or her constituents, even if the entire body is composed of fools and knaves. The status incentive encourages such a juxtaposition in that it reinforces the individual's behavior as well as enhancing the election prospects of the incumbent.

Once we bring incentives into a consideration of motivations, it is no great reach to include legislators' goals. Research from the 1960s on legislative roles bears directly on the question of legislators' goals. In *The Legislative System*, John Wahlke et al. directly asked a sample of state legislators in four states about their goals in seeking office. Taking the responses at face value poses some real dangers, but legislators generally expressed their goals in terms of service or pursuit of ideals as much as they cited status, financial gain, or even enjoyment. At the same time, legislators' goals were shaped by differing state contexts; one suspects that this would remain the case in the future, with increasing variation among state legislatures in their levels of professionalism.

Any consideration of legislators' goals surely means moving closer to some kind of rational calculus, as opposed to a more Lasswellian approach, but it also means moving toward the dominant paradigm in the contemporary study of legislative behavior. Two related perspectives deserve special attention.

First, Richard Fenno, in *Congressmen in Committees*, has noted that the basic legislative goals espoused by members of Congress include reelection, framing good policy, power, advancement to higher office, and material gain; in general, his work has emphasized the first three of these goals. This elementary, yet multifaceted, approach to goals allows for explorations into a wide range of legislative activity; it also is consistent with the ways in which members of Congress think about their work and how their thinking may change over time.

In contrast, a second goal-based perspective draws heavily on the two-year terms of members of the U.S. House of Representatives. David Mayhew and Morris Fiorina, in their analyses of the Congress and especially the House, focus almost exclusively on the reelection goal. To an extent, this concentration is artificial, to be employed only in constructing a useful way to understand the legislature. Mayhew, for example, states:

> I shall make a simple abstract assumption about human motivation and then speculate about the consequences of behavior based on that motivation. Specifically, I shall conjure up a vision of United States congressmen as single-minded seekers of reelection, see what kinds of activity that goal implies, and then speculate about how congressmen so motivated are likely to go about building and sustaining legislative institutions and making policy. (*Congress: The Keystone of the Washington Establishment* [New Haven, Conn., 1977], p. 5)

Although Mayhew and Fiorina owe more to economics than to psychology in formulating the implications of their motivational assumptions, the research that has followed their initial works has proved powerful in generating insights into legislative behavior. Perhaps most interesting is that the motivational assumption of a dominant reelection goal is confirmed not by any definitive survey, interview, or observations of participants. Rather, the reelection goal is most significant in building a framework for understanding the choice of committee assignments, the attention to specific legislative tasks, the building of office-based congressional "enterprises," and a host of other forms of behavior that tend to promote the legislator's reelection chances, often at the expense of the institution as a whole.

Ironically, the very power of the "single-minded seekers of re-election" premise, in terms of comprehending the Congress as a whole, makes the notion altogether too simplistic in examining actual motivations. Indeed, the economics-related assumption of a reelection-goal orientation that Mayhew and Fiorina employ provides us with almost no insight into legislators' operating motives. Multiple motivations surely coexist in complex, perhaps unique, combinations; likewise, motivations may change over time, either as legislators' careers evolve or as they react to the legislature's institutional arrangements. For example, Senate careers may be seen in terms of alternating seasons of campaigning and governing, when differing motivations—for reelection, power, and good policy—may come to the fore. Thus, as a senator, Dan Quayle (R.-Ind.) was highly motivated to demonstrate to his peers that he could function as an effective policy entrepreneur. His efforts in sponsoring a major jobs bill in 1982 eventually garnered him reelection, but his performance as a competent legislator had career payoffs beyond simply helping him retain his Senate seat.

Besides the specific example of a single U.S. senator, many legislators revel in the capacity to affect the processes and outcomes of policy-making. Although reelection is an essential instrumental goal, most legislators see it as a means to an end—of affecting policies or, in somewhat fewer instances, exercising power over an institution. Two of the strongest House speakers of the modern era—Texas Democrats Sam Rayburn and Jim Wright—having once obtained this powerful position, used it to further the policy goals of a conservative body (in the case of Rayburn) and the Democratic majority (in the case of Wright).

The postreform House and Senate of the 1980s and 1990s, along with many state legislative bodies, have allowed large numbers of lawmakers to participate fully in policy-making. At the same time, congressional electoral victory margins have increased, which has allowed leg-

islators to focus more attention on affecting policy at early stages in their careers. Policy-based motivations can be fulfilled quickly and thus have more relevance in the motivational mix for members of Congress in the 1980s and 1990s than for those who served in the 1950s, as John Hibbing observes in his work on the shape of congressional careers, *Choosing to Leave* (1982).

Motivations may well change in systematic ways during the course of a legislative career. Although data to that effect are sketchy at best, the notion of a sequence of goals makes sense. In the electoral arena, for example, Fenno speculates and provides some evidence that careers tend to change from "expansionist" to "protectionist" as House members become more secure in their electoral contexts and take on more responsibilities within the chamber. Much more elaborate is Lawrence Dodd's framework that postulates a sequence of "mastery" goals, moving from reelection to policy-making, then to influence, and finally to institutional control. The career cycle of seeking mastery may lead to frustration, in that party leaders will seek to limit the opportunities to fulfill individual legislators' goals. Indeed, the continuing long-term minority status of Republicans may prevent them from obtaining the capacity to "master" control of the House in the foreseeable future.

One possible motivation that links reelection and policy incentives is that of expanding one's range of discretionary actions. As careers go forward, legislators desire to explore more options—not just seeking reelection but also influencing policy, running for higher office, and so forth. Dodd sees this as a series of stages, but it could just as easily be viewed as widening one's range of choices. Thus, the desire for discretion would be different for each individual legislator, although patterns would likely emerge along the lines suggested by Fenno and Dodd.

Private Gain

Reelection, policy, and power goals are usually expressed within the ordinary legislative context. The ambition motivation (see below) takes a legislator beyond his or her current legislative body; in a similar vein, the motive of private enrichment—ordinarily not considered in research or in theoretical frameworks—moves analysis outside the legislature to the private lives of those who serve. Political scientists have not done much work in exploring the implications of the private gain motivation. This may be shortsighted, in that both state and national legislators do their work within environments that are increasingly populated by the affluent—ranging from corporate executives to high-powered lobbyists to many wealthy peers with similar backgrounds and experiences (especially in the Senate).

Seeking private gain beyond the bounds of congressional rules and/or legal restrictions has proved politically fatal to substantial numbers of legislators in all eras; Congress became more sensitive to conflicts of interest in the 1980s—with the ABSCAM sting operation (the FBI's undercover investigation of members of Congress), the resignations of Speaker Jim Wright and party whip Tony Coelho (D.-Calif.), and the assorted financial ethics problems of senators David Durenberger (R.-Minn.), Mark Hatfield (R.-Oreg.) and Alfonse D'Amato (R.-N.Y.). In many ways, state legislatures have presented more illustrations of the manifestations of private-gain motivations. Although only eight state legislatures are truly full-time institutions, with commensurate pay levels, most other state bodies have experienced great increases in work loads and demands since the 1960s.

In effect, many state lawmakers must work at two full-time jobs—their legislative endeavors and their private means of support. This creates built-in conflicts of interest for many lawmakers, some of whom may seek to take advantage of their public positions to reap private reward. For example, one state legislator who headed a judiciary committee wrote to corporations suggesting that they engage his services, given his access to key information. Crucial to this development is the basic movement of most state legislatures toward effective full-time status. As the stakes of state politics have grown, along with the responsibilities of the legislative job, compensation levels have not kept pace.

One upshot of these trends has been that many state legislators—in South Carolina and Arizona especially, but not exclusively—have become vulnerable to sting operations, in which bribes are offered and often accepted.

The private-gain motivation may not dominate the thinking of most legislators, but to discount it is myopic in both theoretical and empirical terms.

Ambition

Aside from the reelection goal, no legislative motivation has received more systematic attention than ambition. Ambition propels individuals into the political arena and provides much of the structure of political careers. The seminal theorist on this topic, political scientist Joseph Schlesinger, posited differing types of ambition: that for a specific office (discrete), for a career at a particular office level (static), and for advancement (progressive). Schlesinger's pioneering work, *Ambition and Politics* (1966), has fostered studies of recruitment and office-seeking in initial attempts to gain House seats, has led to a thorough analysis of high-level "amateurs" running for the Senate, and has provided a basis for understanding the behavior of such individuals once they take office.

Perhaps most notable, various students of political ambition have built upon Schlesinger's solid foundations to develop models of decision-making used by legislators when considering a bid for higher office. Both the value of one's present position (e.g., in the House) and that of a potential slot (e.g., in the Senate) are crucial to a "strategic" politician's calculation. At the same time, one central factor is the willingness (or reluctance) of a potential candidate to take the risk of running for higher office when a particular opportunity arises. For example, two members of Congress from California and South Dakota, respectively, may harbor similar senatorial ambitions, but their structures of opportunity are very different. South Dakota's single member of the House can run for either of two Senate positions in the same statewide constituency as his House seat's. In California, a legislator is only one of fifty-two members, each of whom represents approximately 2 percent of the entire population of the state. The opportunity structure therefore works against virtually all of California's and other large states' members of Congress who seek to advance, and the ground is littered with the political corpses of those members of the House who have sought to advance in those states.

Ambition may be most important in the assessment of who initially runs for the legislature and why. Given their dominance of the House since 1955, Democrats appear more career-oriented than Republicans, at least in that body, which has been the focus of much of the research on the motivational base of office-seeking.

More broadly, context is extremely important in understanding how ambition plays out. First, and most important, for ambition to flower, conditions must be right; without opportunity, ambition cannot be expressed. In that House seats turn over infrequently (five or more terms is the average length of service), Senate terms are lengthy and state legislative elections increasingly return large numbers of incumbents, the question of opportunity is very real. Mounting a challenge to an incumbent is always a possibility, but open seats offer a much better chance for a would-be legislator. Moreover, district population patterns, name recognition, availability of funds, and any number of personal variables (age, job requirements, children's ages and needs, other family concerns, and so on) all affect the decision to run. Perhaps most important are the ambitions of other potential candidates, and a prospective candidate's information in that regard is usually incomplete, if not downright inaccurate.

The costs—both financial and personal —of seeking election to the Congress and to a lesser extent, state legislatures, are great, and they limit the number of actual candidates from the many potential office-seekers. This means that strong congressional candidates must possess a powerful desire to serve on Capitol Hill. This harkens back to James Madison's emphasis on the virtues of ambition, which he believed ties representatives to their districts "by motives of a more selfish nature" than simply the desire to serve. Again, Democrats hold a substantial advantage in this respect, given their pool of candidates who would find legislative compensation adequate and who would express greater willingness to view the government as offering useful opportunities for resolving serious social problems.

Even among Republicans the fires of ambition burn strongly enough that the Congress and state legislatures are generally faced with no shortage of candidates when opportunities do present themselves. In many ways, the era

from 1970 to the early 1990s has become one in which personal ambition has come to dominate legislative office-seeking, even in states like Illinois, where parties controlled the candidate-selection process into the mid-1960s. But by the next decade the extent of party control had eroded, even in states where party organizations traditionally had been strong. Most of those who ran for Congress, and increasing numbers of those who sought state legislative seats, were self-starters who understood the costs of serving and, once in office, stayed because they enjoyed the job.

The domination of self-starters, who owe little to party or other broad-based organizations, has cut out a substantial proportion of would-be candidates from seeking legislative office. No longer do community elites groom potential candidates; rather, candidates decide if and when to present themselves. Alan Ehrenhalt argues that these ambitious individuals are no more or less healthy emotionally than those who run for more policy-oriented reasons. In any event, legislative life has come to be dominated by careerist professional politicians—not just on Capitol Hill but in most state legislatures as well.

Enjoyment/Self-gratification

In an era of policy gridlock and divided government, such sentiments as a sense of fun and accomplishment seem out of place. Yet these are the driving forces behind the efforts of many legislative policy entrepreneurs, who often absorb both financial and personal costs in order to continue to play the "policy game" at a high level. Placing substantial importance on the reelection motive makes a great deal of sense when legislators are driven by their enjoyment of the legislative game. At the same time, when they stop enjoying themselves, lawmakers may decide the costs are far too high, despite levels of compensation and regardless of position or the relative certainty of reelection.

Amateurs

Despite the general trend toward greater professionalism in political life, a minority of legislators can accurately be labeled amateurs whose motivations are sometimes distinct from their careerist peers. Amateurs are those without significant political experience who run for office. David Canon differentiates among amateurs, placing them in three categories: the ambitious, the policy-oriented, and the hopeless (those running against great odds). Ambitious amateurs resemble their professional colleagues; indeed, they seek to become professional politicians. Policy-oriented amateurs are somewhat less motivated by the desire to be reelected than by the desire to shape policies. Hopeless amateurs have a mix of motives, but since they are usually challenging entrenched incumbents, when they occasionally win a seat, they are often ill-suited to engage productively in legislative life.

State legislatures are institutions that turn many amateurs into professional politicians. This is where the foundations of political careers are built; inexperienced politicians can find out if they are adequately motivated to pursue a legislative career. In the Congress, conversely, amateurs have become increasingly the exception, although there remain significant numbers of wealthy (e.g., Senator Herbert Kohl, D.-Wis.) or well-known (e.g., former astronaut Senator John Glenn, D.-Ohio) individuals who move directly into the Congress. Given their ambition, however, they act in ways very similar to those of legislators who have entered Congress after conventional, extended political careers.

In short, fewer and fewer legislators are coming to their institutions without substantial political experience; amateurs have been urged on by a mix of motivations that may well be missed, as legislatures become careerist bodies where the reelection motivation tends to dominate.

MOTIVATIONS: THE QUESTION OF EVIDENCE

If political scientists and other scholars have not progressed very far in systematically exploring the motivations of legislators, where might adequate information be found? One possibility is to examine biographies and autobiographies, especially those that have a special sensitivity to motivations. Unfortunately, legislators are not ordinarily the target of extensive, skillfully executed biographies, although there are some exceptions, with Lyndon Johnson probably being the leading documented example. Not only are there careful examinations of Johnson's legislative career, but at least one biography also employs a psychological framework in sorting through hours of personal conversations. Johnson may well have been sui generis as a political figure, but his larger-than-life style reflects motivations that are common to many, if not all, career politicians.

In fact, the central debate over Lyndon Johnson's life revolves around his motivations: Was he driven to seek power and control merely to satisfy his own ambitions, or was he motivated to do good for the dispossessed and the country as a whole? This debate is surely somewhat overblown, but it strikes at the core of almost all political careers, as personal ambition mingles with the related desires to lead and to produce policy results. Johnson's ego-fed ambition was so great and his policy goals so far-reaching that the resulting conflict affected large numbers of people from early in his career, as with his direction of the Democratic Congressional Campaign Committee in 1940.

In her psychopolitical biography of Johnson (*Lyndon Johnson and the American Dream* [New York, 1976]), Doris Kearns places these motivations in the immediate context of his parents' wishes, those of the failed politico father and strong mother. Especially important was his mother's force of will. Kearns writes

> The image of Rebekah Baines Johnson that emerges [is that] of a frustrated woman with a host of throttled ambitions, trying, through her first-born son, to find a substitute for a dead father, an unsuccessful marriage, and a failed career.... The son would fulfill the wishful dreams she had never carried out, he would become the important person she had failed to be. (p. 24)

Johnson translated this maternal longing, according to Kearns, into a "process of conquest and control," which also reflected his father's demand "to make himself great among men whose company he shared" and which conflicted directly with his mother's dream for him "to do good for others."

Although Johnson fought these inner battles throughout his life, most publicly as president, they greatly affected his actions as a legislator. His ambitions propelled him to run for the House at an early age and to seek a Senate seat as soon as he reasonably could, at age 33 in 1941. His desire to address the poverty of his roots was almost equal to his motivation to rise to higher and higher office. One problem with the Congress—whether as a freshman congressman or later as the powerful Senate majority leader—was that even in his leadership position Johnson was simply one among many. Despite his generally accepted standing as the strongest floor leader in Senate history, complete control eluded him, as it must any leader in any legislative body. Of course, the presidency cannot provide much more of an opportunity to control events and other actors, even though it offers the promise of such power.

Given the richness of Johnson's life and the biographies it has spawned, it is likely that more and more will be learned about how motivations affect legislative life, at least in his case. Such a study would offer at least two distinct benefits. First, there could be an examination, in at least one important case, of the relationships among motivations, actions, and institutions. Second, it might provide insights that can be pursued using other biographical evidence, especially among politicians of the recent past.

THE LOSS OF MOTIVATION: LEAVING THE LEGISLATURE

As electoral defeat among incumbent U.S. congressmen and, to a lesser extent, senators has become increasingly rare, voluntary retirements account for greater numbers of legislative exits. Although voluntary retirements from the House rose during the late 1960s and 1970s, it is unclear exactly why. Among the reasons put forward was a growing frustration with the legislative process. Many members said that serving in the House just "wasn't fun" anymore. From 1984 to 1990, however, retirements leveled off; indeed, careerism before the 1992 reapportionment of seats stood at an all-time high in the House. Although voluntary retirements continue to occur, the fact remains that House service is highly valued, as evidenced by the high rate of members of Congress running for reelection.

Still, U.S. congressmen and senators do retire; some seek financial rewards in other fields, often in combination with generous retirement benefits. And the overall opportunity structure in the House has changed so that the benefits of accumulating seniority have become less substantial in the post-reform era than they were before the 1970s. In addition, there are some significant partisan differences in the House that are tied to motivations. Given their minority status in the House (and ordinarily in the Senate) since 1955, Republicans tend to serve for periods somewhat briefer than those of their Democratic counterparts and appear more willing to run for the Senate, even in the face of difficult odds.

CONCLUSION

There is a continuing irony in considering the motivations of legislators. Scholars have built major bodies of work by assuming the influence of such motivations as reelection and ambition. Observation has often seemed to confirm the power of these motivations, yet there has been little differentiation made within the general incentive to remain in office and/or the ambition for advancement. Motivational assumptions have served as the bedrock for much of the scholarly literature modeling Congress, but this has not meant that knowledge about legislative motivations has expanded greatly—quite the reverse. To the extent that motivational assumptions are made, empirical investigation into their nature is reduced.

In the early days of behavioral analysis of political life, psychological approaches to the study of elites held out some promise of furthering our understanding of politicians and their motives. Since the mid-1960s, however, large-scale attempts to come to terms with motivations have virtually ceased. The evidence that we have often comes from individual case studies, such as Fenno's series of book-length narratives on five U.S. senators or the increased biographical interest in Lyndon Johnson.

Some students of ambition have sought to understand legislators and candidates within complex personal and institutional contexts; others have sought to sort out the mix of the goals that motivate legislators. For the most part, however, motivations have fallen into the realm of assumptions rather than that of empirical analysis. There certainly has been no cumulative scholarship produced since the 1960s. And there is little reason to believe that legislators will allow much more systematic examination of their motivations in years to come, despite the increasing professionalization of legislative politics in the United States.

BIBLIOGRAPHY

Early Research
The pioneering works on motivations include those by HAROLD D. LASSWELL, *Psychopathology and Politics* (Chicago, 1930) and his *Power and Personality* (New York, 1948), and JOHN B. MCCONAUGHY, "Certain Personality Factors of State Legislators in South Carolina," *American Political Science Quarterly* 45 (1950): 897–903. Later, JAMES L. PAYNE, *The Motivations of Politicians* (Chicago, 1984), specifically addresses the motivational basis of political action.

Some key early behavior research was reported in JOHN C. WAHLKE, HEINZ EULAU, WILLIAM BUCHANAN, and LEROY C. FERGUSON, *The Legislative System: Explorations in Legislative Behavior* (New York, 1962); JAMES DAVID BARBER, *The Lawmakers: Recruitment and Adaptation to Legislative Life* (New Haven, Conn., 1965), and FRANK J. SORAUF, *Party and Representation* (New York, 1963). A crucial overview on one aspect of motivations, ambition, is JOSEPH A. SCHLESINGER, *Ambition and Politics: Political Careers in the United States* (Chicago, 1966). For the U.S. Senate, DONALD R. MATTHEWS, *U.S. Senators and Their World* (Chapel Hill, N.C., 1960), is the benchmark work.

Recent Studies
In the 1980s and early 1990s, numerous books that touch on political motivations have been published. These include JOHN HIBBING, *Choosing to Leave: Voluntary Retirement from the U.S. House of Representatives* (Washington, D.C., 1982), and *Congressional Careers: Contours of Life in the House of Representatives* (Chapel Hill, N.C., 1991). Focusing on ambition are LINDA FOWLER and ROBERT MCCLURE, *Political Ambition: Who Decides to Run for Congress* (New Haven, Conn., 1989); ALAN EHRENHALT, *The United States of Ambition: Politicians, Power, and the Pursuit of Office* (New York, 1991); and BURDETT A. LOOMIS, *The New American Politician: Ambition, Entrepreneurship, and the Changing Face of Political Life* (New York, 1988). More specifically, DAVID CANON explores the motivations of those who run for office with no political experience in *Actors, Athletes, and Astronauts: Political Amateurs in the United States Congress* (Chicago, 1990). A developmental overview of changing motivations is LAWRENCE C. DODD, "A Theory of Congressional Cycles: Solving the Problem of Change," in GERALD C. WRIGHT, LEROY N. RIESELBACH, and LAWRENCE C. DODD, eds., *Congress and Policy Change* (New York, 1986).

Finally, no single political scientist has contributed more to understanding legislators' motivations than RICHARD F. FENNO, JR. His relevant works include *Congressmen in Committees* (Boston, 1973); *Home Style: House Members in Their Districts* (Boston, 1978), and his series of books on senators: *The Making of a Senator: Dan Quayle* (Washington, D.C., 1989); *The Presidential Odyssey of John Glenn* (Washington, D.C., 1990); *The Emergence of a Senate Leader: Pete Domenici and the Reagan Budget* (Washington, D.C., 1990); *Learning to Legislate: The Senate Education of Arlen Specter* (Washington, D.C., 1991); and *When Incumbency Fails: The Senate Career of Mark Andrews* (Washington, D.C., 1992).

SEE ALSO The Historical Legislative Career; Modern Legislative Careers; AND The Social Bases of Legislative Recruitment.

WOMEN IN LEGISLATURES

Joyce Gelb

The first women to serve as American state legislators began their terms almost a century ago, in 1894, when three Republican women were elected to the Colorado House of representatives. The first state senator, Democrat Martha Hughes Canon, was elected to the Utah state senate shortly thereafter, in 1896.

Serious analysis of women's participation in state legislative politics began soon after the feminist movement of the 1960s and 1970s focused scholarly attention on changing gender roles at all levels of American society and politics. Early studies found that most women who entered politics up to 1970 served out the unexpired terms of male family members. It was also clear that women were more likely to be elected to the lower houses of state legislatures (in 1974 women were 9 percent of the lower houses and 5 percent of the upper ones) and to those that paid low salaries.

Students of state legislative politics have pointed to the importance of the concept of "political culture" in helping understand the potential role of women. From this perspective, those states defined as "moralistic," with a sense of politics as a public good, and "individualistic," with intense competition for public office, were seen as more apt to produce gains for women seeking political office than those defined as "traditional." The latter, under elite control and most often found in the South, were seen as less hospitable to representation by women. Initially, states that were urban and populous were less likely to produce significant gains in legislative officeholding for women, though the reasons for this are not entirely clear. In the period that followed the emergence of the second wave of feminism in the 1960s, elected women state legislators tended to be Republicans from states with "moralistic" cultures.

While some early analyses reported that few women in public office had family responsibilities and that they were more likely to be widowed or divorced than their male counterparts, most women in state legislatures were, in fact, married. However, they had fewer children and most assumed legislative positions later than men, first running for office at age 40 or more, when their children were grown (Kirkpatrick, pp. 44, 55, 65). Women also had less and different political experience and were less likely to have been college educated or hold professional degrees.

Women who could be expected to enter state legislative politics tended to be married to politically active and supportive husbands and were more often unemployed housewives. (Diamond, p. 37). If employed, they were usually found in low-status occupations (only slightly more than 5 percent were in the professions, compared with 53 percent of men).

Women's political experience also varied from that of men. Their history was more likely to be in the context of volunteer activity, although four-fifths in one study reported some kind of political party experience, not usually in elective office. Female state legislators combined community political service and political work to a greater extent than men. Women perceived that they both worked harder and needed to do so in order to get ahead in politics (Kirkpatrick, p. 66).

Studies of early female legislators found them to be more liberal (most, for example, actively supported the Equal Rights Amendment), though not likely to belong to feminist organizations or to introduce women's issues into campaigns. They were more apt to hold committee positions in areas related to traditional women's concerns, such as health, welfare, and education (though many served on ways and means and judiciary committees as well).

Women enjoyed advantages and disadvantages based on their gender. On the positive side, they received favorable press coverage and considerable interest because of their relative novelty as officeholders. They were less likely to be troubled by lobbyists and more able to behave in a direct manner, with fewer sanctions for breaking the "rules of the game." On the debit side, they faced the perception of role conflict between family and political responsibilities, the view held by constituents that they were always available, the need to prove their competence, and explicit channeling into specifically traditional female-oriented areas of expertise. Although some early studies emphasized that female candidates for legislative office were adventurous and had a high level of confidence and a strong sense of their ability to effect change (Kirkpatrick, p. 220), others stressed a relative lack of ambition for higher office and political power among women legislators. Obstacles to full participation and leadership, including lack of self-confidence and a fear of discrimination, were cited by several authors (Carroll and Strimling, p. 7).

In this article more recent patterns of recruitment and representation will be explored in order to assess the progress that women have made in state legislative politics. The evidence for increased power and participation by women in state legislative politics as well as the continuing problems and limitations related to their exercise of influence will also be assessed.

WOMEN AS STATE LEGISLATORS

Recruitment and Representation

Since the late 1960s, when research on women in legislative politics began in earnest, the representation of women in state legislatures has quadrupled. In 1993, women made up 20.2 percent of the more than 7,000 state representatives. The pattern of higher representation in the lower houses has continued; in 1993, women were 16.7 percent of state senators and 21.5 percent of state representatives; 60.7 percent of the female representatives were Democrats, 38.4 percent were Republicans. Nine states have legislatures made up of more than 25 percent women—they include Vermont, Maine, New Hampshire, Arizona, Washington

and Colorado. Of the states with the lowest representation by women, most, except for Pennsylvania, are in the South. Kentucky in 1993 had the lowest percentage, with a total of 4.3 percent. In 1989, 1.1 percent of female representatives were Hispanic, 8.3 percent were black (Center for the American Woman in Politics, "Fact Sheet," 1993).

It should be cautioned, however, that state legislatures vary significantly in terms of professionalization, length, and frequency of sessions, competition for office, salary, and size of constituency, so the importance of holding state office may vary as well. Women may get support from male leaders for jobs men do not want—for example, in New Hampshire, where the pay is low and the legislature has little power in contrast with New York, where the legislature is smaller, more powerful, and well paid. This is partly borne out by states in which female legislative representation has been high; in addition to New Hampshire, Washington, Vermont, and Colorado have part-time low-paid legislatures. However, the inverse relationship between legislative salaries and recruitment of women to state houses diminished significantly in the 1970s and later.

Changes in reapportionment, the emergence and expansion of the women's movement, a stronger alliance of women with the Democratic party, which has been represented by the tendency toward the "gender gap," an indication of partisan and other differences in voting behavior between men and women—all of these factors have worked to open the political opportunity structure as it relates to women's opportunities in state legislative politics. Women's access to legislative officeholding has become less concentrated geographically and, as suggested above, Republican women have been less dominant as officeholders. Women are still likely to be underrepresented in more populous states but more apt to be elected from states that reflect a more individualistic or competitive political culture.

Changing Background and Characteristics

Women state legislators in the 1990s have shared many characteristics with their predecessors of the 1970s and 1980s although they have far more resembled their male counterparts than was true earlier. Fewer gender-based differences between women and men regarding previous political experience and other characteristics have been evident, although women have still been more likely to work their way to higher political office by combining civic and community organizational activity with party activity. As the data above suggest, women legislators are predominantly white and mostly middle class. They are now more likely to be college graduates but hold fewer graduate degrees than their male counterparts. Still fewer women hold paid jobs, and when they do, they are more likely to be in traditionally female areas of employment—teaching, nursing, social work and the like. More are professionals than in the past, though their numbers are fewer than men. Reflecting new trends in labor-force participation, fewer are housewives. The eligibility pool of women in professions congruent with politics has widened. For example, in 1975, 3 percent of all women legislators were lawyers; today the number has expanded to 20 percent. Similarly, the number of female managers and administrators has increased dramatically to one third. Increasingly, women legislators are found in two-income families, which may bring them into relatively high income brackets; however, a significant number are in the lowest-income categories in comparison with male colleagues.

Women continue to be older entrants into the political arena, assuming office in middle age, and are still somewhat less likely than men to be married and have children. Nonetheless, in 1992, more than three-quarters of women legislators were employed, married, and had children. Studies of female legislators stress the importance of a supportive spouse for women who hold office. Women are more likely to be running for elective political office for the first time when they enter state legislative politics. They are more likely than men to have held appointive office before entering state politics and to have worked in a campaign or staff position. These findings suggest that despite significant changes in background and experiences, women's state legislative careers continue to be more limited by private, familial responsibilities and other societal constraints.

A major and important difference between the elected men and women in state legislatures is the high percentage of female legislators who are members of women's organizations; they number three-quarters of female state legislators. Fifty-eight percent of female state senators and 46 percent of state representatives belong to at least one out of five organizations: the American Association of University Women, the Federation of Business and Professional Women, the League of Women Voters, the National Organization for Women, and the National Women's Political Caucus. Women often indicate that they received leadership training (for example, experience in public speaking), encouragement, and important support, including volunteers and financial assistance, from these groups in their campaigns for state office. Such support is often crucial because women running for office are less likely to be members of prestigious occupational groups, such as the American Bar Association (although they are more apt than men to belong to such groups as the National Education Association, a leading teachers' group). In addition, a large number of women legislators report that their entrance into politics was facilitated by female role models and mentors.

Factors that help determine women's recruitment for state office and their success in contesting elections may be characterized as the "political opportunity structure." Among the factors that may limit opportunities and inhibit access to office for women are the high cost of campaigning, the power of incumbency, and the possibility of continued discrimination by party leaders. The type of election and the desirability of holding state office also may affect outcomes. While earlier studies emphasized the inaccessibility of higher office to female politicians, recent analysis suggests that many, if not all, structural barriers to state legislative office for women have fallen. In the past, some evidence suggested that female candidates were being selected as "sacrificial lambs" who had little chance to win. Even so, it was argued that such candidates could gain name recognition and acceptance of the idea that it was legitimate to nominate women for high office.

There is some disagreement regarding the likelihood that women candidates will be selected to run for legislative office. Ruth Mandel has contended that women are still less likely to be selected and Marianne Githens has suggested that women have an easier time getting elected than gaining nomination. Others, including R. Darcy, Susan Welch, and Janet Clark, have argued that while evidence for the sacrificial lamb theory is not clear, because women are less likely to be incumbents, they inevitably face more competition in gaining electoral office. Susan J. Carroll has found that Republicans, more than Democrats, were more likely to encourage women to run as sacrificial lambs (one-half of the former compared with one-quarter to two-fifths of the latter). Primaries, rather than general elections, may still be a more critical battleground for female candidates; over half of the women who ran for state office in 1976 were defeated in primary races.

Although the role of parties in state and national politics has weakened in recent years, female candidates continue to view the support of parties as crucial to electoral aspirations. Researchers have reported that women say they are often recruited by party leaders and even encouraged to run by them. It has already been suggested here that the strong ties of many female legislators to organizations have provided them with assistance that may be particularly valuable in situations where party support is not readily forthcoming, and in addition to it as well.

In general, those who study women in state legislative politics have agreed that women are equally, if not more, successful in electoral outcomes and that gender has little impact on voter choice. Women have gained considerable ground in running for winnable seats and garnering a broad cross section of support from voters.

A factor that continues to constrain women's state electoral opportunities is the prevalence of single-member, as opposed to multi-member, districts for state legislative office. Most studies have found that women running in multimember districts have been more likely to win than those in single-member districts, regardless of whether the race is for the state assembly or senate. In the 1960s, fifty-five of ninety-nine state legislators were elected from multimember districts; by 1975, with an increase in single-member districts, the number dropped to thirty-five. The reduction and conversion of multimember districts, which have been far more favorable to women's state legislative aspirations than single-member districts, is an adverse development in the political opportunity structure for women.

Other factors related to the political opportunity structure include incumbency and resources to meet the high cost of campaigning for office. The advantages of incumbency are considerable, ranging from visibility and access to financial resources to opportunities to campaign continually during one's term in office. Since women occupy fewer incumbent seats, it is more difficult for them to gain entry to state legislative politics than it is for men. Incumbency and lack of turnover in state legislative politics means that relatively few seats are open to newcomers in a given election. Incumbents win reelection at a far higher rate than challengers, and the fact that far fewer women than men are incumbents limits new opportunities for electoral success. Perceived problems related to gender loom large for challengers while they vanish for female incumbents.

Nonetheless, the rate of voluntary turnover is far greater in state politics than at the national level. The lure of private business and the pull of higher office does create more seat vacancy in state politics than in the U.S. Congress. Approximately 16 percent of lower-house members vacated state seats in election cycles leading up to 1987, compared with 10 percent for the U.S. House of Representatives, thus permitting somewhat greater access for newcomers at the state level. While candidates of both sexes experience extraordinary difficulty in defeating incumbents, women do better than men in running for open state legislative seats. Women may be more likely to follow other women in running for the same seats.

With regard to campaign finance, some earlier analysis suggested that women experience greater reluctance in soliciting funds than men. However, there is little evidence in the early 1990s that women have more difficulty raising funds than men; in fact, some studies suggest that they may actually raise and spend more than men. Nonetheless, political action committees (PACs) are somewhat less likely to make large contributions to women than to men; male candidates, in general, raise more money from large contributors (Carroll, pp. 50, 56–59). As suggested above, women are often excluded from the powerful networks of campaign support based in labor, business, and professional associations that tend to support incumbents and established power relationships. Again, women may partly compensate by using people-based resources from community groups and women's organizations. One relatively new development that may enhance future prospects for women at the state level is the creation of PACs (political action committees) that raise money specifically targeted at female candidates; most women's PACs, an extension of the feminist movement, were founded during the 1980s. On a less positive note, women candidates are less likely to have professional managers or to do large-scale campaign planning.

Summary

Analysis suggests that women's recruitment to and representation in state legislative politics has undergone considerable change during the past two decades, when these processes have been studied intensively. The vast majority of women legislators in the 1990s are married, have children, and have college degrees. Gender is perceived to be as much an advantage as a disadvantage for women state legislative candidates (Carroll, 1985). Gender differences in political ambition, seen as barriers to women's continued electoral success, have been reduced, and surveys identify large majorities of female state legislators who say they would like to run for higher office. Increasingly, women appear to seek political power and prestige to the same extent as men. Factors related to role conflict engendered by family obligations and lack of party support to run for legislative office seem to have been moderated, if not eliminated. The eligibility pool for prospective female state legislative candidates, based on higher education and a greater degree of professionalism, has expanded considerably, although women still run for political office in far fewer numbers than men. Electoral outcomes, at least at the general election level, appear to be unrelated to gender.

Nonetheless, gender-based differences in recruitment and representation for state legislative office persist. Women legislators report far more reliance on organizational support, largely from women's groups, in encouraging them to run and providing campaign assistance. Women are still likely to enter state legislative politics at a later age and, according to one study, to be less apt to return to their legislative positions (Darcy, Welch and Clark, p.

138). They are, however, closer to their male counterparts in education and previous political experience than was true two decades ago. Women still come up against the entrenched positions of incumbent male legislators and may have difficulty attracting large campaign contributions. The lack of turnover and the high success rate of incumbents, often based on patterns of contributions to campaigns, often result in an entrenched system of power, permitting only incremental and gradual increases of women in state legislative ranks. Thus, political and economic resources continue to be skewed by gender, limiting electoral opportunities for would-be women legislators.

Women may also have some advantages based on gender, including people-oriented skills, visibility and publicity due to their relative novelty, and, if married, less pressure to maintain full-time outside employment.

Examined below is the question of whether the increased recruitment and representation of women in state legislative office has brought them into positions of leadership and altered the policy agendas within state politics to reflect greater concern for women's issues.

WOMEN AS LEADERS AND POLICYMAKERS IN STATE LEGISLATURES

In the last decade of the twentieth century, women's representation in state legislatures has ranged from a low of 2 percent in Louisiana to more than 30 percent in Arizona, Maine, Vermont, and New Hampshire. As of 1989, women held 16 percent of the leadership positions in American state legislatures. As is true for female representation in state politics generally, women are better represented as leaders in the less prestigious lower houses, holding 12 percent of state senate leadership positions and 18.8 percent of those in the statehouses. It is not surprising to find that women in leadership positions are most commonly found in state legislatures that have a large percentage of women. In 1991 three women served in the highest-ranking positions in state senates: Senate President Pro-Tempore Ellen Craswell (R.-Wash.), Senate President Pro-Tempore Bonnie Heinrich (D.-N.Dak.), and Senate President

Gwen Margolis (D.-Fla.), a record number serving simultaneously in such posts. Three women held such positions in the past: Vera Davis (R.-Del.), 1949–1950; Jan Faiks (R.-Ark.), 1987–1988; and Mary McClure (R.-S.Dak.), 1979–1989. One woman served as Speaker of the House in 1991: Jane Hull (R.-Ariz.). Six other women have served in similar capacities; several women have served before the advent of the second wave of feminism: Minnie Craig (R.-N.Dak.), 1933, and Consuelo Bailey (R.-Vt.), 1953.

Women in 1991 served as 12.5 percent of the chairs of standing committees—10.2 percent in state senates and 14.3 percent in state houses. They have chaired committees in thirty-four state senates and all but two state houses; only in Louisiana and Tennessee have they not been represented as committee chairs in either state legislative chamber. (One state, Nebraska, has a unicameral legislature.) As suggested above, women are increasingly likely to serve as chairs of standing committees dealing with diverse matters, although they are still more likely to serve as heads of committees dealing with what are viewed as traditional female interests, such as health, education, and welfare. Slightly fewer women chair business-related committees. Women in the early 1990s have been more likely to obtain committee assignments reflecting a broad range of subjects; fewer have served on health and welfare committees and more on finance and economic committees. While women are still found more often on committees dealing with health and human services, this appears to be the product of choice more than coercion.

Chairmanships are distributed fairly evenly by party in the state legislatures, although Republican women held 17.2 percent of state house chairs in comparison with 13.5 percent of the Democratic chairs in 1989. As is true for other leadership positions, women leaders are usually found in states with a high percentage of women serving in the legislature. Women seeking high-level legislative positions may have some disadvantages stemming from their relatively late entrance into public office and affecting their seniority, although they are beginning to catch up. Women who hold legislative leadership positions or who are political party insiders are as likely as their colleagues to work on women's legislative concerns and are far more likely than men in similar roles to do so. Women officeholders tend to encourage other women to run for political office, support other types of political activity, and, of particular note, hire women as key members of their legislative staffs.

Do Women Make a Difference?

One possible consequence of the growing representation of women in state legislative politics is a different orientation to issues concerning women. Do women legislators vote differently from men? Do they represent women's interests? Does the presence of women in office make a difference?

Early studies of women legislators found that women felt that to espouse women's issues overtly would limit their electability. Women in the early years, therefore, were less apt to hold membership in feminist organizations. Women legislators tended to eschew the labels women's liberation and feminist and to downplay women's issues in campaigning; however, they did support feminist issues in legislative policy-making. In Jeane Kirkpatrick's analysis (*Political Woman*, 1974), for example, a large majority of women legislators support the Equal Rights Amendment (ERA); the Center for the American Woman and Politics noted that in fifteen states that did not ratify the ERA, an enormous 40-percent gender gap separated the 76 percent of women who supported the amendment versus only 36 percent of men who did.

Since the late 1970s, studies have shown that women have different attitudes from men on political issues, differences that become even more pronounced where women's issues are concerned. The greatest differences between men and women holding elective office are found at the state legislative level. In addition to the ERA, differences are apparent on policies related to government regulation, the death penalty, and a proposed constitutional amendment banning abortion. Social Security for homemakers and equal opportunity for women are among the other issues that enjoy near-universal support from female legislators. Although Democratic representatives tend to endorse feminist positions more often, female

Republican liberals are also likely to share women-centered views despite their partisan affiliations.

It is likely that a factor in creating these changed trends is the role of the women's movement. A stronger relationship has developed between female state legislators and women's organizations, affecting issue orientation and policy agendas. More than their male counterparts, women legislators have reported that organizations other than political parties were instrumental in affecting their political career decisions and electoral outcomes. It has already been suggested that in contrast to the results of earlier surveys, women officeholders today are likely to belong to a women's and/or feminist organization. Close to three-quarters of state senators (74.4 percent) and state representatives (72.4 percent) belong to the National Organization for Women (NOW) or the National Women's Political Caucus, League of Women Voters, Association of American University Women (AAUW), or Business and Professional Women (BPW) (Carroll, 1992, p. 32). Democratic women are more likely to belong to such groups than Republican women. Female legislators have stressed the encouragement to run for office they have received from women's organizations. The League of Women Voters has proved especially helpful in motivating women's legislative candidacies; close to half of women state legislators report League membership. Women state legislators most frequently name their state women's political caucus as encouraging their candidacies and supporting them during their campaigns.

Substantial numbers of women legislators indicate a strong desire to represent women in office. Women do, in fact, vote differently from men and devote more energy and attention to issues related to women. One study by Susan J. Carroll finds that among women state legislators, one-fifth to one-third are both "attitudinal" and "behavioral" feminists. Most of the others might best be classified as "closet" feminists, who are not publicly identified, particularly in campaigns, with feminist perspectives, but who are committed to women's issues and feminist goals (1985, pp. 152–154). Only one study, of the California state assembly, found that while women were more likely to support women's issues in the state assemblies, they

were not necessarily more liberal than male legislators (Thomas, 1989, pp. 43–56). Other analyses of gender differences in issue orientation and legislative priorities note that women do indeed behave differently according to their sex; they are likely to be both liberal and supportive of women's issues. Gender consciousness and feminism are the key variables interacting to influence and structure women's legislative priorities and actions.

Women legislators do more for women than men do; they more often support and work for women's concerns. This is true even for self-labeled conservative women. On two indices of social policy constructed by the Center for the American Woman and Politics, female legislators were found to be about twice as likely as men to express support for feminist policy positions. Four of five women in contrast to three of five men mention at least one women's concern as being among their top three legislative priorities. Women also tend to act on their policy predispositions and prioritize and actively press for legislative passage of issues related to women and children. (They are also less attentive to business-related issues.)

These findings appear to hold true regardless of the state and legislature in which women participate. Feminist and nonfeminist women alike influence the legislative consideration of bills that affect women as a group, help set expenditure priorities for the states, and help pass a large number of bills specifically dealing with women's issues. They are far more likely than men to act in feminist and women's interest areas; in one Arizona study, such behavior characterized 28.5 percent of female legislators' behavior and only 12.9 percent of male legislative behavior.

Women have been aided in their legislative activities by women's caucuses, which highlight concerns and have developed strategies for the passage of legislation that now exist in state legislatures; more than three-quarters of women legislatures report such activity in their state legislatures (Carroll, 1992, pp. 33–34). But even when networks are more informal than formal, women's issues are emphasized by female legislators.

Other factors may affect the possibilities for effective intervention in the policy process.

These include what some have referred to as the "threshold" effect; the presence of 15% or more female legislators, an outcome of increased recruitment and representation, may prove especially helpful to the passage of legislation that concerns women. Large numbers help ensure that women's interests pervade the legislative institutional environment and may ease passage of satisfactory bills. But even when there are relatively few female legislators, perhaps because their small numbers give them a special sense of responsibility and increased visibility, they are also likely to support women's issues. Women thus initiate more bills related to women's issues than men and those bills that seek to improve women's status. Nearly one out of every ten women (three times the number of men) introduced a top-priority bill related to women, as reported in a 1988 survey.

While women introduce slightly fewer bills than men, they appear to be somewhat more successful in passage of legislation. Two of three legislators indicate that legislation related to women's issues passed in satisfactory form. Female legislators are therefore as likely as men to achieve their policy goals, although men may be slightly more successful than their female colleagues in gaining passage of bills that challenge women's traditional roles and status.

One final aspect of women's legislative role needs to be considered. This aspect relates to their perception of the type of work they do and the process by which they do it. Earlier analyses suggested that women are more motivated by "public serving" values and more concerned with the internal affairs of the political system than their male colleagues. Female legislators today seem to support the view that they are more publicly minded than their male counterparts and think that they work harder as well. They indicate that they spend more time in problem-solving and constituent-related work and less time interacting with lobbyists. However, a gender gap in perception appears to exist with regard to the notion that female legislators represent a distinctive approach to political processes. Male legislators tent to perceive the activity of their female colleagues differently; they do not see women as producing more legislation in the public view, spending less time with lobbyists, or being more involved in constituent work. However, men think women are less politically astute and well trained. Thus, the belief in the existence of a distinctive women's approach to political activity differs considerably according to gender.

With regard to policy concerns and priorities, it is evident that women have greatly altered the agenda of policy in state legislatures and have had considerable success in addressing new issues. Of course, female legislators continue to be subject to the larger political context in which they operate, including many institutional and psychological constraints. Nonetheless, two decades of increased recruitment and representation has produced a breed of female legislators who are less likely to be political outsiders and more likely to be active participants in the political process. Younger-generation male and female officeholders are more sensitive to gender-related concerns, which augurs well for future legislative policy-making in this area.

SUMMARY

A key and unanswered question is whether the distinctive legislative attitudes and behavior of women in state legislative politics are likely to continue with increased representation and the expansion of other opportunities. But it is clear that state legislative politics will remain the main locus for domestic policy-making in the United States. State legislatures continue to serve as key policy-making entities, particularly in an era of federal retrenchment, enacting important and often innovative social policies. Already, under the influence of female legislators, they have been at the forefront of such issues as wife abuse and violence against women; comparable worth and pay equity; policies affecting the welfare of children and mothers; reproductive rights; and divorce, child custody, and division of joint property.

State legislatures also serve as stepping-stones to higher office for women (one-third of female members of the House of Representatives are drawn from state legislative ranks), and it may be that one explanation for the phenomenon mentioned earlier—the failure of female legislators to return to their seats in expected numbers—is related to the fact that since they have high visibility, they are likely to be tapped for other, higher-level political positions. Finally, because recruitment and representation of **women** has increased far more at the state **legislative** level in American politics than at the national level, albeit in a slow and incremental manner, state legislatures are likely to remain as key instruments in the realization of women's political aspirations in the future.

Women in Congress

Although women have made up half or more of the electorate since they attained suffrage in 1920, their representation in the U.S. Congress has never been more than a mere fraction of the total membership. Particularly notable is the low number of female senators; prior to 1992 the highest representation ever achieved (three) was in 1937–1938. In the 1992 election a record five female senators were elected, bringing the total to a new record high of six in all. Even more significant, though modest, headway has been made in the House, where the number of female candidates receiving major nominations from their respective parties and contesting office has increased from twenty-five in 1970 to a record one hundred and six in 1992. The 1992 Congress had forty-seven women in the House (up from twenty-nine just two years before). The women's delegation in the House in 1992 included twenty-three incumbents, twenty-two candidates who successfully won open seats, and just two who upset incumbents. Twelve women in the House are women of color. With women as 11 percent of the representatives and 6 percent of Senators as of the 1992 election, the record of the United States in elective representation of women at the national level is still among the lowest in democratic countries. Until 1992, the limited increase from 2 percent in 1920 to the present small percentage suggested that the U.S. national legislature was largely immune to the patterns of changing representation that we have described at the state level. An examination of patterns of recruitment and participation for women in Congress before and in 1992 and an assessment of their role in the policy-making process follows.

Recruitment and Representation

During the years 1916–1940, 56 percent of women elected to the House were widows of congressmen who had served in that district, by the 1980s, this was true of only 9 percent of female representatives. However, in 1986, Barbara Mikulski, previously a congresswoman from Maryland, became the first Democratic woman elected to the Senate without having served out her husband's term first. Today, women are likely to run in their own right. They apparently suffer few disadvantages attributable to their gender, related to the nominating process, fund raising, and vote mobilization. To the extent that male candidates have an electoral advantage, it appears to be related more to their incumbency than to antifemale attitudes. When female incumbents run, they almost always win, while when female candidates face incumbents, they almost always lose, particularly in nonprimary elections. Since relatively few women until 1992 have been incumbents, their prospects for electoral success are limited. These factors appear to have a more significant impact on women's electoral prospects than do other variables, including previous electoral experience, nontraditional sex-role attitudes, and the inadequacy of such resources as money, time, and campaign workers. However, relatively few women have aspired to congressional officeholding, another factor limiting more equitable representation. The growing numbers of women entering politics at the state level may serve as an expanding pool for future candidacies, indeed, this appeared to be the case in 1992.

Nineteen ninety-two was characterized by the news media as the "year of the woman" because of the unusual success of women candidates, particularly at the congressional level. Factors responsible for the large increase in women's victories included redistricting, a large number of congressional retirements due to scandal and voter dissatisfaction, and an anti-incumbency stance among the public. As a result women candidates contested a large number of open seats—twenty-two that year, in contrast to four in 1990—providing clear evidence for changes in the "political-opportunity structure." Women may also have been perceived as the ultimate "outsiders" in this time of anti-incumbency, making them especially appealing choices in 1992. The Clarence Thomas–Anita Hill Supreme Court–confirmation hearings on Capitol Hill outraged many women and may have encouraged more women to enter the political arena because of their anger at the political process. Women's groups such as the National Women's Political Caucus and Emily's List found their fund-raising ability greatly enhanced; in 1992, Emily's List was the largest single donor to congressional campaigns (Marian Palley, "Election 1992 and the Thomas Appointment," *PS: Political Science and Politics* 26:1(March 1993).

Impact

As is true at the state legislative level, female congressional candidates reflect overwhelming support for feminist attitudes and positions on such issues as abortion, child care, and ratification of the ERA. Specifically, women legislators have been supportive of the Economic Equity Act, which was first introduced in 1981 and had nine provisions added in the 101st Congress; the Family and Medical Leave Act; the Civil Rights Act of 1991; and other measures regarding child care and parental leave. Women running as Republican congressional candidates have been somewhat less supportive of positive attitudes toward the women's movement than their Democratic counterparts—64 percent to 94 percent in 1987, respectively. At the congressional level, a "congresswoman's caucus" was formed in 1977 in order to activate support and express mutual concern on important feminist issues, including the ERA, equal employment, economic and pay equity, domestic violence, and parental leave. Since 1981, the group has been known as the Congressional Caucus on Women's Issues, and while it now admits male members, men cannot hold office, vote on policy matters or elect officers, or serve on the executive committee. While more Democratic than Republican women belong to the group (twenty Democratic and six Republican women served on the executive committee in 1991, limiting its overall effectiveness), it does highlight issues, act as a forum for discussion and advocacy, provide important information updates on the status of legislation and implementation, as well as maintain contact with key interest groups, the media, and administrative officials.

Women in Congress continue to work in an atmosphere of male domination and often cannot vote as a bloc because they are divided by party as well as by constituency. Nonetheless, as is true for their state counterparts, they appear to be more consistently liberal, particularly on issues related to women and consumer protection. Republican women and men in Congress differ on such issues as abortion rights, child benefits, and the ERA, and female legislators, in general, favor decreased arms-control and defense spending, regardless of party. Moreover, the increasingly large group of female congressional staff members have often played an important role in rallying support for women's issues in the Congress.

BIBLIOGRAPHY

Women as Candidates for Legislative Office
Texts discussing women who run for legislative office include BARBARA BURRELL, "The Presence of Women Candidates and the Role of Gender in Campaigns for the State Legislature in an Urban Setting: The Case of Massachusetts," *Women and Politics* 10:3 (1990): 85–102; SUSAN J. CARROLL, *Women as Candidates in American Politics* (Bloomington, Ind., 1985); SUSAN J. CARROLL and WENDY S. STRIMLING, *Women's Routes to Elective Office: A Comparison with Men's* (New Brunswick, N.J., 1983); and R. DARCY and

SARAH SLAVIN SCHRAMM, "When Women Run Against Men," *Public Opinion Quarterly* 41 (Spring 1977): 1–13.

Women in Party Leadership
A general study of traits and career progression of women legislators is found in EDMOND CONSTANTINI and KENNETH H. CRAIK, "Women as Politicians: The Social Background, Personality, and Political Careers of Female Party Leaders," *Journal of Social Issues* 28:2 (1972): 217–236. See also CAROL NECHEMIAS, "Changes in the

Election of Women to U.S. State Legislative Seats," *Legislative Studies Quarterly* 12:1 (1987): 125–142, for a discussion restricted to the state level of politics. In addition, M. KENT JENNINGS and BARBARA FARAH, "Social Roles and Political Resources: An Over-Time Study of Men and Women in Party Elites," *American Journal of Political Science* 25 (August 1981): 462–482 and M. KENT JENNINGS and NORMAN THOMAS, "Men and Women in Party Elites: Social Roles and Political Resources," *Midwest Journal of Political Science* 12 (November 1968): 462–482, offer analyses on gender differences in political-leadership positions.

Women in State Legislative Politics

A helpful work providing a general overview of women in state legislatures is MARIANNE GITHENS, "Women and State Politics: An Assessment," in JANET FLAMMANG, ed., *Political Women: Current Roles in State and Local Government* (Beverly Hills, Calif., 1984). Statistical information on women in state legislative politics is periodically updated in CENTER FOR THE AMERICAN WOMAN AND POLITICS (CAWP), "Fact Sheet" (New Brunswick, N.J., 1987–). For works on women's contributions to legislative agendas, see SUE THOMAS, "The Impact of Women on State Legislative Policies," *Journal of Politics* 53 (November 1991): 958–976 and DEBRA D. DODSON and SUSAN J. CARROLL, *Reshaping the Agenda: Women in State Legislatures* (New Brunswick, N.J., 1991).

Other studies of the impact of gender on state legislatures include SUE THOMAS and SUSAN WELCH, "The Impact of Gender on Activities and Priorities of State Legislators," *Western Political Quarterly* 44 (June 1991): 445–456; IRENE DIAMOND, *Sex Roles in the State House* (New Haven, Conn., 1977); PATRICIA FREEMAN and WILLIAM LYONS, "Legislators' Perceptions of Women in State Legislatures," *Women and Politics* 10:4 (1990): 121–132; and JEANE KIRKPATRICK, *Political Woman* (New York, 1974). Two studies that are restricted to the activities of a particular state legislature are SUE THOMAS, "Voting Patterns in the California Assembly: The Role of Gender," *Women and Politics* 9:4 (1989): 43–56 and MICHELLE SAINT-GERMAIN, "Does Their Difference Make a Difference?: The Impact of Women on Public Policy in the Arizona Legislature," *Social Science Quarterly* 70:4 (1989): 956–968.

General Works on Women and Politics

A historical view of the progress in the area of women's rights is found in NANCY MCGLEN and KAREN O'CONNOR, *Women's Rights: The Struggle for Equality in the Nineteenth and Twentieth Centuries* (New York, 1983), while JOYCE GELB concentrates on the influence of the feminist movement in *Feminism and Politics* (Berkeley, Calif., 1989). The role of power in particular is the subject of CYNTHIA FUCHS EPSTEIN, "Women and Power: The Roles of Women in Politics in the United States," in CYNTHIA FUCHS EPSTEIN and ROSE COSER, eds., *Access to Power: Cross-National Studies of Women and Elites* (London, 1981). See also SUSAN TOLCHIN and MARTIN TOLCHIN, *Clout: Womanpower and Politics* (New York, 1974); and KATHY A. STANWICK and KATHERINE E. KLEEMAN, *Women Make a Difference* (New Brunswick, N.J., 1983). Finally, RUTH MANDEL, "The Political Woman," in SARAH RIX, ed., *The American Woman 1988–89: A Status Report* (New York, 1988), and R. DARCY, SUSAN WELCH, and JANET CLARK, *Women, Elections, and Representation* (New York, 1987), give comprehensive accounts of women in politics.

SEE ALSO Legislatures and Civil Rights; Legislatures and Gender Issues; AND Modern Legislative Careers.

AFRICAN AMERICAN LEGISLATORS

Milton D. Morris

African Americans have a growing presence in the Congress and state legislatures of the country. Their numbers have grown briskly in the latter half of the twentieth century after a history of tortuously slow growth that mirrors the broader struggle by African Americans for full access to the political system. In this article describes the pattern of growth in the ranks of black legislators, the factors contributing to that growth, and the impact of their presence. Most of the attention to black legislators has focused on those in Congress. In this article we look beyond the Congress to the state legislatures, where the black presence has been no less prominent or important.

African Americans have had two distinct experiences in U.S. legislatures. One is the Reconstruction era, the relatively short-lived experience commencing immediately after the Civil War and lasting until about 1901. The other began in the mid-1920s, on the eve of the Great Depression. While some elements are common to the two experiences, there are profound differences as well.

During the Reconstruction era, the involvement of blacks in the political process was a distinct product of a broader national political struggle in the aftermath of the Civil War. That struggle was to determine not only the character of the reconstruction effort in the South but the fortunes of the two political parties as well. The Republican-controlled Congress had made enfranchisement of the black population a condition for readmitting the Southern states to the Union. The newly enfranchised black voters were overwhelmingly Republican and so their numbers strengthened that party's hold on power in the South and the nation. The white majority acquiesced reluctantly to blacks as voters and officeholders. When a fearful white majority in Georgia expelled black legislators and curtailed black participation, Con-

gress intervened to force reversal of these actions.

Clearly, post–Civil War political participation by blacks did not reflect anything approaching a consensus among whites about the right of blacks to full political participation. Although hundreds of blacks won seats in several southern state legislatures, twenty in the House of Representatives, and two in the Senate, the legitimacy of their presence remained unsettled.

MEMBERS OF CONGRESS

The Reconstruction Era

Joseph H. Rainey (R.-S.C.) and Jefferson F. Long (R.-Ga.) became the first black members of the House of Representatives when they took their seats in 1870. Hiram R. Revels took his seat in the Senate that same year as the first black senator, representing Mississippi. Over the next thirty years, nineteen other African Americans were to serve from seven southern states. South Carolina had the largest number of representatives with nine while Alabama, North Carolina, and Mississippi had three each. Reflecting Republican party leadership of the Civil War and Reconstruction efforts, blacks overwhelmingly supported that party and all elected black officials were Republican (see Table 1).

These senators and representatives had widely varying backgrounds. Some were former slaves; about half had held public office in their states, notably in state constitutional conventions and state legislatures. For example, Republican senator Hiram Revels of Mississippi (1870–1871) was a "free Negro," educated at Knox College in Illinois, a minister and schoolteacher, and a recruiter and chaplain in the

Table 1
BLACK MEMBERS OF CONGRESS, 1870–1992

Reconstruction-Era Senate			
Name	Party/ State	Dates of Service	Years
Hiram R. Revels	R.-Miss.	1870–1871	1
Blanche K. Bruce	R.-Miss.	1875–1881	6

Reconstruction-Era and Late Nineteenth-Century House of Representatives			
Name	Party/ State	Dates of Service	Terms
Joseph H. Rainey	R.-S.C.	1870–1879	5
Jefferson F. Long	R.-Ga.	1870–1871	1
Robert C. De Large	R.-S.C.	1871–1873	1
Robert Brown Elliott	R.-S.C.	1871–1875	2
Benjamin S. Turner	R.-Ala.	1871–1873	1
Joseph T. Walls	R.-Fla.	1871–1873	
		1873–1877	3
Richard H. Cain	R.-S.C.	1873–1879	3
John Roy Lynch	R.-Miss.	1873–1877	
		1882–1883	3
Alonzo J. Rainsier	R.-S.C.	1873–1875	1
James T. Rapier	R.-Ala.	1873–1875	1
Jeremiah Haralson	R.-Ala.	1875–1877	1
John Adams Hyman	R.-N.C.	1875–1877	1
Charles E. Nash	R.-La.	1875–1877	1
Robert Smalls	R.-S.C.	1875–1879	
		1882–1883	
		1884–1887	5
James E. O'Hara	R.-S.C.	1883–1887	2
Henry P. Cheatham	R.-N.C.	1889–1893	2
John Mercer Langston	R.-Va.	1890–1891	1
Thomas E. Miller	R.-S.C.	1890–1891	1
George W. Murray	R.-S.C.	1893–1897	2
George H. White	R.-N.C.	1897–1901	2

Black Members of Congress: Twentieth Century

Senate			
Name	Party/ State	Dates of Service	Years
Edward W. Brooke III	R.-Mass.	1967–1979	12
Carol Moseley-Brown	D.-Ill.	1993–date	

House of Representatives			
Name	Party/ State	Dates of Service	Terms
Oscar S. De Priest	R.-Ill.	1929–1935	3
Arthur W. Mitchell	D.-Ill.	1935–1943	4
William L. Dawson	D.-Ill.	1943–1970	14

Table 1 (continued)

House of Representatives

Name	Party/State	Dates of Service	Terms
Adam Clayton Powell	D.-N.Y.	1945–1967	
		1969–1971	13
Charles C. Diggs Jr.	D.-Mich.	1955–1980	13
Robert N. C. Nix Sr.	D.-Pa.	1958–1979	11
Augustus F. Hawkins	D.-Calif.	1963–1991	14
John Conyers Jr.	D.-Mich.	1965–*date*	14
Shirley A. Chisholm	D.-N.Y.	1969–1983	7
William L. Clay	D.-Mo.	1969-*date*	12
Louis Stokes	D.-Ohio	1969–*date*	12
George W. Collins	D.-Ill.	1970–1973	2
Ronald V. Dellums	D.-Calif.	1971–*date*	11
Ralph H. Metcalfe	D.-Ill.	1971–1978	4
Parren J. Mitchell	D.-D. Md.	1971–1987	8
Charles B. Rangel	D.-N.Y.	1971–*date*	11
Walter E. Fauntroy	D.-D.C.	1971–1991	10
Yvonne B. Burke	D.-Calif.	1973–1979	3
Barbara C. Jordan	D.-Tex.	1973–1979	3
Andrew J. Young Jr.	D.-Ga.	1973–1977	3
Cardiss Collins	D.-Ill.	1973–*date*	10
Harold E. Ford	D.-Tenn.	1975–*date*	9
George W. Crockett Jr.	D.-Mich.	1979–1991	6
Julian C. Dixon	D.-Calif.	1979–*date*	7
G. T. (Mickey) Leland	D.-Tex.	1979–1989	6
Melvin H. Evans	R.-V.I.	1979–1981	1
William H. Gray III	D.-Pa.	1979–1991	7
Bennett M. Stewart	D.-Ill.	1979–1981	1
Mervyn M. Dymally	D.-Cal.	1981–1993	6
Gus Savage	D.-Ill.	1981–1993	6
Harold Washington	D.-Ill.	1981–1983	2
Katie B. Hall	D.-Ind.	1982–1985	2
Charles A. Hayes	D.-Ill.	1983–1993	5
Major R. O. Owens	D.-N.Y.	1983–*date*	5
Edolphus Towns	D.-N.Y.	1983–*date*	5
Alan D. Wheat	D.-Mo.	1983–*date*	5
Alton R. Waldon Jr.	D.-N.Y.	1986–1987	1
Mike Espy	D.-Miss.	1987–*date*	3
Floyd H. Flake	D.-N.Y.	1987–*date*	3
John R. Lewis	D.-Ga.	1987–*date*	3
Kweisi Mfume	D.-Md.	1987–*date*	3
Donald M. Payne	D.-N.J.	1989–*date*	2
Craig A. Washington	D.-Tex.	1990–*date*	2
Barbara-Rose Collins	D.-Mich.	1991–*date*	1
Gary A. Franks	R.-Conn.	1991–*date*	1
William J. Jefferson	D.-La.	1991–*date*	1
Eleanor Holmes Norton	D.-D.C.	1991–*date*	1
Maxine Waters	D.-Calif.	1991–*date*	1
Lucien Blackwell	D.-Pa.	1991–*date*	1

Nonvoting Delegates: Fauntroy (D.-D.C.), Evans (R.-V.I.) and Norton (D.-D.C.).

Source: Adapted from Bruce A. Ragsdale and Joel D. Treese, *Black Americans in Congress, 1870–1989* (Washington, D.C.: Office of the Historian, U.S. House, 1990).

Union army. Senator Blanche K. Bruce, the second black senator, also a Republican from Mississippi, was a former slave who escaped, studied in the North, and on returning to Mississippi worked as a tax collector, a sheriff, and a county school superintendent before serving in the Senate (1875–1881).

Among representatives, a number had held public office previously. Alonzo Ranier, for example, had been a member of South Carolina's constitutional convention and served as lieutenant governor before being elected to Congress. John Hyman, of North Carolina, served in the state legislature for six years before his election to Congress in 1875. Robert Smalls, of South Carolina, had not held office but was a war hero, having seized the Confederate ship *Painter* and delivered it to the Union navy. John R. Lynch was born a slave in Louisiana but became a leading figure in the Mississippi state legislature and the Republican party. He served as speaker of the Mississippi state legislature, as chairman of the executive committee of the Republican party, as a three-time delegate to the party's national convention, and in 1884 became the first black to preside over the Republican National Convention.

The number of blacks who served tends to overstate the level of a black presence in Congress. Half the black representatives served for only one term, and only two, Joseph Rainey and Robert Smalls, both of South Carolina, served through five sessions. One of the two senators served for just one year and the other one term. The era of black congressional participation ended with Representative George White in 1901 after two terms of service.

Relatively little has been done to appraise the impact of black members of Congress up to 1901. Their greatest impact was symbolic. They were evidence of Northern Republican reconstruction of the South, and of the extension of citizenship to the former slave population. To many blacks government representation was a source of pride and a symbol of things to come for full citizens.

Black legislators were not only symbols. In practice they attempted to protect the precarious position of blacks in Southern political life, especially as Northern commitment to Reconstruction waned and political deals began to result in the withdrawal of the protective federal presence. By their presence and activities, black members of Congress played a lonely and eventually futile rearguard action. They were active advocates of a wide range of policy concerns, most dealing with civil and human rights, and educational opportunities for blacks. Notably, James E. O'Hara (R.-N.C.) became the first legislator to use the federal government's power to regulate interstate commerce as a basis for requiring equal public accommodations when he attached an amendment to that effect to an interstate-commerce bill.

The Twentieth-Century Experience

A long absence of blacks from the Congress that began in 1902 was broken in 1929, when Illinois voters sent Oscar DePriest, a wealthy Chicago Republican, to fill the vacant congressional seat of Martin B. Maddew, who had died suddenly in office. DePriest's election marked a critical juncture in black politics on several counts. He was the first black member of Congress elected outside the South. He ushered in an era in which black political participation shifted to the major cities of the Midwest and Northeast after having been drastically curtailed in the South. He was the last of the prominent elected black Republican officials and a bridge to the era of black Democratic party involvement. After uncomfortably straddling the party fence between 1929 and 1934 by voting Republican in Congress while supporting some Democratic candidates locally, DePriest lost his bid for reelection in 1934 to Arthur W. Mitchell, the first black Democrat to serve in Congress.

Mitchell defeated DePriest narrowly by riding the wave of popular support for both the Democratic party and President Franklin D. Roosevelt's New Deal. When he retired in 1942, Mitchell was followed by fellow Chicagoan William L. Dawson. Three years later, in 1945, Dawson was joined in Congress by Adam Clayton Powell, Jr., of New York, whose presence almost immediately highlighted the incongruities of black members of Congress as victims of widespread discrimination within and outside the Congress. A decade later, Michigan Democrat Charles Diggs, Jr., became the third black Democrat to take a seat in Congress.

In 1965, the year Congress enacted the Voting Rights Act, there were a total of five black members of Congress, Augustus Hawkins (D.-Calif.) and John Conyers (D.-Mich.) having joined. The pace of new entrants quickened substantially in the 1970s, when fifteen African Americans entered Congress. These included the first southern Democrats, Barbara Jordan (D.-Tex.) and Andrew Young (D.-Ga.) in 1973 and George "Mickey" Leland (D.-Tex.) in 1979, and the first nonvoting delegate from Washington, D.C., Walter Fauntroy in 1971. Another fifteen blacks entered in the 1980s, and in 1991, Representative Gary Franks (R.-Conn.) entered the Congress as the first black Republican since Oscar DePriest. When the 102d Congress drew to an end, there were twenty-five black voting members and one nonvoting delegate from the District of Columbia. This was just over 5 percent of the total membership of the House of Representatives. In the 103d Congress, forty African Americans were seated in the House.

In the twentieth century only two African Americans, Edward Brooke (R.-Mass.) and Carol Moseley-Braun (D.-Ill.), have managed to win seats in the Senate. Brooke, a native of Washington, D.C., first won the position of Massachusetts attorney general, defeating Franks in 1962. Four years later, he defeated former governor Endicott Peabody to win the Senate seat and was reelected in 1972. He returned to private life in 1978 after losing a bid for a third term.

During the 1980s and 1990s, African Americans in Congress have been at the vanguard of a broad-based process of empowerment of the African American population. Their presence has grown in response to several major developments that occurred during and after World War II. One was demographic. Mass migration from the South to the urban centers of the Midwest and Northeast, and relatively rapid black-population growth nationwide resulted in the black-majority districts sending black members to Congress. Growth of the Latino population also facilitated the election of black representatives to Congress as many have thrown their support behind black candidates. Another development was the expansion of voting rights for blacks and Latinos through the Voting Rights Act and related court decisions. These actions expanded the black electorate in the South and increased demands for majority-black districts everywhere that population size

permitted. Seventeen of the twenty-six districts represented by African Americans have black-population majorities. Another six districts have combined black-Latino majorities. Only three of the black U.S. Representatives—Gary Franks (R.-Conn.), Alan Wheat (D.-Kans.), and Ronald Dellums (D.-Calif.)—are from white-majority districts, which are 96-, 75-, and 60-percent white, respectively.

As the number of African Americans has grown, so has their influence within the Congress and the political system. This growing influence is related to the link between seniority and power in Congress in spite of significant changes in the seniority system in recent years. While some black representatives have had short stays—no more than two terms—most have had relatively long tenures that enhance opportunities for leadership.

The highest Congressional leadership role was attained by Representative William Gray (D.-Pa.). He was selected to chair the House Budget Committee from 1984 to 1988, a position not determined by seniority. In 1988, Gray won the chairmanship of the House Democratic Caucus, and in 1990 he became majority whip. He retired from Congress in 1991 to become president of the United Negro College Fund. Congressman John Lewis (D.-Ga.) started up the leadership ladder with his appointment as deputy whip in 1991.

Committee and subcommittee chairs are still important leadership positions with substantial influence, and African Americans have held a number of such chairmanships (see Table 2). Perhaps the most notable was Representative Adam Clayton Powell, Jr., who chaired the Committee on Education and Labor from 1961 to 1967 and also led the way for the writing and passage of an array of bills during the 1960s that were at the heart of President Lyndon Johnson's War on Poverty. Earlier, Representative Robert Dawson became the first black member of Congress to chair a major committee when he served as chair of the Government Operations Committee from 1949 to 1953 and again from 1955 to 1970. When Congressman Diggs was named chairman of the Committee on the District of Columbia, the long history of white congressional control of the District of Columbia, a jurisdiction with a black-majority population, came to an end.

In the early 1990s African American mem-

Table 2
BLACK MEMBERS WHO HAVE CHAIRED U.S. HOUSE COMMITTEES

Black Members	Party/ State	Chaired
William L. Dawson	D.-Ill.	Expenditures in the Executive Departments, 1949–1952; renamed Government Operations, 1952–1953, 1955–1970
Adam Clayton Powell	D.-N.Y.	Education and Labor, 1961–1967
Charles C. Diggs Jr.	D.-Mich.	District of Columbia, 1973–1979
Robert N.C. Nix	D.-Pa.	Post Office and Civil Service, 1977–1979
Louis Stokes	D.-Ohio	Assassinations (Select), 1977–1978
		Standards of Official Conduct, 1981–1985; 1991–date
		Permanent Select Intelligence, 1987–1989
Ronald V. Dellums	D.-Calif.	District of Columbia, 1979–date
Augustus F. Hawkins	D.-Calif.	House Administration, 1981–1985
		Joint Committee on Library, 1981–1983
		Joint Committee on Printing, 1983–1985
		Education and Labor, 1985–1991
Parren J. Mitchell	D.-Md.	Small Business, 1981–1985
Charles B. Rangel	D.-N.Y.	Narcotics Abuse and Control (Select) 1983–date
G.T. Mickey Leland	D.-Tex.	Hunger (Select), 1984–1989
William H. Gray III	D.-Pa.	Budget, 1985–1989
		Majority Whip, 1989–1991
Julian C. Dixon	D.-Calif.	Standards of Official Conduct, 1985–1991
John Conyers Jr.	D.-Mich.	Government Operations, 1989–date
William L. Clay	D.-Mo.	Post Office and Civil Service, 1991–date

Source: Garrison Nelson, *Directory of Committee Assignments in the U.S. Congress, 1947–1992* (Washington, D.C.: Congressional Quarterly, 1993).

bers of Congress held five major committee chairmanships and about sixteen subcommittee chairmanships (see Table 3). The Committee on Government Operations is chaired by Representative John Conyers, Jr., (D.-Mich.); Committee on the Post Office and Civil Service by Representative William Clay, (D.-Mo.); Committee on the District of Columbia by Representative Ronald Dellums, (D.-Calif.); and the Committee on Standards of Official Conduct by Representative Carl Stokes, (D.-Ohio); and Representative Charles Rangel (D.-N.Y.) chairs the Select Committee on Narcotics Abuse and Control. These, and the sixteen subcommittee chairmanships constitute a strong base of political influence in Congress.

In addition to the routine influence that committee and subcommittee chairmanships provide, some black legislators have been especially adept at utilizing the powers of their committees or subcommittees in exerting influence on public policy. One noteworthy example of this is former Representative Charles Diggs, who used the chairmanship of the Africa subcommittee of the House Foreign Relations Committee as a powerful instrument for mobilizing interest in and support for African affairs at a time when Americans exhibited very little

Table 3

AFRICAN AMERICAN MEMBERS OF CONGRESS AND COMMITTEE
ASSIGNMENTS, 102D CONGRESS

Member	Party and State	Member Since	Committee Assignments

Lucian Blackwell	D.-Pa.	1991	Public Works and Transportation
			  Subcommittee on Surface Transportation
			  Subcommittee on Water Resources
			  Subcommittee on Investigations and Oversight
			Committee on Merchant Marine and Fisheries
			  Subcommittee on Merchant Marine

William L. Clay	D.-Mo.	1969	*Chairman,* Committee on Post Office and Civil Service
			  Chairman, Subcommittee on Investigations
			Committee on Education and Labor
			  Subcommittee on Labor-Management Relations
			  Subcommittee on Labor Standards
			Committee on House Administration
			  Chairman, Subcommittee on Libraries and Memorials

Barbara Rose-Collins	D.-Mich.	1991	Committee on Public Works and Transportation
			  Subcommittee on Aviation
			  Subcommittee on Economic Development
			  Subcommittee on Water Resources
			Committee on Post Office and Civil Service
			  Subcommittee on Postal Personnel and Modernization
			Select Committee on Children, Youth and Families

Cardiss Collins	D.-Ill.	1973	Committee on Energy and Commerce
			  Chairwoman, Subcommittee on Commerce, Consumer Protection and Competitiveness
			  Subcommittee on Transportation
			Committee on Government Operations
			  Subcommittee on Commerce, Consumer, and Monetary Affairs
			Select Committee on Narcotics Abuse and Control

John Conyers	D.-Mich.	1965	*Chairman,* Committee on Government Operations
			  Chairman, Subcommittee on Legislation and National Security
			Committee on Judiciary
			  Subcommittee on Civil and Constitutional Rights
			  Subcommittee on Economic and Commercial Law
			Committee on Small Business
			  Subcommittee on S.B.A. and the General Economy and Minority Enterprise Development

Ronald V. Dellums	D.-Calif.	1971	*Chairman,* Committee on District of Columbia
			  Subcommittee on Fiscal Affairs and Health
			Committee on Armed Services
			  Chairman, Subcommittee on Research and Development
			  Subcommittee on Investigations
			Permanent Select Committee on Intelligence

(continued)

371

Table 3 (continued)
AFRICAN AMERICAN MEMBERS OF CONGRESS AND COMMITTEE
ASSIGNMENTS, 102D CONGRESS

Member	Party and State	Member Since	Committee Assignments
Julian Dixon	D.-Calif.	1979	Committee on Appropriations *Chairman,* Subcommittee on the District of Columbia Subcommittee on Defense
Mervyn Dymally	D.-Calif.	1981	Committee on District of Columbia *Chairman,* Subcommittee on Judiciary and Education Committee on Foreign Affairs *Chairman,* Subcommittee on Africa Committee on the Post Office and Civil Service Subcommittee on Census and Population Subcommittee on Postal Personnel and Modernization
Mike Espy	D.-Miss.	1987	Committee on Agriculture Subcommittee on Domestic Marketing, Consumer Relations and Nutrition Subcommittee on Cotton, Rice and Sugar *Vice Chairman,* Subcommittee on Conservation Credit and Rural Development Committee on the Budget Economic and Trade Task Force Human Resources Task Force *Chairman,* Natural Resources, Community and Economic Development Task Force Select Committee on Hunger *Chairman,* Task Force on Domestic Hunger
Floyd Flake	D.-N.Y.	1987	Committee on Small Business Subcommittee on Regulation, Business Opportunities and Energy Committee on Banking, Finance and Urban Affairs Subcommittee on Housing and Community Development Subcommittee on General Oversight and Investigation Subcommittee on Financial Institutions Supervision, Regulation and Insurance Subcommittee on International Development Finance, Trade and Monetary Policy Select Committee on Hunger
Harold E. Ford	D.-Tenn.	1975	Committee on Ways and Means *Chairman,* Subcommittee on Human Resources Subcommittee on Oversight Select Committee on Aging Subcommittee on Retirement Income and Employment Subcommittee on Housing and Consumer Interest

Table 3 (continued)

Member	Party and State	Member Since	Committee Assignments

Gary A. Franks	R.-Conn.	1991	Committee on Armed Services
			  Subcommittee on Readiness
			  Subcommittee on Personnel
			  Subcommittee on Investigations
			Committee on Small Business
			  Subcommittee on S.B.A., the General Economy and Minority Enterprise Development
			  Subcommittee on Exports, Tax Policy, and Special Programs
			Select Committee on Aging
			  Subcommittee on Retirement Income and Employment

Charles Hayes	D.-Ill.	1983	Committee on Education and Labor
			  Subcommittee on Postsecondary Education
			  Subcommittee on Elementary, Secondary, and Vocational Education
			  Subcommittee on Labor-Management Relations
			  Subcommittee on Health and Safety
			Committee on Post Office and Civil Service
			  Chairman, Subcommittee on Postal Personnel and Modernization

Eleanor Holmes-Norton	D.C.-Delegate	1991	Committee on Public Works and Transportation
			  Subcommittee on Surface Transportation
			  Subcommittee on Investigation and Oversight
			Committee on Post Office and Civil Service
			  Subcommittee on Civil Service
			  Subcommittee on Postal Operations and Services
			Committee on District of Columbia
			  Subcommittee on Judiciary and Education
			  Subcommittee on Fiscal Affairs and Health

William J. Jefferson	D.-La.	1991	Committee on Education and Labor
			  Subcommittee on Elementary, Secondary, and Vocational Education
			  Subcommittee on Postsecondary Education
			  Subcommittee on Select Education
			Committee on Merchant Marine and Fisheries
			  Subcommittee on Fisheries and Wildlife, Conservation, and the Environment
			  Subcommittee on Merchant Marine and Fisheries

John Lewis	D.-Ga.	1987	Committee on Public Works and Transportation
			  Subcommittee on Public Buildings and Grounds
			  Subcommittee on Aviation
			  Subcommittee on Surface Transportation
			Committee on Interior and Insular Affairs
			  Subcommittee on Insular Affairs
			  Subcommittee on National Parks & Public Lands
			Select Committee on Aging

(continued)

Table 3 (continued)
AFRICAN AMERICAN MEMBERS OF CONGRESS AND COMMITTEE
ASSIGNMENTS, 102D CONGRESS

Member	Party and State	Member Since	Committee Assignments

Kweisi Mfume	D.-Md.	1987	Committee on Banking, Finance and Urban Affairs
			  Subcommittee on Housing and Community Development
			  Subcommittee on Financial Institutions Supervision
			Committee on Small Business
			  Subcommittee on Procurement, Tourism, and Rural Development
			  Subcommittee on S.B.A. and the General Economy and Minority Enterprise Development
			Select Committee on Narcotics Abuse and Control

Major Owens	D.-N.Y.	1983	Committee on Education and Labor
			  Chairman, Subcommittee on Select Education
			  Subcommittee on Labor-Management Relations
			Committee on Government Operations
			  Subcommittee on Government Activities and Transportation

Donald M. Payne	D.-N.J.	1988	Committee on Education and Labor
			  Subcommittee on Labor-Management Relations
			  Subcommittee on Postsecondary Education
			  Subcommittee on Select Education
			Committee on Government Operations
			  Subcommittee on Human Resources and Intergovernmental Relations
			Committee on Foreign Affairs
			  Subcommittee on Africa
			Select Committee on Narcotics Abuse and Control

Charles B. Rangel	D.-N.Y.	1971	*Chairman,* Select Committee on Narcotics Abuse and Control
			Committee on Ways and Means
			  Chairman, Subcommittee on Select Revenue Measures
			  Subcommittee on Oversight

Gus Savage	D.-Ill.	1981	Committee on Public Works and Transportation
			  Chairman, Subcom. on Public Bldgs and Grounds
			  Subcommittee on Economic Development
			  Subcommittee on Aviation
			Committee on Small Business
			  Subcommittee on S.B.A. General Economic and Minority Business Enterprise Development
			  Subcommittee on Procurement, Tourism, and Rural Development

Louis Stokes	D.-Ohio	1969	*Chairman,* Committee on Standards of Official Conduct
			Committee on Appropriations
			  Subcommittee on District of Columbia
			  Subcommittee on VA, HUD, & Independent Agencies
			  Subcommittee on Labor-Health and Human Services-Education

Table 3 (continued)

Member	Party and State	Member Since	Committee Assignments
Edolphus Towns	D.-N.Y.	1983	Committee on Government Operations 　Subcommittee on Energy and the Environment 　Subcommittee on Government Information, Justice, and Agriculture Committee on Energy and Commerce 　Subcommittee on Health and the Environment 　Subcommittee on Energy and Power 　Subcommittee on Commerce, Consumer Protection and Competitiveness Select Committee on Narcotics Abuse and Control
Craig Washington	D.-Tex.	1991	Committee on Education and Labor 　Subcommittee on Elementary, Secondary, and Vocational Education 　Subcommittee on Postsecondary Education 　Subcommittee on Labor-Management Relations Committee on the Judiciary 　Subcommittee on Civil and Constitutional Rights 　Subcommittee on Crime and Criminal Justice Select Committee on Narcotics Abuse and Control
Maxine Waters	D.-Calif.	1991	Committee on Banking 　Subcommittee on Consumer Affairs and Coinage 　Subcommittee on Housing and Community Development 　Subcommittee on General Oversight & Investigations 　Subcommittee on International Development and Finance, Trade, and Monetary Policy Committee on Veterans Affairs 　Subcommittee on Oversight and Investigations
Alan Wheat	D.-Mo.	1983	Committee on Rules Committee on District of Columbia 　*Chairman,* Subcommittee on Government Operations and Metropolitan Affairs Select Committee on Hunger Select Committee on Children, Youth and Families

of either and the government seemed indifferent to, or misguided about, many of the African continent's problems.

Black members of Congress historically have viewed their role as larger than that of district representatives, seeing themselves as representatives of the national African American population. One means for exercising that broader leadership role was through the Congressional Black Caucus (CBC), an informal organization of all black representatives established in 1971 under the leadership of Representative Diggs. While the CBC has been a means of coordinated efforts to influence decisions within the House on some issues, the most prominent such effort being the CBC's annual alternative budget proposal, it has not been a notable center of policy influence. One reason is that even without the CBC, African American representatives are an unusually cohesive group, they represent very similar constituencies, share a strong racial identity, and with the exception of Representative Frank, the sole Republican, who arrived in 1991, have all been associated with the Democratic party. Another is that the CBC has remained highly sensitive to the independence of each of its members, and so has never sought to be more than an informal means of coordinating and sharing information and ideas. Its most influential role has been as an informal link between the black electorate and Congress.

The State Legislatures

The number of African Americans serving in state legislatures increased by 274 percent between 1970 and May 1992, going from 168 to 463 (see Figure 1). The increases occurred in both houses of state legislatures and in all regions of the country. In the house the number of blacks grew from 137 to 360, and in the Senate from 31 to 103. Not surprisingly, growth has been fastest in the South, going from 32 in 1970 to 226 in 1992, an 894-percent increase. This is the region with both the largest share of the black population (53 percent) and the one that had the most extensive barriers to black political participation prior to 1970.

Black women have been especially successful in winning seats in state legislatures, and they are a steadily increasing proportion of black legislators. The first black woman legislator was Crystal Byrd Fauset, who was elected to the Pennsylvania state legislature in 1935. Very few others followed. In fact, by 1970 there were only 15 black women, or just under 10 percent of all black state legislators. However, by 1992 their numbers had increased by more than 870 percent, from 15 to 131, substantially faster than their male counterparts. Of these, 108 were in the lower houses and 23 in the

Figure 1
BLACK STATE LEGISLATORS, 1970–1992

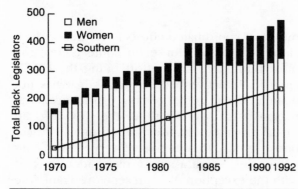

Source: The Joint Center for Political and Economic Studies

senates. Altogether, black women made up 28 percent of all black state legislators and 9.5 percent of all female legislators in 1992.

Although growth in the number of African American state legislators between 1970 and 1992 was substantial, viewed in a larger historical perspective that growth was slow and reflects the pace of the broader black struggle for full inclusion in the political system. Unlike membership in Congress, black representation in state legislatures did not begin in the South. It began 156 years ago when Alexander Lucius Twilight, the first black state legislator, was elected to the Vermont House of Representatives. Immediately after the Civil War, voters in Boston elected two blacks, Edward G. Walker and Charles L. Mitchell, to the Massachusetts House of Representatives. At this time very few blacks outside the South had the right to vote, and there were few jurisdictions where a significant number of white voters were likely to vote for black candidates.

In the immediate post–Civil War South, blacks participated extensively in the Reconstruction-era governments, and several hundred served in southern legislatures, many in leadership positions. In South Carolina a majority, 87 blacks to 40 whites were in the House of Representatives, and blacks were made up about 15 and 40 percent of the membership in several other state legislatures. Many of these black legislators had served in state constitutional conventions and a few moved into other public leadership roles before serving in the legislatures. The early post–Civil War years were turbulent ones for the southern states and state legislative performances were very uneven. There were instances of corruption and imprudent and even reckless spending. A large number of these problems later came to be attributed to the black representatives. Blacks were quickly driven from the political arena as voters and officeholders by the region's white population as the federal government withdrew its protective presence, bringing the Reconstruction era to an abrupt close. By 1902 all but a handful of blacks had been disenfranchised, and no black state legislators were serving anywhere in the South.

Blacks began a slow comeback in winning elective office outside the South during the 1920s. By 1932 a handful were serving in state legislatures in California, Illinois, Indiana, Kansas, Kentucky, New Jersey, New York, Ohio, Pennsylvania, and West Virginia. In 1946, there were thirty of these legislators in ten states. In 1964, at the height of the civil rights movement, there were just 94 black state legislators, 16 of whom were in the South. By 1970, five years after the Voting Rights Act enabled southern blacks to vote, 70 of the 198 black state legislators then served in southern legislatures. States like Alabama, Arkansas, and South Carolina had large black populations but no black legislators, while Florida, Louisiana, Mississippi, and North Carolina had one each. In 1992, the 464 black state legislators served in forty states including all the southern states. Of the ten states without black state legislators the black voting population was less than 1 percent of the total in seven. (See Tables 4 and 5.)

In 1992 the states with the highest level of black legislative representation were in the South. Georgia, with a total of 36, was first, followed by Louisiana with 32. Maryland was third with 31 members. However, Louisiana has the highest percentage of black legislators with 22 and 20 percent in the House and Senate, respectively.

Although the percentage increases in the number of black state legislators have been dramatic, those high percentages are products of the very small base from which blacks were starting. In 1992 blacks were still only about 7 percent of the approximately 7,461 state legislators in the country, and 4.8 percent of state senators, substantially below the percentage of blacks (11 percent) in the voting-age population.

FACTORS FACILITATING GROWTH IN THE NUMBER OF AFRICAN AMERICAN LEGISLATORS

The pace and pattern of growth in the number of black legislators is the product of sweeping legal, political, and demographic forces that have combined to enable blacks to overcome their exclusion from the political system and gain a degree of political influence.

The Voting Rights Act

Easily the most important of the system changes was the enactment of the Voting Rights Act of 1965 and its subsequent amendments. That act opened the voting booths of the South to the hundreds of thousands of previously excluded blacks of voting age. Not only did it remove the numerous direct and indirect obstacles to political participation by blacks, it established procedures for preventing introduction of new obstacles. Furthermore, in accomplishing these objectives the law had a powerful mobilizing effect, reflected in dramatic increases in voter-registration rates for blacks in the South following its enactment. These new black voters quickly became the basis for the election of black candidates to offices at all levels of government in the South, aided by critical amending legislation such as Title II of the 1982 amendment to the Voting Rights Act. This provision prohibited electoral arrangements in jurisdictions covered by the act when those arrangements had the "intent" or "effect" of diluting the vote of minorities. Although there have been indications that increasing numbers of white voters are willing to vote for black candidates for office, majorities of black voters have been the pillar of black electoral success in congressional and state legislative races as they have for virtually all other elective offices.

Ensuring the Effective Ballot

A second, closely related system change is the expansion of the concept of fair representation by the courts and Congress. Gradually, fair representation has come to mean not only the right to vote but the right to cast an "effective ballot." In operational terms this has meant the right to a fair opportunity to elect candidates of one's own race or ethnic group whenever population size and distribution permit.

Politicians and analysts have long recognized the relationship between electoral structure and the success of minority candidates for office. This recognition led several southern states to enact legislative districting arrangements that would prevent those blacks permitted to vote from electing candidates of their own race as early as 1868. According to historian Morgan Kousser, that practice became widespread throughout the South between 1902 and 1920. Several southern states resorted to such arrangements immediately after the Voting Rights Act of 1965 in a final effort to

Table 4

BLACK STATE LEGISLATORS IN THE LOWER CHAMBERS AND BLACK POPULATION BY STATE, 1992

State	Total Number of State Legislators	Total Number of Black Legislators	Percent Black Legislators	Percent Black Population
Alabama	140	19	18.1	22.0
Alaska	60	1	2.5	3.8
Arizona	90	4	6.7	2.4
Arkansas	135	9	9.0	12.0
California	120	7	8.8	6.0
Colorado	100	3	4.6	4.0
Connecticut	187	8	5.3	3.9
Delaware	62	2	4.9	13.8
Florida	160	12	10.0	13.0
Georgia	236	27	15.0	31.0
Hawaii	76	0	0.0	2.1
Idaho	105	0	0.0	0.1
Illinois	236	14	11.9	16.0
Indiana	150	6	6.0	9.0
Iowa	150	1	1.0	1.2
Kansas	165	3	2.4	5.0
Kentucky	138	2	2.0	5.0
Louisana	144	24	22.9	27.0
Maine	184	0	0.0	0.2
Maryland	188	24	17.0	24.0
Massachusetts	200	5	3.1	4.0
Michigan	148	12	10.9	13.0
Minnesota	201	1	0.7	1.2
Mississippi	174	21	17.2	52.2
Missouri	197	13	8.0	10.0
Montana	150	0	0.0	0.2
Nebraska	49	–	–	2.7
Nevada	60	2	4.8	4.8
New Hampshire	424	2	0.5	0.4
New Jersey	120	10	12.5	12.0
New Mexico	112	0	0.0	1.6
New York	210	17	11.3	13.0
North Carolina	170	14	11.7	21.0
North Dakota	150	0	0.0	0.4
Ohio	132	11	11.1	9.0
Oklahoma	149	3	3.0	6.0
Oregon	90	1	1.7	1.2
Pennsylvania	253	15	7.4	8.0
Rhode Island	150	7	7.0	2.4
South Carolina	170	16	12.9	26.0

Table 4 (continued)

State	Total Number of State Legislators	Total Number of Black Legislators	Percent Black Legislators	Percent Black Population
South Dakota	105	0	0.0	0.2
Tennessee	132	10	10.1	15.0
Texas	181	13	8.7	11.0
Utah	104	0	0.0	0.6
Vermont	180	2	1.3	0.3
Virginia	140	7	7.0	18.0
Virgin Islands	15	–	–	–
Washington	147	2	2.0	2.4
West Virginia	134	2	2.0	3.1
Wisconsin	132	5	5.1	5.0
Wyoming	92	0	0.0	0.0
TOTAL	7,497	347		
AVERAGE		7	6.3	8.6

Source: The author.

prevent election of blacks to public office. In his book *Black Votes Count,* veteran civil rights attorney Frank Parker vividly describes Mississippi's "massive resistance" to black electoral success following the Voting Rights Act by making widespread changes in the state's electoral structure, a strategy also used in many other southern states.

The "racial gerrymander"—the drawing of district boundaries so as to dilute potential black majorities—as well as at-large and multimember districts adopted with the same intent, have now been outlawed by the courts. In 1960 the U.S. Supreme Court outlawed the racial gerrymander in *Gomillion* v. *Lightfoot,* and 13 years later in *White* v. *Regester* it held that at-large electoral arrangements were unconstitutional when they diluted black and Latino votes. In 1980, the Supreme Court, in *Bolden* v. *City of Mobile,* ruled that multimember districts were unconstitutionally discriminatory only when it could be shown that discrimination was the "intent" of government, not merely because the action had the "effect" of discriminating. However, shortly thereafter, Section 2 of the 1982 amendment to the Voting Rights Act undid *Bolden* v. *Mobile* by prohibiting districting arrangements that had the "effect" of discriminating, whether or not intent to discriminate could be shown. In *Thornburg* v. *Gingles* (1986) the Supreme Court applied that "effect" standard in invalidating North Carolina's multimember districts. Much of

the legislative success blacks enjoyed in the 1980s and the prospects for future gains rest on successful implementation of the effective ballot principle.

Demographic Change

Demographic trends, especially when combined with the new electoral standards, have also contributed to the rapid growth in the number of black legislators. Black population growth at rates higher than that for whites, and relatively brisk migration from heavily concentrated inner-city districts to suburban ones and from rural to metropolitan areas, have increased the number of black-majority jurisdictions and with that the election of black legislators. The early redistricting decisions based on the census of 1990 illustrate the impact of population growth and migration trends. In Louisiana, one of the few southern states where state legislative elections based on the 1990 census had been held by the fall of 1991, the number of black legislators increased by 60 percent—from 18 to 32. As a result of redistricting decisions made by the spring of 1992, nearly 100 new black-majority state legislative districts were created, allowing for probably a 20-percent or more increase in the number of black state legislators nationwide. About eleven black-majority congressional districts were created as well, and these were ex-

379

Table 5
BLACK STATE LEGISLATORS IN THE UPPER CHAMBERS AND BLACK
POPULATION BY STATE, 1992

State	Total Number of State Legislators	Total Number of Black Legislators	Percent Black Legislators	Percent Black Population
Alabama	140	5	14.3	22.0
Alaska	60	0	0.0	3.8
Arizona	90	0	0.0	2.4
Arkansas	135	3	8.6	12.0
California	120	2	5.0	6.01
Colorado	100	1	2.9	4.0
Connecticut	187	3	8.3	3.9
Delaware	62	1	4.8	13.8
Florida	160	2	5.0	13.0
Georgia	236	9	16.1	31.0
Hawaii	76	0	0.0	2.1
Idaho	105	0	0.0	0.1
Illinois	236	7	11.9	16.0
Indiana	150	2	4.0	9.0
Iowa	150	0	0.0	1.2
Kansas	165	1	2.5	5.0
Kentucky	138	1	2.6	5.0
Louisana	144	8	20.5	27.0
Maine	184	0	0.0	0.2
Maryland	188	7	14.9	24.0
Massachusetts	200	1	2.5	4.0
Michigan	148	3	7.9	13.0
Minnesota	201	0	0.0	1.2
Mississippi	174	2	3.8	52.2
Missouri	197	2	5.9	10.0
Montana	150	0	0.0	0.2
Nebraska	49	1	2.0	2.7
Nevada	60	1	4.8	4.8
New Hampshire	424	0	0.0	0.4
New Jersey	120	2	5.0	12.0
New Mexico	112	0	0.0	1.6
New York	210	5	8.2	13.0
North Carolina	170	5	10.0	21.0
North Dakota	150	0	0.0	0.4
Ohio	132	2	6.1	9.0
Oklahoma	149	2	4.2	6.0
Oregon	90	2	6.7	1.2
Pennsylvania	253	3	6.0	8.0
Rhode Island	150	1	2.0	2.4
South Carolina	170	6	13.0	26.0

Table 5 (continued)

State	Total Number of State Legislators	Total Number of Black Legislators	Percent Black Legislators	Percent Black Population
South Dakota	105	0	0.0	0.2
Tennessee	132	3	9.1	15.0
Texas	181	2	6.5	11.0
Utah	104	0	0.0	0.6
Vermont	180	0	0.0	0.3
Virginia	140	5	12.5	18.0
Virgin Islands	15	–	–	–
Washington	147	0	0.0	2.4
West Virginia	134	0	0.0	3.1
Wisconsin	132	1	3.0	5.0
Wyoming	92	1	3.3	0.6
TOTAL	7,497	102		
AVERAGE		2	4.9	8.6

Source: The author.

pected to boost black representation to about 36 in 1993, a dramatic increase. This level of change far exceeds what would have resulted from routine demographic change alone. In large measure the 1990s redistricting provided the first opportunity to implement the spirit and letter of the antivote dilution standards that evolved during the 1980s.

Black Political Influence

The substantial gains achieved in the number of black legislators was due in part to the growing influence of black legislators in the redistricting process and to the growing experience of black activists with redistricting and other electoral matters. In his 1982 article "Racial Gerrymandering: Its Potential Impact on Black Politics in the 1980s," John O'Loughlin suggested that the best strategy for blacks in the reapportionment process "is to attempt to gain representation on the election and reapportionment committees of the legislature." A decade later, blacks seemed to have well followed that advice. Of the 464 black state legislators in 1992, 80 served on legislative committees dealing with election and redistricting matters in twenty states, and two blacks chair such committees, according to a study by the Joint Center for Political and Economic Studies.

During the early 1990s, several black legislators had even greater opportunities to influence redistricting decisions from other leadership positions within legislatures, in state governments, and in the Democratic party. In the 1990s, for example, black state house speakers Willie L. Brown Jr., of California and Daniel Blue of North Carolina reportedly played key roles in shaping the redistricting decisions of their states. In Virginia, Democratic governor L. Douglas Wilder used his position to obtain a more generous outcome for blacks from the states' redistricting decisions than was initially provided by the legislature with the creation of several new black-majority state legislative districts and a congressional district. In addition, other public officials, as well as civil rights and civic leaders, became attentive to, and knowledgeable about, the redistricting process and seek by participating in the process to create maximum electoral opportunities for blacks. One may then expect that as black political influence increases, so will the number of legislative districts conducive to the election of black representatives.

IMPACT OF THE INCREASE IN BLACK LEGISLATORS

A persistent question by black political analysts and political advocates has been: What difference does electoral success make for the African American population? The assumption that

381

election of African Americans to public office would confer tangible benefits to the African American community has been a major motivation in the struggle for political rights. However, identifying and measuring the impact of black elected officials on policy decisions affecting the African American community has been difficult. Although there is only a modest body of literature and little empirical evidence of this impact, there has been a strong consensus among analysts that winning elective office is important in at least three respects: as a symbol of inclusion, as a form of leadership recruitment, and as a means of influencing group-relevant policy. Black legislators reflect all of these benefits.

The Symbolic Value

Growth in the number of black legislators, as of all elected officials, is of critical symbolic importance to African Americans. Such gains are among the clearest, strongest indicators of the progress African Americans have made in moving from a marginal status in the political system to the political mainstream. Political exclusion was both a reflection and a means of black subordination historically. Depriving blacks of the right to vote was an attempt to affirm their inferior, and second-class, status, and it simultaneously denied them the principal instrument for changing their status. Every gain in political participation, therefore, reaffirms their status as fully vested members of society. For African Americans that reaffirmation is especially great in view of their unique history of bondage and subordination and the extent to which the struggle against these conditions centered on the political arena. Because the treatment of blacks and their access to the political system has varied from state to state, state legislative success is a distinctly important symbol of progress locally.

Inclusion of blacks in mainstream politics and governance has symbolic value for the political system as well. It affirms the continuing expansion of the democratic process to reflect racial, ethnic, and gender diversity. The changes brought about in response to black efforts at inclusion have been extended gradually to other minorities and to women. Another dimension of the symbolic value of black state legislators is linked to the concept of "descriptive representation" suggested in 1967 by Hanna Piktin. This concept views representation in terms of the characteristics of the representatives in relation to the represented. The presence of black legislators in some measure of reasonable proportion to their numbers in the population symbolizes their adequate representation. To a great extent, the law and politics of minority representation reflected in the Voting Rights Act, court decisions supporting an "effective vote," and redistricting decisions are all based on accomplishing this symbolic, descriptive representation.

By virtually all statistical measures, in the early 1990s, African Americans continued to be underrepresented in Congress and the state legislatures when viewed in descriptive terms. Nationally and in most states blacks were a smaller percentage of the population of state legislators than they were in the population. Yet, that situation was clearly improving rapidly.

Leadership Recruitment Value

State legislatures are important arenas for leadership recruitment and development; this is especially true for black politicians. A substantial number of blacks have moved from state legislative seats to higher public office. In a 1992 study in *Black State Legislators* by David Bositis of the Joint Center for Political and Economic Studies, it is noted that among the black legislators serving in 1970 were such later nationally prominent politicians as Harold Washington, the late mayor of Chicago; Ernest Morial, the late mayor of New Orleans; Coleman Young, mayor of Detroit; U.S. Representative Barbara Jordan, (Ret.); U.S. Representative Charles Rangel (D.-N.Y.); and L. Douglas Wilder, who later became governor of Virginia. For these individuals, as for scores of others, the state legislature was an important stepping-stone to higher office within the state or at the national level. Viewed in this way, the increasing number of black state legislators holds out the prospect of a growing pool of experienced politicians from which future political leaders will emerge.

Just as important as the movement of black state legislators into higher office has been their upward mobility within the legislatures. Even among the handful of black state legislators elected prior to 1964, several attained important leadership positions. One example is state representative K. Leroy Irvis who became speaker of the Pennsylvania House of Representatives in May 1975, having first been elected in 1958 and holding a number of other leadership roles. Irvis was elected speaker again in 1985. Nearly half of the population of the black state legislators, 228 (out of a total of 464), are committee or subcommittee chairs; two are state senate majority leaders—Senators Clarence Blount (D.-Md.) and J. B. Banks, (D.-Miss.); two are house speakers—Willie L. Brown, Jr. of California and Daniel Blue, (D.-N.C.). There have been also three majority whips and one minority whip.

This upward mobility by black state legislators is partly a result of their relatively high longevity having once been elected. Black officials, once elected, are much more likely than their white counterparts to be reelected. A 1982 study by John O'Loughlin, a review of 1,236 elections involving blacks, reveals that "non-contests (no challengers) increased in frequency over time as the method of electing black legislators." Anecdotal evidence also suggests that turnovers are much lower in districts represented by black legislators than their white counterparts.

Partisanship has been also a significant factor in the accession of blacks to leadership roles. All but one black member of Congress has been associated with the Democratic party and thus has benefitted from the party's majority status in Congress. All but four of the 464 black state legislators are Democrats, and in twenty-nine states, both chambers of the legislatures have had Democratic majorities. This means that blacks have much greater opportunities to obtain leadership posts because of their attachment to the Democratic party.

While the leadership recruitment benefit is viewed almost entirely in the context of the political system, its impact goes well beyond that arena. Elective office has become one of the principal channels through which leadership of the African American community emerges. Indeed, as the civil rights movement accomplishes its main mission and the principal institutions and leaders disappear, political leaders appear to be the new leadership cadre.

Policy Influence

In Congress, African Americans have been about as influential as any small group of members can be acting individually or as a group. They have used widely differing bases to exert influence in specific areas in addition to their routine activities. As the chairmen of major committees some individual members, such as Adam Clayton Powell and Gus Hawkins, have made substantial contributions to broad areas of domestic public policy. Others, such as Charles Diggs, used the chairmanship of the relatively minor Africa subcommittee to publicize shortcomings of U.S. policies in Africa and to press for changes. Parren Mitchell used the chairmanship of the Committee on Small Business to lead efforts on behalf of minority businesses through various programs that have been set aside. Others influential African Americans on key subcommittees have been equally effective. For example, Congressman William Gray obtained passage of legislation requiring the Agency for International Development (AID) to obtain minority business participation in its contracts.

As a group, black members of Congress have sought to be influential through the congressional Black Caucus. There is no clear evidence of influence beyond routine advocacy and/or a contact point for the interested black public, but as a vehicle for articulating positions held by all African American members of Congress it almost certainly strengthens their voice on selected issues.

At the state level there have been some indications of significant and growing influence. During the 1980s blacks gained strength in state legislatures at a time when those legislatures appeared to have a growing role in governance, especially in providing those benefits directly related to quality of life such as health care, education, and welfare assistance. For more than two decades, Republican presidents have advocated a "new federalism" in which the role of state and local governments would increase and that of the federal government would decrease in domestic affairs. Although President Richard Nixon initially adopted this as a major objective, it was under President Ronald Reagan that major steps were taken to shift programs and responsibilities to states and localities. President Nixon inaugurated a program of block grants (unrestricted federal grants) to states and localities, and President Ronald Reagan advanced that approach starting with the Omnibus Budget Reconciliation Act of 1981.

With this emphasis on devolution, state governments had to assume larger roles in planning, financing, and implementing a variety of major domestic policies. Advocacy of such devolution of responsibilities to states rested mostly on ideological grounds as conservatives saw this process as a means of reducing the size and role of the federal government. However, devolution occurred mainly because of a sharp decline in presidential leadership on domestic policy issues and severe fiscal constraints on the federal government. States were forced to fill both the leadership and financial shortfall. It is noteworthy that liberals, including most blacks, had been advocates of a strong federal role in domestic policy and in empowering local governments and community-based organizations as participants in social policy areas. They were skeptical of state governments, particularly about their capacity to equitably implement social policies vital to minorities and central cities. Thus, the Reagan administration's state-oriented devolution, first seen as a threat to black interests, might have provided opportunities for significant black influence through their growing cadre of representatives.

One of the few studies seeking to ascertain the extent to which state legislatures actually respond to African Americans was conducted in 1988 by Mary Herring. Her study of roll-call voting in Alabama, Georgia, and Louisiana focused on three broad categories of issues: redistributive, civil rights and liberties, and race-specific issues. She found that black voting strength had a significant positive effect on the decisions of state legislators. However, she found also that the presence of black legislators substantially influenced the level of responsiveness to black interests over and above any other impact of their vote. She concluded, therefore, that "to a large extent, responsiveness to black interests is dependent on the election of a black to office." In short, while the behavior of white legislators will be influenced somewhat by the presence of large numbers of black voters in their districts, that influence is substantially greater when elected black officials are also present.

Frank Parker's 1990 study of the effects of black votes on Mississippi politics also underscores the considerable difference in influence that resulted from the arrival of black members in the state legislature. He noted that there is a consensus among Black Caucus members of the Mississippi legislature and veteran white legislators that when black members are in agreement on an issue and vote as a bloc they can determine the fate of major legislation. Parker also observed that "the black members of the Mississippi legislature have made the legislature more responsive to black needs in the enactment of legislation for educational reform, establishment of state-financed kindergartens, improvement in state education financing, salary increases for schoolteachers, improvements in health care under medicaid, and defeating a state sales tax." Finally, he notes that black legislators have been especially influential in blocking actions likely to be injurious to blacks.

It is likely that the kind and level of influence that black state legislators in the South have demonstrated has been experienced by their colleagues elsewhere in the country. Furthermore, that influence will grow as the number of black legislators increases. Yet, there are troubling questions about the efficacy of race-based districting as a means of long-term growth in influence, and about the limits of descriptive representation.

Some analysts have expressed concern that reliance on the creation of black-majority districts as a base for future increases in black legislators might result in a net diminution in black political influence. This might occur because the approach encourages the clustering of black voters into a few districts, thus removing them from other districts where their presence would be substantial and their influence on representatives could be strong and vital. This issue has arisen with particular force where districting to achieve a black-majority district has resulted in advantages for the opposition party or for candidates likely to oppose the interests of blacks. No systematic study has yet been done about the costs of this strategy for black interests, but that will probably change in light of post-1990 redistricting.

Another source of concern is that emphasis on the creation of black-majority districts will inevitably impose a low ceiling on the number or proportion of legislative seats held by African Americans. Demographic realities have been that since blacks constitute about 11 percent of the voting-age population, spread unevenly across states and nation, the number of opportunities for more black-majority districts have been very limited. Strategies that emphasize biracial or multiracial alliances are likely to hold out increased opportunity for future growth and for greater influence on policy decisions. Such alliances have begun to appear in some situations but most certainly will require

significant changes in the style and issue content of black politics. The legislative arena offers a particularly attractive opportunity to African Americans for this next step in establishing themselves in the political mainstream.

BIBLIOGRAPHY

There are relatively few book-length sources for information on African American legislators. Most of the material on the topic may be found in professional journals and news articles.

The Office of the Historian of the U.S. House of Representatives has updated its pictorial compilation of African American Members of the U.S. Congress in BRUCE A. RAGSDALE and JOEL D. TREESE, *Black Americans in Congress, 1870–1989* (Washington, D.C., 1990).

The historical role of the Reconstruction-era African American Members of Congress may be explored in JOHN HOSMER and JOSEPH FINEMAN, "Black Congressmen in Reconstruction Historiography," *Phylon* XXXIX (June 1978): 97–107.

Studies on Congressional Black Caucus
Research on the Congressional Black Caucus in the U.S. House of Representatives has been extensive. Among the studies of the caucus are MARGUERITE ROSS BARNETT, "The Congressional Black Caucus," in HARVEY C. MANSFIELD, ed., *Congress Against the President,* (New York, 1975): 34–50; MARGUERITE ROSS BARNETT, "The Congressional Black Caucus and the Institutionalization of Black Politics," *Journal of Afro-American Issues* V (Summer 1977): 201–227; CHARLES P. HENRY, "Legitimizing Race in Congressional Politics," *American Politics Quarterly* V (April 1977): 149–176; JAKE C. MILLER, "Black Legislators and African-American Relations, 1970–1975," *Journal of Black Studies* X (December 1979): 245–261; ARTHUR B. LEVY and SUSAN STOUDINGER, "Sources of Voting Cues for the Congressional Black Caucus," *Journal of Black Studies* VII (September 1976): 29–46; and CHARLES E. JONES, "Testing a Legislative Strategy: The Congressional Black Caucus's Action-Alert Communications Network," *Legislative Studies Quarterly* XII (November 1987): 521–536.

Policy Studies
Policy linkages are explored in MICHAEL B. PRESTON, "Black Elected Officials and Public Policy: Symbolic or Substantive Representation?" *Policy Studies Journal* VII (Winter 1978): 196–201; and MARIETA L. HARPER, "Black Women and the Development of Black Politics," *Journal of Afro-American Issues* V (Summer 1977): 276–284.

State Legislature Studies
The legal and political aspects of African American representation issues in state legislatures are addressed in *Minority Vote Dilution,* CHANDLER DAVIDSON (Washington, D.C., 1984); PAUL W. JACOBS II and TIMOTHY G. O'ROURKE, "Racial Polarization in Vote Dilution Cases Under Section 2 of the Voting Rights Act: The Impact of *Thornburg* v. *Gingles*," *Journal of Law and Politics* III (Fall 1986): 295–353; BERNARD GROFMAN, MICHAEL MIGALSKI, and NICHOLAS NOVIELLO, "Effects of Multimember Districts on Black Representation in State Legislatures," *Review of Black Political Economy* XIV (Spring 1986): 65–78; ROBERT A. HOLMES, "Reapportionment Politics in Georgia: A Case Study," *Phylon* XLV (September 1984): 179–187; LEE SIGELMAN and ALBERT K. KARNIG, "Black Representation in the American States: A Comparison of Bureaucracies and Legislatures," *American Politics Quarterly* IV (April 1976): 237–246; JOHN O'LOUGHLIN, "Black Representation Growth and the Seat-Vote Relationship," *Social Science Quarterly* LX (June 1979): 72–86; BERNARD GROFMAN and LISA HANDLEY, "Black Representation: Making Sense of Electoral Geography at

Different Levels of Government," *Legislative Studies Quarterly* XIV (May 1989): 265–279; PAMELA S. KARLAN, "Maps and Misreadings: The Role of Geographical Compactness in Racial Vote Dilution Legislation," *Harvard Civil Rights–Civil Liberties Law Review* XXIV (Winter 1989): 173–248; and C. ROBERT HEATH, "Managing the Political Thicket: Developing Objective Standards in Voting Rights Litigation," *Stetson Law Review* XXI, (Summer 1992): 819–846.

State legislative voting behavior for African Americans is explored in GARY MONCRIEF, JOEL THOMPSON, and ROBERT SCHUMANN, "Gender, Race, and the State Legislature: A Research Note on the Double Disadvantage Hypothesis," *Social Science Journal* XXVIII (1991): 481–487; MARY HERRING, "Legislative Responsiveness to Black Constituencies in Three Deep South States," *Journal of Politics* LII (August 1990): 740–758; and FRANK PARKER, *Black Votes Count* (Chapel Hill, N.C., 1990). State legislative black caucuses have received less attention from journalists and academics, but see CHARLES W. DUNN's study of Illinois, "Black Caucuses and Political Machines in Legislative Bodies," *American Journal of Political Science* XVII (February 1973): 148–158. See also AMY PLUMER's report on the New York Assembly, "The Pains of Growing Minority Power: Black and Puerto Rican Caucus," *Empire State Report* I (June 1975): 207–209 and 229–233; and CHERYL M. MILLER's study of North Carolina, "Agenda-Setting by State Legislative Black Caucuses: Policy Priorities and Factors of Success," *Policy Studies Review* IX (Winter 1990): 330–354.

The most extensive enumeration of black state legislators and the positions they occupy is DAVID BOSITIS, *Black State Legislators* (Washington, D.C., 1992).

LEGISLATIVE REDISTRICTING

Bruce Edward Cain

Most American legislators are elected in geographically defined, equally populated districts. The exceptions, however, are significant. U.S. senators, for instance, are elected from unequally populated states, and seven small states—Alaska, Delaware, Montana, North Dakota, South Dakota, Vermont, and Wyoming—will elect a single, at-large member of Congress during the 1990s. Also, in many local governments and special districts, members are selected on an at-large basis, although this practice has increasingly been challenged in areas with large numbers of racial and ethnic minorities.

The legal requirement that districts at all levels—federal, state, and local—must be equally populated (except for the U.S. Senate) forces the periodic adjustment of their geographical boundaries. At the beginning of every decade, the United States conducts its census, and when that task is completed, the populations of legislative districts at each level are recalculated. The subsequent adjustment of the old district lines to achieve the new ideal populations is the essence of redistricting, or as it is sometimes called, reapportionment.

For Congress, the process occurs in two stages. In the first stage, apportionment, the Census Bureau calculates the allocation of congressional districts to each state based upon a priority formula invented by Harvard professor Edward Huntingdon. In the second stage, redistricting, the congressional boundaries within each state's border are adjusted to achieve near equality in district populations. It is important to realize that this procedure makes congressional-district populations equal within states but unequal across states. In 1980, Nevada, with its population of 787,000, and Maine, with 1,125,000, were each apportioned two seats, while South Dakota, with 690,000, was assigned only one, producing very unequal district sizes. Congressional districts in Maine

had an ideal population (that is, if each district within a state has the same population) of 563,000, while Nevada's had 393,000 and South Dakota's had 690,000.

In contrast to the case of the U.S. House of Representatives, the redrawing of state and local government districts has only the redistricting stage—no reapportionment is involved. When states and local jurisdictions receive their new population figures, they have all the information they need from the federal government to do their task. The redrawing of state and local district boundaries is also sometimes referred to as reapportionment, even though, strictly speaking, there is no apportionment phase at the state and local levels. While some experts dislike the fact that the terms *redistricting* and *reapportionment* are popularly regarded as synonymous, this equivalence can be justified in a very important sense: the process of adjusting district boundaries at least implicitly reallocates, or reapportions, political representation over the various areas and interests in a state or local jurisdiction. The term *reapportionment* reminds us that however technical and arcane boundary adjustments may seem, they are in their effects, if not always in their procedures, profoundly political acts.

MALAPPORTIONMENT AND EQUAL POPULATION

The principle of equal population has always applied to congressional districts. The authority for the apportionment of congressional districts resides in Article I, Section 2, of the Constitution, which provides that "Representatives . . . shall be apportioned among the several States . . . according to their respective numbers." Until 1910, Congress expanded its membership to accommodate new states and population increases. Since then the House membership has been frozen at 435. Initially there was one seat for each 33,000 of population. By 1990 the ratio was, on average, one seat per 570,000 of population.

Since 1790 there has been considerable controversy over, and five changes in, the method by which congressional seats are allocated to the states. All of these methods have produced roughly similar and proportionate outcomes. But to a small degree, each formula treats a few states differently, and therein lies the political controversy. The Huntingdon formula, which has been used since 1950, has for the most part reduced objections to a minimum, although critics maintain that it favors small states over large ones.

There have been some spectacular swings in the sizes of state delegations. New York had ten seats in 1790, forty in 1830, thirty-one in 1860, forty-five in 1930, and thirty-one in 1990. California, by contrast, has grown steadily from eleven seats in 1910 to fifty-two seats in 1990. The original thirteen states have gone from constituting 100 percent of Congress in 1790 to comprising 42 percent in 1870 and 33 percent in 1990. Between 1949 and 1992, almost sixty seats shifted from the Frostbelt states to the Sunbelt.

Even prior to the "one person, one vote" decisions of *Baker* v. *Carr*, 369 U.S. 186 (1962), and *Reynolds* v. *Sims*, 377 U.S. 533 (1964), Congress on several occasions made clear its adherence to the equal-population redistricting principle. In 1842 it passed legislation stating that representatives should be "elected by districts of contiguous territory equal in number," with "no district electing more than one representative." The Reapportionment Act of 1872 declared that districts should contain "as nearly as possible an equal number of inhabitants." The mandate for congressional districts derives from an explicit constitutional provision, and the apportionment every ten years of congressional seats among states inevitably forces changes in congressional-district boundaries within states; therefore congressional malapportionment prior to the legal revolution of the 1960s was relatively moderate. In 1960 all but 40 of the 435 congressional districts had populations within 15 percent of the national average.

By comparison malapportionment was at that time a more serious problem at the state legislative and local government level. There were really two kinds of malapportionment. The first was constitutionally sanctioned and deliberate. The compromises necessary for the formation of certain boundaries between states led to negotiated understandings about the relative power of rural as opposed to urban areas; these were perpetuated by constitutional arrangements that exempted some state upper houses from equal-population requirements or that made counties the basic building blocks of redistricting.

But a great deal of malapportionment at the state level was caused by the unwillingness of state legislatures to follow the provisions of their own state constitutions. Alabama, Tennessee, and Delaware did not alter the boundaries of their state legislative districts during the first sixty years of the twentieth century, and nine other states made no changes between 1930 and 1960. In the state legislatures of Vermont, Connecticut, New Hampshire, and Georgia, certain state districts contained one hundred times the population of others.

Prior to 1962 the Supreme Court repeatedly refused to tackle the problem of malapportionment. In *Wood* v. *Brown*, 287 U.S. 1,8 (1932), the Supreme Court decided not to overturn a Mississippi law that created unequal congressional districts. In 1946 the Court was given another chance to intervene when a Professor Colgrove of Northwestern University brought suit against the state of Illinois, arguing that the gross disparities in district populations violated the equal-protection clause of the Fourteenth Amendment. As before, the Court refused by a four to three vote to take up the case of *Colgrove* v. *Green*, 328 U.S. 549 (1946), because the issue was, in Justice Felix Frankfurter's words, "of a peculiarly political nature and therefore not meant for judicial interpretation."

The Court's approach changed dramatically with its ruling in *Baker*. The plaintiffs had argued that the malapportionment of the Tennessee state assembly violated both the state and federal constitutions. The Supreme Court, by a vote of six to two, decided that it had jurisdiction, despite Justice Frankfurter's objection that the decision would "catapult the Courts into a mathematical quagmire." In *Wesberry* v. *Sanders*, 376 U.S. 1 (1964), and *Reynolds*, the Court applied its "one person, one vote" principle to congressional and state legislative districts, respectively. This principle holds that a person's right to vote is not equal if people vote in unequally sized districts. A vote in a large district, the Court reasoned, has less value than a vote in a small district, because the weight of a vote varies inversely with the electorate's size.

Given that an equally weighted vote was the ideal, the critical question was how close to exact equality did the new district populations have to be in order to meet the Court's expectations? In the case of the Congress, the Court ruled that "as nearly as practicable," one person's vote should be worth as much as another's, and in *Kirkpatrick* v. *Priesler*, 394 U.S. 526 (1969), it held that states should make a good-faith effort to achieve exact mathematical equality.

The threat that the Court might strike down a legislature's congressional-redistricting plan if one with smaller deviations was possible was realized in *White* v. *Weiser*, 412 U.S. 783 (1973), a case involving Texas congressional districts. The Court rejected a plan with population deviations from exact equality of less than 5 percent in favor of a plan with a total maximum variation—the proportion by which the largest district's population exceeds that of the smallest—of only .149. A decade later the Court in effect made the equal population requirement even stricter when, in *Karcher* v. *Daggett*, 426 U.S. 725 (1983), it turned down a New Jersey congressional plan with trivial population differences (.69 percent) among districts in favor of a plan with even smaller deviations. Simply stated, the Court's standard of population equality for congressional redistricting has become extremely exact and inflexible.

In contrast the Court's population standard for state legislatures has been somewhat looser and more flexible. The initial state malapportionment cases dealt with very substantial population inequalities. For instance, in *Reynolds*, the range in the district populations was sixteen to one for the Alabama state house and forty-one to one for the state senate. But after striking down the gross disparities of malapportioned districts in the 1960s, the courts seemed to settle on an informal standard of 10 percent deviation from exact equality, as in *Gaffney* v. *Cummings*, 412 U.S. 735 (1973). In a few cases, the Court has even shown a willingness to allow deviations above 10 percent where they serve legitimate state purposes. In *Mahan* v. *Howell*, 410 U.S. 315 (1973), for example, the Court upheld a redistricting plan for the Virginia state legislature that produced population deviations of 16 percent in order to allow the district lines to follow local political subdivision boundaries more closely. In *Brown* v. *Thomson*, 426 U.S. 835 (1983), the Court permitted a plan with population deviations close to 90 percent for similar reasons.

VOTE DILUTION AND THE EVOLVING CONCEPT OF EQUITY

The essential concept behind the "one person, one vote" decisions was that every eligible voter had the right to an equally weighted vote. When districts are unequally sized, the logic goes, people voting in the larger districts have less voice in and influence over the outcome of an election than do those in smaller districts. In addition, malapportionment gives more representation to some areas of a political jurisdiction than other areas.

With the passage of the Voting Rights Act of 1965 and the growing clamor over political gerrymandering (the manipulation of district boundaries for political gain), the Court was forced to consider an additional right beyond the equal right to the vote or the right to an equally weighted vote—namely, the right to a meaningful or undiluted vote. The logic of a vote-dilution claim is as follows: even if an individual has an equal right to an equally weighted vote, that right is diminished if the district lines are drawn in such a manner as to dilute the votes of a group to which that individual belongs and enhance the votes of another group. The Supreme Court has examined two types of vote-dilution claims—political and racial or ethnic.

Political Vote Dilution

In the first type, involving political gerrymandering, the plaintiffs claim that districting arrangements unfairly favor a particular political party over another (the so-called partisan gerrymander, usually benefiting the majority over the minority party) or favor incumbents over challengers (the so-called bipartisan-gerry-mander problem). To date the Court has been extremely cautious in its treatment of partisan gerrymandering cases. Until its ruling in *Davis* v. *Bandemer*, 478 U.S. 109 (1986), for instance, there was no clear indication that partisan ger-rymandering was even a justiciable issue, or an issue within the courts' purview. The Court hinted at its disapproval of partisan districting plans in *Kirkpatrick* and *Karcher* but did not explicitly rule that a partisan-gerrymandering claim based on the equal-protection clause was justiciable until 1986.

In considering the allegation by Indiana's Democrats in *Davis* that the Republican-controlled legislature diluted their voting strength and caused disproportionate gains for Republican candidates, the Supreme Court ruled six to three that a political-gerry-mandering claim was justiciable. However the Court at the same time cast considerable doubt on whether this would have any practical sig-nificance by overruling the lower court's deci-sion to strike down the Indiana legislature's plan. It is possible that a partisan-gerry-mandering claim will only be won by political parties that can show they have suffered exclu-sion and discrimination comparable to that ex-perienced by racial minorities, which virtually rules out the two major political parties, the Democrats and Republicans.

At the end of the decade, the Supreme Court further indicated its intention to require a high level of discrimination before acting in political-gerrymandering cases when it af-firmed a lower court ruling in *Badham* v. *Eu*, 109 U.S. 829 (1989). The Court refused to over-turn the infamous Burton congressional redis-tricting plan, holding that Republicans had many avenues of political redress (including the initiative and referendum process) and could not be said to be in a position of politi-cal exclusion, since they had held a number of statewide offices throughout the 1980s.

Another form of political gerrymandering is the so-called bipartisan, or incumbent-protection, gerrymander. The courts have taken a more benign view of explicitly bipartisan than of partisan plans. In *Burns* v. *Richardson*, 384 U.S. 73 at 88 (1966), and *White*, the Court held that drawing lines to minimize contests between sitting incumbents does not in and

of itself establish "individiousness." And in *Gaffney* the Court upheld a purposely political plan that attempted to create proportionate shares of districts for the two political parties based on voting results in the previous three elections. With the growing clamor over the in-cumbency advantage, the Court may find it harder to bless bipartisan gerrymanders in the future.

Racial and Ethnic Fairness

The other type of vote-dilution case centers on racial and ethnic groups in the electorate. The critical legislation in this regard is the Voting Rights Act (VRA) of 1965 and its subsequent amendments. Although most VRA litigation consists of challenges to the use of multi-member districts, sections 2 and 5 of the act also apply to the arrangements of constituency boundaries in single-member district jurisdic-tions. Areas of the country that are covered by Section 5 of the VRA must preclear any changes in district boundaries with the Justice Department or the District of Columbia District Court. The critical issue in preclearance is whether the proposed changes cause a de-crease in the voting power of minorities in areas with a history of vote discrimination and low voting participation.

Areas that are not covered by Section 5 still must meet the standards of Section 2, which states that "No voting qualification or prere-quisite to voting, or standard, practice, or pro-cedure shall be imposed or applied by any State or political sub-division to deny or abridge the right of any citizen of the United States to vote on account of race or color." Sec-tion 2 was interpreted in *Mobile* v. *Bolden*, 446 U.S. 55 (1980), to apply only to districting ar-rangements that intentionally diluted the votes of disadvantaged minorities. The VRA was amended in 1982 so that any plans that had the effect of diluting minority votes, whatever the intention, were in violation of the VRA. In *Thornburg* v. *Gingles*, 478 U.S. 30 (1986), a case involving state legislative districts in North Carolina, the Court singled out three criteria as the most important in deciding whether a juris-diction has complied with the provisions of the Voting Rights Act: Is a minority group suffi-ciently large and compact to constitute a majority of a district? Is it politically cohesive? Is there evidence of racially polarized voting against candidates from its community?

At a minimum, the protection afforded by the VRA prevents the exclusion of groups from opportunities to elect representatives of their own choice. However, a number of critics maintain that the VRA is being interpreted more expansively by some plaintiffs as a right to proportional representation, a right that the Supreme Court has on several occasions explicitly denied.

More generally, the right to an undiluted vote is problematic in a system that employs single-member, simple plurality (SMSP) rules. The logic of such a system is that it exaggerates the share of seats won by the party with the most votes and minimizes the share the others parties win. This outcome is touted by SMSP proponents as an advantage over that of proportional-representation systems, because it eases the task of creating a governing majority in the legislature. If the right to an undiluted vote is interpreted to mean anything more than the right to nonexclusion, it puts the courts in the uncomfortable position of enforcing remedies for a right—proportional representation for racial or political groups—that it explicitly denies.

COMMON CRITERIA FOR REDISTRICTING

There are two broad types of criteria that are commonly applied when assessing the quality and fairness of a redistricting. The first involves considerations of form and the second of outcome.

Formal Criteria

The most important of the considerations of form are equal population, natural communities of interest, compactness, and contiguity. Equal population has already been discussed. It is sometimes referred to as one of the primary criteria, meaning that considerations of population equality must be satisfied absolutely even if they conflict with other considerations of fairness.

By comparison, respect for natural communities of interest is not one of the primary criteria. In the broadest sense, this term encompasses many types of entity, including agricultural areas, mountainous counties, desert regions, coastal land, and the like. The political interests associated with these geographical areas may be occupational (e.g., farming), sociological (e.g., areas within one media market), or policy-oriented (e.g., the predilection of coastal areas for environmentalism). The assumption is that district boundaries should respect these natural community boundaries so that important socioeconomic interests are clearly articulated within the representative body. Opponents of a community-of-interest approach worry that districts so drawn encourage parochialism and factionalism.

A variant of the communities-of-interest criterion is respect for city, county, and local government boundaries. Prior to the "one person, one vote" decisions, several states required that state legislative districts follow county boundary lines exactly. The equal-population standard now requires that district boundaries stray from local-government jurisdictions when necessary to achieve the target population figure. Assuming the satisfaction of the "one man, one vote" principle, a number of states mandate that districting arrangements minimize the splitting of city and county boundary lines to the degree feasible.

The last of the formal criteria are contiguity and compactness. Contiguity means that all parts of the district must be connected at a point, or in other words, that a district cannot consist of unconnected tracts or "islands" surrounded by tracts from another district. However, contiguity can sometimes be at a point in the water, as when offshore islands are grouped with an onshore district. Contiguity, rarely violated, is a primary criterion.

By contrast, compactness is not a primary criterion and is often violated. Compactness can be measured in a variety of technical ways, but the essential notion behind any compactness measure is that districts should have relatively geometrical shapes, without many branches, dips, or jagged edges. At a minimum, compactness is thought to be a virtue because it constrains attempts to gerrymander by means of contorted shapes drawn to favor one particular party, group, or candidate over another. But some proponents of compactness also believe that it protects political interests stemming from geographic propinquity. In reality, however, districts are often noncompact, sometimes because this serves particular political interests, but frequently because compactness conflicts with other redistricting guidelines, such as protecting communities of interest or complying with the Voting Rights Act.

Outcome Criteria

In sum, the so-called formal criteria—population equality, natural communities of interest, compactness, and contiguity—focus on the size, shape, and geography of ideal districts, but not on their desired political and ethnic makeup. These latter considerations are covered by outcome criteria such as fairness among political parties, fairness to racial and ethnic groups, and competitive districts.

Political Fairness   At a minimum, fairness among parties means that the party receiving a majority of the votes should also receive a majority of the seats. With the elimination of gross malapportionment, this majoritarian condition is rarely violated by even the most outrageous partisan gerrymanders. More often, what people mean by partisan fairness is something beyond the violation of the majority principle—namely, that a party's share of seats should match its share of votes as closely as possible, a condition of at least rough proportionality.

There are a number of problems with this standard. To begin with, single-member, simple-plurality district systems do not yield proportional outcomes in most situations. One of the characteristic features of SMSP systems is that on average they enhance the seat share of the majority party and diminish the seat share of minority parties. So even if a redistricting plan is free of any attempt to gerrymander for partisan advantage, it will likely lead to nonproportional seat-vote allocations. Furthermore, the Court and Congress have explicitly acknowledged that there is no right per se to proportional representation; as a result, popular expectations of fairness and legal requirements are at odds with each other. Finally, the best way to achieve proportional outcomes would

be to abandon the existing system of single-member districts for some form of proportional or semiproportional rules. But while there is evidence of a limited degree of experimentation with such systems in certain southern jurisdictions under the threat of Voting Rights Act litigation, there has historically been little enthusiasm in the United States for European electoral systems based on proportional rules.

In response to this dilemma, political scientists have tried to develop alternative ways of measuring fairness in single-member systems. For instance, some contend that fairness really consists of symmetry among parties. This means that if party A gets a given share of the seats for a given share of the votes, then party B in a symmetric system would get an identical share of seats for that same share of votes. In other words a fair system treats the parties in the same way, even if it does not yield proportional outcomes. This notion of partisan fairness is conceptually much closer to the spirit of single-member, simple-plurality systems than is proportional representation. Unfortunately it is difficult to implement, since it requires knowledge of counterfactual conditions—namely, what share of seats a party would have received had it won a different share of the votes.

Racial and Ethnic Fairness   The idea that redistricting should be fair to all or to as many political parties as possible seems intuitively appealing. Unfortunately it is hard to implement partisan fairness in the American electoral system. The same difficulty underlies the concept of racial and ethnic fairness. As with partisan fairness, there are two approaches. At a minimum, racial fairness means that significantly sized minority groups should not be excluded from representation in the political system. A stronger and more widely held version of racial and ethnic fairness is that there should be rough proportionality between population strength and a group's share of elected officials—in short, proportional descriptive representation.

The critical factors for the electoral success of racial and ethnic groups under a single-member, simple-plurality system are that they must be sufficiently large in number and concentrated in distribution to constitute a viable voting bloc in a given district. At best the treatment of groups in an SMSP system is arbitrary.

Groups optimally concentrated—neither too dispersed nor too packed together—and of sufficient size are most likely to be treated advantageously by the electoral system. Nongeographical groups whose members are distributed throughout the population randomly, such as women or left-handed people, usually cannot hope to win representation by virtue of constituting a majority of the voters in a particular district. Quasigeographical groups are those that are loosely clumped together and can be formed into districts by racially sensitive boundary-line drawing. Much of the current dispute over racial and ethnic gerrymandering centers on the quasigeographical category. In essence, the issue concerns how far the legal obligation of the state legislature or other redistricting body extends under the Voting Rights Act to draw boundaries that unite geographically disparate minority neighborhoods into minority districts.

In a series of decisions prior to 1982, the federal courts ruled that electoral rules and institutions, including redistrictings, could not intentionally dilute the voting strength of minority communities. Jurisdictions covered under Section 5 of the VRA had to propose new district boundaries to the Justice Department or the District of Columbia District Court for approval. In 1982 the language of Section 2 of the VRA was amended to cover redistrictings that may not have the intent to discriminate but do have the effect of denying protected minority groups (blacks, Latinos, and Asians) the equal opportunity to elect a representative of their own choice. The meaning of this was elaborated in 1986 by the Supreme Court in *Thornburg*. If a protected group can show that it is sufficiently numerous in a given area to constitute a majority of a potential congressional district, that it tends to act as a politically cohesive force, and that there has been a pattern of racially polarized voting against them, then districting lines that divide its neighborhoods may be invalidated under the amended VRA. Proponents of the Voting Rights Act proudly point to the significant increase in black and Latino elected officials as a result of VRA litigation. Opponents argue that the VRA has created a special right to proportional representation for some racial and ethnic groups in America but not others, and that descriptive representation (electing representatives from one's own racial and ethnic group) does not necessarily serve minority communities well.

Competitive Districts   The third and last of the outcome criteria is that districts should be formed to create as many competitive districts as possible, which in effect means maximizing the number of marginal seats that candidates from either party have a chance to win. The aim of creating competitive districts is also referred to in political science literature as the goal of responsiveness. A responsive system is one in which small changes in the vote result in relatively large changes in parties' seat shares.

Competitiveness is valued as a redistricting goal because it means that changes in preferences between elections can be translated into changes in policy. For example, if support for more social spending increases in the period between elections 1 and 2, then candidates who support those policies should, in a responsive system, do better in the second election and those who oppose them should do worse. Changes in policy preference should ideally lead to changes in the partisan and ideological composition of the government.

In reality, while the competitiveness of districts is certainly shaped by redistricting, there are a number of nonredistricting factors that are also important. Disparities between candidates' money or name recognition, for example, often dampen district election outcomes' responsiveness to shifting public opinion. But in principle, districts could be drawn to make the underlying distribution of partisan allegiance as even as possible so that on average, districts are more competitive. The chief problem with implementing this criterion is the difficulty of securing an agreement from the various concerned parties over how to measure and define a competitive seat. Should it be measured by using party registration data or averages of previous statewide or district race outcomes? What are the cutoff points between competitive and safe districts? The inability to answer these basic questions has relegated competitiveness to the category of a goal for which there is much lip service but usually little practical effort.

These are the most frequently listed criteria for assessing redistricting plans. What makes redistricting so contentious as a political issue is the fact that these criteria frequently conflict with one another, forcing those who draw district lines to make choices. Making tradeoffs between competing values requires an implicit or explicit ordering of those values, and to some degree, the courts have provided guidance in this regard. Equal population, contiguity, and compliance with the VRA and the provisions of the Fourteenth Amendment form the primary criteria—none of them can be violated for the sake of other criteria. Moreover, while it might be possible to do better with respect to one of the primary criteria by violating another, such criteria are treated as forming binding constraints on one another. Districts that satisfy the VRA must therefore be equally populated and contiguous, even though in theory many unequally populated and discontiguous districts might also comply with the VRA even better.

As for the nonprimary criteria, the examples of potential and real conflicts between them are too numerous to list. The most-common problems arise from clashes between fairness of outcome and formal criteria. In some cases there is simply no logical connection between the two. In some circumstances they are compatible; in others they are not. For instance, compactly drawn districts can be designed to produce politically fair or unfair districts, to lessen or increase the number of minority-controlled districts, and to discourage or promote political competitiveness. Compactness might serve the cause of one criterion or another in a particular political jurisdiction but have the opposite effect in another jurisdiction because of different political and demographic circumstances.

THE PROCESS OF REDISTRICTING

The collection of the decennial census triggers the subsequent redrawing of congressional, state legislative, and local-district boundaries. The Census Bureau is directed by law to begin its national enumeration by April 1 of the first year of each decade and to complete it in nine months, reporting the results to the president of the United States by December 31 of the census year. The allocation of congressional seats based on the census data is a purely mechanical exercise based on a method-of-equal-proportions formula that ranks each state's priority of seat assignment by population, adjusted by the number of seats already allocated to it.

In recent years the quality of the census has been questioned by cities, states, and various ethnic and racial groups that believe they have been undercounted as a proportion of the total population. In fact the Census Bureau acknowledges that in every decade there has been such a differential undercount of blacks, Latinos, and to a somewhat lesser degree, American Indians and Asians. In the 1990 Census, in particular, blacks and Latinos were undercounted by approximately 5 percent.

The differential undercount lowers the apportioned share of congressional seats in states with high minority populations and causes malapportionment in inner-city minority districts as compared to suburban or rural nonminority districts. In anticipation of another undercount in 1990, the Census Bureau designed and then tested a postenumeration survey for the purpose of adjusting the enumerated figures to correct for the undercount bias. The Commerce Department sought to end the funding of the survey in 1987, and in July 1991, Secretary of Commerce Robert A. Mosbacher overturned the Census Bureau director's recommendation in favor of adjustment. It seems likely, however, that future censuses will utilize samples and statistical techniques to improve upon the data collected by enumeration alone.

Once the apportionment of congressional districts among states is completed, the second phase—the adjustment of boundaries within states—can occur. By April 1 of the year after a census is taken, the secretary of Commerce is required by law to hand over population counts at the census-tract and census-block levels to the states. A critical aspect of this second phase of the reapportionment cycle is the limited timetable within which states must complete their task: the new district lines must be in place for the primaries the year after the data are received. In large states especially, this means that a complex process must be performed very quickly.

For the most part, redistricting remains an exercise in state action, although the states' autonomy in these matters has been diminished to a significant degree by three decades of court decisions. States are still free to decide such matters as whether to let legislators draw their own boundary lines or to give the task to a commission, whether to require a simple majority or a supermajority for passage of redistricting bills, and whether to apply additional criteria beyond those mandated by the courts. These choices inevitably affect the nature of the redistricting politics that ensues.

A unique feature of the American political system is that while state legislators in most states draw their own district boundaries, members of Congress never do. This most sensitive task is in all but three instances delegated to state officeholders. The typical redistricting procedure in the states treats the redrawing of district boundaries like any other piece of legislation. Legislative leaders, including the chairs of the committees with jurisdiction over election law and reapportionment, fashion a plan after consultation with some or all incumbent members of Congress, interested legislators, and sometimes, critical interest groups such as the Mexican-American Legal Defense Fund and the NAACP Legal Defense Fund. They then fashion one or more proposals.

A redistricting plan usually consists of "metes and bounds"—detailed street-by-street descriptions of district boundaries—or a list of census tracts and blocks composing each district. In addition the legislature usually produces maps of the new lines and supporting data that provide ethnic and racial breakdowns as well as district population. Where available, states may also provide party-registration figures and data from past political races that give some indication of the likely competitiveness of the district. Like any other piece of legislation, redistricting bills are reported out of committee and onto the floor of the two houses of the legislature, where they are debated and sometimes amended. In the great majority of states, the legislation must then be sent to the governor for approval (in some states, gubernatorial approval is not required). The governor can either sign or veto the bill, and in the event of the latter, the veto can be overridden only with a supermajority legislative vote. The supermajority vote needed to override the governor's veto is a critical barrier to a majority party's attempt to draw partisan district lines. Except in one-party-dominant areas such as the South, the majority party normally lacks the votes to override the veto. So if the minority party gains control of the governor's office, it

can force a better deal from the legislature or cause the matter to be resolved by the courts.

After *Baker*, a number of states sought to escape the inevitable controversies arising from redistricting by referring that issue to a commission or some other neutral agency. Three states have pure commission systems: Hawaii, Montana, and Washington give their commissions the sole right to decide congressional district boundaries. In Connecticut, redistricting is given to a nine-member commission only in the event that an eight-member legislative commission, drawn evenly from both parties, cannot reach agreement. Iowa gives the task of changing congressional boundaries to its nonpartisan Legislative Services Bureau, although final approval is reserved to the legislature.

The courts are involved in redistricting in several ways. They sometimes have to take over the process because of a political impasse at the state level. This is most likely to occur when control of a state is split between two parties. People commonly expect that the party that appointed the judges to the bench will get a more favorable plan than the other party. In fact it often works the other way. In Illinois during the 1980s, for instance, the task of redistricting was given over to a three-judge panel that had a two-to-one majority of Republican appointees; yet to the dismay of Illinois Republicans, the court chose a plan devised by the Illinois house Democratic leader. In short, when the courts assume the responsibility of drawing district boundaries themselves, it is hard to predict what they will do and whom they will favor.

In a majority of instances, however, the courts are simply asked to review the constitutionality of district lines drawn by a state legislature. Several kinds of cases come up most frequently. The most common type involves claims of racial- and ethnic-minority vote dilution, usually under the relevant provisions of the Voting Rights Act. During the 1980s redistrictings, the courts overturned parts of the legislature's redistricting plans in Georgia, Louisiana, and Mississippi in order to strengthen the electoral power and representation of black constituents. Latinos also obtained victories in the courts, most notably in Texas.

In addition to reviewing vote-dilution cases, the courts overturned several redistricting plans in the 1980s—New Jersey's, for example—that had excessively large population deviations among districts. The evolution of these cases, as discussed earlier, has been toward an increasingly strict application of the "one person, one vote" principle, especially in cases where deviations from exact equality of population have seemed to be coupled with political unfairness.

The third, and as yet least frequent, form of constitutional review involves partisan gerrymandering. The definitive statement of the Supreme Court on this subject to date is the decision in *Davis*, a case involving Indiana's state legislative districts. The Court held that political gerrymandering was justiciable, but it was less clear regarding the standard it would apply to determine whether partisan gerrymandering had in fact occurred. Whether this case signals a more activist posture by the courts in this area in the future is a subject of some controversy.

Part of the Court's reluctance to get deeply drawn into this matter, aside from the potential danger of further politicalization of the judiciary and the absence of clear standards, is that there is no evidence that the electoral system suffers from systematic partisan bias. This is not to deny that majority parties seek, sometimes successfully, to gain advantage through redistricting, but only to say that the net effects even out over the country as a whole. The most common measure of electoral bias used by political scientists is the share of seats a party would receive if it were to get 50 percent of the vote. According to one estimate, 50 percent of the vote would have given the Democrats 52.1 percent of the seats between 1946 and 1964 and 53.9 percent between 1966 and 1988. Correcting for the inflated percentages that result from uncontested seats, the Democrats would have received 42.8 percent of the seats before 1966 and 50.6 percent after 1966 with 50 percent of the vote. Another study concluded that only four of the twenty-six congressional losses sustained by the Republicans in 1982 could be attributed to redistricting. In short there is little or no bias in the system, even though the Democrats control the vast majority of state legislatures.

Nonetheless, the quest continues for a better way to carry out redistricting. Reformers frequently argue that it is an unacceptable conflict of interest to allow state legislators to vote on their own district lines. Some point to the success of the Australians, Canadians, and British in removing redistricting from politics, but others note that this is easier to achieve in parliamentary systems, where there is no residency requirement, the civil service and the judiciary are less politicized, and incumbency matters less.

The inability to agree on a better process occurs at a time when more is expected of redistricting. Minority groups look for redistricting to remedy decades of underrepresentation. The political parties seek to use redistricting to break the logjam of divided government by restoring government to single-party control. Good-government advocates envision better redistricting as a means of lessening the incumbency advantage. All of this ensures that redistricting will remain a controversial topic in the future.

BIBLIOGRAPHY

General Accounts

The topic of redistricting covers so many subfields, that there is no one definitive study of the subject. The most comprehensive work on the early evolution of legal thinking about malapportionment and vote dilution is ROBERT DIXON, JR., *Democratic Representation: Reapportionment in Law and Politics* (New York, 1968), a prize-winning work. Excellent up-to-date descriptive material on state redistricting procedures and recent legal opinions can be found in two monographs issued in October 1989 by the NATIONAL COUNCIL OF STATE LEGISLATURES REAPPORTIONMENT TASK FORCE entitled *Redistricting Provisions: 50 State Profiles and Reapportionment Law: The 1990s* and *Reapportionment Law in the 1990s*. CONGRESSIONAL QUARTERLY provides a useful historical summary in its *Guide to U.S. Elections*, 2d ed. (Washington, D.C., 1985). A recent publication by BRUCE CAIN and DAVID BUTLER, *Congressional Redistricting: Comparative and Theoretical Perspec-*

tives (New York, 1992), provides an overview of the process of congressional redistricting, including comparisons with procedures in other single-member political systems throughout the world.

Apportionment

The issues of apportionment are discussed in a number of classic studies. The debate over apportionment formulas for Congress is discussed in MICHEL L. BALINSKI and H. PEYTON YOUNG, *Fair Representation: Meeting the Ideal of One Man, One Vote* (New Haven, Conn., 1982), and EDWARD V. HUNTINGDON, *Methods of Apportionment in Congress* (Washington, D.C., 1940). The problems and policy effects of malapportionment are the subject of GORDON E. BAKER, *The Reapportionment Revolution* (New York, 1967), a classic study; ALFRED DE GRAZIA, *Apportionment and Representative Government* (Washington D.C., 1963); TIMOTHY G. O'ROURKE, *The Impact of Reapportionment* (New Brunswick, N.J., 1980); and NELSON W. POLSBY, ed., *Reapportionment in the 1970s* (Berkeley, Calif., 1971). A number of these issues are discussed in BERNARD GROFMAN et al., *Representation and Redistricting Issues* (Lexington, Mass., 1982).

Gerrymandering and Vote Dilution

Gerrymandering and vote dilution are major topics in ethnic-politics and political representation literature. Minority-vote dilution is discussed in CHANDLER DAVIDSON, ed., *Minority Vote Dilution* (Washington, D.C., 1984), and LORN S. FOSTER, ed., *The Voting Rights Act: Consequences and Implications* (New York, 1985). A controversial critique of the Voting Rights Act can be found in ABIGAIL M. THERNSTROM, *Whose Votes Count?: Affirmative Action and Minority Voting Rights* (Cambridge, Mass., 1987). More generally, the issues of political fairness and redistricting are discussed in BRUCE CAIN, *The Reapportionment Puzzle* (Berkeley, Calif., 1984), and "Symposium: Gerrymandering and the Courts," *UCLA Law Review* 33 (October 1985): 1–281; BERNARD GROFMAN, ed., "Political Gerrymandering: *Badham* v. *Eu*, Political Science Goes to Court," *PS: Political Science and Politics* 18 (Summer 1985): 537–581; GARY KING, "Representation Through Legislative Redistricting: A Stochastic Model," *American Journal of Political Science* 33 (November 1989): 787–824; and RICHARD G. NIEMI and JOHN DEEGAN, JR., "A Theory of Political Districting," *American Political Science Review* 72 (December 1978): 1304–1323.

CONSTITUENCIES

Linda L. Fowler

Legislatures in the United States are more at-tuned to constituency needs and more open to constituency influence than those in any other democratic society. Rooted in the American constitutional system and reinforced by a tradition of weak political parties, the orientation of U.S. legislatures toward their constituencies produces highly personal relationships between elective officials and citizens and generates exceptional sensitivity to local concerns. An examination of the characteristics of legislative constituencies, their connections to elected representatives, and their impact on legislative decision-making reveals how tightly constituency concerns are woven into the fabric of American legislative life.

CONSTITUENCIES AND THE AMERICAN TRADITION

American democracy is based on the "republican principle," a term James Madison used to describe a system in which citizens elect representatives to deliberate and legislate on their behalf. Although some governmental decisions in the United States involve citizens directly—such as the New England–style participatory town meeting, the referendum and initiative, and the widespread requirement for voter approval of state and local bond issues or tax levies—most public business is conducted by elected representatives without active citizen participation.

As constituents, citizens are consulted only intermittently through elections or informally through letters and meetings. Their policy input is minimal, and individual desires are incorporated into a broader collective interest. For this reason, representative democracies have always struggled with issues of constituency definition and control: What is the constituency? What are its interests? How much

leeway does it grant its elective agents? How does it relate to other constituencies and to the national welfare?

These questions have occupied politicians and analysts since the founding of the American republic in 1789, and they were particularly salient in the debate over the drafting of and ratification of the U.S. Constitution. Supporters (Federalists) and opponents (anti-Federalists) of the new governmental structure held different views about the proper relationship between constituents and elected representatives. At issue were how much authority citizens should cede to the elected representatives of a strong national government and how much direct control they should exercise over legislators' deliberations.

The anti-Federalists subscribed to the ideals of classical Greek democracy, in which civic virtue was cultivated through constant public discussion and public officials were controlled by continuous scrutiny and frequent rotation in office. They believed that such high levels of participation and accountability could only be sustained in relatively small, homogeneous constituencies operating in close proximity to the seat of governmental power. Consequently, they concluded that the House constituencies of thirty thousand citizens outlined in the Constitution were too large, the two-year terms of office were too long, the character of the Senate was too aristocratic, and the powers of the central government were too extensive and too far removed from direct citizen oversight. In sum, they feared that individual constituents would be remote from the new government and that they would lose their capacity for democratic discourse and control.

The Federalists were less enthusiastic about the extent of popular participation espoused by the anti-Federalists. Small constituencies, they contended, would be factious and less inclined to support a broad view of the public interest. Indeed, Madison argued in *The Federalist*, no. 10, that a large, diverse nation composed of many different and complex constituencies would be more stable than the union envisioned by the anti-Federalists because factions would be less able to unite and carry out oppressive acts.

The Federalists also defended the two-year terms in the House, arguing that members needed time to learn the complexities of the nation's business and to gain an understanding of other constituencies. In this respect, they differed from the anti-Federalists in thinking that government required more in the way of knowledge and experience than the ordinary constituent would be likely to possess. Furthermore, they hoped that indirectly elected senators serving staggered, six-year terms would interject a broad, statesmanlike perspective on constituency interests to counteract any tendencies toward parochial, factious rule in the House. At the same time, they expected senators to protect the primacy of the states in the realm of domestic policy. Finally, the Federalists feared that greater citizen involvement in governmental decisions was not only inefficient, but also potentially dangerous. In Madison's words, the whole point of the republican principle was to "refine and enlarge the public view," particularly in promoting national unity, prosperity and security.

The debate over constitutional provisions thus reflected the fundamental questions inherent in representative government: how much say ordinary citizens should have in the formulation of public policy and how much weight local constituencies should carry in decisions about the national welfare. The Federalist views prevailed, but the anti-Federalist fears that the new constitution would create a government insulated from constituency control did not materialize. Indeed, many of the Constitution's features have worked to enhance constituency influence in the legislative process—so much so, that observers of American politics often fault the legislature for being overly responsive to local citizen concerns at the expense of the general good. For example, the requirement that senators and House members live in the state that they represent insures that legislators identify strongly with their local communities. Biennial election to the House also keeps representatives in close touch with constituency preferences, and the Seventeenth Amendment's provision for direct popular election to the Senate in 1913 heightened senators' sensitivity to individual state interests. In addition, federalism has promoted the delegation of administrative responsibility for many federal programs to state and municipal governments, an arrangement that has given national policies a decidedly local flavor.

The primary factor in fostering constituency influence in legislative politics, however, has been the overall decentralization of power in the U.S. system. By fragmenting legislative authority in two chambers, subjecting the executive to numerous checks, and reserving significant powers to the states, the Federalists created a central government that is subject to minority veto and able to act only in the presence of large majorities. Equally important, by neglecting the formation of disciplined mass parties, they made it difficult to create a more unified government through external political organizations. Given such a power vacuum at the center, legislators can be held individually accountable for their decisions, but they cannot be judged collectively for their institution's performance. They have few incentives, therefore, to look beyond their immediate constituencies for policy guidance and little fear of displeasing anyone other than the state and district voters who elect them.

DEFINING LEGISLATIVE CONSTITUENCIES

Constituencies are both legal and political entities, defined by state law in accordance with constitutional principles. Constituencies differ widely in size, demography and political orientation, and their formation inevitably confers advantages on some groups in society at the expense of others. Thus, the process of establishing constituencies, by determining what interests get represented in the legislature, often generates intense political conflict.

The Legal Constituency

Federal and state legislative constituencies in the United Sates are based on the Anglo-Saxon tradition of single-member districts that elect representatives in accordance with a plurality, first-past-the-post system of voting (which assigns victory to the candidate with the most votes and does not require a runoff election to produce a majority winner). Their boundaries are established on the basis of the national census every ten years by the legislators and governors of the respective states, with the exception of senatorial constituencies, which take states as the unit of representation irrespective of population. Constituencies, thus, are legal constructs rather than natural political communities; they are based on geography rather than partisan or ideological ties.

This method of defining constituencies contrasts with the systems used in many democracies which typically assign legislative seats to parties according to their proportion of the vote. In the system of proportional representation that one finds in Israel or the Netherlands, for example, parliamentary elections are held on a nationwide basis, and parties designate as many legislators from their list as their percentage of the party vote permits. In Germany both types of constituency are used: the parties nominate candidates to run in geographically defined single-member districts and also select lawmakers from their national list of candidates until their total number of seats in the Bundestag, or Parliament, is equivalent to their proportion of the national vote. In Japan, each district elects between three and five members according to their percentages of the total district vote.

In contrast, the American system promotes large, broad-based parties and penalizes small, narrowly based parties because a candidate must actually obtain a plurality of votes *inside* his or her district to secure a seat. Minor parties dedicated to such issues as the environment, opposition to abortion, or various left- and right-wing causes seldom gain positions in American legislatures, even though they may win the support of 5 to 10 percent of the electorate. Moreover, ethnic constituencies that are a significant minority within the United States, such as Poles, Italians, Latinos, Jews, or African Americans, cannot gain representation in the federal or state legislature unless they are sufficiently concentrated in particular districts to make up a majority of the electorate there. Some scholars, such as Darcy, Welch, and Clark, believe that single-member districts

make it harder for women to win seats in the legislature. In countries with proportional representation, women are far more visible in the national legislature because gaining a place on the party's list of candidates guarantees their election if the party does well enough to take several candidates from its list. For all these reasons, legislatures in the United States contrast strongly with those in most other democracies by their inability to reflect aggregate constituency sentiment accurately or to mirror the full range of partisan, ideological, ethnic, and gender-related interests within the electorate.

Although the geographic basis of constituencies typically produces legislatures that underestimate the public sentiment overall, the House is nonetheless quite responsive to population shifts. Constituency boundaries are reshaped within states after each ten-year census, and until the House fixed its size at 435 seats in 1912, population growth was accommodated by the steady expansion of the House membership and the regular addition of two senators for each new state. Since then, federal districts have been regularly reallocated among the states to reflect demographic trends, and in recent decades reapportionment has greatly expanded the number of seats allotted to states in the Sunbelt at the expense of the Frostbelt. According to data presented in *Vital Statistics On Congress* by Ornstein et al., the ten northeastern states have suffered a net decline of thirty-five seats since 1910, and in 1992 California alone held fifty-two seats, the largest number of seats any state has enjoyed in the history of the House of Representatives.

The reliance on geography as a basis for representation leads to considerable variation in the makeup of federal and state constituencies across the nation. Some small states with relatively small populations, such as Delaware, Hawaii, and Utah, have twenty to thirty senatorial districts, each representing a different constituency. Other states, such as Georgia, Illinois, Minnesota, or New York, have fifty or more constituencies even though they differ substantially in terms of total population. Some states' lower chambers have as few as forty members (Alaska) or as many as 400 (New Hampshire), although information published by the Council of State Legislatures indicates that the average is about 112. Nebraska has only one legislative chamber and hence only one set of state constituencies.

These differences make it difficult to generalize about the appropriate ratio of legislators to constituents. A U.S. senator, for example, may represent as few as 550,000 constituents (Alaska) or as many as 29 million (California). As of 1993, House members have constituencies averaging 573,000 inhabitants. These are vast in comparison to the tiny 6,000-person constituencies of New Hampshire's lower house, but comparable in size to the constituencies represented by state senators from Texas and actually smaller than those from California. Similarly, the size of the real estate encompassed by a constituency's borders can vary significantly: Montana's single House district includes the entire state, whereas New York's Fifteenth District covers only a portion of Manhattan. Other states with only one representative in the House include Alaska, Delaware, North Dakota, South Dakota, Vermont, and Wyoming.

Within rather broad parameters, however, some common rules apply to the definition of constituencies. Since the Supreme Court's 1962 ruling of "one man, one vote" in *Baker* v. *Carr*, 369 U.S. 186 (1962), which subsequent court decisions have applied to all levels of government, legislative constituencies must be substantially equivalent in population, and they must be compact and contiguous to the highest possible extent. Until the Court's rulings, state and federal districts were typically drawn in accordance with county lines, which gave rural communities a disproportionate voice in state legislatures and in Congress. Over the past two decades, however, the requirement of numerical equivalence has given urban and suburban constituencies greater influence in the legislative process. Indeed, more that half of the constituencies represented in the 103rd Congress are suburban.

Although reapportionment, or redistricting, has been instrumental in promoting more equal representation on the basis of population, some political observers believe it has also fostered the creation of constituencies that discourage competition between different parties and interests. Under the Supreme Court's guidelines, state legislatures enjoy considerable discretion either to combine like-minded communities together or to tear them apart.

When boundaries are drawn for the benefit of a particular party, the practice is pejoratively labeled "gerrymandering." Gerrymandering has occurred in American politics since 1812, when Massachusetts governor Elbridge Gerry created a salamander-shaped district to benefit one of his cronies; but many contemporary observers think gerrymandering is more prevalent and sophisticated in the late twentieth century. Armed with computer printouts of local voting habits, state legislators can carve out chunks of cities or counties in order to create safe seats for Democrats or Republicans. They may combine neighborhoods to create ethnic enclaves, a practice called *packing*. Or, they may scatter politically significant groups in order to diffuse their voting strength, a practice called *cracking*.

Some political analysts believe that gerrymandering has been used to counteract the growing strength of the Republican party within the electorate, thus insuring continued Democratic control of the House of Representatives despite landslide Republican victories in presidential elections in 1980, 1984, and 1988. They cite as evidence the fact that Democratic candidates as a group averaged 53 percent of the national congressional vote during the 1980s but won 59 percent of the seats. And they note the significant drop of Republican representatives elected in California immediately following the adoption of a 1982 redistricting plan drafted by Democrats.

To challenge the practice of gerrymandering, in 1986 the national Republican Committee joined with local Indiana Democrats in a lawsuit to contest a Republican plan that had been drawn to the disadvantage of Democratic incumbents. The Republicans' national leadership wanted to put an end to a practice which it considered detrimental to its efforts to gain control of the House, even though it meant conflict with its state affiliate. Until this lawsuit, the Supreme Court had been reluctant to interfere with apportionment schemes that advantaged a particular party on the grounds that such political questions are generally beyond the purview of the judiciary. The Court's review of the Indiana case, *Davis* v. *Bandemer*, 478 U.S. 109 (1986), thus opened the door to challenges aimed at partisan gerrymandering, although it did not specify what degree of partisan bias might be unconstitutional. Nor did the Court provide guidelines for resolving disputed apportionment plans in the future, in that it let the existing plan stand.

Although the *Davis* case raised the likelihood that reapportionment plans for the 1992 elections would be challenged in court, it also provided a telling example of how difficult it would be to establish politically neutral rules for redistricting. The Indiana legislature's scheme, seemingly so prejudicial against the Democratic party, actually left the Republicans with fewer House seats after the election than it had held previously.

If the political impact of gerrymandering is uncertain in specific cases, as the experiences of California and Indiana suggest, it is even more problematic in the aggregate. Research on this question, summarized in a 1991 book by Butler and Cain, generally has failed to uncover evidence of systematic increases in electoral safety in keeping one's seat resulting from redistricting, either for incumbents or for particular parties. In the 1970s, for example, research by Ferejohn indicated that there was no difference in the competitiveness of House districts that had been redistricted and those that had not. Moreover, the U.S. Senate, which never experiences reapportionment, has been dominated for most of the postwar era by Democrats, calling into question the Republicans' contention that they have been redistricted out of office in House elections. Similar patterns of Democratic dominance in the nation's governships and state legislatures further support the assertion that the Republicans' inability to capitalize on their control of presidential elections is not caused by discriminatory districting practices for the House.

Analysis of the 1982 congressional election by Abramowitz, however, revealed that redistricting had a small effect on incumbent reelection success, and several case studies of particular states also uncovered evidence of partisan bias attributable to redistricting. These results are counterbalanced by the recent work of other scholars such as Jacobson, Fiorina, and King and Gelman. Indeed, Jacobson's study of the underlying causes of divided government demonstrated that, prior to the mid-1960s, there was a substantial bias favoring the Republican party at the district level that has gradually disappeared. According to his measure of the responsiveness of changes in seats to changes in votes—the swing-ratio—neither party today is either hurt or hindered by the existing procedures for drawing congressional constituencies.

Extensive analysis of three decades of districting patterns for state legislatures conducted by Niemi and Jackman also reveals little evidence of partisan or incumbent bias, with the exception of some modest advantages conferred on Republicans in the 1970s. These results held, regardless of whether party control of state government was united or divided. They are compelling because one would expect politically biased gerrymandering to be more prevalent and more effective when state lawmakers were drawing their own district lines. In sum, the marginal advantages attributable to redistricting seem to be confined to a relatively small number of states and often do not produce a lasting benefit to a particular party.

There are a variety of reasons for this seeming contradiction between what many practicing politicians believe and what the research supports. First, very few state governments in recent years have experienced single-party dominance of both legislative chambers and the governorship, forcing bipartisan cooperation over redistricting. Second, voters are becoming less loyal toward particular parties, making it difficult to predict whom they will elect. With the growth of registered independents and the increase of split-ticket voting, many communities are no longer reliably Democratic or Republican. According to Jacobson, a third of all congressional districts, and sometimes as many as half, votes for a presidential candidate of one party and a House candidate of the other. Similarly high incidences of split results occur for contests involving governors, senators, and House members. In such a politically volatile environment, it is hard to see how either party could legislate a lasting advantage for itself through redistricting. Nonetheless, Democratic control of more than half the state legislatures in the 1992 reapportionment is sure to spark new Republican efforts to change the rules for drawing constituency lines.

Whatever the partisan effects of gerrymandering, several decades of reapportionment have robbed many constituencies of a coherent political identity. By my calculation, more than 40 percent of all House districts during the

1980s contained six or more counties, and fewer than 20 percent were based on a single county. This is extremely important in shaping the relationship between constituents and representatives because districts encompassing multiple political jurisdictions tend to have many different media markets. Studies by Niemi et al. and Campbell et al. indicate that voters have difficulty recognizing candidates when media markets are either dispersed so that candidates must advertise in many places or inefficient so that candidates spend advertising dollars on non-constituents. Thus, diffuse districts may be less able to hold their legislators accountable.

But even when districts are drawn from a single metropolitan area, they may lack coherent communication networks. The absence of good information about the representative occurs because the total audience for the local news media is so large. The press finds it impossible to give wide coverage to any particular legislator, and advertising rates are so expensive in major cities that few candidates can afford to purchase television or radio spots or buy space in the local papers. In short, the constant redefinition of constituencies to reflect population shifts has done nothing to enhance and may even have hindered the interaction between citizens and their elected representatives.

The most important effect of reapportionment, however, has been its linkage with efforts to increase the representation of ethnic minorities in American legislatures. In recent years, the federal courts have interpreted 1960s' civil rights laws as prohibiting schemes that provide for at-large representation in which multiple legislators are elected in the same community or that divide significant concentrations of African American citizens, on the grounds that such plans dilute black voting strength. In the 1980s, they have gone further and required the redrawing of district lines to create constituencies with an African American voting majority. As a result, about 60 percent of the twenty-six black House members in 1992 came from districts that had a black majority, and no districts that had an African American population greater than 35 percent were represented by white legislators.

The deliberate drawing of district lines to promote representation along racial lines in legislatures has produced a curious result, according to research published by Grofman and Handley. Most black members of Congress come from districts in the North, a region with a relatively small, but heavily concentrated African American population. Most black state legislators, conversely, are located in the South, a region with a significant, but more dispersed African American population and few large cities. With the exception of Atlanta and Miami and the handful of rural areas with substantial black majorities in Mississippi and Alabama, few areas in the South lend themselves to assimilating the districting patterns that exist in Chicago, New York, Philadelphia, Los Angeles, or Detroit. Thus, it is unlikely that court-ordered districting plans after 1992 will create significant numbers of new black congressional constituencies, particularly in light of the decline in seats allocated to northern states. Future increases in black representation in Congress, therefore, probably will depend upon the ability of African American candidates to gain support among white constituencies that have a significant minority of black voters.

The use of court-ordered districting plans to end racial bias in legislatures has had the added impact of placing African American constituencies in direct conflict with other ethnic groups, principally Latinos. In many large cities, these groups are concentrated in the same or adjacent neighborhoods. Drawing lines to promote the election of a Latino legislator thus comes at the expense of African American representatives. After the 1990 census reapportionment, competition between these groups became quite intense, but neither the federal courts' one-man-one-vote rule, nor their readings of the 1964 Voting Rights Act provides clear and consistent constitutional guidelines to resolve these differences.

In general, then, the legal definition of constituencies is shaped by the Anglo-Saxon tradition of single-member districts, the constitutional interpretations of the federal courts, and the distinctive differences among the fifty states. These factors, in turn, have had considerable impact on the types of interest that are represented in the legislature and the racial composition of its members. They also have affected patterns of electoral competition and the linkage between lawmakers and constituents.

CONSTITUENCIES

The Political Interests of the Constituency

Given the potential for diverse districting practices among states, it is hardly surprising that constituencies should assume very distinctive political orientations. Not only are the socioeconomic characteristics of American legislative constituencies extremely diverse, but the political coalitions that form within them are also varied. Such differences are not easily accommodated under the broad Republican and Democratic umbrellas, nor do they permit clear-cut assessments of the responsiveness of legislators to constituency interests.

State and district constituencies derive their identities from a mix of geographic features, ethnic groups, economic interests, and historical developments. These factors produce unique patterns of voter turnout, partisan attachment, and political tradition. The low average-participation rate of 38 percent in midterm congressional elections, for example, masks turnout as little as 15 percent in New York's poor, urban Twelfth District and as great as 70 percent in its suburban, upstate Thirtieth District. Other contrasts are found between coastal communities that depend heavily upon public-works projects to develop their rivers and ports and inland agricultural regions that demand subsidies for agricultural products; or between declining industrial areas, such as Detroit, seeking protection from foreign competition and financial centers, such as San Francisco, that want to reduce international trade barriers. Similarly, we might find descendants of Scandinavian immigrants in Wisconsin requiring a higher standard of personal conduct from politicians than Cajuns expect in Louisiana.

Legislators bring these community differences to their state capitals or to Washington, adding both color and conflict to legislative life. These disparate viewpoints must be accommodated in either the Democratic or Republican party because of the American use of single-member districts. Consequently, legislators with the same party label can come from constituencies which are very distinctive from each other, a situation that divides the parties internally on many issues. For example, Democrats in New York's legislature and congressional delegation are often divided in Albany and Washington because members from New York City reflect political and cultural values very different from those of legislators from rural and suburban areas upstate. Republican members of Congress from Minnesota, who harken back to the Progressive tradition of Robert La Follette, find themselves at odds with the economic and social conservatism of their fellow Republicans from California.

The distinctive cast of local constituencies was perhaps most evident in the congressional delegations of the thirteen states of the old Confederacy. The South's experience with Reconstruction and the realigning election of 1896 led to the exclusive election of Democrats from the region for much of the twentieth century. These legislators brought an idiosyncratic mix of populism and racism to Washington that enabled Congress to pursue some liberal New Deal policies in the 1930s, such as the Tennessee Valley Authority, a massive government-sponsored physical, economic, and social development of the Tennessee River Valley, or the restructuring of the banking system, but prevented the enactment of civil rights and social-welfare legislation. Fearing that federal aid to education or expanded social-welfare programs would be accompanied by federal interference with the system of legal segregation in the region, southern Democrats often defected from the party's congressional majority and opposed liberal policies. By voting with Republicans, they formed what came to be called the Conservative Coalition, which first appeared in the late 1930s and dominated the congressional agenda in the 1950s and early 1960s. Only with extraordinarily large majorities, such as the Eighty-ninth Congress in 1965–1966, could congressional Democrats enact their liberal agenda.

With the revitalization of the Republican party and the enfranchisement of black voters during the 1960s in the South, southern constituencies have moved closer to the ideologies of the two parties. After a brief flirtation with President Ronald Reagan's domestic agenda in 1981, southern Democrats elected to Congress have become more in tune with their northern colleagues on social issues, although they remain far more conservative on questions of national defense—in part because of the presence of numerous military installations there. Similarly, southern Republicans, some of whom were formerly Democrats, tend to be close to the conservative members of their party. Many observers believe that this transformation of southern constituencies is responsible for increased voting unity within both parties in Congress during the 1980s.

Despite the enormous diversity of legislative constituencies in the United States, it is possible to generalize about their characteristics in terms of their relative homogeneity or heterogeneity. The more economic, social, and ethnic similarities found within a district's population and the more geographic features tying it together, the more voters will likely share partisan and ideological viewpoints. The pervasiveness of these bonds, in turn, has important consequences for the style of representation practiced by legislators. Large constituencies, with the exception of some of the big, thinly populated western states, typically have more diverse populations, more complex economies, and more media markets. Lawmakers in such constituencies, therefore, are more likely to perceive conflict among voters and are expected to satisfy more varied needs. At the same time, they have fewer opportunities for face-to-face contact with their constituents and more difficulty obtaining press coverage of their activities. Even when diverse districts are small, citizens may still lack a common denominator when, for example, a suburban area and a portion of the inner city are combined in what Richard Fenno has termed a "segmented district."

Some scholars think that heterogeneity makes the legislator's job more difficult and, in turn, leads to more frequent turnover in elections. Morris Fiorina has demonstrated both formally and empirically that heterogeneous constituencies lack stable majorities that persist from one election to another. Similar patterns have been observed by James Kuklinski and Donald McCrone for state legislators.

Primary and Reelection Constituencies

Legislators cope with the many facets of their constituencies by constructing mental maps of their districts' political, economic, and social features. According to Fenno, they subdivide their legal, geographic constituency into politically significant units, the most important of which are the primary and reelection constituencies. Thus, for the purposes of representation, the constituency is a unique blend of objective conditions and subjective impressions.

In the legislator's eyes, Fenno noted that the primary constituency consists of his or her "strongest supporters"—those citizens who provided time, money, endorsements, and general encouragement for the first election and who serve as the legislator's bulwark against a future primary challenge. These are the most attentive and demanding constituents, and they command a disproportionate level of responsiveness from the legislator because of their strategic value.

The reelection constituency typically includes the citizens who voted for the lawmaker "last time" and is more loosely connected to the legislator through ties of shared party philosophy, casework, and governmental pork barrel projects. This segment of the constituency typically can be counted on to continue its support so long as the legislator avoids major political mistakes and provides reasonable access.

Lawmakers' tendency to differentiate a constituency in this manner has several implications for the type of representation they provide. First, legislators' definition of the constituency in subjective, perceptual political terms makes it impossible to measure objectively, using census or economic data, whether legislators truly represent their constituents' interests. This has made it extremely difficult for scholars to develop techniques that can be used to analyze members' voting records for their level of responsiveness to constituency interests.

One of the most sophisticated studies to measure the impact of constituency interests on congressional decision-making was conducted by Jackson and King. They constructed measures of constituents' preferences from extensive survey data and census information about average levels of education and income in the district. Their results show some relationship between congressional roll-call votes on the 1978 tax bill and citizens' attitudes, specifically the citizens' average preference about their personal economic situation and their support for governmentally sponsored income redistribution. But the statistical parameters are relatively small and not always significant. In addition, the major factor explaining legislators' decisions was loyalty to their party, especially to the Republican party. The authors concluded, "It would take considerable constituency influences or personal influences to induce a Republican to vote against the tax reforms or a Democrat to vote for them" (p. 1158).

Can such studies be taken as evidence that lawmakers ignore their constituents' opinions? The answer is yes only if one accepts Jackson and King's assumption that the average preferences of a representative constituency sample are identical to the legislators' perceptions of the average preferences of his or her political constituency. In a study of Senate roll-call votes on selected environmental issues in 1978, Fowler and Shaiko demonstrated that the preferences of environmental activists within a state had an effect on senators' decisions when other influences were taken into account, and that this influence was heightened when the activists' party loyalty was the same as that of the senator. Thus, when scholars try to measure what interests the legislator serves, they are inevitably faced with the problem of differentiating the interests of the geographic constituency, from the the interests of the politically significant elements of the primary and reelection constituency.

Second, when defining their constituencies subjectively, legislators can never be sure that their perceptions of the constituency are politically accurate, and so, according to Fenno, even the most experienced among them feel uncertainty about what is going on back home. Feelings of unease can become acute even for senior lawmakers, who often wonder if their Washington responsibilities are pulling them too far from home or if the mood of the constituency is changing without their being aware of it. These fears are the prime reason, in Fenno's view, why they spend so much time at home and devote so many staff resources to servicing the constituency. They are also the driving force behind members' constant concern with explaining their Washington activity to their constituents. If Fenno is correct about the high anxiety among legislators, it appears to impose a level of accountability on their behavior that is independent of their apparent lack of electoral opposition.

Third, a legislator's subjective assessments of his or her constituency lead to selective treatment of its members: some constituents inevitably command greater access and count more heavily in deliberations about public policy. As Fenno noted, some House members identified places in their districts that they never visited, because they were unlikely to win supporters and might alienate existing backers by becoming identified with the "outside" group.

This bias is inevitable in a representative system, but it has been accentuated in recent years by two very different phenomena that are examined in a study by Fowler. Legislators have witnessed an increase in the number of citizens who are politically active in joining interest groups, in writing letters, and in contributing to election campaigns. Such activity in the past was limited to no more than 10 percent of the population, but today it ranges from about 13 to 25 percent depending upon the activity involved. Yet voter turnout has declined substantially, especially in nonpresidential election years when members of Congress and state legislatures are typically up for election. With voting participation at a historic low of 36 percent in 1990, activists now make up a disproportionately large portion of the electorate relative to the population as a whole.

Under such circumstances, legislators must be even more attentive to their primary constituents than they have in the past because alienating the activists not only means losing campaign contributions, endorsements, and volunteer assistance, but could also cost votes in the general election, which would be very noticeable given the low turnout. Legislators are thus caught between the demands of intense, vocal, and highly mobilized constituencies drawn from the affluent and educated citizenry and the concerns of the disengaged, often inattentive majority in their state or district.

A telling example of this dilemma occurred in 1988 when upper-income senior citizens thronged Washington to urge the repeal of a major reform in Medicare coverage. The bill that they opposed, the Catastrophic Health Insurance Act of 1988, protected the elderly from catastrophic health costs but was funded largely by premium increases among the most affluent retirees. For members choosing between the politically attentive seniors and the ordinary citizens in their constituency, the choice was painfully obvious. Consequently, what had been hailed as a triumph of bipartisan cooperation between the Democratic Congress and the Reagan White House to produce a fiscally sound solution to a major health issue for the elderly was rescinded before it ever took effect.

CHARACTERISTICS OF LEGISLATORS

Despite the fact that legislators represent constituencies of striking diversity, representatives are remarkably homogeneous in socioeconomic terms. The constituency may be predominantly suburban or urban, agricultural or industrial, affluent or poor, WASP or ethnic, Protestant or Catholic, Republican or Democratic, liberal or conservative, politically active or apathetic—but whatever its disposition, it will in all likelihood elect a white, middle-aged, upper-income male to the legislature.

The underrepresentation of citizens with working-class backgrounds and the relative dearth of women and ethnic groups, such as Latinos and African Americans, in the nation's legislatures is more pronounced in the United States than in Europe. Many political observers attribute this pattern to the U.S. party system which lacks a strong labor or social-democratic tradition. Others believe that the decentralized, candidate-centered campaigns typical of American elections place such a heavy burden on prospective lawmakers to raise their own money and create their own electoral organizations, that only wealthy individuals or those with access to activists and wealthy individuals can run. Coincidentally, the reluctance of the typical American voter to support female or minority candidates until the 1980s and the lower-than-average turnout rates among ethnic minorities all have inhibited the recruitment of legislators from underrepresented groups.

Whatever the particular reasons for the underrepresentation of significant groups within society, the numbers are striking. In 1991 women made up just over 50 percent of the population, but constituted just 6 percent of the members of Congress and about 18 percent of state legislators. African Americans comprised 12.5 percent of the population in 1991, but they held only 5 percent of the congressional seats and 6.5 percent of the state legislative

seats. Latinos numbered roughly 8 percent of the population but held just 2.4 percent of the seats in the House of Representatives, and Asian Americans constituted roughly 3 percent of the population but won just a half percent of the seats in Congress. These figures demonstrate that U.S. lawmakers are slowly but surely becoming more representative. However, at the current slow rate of increase of legislators from traditionally disadvantaged groups, it will be many generations before full parity is achieved. Indeed, some researchers, such as Darcy, Welch, and Clark, estimate that if things continue at their current pace, it will take more than two-hundred years before the membership of the House of Representatives is 50-percent female.

In the aftermath of the 1992 election, representation of women and ethnic minorities increased significantly in the House and improved slightly in the Senate. With the election of nineteen women in the House and four women in the Senate, the percentage of female lawmakers in both chambers rose to 10.5 percent and 6 percent, respectively. Impressive gains were also posted for African American and Latino legislators—a rise to 8.7 percent for the former group and 3.9 percent for the latter. A Native American also took a seat in the Senate for the first time in many years.

However, this change resulted from several unique circumstances that will probably not recur in the next few election cycles. A record number of retirements and primary defeats in 1992 created an unprecedented number of open seats; this produced numerous opportunities for women and members of ethnic minorities to run competitive races. Reapportionment, particularly in California, New York, Texas, Florida and other parts of the South, resulted in a significant increase in "majority minority" districts, a trend that also contributed to the changing demography of Congress. Yet although the Congress is more representative of the population in terms of gender and ethnicity than at any time in this branch's history, further improvement is likely to proceed at a more modest pace in the near future.

The socioeconomic bias is even more pronounced when one considers the backgrounds of the men and women who serve in Congress as listed in Ornstein et al. In the 101st Congress, only two members had previously held leadership positions in the labor movement. There were a handful of sports figures and entertainers, a few law-enforcement officials, more than twenty farmers, and several members of the clergy. The rest were in business and banking (31 percent) or other professions—aeronautics and engineering (9 percent), education (10 percent), journalism (5 percent), and, of course, law (46 percent). The number of lawyers in the House has dropped by nearly 10 percent since the 1960s, but it remains the most common occupation among legislators.

Lawmakers are usually so unlike their constituents, in terms of their social and economic situations, that they must make extraordinary efforts to create the personal bonds that are the foundation of political representation in the United States. American legislators must earn the trust of the citizenry by establishing a sense of identification and empathy with the people they serve. At the same time, they must maintain a personally loyal political constituency within districts that may or may not be homogeneous. They accomplish this through very high levels of personal attentiveness to their constituencies and through legislative action that serves local concerns.

RESPONDING TO THE CONSTITUENCY'S INTERESTS

Given the extreme degree of local orientation and weak central authority characteristic of American legislative politics, it is hardly surprising that lawmakers are exceptionally responsive to their constituents. The pattern emerged early in the nineteenth century when legislators began sending circular letters home, sponsoring private bills, and securing canals and post offices for their districts. It has distinguished every type of legislative behavior since.

Although most lawmakers strive to represent their constituency's interests, they go about it in different ways. Among the means legislators use to demonstrate their responsiveness are the following, voting according to constituency preference, trouble-shooting on their constituents' behalf, competing with other lawmakers for federal government dollars, and trying to identify and empathize with their con-

stituents' needs. These are respectively termed policy congruence, casework, acquisition of resources, and symbolism. According to Eulau and Karps, each of these types of representation concerns a different definition of interest attached to the constituency, and each calls for a specific type of action. Thus, when one discusses constituency interests, it is important to ask what kind of interest is involved and what level of response is appropriate.

Policy congruence on issues is the most widely debated and studied form of representation. It concerns the extent to which the lawmaker votes in accordance with constituency preferences or uses some other criterion, such as party loyalty, support of the executive, personal conscience, or the general welfare. Casework involves legislators in trying to resolve their constituents' personal problems with the government, such as Medicaid eligibility, federal tuition assistance, or veterans benefits. Acquisition of resources involves the legislator in competition with other lawmakers to obtain a share of governmental revenues for the state or district—what are typically termed pork barrel projects. Symbolic responsiveness depends upon the level of identification and empathy between legislators and constituents, often in terms of ethicity or roots in the local community.

Representatives can adopt a mix of these four types of responsiveness, and each member's particular orientation reflects a unique combination of personal style and career aspirations, which Fenno defines as a legislator's "home style." In deciding how they will present themselves to the constituency, lawmakers must figure out what fits them as politicians. Some are more comfortable with issues, while others naturally gravitate toward casework. Some stress their personal ties to the district, while others emphasize their legislative influence in the Capitol. However they present themselves to the constituency, lawmakers all try to convey the three key ingredients that Fenno found were common to many different legislative home styles: qualification, identification, and empathy.

Legislators establish their qualification for the job through a mix of past experience in public office, community service, professional credentials, and discourse on public issues. They identify with the constituency through ethnic pride, symbolic gestures, family ties, and other signals that they are "like" the people who elect them. Finally, lawmakers convey empathy by making themselves accessible through personal appearances, television and radio spots, newsletters, district offices, questionnaires, and so forth—all of which are intended to show their concern for and understanding of the constituency. Each of these stylistic elements, Fenno argues, helps lawmakers gain the trust of their constituents, although some are more effective than others.

Policy Congruence

Lawmakers' voting records on legislation reveal very strong connections to constituency interests, although such patterns are difficult to assess for several reasons. Constituent opinion, as Bernstein notes, is not well formed on many issues and is seldom measured in ways that correspond to the actual policy choices lawmakers confront on specific bills. In addition, legislators usually try to anticipate what their constituents want, in order to avoid having to explain or justify themselves. Consequently, they may not appear to be directly responding to constituent sentiment because their voting records have succeeded in preventing such sentiments from surfacing. Furthermore, strong associations between constituency preferences and party attachments sometimes mask the scope of constituent influence over lawmakers. When a constituency is strongly oriented toward one party, the lawmaker may have a strong record of support for both that party's leadership and its president—not because they have obtained his or her loyalty at the expense of the district but because party positions and constituency preferences are in harmony. For example, members of the Congressional Black Caucus, the organization of African American members of Congress, who frequently are at odds with the party establishment in Washington, nonetheless have very strong party unity because their predominantly black constituents tend to be extremely loyal Democrats.

Scholars, such as Turner and Schneier, Froman, and Mayhew, first became interested in measuring the extent to which lawmakers vote according to their constituents' preferences because they were interested in ascer-

taining the extent of conflict between party loyalty in Washington and responsiveness to local concerns. Because lawmakers' party label is such a strong predictor of role-call voting, it was natural to assume that members slighted their constituencies when they went to Washington in order to gain influence and favor with party leaders and the president. Yet these early studies, conducted before redistricting and voter detachment from both parties had transformed the political complexion of constituencies, revealed that most legislators experienced relatively little conflict between their district and partisan loyalties. Democrats in Congress tended to come from districts with strong Democratic traditions and therefore were able to satisfy both interests. A similar pattern held for Republicans, although in the cases of both parties, when a conflict of interest arose, legislators tended to favor the constituency. In the 1950s, for example, Republicans from agricultural constituencies found themselves torn between the market-oriented farm policies of the Eisenhower administration and the need for price supports for their farming constituents. Many of those who supported the president lost their reelection bids in the 1958 House elections.

Complementing these overall patterns of constituency responsiveness is a variety of research that employs diverse measures and methods to assess the impact of the constituency on roll-call behavior. Those studies relying on interview data include Dexter's work on tariffs in the 1950s and Jones's examination of policy-making in the Agriculture Committee during the 1960s. Those relying on studies of voter attitudes include Miller and Stokes's classic study of the relationship between citizens' preferences on governmental activism, foreign affairs, and civil rights and House members' policy orientations and their roll calls; Erickson's reformulation of these same data; and Kuklinski and McCrone's research on voter referenda and decisions by state legislators. Others, such as Kau and Rubin and Peltzman, have relied on census data to predict roll-call voting, or in the case of Jackson and King noted above, a combination of survey and census data to assess the connection between constituents and legislators. In some of these studies, constituency opinion strongly influenced legislative decisions, while in others it was less significant depending upon the issue involved. Indeed, the Miller and Stokes's study found virtually no relationship between citizen attitudes on foreign affairs and legislators' opinions or eventual decisions.

The most compelling demonstration of the responsiveness of legislators to their constituencies is found in Kingdon's study of legislators' voting decisions on salient issues in the Ninety-first Congress (1969). Kingdon interviewed 222 legislators on the floor of the House right after they had cast their votes and asked them what factors had been most influential in their decision. The constituency was mentioned spontaneously in 37 percent of the decisions and cited in response to a specific question in 50 percent of the cases. In only 13 percent of the decisions was the constituency not involved in a House member's calculation about his or her vote.

Of the other potential influences on roll-call votes—fellow House members, party leaders, interest groups, members of administration, staff, and newspapers—only fellow members were more important than the constituency. In exploring the nature of these influences, Kingdon found that fellow members provided important voting cues because of their reputations for expertise or their particular ideological and partisan orientations. But such characteristics were often interpreted in light of constituency concerns: lawmakers often turned to cue-givers who had comparable constituencies and therefore could be trusted to view issues similarly.

Scholars have also developed evidence that legislators are more likely to be attentive to constituency preferences on highly salient issues, such as civil rights (Miller and Stokes) or the environment (Kau and Rubin; Fowler and Shaiko). They must constantly be wary of voting decisions that might turn constituents against them. In the wake of the Watergate scandal, for example, Wright found that Republicans on the House Judiciary Committee who opposed President Richard Nixon survived the general backlash against their party, while those who supported Nixon were defeated in the 1974 election.

Such sensitivity to constituency sentiment has several important consequences when con-

troversial legislation is before the legislature. First, lawmakers often agree to complex institutional rules and agreements worked out by party leaders. These compel them to vote for necessary but unpopular legislation, so they often demand that controversial provisions be packaged in broad, omnibus legislation that enjoys overall public approval. Second, they tend to be more responsive to the president when he can demonstrate that the issue is important to their constituency. Third, they are most susceptible to interest groups, such as the American Association of Retired Persons, which can effectively mobilize at the grass roots.

Despite the weight of this research, one ought to bear two caveats in mind before accepting the existence of a strong connection between citizen policy preferences and legislators' policy decisions. First, telling criticisms have been leveled at some of the ways in which the relationship between constituency opinion and legislators' voting decisions has been measured—particularly analyses based on correlation coefficients, such as that by Miller and Stokes. Second, Achen has argued that models of constituency congruence depend upon normative assumptions about the direction of this relationship. Regression analysis, the most common technique, assumes that representation takes a particular, mathematical form and that changes in citizen preferences produce direct changes in legislators' positions. This is an explicit adoption of the notion of the legislator as a delegate who does the constituency's bidding. But Achen makes a plausible case for thinking about representation as the act of minimizing the distance between the legislator's and constituents' positions, in which case one would use a different statistical model to assess representation. Similarly, some scholars, such as Fenno, suggest that a legislator is most responsive to constituency interests when he or she educates them to adopt his or her point of view as being more in tune with their long-term interests.

These questions all center on the relative independence of legislators to exercise judgment for the public good, and they remain a matter of dispute many generations after Edmund Burke first described the dilemma of the representative as involving a choice between acting as a delegate or a trustee. The tension in the relationship between legislators and constituents is best summarized by Pitkin:

> The representative must act independently; his action must involve discretion and judgement.... And, despite the resulting potential for conflict between representative and represented about what is to be done, that conflict must normally not take place.... He must not be found persistently at odds with the wishes of the represented without good reasons in terms of their interest, without good explanation of why their wishes are not in accord with their interest. (p. 210)

In assessing the nature of policy congruence as a criterion for evaluating representation, therefore, one must remember that this is a highly complex and controversial issue.

Equally problematic is the capacity of the electorate to evaluate when and if policy congruence has taken place. Several generations of survey researchers have demonstrated that very few constituents have well-formed opinions on issues or keep track of how their representatives vote on legislation. In a summary of these findings, Bernstein disputes the feasibility of policy congruence as a test of legislators' responsiveness, arguing that only a very small segment of the electorate is able to make such judgments. Similarly, Fenno has observed that lawmakers have considerable leeway on many bills, so long as they can explain their reasons for a particular decision. Kingdon, too, found that on particular issues, lawmakers may disregard constituency sentiment and that their primary aim is to avoid a "string of wrong votes on a few salient issues."

Casework

If the nature and extent of policy congruence remains open to interpretation, there is little doubt about the extent of legislators' attentiveness to constituency service. According to a 1988 survey conducted by the Center for Responsive Politics, a public interest group, almost 80 percent of House members name casework as an extremely important part of their job. Although no nationwide surveys of state legislators' attitudes have been conducted, lawmakers in states whose legislatures have been studied in depth by Jewell reveal an equally strong, or even stronger, orientation of attentiveness to individual constituents and to their districts as a whole.

Voters seem to require this concern from both federal and state lawmakers. Jacobson notes that when asked what they like about their U.S. Representatives, for example, citizens consistently rank constituency attention as the most favored trait of incumbent House members, and an overwhelming majority perceive them to be helpful in resolving constituent problems and concerned about the people in the district. They also expect members of Congress to adopt the constituency point of view when there is a conflict between local and national interests. Similarly, Jewell demonstrates that a majority of the public expects state legislators to give their highest priority to district needs, and voters generally value constituency attentiveness more highly than any other attribute except honesty.

Legislators act on these perceptions about how they should allocate their time and resources. The congressional calendar includes frequent recesses so that lawmakers can return to the constituency, and the time members spend away from Washington has increased steadily since the mid-1960s. In the Eisenhower era, according to data compiled by Parker, the members of both houses of Congress averaged 2 or 3 days per month back in their constituencies; but during the past decade the average representative spent roughly eleven days per month in the district, while the average senator spent seven days of every month in the state. No comparable data exist for state legislatures, but fewer than half are in session year-round, ensuring that legislators spend the bulk of their time at home.

The same attention to the district is borne out by lawmakers' allocation of resources. According to figures in Ornstein et al., in the past two decades legislators have doubled the size of their personal staffs so that they can be more attentive to their constituencies. House members assign roughly 40 percent of their staffs to district offices, whereas senators locate about 34 percent of their staff to state offices. For those staffers working in Washington, much of the time is devoted to sending out newsletters, press releases, and others types of communication with constituents, as well as processing requests for casework. The volume of this communication is staggering: about seven-hundred million pieces during election years and about six-hundred million pieces in nonelection years.

State legislators, of course, have fewer resources and less time to devote to their constituencies. But in recent years, there has been a steady increase in the availability of staff resources for state lawmakers. According to figures for the early 1980s compiled by a nonprofit research organization, the National Conference on State Legislatures, about two-thirds of all states now allocate personal assistants to lawmakers' district offices, and these locally based staffers constitute about 20 percent of all legislative personnel.

The success of this approach is evident in the extraordinarily high approval ratings that lawmakers enjoy: typically in the range of 80 to 90 percent. Furthermore, survey data compiled by Jacobson indicate that the highly personal nature of legislative home style leads to an exceptional level of contact between constituents and lawmakers. For example, 90 percent of American voters report having had some contact with their representative in the U.S. House and 94 percent report having had contact with their U.S. senator. A surprisingly large proportion of this contact was personal—20 percent had met their House member, while 9 percent had met their senator. And much of it arose from attendance at group meetings with their federal lawmakers—18 percent had participated in meetings with their House member and 10 percent had been at meetings with a senator. Furthermore, fully three-quarters of voters had received mail from their House member and more than half had received mail from their senator. Such levels of interaction are far higher than those found by Cain, Ferejohn, and Fiorina in Great Britain, despite the fact that American constituencies are considerably larger.

Legislators command considerable resources to maintain such high levels of contact. Parker's analysis of district-level staffs, trips home, and mail to the district, for example, indicates that few lawmakers neglect such activities and that all such means of establishing linkages have increased substantially since the 1960s. Moreover, survey research conducted by Cover and Brumberg indicates that personal communication has a positive impact on constituents' attitudes toward their lawmaker.

Despite the extraordinary amount of effort and resources devoted to casework, some doubt remains about its overall impact on the electoral fortunes of House members. Research by Johannes and by Johannes and McAdams indicates that the impact of casework may be limited because citizens have come to expect such services from whoever holds the office. But work by Fiorina, Yiannakis, and Fiorina and Rivers, however, has demonstrated that when citizens are satisfied with the casework they or their family and friends have received from House members, they respond positively at the polls.

Resource Allocation

The oldest political wisdom in American politics holds that bringing home the "bacon" in terms of governmental projects and grants is a foolproof method of securing reelection. Political folklore is rife with stories of powerful committee chairs who secured military bases for their districts or obtained funds for improving harbors or highways in the districts. Among contemporary observers, New York's Senator Alfonse D'Amato has come to epitomize this type of constituency responsiveness, earning the nickname "Senator Pothole" in the process.

Theorists, such as Ferejohn or Shepsle and Weingast, have demonstrated the powerful pull of the pork barrel as a means of wooing the constituency, and they argue that such incentives foster a distinctive type of bargaining and coalition building inside the legislature so that lawmakers can maximize the electoral return from federal dollars. Such strategies are optimal for individual constituencies, and of course for lawmakers, but they have the perverse effect of making the nation worse off by fostering higher tax rates and economically inefficient projects.

Maximizing the distribution of federal resources to individual constituencies is facilitated by the internal organization of Congress, according to Mayhew. Party leaders in Congress lack the resources to enforce party discipline on the floor, thus enabling individual members to vote with their constituencies when conflict between the two arises. Powerful and specialized committees in the House and Senate further enable members to act as policy entrepreneurs on behalf of their constituencies. Although, Arnold notes, a variety of institutional arrangements and codes of behavior constrain members' ability to raid the federal treasury for their constituents' benefit, the organization nonetheless enables lawmakers to set a policy agenda that is sensitive to state and local concerns.

Legislators from farm states in the Midwest, for example, typically seek assignments to the Agriculture Committees where they endeavor to promote agricultural interests. Similarly, members with large military installations in their constituencies seek access to the Armed Services Committees, while those from the West often obtain seats on the House Interior or Senate Environment and Public Works Committees. In an earlier study, Arnold demonstrated that membership on Armed Services was not quite so lucrative for the district as some might think, but it did have a marginal impact on local concerns, such as base closings. More important, lawmakers' desire to secure funds for their constituencies can provide the executive branch with leverage over them, which it uses to gain support for administration programs. The Model Cities program, an experimental urban renewal program initiated in the 1960s, Arnold argues, was tailored to distribute demonstration projects to key committee members and to win over opponents of the program.

In state legislatures, individual lawmakers typically lack the power to deliver constituency benefits because governors and party leaders exercise more control over legislation than is the case in the Congress. But beginning in the mid-1970s committees have developed more autonomy to promote constituency interests in the professionalized legislatures of states, with their low turnover and relatively high salaries, such as New York, Michigan, and California.

Symbolic Representation

Many lawmakers represent their constituencies in less tangible ways. They express solidarity with identifiable groups in a variety of ways and evoke images that are highly symbolic to the targeted audience. Legislators with large Jewish constituencies, for example, make pilgrimages to Israel; those with substantial numbers of African American citizens join their colleagues in the Congressional Black Caucus to press for the end of apartheid in South Africa. Many supported legislation in a show of patriotism to ban desecration of the American flag, despite personal doubts that the statute proposed in the 1988 election campaign violated the First Amendment of the Constitution, which upholds the right of freedom of expression.

David Mayhew charges that symbolic action has become more pronounced in Congress because reelection-minded legislators are eager to claim credit, take positions and advertise their attentiveness to the constituency. In such an environment, he asserts, it is more important to take the right side than to produce workable programs, to appear responsive than to get actual results.

Although lawmakers are well aware of the political advantages deriving from personal connections with the constituency, over the course of their political careers they may alter the principal components of their home style, by spending less time at home or on casework. Fenno notes that when legislators are first elected, they may choose to spend a lot of time making themselves accessible to the constituency through town meetings, district offices, and aggressive advocacy of local interests in the capital. This expansionist phase of a legislative career solidifies electoral support among voters and deters prospective opponents from challenging them. Having secured a strong political base, lawmakers then may enter a more protectionist mode in which they do not actively seek new supporters, in order to concentrate greater attention on legislative business, particularly the pursuit of institutional power. In compensation to the constituency for diminished attentiveness, they utilize their greater influence to acquire governmental benefits for the state or district.

Some lawmakers also may gear their home style to plans for higher office—for example, a move from the state legislature to the House of Representatives or a transfer from the House to the Senate. If they develop such progressive ambition, they may once again shift the balance among the elements of their legislative style in order to appeal to a new and broader constituency. But whatever the personal objectives of legislators, the overriding expectation governing their behavior is the public's desire that there be a close, personal bond between citizens and their elected representatives.

CONSTITUENCIES AND THE NATIONAL INTEREST

That connections between legislators and their constituents are highly personalized has major implications for the practice of democracy in the United States. On the positive side, it means that ordinary Americans have an unusual degree of contact with their elected representatives in comparison to other countries. However, not all citizens enjoy equal levels of responsiveness from lawmakers, as noted earlier; nevertheless, their access to the legislative branch is sufficiently open and widespread that some scholars believe it accounts for the relatively high degree of efficacy and support Americans express toward their government compared to citizens in other countries.

Legislators' attentiveness leads citizens to believe that their representatives will be sympathetic intermediaries in dealing with federal and local bureaucracies and will be able to get results should they ask for help. Moreover, the legislators' need to communicate with citizens and explain policy choices imposes a level of constraint on their decisions which the average citizen could not enforce through the electoral process. As these relationships deepen over time, lawmakers gain such extensive knowledge of the constituency, that they can anticipate citizens' preferences. Finally, when lawmakers obtain financial resources from the central government, they typically enable local constituencies to exercise discretion over how these revenues are employed within the community.

The trust lawmakers acquire through their personal connections to the constituency has the added advantage of giving them leeway to balance competing local and national interests. Lawmakers have the opportunity to explain decisions of which constituents might initially disapprove, and their personal reputations may insulate them from the occasional vote which the party and presidential politics require. Furthermore, Fenno argues that the unusual degree of confidence between constituents and representatives promotes consensus in the society. When constituents feel that their legislators are paying attention to them, he contends, they will be more likely to think decisions are fair and to support painful reallocations of resources.

On the negative side, the close relationship representatives create with their constituents often interferes with the performance of the legislative branch as an institution. The attention lawmakers lavish on their constituents consumes a disproportionate amount of their time and resources, and many lawmakers believe that their frequent trips home conflict with their legislative duties in Washington. Even when they remain at the Capitol, they and their staffs expend a large percentage of their energies on constituency business. To meet the myriad demands of both home and Washington, then, lawmakers lead a life that can only be described as frantic.

Furthermore, the hypersensitivity among lawmakers toward their constituents' preferences has the added drawback of making it difficult for them to support policies that are unpopular locally but advantageous over the long run to society as a whole. Too often, critics of the legislature charge, policies are adopted that are more symbolic than real, or that tend to focus on short-term solutions that have high costs in the long term. At the same time, members of the legislature may be so determined to secure their constituency's fair allocation of resources that they fund programs in ways that are grossly inefficient. If every community is to retain a military base or get its share of education aid, for example, it becomes impossible to streamline the defense budget or to direct resources to areas with the greatest need.

An added disadvantage of the highly personal connections between elected representatives and their constituents is the propensity of the legislature toward deadlock. Members can become so sensitive to constituency concerns that the institution finds itself unable to act or locked in conflict with the president. The inevitable stalemate that arises eventually reduces public confidence in the government as a whole. The individual responsiveness of lawmakers and the collective irresponsibility of the legislative branch thus create a paradoxical situation in which constituents approve of their own representatives but denigrate the institution of which they are a part.

Most important in the eyes of some political observers is the disjunction between what constituents want from their lawmakers and what they desire from the legislature as an institution. To the extent that citizens judge their representatives purely on the basis of attentiveness to local concerns, they may end up voting for legislators who do not necessarily reflect their views on broader, more national issues. In recent years, for example, roughly 40 percent of House districts have supported the candidate of one party for the House and the opposite party for the presidency. A similar, though smaller, discrepancy occurs for House-Senate voting. Nationwide, this pattern has produced the phenomenon of divided government, in which Republicans frequently capture the White House but are unable to hold the Senate or gain control of the House.

Viewed from this perspective, legislators' intense cultivation of their constituencies is indistinguishable from a permanent election campaign, in which the high rates of approval enjoyed by incumbent legislators lead to reduced competition and turnover in both state and federal legislatures. For example, the number of uncontested House races has increased over the past decade, reaching 20 percent in 1990, and at the same time, the number of experienced challengers has precipitously declined, particularly in the Republican party. With reelection rates running at 98 percent in the last several House elections, many critics charge that incumbents have made themselves so popular that they are now beyond electoral control. Ironically, the very responsiveness which earns lawmakers such high marks from citizens may lead to irresponsible and unaccountable lawmaking.

BIBLIOGRAPHY

For general data and perspectives on Congress see DAVID R. MAYHEW, *Congress: The Electoral Connection* (New Haven, Conn., 1990); and NORMAN J. ORNSTEIN, THOMAS E. MANN, and MICHAEL J. MALBIN, *Vital Statistics on Congress, 1991–1992* (Washington, D.C., 1990).

For an overview of state legislatures, see MALCOLM E. JEWELL, *Representation in State Legislatures* (Lexington, Ky., 1982); and SAMUEL C. PATTERSON, RONALD D. HEDLUND and G. ROBERT BOYNTON, *Representatives and Represented* (New York, 1975).

Representation
For discussions of the politics of representation see CHRISTOPHER H. ACHEN, "Measuring Representation," *American Journal of Political Science* 22 (1978); R. DOUGLAS ARNOLD, *The Logic of Congressional Action* (New Haven, Conn., 1990); ROBERT A. BERNSTEIN, *Elections, Representation, and Congressional Voting Behavior* (Englewood Cliffs, N.J., 1989); LEWIS ANTHONY DEXTER, "The Representative and His District," in ROBERT L. PEABODY and NELSON W. POLSBY, eds., *New Perspectives on the House of Representatives* (Chicago, 1977); ROBERT S. ERICKSON, "Constituency Opinion and Congressional Behavior: A Reexamination of the Miller-Stokes Representation Data," *American Journal of Political Science* 22 (1978); HEINZ EULAU and PAUL D. KARPS, "The Puzzle of Representation: Specifying Components of Responsiveness," *Legislative Studies Quarterly* 2 (1977); RICHARD F. FENNO, JR., *Home Style: House Members in Their Districts* (Boston, 1978); MORRIS P. FIORINA, *Representatives, Roll Calls, and Constituencies* (Lexington, Mass., 1974); LINDA L. FOWLER and RONALD G. SHAIKO, "The Grass Roots Connection: Environmental Activists and Senate Roll Calls," *American Journal of Political Science* 31 (1987); and LINDA L. FOWLER, "The Attentive Constituency and Congressional Politics" (1992, unpublished manuscript).

See also LEWIS A. FROMAN, JR., *Congressmen and Their Constituencies* (Chicago, 1963); JOHN E. JACKSON and DAVID C. KING, "Public Goods, Private Interests, and Representation,"

American Political Science Review 83 (1989); JAMES KAU and PAUL RUBIN, *Congressmen, Constituents, and Contributors: Determinants of Roll Call Voting in the House of Representatives* (Boston, 1982); JOHN KINGDON, *Congressmen's Voting Decisions* (New York, 1973); JAMES KUKLINSKI and DONALD McCRONE, "Electoral Accountability as a Source of Policy Representation," in NORMAN LUTTBERG, ed., *Public Opinion and Public Policy: Models of Political Linkage*, 3d ed. (Itasca, Ill., 1981); DAVID R. MAYHEW, *Party Loyalty Among Congressmen* (Cambridge, Mass., 1966); and WARREN E. MILLER and DONALD E. STOKES, "Constituency Influence in Congress," in ANGUS CAMPBELL et al., eds., *Elections and the Political Order* (New York, 1966).

See also SAM PELTZMAN, "Constituent Interest and Congressional Voting," *Journal of Law and Economics* 27 (1984); HANNAH F. PITKIN, *The Concept of Representation* (Berkeley, Calif., 1967); WALTER STONE, "The Dynamics of Constituency: Electoral Control in the House," *American Politics Quarterly* 8 (1980); JULIUS TURNER and EDWARD SCHNEIR, *Party and Constituency: Pressures on Congress*, rev. ed. (Baltimore, 1970); and GERALD C. WRIGHT, JR., "Constituency Response to Congressional Behavior: The Impact of the House Judiciary Committee Impeachment Votes," *Western Political Quarterly* 30 (1977).

Reapportionment and Redistricting

For discussion see ALAN ABRAMOWITZ, "Partisan Redistricting and the 1982 Congressional Elections," *Journal of Politics* 45 (1983); DAVID BUTLER and BRUCE CAIN, *Congressional Redistricting* (New York, 1991); BERNARD GROFMAN and LISA HANDLEY, "Black Representation: Making Sense of Electoral Geography at Different Levels of Government," *Legislative Studies Quarterly* 14 (1989); and RICHARD G. NIEMI and SIMON JACKMAN, "Bias and Responsiveness in State Legislative Districting," *Legislative Studies Quarterly* 14 (1991).

Congressional Elections

See BRUCE CAIN, JOHN FEREJOHN, and MORRIS FIORINA, *The Personal Vote* (Cambridge, Mass., 1988); JAMES E. CAMPBELL, JOHN R. ALFORD, and KEITH HENRY, "Television Markets and Congressional Elections," *Legislative Studies Quarterly* 9 (1984); MORRIS P. FIORINA, *Divided Government* (New York, 1991); GARY KING and ANDREW GELMAN, "Systemic Consequences of Incumbency Advantage in U.S. House Elections," *American Journal of Political Science* 35 (1991); GARY C. JACOBSON, *The Electoral Origins of Divided Government* (Boulder, Col., 1990); GARY C. JACOBSON, *The Politics of Congressional Elections*, 3d ed. (New York, 1992); and RICHARD G. NIEMI, LYNDA W. POWELL, and PATRICIA L. BICKNELL, "The Effects of Congruity Between Community and District on the Salience of U.S. House Candidates," *Legislative Studies Quarterly* 11 (1968).

Constituency Service

For discussion see CENTER FOR RESPONSIVE POLITICS, *Congressional Operations: Congress Speaks —A Survey of the 100th Congress* (Washington, D.C., 1988); ALBERT D. COVER and BRUCE S. BRUMBERG, "Baby Books and Ballots: The Impact of Congressional Mail on Constituency Opinion," *American Political Science Review* 76 (1982); JOHN R. HIBBING, "The Liberal Hour: Electoral Pressures and Transfer Payment Voting in the U.S. Congress," *Journal of Politics* 46 (1984); JOHN R. FEREJOHN, *Pork Barrel Politics* (Palo Alto, Calif., 1974); JOHN R. JOHANNES, *To Serve the People: Congress and Constituency Service* (Lincoln, Neb., 1984); JOHN R. JOHANNES and JOHN C. McADAMS, "The Congressional Incumbency Effect: Is It Casework, Policy Compatibility, or Something Else?," *American Journal of Political Science* 25 (1981); CHARLES O. JONES, "Representation in Congress: The Case of the House Agriculture Committee," *American Political Science Review* 55 (1961); GLENN R. PARKER, *Homeward Bound* (Pittsburgh, 1986) and his "Members of Congress and Their Constituents: The Home Style Connection," in LAWRENCE C. DODD and BRUCE I. OPPENHEIMER, eds., *Congress Reconsidered*, 4th ed. (Washington, D.C., 1989); DOUGLAS RIVERS and MORRIS P. FIORINA, "Constituency Service, Reputation, and the Incumbency Advantage," in MORRIS P. FIORINA and DAVID W. ROHDE, eds., *Home Style and Washington Work* (Ann Arbor, 1989); KENNETH A. SHEPSLE and BARRY R. WEINGAST, "Legislative Politics and Budget Outcomes," in G. MILLS and J. L. PALMER, eds., *Fed-*

eral Budget Policy in the 1980s (Washington, D.C., 1984); and DIANA EVANS YIANNAKIS, "The Grateful Electorate: Casework and Congressional Elections," *American Journal of Political Science* 25 (1981).

Women and Representation
For discussion of the representation of women see R. DARCY, SUSAN WELCH, and JANET CLARK, *Women, Elections, and Representation* (New York, 1987).

SEE ALSO Elections to the U.S. House of Representatives; Elections to the U.S. Senate; Elections to the State Legislatures; Legislative Redistricting; Representation; **AND** Women in Legislatures.

THE RESPONSIBILITY OF THE REPRESENTATIVE

Eugene J. Alpert

In 1991, Congressmen Dick Armey (R.-Tex.) and Pete Geren (D.-Tex.) represented two adjoining congressional districts in their state's north-central area. Both were among the most conservative members of Congress, voting frequently for a strong national defense and reduced government spending for domestic programs and also favoring a balanced federal budget. But when Dick Armey helped pass legislation in the Congress to reduce the federal deficit by closing certain unnecessary military bases, he was roundly criticized by constituents for being against the economic interests of his district and the region, which were heavily dependent on the defense industry.

When a bipartisan commission recommended the closing of Carswell Air Force Base, a major Strategic Air Command facility on the outskirts of Fort Worth, the political skills of Pete Geren were put to the test as he unsuccessfully tried to persuade the commission and the secretary of defense to reverse the decision and keep the base open. President George Bush eventually approved the list of base closings and sent the list to Congress with no effective opposition. (In 1992, Armey and Geren each received his respective party's nomination to run for reelection in newly redrawn congressional districts.)

The example of Armey, who acted according to his strong conservative beliefs, contrasts sharply with that of Geren, who, despite his own conservative orientation, tried to protect the immediate well-being of his constituents. The responsibility of a representative is therefore a complicated matter that often depends upon both the values of that legislator and whether he sees the need to consider the short- or long-run prospects for his district and the nation.

The view of a legislator's responsibility is sometimes reflected in the particular style that the lawmaker brings to office. In the early 1990s the so-called Keating Five senators were investigated by the Senate Ethics Committee for their efforts on behalf of a campaign contributor, Charles Keating, who was involved in the savings-and-loan scandal. Senators Alan Cranston (D.-Calif.), Dennis DeConcini (D.-Ariz.), John Glenn (D.-Ohio), John McCain (R.-Ariz.), and Donald Riegle, Jr. (D.-Mich.), came under severe scrutiny for doing what they said many of their constituents expected them to do—provide assistance by contacting federal regulatory officials in order to ensure an adequate hearing of their concerns. The problem, as the committee and the public saw it, was that Keating had poured thousands of dollars into the campaign war chests of these senators.

The appearance of a conflict of interest was considerable. In his defense, Cranston said that he was doing what many of his colleagues regularly do to help constituents and that assisting contributors like Keating was a way of life in the Senate. Apparently, the role of the representative has its ethical limits, but these are not always clear and well defined, posing a dilemma for legislators who are concerned not only about the duties of representation but also about how to help those on whom they rely for necessary financial and political support. This essay examines some of the dimensions of this debate and its likely impact upon public policy and representation in America.

BACKGROUND

Unlike most legislative bodies around the world, the U.S. Congress and state legislatures are able to modify proposals as well as approve or disapprove those presented to them by the president or a governor. In a parliamentary democracy legislators may represent various constituencies, but their loyalties are expected to remain with their party leadership. Therefore, the lack of a responsible, party-centered system in the United States means that individual legislators must shoulder a greater responsibility to make public-policy decisions that are more representative of their individual constituencies. There is, however, a philosophical and empirical debate about the nature of this responsibility.

Edmund Burke, elected a member of the British House of Commons in 1774, was influential in the philosophical discussion of what that responsibility should be. His view was that elected representatives should be free to vote in ways they think are best. The role of trustee, Burke suggested, would help ensure that a representative would vote to support national policy instead of focusing on narrow local interests. Alternatively, he feared, a representative acting as a delegate by representing the local interests of constituents would lead to bad national policy. Thus, Burke, conceding certain defeat at the polls by a Protestant majority for his advocacy of toleration of Catholics, withdrew his candidacy for reelection, providing a lesson about the importance of following majority opinion that many future legislators have prudently heeded.

But the problem for representatives who seek a role as delegate is that constituency opinion is unclear, changing, and often nonexistent on the wide range of complicated questions that face legislators. The Keating Five would also acknowledge changing ethical concerns as well. Consequently, what is known about the philosophy of individual legislators with regard to representing constituency interests has a lot to do with their style of representation. For example, while most legislators act as if they are delegates, they demonstrate this not by simply casting a vote on behalf of their constituency's interests, but by providing policy support to district concerns; working to ensure a reasonable allocation of government benefits to their districts; providing constituency service to individuals, groups, and businesses; and engaging in symbolic representational actions. The activities associated with these efforts are called a representative's "home style." In many ways legislators' home styles reveal as much about their sense of representative responsibility toward their districts as their approach to voting on particular issues does.

The responsibility of the representative therefore involves a linkage between the philosophy of representation and the practical approach each legislator takes toward fulfilling the expectations of that philosophy. This essay examines that philosophy and what is known about how legislators act to fulfill their responsibility as representatives.

THE CONCEPT OF REPRESENTATION

According to Hanna Pitkin in her book *Representation*, the modern concept of representation began to emerge during the Middle Ages as kings created and enlarged their advisory councils to include individuals from the many newly emerging societal and clerical groups. One of the English councils, Parliament, at first served mostly as a high court and as a ratifier of special taxes imposed by the king, not as a lawmaking body. These functions promoted greater communication with the commoners, and eventually, those who entered Parliament began to think of themselves as "members" of Parliament. Some were even paid by their local communities to report on their activities in Parliament.

By the late sixteenth century, as the power of Parliament evolved and its identity as a decision-making body became more evident, the commoners in Parliament were thought of as agents for their communities, but not yet as true representatives with authority to act without prior consent. In the middle of the seventeenth century, the idea of representation came to full fruition as the English civil war created a parliament that governed without a king. The revolutions of the late eighteenth century in America and France and reforms in the ensuing centuries that extended universal suffrage made governing executives more accountable to representative bodies. They replaced hereditary or appointed councils with elected ones and thus established representative government as a widely accepted political concept. Additionally, the American doctrine of popular sovereignty advanced the idea that representatives should act as agents of their constituents by expressing the constituents' opinions and being accountable to the voters for their actions.

Questions about representation have since focused on how to create a system of representation to ensure efficient and effective representation within a political system. Debates in the United States still occur on such issues as the indirect election of the president through the electoral-college system rather than through popular election, the methods and requirements of voter registration, access to the ballot by third parties and independent candidates, and term limitations for legislators.

A number of political philosophers have expressed their views on the role of a representative. According to Thomas Hobbes, a representative is a person who is free to do as one chooses. Others—such as John Stuart Mill, who wrote that a legislator should be more of an agent than a trustee—believe that a representative must be held accountable for his views. In addition, Jean-Jacques Rousseau stated that representation is tyranny unless there is some guarantee that the views of the representative coincide with the views of the representative's constituents. That, of course, is not possible in all circumstances.

Instead, the best a society might strive for is to have an institution that is composed of people who are similar to those for whom it purports to stand. Thus, as Hanna Pitkin suggests in *Representation* (1969), "representation" means "re-presentation," a making-present of something absent (p. 8). Representation does not have to be literally present, but it must be made present in some sense or in some form. Accordingly, Pitkin accepts the notion that the concept of representation sets some outer limits within which a wide range of actions concerning a representative's role in relation to one's constituents is acceptable. Thus, a legislator could move between representational roles as a delegate or a trustee as if representation were a sliding scale. Those who do so are referred to as "politicos" by John Wahlke, Heinz Eulau, William Buchanan, and LeRoy Ferguson in their book, *The Legislative System* (1962).

Support for the delegate, trustee, or politico role often depends on the importance or presence of particular political issues. These might include the nature of the political issues of the society, the relative capacities of the representative and the represented, the relationship between a nation and its political subdivisions, and the role of political parties and elections in the political system. The degree of representation in a legislature on any particular issue is therefore of variable concern.

TYPES OF REPRESENTATION

There are certain dimensions of representation that fall within the context of the legislative role, as suggested by Pitkin. These include the formal, the descriptive, the symbolic, and the substantive, each of which affects the approach that representatives adopt to fulfill their legislative responsibilities.

Formal representation involves the constitutional or other legal means by which one person or a set of persons is said to represent others. The degree of accountability through election laws that affect the voting process such as the franchise, the voter-registration system, and the apportionment rules would determine the degree of formal representation that exists in a political system.

Descriptive representation involves the extent to which the important characteristics of the populace—including race, gender, religion, and economic or ethnic background—are reflected in the legislature. In that Congress and most state legislatures are composed of political elites, they are often not demographically representative of the population at large. The membership of Congress, for example, is better educated, has greater wealth, is more likely to be white and male, and contains a greater proportion of lawyers than the general population. Pitkin and others argue that this is a less important form of representation, since it involves more an activity than a set of characteristics. Also, with free elections and competing political parties, the legitimacy of U.S. representative institutions that lack full descriptive representation has not been widely disputed.

Symbolic representation includes the ways in which representatives convey their concern for the wishes of their constituents and how this concern is perceived. These actions may or may not actually affect public policy outcomes, but may in some way convey the accessibility and responsiveness of representatives to their constituents. Examples of symbolic representation include cases in which legislators introduce or cosponsor bills and amendments that have no chance of passing. The purpose of such actions is to demonstrate support for one's constituency, but not necessarily to take the responsibility of working to enact them. In cases in which such proposals do happen to come up for a vote, legislators have sometimes been found to vote against their own legislation. The trend in the 1980s was for Congress to avoid voting on specific budget cuts of popular programs and instead to support the call for deficit reduction by permitting across-the-board cuts within certain areas, such as defense and social programs.

Symbolic representation has at least two facets: one that focuses on policy issues within the context of the legislature and one that reflects on the personal qualities of the representative. Thus, any consideration of the nature of the representative's responsibilities must examine his actions not only in the context of the legislature but also in his district, where his constituents can develop a perception of the kind of individual who represents them.

It is difficult to expect constituents to be able to evaluate the representative behavior of a legislator objectively without fully understanding the legislative environment of the institution. Therefore, symbolic action through personal interaction becomes a convenient way for a legislator to develop a level of trust between the representative and the represented. Pitkin deems this to be one of the crucial tests of political representation. If people at least believe that their representative stands for them from both a policy and a personal perspective, then they can accept that person as their true representative.

Substantive representation is the idea that individuals act in the interests of the represented and are in some manner responsive to them. This means that representatives should be evaluated on the basis of what they do on matters of public policy. According to Pitkin, substantive representation goes to the heart of political representation because this means that legislators need to be evaluated primarily on the basis of how they represent others and not on other criteria, such as how they are selected.

FORMS OF SUBSTANTIVE REPRESENTATION

There are many ways in which evaluation of representation can be accomplished. As Heinz Eulau and Paul Karps have defined substantive representation, it includes the congruence of policy with constituents' policy preferences, the delivery of constituency service, and the allocation of government benefits to constituents.

The first aspect of substantive representation, involves representatives actively supporting and voting for policies that are believed to be supported by a majority of constituents in their district. Constituents and various organized groups in the district often monitor the degree of congruence between the positions representatives say they support and how they actually support the policies through legislative action.

Constituency service involves providing assistance to constituents, often on a personal basis. These activities involve sending congratulatory or condolence letters, speaking to local organizations and groups, keeping constituents informed through newsletters, and meeting with voters. Specific mail requests include information about legislation and government publications. Members of Congress also receive requests for help obtaining a government job or for an appointment to a military academy.

A major aspect of constituency service also involves casework, which enhances the role of the legislator as an "ombudsman." The ombudsman, a Swedish invention that originated in the early nineteenth century, is an official of high prestige appointed to assure justice to citizens and government employees who have complaints against the government. Steve Frantzich, in *Write Your Congressman*, demonstrates the great lengths to which members will go to encourage casework and respond to demands to cut through bureaucratic red tape and address administrative abuses.

In *Congress, Keystone of the Washington Establishment*, Morris Fiorina presents a critical argument that the growth of the federal bureaucracy did not happen by chance. His book presents evidence to indicate that the increasing safety of congressional incumbents from serious political opposition is the result of a conscious effort to create a governmental system so large and complicated that people would turn to their government ombudsman—their senator or representative—for help. Members of Congress, in turn, are more willing to provide them with this kind of assistance than to be responsible for dealing with the more difficult economic and social problems of the nation. In this situation, it is not surprising that corporations have increasingly sought assistance from members of Congress and state legislatures. This is most evident by the growth in Washington and in state capitals of lobbying organizations, many of which actually draft legislation for a representative. In recent decades, savings-and-loan executives, military contractors, and automobile companies, in particular, have sought relief from federal enforcement of certain laws by asking their government representatives to support or introduce legislation to authorize exemptions or changes in standards or regulations.

There is also the expected demand by constituents that members of Congress secure a share of the allocation of government benefits, including government contracts, projects, and grants, sometimes regardless of whether the money will be efficiently used or is actually needed. In many cases, members seek certain committee assignments that will allow them to be in an advantageous position to influence the distribution of these benefits. For example, legislators from states with high agricultural production have traditionally disproportionate representation on the congressional agriculture committees. Congressional delegations from large states, such as California and Texas, work together to ensure that there is at least one representative from their state (and often each party) on every important congressional committee. In most congressional committees, there is also an unwritten rule of reciprocity that if a member of the committee has a bill that affects his or her constituency and wants it reported out of committee, the other members will oblige, often regardless of political party affiliation.

Since the mid-1980s, Congress, acting in the national interest to reduce huge federal deficits, has sought ways to curb these allocations to congressional districts, called "pork barrel" legislation. In the case of the closing of military installations, Congress passed the Defense Base Closure and Realignment Act of 1990, which specified a series of complicated executive review procedures and recommendations that the president must either accept or reject as a whole. Only House and Senate passage of a joint resolution disapproving the entire list can block the closings. However, the president can still veto the resolution, thus shielding members of Congress from constituent fury. This procedure effectively absolves legislators from having to vote against important constituency interests but at the same time allows them to protect national economic concerns.

A prime example is the Gramm-Rudman deficit-reduction act of 1985, enacted because of political pressure not to cut programs through normal legislative procedures. If legislators did not make the cuts themselves, automatic across-the-board cuts would go into effect, a process called "sequestration." Thus, they would not have to go on record supporting cuts in any one particular area. Many senators reacted strongly to the legislation, from cosponsor Warren Rudman (R.-N.H.), who called it "a bad idea whose time has come," to J. Bennett Johnston (D.-La.), who named it a "legislative Armageddon." Nevertheless, it enabled Congress to represent the national interest when political circumstances often dictated otherwise.

The quest, however, to serve their constituents in some tangible way goes on. From immigration and tax matters to lost Social Security checks and veterans' benefits, these efforts are often perceived as a troublesome but worthwhile part of legislators' responsibilities. In the end, the gain of goodwill, as tangible or as symbolic as it may be, is perceived by legislators as essential to gaining the maneuverability they sometimes need when their position may be in conflict with the views of important components of their constituencies.

Constituency service is but one reason why constituents express so much support for their own representatives but so little support for the Congress itself. Surveys indicate that the reason for this is that people believe that Congress is unresponsive to the will of a majority of the people and more responsive to the views of "special-interest groups."

As Richard Fenno has described in his studies of representatives' home style, members of Congress run for Congress by running against Congress. On the campaign trail, legislators tend to emphasize their service to the district and distance themselves from the policy decisions of Congress. Actually, Congress as an institution tends to favor the articulation of local interests, since each representative and senator is elected from a distinct political entity, a congressional district or a state, and is politically accountable to the local or state constituency. However, the rules of congressional decision-making force the members of Congress to become aggregated to meet national policy needs; otherwise, nothing is accomplished. When this happens, people continue to support the efforts of their own representative, but are sometimes disappointed when Congress actually responds to problems at a national level of policy-making when it comes at the expense of a particular district's interests. The base-closing legislation is a good example of this.

THE DELEGATE-TRUSTEE ROLE

Burke's theory of representation recognized how individual representation of constituency would affect national interests through representation of the whole. Burke's interpretation of representation depended on whether representatives should do what their constituency wants or expects (the delegate role) or do what they think is best according to their abilities or independent judgment (the trustee role). Representatives thus have the responsibility to balance the wishes of the constituency with the needs of the constituency, given whatever political sanctions exist. With the increasing complexity of modern government, the representative linkage between legislator and constituency cannot be assured, nor can the representative be safe in assuming that constituents will provide the flexibility he or she needs to vote his conscience, even if his or her efforts at symbolic or substantive representation are successful.

The questions about the linkage of role and constituency representation have generated research at both the state and national levels. The emphasis has been on both representational role and areal-focal orientations as empirical concepts. The first examines whether these forms of representation help establish a more or less responsive style of representation; the second relates to the focus or distinctive nature of the electoral unit or group being represented in the legislative decision-making process.

ROLE AS AN EMPIRICAL CONCEPT

For one to be a delegate and to follow the opinion of one's district, certain conditions must be present. First, the constituency must be well informed on the issues, including those which may be brought up at any time during a legislative debate. Second, the constituency must have a preference ordering for the various alternatives being offered for consideration. Preference orderings are rankings based on the aggregate opinions of a majority of the constituents in a district. These rankings must remain relatively constant during the time in which the issue is being considered. It is also important that constituency opinion remain stable after consideration of the issue, for the representative may experience a backlash if circumstances indicate a shift of support among the electorate. Third, one must know what constituency opinion is. The most vocal constituents are not always the majority of the voters in a district. Some issues cut across so many different interests in a district that constituents themselves are confused or unsure about how they feel about an issue. One example is foreign aid, particularly to newly emerging democracies. While some would prefer to spend the money at home (or not at all), others see both short- and long-term economic benefits to the United States. Also, important ethnic ties, especially in districts with diverse ethnic populations, may further complicate a representative's view of majority opinion.

A particular problem exists when constituency views are contradictory. Public-opinion polls in the early 1980s indicated that a majority of Americans supported President Ronald Reagan's proposed domestic-spending cuts, but when asked to identify specific programs, the public was often in support of more spending, and not less.

Even legislators' mail provides only a small amount of information about district opinion. Letters often are general in content and poorly express the views of individuals on specific issues. Most letter-writing campaigns that are organized by special interests and rely upon preprinted forms and postcards tend to be discounted, unless they are followed by individualized constituent communications.

Legislators must therefore be prepared to

vote their own views on legislative questions or to depend upon specific cues from other reliable sources. The trustee role and the combination of both delegate and trustee roles—the politico role—are thus quite viable options for legislators.

As David Mayhew has suggested, legislators' primary interest is in getting reelected. This "electoral connection" is often what drives legislators to pay close attention to district concerns, especially representatives who come from "marginal," as opposed to "safe," districts.

The most experienced and talented legislators tend to spot which issues are the most important and relevant to constituent interests. It is on these issues that they are most likely to be seen as active and supportive. However, a certain paradox arises, especially in the U.S. Senate, where states are represented by two individuals whose votes may frequently cancel out, even though they each purport to represent the same constituency. The liberal Democrat Daniel Patrick Moynihan and the conservative Republican Alphonse D'Amato, senators of New York, provide classic examples of this. The research of Catherine Shapiro and her colleagues casts some light on this by demonstrating that especially in the most heterogeneous states, senators are more likely to vote according to their perception of the views of constituents in their own party. Nevertheless, the question of who is being represented when, and on what issues, remains a focus of concern.

Attempts to ask members of Congress or state legislatures what role each has adopted and to correlate the response with the actual voting records have shown little success. Also, some research has found that legislators identified as trustees are more aware of, and are more responsive to, the views of their constituency than are those identified as delegates. It is thought that delegates, being more open to hearing district opinion, become less sure of true district opinion and are then unable to vote according to their perceptions and so vote on the basis of what they think is best. Consequently, identification of a legislator by a particular role or style of representation is not expected to be a good predictor of his or her behavior, at least on the basis of self-reporting of role orientation.

Malcolm Jewell, in *Representation in State Legislatures*, concurs by stating that "developing simple stereotypes of roles from interviews or questionnaires does not provide a full enough understanding of the complex process of representation to make possible useful predictions about behavior" (p. 97). He prefers to investigate the different ways in which legislators exhibit behavior indicative of representation and to whom they appeal for votes.

The problem is that the concept of a legislative role as a trustee or delegate, for example, is actually an "ideal" style that is often not practical to follow in the midst of complicated legislative actions. It is mostly avoided by political scientists as a predictive concept. In *The Legislative System*, John Wahlke and his coauthors do not claim that delegates are necessarily any more representative of constituency opinion than trustees. They also make the argument that by virtue of a delegate's interest and availability for instructions from many different interests in a district, the delegate might be more likely to follow the views of a highly vocal or influential group within the constituency. In contrast, the trustee, setting himself at a distance from constituency interests, might be better prepared to resist these pressures and consider the overall interests of the constituency rather than listen to the more vocal interests within the district.

To elaborate on what happens when there is a conflict among competing views, research was done by Samuel Patterson, Ronald Hedlund, and G. Robert Boynton, who found that when district interests are in conflict with political-party or interest-group positions, legislators are more likely to take the district view. They also found that legislators believe they ought to give their highest priority to following their own judgment, with constituency interests ranked second, party positions third, and interest-group positions fourth.

In general, legislators are more likely to follow district opinion when that opinion is clear, loud, and intense. Such instances usually involve economic issues and occasionally high-visibility social issues, such as the death penalty and abortion rights. In some circumstances, a very vocal minority may exercise considerable influence, especially when there are no opposing or organized groups within the district. Encouraged, in part, by the independent presidential campaign of Ross Perot and "hot-button" issues such as congressional pay raises and term limitations fueled by radio talk shows and viewer call-in programs, the opportunities for vocal minorities to influence public policy have been significantly enhanced. For example, witness the immediate negative public reaction and response by the Senate Judiciary Committee to President Bill Clinton's first nominee for attorney general, Zoë Baird, when it was learned she had hired an illegal immigrant couple as her domestics. No statewide vote was taken, but the telephone and fax messages from their constituents were the determining factors in legislators' opposition and her withdrawal as a nominee.

Organized interests must especially take care to be well informed, well organized, and able to articulate their views clearly and precisely. Otherwise, legislators may need to rely on their own experience and judgment regarding how to vote. This is especially true if the groups support views that a legislator may perceive are against the best interests of the district. In this case, the legislator may rely on his or her own judgment, and that judgment may actually coincide with the best interests of the district and not with the most vocal group in the district.

If a district is relatively homogeneous, there is a greater likelihood that a representative will share the views of a majority of constituents. Often lifelong residents or well-established businessmen, legislators are generally products of their district. They are usually well aware of their constituents' voting habits in past elections, which can provide an important indication of constituents' preferences. They also engage in sufficient campaigning to learn about voters' concerns and seek to reflect those concerns in their position statements. Regardless of the role they may attempt to attain in the ideal, they are very likely to respond as if they were delegates, simply because they were elected by a majority of individuals whose views they already share.

Legislators who adopt a role resembling that of a trustee often defend their actions by explaining that it is the duty of legislators to provide leadership to their constituencies. The constituencies thus expect legislators to educate them about the issues and to explain votes accordingly. Since hundreds of votes are cast in a legislative session, a representative must decide which to emphasize.

The process of educating one's constituency is really an opportunity to convince constituents that the representative acts in their best interest. This proactive stance serves to convince voters and potential critics of the legislator's point of view and may neutralize opponents by appearing to be knowledgeable, sincere, and honest.

Richard Fenno describes the process of explaining one's vote as the description, the interpretation, and the justification of legislative behavior. The object of the explanation is to invoke a greater sense of trust between the legislator and the constituent so that even a constituent who disagrees with the legislator's position will at least respect the honesty of the legislator. This trust of course does not prevent a tough reelection battle, for there are a sufficient number of well-known congressional leaders who have been defeated when they espoused highly visible, unpopular views to confirm this.

The most noteworthy examples of this include the chairs of the Senate Foreign Relations Committee. Constitutents, having seen their senators on the national scene expressing views about international issues, wonder whether proper attention is being devoted to the affairs of a certain state—their own. In the 1970s, Senate Foreign Relations chairmen J. William Fulbright (D.-Ark.) and Frank Church (D.-Idaho) were well-entrenched senior senators who were defeated for reelection. In 1984, despite his recognition of this problem, Senator Charles Percy (R.-Ill.) lost his seat and chairmanship for much the same reason.

Often legislators adopt a mixture of views and present themselves as politicos. Especially when they have been elevated to positions of leadership within the ranks of the legislature, they are expected to be more representative of their party's views than otherwise. Members from safe districts have greater flexibility in this regard, but by pursuing a visible agenda that transcends the interests of one's constituencies, legislators run the risk of appearing aloof and being called "out of touch" with their districts by their opponents.

Interestingly, John Hibbing and John

Alford, in an analysis based on the 1988 National Election Study, found that despite differences in population between large and small states, constituents in large states, such as California, New York, and Illinois, did not see their senators as being out of touch. Apparently, the constituents in these states seemed more forgiving of the lack of a personal touch. Hibbing and Alford also found that often the senators were helped by the difficulty that challengers had in gaining media attention.

IDENTIFYING THE CONSTITUENCY

Implied in this discussion is that representatives know to whom they are being responsive; yet there are obvious problems with identifying exactly who constitutes one's constituency. Constituencies are not always readily defined or knowledgeable about the issues, and are unlikely to consider all issues to have the same degree of saliency.

Fenno's concept of a representational constituency involves a series of concentric circles that representatives think about when they consider whom they represent. From largest to smallest, they are the geographical constituency, the reelection constituency, the primary constituency, and, finally, the personal constituency.

The geographical constituency is defined by the political boundaries of one's district. It may be fairly heterogeneous or homogeneous, depending on the size or the way in which the district has been drawn. The reelection constituency is composed of the people who support the representative through voting and other ancillary activities. The primary constituency forms the strongest and most loyal, reliable, and active supporters of the representative—those who are often instrumental in the primary-election campaign to win the nomination. The personal constituency includes the inner circle of the representative's supporters, including close friends and advisers.

Also, a legislator may be responsive to a statewide or national constituency that supersedes the geographical boundaries of the district. Consequently, one may be responsive to different constituencies to varying degrees, depending on the issue at hand.

Research has indicated that legislators' primary focus is on their districts, but at least one-fourth of the congressmen interviewed by Roger Davidson in his book *The Role of the Congressman* indicated a national orientation as well. The smaller and closer the constituent circle is to the congressman, the more attention he will likely pay to its members. This often results in congressmen spending more of their time with their friends and close associates, people who are often more like themselves and who tend to reinforce a congressman's own beliefs.

State legislators are less likely to view their constituencies in the way members of Congress do. Their districts are often more homogeneous and the competition in them is less organized than that in larger congressional districts. However, it is also likely that state legislators may be viewed as representatives of areas that transcend their immediate boundaries, especially in large urban and suburban areas where city and county concerns overlap. This often results in representatives, sometimes from different parties or ideological viewpoints, who work together on behalf of a larger geographical region.

In *Representation in State Legislatures*, Malcolm Jewell confirmed the different view that state legislators take of their constituencies. For example, he found that the legislators interviewed were more likely to be vague about defining their reelection constituency, referring mostly to voting support on the basis of party registration, voting statistics, and places where they had strong personal contacts. Often they said they represented "the entire district," not just particular segments. Jewell thought perhaps that this response was reflective of the smaller size of the state legislative district, compared to a congressional district, and the lessened need (or even lower ability) to identify one's reelection constituency.

Delegates are more likely to believe that what is best for a majority of districts is best for the national (or state) interest. In the mind of the delegate, he or she is always acting for a higher interest than the district. Alternatively, a trustee considers the strength of the collective interest of the larger unit as a determinant of the interests of the district. Thus, a trustee is more likely to consider the views of the president or governor and his political party as important factors when determining whether to support certain policies and legislative actions.

However, Wahlke and his coauthors of *The Legislative System* showed that areal focus of representation at the state level is related to the dynamics of the political system. In the early 1960s in the state of Tennessee, which at the time had a predominant one-party system, state representatives indicated less interest in district areal role orientation than those from states with greater two-party competition. Also, when the authors examined the relationship between the political character of districts (competitive, semicompetitive, and one-party) in California, New Jersey, and Ohio with areal role orientation, they found that in competitive districts, compared to semicompetitive districts, the areal role orientation was closer to the district level than to the district-state and state levels. In one-party districts, legislators did not show a preference for areal role orientation.

Another result was that state-oriented representatives were more likely to be trustees than district-oriented representatives, who were in turn more likely to be delegates. It was also found that a district-oriented legislator was just as likely to be a delegate as a trustee, but state-oriented representatives were more likely to be trustees than delegates. Those in the category of state-district–oriented legislators were more likely to favor the role of a politico.

THE IMPACT OF CONSTITUENCY OPINION ON POLICY

Even if a representative feels pressure to follow constituency opinion and act according to the delegate role, there is no guarantee that a correspondence in voting behavior will actually occur. Also, different issues evoke different constituencies and different levels of saliency, which may allow a representative greater flexibility to vote according to other criteria, such as party influence and personal political goals. These personal goals may involve gaining greater power and influence within the legislative body, a power that in the long run will serve the best interests of the district, particularly on matters involving the allocation of government benefits. Consequently, the nature of

legislative action makes a valid roll-call-voting analysis questionable, since vote trading frequently occurs, especially on these kinds of issues.

When researchers try to measure the opinions of citizens in the district to determine the relationship between legislative voting and majority opinion, they run into problems. Measures of roll-call behavior are by their nature imprecise because they often miss the subtleties of the legislative process. Measures of a constituency's demographic characteristics confront considerable problems because it is unclear what is really being measured and what their relevance is for a particular legislator's decision. Here again is the question of which constituency is represented, for as Richard Fenno points out, there are many to consider. Knowing which is important on any particular issue is difficult to determine from afar.

The available information about the linkage between constituency opinion and policy outcomes originated in a landmark 1958 national election study in which both constituents and congressional candidates, including incumbents, were interviewed. Researchers Warren Miller and Donald Stokes attempted to determine the degree of responsiveness to district opinion by members of Congress.

Miller and Stokes hypothesized that constituency control of a representative's actions can be exerted in two different ways. The first is through a representative's own policy preferences. If a legislator's positions are already reflective of district opinion, the constituency's views will be well represented. However, this hinges on a representative's actually voting according to these preferences. This may not occur because of other influences, such as political-party pressures and the absence of a voting alternative that accurately reflects his own and his district's position.

The second is through a representative's perceptions of district opinion. If, in order to win reelection, a legislator attempts to keep in close touch with majority opinion in the district and so develops an accurate perception of district opinion, then constituency control will occur in this manner. This again assumes favorable conditions for such voting opportunities to occur.

Miller and Stokes examined the correspondences between constituency opinion, congressional perception of district opinion, and congressional voting behavior on foreign policy, social welfare, and civil rights issues. The strongest congruence found between constituent opinion and congressional votes was in the area of civil rights, the weakest in foreign policy. The strongest path of constituency influence was through a representative's perception of constituency opinion rather than through his own attitude. In contrast, a study by Edith Barrett and Fay Lomax Cook based on interviews with House members indicated a strong relationship between members' votes on social-welfare issues and their personal views. At the same time, party affiliation appeared to have a strong effect on voting by committee leaders.

These findings indicate that, in the words of Miller and Stokes, "no single tradition of representation fully accords with the realities of American legislative politics" (p. 56). It is instead a mixture of styles and philosophies, with the Burkean trustee model, the instructed-delegate model, and the responsible-party model contributing to the nature of American political representation, with policies—or at least the saliency of these policies—being an important determining factor in the linkage between constituency opinion and representation.

Aage Clausen investigated the influence of policy dimensions further by identifying and examining five major policy dimensions that were affected by issues of party and constituency concern. He found that party voting was strongest on those votes which involved fiscal and tax matters, public works, and other government management issues. Constituency influence was found to be most important in regard to civil rights issues, while both party and constituency factors were relevant to social-welfare and agriculture issues. On foreign policy, voting was not related to either party or constituency characteristics. Additional evidence that constituency opinion is influential in determining the voting behavior of congressmen is found in John Kingdon's *Congressmen's Voting Decisions.*

Besides looking at perceptions of district opinion, one may look at the impact of constituents' interests on congressional attitudes and behavior to examine the characteristics of individual districts with aggregate data, rather than survey data, and to correlate these characteristics with the voting behavior of a district's representative.

The results of this method indicate that certain types of districts tend to favor the election of a candidate from one party over the other. In these studies, including Lewis Froman's *Congressmen and Their Constituencies*, party affiliation is often more important than constituency characteristics in determining a congressman's vote. However, this does not necessarily discount the importance of constituency influence, because the measure of constituency opinion using the demographic characteristics of a district may not be valid.

The underlying factor here is the saliency of the issue. It appears that the greater the degree of interest in a district on an issue, the more likely a representative will vote on the basis of what he or she perceives to be the majority opinion in that district. However, various research has qualified this statement. For example, in a study of Senate voting, Catherine Shapiro and her associates found a relationship between policy and constituency opinion in the areas of economic and foreign policy that showed senators voting most often with the preferences of constituents from their own party.

Also, there is no clear difference between how Democrats and Republicans tend to follow constituent opinion. Even the marginality of the district or the safeness of the district will occasionally have an effect on the responsiveness of the legislator to district opinion, but findings in this area have tended to be inconsistent. Roger Davidson, for example, found that congressmen from marginal districts are likely to view themselves as delegates and take a district-oriented view, while those elected with more than 60 percent of the vote from safer districts are more likely to be trustees and to pay particular attention to issues of national importance.

It is not clear whether marginal representatives are more likely to support party or constituency when there is a conflict of views on an issue. There is some evidence, however, from James Kuklinski and Richard Elling's research that senators are more likely to be responsive to state interests during election years than during nonelection years.

The measurement of the effect of constituency opinion on public policy is of considerable interest among researchers, especially with new methodological techniques that relate characteristics of the congressmen and their districts to their voting behavior on a series of related roll-call votes. Larry Bartels, for example, found that congressmen's votes on the defense budget for Fiscal 1982 were related to constituency opinion about defense spending in the 1980 presidential campaign. What was particularly interesting about this study was that even congressmen from safe districts were as moved by constituency opinion as those from marginal ones. Marvin Overby also found that constituency opinion influenced congressional voting on the nuclear-freeze issue in 1983.

PERCEPTIONS OF DISTRICT OPINION

Legislators may be concerned about following district opinion, but their perceptions may be inaccurate. Often expression of district opinion comes from those who already agree with the representative. In some cases, a representative will hear what he wants to hear, filtering out expressions of criticism or disagreement. By the nature of the electoral process, though, representatives tend to be already representative of a good proportion of their constituency, and according to Davidson's study, this is what many of them believe.

To alleviate uncertainty about district opinion, legislators engage in various kinds of behavior to become more informed about district opinion. While some merely rely on their own intuition or on discussion with a small group of individual constituents whose views, on the basis of experience, they trust and respect, others conduct scientific polls or base their assessments on questionnaires in their periodic newsletters. As John Johannes points out, some members even use the requests for casework assistance as a measure of constituency attentiveness.

Legislators' mail is also important, but less so when it is clear that an orchestrated writing campaign is being conducted by a special-interest group rather than through personal letters. Nevertheless, constituents are encouraged to write to their congressmen and senators for no other reason than to be placed on a computer list for future correspondence. As a reelection strategy, legislators use their franking privilege to communicate with constituents to inform them about matters of interest to them. This is less frequently done at the state level, where legislators have small staffs and fewer computer resources. However, with smaller state-legislative districts, other methods, including greater personal contact, sometimes accomplish the same goal.

Congressmen and senators have been able to engage in more constituency contact than in the past because of changes in House rules and office-fund allocations and legislative scheduling. Advances in communication technology over the past twenty years have also enabled members to pay greater attention to constituency matters.

In a study of district attentiveness, Glenn Parker found a major difference between House and Senate members. Senators pay less attention to their constituencies than House members do, although senators are more active after they are first elected and when their reelection campaign is drawing near. The larger size of their constituencies makes it more difficult for senators to rely on personal contact. However, senators enjoy higher visibility and encourage greater constituency contact through such methods as correspondence and casework. Overall, most representatives base their assessments on a mixture of these methods.

The nature of representation flows not only in the direction from constituent to representative. Legislators, especially those whose role-orientation approaches the trustee model, are often involved in an important educational function: to explain their vote and to lead district opinion rather than to respond to what may be mixed signals from constituents. Representatives devote a considerable amount of time to this effort by promoting newspaper, television, and radio coverage of their activities, publishing newsletters, writing newspaper columns, sending committee reports and government publications to interested individuals, speaking at public functions, sending letters of congratulations and condolences, and acting as personal hosts for visitors.

THE RESPONSIBILITY OF THE REPRESENTATIVE

LEGISLATORS' RESPONSIBILITIES TO THEIR DISTRICTS

Especially for legislators from marginal districts, constituency service is of the utmost priority. As Bruce Cain, John Ferejohn, and Morris Fiorina reported, representatives believe that casework has both a positive and a negative impact on their reelection chances. They can gain more votes by making an extra effort, but they can also lose votes by not living up to expectations.

In contrast, their research also indicated that constituents in the United States ranked keeping in touch with the people about what the government is doing as the most important representative role. Second in importance was working on bills concerning national issues. Interestingly, those who thought keeping in touch with constituents was most important strongly favored the delegate over the trustee role for their representatives. Those who thought paying attention to policy issues was most important favored the delegate role by a much smaller margin. Clearly, representatives are correct in assuming that working on behalf of constituency problems is important for reelection.

HOME STYLE

Home style, as defined by Richard Fenno, involves how legislators are involved in symbolic communication with their constituents in order to gain their trust and to demonstrate their identification and empathy with those they represent. As a measure of representation, this might suggest that attentiveness to district concerns is a way of expressing an interest in assessing district opinion.

However, the effectiveness of home style depends on some basic assumptions. First, representatives must assure their constituents that they have the necessary capacity and understanding to carry out the responsibilities of a legislator. Second, they must be able to demonstrate that they can identify with their constituents, perhaps by having certain descriptive or demographic qualities representative of the constituency. Third, they should be able to show that they understand their constituents' points of view when they make decisions.

Fenno found that this presentation of self helps to form the link between constituency and representational activity. For example, a legislator may project different images or discuss different themes with various audiences to help define himself or herself according to how one's constituents expect the representative to act. Some, for example, may project an image of a national leader with "insider" status, a legislative strategist, a reformer running against the system, or even just a down-home guy.

If accountability is based on perceptions of constituency, then there is perhaps room for maneuverability in the education of one's constituency or in the definition of the constituency. The trust from one's constituents, Fenno says, should be viewed as "working capital" to be used for the benefit of the institution and not just for the benefit of the member.

CONCLUSION

Questions remain about the true nature of representation and how it can be determined. When constituents are uninformed, when there is a lack of control over the legislative agenda, when problems become more complex, and when communication becomes increasingly more difficult and expensive, the nature of representation becomes distorted. Also, with increased lobbying activities and techniques, questions arise about who is being represented and in what way.

The nature of modern legislative institutions and the speed with which information is distributed make it more difficult for a legislator to expect that voting is the only form of representation expected by constituents. Today, constituency service is a high expectation, along with legislative work. The quest today for a legislator is to gain the necessary latitude to follow either perceived constituency opinion or another point of view. Thus, what follows is often a less clear choice and therefore less responsiveness. But one is unable to know for certain unless one knows what the constituency is and the constituency itself knows what it wants.

Often relying on symbolic rather than substantive information, voters continue to reelect incumbents. Symbolic actions are less costly and are easier to effect and to publicize to a constituency than trying to explain one's vote. So much attention to making constituents feel confident about the symbolic quality of their representation in Congress perhaps explains why constituents love their congressmen, but are so highly critical of their Congress.

The U.S. Congress, with its decentralized decision-making process, is well equipped to make legislators more responsive to district

opinion through the establishment of multiple linkages. However, the effectiveness of this linkage must be measured by the extent to which, according to Pitkin, "the people of a nation are present in the action of its government" (Pitkin, 1967, p. 235). The challenge, then, is to give people the feeling not only that their views are being represented, but also that they are being well served as a nation in the process. That is the responsibility of the representative.

BIBLIOGRAPHY

General Studies
A compilation of EDMUND BURKE's most important writing is W. J. BATE, ed., *Selected Works* (New York, 1960). The study of representational role should begin with HANNA F. PITKIN, *The Concept of Representation* (Berkeley and Los Angeles, 1967), and PITKIN, ed., *Representation* (New York, 1969), followed by an examination of the first major empirical research on the topic at the state level, JOHN C. WAHLKE, HEINZ EULAU, WILLIAM BUCHANAN, and LEROY C. FERGUSON, *The Legislative System* (New York, 1962). A discussion of the types of representational responsiveness is presented in HEINZ EULAU and PAUL D. KARPS, "The Puzzle of Representation: Specifying Components of Responsiveness," *Legislative Studies Quarterly* 2 (1977). A collection of articles that review the impact of this research and related studies of representation is HEINZ EULAU and JOHN C. WAHLKE, eds., *The Politics of Representation* (Beverly Hills, Calif., 1978).

State and Congressional Role Behavior
Books that focus on state-legislative role behavior are MALCOLM E. JEWELL and SAMUEL C. PATTERSON, *The Legislative Process in the United States*, 3d. ed. (New York, 1977); JEWELL, *Representation in State Legislatures* (Lexington, Ky., 1982); and SAMUEL C. PATTERSON, RONALD D. HEDLUND, and G. ROBERT BOYNTON, *Representatives and Represented: Bases of Public Support for the American Legislatures* (New York, 1975).

In the congressional arena, CHARLES L. CLAPP, *The Congressman: His Work as He Sees It* (Washington, D.C., 1963), was one of the first to examine empirically the congressional-constituency relationship from the point of view of a member of Congress. ROGER H. DAVIDSON's classic study of congressional behavior, *The Role of the Congressman* (Indianapolis, 1969), for the first time presents data about representational role at the national level.

Efforts to find the linkage between constituency and congressional behavior were first advanced in WARREN MILLER and DONALD E. STOKES, "Constituency Influence in Congress," *American Political Science Review* 57 (1963). Further efforts to link constituency characteristics with roll-call voting are reviewed in JAMES KUKLINSKI, "Representative-Constituency Linkages: A Review Article," *Legislative Studies Quarterly* 4 (1979). For House voting, see also EDITH J. BARRETT and FAY LOMAX COOK, "Congressional Attitudes and Voting Behavior: An Examination of Support for Social Welfare," *Legislative Studies Quarterly* 3 (1991), LARRY M. BARTELS, "Constituency Opinion and Congressional Policy Making: The Reagan Defense Buildup," *American Political Science Review* 2 (1991), and L. MARVIN OVERBY, "Assessing Constituency Influence: Congressional Voting on the Nuclear Freeze, 1982–83," *Legislative Studies Quarterly* 2 (1991). For Senate-voting linkages, see RICHARD C. ELLING, "Ideological Change in the U.S. Senate: Time and Electoral Responsiveness," *Legislative Studies Quarterly* 7 (1982); JOHN R. HIBBING and JOHN R. ALFORD, "Constituency Population and Representation in the U.S. Senate," and CATHERINE R. SHAPIRO,

THE RESPONSIBILITY OF THE REPRESENTATIVE

DAVID W. BRADY, RICHARD A. BRODY, and JOHN A. FEREJOHN, "Linking Constituency Opinion and Senate Voting Scores: A Hybrid Explanation," both in *Legislative Studies Quarterly* 4 (1990). These articles provide additional references for further insights into this research.

Constituency-Representative Relationships
Works that investigate the constituency-representative relationships are extensive and include such seminal books as DAVID R. MAYHEW, *Congress: The Electoral Connection* (New Haven, Conn., 1974); JULIUS TURNER and EDWARD V. SCHNEIER, JR., *Party and Constituency: Pressures on Congress*, rev. ed. (Baltimore, 1970); LEWIS A. FROMAN, *Congressmen and Their Constituencies* (Chicago, 1963); W. WAYNE SHANNON, *Party, Constituency, and Congressional Voting* (Baton Rouge, La., 1968); JOHN KINGDON, *Congressmen's Voting Decisions* (1973); AAGE R. CLAUSEN, *How Congressmen Decide: A Policy Focus* (New York, 1973); and MORRIS P. FIORINA, *Representatives, Roll Calls, and Constituencies* (Lexington, Ky., 1974) and *Congress, Keystone of the Washington Establishment*, 2d. ed. (New Haven, Conn., 1989).

The study of home style and congressional-district relations is described in RICHARD F. FENNO, *Home Style: House Members in Their Districts* (Boston, 1978) and his "U.S. House Members in Their Constituencies: An Exploration," *American Political Science Review* 77 (1977); STEPHEN E. FRANTZICH, *Write Your Congressman: Constituent Communications and Representation* (New York, 1986); MORRIS P. FIORINA and DAVID W. ROHDE, eds., *Home Style and Washington Work: Studies of Congressional Politics* (Ann Arbor, Mich., 1989); GLENN R. PARKER, *Homeward Bound: Explaining Changes in Congressional Behavior* (Pittsburgh, 1986); JOHN R. JOHANNES, *To Serve the People: Congress and Constituency Service* (Lincoln, Nebr., 1984); and BRUCE CAIN, JOHN FEREJOHN, and MORRIS P. FIORINA, *The Personal Vote: Constituency Service and Electoral Independence* (Cambridge, Mass., 1987).

SEE ALSO Constituencies AND The Role of Congressional Parties.

ELECTIONS TO THE STATE LEGISLATURES

Anthony Gierzynski

State legislative elections—and state legislatures in general—have been the "poor sister" of legislative research. While volumes of research have been published on congressional elections in the past several decades, state legislative elections have been the focus of only a few researchers. This neglect is due in part to the difficulty of obtaining good information and data from the states. It is also due to the fact that to many observers of politics, state legislative elections appear simply as congressional elections on a smaller scale. The fact of the matter is that they are not. While most state legislative elections do share some characteristics with congressional elections, including the high reelection rates of incumbents and the importance of campaign expenditures, there are significant differences between the two in district size, constituency size, competitiveness, campaign strategies, campaign-finance laws, the involvement of party organizations, the number of seats per district, and the length of terms.

State legislative elections also differ from congressional elections in one other very important way. Congressional elections are merely to one legislative body, but state legislative elections are to fifty separate legislative bodies. These fifty bodies represent a large number of cases—ninety-nine if one counts each chamber separately—that share the same basic structure but vary greatly with regard to practices and characteristics. State legislative elections therefore offer the perfect conditions for comparative research of legislative elections. Studying elections comparatively allows researchers to determine how the different characteristics of elections have an impact on the nature and the outcomes of elections and, ultimately, how the differences in elections have an impact on matters of public policy. This advantage of studying state legislative politics, along with the increased importance of the role of state gov-

ernments as a result of the policies of the Reagan years, has resulted in a greater interest in legislative elections among researchers and politicos. In 1990 a very basic set of information, comprehensive election returns, was available to researchers for the first time. Since the release of the election-returns data, there has been an explosion of research on state legislative elections as political scientists have combined the election returns with other data, such as campaign-finance data, to explore the rich variation among state legislatures.

The purpose of this essay is to provide the reader with a general overview of the issues in state legislative elections and convey the basic substance of what legislative researchers have found to date about these elections. The first part focuses on the role of two institutional characteristics in legislative elections—districts and terms. The second part concentrates on competition in state legislative elections, and the final section is concerned with the nature of state legislative campaigns.

STATE LEGISLATIVE DISTRICTS

One of the important ways in which state legislative elections differ from congressional elections is in the characteristics of the legislative districts. And what legislative elections are like depends a lot on the nature of the legislative districts. State legislative districts differ in population, in the number of legislators elected to represent the district, and in geographic size, whereas U.S. House districts vary only in terms of geographic size. As Table 1 shows, the population of state legislative districts varies greatly from state to state. State house districts average about 50,900 persons and state senate districts average about 122,700 persons. These averages are significantly less than the approximately 500,000 persons in districts of the U.S. House.

Table 1
POPULATION OF STATE LEGISLATIVE DISTRICTS AND LENGTH OF TERMS

	Senate			House		
	Seats	District Population[a]	Term (years)	Seats	District Population[a]	Term (years)
Alabama	35	115,450	4	105	38,480	4
Alaska	20	27,500	4	40	13,750	2
Arizona	30	122,170	2	60	122,170[b]	2
Arkansas	35	67,160	4	100	23,510	2
California	40	744,000	4	80	372,000	2
Colorado	35	94,130	4	65	50,680	2
Connecticut	36	91,310	2	151	21,770	2
Delaware	21	31,720	4	41	16,250	2
Florida	40	323,450	4	120	107,820	2
Georgia	56	115,680	2	180	35,990	2
Hawaii	25	44,330	4	51	21,730	2
Idaho	42	23,970	2	84	23,970[b]	2
Illinois	59	193,740	4	118	96,870	2
Indiana	50	111,080	4	100	55,540	2
Iowa	50	55,540	4	100	27,770	2
Kansas	40	61,940	4	125	19,820	2
Kentucky	38	96,980	4	100	36,850	2
Louisiana	39	108,200	4	105	40,190	4
Maine	35	35,080	2	151	8,130	2
Maryland	47	101,730	4	141	33,910	4
Massachusetts	40	150,410	2	160	37,600	2
Michigan	38	244,610	4	110	84,500	2
Minnesota	67	65,300	4	134	32,650	2
Mississippi	52	49,490	4	122	21,090	4
Missouri	34	150,500	4	163	31,390	2
Montana	50	15,980	4	100	7,990	2
Nebraska	49	32,210	4	—	—	—

(continued)

Only the California and Texas state senate districts have populations greater than U.S. House districts. At the other extreme, seven states— New Hampshire, Vermont, North Dakota, Wyoming, Montana, Maine, and South Dakota— have house districts with populations under 10,000. State legislative-district populations can differ to great extremes, as illustrated by the fact that the population in one of California's state senate districts is equal to that in about 268 of New Hampshire's state house districts! The great range in population of state legislative districts means that state legislative elections are characterized by a wide variety of campaign techniques and that their outcomes are affected differently by the factors that are important in legislative elections.

The number of persons in a district affects the type and style of campaigns. Elections in districts with small populations allow legislators to campaign largely on a personal, door-to-door basis. Candidates for the New Hampshire House of Representatives, for example, have little trouble in meeting most of their approximately 2,800 constituents. In districts with large populations, however, candidates must use the impersonal means of the electronic and print media to reach voters. It is unimaginable that a state senate candidate in California, for example, could meet even most of the approximately 750,000 constituents in his or her district.

The style of campaigning employed, whether door-to-door or by mass media, is important

Table 1 *(continued)*
POPULATION OF STATE LEGISLATIVE DISTRICTS AND LENGTH OF TERMS

	Senate			House		
	Seats	District Population[a]	Term (years)	Seats	District Population[a]	Term (years)
Nevada	21	57,230	4	42	28,620	2
New Hampshire	24	46,210	2	400	2,770	2
New Jersey	40	193,260	4	80	193,250[b]	2
New Mexico	42	36,070	4	70	21,640	2
New York	61	294,930	2	150	119,940	2
North Carolina	50	132,570	2	120	55,240	2
North Dakota	53	12,620	4	106	12,620[b]	2
Ohio	33	328,700	4	99	109,570	2
Oklahoma	48	65,530	4	101	31,140	2
Oregon	30	94,740	4	60	47,370	2
Pennsylvania	50	237,630	4	203	58,530	2
Rhode Island	50	20,070	2	100	10,040	2
South Carolina	46	75,800	4	124	28,120	2
South Dakota	35	19,890	2	70	19,890[b]	2
Tennessee	33	147,790	4	99	49,260	2
Texas	31	547,950	4	150	113,240	2
Utah	29	59,410	4	75	22,970	2
Vermont	30	18,760	2	150	3,750	2
Virginia	40	154,680	4	100	61,870	2
Washington	49	99,320	4	98	49,660	2
West Virginia	34	52,750	4	100	17,940	2
Wisconsin	33	148,240	4	99	49,410	2
Wyoming	30	15,120	4	64	7,090	2

[a] Population is given for single-member districts in states with mixed district types. District populations were calculated by dividing the 1990 population of the state by the number of seats.
[b] Population for districts with 2 seats.

Source: Council of State Governments, *State Elective Officials and the Legislatures, 1991–92* (Lexington, Ky., 1991), p. v.

because it affects other aspects of the election such as the content of campaign messages and the importance of money in legislative elections. Candidates' messages given in media "sound bites" or thirty-second television advertisements are not going to contain the same detail or involve the same level of personal interaction that are characteristic of one-on-one or small-group situations. Money is more important in large districts because the means of communicating with voters—the electronic and print media—are more expensive. Furthermore, if a candidate wants to get a feel for a district with a large population, he or she will have to conduct polls, another expense that makes the amount of money a candidate has an important factor. The difference between large

and small districts is analogous to the differences found in the presidential primary system; some legislative elections are like the New Hampshire presidential primary and others are like Super Tuesday (when several states in the South hold their primaries simultaneously).

The size of the population of legislative districts affects more than the style of campaigning. It also affects the issues that are important in a legislative campaign as well as the level of competition. General elections in small districts are neither likely to involve serious policy disputes nor to be very competitive, because districts with few people are likely to be politically homogeneous (that is, they consist of citizens with similar views on politics). The reason for this is simply a matter of geography. People who live in close proximity to each other tend to share many of the same beliefs. Generally, the smaller the geographical region, the greater the similarity of its inhabitants. Competition, when it does occur in small, homogeneous districts, is often limited to the primary election of the dominant party in a district.

Large districts are likely to be more heterogeneous when it comes to public opinion. Legislative races in these districts may be characterized by candidates who build coalitions among various segments of the constituency based on policy preferences. Larger districts do not, however, automatically lead to legislative races based on issues. Legislators, who redraw the legislative districts every ten years, usually draw as few competitive districts as possible. Furthermore, studies of congressional elections have shown that incumbent members of Congress are very adept at using ombudsman services to constituents and to the district in order to keep legislative elections from turning on policy issues. It is unlikely that state legislators have failed to follow suit. The need to use the mass media to communicate with voters also, as discussed above, limits the breadth and depth of policy discussions in the campaign. Thus the potential for greater competition in large districts is not always realized.

The only differences in district population within states are the differences between senate and house districts and between single-member and multimember districts. This was not always the case. Prior to the 1962 landmark case of *Baker* v. *Carr*, 369 U.S. 186 (1962), state legislative districts varied greatly in population. Because population growth is slower in rural areas, their districts had small populations, while urban areas had districts with much larger populations—an imbalance that translated into an imbalance in political power in favor of the disproportionately well-represented rural areas of the states. With the exception of a few states, it was possible for a small percentage of a state's voting population to elect a majority of its legislators. In Nevada, for example, malapportionment (unequal district populations) made it possible for 8 percent of the state's population to elect a majority of the state's senators in 1962. Also that year, as little as 12 percent of the population could elect a

majority of the house in Connecticut, Florida, and Vermont.

In *Baker* v. *Carr*, the U.S. Supreme Court ruled that the issue of legislative malapportionment was a justifiable question (one in the Court's purview) and that legislative malapportionment violated the equal-protection clause of the Fourteenth Amendment. This decision led to subsequent rulings that forced state legislatures to follow the principle of "one person, one vote"—that is, to draw their state legislative districts so that all of the districts in the state have equal representation. This principle was extended to state senates in *Reynolds* v. *Sims*, 377 U.S. 533 (1964). So with the exception of multimember districts, all candidates for a chamber of a particular state legislature must campaign in districts of roughly the same population.

In order to maintain the "one person, one vote" principle, states must redraw the legislative districts (both congressional and state) every ten years after the official U.S. decennial census. Thus every ten years, the potential exists for legislators to find themselves in districts that include new constituents and new territory; sometimes when that is the case, they must vie with other incumbent legislators for the same seat. Redistricting thus affects state legislative elections just as it does congressional elections, for it sets a cycle of elections that repeats every ten years. Elections held at different points in that cycle differ in competitiveness and in the relative importance of party, incumbency, and money in shaping the outcome of legislative elections.

In elections just prior to redistricting, party involvement and competition for control over the legislature is at its highest because, for most states, the party that controls the state government is the party that draws the state legislative and congressional maps. And the party that draws the maps can do so to its advantage by maximizing the number of districts that its candidates can win easily. This practice is called gerrymandering. Legislative scholars point to a number of states, including California and Indiana, where this was clearly the case in the 1980s. But on the whole, the evidence on the effectiveness of partisan gerrymandering is mixed. New computer technology which allows state organizations to utilize election returns from previous years to measure the partisanship of the districts they draw, may or may not make gerrymandering more effective in the future. It also remains to be seen how the courts will react to future partisan-gerrymandering cases. In an Indiana case, *Davis* v. *Bandemer*, 106 S. Ct. 2810 (1986), the Supreme Court ruled for the first time that partisan gerrymandering was a justiciable question. The Court, however, rejected the Democrats' claim that the Republican-drawn Indiana legislative map was a case of gerrymandering.

Redistricting is less of a partisan issue in states that use a commission to draw the legislative maps. Eight states use commissions appointed by party leaders to draw state legislative districts; one of them, Iowa, uses its Legislative Service Bureau. In addition, Illinois utilizes a commission for redistricting, but only if the legislature and governor fail to agree on a legislative map. The partisan balance of the commission is decided by a lottery. The commission was necessary in 1980 and 1990, with the Democrats winning the lottery in 1980 and the Republicans winning in 1990.

In elections prior to redistricting, at least in states where a change in party control of the legislature is a possibility, a great deal of party activities and resources are devoted to winning enough seats to take control of the legislature. An indication of the level of party involvement in the elections just prior to redistricting is the involvement of the national and congressional parties in state legislative elections. In 1978 the Republican National Committee spent approximately $1.7 million on state legislative elections. In 1988 the Republican National State Elections Committee contributed ninety-four thousand dollars to state legislative candidates and the campaign committees of the senate and assembly Republicans in California. In 1990 the Republican National Committee contributed eighty-thousand dollars to the campaign committee of the Republicans in Oregon's house.

In elections immediately following redistricting, party involvement is still high as the parties attempt to win in the adjusted districts. These elections are also the most competitive. Many incumbent legislators decide to retire instead of running for reelection in what may be a radically altered district. This increases the number of open seats and consequently the amount of competition, in that races for open seats are the most competitive. A number of incumbents sometimes face off against each other, eliminating the advantage of incumbency. The 1990 round of redistricting in Iowa, for example, put 20 of the 50 incumbent senators and 40 of the 100 incumbent representatives in districts with other incumbents. Aside from the possibility of competition among themselves, incumbents who run for reelection in districts with new territory are more vulnerable because the new constituents are not familiar with the incumbent and his or her record. Because of the relative weakness of incumbents in new territory and the high level of competition, money plays a greater role in elections immediately following redistricting. (The elections that fall in the middle of the redistricting cycle see less competition, as incumbents have established their hold over their districts, and so quality challengers wait for the next redistricting to make their move.)

Another property of districts that varies in state legislative elections but not in congressional elections is the number of legislators elected per district. As Table 2 shows, seven state senates and fifteen state houses had multimember districts in 1988. The number of multimember districts has declined in recent years because authorities in some states, particularly in the South, used them to dilute minority voting strength. Multimember districts do serve other purposes, however—purposes the courts have recognized as legitimate, such as maintaining local boundaries or enhancing representation of dispersed minority groups. Thus, multimember districts are likely to remain an aspect of state legislative elections.

There are four different types of multimember districts in the states: multimember districts with posts; free-for-all multimember districts; alternating-elections multimember districts; and floterial multimember districts. In multimember districts with posts, such as those in Alaska and Arkansas, candidates vie for separate seats. Voters select from one set of candidates for one seat and another set of candidates for the other seat. Free-for-all multimember districts, such as those in Arizona and Indiana, pit all candidates against each

Table 2
STATES WITH MULTIMEMBER DISTRICTS

	Senate			House		
	#	Seats per District	Type	#	Seats per District	Type
Alaska	6	2	Alternating	13	2	Posts
Arizona				30	2	Free
Arkansas				4	2	Posts
				6	3	Posts
Georgia				8	2	Posts
				5	3+	Posts
				2	1	Floterial
Idaho	3	2	Posts	27	2	Posts
	3	2	Posts	3	4	Posts
				3	6	Posts
Indiana				9	2	Free
				7	3	Free
Maryland				7	2	Free
				38	3	Free
Nevada	7	2	Alternating			
New Hampshire				40	2	Free
				35	3	Free
				29	4+	Free
New Jersey				40	2	Free
North Dakota	1	2	Alternating	49	2	Free
	1	2	Free	2	4	Free
South Dakota				35	2	Free
Vermont	6	2	Free	44	2	Free
	4	3+	Free			
Washington				47	2	Posts
West Virginia	16	2	Alternating	14	2	Free
				12	3+	Free
Wyoming	4	2	Alternating	6	2	Free
	3	4	Alternating	9	3+	Free

Source: State Legislative Election Returns in the United States: 1968–1989 (ICPSR 8907). Free = free-for-all districts, Posts = districts with posts, Floterial = overlapping districts, Alternating = members elected in alternating years. Shaded areas indicate multimember districts exist in only one chamber in the state.

other. If there are three seats in the district, the top three vote getters are awarded the seats. Voters may cast as many votes as there are seats. Alternating-elections multimember districts, such as those in Alaska and Nevada, are used only for senate districts. In these districts two senate candidates are elected for four-year terms from the same district but in alternating elections. Floterial districts, found only in Georgia in 1988, are districts that share territory with another district of the same chamber. Voters in the areas of the districts that overlap have the opportunity to vote in the races in both districts. Before 1982 one other type of multimember district, found only in Illinois, had three-member districts with a proportional-representation system. Voters could cast all three of their votes for one candidate or divide their vote among two or three candidates. The system guaranteed minority representation in each legislative district. A unique system, it was discontinued by Illinois voters as part of an initiative to cut the size of the state house.

Most multimember districts elect two legislators. Many districts, however, have three or more members. In the 1980s the most legislators elected in a district was twelve, in West Virginia house district 23. One New Hampshire district, the 147th, elected ten, and two house districts in Wyoming, the 11th and 15th, elected nine.

There are some differences in elections between multimember and single-member districts. The effort required to be an informed voter is greater in multimember districts, since voters must keep up with more than one incumbent and familiarize themselves with more than one challenger. Multimember districts have slightly higher turnover rates than single-member districts. The presence of free-for-all multimember districts is an advantage for women and a disadvantage for African American candidates. Multimember and single-member districts do not differ, however, regarding the reelection success of incumbents.

The nature of elections is also affected by the geographic size of the district. Since state legislative elections are held in districts based on population, they vary dramatically in the amount of territory that they cover within states as well as between states. State legislative elections share this characteristic with congressional elections, but because the range in the population of state legislative districts is greater than it is for congressional districts, the range in geographic size is also greater. Some statistics on state legislative district size for selected state houses are presented in Table 3. In this sample, state legislative districts range in size from one square mile (2.6 square kilometers) to just under twenty-nine thousand square miles (75,400 square kilometers).

Districts covering large territories make both personal campaigns and campaigns via the electronic media difficult and increase their cost. Large districts require a great deal of travel, making it difficult for candidates to have personal contact with the voters. Large districts also pose problems for the use of the electronic media in reaching voters, because the reach of radio and television channels is unlikely to extend over the entire district. As a result, it is necessary to purchase airtime in a number of different media markets, which means additional campaign expenditures. The same holds true for the use of newspaper advertisements in large districts. Research con-

Table 3
HOUSE DISTRICT SIZE FOR SELECTED STATES (IN SQUARE MILES)

	Average Size	Smallest District	Largest District
California	1958	18	28,991
Colorado	1594	6	12,916
Indiana	552	56	4533
Iowa	563	39	1964
Kentucky	392	14	1052
Michigan	518	13	6063
Minnesota	594	6	4760
Missouri	423	3	2985
New York	316	1	4731
Oregon	1603	21	28,286
Washington	1321	105	12,403
Wisconsin	550	6	4226

Sources: Calculated by author using information on county size from the U.S. Department of Commerce, Bureau of the Census, *County and City Data Book, 1988* (Washington, D.C., 1988) and the State Legislative Elections Returns, 1968–1989 (ICPSR 8907).

ducted by the author has uncovered a sizable number of lower-chamber districts that contain two or more separate television markets.

Districts that cover a small amount of territory, like districts with small populations, make campaigning door-to-door easy. Use of the electronic media, however, is as problematic for very small districts as it is for very large ones, but for the opposite reason. In very large districts, the problem with using radio or television is being unable to reach all constituents with one station. In very small districts, the problem with using the electronic media is the inability to exclude constituents who are not in the candidate's district. This might not be a problem if the candidates were charged for airtime based on whom they wanted to reach. They are charged, however, based on whom the stations do reach, and because small districts exist in large urban areas, candidates there have to pay for reaching a lot of people who will not participate in their election.

TERMS

Table 1 lists the terms for each chamber in the fifty states. No state senator is elected for a term as long as that of a U.S. senator. Thirty-eight states allow their senators four-year terms. (In three of these states, Illinois, Montana, and New Jersey, every third term is two years in order to adjust for the ten-year redistricting cycle.) Twelve states require that state senators run for reelection every two years. State representatives in four states serve four-year terms. The rest of the states have two-year terms for their representatives.

Until recently there were no limits on the number of times state legislators and members of Congress could run for reelection. Voter dissatisfaction with the responsiveness of national and state governments to popular will has changed this. In 1990 voters in California, Colorado, and Oklahoma voted to limit the number of terms that their state legislators could serve. California's Proposition 140, which was upheld in a ruling by the California Supreme Court, limited members of the state assembly to three two-year terms and state senators to two four-year terms. Colorado limited its legislators to eight years of consecutive service per chamber and also limited the terms its members of Congress can serve. Oklahoma limited its legislators to a total of twelve years of service in either chamber. In 1992, twelve additional states passed initiatives to limit the number of terms that their state legislators can serve. Included among these states was Washington, whose voters had just rejected term limits in the 1991 election.

What effect will term limits have on state legislative elections? A study by Moncrief, Thompson, Haddon, and Hoyer (1992) indicates that twelve-year term limits will have little impact on turnover in state legislatures because only a small percentage of legislators stay there for that many years. This is especially true of citizen-type legislatures, composed of part-time legislators with low pay, no staff, and who meet infrequently. Considering the dynamics of legislative elections, the effect of term limits on incumbency success and competition in state legislatures is likely to be limited. With term limits there will be more races without incumbents, but there is no evidence to indicate that the races with incumbents will be any more competitive than before term limits. In fact, elections between terms might even be less competitive, since strong candidates might concede elections to incumbents and

wait for seats to become open. Competition between the parties is unlikely to increase with term limits, since lack of competition in legislative elections before limits is as much a function of the way the districts are drawn as it is of the strength of incumbents. Districts that are dominated by one party will elect candidates from that party regardless of term limits. Comparative state research will be able to assess more concretely the effect term limits have on legislative elections and on the functioning of legislative bodies as the limitations take effect.

COMPETITION

Competitive elections have long been one of the linchpins of a democratic system. When it comes to legislatures, competition in elections can be thought of in two different ways: (1) competition for control of the legislature and (2) competition in the legislative districts. In the past several decades, the U.S. House of Representatives has seen a decline in both types of competition; the Republicans have failed to threaten the Democrats' hold over the House, and the margin of victory for House incumbents has increased. Competition in state legislative elections in the late twentieth century has not followed the same pattern. District-level competition has decreased, but competition for the control of legislatures has actually increased in many states as the historical dominance of the Democrats in the South and the border states and of the Republicans in the Midwest, West, and New England has declined. This is demonstrated in Figure 1, which charts the average difference in the percentage of seats held by Democrats and Republicans in lower chambers of state legislatures from 1950 to 1990, with the states grouped by region. The figure shows that the average differences between the percentage of Democratic and Republican seats has moved closer to zero (completely competitive) in all regions, though the Republicans still have a ways to go before they can be considered serious challengers for control of the South's legislatures. Harvey J. Tucker and Ronald E. Weber (1992) found similar trends of increasing competition for control of state legislatures in a sample of eighteen states. The trend is also reflected in changes in the measure of two-party competition developed

ELECTIONS TO THE STATE LEGISLATURES

Figure 1

MEAN PERCENT DIFFERENCE BETWEEN NUMBERS OF DEMOCRATS AND REPUBLICANS IN STATE HOUSES

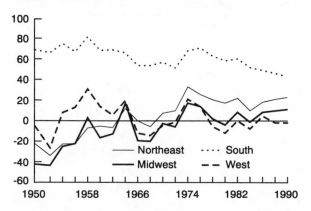

Source: Constructed by the author from data provided by the Social Science Research Institute, Northern Illinois University.

by Austin Ranney, as seen in Bibby, Cotter, Gibson and Huckshorn (1990).

While competition for control of legislatures has increased, competition within the individual districts has declined. The decline in district-level competition is apparent from a number of different perspectives. The percentage of marginal, or competitive, seats has declined; the percentage of seats contested by both parties has declined; incumbent candidates are winning by larger margins; and membership turnover has decreased.

The decline in marginal districts has been noted by a number of political scientists. Weber, Tucker, and Brace (1991) calculated the average percentage of competitive seats from 1950 to 1986 for a sample of twenty states. At the low end of the scale were states like Tennessee and Massachusetts; fewer than 25 percent of their lower-house legislative districts were competitive between 1950 and 1986. At the high end of the scale were Iowa, Colorado, New Jersey, and Wyoming; more than 55 percent of their districts were competitive. The percentage of competitive seats for the same time period for the U.S. House of Representatives was 35.5 percent. All but two of the states that were studied showed a decline in the percent of competitive seats. Ray and Havick (1981) found the same decline in marginal elections for eight states from 1892 to 1972. Evidently the marginals are vanishing in state leg-

islative elections as well as in congressional elections.

The decline in the percentage of state legislative elections that are contested by both parties is also well documented. While fourteen out of twenty states examined in Weber, Tucker, and Brace's sample had contested elections in 80 percent or more of their lower-house districts in the period between 1950 and 1986, the percentage of contested seats declined in sixteen of the twenty states studied. There has been a significant increase in contested seats in California and Tennessee. The increase in California is partially the result of increasingly divisive partisanship and the activities of the assembly caucus campaign committees. One of the goals of the Assembly Democrats was to have a Democrat running in every district, and they accomplished this goal in 1988. The increase in contested seats in Tennessee, the only southern state in the sample of Weber, Brace, and Tucker, is probably due to the increase in competitiveness of the Republican party in the South. An analysis of the trends in other southern states, however, is needed to test this notion further.

As one might suspect, an increase in the winning margin of incumbent candidates has accompanied the decline in marginal and contested seats. Examining incumbents' votes in sixteen state houses and senates between the years 1968 and 1986, Garand (1991) found that the average vote for incumbents in state house contests was 70.7 percent, and the average vote for incumbents in state senate contests was 68.4 percent. In fifteen of the sixteen states he examined, the incumbents' vote percentage increased between 1968 and 1986.

Interestingly, this trend has not made incumbents any safer from electoral defeat. Just as with congressional incumbents, the higher vote totals for incumbents has not translated into higher probabilities of winning reelection. One explanation for this is that the percentage of incumbents winning reelection was already so high, around 90 percent, that there was no room for improvement. Table 4 presents the percentage of incumbents winning reelection over two time periods, 1968–1976 and 1978–1986, for fourteen states. An increase in the magnitude of vote swings between elections—an explanation given for the same phenomenon observed in congressional elec-

Table 4
PERCENTAGE OF INCUMBENTS WINNING REELECTION

	Upper Chamber		Lower Chamber	
	1968–1976	1978–1986	1968–1976	1978–1986
California	93%	93%	95%	97%
Colorado	87%	96%	91%	89%
Connecticut	81%	78%	82%	87%
Delaware	92%	94%	93%	89%
Pennsylvania	89%	94%	93%	97%
Iowa	77%	89%	89%	92%
Kentucky	79%	96%	92%	96%
Michigan	89%	99%	96%	95%
Missouri	89%	99%	93%	98%
New York	97%	98%	90%	95%
Ohio	82%	83%	94%	96%
Rhode Island	95%	93%	92%	96%
Utah	90%	81%	85%	84%
Wisconsin	87%	92%	90%	93%

Source: Malcolm E. Jewell and David A. Breaux, "The Effect of Incumbency on State Legislative Elections," *Legislative Studies Quarterly* 13 (November 1988): 501. Reprinted with permission of the Comparative Legislative Research Center, the University of Iowa.

tions—provides another plausible reason why incumbents' increased vote margins have not translated into safer seats.

The decreasing turnover rate in state legislatures also reflects the decline in competition over legislative districts. Turnover was probably the first aspect of state legislative elections tracked on a systematic basis. As early as the turn of the century, Haynes (1906) was interested in turnover rates of state legislatures, primarily because of its implications for the election of U.S. senators by state legislatures. Turnover rates were tracked later by Hyneman (1938) and Rosenthal (1974). Patterson (1990) presents data on turnover up to 1987.

Legislative turnover, measured by the percentage of new members, reached a low around 20 to 25 percent in the 1980s, compared to a level between 30 and 40 percent in the early 1960s. Turnover rates fluctuate significantly, often increasing significantly following redistricting. As discussed above, states that have adopted limitations on the number of terms that legislators can serve should not see a return to high levels of turnover unless the term limitations are severe. In the time span of twelve years, the length of time a legislator can serve under the Oklahoma term-limitation law, about three-quarters of the legislators leave even without term limits. However, California's limit of six years for members of the assembly is severe and should substantially increase turnover in that state.

Turnover captures much more than electoral competition. The decline in turnover also reflects a decline in those leaving the legislature voluntarily. The attractiveness of legislative service has increased since the movement to professionalize legislatures that began in the 1960s. Since then, legislators in professional legislatures have received better staff support, higher pay, and have been part of a body that is more independent and more of an equal partner with governors in running the states. In addition to professionalism, the opportunities for legislators to advance their careers by running for higher offices also affect turnover by increasing voluntary departures. States with greater opportunities for political advancement, which basically are states with many state senate and congressional seats, have higher turnover rates as measured by average years of service.

In sum, the picture of competition in state legislative elections is not a simple one. Competition for control of legislatures has increased in many states, while competition in the districts is on the decline and turnover is much lower than in the past. How can such opposite trends be occurring at the same time?

No one has yet provided a convincing answer. One possible explanation is that competition in state legislative elections is becoming relegated to a few districts in each state. The number of contested elections has declined in most states, and legislative redistricting and the allocation of campaign resources are probably concentrating competition in a few districts. Legislators in control of the redistricting process seek to do two things: (1) strengthen their own districts by increasing the strength of their party in the district and (2) concentrate the opposition party into fewer districts by packing them with opposition-party voters. This results in legislative maps with a large number of uncompetitive districts and just a handful of competitive ones. In addition to the redistricting process, there is substantial evidence that political parties and party leaders have been channeling campaign resources into competitive districts, often redistributing money contributed by political action committees, corporations, and individuals.

The implications of these trends are already being felt. Increased party competition for control of the legislatures as well as for the control of the governors' mansions has increased the frequency of split control of state government. The resulting battles and stalemates between the two branches, along with the high reelection rates of incumbents, is probably an important source of the public frustration that has manifested itself in the popularity of the term-limitation movement.

CAMPAIGNS

The typical state legislative election attracts little attention from the public; turnout is even lower than in U.S. House elections. Voters, who have little information about congressional candidates, are likely to have even less on the policy positions and backgrounds of state legislative candidates. In many states the traditional mechanism for disseminating information about candidates, the state and local political party organizations, no longer provides that service. Party grass-roots organizations weakened early in the twentieth century because candidates found it necessary to build their own organizations in order to win the increasingly common primary elections. The spread of the primary and the weakening of the political parties has resulted in the candidate-centered campaigns that characterize elections throughout the American political system. Given these conditions of state legislative elections, factors such as partisanship, incumbency, and money are likely to be at least as important as they are in congressional elections.

The candidates' party affiliation is important in state legislative elections for much the same reason as it is in congressional elections. It is the one piece of information that is available to voters in the voting booth. For voters who know little or nothing of the candidates, the party label provides some general idea of the candidate's basic political philosophy as well as his or her stands on a number of issues. Since most voters feel some attachment to one of the parties, that attachment, or partisanship, will affect their vote. Though the lack of polling data on state legislative elections prohibits scholars from drawing any conclusions about how party affects voters' decisions, there is strong district-level evidence that partisanship plays an important role in state legislative elections. The party vote in state legislative districts is strongly related to strength of the party in the district as measured by party registration, the previous vote in the district, and the average party vote in the district.

Incumbency plays as large a role in state legislative elections as it does in congressional elections. Table 4 indicates just how important incumbency is in state legislative elections. The states that have been studied vary little with regard to the success rates of incumbents. As in congressional elections, legislative candidates for states' lower chambers are successful in their reelection bids around 90 percent of the time or better. In contrast with the U.S. Senate, state-senate reelection rates are very close to those of the state house incumbents. In 1986, 100 percent of the incumbents running for reelection to the Rhode Island, Delaware, New York, Michigan, Iowa, Wisconsin, Missouri, and California senates were successful. One hundred percent of all state house incumbents were successful in California and Ohio in 1986.

The effect incumbency has on the vote in state legislative elections is similar to the effect observed in congressional elections. As mentioned above, the margins by which state legislative incumbents win have increased. There is also strong evidence of a sophomore surge and retirement slump. Incumbent state legislative candidates experience an increase in their electoral margin in their second race, known as the "sophomore surge." The magnitude of this surge has been found to be related to the resources available to legislators, such as staff. Because staff and other resources are used primarily for constituency service, this association between resources and the magnitude of the sophomore surge is an indication that constituency service may be partially responsible for the high rate of incumbent success among state legislators as well as among members of Congress. Furthermore, the vote for an incumbent's party declines in districts following the retirement of an incumbent, which is termed the "retirement slump."

State legislative elections, particularly those in districts with moderate or large populations, are elections in which money plays an important role. The costs of legislative campaigns has increased dramatically. For example, between 1978 and 1986, the amount of money spent in Oregon and California state-senate races increased 135 percent and 89 percent, respectively, controlling for inflation. For the sake of comparison, the cost of U.S. Senate races increased by 39 percent and the cost of U.S. House races increased by 20 percent over the same period. As Table 5 indicates, the costs of legislative campaigns vary widely from state to state.

Candidates need money in order to communicate with voters, and the need for money has increased as the costs of communicating with them has increased. Candidates communicate via grass-roots organizations, the news media, and campaign material. The candidate who has money can build a campaign organization, purchase radio and television air time, cover the district with name advertisement in the form of yard signs and bumper stickers, and mail campaign material directly to potential voters. With the exception of small districts, the candidate with little money to spend has difficulty getting his or her message across and consequently fails to appeal to voters.

Several studies have found a significant relationship between money spent on campaigns and votes received in state legislative elections. Money has also been found to play an important role in state legislative primary elections.

Table 5
AVERAGE EXPENDITURES FOR STATE HOUSE CANDIDATES IN 1988

	Average Expenditures
California	$370,722
Idaho	$4,425
Maine	$2,368
Minnesota	$13,244
Missouri	$9,618
Montana	$2,692
North Carolina	$12,085
New Jersey	$48,033
Oregon	$35,982
Pennsylvania	$18,462
Washington	$25,811
Wisconsin	$14,868

Sources: Compiled by David Breaux, William Cassey, Anthony Gierzynski, Keith Hamm, Malcolm Jewell, Gary Moncrief, and Joel Thompson from various state agencies. Data from Maine were made available by Senator Charles Pray.

The relationship between money and the vote follows one of the patterns that has been observed at the congressional level—money is more important to challengers than to incumbents. Higher levels of spending also result in higher levels of voter turnout in state legislative elections.

State legislative candidates are not completely without assistance for their campaigns today. Many legislative candidates receive help from a relatively new political party organization, the legislative party campaign committee. Legislative party caucuses in a large number of states have formed campaign committees, much like the Democratic Congressional Campaign Committee and the National Republican Congressional Committee. These caucus campaign committees raise money and help legislative candidates by providing television and radio studios and media experts, conducting public-opinion polls, running phone banks, registering voters, and sending out mass mailings of campaign literature on behalf of their party's legislative candidates. Legislative party campaign committees are effective because they often work in tandem with other contributors, including political action committees and legislative party leaders (who also contribute significant amounts of money to other legislative candidates). They are also effective because they concentrate their efforts on close races.

The regulation of campaign finance is another area of state government where there is a great deal of diversity. The federal government limits the amounts that individuals, political action committees, and political parties can give to congressional candidates. Federal law prohibits corporations from giving contributions directly to congressional candidates. State legislative candidates, however, are not regulated by federal campaign-finance laws. Instead they have to follow state regulations, which vary in strictness. Some states have limits on contributions and expenditures. Two states, Minnesota and Wisconsin, have public financing for state legislative elections. Legislative candidates in these states are awarded public grants if they meet certain requirements, which include limitations on contributions and expenditures. Other states have much more lax campaign laws: some allow corporations to contribute directly to candidates, and many place no limits on what individuals or groups can contribute.

In sum, the three factors that appear to play the dominant role in shaping the outcome of state legislative elections are party, incumbency, and money. Studies have found that state legislative elections are also responsive to national and state political trends. There is evidence of both presidential and gubernatorial coattails effects on legislative elections; seat changes in state legislative elections are sensitive to the presidential and gubernatorial vote. The president's party typically experiences midterm losses in state legislative seats. And there is some evidence that seat changes in state legislative elections are related to national economic trends.

CONCLUSION

There is still much to learn about state legislative elections. This knowledge constitutes one of the most critical gaps in our understanding of voting behavior. We can only speculate that voters make their decisions for state legislators much in the way they do for members of Congress. But as we have seen in this essay, state legislative elections differ from congressional elections in a number of important ways, and these differences could alter the decision-making process for voters. Another critical gap in our knowledge is in the area of campaign finance at the state level. Comprehensive data on candidate revenues and expenditures, for instance, are limited.

Fortunately it appears that many of our gaps of knowledge regarding state legislative elections will continue to be filled in the coming years, since the attention scholars have been giving to state legislative elections is not likely to fade. State politics and, as a consequence, the election of state policymakers, has become more important as states have taken on more responsibilities since the beginning of the Reagan presidency. The opportunity for comparative research to determine the impact of innovations such as public funding, term limitations, and campaign-finance reform, as well as the effect that different factors have on the outcome of state legislative races, is also likely to keep scholars focused on state legislative elections. States are indeed the experimental laboratories of democracy, but as far as legislative elections are concerned, only since the late 1980s has anyone bothered to collect and analyze the data from their experiments.

BIBLIOGRAPHY

Incumbency
The effect of incumbency on the vote has been addressed in a number of recent articles, including DAVID A. BREAUX, "Specifying the Impact of Incumbency on State Legislative Elections: A District-Level Analysis," *American Politics Quarterly* 18 (July 1990): 270–285; MALCOLM E. JEWELL and DAVID A. BREAUX, "The Effect of Incumbency on State Legislative Elec-

tions," *Legislative Studies Quarterly* 13 (November 1988): 495–514; and THOMAS M. HOLBROOK and CHARLES M. TIDMARCH, "Sophomore Surge in State Legislative Elections, 1968–1986," *Legislative Studies Quarterly* 16 (February 1991): 49–63. On the impact of incumbency in primary elections, see MALCOLM E. JEWELL and DAVID A. BREAUX, "Southern Primary and Electoral Competition and Incumbent Success," *Legislative Studies Quarterly* 16 (February 1991): 129–143.

Turnover
For an early study on turnover in state legislatures, see CHARLES HYNEMAN, "Tenure and Turnover of Legislative Personnel," *Annals of the American Academy of Political and Social Science* 23 (January 1938): 21–31. For more recent studies on turnover, see ALAN ROSENTHAL, "Turnover in State Legislatures," *American Journal of Political Science* 18 (August 1974): 609–616 and RICHARD G. NIEMI and LAURA WINSKY, "Membership Turnover in U.S. State Legislatures: Trends and Effects of Districting," *Legislative Studies Quarterly* 12 (February 1987): 115–123. PEVERILL SQUIRE, "Career Opportunities and Membership Stability in Legislatures," *Legislative Studies Quarterly* 13 (February 1988): 65–82, examines two factors that affect turnover: legislative professionalism and opportunities for higher office. On the impact of term limits on membership turnover, see GARY MONCRIEF, JOEL THOMPSON, MICHAEL HADDON, and ROBERT HOYER, "For Whom the Bell Tolls: Term Limits and State Legislatures," *Legislative Studies Quarterly* 17 (February 1992): 37–47.

Competitiveness
For competition at the district level, see JAMES C. GARAND, "Electoral Marginality in State Legislative Elections: 1968–86," *Legislative Studies Quarterly* 16 (February 1991): 7–28; RONALD E. WEBER, HARVEY J. TUCKER, and PAUL BRACE, "Vanishing Marginals in State Legislative Elections," *Legislative Studies Quarterly* 16 (February 1991): 29–47; and DAVID RAY and J. HAVICK, "A Longitudinal Analysis of Party Competition in State Legislative Elections," *American Journal of Political Science* 25 (February 1981): 119–128. HARVEY J. TUCKER and RONALD E. WEBER examine differences between state-level and district-level competitiveness in "Electoral Change in U.S. States: System Versus Constituency Competition," in GARY F. MONCRIEF and JOEL A. THOMPSON, eds., *Changing Patterns in State Legislative Careers* (Ann Arbor, Mich., 1992). RICHARD G. NIEMI, SIMON JACKMAN, and LAURA R. WINSKY focus on competition in multimember districts in "Candidacies and Competitiveness in Multimember Districts," *Legislative Studies Quarterly* 16 (February 1991): 91–109.

See CHARLES M. TIDMARCH, EDWARD LONERGAN, and JOHN SCIORTINO, "Interparty Competion in the U.S. States: Legislative Elections, 1970–1978" *Legislative Studies Quarterly* 11 (August 1986): 353–374, for discussion of competition at the state level.

Campaign Finance
RUTH S. JONES, "Financing State Elections," in MICHAEL J. MALBIN, ed., *Money and Politics in the United States: Financing Elections in the 1980s* (Chatham, N.J., 1984), and chap. 9 of FRANK J. SORAUF, *Money in American Elections* (Glenview, Ill., 1988), provide general overviews of campaign finance in state legislative elections. On the role of money in the outcome of elections, see HARVEY J. TUCKER and RONALD E. WEBER, "State Legislative Election Outcomes: Contextual Effects and Legislative Performance Effects," *Legislative Studies Quarterly* 12 (November 1987): 537–553; MICHAEL W. GILES and ANITA PRITCHARD, "Campaign Expenditures and Legislative Elections in Florida," *Legislative Studies Quarterly* 10 (February 1985): 71–88; and GREGORY A. CALDEIRA and SAMUEL C. PATTERSON, "Bringing Home the Votes: Electoral Outcomes in State Legislative Races," *Political Behavior* 4, no. 1 (1982): 33–67. For a multistate study of the role of money in the outcome of general elections, see ANTHONY GIERZYNSKI and DAVID A. BREAUX, "Money and Votes in State Legislative Elections," *Legislative Studies Quarterly* 16 (May 1991): 203–217. For a multistate study on the role of money in primary elections, see DAVID A. BREAUX and ANTHONY GIERZYNSKI, "'It's Money That Matters': Campaign Expenditures and State Legislative Primaries," *Legislative Studies Quarterly* 16 (August 1991): 429–443. For differences between party and PAC contributions, see RUTH S. JONES and THOMAS J. BORRIS, "Strategic Contributing in Legislative Campaigns: The Case of Minnesota," *Legislative Studies Quarterly* 10 (February 1985): 89–105.

Turnout
ERIK W. AUSTIN, JEROME M. CLUBB, WILLIAM H. FLANIGAN, PETER GRANDA, and NANCY H. ZINGALE examine turnout in state legislative elections, comparing it with turnout for other elections in "Electoral Participation in the United States, 1968–86," *Legislative Studies Quarterly* 16 (February 1991): 145–164. See HARVEY J. TUCK-

ER, "Contextual Models of Participation in U.S. Legislative Elections," *Western Political Quarterly* 39 (March 1986): 67–78, for a study examining the factors affecting turnout in state legislative elections in Texas.

National and Statewide Forces
JAMES E. CAMPBELL, "Presidential Coattails and Midterm Losses in State Legislative Elections," *American Political Science Review* 80 (March 1986): 45–63 and JOHN E. CHUBB, "Institutions, the Economy, and the Dynamics of State Elections," *American Political Science Review* 82 (March 1988): 133–154, examine the effect of national and statewide forces on the vote in state legislative elections.

On the role of national parties in state legislative elections, see JOHN F. BIBBY, "Political Parties and Federalism: The Republican National Committee Involvement in Gubernatorial and Legislative Elections," *Publius* 9 (Winter 1979): 229–236; JOHN F. BIBBY, CORNELIUS P. COTTER, JAMES L. GIBSON and ROBERT J. HUCKSHORN, "Parties in State Politics," in VIRGINIA GRAY, HERBERT JACOB, and ROBERT B. ALBRITTON, eds., *Politics in the American States: A Comparative Analysis*, 5th ed. (Glenview, Ill., 1990), provide a discussion of the role of political parties in state legislative elections as part of their discussion of state parties. For the role of state legislative party-campaign committees in legislative elections, see ANTHONY GIERZYNSKI, *Legislative Party Campaign Committees in the American States* (Lexington, Ky., 1992); ANTHONY GIERZYNSKI and MALCOLM E. JEWELL, "Legislative Caucus and Leadership Campaign Committees," in GARY F. MONCRIEF and A. JOEL THOMPSON, eds., *Changing Patterns in State Legislative Careers* (Ann Arbor, Mich., 1992); and JEFFREY M. STONECASH, "Working at the Margins: Campaign Finance and Party Strategy in New York Assembly Elections," *Legislative Studies Quarterly* 13 (November 1988): 477–493.

State Legislatures: General Works
There are a number of studies focusing on state legislatures in general that provide insights into state legislative elections. These include ALAN ROSENTHAL, *Governors and Legislatures: Contending Powers* (Washington, D.C., 1990); THOMAS R. DYE, "State Legislative Politics," in HERBERT JACOB and KENNETH N. VINES, eds., *Politics in the American States: A Comparative Analysis*, 2d ed. (Boston, 1971); MALCOLM E. JEWELL and DAVID M. OLSON, *Political Parties and Elections in American States*, 3d ed. (Chicago, 1988); and SAMUEL C. PATTERSON, "State Legislators and the Legislatures," in VIRGINIA GRAY, HERBERT JACOB, and ROBERT B. ALBRITTON, eds., *Politics in the American States: A Comparative Analysis*, 5th ed. (Glenview, Ill., 1990).

Miscellaneous Works
On women candidates see ROBERT DARCY, SUSAN WELCH, and JANET CLARK, "Women Candidates in Single- and Multi-Member Districts," *Social Science Quarterly* 66 (December 1985): 945–953. On divided government, see MORRIS P. FIORINA, *Divided Government* (New York, 1992), and for one of the earliest studies at least partially concerned with state legislative elections (because of their role in electing U.S. senators), see GEORGE H. HAYNES, *The Election of Senators* (New York, 1906).

SEE ALSO Legislative Incumbency and Insulation; Political Parties in State Legislatures; AND Women in Legislatures.

ELECTIONS TO THE U.S. HOUSE OF REPRESENTATIVES

Alan I. Abramowitz

The 1992 election produced one very predictable result and one somewhat surprising one. Despite the following factors—redistricting, the largest number of congressional retirements in 50 years, and widespread anti-incumbent sentiment in the electorate fueled by the House Bank scandal—the Democratic party predictably maintained control of the House of Representatives. More surprising, the Democratic presidential challenger, Bill Clinton, rode a wave of voter discontent with the economy to a decisive victory over the Republican incumbent, George Bush, thus breaking the twelve-year Republican hold on the White House. For the first time since 1980, one party, the Democrats, would control the executive and legislative branches of government.

Divided government, once rare, has become an accepted fact of American political life. Every Republican president between World War II and 1992 had to deal with a Democratic Congress. In 1980 the Republicans did manage to gain a majority of seats in the Senate—an advantage they maintained until the 1986 midterm election. Since 1955, however, the House has been firmly controlled by the Democratic party—the longest period of one-party rule in any branch of government in American history.

The Democratic grip on the House of Representatives has several explanations. Despite the success of Republican candidates in presidential elections, the Republican party has had difficulty gaining the enduring loyalty of most American voters. Throughout the 1960s and 1970s, far more Americans identified with the Democratic party than with the Republican. As recently as 1980, according to a CBS News–New York Times exit poll, Democratic identifiers outnumbered Republicans, 46 percent to 30 percent. The Democratic edge in party identification gave Democratic candidates a significant advantage in most Senate and House contests. Party identification is an important factor in evaluating information about candidates for public office. In addition, many voters, if they know little or nothing about the candidates, simply vote along party lines. Of course, this situation is much more common in Senate and House races than in presidential elections, where the media are saturated with information about the candidates.

The Democratic advantage in party identification does not in itself explain the Democrats' long-term domination of the House of Representatives. During the 1980s, the Republican party made significant gains in voter identification. According to CBS–New York Times exit polls, the overall Democratic advantage in party identification slipped from 16 percentage points in 1980 to only 3 percentage points in 1988. By 1988, a plurality of white voters identified themselves as Republicans. Only the Democrats' huge advantage among black voters allowed them to maintain a slim lead in the total electorate.

The erosion of the Democratic party's advantage in voter identification after 1980 did not adversely affect the Democrats' strength in Congress because there has also been a substantial decline in party-line voting in congressional elections since the 1950s. According to survey data collected by the Center for Political Studies at the University of Michigan, the percentage of voters casting their ballots along party lines in House contests fell from 84 percent in 1958 to only 69 percent in 1978; conversely, during these years the percentage of voters defecting to the opposition party rose from 11 percent to 22 percent. Party-line voting has actually been more prevalent in presidential elections than in House or Senate elections. In 1988, according to the American National Election Study, 82 percent of voters cast their ballots along party lines in the presidential contest, compared with only 74 percent in House contests and 73 percent in Senate contests.

The decrease in party-line voting in House elections since 1958 is almost entirely attributable to the growing advantage of incumbency in House elections. In the 1978 elections, voters who crossed party lines in House races favored the incumbent over the challenger by a ratio of eight to one. The growing advantage of incumbency was the main reason the Democratic party was able to maintain its grip on the House of Representatives after 1980, despite substantial GOP gains in voter identification. In the five elections between 1982 and 1990, only 23 Democratic incumbents running for reelection were defeated in more than twelve-hundred contests.

The outcome of the 1992 election underscored the advantage of incumbency in congressional elections. Despite widespread public discontent with the performance of Congress and media reports of an anti-incumbent mood in the electorate, excluding incumbents running against other incumbents, only 17 out of 337 House incumbents running for reelection were defeated. The 95-percent success rate of House incumbents represented only a slight drop from the 96-percent reelection rate of House incumbents in 1990. On the Senate side, incumbents also fared well in 1992. Twenty-three of the twenty-seven senators seeking another term were reelected.

The success of incumbents in the 1992 congressional elections continued a long-standing pattern. Between the end of World War II and 1992, the reelection rate for House incumbents averaged well over 90 percent. The rate for Senate incumbents has been somewhat lower—about 80 percent. In the 1980s, the reelection rate for incumbents in House elections reached an all-time high of almost 96 percent.

Not only did more House incumbents win, but they did so by bigger margins. The percentage of incumbents winning by at least 20 percentage points rose from around 60 percent during the 1950s to almost 80 percent during the 1980s. As a result of the growing advantage of incumbency, there are fewer and fewer "marginal" (closely contested) seats in the House of Representatives. The 1990 midterm election did represent a break in this pattern. For the first time since World War II, both Democratic and Republican incumbents saw their victory margins reduced: only 59 percent of incum-

bents in contested races won by a margin of at least 20 percentage points. However, 84 House incumbents and 5 Senate incumbents had no major-party opponent in 1990. This was the largest number of unopposed incumbents since the emergence of two-party competition in the South during the 1960s.

Americans have come to take the advantage of incumbency for granted, but it was not supposed to be that way. The framers of the Constitution intended the House of Representatives to be the branch of government closest to the people. Unlike the president or members of the Senate, representatives were to be directly elected by the voters for a term limited to two years, instead of four or six years. Direct election and the two-year term were expected to produce a relatively high rate of turnover in the membership of the House so that the lower chamber would be responsive to shifts in public sentiment.

Throughout the nineteenth and early twentieth centuries, the membership of the House of Representatives was indeed subject to rapid turnover. National electoral tides frequently swept large numbers of House members out of office. In the 1894 midterm election, for example, the Democrats lost 116 seats in the midst of a severe recession; as recently as 1948, the Republican party lost 75 seats in the House, including 68 seats held by incumbents. Shifts in party control during these years were commonplace. Between 1877 and 1955, party control of the House changed twelve times and the longest period of one-party rule was sixteen years. From 1955 to 1992, despite the election of four Republican presidents, the Democrats maintained continuous control of the House. Between 1955 and 1992 the number of Democrats in the 435-member House did not fall below 232, and between 1960 and 1992 the Democrats never held fewer than 242 seats in the House.

The major explanation for the decline in party turnover of House seats since the 1950s is the growing electoral advantage of incumbency. Because there are fewer marginal seats, the swing in the national popular vote changes party control in fewer seats than in the past. Between 1946 and 1966 the average net shift in party control was 33 seats; between 1968 and 1988 the average was only 16 seats. In the Senate, where only one-third of the members are elected every two years, the decline was not so dramatic—from an average of just over 5 seats between 1946 and 1966 to just under 4 seats between 1968 and 1988.

With more and more House incumbents being effectively insulated from real competition, relatively few seats can be captured by the minority party, even when it is favored by national political conditions. In 1980, for example, the electorate expressed its frustration over double-digit inflation, rising unemployment, and the Iranian hostage crisis by replacing Jimmy Carter with Ronald Reagan in the White House and giving the Republican party a majority of seats in the Senate. In the House, however, the best the GOP could do was a 33-seat gain, which left the Democrats with 243 seats, still a comfortable majority. Four years later, despite Ronald Reagan's landslide victory over Walter Mondale in the presidential race, only 13 Democratic incumbents lost their seats. President Reagan began his second term with Democrats enjoying a 71-seat majority in the House of Representatives. It is no wonder that Reagan's second term was characterized by political gridlock.

Divided party control is only one of the problems caused by the growing advantage of incumbency in House elections. Even when the president's party does control a majority of seats in the House, entrenched incumbents may feel little or no obligation to support the president's legislative program. Jimmy Carter's difficulties dealing with Congress were not all due to political inexperience and ineptness. Carter began his term with large Democratic majorities in the House and Senate after the 1976 elections. However, very few Democrats in the House or Senate felt that they owed their seats to Jimmy Carter or that their fate depended on the success of his program.

Not surprisingly, most members of Congress see nothing wrong with the high reelection rate of House incumbents. After all, despite the success of incumbents, the House has had a considerable infusion of new blood over the years. More than half of the membership of the House changed between 1980 and 1989, and more than 80 percent of the representatives serving in the 101st Congress (1989–1991) had been elected after 1974.

There was a considerable amount of turnover in the membership of the House of Representatives during the 1970s and 1980s, but turnover and competition are not the same thing. In recent decades, most of the turnover in House seats has been the result of death, voluntary retirement, or members who decide to run for higher office. Only a small proportion of the membership changes have resulted from incumbent defeats, and most of the changes have not involved a turnover in party control. In 1988, for example, 33 new members were elected to the House, but only nine of these new members came from a party different from their predecessors'.

Some political scientists have defended the lack of competition in House elections by arguing that, despite high reelection rates, most incumbents feel insecure and therefore work very hard at representing their constituents. According to these scholars, the advantage of incumbency is the result of hard work by representatives in cultivating their constituencies and building a personal base of support in their districts. Thus, Richard Fenno has argued that "incumbency is not an automatic entitlement to a fixed number of votes or percentage points toward reelection. . . . The power of incumbency is whatever each member makes of the resource and the opportunity" (1978, p. 211).

It is undoubtedly true that most representatives work very hard at cultivating their constituencies. They answer their mail, travel to their districts regularly, hold frequent meetings with groups of constituents, and assist citizens who have problems with government agencies. The problem with the House of Representatives today is not that incumbents ignore their districts or take their constituents for granted. The problem is that constituents only learn what the incumbent wants them to know about his or her performance. The most important reason for the increasing advantage of incumbency in House elections is the increasing ability of incumbents to control the flow of information to constituents.

INFORMATION AND THE INCUMBENCY ADVANTAGE

In an earlier political era, information was not so crucial a resource in congressional elections. This is because political parties were the main combatants in the electoral arena during the late nineteenth and early twentieth centuries. Voters' preferences in congressional elections were closely linked to their evaluations of the national parties and their leaders; the individual candidates were, in most cases, relatively unimportant. Between 1929 and 1933, for example, following the onset of the Great Depression, the Republican party went from 267 seats in the House of Representatives to only 117 seats, a net loss of 150 seats in two elections.

The personal advantage of incumbency in House elections is a relatively recent phenomenon. During the nineteenth and early twentieth centuries, any electoral advantage enjoyed by House incumbents depended on the distribution of party loyalties among the voters in their districts. A "safe district" in those days meant a district in which the large majority of voters supported a particular party. The district was safe for any candidate from that party.

There are still many House districts that are so overwhelmingly Republican or Democratic that they can be considered safe for one party or the other. However, there are many more districts that are safe only for a particular incumbent who has established a personal following through his or her own activities. In such districts, the party division of the vote can change drastically when the incumbent retires.

In order to separate the personal advantage of incumbency from the advantage that House incumbents derive from the party loyalties of the electorate, in 1990 David Brady calculated the average size of the "sophomore surge" and "retirement slump" in all contested House races between 1846 and 1986. The "sophomore surge" refers to the expected increase in the vote for a party when its candidate is running as an incumbent for the first time; the "retirement slump" refers to the expected decrease in the vote for a party in the first election after its incumbent has retired or died. Before 1946, Brady found no evidence of any personal advantage of incumbency: the average values for both the sophomore surge and the retirement slump were close to zero. Since the end of World War II, however, and especially since the 1960s, the average values for the sophomore surge and the retirement slump had diverged sharply from zero. In 1986, for example, the average sophomore surge was

+6.4 percentage points while the average retirement slump was −9.3 percentage points.

Brady's findings regarding the emergence of a personal incumbency advantage reflect the dramatic transformation of the American electoral process since the end of World War II. The development of mass media, and especially television, has allowed individual officeholders and candidates to take their messages directly to the voters, without depending on the local, state, or national party organizations. As a result, the focus of most political campaigns has shifted from the parties to the individual candidates.

Along with the shift from party-centered to candidate-centered campaigns, there has been a decline in party loyalty among the electorate. Fewer voters consider themselves strong partisans than in the past, and more voters consider themselves independents. Moreover, even among those who identify with a party, there is a greater willingness to vote for candidates of the opposing party. Defections have increased, and so has split-ticket voting. As a result, the fortunes of congressional candidates are not as closely linked to the fate of their party or its leaders.

Though once unusual, split results between presidential and House races have become commonplace. In the twelve presidential elections between 1900 and 1944, an average of only 11 percent of House districts split their vote to support a presidential candidate of one party and a House candidate of the opposing party. In the eleven presidential elections between 1948 and 1988, the average was 31 percent, and in 1984 a record 45 percent of House districts produced a split result. The main reason for the increase in ticket-splitting was the growing advantage of incumbency in House elections: the vast majority of these split outcomes were the result of voters supporting a presidential candidate of one party and a House incumbent from the opposing party. In the 1988 election, 34 percent of all House districts produced a split result. Of the 297 House districts carried by George Bush, 135 elected a Democratic representative. A little more than half of the Democrats elected to the House came from districts carried by George Bush, and all but 9 of these Democrats were incumbents. Likewise, 12 of the 13 Republican representatives elected in districts carried by Michael Dukakis were incumbents.

As the candidates have become more important in congressional elections, information has become an increasingly important resource. What, as well as how much, voters know about the candidates is crucial, and incumbents have an enormous advantage in this area. For two years between elections, incumbents have a virtual monopoly over the information that constituents receive about their performance. Few local newspapers or television stations are willing to devote much space or time to the routine activities of members of Congress. Crimes, fires, and human-interest stories are regarded as much more interesting to most readers and viewers. Barring a scandal, the local news media generally pay little or no attention to the activities of members of Congress, especially members of the House. This is particularly true in metropolitan areas, which include a large number of House districts. What little coverage is devoted to members of the House is usually instigated by the members themselves through such activities as press releases and visits to the district. Not surprisingly, the tone of this coverage is overwhelmingly positive.

Since the news media devote very little coverage to members of Congress, most of the information constituents do receive is provided by the members themselves. The political scientist David Mayhew, in *Congress: The Electoral Connection*, described three techniques that are used by members of Congress to publicize their activities between elections. These techniques are advertising, credit-claiming, and position-taking.

Advertising, according to Mayhew, involves gaining favorable publicity through noncontroversial activities, such as attending ribbon-cutting ceremonies, sponsoring commemorative resolutions, giving patriotic speeches, and assisting citizens who have problems with federal agencies. These activities have little or no policy content. However, even such a seemingly innocuous activity as mailing free baby-care books to new parents can help to build name recognition and a positive image.

Credit-claiming involves taking responsibility for government programs or projects that benefit constituents. The important thing here is not actual responsibility for the project or program but the appearance of responsibility. Thus, members of Congress can claim credit by announcing the awarding of federal grants or contracts to organizations or companies in their districts even if their actions had nothing to do with the award. Members can also claim credit for trying to prevent cutbacks in federal programs, even if they fail to prevent the cutbacks from taking place. Putting up a good fight, even in a losing cause, can have very positive results.

Credit-claiming is greatly facilitated by the congressional committee system. Most of the work of Congress is done in its specialized standing committees and members are generally assigned to committees that deal with the issues of greatest concern to their constituents. Members of the Armed Service Committee, for example, are drawn overwhelmingly from districts with major military installations or defense contractors. Similarly, members of the Agriculture Committee tend to represent rural districts with large numbers of farmers, and members of the Interior and Insular Affairs Committee tend to represent western districts in which the federal government has large landholdings. Thus, the committee system enables members to exercise disproportionate influence over those government agencies and programs which have the greatest impact on their constituencies.

Mayhew's third activity, position-taking, involves publicizing popular stands on issues of importance to one's constituents. The issues selected depend on the demographic and political makeup of the district, but they should always be issues that unite rather than divide voters. Controversial issues, such as the Vietnam War during the late 1960s or abortion during the 1980s, are generally avoided because whatever position a representative takes is bound to alienate a large number of voters. As in the case of credit-claiming, success in position-taking does not require legislative action. What matters is publicizing a popular position rather than producing any legislative results.

Position-taking is facilitated by a party system that places few demands for loyalty on members of Congress. Party discipline in Congress is quite lax, and members are rarely punished for voting with the opposing party. In 1981, for example, Ronald Reagan was able to win House approval for his program of domestic-spending and tax cuts by gaining the votes of a large number of conservative southern Democrats. None of these so-called boll weevils received any punishment for voting with the Republicans; they retained their membership in the Democratic caucus, their committee assignments, and their seniority. The only boll weevil who was punished for his actions was Phil Gramm of Texas, who had cosponsored the Reagan spending cuts in the House. Gramm was removed from the House Budget Committee in 1983. He subsequently resigned from the House, changed parties, won a special election for his old seat as a Republican, and in 1984 was elected senator.

Lack of party discipline encourages members of Congress to "vote their districts" and follow the views of their constituents, even if these views conflict with the position of their party's leaders in Congress. This is especially important for members who represent districts that are atypical for their party, notably Democrats from conservative districts in the South and Republicans from liberal districts in the Northeast. In 1988, for example, two Texas Democrats, Ralph Hall and Charles Stenholm, voted with the Republicans on more than half of the party divisions (votes on which a majority of Democrats voted against a majority of Republicans); five Republicans—Constance Morella of Maryland, Silvio Conte of Massachusetts, Frank Horton of New York, Claudine Schneider of Rhode Island, and Jim Jeffords of Vermont—voted with the Democrats on more than three-fifths of the party divisions. Moderate-to-liberal Republicans who frequently desert their party on key votes are known by the nickname "gypsy moths."

As a result of lax party discipline, cross-party coalitions are common on congressional votes. The most important such cross-party coalition, the "conservative coalition" of Republicans and southern Democrats, has formed regularly since the 1950s on issues ranging from civil rights and criminal justice to labor relations and social welfare. The coalition has been somewhat less prevalent in recent years, but when it does form, it remains a potent force in the House.

Advertising, credit-claiming, and position-taking are all greatly facilitated by the ability of incumbents to control the flow of information to constituents. Since the vast majority of citizens receive no independent information about their congressman's voting record, his work in committee, or any other aspect of his performance on the job, it is not the actual performance of the member that matters but what the member tells constituents about that performance.

Incumbents are provided with many resources that allow them to control the flow of information to constituents. Perhaps the most valuable such resource is the franking privilege. This is the ability of members of Congress to send out mail under their signature, without paying for the postage. The stated purpose of the franking privilege is to allow members of Congress to carry out their official responsibilities. In practice, however, the franking privilege is used mainly for political propaganda in the form of newsletters and questionnaires. In addition to answering letters from constituents and conducting legitimate legislative business, House members are allowed to send out up to six bulk mailings per year to all postal patrons in their districts. Not surprisingly, the volume of congressional mail swells considerably during election years and shrinks during nonelection years. Moreover, in addition to free postage, members of Congress receive a generous allowance to cover the cost of paper and printing.

The volume of franked mail has increased dramatically over time. In 1954, members of Congress sent out 43.5 million pieces of franked mail; in 1984, a record 924.6 million pieces of franked mail were sent out at an estimated cost of more than $117 million. This works out to an average of more than 1.7 million pieces of mail at a cost of over $200,000 per member. Until relatively recently, however, no record was kept of the amount of mail sent out by individual members or the cost to the taxpayers. In 1988 the Senate voted to require individual members to report their spending on franked mail. Thus far, however, the House has refused to go along with this requirement. A new law reducing the number of bulk mailings permitted each year is unlikely to have much impact on the volume of congressional mail, since members are increasingly using computer-generated personalized first-class mailings to reach constituents. To supplement their mailings, many members of Congress also record television and radio programs to be sent to stations in their districts. Members are provided with fully equipped recording studios on Capitol Hill, for which they are charged far less than the actual cost to the taxpayers.

The personal staffs of members of Congress have increased dramatically in size. Between 1947 and 1986, the personal staffs of House members increased from 1,440 to 7,920, an average of 18 staffers per representative, while senators' personal staffs increased from 590 to 3,774, an average of 38 staffers per senator. In addition to the overall increase in the size of members' staffs, an increasing proportion of the staff have been assigned to members' district offices. Between 1972 and 1986, the proportion of House members' staffs assigned to district offices almost doubled, from 22.5 percent to 43.6 percent, while the proportion of senators' staffs assigned to district offices almost tripled, from 12.5 percent to 34.1 percent. Thus, it appears that members of Congress have been using their staffs increasingly to provide direct services to constituents.

Despite the increase in staff members assigned to district offices, few members of Congress are content to stay in Washington and let their staff handle matters in the district. Instead, they travel regularly to their districts to meet and speak with constituents. These trips are, of course, paid for by the taxpaying public. Between 1962 and 1977, the number of trips allowed at public expense was increased six different times, from three to thirty-three. Since 1978, members have been allowed to take an unlimited number of trips and pay for them out of a general office-expense budget (Jacobson, 1987, p. 39).

In 1981, the perquisites given to members of Congress were estimated to be worth more than $1 million annually per member, and their value has undoubtedly increased considerably since then. These perks allow members of Congress to conduct what amounts to a continuous campaign for reelection. By the time the official election campaign begins, House districts have already been saturated with the incumbents' propaganda for at least two years. The best thing about the campaign between elections for incumbents is that they have no competition and almost complete control over the information received by constituents.

CONGRESSIONAL CHALLENGERS AND CAMPAIGNS

Given the lack of independent coverage of members of Congress by the news media, there is only one potential source of critical information available to most voters—the challenger. The task confronting the challenger is a daunting one. In the first place, the incumbent has had at least a two-year head start in persuading the voters that she or he is doing a good job. The challenger usually has only a few months to counteract the incumbent's propaganda and convince voters that he or she could do a better job.

Not only does the challenger have very little time in which to convince voters to abandon the incumbent, but he or she usually has to convince a skeptical audience that consists disproportionately of supporters of the incumbent's party. Although voters' party loyalties have become weaker over time, most Americans continue to identify with one party or the other, and these loyalties condition their reactions to the information that they receive during political campaigns. The tendency of voters to interpret political information in partisan terms is probably stronger during a political campaign than it is between campaigns, when they are not expecting to receive partisan propaganda.

Aside from voter skepticism, the main problem confronting the challenger is simply getting the voters' attention. The level of public interest in congressional campaigns is not very high to begin with. The challengers' problems are compounded by the fact that, barring a scandal, the news media generally pay little attention to House campaigns. Therefore, opportunities for the challenger to receive free media coverage are extremely limited. The problem is especially severe in large metropolitan areas, which include many House districts. The New York metropolitan area, for example, includes thirty-two House districts; the Los Angeles metropolitan area includes twenty-three House districts. Even closely contested House races generally receive little or no coverage on local television news programs or in the major newspapers.

Given all of the difficulties that challengers confront in communicating with the electorate, it is not surprising that very few are successful. To counteract all of the resources that are given to incumbents, challengers have to rely primarily on one resource—money. Incumbents can use the perquisites of office to gain recognition and build a positive image; challengers have to spend a great deal of money to have any chance at all of unseating an incumbent. In the 1986 and 1988 elections, the average successful challenger spent more than $500,000. Unfortunately, the current system of financing congressional campaigns makes it very difficult for a challenger to raise enough money to wage a competitive race, let alone seriously threaten to unseat an incumbent.

Since the Federal Election Campaign Act legalized corporate political action committees (PACs) in 1972, PACs have come to play a larger and larger role in financing congressional campaigns. PACs are political fund-raising organizations sponsored by interest groups such as labor unions, corporations, trade associations, and ideological groups. Their number has increased from about six hundred in 1974 to more than four thousand in 1988. In 1974, PACs gave just over $10 million to congressional candidates; in 1988 they gave almost $150 million. In 1974, PACs accounted for 17 percent of all contributions to House candidates and 11 percent of all contributions to Senate candidates; in 1988 they accounted for 37 percent of all contributions to House candidates and 23 percent of all contributions to Senate candidates.

Most PACs, especially those sponsored by corporations and trade associations, view campaign contributions as an investment in political influence, and incumbents represent a much safer investment than challengers. PACs give the lion's share of their contributions—more than 80 percent in 1988—to incumbents, because they expect incumbents to win. But this belief becomes a self-fulfilling prophecy. Because challengers are given little chance of winning, PACs will not contribute to their campaigns and because PACs will not contribute to their campaigns, the challengers have little chance of winning. There is nothing new about this situation, but it has gotten worse as the role of PACs in financing congressional campaigns has increased. Between 1974 and 1980, House incumbents outspent challengers by a ratio of approximately 1.5 to 1. By 1988, how-

ever, the ratio of incumbent-to-challenger spending was greater than 3 to 1 and in 1990 it was almost 4 to 1. Accounting for inflation, challenger spending decreased by more than 40 percent between 1980 and 1990, while incumbent spending increased by almost 50 percent.

As members of a party that has been in the minority since 1955, House Republican challengers have had particular difficulty in raising money from PACs. During his reign as chairman of the Democratic Congressional Campaign Committee, Congressman Tony Coelho (D.-Calif.) actively sought to dissuade business PACs from contributing to Republican challengers and thereby offending Democratic incumbents who chaired vital committees and subcommittees in the House. Evidently Coelho was quite persuasive. In 1988, PACs contributed approximately twenty times more money to House Democratic incumbents than to Republican challengers. The average Democratic incumbent raised $413,000, of which more than $200,000 came from PAC contributions. The average GOP challenger raised $102,000, of which less than $12,000 came from PACs. Democratic challengers in 1988, although greatly outspent by Republican incumbents, fared somewhat better with PACs than GOP challengers. The average Democratic challenger raised $146,000, of which almost $50,000 came from PACs; the average GOP incumbent raised $442,000 and received more than $150,000 in PAC contributions. These figures actually understate the financial problems of most House challengers. The average spending of House challengers is pulled up considerably by a few challengers who spend large sums of money. In 1988, for example, the average level of spending for challengers to the House was $119,000, but the median was only $37,000. Half of the challengers spent less than $37,000 —a truly pitiful sum.

While challengers' fund-raising has not kept pace with inflation, many of the costs involved in running a political campaign have skyrocketed. This is especially true of media costs. The cost of advertising time on radio and television has increased at a rate more rapid than the overall rate of inflation. The prices charged by political consultants for services such as polling, canvasing, and fund-raising have also increased dramatically. While these increases in campaign costs have affected all candidates, they have had a much more severe impact on challengers because they have much less money to spend and depend on the campaign to get their message across to voters.

The increasing cost of campaigning and the decreasing ability of House challengers to raise campaign funds mean that fewer and fewer challengers are able to reach voters with their messages. In 1978, for example, only 37 percent of eligible voters in a national survey reported having had any contact with the House challenger during the campaign. Increasingly, incumbents are able to control the flow of information to constituents during the campaign as well as between campaigns, and without any competing sources of information, voters have little choice but to accept the information provided by incumbents.

The results of the 1990 House elections serve to underscore the difficulties faced by challengers in getting their message across to the voters. As a result of widespread public discontent with the performance of Congress, for the first time since World War II both Democratic and Republican incumbents saw their victory margins shrink between 1988 and 1990. Only fifteen incumbents were defeated, but seventy-four won with less than 60 percent of the major-party vote. Many incumbents won marginal victories, despite facing inexperienced and inadequately financed challengers. Only 11 percent of House challengers in 1990 had ever held elective office—the smallest proportion of experienced challengers since World War II—and challenger spending declined by more than 15 percent in real dollars between 1988 and 1990. The average House challenger spent about $110,000 in 1990, but this average was pulled up by a few challengers who spent large sums on their campaigns. More than half of the House challengers spent less than $50,000.

In 1990 a total of forty-seven House incumbents won marginal victories (winning with less than 60 percent of the major-party vote) against challengers who spent less than $200,000, and thirty-one of these incumbents were held to under 60 percent of the vote by challengers who spent less than $100,000. By contrast, in 1988 only nine House incumbents won marginal victories against challengers who spent less than $200,000, and only two incum-

bents were held to under 60 percent of the vote by challengers who spent less than $100,000.

It appears that many House incumbents of both parties escaped defeat in 1990 only because of the financial weakness of their challengers. Among those who probably could have been defeated by better-financed challengers were the Democratic majority leader, Richard Gephardt of Missouri, who outspent his GOP challenger, $1,456,000 to $82,000, but received only 56.8 percent of the vote; the chairman of the House Republican campaign committee, Guy Vander Jagt of Michigan, who outspent his Democratic challenger, $453,000 to $22,000, but received only 54.7 percent of the vote; and the Republican whip, Newt Gingrich of Georgia, who outspent his Democratic challenger, $1,539,000 to $334,000, but received only 50.3 percent of the vote. Perhaps the luckiest survivor of the 1990 House elections was Democrat Bernard Dwyer of New Jersey. Dwyer managed to win 52.2 percent of the vote against a Republican challenger who spent less than $9,000 on his campaign. In Dwyer's case, the Republicans almost disproved the old adage that "you can't beat somebody with nobody." Given adequately financed challengers, it is almost certain that Dwyer and a good many other House incumbents would have been sent packing by the voters.

The results of the 1990 House elections suggest that despite all of the perquisites of office, a lot of House incumbents are far from invulnerable. The extraordinarily high reelection rates normally enjoyed by House incumbents are attributable to weak opposition as much as to the political skills of the incumbents.

A COMPARISON WITH SENATE ELECTIONS

Senators have less control than do representatives over the information that constituents receive about their performance, and this helps to explain why Senate incumbents have had less success winning reelection. Because there are only a hundred senators and because each senator represents an entire state, their activities are more likely to be reported by the news media than those of representatives. Even between elections, therefore, citizens do not have to rely entirely on information provided by the incumbent to judge the incumbent's performance.

The most important difference between Senate and House elections, however, is the visibility of the challenger. Many Senate challengers have held a major elected office. The most common office has been U.S. representative, but several governors, lieutenant governors, and other statewide elected officials have been found among the ranks of Senate challengers in modern elections. These challengers often begin their campaigns with a high level of visibility. They also find it relatively easy to attract media coverage.

Just as senators generally receive more extensive coverage in the news media than representatives, Senate campaigns are generally covered more extensively than House campaigns. There is only one Senate campaign in a state, so newspapers and television stations in that state can afford to be much more generous with time and space than they can in covering House campaigns. Thus, it is usually much easier for a Senate challenger to obtain free media exposure than it is for a House challenger.

Finally, Senate challengers generally raise much more money than House challengers. It is more expensive to run a Senate campaign than a House campaign, in part because the average state includes about nine House districts. Because of fixed costs and economies of scale, a Senate campaign in an average state probably costs considerably less than nine times as much as an equivalent House campaign. In 1988 the average Senate challenger spent over $1.8 million—more than fifteen times as much as the average House challenger. Moreover, although Senate challengers were greatly outspent by incumbents during the 1980s, they did manage to stay ahead of inflation: between 1980 and 1990, spending by Senate challengers increased by almost 50 percent in real dollars and spending by House challengers decreased by over 40 percent. This has allowed many Senate challengers, unlike their House counterparts, to make extensive use of television advertising in their campaigns. The higher spending of Senate challengers and the greater willingness of the news media to cover Senate campaigns means that voters in Senate elections are much less dependent on incumbents for information than voters in House elections.

In 1978, for example, 70 percent of eligible voters reported having had some contact with the Senate challenger during the campaign, but as noted above, only 37 percent reported having had some contact with the House challenger.

As a result of the greater visibility of challengers, Senate elections have been much more competitive than House elections. In the five elections between 1980 and 1988, 18 percent of Senate incumbents were defeated, compared with 4 percent of House incumbents. In the 1986 elections, more Senate incumbents (seven) than House incumbents (six) were defeated, even though more than ten times as many House seats were at stake. Contrary to the intent of the framers of the Constitution, the House of Representatives now appears to be more insulated from shifts in public sentiment than the Senate. Between 1980 and 1988, the average net shift in party control was 4.8 percent of Senate seats, compared with only 3.8 percent of House seats, despite the fact that only one-third of the Senate's seats were contested in each election.

THE ELECTORAL CYCLE AND STRATEGIC POLITICIANS

A congressional election is more than a collection of 435 separate House contests and 33 or 34 separate Senate contests. It is also a national election, and despite Tip O'Neill's well-known statement that "all politics is local," the outcomes of House and Senate elections are affected by such national issues as the state of the economy and the popularity of the incumbent president. These issues influence voters' candidate preferences in individual races as well as the aggregate outcomes of House and Senate elections. The more prosperous the economy and the higher the president's approval rating at the time of an election, the more support voters give to Senate and House candidates of the president's party. Thus, congressional elections constitute a kind of referendum on the performance of the president, even when there is no presidential contest on the ballot.

The outcomes of congressional elections are also affected by the peculiarly American electoral cycle—the rhythm of surge and decline that reflects the alternation of presidential and midterm election years. In a presidential election year, voter turnout surges and the party capturing the White House normally gains seats in the House and Senate as congressional candidates ride the winning presidential candidate's coattails into office. Two years later, without the excitement of a presidential contest to lure voters to the polls, turnout declines, voters return to their normal partisan voting habits, and the party holding the White House almost always loses seats in the House of Representatives and usually loses seats in the Senate (although any Senate seats gained in the preceding presidential election will not be vulnerable until four years later). The size of this midterm loss varies considerably, depending on the popularity of the incumbent president, the state of the economy, and the number of seats the president's party has to defend in the House and Senate. Although the existence of this alternating rhythm of surge and decline is indisputable, the precise mechanism by which it occurs has been the subject of scholarly debate since the publication of Angus Campbell's pioneering 1960 study (e.g., Wolfinger, Rosenstone, and McIntosh; and Cover, 1983).

One of the consequences of surge and decline, presidential coattails, appears to be declining in importance in congressional elections, although the extent of this decline is a matter of dispute. Shrinking presidential coattails may help to explain why the Republican party was unable to translate its dominance of presidential elections between 1968 and 1988 into lasting gains in the House of Representatives. In 1988, George Bush became the first presidential candidate in the twentieth century to capture the White House even as his party lost seats in both the House and Senate. Likewise, in the same period the size of the midterm losses by the president's party in the House were minimal: in the 1986 and 1990 elections the Republicans lost only five and eight House seats, respectively. While not entirely absent, the rhythm of surge and decline has been rather muted since 1980.

One explanation regularly offered by Republican strategists for their party's failure to translate its presidential successes in the 1980s into gains in the House of Representatives—Democratic gerrymandering of House district boundaries following the 1980 census—can be

safely dismissed. In the first place, the Democrats only completely controlled the redistricting process in a minority of states. Only where the Democrats controlled the governorship and both houses of the state legislature did they reap any gains from the redistricting process. Furthermore, whatever benefits a party receives from partisan control of redistricting appear to be short-lived. One must look elsewhere for an explanation of the Republican's failure to make inroads into the Democrats' House majorities during the 1980s.

Gary Jacobson and Samuel Kernell provided an explanation for the shrinking influence of national issues and the electoral cycle on the outcomes of House elections and, indirectly, the inability of the Republican party to convert its presidential victories into meaningful gains in the House. In addition to influencing voters, national issues and the electoral cycle can affect each party's ability to recruit well-qualified, well-financed candidates to run in Senate and House elections. The more these conditions favor a party, the easier it should be for that party to convince well-qualified candidates to challenge the opposing party's entrenched incumbents and the easier it should be for these challengers to convince PACs and individual contributors to finance their campaigns. Thus, the strategic decisions of candidates and contributors mediate the effects of national issues and the electoral cycle on the outcomes of House and Senate elections. Moreover, in an era of candidate-centered campaigns, the impact of these strategic decisions on the electoral cycle may be increasing.

Why, then, has the average seat swing in House elections diminished over time? It is not that voters have become less concerned about economic conditions or presidential performance. Rather, the electoral cycle and national issues only provide a party with an opportunity, and the ability of a party that is favored by these conditions to convert this opportunity into substantial seat gains in the Senate and House depends on its ability to recruit well-qualified, well-financed challengers who can convince voters to "throw the rascals out." In the 1980s both parties, but especially the Republicans, frequently failed to take advantage of their opportunities by recruiting inexperienced and inadequately financed challengers, especially in House elections. Thus, in 1984 the Republicans might have defeated a lot more than thirteen Democratic House incumbents if the party had recruited more qualified challengers and had provided its challengers with greater financial support. In 1990 both parties failed to take advantage of numerous opportunities to defeat vulnerable incumbents, because they nominated challengers who could not wage creditable campaigns.

Aside from its inability to recruit well-qualified and well-financed challengers, the Republican party of the 1980s suffered from an additional liability in congressional elections— its control of the White House. Public satisfaction with the state of the nation contributed to the reelection of Ronald Reagan in 1984 and the election of Vice President George Bush to succeed Reagan in 1988. However, voter contentment with the status quo provided Republican challengers with little ammunition to use against Democratic congressional incumbents in either year. After all, as the majority party in Congress, or half of Congress in 1984, the Democrats could claim partial responsibility for the status quo. Similarly, in 1990, when the public mood turned sour, the Democrats had to share the blame for the status quo.

Since World War II, most of the elections that have produced dramatic shifts in party control of seats in Congress have occurred when voters were dissatisfied with the performance of an incumbent president and took out their wrath on his party's congressional incumbents. Of the seven elections that produced the largest net shifts in party control of seats, five (the 1946, 1958, 1966, 1974, and 1980 elections) involved voters punishing the party controlling the White House for poor performance, while only two (the 1948 and 1964 elections) involved voters rewarding the party controlling the White House for good performance. This suggests that as long as the Republicans maintained control of the White House, there was little chance of the GOP capturing control of Congress. Indeed, the voters seemed to be very comfortable with this division of power, despite their dissatisfaction with the way both Congress and the White House were dealing with the nation's problems. According to public-opinion polls of the early 1990s, most Americans preferred having Congress and the presidency controlled by different parties to having one party in charge of both branches,

apparently feeling that divided control of the legislative and executive branches serves as a check on policy excesses by either side.

The greatest threat to continued Democratic control of Congress could be the presence of a Democrat in the White House. If Bill Clinton's popularity declines far enough, voters might turn against Democratic congressional incumbents, just as they did in 1980. In that year, voters expressed their dissatisfaction with Jimmy Carter's handling of the economy and the Iranian hostage crisis by voting him out of the office along with twenty-seven Democratic representatives and nine Democratic senators. Democrats suffered a net loss of thirty-four seats in the House and twelve seats in the Senate.

THE PUZZLE OF DECLINING TURNOUT

The declining responsiveness of congressional elections to national electoral forces has been accompanied by a decline in voter turnout in congressional elections. In part, this decline simply reflects the decline in voter interest in presidential elections since 1960. With fewer voters attracted to the polls by the presidential contest, turnout in House and Senate elections has been correspondingly smaller. Between 1960 and 1988, turnout in presidential elections fell from 63 percent of the voting-age population to just over 50 percent. But declining turnout has not been confined to presidential elections; turnout in midterm elections fell from 45 percent of the voting-age population in 1962 to less than 35 percent in 1990. Voter turnout has fallen since 1960, despite rising levels of education in the electorate, the enfranchisement of millions of southern blacks by the Voting Rights Act of 1965, and a general liberalization of voter-registration requirements. And only a fraction of the decline is attributable to the Twenty-sixth Amendment's addition of eighteen-to-twenty-year-olds to the electorate in 1972. Hence, the puzzle of declining turnout.

Although political scientists have not been able to solve the puzzle, they have provided some clues to the solution. Two trends in the political attitudes of American citizens appear to explain a good part of the decline in voter participation since the 1960s—decreasing party identification and decreasing political efficacy. Fewer Americans identify strongly with a political party than in the past, and fewer Americans believe that elected officials are responsive to their needs and desires. Since, controlling for demographic characteristics, citizens who have a strong attachment to a political party and citizens who feel that elected officials care about their needs and desires are more likely to vote, both of these trends have had the effect of depressing voter turnout.

The conclusion that declining turnout is attributable to a growing detachment from political parties and a decreasing sense of political efficacy raises the question of what explains these trends in political attitudes. While there is no definitive answer to this question, it seems reasonable to assume that declining public confidence in two of the central institutions of democracy—political parties and elections—reflects frustration with the failure of these institutions to provide a measure of collective accountability for policy outcomes. Political parties are viewed as increasingly irrelevant to the determination of public policy. Why bother going to the polls if you do not think it is possible to change the direction of public policy by putting a different party in charge?

ONE-PARTY RULE AND ELECTORAL ACCOUNTABILITY

One of the hallmarks of a democratic political system is alternation in power by political parties. Many authoritarian regimes hold elections. Often the voter turnout in these elections is extremely high. But these elections are a sham because only one party's candidates are allowed to run or campaign. Unless the opposition party has a realistic chance of replacing the governing party in power, the governing party and its leaders cannot be held accountable for their actions.

In the House of Representatives in the 1990s, individual members have, with some difficulty, been held accountable for their actions, but the governing party and its leaders have not. A representative who has shirked his duties, ignored his constituents' views, or violated public standards of morality risks attract-

ing a strong opponent and losing his seat. But this sort of behavior has been relatively rare and represents no threat to the majority party's control.

One-party rule has had serious negative consequences for the House of Representatives and the American political system. Within the Democratic majority, one-party rule has encouraged arrogance and abuse of power. Within the Republican minority, one-party rule has led to growing frustration and a preference for partisan guerrilla warfare over legislative results. The result has been an increasingly confrontational style of politics in the House. The resignations of the House Speaker Jim Wright and the Majority whip Tony Coelho and the election of Newt Gingrich as minority whip in 1989 were all products of this political climate.

Perhaps the most dangerous consequence of one-party rule is that it undermines a sense of collective responsibility on the part of members of Congress. As long as Democrats have no fear of losing their majority status and Republicans have no hope of overcoming their minority status, members have no reason to place the interest of their party ahead of self-aggrandizement. Without any sense of party responsibility, national issues and problems have continued to be ignored while members attend to the parochial concerns of their individual constituencies.

The tendency of members of Congress to place their personal electoral interests ahead of the welfare of their party and the nation was clearly evident during the wrangling over the federal budget deficit in October 1990. After long and difficult negotiations, the Bush administration reached an agreement with Democratic and Republican congressional leaders on a package of tax increases and spending cuts to reduce the deficit. The package included major concessions by both sides: President Bush agreed to abandon his "no new taxes" pledge, and Democratic congressional leaders agreed to cuts in some domestic social programs. The plan was then presented to the House of Representatives, but despite intense lobbying by the Bush administration and by Democratic and congressional leaders, a majority of Republicans, along with a large minority of Democrats, voted the plan down. Among the Republican representatives voting against the budget package was the Republican House whip, Newt

Gingrich. A watered-down deficit-reduction package was later passed by the House and Senate.

Gary Jacobson's 1991 analysis of both the House and Senate votes on the deficit-reduction agreements demonstrated that the probability of a member of Congress opposing the agreements was directly related to his or her personal political vulnerability. The large majority of members who were not running for reelection or running unopposed voted for the deficit-reduction agreements. The large majority of members involved in difficult reelection battles voted against the agreements. In such an electoral environment in Congress, with its emphasis on individual over collective accountability, competition encourages members to behave irresponsibly.

Most Americans are dissatisfied with the collective performance of Congress. According to a CBS News–*New York Times* poll conducted in October 1990, only 23 percent of Americans approved of the job that Congress was doing, while 69 percent disapproved. Unless something is done to restore meaningful interparty competition in congressional elections, little change is possible. A few corrupt or incompetent incumbents may lose their seats, but the overwhelming majority will be reelected with little or no difficulty, and divided government will continue. The inability of Congress to come to grips with the budget deficit is just one symptom of the absence of collective accountability in congressional elections.

The fundamental problem underlying the inability of Congress to come to grips with the major problems facing the nation is the excessive localism inherent in the current electoral system. Members of Congress feel very little responsibility for dealing with national problems, because they are elected or defeated almost entirely on the basis of their responsiveness to local interests and concerns. By servicing their individual constituencies, members of Congress are able to escape responsibility for national problems. Such reform proposals as campaign-spending ceilings and term limits do not address the fundamental problem of excessive localism in congressional representation. These reforms would do little to increase competition for individual seats and nothing to increase members' sense of collective accountability for national policies. Short of major constitutional reforms, which appear highly unlikely, the most promising way to reduce excessive localism and encourage a greater sense of collective responsibility for national policy among members of Congress would be to strengthen the role of political parties in the electoral process.

BIBLIOGRAPHY

General Works
See ROGER H. DAVIDSON and WALTER J. OLESZEK, *Congress and Its Members* (Washington, D.C., 1981); GARY C. JACOBSON, *The Politics of Congressional Elections*, 3d ed. (New York, 1992) and NORMAN J. ORNSTEIN, THOMAS E. MANN, and MICHAEL J. MALBIN, *Vital Statistics on Congress, 1991–1992* (Washington, D.C., 1992).

The Advantage of Incumbency
DAVID W. BRADY, "Coalitions in the U.S. Congress," in L. SANDY MAISEL, ed., *The Parties Respond: Changes in the American Party System.* (Boulder, Colo., 1990); ALBERT D. COVER, "One Good Term Deserves Another: The Advantage of Incumbency in Congressional Elections,"

American Journal of Political Science (1977): 523–542; JOHN A. FEREJOHN, "On the Decline of Competition in Congressional Elections," *American Political Science Review* 71 (1977): 166–176; and THOMAS E. MANN, *Unsafe at Any Margin: Interpreting Congressional Elections* (Washington, D.C., 1978).

Redistricting
ALAN I. ABRAMOWITZ, "Partisan Redistricting and the 1982 Congressional Elections," *Journal of Politics* 45 (1982): 767–770; RICHARD BORN, "Partisan Intentions and Election Day Realities in the Congressional Redistricting Process," *American Political Science Review* 79 (1985): 304–319; and ROBERT S. ERIKSON, "Malappor-

tionment, Gerrymandering, and Party Fortunes in Congressional Elections," *American Political Science Review* 66 (1972): 1234–1245.

Campaign Finance

ALAN I. ABRAMOWITZ, "Incumbency, Campaign Spending, and the Decline of Competition in U.S. House Elections," *Journal of Politics* 53 (1991): 34–56; BROOKS JACKSON, *Honest Graft: Big Money and the American Political Process* (New York, 1988); GARY C. JACOBSON, *Money in Congressional Elections* (New Haven, Conn., 1980); DAVID B. MAGLEBY and CANDICE J. NELSON, *The Money Chase: Congressional Campaign Finance Reform* (Washington, D.C., 1990); MICHAEL J. MALBIN, ed., *Money and Politics in the United States* (Chatham, N.J., 1984); and FRANK J. SORAUF, *Money in American Elections* (Boston, 1988).

House vs. Senate Elections

ALAN I. ABRAMOWITZ, "A Comparison of Voting for U.S. Senator and Representative," *American Political Science Review* 74 (1980): 633–640 and ALAN I. ABRAMOWITZ and JEFFREY A. SEGAL, *Senate Elections* (Ann Arbor, Mich., 1992); BARBARA HINCKLEY, "House Re-elections and Senate Defeats: The Role of the Challenger," *British Journal of Political Science* 10 (1980): 441–460.

Elections, Representation, and Congressional Decision-making

RICHARD F. FENNO, JR., *Home Style: House Members in Their Districts* (Boston, 1978); MORRIS P. FIORINA, "The Decline of Collective Responsibility in American Politics," *Daedalus* 109 (1980): 25–45; and DAVID R. MAYHEW, *Congress: The Electoral Connection* (New Haven, Conn., 1974).

Congressional Campaigns

PETER CLARKE and SUSAN EVANS, *Covering Campaigns: Journalism in Congressional Elections* (Stanford, Calif., 1983) and EDIE GOLDENBERG and MICHAEL TRAUGOTT, *Campaigning for Congress* (Washington, D.C., 1984).

National Trends and Issues

ALAN I. ABRAMOWITZ, "National Issues, Strategic Politicians, and Voting Behavior in the 1980 and 1982 Elections," *American Journal of Political Science* 28 (1984): 710–721; and his "Economic Conditions, Presidential Popularity, and Voting Behavior in Midterm Congressional Elections," *Journal of Politics* 47 (1985): 31–43; RICHARD BORN, "Reassessing the Decline of Presidential Coattails: U.S. House Elections from 1952–1980," *Journal of Politics* 46 (1984): 60–79; RANDALL L. CALVERT and JOHN A. FEREJOHN, "Coattail Voting in Recent Presidential Elections," *American Political Science Review* 77 (1983): 407–419; ANGUS CAMPBELL, "Surge and Decline: A Study of Electoral Change," *Public Opinion Quarterly* 24 (1960): 397–418; JAMES E. CAMPBELL, "Predicting Seat Gains from Presidential Coattails," *American Journal of Political Science* 30 (1986): 165–183; MILTON C. CUMMINGS, JR., *Congressmen and the Electorate* (New York, 1966); JOHN A. FEREJOHN and RANDALL L. CALVERT, "Presidential Coattails in Historical Perspective," *American Journal of Political Science* 28 (1984): 127–146; MORRIS P. FIORINA, *Retrospective Voting in American National Elections* (New Haven, Conn., 1981); GARY C. JACOBSON, *The Electoral Origins of Divided Government: Competition in U.S. House Elections, 1946–1988* (Boulder, Colo., 1990); and GARY C. JACOBSON and SAMUEL KERNELL, *Strategy and Choice in Congressional Elections*, 2d ed. (New Haven, Conn., 1983).

Voter Turnout

CAROL A. CASSEL and DAVID B. HILL, "Explanations of Turnout Decline: A Multivariate Test," *American Politics Quarterly* 9 (1981): 181–195 and CAROL A. CASSEL and ROBERT C. LUSKIN, "Simple Explanations of Turnout Decline," *American Political Science Review* 82 (1981): 1321–1330.

SEE ALSO Constituencies; Elections to the U.S. Senate; Legislative Incumbency and Insulation; AND Legislative Redistricting.

ELECTIONS TO THE U.S. SENATE

Barbara Hinckley
Edward Muir

Senator Thruston Morton (R.-Ky.) once remarked that he had noticed certain "common denominators" in his varied experience of successful Senate contests. "These are: stature, intimate awareness of the problems of the states, a good sense of public relations and in most cases, previous political experience." Morton's comment was made in the 1960s, but it calls attention to themes important in the selection of Senate candidates from early American congressional history to the present day.

HISTORY

Establishing the Senate

The United States Senate was born in compromise. It was the result of the so-called Great Compromise between the interests of large and small states worked out in the Constitutional Convention of 1787. The small states wanted equal representation in Congress, fearing domination by the larger states if elections were based solely on population. Representatives of the large states argued that elections based on population size were the only acceptable basis for the new democracy. Small-state interests were represented by the New Jersey Plan, in which all states would have an equal vote in a one-house legislature. Large-state interests were accommodated in the Virginia Plan, which proposed a two-house (bicameral) legislature, with the lower house chosen directly by the electorate and the upper house chosen by the lower house. "Can we forget for whom we are forming a government?" one delegate argued heatedly. "Is it for *men*, or for imaginary beings called *states?*"

The issue was so emotionally charged that it seemed the convention would not survive the controversy. One small-state delegate an-

nounced he would "sooner submit to a foreign power than . . . be deprived of an equality of suffrage and thrown under the domination of the large states." A large-state representative countered that he "preferred doing nothing rather than to allow an equal vote to all States." Benjamin Franklin proposed that if each session was opened with a prayer, they could "implore the assistance of heaven" in reaching a compromise.

The problem was finally resolved in what a Senate historian calls "one of the most difficult engineering feats in the whole history of the Convention." According to the Great Compromise, a bicameral, or two-house, legislature would be created in which the lower house would represent the nation by population and the upper house would give equality to the states. The Senate, the upper chamber, would consist of members chosen equally by the states, two Senators from each state.

There was also conflict about the length and nature of Senate terms. Suggestions of four-, five-, six-, seven-, and nine-year terms were all put forward. Gouvernor Morris of New York even proposed that "members of the upper chamber should be appointed by the executive, that they should serve for life, and without pay." George Read of Delaware wanted the term of service to be "during good behavior," as in the case of Supreme Court justices. These proposals, however, met with little favor. The delegates finally agreed on a six-year term.

As a result of these compromises, the Senate would not only represent the states, but it would also represent the state governments since senators would be appointed by the state legislators. While some delegates, including James Madison, opposed the provision, others wanted the state governments to have this potential power to check the actions of the na-

467

tional legislature. In this way the Senate could veto policy that appeared to threaten the interests of the states. The senators, selected by the state legislatures, were considered by many as the states' ambassadors to the federal government.

As the government developed, some state legislatures would take this point so seriously that they instructed their senators how to vote on legislation before the Congress. Indeed, several senators in the nineteenth century resigned when their own views were too sharply opposed to their respective state legislature's instructions. In several states the practice came into being of dividing the state geographically: for example, one senator would be appointed to represent the eastern half of the state and one its western half. This practice shows how strongly senators were expected to bring to the national government the interests of the states.

At times, elections for U.S. senators in the state legislatures were very contentious. Delaware, for example, caught in factional battles within and between the parties, had no representation in the Senate between 1901 and 1903. In more successful years the state took 217 ballots (in 1895) and 113 ballots (in 1899) to elect its senator. It is also worth remembering that the fierce Lincoln-Douglas debates in 1858 that so captured the public imagination and dramatized the national conflict over slavery were actually hard-fought attempts to influence a state legislative election. The members of the state legislature of Illinois would be deciding whether the Democratic Douglas or the Republican Lincoln would be their state's senator in the Congress.

One other characteristic of senators was deemed important at the time of the convention. They were to be an elite group who could check the lower, more democratic chamber which might be too swayed by popular opinion. In James Madison's words, recorded in *The Federalist*, no. 62, the Senate could check the House, which might "yield to the impulse of sudden and violent passions and be seduced by factious leaders into intemperate and pernicious resolutions." The Senate, in contrast, was described by Madison in his *Notes of Debates in the Federal Convention of 1787*, as a group of "enlightened citizens, whose limited number and firmness might reasonably interpose against impetuous councils." This elite group

of sober, responsible citizens would be aided in taking the long view by being elected for a six-year term, as opposed to the two-year term in the House.

With Shays's Rebellion in Massachusetts fresh in the delegates' minds, a body of men who would protect the interests of wealth and property was appealing to many. The people appointed by the state legislatures did in fact show this elite character. As one historian summarizes, "The Senate roll sounded almost like a 'Who's Who' of the wealthy and socially prominent of the day. Not only were the majority of the first . . . Senators men of handsome fortune, but this practice of sending wealthy individuals to the Senate extended to all parts of the country . . . and to both parties." The practice continued and by 1906, twenty-five of the ninety sitting senators officially qualified as millionaires.

Thus the Senate, a body that could be expected to watch the interests of property and of the states, came into being. As part of the checks and balances of the Constitution, it would be powerful enough to check the executive and the actions of the House. Each house of the legislature would differ from the other in its constituency, its form of election, the length of its term, and the members who were expected to fill each chamber.

At the same time the Senate came to be known as an assembly of individuals, complementing the notion that each senator was an ambassador from a sovereign state. It included such nineteenth-century orators and statesmen as Henry Clay, Daniel Webster, and John C. Calhoun. It witnessed a debate in 1850 that became so acrimonious that one member drew a pistol to rebuff the hostile advances of the other. The two men were restrained, the pistol was captured, and the Senate subsequently issued a mild reprimand in disapproval of personal fights on the floor. Several of the early nineteenth century senators had engaged in duels, and had killed their opponents. One sitting senator, David Broderick of California, was himself killed in a duel.

The tradition of Senate individualism continued into the twentieth century, producing such political mavericks as Robert La Follette of Wisconsin and Wayne Morse of Oregon and unique personalities like Lyndon Johnson of Texas and Margaret Chase Smith of Maine. As

Smith rebuffed presidents and party leaders alike for presuming to influence her votes, she developed visibility and respect. In the words of Ralph Huitt, a scholar and close observer of Congress, "the Senate is of all official bodies perhaps the most tolerant of individualistic, even eccentric, behavior." The role of the outsider, or maverick, became a distinct—and acceptable—Senate style.

Direct Election of Senators

By the end of the nineteenth century the appointment of senators by the state legislatures came increasingly under fire. State legislative conflict produced deadlocks, in some cases so severe as to leave the Senate seat unfilled. Indeed, during the last decade of the century, a total of eleven Senate seats were left empty. Charges of bribery and other illegal practices in several states made the situation worse. Most important, the selection system became the target of Progressive reformers, who argued that the Senate, like the House, should be directly elected by the people. As Senate historian George Haynes summarized, people "had lost faith in a filtration which does not filter, a refinement which does not refine."

Momentum built for a constitutional amendment that would cause the Senate, like the House, to be elected by popular vote in the states. Five times the House passed the amendment, but as might be expected, it was defeated in the Senate. Some states—Oregon for example—passed laws calling for popular elections that would provide the state legislatures with nonbinding preferences for senator (that is, an election would name the most popular candidate, who might or might not then be selected by the state legislators). While some state legislatures continued to ignore the popular vote, several of them accepted it. In 1908, the Republican-dominated Oregon legislature elected Democrat George Chamberlain to the Senate because he had won the popular election in the state.

As the Progressive movement in both parties gained strength, the momentum for reform continued. Some newly appointed Senate candidates pledged to support the direct election of senators. Reformers also threatened to convene a special constitutional convention to ensure the successful passage of the amendment

if it continued to be blocked in the Senate. The Senate finally passed the amendment in June 1911 by a vote of sixty-four to twenty-four. The House followed and the Seventeenth Amendment was ratified by two-thirds of the states and became part of the Constitution in 1913. Thenceforth senators were directly elected by the voters of the states.

Other requirements for election remained the same as under Article I of the Constitution. Senators must be thirty years of age, a United States citizen for at least nine years, and at the time of the election, a resident of the state. (In a notable exception, Henry Clay was seated at the age of twenty-nine with full rights and privileges of the office, in contravention of Article I.) The Senate continued to be divided by thirds into classes, each serving staggered six-year terms arranged to ensure that all senators do not face simultaneous reelection. In other words, the classes are staggered so that one class comes up for reelection every second year, with the remaining two-thirds of the Senate not subject to reelection in that year. The two senatorial elections within each state are also staggered; hence, a state might have only one senatorial election in an election year or it might have none. The provision for staggered terms, as explained at the Constitutional Convention of 1787 by Edmund Randolph of Virginia, should be "favorable to the wisdom and stability of the Corps [the Senate body]." Like the extended six-year term, the staggered-selection system produced continuity. The Senate, as its members remind the House and the White House, is a continuing body.

The method of filling Senate vacancies also remained similar. Before the enactment of the Seventeenth Amendment, a state's governor could appoint a senator to fulfill a vacancy when a sitting senator died or retired, so long as the vacancy occurred when the state legislature was not in session. The appointed senator's term would last until the state legislature returned and selected its own candidate. After the Seventeenth Amendment, governors continued to make the appointments, with the appointed senator's term lasting until a special election could be held. Special elections are usually held in November of an even-numbered year, although some states provide for them to take place soon after the vacancy occurs. The appointees are not necessarily interested in a long-term Senate career, although some are. At times, governors interested in trading a state office for a national office have appointed themselves, then run for reelection as an incumbent when the special election is held.

For all its importance, the Seventeenth Amendment brought little change in the composition of the Senate. Every one of the twenty-three senators who were running for reelection and who had been previously appointed by their state legislatures was returned to Congress. In other ways, too, the special characteristics of the Senate continued. Senators continued in large part to be wealthy, highly individualistic, and closely tied to the politics of the various states.

THE ROAD TO THE SENATE

The Social Background of Senators

Although the patterns of recruitment to the modern Senate vary somewhat by state and region, there are common features. Overall senators are much wealthier and more highly educated than members of the House, although members of both chambers are wealthier and more educated than the population as a whole. Senators' occupations along with their past political careers are typical of this socioeconomic elite. During the 1980s about half (53 percent) of the Senate membership listed a past career in law. Twenty-one percent listed business as a past career, while occupations in education, journalism, and agriculture were each listed by 7 percent of senators. However, there were few actually working journalists or farmers among these groups. Typically, they primarily had been broadcasting executives or heads of large agribusinesses. The following occupations were listed once: naval officer, social worker, airline pilot, professional basketball player, and congressional aide. There were also two astronauts.

The high percentage of attorneys in the Senate has existed since the beginning of American history. The proportion of lawyers has been even higher, at times surpassing 75 percent of the membership. In the First Congress, convening in 1789, 56 percent of the Senate had been attorneys. There were also three merchants, two professional soldiers, two farmers, and one each in the professions of miner, doctor, miller, surveyor, and justice of the peace. In the Congress meeting in 1850, 83 percent of senators were attorneys, the rest being merchants, soldiers, planters, doctors, and editors. The Senate of 1950, similar to that in more recent years, also had a high percentage of legal professionals. A total of 57 percent were attorneys that year, although many had been in business, education, and publishing. There was also one dentist, one entertainer, and an engineer.

Members of the modern Senate are also much more likely to be white and male compared to the House and to the population as a whole. In the 1950s, before the Women's Movement, there were at most one or two women in the Senate at any one time. This was also true of the more recent Congresses up to 1991. After the 1992 election, a record number of six out of one hundred held Senate seats. However, women do slightly better than African Americans. The only African American senator in recent American history until the election in 1992 of Carol Moseley-Braun (D.-Ill.), was Edward Brooke (R.-Mass.), who served in the Senate from 1966 to 1978. (African American activist Jesse Jackson was elected "Shadow Senator" from the District of Columbia to act as an advocate of a constitutional amendment to give the District statehood; however, this nongovernmental position does not entail sitting or voting as part of the Senate.)

The original Senate was supposed to be an elite body selected by the state legislatures. Despite the Seventeenth Amendment's passage, present-day senators still comprise an elite group, as measured by their social and economic characteristics and exemplified by the exclusion of particular social groups. The *World Almanac* of 1902 listed eighteen of the ninety senators as millionaires, and in 1906 a writer listed twenty-five. By 1978, after many years of direct elections, about one-third of the senators could claim a net worth of $1 million or more, according to *Congressional Quarterly.* Thus, the proportion of millionaires appears to have increased from the turn of the century from one-fifth to about one-third.

In addition to being wealthy, senators often came from famous political families. Over the past twenty years, many states have elected at least one such "favorite son" or "daughter" to the Senate. Beyond the most famous political families—the Kennedys of Massachusetts and other states, the Longs of Louisiana, and the Byrds of Virginia and West Virginia—Al Gore, Jr.; Robert Taft, Jr.; Adlai Stevenson III; Hubert Humphrey III; and John D. Rockefeller IV, have all received Senate nominations. Christopher Dodd succeeded his father as senator from Connecticut while Alan Simpson's father, Milward Simpson, was governor of Wyoming. Sam Nunn of Georgia is Representative Carl Vinson's nephew, while Nancy Kassebaum is daughter of the 1936 Republican presidential candidate, Alf Landon.

The Political Background

In addition to their occupations in the private sector, senators have impressive past political experience. A study of senators in office between 1972 and 1988 shows that the large majority served in either a major state office or the House of Representatives. The breakdown is as follows:

U.S. Representative	32%
Governor	14%
State Legislature	12%
State Judicial Office	9%
Municipal Office	7%
Other	18%
No Political Office	9%

The House is therefore clearly the primary route to the Senate in recent years, with about one-third of the senators coming from the lower chamber. Representatives who have built a political base in a district expand their efforts to encompass the state. Why should they do this, however, since they are already in Congress and in more secure seats than the ones they are seeking? The answer seems to lie in the difference between static and progressive ambition found among politicians. While some House members have static ambition, desiring to hold their office indefinitely and gain power within the lower chamber, others have progressive ambition and desire to move to higher office despite the entailed risks. The Senate, not the House, is typically the base for those with presidential or vice-presidential ambitions and

is seen as more prestigious, at least in one's home state if not in Congress. Former Speaker of the House Tip O'Neill tells a story that nicely illustrates the point:

> There's a banquet in my state, and I'm sharing the platform with our two state senators, who are, of course, famous. Afterward 200 people come up and ask for Ted Kennedy's autograph; 200 come up and ask for Ed Brooke's autograph; and 18 come up and ask me for a favor. (quoted in Fenno, *Bicameral Perspective*)

Former governors and state legislators comprise the next largest groups among senators. There are a few state judicial officers—attorneys general and district attorneys—a few municipal officers—mayors, commissioners, and city council chairs—as well as some judges, party officials, bureaucrats, and others. Altogether, only 9 percent of the senators between 1972 and 1988 had no prior political office.

Many of those with no past political experience who have been elected to the Senate had compensating fame or fortune or both. In this category are ex-astronaut John Glenn, ex-basketball player Bill Bradley, basketball team owner and millionaire Herbert Kohl, and the late ketchup-and-pickle heir John Heinz. On the other hand, astronauts and millionaires have also lost Senate elections. While nonpolitical fame or fortune does appear to be an alternative route to the Senate, it is neither common nor particularly promising.

Political Precedent Again, history shows similarities between various eras. All of the members of the First Congress had some political background. Many were delegates at the Constitutional Convention and at their state ratifying conventions. Twenty had been members of one of the Continental Congresses. There were also several state legislators, four judges, and one governor. It is interesting to note that some members were elected to serve simultaneously in federal and state senates, a practice that continued into the nineteenth century. In the Senate that met in 1850, only 4 percent of members had no past political office; 20 percent had been representatives, and 16 percent were governors. This Congress also boasted a past president of the Republic of Texas, Sam Houston, and a chief justice, also of the Republic of Texas. Several senators had experience as former U.S. Cabinet members. Eleven percent of the Senate that met in 1950 had no prior political experience, a figure close to that in more recent years. Former governors led in that Congress with 26 percent of the senators, former members of the House, with 23 percent: the rest had held other state and local positions. One senator, for example, had been a one-man grand jury of Wayne County, Michigan.

The similarities across time appear more striking than the differences. Most senators come to office with past experience in a major political office, usually an elective one. Although the modern Senate is more likely to include those with no past experience, the differences are not great.

State Ties

Both houses of Congress are similar to other national legislatures in that they overrepresent an educational and social elite. In education, wealth, and social status, most legislatures in Western democratic nations are unlike the population they represent. The members of Congress, however, *are* like their constituents in one important regard. In their birthplace, place of education, and workplace, they have grown up with their constituents and share much of the same home-state socialization in local customs and culture. Typical senators were born in the state they represent, received some higher education (college or law school) in that state, and have previously worked in politics within that state in an appointive or elective position. About two-thirds of senators in the 1980s, for example, were born in the state they came to represent, two-thirds had some higher education in the state, and two-thirds had held a political office within the state or had been elected to the House from a district within the state. Fewer than ten members had none of these characteristics. These are the few modern "carpetbaggers," a term evoking the Reconstruction Era, in which Northerners moved to the South to seek their political fortunes.

It is often said that the modern campaign, with its emphasis on personal style and the candidate's own organization, makes state political ties less important. This may be so, and yet it is interesting to see how many senators have preserved their home-state ties and been rewarded for it by their party's nomination. Even the astronauts who won election did so by returning from outer space to the politics of their original home state.

The proportions of home-state characteristics are similar for the Senate that met in 1950. However, the nineteenth-century pattern is much less parochial at times because of the movement across the American frontier. In the 1850 Senate, for example, slightly less than half of the senators were born in the state they came to represent. Still, these outsiders apparently moved to the state early, since most held prior elective office in their adopted state. One of the original purposes of the Senate—to represent the various interests of the states—does not appear to have been weakened by the change to direct elections. Senators under both selection systems can claim they are well acquainted with the problems of the state.

The Candidates

The relative advantage of the various characteristics in winning a Senate seat can be seen by looking at all candidates—those who lost as well as those who won. In the pool of all Senate candidates between 1972 and 1988, people with backgrounds in law constituted 51 percent, candidates in business made up 23 percent, and those in scattered professorial, agricultural, and media fields were about 6 percent. There is little difference, then, in occupational backgrounds between those nominated by their party and those who actually win the seat. A few additional professions were listed for the losing candidates, including six ministers, eight teachers (below college level), three doctors, and two veterinarians. It is interesting that with the exception of a few individuals, service professionals are not elected to the Senate.

The most discernable difference between the winning senators and the entire pool of candidates is seen in their political backgrounds. Whereas former representatives and governors together comprised almost half of the winning senatorial group, they made up only about one-third of all the candidates. At the other extreme, those with no prior experience made up 9 percent of the winning senators, but comprised 14 percent of the entire pool. People with other state and local positions were also more heavily represented in the total pool of candidates than they were among the winning group. Although these are marginal differences at most, they suggest that political background does help distinguish the winners from the losers.

Additional evidence for the importance of political background is seen by comparing the candidates' ability to defeat incumbents. This is a difficult political hurdle to overcome, as will be discussed below. Whereas all candidates running against incumbents win about 20 percent of the time on the average, those with backgrounds in the House win about 40 percent of the time: they won sixteen challenges and lost twenty-three between 1972 and 1978. Those with backgrounds as governor win about 30 percent, having won in three races and lost in nine during the same period. Those from minor state and local positions have the lowest victory record—lieutenant governors were zero for six, for example, and state secretaries zero for four—while those with no prior experience won about 20 percent of the time.

This does not necessarily mean that political stature itself is important to voters, although it might be so. Representatives and governors, already well-placed politically, may be better able to pick the contests that can be won, leaving the hopeless races to unknowns or minor state officials. In addition, representatives and governors have a past track record and experience that make them attractive to potential campaign contributors. They can thus raise more money than the relative unknowns, a factor of major importance in the expensive Senate campaigns. All of these factors reinforce each other. Therefore, candidates who have already won a major office have a certain degree of momentum working for them that the other candidates do not possess.

One anomaly in recent recruitment patterns is found with women candidates. Although women have not been elected at higher rates overall in the 1980s compared to the 1950s, they do run more often as candidates in Senate contests than before. A total of ten women candidates ran during the period 1950–1970, while thirty-one ran between 1972 and 1988. Of this latter group, however, most ran as challengers against very strong incumbents: their opponents included such well-entrenched senators as John Warner (R.-Va.), Pete Domenici (R.-N.Mex.), Spark Matsunaga (D.-Hawaii), Jennings Randolph (D.-W.Va.), Charles Mathias (R.-Md.), and Clayborne Pell (D.-R.I.). The three women who won during this period did so in open-seat contests when no incumbents were running; four women lost open-seat contests in the same period. Studies show that women do as well in raising money and gaining votes as men do, when one controls for such factors as incumbency and the competitiveness of the state. It does not seem to be the voters then, who are controlling the number of women in Congress. The hurdle appears to be the nomination process and the lack of women in the key offices from which senators successfully launch campaigns. While there are more women in the House than in the Senate (about 40 of 435 as of 1992), their numbers nonetheless put them at a disadvantage in gaining the nomination for the choicest races—the few open-seat contests or contests where the incumbent is weak. Although it may appear as if the women's political fortunes are improving because of the increase in numbers running, in fact the number of women in the Senate remains low.

PATTERNS OF SENATE ELECTIONS

Senate electoral patterns are similar to those found for other major state and national offices. Like elections for president and the House of Representatives, Senate elections are decided by a mix of factors including the number of partisans voting in the state, the activities of the candidates, and the issues raised in the campaign. The more information available to the voters—as in a presidential election and some Senate elections—the more likely candidates or issues will be important. When the information available to the voter is minimal—as in many House races and some Senate contests— voters usually choose candidates based on party affiliation or because the candidate is already in office. It is not surprising, then, that Senate elections are in some ways both like and unlike presidential and House contests.

Incumbency in the Senate

The advantage of incumbency helps both senators and representatives win reelection. Congress provides perks, or material support, that come with the job, including the franking privilege which allows free mailing to constituents and local media, a paid staff for Washington and district offices, and distribution of government publications. Congress also provides a forum where members can announce a new federal project in their state or district. It encourages them to work on committees that help the home constituency and provides access to the government bureaucracy to do further constituency service. Although constituency service as a reelection tool is most often associated with House members, many senators, such as Alphonse D'Amato (R.-N.Y.) and Larry Pressler (R.-S.D.), have made a career out of constituency advocacy. Members can also select the issues they will take positions on, avoiding or downplaying others. Because there are so many more representatives (435) than senators (100) in the present-day Congress, senators cannot be held responsible for everything that happens in government. Unlike governors, who are also elected by a state's voters, senators are not blamed if a bill does not pass or if taxes are increased. In addition, incumbents in both House and Senate are able to raise more money for their campaigns than their challengers, since both political action committees and private fundraisers are more willing to give their money to candidates who have a record of electoral success. This advantage in fundraising can be critical in a modern Senate campaign, which typically costs more than one million dollars.

Although many of the advantages for reelection are similar in the Senate and House, the fact that more information is available to voters in Senate campaigns suggests that the reelection rate for incumbents be lower in the Senate than in the House. Senators overall face a higher quality of challenge than do House incumbents. Senators also face a greater reelection challenge because their opponents have frequently served in the House or as governor, while a much larger portion of House challengers have no previous political experience. These differences are seen in the reelection

rates. Whereas typically more than 90 percent of House incumbents seeking reelection have won their contests in the years since 1946, the reelection rate for Senate incumbents is closer to 80 percent. Note that the difference is not so great as some popular commentaries on congressional elections suggest. These figures include victories in both the primaries and general election; usually only one or two senators are defeated in primaries in any year. However, no senators were defeated in primaries from 1982 through 1988.

Senators do retire, of course, at the rate of about five or six in every election year. Some of these retirees may have read the writing on the wall and known that they could not be reelected. Others may simply have reached advanced age or decided to run for another office. Overall, of some thirty-three senators facing reelection in a given election year, about two-thirds return to the next Congress. Defeats for Senate incumbents in general elections have been somewhat erratic, with the highest aggregate number of such defeats in any recent decade at thirty-four in the 1950s, and the lowest number at fifteen in the 1960s. A total of twenty-nine senators were defeated during the elections of the 1970s and a total of twenty-five lost in the 1980s. Overall, the success rate for senators running in the general election is as follows:

1950s	78%
1960s	94%
1970s	79%
1980s	83%

As the figures show, no chronological trend is evident that favors or disfavors incumbents.

No trend is apparent in Senate retirement rates either. The rates were low in some of the years of the 1960s: only two senators retired in 1964, and three did so in 1966. The rates were high at points in the 1970s: eight retired in 1976, ten in 1978. The 1980s, however, showed a return to more average retirement rates. Incumbents clearly have an advantage, but the game is nowhere nearly so one-sided as in the House.

While only one incumbent senator was defeated in 1990, to take an example from one election year, there were several close contests. The National Republican Senatorial Committee invested millions of dollars in six races where Republican House members were thought to have a good chance of defeating sitting Democratic senators. Other conservative groups also targeted these and similar races. All of the Democrats won, however. But a race thought to be safe for Senator Bill Bradley (D.-N.J.) against a little-known public utilities commissioner, Christine Todd Whitman, was won by him by a very tight margin, with 51 percent of the vote. The one defeat for an incumbent was also a surprise. It occurred in Minnesota where Paul Wellstone, a college professor with a colorful personality, upset the Republican incumbent, Rudy Boschwitz. While Boschwitz outspent his opponent by more than 7 to 1, he suffered from conflicts within the state Republican organization and a late start in the campaign.

Party and Presidential Trends

The erratic component seen in Senate election results can best be explained by partisan voting and the staggered nature of the six-year terms. Some senators might run for reelection in a good year for their party, running again six years later in another favorable year. Their reelection rate would be understandably higher than those running when the national mood favored the other party. So, senators winning in the "Democratic" year of 1974, following the Watergate scandal and resignation of Republican president Richard Nixon, had to run for reelection in 1980 against a Republican trend. Nine incumbents were defeated that year, all of them Democratic. The 1974–1980 class would therefore show higher incumbency-defeat rates than many other classes.

The impact that national trends have on Senate elections can be seen in another way. In presidential-election years the president's party in the Senate generally picks up a few seats: the average gain between 1952 and 1984 was 2.1 seats. In the off-year elections held halfway through the president's term, the president's party loses a few seats on the average in the Senate: the average loss in the period 1952–1984 was 2.5 seats. Since the same senators are not up for reelection in two consecutive elec-

tions, the results do not mean that the same seat is swinging back and forth between parties. Rather, a small trend, probably due to presidential politics, appears to be at work in both kinds of election. The same trend is seen in the House where the president's party has lost an average of 27.5 seats in off-year elections during the same period, and has gained an average of 11 seats in the presidential-election year. The average loss in both chambers in off-year elections is about 6 percent of the seats up for reelection. Each election year varies greatly, of course, and many senators are fairly well insulated from these trends because of incumbency or favorable partisan voting in a state. Nevertheless, the predominant pattern is that a few Senate seats are lost or gained for a party depending on when the election occurs in the presidential term. A recent study confirms that a modest pull from the presidential vote in presidential-election years probably affected Senate outcomes in twelve cases between 1972 and 1988.

While many voters split their tickets, voting for candidates of different parties on the same ballot, party voting has not disappeared from American politics, as several studies point out. Even in the last quarter of the twentieth century, about two-thirds of Americans say they identify with one of the two major parties, and many use that identification in deciding how to vote. This means that, depending on the partisan makeup of the state, some senators have an easier time gaining reelection than others.

This trend can be illustrated by looking at the South, which for years has elected Democratic senators to Congress. For these candidates the only obstacle to being elected was their party's nomination—not the general-election campaign. While nominations in the South have become increasingly competitive, even swinging to the Republicans in presidential voting, Democrats in several states continue to dominate state and local elections. These traces of the old "Solid South" are still evident in Senate races. Arkansas and Louisiana elected no Republican senators in the years between 1950 and 1988, while West Virginia, Alabama, and Georgia have each seen Republicans win in only one election. West Virginia elected fourteen Democrats and one Republican, while the record for Alabama and Georgia was thirteen and one. Some commentators felt that the Reagan landslide of 1980, which carried Republicans into the Senate from the southern states where they had never won before, marked the end of this phenomenon. However, these views may have been exaggerated because these same new southern Republicans, such as Jeremiah Denton (Ala.), Paula Hawkins (Fla.), and Mack Mattingly (Ga.), were all unable to win reelection following their first terms.

Other states showing lopsided margins for one of the two parties include Kansas, with a record of 14 and 0 in electing Republicans; and Montana, with a record for Democrats of 12 and 1. These are not, by the way, merely products of safe incumbents winning one election after another. When an open-seat race appeared in each of these states, a candidate of the same party as the retiring senator won the seat.

At the other extreme, six states show close competitive margins between the parties for Senate contests, electing the same number—minus one—of Democrats as Republicans. Illinois is the only state that between 1950 and 1988 showed a perfect balance between the parties, with seven Democratic and seven Republican victories. During the same period, the state elected Republicans Everett Dirksen and Charles Percy and Democrats Paul Douglas, Adlai Stevenson III, Alan Dixon, and Paul Simon. Since senators can build their own electoral base, even in races where the other party has a majority of the voters, states will often be represented by two senators of opposite parties. In the 102d Congress, elected in 1990, twenty-two of the states had senators from opposite parties, while twenty-eight states had senators from the same party.

The Role of Minor Parties

The impact of minor parties in Senate elections in the late twentieth century is similar to that found in presidential races. While most of the Senate candidates run and win as Democrats or Republicans, minor parties can make a difference. It is true that some of the minor parties have made a very small political impact. The Courage party in one New York State Senate race mustered only 7,459 votes. The People Be-

fore Politics party in an Arizona race garnered only 3,608 votes, while the Destroy Drug Devils party in New Jersey corralled only 6,066 votes. Nevertheless, between the middle of the 1950s and 1988, candidates running solely on the tickets of minor parties won more than 50,000 votes in thirty-seven different Senate contests. There were twenty-six occasions in which the votes for a minor-party candidate exceeded the margin of victory recorded between the two major parties. In other words, the votes for the minor-party candidate could have made the difference between who lost and who won. The high point for these pivotal minor-party races occurred with seven such contests in 1974. Altogether, three senators in this time period won election as third-party members: Harry Byrd of Virginia and Strom Thurmond of South Carolina as Independents, and James Buckley of New York as a Conservative. Thurmond incidentally won his election in 1954 by a write-in vote and eventually identified himself as a Republican.

Candidates, Issues, and the Use of Media

Although many influences contribute to the outcome of Senate elections, survey studies show that the most important are the characteristics of the candidates, in particular the relative experience and the quality, or stature, of those running in the race. Incumbents win, in part, because they are seen as more experienced and more qualified than their challengers. Because of this, much depends on the quality of the challenger, as studies by Abramowitz, Westlye, Squire, and Waterman all point out. While many Senate contests are hard-fought, there is a substantial proportion of low-key races where only one candidate is known and the other lacks the resources to make a real challenge. Some states do appear to present a larger pool of qualified candidates than others. The quality of the challenger matters partly because higher-quality opponents are able to raise more campaign money, even though this influence affects the vote independently of the amount of money spent on the campaign. Seen in this light, House and Senate races show the same influences are at work, but the Senate attracts a higher quality of challenger than the House does.

The impact of issues on Senate elections is less clear-cut. Studies show that the ideological positions of candidates, as well as the voting records of incumbent senators, have a significant impact on the vote. Studies also show that, when questioned about how they voted, citizens are more likely to mention issues as important in Senate races than they do in House races. Issues can have a hidden effect as well, prompting groups to support particular candidates and target others for defeat. Pro-choice and pro-life groups with rigid stances on the abortion issue have been active in recent Senate campaigns.

It is interesting to see the issues listed in *Congressional Quarterly*'s index between 1980 and 1990 under the topic of congressional elections. Only two issues appear consistently throughout that decade: the budget and the federal deficit in all years except one; and abortion in all years except two. On average, seven to eight issues are deemed noteworthy enough to be discussed by that publication for each election year, although they are not necessarily the same ones from year to year. (The lowest number appeared in the presidential-election year of 1988.) Among the issues that gained prominence in the early 1990s are ethics, the banking crisis, and the environment. Education and cities, on the other hand, have not been listed as issues since 1982. Some issues appear in the index for only one election year: policy towards South Africa in 1986, the Nicaraguan contras in 1984, and the New Right in 1982.

Nevertheless, critics point to a lack of substantive issues in Senate campaigns and negative campaigning in the form of personal or slanted attacks against the opponent. In the 1990 Bradley-Whitman race in New Jersey, for example, Whitman campaigned against the Democratic senator by using the issue of an unpopular tax raise the Democratic governor had called for. However, while serving in the Senate, Bradley had nothing to do with the making of the state of New Jersey's tax policy. The Bayh-Quayle race of 1980 in Indiana was marked by unusually visceral tactics of pro-life groups campaigning against longtime incumbent Birch Bayh, including the distribution of

pictures of aborted fetuses with a caption stating Birch Bayh had killed them. In 1984 another famous case of negative campaigning occurred in the North Carolina race between Republican incumbent Jesse Helms and the state's governor, Jim Hunt. Using the highest professional public-relations skills, the campaigns produced 7,000 advertisements in the final five weeks of the campaign in which the candidates accused each other of being a liar or a bigot.

The Role of the Media Senate and House races differ in the much greater use of the media in Senate campaigns, at least in part because of the greater number of voters that senatorial candidates usually must reach and the greater distances they often have to cover. Campaigning House candidates, according to Richard Fenno, ask, "How many people did we meet today?" The Senate candidates ask, "What kind of coverage did we get?" Media coverage of the campaign is at best a mixed blessing for incumbent senators, for the coverage means that the challengers will be made more visible, too. Studies show that citizens residing in states with fragmented television markets (those more costly and less efficient to reach through media campaigns) are also more likely to vote for the incumbents. Nevertheless, the search for coverage goes on. Modern senators are expected to have good public-relations skills. It is the reliance on media that contributes to the huge cost increase of Senate campaigns.

Many senators do not limit their pursuit of media outlets to the campaign, but seek them throughout their term. Holding formal positions in the Senate, announcing a presidential bid, or taking the lead on newsworthy issues can all increase media coverage and thus enhance a senator's visibility in the state, although it need not increase his or her popularity with the voters. Senators volunteer for the Sunday talk shows and line up at the Capitol Hill microphones, hoping to be caught with a notable line for the evening news. Senators also keep in touch with their constituents in the more traditional ways that House members also use, such as making regular visits home to conduct fundraising and to be seen by the voters. Senatorial trips home are less frequent, however, than the House members' trips, and they are most heavily scheduled in the year or two before their reelection.

The Impact of Money on Senate Elections

As political scientist Charles Stewart observed, if an army travels on its stomach, a Senate campaign travels on the funds its candidate can raise. Money is critical, given the need for visibility and the importance of media. It is especially critical for challengers who are not governors and who have a low profile to try to equal the visibility of the senators already in the public eye. The success of challengers in both the House and Senate is directly influenced by how much money they can raise, which in turn appears to be affected by the perceived quality of the candidates, especially in terms of past political experience, and by perceptions of how close the outcome is likely to be. Hence candidates seem bound by the self-fulfilling prophecy whereby perceptions that one is likely to lose increase the chance that one will lose; a close race inspires more people to provide the funds that make a race even closer. Fundraising by incumbents appears to be most affected by how much the challenger spends and how close the outcome is expected to be.

Senate campaign spending has increased steadily since the early 1970s. Few candidates now can make the boast of former Senator William Proxmire (D.-Wis.), who once reported his $50 spent on his campaign. In the 1988 election the average spending for incumbents was $3.9 million; for challengers, $1.8 million; and for open-seat candidates, $2.9 million. The increase between 1974 and 1988 in the mean expenditure in dollars for all major candidates in Senate campaigns was as follows:

1974	$437,482
1976	$595,449
1978	$951,405
1980	$1,106,920
1982	$1,781,815
1984	$2,327,250
1986	$2,789,360
1988	$2,802,118

Source: Norman I. Ornstein, Thomas E. Mann, and Michael J. Malbin, eds., *Vital Statistics on Congress* (Washington, D.C., 1990), adapted from pp. 82–83.

Top spenders in 1988 were Pete Wilson (R.-Calif.) with 10.9 million and George Voinovich and Howard Metzenbaum (D.-Ohio) with $7.2 million and $7.1 million, respectively. Despite the similarity in spending, the incumbent Metzenbaum beat the Republican Voinovich soundly. Ed Zschau, U.S. Representative and high-tech entrepreneur, also found that money did not ensure success in the California Senate race of 1986, in which he spent $11.7 million but lost to an equally well-funded Alan Cranston, the Democratic incumbent. Approximately 20 percent of the funds raised since the 1980s are supplied by political action committees, with another 10 percent being raised by party committees. The remainder, or close to 70 percent, is contributed by individuals, including the candidates themselves.

These facts produce a quandary for reformers. If one limits the funds that can be spent—hence limiting the pressure for raising money—one benefits the incumbents, who need less visibility than their challengers do. If, however, one allows campaign spending to continue to escalate, one might make the Senate only the province of millionaires or those who are friends of millionaires. This is presumably not the kind of elite that modern citizens desire for the upper chamber of the Congress.

BIBLIOGRAPHY

Overviews
Useful historical overviews of the formation and early development of Senate elections are found in CONGRESSIONAL QUARTERLY, *Guide to U.S. Elections,* 2d ed. (Washington, D.C., 1985); BOB DOLE, *Historical Almanac of the United States Senate* (Washington, D.C., 1989); GEORGE HAYNES, *The Election of Senators* (New York, 1906), and *The Senate of the United States* (Boston, 1938); and CLINTON ROSSITER, *The Grand Convention* (New York, 1966). Comments on the delegates' positions in the Con-

stitutional Convention are also found in JAMES MADISON, *The Federalist,* nos. 62 and 63 (New York, 1961); and MADISON'S *Notes of Debates in the Federal Convention of 1787* (New York, 1987).

Valuable essays on the Senate, including one quoted in this article, have been written by RALPH HUITT and collected in RALPH HUITT and ROBERT PEABODY, *Congress: Two Decades of Analysis* (New York, 1969). Also worth reading is NATHANIEL STONE PRESTON, ed., *The Senate Institution* (New York, 1969), which provides insights by senators themselves on the institution and its history.

Biographical Information
Biographical data on members of Congress is found in a variety of available sources, including *The Biographical Directory of the American Congress, 1774–1971* (Washington, D.C., 1971). Data on all candidates, both winners and losers, are more difficult to find, but can be gathered from issues of CONGRESSIONAL QUARTERLY, *Weekly Report* (Washington, D.C., published immediately before and after elections), as well as in MICHAEL BARONE, GRANT UJIFUSA, and DOUGLAS MATTHEWS, eds., *The Almanac of American Politics* (various publishers, 1972–1990). Information on reelection and retirement rates as well as campaign spending is conveniently summarized in NORMAN J. ORNSTEIN, THOMAS E. MANN, and MICHAEL J. MALBIN, eds., *Vital Statistics on Congress* (Washington, D.C., 1990).

Senate Elections
Key studies of Senate elections can be found in ALAN ABRAMOWITZ, "Explaining Senate Election Outcomes," *American Political Science Review* 82 (June 1988): 385–403; JAMES E. CAMPBELL and JOE A. SUMNERS, "Presidential Coattails in Senate Elections," *American Political Science Review* 84 (June 1990): 513–524; BARBARA HINCKLEY, "House Reelections and Senate Defeats: The Role of the Challenger," *British Journal of Political Science* 6 (October 1987): 441–460; ARTHUR MILLER, "Public Judgments of Senate and House Candidates," *Legislative Studies Quarterly* 13 (November 1990): 525–542; PEVERILL SQUIRE, "Challengers in U.S. Senate Elections," *Legislative Studies Quarterly* 14 (November 1989): 531–547; CHARLES STEWART III, "A Sequential Model of U.S. Senate Elections," *Legislative Studies Quarterly* 14 (November 1989): 567–601; RICHARD WATERMAN, "Comparing Senate and House Electoral Outcomes: The Exposure Thesis," *Legislative Studies Quarterly* 14 (February 1990): 99–114; and MARK C. WESTLYE, "Competitiveness of Senate Seats and Voting Behavior in Senate Elections," *American Journal of Political Science* 27 (May 1983): 253–283.

RICHARD FENNO, JR., *The United States Senate: A Bicameral Perspective* (Washington, D.C., 1982), compares senators and House members on the campaign trail. The search for media visibility is analyzed in BARBARA SINCLAIR, "Washington Behavior and Home-State Reputation: The Impact of National Prominence on Senators' Images," *Legislative Studies Quarterly* 14 (November 1990): 475–494 and CHARLES STEWART III and MARK REYNOLDS, "Television Markets and U.S. Senate Elections," *Legislative Studies Quarterly* 14 (November 1990): 495–524.

SEE ALSO Constituencies; Elections to the U.S. House of Representatives; The Historical Legislative Career; Legislative Incumbency and Insulation; AND Modern Legislative Careers.

THE HISTORICAL LEGISLATIVE CAREER

Jerome M. Clubb

Considerable effort has been directed to systematic, empirically based investigations of the characteristics of legislators and the nature of legislative service. Much of this effort, however, has been concentrated on Congress in the post–World War II era. With important exceptions, the historical literature on Congress tends to be episodic and concerned with particular issues. Efforts to identify and investigate long-term patterns of change and continuity in congressional careers have been infrequent. Additionally, the methods and approaches in these studies vary widely, making comparisons difficult. In general, the historical literature is less rich than that for the more recent period.

An extensive literature concerned with state legislative service has also appeared, but research in this area has focused even more narrowly upon the post–World War II era. Systematic and empirically grounded historical studies of state legislatures remain relatively few in number, and tend to be confined to particular periods and states. Here again, the studies that have been conducted often pose problems of comparability, since methods and approaches vary from study to study. Thus, forming generalizations about the history and development of state legislative service presents major difficulties. In these terms, the state legislatures remain a largely unexploited scholarly opportunity. If we shift our attention to other legislative bodies —city councils, county boards of supervisors, and the like—the historical dimension is almost completely lacking.

This essay reflects these characteristics of work in the field. It is largely concerned with Congress and the congressional career. The treatment of historical state legislators is much more skimpy. While generalizations are offered, these should be taken more as hypotheses and suggestions for needed research than as established knowledge. The other legislative bodies are not considered.

Historical studies of legislative service are further limited by the nature of available source material as well as the sheer magnitude and complexity of the research involved. To a marked degree these studies do not, and cannot, directly address many questions of interest. We would like to know more about how members of Congress and other legislative bodies viewed their roles, and whether or not legislators differed from other officeholders (or from those who did not enter public service in terms of personality and psychology).

In the main, however, historical source materials do not address such attitudinal and motivational questions in any direct sense. It is true, of course, that the personal papers of many legislators who served for more or less extended periods have been preserved. Materials of this sort sometimes give more direct indications of motivations and underlying attitudes, and they certainly provide much information on the intimate details of individual lives. On the other hand, since the First Congress convened in 1789, more than 11,200 individuals have served in the two chambers— more than 1,740 in the Senate and more than 9,480 in the House of Representatives—and while personal papers, autobiographies, and the like are numerous, they are available from only a minority of these individuals, and it is questionable whether they provide a valid representation of all members.

Limited data are available that allow development of a reasonably systematic and comprehensive view of the demographic, social, and economic characteristics of members of Congress, and to a lesser degree, certain of their behavioral characteristics. Various biographical directories, particularly the *Biographical Directory of the American Congress, 1774–1961,* Eighty-fifth Congress, 2d sess., 1961, H. Doc. 442, although certainly flawed and limited in their own ways, provide a mine of consistent

481

and comprehensive information. On the basis of these data, a good bit can be learned about the social and economic backgrounds of members of Congress, their careers in public service before entering Congress, the length of their service in Congress, and their reasons for termination of service. These data permit construction of a limited collective portrait—"sketch" is a more accurate term—of senators and representatives from the First Congress to the early 1990s. This sketch, in turn, provides a partial and heavily inferential view of the changing congressional career.

Essentially similar data are also available in the form of state "blue books," legislative manuals and the like, for the legislators of an unknown but probably large number of states across a substantial part of American history. In this case, however, the scale of research is even more daunting. In 1840, for example, more than 4,500 individuals were serving in the upper and lower houses of state legislatures; by 1880 the number had grown to 5,700; by 1916, to 7,300. In the early 1990s, the state legislatures of the nation had approximately 7,500 members. No estimate is available of the total number of individuals that have served in state legislatures since Revolutionary times, but the number surely ranges in the hundreds of thousands. The scattered nature of the sources and the magnitude of needed research have allowed us only occasional snapshots of the legislators and legislatures of a few states in certain periods.

However understandable, the fact is nonetheless unfortunate. The state legislatures constitute a major opportunity for comparative research across both time and space. The varied nature of the states, the differing patterns which they have followed during their histories, and their diverse social and economic characteristics afford signal opportunities for research into the ways in which legislatures (and government in general) have developed and into the factors which have shaped that development.

Despite gaps and imbalances in the historical knowledge of American legislatures, a great deal is known. By considering the patterns of change that the nation has undergone, a variety of plausible surmises can be readily made on the historical changes and continuities in the legislative career. Indeed, these surmises are so obvious that to elaborate them hardly seems necessary. However, they concern changes in the size and complexity of the nation, shifts in the distribution of governmental power and authority, and the resulting changes in the status of particular offices and levels of government.

It would be possible to think of these patterns of change in terms of such concepts as modernization, political development, or institutionalization. However fruitful these concepts are for many purposes, they introduce levels of abstraction that are beyond this essay's needs. It is sufficient to think in terms of growth of complexity and governmental centralization. While these patterns are not necessarily unidirectional or progressive, they do suggest patterns of change in both congressional and state legislative careers.

Stated with only a little exaggeration, Congress was of relatively limited interest and importance during the later eighteenth and early nineteenth centuries. Neither the demands upon Congress nor the status of senators or representatives were particularly great. In the early Republic, the state governments were clearly the loci of action, with the legislatures being the dominant elements. State legislatures made decisions concerning local improvements, chartering corporations, transportation facilities, and a host of other developmental activities.

The legislative history of the United States, from the nation's founding through the middle decades of the twentieth century can be summarized in terms of the long-term growth in the power and centrality of Congress. With that growth came change in congressional service patterns. Service in Congress shifted from short- to long-term and from a part-time to a full-time occupation. However, the role and importance of the state legislatures generally declined during the later nineteenth and early twentieth centuries.

SOCIAL AND ECONOMIC CHARACTERISTICS

Congressional Members

Longitudinal studies of Congress often emphasize patterns of long-term change, and certainly the institution has undergone massive changes since the early years of the nation. In many respects, however, the institution remains much the same as at the time of the founding. Continuity also provides the best description of the social and economic characteristics of members. As numerous researchers have noted, members of Congress have never been simply "ordinary Americans." Rather the indications are that they came disproportionately from the higher status, the economically better off, and the more privileged segments of society, although the majority were probably not born to wealth or aristocratic status.

Little convincing evidence exists that links the background characteristics of members of Congress, or other legislative bodies, to differences in legislative behavior or policy positions. Even so, it is clear that however members of Congress may have been selected, or how they selected themselves, they have never represented a cross-section of the population at large.

Three indicators of social status are available for members of Congress for the period from 1789 to the 1950s: college attendance, the nature of military service, and prior non–public service occupations. None of the three yield surprising results; in all respects, congressional members appear of higher status than the national population.

College Attendance   Across the entire period, members of the House of Representatives appear better educated then the average citizen. Through the decade of the 1830s more than a third of the members who entered the House since its origin in 1789 had attended college. The percentage rose to over 60% by the 1880s and to over 90% by the 1950s. During most of the nineteenth century, senators were better educated, with over 50% having attended college through the 1870s. Thereafter, the differences between members of the two chambers diminish.

Systematic historical data on the educational attainments of the national population are not readily available. However, as late as 1959, only 18.2% of men and 14% of women 25 years of age or older had some college education. The equivalent figures for 1940 were 10.3% and 9.7%. In contrast, more than 85% of those who entered the House and Senate in the 1940s and over 90% of those entering in the 1950s had attended college. In short, during

these years, members of Congress were substantially better educated than the population at large. There can be little doubt that differences of this sort were also present prior to the 1940s.

Military Service   Service in the military, and particularly whether service was in the commissioned or noncommissioned ranks, provides a further indication of social and economic status. Once again, the available data suggest that members of Congress were of higher status. In both houses, the majority of those who were veterans served all or part of their military careers as commissioned officers. Of those entering Congress with previous military service in most decades from 1789 to 1959, more than 60% had served as commissioned officers. For some decades between 1759 and 1900 the percentages were in the high 80s or the 90s. In general, however, the percentage of members who served as commissioned officers declined between 1900 and 1950.

Information on the number of veterans in the national population who had served as commissioned officers is not available. It is likely, however, that former commissioned officers never constituted more than a small minority of all veterans. From the 1790s to the early 1990s, commissioned officers never exceeded 15% of the military personnel on active duty and usually constituted fewer than 10%, although the percentages varied from one branch of service to the other. To the degree, then, that commissioned military service can be taken as a mark of higher social status, members of Congress were unrepresentative of the larger national population.

Occupation   The occupations of members of Congress provide a third indicator of social and economic status, and here again, senators and representatives historically do not appear as drawn from the ranks of ordinary Americans. Lawyers have always constituted the largest single occupational group in both the House and Senate. Historically the proportion of senators who were lawyers was somewhat greater than that of representatives. In any given decade, half or more of those entering the senate were lawyers. In most decades lawyers accounted for more than two-thirds of the entering members. Of those entering in the 1820s, 1830s, and 1840s, more than 80% were lawyers. Thereafter the percentage of senators who were lawyers declined, ranging between percentages in the high 70s and the mid-50s from the 1860s to 1950. Almost 45% of the representatives entering Congress in the 1790s were lawyers. This figure rose to more than two-thirds by 1850, and declined afterward. During the 1910s, however, more than 60% of entering representatives were lawyers, and from the 1920s to the 1950s, the proportion that were lawyers never fell below 50%.

Other professions—such as education and medicine—were also represented in the House and Senate. Taken in combination, lawyers and other professionals consistently accounted for more than two-thirds of those entering the Senate, and the percentages were often in the 80s through 1959. At the lowest, more than 50% of entering House members were professionals, and in most decades the percentages were in the 60s and 70s. Members of the House and Senate were disproportionately individuals with some form of professional training and experience, particularly in the law. The prior occupations of the bulk of the remainder were in agriculture and business with the former decreasing and the latter increasing over time.

It is true, of course, that in the nineteenth century and well into the twentieth, professional occupations did not involve the same level or kind of education, hold the same connotations of higher social status, or confer the degree of economic advantage that is now the case. Even so, the occupational backgrounds of members of Congress were not those of the population at large.

All three indicators suggest, then, that members of Congress have consistently come disproportionately from higher-status segments of society. Moreover, the indicators provide little evidence of major change. In terms of education, members of Congress more closely resembled the nation's adult population in later years. But this reflected rising educational levels among the population at large rather than a decline in congressional college attendance. In later years the proportion of former commissioned officers elected to the House declined, although that proportion probably far exceeded national averages. In terms of occupation, both Houses remained disproportionately professional in their backgrounds.

But however useful, these data provide, at best, a surface picture of historical members of Congress and fall far short of telling the entire story. Not all lawyers, after all, are the same. A small-town lawyer was undoubtedly a different person from a member of a Wall Street legal firm. The data also do not tell us how members of Congress attained higher social and economic status. Some evidence indicates, as an example, that as many as 40% of the senators serving between 1870 and 1900 came from humble origins and could justifiably be described as "self-made." While the majority of senators and representatives were comparatively well educated, relatively well-off, and held more prestigious occupations, many of them did not begin life in those circumstances. These are questions that suggest gaps in historical knowledge. Yet we do know that entering members of Congress tended to be people of higher social and economic status, however that status was attained.

State Legislators

It is risky, indeed, to generalize about state legislators. The terrain is vast and its contours varied. Relatively few systematic studies have been carried out, and classifications also vary. It is difficult to know, for example, whether a classification such as "of moderate means" in one study signifies the same thing as it does in another. Even so, it is safe to say that state legislators, especially during the late eighteenth and the first half of the nineteenth century, also tended to be drawn from the upper social and economic segments of their constituencies. On average, state legislators probably did not enjoy the same status as members of Congress. It is likely, however, that in these terms they still differed from their constituents.

The Early Republic   The post-Revolutionary legislatures tended to be more democratic, in terms of the social and economic characteristics of their members, than those of the colonial era. Even with many variations from state to state, the wealthy and the old colonial families were still represented in the new state legislatures, but in diminished numbers. Particularly as the legislatures grew in size and western areas gained representation, the number of farmers, lawyers, lesser merchants, and even artisans in general increased and, in some cases, grew to majorities. Thus the legislatures came to be more representative of the population at large than in the colonial era. Even so, change apparently tended to be from the wealthy to the well-to-do and to those of moderate means rather than to the poor, the landless, and the laboring classes.

An examination of the New Jersey legislature during the period 1829–1844 suggests the point. Of the legislators who served and whose occupations are known, some 43% were farmers (as befitted the agricultural nature of the state), 18% were businessmen, 14% were lawyers, 4% were doctors, and only 1% artisans. Scattered evidence suggests, moreover, that the legislators were men who had sufficient means to allow them to "live comfortably."

A somewhat similar impression is conveyed by studies of the fourteen states of the upper and lower South in the 1850s. More than half of the legislators of the lower South (South Carolina, Georgia, Florida, Alabama, Mississippi, Louisiana, and Texas) were farmers or planters, approximately one-fourth were lawyers, and about one-fifth represented a variety of other occupations including a few laborers. The large majority were born in the lower South if not in the same state in which they resided as adults. Most appear to have been men of substantial means, and many were slaveholders. There was some tendency for legislators in 1860 to hold greater numbers of slaves and wealth than their counterparts in 1850.

In the upper South (Virginia, Maryland, North Carolina, Kentucky, Tennessee, Missouri, and Arkansas), state legislators in the 1850s appear somewhat more representative of their constituencies than those in the lower South. While more than half of the legislators in the upper South were slaveholders, most held twenty or fewer slaves. The majority were planters, farmers, or lawyers, and although not necessarily wealthy, most were property owners. As in the lower South, the property holdings of legislators in 1860 were greater than of those in 1850. Except in Kentucky, the number of planters also increased as did, in most but not all states, the percentage of slaveholders.

The Late Nineteenth Century   In the early 1800s, state legislatures were at their peak in importance, due largely to their role in resisting the crown. During this time they played a primary role in national development.

After the Civil War, however, state government, and particularly the state legislatures, faced allegations of graft, corruption, and subservience to the special interests. However exaggerated they were, such charges took promi-

nence in the public mind, and legislatures were often the targets of journalists and reform-minded elites.

In part as a consequence, the power and position of the state legislatures tended to be reduced. Biennial sessions replaced annual sessions in many states, limitations on the length of sessions were imposed, and powers that once belonged to the legislatures were shifted to the governors or other agencies.

These developments suggest obvious hypotheses. Given the bad reputation, which was their lot, and the reduction in their roles, it might be expected that the prestige of legislative office would also have been diminished. Thus it might be inferred that the social and economic characteristics of legislators would also change as higher-status candidates increasingly rejected state legislative service. Unfortunately, such hypotheses cannot be readily subjected to direct tests. The problem is that data, comparable to that available for the antebellum years, have not been assembled.

Whether or not the social and economic characteristics of legislators declined in the latter decades of the nineteenth century, legislators probably continued to be drawn from the middle and upper segments of their constituencies. Describing the legislatures of Illinois, Iowa, and Wisconsin during these years, Ballard C. Campbell, in *Representative Democracy* (1980), indicated that "both Democrats and Republicans recruited their delegations mainly from the more eminent citizens of small-town and rural America, not from men of great wealth or nationally recognized professional achievement, or from the lowest rungs of the occupational ladder" (p. 39).

At first glance, Samuel P. Orth seemed to contradict the point in his article "Our State Legislatures" (*Atlantic Monthly*, 1904), which examines the legislators of turn-of-the-century Vermont, Ohio, Indiana, and Missouri. Although the proportions varied from state to state, relatively few had attended college or other institutions of higher education, and many had only attended public school. In general, Orth found the occupational backgrounds of these individuals as not conducive to the training and experience required for the complex tasks of legislation.

Whatever their education or personal experience, these individuals were probably nonetheless drawn from the more eminent elements of their districts. The legislatures included few artisans and laborers and some of these few were apparently union officials and not rank-and-file workers. On the other hand, legislators were probably representative of the more substantial citizens of their districts. It is unlikely that the population of rural and small-town America included large numbers of people with the characteristics that Orth felt legislative service required.

The Twentieth Century   No sharp patterns of change in the social and economic characteristics of state legislators are apparent across the first half of the twentieth century. Sketchy evidence suggests that the proportion of legislators who had attended college increased modestly as would be expected, given general increase in national education levels. The proportion of legislators with business occupations also grew. The proportion of legislators who were lawyers may have increased modestly. Even so, in 1935 and 1937, 24% of all state legislators were lawyers, as compared with 22% in 1949. In general, the members of state senates probably were better educated and included more lawyers than the members of the lower houses.

It is likely, however, that the most defensible generalizations would note the diversity of state legislatures during these years. For example, in 1933, 21% of Pennsylvania legislators were lawyers, as compared to almost 45% in New York and 49% in New Jersey. Of all state legislators in the nation in 1933, 24% were lawyers. It is possible that the legislatures of the more urban and industrial states were, in general, better developed than those of the predominantly rural and agricultural states. The evidence to support such a generalization is limited at best, and there were undoubtedly many exceptions.

POLITICAL CAREERS

In longitudinal studies the history of Congress is sometimes divided into three periods: The pre–Civil War years, the years from the Civil War through approximately 1910, and the twentieth century. As with any periodization, this one is subject to question. It is certainly questionable whether the entire twentieth century should be seen as a single period, and the present discussion will be carried only through

the 1950s. Boundary dates are, however, inevitably imprecise and depend in some degree upon the particular characteristics under consideration. Even so, this periodization has some justification and will be used here.

The Antebellum Years

American legislatures during much of the history of the nation have often been described as little more than bodies of "amateurs." The generalization is most accurate for the pre–Civil War period. Indeed, during these years it is something of a misnomer to speak of Congressional "careers." Service in Congress tended to be brief; one or two two-year terms in the House, or a single six-year term in the Senate, was the rule rather than the exception. As far as is known, members of Congress generally ended their service voluntarily, rather than because of death in office or political defeat. For many members during these years, service in Congress was probably seen as the nonrecurring obligation of the good citizen. As will be seen, though, all of these generalizations require qualification.

Political Experience   While the period of congressional service tended to be brief, most new members had more or less extensive experience in other offices before entering Congress. Of the 506 individuals who entered the Senate during the years from the first Congress through the thirty-sixth (which adjourned in March 1861), the *Biographical Directory of the American Congress, 1774–1971* mentions no prior public office-holding experience in approximately 6% of the cases. More than 80% had held at least one state office, more than 58% had served in state legislatures, and more than one-third had served in at least one local office. Some 30% had held office at two or three levels of government (local, state, or federal), in addition to serving in Congress. Approximately 35% of those entering the Senate during these years had previously served in the House of Representatives. For significant numbers, moreover, governmental service did not end with Senate tenure. After leaving the Senate, approximately 7% served in local office, 27% in state office, and 25% held federal office.

Most entering members of the House were men with political and governmental experience, although they were somewhat less experienced than senators. Only 19% of the representatives entering the House during this period presumably held no prior public office; approximately one-third had held at least one local office, two-thirds had served in one or more state offices, and more than 55% had served in state legislatures. More than half had served at one level of government and almost one-fourth at two levels. Here again, departure from the House did not necessarily mean the end of political careers. Of the representatives entering in this period, approximately 13% subsequently served in local office, 30% served at the state level, and 18% held federal office, in addition to those that went on to the Senate.

Congressional Service Consideration of congressional careers, taken alone, works to exaggerate the degree to which the House and Senate were collections of political amateurs. Most members during these years had more or less extensive governmental experience at the state and local levels before coming to Congress. Congressional service, as noted before, was usually brief, and this may have also been true of service in other offices. Two general factors help account for the brevity of congressional service. One was the desirability with which service was seen and the other the prospects of continuing in office. In both respects the pre–Civil War years, particularly the earlier decades of that period, appear biased against extended legislative service.

In the first place, service in Congress, especially the Senate, was probably not seen as highly attractive. While sessions of Congress were shorter than they would become, they still required for most members uncomfortable and arduous travel over long distances, extended periods away from home, and living in temporary and often inadequate accommodations. Service in Congress was also not a full-time occupation, and the pay was not sufficient to support the member in the absence of other income. The large majority of members had to maintain another occupation, and congressional service required neglecting that occupation. The consequence was undoubtedly personal sacrifice. It may be as well that service in Congress—and again especially in the Senate—was not seen by many members as of great interest or importance in terms of power, status, or the opportunity to contribute constructively to the life of the nation. It is likely that the state legislatures were seen as accom-

plishing more, particularly during the earlier decades.

An extended career in Congress, as any elective office, is obviously dependent upon renomination and reelection. The principle of rotation in office also limited the possibility of extended service during the nineteenth century. Limitation of service to one or two terms—one term in the case of the Senate—was seen as a device of popular representation. Through rapid rotation in office, more citizens could participate in government and the goal of representative democracy was thereby served. This principle was made law in the Articles of Confederation, which limited members of the Continental Congress to no more than three years of service every six years. Rotation in office was an important tenet of Jeffersonian and Jacksonian democracy. The available data give the impression that, at least during the earlier decades of the period, rotation contributed more to brevity of service than defeat for reelection or denial of renomination.

Whatever the relative balance between rotation and the unattractiveness of office, both contributed to brevity of service in Congress. Among senators leaving office during the pre–Civil War years, the median period of service was five years, with almost 70% serving a single six-year term or less. As might be expected given their shorter terms, the median service of representatives leaving office was three years. Forty-six % served two years or less, and 76% served four years or less.

Termination of service was usually not due to death, defeat, or refusal of renomination, although the reasons for ending service are unknown for many House and Senate members who served during the antebellum years. Of the senators whose reasons for leaving office are known, however, some 56% either resigned or did not seek reelection, only 9% were refused renomination or defeated for reelection, and 14% died in office. The pattern for the House of Representatives was much the same. Of those whose reason for termination of service is known, approximately 58% resigned or did not stand for reelection, some 29% were defeated or refused renomination, and 9% died in office.

However, these figures may also exaggerate the "amateur" nature of Congress during these years. In addition, some changes in service patterns can be observed, although the trends are faint and not entirely consistent. On a decade-by-decade basis, the median service of senators leaving office crept upward from three-and-one-half years in the 1790s to five-and-one-half in the 1850s, and the percentage of those serving only a single six-year term fell from approximately 80% in the first decade to 63% in the 1850s. Moreover, while most senators were short-termers, there was also a small cadre of long-term members. Of those ending service in the 1840s and the 1850s, approximately 13% had served two terms or more and a few had served more than three terms. The proportion of senators who resigned from office declined moderately, as did the proportion who did not seek reelection, although quite irregularly.

The House was also characterized by a small cadre of relatively long-term members. Here, the trends are at least compatible with the view that competition for office increased. From 1801 through 1840, between 26% and 33% of those whose service terminated had served for more than four years, and between 11% and 16% had served for more than six years. In the 1840s and 1850s, however, these percentages declined as did median service, which declined from four years in the 1820s and 1830s, to approximately three years in the 1840s, and to about two years in the 1850s. At the same time the number who resigned tended to decline, while the number who either were defeated for reelection or were not renominated increased from approximately 6% in the 1790s to about 24% in the 1850s.

It would not be accurate, then, to conclude that the members of the pre–Civil War Congresses were little more than political neophytes. Many of them had broad and diverse political and governmental experience, and this diversity is almost certainly understated in the preceding paragraphs. While service in Congress was usually brief, both houses included at least a sprinkling of more experienced members from the early 1800s onward. Rather than describing these members of Congress as having limited experience, it would be better to see them as having different experience than their successors.

State Legislative Service It is much more difficult to generalize about state legislatures and legislators. Less has been written, and although source material exists, its extent

and scattered nature have prevented effective use. However, it is plausible to believe that some of the same generalizations that apply to the state legislatures also apply to Congress.

In most, if not all, states of the early nineteenth century, the legislatures were the central elements of government. In many instances, their powers extended to the appointment of governors and other state officers, and even local officials. Prior to the Civil War, legislative powers in some states were reduced. The eclipse that they experienced in the late nineteenth century may have begun much earlier.

It is highly probable that in most states during the early nineteenth century, the principle of rotation in office was as strongly adhered to in state legislatures as in Congress. Studies of the upper and lower South indicate that the typical pattern for both houses was a single term of service. On the other hand, these studies also show variation in service patterns from state to state, indicating that most state legislative bodies included at least a few members with relatively extended experience.

Little systematic information is available concerning the prior and subsequent experience of state legislators during these years. Here again, there is indication that at one time, state legislative service was seen as necessary preparation for service in federal office, and we know that more than half of the members of pre–Civil War Congresses had served in state legislatures. It appears that in the upper South during the latter decades of the period, a single term marked the end of the political careers of most legislators. It is likely that many southern state legislators also served, sometimes concurrently, in local office. Given the plethora of local offices characteristic of the nation during these years, and the service patterns of members of Congress, it is at least plausible to believe that legislators in other states also often served in local office.

Examination of patterns of legislative service during the pre–Civil War years does not suggest intensive or specialized experience. The national and state legislatures were, however, parts of a rich political culture that afforded numerous opportunities—and, perhaps, obligations—to participate in government and politics, and many participated. If legislative experience was neither specialized nor intensive, it was also the case that the tasks of government were not seen as requiring that form of experience.

The Late Nineteenth and the Early Twentieth Centuries

The politics and government of the late nineteenth and early twentieth centuries have often been described in far less than laudatory terms by both contemporary observers and later students. Rather, corruption in government, machine and boss dominance, and service to special interests have been seen as the hallmarks of the period. The national and state legislatures have been particular targets of criticism.

The degree to which these years were so characterized has probably been exaggerated. On the other hand, corruption in diverse forms—venality, misuse of government office, and so forth—was certainly present and may have been more marked than in other eras. Even so, it is probably more useful to see the later nineteenth century as a period during which the machinery of government proved inadequate for the needs of a changing and increasingly complex society and economy. These were years of rapid industrialization and urbanization, increasing concentration and centralization of economic power, and pronounced inequality. Governmental structures did not develop rapidly enough to meet the complex problems and issues that these societal and economic changes produced. The nation's legislatures are not exempt from these generalizations.

As a consequence of these demands and pressures, Congress and the state legislatures underwent rapid change, albeit in somewhat divergent directions. In both houses of Congress, organization became more effective. The committee system underwent further development and seniority became increasingly important in the selection of members to positions of power. Political parties grew in strength and they became the dominant elements in organizing, governing, and determining the business of both houses of the national legislature. Power became increasingly concentrated in the hands of the party leaders, particularly the Speakers and the chairs of the major standing committees.

Change in Congress mirrored change in the larger political universe. These years are usually described as characterized by intense partisanship and high levels of political involvement on the part of the electorate at large. Party organization was strengthened at all political and governmental levels and assumed more hierarchical form. Access to congressional office, and to positions of power once there, was increasingly dominated by party organizations, and success in growing degree was dependent upon party service and loyalty. Party service, in turn, provided security. Service in Congress might not continue, but for loyal partisans, continuation in some public or party office was likely.

It is sometimes argued that this pattern of change brought a different kind of person into Congress. Prior to the Civil War, leadership roles could be gained and played to a greater degree on the basis of such characteristics as personal charisma, debating skill, intellectual capacity, and expertise in a particular area, and often it appears by newcomers to Congress who possessed these characteristics. Following the Civil War, leadership roles tended to shift toward men with organizational skills and experience, who were less motivated by causes or ideologies, and who operated in less visible ways. For these reasons, the Congresses of the late nineteenth century have been described as dominated by "careerists" as compared to the amateurs of the pre–Civil War years.

Prior Experience These processes of change cannot be directly examined using the data that are readily available. On the other hand, observable changes in career patterns are at least compatible with these underlying processes. Between 1870 and 1910, the percentage of entering congressmen who had served in local office grew slightly. This probably reflected the growing importance of both the cities and local party organizations. During the 1870s approximately 42% of the entering House members had served in at least one local office; in the first decade of the new century slightly over 50% had served in local office. Of entering senators, 27% of the 1870s cohort had served in at least one local office, compared to 43% of those entering between 1901 and 1910.

Prior experience in state office—particularly service in state legislatures—declined, suggesting the lower repute to which state legislatures fell during these years. Approximately 60% of House members entering in the 1870s had served in at least one state office, and at least 47% had served in a state legislature. In the period 1901–1910, however, at least 49% had served in state government, and at least 35% in state legislatures. The decline in importance of state office-holding was even more pronounced in the Senate. Of the senators entering in the 1870s, more than 75% had served in state office; of those entering between 1901 and 1910, only about 66% had held state office. Decline in service in state legislatures was, if anything, even more pronounced. Of entering senators in the 1870s, at least 57% had served in state legislatures as compared to more than 25% of those entering in the years 1901 to 1910.

Congressional Careers   After the Civil War, the average congressional career lengthened, and the circumstances under which those careers ended changed. These patterns suggest that service in Congress had become more attractive and that the possibility of an extended career had increased. From the 1840s through the 1860s, rotation in office was still widely adhered to, both as a matter of ideological principle and as a means to reconcile competition between local factions. As the century wore to a close, however, the rotation rule declined in importance.

In the House, the median service of those leaving office in the 1870s was three years; of those leaving during the period 1901–1910, median service was five years. The median service of those leaving the Senate also increased from six years in the 1870s to eight years in the latter period.

These figures, however, understate change in service patterns. Of those ending service in the House in the 1870s, some 21% had served for more than four years and 10% had served for more than six. Between 1901 and 1910, the corresponding figures were approximately 51% and 37%. Of senators departing in the 1870s, 72% had served a single six-year term and 16% had served two or more. The comparable figures for the years from 1901 through 1910 were 44% and 39%.

Termination of Congressional Service Change in the reasons given for leaving con-

gressional service also suggests that both the attractiveness and the possibility of extended service had increased. The percentage of incumbent representatives who sought to remain in office but either were not renominated or were defeated for reelection increased modestly, from approximately 33% in the 1870s to some 40% during the period 1901–1910. Although the increase was modest, the incidence of defeat was well above the levels of the pre–Civil War years and the Civil War decade. The percentage who did not stand for reelection declined, from more than 40% to 32%, while the percentage who died in office rose from approximately 4% to 11%. Between 1871 and 1910, in contrast to the pre–Civil War years, few resigned, never more than 3% in any decade.

The Senate was marked by a similar pattern. Among those for whom the reason for ending service is known, death in office rose steadily from 15% to 30%. The percentage who did not seek reelection dropped from approximately 52% to 32%. Slightly more than 30% of those whose service ended during this period had been either defeated or not renominated. In the 1870s the percentage who resigned dropped below 10% for the first time in the history of the nation, and it stayed below 5% throughout the remainder of the period.

The data also suggest that for growing numbers, particularly senators, termination of congressional service signified the end of political careers. The percentage of senators for whom no subsequent office is listed in the *Biographical Directory* rose from 58% in the 1870s to 79% in the 1890s, dropping to 72% in the following decade. A modest increase in the age of departing senators suggests a similar conclusion. Across the period the median age of those ending service increased from fifty-four years to sixty-two. Of those who ended service in the 1870s, 70% were aged fifty or older, compared to 81% in the period 1901–1910. (During the pre–Civil War years, approximately 50% of senators were fifty or older at the close of their service.)

Similar changes among representatives were less marked. For about 59% of those ending service in the 1870s, no subsequent officeholding is reported. Of those ending service between 1901 and 1910, the corresponding figure is 65%. The ages of departing representatives also increased. Slightly more than 46% of those ending service during the 1870s were aged fifty or older, compared to 57% in the last decade. (Only about 30% of those ending service in the House during the pre–Civil War era were fifty or over.)

During the late nineteenth and early twentieth century, Congress increasingly became the target of reformers. Despite this, there can be little doubt that the status and power of Congress and, certainly, the attractiveness of Congressional office grew. The relative status of the two houses also changed, and the Senate became the more prestigious body, reversing the pattern of the Republic's early years.

State Legislative Service While the power and prestige of Congress increased, that of the state legislatures declined over the last half of the nineteenth century, and they came to be viewed with mistrust. In his article "Our State Legislatures" (*Atlantic Monthly*, December 1904), Samuel P. Orth wrote, "Their convening is not hailed with joy, and a universal sigh of relief follows their adjournment. The utterances of the press, the opinions of publicists and scholars, and the sentiments of the street and the marketplace are quite at one in their denunciation of the legislature. Our representatives are the subject of jest and ridicule, of anger and fear" (p. 728). Reflecting these views, steps were taken to reduce the powers of the legislatures. In many states, annual sessions were changed to biennial, limitations were placed on the length of sessions, and powers were shifted to governors, a burgeoning executive establishment, and to the courts.

The most consistent generalizations made about state legislative service during these years are that it was brief and that the incidence of reelection had declined since the earlier decades of the century. Although marked by some of the characteristics of the muckraking press, Orth's 1904 survey of four contemporary state legislatures provides detailed information about service and governmental experience. Although brevity of service was the general rule, there was substantial variation from state to state. In Vermont, only 7% of the 282 legislators serving at the time of Orth's survey had served in a previous legislature. In the Ohio Senate 18% had prior legislative service; in the House, 25%. In Indiana, one-third of the

sitting senators and one-fourth of the representatives had served previously. Two-thirds of the Missouri Senate and one-third of the Missouri House had served in earlier legislatures.

Other studies show somewhat similar service patterns. In the late-nineteenth century legislatures of Illinois, Iowa, and Winconsin, the majority served only a single term. Only an average of one-fourth of the members of any session returned to the next. Of Pennsylvania state senators serving at the beginning of each decade from 1881 through 1911, between one-fourth and one-third had no prior service, and only an average of 5% had served in more than five regular sessions. In the state House of Representatives, those without previous legislative service declined from 63.9% to 52.5%, while the percentage with experience in more than five sessions fluctuated between 0% and 2%.

It appears, however, that while service in state legislatures tended to be brief, legislators were not necessarily without political experience. At the turn of the century, virtually all Vermont's legislators had served in other offices, not at all surprising given the nature of town government in the state. Two-thirds of Indiana's legislators and the large majority of Missouri legislators had held public office before serving in the legislature. One-half of Ohio's senators and two-thirds of its representatives had held other public offices.

The political experience of legislators during the later nineteenth and early twentieth centuries was, at best, broad rather than intensive. In these terms, legislators probably resembled their colleagues of the pre–Civil War era. Whether the extent of prior experience and the length of legislative service actually declined over the course of the nineteenth century, as many later students and contemporary commentators suggest, is not clear. Whatever the case, observers at the turn of the century did not consider legislators' experience and education adequate to the needs of the time.

The Early Twentieth Century

The dominant trends during the latter decades of the nineteenth century were toward centralization of both houses of Congress and concentration of power in the hands of the congressional party leaders. As the twentieth century began, the trend was reversed. By the late 1920s, according to one estimate, power in the House that had once been concentrated in the hands of four or five members, particularly the Speaker, had passed to more than sixty members of the majority party. A Congress that had been highly centralized and efficient, albeit authoritarian, in its organization became, in the following decades, progressively more decentralized and "democratic," in at least some senses of that word—and, possibly, less efficient.

Political Organization   It can be argued that the reversal of the centralizing trend actually began in the first decade of the new century, if not earlier, with the rise of the "progressive" reform movement and the attacks upon machine and partisan politics, boss rule, and the special interests that Progressivism involved. The 1910 "Insurgent Revolt" against Joseph G. "Uncle Joe" Cannon (R.-Ill.), then–Speaker of the House of Representatives, and the resulting reduction of the powers of that office, was surely a primary element and a striking symbol of that reversal.

The explanation for this reversal is less clear and has been the subject of some scholarly debate. It is probable, however, that several factors were involved. The protest movements and the shifts in partisan control of government of the 1890s worked to reduce electoral competition in the nation and created an increased number of safe seats in both the House and Senate. The occupants of these seats were less in need of party organization in their quest for renomination and reelection. Hence, they could afford greater independence from the party leaderships in Congress. The initiation of the direct primary election, as well as other general efforts to reduce the power of the party machinery, undoubtedly had similar consequences. These efforts included such ballot reform measures as the introduction of the Australian ballot, which listed all the nominated candidates and was marked in secret by voters. As the strength of the party organization decreased, seniority became a primary factor in determining selection for committee appointments. This further increased the autonomy of individual members.

Passage of the Seventeenth Amendment to the U.S. Constitution in 1913, which replaced "indirect" election of senators by state legislatures with "direct" election by popular vote, both contributed to and reflected this trend. Direct election did not result in the wholesale replacement of serving senators as some supporters and opponents may have hoped or feared. In some states, something akin to direct election was already in practice. Aspiring senators seeking election, or reelection, often actively campaigned for election of state legislators who were pledged to support their aspirations. On the other hand, direct election of U.S. senators undoubtedly contributed to weakening organizational and partisan linkages, and, hence, also contributed to the senators' autonomy and independence.

It is less certain that we can also say that shifts in the occupational patterns of the nation during the early decades of the century worked to produce a new and more entrepreneurial and independent breed of congressional candidate. Whether as cause or consequence, it does appear that the characteristics of members of Congress and of the Congressional role did shift in more independent and autonomous directions.

Congressional members could build their own power bases and increase their perquisites, which made extended service both more feasible and more attractive. Members could now specialize in areas of interest for themselves and their constituents', and it is possible to speak of a more professionalized congressional career.

The Professional Career   In general, the career patterns characteristic of turn-of-the-century congressmen continued through the 1930s and 1940s, with some deviation in the 1950s. During that period, fewer entering congressmen probably had experience in state legislatures, although the magnitude of decline cannot be established with any degree of precision. Through the 1930s the percentage of entering senators with prior service in state office remained at about 63%, roughly the same level as at the beginning of the century, but declined to 42% in the 1950s. The incidence of service in state legislatures probably also declined. In contrast, the increase of prior service in local office that marked the late nineteenth century continued, although at a modest rate. The frequency of prior service in state office by entering House members had fallen to approximately 43% by the 1930s but rose again to 51% in the 1950s.

Congressional careers continued to lengthen, apparently for different reasons than during the later nineteenth century. From the 1910s to the 1950s, median years served at termination of service in the House rose from five years to eight years, and in the Senate from six years to eleven. The medians, of course, tell only part of the story. Of those leaving the House in the 1950s, approximately 44% had served for more than eight years, compared to 28% in the 1910s. The percentage with eighteen years of service or more rose from 4% in the 1910s to 15% in the 1950s. The pattern for the Senate was much the same. In the 1910s, 58% of those leaving the Senate for the last time had served six years or less while approximately 10% had served eighteen years or more. In contrast, of those leaving in the 1950s, only 32% had served six years or less and 19% had served eighteen years or more.

In other respects, the evidence also suggests that congressional service became more attractive during the first half of the twentieth century and that the possibility of extended service increased as well. In both the House and the Senate, the incidence of voluntary termination of service declined over the period 1901–1940 but rose again in the 1940s and 1950s. Termination of service as a consequence of electoral defeat or denial of renomination increased in the period 1901–1940 and then decreased in the 1940s and 1950s. Of the House members whose service ended in the period 1901–1950, between 11% and 17% died in office. The equivalent range for senators was from 26% to 32%.

For whatever reason, members of Congress were also ending service at an older age in the twentieth century than in the late nineteenth century. The median age of those ending House service rose to fifty-seven in the 1950s from fifty-one during the period 1901–1910. The median for senators ending service during these years ranged from sixty to sixty-three. Between 1891 and 1900, some 53% of the representatives whose service ended were fifty years of age or older; in the 1950s, 70% were of that age. More than 80% of the senators ending their service in the 1950s were fifty or older.

For most, termination of congressional service was the end of their political careers. Almost two-thirds of the House members ending service in the 1950s apparently held no further political office, and of those ending Senate service in the 1950s, more than 70% did not hold public office again. Of those who did, the large majority served in federal office; few returned to state or local service.

The evidence, then, is at least compatible with the view that by the 1950s, service in Congress was, for many members, an end in itself, a profession—in a sense of the word—that was usually not given up voluntarily. Congressional service was no longer merely one element of a political career or the onetime obligation of a good citizen. Rather, congressional service had itself become a career.

Development of State Legislatures

State legislative service had not yet become a career, although movement in this direction can be observed. Contemporary commentators expressed concern over the brevity of such service. They noted that few legislators served long enough to accumulate the experience and knowledge that were vital to the effective conduct of legislative business. According to some, moreover, brevity of service did not result from defeat at the polls or failure to gain renomination. Instead, it resulted from an unwillingness to serve, which reflected the unattractive nature of state legislative service.

One examination of the length of legislative service in ten northern states (California, Illinois, Indiana, Iowa, Maine, Minnesota, New Jersey, New York, Pennsylvania, and Washington) between 1925 and 1935 indicated that 39.6% of those serving in lower houses were in their first terms, and only 15.9% had served five terms or more. State senators tended to be more experienced. In the ten states, 20.3% of the senators were in their first terms, and 34.2% had served five terms or more. However, length of service varied widely between states. At one extreme, 60.1% of Indiana's representatives and 29.3% of its senators were in their first terms, compared to 3.2% and 17.3%, respectively, of representatives and senators who served five terms or more. New York was at the opposite extreme, with only 17.7% of its representatives and 12.1% of its senators in their first terms. On the other hand, 41.5% of its representatives and 69.2% of its senators had served five terms or more.

The indications are, however, that from 1900 to 1950 the length of legislative service increased, although the evidence is not as extensive as could be wished. In Missouri and Pennsylvania the length of legislative service increased progressively, and by the 1930s legislators in both states were generally more experienced than their predecessors. In Pennsylvania, however, the trend was temporarily reversed when veteran Republican legislators were decimated by the New Deal realignment, the shift from 1932 through 1936 from Republican to Democratic control of national government.

The trend continued through the 1940s. Of the senators serving in the ten northern states between 1925 and 1935, approximately 20% were serving their first term and 34% had served five terms or more. The comparable figures for senators serving in the same states in 1950 were 15% and 45%. Representatives in these states were somewhat less experienced. Of those serving from 1925 to 1935, approximately 40% were in their first terms, and only 15% had served more than four terms, compared to 29% and 27% in 1950.

Here again, the states varied widely. As examples of that variation, in 1950 the lower houses of New York and Mississippi, each with approximately 1% of their members serving their first terms, were the most experienced. In contrast, more than 48% of the lower-house members in Delaware, and 47% of those in Vermont, were gaining their first legislative experience. Of the senators, approximately 32% in Delaware and Nebraska were first-termers, compared to 1% in Minnesota and Mississippi.

Other changes accompanied the increase in length of legislative service, perhaps as both cause and consequence. In a number of states, reference services for legislators were created, and in other ways supporting services for the conduct of legislative business were improved. In some states compensation was also increased. These steps made legislative service more attractive, leading toward its professionalization in some states.

Even so, there were still wide variations from state to state. It is sometimes suggested that these variations can be explained by the differing economic and social characteristics of the states. Urban and industrial states presented larger and more grievous problems than predominantly rural and agricultural states. Consequently, urban states provided better compensation and other rewards for legislators. Between its challenges and rewards, legislative service in urban states became increasingly attractive, inducing legislators into longer service.

Certainly such states as New York, Illinois, New Jersey, and Pennsylvania, all with larger proportions of long-term members, seem to fit this theory. But it does not readily explain the comparatively greater experience of legislators in such states as Minnesota, Mississippi, and Wisconsin—states usually not thought of as either predominantly urban or industrial. Clearly, other factors, including the presence of entrenched political machines in various southern states, were also relevant.

CONCLUSION

By the mid-twentieth century the congressional career had become highly professionalized. Members enjoyed a good deal of individual autonomy and independence. Power was widely shared. Members could become recognized by their colleagues as experts in areas relevant to their own specialized interests and those of their constituents. A congressional career was not, and would never be, for everyone. Some continued to leave out of choice after brief service. Others, whatever their ambitions, left involuntarily through electoral defeat or failure to gain renomination.

The evidence suggests, however, that most members preferred to continue congressional service once elected. Certainly, representatives were sometimes lured away by a senate seat or a governor's mansion. Senators might be drawn away by presidential or vice-presidential nominations, by a seat on the Supreme Court bench, or perhaps by a cabinet post. But even these siren songs apparently became less enticing as the twentieth century wore on. In addition, the number of members who returned to state legislatures or other state and local offices was small compared to that of the nineteenth century.

Members also enjoyed increased security. Attaining power within Congress opened the doors to greater power. Incumbents enjoyed an increasing degree of security against defeat at the polls or denial of renomination. In short, extended service became both more attractive and more possible, and service in Congress became a career in its own right.

Signs of similar change in state legislatures can also be observed. In some states, legislative service had become, or was becoming, a full-time occupation. Legislators were serving more terms as the legislative role increasingly demanded both experience and specialized expertise. By the 1950s, it was possible to speak in some states of careers as professional legislators, just as in Congress. But change along these dimensions was by no means uniform. Some states lagged far behind others, and some legislatures changed very little.

Why the development and history of legislative bodies and the careers of legislators in the United States took the form that it did remains to be fully explained. It is obvious that differential changes in the national society and economy were of major importance in shaping that development. However, other factors were clearly relevant as well, including differences in the party systems of various states, and perhaps the persistence of a strong ideal of good government in such states as Minnesota and Wisconsin. For the purposes of these and related questions, a systematic investigation of the history and development of state legislatures would be well repaid.

BIBLIOGRAPHY

Useful surveys of the literature and bibliographies are DONALD R. MATTHEWS, "Legislative Recruitment and Legislative Careers," and MARGARET SUSAN THOMPSON and JOEL H. SILBEY, "Historical Research on 19th-Century Legislatures," both in GERHARD LOEWENBERG, SAMUEL C. PATTERSON, and MALCOLM E. JEWELL, eds., *Handbook of Legislative Research* (Cambridge, Mass., 1985); BALLARD C. CAMPBELL, "The State Legislature in American History: A Review Essay," *Historical Methods Newsletter* 9 (Sept. 1976): 185–194; and JOEL H. SILBEY, "'Delegates Fresh from the People': American Congressional and Legislative Behavior," *Journal of Interdisciplinary History* 13 (Spring 1983): 603–627.

Congress
A number of articles are of major value for an understanding of the development of Congress and the congressional career. These include NELSON W. POLSBY, "The Institutionalization of the U.S. House of Representatives," *American Political Science Review* 62 (March 1968): 144–168; NELSON W. POLSBY, MIRIAM GALLAHER, and BARRY SPENCER RUNDQUIST, "The Growth of the Seniority System in the U.S. House of Representatives," *American Political Science Review* 63 (September 1969): 787–807; H. DOUGLAS PRICE, "The Congressional Career: Then and Now," in NELSON W. POLSBY, ed., *Congressional Behavior* (New York, 1971); also by PRICE, "Congress and the Evolution of Legislative Professionalism," in NORMAN J. ORNSTEIN, ed., *Congress in Change: Evolution and Reform* (New York, 1975); by the same author, "Careers and Committees in the American Congress: The Problem of Structural Change," in WILLIAM O. AYDELOTTE, ed., *The History of Parliamentary Behavior* (Princeton, N.J., 1977); and MORRIS P. FIORINA, DAVID ROHDE, and PETER WISSEL, "Historical Change in House Turnover," in ORNSTEIN, ed., *Congress in Change*.

Important articles also include GARRISON NELSON, "Change and Continuity in the Recruitment of U.S. House Leaders, 1789–1975," in ORNSTEIN, ed., *Congress in Change*; by the same author, "Partisan Patterns of House Leadership Change, 1789–1977," *American Political Science Review* 71 (1977): 918–939; SAMUEL KERNELL, "Toward Understanding 19th Century Congressional Careers: Ambition, Competition, and Rotation," *American Journal of Political Science* 21 (November 1977): 669–693; and PETER H. SWENSON, "The Influence of Recruitment on the Structure of Power in the U.S. House, 1870–

1940," *Legislative Studies Quarterly* 7 (February 1982): 7–36.

The discussion of the House of Representatives in the present chapter draws heavily upon ALLAN G. BOGUE, JEROME M. CLUBB, CARROLL R. MCKIBBIN, and SANTA A. TRAUGOTT, "Members of the House of Representatives and the Processes of Modernization, 1789–1960," *Journal of American History* 63 (September 1976): 275–302. This article and the discussion of the Senate above are based upon INTER-UNIVERSITY CONSORTIUM FOR POLITICAL AND SOCIAL RESEARCH and CARROLL R. MCKIBBEN, *Roster of United States Congressional Office Holders and Biographical Characteristics of Members of the United States Congress, 1789–1991: Merged Data [Computer File]*, 8th ICPSR ed. (Ann Arbor, Mich., 1991). DAVID J. ROTHMAN, *Politics and Power: The United States Senate, 1869–1901* (Cambridge, Mass., 1966), is also useful.

State Legislatures

The discussion of state legislators in this chapter draws upon several studies. These include JACKSON TURNER MAIN, "Government by the People: The American Revolution and the Democratization of the Legislatures," *William and Mary Quarterly* Third Series 23 (1966): 391–407; PETER D. LEVINE, *The Behavior of State Legislative Parties in the Jacksonian Era: New Jersey, 1829–1844* (Rutherford, N.J., 1977); RALPH A. WOOSTER, *The People in Power: Courthouse and Statehouse in the Lower South, 1850–1860* (Knoxville, Tenn., 1969); also by WOOSTER, *Politicians, Planters and Plain Folk: Courthouse and Statehouse in the Upper South, 1850–1860* (Knoxville, Tenn., 1975); MORTON KELLER, *Affairs of State: Public Life in Late Nineteenth Century America* (Cambridge, Mass., 1977); BALLARD C. CAMPBELL, *Representative Democracy: Public Policy and Midwestern Legislatures in the Late Nineteenth Century* (Cambridge, Mass., 1980); and SAMUEL P. ORTH, "Our State Legislatures," *Atlantic Monthly* 94 (1904): 728–739. The January 1938 issue of *The Annals of the American Academy of Political and Social Science* was devoted entirely to state legislatures. Particularly useful studies are CHARLES S. HYNEMAN, "Tenure and Turnover of Legislative Personnel"; WILLIAM T.R. FOX, "Legislative Personnel in Pennsylvania"; HOWARD B. LANG, JR., "They Legislate for Missouri"; and DEAN E. MCHENRY, "Legislative Personnel in California."

Information on legislative-service patterns in the late 1940s and early 1950s is provided by BELLE ZELLER, ed., *American State Legislatures: Report of the Committee on American Legislatures, American Political Science Association* (1954); and for a more extended period by KWANG S. SHIN and JOHN S. JACKSON, III, "Membership Turnover in U.S. State Legislatures: 1931–1976," *Legislative Studies Quarterly* 4 (1979): 95–104.

SEE ALSO The Motivations of Legislators.

MODERN LEGISLATIVE CAREERS

John R. Hibbing

Legislative bodies in the United States are unusually powerful. They possess far more independence and influence over policy than legislatures in most other parts of the world. The U.S. Congress and its legislative counterparts in the fifty states are not usually referred to as "parliaments" (though this term is common elsewhere), but rather as "legislatures," thereby reflecting an emphasis on lawmaking and legislating rather than the "parlor" debates seen and heard elsewhere in the world. Thus, the nature of the membership of legislative bodies in the United States takes on more significance than it does in parliaments, where party loyalists replace party loyalists with no major consequence. It is therefore necessary to understand who these American legislators are, where they come from, how they grow as legislators, where they go, and where they would like to go. The purpose of this essay is to discuss these matters as they pertain to the modern era (after 1870), thereby complementing Jerome Clubb's essay concerning legislative careers in historical context.

The essay is organized into three main sections: entry to legislatures, careers inside legislatures, and departure from legislatures. Each section will in turn contain information about each house of the U.S. Congress as well as about the state legislatures. Summarizing information on the states is especially difficult, since state legislatures vary tremendously among themselves. But this variance is particularly marked with regard to careers; when compared to the poorly paid and part-time legislatures of South Dakota and Wyoming, the highly professionalized state legislatures of California and New York produce vastly different types of members, motivations, behaviors, and aspirations. Any generalized statement about state legislatures should therefore be interpreted with this caveat in mind.

LEGISLATIVE ENTRY

Just as it is frequently said that "we are what we eat," legislatures, to a large extent, are composed of those who walk through the doors of the chamber to serve. Who is attracted to service in U.S. legislatures? Where do these people come from, and how do they end up in office? What qualifications or traits seem to facilitate legislative entry?

Recruitment to State Legislatures

The United States is unique in the number of elected local positions that exist, including, among many others, those of sheriff, mayor, alderman, supervisor, registrar of deeds, and seats on city councils, weed commissions, "natural-resource-district" panels, boards of education, and boards of regents. These positions naturally suggest themselves as possible launching points for attempts to enter state legislatures. After all, experience at the local level would seem to be the first step up the ladder to state government, particularly a seat in the state legislature.

This expectation is not totally incorrect, but it perhaps is a little less true than might be anticipated. The proportion of state legislators with previous experience in elective positions is more than 50 percent in some states, such as Massachusetts, North Carolina, and especially Connecticut, but in such states as Oregon, Utah, Minnesota, and Washington it is only in a range of 30 to 40 percent. One reason for the variance appears to be the way candidates are nominated for seats in the state legislature. Where political parties call the shots in selecting candidates through "restrictive" nominating systems, previous political experience is valued more highly than in states with relatively open nomination practices.

The important point is that many state legislators have not previously served in any elective capacity. In other words, for many people a seat in the state legislature becomes a baseline elective office, the experience gained from which can prove useful if a higher elective office is later attained. To be sure, many of these individuals are not political novices. A growing percentage, particularly in states with highly professionalized legislatures, have experience as state legislative staffers. For example, almost one-third of all members of the California assembly, the lower house of the state's legislature, have served as legislative aides or interns. Growing numbers of former staffers can also be seen in New York, Illinios, Michigan, Minnesota, and other states. Still other state legislators have been active in party politics, campaign politics, interest-group politics, or community-action groups, even though they have never held a formal elective position or served as a staffer. Thus, a majority of state legislators possess previous political experience in some shape or form.

A significant and interesting minority are true political amateurs, however, listing on their résumés nothing that would seem to indicate the foundations of a political career. The desirability of political amateurs serving in legislative bodies is an issue that has been pushed to the fore by the debate over legislative-term limitations and the relative worth of legislative expertise as opposed to the value of "new blood"; this contentious matter is discussed below.

Regardless of whether a state legislative seat is the first, second, or third stop on a political career, it is likely that the prepolitical occupation of the new member had something to do with either business or the law. These two careers are well suited for political endeavors. Law practices are frequently flexible enough that one of the partners of a firm is able to withstand the disruptions of service in a part-time legislature; moreover, an emphasis on legal matters and verbal skills applies equally to attorneys and legislators. Those in business, particularly the self-employed, also have flexibility and may have special, policy-based motivations to become involved in legislative activities. But the fastest-growing occupational group among state legislators is educators, though they still constitute only about 10 percent of the total membership. Manual laborers are severely underrepresented in state legislatures, as they are in most legislative bodies worldwide.

Also underrepresented in state legislatures are blacks, although there is great variance here. Michigan has almost achieved proportional equality, with 11.5 percent of its legislature being black, compared to 12.9 percent of the state's population. In contrast, the population of Mississippi is more than 35-percent black, but the state legislature is only 9.8-percent black. The number of women in state legislatures is growing but still has a long way to go before it approaches the proportion of women in the overall population. In the 1980s the national average for women in state legislatures was about 18 percent, ranging from a low of 2 percent in Louisiana to a high of 34 percent in Arizona. The presence of females in state legislatures nationwide has been growing by about 1 percent per year. On the whole, state legislators are far more educated and are significantly more likely to be male, white, Protestant, and well-off than the general population.

In the early 1990s, trends were toward younger state legislators, with increasing numbers of members under forty, and sometimes under-thirty years of age. Younger people may not be bothered as much as older people by the disruptive schedule and poor pay of many state legislatures. But these same young members tend to be quick to look beyond the state legislature. In fact, many see the legislature as a springboard to higher office or as a credentialing device for their other occupations. The fact that legislative careers are beginning at earlier ages thus should not lead to the conclusion that careers in state legislatures are becoming significantly longer. Typically, each biennium has brought about 25–45 percent new members into the various state legislatures. The fifty-state average as of the mid-1980s was 32 percent in state senates and 37 percent in state houses. Members with exceedingly long tenure are still rare. Alan Rosenthal's 1981 study surveyed eighteen state legislative bodies and discovered that in only three were at least one-third of the members veterans of at least ten years of service.

In sum, it is now fairly typical that state legislative careers begin and end at early ages; that newly elected members are either fresh out of school or have been drawn from occupations related to business or the law; that there is a bias toward WASPs (white, Anglo-Saxon Protestants) with much education; and that, while most new members have some sort of political experience on which to build, for many it is not elective political experience, and for a minority previous experiences include nothing particularly political. Can these same statements be made about the U.S. Congress?

Recruitment to the U.S. Congress

For many politicos in the United States, a stay in Congress is the ultimate dream. Such service provides an entourage of doting staffers, a six-figure salary, a lucrative pension plan, and an enticing array of additional perquisites, not to mention substantial visibility and policy clout. The chance to be on the nightly news, to be courted by the president, and to be close to the vortex of power are the goals of many politically oriented citizens.

There is no shortage of people who wish to serve in Congress. It may not seem necessary to make this obvious point, but it is. Several scholars have explained the tremendous success of incumbent representatives at securing reelection by pointing to the poor quality of their challengers. Occasionally, the sense left by this literature is that the position needs to be made more desirable so that high-quality candidates will run against, and sometimes defeat, incumbents. Of course, the obvious point here is that high-quality candidates decide against running because they are smart enough to know about the very high incumbent-reelection rate. Their calculus has little to do with the desirability of the office and much to do with the chances of actually securing the office. Despite complaints that congressional service is not fun anymore, there is no dearth of people ready to jump at the opportunity to serve.

But just what kind of person enters the U.S. House or the Senate? Where do these people come from, and what have they experienced on their way to Congress? Congress, even more than the state legislatures, might be expected to have new members with some previous political experience, probably in elective public office. This expectation is generally warranted. The most reliable data indicate that

from the New Deal to the early 1990s, approximately 75 percent of all new members of the U.S. House previously had held some public office. The most common previous office is a seat in the state legislature. In fact, state legislative service established itself as the norm over the course of this period. About 30 percent of newly elected members in the 1930s and early 1940s had state legislative experience, while by the 1980s nearly half were state legislative veterans, with many going to Congress directly from the statehouse.

The professionalization of state legislatures appears to have positioned these institutions as logical stepping-stones to service in the U.S. House. The House, in turn, is usually seen as the logical stepping-stone to service in the U.S. Senate. Between 1960 and 1990, almost 40 percent of new senators came from the U.S. House, compared to about 14 percent who moved to the Senate from a governor's mansion. At times, especially in the late 1970s, there has been a significant increase in the number of political amateurs who have run for, and won, seats in the U.S. Senate. But since 1984, nearly all (95 percent) new senators had either previous legislative or previous executive experience, so it may be a mistake to overemphasize the presence of a few political novices. Although previous political experience is the norm, there occasionally are members who enter Congress after achieving notoriety as astronauts, actors, or athletes, or after participating in some other largely nonpolitical arena.

Special interest has been shown in explaining why some members of the House opt to run for the Senate, while other Representatives are content to stay in "the lower House." Research resulting from this interest has determined that the typical representative who runs for the Senate is between the ages of forty and forty-eight, lacks a formal leadership position in the House, is reasonably safe in an electoral sense, is a Republican (probably because at the time of the research that party had poor prospects of becoming the majority party in the House), and is predisposed to taking risks. Mostly, it seems, the decision to leave the House and run for the Senate is based on the perceived chances of winning the Senate seat. Is the Senate seat open (that is, is the incumbent not seeking to retain it)? If the seat is not open, is the incumbent vulnerable? Are other worthy challengers eager about the prospects of entering the Senate race? Does it appear to be a good year for one's particular party? These factors are likely to be crucial as representatives ponder a Senate campaign, and they may explain why only about 5 percent of all representatives with the opportunity to run for a Senate seat in any given year do so.

Despite the interest generated by such high-visibility previous occupations as acting and athletics, one should not lose sight of the other previous occupations listed by those roaming the halls of Congress. Perhaps an illustration of the diversity of previous occupations will best be achieved by focusing on the 102d Congress (1991–1993). In one survey, the 535 members of Congress listed 560 occupations (obviously a few listed more than one): 244 claimed law as an occupation; 188, business; 67, education; 65, public service; 35, journalism; 28, agriculture; 7, engineering; 5, law enforcement; 5, medicine; 4, professional athletics; 3, a religious calling; 3, labor; 2, entertainment; 2, the military; and 2, aeronautics. Lawyers with previous political experience certainly abound, but a rather generous sprinkling of alternative previous occupations is clearly present. Moreover, while previous service in state legislatures is becoming more common for members of Congress, law backgrounds are actually becoming less common: the high was 316 in 1963, compared to 244 in 1991. The Senate has held firm at about 60–65 percent lawyers since World War II, so the drop has been confined to the House.

In the 102d Congress, 29 of the 435 representatives and 2 of the 100 senators were women. There were 26 blacks and 12 Hispanics in the House and none in the Senate; 5 Asians and Pacific Islanders were in the House, and the 2 in the Senate were both from Hawaii. These figures mean that in Congress, as in the case with state legislatures, women and minorities are significantly underrepresented. Blacks, for example constitute approximately 12 percent of the U.S. population, so there should be 52 blacks in the House (twice as many as in 1992) and 12 in the Senate (there has not been a black senator since Republican Edward Brooke of Connecticut was defeated in 1978). Women, of course, are by far the most underrepresented, with well over 50 percent of the

U.S. population but only 5.8 percent of the membership in Congress, far below even their 18-percent share of state legislative seats. The 1992 elections changed these situations only marginally. The number of female legislators increased to 48 in the U.S. House and to 6 in the Senate. Blacks increased from 26 in the 102d House of Representatives to 39 in the 103d and Latinos grew from 12 to 19.

Viewed over time, the picture seems slightly less gloomy. Women and minorities have made steady but glacial movement into Congress. The first Congress after World War II had 2 blacks and 8 women, by 1965 there were 5 blacks and 13 women, and in 1981 there were 17 blacks and 20 women. Women and minorities are therefore gaining entry to Congress more than in the past, but the increases have been surprisingly small. The growing numbers of women and minorities in the state legislatures, the common stepping-stone to Congress, are encouraging, but of course the difficulty of unseating sitting members of Congress restricts the opportunities for the promotion of these individuals to the national legislature.

The average age of members of Congress has followed a peculiar pattern. It had been increasing for decades in conjunction with the lengthening tenure of members and the general aging of the nation's population. But then, with the reasonably large entering classes of the 1970s, the mean age dropped, so that by the Ninety-eighth Congress (1983–1984) the average age was the lowest it had been since World War II. But since 1984 the historical trend has reasserted itself, and by the 102d Congress the average age of members of Congress overall was 53.6 years, the oldest since 1957–1958. In 1991 the average age for senators was 57.2, and for representatives, 52.8.

As mentioned, the basic trend has been toward a congressional membership that is staying longer in Congress, but perhaps not so long as is suspected by many citizens—particularly the 70 percent who support term limits for members of Congress. In the 102d Congress, members of the House had been in that body, on average, 11.6 years, less than the 12 years that many propose as a mandatory maximum length of service. Only 146 of the 435 representatives and 20 of the 100 senators had served more than 12 years (the mean length of service in the Senate is actually shorter than in the House, though not by much). So the caricature of congressional membership as entrenched, ancient, and unvarying is not totally accurate. By historical standards, careers in Congress are now quite long, but since 1955 the change has been modest, for the mean length of stay in the House has increased by about a year and the mean length of stay in the Senate has increased by about 1.5 years.

From where do American legislators come? It would be a mistake to suggest that there is only one path to legislative service; there is not. But we can identify a typical legislator as a white male of some years and means, with a legal or business background, who has served as an apprentice in some type of politically relevant activity, preferably elective office but possibly involvement in party, campaign, or staff work. The system has become more open to diversity since World War II, although the rate of change appears to have been slowed in Congress, though not in most state legislatures, by the desire and ability of incumbents to serve relatively lengthy careers in the legislature.

LEGISLATIVE SERVICE

Most research on political careers focuses on the comings and goings of members, but in between the entry to, and the exit from, a legislature is the most crucial element of legislative careers and the element that has in previous research been given all too little attention: that portion of the legislative career during which members actually serve in the legislature. Do they progress through the maze of committee and party leadership positions? At what rate? Do their activity levels change? Their ideological predisposition? Their relations with constituents? Is there a "learning curve" for those engaged in legislative service? Are there life-cycle effects? Do members change while they are in the legislature? If so, how?

State Legislative Service

Unfortunately, not much can be said about the features of internal legislative careers in state legislatures. Part of the reason for this is the scarcity of earlier research on how state legislators change. One study that relied on surveys of state legislators in a single state was able to determine that it generally took members of the California Assembly at least two years to learn the legislative process. Since of all states California has one of the most truly full-time legislatures, it has been estimated that in other state legislatures six or more years of in-session experience would be required to become familiar with the legislative process at a comparable level. But beyond this, little is known about the evolution of state legislators while they are serving. The major reason for the lack of research is that it is difficult to study change over time when members only stay, on average, a few years. With such short stays, how is it possible to get an accurate sense of a legislator's evolution over time? Thus, as is only logical, this section is primarily devoted to a discussion of change over time displayed by members of Congress rather than by state legislators.

Congressional Service

With members of Congress typically serving ten to twelve years, it is possible to conduct research that will lead to generalizations about change over the course of a congressional career. In fact, with the growing amount of careerism in Congress—and with growing concern over the advantages and disadvantages of careerism—establishing generalizations about how members change during their congressional service would seem to be vital.

What is known about how legislators evolve as they move through careers in Congress? Careers within legislatures have many aspects, not the least of which involves the range of formal positions available to members. The most institutionalized of these positions are connected with the political parties within Congress or with the highly developed system of standing committees. The modern Congress is awash with formal positions. It sometimes seems as though every member, save the true novice, possesses some committee or party position. The number of party positions has increased markedly since the early 1970s. In addition to the Speaker of the House, the party leader, the whip, deputy whips, the caucus chair, the Campaign Committee chair, Steering and Policy Committee members, and members of the Speaker's task forces, there are a variety of ancillary positions. On the committee side of the ledger, the number of full committees (and therefore the number of full-committee chairs) has stayed reasonably constant since the 1950s, but the number of subcommittees has increased dramatically, so that now some very junior members of the majority party have a chance to chair a subcommittee.

For most members, these party and committee positions provide an identity and would appear to shape the nature and extent of legislative and constituency-oriented activities. They can provide formidable bases of power for some members, and the lack of such positions can make it difficult for other members to be taken seriously. Thus, it is important to note any patterns that might exist in the movement of members into, and perhaps out of, these positions.

But generalizing about career paths even within a single legislative body, such as the U.S. House of Representatives, is a hazardous endeavor. There are about as many paths in the House as there are representatives. Some members display formal position careers that are extraordinarily stable. James Delaney (D.-N.Y.), for one, entered the House in 1949 and immediately went on the powerful Rules Committee. He spent the next twenty-eight years there, never serving on another committee and never assuming any other party or committee position, except in his last term, when he chaired the Rules Committee on which he had served for so long.

Delaney's position stability stands in stark contrast with the House career of Olin Teague (D.-Tex.). Teague was first elected in 1946 in a freshman class that included John F. Kennedy, Richard Nixon, and future Speaker Carl Albert, and he immediately took a seat on the Veterans Affairs Committee, an important committee in the wake of World War II. By 1955, Teague had worked his way up to committee chair, but he also had taken a spot on the District of Columbia Committee. In fact, he had a subcommittee chair on the latter. In addition, Teague was a charter member of the Science and Astronautics Committee, and he subsequently chaired the Manned Space Flight Subcommittee. In 1971, Teague became chair of the Democratic Caucus. Two years later, he traded his Veterans Affairs chair (while retaining the number-two ranking) for the top position on Science and Astronautics, and two years after that, he rotated

out of the caucus chair, as is required by caucus rules, later adding several terms of service on the Ethics Committee to his continuing positions on Science and Astronautics and Veterans Affairs.

The position careers (as measured by committee and partisan duties) of most House members fall between the stability of Delaney and the fits and starts of Teague, but the point is that generalizations are unable to capture the rich variety of moves made possible in the modern Congress by the plethora of positions and motivations. With this caveat in mind, what can be said about career moves within Congress?

With regard to party positions, the kind of individual most likely to acquire a formal leadership position is an ideological moderate (able to appeal to all, or at least most, elements of the party), the owner of a safe seat (able to take tough and possibly unpopular stands), reasonably senior (a proven commodity), and the possessor of skills valued by the party (perhaps bargaining, speaking, or media skills). But exceptions to these statements abound. Newt Gingrich (R.-Ga.), the minority whip in the 103d Congress, was mellowing but was certainly not an ideological moderate when he was selected to the number-two party position by Republicans in the House. The number-one Republican in the House, Robert Michel (Ill.), despite his position, received a serious electoral scare in 1982. And Tony Coehlo (D.-Calif.) and Gingrich in the House, and Lyndon Johnson and Howard Baker in the Senate, all moved into leadership positions without first acquiring a great deal of seniority. Thus, moderation, security, and seniority are desirable, but not required, for entry into the party leadership.

Particularly in the House, a leadership ladder exists, with the Speaker likely to move up from majority leader, the majority leader from majority whip, and the majority whip perhaps from caucus secretary or possibly chair of the Campaign Committee. Requisite skills for these various positions have evolved along with American politics. Whereas the quiet, behind-the-scenes, negotiating style of longtime Speaker Sam Rayburn (D.-Tex.) was suitable in the 1950s, more recent Congresses would appear to require leaders with the ability to project well on television. This factor was ostensibly one of the reasons Senate Democrats selected George Mitchell (D.-Maine) in 1989 as majority leader.

The progression to positions of leadership within committees is structured quite differently. The so-called seniority rule, which is not really a rule but rather a tradition, holds that the majority-party member with the longest continuous service on a committee is entitled to chair that committee. Seniority is usually accompanied by the right to have first pick of subcommittee assignments and, on the minority side, to become the ranking minority member on a committee. During the early 1970s, the seniority norm was weakened. In a well-publicized series of events culminating in 1975, three longtime committee chairs in the House were replaced by less-senior committee members. Other "violations" of the norm at both the committee and the subcommittee levels have occurred since then, even though chairs are still the most senior members more often than not.

Still, the behavior of committee chairs is no longer beyond challenge. The days of the autocratic, condescending, and ideologically out-of-step chairs have ended. Chairs are now much more likely to be in the behavioral and ideological mainstream, since the seniority system no longer serves as a guarantor. The only exception in the 102d Congress, for example, was G. V. ("Sonny") Montgomery (D.-Miss.), who chaired the Veterans Committee and was an old-style fiscal conservative on most issues but a strong advocate for veterans' programs. For those now wishing to become a committee chair, the best strategy is not only to stay on a particular committee for a long time but also to demonstrate subject-matter mastery, thoughtfulness, a willingness to compromise, and a respectful attitude toward other members. Many of these traits may have been lacking in the 1950s and 1960s when extended tenure could insulate committee chairs to such an extent that the seniority rule was sometimes derisively referred to as "the senility rule."

Every two years, at the beginning of each Congress, returning members are free to request committee transfers, just as new members request initial committee assignments. Transfers are not widespread, since they usually involve a loss of accumulated committee seniority. Still, some members are dissatisfied with their initial committee assignments and eagerly attempt to move at the earliest opportunity. Others, such as Teague, find their interests changing or certain opportunities presenting themselves. Members of the House are limited to one committee and one subcommittee chair each, though the average member serves on two committees and a total of four subcommittees. This restriction on chairmanships, combined with the enlargement of key committees, the growth in the number of subcommittees, and the surge in the number of party positions, has led to a Congress that appears on the basis of formal positions to have distributed power more equitably than was the case a few decades ago. (Moreover, the Senate usually follows the so-called Johnson Rule, which guarantees every member at least one good committee assignment.) But formal positions and power are not always identical. Several scholars believe that since the early 1980s many subcommittees have become all but irrelevant and that a new power oligarchy has formed, consisting not of committee chairs but of the membership of a few key committees, particularly Ways and Means, and Appropriations.

Note should be taken here of some important changes in the speed with which formal positions are acquired in Congress, especially in the House, where formal positions are more meaningful than they are in the Senate. Formal positions used to come to representatives usually only after several terms of service. Now they come much more quickly; sometimes a subcommittee chair is obtained after only a couple of terms. Whereas in years past the typical graphical pattern of position acquisition was concave (with large increases coming late in a career), the typical pattern is thus now convex, with rapid rises coming early and then a flattening of the acquisition of new committee positions. This shift may have caused some members to be slightly disillusioned with House service, since after a few terms they probably had as much in the way of formal positions as they were likely to acquire for quite some time. But of course the old-style congressional career also led to substantial disillusionment because many members had to think seriously about whether they wanted to wait around for twenty years to get a crack at their first committee chair.

But there is more to congressional life

than formal positions. How do these other facets of the congressional career evolve during what are now frequently lengthy stints in the House? Electorally, it used to be the case that senior members were much more secure than junior members. A typical pattern was for the first-time winner to squeak through the first election, survive a couple of tough races early, and then build the seat into an electorally safe one. For example, in the 1950s, incumbents seeking their first reelection to the House were successful about 80 percent of the time and captured an average of approximately 60–65 percent of the vote. After a few more terms, they were successful nearly 95 percent of the time and received around 70 percent of the vote. Such variance across tenure levels is not common anymore, though. By the 1980s, incumbents seeking their first reelection to the House were successful approximately 93 percent of the time and averaged 68 percent of the vote. But after a few terms representatives seem to be in virtually the same spot, with reelection rates around 93 percent and share of the vote still averaging less than 70 percent. In the modern House, senior members are not significantly electorally safer than their junior colleagues. To the extent that electoral concerns influence the activities of members of Congress, this situation represents an important change from just a few decades ago.

Senators, too, used to see their electoral support improve during their careers. One study concluded that (excluding unopposed races) first-term senators were successful 69 percent of the time; second-term senators, 73.5 percent of the time; and third-term senators, 82.5 percent. Those who ran for a fourth term tended to be less electorally successful than third-term senators, but so few did this that it is difficult to form conclusions. Though no study of more recent Senate electoral careers exists, it appears that variation across careers is not so great as it used to be, as in the House.

This variation leads to the crucial matter of the actual behavior of members of Congress and the extent to which this behavior changes with the passage of the years. For organizational reasons, behavior will be divided here into *legislative behavior* (introducing bills, giving speeches, casting roll-call votes, etc.) and *constituency-oriented behavior* (traveling

home, assigning staffers to district rather than Washington offices, etc.).

An anonymous former representative once attempted to communicate the seriousness with which the apprenticeship norm (the expectation that junior members should not be full congressional participants) used to be taken in Congress:

> When I came to Congress in 1960, Carl Vinson [D.-Ga. and longtime chair of the Armed Services Committee] had a rule that first-term committee members were permitted one question in all the deliberations that took place during that term; that's it—one question in an entire term; they were permitted two questions in their second term; three in their third; and so on.

Another anonymous former member stated that the major changes in his legislative activity were produced less by what he was permitted to do than by his understanding of what was possible and what was not. To illustrate, he related the following incident:

> When I was young I offered an amendment to a bill we were considering in the Interior Committee. Well, all this amendment did was make [committee chair and dominant force Wayne] Aspinall [D.-Colo.] mad as hell. The amendment was adopted but this in turn doomed the bill. I would never have done that years later.

These quotations provide anecdotal evidence that legislative activity changes with the passage of years, but more systematic evidence would be helpful, particularly since the relative legislative contributions of junior and senior representatives is at the heart of the ongoing debate on limiting the terms of members of Congress.

Research has provided some information on how legislative activities change with the passage of time. Members do become more legislatively active the longer they stay, as measured by the introduction of bills, the offering of amendments to bills, and the number of speeches given on the floor of the House. In addition, the more tenure possessed by a representative, the more likely he or she is to have a focused and successful legislative agenda (that is, an agenda that concentrates on just one or two topics and that is more likely to become law, or at least partially so). Younger members may have an agenda that is all over the lot and that stands very little chance of being passed. Thus, the argument that it takes a while to learn the ropes of the legislative process seems to be supported empirically. Moreover, the gap between the legislative contributions of junior and senior members has actually grown in the last few decades, despite much talk of the death of the apprenticeship norm and despite the growing number of formal positions, which should give junior members more of a chance to develop.

At the same time, increasing tenure does not seem to have much effect on roll-call behavior. As members stay longer, there is a slight tendency for them to miss more roll-call votes, to be just a little more conservative (or less liberal), and to be less supportive of their party; but these changes are modest. For the most part, a longitudinal analysis of roll-call behavior suggests stability rather than movement. How a member votes early in his or her career is a good indicator of how that member will vote late in that career, and this stability is stronger in the modern Congress than it was decades ago.

But purely legislative activity is just part of what members of Congress are required to do; they also represent diverse constituencies, and actions within these constituencies can be even more time-consuming than actions back in Washington. Political-science research ignored constituency-oriented activity for a long time, but since about the mid-1970s there has been a surge of interest. Thus, some comments are possible about constituency-oriented activities and how they may change as careers progress.

Naturally, it is more difficult to measure interactions with constituents than it is to measure legislative activity. Richard Fenno's book *Home Style* (1978) describes in vivid detail the range of styles with which members relate to their constituents. It is impossible to capture this same detail with objective data. Scholars have turned to poor substitutes: variables such as the number of times a member travels from Washington to the home district and the number of staffers assigned to home-district offices (district-based staffers are likely to be concentrating on casework, directly servicing constituents, rather than legislative activities). And over

the course of a career in the U.S. House, members' attention to constituents, as measured by traveling home and assigning staffers to the district, tends to decline. Other things being equal, senior members spend less time doting on constituents than do junior members. This is true in both the House and the Senate.

Now that the changes occurring in isolated aspects of the congressional career have been noted, it is time to try to see the entire picture of the internal congressional career. For decades, it has been commonly assumed that congressional careers followed a political life-cycle pattern. This pattern began with a newly minted, electorally insecure member who was legislatively inconsequential but eager to service constituents and claimed to have an agenda pleasing to everyone. As the years passed, the member began acquiring electoral security, quality formal positions within the House or Senate, and well-focused legislative interests. These serious legislative positions and interests made it difficult for the member to devote substantial time to purely constituent matters. After several years, constituents eventually turned on the legislator, perhaps feeling that he or she had contracted "Potomac fever."

Research suggests that such variations in the political life cycle are no longer common. Relative to their junior colleagues, senior members do more legislative work and less constituency-oriented work. But with respect to several other variables, the gap between junior and senior members was smaller in the 1980s than it was in the 1950s. Cyclical patterns have frequently been replaced by career stasis. The big exception to this statement is legislative activity. Here, the political life-cycle pattern, consisting of limited legislative contributions early and substantial contributions late in a career, is now more applicable than it has been in the last several decades.

LEGISLATIVE EXIT

While it is true that legislative careers are longer now than they have ever been, they do still end. And the ending of a legislative career means membership turnover—a topic that has been of special interest to students of political institutions. This interest stems from the fact that turnover is intimately related to representation. If representatives were completely malleable and attuned to constituent concerns, membership change would not be necessary, since representation would occur by way of changes on the part of the sitting member. But it does not usually work this way, and most times legislative change, if it is to come at all, comes by way of member replacement rather than member conversion to another point of view. For those who desire a fundamental alteration in the status quo, the best hope is to inject the legislature with new people rather than to try to convert those already serving in the legislature. Thus, membership turnover takes on added significance.

Why, then, is it that members occasionally depart from a legislature? There are four basic reasons: first, electoral defeat; second, progressive ambition on the part of a member (the desire to run for a higher office); third, discrete ambition (the desire to run for a lower office or to get out of politics altogether); and fourth, death or a sudden resignation. The last category will not be addressed here. In another time, sudden resignation was common—and not always for serious reasons—but in the modern era such actions are rare, largely ideosyncratic, and not amenable to systematic analysis. But the other three sources of exit will be discussed, first for state legislatures and then for the U.S. Congress.

Exit from State Legislatures

Most departures from state legislatures are voluntary. In other words, departures result from someone wanting to leave rather than the voters wanting that person to leave. Of course, the usual caveats must be made about variance from legislature to legislature, depending upon the level of professionalization and the like. But on the whole, close to 90 percent of the state legislators who seek reelection are successful. Of those who lose, about a quarter are defeated in the primaries, while the rest lose in general elections. But, for the most part, state legislative incumbents, like incumbent members of Congress, win when they want to win. A study of thirty states from 1966 to 1976 found that the lowest success rate was in West Virginia, and even there, incumbent state legislators won about 80 percent of the time. There is

no indication of a substantial drop in reelection rates since 1976, so it is safe to conclude that electoral defeat in state legislatures is rare in the modern era.

What is not so rare is a member who decides it is not worth running for another term in the state legislature. Some of the people who arrive at this decision want to get out of elective politics altogether; others want to run for another, more lucrative office. All told, every two-year cycle sees about one in five state legislators voluntarily departing. This figure is down markedly from the 1960s, when nearly two out of five exited voluntarily every two years. Voluntary turnover tends to be higher in the upper houses of state legislatures than in the lower houses, whereas electoral defeat is more prevalent in lower houses, no doubt because of the shorter terms. And voluntary turnover tends to be higher in states with less professionalized legislatures (that is, legislatures offering low pay, small staffs, and short sessions).

As a result of a voluntary-turnover rate that is fairly high, though lower than it used to be, plus the occasional electoral defeat, the mean length of service in state legislative bodies is only about four years. Some observers worry that this figure is too low and that more incentives need to be provided to keep experienced members. But as the burgeoning movement to limit the terms of state legislators suggests, many other citizens, observers, and activists feel a rapidly changing membership is a good thing, fostering citizen legislators who are sensitive to constituent concerns.

The limitation of terms is a controversial matter, and the perceived pros and cons of the idea are not central to this essay. It is important to note, however, that in 1990 the citizens of California, Oklahoma, and Colorado voted to limit the number of years a person is permitted to serve in the legislatures of these states. The limit in Oklahoma is twelve years and in Colorado is eight; in California it is eight for the senate and six for the assembly. In 1992, fourteen more states, including populous states such as Michigan, Ohio, and Florida, passed term-limitation provisions. Many states are attempting to apply limits to their U.S. legislators as well. This is a matter on which the courts will rule. Seventy percent of the American public supports the term-limit concept, and the proposal is likely to be the major legislative-reform idea of the 1990s. In some respects, implementation of term limitation would add a new category of legislative turnover—involuntary but nonelectoral turnover. It would assure a steady infusion of new legislators, although since the average stay is only about four years, mandatory limits of eight to twelve years may not stimulate as much additional turnover as some supporters think.

Setting aside involuntary turnover produced by either electoral defeat or mandated rotation, why do so many members of state legislatures leave voluntarily? Some leave the state legislature to make a run for higher office, often in the U.S. Congress. It is safe to say that most state legislators harbor progressive ambition. A study of 150 state legislators from across the nation concluded that about two out of three were progressively ambitious. But politicians are generally astute and not lacking in ego. Acting on the basis of progressive ambitions is much less common than is the mere presence of these ambitions. Most wait for a good opportunity—perhaps an open seat in the U.S. House—and many find the wait tiring. Still, one study indicated that, as of the late 1970s, at one time or another almost 40 percent of all state legislators did seek some other elective office. Those who do run for higher office tend to be younger, tend not to be in the power elite of the state legislature (by having a party leadership position or being a member of a tax or appropriations committee), and tend to be legislatively active.

But more than half of those retiring voluntarily do not immediately seek other elective positions. These are the people who are best classified as having discrete ambition. Why do so many state legislators depart of their own free will and for reasons other than a desire to move up the political ladder? The low pay, high demands, and inconvenient, part-time schedule of many state legislatures render the high retirement rate less surprising than it might initially appear. Surveys of former state legislators who displayed discrete ambition usually uncover concern over their nonpolitical occupations, their families, and their own age or health, and dissatisfaction with the legislative process and politics generally and with the demands deriving from fund-raising and frequent elections. A detailed study of retirees from the Arkansas legislature concluded that family concerns were of primary importance generally, overwhelmingly so among the subset of female legislators. But other studies note that there may be a tendency for retirees to mention family concerns even though other factors, perhaps electoral fears or the desire to make more money, may also be involved. Regardless, voluntary departure from state legislatures with the intention of leaving public office, at least for a time, is the single major reason for exit from state legislatures.

As might be expected, aggregate turnover levels (adding electoral defeats to voluntary departures and the residual category) vary widely from state legislature to state legislature. Some of this variance is caused by different levels of professionalization, but there is more to the story. California's legislature, for example, though the most highly professionalized according to many measures, has tended to have fairly high levels of membership turnover. One recent study suggested that extreme cases can be explained by the fact that some legislatures (including California's) tend to be "springboards"; others tend to be "dead ends"; and still others tend to be "careerist." A major reason for the different types of legislatures, aside from levels of professionalization, involves the political career structure of a state, which in turn involves such matters as how a seat in the state legislature is perceived by candidates and incumbents and the number of other political opportunities existing in the state.

Exit from the U.S. Congress

The organizational scheme employed for state legislative exit can be used for departures from Congress; thus, discussion in this section will address electoral defeat, voluntary retirement due to progressive ambition, and voluntary retirement due to discrete ambition. A few preliminary comments about membership turnover levels in the modern Congress may be in order.

Total departures from Congress reached an all-time low in the 1980s. In 1988, only thirty-three new members entered the U.S. House and ten the Senate. In 1990 there were forty-four new House members and only five new senators. Turnover in the 1980s was down about 22 percent from what it had been in the 1970s, when a high rate of retirement combined with the volatile election of 1974 to provide an influx of new members. In some respects, the 1980s were more like the 1960s, when voluntary retirements were rare and electoral turnover (especially in the last half of the 1960s) was also becoming less common. Since about 1980, every two years sees, on average, about 10 percent of the congressional membership turning over. Historically speaking, the modern House is characterized by low turnover and by long careers. To illustrate this point, one can see that in January 1992, Jamie Whitten (D.-Miss.) broke the record of Carl Vinson (D.-Ga.) for the longest House service of any person in the country's history (fifty-two years).

When congressional departures do occur, it is more often than not for some reason other than electoral defeat. Of the 407 representatives who sought reelection in 1990, only 15 lost in the general election and only 1 in a primary. In 1988, 401 of 408 incumbents were successful in securing reelection. Never before had the country returned more than 400 incumbent representatives in a single election. These 96-percent and 98-percent reelection rates are not atypical for other elections since the 1970s. Even in 1992, which was supposed to be the year of anti-incumbency, just short of 90 percent of all incumbents who sought reelection were successful. It is true that an unusually large group of incumbents (sixty-six) chose not to seek reelection. Many were concerned with changes in their district boundaries or the vagaries of a contentious presidential election year, but most were scared off by the so-called check-kiting scandal (the average number of checks kited for nonretiring members was forty while for retirees it was one hundred five). But those who did run for reelection did amazingly well. Only twenty-four lost in the general election and five of those losses came to other incumbents (when redistricting threw two incumbents into the same district).

The story is not much different in the Senate. In 1990, 97 percent of Senate incumbents up for reelection won (31 of 32), the highest reelection rate since direct elections to the Senate were initiated following ratification of the Seventeenth Amendment in 1913. But the 85-percent reelection rate for incumbent sena-

tors in 1988 (23 of 27) is more typical of recent elections. Senate incumbents are generally not quite as safe electorally as their counterparts in the House.

Throughout the post–World War II years, House incumbents were a good bet to win reelection, but their seats became even safer around the mid-1960s. The percent reelected did not increase so much as the average share of the vote for all incumbents. What this means is that as of the mid-1960s, in addition to almost always winning, incumbents began routinely winning by reasonably large margins. On average, incumbents now win by more than a 2 to 1 ratio over their challengers. This has led to much discussion of the "vanishing marginals" and "incumbency advantage," topics that are addressed in this encyclopedia. Average Senate victory margins generally vary more erratically from year to year because of the smaller number of races and perhaps the more personalized nature of Senate campaigns.

A final point about congressional elections is that the few exits caused by electoral defeat are not as they were years ago. In the old days, defeats were mainly due to the large partisan fluctuations that regularly swept the country. Big swings of forty, fifty, sixty, and seventy seats from one party to the other occurred in election years such as 1942, 1946, 1958, 1966, and 1974. Even larger swings occurred in earlier eras. Whether it was a good year or a bad year for a party made all the difference in the world to the precise composition of the exiting group. Such partisan-centered swings are rare today. Congressional elections are candidate-centered rather than partisan-centered. Many incumbents seem to be buffered from national forces.

Losers are now more likely to be individuals who have been tinged by scandal rather than undercut by a bad year for their party. In 1988, to take the extreme example, six of the seven incumbents who lost their House reelection bids were tied to some form of scandalous revelation. In 1990 the only incumbent to lose a primary was Donald E. ("Buzz") Lukens (R.-Ohio), who had been convicted on a charge of having sex with a minor. Another source of electoral difficulty is unfavorable redistricting, but again this is a localized, not nationwide, occurrence. Recent national partisan swings have been modest by historical standards, and most defeats now have a special, candidate-centered explanation.

Given the lack of competition facing most incumbents in the modern Congress, it will probably come as no surprise that voluntary departure, as was the case with the state legislatures, is the major source of membership turnover. Some of this voluntary turnover is the result of progressive ambition—representatives running for the Senate and senators running for the presidency—and some is the result of discrete ambition. The factors involved with representatives running for the Senate have been addressed earlier in this chapter, since this act constitutes not just an act of exit but also an act of attempted entry. Senatorial bids for the presidency seem to be encouraged by middle-aged status, some senatorial experience, a psychological tendency to take risks, and the opportunity for a free try—that is, a situation in which the Senate term does not expire at the same time as a presidential bid (although this would not matter in Texas, where Lyndon Johnson assured through a constitutional amendment that both races could be safely undertaken simultaneously). These tendencies are merely extensions of those on virtually every rung of the legislative ladder in the United States.

But what about those members who voluntarily retire with no intention of running for other elective office? In light of how most people view the motivations of politicians and given the degree to which positions in the U.S. Congress are coveted, blatant displays of discrete ambition on the part of members of Congress are indeed surprising. Yet, since the 1970s or so, the desire to leave the world of elective office altogether has accounted for nearly as many congressional exits as all the other sources of turnover combined. What are the facts behind this somewhat surprising situation?

Voluntary departures from Congress for purposes other than running for a different public office, or voluntary retirements, were extremely common in the early nineteenth century, but gradually declined, with only modest interruptions, all the way through to the 1960s, by which time they were anything but common. This trend is seen as part and parcel of the "institutionalization" of Congress into an established, professional, full-time body with recognized norms and a clear identity. This long-term trend toward less voluntary turnover reversed course in the 1970s. The number of voluntary retirements increased from 81 in the entire decade of the 1960s to 153 in the 1970s. This reversal led to loose and, as it turns out, premature talk about the "deinstitutionalization" of the House.

But it is now clear that the 1970s were an abberation. In the 1980s the trend reversed course again, and voluntary retirements became rarities, just as they had been in the 1960s. Either it suddenly became "fun" again to serve in Congress, or there are other explanations for the high rate of voluntary retirements in the 1970s. Given the confusion on this matter, given the instability of the House pattern relative to the Senate pattern (the number of Senate retirements has been basically constant), and given that voluntary retirements constitute one of the most common sources of congressional exit, the motivations behind voluntary retirements are worth additional attention.

Obviously, some retirements occur because members are elderly or enfeebled. It is unlikely, though, that these factors are variable enough to explain the fairly wild fluctuations in House voluntary-retirement rates since the 1960s. Interviews with retired members usually become a litany of horror stories about congressional service. The long sessions and the unceasing travel back and forth between Washington and the home district make family life stressful. Members are not able to have much in the way of private lives under the scrutiny of the media. Ethics requirements force members to be on their toes or face the chance of paying a price. Many members feel they spend more time running errands and doing casework than working on real legislation. Members of Congress are not well respected by the public and this makes congressional service less desirable. The constant need to campaign and to raise funds can be wearing, even for those members whose seats appear to be reasonably safe. And the nature of the modern congressional process, with its simultaneous committee and subcommittee meetings, with its generally unproductive plenary sessions, and with the presence of a group of members who are alleged to be acerbic and supercilious, does not encourage lengthy service.

These, then, are some of the reasons members complain about congressional service. They are undoubtedly valid complaints, but the events of the 1980s raise questions about the extent to which these complaints actually translated into voluntary retirements. More careful inspection of the data reveals that most of the retirees in the 1970s were actually senior members, many of whom were well into retirement age. If the "no fun" explanation were valid, it seems unlikely that retirements would have been inordinately tilted toward this particular age bracket. It is clear that the 1970s surge in voluntary retirements was due to the unusual number of elderly members present at the time (many had entered with the large classes in the late 1940s and were thus quite senior by the 1970s) and to the devaluation of seniority. Senior members would be the most bothered by seniority reforms. Many of them perceived the younger reformers as haughty and were displeased with the new environment, in which it was less likely that substantial deference would be given to senior members. With this altered mood, it is not surprising that many senior members decided they had had enough.

By the 1980s the glut of senior legislators was gone, and most of the remaining members had either grown up with or had accommodated themselves to the new system, in which seniority was a less than automatic ticket to committee leadership posts. There continue to be reasons to complain about congressional service—indeed, the problems listed earlier are still very much present—but few members retire. The 1970s retirements did not result from the perception that service was no longer any fun, just as the 1980s dearth of retirements did not result from the perception that service was suddenly fun again. And the fact that retirees in 1992 were primarily members who had kited checks and/or been redistricted suggests blanket disaffection is not the reason for the record number of voluntary retirements in that year. Whether they want to admit it or not, most members of Congress are aggressive personalities who would probably be leading an overscheduled life even if they were not in Congress. The demands of Congress are intense and undeniably lead to the premature burn-out of some, but variations in the aggregate number of voluntary retirements are probably best explained by the other, more temporally appropriate variables mentioned here.

This is why of late there have been few retirements to explain in either the House or the Senate.

CONCLUSION

Legislators enter, serve, and leave. Each of these stages reveals much about American legislatures, about legislative behavior, about the location of various legislatures in the American political system, and about the political motivations and actions of American politicians. This essay has presented information on entry, service, and departure in the state legislatures, the U.S. House, and the U.S. Senate. Comparing careers in different U.S. legislative bodies can be revealing. To illustrate, consider the differing aspects of modern House and Senate careers—a comparison that has long been of special interest to political observers.

The Senate is simply one or two rungs up the political ladder from the House. Senators enter later and have different pre-Senate political careers. About half of them have served in the U.S. House, while it is now extremely rare for a member to leave the Senate to run for the House (this has not always been the case). In fact, it is now more common for a governor to run for the Senate than for a senator to run for the governorship. A position in the Senate is truly a career capstone for most who make it that far, since, unlike the House, there are few outlets for progressive ambitions, apart from cabinet appointments or presidential and vice-presidential nominations.

These facts might lead one to think that the Senate would be a more sedate institution. After all, this is what the founders intended, and many upper houses around the world are indeed less easily upset than lower houses. But the Senate has evolved into a politically sensitive—some say hypersensitive—body. On average, Senate careers are now actually shorter than House careers. Senators are more likely than representatives to suffer electoral defeat, and those who win are less likely to win by large margins. Even with the longer, six-year term, membership turnover in the Senate is nearly as great as it is in the House. Internally, the Senate is messy, argumentative, involved in the details of legislation, and attuned to constituent groups. In short, career analysis gives some support to the belief that the Senate, for better or worse, has ceased performing many of the functions traditionally associated with the term *upper house* and has become a second lower house.

Legislative-entry studies have the potential for informing us about the kind of individual attracted to legislative service and the kinds of traits, occupations, and preparatory activities that increase the chances of gaining entry. More specifically, a review of the scholarly literature and the facts indicates that American legislative careers are diverse. There is no single set of hoops through which one must jump in order to qualify. Still, there does seem to be a lingering bias toward certain occupations and individuals and toward a polite and orderly movement up the ladder from local office to state legislature, and then Congress. Lateral entry of political amateurs and the presence of women and minorities in legislatures still constitute exceptions to standard entry patterns.

The study of legislative service, when viewed from the perspective of careers, has a tremendous amount of potential to inform. Most research on legislative careers stresses the comings and goings of legislators rather than what they do after they come and before they go. But this very stage is at the core of legislative careers. Analysis of this stage is made difficult in American state legislatures by the short stays that characterize service in those bodies. It is difficult to draw generalizations when the length of stay about which one can generalize is only a few years. Congress is another story. The reasonably lengthy careers allow inspection of patterns formed over time in the acquisition of formal positions, in electoral success, in legislative activity, and in constituency-oriented activity. For the most part, life-cycle patterns in these various aspects of the congressional career have diminished, so that there are not as many differences between junior and senior members as there used to be. An exception to this statement is legislative activity, in which senior members are carrying the legislative burden to a greater extent than was the case a few decades ago.

Finally, examining legislative exit can provide scholars a plethora of implications, even for the theoretically central issue of political representation. In *Ambition and Politics* (1966), Joseph Schlesinger noted that "a political system unable to kindle ambitions for office is as much in danger of breaking down as one unable to restrain ambitions. . . . The desire for election and, more important, for reelection becomes the electorate's restraint upon its public officials" (p. 2). If Schlesinger is correct, some concern may need to be directed at the state legislatures. Voluntary departures from these institutions occur with some regularity—though less than was the case even a few decades ago. In Congress, despite a slight surge in the 1970s, voluntary departures are not all that common. Of course, the American public is now more worried that too many incumbents are seeking reelection than it is that an insufficient number are seeking reelection. The desire to limit terms is based on the belief that frequent legislative turnover is a good thing and that Schlesinger is incorrect about the need for politicians who are eligible for, and ambitious to continue in, elective office.

This is not the place to take a position on legislative term limits or any other controversial reform proposal. Suffice it to say that this issue cuts to the heart of the representative process and that positions on this issue should be driven not just by philosophical predispositions, but also by a thorough understanding of the current nature of legislative careers in the United States. Sometimes opinions on where we need to go are based on a faulty understanding of where we are.

BIBLIOGRAPHY

General Works
JAMES DAVID BARBER, *The Lawmakers* (New Haven, Conn., 1965), provides an imaginative inspection of different legislative styles present in the Connecticut legislature. In *Actors, Athletes, and Astronauts* (Chicago, 1990), DAVID T. CANON describes the phenomenon of political amateurs entering legislative office and offers

some views on the pros and cons of this career path. *Congress and Its Members*, 3d ed. (Washington, D.C., 1990), by ROGER H. DAVIDSON and WALTER J. OLESZEK, is a textbook treatment of the two worlds that members of Congress must inhabit simultaneously—Washington, D.C., and their respective home districts. RICHARD F. FENNO, JR., *Home Style* (Boston, 1978), is an extremely influential account of how members spend their time back in their districts. A detailed case study of the decision to run (or not to run) for the U.S. Congress is found in LINDA L. FOWLER and ROBERT D. McCLURE, *Political Ambition* (New Haven, Conn., 1989).

JOHN R. HIBBING, *Congressional Careers* (Chapel Hill, N.C., 1991), traces the changing contours of the "internal" congressional careers, including positions held, electoral success, legislative activity, and constituency-oriented activity. The best overview of congressional elections is found in GARY C. JACOBSON, *The Politics of Congressional Elections* (Boston, 1987). A few years earlier, JACOBSON, with SAMUEL KERNELL, in *Strategy and Choice in Congressional Elections*, 2d ed. (New Haven, Conn., 1983), provided a widely cited and deservedly influential account of how legislators (and others) make "strategic" decisions that are intimately related with their careers. MALCOLM E. JEWELL and SAMUEL C. PATTERSON, *The Legislative Process in the United States*, 4th ed. (New York, 1986), is a textbook with a wealth of valuable information and interpretations on both the congressional and the state legislative levels. WILLIAM J. KEEFE and MORRIS S. OGUL, *The American Legislative Process*, 7th ed. (Englewood Cliffs, N.J., 1989), does much the same thing as JEWELL and PATTERSON's text, with perhaps a little more detail.

BURDETT A. LOOMIS, *The New American Politician* (New York, 1988), traces the careers of the large group of people who first began their service in the U.S. House in 1975 after the first post-Watergate elections. DONALD R.

MATTHEWS, *U.S. Senators and Their World* (Chapel Hill, N.C., 1960), is the classic account of life in the Senate; it is now somewhat dated but still provides many valuable insights about the political life cycle and other matters relevant to modern legislative careers. MATTHEWS also penned a helpful review article on legislative careers: "Legislative Recruitment and Legislative Careers," *Legislative Studies Quarterly* 9 (November 1984): 547–586. L. SANDY MAISEL, *From Obscurity to Oblivion* (Knoxville, Tenn., 1982), is a novel account of the early stages of a race for a seat in Congress, based partially on the author's own efforts in a primary campaign. DAVID R. MAYHEW, *Congress: The Electoral Connection* (New Haven, Conn., 1974), is stylish essay on how the desire for reelection influences all aspects of congressional life, including career contours.

NORMAN J. ORNSTEIN, THOMAS E. MANN, and MICHAEL J. MALBIN, *Vital Statistics on Congress, 1989–1990* (Washington, D.C., 1992), one in a series of data compendiums documenting many aspects of congressional life, is a valuable source of information. GLENN R. PARKER's book on legislators traveling back to their home districts is entitled *Homeward Bound* (Pittsburgh, 1986). DAVID ROHDE's article on progressive ambition, "Risk-Bearing and Progressive Ambition," *American Journal of Political Science* 23 (February 1979): 1–23, provides a valuable analysis of why some representatives run for the Senate. ALAN ROSENTHAL, *Legislative Life* (New York, 1981), which brings together an immense amount of information and data on both state legislatures and state legislators, is the best book-length treatment of those topics. JOSEPH A. SCHLESINGER, *Ambition and Politics* (Chicago, 1966), provides the classic account of the political-career ladder in the United States, with substantial emphasis on the legislative component of that ladder as a source of opportunity and as an object of ambition.

SEE ALSO Constituencies; Legislative Incumbency and Insulation; The Motivations of Legislators; Parties, Elections, Moods, and Lawmaking Surges; AND The Responsibility of the Representative.

LEGISLATIVE INCUMBENCY AND INSULATION

Morris P. Fiorina
Timothy S. Prinz

Over the course of its two-hundred-year history, Congress has changed in myriad ways. Some of the most significant changes involve the composition of the institution—specifically, the kinds of people who serve and how they earn the right to serve. This chapter surveys two important changes pertaining to the membership: the shift from an "amateur," impermanent body to the most professionalized legislative body in the world and the shift from a body greatly at the mercy of national electoral forces to a body whose electoral fate depends mostly on individual records and achievements. This choice of subjects is not accidental, for in our view, the changes are interconnected. The decline of electoral threat allows members to consider service in the national legislature as a career option. Conversely, there is every reason to believe that careerist members purposely seek to insulate themselves from national forces and other uncontrollable factors that might upset their career plans. There is a bit of a chicken-and-egg problem here, but we will make no attempt to resolve it. Suffice it to say that motive and capability interact. As the discussion will note, the two changes discussed here are major contributing factors to other aspects of congressional evolution discussed elsewhere in this volume.

FROM AMATEUR TO PROFESSIONAL

The framers of the U.S. Constitution anticipated a Congress composed of citizen legislators who would represent their states and districts for a time and then return to their primary occupations in commerce, the professions, and agriculture. To be sure, they anticipated that the Senate would be a more stable body than the House, but they did not foresee that either body would be composed of professionals—members who would make careers of congressional service. For a time the framers' expectations were met with a vengeance: more than 40 percent of the members of the First House did not return for the Second, and turnover exceeded 50 percent as late as the Fifty-fourth Congress (1895–1897). In the Senate, turnover was high at the beginning—in the first decade of the Republic one-third of the senators declined to serve out their full six-year terms—but a major decline was evident by the end of the Jacksonian era.

House Turnover

The first task in charting the dramatic changes in membership stability is to select a measure of turnover. In his seminal article on the institutionalization of the U.S. House of Representatives, Nelson Polsby reported the percent of first-term members in each Congress. At times, this straightforward measure slightly overestimates turnover, since the House regularly added new seats in the nineteenth century, particularly after the decennial censuses (the House did not reach its present size of 435 until 1913). Thus, Morris P. Fiorina, David W. Rohde, and Peter Wissel calculated a modified measure of turnover that accounts for the freshmen from newly created seats (see Figure 1).

The movements of House turnover show suggestive connections to significant periods in American history. For one, notable changes in turnover are associated with different party systems discussed by political historians. Turnover increases with considerable fluctuation until about 1825, when it takes a 15 percent drop, a change that roughly corresponds to the demise of the first American party system. Turnover then resumes a more or less upward path until about the early 1850s, when the Jacksonian party system splinters, and then it levels off and

Figure 1
PERCENT OF HOUSE MEMBERSHIP REPLACED

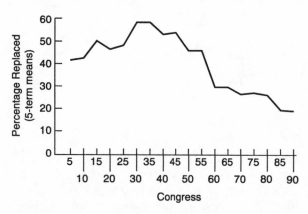

Source: Morris P. Fiorina, David W. Rohde, and Peter Wissel, "Historical Change in House Turnover," in Norman J. Ornstein, ed., *Congress in Change: Evolution and Reform* (New York: Praeger, 1975), p. 32. Reprinted by permission.

begins a ragged decline that persists throughout the third party system. Turnover peaks at the election of 1894 and then drops significantly after the 1896 election and the advent of the fourth party system. After somewhat heightened turnover in the New Deal period, turnover declines again and, by the late 1960s, plateaus at the familiar contemporary low.

Within these broad secular movements, turnover rises and falls with national economic conditions. The panic of 1873 was followed by a sharp increase in turnover. Turnover also jumps in both 1894 and 1932, elections that followed major economic setbacks. Even the recession of 1958 is followed by a sizable rise in turnover. Other more particular effects are also evident. For example, turnover for the Fifteenth Congress is 15 points greater than that for the Fourteenth and Sixteenth Congresses, the apparent result of an ill-advised decision by members to vote themselves a pay raise.

Beneath these aggregate turnover patterns lie important regional and state variations in turnover. For much of the nineteenth century the practice of rotation was common in many states. Political organizations might nominate a representative to serve for a term or two and then bestow the favor on another. Rotation was also used as a compromise between political factions: the two sides would agree to allow one person to serve a specified number of terms and then be replaced by a factional rival.

Some party organizations even followed a strict "one term and out" rule. Significantly, rotation was common in every region but the South, creating markedly lower turnover for that region's members of Congress. Generally, turnover was around 10 percentage points higher in other regions of the country (see Table 1). Some scholars speculate that southern slaveholders appreciated the value of having experienced members in Congress, while less-threatened regions did not. Other scholars suggest that southern politicians simply were more attracted to Congress because alternative careers were less available in the economically and politically undeveloped South. Whatever the underlying causes, the data clearly show that southerners returned to Congress at significantly higher rates than northerners during the nineteenth century.

Senate Turnover

Senate turnover was initially very high, largely because state politics was the place for ambitious politicians. The early Senate was largely a "do-nothing" chamber; most of the major political activity in the new national government began in the House of Representatives. When comparing turnover in the House and Senate, it is also important to keep in mind that turnover figures are not strictly comparable, since senators were officially elected by state legislatures until adoption of the Seventeenth Amendment in 1913. An element of popular selection had emerged in some states by the mid-nineteenth century, however; for example, state legislative

Table 1
AVERAGE AMOUNT BY WHICH EASTERN TURNOVER EXCEEDS SOUTHERN TURNOVER

Party System	Average Eastern Excess
1789–1822	10.2%
1824–1852	14.4
1854–1894	6.6
1896–1930	11.4
1932–1970	6.9

Source: Morris P. Fiorina, David W. Rohde, and Peter Wissel, "Historical Change in House Turnover," in Norman J. Ornstein, ed., *Congress in Change: Evolution and Reform* (New York: Praeger, 1975), p. 35. Reprinted by permission.

candidates might run as committed supporters of particular senatorial candidates.

Early in the nineteenth century, powerful political figures such as Henry Clay, John C. Calhoun, and Daniel Webster gravitated to the Senate and made it the seat of debate over the great issues of the day. After the Civil War and Reconstruction, the Senate rose to the height of its influence in the national government. Senators were major figures in state and local party machines and greatly influenced federal patronage. During this same period, the presidency was at a low ebb, and the federal government was increasingly involved in critical policy matters such as trade and finance, matters that were quite often settled in the Senate. As a result, the Senate became an attractive place for a politician to be, and senators began to remain in the chamber with much greater regularity. By the mid-1880s, Senate turnover had fallen to about 20 percent.

Congressional Tenure

Congressional tenure is closely related to turnover, although similar turnover rates are logically compatible with considerably different tenure rates. The closeness of the relationship between tenure and turnover depends on whether the turnover occurs repeatedly in the same seats or is spread across all seats. For example, if a legislature has 25 percent newly elected members serving their first term and 75 percent veterans serving their tenth, average tenure is 7.75 terms. But if another legislature with the same 25 percent newly elected members has 25 percent second-term members, 25 percent third-term, and 25 percent fourth-term, it will have average tenure of only 2.5 terms. Thus, tenure figures provide another indicator of the overall stability of a legislature's membership over time. These figures track the turnover data reasonably closely, although they do not show the striking shifts apparent in the turnover measure (see Figure 2). Once again, regional differences in the time series emerge: southerners had longer tenure than northern members from the 1830s on.

Changes in Turnover Patterns

Many scholars have sought to explain the large historical changes in turnover and tenure patterns. H. Douglas Price attributes the striking changes in turnover around the turn of the century to the events surrounding the election of

Figure 2
HOUSE TENURE, 1790–1990

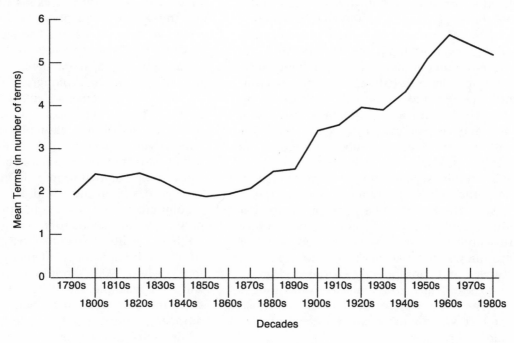

1896 and William McKinley's landslide victory over William Jennings Bryan. That election produced a political realignment that reduced the number of competitive seats and allowed incumbents to return to the chamber more easily. The broad outlines of the data are consistent with this thesis. Figure 1 shows that average turnover for the five Congresses prior to the turn of the century was about 44 percent, whereas the average for 1901–1909 dropped to 27 percent.

Whether entirely due to the sectional realignment of the 1890s or not, the decline in electoral competition for congressional seats undoubtedly made both the House and the Senate more attractive career options. No matter how attractive the work, great electoral uncertainty detracts from the career possibilities of the job. Conversely, no matter how uncompetitive the system, if the position is unattractive, politicians will voluntarily opt out. But with electoral uncertainty dropping and the power and importance of the federal government increasing at the same time, long and continuous service in Congress became both possible and desirable. Samuel Kernell's research is consistent with this thesis; he concludes that the increasing attractiveness of careers in the House was largely responsible for the secular decline in turnover at the end of the nineteenth century.

Although research is scanty, several other related factors also probably contributed to the emergence of an increasingly stable congressional membership. First, with the weakening of the party leadership the membership became more autonomous and presumably service became more satisfying. Second, as committee power and autonomy increased, the influence of individual members increased. Third, the rise of seniority as the basis for awarding committee and subcommittee chairs ensured that those who remained in Congress would accrue and maintain power and prestige; a seniority system gives legislators "property rights" in their committee assignments, essentially guaranteeing a committee seat in future terms unless a transfer is requested. Each of these interrelated changes increased the worth of service and consequently encouraged members to stay. Thus, lower turnover and longer tenure were probably associated as both cause and effect with the increasing internal differentiation of Congress.

The Era of the Incumbency Advantage

Over time, then, legislative tenure in the House and Senate has gone from brief periods of service, often interrupted, to long, continuous service. Interestingly, the most current analyses of turnover and tenure suggest that over the course of the post–World War II era there have been further developments in this regard. One of the logical difficulties with measuring the average tenure for a recent Congress is that most members' terms are not yet complete. Indeed, some representatives stay in office for a long time, so that the actual tenure of the members of a Congress might not become apparent until some decades later. Economists W. Robert Reed and D. Eric Schansberg used techniques from the labor-market literature to estimate the expected tenure of currently serving members and then incorporated these estimates into the calculation of mean tenure for each Congress. They found that tenure for Congresses has increased substantially: mean completed tenure for members who entered after 1975 is 20 percent to 40 percent greater than mean completed tenure for those who entered Congress between 1953 and 1975. Reed and Schansberg argue that increased tenure in the contemporary House is due to the increasing effectiveness of the incumbency advantage. There is no obvious reason why the attractiveness of congressional office should have increased in the last decades of the century, but the ability of members to remain in office seems to have increased. The latter is the subject of a far-flung literature on the incumbency advantage, perhaps the most noteworthy feature of contemporary congressional elections.

The "incumbency advantage" refers to that portion of the candidate's vote total that is due solely to his or her particular characteristics and activities. It is that part of the vote that is not of party, region, national conditions, and so forth. In operational terms, the incumbency advantage has been measured as that part of the incumbent's vote beyond his or her baseline party vote in the district. Using a variety of methods, political scientists have pinpointed a surge in the advantage of incumbency in the mid- to late 1960s. Andrew Gelman and Gary King, for example, calculated that in elections since the mid-1960s incumbents gained an additional 5 percent to 12 percent in their vote totals simply by virtue of being incumbents.

LEGISLATIVE INCUMBENCY AND INSULATION

Actual reelection rates, always high in the twentieth century, never fell below 88 percent between 1966 and 1990, and were generally well above 90 percent (see Table 2). In 1986 and 1988, incumbent success rates reached all-time highs of 98 percent.

David R. Mayhew's histograms provide the most graphic illustration of how the incumbency advantage has increased over time; they also provide a good introduction to our second argument. Mayhew plotted the changing distributions of the House vote in incumbent races, paying special attention to the declining percentage of marginal districts—those commonly identified by winning percentages of less than 55 percent or 60 percent. In Figure 3, the horizontal axis indexes the Democratic percentage of the vote in the election and the vertical axis depicts the percentage of all elections receiving that percentage. Before the mid-1960s the distributions of outcomes were unimodal, like 1948, with most of the elections occurring in the marginal range. By 1972, a significant

change had occurred: the distributions assumed a distinctly bimodal character as most of the elections moved out of the marginal range. This bimodal pattern has continued.

Much research has sought to identify the causes of the House incumbency advantage. A number of early studies eliminated some possibilities. John A. Ferejohn concluded that redistricting could not explain the incumbency advantage, since incumbents from redistricted areas in the late 1960s were no more likely to win reelection than incumbents from districts that had not been redistricted. Succeeding research has consistently failed to implicate redistricting as the basis of incumbent success. No one denies that redistricting can dramatically affect the partisan base in a district, but it does not appear to be a major component of the incumbency advantage.

Other scholars sought to explain the incumbency advantage by reference to changes in the voting behavior of the American electorate. Voters were no longer following party

Table 2
INCUMBENT REELECTION RATES, 1946–1990

Year	Sought Reelection	Defeated in Primary	Defeated in General	Percent Reelected
1946	398	18	52	82
1948	400	15	68	79
1950	400	6	32	91
1952	389	9	26	91
1954	407	6	22	93
1956	411	6	16	95
1958	396	3	37	90
1960	405	5	25	93
1962	402	12	22	92
1964	397	8	45	87
1966	411	8	41	88
1968	409	4	9	97
1970	401	10	12	95
1972	390	12	13	94
1974	391	8	40	88
1976	384	3	13	96
1978	382	5	19	94
1980	398	6	31	91
1982	393	10	29	90
1984	409	3	16	95
1986	393	2	6	98
1988	408	1	6	98
1990	406	1	15	96

Source: Norman J. Ornstein, Thomas E. Mann, and Michael J. Malbin, *Vital Statistics on Congress, 1991–1992* (Washington, D.C.: Congressional Quarterly, Inc., 1992), Tables 2–8.

Figure 3
DECLINE IN MARGINAL HOUSE DISTRICTS

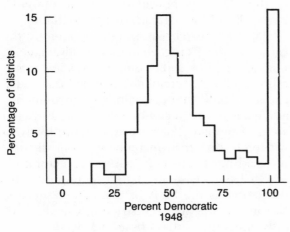

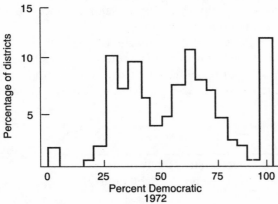

Source: Morris P. Fiorina. *Congress, Keystone of the Washington Establishment,* 2d ed. (New Haven, Conn.: Yale University Press, 1989), Figure 1.

lines to the extent they previously had, and they were voting for incumbents more than they previously had. Perhaps incumbency voting had replaced party voting as a rule of thumb for some voters. But that left the question of why. In an era of growing distrust of government, why would the decline of party not be at least as likely to lead to anti-incumbent voting as incumbent voting?

To answer that question, scholars began to focus on changes in the behavior of incumbents. Members of Congress have a large pool of resources that can be used for reelection purposes. They can employ both the congressional franking privilege and free media coverage to communicate directly with constituents in the district and enhance their visibility. Greater exposure (unless the result of a scandal or a grave political faux pas, of course) gen-erally produces a boost at the polls. Another argument focuses on a change in the mix of incumbent activities. Incumbent representatives can deliver low-cost, high-profile constituency service; they can procure, or at least claim credit for, federal projects and grants, and they can create federal programs for constituents and then assist them in obtaining the benefits of those programs. There is little downside to either activity, and the expanded federal role gives members of Congress more opportunities to engage in both.

A final explanation for the incumbency advantage focuses also on incumbents, but compares them to their opponents in congressional elections. Studies of congressional voting show that incumbents have much greater visibility and popularity than challengers; much of the reason incumbents do so well is because challengers do so poorly. This explanation is incomplete in that it says little about why incumbents do well in comparison with challengers. Gary Jacobson and Samuel Kernell maintain that this outcome can be partly explained by reference to the strategic behavior of politicians. They argue that high-quality challengers, such as those who already hold elective office, wait for the right opportunity to run against incumbents, preferring to remain in their present position rather than risk losing it and losing to the incumbent at the same time.

Yet another reason for the lack of strong challengers lies in larger changes that have taken place in the mid-twentieth century. With local party organizations in decline, there is less organized effort to recruit strong challengers. Similarly, those organizations are less able to promise challengers consolation prizes of other offices, should they lose. And, finally, campaigns have become much more expensive. In the last quarter of the twentieth century a campaign has come to require the commitment of one's entire net worth and whatever could be borrowed against it. Not surprisingly, many potential challengers may decide that the risks exceed the benefits.

NATIONAL FORCES AND CONGRESSIONAL ELECTIONS

In the midterm elections of 1894 the Democrats lost 116 seats. The Republicans dropped

75 in 1922. Even in more recent times, large seat swings were common: in 1946 the Democrats lost 56 seats, and in 1958 the Republicans lost 49. Such swings have not been seen since the rise of the incumbency advantage, however. In contrast to 1946, in 1978 a Democratic administration widely thought to be beyond its depth lost a mere 15 seats. And in contrast to 1958, in 1982 a Republican president presiding over a severe recession saw his party lose only 26 seats.

In on-year elections the picture is similar. In 1920, James M. Cox helped make his party 59 House seats poorer, and in 1932, Herbert Hoover presided over a Republican loss of 101 seats. In contrast, the Democrats dropped only 12 seats in the 1972 George McGovern defeat, and even in the great "turn to the right" of 1980 lost only 33. Presidential coattails and midterm referenda were major electoral phenomena for the first century and a half of American history. Today they are marginal influences on congressional elections.

The insulation of contemporary Congresses from national forces has been extensively discussed by Walter Dean Burnham. Nineteenth-century members had every reason to worry about the performance of their presidents and their parties; late-twentieth-century members had relatively little reason to worry. Therefore, modern presidents have less leverage over their partisan allies in Congress, and other things being equal, party cohesion in the Congress is relatively more difficult to achieve.

The reasons for the declining importance of national forces in congressional elections are implicit in our earlier discussion. Recall Mayhew's histograms (see Figure 3). If many districts fall in the marginal range, as in the 1948 diagram, then a national swing against a party will cause many of its seats to fall to the other party. But if few seats fall in the marginal range, as in the 1972 diagram, a similarly strong national swing will affect fewer seats. Larger margins insulate incumbents against shocks to the system.

The standard way of measuring the sensitivity of seat changes to vote changes is via a concept called the "swing ratio," which gives the expected percent change in seats as a function of a 1-percent change in votes. There are a variety of ways of calculating this measure, and researchers disagree on numerous particulars, but

there is a general consensus that the swing ratio has declined over the past century. Table 3 presents one set of calculations. The figures indicate that if a party's average vote share dropped 1 percent in 1880, then about 4 percent of the party's representatives in the House could anticipate defeat. In the present era, only about 1.5 percent need feel so threatened by a 1-percent swing. The responsiveness of congressional-party fortunes to national forces has clearly declined. Recessions, scandals, foreign-policy disasters, or other negative events and situations are never helpful to a party, but they threaten modern members of Congress much less than they did their predecessors.

Moreover, a second linkage between national forces and congressional outcomes also has declined. Not only do swings in the congressional vote not hurt as much as previously, but swings in the congressional vote are not as likely to accompany swings in the presidential vote. As the incumbency advantage has increased, split-ticket voting has increased. Between 1960 and 1988 a quarter or more of the electorate cast a vote for the presidential candidate of one party and the House candidate of the other. About one-fifth of the electorate split their ticket between president and Senate choices. Incumbent visibility, constituency service, the increased importance of the media, weak challengers, and other factors have all served to weaken the link between presidential and congressional voting, to the point where scholars of the presidency now write of the "disappearance" of presidential coattails. Thus, a swing in the presidential vote is now not as likely to translate into a swing in the congressional vote as it did in the nineteenth century,

Table 3
SWING RATIOS: HYPOTHETICAL
(BUTLER) METHOD

Period	Swing Ratio
1868–1892	4.23
1896–1928	2.45
1932–1948	2.65
1952–1964	2.13
1968–1980	1.58

Source: Calculated from David W. Brady and Bernard Grofman, "Sectional Differences in Partisan Bias and Electoral Responsiveness in U.S. House Elections, 1850–1980," *British Journal of Political Science* 21 (1991): 252–253. Reprinted by permission.

and a swing in the congressional vote is not as likely to translate into a swing in congressional seats. Both links in the chain of party accountability or system responsiveness have weakened.

The declining connection between presidential and congressional outcomes has multiple causes—the decline of party, an increasingly educated and independent electorate, the growing importance of the media, to name some exogenous factors. But there is little doubt that the weakened connection is what members of Congress want and what their actions have collectively helped to bring about. Members who are highly visible, who provide all manner of services to their districts, who use their committee positions to establish independent issue identities, and who provide their own campaign organizations and financing are members who have independent bases of support. They are personally accountable, not collectively accountable. This is as they prefer: careerists wish to control their own fates, not to be subject to the fate of larger collectivities.

DANGERS OF CAREERISM

While scholars view a professionalized membership and a large incumbency advantage as important features of Congress that require explanation, observers outside of academia often view the same features as undesirable developments that require reform. In their view, careerism and high reelection rates indicate an electorally insulated Congress composed of professional officeholders, most of them Democrats, insufficiently concerned for the general welfare. As David Broder, the American political columnist, asked, "How about a little *glasnost* for the one-party House of Representatives?"

The equation of careerism and high reelection rates with insulation and unresponsiveness is questionable. The incumbency advantage probably makes the composition of Congress less responsive to national forces, as noted above, but as Richard Fenno, Gary Jacobson, and others have noted, there is good reason to believe that high reelection rates indicate that members work hard to be responsive to their individual constituencies, a point discussed below. Nonetheless, taking the equation for granted, reformers have proposed

major changes in the conduct of contemporary congressional elections. The first, campaign-finance reforms, seeks to lessen the advantage that congressional incumbents have over their challengers. The second, term limitations, seeks to take an ax to the Gordian knot of professionalism.

CAMPAIGN FINANCE

When it comes to congressional elections, few aspects have been treated more extensively by popular commentators than campaign financing, and seldom has that treatment been so one-sided. Few journalists will defend the current system of financing elections, and few will hesitate to endorse any of myriad proposed reforms. Academic research, however, provides little basis for such a popular consensus. In the first place, it is not clear that campaign spending is the principal part of the advantage that incumbents have over their challengers. And, in the second place, the importance of contributions for influencing behavior is a matter of considerable dispute.

Money and Congressional Elections

Research on money in congressional elections is based on the Congresses that have sat since the mid-1970s, for the simple reason that reliable data have only been available since passage of the Federal Election Campaign Act (FECA) and its amendments in the early 1970s. Research based on these Congresses presents a cloudy picture. There is no denying that congressional elections have become much more expensive contests: an average House race that cost $50,000 in 1976 cost about $275,000 in 1990, and even a small state-Senate race now costs in the millions. (Figure 4 details the costs of congressional campaigns from 1974 to 1988 in millions of dollars.) Nor is there any denying the explosive growth of political action committees (PACs)—a classic "unintended" consequence of the 1970s reforms (see Table 4). A relatively rare species in the political arena of the 1970s, PACs now roam the political savanna in veritable herds and provide an increasing proportion of total expenditures in congressional races (see Table 5).

LEGISLATIVE INCUMBENCY AND INSULATION

Figure 4
CAMPAIGN SPENDING, 1974–1988

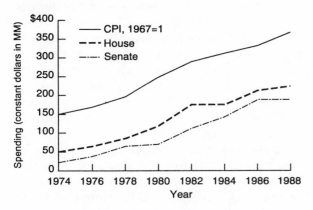

Source: Norman J. Ornstein, Thomas E. Mann, and Michael J. Malbin, eds., *Vital Statistics on Congress, 1987–1988* (Washington, D.C.: Congressional Quarterly, Inc., 1987), Tables 3–1, 3–4, and 5–9.

But insofar as providing an explanation for the incumbency advantage in House elections, the developments in campaign finance have been mistimed. Recall that the incumbency advantage grew sharply in the mid-1960s. The growing cost of congressional elections and the growing number of PACs, however, are developments of the mid-1970s and later. Logically, developments in campaign finance might reinforce an already existing incumbency advantage, but apparently they do not contribute much to an explanation of why it arose in the first place.

Moreover, there is more than a little debate about the extent to which campaign financing really works to the advantage of the incumbent. In his seminal 1978 work on congressional campaign financing, Gary Jacobson propounded the provocative conclusion that "the more incum-bents spend, the worse they do." Jacobson's statistical analyses of 1970s elections show that while campaign spending had a significant positive impact on the challenger's fortunes, the impact of spending on incumbent fortunes was nonexistent or negative.

This surprising statistical relationship was not to be taken literally, of course: spending more did not actually hurt incumbents. Rather, two plausible processes underlay the curious statistical pattern. First, there is the well-known law of diminishing returns. All members of Congress receive personal staff, district office space, the frank and various types of communications and audiovisual assistance. Estimates of the market value of such perquisites of office are as high as one million dollars per year. Not all such "perks" are used entirely in the quest for reelection, of course, but if even as little as 50 percent are so employed, then incumbents receive as much as a million dollars of electoral resources over a two-year term. In that light, a few hundred thousand dollars of additional campaign funds is more or less gilding the lily. Given that members already enjoy almost universal name recognition and overwhelmingly positive reputations, campaign spending cannot add much to their already high base.

While diminishing returns may explain why campaign spending has little impact on incumbent fortunes, it does not explain why spending may appear to have a negative impact, as some analyses have found. Here, a more subtle process appears to be at work. Rather

Table 4
GROWTH OF PACs

Type	1974	1978	1982	1986
Corporate	89	784	1,467	1,744
Labor	201	217	380	384
Nonconnected	—	165	746	1,077
Other	318	487	778	952
TOTAL	608	1,653	3,371	4,157

Source: Norman J. Ornstein, Thomas E. Mann, and Michael J. Malbin, eds. *Vital Statistics on Congress, 1987–1988.* Washington, D.C.: Congressional Quarterly, Inc., 1987, Tables 3–15.

Table 5
SOURCES OF CONGRESSIONAL CAMPAIGN FUNDS

	1974	1978	1982	1986
HOUSE				
Party	4%	7%	6%	4%
PACs	17	24	31	36
Individual	79	69	63	60
SENATE				
Party	6	6	10	8
PACs	11	13	17	22
Individual	83	81	73	70

Source: Norman J. Ornstein, Thomas E. Mann, and Michael J. Malbin, eds., *Vital Statistics on Congress, 1987–1988* (Washington, D.C.: Congressional Quarterly, Inc., 1987), Tables 3–11.

than spending being the cause of the election result, in some cases spending may be the effect of the (feared) result; that is, an incumbent may spend a great deal because he or she is involved in a tough race with an experienced challenger who has adequate financing. If the incumbent narrowly wins—or even loses—that does not indicate that his or her spending had a negative impact; it only reflects the gravity of the challenge. Presumably, in the absence of spending, the incumbent would have received even fewer votes. The effect of spending is positive, but that effect is swamped by other effects.

As more data have become available and more advanced statistical methods have been brought to bear, the effects of incumbent spending have become somewhat clearer. Several studies report a positive impact of incumbent spending on incumbent vote, and Jacobson reported a positive impact in a pooled data set that includes all contested elections from 1972 to 1988. All studies, however, continue to report a much bigger "bang for the buck" for challenger spending than for incumbent spending. Challengers start from such a low base that few ever reach the point of diminishing returns from which incumbents begin.

Of course, there are some possible effects of money that are difficult to study statistically. For example, if an incumbent's large war chest deters a strong challenger from entering the race and the incumbent overwhelms a sacrificial lamb instead, then (potential) campaign spending had a major effect, but one that by its nature cannot be directly observed. Standing against this possibility is research showing that the quality of challengers does not seem to bear much relation to an incumbent's spending.

Money and Congressional Behavior

Among followers of the consumer advocate Ralph Nader and the public-interest group Common Cause, there appears to be little doubt that campaign contributions pervert the democratic process. Special interests give money in exchange for special favors. The contribution process is simply a quid pro quo. Public-interest groups regularly produce reports showing that PACs give disproportionately to people who vote in favor of PAC-supported legislation and to the members of committees who handle such legislation. Most members of Congress, of course, indignantly reject any suggestion that they are bought (or rented) by campaign contributions. They reverse the causal relation asserted by public-interest groups, and claim that contributions follow their votes rather than cause them. Contributors give to those who have already indicated their support, rather than give to purchase future support. At most, members of Congress admit that contributions result in access that groups might otherwise find it more difficult to gain, for a member is more likely to make room in a busy schedule to hear the case of a previous contributor than an unknown petitioner.

Again, research yields a cloudy picture. Analysts agree with members that an association between contributions and votes provokes suspicion but proves nothing. One does not need to point to dairy co-op contributions to explain why Wisconsin representatives vote for milk-price supports or to steel PAC contributions to explain why Pennsylvania senators support legislation to prohibit foreign steelmakers from selling below cost in the United States. Numerous studies that attempt to relate campaign contributions to roll-call voting produce conflicting conclusions, with some reporting positive evidence and others reporting negative.

On the other hand, why would interest groups continue to contribute if there was nothing to gain from doing so? And certainly contributors seem to be instrumental in their giving. Ideological PACs may indulge their preferences, but business PACs often allow Republican challengers to go begging while giving to incumbents and to subcommittee chairs, more often than not Democrats. It may be the case that research so far has focused on the wrong arena; floor voting is the most visible of all congressional behavior and thus the arena in which members must be the most careful of what they do. Some work by Richard L. Hall and Frank W. Wayman reports strong effects of PAC contributions at the committee stage. If these findings are replicated for other committees and other issues, the public-interest critique will gain force.

Campaign-Finance Reforms

Proposals to alter the campaign-finance process fall into three broad categories. The first, expenditure limits, attempts to reduce the role of money, whether to lessen the advantage of incumbents, who normally can raise far more than challengers; to weaken the influence of special interests, who will be unable to contribute to "maxed-out" incumbents; or to satisfy an inherent distaste for high spending. The second category, public financing, obviously changes the source of campaign funds and presumably lessens the influence of special interests. The third category, an enhanced party role in the financing process, also alters the source of funds and thereby strengthens a more-encompassing interest (party) over less-encompassing ones (PACs and individuals).

Researchers are generally skeptical of expenditure limits, fearing that in practice they will amount to incumbent-protection acts. The reason is that alluded to earlier: incumbents already receive as much as $2 million per term in electorally fungible perks of office. They would probably be willing to eliminate all campaign spending in congressional elections, leaving them with their perks and the challenger with nothing. Since campaign expenditures help incumbents much less than they do challengers, expenditure limits would hurt incumbents correspondingly less. Incumbents can appear to be proreform by supporting spending limits while actually supporting their electoral self-interest.

Public financing receives much more support among academic analysts, provided that the support levels are set high enough. Therein lies the rub. Researchers estimate that a contemporary challenger needs $300,000 to $400,000 to make a credible race against a House incumbent. Thus, public financing that provided, for example, $100,000 to every candidate would largely waste $43.5 million on House challengers for whom it would be insufficient and a similar amount on incumbents for whom it would be unnecessary. But what are the odds that public financing of $400,000 per candidate could be sold politically—especially to incumbents, most of whom currently face challengers with far less funding?

The third category of reforms is part of a far broader effort to rejuvenate American political parties. Many political scientists favor stronger parties as means of increasing cohesion in government and accountability in elections. Doing whatever is constitutionally permissible to restrict contributions to individual candidates while loosening restrictions on contributions to parties would enhance the parties' role in financing elections and therefore enhance party influence over their candidates who win office. The more or less explicit belief is that party influence is preferable to interest-group influence.

Republicans share many professors' enthusiasm for stronger parties. Democrats demur. With a superior national party organization that regularly raises far more money than the Democrats, the Republican party (though not all its congressional incumbents) is favorably disposed toward reforms that enhance the role of party. Moreover, since PACs give so much to incumbents, most of whom are Democrats, Republicans are favorably disposed toward restrictions on PACs. Democrats, faring quite well under the status quo, have little to gain by strengthening the parties' role or by restricting their PAC contributors. Their preference is for expenditure limits that hurt challengers. Both parties favor reform so long as it is the kind of reform that benefits them.

TERM LIMITATIONS

Some citizen activists have become so frustrated by the rise of legislative careerism that they have begun to attack the perceived problem directly by promoting statutes or constitutional amendments that prohibit it. In the 1990 elections, for example, the voters of Colorado imposed a limit of eight consecutive years on service in both houses of the state legislature and limited congressional service to twelve years. California and Oklahoma have also passed limitations on state legislative service. A national group is currently campaigning for a six-year congressional limit.

State-imposed limits on congressional terms are of questionable constitutionality and may be disallowed by the courts, but the movement is worth considering nonetheless, given that it represents a significant degree of public frustration. The case for term limitations appears to be based on three premises. First, there is a widespread impression that incumbent legislators are virtually unbeatable; the 95–98 percent reelection rates of U.S. representatives in the four elections between 1984 and 1990 contribute to that impression. Second, there is a widespread impression that incumbent success is somehow illegitimate; the large war chests of PAC funds amassed by incumbents contribute to that impression. Third, there is a widespread feeling that legislatures are not performing well, although this belief is a relatively constant feature of American public opinion. Unlike the public, academic specialists tend not to support terms limitations, believing that however well-meaning, the term-limitation movement is premised on inaccurate impressions. Moreover, they fear that this reform, like most, will have consequences other than those expressly sought by its proponents.

Incumbents in many states and in Congress are tough to beat, but they are not invulnerable. Jacobson and others have argued that members of the House win 95 percent of the time not because they are unbeatable but because they work very hard at it. Huge war chests surely are a means to victory, but they also signify how worried members are—even with no serious challenge in sight. Those who have studied these members most closely agree that members of Congress "run scared." To the outside observer, a 95-percent success rate means representatives have nothing to worry about, but not being statisticians and with their careers at stake, members focus on the exceptions—those few who lose—not the rule. And because the exceptions are so unpredictable, members are subject to what Robert Weissberg calls "random terror." Rather than being unresponsive, the problem is, if anything, the opposite: members are regularly accused of crossing the line from responsiveness to pandering. Why would invulnerable politicians pander?

If 95-percent reelection rates do not necessarily indicate invulnerable, unresponsive members, neither do they necessarily indicate an ossified, unresponsive institution. If turnover was concentrated in the same 5 percent election after election, there would be cause for worry. But as Robert S. Erikson pointed out long ago, a surprisingly large proportion of members come to Congress by defeating the previous incumbent in a primary or general election (more than one-third) and leave via their own primary or general-election defeat (more than one-third). By the late 1980s, these proportions had fallen somewhat, but many members have electoral close shaves that remind them and their colleagues of their potential vulnerability. A much larger proportion of the membership of the House has some personal acquaintance with electoral vulnerability than overall reelection rates would suggest. All things considered—defeats, deaths, and resignations—there is not much basis for worries about the petrification of Congress: more than one-half of the 1990 membership had been elected since 1980 and average length of service was only a bit over five terms.

What about the third impression—that America's national and state legislatures are failing in their jobs? In an era of runaway federal deficits and widespread state fiscal crises, it is easy to assume that legislatures are not functioning properly. But as political scientists pointed out long ago, a considerable portion of legislatures' poor performance stems directly from legislators' conscientious efforts to serve their constituents. Members of Congress, for example, do not hesitate to fight for failing savings and loans, billion-dollar weapon boondoggles, and ineffective programs of all types so long as the waste (and worse) such programs entail accrues to the benefit of their local economies. Of course, the inevitable result of the representatives of 435 individual districts and fifty states seeking to benefit their own is that the nation suffers. If every district tries to benefit at the expense of others, then on balance none will benefit. If no district will bear any costs for the national good, then the national good will not be achieved. Ironically, as Richard Fenno has observed, if legislators were less responsive, they might be more willing to make tough but nationally beneficial decisions, and the people would probably rate their legislatures more highly.

If the only problem with the term-limitation movement was that it misread the situation, professional legislators would be the only ones with cause for worry. But the likely consequences of term limitations should give pause to ordinary citizens as well. Reform movements typically assume naively that if power can be taken from the special interests who are the objects of the reforms, it will devolve to ordinary citizens. Unfortunately, reality is such that when one special interest loses power, a different one generally gains. Term limitations may well have that effect.

In the first place, within the legislature, power would probably flow to the staff. Members would have less time to acquire technical expertise and that intangible "institutional memory" which is vital in any organization. Of course, many reformers also wish to do away with the permanent staff and allow legislators to manage, along with a few secretaries, to answer mail and the phones. Aside from impairing the ability of members to service their districts, the likely result would be that power would shift to the executive branch, where the permanent bureaucracy would become the principal source of expertise and experience. Assuming that the bureaucracy cannot be eliminated, the only way for an amateur legislature to avoid reliance on the executive would be to rely more heavily on interest groups than it presently does. These groups undoubtedly would be happy to provide the expertise legislators need. Whether this would improve on the present situation is highly questionable.

Perhaps the most serious negative consequence of term limitations would be its effect on legislator incentives. Members of Congress currently have the option of planning a career in Congress. Not all will: some will opt to try for higher office, some will quit, and a few will be defeated. Those few who leave with useful years remaining usually have the option of taking executive appointments or lucrative jobs as Washington lobbyists. But if terms were limited, what would happen? Soon after taking office all members would begin thinking about where their income would be coming from six to twelve years hence. Their situation would force them to begin planning the next move immediately—to a higher office (these are scarce), to an appointive position (high-level ones are also scarce), or to a lucrative position in the private sector (most likely). Some do that now, as mentioned above, but everyone would be looking ahead if there were term limitations. Such a reform almost certainly would enhance the power of interest groups, inasmuch as all legislators would be thinking of themselves as potential job applicants.

There is yet another probable conse-

quence of term limitations, the evaluation of which depends on the political predispositions of the reader. What proponents of term limitations refer to as "citizen legislatures" are what political scientists call "amateur legislatures." Severely constrained in terms of session length, lacking staff, paid but a pittance, their membership turns over at rates as high as 40 percent per term. This is the vision held by proponents of term limitations, of course. But whether they consciously appreciate it or not, an additional element of citizen legislatures is that these legislatures are Republican; empirically, Republican candidates do relatively better in elections to amateur legislatures than to professional ones.

The logic is not complicated. The California initiative, since upheld by the California Supreme Court, provides that legislative pensions be eliminated, salaries be cut, and terms be limited to six (House) or eight (Senate) years. What kinds of people will seek the office then? Will schoolteachers and other public employees give up job security and seniority to serve short stints in the legislature? Probably not. Conversely, large law firms and corporations may well encourage junior partners and vice presidents to serve as legislators. Rather than lobby legislators, interest groups can simply pay employees to serve. In all likelihood, the changes in California will lower the proportion of Democrats eager to serve and raise the proportion of Republicans. And if Republicans gain strength in the state legislatures, it will be only a matter of time until they begin fielding stronger candidates for Congress.

The history of congressional reform demonstrates that reforms are never neutral. Some win, some lose. The likely gainers under term limitations are Republicans, the executive, and interest groups. The likely losers are Democrats and Congress.

CHANGES IN THE ELECTORAL CALENDAR

While the idea of term limitations has captured the lion's share of the contemporary debate about the structure of congressional elections, there is also an ongoing debate about the wisdom of altering the length and timing of congressional terms. Many observers have noted that members of the House, in particular, are engaged in a perpetual campaign. With a two-year term, there is virtually no breathing time for serious consideration of issues where an election is not looming. Some observers argue that the difficulties of accomplishing anything in an election year mean that half the time there is no real chance of productive activity in the House. One might think that with six-year terms senators are different, but journalistic accounts claim that Senate races have become so expensive that senators are forced to engage in serious fund-raising throughout their six-year tenure. (On average, a successful Senate campaign costs about $4 million. This implies that a senator must raise an average of $15,000 per week every week for six years.) Such claims probably are exaggerated, but they contain more than a grain of truth.

Seeing one fairly simple means of improving this situation, some reformers advocate four-year terms for representatives and, less important, eight-year terms for senators. This would presumably alleviate some electoral pressure, especially in the House. The opposing argument, of course, is that the framers deliberately set term lengths in the House to impose electoral pressure. How, then, can one determine whether the efficiency gains from lengthening terms would exceed the responsiveness losses from doing so?

From a practical standpoint, there is not much reason to dwell on such a question. In the first place, in an era in which term-limitation proposals are increasingly being placed on state ballots, proposals to lengthen terms are swimming against a strong current. In the second place, supporters of lengthened terms divide when it comes to timing the elections for such lengthened terms. Most reformers wish to hold congressional elections concurrently with presidential elections. By retaining presidential coattails while eliminating the midterm penalty, this would presumably give presidents more support in Congress and

lessen the chances of the division of control that has come to characterize national government since 1968. Careerist members of Congress, of course, feel just the opposite. They have no wish to tie their fates to executive candidates of their party. If anything, they would prefer to have all elections held in the off years so that the outcomes would be more likely to turn on the personal record and characteristics of the members.

Any attempt to alter the Constitution faces a tough fight. Even if there is universal dissatisfaction with the status quo, if the proponents of change are not united on the specifics of what they wish to accomplish, the probability of change is correspondingly lessened. Such appears to be the case for term lengths. Two-year terms for representatives and six-year terms for senators will continue to characterize Congress; the only question will be how many terms they will be permitted to serve.

CONCLUSION

Some believe that every significant social action provokes a reaction. The development of a professional Congress—and professional legislatures more generally—may be a case in point. If members enhance their prospects of making a career out of congressional service by acting to increase their electoral resources and insulate themselves from larger national forces, their very success may bring about a reaction. Believing rightly or wrongly (in my view wrongly) that low turnover, high tenure, high incumbent success rates, and independence of national forces imply that legislators are professional politicians, unresponsive to constituents and beholden to special interests, citizens may move to limit—actually, to eliminate—congressional careerism. Such actions would restore Congress to the kind of body envisioned by the framers. Whether it would be advisable is highly debatable. That it would mark a new era in the evolution of Congress is certain.

BIBLIOGRAPHY

Congressional Elections

The literature on congressional elections is rather extensive. Significant sources on the incumbency advantage include JOHN R. ALFORD and DAVID W. BRADY, "Personal and Partisan Advantage in U.S. Congressional Elections, 1846–1986," in LAWRENCE C. DODD and BRUCE I. OPPENHEIMER, eds., *Congress Reconsidered,* 4th ed. (Washington, D.C., 1989); WALTER DEAN BURNHAM, "Insulation and Responsiveness in Congressional Elections," *Political Science Quarterly* 90 (Fall 1975): 411–435; ALBERT D. COVER, "One Good Term Deserves Another: The Advantage of Incumbency in Congressional Elections," *American Journal of Political Science* 21 (1977): 523–542; ROBERT S. ERIKSON, "The Advantage of Incumbency in Congressional Elections," *Polity* 3 (1971): 395–405; JOHN A. FEREJOHN, "On the Decline of Competition in Congressional Elections," *American Political Science Review* 71 (1977): 166–176; MORRIS P. FIORINA, *Congress: Keystone of the Washington Establishment,* 2d ed. (New Haven, Conn., 1989); ANDREW GELMAN and GARY KING, "Estimating Incumbency Advantage Without Bias," *American Journal of Political Science* 34 (1990): 1142–1164; GARY C. JACOBSON, *The Politics of Congressional Elections,* 3d ed. (New York, 1992); GARY C. JACOBSON and SAMUEL KERNELL, *Strategy and Choice in Congressional Elections,* 2d ed. (New Haven, Conn., 1983); and DAVID R. MAYHEW, "Congressional Elections: The Case of the Vanishing Marginals," *Polity* 6 (1974): 295–317.

On the role of money in congressional elections, see GARY C. JACOBSON, "The Effects of Campaign Spending in Congressional Elections," *American Political Science Review* 72 (June 1978): 469–491, and his *Money in Congressional Elections* (New Haven, Conn., 1980); DONALD P. GREEN and JONATHAN S. KRASNO, "Salvation for the Spendthrift Incumbent: Reestimating the Effects of Campaign Spending in House Elections," *American Journal of Political Science* 32 (1988): 884–907; GARY C. JACOBSON, "The Effects of Campaign Spending in House Elections: New Evidence for Old Arguments," *American Journal of Political Science* 34 (1990): 334–362; and RICHARD L. HALL and FRANK W. WAYMAN, "Buying Time: Moneyed Interests and the Mobilization of Bias in Congressional Committees," *American Political Science Review* 84 (1990): 797–820.

Congressional Careers: Turnover and Tenure

See MORRIS P. FIORINA, DAVID W. ROHDE, and PETER WISSEL, "Historical Change in House Turnover," in NORMAN J. ORNSTEIN, ed., *Congress in Change: Evolution and Reform* (New York, 1975); JOHN R. HIBBING, "Contours of the Modern Congressional Career," *American Political Science Review* 85 (1991): 405–428; SAMUEL KERNELL, "Toward Understanding the 19th Century Congressional Career: Ambition, Competition, and Rotation," *American Journal of Political Science* 21 (1977): 669–693; NELSON W. POLSBY, "The Institutionalization of the U.S. House of Representatives," *American Political Science Review* 62 (1968): 144–168; NELSON W. POLSBY, MIRIAM GALLAGHER, and BARRY S. RUNDQUIST, "The Growth of the Seniority System in the U.S. House of Representatives," *American Political Science Review* 63 (1969): 787–807; H. DOUGLAS PRICE, "The Congressional Career: Then and Now," in NELSON W. POLSBY, ed., *Congressional Behavior* (New York, 1971); and his "Careers and Committees in the American Congress: The Problem of Structural Change," in WILLIAM O. AYDELLOTTE, ed., *The History of Parliamentary Behavior* (Princeton, N.J., 1977).

On tenure, W. ROBERT REED and D. ERIC SCHANSBERG, "How Long Do Congressmen Stay in Office?" *Economics and Politics* 2 (1990): 173–191 and "A Comparison of Alternative Measures of Turnover" (mimeo 1991) provide the most recent work. Two very good historical surveys of the development of the House and Senate are DAVID J. ROTHMAN, *Politics and Power: The United States Senate, 1869–1901* (Cambridge, Mass., 1966) and JAMES STERLING YOUNG, *The Washington Community, 1800–1828* (New York, 1966).

SEE ALSO Modern Legislative Careers; The Motivations of Legislators; PACs and Congressional Decisions; AND The Role of Congressional Parties.

ELECTORAL REALIGNMENTS

Patricia A. Hurley

Electoral realignments are major turning points in American political history. They are periods of transition from one political-party system to the next and involve a series of critical congressional and presidential elections. Such elections are accompanied by the rise of cross-cutting issues of national importance and ideological polarization of the political parties. This polarization leads immediately to shifts in mass voting behavior and ultimately to changes both in the partisan preferences of the mass public and in the nature of public policy as government crafts solutions to the fundamental problems that precipitated electoral change.

There is a general consensus among historians and political scientists that the presidential election years of 1800, 1828, 1860, 1896, and 1932 were critical ones, each marking the beginning of a new period of partisan competition or party system. A party system is defined both by a particular set of issues that underlie opposition between parties as organizational and governmental entities and a relatively stable distribution of partisan preference among the mass public. Empirical research has established that individuals are highly influenced in their candidate choices by their preexisting partisan identifications. Consequently, the distribution of party identification in any given party system has major implications for the outcomes of elections at all levels of government, and the party with the greatest number of identifiers in the electorate is considered the majority or dominant party in any party system.

During periods of electoral realignment, party identification within the electorate and party organizations are in a state of flux. New issues arise that cannot be integrated neatly into existing party philosophy. Party organizations may choose to ignore such issues owing to their internally divisive character, but if an issue is important enough, a new, third party is likely to arise and exploit the critical issue.

This new party may attract adherents from the existing parties, leading to the demise of one or both of those parties. Or the existing parties may react quickly to the threat of competition from the new party and adopt positions of their own on the critical issue. This would lead to the absorption of the third party into the pre-existing party that adopted its stance on the issue. Alternatively, one or both of the established parties may confront the new issue directly rather than being forced to do so by a third party. This can lead to temporary internal disunity, followed by the emergence of new party-platform positions and important new organizational actors, or prominent individuals within the party organization. (For a more detailed description of these scenarios, see Sundquist.)

Voters react to the changed party positions by altering long-standing patterns of electoral behavior, thereby ushering in a new set of elected officials who can take policy action to address the issues that precipitated the critical election. A hallmark of such election outcomes is unified control of the national government: the White House, the Senate, and the House of Representatives must all be controlled by the same political party, although control of any one of these may have shifted prior to the election identified as critical.

If voters react favorably to the new course of action pursued by the government, new patterns of voting behavior will be established, creating a rearrangement of partisan loyalties within the electorate. Voting in subsequent elections will be influenced by the new party identification, allowing the newly constituted majority party sufficient time in office to complete its agenda of policy change. As time passes, however, the critical election and the issues associated with it become less salient for individual voters. Even voters identifying with the majority party may stray from the candidates nominated by their party, allowing the minority party to control the government temporarily. Partisan control of the government will alternate (although the majority should win more often than not) until a new set of issues arises to engender another electoral realignment. In the past, this process has generally been repeated cyclically, approximately once per generation.

The preceding discussion omits the details and complexities of each historical party system of electoral realignment. It ignores, as well, the particular mechanisms through which changes in voting behavior are translated into new directions in public policy. While early research focused on presidential elections and policy leadership from the White House, more recent scholarship has identified the pivotal role of Congress in the realignment process. The remainder of this essay will consider the precise nature of the congressional role, with particular emphasis on the electoral realignments marked by the critical elections of 1860, 1896, and 1932. This explanation will be followed by a discussion of the factors that distinguish periods of temporary electoral upheaval from the more exceptional periods of critical realignment. Finally, because the generational or cyclical theory of realignment suggests that the United States is long overdue for an electoral realignment as of the early 1990s, the essay will conclude with an examination of contemporary barriers to critical elections at the congressional level.

Before proceeding, however, a few words are in order about the relatively little attention given to the first two party systems and the critical elections of 1800 and 1828. The critical election of 1800, which sent Thomas Jefferson to the White House and his Republican party to Congress, was not, strictly speaking, an electoral realignment. Instead, this election should be understood as the beginning of the first party alignment following the decade of formation of the Republican and Federalist parties in the 1790s. By modern standards, the Republicans and Federalists were hardly deserving of the term *party*. Most politicians were amateurs rather than professionals, and turnover in office was frequent. Moreover, Paul Goodman (Chambers and Burnham, eds., p. 86) notes that in the early nineteenth century it was often difficult to determine the partisan affiliation of pol-

iticians. Probably because of its underdeveloped character, the first party system collapsed sometime between 1815 and 1824. Consequently, it would be risky to draw inferences about the behaviors and preferences of individuals within the electorate on the basis of aggregate voting statistics and election outcomes during this period.

It was during the lifetime of the second party system that party organizations worthy of the name emerged. But they did not suddenly appear with the contest of 1828; rather, they developed gradually until conflict between Democrats and Whigs was institutionalized in the latter part of the 1830s and the early part of the 1840s. It is highly unlikely that persistent partisan loyalties developed in the electorate until after the emergence of the competing party organizations. Within this context of emerging party organizations and loyalties it is difficult to isolate the effects of electoral realignment on Congress and on national policy changes.

The character of federalism during the first half of the nineteenth century also was such that the national government—and therefore the Congress—was less important than the governments of the states. Yet the debate over slavery assumed national proportions in the 1850s, setting the stage for an electoral realignment with major consequences for national policy in which Congress was a key player.

CONGRESSIONAL ELECTIONS AS CRITICAL ELECTIONS

Because realignments are electoral phenomena, an examination of the role of Congress must begin with congressional elections. Congressional-election outcomes alone, however, are insufficient indicators of whether a realignment has occurred, for they must be considered in conjunction with the outcomes of presidential voting. A single party must control the House of Representatives, the Senate, and the White House for an electoral realignment to occur, and this control must be retained long enough to allow that party to put its policy agenda into place. Only if elections yield such sustained, unified control of the government are the preconditions for a realignment met. This means that congressional elections are also good indicators for distinguishing temporary electoral upheaval from realignments. If a particular election results in unified control of the government, it may have the initial appearance of a realignment, but a seat loss by the controlling party two years later that shifts the partisan majority in the House or the Senate is evidence that the initial election was not a realigning one.

Elections for the U.S. House of Representatives are most important for finding clues to whether realignment is taking place, for three reasons. First, according to the original design in the Constitution, only the members of the House were to be directly elected by the people. Second, the term of office there is only two years. Third, the entire institutional membership is subject to biennial review by the electorate, allowing for abrupt shifts in party fortunes if the nation's electorate undergoes a systematic change of preference. As a result, any changes in mass voting behavior should first be observable in the collective outcome of House elections, possibly even in House elections that preceded the critical presidential election year. Changes in the distribution of partisan seats in the Senate, as was particularly true during the nineteenth century, may sometimes follow, rather than accompany, those in the House. This is because the staggered character of elections to the Senate and the selection of senators by state legislatures prior to the ratification of the Seventeenth Amendment in 1913 have served as structural barriers to rapid institutional change in the upper chamber. Yet, if new patterns of electoral behavior persist, which by definition they do in a realignment, the Senate will be affected.

All five realigning periods in the United States share a common electoral pattern. Each led to a sustained period of unified control of the government, and the early years of each were marked by seat switches from one party to another in Congress that disproportionately benefited the ascendant party. In other words, the pattern of switched seats is not a random one in which one party's gains and losses are negated by the gains and losses of the opposition. Random patterns would be expected if voters reacted to congressional elections as purely local events. Instead, the historical record suggests that national forces were the predominant influence on voting behavior in crucial elections and that candidates for House elections were evaluated within the context of their national party's position on the issues central to the realignment. Because the national parties are polarized on the most salient issues during a realignment phase, the policy implications of electing one candidate rather than the other are easier than usual for voters to discern. And precisely because issues are salient at these times, they influence voting for all offices on the same ballot. That is, voters are more likely to cast a straight party ballot during critical elections than they are at other times. While the institutional structure of the American national government and the nature of the election calendar enhance the prospects for divided partisan control of the government, it is the incidence of straight-ticket voting that eventually leads to unified control of the government.

Issues and Outcomes in Critical Congressional Elections

So far, little has been said in this essay about the nature of the specific issues that were associated with particular realignments, but a brief discussion of those issues is necessary for understanding how they affected congressional elections. The role of issues is most clear, and has received the most scholarly attention, for the realignments of the 1850s, the 1890s, and the 1930s. However, it is also possible to identify the issues that led to the alignment of 1800. Voting in the 1820s and 1830s was less clearly driven by responses to issues.

Controversy over issues with national implications led to the formation of political parties in the United States. The first party (albeit a very underdeveloped one), the Federalists, formed around Alexander Hamilton and his policies that were designed to advance the United States economically. These economic policies were especially appealing to the wealthier segments of society. The Federalists also advocated a relatively strong national government as necessary to the economic success of the United States. Because George Washington endorsed Hamilton's policies and came increasingly to rely on him, the Federalists can be considered to have controlled the White House during the Washington administration, and such control continued with the election of John Adams to the presidency in 1796.

The original opposition to Federalist economic policies came from James Madison within the Congress and Thomas Jefferson within the cabinet, although disagreement with the Federalist position could be found outside the capital as well. The bases for disagreement were that Federalist policies were inhospitable to agricultural interests and that the push for a stronger central government was too similar to the British system that had recently been repudiated. After his resignation from the cabinet at the end of 1793, Jefferson and others sought to mobilize popular opinion and electoral support against the Federalists.

The success of Jefferson's enterprise can be seen in the changed composition of the government that marks the formal beginning of the first party system. Because it was an elitist organization formed from within the government, the Federalist party controlled the Senate and the presidency during the first decade of U.S. history, and only once, in the Third Congress (1793–1795), did it fail to control the House of Representatives. But the Federalists never developed a mass power base within the electorate. In contrast, those in the opposition party, known variously as the Democratic-Republicans or the Jeffersonian Republicans, were required to gain the support of the electorate if they hoped to take control of the government from the Federalists.

When the Democratic-Republicans advanced Thomas Jefferson as their candidate for the presidency for the second time, in 1800, the party was strikingly successful. His party enjoyed a 66-percent majority in the House and a 58-percent majority in the Senate in the Seventh Congress (1801–1803)—a marked contrast to the 40 percent and 41 percent of the seats that they had held in the two chambers during the Sixth Congress. These extraordinary margins of control in Congress persisted throughout the first party system. The smallest margin the party held during this period was 62 percent of House seats in the Thirteenth Congress (1813–1815). The delayed effects of the alignment of 1800 on the Senate are observable if one contrasts the 58-percent majority in the Seventh Congress with the percentage of Senate seats held by the Democratic-Republicans in subsequent Congresses. The margin increased to 74

percent in the Eighth Congress (1803–1805), 79 percent in the Ninth Congress (1805–1807), 82 percent in the Tenth (1807–1809) and Eleventh Congresses (1809–1811), and 83 percent in the Twelfth Congress (1811–1813).

The large majorities in Congress enjoyed by the Democratic-Republicans are remarkable only while the Federalists were a viable opposition party. But the Federalists' support fell so low after 1815 that they effectively ceased to function as a party. Without an opposition against which to coalesce, the Democratic-Republican party was fraught with internal strife and competition between personalities, and itself was dead by 1824.

The second party system grew out of popular attachments to political personalities rather than issues, and it was characterized by competition between the Jacksonian Democrats and ultimately, the Whig party. Opposition to the Jacksonian Democrats was slow to develop, owing both to the widespread popularity of Andrew Jackson and to the inability of the opposition to unite behind any one individual in the 1830s. While Jackson had only a single opponent, incumbent President John Quincy Adams, in the election of 1828, he faced three candidates in 1832. That year, Henry Clay ran as a National Republican, William Wirt represented the Anti-Masonic party, and the independent John Floyd carried the banner for the nullifiers. All were easily defeated by Jackson, who received 55 percent of the popular vote.

Jackson's successor, Martin Van Buren, did not inherit the popularity of "Old Hickory," but the opposition, now known as the Whigs, was still unable to produce a single candidate. In the election of 1836, Van Buren ran against William Henry Harrison, Hugh L. White, and Daniel Webster, all three of whom were identified as Whigs, and Willie Person Mangrum, as an independent democrat. Voting patterns in that election were quite different from those observed for the two Jackson elections, especially in the South. Still, Van Buren won, although by a narrow margin. In 1840, however, when the Whigs ran only one candidate, William Henry Harrison, they were victorious.

While the Democrats are commonly considered to have been the majority party during this system, the latter part of the second party system was characterized by extremely well developed partisan competition, as evidenced by

House election outcomes. But the party of Jackson held the initial advantage, and that advantage preceded Andrew Jackson's election to the presidency in 1828. Candidates of the Jacksonian party were able to capture 48 percent of the House seats and 44 percent of the Senate seats in the Nineteenth Congress following the election of 1824. These healthy minorities increased to substantial majorities of 56 percent and 58 percent in the House and Senate, respectively, in the Twentieth Congress (1827–1829). The critical election of 1828 increased the party, now under the name Democrats, to a 65-percent majority in the House, and it maintained control of the lower chamber, as well as the Senate, until the Twenty-seventh Congress (1841–1843), although occasionally the majorities were very thin in both chambers. The historical record suggests that two-party competition was extremely keen until the 1850s.

The issue that precipitated the 1850s realignment was slavery. While the issue of slavery was not new in the 1850s (indeed, it lurked beneath the surface throughout the second party system), the extent to which it was debated in moral terms was. Controversies surrounding this issue were frequent in the 1850s and included continued intense debate on whether new states should be admitted to the Union as slave or free states, public shock outside the South at the return of runaway slaves and the Supreme Court's Dred Scott decision ruling that slaves were not accorded the rights of citizenship, John Brown's raid on Harper's Ferry, and even physical attacks in the U.S. Senate in the heat of discussion over the issue. While both the Democrats and the Whigs contained pro- and antislavery elements, neither party clearly faced the issue. But within the Democratic party, the Southern faction was eventually able to dominate the party's position. Sectional disagreements within the Whig party were so intense that they led to the collapse of that organization. Against this backdrop, the Republican party emerged in 1854 as an antislavery party, steadily gaining in congressional strength. The polarization between the Democrats and Republicans on this issue was readily apparent. Southern reaction to the Republican national victory in the critical election of 1860 was so strong that South Carolina seceded from the Union in December of that year, and the remaining ten states of the Confederacy did so within six months.

The congressional elections of the 1850s signaled the coming of the Civil War party system. The elections of 1854 resulted in a House with 46 percent Republicans—a new political party. While not an absolute majority, this was a plurality of seats in the Thirty-fourth Congress. In contrast, the 25 percent of Senate seats garnered by Republicans in that Congress was substantially below the 67 percent held by the Democrats. The share of Republican seats grew in subsequent Senates until it reached a significant majority, 63 percent, following the election of 1860. House elections in 1856 resulted in a setback for the Republican party, but it gained strength in 1858 and held a clear majority, 59 percent, in the Thirty-seventh Congress, elected in 1860. The election of Abraham Lincoln to the presidency that year marks it as the critical election. In part because of the secession of the Southern states, the Republicans maintained extremely large majorities in both the House and the Senate until the end of Reconstruction.

The Civil War, as well as congressional policy-making, led to the eventual resolution of the controversy over slavery. With this issue removed from the agenda, the two parties were relatively indistinguishable on policy matters after 1876. Following the return of all Southern states to the Union, partisan control of the Congress and the presidency alternated, and control of the government was frequently divided, with one party occupying the White House and the other holding one or both chambers of Congress. In the Senate, where members were appointed by state legislatures, the Republicans were generally in control, losing majority status only twice during the last quarter of the nineteenth century. Democrats were more successful in retaining control of the popularly elected House of Representatives, which they only lost twice between the elections of 1874 and 1892 (in 1880 and in 1888).

As the slavery question faded, new issues arose associated with the effects of industrialization, corporate capitalism, and urbanization on what had once been a predominantly agrarian society. The economic security of farmers was especially threatened, and they agitated for a variety of policies to gain relief, especially an expansion of the money supply. But throughout the 1870s and 1880s, both the Democratic and Republican parties took sound-money stands, advocating anti-inflationary policies such as limiting the money supply and tying the dollar to the gold standard. For this reason, the Populist party was organized in May 1891 at a Ohio convention, advocating positions supported by the farmers, which helped it gain some seats in Congress. Of additional importance in explaining the appearance of the Populists, as well as congressional election outcomes in the 1890s, is the McKinley Tariff Act, passed in 1890 under Republican rule. This act established extremely high tariffs, and the rise in prices was so immediate that the Republicans were reduced to only eighty-eight seats in the House of Representatives following the 1890 elections and lost the presidency in 1892. But economic hard times continued, and the Republicans regained control of the House in 1894.

This "Era of No Decision," as it is sometimes called, came to a halt in 1896, when the Republican party was able once again to take complete control of the government, which it maintained throughout the first decade of the twentieth century. In 1896 the Democratic and Republican parties were offering the voters clear policy alternatives with nationwide implications. Factions advocating the unlimited coinage of silver had taken control at the Democratic national convention that year and nominated William Jennings Bryan as that party's presidential candidate following his famous "Cross of Gold" speech. Bryan was also nominated by the Populist party, and in many states voters were presented with slates fusing the candidates of the two parties, leading to the absorption of the Populists into the Democratic ranks. In contrast, the Republican party, which advanced William McKinley as its candidate, took the alternative stand on the question of monetary policy, preferring sound money to free silver. The Republicans were also in favor of high protective tariffs to promote developing American industry, a position opposed by Democrats on the grounds that the resultant high prices would hurt farmers and other nonmonied interests. Superimposed on these domestic disagreements was the issue of foreign policy. The Republican party was interested in pursuing an expansionist foreign policy, in part to create new markets for U.S. goods, while the

Democrats had little interest in developing a role for the United States in international affairs.

The Republican presidential victory in 1896 was foreshadowed by the House elections of 1894. Despite the presidential victory of 1896, the Republicans actually lost seats in the House, although their margin of control there remained a sizable 57 percent. Again, the Senate shows a lagging pattern. The Republicans gradually increased their share of Senate seats from 53 percent in the Fifty-fifth Congress (1897–1899) to 66 percent in the Sixtieth (1907–1909). The Republican gains in the Senate cannot be attributed to the seven western states that had been admitted to the Union between 1889 and 1896, and they hence are all the more impressive. In the latter half of the 1890s, the majority of these states sent senators of differing parties to Washington, and only a bare majority of the fourteen new seats were held by Republicans. Republican strength was concentrated in the northeastern portion of the country. Following an interlude of Democratic government beginning in 1912 (1910 in the House), the Republicans regained Congress in 1918 and controlled both elected branches of the national government throughout the 1920s.

The realignment of the 1930s was brought about by the Great Depression and the limited response of the incumbent Republican party to its domestic consequences. President Herbert Hoover, following traditional economic thinking, took the position that economic downturns were self-correcting and that federal intervention in the economy was unnecessary and inappropriate. While the Reconstruction Finance Corporation, created in 1932, offered some aid to business, relief for other sectors of the economy was left to private organizations or the state governments. Hoover maintained these positions when he ran for reelection in 1932 and was soundly defeated by the Democratic candidate, Franklin Roosevelt. While Roosevelt promised very little in terms of specific policy actions, he did commit the Democratic party to federal intervention in the economy.

The outcome of the critical election of 1932 was foreshadowed by the outcomes of the House elections of 1930. The Democratic party increased its share of seats by 12.5 percent as voters reacted to the economic hardships of the Great Depression by voting against the party of the president. This increase allowed the Democrats in the Seventy-second to organize the House, albeit by the slim margin of only seven seats—50.5 percent of the entire House membership. The 1932 House elections boosted this margin considerably, to a 72-percent majority, and the elections of 1934 and 1936 resulted in incremental seat gains for the Democratic party. While the Democrats lost ground in the House after 1938, they retained majority status in the chamber until the Eightieth Congress, seated after the elections of 1946.

Ratification of the Seventeenth Amendment in 1913, which allowed for the popular election of senators, increased the potential for direct electoral impact on the Senate in the 1930s realignment, relative to realignments of the nineteenth century. Since both houses of Congress have been directly elected, divided control of Congress has rarely occurred. Still, Democratic gains in the upper chamber followed those in the House in the 1930s. The Democrats gained seats in the Senate after the 1930 elections, but the increase was insufficient to give them control of the institution. Control did follow the critical election of 1932, which gave the party of Roosevelt 63 percent of the Senate seats. In that chamber, as in the House, the Democrats increased their share of seats in the elections of 1934 and 1936, and their losses began in 1938 and continued until the Republicans won a 53-percent majority in 1946.

Critical Elections and Party Constituencies

To understand the effects of these elections on subsequent congressional behavior, their implications for the constituency bases of the party—particularly the advantaged party—must be considered. In *Critical Elections and Congressional Policymaking*, David Brady demonstrated that the effect of the systematic seat switches characteristic of electoral realignments was to transform the constituency bases of the parties from demographically or regionally heterogeneous units to homogeneous ones. In other words, prior to a realignment, the characteristics of one House district held by a Democrat, for example, might have little in common with another House district also

represented by a Democrat. And both of those districts might be similar to other districts held by Republicans. Under these conditions, each party holds districts that are demographically dissimilar, resulting in intraparty heterogeneity. The effect of seat switching is to align the districts held by a single party, so that intraparty homogeneity on demographic characteristics relevant to the realigning issues is enhanced. This creates interparty differences in the electoral bases of the parties, as can readily be seen in the 1850s, 1890s, and 1930s. This phenomenon is far more difficult to document for the first party system because members of Congress were often elected at large or from multimember, not single-member, districts.

The realignment of the 1850s produced constituencies based on regional similarities, as is indicated by the growing proportion of Southern congressional seats held by Democrats and, more dramatically, by the rise of the Republican party outside the South. The Democrats had been competitive with the Whigs in New England in the early 1850s, but by 1856 the ratio of Republican-to-Democratic seats there was 11 to 1, and by 1858 it was 21.5 to 1. While the transformation is most dramatic for New England, other non-Southern areas also show a pattern of increasing Republican dominance. Even after the setback for the Republican party in the 1862 election, the result of negative voter reaction in the Union to the continuing Civil War, the ratio of Republican to Democratic seats remained high (see Brady, 1988, pp. 37–38). The Democrats remained highly uncompetitive outside the South until after Reconstruction. In the 1880s, however, with the slavery issue off the agenda, Democrats once again successfully contested House races outside the South.

The important divisions for the parties in the 1890s were between agricultural and industrialized districts and between rural and urban districts. The Republican positions were far more appealing in the urbanizing, industrializing areas of the country, and they appealed to blue-collar labor, as well as to corporate and financial interests, because they were more likely to produce jobs for labor. In contrast, the Democrats were more attractive to voters in rural agricultural areas. Between 1892 and 1896 the Republican party's share of districts with higher-than-average concentrations of industrial labor increased from 44 percent to 79 percent, and after 1896 the Republicans held only 33 percent of the heavily agricultural House districts. Translating this change into regional terms, the Democrats lost much of the ground they had regained in the 1880s in New England, the Northeast, and the north-central states, and they increased their share of the seats from the South and border region. In some senses, the realignment of the 1890s restored the regional aspects of the fading Civil War system, but regionalism per se was not as important as the conflict between agricultural and industrial interests. As a product of historical accident, the latter division coincided with the former.

While the 1920s constituted a decade of prosperity for almost everyone except farmers, and particularly southern farmers, the negative effects of the Great Depression were felt in diverse economic quarters. When voters retaliated against the Republican incumbents, Democrats gained seats in a variety of district types. Most dramatic were the gains in areas where they had been defeated in the 1890s—industrialized, urban, and blue-collar districts outside the South, where they increased their seat share from about one-third to two-thirds. The Democrats also showed gains in rural districts with relatively low levels of labor and industry, but they had enjoyed strength in these areas prior to 1932 (see Brady, 1988, pp. 100–102). While it can hardly be argued that a coalition including agriculture as well as labor, rural as well as urban, and southern as well as non-southern elements is homogeneous, these disparate districts had in common their need for government action to address the hardships brought on by the Great Depression. At least temporarily, this common concern transcended all others.

To summarize, congressional elections during periods of realignment lead to unified control of the government for a sustained period (which is itself accomplished through straight-ticket voting influenced by issues that divide the parties nationally), and they unify the constituency bases of the respective parties. These relatively unusual conditions affect partisan behavior within Congress in ways that produce the major transformations in public policy associated with electoral realignment.

CRITICAL ELECTIONS AND CONGRESSIONAL PERFORMANCE

Critical elections lead most immediately to personnel turnover in Congress. Incumbents of the disadvantaged party lose their seats as voters shift to the advantaged party, and a new partisan majority emerges. These changes have important consequences for the business before Congress. The new majority is also largely a young majority; that is, many of its members are serving in Congress for the first time. These first-term members are especially likely to be loyal to their party's platform positions for several reasons. During a period of electoral realignment, a party commits itself to a new philosophy or a new course of action, often after severe intraparty disagreement. Any former member of the party unhappy with the alteration of party positions is likely to leave the party. Those who remain and allow themselves to be advanced as candidates for Congress are in sympathy with the new mission of the party. And because this new mission is national in scope, regional or ideological differences between members of the same party are not as important as the members' common commitment to the new policy agenda.

The general membership turnover, coupled with the change in partisan control, has a substantial effect on the committee system. Because committee chairs are always members of the majority party, old committee chairs are replaced with new ones. These new chairs have policy concerns that are at sharp variance with the priorities and preferences of the chairs they replaced. The new chairs are aided in the pursuit of these concerns by the presence of the large number of new members of their own party that serve with them on the committees. The legislation that emerges from the committees to be considered by the full House or Senate reflects the agenda of the ascendant party.

The situation on the floor of the full House in Congresses following critical elections also works to the advantage of the ascendant party. Committee bills are likely to fare well because the cohesion of the majority party allows them to pass fairly easily. A highly cohesive majority party would always be able to outvote the minority, but during an electoral realignment the majority is doubly advantaged, for not only is party unity higher than normal, but the size of the party's margin of control is also larger than normal. Overly large, unified majorities cannot be obstructed easily by activities of the minority party, such as the offering of unfriendly amendments or parliamentary maneuvering designed to kill legislation. Highly partisan floor voting is bolstered by the homogeneity of the constituency bases of each party documented above. The party-constituency cross-pressuring that can arise from a diversified constituency base is absent during periods of electoral realignment. Members of the same party can simultaneously vote with their party leadership and for measures that serve the interests of their constituencies because party goals and constituency goals are one and the same.

Under conditions of partisan voting, the majority party's agenda can easily clear both the House and the Senate. Because the presidency is also held by the same party, the new legislation is signed into law, thus leading to major redirections in the course of public policy. Yet the sustained period of unified control of government detailed above is essential to the long-term survival of these new policies. If control of government were to revert to the opposition party in the next election, it would be an easy task for that party to dismantle the work that had just been done. But when policies have been in place for a number of years, no matter how novel or radical they seemed at the time of enactment, they are far harder to dismantle when the opposition finally gains control of government. By then, the policy changes that follow electoral realignments have become institutionalized.

This general process is easily illustrated by the behavior of Congress, especially the House of Representatives, for the realignments of the 1850s, 1890s, and 1930s. Brady has performed the most extensive quantitative analysis of committee turnover in each of these periods. During the Thirty-second and Thirty-third Congresses (1851–1855), the average percentage of new members on the influential House Ways and Means Committee was 38.5, but this figure rose to 61.3 percent for the Thirty-fourth through the Thirty-seventh Congresses (1855–1863). Other House committees had even more remarkable membership replacements. The Public Lands and Public Expenditures committees showed 78 percent new members in the Thirty-fourth Congress (1855–1857), while the Agriculture Committee and the Roads and Canals Committee experienced complete membership replacement in the Thirty-fourth Congress (see Brady, 1988, pp. 40–41).

Similar patterns affected the committee systems of the 1890s and 1930s. Following the election of 1894, the average rate of turnover for House committees rose, primarily as a consequence of the defeat of House members in the critical elections. Brady's examination of thirteen selected committees shows that the percentage of new members ranged from a low of 65 percent on Appropriations to a high of 100 percent on Agriculture in the Fifty-fifth Congress (1897–1899). The extremely powerful House Rules Committee showed 80 percent turnover, replacing four of its five members between 1893 and 1897, while the comparable figure for Ways and Means was 77 percent. Nearly identical changes occurred in the early 1930s, when turnover ranged from 64 percent on Commerce to nearly 96 percent on both Public Lands and Mines and Mining between the Seventy-first (1929–1931) and Seventy-third (1933–1935) Congresses. The triumvirate of power committees—Appropriations, Rules, and Ways and Means—had 74 percent, 67 percent, and 80 percent new members, respectively, for the comparable time periods.

To reiterate, the advantage of populating committees with new members elected to office in critical years is that these new members are committed to the national party's position on the important issues. Because congressional committees have the power to sit on bills almost indefinitely, never submitting a proposal to the full chamber, they can easily become "black holes" for innovative new ideas. But a committee composed of individuals committed to new ideas will incorporate policy innovation into legislation and move it quickly from committee to floor, where its fate will be determined by the full house.

Because Congress keeps records of how specific members voted on roll calls, it is possible to observe the extent to which partisan floor voting led to the enactment of significant new legislation during realigning eras. Yet the extent of partisan voting in each realigning period must be evaluated in the context of long-term trends. Using slightly different data and time spans, studies by Clubb, Flanigan, and Zingale and by Brady, Cooper, and Hurley demonstrate that there has been a long-term decline in party voting in the House from the nineteenth to the twentieth century. The work of Clubb and his colleagues shows that opposition between the two parties increased during the 1850s, 1890s, and 1930s. Using an analysis of the percentage of times a majority of the members of one party voted in opposition to a majority of members of the other party, Brady and his associates show a very sharp rise in the overall level of party voting in the 1890s, from an average of 45 percent in the Fifty-second and Fifty-third Congresses (1891–1895) to an average rate of 75 percent in the Fifty-fourth through the Fifty-sixth (1895–1901). Between the Seventy-second and Seventy-third Congresses, elected in 1930 and 1932, party voting rose from 58 percent to 71 percent of all recorded votes. This high rate of 71 percent was not sustained in the next two Congresses, but the Democratic majority was by then so large that it could easily afford voting defection by some of its members.

Perhaps more important than the extent to which party determined voting on all matters is the extent to which it determined voting on the specific matters germane to each realignment. Several scholars have grouped roll calls by subject matter and examined the effects of party separately for different issue areas. The paramount issues for the Civil War party system were, of course, slavery, secession, and civil rights. Statistical analysis reveals that in the House partisanship was only modestly important on these matters in the Thirty-third and Thirty-fourth Congresses (1853–1857), but party voting in these issue areas became extremely high in the Thirty-fifth through Forty-second Congresses (1857–1873). Similar but far less dramatic patterns are in evidence for voting on public works, railroad and telegraph construction, tariffs, procedural matters, and a new issue dimension, federal control over money and banking (see Brady, 1988, pp. 42–45).

The three most important issues for the electoral realignment of the 1890s were currency, expansionism, and tariff policy. Both currency and expansionism show much higher levels of party voting in the second half of the 1890s than they did in the first portion of the decade. In contrast, tariff matters divided the parties even before the realignment. What is remarkable is that the tariff dimension does not even appear in the Fifty-sixth and Fifty-seventh Congresses (1899–1903), suggesting that the tariff legislation passed during the special session of the Fifty-fifth Congress gave early resolution to this controversy (see Brady, 1988, p. 76).

The policy changes of the 1930s constituted the legislation that became known as the New Deal. The most important components of the New Deal were agricultural assistance, social welfare, and government management of the economy. Agricultural-assistance and social-welfare policy best exemplify the pattern of increasing partisan diversity in new areas. Social-welfare votes do not even appear until the Seventy-second Congress (1931–1933) and are highly partisan when they do. Prior to the Seventy-first Congress (1929–1931), voting on agricultural policy is virtually unrelated to partisanship, but is very much so in the Seventy-second and throughout the remainder of the 1930s. The House of Representatives took recorded votes on government management of the economy prior to the New Deal legislation, and this issue shows two distinctive partisan positions both before and after the critical elections of the 1930s. Inspection of the details of bills in this dimension, however, demonstrates that "while the gross voting response remained stable, the content of the measures included in the government management dimension changed with the coming of the New Deal" (Sinclair, p. 22).

Partisan voting in the Senate has received far less scholarly attention than it has in the House. A longitudinal analysis (or time-series analysis) of the Senate covering the period 1876–1986 shows that partisan voting in the Senate rose between the Fifty-fourth and Fifty-fifth Congresses (1895–1899) and remained consistently high for the next four Congresses. This consistent partisanship was a marked contrast to the widely fluctuating patterns of voting observed in the Senate between 1876 and 1896. Such fluctuation had returned by the 1920s, but the New Deal period shows a fairly consistent pattern of partisanship in the Senate for several Congresses following the 1932 elections (Hurley and Wilson, p. 229). Bogue's work on the Civil War Senates demonstrates that while the Republican party did experience some internal divisions, party was an important cue for Senate voting behavior in that era as well (1973, p. 461).

In sum, similar conditions in the several Congresses following the critical elections of the 1850s, 1890s, and 1930s led to some of the most comprehensive policy changes in American history. The passage of the Thirteenth, Fourteenth, and Fifteenth amendments had a profound and continued impact on individuals and state governments. The policies of the late 1890s assured the development of the United States as a major industrial power. And the New Deal permanently changed attitudes as well as policies, institutionalizing the federal government's responsibility for the economic health of the nation and for providing citizens with a minimum standard of living. These policy innovations would not have been possible had not critical elections altered the composition and thus the behavior of Congress.

DISTINGUISHING REALIGNMENTS FROM TEMPORARY ELECTORAL CHANGE

This essay has documented the special role of Congress in the process of electoral realignments. The research literature suggests that representatives of the emerging majority party respond to constituency signals for change and do so in accord with constituency preferences, which during realignments are relatively uniform throughout the nation. Since the only acknowledged realignments took place prior to the advent of modern-day opinion surveys, the true extent of opinion-policy congruence, or representation, during realignments remains a matter of inference.

Yet the nature of opinion-policy congruence between parties in the electorate and parties in government is likely to be a fundamental factor in transforming what might otherwise be short-term electoral change into durable new patterns of voting and partisan preference. While the electorate creates the conditions for realignment, it can only be realized if the advantaged partisan elite pursues policies "that win the long-term support of newly eligible, weakly identified or unidentified, and formerly apolitical members of the electorate" (Clubb, Flanigan, and Zingale, p. 268).

In other words, realignments simultaneously involve mass public-to-government elite and elite government-to-mass public linkage processes: the connections between opinion and policy are bidirectional during a realigning sequence. The electorate, dissatisfied with the status quo, votes into Congress large numbers of members who represent a party different from that of the defeated incumbents, leading to a new majority or a greatly altered margin of control for the existing majority. In such times, a realignment may occur, but whether it will occur depends on whether the advantaged party continues to represent successfully those who identify with it while providing the nonaligned portion of the mass public with more policy satisfaction than does the disadvantaged party. The popularity of the advantaged party's program should be a key factor in distinguishing short-lived changes in voting behavior that have the initial appearances of realignments, such as in 1912, 1964, or 1980, from more enduring changes, such as those of the 1850s, 1890s, and 1930s. Thus, a process one might call partisan representation should be essential to the culmination of a realignment. Partisan representation is the extent of opinion-policy congruence between identifiers with the major parties and independents in the mass public, as groups, and the respective congressional parties, as groups.

Specific patterns of partisan representation should hold for the advantaged party during a realigning sequence. The congressional elite of this party should be especially representative of its own followers and should stay representative of them over a period of several Congresses. The partisan preferences of the mass of this group, and especially those of any recent converts to it, need positive policy reinforcement. In other words, partisan preferences will be reinforced if the policies of the advantaged party are popular. During this period, the advantaged party should also be more attuned than the opposition to the preferences of independent members of the electorate. Some large portion of these independents is presumably voting for candidates of the advantaged party. They need to be mobilized into active identification with it through the process of positive policy reinforcement.

Yet, this situation is awkward for the advantaged party. As the party in the electorate grows larger it may become more heterogeneous and thus more difficult to represent. Ultimately, this will always be a problem for the majority party. Yet it should not be a problem immediately after the realignment. To preclude this circumstance, the advantaged party may need to bring opinion of its rank-and-file members into line with the policy positions of the party. Opinion persuasion by a popular president would be an important mechanism for bringing this about; perceived substantive policy success would be another. Thus, during a realignment, the process of partisan representation should be reciprocal: opinion-policy congruence results both from the party in government responding to the party in the electorate and from the party in the electorate moving toward the party in government because its policy efforts are viewed favorably in retrospect. Public opinion and elite policy behavior must go through several iterations until the two converge.

An ideal test of this proposition requires public-opinion data from a period that scholars agree was one of realignment. Unfortunately, reliable data on public opinions on issues are not available prior to 1936. Yet the test has been approached from another angle: examining realignments that might have been, or short-term periods of electoral change that did not become permanent. In such cases, one should expect to observe no convergence between the policy preferences of the majority of the electorate and the programs advocated by the party that profited from short-term shifts in voting behavior.

Two test cases for which public opinion data are available are the 1960s and the 1980s. Both the 1964 and 1980 elections had many of the hallmarks of critical elections at both the presidential and congressional levels. Subsequent election outcomes, however, made it clear that neither of these periods resulted in an electoral realignment similar to those of the 1850s, 1890s, and 1930s. An examination of the correspondence between public preferences and congressional policy-making behaviors suggests that these potential realignments were aborted, at least in part, by the failure of the Democratic and Republican congressional parties in 1964 and 1980, respectively, to provide the necessary level of partisan representation.

While a number of scholars have attributed Lyndon Johnson's 1964 victory over Barry Goldwater to voters' greater preferences for Johnson's policy positions, public-opinion data show that even in 1964 the Democratic members of the public were highly divided on such critical issues as government support of social welfare, federal aid to education, and civil rights, and they remained split on these matters even as the congressional Democrats expanded federal efforts in these program areas during the Eighty-ninth and 90th Congresses (1965–1968). Further, the preferences of the independent members of the public were generally better represented by the Republicans in Congress in the mid 1960s. Not only did independent opinion fail to follow the policy direction taken by the Democrats, but that policy direction actually reduced the commitment to expanded federal programs among independents.

During the Ninety-seventh Congress (1981–1982), the Republican House delegation was considerably closer to both its own identifiers and the independents than was the Democratic party elite. By the Ninety-eighth Congress (1983–1984), the situation had been reversed, with the Democratic House contingent closer to its followers as well as to independents on a number of important issues. Patterns of opinion-policy agreement for the Senate are almost identical to those observed for the House: the differences between Senate Republicans and the Republican and independent members of the mass public were much smaller in 1980 than they were in 1986, when control of the Senate reverted to the Democratic party.

A second aspect of the representational process that may distinguish true electoral realignment from temporary aberrations in voter behavior concerns the types of issues involved. Realignments have been said to turn on moral issues to which voters react emotionally, and on which they are unlikely to accept policy compromises, thus simplifying their choices between candidates of opposing parties. Such issues have also been called "easy issues," in contrast to "hard issues," which are technical rather than symbolic or emotional and are more likely to involve conflict over policy means than policy goals. Extrapolating from James Kuklinski's work on representation, one can infer that opinion-policy congruence should be greater on easy issues than on hard issues, because legislators have greater incentives to attend to constituency preferences on easy issues. Constituency preferences are also better defined and more clearly communicated on easy issues. The prominant role of easy issues in realignments increases the probability that the high level of representation by the advantaged party necessary to produce a new party system will be achieved. In cases of short-lived electoral upheaval, easy issues are either absent or insufficiently dominant to sustain a realignment.

Elections are relatively crude devices for registering the policy preferences of voters most of the time. Yet this is less true in critical elections than it is at other occasions. The polarization between the parties offers the voters a relatively clear choice of prospective policy directions. The specific details of policies are not necessarily clear at the moment ballots are cast. Because voters are pragmatic, long-term commitments to new policies are made retrospectively and are signaled by the voters' willingness to allow the new majority to continue in office. Without this retrospective approval, the policy innovations of the new majority party would not be permanent.

CONTEMPORARY BARRIERS TO REALIGNMENT

The cyclical theory of electoral realignments predicts that the phenomenon will occur approximately once every generation. According to this view, the United States is long overdue for a major restructuring of partisan competition and has been since the mid-1960s. But no electoral realignment has been forthcoming. Several facets of contemporary American politics may be working to limit the prospects for such change. These include structural changes in the electoral system, changes in the way presidential and congressional campaigns are conducted, and the behavioral responses of voters.

Political parties no longer have the control over the electoral process that they once enjoyed. Rather than being selected through a process of peer review, would-be presidential candidates compete against others of the same party in a series of primary elections, which

have a major impact on whom the party eventually nominates. But the process can lead to highly public intraparty friction that lessens the ability of parties to present themselves to voters as coherent organizational entities. Parties also have virtually no control over the individuals who choose to run for a seat in Congress under the party's banner. If an individual can win a district's primary election, he or she becomes the nominee. This system of presidential and congressional primaries greatly reduces the role of national forces in elections, particularly congressional elections. Rather than reacting to an entire party ticket, voters react to what they perceive as a series of discrete races that happen to be on the same ballot. The forces that shape a voter's choice for president may be completely unrelated to that same voter's reasons for selecting a particular candidate for the House or Senate.

A number of other mutually reinforcing trends also contribute to the declining importance of national forces in congressional elections. First, voters are less likely to have a partisan preference than they were in the 1950s and earlier, and even those who do are likely to hold that preference more weakly than did voters a generation ago. Consequently, appeals by candidates to the partisanship of the voters are not likely to be effective campaign tactics. Voters are far more likely to split their tickets, voting for candidates of both political parties in the same general election. This split-ticket voting increases the chances for divided control of the government. In fact, divided government was the rule for more than two decades after 1968, with the only exception being the administration of Jimmy Carter. As long as sufficient numbers of voters split their tickets, the unified control of the government necessary to a realignment will not occur.

The Democratic advantage in congressional elections is the second trend that works against the likelihood of electoral realignment. The Democrats' continued success in the late twentieth century can be traced to what scholars have called the incumbency advantage in congressional elections. Incumbent members of Congress, especially of the House of Representatives, have at their disposal several tools that position them more favorably than their opponents at election time. Because they already hold office, incumbents are more likely to have name recognition, and they can use their franking privileges to make sure that residents of their respective districts see their names often by sending favorable mailings at no postage cost. Incumbents can also use their positions to gain favor by responding to appeals from constituents for help with bureaucratic problems and by delivering federal largesse to their respective districts. All of this behavior is nonpartisan, and it may lead constituents of the opposition party to support an incumbent simply because he or she is good for the district. Consequently, the election contest is perceived in terms of local forces rather than as a debate over national policy directions. And if a high number of voters do not even hold a partisan preference at all, the weight of the local forces is even greater.

Incumbents are also better positioned than challengers when it comes to funding. Those who give money to congressional candidates would like a return on their investment: they would like to see their candidate win. Consequently, money is most likely to flow to incumbents because they are more likely to win than challengers. This contribution strategy is especially characteristic of political action committees (PACs). Such a contribution strategy also creates something of a self-fulfilling prophecy: incumbents receive contributions because they have the best prospects of winning, but the prospects of winning are enhanced because they have the most campaign money. Promising challengers may be deterred by the almost inevitable loss to the well-funded incumbent, and those who are willing to make the race will be too underfunded to make that race effective. While the incumbency advantage accrues to both Democrats and Republicans, the Democrats benefit disproportionately. Democrats held the majority of House seats when the value of incumbency increased in the 1960s, and they have continued to maintain that advantage.

The nature of the 1930s realignment may also be inhibiting realignment today. Changes in voting behavior in the 1850s and 1890s were the product of both interactive and across-the-board partisan change. Interactive change occurs when partisans essentially change places: one party's losses are the other party's gains and vice versa. Across-the-board change involves movement in one direction only: the as-

cendant party gains and the descendant party loses. When realignments involve both types of change, the party system remains competitive, even though one party has an advantage. But if a realignment is dominated by across-the-board change, it can have an adverse effect on the overall level of party competition. Clubb, Flanigan, Zingale (1980), and Brady (1988) demonstrate that the 1930s realignment was largely the product of across-the-board change toward the Democratic party. Consequently, the Democrats in the 1930s benefited more than had the emerging majority party in previous realignments.

The result of the contemporary trends overlaid on the party system that developed in the 1930s is that competition in congressional elections has been considerably reduced from what it was at the time of any of the critical elections discussed in this essay. In any given election, more than 90 percent of the House incumbents can be expected to retain their seats, regardless of the outcome of the accompanying presidential contest. More important, they win by large margins, usually more than 60 percent of the vote. It is these large margins that make incumbents relatively impervious to any nationwide vote swings that do occur. Imagine a uniform movement in the nationwide vote of 5 percent away from the Democrats toward the Republicans. The effect would be simply to reduce an incumbent Democrat's vote margin from 60 percent to 55 percent. In either case, the incumbent Democrat wins. In contrast, if elections were highly competitive, with contests decided by narrow margins—say, 53 percent to 47 percent—a nationwide swing of 5 percent would produce a number of electoral upsets: many incumbents would be defeated by challengers, resulting in large numbers of switched seats and a new majority in the House. Thus, for example, in the 1980s the magnitude of the swing toward the Republicans that would be necessary to alter the majority would be well over 10 percent. The electoral realignments of the past were accomplished with considerably smaller movements in nationwide voting behavior.

At the extreme, the advantage held by House incumbents may be large enough to preclude any future realignment in American politics unless competition is restored to House elections. At a minimum, the lack of competition in House elections means that the lower chamber will no longer serve as a harbinger of realignments as it did in the past. Instead, change in control of the Senate, the members of which are more electorally vulnerable, may signal a possible realignment. In fact, in 1980 it was the Republican victories in Senate races, rather than at the presidential level, that led observers to forecast a possible realignment, even though that forecast was ultimately proven in error by subsequent events.

CONCLUSION

The Founding Fathers designed the American political system with the intention of thwarting quick action by popular majorities. Incrementalism was preferred to innovation in matters of public policy, and a number of structural barriers to the latter ensure that the former is "politics as usual" in the United States. These structural barriers include a president who is elected separately from the members of the legislative branch; a bicameral Congress; differing lengths of terms for presidents, representatives, and senators; and staggered terms in the Senate. Because legislation must generally pass through the House, the Senate, and the president's office before becoming law (even when a presidential veto has been overridden by Congress), any one of these institutions can effectively block policy action. This institutional structure imposes severe constraints on the ability of American political parties to function as responsible parties. Parties were no more preferred by the framers of the Constitution than was hasty policy action.

A responsible party system is one in which the party favored by the majority of voters (as evidenced by election outcomes) gains control of the government and implements the policies that the party promised during the election campaign. If the policies are successful, the voters will reward the party with another term in office at the next election; if the policies prove to be failures or the party fails to keep its promises, the voters will replace the party with the opposition. In such a system, voters make prospective evaluations of policy directions and retrospective evaluations of policy success, and these evaluations influence their choices for all offices on the ballot. In a truly responsible party system, divided control of the government would never occur. But the character of the American system is such that voters make evaluations of the candidates for the separate institutions at different points in time and often on the basis of separate criteria. Under these circumstances, the prospects for divided government are great and the prospects for parties to behave responsibly are limited.

During periods of electoral realignment, a confluence of conditions overcomes the inherent limitations of the American political structure, and the nation approximates the responsible party model of government. Party candidates, voters, and those elected to office all live up to their respective parts of the responsible-party bargain. Candidates of opposing parties offer voters clear policy choices on issues of national importance. Voters make their electoral selections on the basis of those choices and cast a straight party ballot, sending the same party to the White House and both chambers of Congress. The elected members of the party make good on their campaign promises. Voters signal approval of the policy actions of the party in power by granting it successive terms in office. The result is not the normal politics of incrementalism and compromise, but is instead the politics of resolution and principle.

BIBLIOGRAPHY

Realignments
General works on the subject of realignment include WALTER DEAN BURNHAM, *Critical Elections and the Mainsprings of American Politics* (New York, 1970); JEROME M. CLUBB, WILLIAM H. FLANIGAN, and NANCY H. ZINGALE, *Partisan Realignment: Voters, Parties, and Government in American History* (Beverly Hills, Calif., 1980); V. O. KEY, JR., "A Theory of Critical Elections," *Journal of Politics* 17 (February 1955);

and JAMES L. SUNDQUIST, *Dynamics of the Party System: Alignment and Realignment of the Political Parties of the United States* (1973; rev. ed., Washington, D.C., 1983). Good treatments of the development of the separate party systems may be found in WILLIAM NISBET CHAMBERS and WALTER DEAN BURNHAM, eds., *The American Party Systems: Stages of Political Development* (New York, 1967; 2d ed., 1975). Especially useful in that volume are PAUL GOODMAN, "The First American Party System"; RICHARD P. MCCORMICK, "Political Development and the Second Party System"; and ERIC L. MCKITRICK, "Party Politics and the Union and Confederate War Efforts." Also useful is WILLIAM NISBET CHAMBERS, *Political Parties in a New Nation* (New York, 1963). For an alternative to the realignment perspective, see EDWARD G. CARMINES and JAMES A. STIMSON, *Issue Evolution: Race and the Transformation of American Politics* (Princeton, N.J., 1989). See also EDWARD G. CARMINES and JAMES A. STIMSON, "The Two Faces of Issue Voting," *American Political Science Review* 74 (March 1980).

More specific analyses of Congress and electoral realignments are DAVID W. BRADY, *Critical Elections and Congressional Policy Making* (Stanford, Calif., 1988), and "A Reevaluation of Realignments in American Politics: Evidence from the House of Representatives," *American Political Science Review* 79 (1985); and BARBARA SINCLAIR, *Congressional Realignment, 1925–1978* (Austin, Tex., 1982). Detailed accounts of the importance of party for congressional behavior in specific periods following realignments include ALLAN G. BOGUE, "The Radical Voting Dimension in the U.S. Senate During the Civil War," *Journal of Interdisciplinary History* 3 (Winter 1973), and *The Congressman's Civil War* (New York, 1989); DAVID W. BRADY, *Congressional Voting in a Partisan Era* (Lawrence, Kans., 1973); and JOEL H. SILBEY, *The Shrine of Party: Congressional Voting Behavior, 1841–1852* (Pittsburgh, 1967). The role of party over time is considered in DAVID W. BRADY, JOSEPH COOPER, and PATRICIA A. HURLEY, "The Decline of Party in the U.S. House of Representatives, 1887–1968," *Legislative Studies Quarterly* 4 (August 1979); and PATRICIA A. HURLEY and RICK K. WILSON, "Partisan Voting Patterns in the U.S. Senate, 1876–1986," *Legislative Studies Quarterly* 14 (May 1989).

The Importance of Party

Explication of the role of partisan representation and the realignment process can be found in PATRICIA A. HURLEY, "Partisan Representation and the Failure of Realignment in the 1980s," *American Journal of Political Science* 33 (February 1989), and "Partisan Representation, Realignment, and the Senate in the 1980s," *Journal of Politics* 53 (February 1991). Useful insights into the process of representation with implications for realignment are JAMES H. KUKLINSKI, "Representativeness and Elections: A Policy Analysis," *American Political Science Review* 72 (March 1978); and DONALD J. MCCRONE and JAMES H. KUKLINSKI, "The Delegate Theory of Representation," *American Journal of Political Science* 23 (May 1979).

The importance of party in shaping voter choice is considered by ANGUS CAMPBELL, PHILIP E. CONVERSE, WARREN E. MILLER, and DONALD E. STOKES, *The American Voter* (Ann Arbor, Mich., 1960), and WARREN E. MILLER and DONALD STOKES, "Party Government and the Saliency of Congress," *Public Opinion Quarterly* 26 (Winter 1962). The notions of party dealignment and the declining importance of partisan identification are treated by numerous scholars. Notable works include WALTER DEAN BURNHAM, "The Changing Shape of the American Political Universe," *American Political Science Review* 59 (March 1965); NORMAN H. NIE, SIDNEY VERBA, and JOHN R. PETROCIK, *The Changing American Voter* (Cambridge, Mass., 1976), esp. chap. 4; and GERALD POMPER, *Voters' Choice: Varieties of American Electoral Behavior* (New York, 1975).

Congressional Elections

On the role of money in congressional elections, see GARY C. JACOBSON, *Money in Congressional Elections* (New Haven, Conn., 1980), and GARY C. JACOBSON and SAMUEL KERNELL, *Strategy and Choice in Congressional Elections* (1981; 2d ed., New Haven, Conn., 1983). There are numerous accounts of the incumbency advantage in congressional elections, but seminal work is that of DAVID R. MAYHEW, "Congressional Elections: The Case of the Vanishing Marginals," *Polity* 6 (Spring 1974), and *Congress: The Electoral Connection* (New Haven, Conn., 1974); RICHARD F. FENNO, JR., *Home Style* (Boston, 1978); and MORRIS P. FIORINA, *Congress:*

Keystone of the Washington Establishment (New Haven, Conn., 1977; 2d ed., 1989). A good overview of the implications of the incumbency advantage combined with other changes in the American political system is MORRIS P. FIORINA, "The Decline of Collective Responsibility in American Politics," *Daedulus* 109 (Summer 1980).

SEE ALSO The Congressional Committee System; Parties, Elections, Moods, and Lawmaking Surges; Elections to the U.S. House of Representatives; Elections to the U.S. Senate; AND The U.S. Congress: The Era of Party Patronage and Sectional Stress, 1829–1881.

RECALL AND EXPULSION
OF LEGISLATORS

Jack H. Maskell

Recall and expulsion are two methods by which legislators may be removed from office before their terms have ended. Although quite distinct in form, procedure, and underlying purpose, both methods attempt to regulate to some degree the behavior and conduct of elected officials through the possibility of an involuntary and premature ending of their terms in office. Normally, members of state legislatures, and members of Congress, have their terms in office ended prematurely by resignation, death, or in some cases, by accepting another public office that is found to be incompatible with their legislative positions. However, legislators may also be removed from office before the end of their terms by way of two extraordinary means: expulsion by the legislative institution; or, in the case of legislators in certain states, through a recall by the electorate.

A *recall* is a procedure whereby the citizens in a jurisdiction may petition for a special election to remove an elected official from office some time before the normal expiration of that official's term. Its proponents primarily see it as a device to assure the responsiveness and continued competency of an elected official or representative through the direct expression of the popular will.

Alternatively, an *expulsion* is an action, by the members of the legislative body itself, removing an individual from membership in that institution. It is primarily a disciplinary measure and a device of institutional self-protection that preserves the integrity of the legislative body as a whole, rather than regulating the responsiveness or effectiveness of a representative.

There is no recall provision for representatives or senators in the Constitution, and most states do not have recall provisions for state legislators. In most instances, therefore, if an electorate or constituency is unhappy with its legislator, the voters must either wait until the next scheduled election to express their displeasure through the ballot box, or successfully petition and convince the legislative body to expel the member.

For public officials who are in either the executive or the judicial branches of government, an involuntary removal from office through an impeachment procedure by the legislature may also apply. The legislatures of the various states, as well as Congress, are generally given the express power and authority to remove from office, through impeachment, civil officers in their jurisdictions who have been found to have committed certain specified offenses, engaged in public corruption, or otherwise abused their official positions. Members of the legislature generally do not impeach one another, but rather remove a fellow legislator from office by means of expulsion.

EXPULSION

The act of expelling a member from a legislative body is one which may be exercised by each house of the legislature acting on its own, without the concurrence of the other house, and without the concurrence of the executive. It is considered an internal housekeeping matter that may be accomplished without all of the requirements that are generally associated with the passing of a law by the legislature, such as bicameralism (approval by both houses) and presentment to the president, or to the governor of the state in the case of state legislation. However, in Congress, as well as in most of the state legislative bodies, an expulsion requires a supermajority, defined as the concurrence of two-thirds of the members.

Legislative bodies in the United States possess both inherent authority to take certain action in their capacity as legislative institutions, as well as express authority granted specifically by constitution or law. In the United States, legislatures are generally considered to possess a large degree of inherent authority to be exercised for their self-protection, including the inherent authority to expel a member of the body. In *Elements of the Law and Practice of Legislative Assemblies in the United States of America* (Boston, 1856), Luther Stearns Cushing described this authority to expel as "naturally and even necessarily incidental to . . . legislative bodies; which, without such power, could not exist honorably, and fulfil the object of their creation" (pp. 250–251).

Although generally an inherent authority of legislatures, the framers of the Constitution, as well as the drafters of the constitutions of all but five of the states, did not leave this expulsion power as merely an unwritten, incidental authority of the legislature, but rather expressly set out the power to expel members of the body within those constitutions. Aware of the fundamental contradiction between the power of expulsion by a legislative body and the concept of a representative democracy, wherein the people are free to choose whomever they wish to represent them in the legislature—the authority to expel was expressly and carefully delineated in those constitutions and has been approached cautiously in its exercise. In this regard, according to Cushing, it has been emphasized that in expelling a member a legislature must be governed by the "strictest justice," for if "a representative of the people [is] discharged of the trust conferred upon him by his constituents, without good cause, a power of control would thus be assumed by the representative body over the constituent, wholly inconsistent with the freedom of election" (pp. 250–251).

Expulsion Versus Exclusion

It is important to distinguish a legislative expulsion from an exclusion. While an expulsion is the removal from membership by the legislature of an individual who is already a member of that body—that is, one who has taken the oath of office and has been seated; an exclusion is an action by the legislative body to bar an individual, who is otherwise duly elected to the office, from being seated as a member of the legislature.

An exclusion involves a judging by the legislature of the specific, required qualifications of an individual for that legislative position, while an expulsion involves a more discretionary judgment by the legislature concerning the conduct or fitness of an individual member. Significantly, a member-elect may generally be excluded because of a failure to meet the express qualifications for office by a majority vote of the body, while an expulsion generally requires a concurrence of two-thirds of the legislative body.

In a landmark case involving an attempted exclusion from Congress, the U.S. Supreme Court, in *Powell* v. *McCormack,* 395 U.S. 486 (1969), found that Congress could not exclude Adam Clayton Powell (D.-N.Y.), who was duly reelected by his constituents, based solely on his past misconduct or lack of fitness for office.

Powell, a powerful black member of Congress who was very popular in his district of Harlem, had been the chairman of the House Committee on Education and Labor. During his tenure as chairman, charges had surfaced—investigated and reported upon by a special subcommittee of the House Administration Committee in the Eighty-ninth Congress—regarding allegations of his misuse of government appropriations and the payment of relatives who neither performed official duties nor resided in his district or in Washington, D.C., as required by law. At the beginning of the Ninetieth Congress, to which Powell was reelected, certain members objected to his being sworn and seated because of his alleged congressional misconduct and his standing convictions for civil and criminal contempt of court in New York judicial proceedings. The matter was referred to a special select committee which, finding that Powell met the qualifications for congressional office and was duly elected, concluded that Powell should be seated by Congress and then censured and condemned for his misconduct, fined by the House, and stripped of his seniority. The full House of Representatives, however, did not agree to the select committee's recommendations, and instead voted to exclude Representative-elect Powell. In overturning this exclusion, the Supreme Court found that Congress may refuse to seat a member-elect only for failure to meet the three qualifications expressly provided in the Constitution for congressional office: age, United States citizenship, and residency in the state from which elected.

The Court noted that in providing for the power of each house of Congress to "be the Judge of the Elections, Returns and Qualifications of its own Members" in Article I, Section 5, paragraph 1, the drafters of the Constitution were concerned that the legislature not be able to "usurp the 'indisputable right [of the people] to return whom they thought proper' to the legislature" (*Powell* v. *McCormack,* at 535). In the deliberations of the Constitutional Convention of 1787, James Madison had spoken against a proposal that would have granted the authority to the legislature itself to establish certain qualifications to office. Instead, Madison supported the concept that qualifications to the legislature should be defined in the Constitution. He argued that allowing the legislature to establish its own qualifications would vest in the institution "an improper and dangerous power," and that the qualifications of the elected "ought to be fixed by the Constitution" so that the legislature could not itself regulate who was elected, and "by degrees subvert the Constitution." Madison believed that the government could be "converted into an aristocracy or oligarchy ... by limiting the number capable of being elected," and warned that with such power in the legislature "qualifications founded on artificial distinctions may be devised, by the stronger in order to keep out partizans of a weaker faction" (quoted in Farrand, pp. 249–250).

Thus, in an exclusion proceeding, the legislature judges a member-elect's qualifications to office and may refuse to seat someone by a simple majority vote, but may do so only on the grounds that the individual does not meet the established qualifications for office. No such restriction or limitation on the grounds for an expulsion action is placed upon the legislative body, in expelling a member, for misconduct or lack of fitness to serve, after the member has been sworn and seated in the legislature—but such action requires in Congress, and generally in the states, a vote of two-thirds of the body.

Expulsion from Congress

The Constitution provides in Article I, Section 5, paragraph 2, that "each House may determine the Rules of its Proceedings, punish its Members for disorderly Behaviour, and, with the Concurrence of two thirds, expel a Member."

The authority to expel is part of the self-protection given to the House of Representatives and the Senate to preserve the integrity of the proceedings and reputation of the institution. Expulsion is considered the most severe of the legislative punishments that the House or the Senate may inflict upon its own members. In addition to expelling a member, the House or the Senate may censure a member for misconduct or disorderly behavior, and may also fine a member. A censure is a formal expression of disapproval of a member's conduct stated in a resolution adopted by a majority vote of the House or the Senate. No specific disability or forfeiture of privileges automatically results from a censure. The House of Representatives has in the past also adopted resolutions reprimanding a member for misconduct, and this expression of disapproval or punishment is considered a milder form of rebuke than is a censure. The Senate has never formally used the term *reprimand* in a resolution adopted by that body.

In addition to preserving the integrity of the proceedings and the reputation of the institution, the power of each house of Congress to punish or expel its own members is, to some extent, a necessary counterpart to the immunity from prosecution that a member of Congress enjoys for his or her legislative acts in the so-called Speech or Debate clause of the Constitution (Article I, Section 6, paragraph 1). Since a member of Congress, under the Constitution's grant of legislative immunity, may not be "questioned in any other Place" regarding his or her official legislative conduct, it is incumbent upon the legislative body itself to possess and internally exercise control over the conduct and behavior of its members in their official legislative capacity; thus, a member may be called to answer for misconduct and may be judged in some forum other than a strictly political one, such as an election.

Constitutional History The power and authority given to each house of Congress by the Constitution to expel a member was drawn from the practice and experience of the English Parliament and the early colonial legislatures. In Parliament, the House of Commons had possessed and exercised extraordinary discretion and authority to expel a member of the body. Expulsion was used frequently in Parliament since the first member was expelled in 1581. Members could be expelled from Parliament as a punishment for a specific offense or as a remedial measure to deal with those deemed by the other members to be unworthy or unfit to serve, regardless of the offense, the timing of the offense, or any connection between the offense and one's official duties. In some cases, members of Parliament appeared to have been expelled merely for expressing political or social views that were considered offensive to the other members.

Shortly before the framers met in Philadelphia to draft the Constitution, the infamous expulsion case of John Wilkes arose in Parliament. John Wilkes was a member of Parliament who had been expelled, under pressure from King George III, for writing "scandalous and seditious libel" about the King. After having been returned to Parliament by his constituents in 1768, he was again expelled for another writing found to have been scandalous and seditious. Wilkes's constituents, however, returned him to Parliament in three consecutive special elections to fill the seat during that Parliament. Each time, Parliament refused to seat Wilkes on the grounds that he had been expelled from, and was ineligible to be seated in, that Parliament. Finally, Wilkes was elected to the next Parliament in 1774 and was seated as a member. In 1782 he had his earlier exclusions expunged from the record, and exclusion was recognized as a dangerous practice that interfered with and abridged the right of the people to choose their own representatives in Parliament.

The framers of the Constitution paid considerable deference to the sanctity of the freedom of the people to choose their own representatives in the legislature, and thus carefully approached the subject of expulsion, as well as the subject of standing qualifications to be a representative. The abuses of Parliament were noted and criticized during the Constitutional Convention, particularly by Madison, but during the Convention, there was no expansive explanation made for the provision allowing each house of Congress to expel members.

The question of expulsion was first raised during the Constitutional Convention by Edmund Randolph of Virginia, who was a member of the Committee of Detail. An early draft of the expulsion clause that came from that committee had included a provision stating that a member could not be expelled "a second Time for the same Offence." The final draft from that committee, however, deleted that particular restriction, and merely provided that in addition to each house having the authority to "punish its members for disorderly behavior," each house of Congress "may expel a member."

Madison then proposed an amendment, which was eventually adopted by the Convention, providing that expulsion must have the votes of two-thirds of the house's members. This was in recognition, as stated by Madison, "that the right of expulsion . . . was too important to be exercised by a bare majority of the quorum: and in emergencies of faction might be dangerously abused" (quoted in Farrand, p. 254). No other restrictions or qualifications on the authority of the legislature to expel were adopted.

The Constitution's final version of the authority and power of each house to expel a member is thus, on its face, unqualified except as to the requirement for a two-thirds vote. The legislative history of the provision indicates no express intent of the framers to limit the power of the legislature to expel. Despite their obvious knowledge of the celebrated Wilkes case in Parliament, and the general criticism of such English practices, the framers of the Constitution did not expressly limit the expulsion power of Congress as to either the offense or its timing, nor did they expressly limit the power to expel to only one time for the same offense. However, they concurrently allowed each house to exclude a member-elect by majority vote, but only for failure to meet the standing qualifications to office expressly established in the Constitution. By doing so, they presumably addressed the excesses of Parliament, and the need for a proper balance between the legislature's right to preserve its own institutional integrity through expulsion versus the right of the people to elect their own representatives to Congress. In this way, a John Wilkes, reelected to Congress after his expulsion, would at least have to be seated by Congress and could not be continuously excluded by a simple majority, as had been the case in Parliament.

Authority to Expel   The general authority and power of each house of Congress to expel a member has been described by the Supreme Court as a very broad and expansive power to which members may be subject when "the integrity and purity of members ... [has] been questioned in a manner calculated to destroy public confidence in the body (*In re Chapman,* 166 U.S. 661, 668 [1897]). In *United States* v. *Brewster,* 408 U.S. 501, 519 (1972), the Court commented that in a disciplinary action in Congress "an accused Member ... is at the mercy of an almost unbridled discretion of the charging body."

Congressional expressions of power and authority in expulsion precedents have also emphasized the broad discretion inherent in the institution in expulsion cases. The House Judiciary Committee in 1914 explained that the power to expel a member "is full and plenary and may be enforced by summary proceedings." It described the action as "discretionary in character, and upon a resolution of expulsion or censure of a Member for misconduct each individual Member is at liberty to act on his sound discretion and vote according to the dictates of his own judgment and conscience" (quoted in Cannon, p. 558).

Grounds for Expulsion from Congress
The Constitution does not specifically establish any grounds for expulsion. It is within the discretion of Congress to determine which offenses merit expulsion. In *In re Chapman,* the Supreme Court, citing the 1797 Senate expulsion case of William Blount of Tennessee, stated that the constitutional authority of either house to expel extends to conduct that, in the judgment of the body, "is inconsistent with the trust and duty of a member" even if such conduct was "not a statutable offence nor was it committed in his official character, nor was it committed during the session of Congress, nor at the seat of government."

It is clear that both houses have the authority to expel a member for conduct that is not necessarily an indictable offense. In cautiously exercising their discretion to expel, however, the House and the Senate have actually employed this most extreme form of discipline only to deal with conduct that has involved perceived disloyalty to the United States government, or criminal conduct relating to the abuse and corruption of one's official position, such as bribery.

Questions have arisen as to the power of Congress to expel a member for past misconduct which was known to the electorate when it voted that individual into office. The Supreme Court indicated, in *Powell* v. *McCormack,* that Congress has questioned its own power to expel for past misconduct. In more recent congressional considerations, it has not been the power to expel that Congress has questioned so much as the wisdom of the policy to expel. In early expulsion cases the power of the institution to expel for past misconduct was regularly questioned by both the House and Senate. In later cases there was a division of opinion concerning this authority, and the opinion subsequently emerged that while the power to expel a member is not expressly restricted by the Constitution—except as to the requirement for a two-thirds vote—policy and precedent has led to congressional restraint in exercising this authority in instances of past misconduct known to the member's electorate before election, or past misconduct not related to one's duties as a member of Congress.

In practice, Congress has generally refrained from exercising its broad power to expel a member whose misconduct was generally known at the time of his or her election. After noting Congress's broad, and almost unlimited, power and discretion to expel, the House Judiciary Committee explained in 1914 that Congress should exercise caution and restraint in such matters: "To exercise such power in that instance the House might abuse its high prerogative, and in our opinion might exceed the just limitations of its constitutional authority by seeking to substitute its own standards and ideals for the standards and ideals of the constituency of the Member who has deliberately chosen him to be their Representative" (quoted in Cannon, p. 558).

Although precedents have shown that Congress has generally refrained from exercising its authority to expel a member for misconduct in a past Congress, particularly if it were known to the electorate at the time the member was sent to Congress, neither house has felt similar restraint in formally censuring a member of the body for past misconduct. In 1954, for example, the Senate censured Joseph McCarthy of Wisconsin for his conduct toward two Senate investigating committees in the previous Congress. The House has exercised similar authority to censure for past misconduct, such as in the cases of Representatives Oakes Ames of Massachusetts and James Brooks of New York in the infamous "Crédit Mobilier" railroad scandal of the 1870s.

Expulsion Precedents and Practice   An expulsion action may originate from a complaint to and investigation by, or from a resolution for expulsion referred to, either the House Committee on Standards of Official Conduct or the Senate Select Committee on Ethics. These standing committees, unlike most other committees in Congress, are made up of an even number of members from both parties to ensure a more bipartisan and nonpolitical approach to ethics and disciplinary questions. These committees' rules provide for a detailed procedure of fact-finding, investigations, and hearings concerning the questioned conduct. After such procedures the committees may recommend action on a particular disciplinary matter to the full House or Senate, including expulsion of the member.

The House of Representatives had expelled only four members by the early 1990s. Three of those members were expelled during the Civil War era for disloyalty to the Union. These were John B. Clark of Missouri, on 13 July 1861; John W. Reid of Missouri, on 2 December 1861; and Henry C. Burnett of Kentucky, on 3 December 1861. Clark was expelled for joining and holding a commission in the so-called State Guard of Missouri under the Confederate Governor of that state. Reid was also expelled for taking up arms against the government. Burnett was expelled for being in open rebellion against the government. He was reportedly the president of a revolutionary convention claiming to be the provisional government of the state; some of the members of this convention were in armed rebellion.

The fourth House member, Michael J. "Ozzie" Myers (D.-Pa.), was expelled on 2 October 1980 for conduct that led to his federal bribery and conspiracy convictions. During the so-called Abscam sting operation conducted by the Federal Bureau of Investigation, Myers had been videotaped receiving cash payments in return for promising to use his influence in Congress on immigration bills.

The Senate had expelled fifteen members in six separate expulsion proceedings by the early 1990s. Fourteen members were expelled during the Civil War era for disloyalty to the

Union, ten of them on 11 July 1861: James M. Mason and Robert M. Hunter of Virginia; Thomas L. Clingman and Thomas Bragg of North Carolina; James Chestnut, Jr., of South Carolina; A. O. P. Nicholson of Tennessee; William K. Sebastian and Charles B. Mitchel of Arkansas; and John Hemphill and Louis T. Wigfall of Texas. The resolution stated that the members were expelled because they were "engaged in said conspiracy for the destruction of the Union and Government, or with full knowledge of such conspiracy have failed to advise the Government of its progress or aid in its suppression." The resolution as it pertained to Senator Sebastian was later revoked and annulled on 3 March 1877, and the unpaid accounts to Sebastian were settled. Four other members of the Senate were later expelled during the Civil War period. John C. Breckinridge of Kentucky was expelled on 4 December 1861 for having "joined the enemies of his country" and for being "in arms against the Government he had sworn to support." Jesse D. Bright of Indiana was expelled on 5 February 1862 for having written a letter of introduction for an arms dealer to Confederate President Jefferson Davis. Although the committee considering the matter found that the facts did not warrant expulsion, the full Senate, after debate, expelled Senator Bright. Waldo P. Johnson of Missouri was expelled on 10 January 1862 for his sympathy with and participation in the rebellion. Trusten Polk of Missouri was also expelled on 10 January 1862 for having written treasonable expressions in a secessionist newspaper, and for having gone within the lines of the enemy then in rebellion against the government.

The other member of the Senate to be expelled was William Blount of Tennessee, on 8 July 1797. President John Adams had forwarded a letter to Congress with documents that purported to show Blount had written a letter to a government interpreter, seeking his aid in a plan to seize Spanish Florida and Louisiana with British and Indian help. A select committee found that Senator Blount's conduct in attempting to incite the Indians against government officials was inconsistent with his public duty, amounted to a "high misdemeanor," and they therefore recommended expulsion.

In addition to those members who were actually expelled by the institution of the House or Senate, a number of members, facing an expulsion action, resigned from the body rather than be expelled. Representatives W. A. Gilbert, Francis S. Edwards, and Orasmus B. Matteson, all of New York, were accused of taking bribes in return for favoring legislation, and an expulsion resolution was issued from the committee investigating the matter in 1857: all three members resigned from the Thirty-fourth Congress before the House voted on the resolution. In 1870 a House committee recommended the expulsion of B. F. Whittemore of South Carolina, who was accused of selling military-academy appointments to West Point. Representative Whittemore resigned prior to the House consideration of the resolution.

In 1981, U.S. Representative Raymond F. Lederer (D.-Pa.) resigned from the Ninety-seventh Congress after the House Committee on Standards of Official Conduct recommended his expulsion to the full House for his part in the Abscam sting operation. Senator Harrison Williams (D.-N.J.) resigned in March 1982 after six days of debate in the full Senate on an expulsion resolution reported from the Senate Select Committee on Ethics for his conduct in the Abscam operation. U.S. Representative John W. Jenrette, Jr., (D.-N.C.) had earlier resigned from the House, on 10 December 1980, while the House Committee considered discipline for his conviction on bribery, conspiracy, and Travel Act charges resulting from the Abscam operation.

Expulsion from State Legislatures

The constitutions of all but five of the fifty states expressly provide for the authority of each house of the legislature to expel a member. Even in those five states without such express authority—Massachusetts, New Hampshire, New York, North Carolina, and South Dakota—the legislative bodies may possess a generally recognized inherent authority to expel a member for the protection and the integrity of the institution.

In Massachusetts, for example, a member of the legislature was expelled in 1855 despite the fact that no express authorization for this action existed in the state's constitution. In *Hiss* v. *Bartlett,* 69 Mass. 468, 472, 473 (1855), the court explained that the legislature's authority to punish its own members is an inherent authority of the institution and may be exercised even without express authorization.

The court found that the legislature's "implied power over their members was full and complete" and was a "necessary and incidental power, to enable the house to perform its high functions, and is necessary to the safety of the State."

Of the forty-five state constitutions that provide for the express authority to expel, forty-three provide that an expulsion require a vote of two-thirds, while the constitutions of Kansas and Vermont do not expressly establish the required majority needed for expulsion. Of the forty-three states requiring a two-thirds majority, sixteen required a vote of two-thirds of all the members elected.

Although the measure that a member of the legislature may not be expelled for the same offense more than once is not incorporated into the Constitution, it is expressly provided for in the constitutions of twenty-six states. These states include Alabama, Arkansas, Colorado, Connecticut, Illinois, Indiana, Iowa, Kentucky, Maine, Maryland, Michigan, Minnesota, Mississippi, Missouri, Nebraska, New Mexico, Ohio, Oregon, Pennsylvania, Rhode Island, South Carolina, Tennessee, Texas, Washington, West Virginia, and Wisconsin.

Specific grounds for expulsion are generally not set out in the constitutions. However, the constitutions of Idaho and Montana do provide that expulsion shall be "for good cause shown," while Utah's constitution states that expulsion shall be "for cause." The Vermont constitution expressly restricts reasons for the legislature to expel to certain past misconduct of a member, providing that the legislature may not expel members for "causes known to their constituents antecedent to their election."

Additional disabilities that are attendant from an expulsion action are expressly provided in six other state constitutions. The constitutions of Alabama, Arkansas, North Dakota, Oklahoma, Pennsylvania, and Wyoming stipulate that if a member is expelled for corruption, that person is no longer eligible for the legislature. In Colorado, if a legislator is expelled for corruption, he or she is no longer eligible for that same general assembly.

RECALL

While expulsion is an inherent authority necessary and incident to the general powers of legislative bodies over their own proceedings and members, the recall procedure is a special process outside of the legislative institution itself, exercised solely by the people. It is often grouped together with two other devices popularly referred to as mechanisms of direct democracy: the initiative and the referendum. The initiative and referendum allow for a direct check and input by the voters over legislation, while the recall allows for a direct check and control over the elected officials themselves by providing the potential for a direct vote on whether or not to remove an elected official from office.

The provisions for recall of state officials in the United States are a legacy and outgrowth of the Progressive reform movement of the late nineteenth and early twentieth centuries. There had been a growing dissatisfaction with municipal machine politics and party bosses by the time of the movement's beginnings, and allegations of undue influence of wealthy corporate industrialists over state and local government officials were prevalent. Populist and Progressive movements, particularly in the western states, began to look for ways to bring back the control of government more directly into the hands of the electorate through initiative, referendum, and recall. Opponents of recall provisions in the early part of the century often criticized these provisions as radical, injurious to the representational form of government, and socialistic; in fact, the recall was part of the Socialist Party platform in the late nineteenth century.

The first formal provision for recall has been attributed to the charter of Los Angeles in 1903, in which city there had been a populist battle against special interests—particularly railroad interests—and their alleged influence over the city government. Shortly after the enactment of the recall provision, a member of the Los Angeles city council was successfully recalled by his constituents for voting to award a favorable public printing contract, at a price significantly above the lowest bidder, to an antiunion newspaper. Within the next several years, twenty-five other cities in California adopted recall provisions.

The first state to adopt a statewide recall provision was Oregon in 1908. Several states followed shortly thereafter, including California in 1911; Arizona, Colorado, Idaho, Nevada, and

Washington in 1912; Michigan in 1913; Kansas and Louisiana in 1914; North Dakota in 1920; and Wisconsin in 1926. The impetus for statewide recall provisions lessened after the 1920s, and only four new states added recall provisions between 1926 and 1992, for a total of sixteen states. Most states, however, allow for local recall elections directed against officials in local jurisdictions.

Pros and Cons of Recall Provisions

The recall is an extension of the electorate's right to chose whom it wishes to represent it in government, as well as a complement to the other direct-democracy mechanisms of initiative and referendum. Supporters of recall provisions see this mechanism as a device to assure regular and close oversight of elected public officials. The persistent threat of a recall election makes elected officials continuously—rather than periodically—responsible and responsive to the will of the electorate. The recall may be used to remove elected officials who have engaged in corruption, malfeasance, or misfeasance in office, or in some cases those who have merely become unresponsive or out of touch with the electorate. With recall procedures available, there is no need for the electorate to have to tolerate such an official until that official's term is over.

Those who oppose recall note that recall petitions generally need a relatively small minority of the electorate to sign the petition to force a recall election. With the threat of a recall ever present, an official may be deterred from, or penalized for, taking strong political positions that could offend even a small but active political group. Such a group could use the recall as a harassment tactic, stymieing government by constantly occupying elected officials with the need to campaign and run in recall elections. The need for continual oversight of the decisions and programs of elected officials has also been brought into question, as complex government programs and policies often need to function and be evaluated in the long run. If constantly threatened with recall, officials may not be able to exercise discretion and use long-term judgments and planning for programs that may not bring immediate, short-term benefits.

Recall of judicial officers has been a particular subject of criticism. Since the protected legal rights of the minority could be infringed upon by mere popular opinion, judges who have rendered unpopular decisions could face recall. This fear of the so-called tyranny of the majority, and of compromising an independent judiciary, led in 1911 to President William Howard Taft's veto of statehood legislation for Arizona because the Arizona constitution had a provision for recall of members of the judiciary (he approved Arizona statehood when the offending provision was removed the following year).

Recall of Members of Congress

There is no provision in the Constitution, or in federal law, for the recall of senators or representatives from Congress, and no senator or representative has ever been recalled. Under the Constitution and following congressional practice, members of Congress may have their service ended prior to the normal expiration of their term by resignation, death, expulsion, or acceptance of another public office deemed incompatible with congressional office. Under the Fourteenth Amendment, members can forfeit their offices for engaging in insurrection or rebellion against the United States, or for giving aid or comfort to the nation's enemies after having taken an oath to support the Constitution.

The recall of senators and representatives was considered during the drafting of the Constitution. In fact, the Articles of Confederation contained a clause providing for the recall of senators by the state legislatures. Article V stated that there would be "a power reserved to each state, to recall its delegates, or any of them, at any time within the year, and to send others in their stead. . . ."

That provision, or one similar to it, was not included in the drafting of the Constitution, however. The ratifying process in the states shows debate over the lack of inclusion of a recall provision. For example, in an address delivered to the Maryland legislature, Luther Martin criticized the pending Constitution because the senators "are to pay themselves, out of the treasury of the United States; and are not liable to be recalled during the period for which they are chosen" (quoted in Farrand, p. 173). In New York, an amendment was proposed in the 1788 ratifying convention that would have allowed the state legislatures to "recall their Senators . . . and elect others in their stead." The failure of these provisions, arguments, and amendments strongly indicates the intent of the framers, in their contemporaneous interpretation of the Constitution at its drafting and ratification, that there exists no right or power to recall a senator or representative from the United States Congress.

The lack of authority to recall a member of Congress is also apparent in the constitutional systems structured for congressional elections, judging the qualifications of members, and the discipline and removal of members, the authority for which is expressly given to each house of Congress. Since the Constitution has supremacy over state laws and provisions, any state law in conflict with and contrary to such constitutional provisions would not prevail.

The right to remove a member of Congress before the expiration of his or her term of office is one which resides in each house of Congress individually, according to the expulsion clause of the Constitution, and not in the Congress as a whole or in the state legislatures. In *Burton* v. *United States,* 202 U.S. 344 (1906), the Supreme Court ruled that a federal law that, on its face, purported to make someone convicted of bribery ineligible to be a U.S. senator, could not force an incumbent senator to leave office, since the Senate could only remove a member by exercising its expulsion power: "The seat into which he was originally inducted as a Senator from Kansas could only become vacant by his death, or by expiration of his term of office, or by some direct action on the part of the Senate in the exercise of its constitutional powers" (*Burton* v. *United States,* at 369).

The Constitution expressly establishes the exclusive qualifications for congressional office. These qualifications may not be altered by either Congress or the state legislatures. The courts have consistently struck down state laws and regulations that attempted to add additional qualifications for congressional office, such as residency within a congressional district, or nonconviction of certain offenses. Allowing for a state to provide a recall of a senator or representative would appear to add an additional, and impermissible, qualification for congressional office.

Finally, a member of Congress is not generally considered a state officer, but rather a federal official who holds office established by and under authority of the Constitution. As a federal official and constitutional officer, a senator or representative is not susceptible to state recall provisions for state officers.

The language of recall provisions in several states may arguably be broad enough to encompass members of Congress. Michigan law expressly includes, and Wisconsin law appears to provide for, the recall of U.S. senators and representatives, while Arizona law provides for an optional pledge by congressional candidates to abide by the results of a state recall election. The attorney general of Wisconsin noted in an opinion on 3 May 1979 that the state election board, upon presentation of a valid petition to recall a member of Congress, had no authority in itself to reject such petition without a ruling from a court. However, a state district court judge dismissed a suit in October 1967 that attempted to compel the Idaho secretary of state to accept petitions recalling Senator Frank Church. In the unreported decision, the judge found that such a recall would violate those provisions of the Constitution giving Congress the authority to judge the elections and qualifications of its own members. In Oregon, the attorney general ruled in an opinion, on 19 April 1935 that the state's recall provisions could not apply to a member of Congress, who is not actually a state official, but a constitutional officer. The opinion also found that such recall provisions would interfere with Congress's exclusively constitutional authority over the elections and qualifications of its own members, noting that the "jurisdiction to determine the right of a representative in Congress to a seat is vested exclusively in the House of Representatives."

Despite the fact that some state laws thus appear to provide for the mechanism for a recall of a member of Congress, a state recall provision could not be legally enforceable. If an election to recall a member of Congress were actually allowed to be held in a state, the effect would be advisory only, having perhaps significant political, but not legal, import.

For a recall provision to be enforceable against a member of Congress, an amendment to the Constitution would need to be adopted authorizing such a procedure. There have been some movements for such an amendment, as well as for national initiative and referendum provisions. Although apparently having some public appeal, no drive for a national recall provision gained sufficient stature and force to begin the lengthy amendatory process in earnest by the early 1990s.

Recall in the States

Sixteen states provided for recall of some or all state officials. Reflecting the trend of the populist and progressive movements in the early part of the twentieth century, most of these states are in the western or midwestern parts of the country. Jurisdictions with statewide recall provisions include the western states of Alaska, Arizona, California, Colorado, Idaho, Montana, Nevada, Oregon, and Washington; the midwestern states of Kansas, Michigan, North Dakota, and Wisconsin; and the southern states of Georgia, Louisiana, and Virginia. In addition to statewide recall provisions in these sixteen states, most states provide for recalls of some local, municipal, or county officials or commissioners.

A recall is generally begun by the filing of a petition signed by a specified percentage of the electorate in the affected jurisdiction. The percentage of required signatures may vary from state to state ranging from a low of 12 percent of the number of votes cast in the last election for that office in California, to 40 percent in Kansas. Most of the states require signatures in a number equaling at least 25 percent of the votes cast for the office at the last election.

The laws providing for recall vary as to the express designation or requirement of a cause for a recall. There has been much criticism put forward of recall-at-will provisions—in which no specific cause for the recall need be certified—since such provisions could arguably be used merely as a harassment tactic by organized political opponents.

Most state recall laws, except those in California and in Washington, provide for a grace period after an official's election during which that official is not subject to a recall. These grace periods range from two months in Montana to one year in Wisconsin, and are usually four or six months in duration. Additionally, four states provide for a cutoff time near the expiration of an official's term during which a recall may not be initiated: 180 days in Alaska, Georgia, and Washington; and 200 days in Kansas.

After the petition is submitted to the appropriate public official or public office, there is generally a specified time period wherein the petition and signatures will be reviewed for conformance to state laws and regulations. After that time, if a sufficient number of signatures are certified, a recall election will be held. In the Commonwealth of Virginia, recall elections are not held. Instead, a petition is first filed with a circuit court; it must be signed by at least 10 percent of the number of persons who voted for the particular office in the last election. Then, a judicial trial will proceed to determine if the official should be removed from office.

Recall statutes may require that the electorate simply choose between the options of recalling or not recalling the official. In some jurisdictions another candidate may actually run against the official subject to recall. After an official is subjected to an unsuccessful recall election, in some states that official may not be subject to another recall election either for a certain period of time, or ever again.

Recalls of statewide officeholders are not common in the United States. Some studies of recall have noted that only one governor has been recalled—Lynn Frazier of North Dakota, in 1922—although Evan Mecham of Arizona seemed about to be successfully recalled at the time he was impeached and removed by the Arizona legislature in 1988. Several state legislators have been recalled, including legislators in California, Idaho, Michigan, and Oregon.

IMPEACHMENT

What is commonly referred to as an impeachment is generally a two-step procedure. One house of the legislature (usually the lower house) votes to impeach, or bring formal charges against, an officer. The other house tries the impeachment and can convict the officer of specified offenses; removing that person from office is part of the remedy imposed in a finding of guilt.

The authority of the legislature to impeach executive and judicial officers is a power patterned after English parliamentary practice, but which also reflected colonial experiences with impeachments. The underlying purpose of allowing impeachments by the legislature—that is, to remove a corrupt or otherwise unworthy public official who may otherwise be protected from removal by the executive, or in England by the crown—is common to both England and the United States. However, the provisions that were eventually accepted in the Constitution, and that are replicated to a great extent in the state constitutions, differ greatly from the impeachment practice in England.

Impeachments in Congress

Constitutional History   Early drafts of the Constitution submitted to the Constitutional Convention during June 1787 had provided for impeachment trials to be conducted by the national judiciary. By September 1787 a committee submitted a proposal that the Senate was to try impeachments, but that it would require a two-thirds vote to convict an officer.

The forum selected for impeachments, as well as the inclusion of the president among the officers who may be impeached, reflected the delegates' colonial experience and greater comfort with legislative bodies and assemblies—which had been made up of the colonists themselves, as opposed to governors and executives sent by the crown from England. In addition to their colonial experiences, the delegates held a continual fear of a president who might turn his power and expansive authority toward monarchy.

Authority and Procedure   The Constitution has several sections that define the authority, the scope, and the basic procedures of impeachments. Article II, Section 4 provides that "the President, Vice President and all civil Officers of the United States, shall be removed from Office on Impeachment for, and Conviction of, Treason, Bribery, or other high Crimes and Misdemeanors."

The House of Representatives has the "sole Power of Impeachment" (Article I, Section 2, paragraph 5); and the Senate has "the sole Power to try all Impeachments" (Article II, Section 3, paragraph 6). The senators must be sworn when sitting for the purpose of impeachment, and no person may be convicted on any article charged without the votes of two-thirds of the senators present (Article I, Section

3, paragraph 6). The judgment for impeachment may extend no further than removal from office and disqualification to hold federal office (Article I, Section 3, paragraph 7), and the president is not allowed to grant pardons in cases of impeachments (Article II, Section 2, paragraph 1).

Grounds for Impeachment The Constitution provides that the president, vice president, judges, and all civil officers may be impeached for "Treason, Bribery or other high Crimes and Misdemeanors." This phrase has engendered as much debate as has any phrase of the Constitution. It is clear that the framers intended to set out certain specified grounds for impeachment so that the president and other executive officers would not, as Madison phrased it, serve merely at the "pleasure of the Senate." However, objections were also raised during the Constitutional Convention at limiting impeachable offenses to treason or bribery, since this would not cover other conduct that some considered to be grounds for impeachment, as well. Congressional precedents have shown that criminal conduct is considered sufficient as an impeachable offense; also, conduct that does not reach the level of an indictable offense may be considered sufficient grounds in the House to impeach a civil officer—particularly a federal judge who, with good behavior, would normally serve a lifetime tenure.

Officers Subject to Impeachment All civil officers of the United States are subject to impeachment by Congress. The precedents have shown that this category clearly includes civil officers in the executive and judicial branches of government, including federal judges. It does not include military officers; however, impeachment may not extend to persons who are considered only employees, and not civil officers, of the government.

There has been substantial debate over whether a member of Congress is a civil officer and therefore subject to impeachment. Although constitutional scholars have interpreted the original intent of the drafters of the Constitution in various ways, the Senate set an early, and largely undisturbed, precedent in the case of Senator William Blount in 1797, by acquitting Senator Blount of impeachment charges on the grounds that a Senator was not a civil officer as set out in the impeachment clause.

Rather than convicting Senator Blount, who had been impeached by the House, the Senate had him expelled on 8 July 1797.

As a practical matter, relying on both houses of Congress to impeach a member is more restrictive than the authority of each house, separately and individually, to remove a member by an expulsion on a two-thirds vote. Furthermore, the Constitution requires a trial in the Senate for an impeachment, while an expulsion proceeding does not. Finally, the Constitution sets out specific grounds for impeachment, while each house of Congress has greater discretion in determining what misconduct would merit an expulsion. Of course, upon conviction in an impeachment, a continuing disqualification from office may be imposed as the penalty, while such a disqualification from holding congressional office could not be imposed as part of an expulsion.

Impeachment Precedents Fifteen impeachment trials took place in the Senate between the founding of the United States and the early 1990s. The federal officials who were impeached by the House of Representatives and tried by the Senate included twelve federal judges, one president of the United States, one cabinet officer, and one U.S. senator.

The fifteen impeachment trials involved the following individuals: William Blount, U.S. senator from Tennessee (impeachment proceedings, 1797–1799); John Pickering, district judge of the United States District Court of New Hampshire (1803–1804); Samuel Chase, associate justice of the Supreme Court (1804–1805); James H. Peck, district judge of the United States District Court for the District of Missouri (1826–1831); West H. Humphreys, district judge for the United States District Court for several districts of Tennessee (1862); Andrew Johnson, president of the United States (1867–1868); William W. Belknap, secretary of war (1876); Charles Swayne, district judge for the United States District Court for the Northern District of Florida (1903–1905); Robert W. Archbald, circuit judge of the United States Court of Appeals for the Third Circuit, serving as associate judge of the United States Commerce Court (1912–1913); George W. English, district judge for the United States District Court for the Eastern District of Illinois (1925–1926); Harold Louderback, district judge of the United States District Court for the Northern

District of California (1932–1933); Halsted L. Ritter, district judge of the United States District Court for the Southern District of Florida (1936); Harry E. Claiborne, district judge of the United States District Court for the District of Nevada (1986); Walter L. Nixon, Jr., district judge of the United States District Court for the Southern District of Mississippi (1988–1989); and Alcee Hastings, district judge of the United States District Court for the Southern District of Florida (1988–1989).

These impeachment trials resulted in only seven convictions and removals from office. Those convicted and removed were all federal judges: Pickering, Humphreys, Archbald, Ritter, Claiborne, Nixon, and Hastings.

There have been a number of other instances in which the impeachment process had been initiated in some form, but for which no trial was held in the Senate. These cases have included inquiries or proceedings concerning forty-one federal judges, nine high-level executive-branch officials, one vice president, and three presidents. One of the more recent and significant impeachment proceedings was against President Richard M. Nixon in 1974. Four Articles of Impeachment were adopted by the House Judiciary Committee and were to be reported to the full House of Representatives for an impeachment vote when Nixon resigned the presidency. The House eventually did vote to accept the committee report on President Nixon.

Impeachment in the States

By 1992, impeachments by the state legislature of certain civil officers were expressly authorized in the constitutions of all but one of the fifty states. Only Oregon did not provide for an impeachment process in its constitution.

In most of the states, an impeachment is initiated upon a vote of the lower body of the legislature—that is, the house of representatives or the house of delegates—and then tried in the upper chamber, or the senate. In Alaska, however, it is just the opposite, with the impeachment being brought in the senate and tried in the house. In Nebraska, which has only one legislative body, the impeachments are initiated in the senate and then tried by the state supreme court, meeting in the capitol. In Missouri, after the house votes for impeachment,

the impeachment is also tried before the state supreme court. In New York, a court for trial impeachment is composed of the president of the senate, a majority of senators, and the judges of the court of appeals.

Although in most states, articles of impeachment may be voted by a simple majority of the initiating legislative body, nine of the states expressly require a two-thirds vote to impeach. These states are Alaska, Delaware, Florida, Indiana, Mississippi, Montana, South Carolina, Utah, and Vermont. Rhode Island requires a two-thirds vote to impeach the governor.

Of the state constitutions that provide for an impeachment process, all but four require a two-thirds vote to convict an impeached officer. Alabama, Massachusetts, and New Hampshire do not specify the number required in their constitutions, while Missouri requires a conviction by five-sevenths of the court trying the impeachment.

As with the Constitution, there may be questions concerning whether or not a legislator may be impeached under a state constitution as a state officer. Some state constitutions—or court decisions interpreting them—expressly stipulate that legislators cannot be impeached and convicted by the legislature, but can only be removed through expulsion by one house of the legislature. However, other provisions may define nonlegislative officers who are expressly subject to impeachment. Other constitutions are silent on the subject and merely provide that state officers may be impeached.

The provisions for impeachment, both in New York and in North Carolina, appear to contemplate impeachment of legislators. It is noteworthy that their constitutions do not provide for an express authority of the legislature to expel its own members; these states apparently rely on an impeachment process to remove a legislator from office.

State legislatures have impeached seven governors between 1789 and the early 1990s. Of these seven, six either were removed from office or resigned. Prior to the impeachment of Evan Mecham in 1988 by the Arizona legislature, the last governor to be impeached was Huey P. Long of Louisiana in 1928. Long became the only governor to survive an impeachment by the lower house when the charges were later dropped.

CONCLUSION

In American legislative institutions, the practical control over a legislator's conduct is still substantially exercised by the traditional mechanisms of the periodic election process, rather than by the more extraordinary methods of expulsion or recall. Although Congress possesses what appears to be an unlimited power to expel a member of either house by a two-thirds vote of that particular body, its exercise of this power has been substantially restrained. Several members of Congress, facing a possible expulsion action, have resigned from Congress before the matter was officially completed. However, other than for the Civil War–era findings of disloyalty of certain members to the Union, the House and the Senate have actually expelled only one member each between the founding of the nation and the early 1990s. There appears to abide in Congress an acceptance of the Founding Fathers' deep suspicion of a political and governmental institution overriding the electorate's choice as their representative to the legislature. An expulsion is seen in Congress more as a measure of self-protection of the institution itself, its integrity, and its proceedings, and not as a method of overseeing the conduct of individual members.

A recall provision may appear on its face to enhance the electorate's oversight of a legislator's conduct and responsiveness once he or she has been elected. However, as of the early 1990s, recall procedures have not gained widespread acceptance in the states for state legislative offices, because of some of this mechanism's practical political disadvantages. Many jurisdictions do use or allow the recall provisions for local elective offices. There is no provision in the Constitution for the recall of members of Congress, and no member of Congress has ever been recalled by the electorate under any state law. A state law purporting to authorize the recall of a member of Congress before the normal expiration of the member's term would be of questionable constitutional validity given the supremacy of the Constitution's qualifications, terms of office, and methods of removal of a member of Congress. Without a constitutional amendment on this issue, the electorate's most effective tool for controlling the conduct or responsiveness of a member of Congress after his or her election to office remains the ballot box.

BIBLIOGRAPHY

Useful sources include CHARLES R. ADRIAN, *State and Local Governments,* 4th ed. (New York, 1976); WILLIAM ANDERSON and EDWARD W. WEIDNER, *State and Local Government in the United States* (New York, 1951); RAOUL BERGER, *Impeachment: The Constitutional Problems* (Cambridge, Mass., 1973); FREDERICK L. BIRD and FRANCES M. RYAN, *The Recall of Public Officers: A Study of the Operation of the Recall in California* (New York, 1930); DORIAN BOWMAN and JUDITH FARRIS BOWMAN, "Article I, Section 5: Congress' Power to Expel—An Exercise in Self-Restraint," *Syracuse Law Review* 29 (1978): 1071; CLARENCE CANNON, *Cannon's Precedents of the House of Representatives of the United States,* 6 vols. (Washington, D.C., 1935); CONGRESSIONAL QUARTERLY, INC., *Congressional Ethics,* 2d ed. (Washington, D.C., 1980); THE COUNCIL OF STATE GOVERNMENTS, *The Book of the States, 1990–1991 Edition* (Lexington, Ky., 1990); THOMAS E. CRONIN, *Direct Democracy: The Politics of Initiative, Referendum, and Recall* (Cambridge, Mass., 1989); LUTHER STEARNS CUSHING, *Lex parliamentaria americana: Elements of the Law and Practice of Legislative Assemblies in the United States of America* (Boston, 1856); LEWIS DESCHLER, *Deschler's Precedents of the United States House of Representatives* (Washington, D.C., 1977); MAX FARRAND, ed., *The Records of the Federal Convention of 1787* (New Haven, Conn., 1911); MICHAEL J. GERHARDT, "The Constitutional Limits to Impeachment and Its Alternatives," 68 *Texas Law Review* 1 (November 1989); ROBERT S. GETZ, *Congressional Ethics: The Conflict of Interest Issue* (Princeton, N.J., 1967); ASSOCIATION OF THE BAR OF THE CITY OF NEW YORK, SPECIAL COMMITTEE ON CONGRESSIONAL ETHICS, *Congress and the Public Trust* (New York, 1970); ASHER C. HINDS, *Hinds' Precedents of the House of Representatives of the United States,* 5 vols. (Washington, D.C., 1907); JOHNNY H. KILLIAN, ed., *The Constitution of the United States of America: Analysis and Interpretation* (Washington, D.C., 1982); ELIZABETH E. MACK, "The Use and Abuse of Recall: A Proposal for Legislative Reform," 67 *Nebraska Law Review* 617 (1988); SIR THOMAS ERSKINE MAY, *The Law, Privileges, Proceedings and Usage of Parliament,* rev. ed. (1946); GEOFFREY W. R. PALMER, "Adam Clayton Powell and John Wilkes: An Analogue from England for the Men in the Marble Palace," 56 *Iowa Law Review* 725 (April 1971); and HERBERT S. SWAN, "The Use of the Recall in the United States," in WILLIAM BENNETT MUNRO, ed., *The Initiative, Referendum and Recall,* (New York, 1912).